INSIDE OLE 2

INSIDE OLE 2

The Fast Track
to Building
Powerful
Object-Oriented
Applications

KRAIG BROCKSCHMIDT

PUBLISHED BY
Microsoft Press
A Division of Microsoft Corporation
One Microsoft Way
Redmond, Washington 98052-6399

Library of Congress Cataloging-in-Publication Data
Brockschmidt, Kraig, 1968–
Inside OLE 2 / Kraig Brockschmidt.
p. cm.
Includes index.
ISBN 1-55615-618-9
1. Object-oriented programming (Computer science) 2. Microsoft Windows (Computer file) I. Title.
QA76.64.B76 1993
005.4'3--dc20
93-34953
CIP

Printed and bound in the United States of America.

1 2 3 4 5 6 7 8 9 AGAG 9 8 7 6 5 4

Distributed to the book trade in Canada by Macmillan of Canada, a division of Canada Publishing Corporation.

Distributed to the book trade outside the United States and Canada by Penguin Books Ltd.

Penguin Books Ltd., Harmondsworth, Middlesex, England
Penguin Books Australia Ltd., Ringwood, Victoria, Australia
Penguin Books N.Z. Ltd., 182-190 Wairau Road, Auckland 10, New Zealand

British Cataloging-in-Publication Data available.

Acquisitions Editor: Dean Holmes
Project Editor: Ron Lamb
Technical Editor: Seth McEvoy

CONTENTS

SECTION II

OBJECT-ORIENTED SYSTEM FEATURES: FILES AND DATA TRANSFER

CHAPTER 5

CHAPTER 6

CHAPTER 7

CLIPBOARD TRANSFERS USING DATA OBJECTS 387

CHAPTER 8

DRAG-AND-DROP OPERATIONS USING DATA OBJECTS 429

SECTION III
COMPOUND DOCUMENTS: OLE

CHAPTER 9

CHAPTER 10

COMPOUND DOCUMENTS AND EMBEDDED OBJECT SERVERS (EXEs) 565

CHAPTER 11

IN-PROCESS OBJECT HANDLERS AND SERVERS 641

CHAPTER 12

MONIKERS AND LINKING CONTAINERS 695

CHAPTER 13

MONIKER BINDING AND LINK SOURCES 753

CHAPTER 14

CONVERSION, EMULATION, AND COMPATIBILITY WITH OLE 1 ... **809**

SECTION IV

COMPOUND DOCUMENTS: IN-PLACE ACTIVATION

CHAPTER 15

VISUAL EDITING: IN-PLACE ACTIVATION AND IN-PLACE CONTAINERS ... **843**

CHAPTER 16

IN-PLACE ACTIVATION FOR COMPOUND DOCUMENT OBJECTS **907**

PREFACE

Give me a fish and you feed me for a day.
Teach me to fish and you feed me for a lifetime.
A proverb

This is a book about fish. But because without knowing how to catch them, you'd eventually starve, it's also about fishing. The fish are all those pieces of information that you need as a developer in order to exploit OLE 2 features in your application. Teaching you to fish involves describing why the specific pieces you are using were designed and what path they lay toward the future. Of course, you always need a reason to keep fishing even if you're currently well fed, so at the beginning of each chapter I will attempt to motivate you enough to read it.

It has been said that authors write books not so that they will be understood, but so that they themselves understand. Certainly this work has been such an experience for me. When I started working with OLE 2 in the middle of 1992 as part of my job in Microsoft's Developer Relations Group, I saw the technology as merely a way to create applications that support what is called "Compound Documents," as OLE version 1 was. This attitude was well accepted at Microsoft because OLE 2 was a refinement of OLE 1; in fact, the OLE 2 design specifications are organized around a Compound Document core with a number of other technologies hanging off the sides to solve the most critical problems exposed in OLE 1.

For a number of months, I plodded through prerelease information about OLE 2 to create some sample applications to demonstrate compound documents. With the help of various members of the OLE 2 development team, with whom I've worked closely for all this time, I gave a number of classes inside and outside of Microsoft to help others use OLE 2 to create Compound Document applications. In the back of my mind something was telling me that there was much more to OLE 2 than I had originally perceived, but it was very hard to break away from equating OLE 2 and Compound Documents because every available piece of documentation made the two terms synonymous.

In the first few weeks of January, 1993, I started to see that, in the process of solving the most important problems in OLE 1, the OLE 2 architects had actually created a much larger system for object-oriented programming under Windows. I began to see that OLE 2 has technologies that are separate from the true Compound Document technologies. In fact, I started to see exactly how one might use those other technologies without ever coming into contact with Compound Documents. I was not the first person to realize this. In fact, OLE 2 was actually designed this way, but this aspect of the design unfortunately was lost somewhere between the minds of the OLE 2 architects and the actual OLE 2 Design Specification. But I was slowly beginning to rediscover the elegant underlying architecture of the entire group of technologies. My position within Microsoft allowed me to explore OLE 2 in depth and even to browse the OLE 2 sources, letting me truly get "Inside OLE 2."

One Sunday afternoon in mid-January, 1993, while doing something totally unrelated to OLE 2, I achieved what Eric Maffei (editor of *Microsoft Systems Journal*) describes as "OLE Nirvana." All the little subtechnologies in OLE 2 fell into place and I saw clearly, after six months of mental fog, what OLE 2 was all about. I realized that you could exploit very small pieces of OLE 2 in incremental steps and that the best way to communicate the entire vision was to write a book. I quickly fired up my notebook computer and spent the next three hours pounding out the outline. The book you now hold follows that original outline closely.

My goal in writing this book was to provide an organization for OLE 2 in such a way that each chapter depends *solely* on information in previous chapters, with no dependencies on later chapters. Because OLE 2 is not a technology for writing whole applications (because we still use many Windows API functions), I had the luxury of concentrating on OLE 2's features and the way you use those features in your applications. I have presented the material a little at a time, in order to help you solidify your understanding of that building block before moving on. I hope the book takes you on an evolutionary path, on which the work you do early in the book will be reusable in work you do in the later stages.

This same idea is present even within any given chapter, where I have provided finely detailed step-by-step instructions for implementing specific features and where each step depends on the prior steps but not on any later step. This sort of process enables you to add a little code, compile your application, and actually see something working! Personally, I find the incremental feedback of this sort of process extraordinarily motivating. In fact, it makes programming fun, and that is refreshing in this day and age of "serious" professional programmers. I got into computers because hacking out some BASIC code was exhilarating. I hope I can bring some of that back through this book.

OLE 2 is the first step in the evolution of Windows from the function call–based operating system we have today to an object-oriented operating system in the future. The object model you will learn in this book will be a part of Windows programming for a long time, and I hope it will help you develop a definite edge in your programming career. Because OLE 2 is a first step, it is going to seem utterly alien much of the time. But you need to learn how to fish sometime if you are ever going to feed yourself. While you are learning the skills of a master angler, this book will help you catch enough fish to keep you from starving.

Who Can Use This Book

I mentioned earlier that OLE 2 is not a technology for writing an entire application. To use OLE 2, you must be familiar with how to write an application for Windows. I will not describe how to use any of the existing Windows API functions, nor will I attempt to describe any intricate details about Windows itself. Our focus in this book is strictly on OLE 2.

Therefore, I assume that you are already familiar with programming in the Windows environment and that you have at least a working knowledge of the Windows API. In addition, because we are talking about object-oriented programming here, a knowledge of C++ is helpful, but not required. In fact, C++ knowledge can at times be a hindrance to understanding the object model in OLE 2. Although the samples in this book are written in C++, I've kept them very much like standard C Windows programs. Chapter 2 contains a short discussion of the C++ I use in all the book's samples, from a C programmer's perspective (which was my own perspective when I started writing this book).

This book is not only for programmers, however. Each chapter is structured so that a person who designs application architectures can read the first few sections and understand how the mechanisms in OLE 2 work without having to work through the details of code. The first 5 to 20 pages of each chapter discuss architecture, leaving exact details about writing code to the latter parts of the chapter. So, if you want an in-depth look at how OLE 2 works, read the first section or two of each chapter.

Some Assembly Required

No, we won't use any *assembly* language, but this book does assume that you have an appropriate software development environment installed that includes the following:

- A C++ Compiler such as Microsoft C version 7 or Microsoft Visual C++ version 1. The make files for the samples in this book are specific to Microsoft compilers, so some adjustment will be necessary for other environments.
- The Windows 3.1 Software Development Kit.
- *And most important*: the OLE 2 Software Development Kit. Be sure that the OLE 2 directory is added to your PATH, INCLUDE, and LIB environment variables before attempting to build any samples in this book. You can obtain the OLE 2 SDK from Microsoft for a $50 charge by calling 1-800-227-4679.

Chapter 2 includes more information on creating the right build environment for the book samples specifically.

On Coding Style

As soon as you start reading some of the code in this book, you'll begin to wonder where I developed my coding style.

My coding style, which is unlike any other widely published standard, is what I've personally developed over a number of years to improve (in my mind) code readability as well as to prevent myself from making certain mistakes. For example, when I want to compare a variable to a constant, I always put the constant first—that is, I'll write *if (0L==m_cRef)* instead of *if (m_cRef==0L)*. Like all C and C++ programmers, I've had my share of bugs because I typed = instead of ==. Putting the constant on the left causes a compiler error when you forget the second equal sign. With the variable on the left, you get a legal assignment statement but a very nasty run-time error.

All other stylistic elements have their justifications as well and are used consistently. I've often heard that people prefer consistency over specific styles, so there you have it. Let me also mention that in many of the source listings in this book, I have eliminated lengthy header comments on files and functions that you will see in the actual disk files. This is done simply to save space. Any code within a function, however, will match exactly what you will find on disk.

Acknowledgments

People who have read drafts of this book have repeatedly asked me where I found my inspiration for writing the way I have. Influence has come from many corners, so let me list those sources as well as offer my thanks to the following groups or individuals who have helped create this tome of OLE:

To all the programmers in the trenches who are usually told to do too much with too little information. Without you, I'd have little incentive to write a book like this.

To all those developers inside Microsoft who took the time to formally review this work: Charlie Kindel, Nigel Thompson, Scott Skorupa, Sara Williams, Vinoo Cherian, Craig Wittenberg, Douglas Hodges, Alex Tilles, Mark Bader, Dean McCrory, and especially Nat "Zoinks" Brown—thanks for all your useful and real-world insights.

To the OLE 2 team at Microsoft for all their answers and input, especially to architects Tony Williams and Bob Atkinson.

To all the developers who devoured my draft copies as soon as I could write them and who sent words of encouragement, including Dominic Kyrie, Marc Singer, Marcellus Bucheit, Lars Nyman, Howard Chalkley, and Jim Adam, a total Python Head who reminded me that it was *Patsy* who actually said Camelot was only a model.

To Burt Harris and Thomas Holaday for setting me straight on the finer points of C++ programming.

To Monty Python, Yoda, the *Harvard Lampoon*, and *MAD Magazine*, as well as authors Donald Norman, Robert Fulghum, Tom DeMarco, Timothy Lister, Douglas Adams, Piers Anthony, Marvin Harris, and Jim Stacey for whatever it is that made me include the crazy things I wrote in this book.

To photographer Dewitt Jones, Lynette Sheppard, and the entire group from our week at HollyHock, who showed me how to enjoy and appreciate doing the crazy things I have in this book. May you always fly with frozen eagles.

To Dean Holmes, Ron Lamb, Seth McEvoy, and all the other people at Microsoft Press, not only for doing the work of publishing this book but also for letting me get away with the crazy things I've done here.

To Bob Taniguchi for helping me get into the position at Microsoft to write this book, and to Viktor Grabner for teaching me what the purpose of making my job obsolete really means and how to be a little crazy in the process.

To Microsoft's Developer Relations Group for allowing me to lock myself in my office undisturbed for months on end while I was doing crazy things.

And, of course, to my wife, Kristi, who was there through what has been the busiest year we've yet experienced.

Road Map

Before we get started, let me give you a word of warning. OLE 2 is big. Very big. If you count the number of new functions in OLE 2, you have more than in Windows 3.0 itself. If you count the number of pages in this book, you'll find it longer than the Windows 3.1 edition of Charles Petzold's *Programming Windows* (no offense, Charles), and I don't list most of the sample code. What does this mean for you? If there ever was a time to heed the warning "Don't bite off more than you can chew," now is the time. Allow me to illustrate.

Pat and Casey each decided to build a cabin at the top of a mountain. Each cabin would have the latest siding, a hardwood floor, and a pressure-treated deck with a great view of the valley.

Pat was so excited about actually having this cabin that she quickly threw some wood and tools into a helicopter and went straight to the summit. "Time is money," Pat philosophized, as she started hammering away. Soon she needed another tool and more materials, so she rushed back down the mountain, grabbed what she needed, and hurried back up. This process repeated itself again and again and again. Pat never had the right things on hand to complete the job efficiently, although on every flight back up the mountain she thought she did. But the progress was impressive.

Meanwhile, Casey did not start so quickly. She carefully planned an approach to the construction, organized all the materials she would need, and arranged for them to be delivered just before they were necessary. She intended to have everything on hand to complete each stage in the project.

When Casey eventually arrived at the summit, she had only enough to build the foundation, but it went perfectly. Pat would often peer over and laugh, touting how much more she had accomplished and how much faster. "Time is money!" she would shout. Casey would quietly think, "If time is money, why are you spending as much time going up and down this mountain as you are building?"

It seemed that Pat would complete the project long before Casey. Pat had an insatiable urge to keep building something, and so she was finishing the floor and building parts of the deck with only half the walls and roof complete. Casey had only a foundation, the frame, and the roof completed on her cabin.

Unexpectedly, powerful monsoons fell upon the two builders. Pat watched in horror as the incomplete walls and roof were torn away in the strong winds. She could only stand there helplessly and get drenched, watching her beautiful wood floors split under the intense pounding. Casey, keeping perfectly dry with a solid roof overhead, continued working through the rains, adding wallboard so that her cabin would withstand the wind and completing a magnificent interior, all the time staying warm and dry.

When the monsoons subsided and the sun returned, Pat cleaned up the wreckage and salvaged what she could. Months later, she completed her cabin—it was finished, but it wasn't what she had imagined. She was just glad that it was finally done.

After the storms, Casey had only to spend a few more weeks on the deck before she finished her cabin. While Pat was painfully recovering what she could, Casey was enjoying a wonderful spring in the mountains.

Catastrophes often occur in software development. A competitor releases a product that has more features than you knew about, sooner than you expected. If your work doesn't stand up to that competition, it has to be scrapped or completely reworked.

The approach taken in this book will help you incorporate technologies of OLE 2 into your application in such a way that you can stop completely at a number of points but will still have a lot to show for your efforts.

Section One, "Windows Objects," discusses the basic architecture of the OLE 2 object model. This in itself does not contain much that will be very visible to your customers, but it is the foundation.

Section Two, "Object-Oriented System Features: Files and Data," describes a new way to read and write disk files that is powerful enough in itself that it might be the only technology you exploit in OLE 2. This new method simplifies features such as incremental saves and transactioning. In addition, Section Two deals with the concepts of Uniform Data Transfer, through which you can gain significant performance benefits, especially within suites of applications. That alone might be enough to satisfy immediate demands of your customers. You might also want to exploit OLE 2's drag-and-drop protocol, on which many features in future versions of Windows will be based.

From there, you can work into Section Three, "Compound Documents: OLE," which explores the concepts and necessary code to support Linked and Embedded objects according to the OLE 2 Design Specification for Compound Documents. Linking-and-embedding support by itself is quite valuable, but you can take embedded objects one step further by implementing a powerful user-interface model called in-place activation, otherwise known as Visual Editing, covered in Section Four.

I encourage you to start by reading Chapter 1 to become familiar with all the OLE 2 technologies and how they fit together. Chapter 1 also details the information that is in all the later chapters. From there, set your goal and map out an approach that helps you first build a foundation on which you build basic structures like walls and roofing. After that, you can add all the finishing touches on the inside, all the time keeping dry when the monsoons come.

Kraig Brockschmidt
Redmond, Washington
September, 1993

Using the Companion Disks

Bound into the back of this book are two 3.5-inch, 1.44-megabyte companion disks containing the source code files for all the sample programs described in the book. The files on the floppy disks are compressed and must be expanded and copied to your hard disk before you can use them.

To copy these programs to your hard disk, place your disk in the A drive of your computer and enter the following at the MS-DOS prompt:

```
A:INSTALL
```

The decompression program on the disk will begin, and you will be told what to do at each step of the unpacking process until all files are copied to the hard disk.

You will need at least 6 MB of space on your hard disk for the sample code that accompanies this book.

Of course, you'll need more than 6 MB of free disk space. The MAKEALL.BAT file in the installation directory will automatically build all the samples for all chapters. The default debug build will consume approximately 80 MB of hard disk space. A "retail" build (type *SET RETAIL=1* at the MS-DOS prompt before running MAKEALL.BAT) will consume considerably less disk space but still requires approximately 50 MB or so. Your compiler is likely to need a megabyte or two extra for temporary files it creates along the way, so be sure you have enough room.

SECTION I

WINDOWS OBJECTS

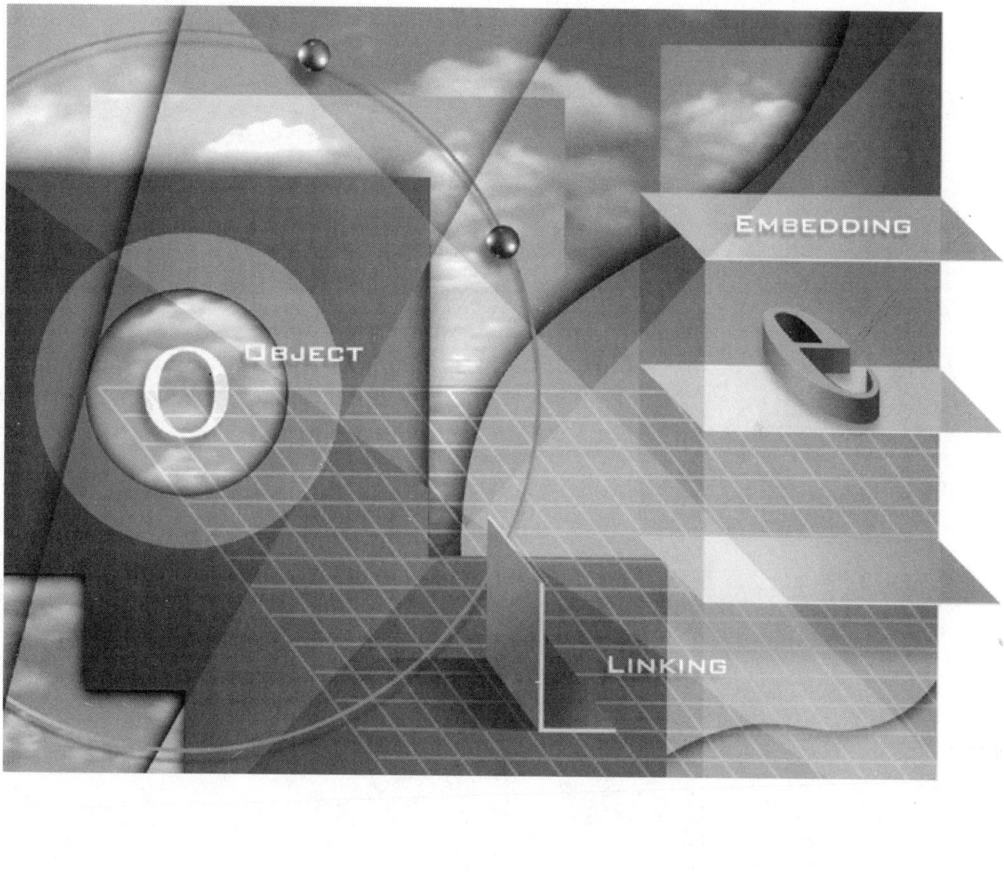

CHAPTER ONE

AN OVERVIEW OF OLE 2

All evolution in thought and conduct must at first appear as heresy and misconduct.

—George Bernard Shaw (1856–1950)

Many years from now, a Charles Darwin of computerdom might look back and wonder how the Microsoft Windows APIs (Application Programming Interfaces) evolved into Windows Objects, an object-oriented operating system. OLE version 2 is the genesis of this transformation—it will change how you program—and eventually how you use—Windows. In the beginning, you'll probably regard it as utterly strange and difficult, no matter what your background. But don't feel too threatened. I won't ask you to throw away any knowledge you've accumulated. Instead, we'll ease into the features of OLE 2 and see how those features, combined with everything you already know, can help you reach new heights in your applications.

Today, Windows' features are exposed to applications through a large—and growing—collection of randomly named API functions. (Remember when you first learned that *DeleteObject* is the opposite of *CreateBrush*?) Every API function is created equal, so to speak, and is accessible from virtually any piece of code, regardless of how useful such access really is. Over the years, many new API functions have emerged, each in its own way describing some new capability of the system, each in its own way providing yet another different set of functions by which an application implements various features, and each with its own naming convention (or lack thereof).

Such an environment is a ripe opportunity for object-oriented tools to flourish. Languages such as C++ and class libraries such as Microsoft's Foundation Classes or Borland's Object Windows Library provide some order in the chaos of the API waters. For example, instead of dealing with a window by means of a handle and numerous API functions spread thinly through the reference manuals, these products shelter a window handle in a C++ object class and directly provide member functions to manipulate the window by means of the object instead of the handle.

In addition, because a member function is always called by means of an object variable, for convenience the names of those functions are located together in the reference manuals, categorized by the object name itself.

In the same manner—and independent of the programming language you choose—OLE 2 exposes system features through what are called "Windows Objects" instead of through API functions. Basically, a Windows Object is a piece of code that exposes its functions through one or more distinct groups of functions. Each group is called an interface. This arrangement provides much-needed order at the system level: Instead of working with disparate handle-based functions, you work with tightly organized system objects. The object model that describes Windows Objects not only describes how the system exposes its functionality to applications but also how applications expose their functionality to the system and to other applications. Realize, too, that the way in which you *expose* an object does not restrict the way in which you can *implement* an object. As we'll see, C++ is the most convenient language in which to express a Windows Object, but you can use other languages just as effectively.

Windows Objects are built on a foundation that also allows an object's code to live anywhere: within a particular application, in a DLL loaded into an application's task, in another application, or even on another machine (in the future, when OLE is network enabled). The object model that OLE 2 introduces lays the evolutionary groundwork for distributed object computing in the years ahead.

OLE 2 exposes a number of key system features, such as the clipboard and the file system, through specific objects. These objects are implemented on top of the existing Windows API functions such as *SetClipboardData* and *OpenFile*. Using these objects today will, of course, cause a decrease in overall performance because you add another layer of function calls to accomplish the same task. For the programmer, however, the overall surface area of API functions is markedly reduced; many of those API functions are moved into member functions of a particular object that you see only when you are manipulating that object. The only globally accessible API functions that remain are a few that initially obtain a pointer to one of the system objects.

Although you will suffer from a performance penalty today, the object implementations of system features will, I believe, gradually become the native expression of those features. The API functions will still be available, but they will be implemented on top of the objects, transferring the performance penalty to those applications that still use the old API functions.

Eventually, the API functions will be provided as some sort of compatibility layer that exists only for the ability to run old applications. All new system features will be provided exclusively by means of objects. Only those applications that have made the transition to using these system objects will be able to benefit from the newest and most powerful features.

This chapter will introduce each specific feature (or technology) of OLE 2, describing briefly how your application might take advantage of it (that is, profit from it) today. By using these features today, you begin to transform your application to more readily take advantage of Windows' future evolution (that is, profit from it tomorrow). The stick that goes along with this proverbial carrot is that you must read this book.

Our latter-day Charles Darwin will then have plenty to say about the origin of a new species of incredibly sophisticated and powerful applications for Windows.

Windows Objects: The Component Object Model

Windows version 1 had about 350 API functions. OLE 2 has over 100. So by measures of new functionality, OLE 2 is roughly one-third of an operating system. By the measure of its impact on your applications, it has appeal as an entire system in itself. It presents as system objects a number of key operating system features such as memory allocation, file management, and data transfer. The huge number of additional features and functions in OLE 2 can be overwhelming. The first step in adopting these new and powerful technologies is to realize that one doesn't learn and exploit a new operating system overnight—there are a few fundamental concepts to learn first. In addition, many higher-level features of any system build on the lower-level features, and OLE 2 is no different. In fact, OLE 2 makes great use of the idea, as shown in Figure 1-1 on the following page.

The first feature is the Component Object Model, which is partly a specification (hence "*Model*") and partly an implementation (contained in COMPOBJ.DLL provided with the OLE 2 SDK). The specification part results from defining a binary standard for object implementation that is independent of the programming language you decide to use. Objects adhering to this standard earn the right to be called Windows Objects. This binary standard enables two applications to communicate through object-oriented interfaces without requiring either to know anything about the other's implementation. For example, you might implement a Windows Object in C++ that supports an interface through which some other code (the user of that object) can learn the names of functions that can be invoked on that object. The

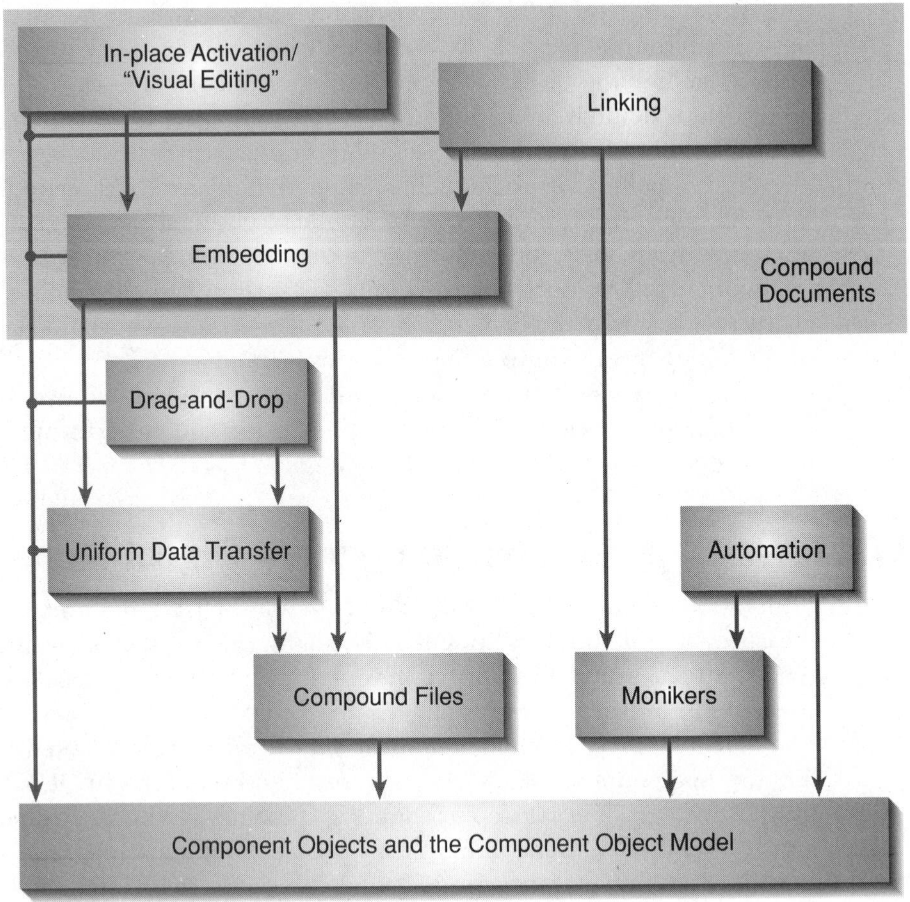

Figure 1-1.
Each feature in OLE 2 builds on lower-level features.

user of this object might be a programming environment such as Visual Basic, or it might be another application written in C, Pascal, Smalltalk, or another language.

The implementation in the component object library (COMPOBJ.DLL) provides a small number of fundamental API functions that allow you to instantiate what is called a *Component Object,* a special type of Windows Object that is identified with a unique class identifier. In return, you are given a pointer to a table of functions (called an interface) that the object implements and through which you can call those functions. This mechanism creates a standard object-creation technique within the system that is independent of the programming language. In addition, this mechanism isolates you from where the actual object is implemented, which could be in a DLL or another EXE. However, you are oblivious to the location because the component object library handles the communication between modules. In the future, the object might live and execute on another machine on your network, an arrangement that would open the way for distributed object architectures under Windows. Although OLE 2 itself does not contain this feature, it has all the necessary mechanisms into which distributed computing will easily fit.

A Windows Object does not always need to be structured as a Component Object in such a way that the API functions in COMPOBJ.DLL can instantiate it. Use of such API functions is merely one way through which you can obtain your first interface pointer to an object.

There are, of course, other API functions and routes in OLE 2 through which you can obtain that first pointer as well—many of the chapters in this book describe how you generally obtain and use a pointer to specific kinds of objects. When implementing an object, how you allow others to get at your object affects your overall code structure. To make objects addressable via the COMPOBJ.DLL API functions, you must "house" them inside either a DLL (dynamic link library) or an EXE (executable) with specific code—that is, specific functions you call and export from your module. The object itself, however, can be independent of the housing, a capability we will explore in Chapter 4.

The other key piece of implementation in COMPOBJ.DLL handles a process called *marshaling*, or passing function calls and parameters across process boundaries. Because an object's code can execute in another process space and eventually on another machine, COMPOBJ.DLL handles translation of calling conventions and 16-bit to 32-bit parameter translation when the object and that object's user are running in different process spaces. For example, an object might be executing in a 32-bit process space, so it treats types such as UINT as 32-bit values. The user of that object might be running in a 16-bit process space and might call a function in the object passing a 16-bit UINT. In the middle sits COMPOBJ.DLL to marshal that UINT from a 16-bit world into a 32-bit world. Other types, such as pointers, memory handles, and so on, are handled in a similar manner: COMPOBJ.DLL makes sure that each side, object and user, sees the other in terms of its own process space. In the future, when the object can execute on another machine, COMPOBJ.DLL will also account for considerations such as byte ordering.

The need for marshaling is not new: OLE 1 also had to move parameters and memory across process boundaries using Dynamic Data Exchange (DDE). A major problem of OLE 1 that resulted from the asynchronous DDE protocol was that a function call made on an object was inherently asynchronous, forcing the caller to sit and wait in a message loop until that function was complete, with all the associated problems of time-outs, error recovery, and blocking other requests on the same object. The marshaling mechanism in OLE 2, Lightweight[1] Remote Procedure Call (LRPC), is inherently synchronous—that is, calls made on objects don't return until completed—simplifying the programming model. Some calls, such as those dealing with event notification, remain asynchronous due to the general uses of those calls.

Objects and Interfaces

A technique that describes a binary standard for objects, such as the Component Object Model, does require some change in typical understanding of what the term *object* really means. *Object* is probably the most overused and ambiguous term in the computer industry. *Object* is used everywhere and often with wildly different meanings; as used in this book the term has a specific meaning. Chapter 3 describes a Windows Object in detail, showing exactly how to implement one in both C and C++. Later chapters illustrate a number of routes by which you can obtain a pointer to a specific type of Windows Object. I warn C++ programmers now that a Windows Object is a little different from a C++ object, although you can effectively use C++ objects to implement Windows Objects.

Another term that requires some explanation here is *interface*, another hackneyed and ambiguous term. The notion of interface that applies throughout this book is defined as "a set of semantically related functions implemented on an object." The word *interface* by itself means the *definition* (or *prototype* or *signatures*) of those functions: The OLE 2 include files contain these definitions. An *instantiation* of what I call an *interface implementation* (because the defined interfaces themselves cannot be instantiated without implementation) is simply an array of pointers to functions. Any code that has access to that array—that is, a pointer through which you can get to the top of the array—can call the functions in that interface, as shown in Figure 1-2. Note that in reality, a pointer to an interface is actually a pointer to a pointer to the function table, but that is a detail we can leave until Chapter 3. Conceptually, however, an interface pointer can be viewed simply as a pointer to a function table in which you can call those functions by dereferencing them by means of the interface pointer.

1. "Lightweight" means "no network"; all calls are made on one machine.

The interface definition allows that code to call functions by name and provides type checking on parameters instead of calling functions by an index into the array. Because it's generally inconvenient to draw function tables in expanded form for every interface, this book and other OLE 2 documentation show each function table as a circle (or a jack) connected to the object, as you can see in Figure 1-2.

A Windows Object implements one or more interfaces—that is, it provides pointers to instantiated function tables for each supported interface. A simple object, such as a data object we'll implement in Chapter 6, supports only one specific interface describing data operations such as *GetData* and *SetData*. More complex objects, such as the compound document objects we'll

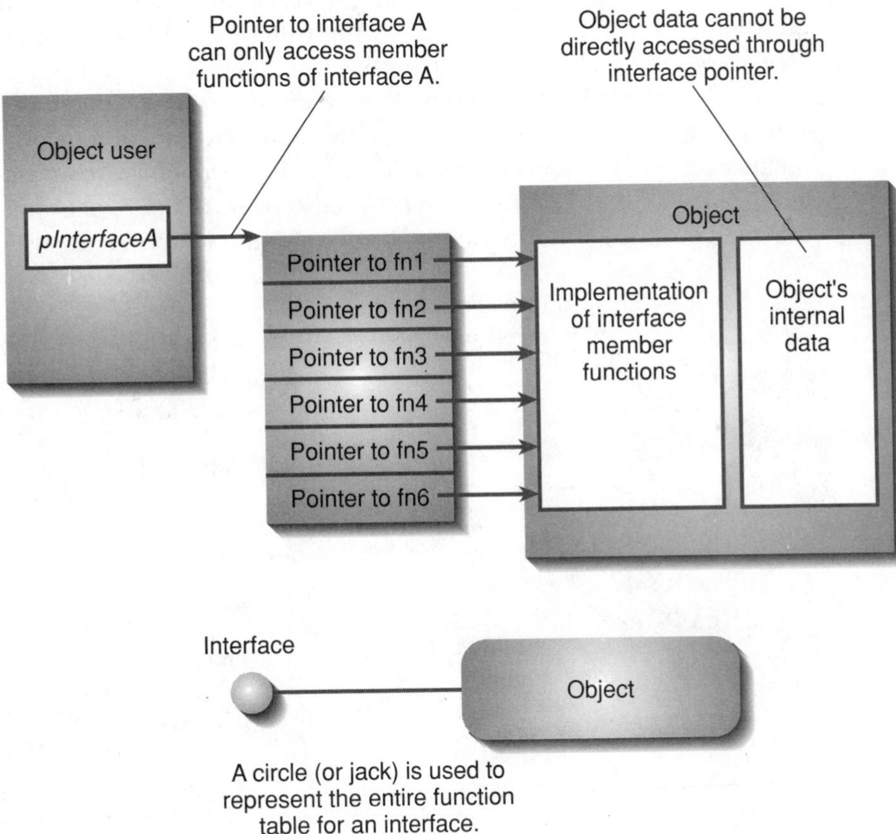

Figure 1-2.
An instantiation of an interface is simply an array of function pointers. A circle (or jack) is a more convenient representation of an interface function table.

implement and use in Chapter 9 and beyond, support at least three interfaces, perhaps more, depending on the features that object implements. Overall, an object is completely described by the collection of interfaces it supports because each separate interface provides the essential manipulation API function to a user of that object.

Whenever the user of some object first obtains a pointer to that object, it has a pointer to only *one interface;* the user never obtains a pointer to the entire object. This pointer allows the user to call only the functions in that one interface's function table, as illustrated in Figure 1-3. Through this pointer, the user has no access to any data members of the object nor does it have any direct access to other interface. In other words, data must be manipulated exclusively through the interface functions, and the interface must have a function through which the caller can obtain a pointer to the object's other interfaces within the object.

Although OLE 2 does not define standard interface functions to access data members of the object, it does define a standard function through which the user of one interface on that object can obtain a pointer to another interface on that object. This function is called *QueryInterface,* as shown in Figure 1-4. We'll examine this function in detail in Chapter 3. When the user queries

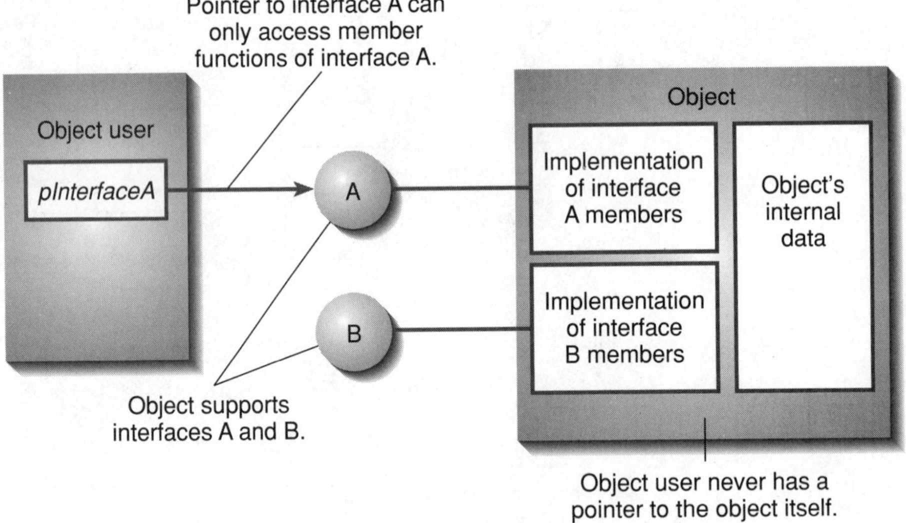

Figure 1-3.
Object users with a pointer to interface A can access only member functions of interface A.

for another interface, it either receives an error (and a NULL pointer), meaning the object does not support the functionality described by the interface, or a valid pointer through which the user might then manipulate the object through that new interface. Because *QueryInterface* is so fundamental, it is part of an interface called *IUnknown* (the *I* stands for *Interface*), which describes the group of fundamental functions that all Windows Objects support, no matter how unknown they are in other respects. All other interfaces in OLE 2 are derived from *IUnknown*, so all interfaces contain the *QueryInterface* function. By implementing one interface on a Windows Object, you automatically implement *IUnknown* because the first few functions in each function table will be those of *IUnknown*, as shown in Figure 1-5 on the following page. (The other two members of *IUnknown* are *AddRef* and *Release*.)

Through *QueryInterface* the user of an object can discover the capabilities of that object at run-time by asking for pointers to specific interfaces. By returning a pointer to that interface, the object is contractually obliged to support the behavior specified for that interface. This enables every object to implement as many interfaces as it wants, so that when it meets a user that

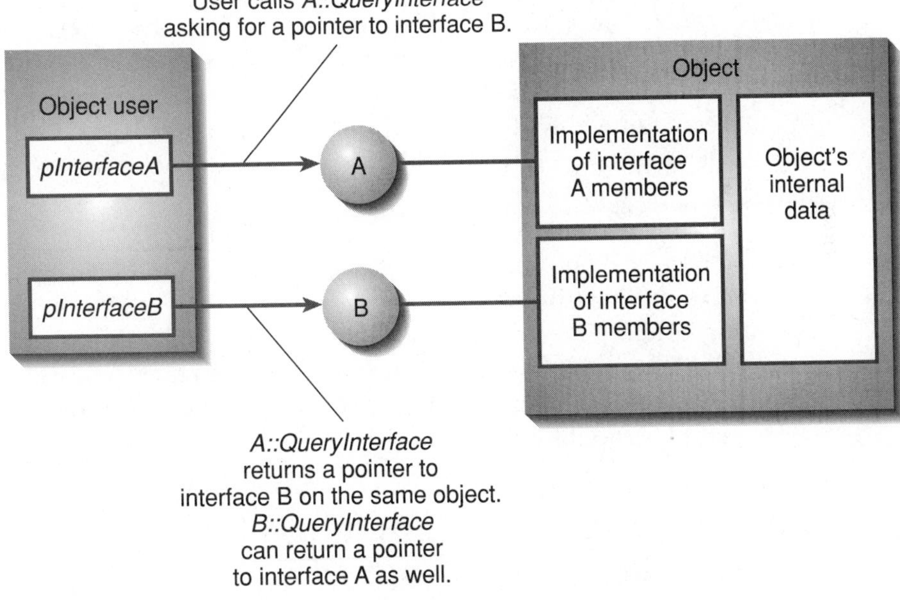

Figure 1-4.
An object user asks the QueryInterface *member of any interface to retrieve pointers to other interfaces on the same object.*

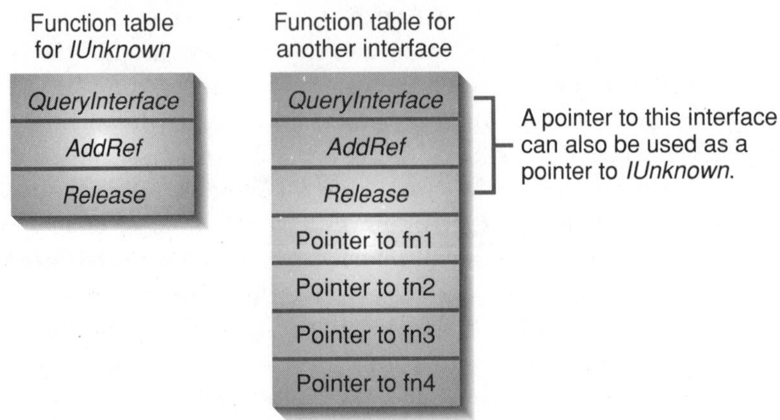

Figure 1-5.
The first few members of any interface are always IUnknown *members. Any interface is therefore polymordial with* IUnknown.

knows how to use many of those interfaces, the two can communicate on a high level. When the object meets a user that knows fewer interfaces, the two can still communicate through the common set of interfaces they both understand—that is, if an object implements interfaces A, B, and C, but the user only knows how to make use of interface B, the object and user can still communicate, but only through interface B. Because all Windows Objects implement at least *IUnknown*, there is always some rudimentary form of possible dialog.

Although OLE 2 defines a large number of standard interfaces, you are free to define and publish your own custom interfaces without requiring any changes whatsoever to the OLE 2 DLLs or any other part of the Windows operating system. The only complication is that you must also provide a DLL for marshaling support because OLE 2's marshaling knows only its own interfaces. But that is a small price to pay for the ability essentially to publish your own new API without having to wait for a system revision from Microsoft.

Structured Storage and Compound Files

The OLE 2 specification defines a number of storage-related interfaces, collectively called Structured Storage. By definition of the term *interface*, these interfaces carry no implementation. They describe a way to create a "file system within a file," and they provide some extremely powerful features for applications. Instead of requiring that a large contiguous sequence of bytes on the disk be manipulated through a single file handle with a single seek pointer, Structured Storage describes how to treat a single file-system entity as a structured collection of two types of objects—storages and streams—that act like directories and files, respectively.

A stream object is the conceptual equivalent of a single disk file as we understand disk files today. Streams are the basic file-system component in which data lives, and each stream in itself has access rights and a single seek pointer. Streams are named by using a text string (up to 31 characters in OLE 2) and can contain any internal structure you desire.

A storage object is the conceptual equivalent of a directory. Each storage, like a directory, can contain any number of storages (subdirectories) and any number of streams (files), as shown in Figure 1-6. In turn, each substorage can contain any number of storages and streams, until your disk is full.

A storage object does not contain any user-defined data—just as a file-system directory cannot—because it maintains only information related to the storage structure—information about the other streams and substorages that live below it. Each storage has its own access rights—as do streams, a feature that is lacking in MS-DOS directories. Given a storage, you can ask it to

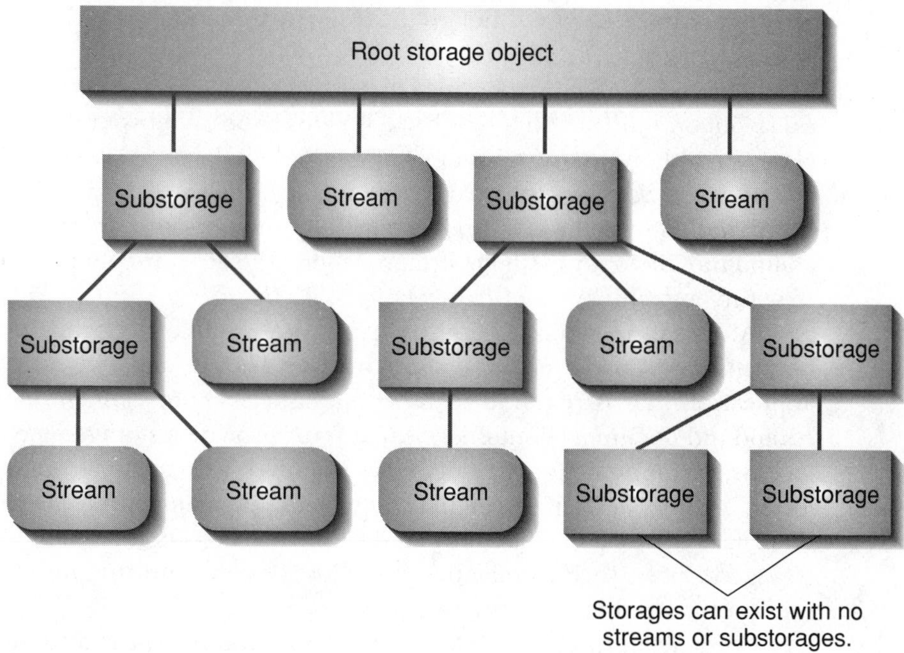

Figure 1-6.
Conceptual structure of storage and stream objects in a compound file.

enumerate, copy, move, rename, delete, or change dates and times of elements within it, providing more than simply the equivalents of MS-DOS commands.

Because Structured Storage is only a specification, OLE 2 provides a complete implementation called Compound Files[2] which you can use to replace a traditional file handle–based API functions such as *_lread* and *_lwrite*. Do not think that the word *compound* as used here means that compound files are useful only to compound document implementations: The compound files technology is completely independent in the OLE 2 package. In fact, it lives independently in STORAGE.DLL and requires only COMPOBJ.DLL to operate. A similar and 100 percent compatible implementation of compound files will also become the native file system in future versions of Windows, and so, as basic technology, it cannot be restricted to high-level integration features such as the Compound Document standard.

Compound files isolate your application from the exact placement of bytes within your file, just as MS-DOS isolates applications from the exact sectors on the hard disk that your file occupies. MS-DOS presents disparate sectors as a contiguous byte array when you access that file by means of a file handle. In the same manner, compound files present information in a stream as one contiguous entity although the exact information in that stream might be fragmented within the actual file itself.

This means that by adopting compound files for your storage, the physical layout of your files on the disk will no longer be under your direct control. However, although you lose control of the physical layout, you still retain control of which data structures are written into which streams within the file. If you don't want to hassle with reorganizing your structures, you can create a compound file with a single stream, where the stream contains the same structure as your existing file format.

Microsoft recognized that changing your on-disk file format might not be an option, so the use of compound files is optional. The only kind of application that is required to use some aspect of this storage model is a compound document container, which must provide a storage object to any contained compound document object. However, you can create a storage object in memory and later write the contents of that memory into your own file format, as detailed in Chapters 5 and 9. Storage objects created on different storage devices, such as memory and disk files, are indistinguishable from one another to the user of those objects.

Aside from future considerations, compound files provide a number of key features that you can use today to make a more powerful application. For

2. Formerly called *DOCFILES*.

example, you could add additional features yourself that would otherwise be too difficult or time-consuming, such as transactioning and incremental saves. Chapter 5 discusses all the features of compound files and demonstrates both simple and complex uses of this technology. All the features can greatly improve an application's design and treatment of storage.

Structured Storage, as well as compound files, is important for a number of reasons, not the least of which is to standardize the layout of pieces of information within a file. Such standardization enables any piece of code, be it the system shell or another application, to examine the structure of the entire compound file. The exact data formats of each individual stream is still private to whatever wrote that data, but anyone can look into a compound file and enumerate the storages and streams it contains. The OLE 2 Software Development Kit (SDK) even contains a tool called DFVIEW.EXE that displays the structure of any compound file and allows you to dump the hex data of any stream.

Further standardization of the names and contents of a few specific streams (but by no means all streams) enables the system shell and other applications to allow end users to search for occurrences of data within files that match attributes such as creation date, author, keywords, and so on. Microsoft is determined to work with other independent software vendors (ISVs) to define standard names and structures for streams that contain information useful in such queries. The long-range goal is to have all information on the file system structured in such a way that end users can browse the contents of many streams using the system shell. This capability is far more powerful, yet easier to use, than requiring the end user to first find a file, then find the application that can load that file, and then use the application to open and browse files to eventually find the data. Structured Storage enables shell-level document searching, an important manifestation of Microsoft's *Information At Your Fingertips* philosophy.

Uniform Data Transfer and Notification

Built on top of both the Component Object Model and the Compound Files technology is a technology in OLE 2 called Uniform Data Transfer, which provides the functionality to represent all data transfers—clipboard, drag-and-drop, DDE, and OLE—through a single piece of code called a *data object.* Such data objects are not restricted to transferring data through global memory either—they can use other mediums such as compound files. In general, a data source can choose the *best* method for data exchange—that is, the most efficient format and medium of transport. End users benefit from better performance. Add that to direct, streamlined capabilities such as drag-and-drop and you have a more usable environment overall.

Up to now, all data transfer between an application and anything external (for example, clipboard, drag-and-drop, DDE, or OLE 1) has used global memory. The specific data format contained in that global memory was described by using a clipboard format such as CF_TEXT or CF_BITMAP. Windows (not to mention the programmer) has suffered immensely from inherent limitations of global memory transfers as well as from having radically different protocols and unrelated API functions for exchanging data via clipboard, drag-and-drop, DDE, and OLE 1.

OLE 2 makes two major improvements. First, it allows you to describe data using not only a clipboard format, but also a specification about how much detail the data contains, what type of device (primarily printers) it was rendered for, and what sort of medium is used to transfer the data. This new method of describing and exchanging data, which we'll examine in Chapter 6, is much more powerful than anything previously available. Instead of simply saying "I have a DIB," I can say "I have a thumbnail sketch of a DIB rendered for a 300 dots per inch (dpi) PostScript printer, and it lives in a storage object." For a source of data, you can choose the best possible medium in which to transfer data, and you can make it the preferred format, providing other mediums as backups (such as global memory, the lowest common denominator). So if you happen to generate 30-MB 24-bit DIBs, you can keep those in disk files or storage objects, even during a data exchange. You don't have to load that entire DIB into memory simply for such a transfer.

Data transfer in OLE 2, therefore, can use a compound file, disk file, global memory, or whatever medium is most preferable for data. Understanding that data transfer works on top of compound files, you can see how this OLE 2 feature builds on a lower feature, much in the way that today's clipboard takes advantage of Windows' kernel memory allocation primitives.

Secondly, OLE 2 separates the means of setting up a data exchange—the protocol—from the actual operation of exchanging data. The problem today is that the four transfer protocols (clipboard, File Manager drag-and-drop, DDE, and OLE 1) use widely different functions and widely different data structures, and each has its own limitations. Under OLE 2, applications use new API functions to transfer a *pointer* to a data object from the data source to the consumer of that data. These API functions form the protocol, as discussed in Chapters 6 through 8. After this pointer has been exchanged, the protocol disappears, and all exchange of data happens through the data object. In other words, the protocol worries about exchanging a data object; the data object standardizes how to exchange data rendered in some medium independent from the protocol. Because the data object does not know anything about protocols, you can write one piece of code to perform an operation such as Paste regardless of how you obtained the data object, hence the "Uniform" in Uniform Data Transfer.

Notification

Consumers of data from an external source are generally interested in when that data changes. OLE 2 handles notifications of this kind through an object called an *advise sink*—that is, a body that absorbs asynchronous notifications from a source. The advise sink not only handles notifications for data changes, but it also is generally used to detect changes in another compound document object, such as when it's saved, closed, or renamed. We'll first see advise sinks in Chapter 6, and we'll see them again in Chapter 9 and beyond.

Data Objects and the Clipboard

Applications can first make use of data objects for Cut and Copy clipboard operations. As Chapter 7 shows, a data object is programmatically similar to common clipboard-handling code. When your data object renders data, you use the same functions you used to generate a handle to pass to *SetClipboardData*. When your data object is asked to enumerate the formats it supports, it does so in the same order your clipboard code always has. In fact, a data object used for Copy and Cut operations can be implemented on top of whatever clipboard-handling code you currently have, with some minor modifications, primarily to handle delayed rendering if you have not already.

Pasting data from the clipboard is a matter of retrieving a data object that describes what data is currently on the clipboard. Instead of asking about availability with *IsClipboardFormatAvailable*, you ask such a data object whether it can render a specific format for whatever device, content, and transfer media you want. If the data object can provide the data, you can, at any time, ask for a rendering through the object instead of through *GetClipboardData*.

Data Objects and Drag-and-Drop

Converting an application so that it uses data objects for clipboard transfers is not much of a benefit in and of itself. However, after you have the data object implemented for the clipboard, you can use that same implementation for drag-and-drop. OLE 2 does not deal with the simplistic drag-and-drop of files from File Manager: OLE 2 provides for *full* drag-and-drop of *any* data that you could transfer through the clipboard. Instead of being limited to files or maybe simply to compound document objects, you can write your application to drag and drop any data that you can describe in a data object.

Think of drag-and-drop as a streamlining your existing clipboard operations by eliminating menus, allowing direct manipulation, and providing dynamic feedback to the user about what data is being dragged and what might happen if the data is dropped. In this model, the source of the drag provides the data object, determines what starts and stops the operation, and controls the mouse-cursor–related user interface. The target of a drag receives the data object, checks for usable formats, and determines what will happen with the data if it's dropped inside the target window.

Drag-and-drop is a tremendous user benefit, and if you implement a data object for the clipboard first, your drag-and-drop implementation is close to trivial, as we'll see in Chapter 8: An implementation will not take more than a few days, depending on how fancy you want to get. For the simplest implementation of a drop source you can copy code straight from this book and probably have it working in under an hour. Targets are a little more complicated, but simple targets could be written in an afternoon. You won't find another feature this powerful and this easy to implement.

Data Objects and Compound Documents

Drag-and-drop is not the end; implementing linking and embedding (what we call Compound Document technology) involves augmenting the data object to handle OLE 2 formats to describe both linked and embedded objects. You will modify your data object code to enumerate and render a few new formats; most of the rendering can be delegated to functions already implemented in the OLE 2 SDK's sample code. We'll examine how the Compound Document technology affects data transfers in various ways in Chapter 9 and beyond.

After you have augmented the data object for OLE 2 formats, you instantly enable transfers of Compound Document objects via clipboard and drag-and-drop because neither mechanism cares what the data object actually contains. In addition, by providing OLE 2 clipboard formats in a data object, OLE automatically generates OLE 1 formats for backward compatibility. With an OLE 2 application, you get such backward compatibility for free by simple virtue of using a data object.

If you are familiar with OLE 1, you need to be aware that exchange of an object's native data is now handled through a storage object that represents the part of the container's compound file that is set aside for the object. In OLE 1, the object was asked to allocate global memory and copy its native data into it. In OLE 2, the object instead is given the storage object pointer through which it writes its native data as if it were writing to a file, resulting in much better performance.

Data Objects and DDE

OLE 2 itself doesn't attempt to address data transfers with DDE by use of data objects, for reasons outlined in Chapter 6. It is possible to design a protocol that you could use to isolate your application from DDE and treat it, again, with a data object just as you would treat any other data transfer. Although such a design is outside the scope of this book, it would allow us to come full circle, supporting the four data exchange mechanisms in Windows by means of data objects, and keeping different protocols to retrieve a data object, but treating that data object uniformly from that point onward.

Compound Documents: Object Embedding

The Component Object Model, Compound File, Uniform Data Transfer, and Drag-and-Drop technologies constitute the bulk of OLE 2 that is not concerned with creating applications to support compound documents. The rest of OLE 2 supports what is known as *linking and embedding*. The Compound Document technology is now only a subset of the OLE 2 functionality[3] which builds on the lower-level technologies, as illustrated previously in Figure 1-1 on page 6. The Compound Document technology is first and foremost a standard for integration between applications that follows the standards provided in the lower layers: the Component Object Model standardizes how an object and object user communicate; compound files standardize file structure; Uniform Data Transfer standardizes data exchange functions.

A compound document is essentially a collection site for data from a variety of other sources (that is, other applications). A word processor document, for example, might contain a chart, a table, a metafile drawing, and a bitmap, all of which were created in different applications. Before Object Linking and Embedding, you created such documents by creating the data in another application, copying it to the clipboard, and then pasting it into the document as what we can generically (and rather loathingly) call an object. The clipboard works very well for creating objects, but it does not work so well for later making modifications to those objects because the pasted data no longer retains any information about the application that created it, and it does not retain any of the native data structures that the application used to create it. So when end users want to modify an object, they first have to remember which application was used to create the object, manually locate and launch that application, and then attempt to copy and paste the object back into that application for editing. Because almost all of the native data

3. A historical note: OLE 1 was concerned only with compound documents and provided no other technologies.

structures used to create that object were lost, what is pasted is not what was originally created or even what was originally in the compound document. In most cases, end users were lucky if they could make this work.

The solution to this before OLE was that the application creating an object—what we call a server—and the application that maintained the compound document—what we call a container—shared some sort of private protocol between them, allowing a higher-fidelity transfer. The problem was that no one wanted to maintain private protocols for every other application on the market, and so there had to be a standard. OLE's Compound Document technology is that standard. The server packages its objects so that they are usable in any container written to understand those packages. Because both applications write to a standard instead of to each other, they can achieve high-fidelity integration without any specific knowledge of the other. They communicate through standard OLE interfaces, which provide for editing (or otherwise manipulating) an object, exchanging an object's data, and storing the object's native data structures somewhere in the compound document itself. Custom interfaces allow two applications to achieve even tighter integration than what OLE itself provides, but the existence of such interfaces does not interfere with the standard interfaces because of the *QueryInterface* mechanism mentioned earlier, in the "Objects and Interfaces" section. For most purposes, OLE's Compound Document technology eliminates most of the need for custom interfaces.

Chapter 9 explores container applications that provide site objects that describe places in which an embedded compound document object can live. These site objects implement at least two interfaces, one of which describes containment functions and another that provides functions through which the container is notified of events in the object. Much of the implementation of a container is user-interface oriented, providing dialog boxes such as Paste Special, Insert Object, and Convert Type (new in OLE 2). Fortunately, various groups at Microsoft have contributed to writing a source code library of these dialog boxes as well as other user interface helper functions that should save you tremendous amounts of time implementing a container.

Chapters 10 and 11 explore compound document objects and how to implement them in either DLL or EXE servers. These chapters deal only with embedded objects, which store their private data structures in a storage object provided by the container. This storage object, which is usually some piece of a larger compound file, is for the object's exclusive use. The object can create any kind of structure within that storage object—that is, as many streams and substorages as you want. When asked to save itself, the object writes into this storage, which is essentially writing directly into the container's file. This means that the object is the only agent that needs to access that storage, and it has the ability to access only as much as necessary. This is a stark contrast to OLE 1's Compound Document technology, in which the container always had to load the entire object's data from a file and pass it to the object via global memory. Under OLE 2, containers only need to pass a pointer to the storage object, resulting in much better performance than OLE 1 could achieve.

You will notice that by Chapter 9 the flavor of this book changes from discussions about specific interfaces and what you *can* do with them into step-by-step guides to compound document interfaces and what you *must* do with them. This reflects the shift from the lower-level and more generic interfaces to those that specifically deal with the Compound Document standard. Standards require predictability, so the step-by-step guides in these later chapters describe how exactly to implement that standard. This is very important because when we talk about compound documents, we're talking about the interaction between two applications that don't know about each other, and that means a certain degree of conformity must be met to prevent a radical increase in entropy.

Compound Documents: Object Linking and Monikers

Enabling container and server applications for linking is a matter of dealing with an additional OLE 2 data format (describing a *link source*) and adding a few more interfaces to the objects that each application implements. The addition of linking capabilities requires very few changes to other compound document code that you implement to handle embedding. Chapters 12 and 13 deal with the necessary changes to support linking in a container and in an object server, respectively.

Linking in OLE 2 affects containers more than it did in OLE 1. Containers are more than just consumers of linked objects—they can become link sources in and of themselves. OLE 2 provides the mechanisms by which a container can provide link source information for objects embedded within their documents. Within the same container, therefore, you can create an embedded object to which another object is linked. Chapter 13 deals specifically with this.

Linked objects have been a significant difficulty for programmers since the beginning of OLE. Because the linked object's data lives in a separate file in the file system, links are easily broken when the end user manually changes the location of that file. OLE 1 depended on absolute pathnames to linked files, so any change in that file's location broke the link, even when the relative paths between the container and the linked file remained the same. In addition, OLE 1 could not describe more than one layer of nested objects. To solve most of the link breakage problems, as well as to provide for arbitrarily deep object nestings, OLE 2 introduces a type of object called a *moniker.*

A simple moniker contains a reference to linked data and code that knows how to "bind" that link. Binding means different things for different types of monikers. For instance, binding can mean launching applications, loading files, and requesting pointers to interfaces. The most common use of monikers is to identify the source data for a linked object in a compound document. This generally requires a reference to a file (such as a filename) and an identification of the part of that file that is the actual source of the link. To accommodate this, OLE 2 provides a simple *file moniker* to manage a filename and an *item moniker* to manage some identification for a portion of a file.

A file moniker contains some sort of pathname, which can be as simple as an eight-character filename (with or without a three-character extension) or as complex as a full pathname, drive letter included. A linked object actually maintains two file monikers (and can have other monikers, as well): one with a full pathname to the linked file (such as C:\STATUS\JUNE\REPORT.DOC) and another with a relative pathname (such as ..\JUNE\REPORT.DOC). When a linked object is asked to bind to its source, it first asks the absolute file moniker to bind, which means launching the application that knows how to load the file (based on the extension). It then asks the application for an interface that knows how to load files, and then it asks that interface to load the actual file. If loading fails, the linked object tries to bind the relative moniker, which executes the same process. Although the absolute pathname is the fastest and most reliable way to get to a file, the relative moniker addresses the cases in which an entire directory tree was moved, breaking absolute links but not relative links. The only case that is not handled is when the user moves a source file to a completely new location. That cannot be solved until the operating system is aware of every such change. When that happens, the system will automatically update the link paths without the application knowing or caring.

An item moniker is simply some sort of name that makes sense only to the application that originally created it and provided it as part of a linked object. Binding to an item moniker means asking the application (presumably loaded through a file moniker already) for an interface that knows how to resolve the name into some sort of pointer to an interface on the actual object.

A linked object generally stores complex references in a composite moniker that is a collection or sequence of other simple monikers. Most links are expressed in a composite of one file moniker and one item moniker. Longer sequences of monikers express more complex notions, such as nested objects in which the composite contains many item monikers. An illustration of a composite moniker that contains a file and an item moniker is shown in Figure 1-7.

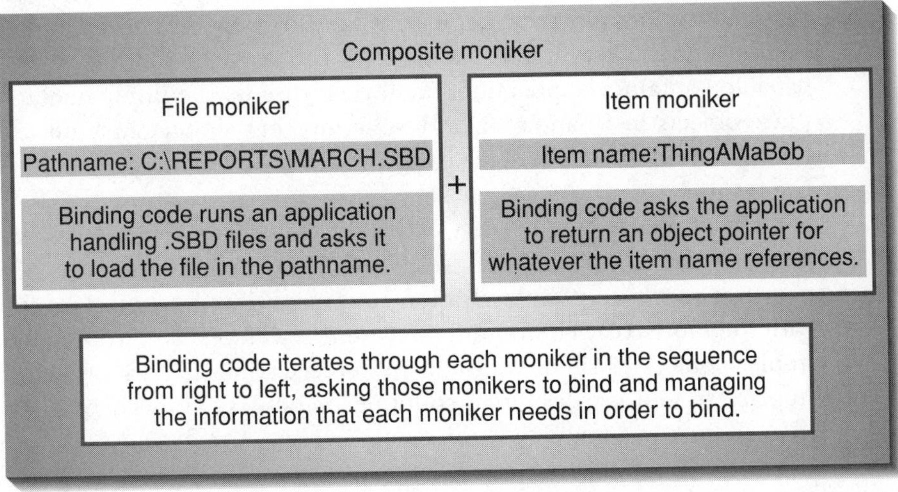

Figure 1-7.
Conceptual file, item, and composite monikers.

Compound Documents: In-Place Activation (Visual Editing™)

The Compound Document technology provides a way to embed an object in or link an object to a container document. The container provides the appropriate functionality to activate the object, which can invoke any number of actions on the object. When the action implies editing, both linked and embedded objects are opened in another window, which provides the editing context, the same model OLE 1 supported.

To stress a document-centric view of computing, OLE 2 provides the ability to *activate* an object in place—inside the container application's window. Editing the object is a subset of the more generic action of activating. Instead of the object opening another window to execute an action, it might choose to provide editing tools or other controls in the context of the container. End users benefit from never having to leave the document context in which they are working—no distractions of other windows and other environments. Instead of seeing two copies of the data, one in the container and one in a separate editing window, end users see only the one in the container, in the full context of its containing document.

Servers, containers, and compound document objects require a number of additional changes and interfaces to support in-place activation, but these build on top of and use much of the compound document implementations that you'll already have done by this time. We'll discuss the mechanisms of in-place activation and the interactions between objects and containers at the beginning of Chapter 15, leading into the implementation of an in-place capable container application. We'll then discuss the implementation of in-place objects in Chapter 16, and we'll end that chapter with an exercise in extrapolation to see where the in-place activation technology might take us in the future.

By implementing in-place activation interfaces, you do not restrict your container or object to being useful only to other in-place applications. The presence of the in-place activation interfaces does not interfere in any way with the more basic compound document interfaces. So if you implement an in-place object, it will be useful to an in-place container, which can activate it in place, as well as to a simpler container, which will always activate the object in a separate window.

Automation

One other key technology that is part of the OLE 2 system but that is completely separate from the rest is OLE Automation. This technology allows an object—any object regardless of other features—to expose a set of commands and functions that some other piece of code can invoke. Each command can take any number of parameters, and automation provides the methods through which an object describes the names and types of those parameters. A full description of this technology, while very rich and exciting, is beyond the scope of this book. In fact, automation is a large enough topic to justify an entire book by itself. These few paragraphs constitute all that I mention in this book about the technology.

The intent of Automation is to enable the creation of system macro programming tools. Such tools will ask automation-enabled objects for lists of their function names and lists of parameters (names and types) that those functions accept. At one point, Microsoft was considering a single system macro programming tool, but this approach would have meant one language and one tool for all end users. Through Automation, OLE 2 allows objects to describe their capabilities to any tool where the tool defines the programming environment. Ultimately this gives the end user the choice of language, vendor, functionality, and so on.

Automation objects generally describe user-level functions on the order of File Open or Format Character; Automation tools display those functions to the user, allowing the user to write macro scripts that span applications.

The major motivation for this mechanism is to pave the way for programming tools that can affect any Automation-enabled object, regardless of whether the system or an application implements that object. When the user chooses an object, such a tool asks the object for its list of function names and exposes to the user the operations that are possible on the object. When the user selects a function to use, the programming tool can further ask the object for the names and types of that function's parameters, and it can provide the environment in which the end user can indicate what to pass in each parameter.

With a system full of such objects from many applications, the end user can use any programming tool that understands Automation to write macros that *could* span applications. A more immediate benefit to your specific application is that such a tool can also write macros that operate only in your application, eliminating the need for you to create your own specific macro language. The end user is then free to choose his or her preferred programming tool, any of which use your Automation interfaces in the same way. The user gains the benefit of having one tool that works with all Automation applications; you benefit from exposing Automation once and letting someone else provide the programming environment.

But it doesn't stop there. Although Automation exposes commands through which external agents invoke your functions, there is no reason whatsoever that you could not invoke those same commands yourself. You might implement Automation on top of your application's message procedure, or you might choose to implement your message procedure on top of Automation. Looking ahead, centralizing such code in the Automation interface might lead to the eventual elimination of message procedures, using instead a more general-purpose and powerful command processing object.

CHAPTER TWO

CONVENTIONS, C++, AND SAMPLE CODE

Throughout this book, we'll watch two applications evolve as we learn how applications can take advantage of the various OLE 2 technologies and what pieces of code are necessary to achieve the apex of in-place activation, which will doubtless be the goal of many readers.

One application will be written from scratch—that is, it will not implement certain features such as file I/O until we can use compound files. This application is suitable to become a container application, but before that time, it will serve to illustrate how to incorporate non-compound-document features.

The other sample is a full-featured application that without doing anything else terribly important uses the traditional Windows API functions from the start, implementing a number of features common to all applications, such as clipboard exchanges and file I/O. As we follow this application through each chapter, we'll replace the use of Windows API functions with the use of OLE 2 technologies, such as converting existing file I/O into compound files. Beginning in Chapter 4, we'll break a piece of this application into a component object DLL and separately develop it into an embedded object capable of in-place activation.

Along the way, we'll also create a number of useful components (either code fragments or DLLs) that you might find helpful in your own implementations.

To C or Not to C (with Apologies to Shakespeare)

The sample code provided in this book is mostly in C++, primarily because the concepts and features of OLE 2 are best expressed in that language. Authoring a book of this sort presents a few philosophical difficulties, such as what language to use, how everything will fit on the companion disks, and how not to alienate a large portion of your audience.

C++ code is smaller and simplifies code reuse, reducing the amount of code I have to write and the amount of code you have to read. C programmers will no doubt be a little put off by this, so in this section I've provided critical explanations of basic C++ concepts and notations that should help the C programmer understand the sample code. While writing the code, I tried to remember that it has to be understandable to a typical C programmer, so I've purposely kept myself from going hog wild about everything C++ can do, such as deep multiple inheritance or long chains of virtual functions. This will no doubt put off a number of C++ programmers, but believe me, it is not as bad as forcing everyone to labor through verbose C.

Another possible source of irritation is that I wrote these samples in C++ using my own class library (called CLASSLIB) instead of a real library such as the Microsoft Foundation Classes, which you might be using and for which you might harbor a religious zeal. The reason is that libraries such as Microsoft Foundation Classes, although very convenient, tend to hide much of what we need to discuss and have a strong tendency to render an application utterly foreign to C programmers, who develop glazed expressions and start asking questions such as "Where is *WinMain*?" and "Where's the window procedure?" All the samples in this book have a *WinMain* (or a *LibMain*) from which you can follow the thread of execution. The class libraries I wrote for this book serve mostly to keep a lot of the basic code for a Windows program out of the way, and they were something I could include on the sample disks.

With the exception of the code to manage the application's data structures, the sample code was originally written in straight C. In fact, these applications were ported from original C versions mostly by changing structures into classes, which represents nearly the extent of my C++ talents. A C programmer briefed on the fundamental rules of C++ should be capable of taking the classes back to structures mostly by means of global search and replace instead of a line-by-line rewrite.

The remainder of this section is intended to be a C++ briefing for C programmers, explaining this newer language from a C perspective so that you can work through the rest of the code in this book. This section does not describe any details about OLE 2 itself but covers the aspects of the C++ language that I used in this book's samples to implement OLE 2 features. (Note that when I use the word *object* in this section I mean a C++ object, not a Windows Object, as I will mean in the rest of the book.) C++ is a matter of convenience and results in much more compact code. I do not claim to be a C++ expert, so please refer to any of the plethora of C++ books available to make more sense out of this language. If you are already comfortable with your C++ knowledge, feel free to skip to the "Sample Code" section of this chapter, which starts on page 41.

User-Defined Types: C++ Classes

Many a C application is built on top of a number of data structures, one of which might be a typical user-defined structure of application variables such as the following:

```
typedef struct tagAPPVARS
    {
    HINSTANCE    hInst;               //WinMain parameters
    HINSTANCE    hInstPrev;
    LPSTR        pszCmdLine;
    int          nCmdShow;

    HWND         hWnd;                //Main window handle
    } APPVARS;

typedef APPVARS FAR *LPAPPVARS;
```

To manage this structure, an application will implement a function to allocate one of these structures, a function to initialize it, and a function to free it.

```
LPAPPVARS AppVarsPAllocate(HINSTANCE, HINSTANCE, LPSTR, int);
BOOL      AppVarsFInit(LPAPPVARS)
LPAPPVARS AppVarsPFree(LPAPPVARS);
```

When another piece of code wants to obtain one of these structures, it calls *AppVarsPAllocate* to retrieve a pointer. Through that pointer, it can initialize the structure with *AppVarsFInit* (which in this case might attempt to create a window and store it in *hWnd*) or access each field in the structure.

By creating this structure and providing functions that know how to manipulate that structure, you have defined a type. C++ formalizes this commonly used technique into a *class* defined by the *class* keyword:

```
class __far CAppVars
    {
    public:
        HINSTANCE    m_hInst;             //WinMain parameters
        HINSTANCE    m_hInstPrev;
        LPSTR        m_pszCmdLine;
        int          m_nCmdShow;

        HWND         m_hWnd;              //Main window handle

    public:
        CAppVars(HINSTANCE, HINSTANCE, LPSTR, int);
```

(continued)

```
        ~CAppVars(void);
        BOOL FInit(void);
    };

typedef CAppVars FAR *LPCAppVars;
```

The name after *class* can be whatever name you want. Although we could have used APPVARS, paralleling the C structure, the name *CAppVars* conforms to a C++ convention of using mixed-case names for classes prefixed with a *C* for *class.* Another convention in C++ classes, at least around Microsoft, is to name data fields with an *m_* prefix to clearly identify the variable as a member of a class.

When another piece of code wants to use this class, it must instantiate a C++ object of this class. In C terms, *CAppVars* is a structure. To use the structure, you still have to allocate one. In C++, we do not need separate functions to allocate the structure, nor do we use typical memory allocation functions. Instead we use C++'s *new* operator, which allocates an object of this class and returns a pointer to it, as follows:

```
LPCAppVars     pAV;

pAV=new CAppVars(hInst, hInstPrev, pszCmdLine, nCmdShow);
```

Because *CAppVars* was declared as *__far, new* allocates far memory and returns a far pointer. If the allocation fails, *new* returns NULL. But this is not the whole story. After the allocation is complete, and before returning, *new* calls the class *constructor* function, which is the funny-looking entry in the following class declaration:

```
    public:
        CAppVars(HINSTANCE, HINSTANCE, LPSTR, int);
```

To implement a constructor, you supply a piece of code in which the function name is *<class>::<class> (<parameter list>)* where *::* means "member function of," as in the following:

```
CAppVars::CAppVars(HINSTANCE hInst, HINSTANCE hInstPrev
    , LPSTR pszCmdLine, int nCmdShow)
    {
    //Initialize members of the object
    m_hInst=hInst;
    m_hInstPrev=hInstPrev;
    m_pszCmdLine=pszCmdLine;
    m_nCmdShow=nCmdShow;
    }
```

The *::* notation allows different classes to have member functions with identical names because the actual name of the function known internally to the compiler is a combination of the class name and the member function name. This allows programmers to remove the extra characters from function names that are used in C to identify the structure on which those functions operate.

The constructor, which always has the same name as the class, can take any list of parameters, but unlike a C function, it has no return value because the *new* operator will return whether or not the allocation succeeded. Because the constructor cannot return a value, C++ programmers typically avoid placing code in the constructor that might fail, opting instead for a second function to initialize the object after it has been positively instantiated.

Inside the constructor, as well as inside any other member function of the class, you can directly access the data members in this object instantiation. The *m_* prefix on data members is the common convention used to distinguish their names from other variables, especially since the names of data members often conflict with parameter names.

Implicitly all the members (both data and functions) are dereferenced off a pointer named *this*, which provides the member function with a pointer to the object that's being affected. Accessing a member such as *m_hInst* directly is equivalent to writing *this->m_hInst*; the latter is more verbose, and so it is not used often.

The code that called *new* will have a pointer through which it can access members in the object just as it would access any field in a data structure:

```
UpdateWindow(pAV->m_hWnd);
```

What is special about C++ object pointers is that you can also call the *member functions* defined in the class through that same pointer. In the preceding class declaration, you'll notice that the functions we had defined separately from a structure are pulled into the class itself. Instead of having to call a function and pass a structure pointer, as follows;

```
//C call to a function that operates on a structure pointer
if (!AppFInit(pAV))
    {
    [Other code here]
    }
```

the caller can dereference a member function through the following pointer:

```
//C++ call to an object's member function
if (!pAV->FInit())
    {
    [Other code here]
    }
```

The *FInit* function is implemented with the same :: notation that the constructor uses:

```
CAppVars::FInit(void)
    {
    //Code to register the window class might go here.

    m_hWnd=CreateWindow(...);    //Create the main app window

    if (NULL!=m_hWnd)
        {
        ShowWindow(m_hWnd, m_nCmdShow);
        UpdateWindow(m_hWnd);
        }

    return (NULL!=m_hWnd);
    }
```

Again, because a constructor cannot indicate failure through a return value, C++ programmers typically supply a second initialization function, such as *FInit*, that performs operations that might be prone to failure.

You could, of course, still provide a separate function outside the class that took a pointer to an object and manipulated it in some way. However, a great advantage of using member functions is that you can only call member functions in a class through a pointer to an object of that class. This prevents all sorts of problems when you accidentally pass the wrong pointer to the wrong function, an act that usually brings about some very wrong events.

Finally, when you are finished with this object, you'll want to perform cleanup on the object and free the memory it occupies. Instead of calling a specific function for this purpose, you use C++'s *delete* operator:

```
delete pAV;
```

delete frees the memory allocated by *new*, but before doing so it calls the object's *destructor*, which is that even-funnier-looking function in the class declaration (with the tilde, ~) but which comes with an implementation like any other member function:

```
//In the class
public:
    ~CAppVars(void);

...

//Destructor implementation
CAppVars::~CAppVars(void)
    {
    //Perform any cleanup on the object.
    if (IsWindow(m_hWnd))
        DestroyWindow(m_hWnd);

    return;
    }
```

The destructor has no parameters and no return value because after this function returns, the object is simply *gone.* Therefore, there is no point in telling anyone that something in here worked or failed because there is no longer an object to which such information would apply. The destructor is a great place—in fact, your only chance—to perform final cleanup of any allocations made in the course of this object's lifetime.

Of course, there are many other ways to define classes and to use constructors, destructors, and member functions than I've shown here. However, this reflects how I've implemented all the sample code in this book.

Access Rights

You probably noticed those *public* labels in the class definition or should, by now, be wondering what they're for. In addition to *public,* two variations of *public* can appear anywhere in the class definition: *protected* and *private.*

When a data member or member function is declared under a *public* label, any other piece of code that has a pointer to an object of this class can directly access those members by means of dereferencing, as follows:

```
LPCAppVars      pAV;
HINSTANCE       hInst2;

pAV=new CAppVars(hInst, hPrevInst, pszCmdLine, nCmdShow);

hInst2=pAV->m_hInst;  //Public data member access

if (!pAV->FInit())      //Public member function access
    {
    [Other code here]
    }
```

When data members are marked as *public,* another piece of code is allowed to change that data without the object knowing, as in the following:

```
pAV->m_hInst=NULL;      //Generally NOT a good idea
```

This is a nasty thing to do to some poor object that assumes that *m_hInst* never changes. To prevent such arbitrary access to an object's data members, you would mark such data members as *private* in the class, as follows:

```
class __far CAppVars
    {
    private:
        HINSTANCE   m_hInst;                //WinMain parameters
        HINSTANCE   m_hInstPrev;
        LPSTR       m_pszCmdLine;
        int         m_nCmdShow;
```

(continued)

```
        HWND        m_hWnd;                 //Main window handle

    public:
        CAppVars(HINSTANCE, HINSTANCE, LPSTR, int);
        ~CAppVars(void);
        BOOL FInit(void);
    };
```

Now code such as *pAV->hInst=NULL* will fail with a compiler error because the user of the object does not have access to private members of the object. If you want to allow read-only access to a data member, provide a public member function to return that data. If you want to allow write access but would like to validate the data before storing it in the object, provide a public member function to change a data member.

Both data members and member functions can be private. Private member functions can be called only from within the implementation of any other member function. In the absence of any label, *private* is used by default.

If a class wants to provide full access to its private members, it can declare another class or a specific function as a *friend.* Any friend code has as much right to access the object as the object's implementation has. For example, a window procedure for a window created inside an object's initializer is a good case for a friend:

```
class __far CAppVars
    {
    friend LRESULT FAR PASCAL AppWndProc([WndProc parameters]);

    private:
        [Private members accessible in AppWndProc]

    ...
    };
```

Any member declared after a *protected* label is the same as *private* as far as the object implementation or the object's user is concerned. The difference between *private* and *protected* manifests itself in derived classes, which brings us to the subject of inheritance.

Single Inheritance

A key feature of the C++ language is code reusability through a mechanism called *inheritance*—that is, one class can inherit the members and implementation of those members from another class. The inheriting class is called a *derived class;* the class from which the derived class inherits is called a *base class.*

Inheritance is a technique to concentrate code common to a number of other classes in one base class—that is, placing the code in a place where other classes can reuse it. Applications for Windows written in C++ typically have some sort of base class to manage a window, as in the following *CWindow* class:

```
class __far CWindow
    {
    protected:
        HINSTANCE    m_hInst;
        HWND         m_hWnd;

    public:
        CWindow(HINSTANCE);
        ~CWindow(void);

        HWND Window(void);
    };
```

The *CWindow* member function *Window* simply returns *m_hWnd*, allowing read-only access to that member.

If you now want to make a more specific type of window, such as a frame window, you can inherit the members and the implementation from *CWindow* by specifying *CWindow* in the class definition, using a colon to separate the derived class from the base class, as follows:

```
class __far CFrame : public CWindow
    {
//CFrame gets all CWindows variables.
    protected:
        //We can now add more members specific to our class.
        HMENU     m_hMenu;

    public:
        CFrame(HINSTANCE);
        ~CFrame(void);

    //We also get CWindow's Window function.
    };
```

The implementation of *CFrame* can access any member marked *protected* in its base class *CWindow*. However, *CFrame* has no access to *private* members of *CWindow*.

You will also see a strange notation in constructor functions:

```
CFrame::CFrame(HINSTANCE hInst) : CWindow(hInst)
```

This notation means that the *hInst* parameter to the *CFrame* constructor is passed to the constructor of the *CWindow* base class first, before we start executing the *CFrame* constructor.

Code that has a pointer to a *CFrame* object can call *CWindow::Window* through that pointer. The code that executes will be the implementation of *CWindow*. The implementation of *CFrame* can, if it wants, redeclare *Window* in its class and provide a separate implementation that might perform other operations, as follows:

```
class __far CFrame : public CWindow
    {
    ...
    HWND Window(void);
    };

CFrame::Window(void)
    {
    [Other code here]

    return m_hWnd;     //Member inherited from CWindow
    }
```

If a function in a derived class wants to call the implementation in the base class, it explicitly uses the base class's name in the function call. For example, we could write an equivalent *CFrame::Window* as follows:

```
CFrame::Window(void)
    {
    return CWindow::Window();
    }
```

In programming, one often finds it convenient to typecast pointers of various types to a single type that contains the common elements. In C++, you can legally typecast a *CFrame* pointer to a *CWindow* pointer, because *CFrame* looks like a *CWindow*. However, calling a member function through that pointer might not do what you expect, as in the following:

```
CWindow * pWindow;
HWND      hWnd;

pWindow=(CWindow *)new CFrame();     //Legal conversion
hWnd=pWindow->Window();
```

Whose *Window* is called? Because it is calling through a pointer of type *CWindow **, this code calls *CWindow::Window*, not *CFrame::Window*.

Programmers would like to be able to write a piece of code that knows only about the *CWindow* class but that is also capable of calling the *Window* member functions of derived class. For example, a call to *pWindow->Window* would call *CFrame::Window* if, in fact, *pWindow* is physically a pointer to a *CFrame.* To accomplish this requires what is known as a *virtual function.*

Virtual Functions and Abstract Base Classes

To solve the typecasting problem described in the previous section, we have to redefine the *CWindow* class to make *Window* a virtual function using the keyword *virtual,* as follows:

```
class __far CWindow
    {
    ...
    virtual HWND Window(void);
    };
```

The *virtual* keyword does not appear in the implementation of *CWindow::Window.*

If *CFrame* wants to override *CWindow::Window,* it then declares the same function in its own class and provides an implementation of *Window,* like this:

```
class __far CFrame : public CWindow
    {
    ...
    virtual HWND Window(void);
    };

CFrame::Window(void)
    {
    [Code that overrides the default behavior of CWindow]
    }
```

Such an override might be useful in a class that hides the fact that it actually contains two windows; the implementation of *Window* would then perhaps return one or the other window handle, depending on some condition.

With *CWindow::Window* declared as *virtual,* the piece of code we saw earlier has a different behavior, as in this:

```
pWindow=(CWindow *)new CFrame();    //Legal conversion
hWnd=pWindow->Window();
```

The compiler, knowing that *CWindow::Window* is virtual, is now responsible for figuring out what type *pWindow* really points to, although the program itself thinks it's a pointer to a *CWindow.* In this code, *pWindow->Window* calls *CFrame::Window.* If *pWindow* really points to a *CWindow,* the same code would call *CWindow::Window* instead.

C++ compilers implement this mechanism by means of a *virtual function table* (sometimes referred to as a *Vtbl*) that lives with each object. The function table of a *CWindow* will contain one pointer to *CWindow::Window.* If *CFrame* overrides the virtual functions in *CWindow,* its table will contain a pointer to *CFrame::Window.* If, however, *CFrame* does *not* override the *Window* function, its table contains a pointer to *CWindow::Window.*

A pointer to any object in certain implementations of C++[1] is really a pointer to a pointer to the object's function table. Whenever the compiler needs to call a member function through an object pointer, it looks in the table to find the appropriate address, as shown in Figure 2-1. So if the virtual

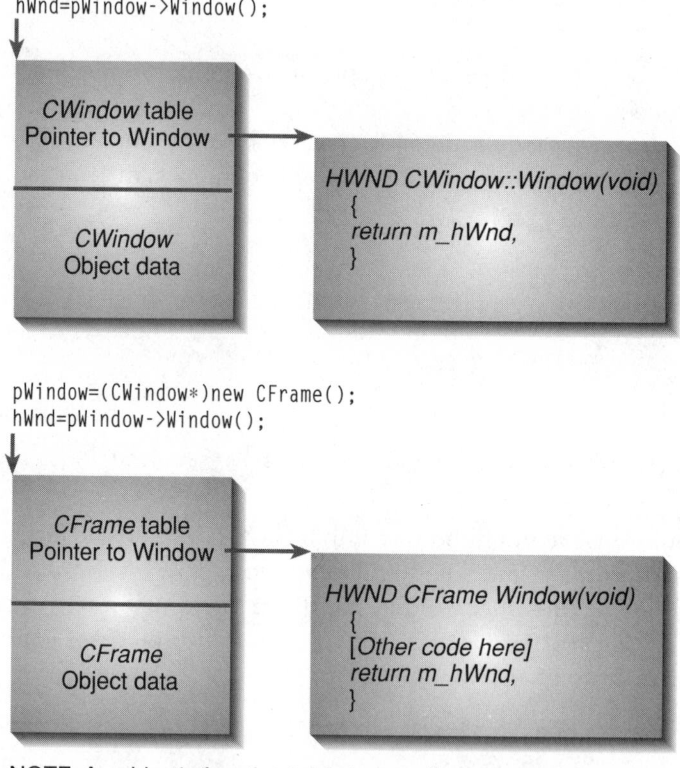

Figure 2-1.
C++ compilers call virtual functions of an object by means of a function table.

1. At least Visual C++ 1.0 and Borland C++ 3.1.

Window of the *CWindow* class and of all derived classes always occupies the first position in the table, calls such as *pWindow->Window* are actually calls to whatever address is in that position.

Virtual functions can also be declared as *pure virtual* by appending *=0* to the function in the class declaration, as follows:

```
class __far CWindow
    {
    ...
    virtual HWND Window(void)=0;
    };
```

Pure virtual means "no implementation defined," which renders *CWindow* into an *abstract base class*—that is, you cannot instantiate a *CWindow* by itself. In other words, pure virtual functions do not create entries in an object's function table, so C++ cannot create an object through which someone might try to make that call. As long as a class has at least one pure virtual member function, it is an abstract base class and cannot be instantiated, a fact compilers will kindly mention.

An abstract base class tells derived classes "You *must* override my pure virtual functions!" A normal base class with normal virtual functions tells derived classes "You *can* override these, *if you really care.*"

You might have noticed by now that an OLE 2 interface is exactly like a C++ function table, and this is intentional. OLE 2's interfaces are defined as abstract base classes, so an object that inherits from an interface must override every interface member function—that is, when implementing an object in C++, you must create a function table for each interface, and because interfaces themselves cannot create a table, you must provide the implementations that will. OLE 2, however, does not require that you use C++ to generate the function table; although C++ compilers naturally create function tables, you can just as easily write explicit C code to do the same.

Multiple Inheritance

The preceding section described single inheritance—that is, inheritance from a single base class. C++ allows a derived class to inherit from multiple base classes and thus to inherit implementations and members from multiple sources. The samples in this book do not use multiple inheritance, although there are no technical reasons preventing them from doing so. They use only single inheritance to remain comprehensible to C programmers who are just beginning to understand the concept. In any case, multiple inheritance is evident in the following class declaration:

```
class __far CBase
    {
    public:
        virtual FunctionA(void);
        virtual FunctionB(void);
        virtual FunctionC(void);
    };

class __far CAbstractBase
    {
    public:
        virtual FunctionD(void)=0;
        virtual FunctionE(void)=0;
        virtual FunctionF(void)=0;
    };

//Note the comma delineating multiple base classes.
class __far CDerived : public CBase, public CAbstractBase
    {
    public:
        virtual FunctionA(void);
        virtual FunctionB(void);
        virtual FunctionC(void);
        virtual FunctionD(void);
        virtual FunctionE(void);
        virtual FunctionF(void);
    };
```

An object of a class using multiple inheritance actually lives with multiple function tables, as shown in Figure 2-2. A pointer to an object of the derived class points to a table that contains all the member functions of all the base classes. If this pointer is typecast to a pointer to one of the derived classes, the pointer actually used will refer to a table for that specific base class. In all cases, the compiler dutifully calls the function in whatever table the pointer referenced.

Of course, there are limitations to using multiple inheritance, primarily when the base classes have member functions with the same names. In such cases, the object can have only one implementation of a given member that is shared between all function tables, just as each function in Figure 2-2 is shared between the base class table and the derived class table.

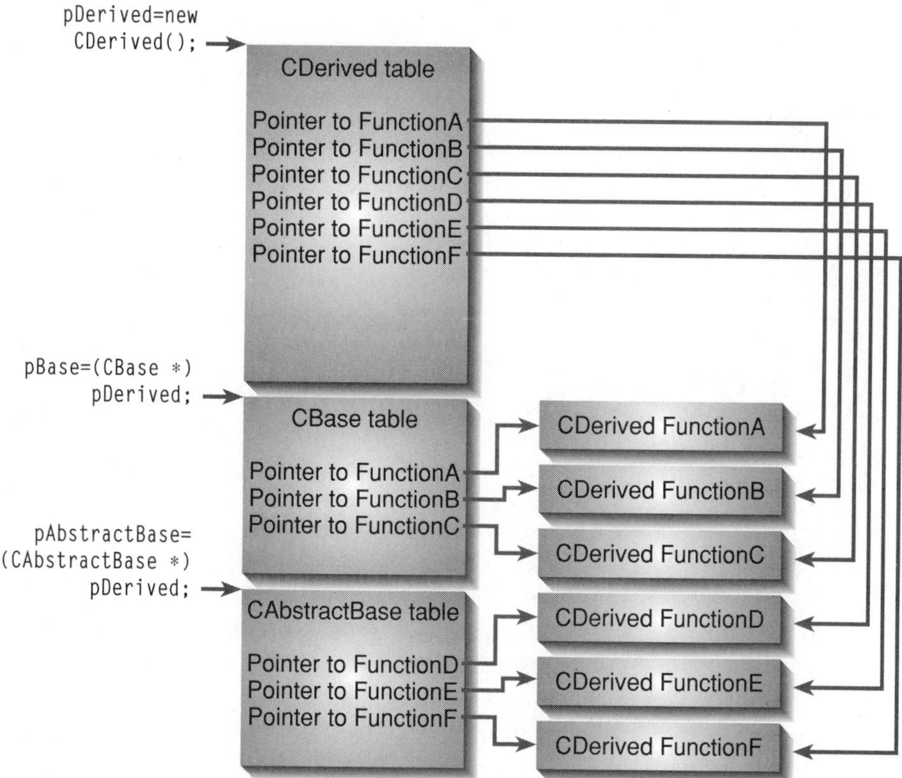

Figure 2-2.
Objects of classes using multiple inheritance contain multiple tables.

Sample Code

In case you have not noticed already, this book contains quite a lot of sample code, enough to require two companion disks. After installing the sample code on your own machine, you will have a number of directories with the contents shown in Table 2-1.

This book follows the development of two applications that you'll find in many CHAP*xx* directories in the sample code: Cosmo and Patron. Both of these applications will compile into single-document or multiple-document versions, depending on the build environment you want. They both make use of a common code base in CLASSLIB, and they use the BTTNCUR, GIZMOBAR, and STASTRIP DLLs to provide user interface components. Most of the sample code depends on the contents of the INC and LIB directories as well, including Cosmo and Patron. To make the purpose of all the code clear, the following sections deal with each directory in detail.

Directory	Contents
INC	Include (.H) files used by more than one sample.
LIB	Libraries (.LIB files) used by more than one sample.
BUILD	A repository for built DLLs and EXEs so that you can include this one directory in your PATH command. Before you build any of the other samples, this directory will contain a build of the OLE2UI library that is shipped with the OLE 2 SDK, customized for the samples in this book (in the file BOOKUI.DLL).
BTTNCUR	Version 1.1 update of the Buttons & Cursors DLL. Compiles into BTTNCUR.DLL.
GIZMOBAR	An implementation of a toolbar, called the GizmoBar, which compiles into GIZMOBAR.DLL.
STASTRIP	An implementation of a status-line control, StatStrip, which compiles into STASTRIP.DLL and includes a small test program in the DEMO directory.
CLASSLIB	A specific C++ class library as used by the more feature-laden samples.
INTERFAC	Template implementations for all the OLE 2 interfaces discussed in this book.
CHAP*xx*	Sample code for Chapter *xx*.

Table 2-1.
Directories created after the companion disks are installed.

Include Files: The INC Directory

The INC directory is a repository for any .H file that is used from more than one application. The files stored in the directory and their use are listed in Table 2-2:

File	Purpose
BOOK1632.H	Macros that isolate the application from Win16 and Win32 differences.
BOOKGUID.H	Definitions of Globally Unique Identifiers (CLSIDs and IIDs) used in all samples in this book, as well as anything else generally useful to all samples, such as OLE 2-related macros.

Table 2-2. *(continued)*
Contents of the INC directory in the sample code.

Table 2-2. *continued*

File	Purpose
BTTNCUR.H	Definitions for BTTNCUR.DLL. Identical to BTTNCUR\BTTNCUR.H.
CLASSLIB.H	Include file for the class library. Identical to CLASSLIB\CLASSLIB.H.
CLASSRES.H	Resource constants for applications using the class library. Identical to CLASSLIB\CLASSRES.H.
DEBUG.H	Macros to facilitate simple debug output.
IENUM0.H	A file shared by both samples in Chapter 3.
IPOLY*x*.H	Definitions for a POLYLINE.DLL from Chapters 4, 5, and 6, where *x* represents the applicable chapter. See the later section titled "Cosmo: A Graphical Editor."
GIZMOBAR.H	Definitions for GIZMOBAR.DLL. Identical to GIZMOBAR\GIZMOBAR.H.
STASTRIP.H	Definitions for STASTRIP.DLL. Identical to STASTRIP\STASTRIP.H.

Note in Table 2-2 that a number of the files in this directory are duplicates of those found in other directories. This is simply to provide you with an environment in which you can immediately compile any of the chapter-specific samples. To build the sample for any chapter, you must add this directory to those listed in your INCLUDE environment variable.

Libraries: The LIB Directory

Like the INC directory, the LIB directory is a repository for any .LIB that is useful to more than one sample. For the most part, the files found here are builds of their respective components, as listed in Table 2-3.

You can, of course, build each of these LIBs from the respective sources at your disposal, but you must first build BTTNCUR to build GIZMOBAR; you must build both of those and STASTRIP to build CLASSLIB; and you must build CLASSLIB to build most of the chapter samples. The builds provided on the companion disks are simply intended to save you the trouble of such interdependencies.

The BUILD Directory

As was mentioned earlier, the BUILD directory is the respository for builds of DLL and EXE samples. After installing the companion disks, this directory will contain the files shown in Table 2-4.

File	Purpose
BOOKUI.LIB	Import library for BOOKUI.DLL.
CLASSMDI.LIB	A Multiple Document Interface (MDI) build of the class libraries in CLASSLIB.
CLASSSDI.LIB	A Single Document Interface (SDI) build of the class libraries in CLASSLIB.

Table 2-3.
Contents of the LIB directory in the sample code.

File	Purpose
BOOKUI.DLL	A build of the OLE2UI library provided with the OLE 2 SDK specifically named for this book.
DATATRAN.DLL	A build of the Data Transfer object from the source code in \CHAP07\DATATRAN.
LNKASSIS.DLL	A build of the Link Assistant object from the source code in \CHAP12\LNKASSIS.

Table 2-4.
Contents of the BUILD directory in the sample code.

You should ensure that the BUILD directory is in your PATH command, because many samples depend on these files at run-time. Note that the versions of BTTNCUR.DLL and GIZMOBAR.DLL provided with the OLE 2 SDK are the same as the ones provided here, so you do not need to worry about the location of the BUILD directory in your path relative to the OLE 2 directory.

NOTE: Before you build any other projects described in this book, be sure to run the MAKEALL.BAT files in the \BTTNCUR, \GIZMOBAR, and \STASTRIP directories so that you have BTTNCUR.DLL, GIZMOBAR.DLL, and STASTRIP.DLL in the \BUILD directory and BTTNCUR.LIB, GIZMOBAR.LIB, and STASTRIP.LIB in the \LIB directory. These files must be built in this order because GizmoBar needs the Buttons & Cursors library. The MAKEALL.BAT file in the installation directory builds these files in the correct order for you.

Three Amigos: BttnCur, GizmoBar, and StatStrip

To fully demonstrate all the user interface affected by in-place activation and to add some spice to the samples, we need a few slick controls, such as a toolbar and a status line. The GizmoBar, whose source code is in the GIZMOBAR directory, is an implementation of a typical toolbar control that builds on code provided in BttnCur, a DLL that draws up to six states (for example, up, down, disabled, and so on) of toolbar buttons from a single bitmap image. The GizmoBar uses BttnCur to draw its buttons, but it is also capable of containing any other standard Windows control. The GizmoBar is not able to hold arbitrary custom controls, however.

NOTE: The code for BttnCur is a version 1.1 refinement of BttnCur 1.0 that was included with *The Windows Interface: An Application Design Guide* from Microsoft Press. Version 1.1 has two major feature enhancements—support for different display resolutions and full color control, which allows the standard black/white/gray buttons to change with the system colors.

The StatStrip control provides a rudimentary message bar that generally is placed at the bottom of frame windows. The StatStrip is capable of managing a number of strings and displaying one of those strings on request. It also provides an almost painless way of tracking menu selections and displaying the appropriate message for each item. If you are interested in this mechanism, please study the sources in the STASTRIP directory.

NOTE: Sources for both BttnCur and GizmoBar are included with the OLE 2 SDK. The source code provided with this book is slightly and innocuously altered from the code in the OLE 2 SDK, but both sources build identical DLLs.

All three of these DLLs are implemented in straight C, mostly because they were projects that I wrote prior to writing this book. As I mentioned earlier, GizmoBar makes use of BttnCur, so you must build the latter to build the former.

Class Libraries: The CLASSLIB Directory

I mentioned earlier that I did not use a real C++ class library or an "application frameworks" to implement these samples. However, I still wanted to keep much of the mundane Windows code out of the way as we work through OLE 2, so I concentrated as much code as was reasonable into my own class library, which you'll find in the CLASSLIB directory. This code will compile into either an MDI version (CLASSMDI.LIB) or an SDI version (CLASSSDI.LIB), builds of which are provided in the LIB directory. The primary *include* file for these libraries is CLASSLIB.H, with resource definitions in CLASSRES.H.

Both Cosmo and Patron, as well as a few other samples in this book, make use of CLASSLIB. CLASSLIB essentially provides the framework for a simple application so that when we need to add a feature or a customization, we only need to override the applicable virtual functions in the default CLASSLIB classes with a more specific implementation. To see how much CLASSLIB provides on its own, you only need to create a "frame window" object, initialize it, and tell it to start spinning in a message loop.

```
#include <windows.h>
#include <classlib.h>

/*
 * WinMain
 *
 * Purpose:
 *  Main entry point of application. Should register the app class
 *  if a previous instance has not done so and do any other one-time
 *  initializations.
 */

int PASCAL WinMain (HINSTANCE hInst, HINSTANCE hPrev
    , LPSTR pszCmdLine, int nCmdList
    {
    LPCFrame        pFR;
    FRAMEINIT       fi;
    WPARAM          wRet;

    //Attempt to allocate and initialize the application
    pFR=new CFrame(hInst, hPrev, pszCmdLine, nCmdShow);

    fi.idsMin=IDS_STANDARDFRAMEMIN;
    fi.idsMax=IDS_STANDARDFRAMEMAX;
    fi.idsStatMin=IDS_STANDARDSTATMESSAGEMIN;
    fi.idsStatMax=IDS_STANDARDSTATMESSAGEMAX;
    fi.idStatMenuMin=ID_MENUFILE;
    fi.idStatMenuMax=ID_MENUHELP;
    fi.iPosWindowMenu=WINDOW_MENU;
    fi.cMenus=CMENUS;

    //If we can initialize pFR, start chugging messages
    if (pFR->FInit(&fi))
        wRet=pFR->MessageLoop();

    delete pFR;
    return wRet;
    }
```

You can find code identical to this in CHAP02\SKEL, which builds a skeletal application based on CLASSLIB, complete with toolbar and status line, using (of course) GIZMOBAR.DLL and STASTRIP.DLL.

With this class library, the code to implement both Cosmo and Patron deals almost exclusively with the special features of each application. In this way, we keep the typical windowing code out of our way to show only the application features and how OLE 2 affects them. Throughout this book, CLASSLIB will remain unaltered—all modifications to accommodate OLE 2 will be made only in the respective application's source code.

All of the C++ classes defined in CLASSLIB are shown in Table 2-5. Note, however, that this class library is not intended to be a basis for your own application (but, of course, there's nothing stopping you). I do not intend to revise this library, and I certainly will not be able to provide the level of product support for this code that you would get with a real class library from a reputable tools vendor. I do encourage you to use a professional development environment in your own endeavors to produce applications.

Class	Purpose
CStringTable	Loads a range of strings from the application's resources into memory and provides an overloaded [ ] (array lookup) operator to access those strings.
CWindow	Base class for other window-related classes.
CGizmoBar	A C++ wrapper class for the control implemented in GIZMOBAR.DLL.
CStatStrip	A C++ wrapper class for the control implemented in STASTRIP.DLL.
CFrame	Creates and manages a frame window that owns a menu, toolbar, and a client window. Compiles differently for MDI and SDI cases.
CClient	Creates and manages a client window identical to an MDI client window for MDI cases. Under SDI, provides a client window that responds to the MDI messages, isolating the rest of the application from many MDI/SDI differences.
CDocument	Creates and manages a document window inside the client window. The window is either an MDI child or a simple child window, depending on the build.

Table 2-5.
C++ classes in CLASSLIB and their uses.

CLASSLIB also contains resource files necessary for building a skeletal application. These resource files are the ones used by CHAP02\SKEL. These are not compiled into the library itself, but reside here as templates for applications using this library.

Note the use of one macro in CLASSLIB.H that might appear odd: *PSZ(i)* where *i* is an integer string identifier, always with an *IDS_* prefix. The *PSZ* macro simplifies the lookup of the string of that index in a *CStringTable* object that manages stringtable resources. When reading the code in this book, read *PSZ* as meaning "this string from the stringtable." A quick look in the .RC file for the relevant sample will show you exactly which string is being referenced.

Interface Templates: The INTERFAC Directory

C++ programmers: Don't get your hopes up. The INTERFAC directory contains a large number of .CPP and .H files—one for each interface—that we'll explore throughout this book. These are not official "C++ templates," rather they are interface templates that are simply source files containing a stubbed or default implementation for each interface. In some cases, a file will contain a complete implementation of a specific type of Windows Object, implemented using a C++ object class. In most other cases, the files simply contain stubbed functions that are meant to serve as a respository for source code from which you can copy and paste into your own applications, an approach that requires much less work than typing all the function headers themselves. You can easily customize this code with a few quick search-and-replace passes in your favorite editor.

Chapter Sources: The CHAP*xx* Directories

The specific source code related to a specific chapter is found in the CHAP*xx* directories, where *xx* ranges from 2 through 16. I will not show the code for any complete sample in any chapters because the code is too long for such a listing. At times I will show the entire contents of a specific file relevant to the discussion, but I will not show much in the way of make files, .DEF files, icons or bitmaps, resource scripts, and even some include files.

Most of the code in the CHAP*xx* directories are different revisions of Cosmo and Patron as they evolve throughout the book. The initial versions of both of these applications are provided in the CHAP02\COSMO and CHAP02\PATRON directories, with each application discussed in more detail later. As these applications evolve throughout this book, we'll modify many small parts of different source files (adding source files as well). These modifications are consistently marked with two comments: *//CHAPTERxxMOD* and *//End CHAPTERxxMOD*, where *xx* is the relevant chapter number. These comment delimiters will help you see which changes I had to make to both header (.H) and source (.CPP) files in our pursuit of OLE 2 nirvana. What I primarily show in each chapter is the code around the blocks, set off with these comments. So, for example, if you want to see which variables I added to a class to support a specific feature, look in the .H file, and you'll see the new ones between these comments.

In addition, most CHAP*xx* directories contain a CHAP*xx*.REG file. These are plain text files containing chapter-relevant entries for the system Registration Database. Some files contain duplicate entries from previous chapters because some samples depend on samples and builds from previous chapters. This redundancy ensures that the proper entries exist if you skip a chapter.

So before attempting to run any sample in a chapter, you must merge the contents of the appropriate .REG file with the existing Registration Database by using the Windows 3.1 REGEDIT program. In some cases, the .REG file from a later chapter will replace some of the entries made with an earlier .REG file, which is why there is not just one master file for the entire book.

Keep in mind as you examine the code that I designed it in such a way that code changes or additions made to accommodate OLE 2 occur in one place. This is the same idea as centralizing drawing code in a window in its WM_PAINT message handling: Any other code that wants to draw something merely changes the state of the data and causes a repaint. This design, as well as other designs in the sample code, are my personal choices and are not meant to represent Truth. "If it's Truth you're interested in," as Dr. Indiana Jones would remind us, "Dr. Tyree's philosophy class is right down the hall."

Cosmo: A Graphical Editor (with Apologies to No One in Particular)

Cosmo is an application with a silly name that does nothing important. Despite its limited value, Cosmo is a typical application that creates some kind of graphical data—in this case, an image called a polyline. The polyline is simply any number of points between 0 and 20 connected by lines, as shown in Figure 2-3, which is managed by a C++ class in Cosmo called *CPolyline.*

The user is able to add up to 20 lines by clicking in the Polyline region—the Polyline adds the points to an array of 20 POINT structures and increments a point count. The user can reverse added points by using Undo, which simply decrements the number of points drawn and repaints. The user can also change both the line and background colors, as well as change the line style, but these operations are not reversible. All commands are available from either menus or the toolbar. Cosmo also sports a simple status line at the bottom of its window.

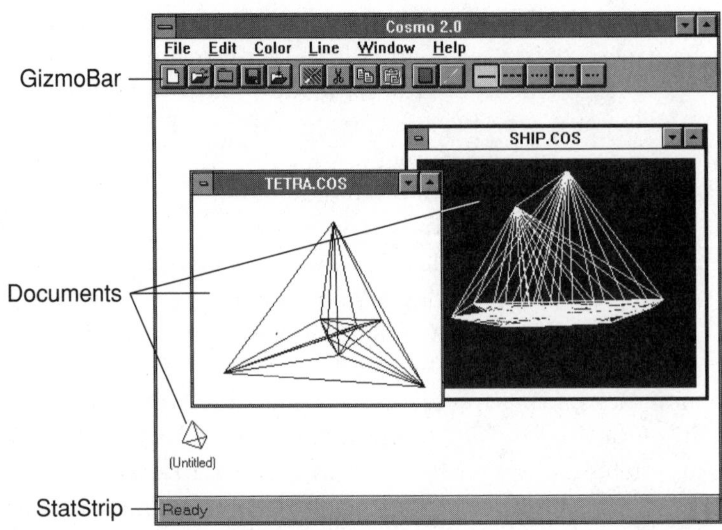

Figure 2-3.
Multiple-document version of Cosmo, with several open Polylines.

I provide two versions of Cosmo for use in illustrating object conversion and emulation between OLE 1 and OLE 2 servers, as discussed in Chapter 14. CHAP02\COSMO contains the source code for the C++ version build on CLASSLIB with a version 2 number. CHAP02\COSMO10 contains the source code for an earlier version written in straight C as an OLE 1 server. Anytime I refer to Cosmo in this book, I'm referring to version 2 unless I specifically state otherwise.

Cosmo performs traditional Windows file I/O, uses the Windows API to support the clipboard, and handles conversion to and from its version 1 file format. Both file formats use the .COS extension. A few sample Cosmo files can be found in CHAP02\COSFILES. In any case, Cosmo certainly lacks a few features (such as printing capability, Help, and maybe some real Undo functionality) that will keep it from being something I could sell. It does, however, maintain those elements that you would typically find in most applications of a higher caliber.

Cosmo will follow a course of evolution that will take it from a standard application for Windows to an OLE 2 application. Starting with Chapter 4, we'll also begin to separately develop a version of Cosmo's *CPolyline* object as an OLE 2 component object in a DLL. We'll also create a separate modified copy of Cosmo called Component Cosmo, or CoCosmo, that will use this component Polyline object so as to appear indistinguishable from the self-contained Cosmo. Using Polyline, we'll explore how various OLE 2 features can affect such a DLL, while at the same time illustrating those features in the self-contained Cosmo .EXE. Both cases are important to illustrate, and both follow paths detailed in Table 2-6.

Chapter	Features
DLL Object Path	
4	Polyline is split from Cosmo into a component object DLL. A version of Cosmo called CoCosmo is created to demonstrate how to instantiate and use such an object.
5	Polyline begins to use compound files. CoCosmo is modified to follow the changes to Polyline.
6	Polyline implements a data object interface to provide uniform data transfer. CoCosmo is modified in Chapters 7 and 8 to use this data object interface to implement clipboard and drag-and-drop support.
11	Polyline is upgraded to a full compound document object that supports embedding. Polyline essentially becomes an embedded object server.
16	Polyline becomes capable of in-place activation.
Application Object Path	
5	Cosmo is converted to use compound files.
7	Cosmo implements a data object and converts clipboard transfers to using data objects.
8	Cosmo adds drag-and-drop functionality.
10	Cosmo is modified to support compound documents as an embedded object server.
11	An object handler DLL is created for Cosmo's embedded objects.
13	Cosmo is capable of providing compound document linked objects.
14	Cosmo becomes capable of converting and emulating OLE 1 objects from Cosmo version 1.
16	Cosmo becomes capable of in-place activation.

Table 2-6.
Evolution of the Cosmo application by chapter.

Polyline will compile into POLY*xx*.DLL, where *xx* is the appropriate chapter number of the build. Likewise, Cosmo will compile into COSMO*xx*-.EXE. This naming scheme is intended to avoid naming conflicts when all the files are copied to the BUILD directory.

Patron: A Page Container (with Apologies to Merriam-Webster)

When I created the first version of this application for OLE 1, we called containers "clients," so a brief encounter with a thesaurus generated the name

Patron. In this case, *patron* is defined as either "one who uses the services of another establishment" or "the proprietor of an establishment (such as an inn)."[2] After all, as a container, Patron will use the implementations of compound document objects and provide a place (a document) in which they stay. Patron seems a better choice than another butchered version of "container," which doesn't fit an 8-character filename anyway. Essentially, Patron is a place to store various objects, such as bitmaps, metafiles, sounds, or spreadsheets—all of which Patron refers to as "tenants."

Patron's documents are pages that match the size and orientation of whatever printer setup you choose. You can add or delete pages and navigate through them, as well as scroll the view of the current page around in the document window. These commands are available from the menu or from a toolbar, as shown in Figure 2-4. Like Cosmo, Patron also sports a status line because we'll eventually make use of it in demonstrating in-place activation.

Aside from features for changing the number of pages or navigating through them, the only meaningful commands that the initial version of Patron (in CHAP02\PATRON) supports are Printer Setup and Print. Printer Setup lets you change size and orientation as you can with any real application. Print will actually pump out a printed page for every page you've created, complete with page number. Patron also draws a rectangle on the page so that you can see the printable boundaries. How exciting can it get?

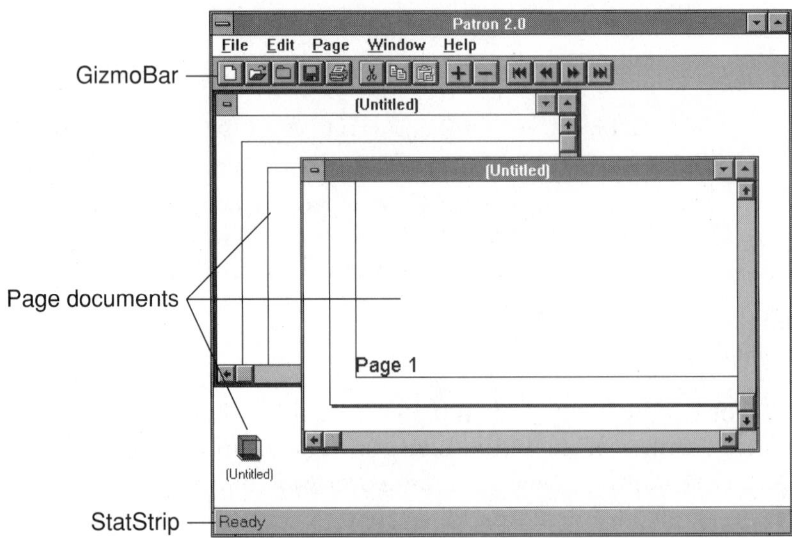

Figure 2-4.
Multiple-document version of Patron with several open documents.

2. *Webster's Ninth New Collegiate Dictionary*, Merriam-Webster, 1987.

Well, features stop there, as you might surmise from the code in CHAP02\PATRON. Patron's only purpose in life is to become an OLE 2 container application. Patron will be used to demonstrate how to write a relatively new application to take advantage of OLE 2 technologies. I did not bother to implement any file I/O for Patron because it will use compound files beginning in Chapter 5. I also didn't bother to make Patron capable of pasting metafiles and bitmaps from the clipboard because that would require a horrendous amount of code to draw those formats and to somehow serialize them to a file; you might call it laziness, but I call it planning.

Because we programmers instinctively try to avoid as much work as possible, we'll use functionality that OLE 2 already provides to add metafile and bitmap capabilities. As we'll see in the chapters ahead, OLE 2 already knows how to display and serialize these formats, so we need not consider writing such code ourselves. How convenient! We then add a little more code to enable Patron to contain compound document objects and work from there to in-place activation. As we progress through the chapters, we'll add various features to Patron, as shown in Table 2-7.

Chapter	Features
5	Patron adds file I/O using compound files.
7	Patron implements clipboard functions using a data object. It pastes metafiles and bitmaps using OLE 2 for drawing and serialization to a compound file.
8	Patron adds drag-and-drop functionality.
9	Patron is made into a simple compound document container for embedded objects only.
12	Patron becomes capable of containing linked objects.
13	Patron handles linking to embedded object stored in its own documents.
14	Patron handles object conversion and emulation.
15	Patron becomes capable of in-place activation.

Table 2-7.
Evolution of the Patron application by chapter.

Like Cosmo, Patron will compile into PATRON*xx*.EXE, where *xx* is the appropriate chapter number of the build. This naming scheme is intended to avoid naming conflicts when all the files are copied to the BUILD directory.

Building and Testing Environment

As I've mentioned before, the sample code in most of the directories depends on various files in the INC and LIB directories. Running the samples require some of the DLLs that are found in the LIB directory, as well. For these reasons, you need to make the following changes to your environment variables:

1. Add the INC directory to your INCLUDE path so that the compiler can locate the book's include files referenced with *#include <file>*.
2. Add the LIB directory to your LIB path so that the linker can find the libraries referenced in various make files.
3. Add the BUILD directory to your PATH so that when you run samples from the chapters they will be able to load the necessary DLLs.

In addition, note that the .REG files included with each chapter do not provide full pathnames to DLLs and EXEs referenced in those Registration Database entries, which is why you should add the BUILD directory to your PATH. Otherwise, you can modify the Registration Database to include full pathnames to each compiled DLL and EXE as needed. For debugging purposes, I recommend the latter approach. If you merely want to compile and run the samples quickly, I recommend the former approach.

There are two environment variables that affect compilations, as shown in Table 2-8. When the SDI variable is set to *1*, builds that are sensitive to that variable (Cosmo and Patron always are) will build into an SDI directory under the relevant source code directory (for example, CHAP02\COSMO\SDI). When the SDI variable is clear, builds will end up in the MDI directory under the relevant source tree. In addition, if you set the RETAIL variable to 1, you will build a nondebugging version in the appropriate SDI or MDI directory for whatever SDI or MDI option is set, wiping out the previous build in that same directory.

Variable	Purpose
SET SDI=1	Sets the SDI flag to build SDI versions.
SET SDI=	Clears the SDI flag to build MDI versions.
SET RETAIL=1	Builds nondebug versions using optimizations and eliminating debugging symbols.
SET RETAIL=	Builds debug versions with symbols and no optimization.

Table 2-8.
Build options controlled through environment variables.

In the sample code on your disk, you will find a number of files called MAKEALL.BAT. In any given directory, the file will completely rebuild all the samples visible in that directory. For example, the MAKEALL.BAT file in BTTNCUR will build BTTNCUR.DLL and a small demonstration program, BCDEMO.EXE. The MAKEALL.BAT in CHAP02\COSMO will build both MDI and SDI versions of Cosmo into CHAP02\COSMO\MDI and CHAP-02\COSMO\SDI. The MAKEALL.BAT in any CHAP*xx* directory will build all the samples—both SDI and MDI versions—for that chapter. For example, the one in CHAP02 will build MDI and SDI versions of Skel, Cosmo, and Patron, as well as the single SDI version of Cosmo version 1.

For your convenience, the MAKEALL files will redirect all error output from any compilation into a file called ERR in the same directory as the build DLL or EXE and will also concatenate all error output from all builds into BUILD\ERR. This provides a convenient record of any compilation problems. In addition, MAKEALL will copy the builds of all the DLLs to the BUILD directory along with MDI versions of all EXEs. SDI versions of EXEs are copied into BUILD\SDI.

Finally, the MAKEALL.BAT in the directory where you installed the sample code will rebuild every sample for the book, including all the DLLs and libraries in both MDI and SDI versions, for whatever debugging or retail version you have indicated through the RETAIL environment variable. It will also install builds to the INC, LIB, and BUILD directories as appropriate.

It's not a bad idea to install the samples at the end of your work day or before lunch and run MAKEALL before you leave your office. It will take some time to compile everything. Plenty of time to have a great lunch.

CHAPTER THREE

OBJECTS AND INTERFACES

object *n* **1** ***syn*** THING, article; ***rel*** doodad; gadget **2** ***syn*** THING, being, entity, individual, material, matter, stuff, substance.[1]

"Objects solve everything," or so you might have heard. If an object is a *thing*, how does one *thing* solve other *things*? The answer is it doesn't. Things don't solve, people solve. The belief that "object virtues" solve all your programming problems is what some friends of mine classify as "objects on the brain." They suggest that you attend meetings of your local OOPaholics Anonymous.

Using object-oriented languages to write applications and operating systems is only a matter of convenience if the ideas you want to express in that code are best done in such a language. But C++ programmers will tell you great stories about how C++ solved many problems they encountered in C but also introduced a whole new class of unique problems. For one thing, your language of choice has never simplified design—it has only made the implementation of many designs faster and more robust. I wrote the code in this book in C++ for such conveniences.

So just what is an object? No doubt everyone reading this book has a different idea about the term *object.* Objects are becoming so commonplace in just about every facet of computing that it has become difficult to understand what the word *object* means in a variety of contexts. Object models appear in places regardless of their relationships to any sort of object-oriented programming model. This chapter will attempt to clarify exactly what we mean by a Windows Object (note the capitalization to make the distinction) and what we mean by the interfaces that such an object supports. The standardized specifications of both are part of OLE 2's Component Object Model.

Windows Objects are slightly different from what C++ programmers might be used to. For instance, Windows objects do not allow direct access to data. Windows Objects can also be used and implemented in C or any other

1. *Webster's Collegiate Thesaurus*, Merriam-Webster, Inc., 1976.

language—that is, an object-oriented language is not necessary, only more convenient, to express object-oriented ideas.

We also have to distinguish between the object implementation and the object user, which this book will refer to as the "user" in programming contexts. The term *user* here should not be confused with the end user, a person who will see only the features you are implementing in your applications and will generally not be aware of your programming constructs.

This chapter will look at objects and interfaces in both C and C++ without delving deeply into OLE 2 itself. The first sets of code we'll see don't even use *#include* in any of the OLE 2 include files, but they still implement what we mean by a Windows Object—that is, something with interfaces. With a solid understanding of these fundamentals, we can move forward into seeing what is required for more complex Windows Objects with more useful capabilities. Note that much of the background, beginning with the section "*IUnknown*, the Root of All Evil," leads directly into Chapter 4.

I want to stress that an object as presented here is not a compound document (linked or embedded) object. We're not yet talking about specific applications such as containers. Much of the information from this point through Chapter 8 deals with topics completely outside the realm of Compound Document technology. So, as Yoda might suggest, "clear your mind of questions" and be prepared to learn what we mean by *object* in the cosmos of OLE 2.

Do objects solve everything? No. Do OLE 2 and its object model solve everything? No. OLE 2 intends to *simplify the expression* of object-oriented ideas under Windows. It does not intend to somehow make application or system design fall freely, like manna, from heaven. If it could, we would not have to worry about the national debt.

The Ultimate Question to Life, the Universe, and Objects (with Apologies to Douglas Adams)

I know a Windows Object exists that is capable of specific functions. How do I obtain a pointer to that object? This question is a central theme in this book: This chapter and those that follow are concerned with specific types of objects, how you get a pointer to one, and what you can do with that object once you have the pointer. Each chapter generally deals with different object types (and how you identify those objects), the interfaces they support, techniques to obtain their pointers (for whatever code uses the object), and the specific functions you can call through those pointers. So the answer to *our* question (which is not "42," as it was in Douglas Adams's books) varies with each subtechnology in OLE 2. Realize as well that a compound document object is only one type of Windows Object and that server applications are not the only object implementors. The fact is that almost all OLE 2 applications, regardless of what technologies they use, are both object users and object implementors.

To fully understand obtaining and using a Windows Object, we must first go back to a few even more fundamental questions. What is an object? To answer that question we must ask: What is an object class? To some, an object class may seem some mighty spiritual force divinely manifested in your include files. In reality, a class (and objects) can be described in terms that anthropologist Marvin Harris would call "practical and mundane,"[2] for in one way or another, a programmer or compiler has to reduce the notion of a class into code.

A *class*, in mundane terms, is the *definition* of a data structure (members) and the functions that manipulate that structure (member functions). The concept can be expressed in any programming language; C++, Smalltalk, and other such languages have merely formalized the notion. For example, C++ classes generally live in include files, such as this one, shown in Chapter 2:

```
class __far CAppVars
    {
    public:
        HINSTANCE     m_hInst;
        HINSTANCE     m_hInstPrev;
        LPSTR         m_pszCmdLine;
        int           m_nCmdShow;
        HWND          m_hWnd;

    public:
        CAppVars(HINSTANCE, HINSTANCE, LPSTR, int);
        ~CAppVars(void);
        BOOL FInit(void);
    };
```

A class is only a definition and carries no implementation, although classes in some languages may define default implementations that are not realized until there is some instantiation of the data structure that contains a function table and the variables of the class. We call that instantiated structure an *object*. In C++, objects are manifested in memory, as shown in Figure 3-1 on the next page.

The object has two components in memory: a function table, containing pointers to each member function (sometimes known as a *method*) defined in

2. In *Cows, Pigs, Wars, and Witches*, by Marvin Harris, Vintage Books, 1974.

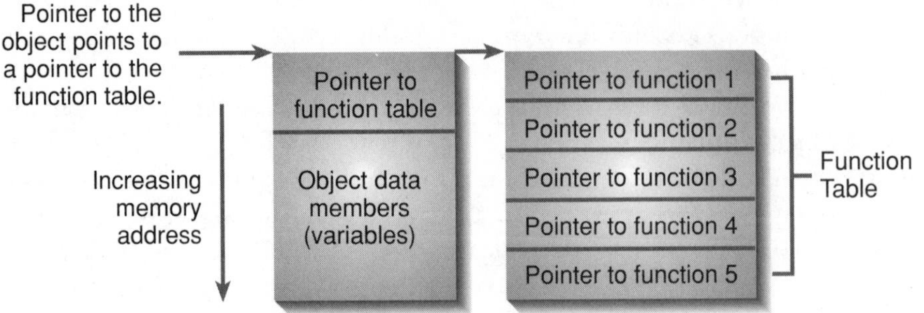

Figure 3-1.
A C++ object in memory is a data structure containing a pointer to the object's function table followed by the object's data. The function table is separate from the object structure itself, so a pointer to the object first points to a pointer to the function table.

the object's class, and a data block, containing the current values for each variable (or data member, sometimes known as a *property*). The user of the object generally has some reference[3] to this chunk of memory, which for the purposes of this book is always a pointer. The user obtains this reference by using some type of function call (direct or implied) in which that function allocates the block in memory, initializes the function table, and returns the reference to that memory to the user.

When the user has the reference to the block of memory, the user can call any of the functions in the object's function table and possibly access the object's variables, depending on the language being used. The single most important benefit is this: To call any of the functions defined in an object class, you must first have a reference to an instantiated object so that the functions have some data on which to operate. Without a reference to the object, you have no way to call one of the object's functions. Even with a pointer, the object can restrict your access to its variables or functions by means of language mechanisms such as *public* and *private* members in C++. In contrast, a non-object-oriented language such as C allows you to call any function with any garbage you want. Given a pointer to a data structure, there is nothing to keep you from partying all over those variables.

The OLE 2 notion of class is even more strict than the preceding general definition because the only accessible members of a class are specific groups of functions called *interfaces*. As mentioned in Chapter 1 and as shown in

3. *Reference* here does not necessarily mean a C++ reference.

Figure 3-2, an interface is a group of semantically related functions that are publicly accessible to the user of a Windows Object. An object's interface can really be viewed as only the function table part of an object in memory.

By themselves, interface definitions in OLE 2 are only virtual base classes, and thus they cannot be instantiated. In other words, they provide a convenient structure to lay over the top of a function table to provide more readable and maintainable names for each function.

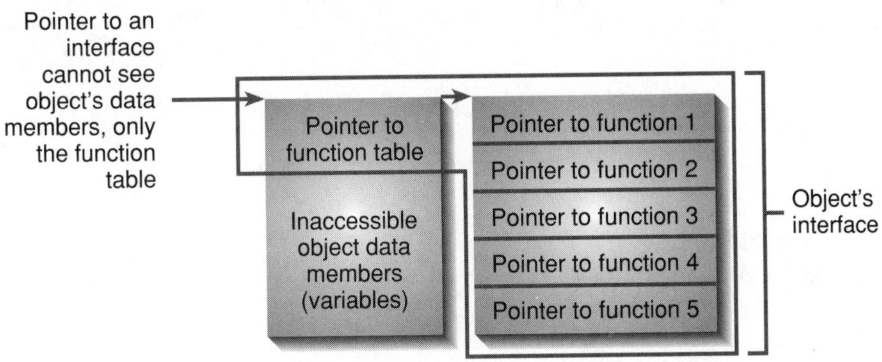

Figure 3-2.
A pointer to an interface can access only member functions in the object's function table.

An interface implementation, in pedestrian terms, is a block of memory containing an array of function pointers—that is, a function table. The interface definition itself simply provides names for each pointer in that table. When a user of a Windows Object obtains a pointer to an interface that an object supports, we say it has a pointer to an interface *on* that object. Again, that pointer does not provide access to the entire object; instead, it allows access to one interface on that object—that is, to one set of functions. Through an indirection on that pointer, the user calls a function of the object, as shown in Figure 3-3 on the next page.

As mentioned in Chapter 1, the user of a Windows Object has access to only one interface through one pointer, even when the object itself actually supports more than one interface—that is, implements more than one set of related functions and provides multiple function tables. Note that when we graphically represent an object with interfaces, we use a circle to represent each interface, as introduced in Chapter 1 and as shown in Figure 3-4 on the next page.

To use functions in a different interface on the same object, the user must obtain a second pointer to that other interface through the *QueryInterface* function, which is present in all interfaces. The section "*IUnknown*, the

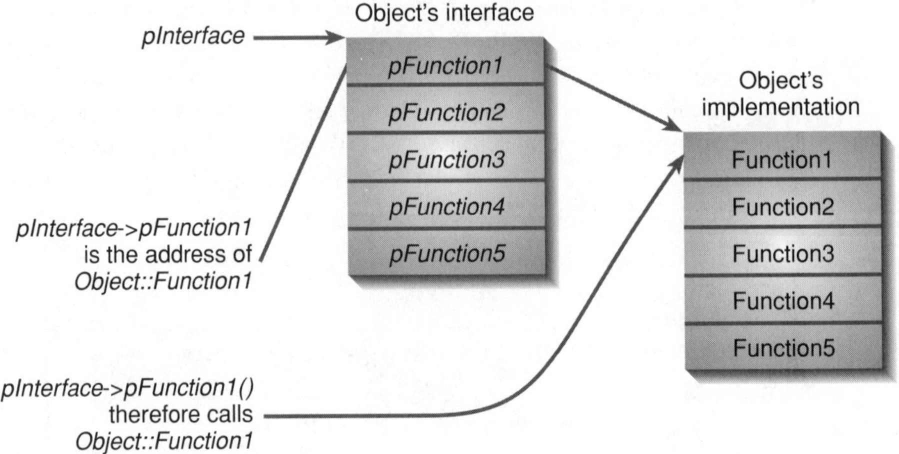

Figure 3-3.
Calling an interface member function. Note that the indirection through the pointer to the function table is not shown because C++ hides this extra step. The indirection is apparent, however, in C.

Root of All Evil'' later in this chapter explores *QueryInterface* in detail. *IUnknown* is a fundamental interface that all Windows Objects must support. (This is why in diagrams it's always placed above the object, as it is in Figure 3-4, instead of to the side, as other interfaces are.)

The function table itself is designed to have a layout that is identical to the one generated by many C++ compilers. Such a layout lets you use a single indirection (->) on the pointer to call an interface function. However, this does not force you to use C++ to program OLE 2; as I said in Chapter 2, C++ is

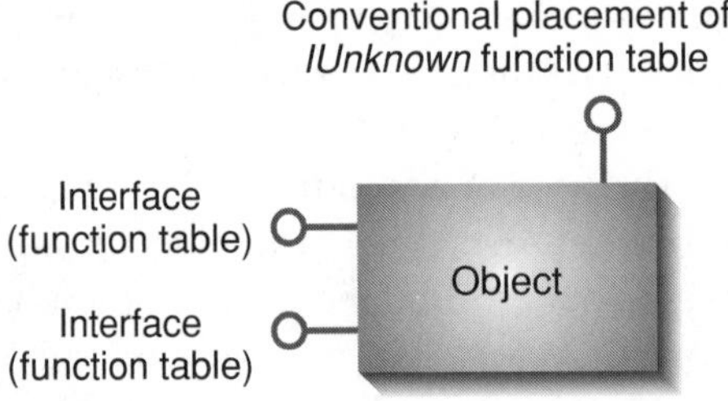

Figure 3-4.
Instead of always showing expanded function tables, interfaces are represented with a circle, or jack. By convention, IUnknown *is on top of the object, and all other interfaces are to the left or right.*

simply more *convenient.* Any object implementation is only required to provide separate function tables for each supported interface. How you choose to create each table will of course be different, depending on your language of choice, as the later section "A Simple Object in C and C++: *RECTEnumerator*" illustrates.

Because neither use nor implementation of a Windows Object is dependent on the programming language used, you can view OLE 2's object model, the Component Object Model, as a *binary standard.* This approach has a major advantage over other proposed object models. You can choose to implement in Visual Basic an object that is still usable from a C or C++ application as long as you can provide a pointer to your interface function tables. Microsoft has done us a wonderful service by not limiting our choice of programming tools or languages.

So back to the Ultimate Question: I know there's a Windows Object, but how do I obtain the first pointer to an interface on that object? The answer greatly depends on how you identify the Windows Object, but it can be reduced to four basic methods in OLE 2 for getting that pointer:

- Call an API function that creates an object of only one type—that is, the function will only ever return a pointer to one specific interface or object type.
- Call an API function that can create an object based on some class identifier and that returns any interface pointer you request.
- Call a member function of some interface that returns a specific interface pointer on another separate object.
- Implement interface functions on your own objects to which other object users pass their own interface pointers.

All these mechanisms are used by both OLE 2 applications and the OLE 2 libraries themselves. OLE 2 implements most of the API functions you'll use to obtain a pointer using the first two methods, but you might implement your own private API functions to accomplish similar ends. You will use the third method when you are the user of some object and have occasion to ask that object to create another object. You will use the fourth method for an object implementor whose user needs to provide the implementor with a pointer to the user's own objects. This last method is how two applications, such as a compound document container and a server, initiate a two-way dialog: Both applications implement specific (and different) objects and pass interface pointers to each other.

Windows Objects vs. C++ Objects

You might wonder why Windows Objects differ in many respects from C++ objects even though C++ is the most widely used object-oriented language for programming Windows. The overriding reason is that in C++ you might use only C++ objects that live and execute within your own application (EXE), possibly within DLLs (but at a price). On the other hand, you can use Windows Objects regardless of where they live and execute, be it in your own EXE, in a DLL (including the operating system itself), or in another EXE. In the future, Microsoft will enable Windows Objects to live and execute on another machine, a capability far out of reach of C++ objects.

Let's Go Traveling

Suppose I'm a C++ application that lives in Rugby, North Dakota (the geographic center of North America), and my application is bounded by the border of the continental United States, as illustrated in Figure 3-5. I can visit freely any of 48 states, no questions asked, by driving along an interstate. Access is fast and easy, although I am subject to the laws of each state I drive through. I can also drive into Canada or Mexico to buy their goods and use their services, but I do have to stop at the border and answer a few questions; travel is a little slower but still quite easy. In programming terms, I can freely use any object class within the boundaries of my application as long as I obey the access rights of those individual objects. I can also use objects implemented in DLLs, but there is more work involved in getting across the DLL boundary, even to my own DLL, such as Alaska.

I might live happily for a long time restricting my travels to a single continent. But there are six other continents and many other countries on the planet that I might want to visit. Getting there is not easy—I have to transfer flights, go through customs, and show my passport. If I want to travel to a distant destination, such as Antananarivo, Madagascar, I would have to fly to Chicago and then to London, switch carriers to get to Nairobi, Kenya, and then catch a final flight to Antananarivo. On each segment of my journey, I will probably fly on a different airline in a different airplane (or I might be forced to travel only by boat or train) and walk through customs offices in three different countries. If I step out of line anywhere, I might find myself in a prison on the other side of the globe.

As a C++ application, I would experience the same difficulty in using C++ objects implemented in other applications (countries) or code that is otherwise separated by a process boundary (oceans), as illustrated in Figure 3-6 on page 66. The best I can hope for is to become intimately familiar with

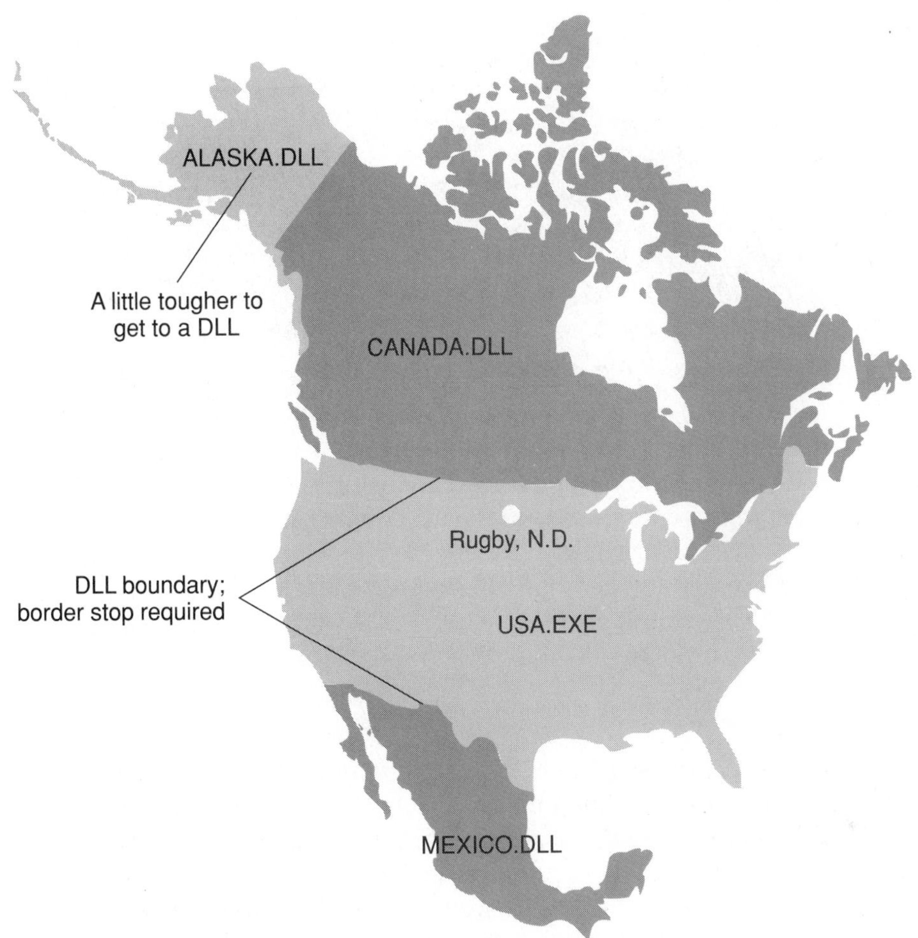

Figure 3-5.
Travel within North America is fairly painless.

the protocols and customs of each application along my way, knowledge that can apply only to those specific applications: When I want to use the services of a different application, I must learn another new interface. If time is not a luxury, I'll probably decide to visit only a few other countries.

OLE 2 offers you membership in the Windows Objects Club, which makes travel abroad much easier. The Windows Objects Club standardizes the protocol for visiting any other country, so you have to learn only one set of rules. The Windows Objects Club offers nonstop flights to many countries (Windows Objects in DLLs) and at worst one-stop flights to any other destination on the planet (Windows Objects in EXE applications). When you are a

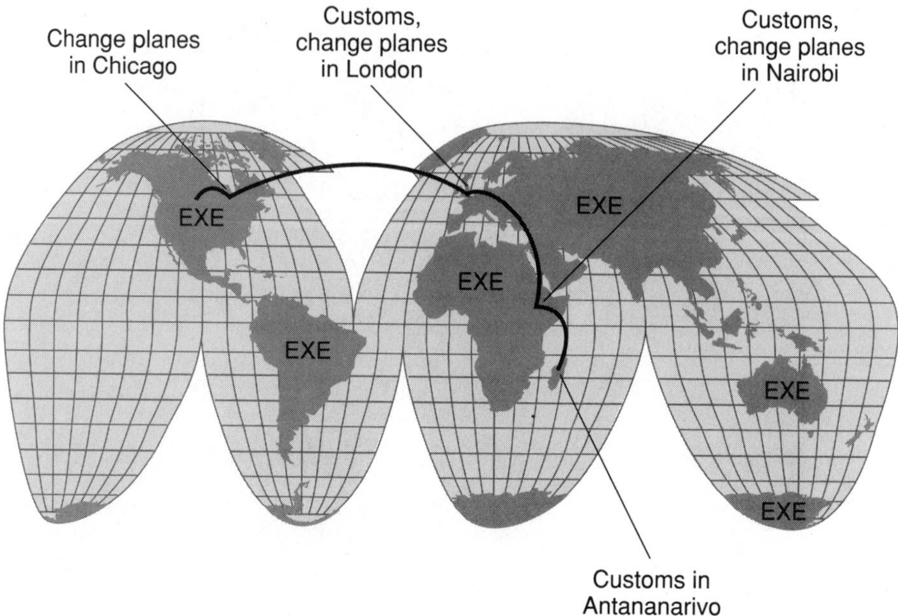

Figure 3-6.
Travel abroad involves much more time, effort, and knowledge.

member of the Windows Objects Club, travel is as easy as showing your membership card and hopping on a plane bound for whatever destination you choose. No matter where you are, the Windows Objects Club has a flight departing to any destination, as depicted in Figure 3-7.

In programming terms, you join the Windows Objects Club by using the various OLE 2 API functions to access specific objects without concern for where that object actually lives. Those API functions form the protocol you learn once; later, in Chapters 9 and beyond, we'll learn more about compound documents, which provide you with the benefit of a personal interpreter in any country you visit or with whom you do business. When we talk about in-place activation, we'll see how the Windows Objects Club can bring the country to you.

The Windows Objects Club today offers easy travel between all countries and continents on our little blue planet. In the future, this club will provide the same benefits to interplanetary and interstellar travel without even requiring you to reapply. More to the point, Windows Objects will become network aware and will allow you to use objects running on other machines, either on your local area network or even on a wide area network. Perhaps

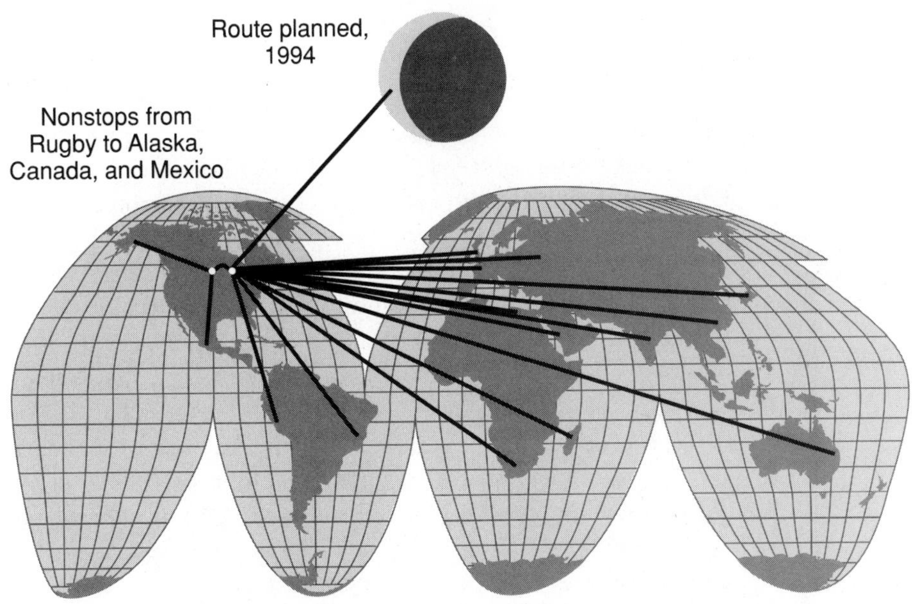
Route planned,
1994
Nonstops from
Rugby to Alaska,
Canada, and Mexico
Fly through Chicago to get anywhere else in the world.
At every destination you treat customs identically;
the Windows Objects Club provides interpreters.

Figure 3-7.
The Windows Objects Club simplifies travel, and someday it will open more routes.

someday we'll have the PLAN (planetary network), letting you use objects that live on the moon, either figuratively or physically.

The purpose of this little exercise was to show that C++ objects are somewhat limited in scope because access to objects, being defined by the language, restricts you to objects that live in your own process space. Windows Objects, being defined by the system, open access to any object anywhere on your machine, and eventually on other machines as well.

Other Differences Between Windows Objects and C++ Objects

Because the location of an object's implementation varies so widely between C++ objects and Windows Objects, there are a number of other key implementation differences that affect programming:

- Class definition
- Object instantiation

- Object references
- Object destruction

Class Definition

C++ defines a class by using the *class* keyword, which generates a user-defined *type*. Members and member functions can be private, protected, or public. Furthermore, a C++ class can inherit from another class, thereby taking on all the characteristics (data and member functions) of that base class with the ability to override or expand select pieces of that base class.

A Windows Object is defined in terms of the interfaces it supports. All objects support at least one interface named *IUnknown*, which is discussed in the later section "*IUnknown*, The Root of All Evil"; support of this one interface qualifies the object as a Windows Object. The object user learns about other interfaces the object supports through member functions of *IUnknown*.

Windows Objects are all, therefore, at least of type *IUnknown* and can be treated as another type by means of a different interface. Because of this mechanism, there is no user-defined type associated with a Windows Object class as there is with a C++ class. In fact, there is no single way to identify a specific object. As we saw earlier, there are four general ways by which you can obtain a pointer to a Windows Object. Each technique has its own way of identifying the object. One of the techniques—identifying a Windows Object using a class identifier—is the closest analogy to a C++ method, but it is only one of the many ways to identify such objects.

Object Instantiation

C++ objects are instantiated by various means, such as declaring a variable of the object's type on the stack, declaring a global variable, or using the *new* operator on that type. Regardless of the actual technique used, C++ eventually calls the object's constructor.

Again, just as there are many ways to identify a Windows Object, there are many ways to instantiate an object. In some cases, you call a function to instantiate the object. In other cases, you don't directly instantiate an object, but you are given a pointer to one that something else already created. One of the most common techniques, described in Chapter 4, is to use a thing called a *class factory object* to instantiate a Windows Object, much as the *new* operator works for C++ objects. A class factory object represents a specific class identifier, is obtained by a specific OLE 2 function, and supports an interface named *IClassFactory*. The *IClassFactory* interface contains a member function named *CreateInstance*, to which you pass an identifier of the interface you want on that object. *IClassFactory::CreateInstance* is the logical equivalent of *new*.

Object References

C++ objects can be referenced through an object variable, an object reference (a special type in C++), or a pointer to the object. Because objects are always local (in your EXEs or DLLs), their instantiations can live anywhere in your process space. Through any variable, the user has access to any public members of the object or to private and protected members if the user and the object are friends.

As I hope I have beaten into your head by now, a Windows Object is *always* referenced through a pointer, not to the object itself but to an *interface.* This means that through a given interface pointer the user can access member functions only in that interface. The user can never have a pointer to the whole object (because there is no definition of *whole object*), so there is no access to data members and no concept of *friend.*

Through the *IUnknown* interface, a user can get at other interfaces that the object also supports, but that means obtaining a different pointer that refers to the same object. Each pointer to an interface points to a function table in the object, and each table contains only member functions for a specific interface, as shown in Figure 3-8 on the next page. Because every interface defined in OLE 2 is derived from *IUnknown,* it is not necessary to have an *IUnknown* pointer to query for other interfaces; you can use any other interface pointer as if it were an *IUnknown.*

When you have a pointer to an object's interface, you can call the interface's member functions just as you can call a member function of a C++ object through a pointer:

```
pObject->MemberFunction([parameters]);
```

Because a pointer to a Windows Object always points to a function table, such a pointer can also be used from C or from assembly code, not only from C++, as described in "A Simple Object in C and C++: *RECTEnumerator.*"

Object Destruction

In C++, you destroy an object created with *new* by calling the *delete* operator on an object pointer. Objects declared as stack variables are automatically freed by virtue of restoring the stack before returning from a function. In either case, the memory that the object occupied is freed, and the object's destructor function is called.

The function that frees a Windows Object and essentially calls its destructor is a member function called *Release.* This function is a member of the *IUnknown* interface, and so it is present in every interface you will ever

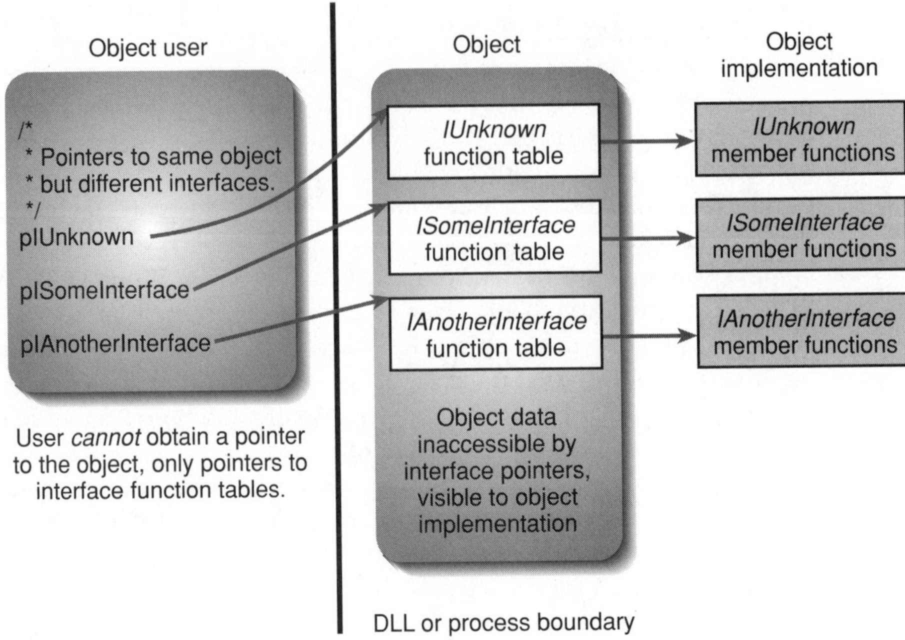

Figure 3-8.
Multiple interface pointers to an object reference unique function tables in the object but never reference the entire object itself.

obtain on any Windows Object. *Release*, however, is not as brutal as the *delete* operator, for as we'll see in the "Reference Counting" section later, the object might not actually be destroyed when *Release* is called. Internally, the object maintains a count of how many references exist to any of its interfaces. Creating an interface pointer increments the reference count, whereas *Release* decrements it. When the count is reduced to zero, the object frees itself, calling its own destructor.

A Simple Object in C and C++: *RECTEnumerator*

Windows Objects really can be written in any language; the most common are C and C++. As with any programming task, you need to choose a language that is well suited to the problems at hand, and C++ is the best suited for expressing the ideas in OLE 2. Therefore, C++ is more natural and definitely more convenient for use in programming with Windows Objects. With a little more overhead, however, you can program just as effectively using C. The differences lie in how you create the function table for the object's interfaces and how you call the functions in those function tables. To illustrate the differences between the two languages, let's implement a type of object called an *enumerator.*

Enumerators are specific objects defined in OLE 2 that are used to communicate lists of information between another object and the user of that object, even when they are in different processes. For example, let's say you're using an object that represents a source of data—call it a data object—and you ask that object what data formats it supports (as we'll see in Chapter 6). The data object would create another independent enumerator that allows the user to iterate through the list of formats supported by the data object. The user of the data object also becomes a user of the enumerator, albeit through a different interface pointer.

An enumerator supports one of a set of interfaces prefixed with *IEnum.* Because the elements of the enumerator's list vary by context, OLE 2 defines a number of *IEnum<type>* interfaces where *<type>* is the name of the specific data structure used for each element in the list. OLE 2 also provides marshaling support for each standard *IEnum* interface. Each *IEnum* interface supports all member functions of *IUnknown* (of course) as well as four additional members to facilitate iteration over the list of elements:

Member	Result
Next	Returns the next *n* elements of the list starting at the current index.
Skip	Skips past *n* elements in the list.
Reset	Sets the current index to zero.
Clone	Returns a new enumerator object with the same state.

For this exercise, let's define a custom interface named *IEnumRECT* with all the functions in the preceding tale except *Clone.* Let's also define an object named *RECTEnumerator,* which implements that interface. The interface is defined in IENUM0.H, as shown in Listing 3-1 on page 73, which you'll find in the INC directory in the sample code. This file compiles differently for C and C++, depending on the *__cplusplus* symbol, which is defined only when you are compiling for C++.[4] The C++ implementation of the *RECT-Enumerator* object, in a program called ENUMCAP, is shown in Listing 3-2 on page 74, and the C implementation, in ENUMC, is shown in Listing 3-3 on page 83. Both samples are in the CHAP03 directory. Do not confuse the name *RECTEnumerator* for this object with the name of anything you might use to implement the object: It's merely a label.

Do ENUMC and ENUMCPP Do Anything?

When you run either ENUMC or ENUMCPP, you'll see no visible output no matter which menu commands you choose. You are *not* going crazy. Both programs are so intentionally boring on the outside that you should really want to run them in a debugger, which is where you can step through the code to see what is actually happening. These samples are intended for use in a debugger to illustrate interfaces in C and C++.

RECTEnumerator and the *IEnumRECT* Interface

The *RECTEnumerator* object supports one interface, named *IEnumRECT*, as shown in Listing 3-1, with the following member functions:

Member Function	Result
AddRef	Increments the reference count on the enumerator object.
Release	Decrements the reference count and frees the enumerator object when the reference count is zero.
Next	Returns the next *n* RECT structures starting at the current index.
Skip	Skips past *n* RECTs in the list.
Reset	Sets the current index to zero.

Because we have not yet examined *IUnknown* and because we want to keep this example as simple as possible, *IEnumRECT* borrows the two *IUnknown* members *AddRef* and *Release* but does not include *QueryInterface.* For the same reasons, we also eliminate the *Clone* member, which is part of standard *IEnum* interfaces.

4. The major C++ compilers, at least, define the __*cplusplus* symbol.

IENUM0.H

```
/*
 * Definition of an IEnumRECT interface as an example of the
 * interface notion introduced in OLE 2 with the Component Object
 * Model as well as the idea of enumerators.  This include file
 * defines the interface differently for C or C++.
 *
 * Copyright (c)1993 Microsoft Corporation, All Rights Reserved
 */

#ifndef _IENUM0_H_
#define _IENUM0_H_

//C++ Definition of an interface.
#ifdef __cplusplus

//This is the interface, a struct of pure virtual functions.
struct __far IEnumRECT
    {
    virtual DWORD AddRef(void)=0;
    virtual DWORD Release(void)=0;

    virtual BOOL  Next(DWORD, LPRECT, LPDWORD)=0;
    virtual BOOL  Skip(DWORD)=0;
    virtual void  Reset(void)=0;
    };

typedef IEnumRECT FAR *LPENUMRECT;

#else   //!__cplusplus

/*
 * A C interface is explicitly a structure containing a
 * long pointer to a virtual function table that we have to
 * initialize explicitly.
 */

typedef struct
    {
    struct IEnumRECTVtbl FAR *lpVtbl;
    } IEnumRECT;

typedef IEnumRECT FAR *LPENUMRECT;
```

Listing 3-1.

The IENUM0.H include file found in the shared INC directory.

(continued)

Listing 3-1. *continued*

```
//This is simply a convenient naming
typedef struct IEnumRECTVtbl IEnumRECTVtbl;

struct IEnumRECTVtbl
    {
    DWORD (* AddRef)(LPENUMRECT);
    DWORD (* Release)(LPENUMRECT);
    BOOL  (* Next)(LPENUMRECT, DWORD, LPRECT, LPDWORD);
    BOOL  (* Skip)(LPENUMRECT, DWORD);
    void  (* Reset)(LPENUMRECT);
    };

#endif  //!__cplusplus

#endif //_IENUM0_H_
```

NOTE: The following files (ENUMCPP.H, ENUMCPP.CPP, IENUM.CPP) are for the C++ implementation of the Enum program.

ENUMCPP.H

```
/*
 * Enumerator in C++ Chapter 3
 * Definitions, classes, and prototypes for enumerator interface
 * example implemented in C++.
 *
 * Copyright (c)1993 Microsoft Corporation, All Rights Reserved
 */

#ifndef _ENUMCPP_H_
#define _ENUMCPP_H_

#include <ienum0.h>        //Found in shared include directory.
#include <book1632.h>

//Menu resource ID and commands
#define IDR_MENU                        1

#define IDM_ENUMCREATE                  100
#define IDM_ENUMRELEASE                 101
#define IDM_ENUMRUNTHROUGH              102
```

Listing 3-2.
The ENUM program implemented in C++.

(continued)

Listing 3-2. *continued*

```
#define IDM_ENUMEVERYTHIRD          103
#define IDM_ENUMRESET               104
#define IDM_ENUMEXIT                105

//ENUMCPP.CPP
LRESULT FAR PASCAL EXPORT EnumWndProc(HWND, UINT, WPARAM, LPARAM);

class __far CAppVars
    {
    friend LRESULT FAR PASCAL EXPORT EnumWndProc(HWND, UINT
        , WPARAM, LPARAM);

    protected:
        HINSTANCE       m_hInst;            //WinMain parameters
        HINSTANCE       m_hInstPrev;
        UINT            m_nCmdShow;

        HWND            m_hWnd;             //Main window handle
        LPENUMRECT      m_pIEnumRect;       //Enumerator interface

    public:
        CAppVars(HINSTANCE, HINSTANCE, UINT);
        ~CAppVars(void);
        BOOL FInit(void);
    };

typedef CAppVars FAR *LPAPPVARS;

#define CBWNDEXTRA          sizeof(LONG)
#define ENUMWL_STRUCTURE    0

//IENUM.CPP

//Number of rectangles that objects with IEnumRECT support (demo)
#define CRECTS        15

/*
 * A class definition, not provided by OLE, then inherits from
 * whatever interfaces it supports.  Multiple inheritance works
 * in this scenario as does the single inheritance shown here.
 */
class __far CImpIEnumRECT : public IEnumRECT
    {
    private:
```

(continued)

Listing 3-2. *continued*

```
        DWORD     m_cRef;           //Reference count
        DWORD     m_iCur;           //Current Enum position
        RECT      m_rgrc[CRECTS]; //RECTs we enumerate

    public:
        CImpIEnumRECT(void);
        ~CImpIEnumRECT(void);

        virtual DWORD AddRef(void);
        virtual DWORD Release(void);
        virtual BOOL  Next(DWORD, LPRECT, LPDWORD);
        virtual BOOL  Skip(DWORD);
        virtual void  Reset(void);
    };

typedef CImpIEnumRECT FAR *LPIMPIENUMRECT;

//Function that creates one of these objects
BOOL CreateRECTEnumerator(LPENUMRECT FAR *);

#endif //_ENUMCPP_H_
```

ENUMCPP.CPP

```
/*
 * Enumerator interface in C++ Chapter 3
 *
 * Copyright (c)1993 Microsoft Corporation, All Rights Reserved
 */

#include <windows.h>
#include "enumcpp.h"

int PASCAL WinMain(HINSTANCE hInst, HINSTANCE hInstPrev
    , LPSTR pszCmdLine, int nCmdShow)
    {
    MSG          msg;
    LPAPPVARS    pAV;

    //Create and initialize the application.
    pAV=new CAppVars(hInst, hInstPrev, nCmdShow);
```

(continued)

Listing 3-2. *continued*

```
    if (NULL==pAV)
        return -1;

    if (pAV->FInit())
        {
        while (GetMessage(&msg, NULL, 0,0))
            {
            TranslateMessage(&msg);
            DispatchMessage(&msg);
            }
        }

    delete pAV;
    return msg.wParam;
    }

LRESULT FAR PASCAL EXPORT EnumWndProc(HWND hWnd, UINT iMsg
    , WPARAM wParam, LPARAM lParam)
    {
    LPAPPVARS   pAV;
    RECT        rc;
    DWORD       cRect;

    COMMANDPARAMS(wID, wCode, hWndMsg);
    pAV=(LPAPPVARS)GetWindowLong(hWnd, ENUMWL_STRUCTURE);

    switch (iMsg)
        {
        case WM_NCCREATE:
            pAV=(LPAPPVARS)((LONG)((LPCREATESTRUCT)lParam)
                ->lpCreateParams);

            SetWindowLong(hWnd, ENUMWL_STRUCTURE, (LONG)pAV);
            return (DefWindowProc(hWnd, iMsg, wParam, lParam));

        case WM_DESTROY:
            PostQuitMessage(0);
            break;

        case WM_COMMAND:
            switch (wID)
                {
```

(continued)

Listing 3-2. *continued*

```
            case IDM_ENUMCREATE:
                if (NULL!=pAV->m_pIEnumRect)
                    pAV->m_pIEnumRect->Release();

                CreateRECTEnumerator(&pAV->m_pIEnumRect);
                break;

            case IDM_ENUMRELEASE:
                if (NULL==pAV->m_pIEnumRect)
                    break;

                if (0==pAV->m_pIEnumRect->Release())
                    pAV->m_pIEnumRect=NULL;

                break;

            case IDM_ENUMRUNTHROUGH:
                if (NULL==pAV->m_pIEnumRect)
                    break;

                while (pAV->m_pIEnumRect->Next(1, &rc, &cRect))
                    ;

                break;

            case IDM_ENUMEVERYTHIRD:
                if (NULL==pAV->m_pIEnumRect)
                    break;

                while (pAV->m_pIEnumRect->Next(1, &rc, &cRect))
                    {
                    if (!pAV->m_pIEnumRect->Skip(2))
                        break;
                    }

                break;

            case IDM_ENUMRESET:
                if (NULL==pAV->m_pIEnumRect)
                    break;

                pAV->m_pIEnumRect->Reset();
                break;
```

(continued)

Listing 3-2. *continued*

```
                case IDM_ENUMEXIT:
                    PostMessage(hWnd, WM_CLOSE, 0, 0L);
                    break;
                }
            break;

        default:
            return (DefWindowProc(hWnd, iMsg, wParam, lParam));
        }

    return 0L;
    }

CAppVars::CAppVars(HINSTANCE hInst, HINSTANCE hInstPrev
    , UINT nCmdShow)
    {
    //Initialize WinMain parameter holders.
    m_hInst     = hInst;
    m_hInstPrev = hInstPrev;
    m_nCmdShow  = nCmdShow;

    m_hWnd=NULL;
    m_pIEnumRect=NULL;

    return;
    }

CAppVars::~CAppVars(void)
    {
    //Free the enumerator object if we have one.
    if (NULL!=m_pIEnumRect)
        m_pIEnumRect->Release();

    return;
    }

BOOL CAppVars::FInit(void)
    {

    WNDCLASS    wc;

    if (!m_hInstPrev)
        {
```

(continued)

Listing 3-2. *continued*

```
        wc.style          = CS_HREDRAW | CS_VREDRAW;
        wc.lpfnWndProc    = EnumWndProc;
        wc.cbClsExtra     = 0;
        wc.cbWndExtra     = CBWNDEXTRA;
        wc.hInstance      = m_hInst;
        wc.hIcon          = LoadIcon(m_hInst, "Icon");
        wc.hCursor        = LoadCursor(NULL, IDC_ARROW);
        wc.hbrBackground  = (HBRUSH)(COLOR_WINDOW + 1);
        wc.lpszMenuName   = MAKEINTRESOURCE(IDR_MENU);
        wc.lpszClassName  = "ENUMCPP";

        if (!RegisterClass(&wc))
            return FALSE;
        }

        m_hWnd=CreateWindow("ENUMCPP", "Enumerator in C++"
            , WS_MINIMIZEBOX | WS_OVERLAPPEDWINDOW
            , 35, 35, 350, 250, NULL, NULL, m_hInst, this);

    if (NULL==m_hWnd)
        return FALSE;

    ShowWindow(m_hWnd, m_nCmdShow);
    UpdateWindow(m_hWnd);

    return TRUE;
    }
```

IENUM.CPP

```
/*
 * Enumerator in C++ Chapter 3
 *
 * Copyright (c)1993 Microsoft Corporation, All Rights Reserved
 */

#include <windows.h>
#include "ENUMCPP.H"

/*
 * CreateRECTEnumerator
 *
```

(continued)

Listing 3-2. *continued*

```
 * Purpose:
 *  Given an array of rectangles, creates an enumerator interface
 *  on top of that array.
 *
 * Parameters:
 *  ppEnum          LPENUMRECT FAR * in which to return the
 *                  interface pointer on the created object.
 *
 * Return value:
 *  BOOL            TRUE if successful, FALSE otherwise.
 */

BOOL CreateRECTEnumerator(LPENUMRECT FAR *ppEnum)
    {
    if (NULL==ppEnum)
        return FALSE;

    //Create the object storing a pointer to the interface
    *ppEnum=(LPENUMRECT)new CImpIEnumRECT();

    if (NULL==*ppEnum)
        return FALSE;

    //If creation worked, AddRef the interface
    if (NULL!=*ppEnum)
        (*ppEnum)->AddRef();

    return (NULL!=*ppEnum);
    }

CImpIEnumRECT::CImpIEnumRECT(void)
    {
    UINT        i;

    //Initialize the array of rectangles
    for (i=0; i < CRECTS; i++)
        SetRect(&m_rgrc[i], i, i*2, i*3, i*4);

    //Ref counts always start as zero
    m_cRef=0;

    //Current pointer is the first element.
    m_iCur=0;
```

(continued)

Listing 3-2. *continued*

```
    return;
    }

CImpIEnumRECT::~CImpIEnumRECT(void)
    {
    return;
    }

DWORD CImpIEnumRECT::AddRef(void)
    {
    return ++m_cRef;
    }

DWORD CImpIEnumRECT::Release(void)
    {
    DWORD       cRefT;

    cRefT=--m_cRef;

    if (0==m_cRef)
        delete this;

    return cRefT;
    }

BOOL CImpIEnumRECT::Next(DWORD cRect, LPRECT prc, LPDWORD pdwRects)
    {
    DWORD       cRectReturn=0L;

    if (NULL==pdwRects)
        return FALSE;

    *pdwRects=0L;

    if (NULL==prc || (m_iCur >= CRECTS))
        return FALSE;

    while (m_iCur < CRECTS && cRect > 0)
        {
        *prc++=m_rgrc[m_iCur++];
        cRectReturn++;
        cRect--;
        }
```

(continued)

Listing 3-2. *continued*

```
    *pdwRects=(cRectReturn-cRect);
    return TRUE;
    }

BOOL CImpIEnumRECT::Skip(DWORD cSkip)
    {
    if ((m_iCur+cSkip) >= CRECTS)
        return FALSE;

    m_iCur+=cSkip;
    return TRUE;
    }

void CImpIEnumRECT::Reset(void)
    {
    m_iCur=0;
    return;
    }
```

NOTE: The following files (ENUMC.H, ENUMC.C, and IENUM.C) are for the C implementation of the Enum program.

ENUMC.H

```
/*
 * Enumerator in C, Chapter 3
 *
 * Definitions, structures, and prototypes.
 *
 * Copyright (c)1993 Microsoft Corporation, All Rights Reserved
 */

#ifndef _ENUMC_H_
#define _ENUMC_H_

#include <ienum0.h>      //Found in shared include directory
#include <book1632.h>

//Menu resource ID and commands
#define IDR_MENU                    1
```

Listing 3-3.
The ENUM program implemented in C.

(continued)

Listing 3-3. *continued*

```
#define IDM_ENUMCREATE              100
#define IDM_ENUMRELEASE             101
#define IDM_ENUMRUNTHROUGH          102
#define IDM_ENUMEVERYTHIRD          103
#define IDM_ENUMRESET               104
#define IDM_ENUMEXIT                105

//ENUMC.C
LRESULT FAR PASCAL EXPORT EnumWndProc(HWND, UINT, WPARAM, LPARAM);

typedef struct tagAPPVARS
    {
    HINSTANCE       m_hInst;            //WinMain parameters
    HINSTANCE       m_hInstPrev;
    UINT            m_nCmdShow;

    HWND            m_hWnd;             //Main window handle
    LPENUMRECT      m_pIEnumRect;       //Enumerator interface
    } APPVARS, FAR *LPAPPVARS;

LPAPPVARS AppVarsConstructor(HINSTANCE, HINSTANCE, UINT);
void      AppVarsDestructor(LPAPPVARS);
BOOL      AppVarsFInit(LPAPPVARS);

#define CBWNDEXTRA            sizeof(LONG)
#define ENUMWL_STRUCTURE      0

//Number of rectangles that IEnumRECT objects support (for demo)
#define CRECTS      15

/*
 * In C we make a class by reusing the elements of IEnumRECT,
 * thereby inheriting from it, albeit manually.
 */

typedef struct tagIMPIENUMRECT
    {
    IEnumRECTVtbl FAR * lpVtbl;
    DWORD           m_cRef;         //Reference count
    DWORD           m_iCur;         //Current position
    RECT            m_rgrc[CRECTS]; //RECTs we enumerate
    } IMPIENUMRECT, FAR *LPIMPIENUMRECT;

/*
```

(continued)

Listing 3-3. *continued*

```
 * In C, you must separately declare member functions
 * with globally unique names, so prefixing with the class name
 * should remove any conflicts.
 */

LPIMPIENUMRECT  IMPIEnumRect_Constructor(void);
void            IMPIEnumRect_Destructor(LPIMPIENUMRECT);

DWORD           IMPIEnumRect_AddRef(LPENUMRECT);
DWORD           IMPIEnumRect_Release(LPENUMRECT);
BOOL            IMPIEnumRect_Next(LPENUMRECT, DWORD, LPRECT
                    , LPDWORD);
BOOL            IMPIEnumRect_Skip(LPENUMRECT, DWORD);
void            IMPIEnumRect_Reset(LPENUMRECT);

//Function that creates one of these objects
BOOL CreateRECTEnumerator(LPENUMRECT FAR *);

#endif //_ENUMC_H_
```

ENUMC.C

```
/*
 * Enumerator in C Chapter 3
 *
 * Copyright (c)1993 Microsoft Corporation, All Rights Reserved
 */

#include <windows.h>
#include <malloc.h>
#include "enumc.h"

int PASCAL WinMain(HINSTANCE hInst, HINSTANCE hInstPrev
    , LPSTR pszCmdLine, int nCmdShow)
    {
    MSG         msg;
    LPAPPVARS   pAV;

    pAV=AppVarsConstructor(hInst, hInstPrev, nCmdShow);

    if (NULL==pAV)
        return -1;
```

(continued)

Listing 3-3. *continued*

```
    if (AppVarsFInit(pAV))
        {
        while (GetMessage(&msg, NULL, 0,0 ))
            {
            TranslateMessage(&msg);
            DispatchMessage(&msg);
            }
        }

    AppVarsDestructor(pAV);
    return msg.wParam;
    }

LRESULT FAR PASCAL EXPORT EnumWndProc(HWND hWnd, UINT iMsg,
    WPARAM wParam, LPARAM lParam)
    {
    LPAPPVARS   pAV;
    RECT        rc;
    DWORD       cRect;

    COMMANDPARAMS(wID, wCode, hWndMsg);

    pAV=(LPAPPVARS)GetWindowLong(hWnd, ENUMWL_STRUCTURE);

    switch (iMsg)
        {
        case WM_NCCREATE:
            pAV=(LPAPPVARS)((LONG)((LPCREATESTRUCT)lParam)
                ->lpCreateParams);

            SetWindowLong(hWnd, ENUMWL_STRUCTURE, (LONG)pAV);
            return (DefWindowProc(hWnd, iMsg, wParam, lParam));

        case WM_DESTROY:
            PostQuitMessage(0);
            break;

        case WM_COMMAND:
            switch (wID)
                {
                case IDM_ENUMCREATE:
                    if (NULL!=pAV->m_pIEnumRect)
                        {
```

(continued)

Listing 3-3. *continued*

```
                pAV->m_pIEnumRect->lpVtbl->Release(pAVM
                    ->m_pIEnumRect);
                }

            CreateRECTEnumerator(&pAV->m_pIEnumRect);
            break;

        case IDM_ENUMRELEASE:
            if (NULL==pAV->m_pIEnumRect)
                break;

            if (0==pAV->m_pIEnumRect->lpVtbl->Release(pAV
                ->m_pIEnumRect))
                pAV->m_pIEnumRect=NULL;

            break;

        case IDM_ENUMRUNTHROUGH:
            if (NULL==pAV->m_pIEnumRect)
                break;

            while (pAV->m_pIEnumRect->lpVtbl->Next(pAV
                ->m_pIEnumRect, 1, &rc, &cRect))
                ;

            break;

        case IDM_ENUMEVERYTHIRD:
            if (NULL==pAV->m_pIEnumRect)
                break;

            while (pAV->m_pIEnumRect->lpVtbl->Next(pAV
                ->m_pIEnumRect, 1, &rc, &cRect))
                {
                if (!pAV->m_pIEnumRect->lpVtbl->Skip(pAV
                    ->m_pIEnumRect, 2))
                    break;
                }
            break;

        case IDM_ENUMRESET:
            if (NULL==pAV->m_pIEnumRect)
                break;

            pAV->m_pIEnumRect->lpVtbl->Reset(pAV
                ->m_pIEnumRect);
            break;
```

(continued)

Listing 3-3. *continued*

```
                case IDM_ENUMEXIT:
                    PostMessage(hWnd, WM_CLOSE, 0, 0L);
                    break;
                }
            break;

        default:
            return (DefWindowProc(hWnd, iMsg, wParam, lParam));
        }

    return 0L;
    }

LPAPPVARS AppVarsConstructor(HINSTANCE hInst, HINSTANCE hInstPrev
    , UINT nCmdShow)
    {
    LPAPPVARS       pAV;

    pAV=(LPAPPVARS)_fmalloc(sizeof(APPVARS));

    if (NULL==pAV)
        return NULL;

    pAV->m_hInst     =hInst;
    pAV->m_hInstPrev =hInstPrev;
    pAV->m_nCmdShow  =nCmdShow;

    pAV->m_hWnd=NULL;
    pAV->m_pIEnumRect=NULL;

    return pAV;
    }

void AppVarsDestructor(LPAPPVARS pAV)
    {
    //Free any object we still hold on to
    if (NULL!=pAV->m_pIEnumRect)
        pAV->m_pIEnumRect->lpVtbl->Release(pAV->m_pIEnumRect);

    if (IsWindow(pAV->m_hWnd))
        DestroyWindow(pAV->m_hWnd);

    _ffree((LPVOID)pAV);
```

(continued)

Listing 3-3. *continued*

```
    return;
    }

BOOL AppVarsFInit(LPAPPVARS pAV)
    {
    WNDCLASS    wc;

    if (!pAV->m_hInstPrev)
        {

        wc.style            = CS_HREDRAW | CS_VREDRAW;
        wc.lpfnWndProc      = (WNDPROC)EnumWndProc;
        wc.cbClsExtra       = 0;
        wc.cbWndExtra       = CBWNDEXTRA;
        wc.hInstance        = pAV->m_hInst;
        wc.hIcon            = LoadIcon(pAV->m_hInst, "Icon");
        wc.hCursor          = LoadCursor(NULL, IDC_ARROW);
        wc.hbrBackground    = (HBRUSH)(COLOR_WINDOW + 1);
        wc.lpszMenuName     = MAKEINTRESOURCE(IDR_MENU);
        wc.lpszClassName    = "ENUMC";

        if (!RegisterClass(&wc))
            return FALSE;
        }

        pAV->m_hWnd=CreateWindow("ENUMC", "Enumerator in C"
            , WS_MINIMIZEBOX | WS_OVERLAPPEDWINDOW
            , 35, 35, 350, 250, NULL, NULL, pAV->m_hInst, pAV);

    if (NULL==pAV->m_hWnd)
        return FALSE;

    ShowWindow(pAV->m_hWnd, pAV->m_nCmdShow);
    UpdateWindow(pAV->m_hWnd);

    return TRUE;
    }
```

IENUM.C

```
/*
 * Enumerator in C, Chapter 3
 * Implements the IMPIENUMRECT structure and functions (an object).
 */
```

(continued)

Listing 3-3. *continued*

```
#include <windows.h>
#include <malloc.h>
#include "enumc.h"

//We have to explicitly define function table for IEnumRECT in C
static IEnumRECTVtbl  vtEnumRect;
static BOOL           fVtblInitialized=FALSE;

/*
 * CreateRECTEnumerator
 *
 * Purpose:
 *  Given an array of rectangles, creates an enumerator interface
 *  on top of that array.

 *
 * Parameters:
 *  ppEnum          LPENUMRECT FAR * in which to return the interface
 *                  pointer on the created object.
 *
 * Return value:
 *  BOOL            TRUE if successful, FALSE otherwise.
 */

BOOL CreateRECTEnumerator(LPENUMRECT FAR *ppEnum)
    {
    if (NULL==ppEnum)
        return FALSE;

    //Create the object storing a pointer to the interface
    *ppEnum=(LPENUMRECT)IMPIEnumRect_Constructor();

    if (NULL==*ppEnum)
        return FALSE;

    //If creation worked, AddRef the interface
    if (NULL!=*ppEnum)
        (*ppEnum)->lpVtbl->AddRef(*ppEnum);

    return (NULL!=*ppEnum);
    }

LPIMPIENUMRECT IMPIEnumRect_Constructor(void)
    {
    LPIMPIENUMRECT      pER;
    UINT                i;
```

(continued)

Listing 3-3. *continued*

```
/*
 * First time through initialize function table.  Such a table
 * could be defined as a constant instead of doing explicit
 * initialization here.  However, this method shows exactly
 * which pointers are going where and does not depend on knowing
 * the ordering of the functions in the table, just the names.
 */

    if (!fVtblInitialized)
        {
        vtEnumRect.AddRef =IMPIEnumRect_AddRef;
        vtEnumRect.Release=IMPIEnumRect_Release;
        vtEnumRect.Next   =IMPIEnumRect_Next;
        vtEnumRect.Skip   =IMPIEnumRect_Skip;
        vtEnumRect.Reset  =IMPIEnumRect_Reset;

        fVtblInitialized=TRUE;
        }

    pER=(LPIMPIENUMRECT)_fmalloc(sizeof(IMPIENUMRECT));

    if (NULL==pER)
        return NULL;

    //Initialize function table pointer
    pER->lpVtbl=&vtEnumRect;

    //Initialize the array of rectangles
    for (i=0; i < CRECTS; i++)
        SetRect(&pER->m_rgrc[i], i, i*2, i*3, i*4);

    //Ref counts always start at zero
    pER->m_cRef=0;

    //Current pointer is the first element.
    pER->m_iCur=0;

    return pER;
    }

void IMPIEnumRect_Destructor(LPIMPIENUMRECT pER)
    {
    if (NULL==pER)
        return;
```

(continued)

Listing 3-3. *continued*

```
    _ffree((LPVOID)pER);

    return;
    }

DWORD IMPIEnumRect_AddRef(LPENUMRECT pEnum)
    {
    LPIMPIENUMRECT      pER=(LPIMPIENUMRECT)pEnum;

    if (NULL==pER)
        return 0L;

    return ++pER->m_cRef;
    }

DWORD IMPIEnumRect_Release(LPENUMRECT pEnum)
    {
    LPIMPIENUMRECT      pER=(LPIMPIENUMRECT)pEnum;
    DWORD               cRefT;

    if (NULL==pER)
        return 0L;

    cRefT=--pER->m_cRef;

    if (0==pER->m_cRef)
        IMPIEnumRect_Destructor(pER);

    return cRefT;
    }

BOOL IMPIEnumRect_Next(LPENUMRECT pEnum, DWORD cRect
    , LPRECT prc, LPDWORD pdwRects)
    {
    LPIMPIENUMRECT  pER=(LPIMPIENUMRECT)pEnum;
    DWORD           cRectReturn=0L;

    if (NULL==pdwRects)
        return FALSE;

    *pdwRects=0L;

    if (NULL==prc || (pER->m_iCur >= CRECTS))
        return FALSE;
```

(continued)

Listing 3-3. *continued*

```
    while (pER->m_iCur < CRECTS && cRect > 0)
        {
        *prc++=pER->m_rgrc[pER->m_iCur++];
        cRectReturn++;
        cRect--;
        }

    *pdwRects=(cRectReturn-cRect);
    return TRUE;
    }

BOOL IMPIEnumRect_Skip(LPENUMRECT pEnum, DWORD cSkip)
    {
    LPIMPIENUMRECT      pER=(LPIMPIENUMRECT)pEnum;

    if (NULL==pER)
        return FALSE;

    if ((pER->m_iCur+cSkip) >= CRECTS)
        return FALSE;

    pER->m_iCur+=cSkip;
    return TRUE;
    }

void IMPIEnumRect_Reset(LPENUMRECT pEnum)
    {
    LPIMPIENUMRECT      pER=(LPIMPIENUMRECT)pEnum;

    if (NULL==pER)
        return;

    pER->m_iCur=0;
    return;
    }
```

When IENUM0.H is compiled for C++, it generates a C++ abstract base class—that is, a base class that defines a set of pure virtual functions (by using *virtual* and *=0*). In addition, IENUM0.H defines a far pointer type for this interface in the conventional form LP<INTERFACE>, where <INTERFACE> is the interface name in all caps excluding the *I* prefix. The C++ implementation of the *RECTEnumerator* object, *CImplEnumRECT* in ENUMCPP.H, inherits these function signatures from this interface and provides each implementation. Instantiating this C++ class will generate an IEnumRECT function table for you.

Defining an interface in C is more work, primarily because you have to construct the function table manually. In ENUMC, the structure *IEnumRECTVtbl*[5] is a structure of function pointers that is exactly what many C++ compilers create internally for C++ classes. The actual interface, *IEnumRECT*, is defined as a structure that contains a pointer to this function table. So when a C application has a pointer to an interface, it really has a pointer to a pointer to a function table. The C implementation of the *RECTEnumerator* object, a structure named IMPIENUMRECT in ENUMC.H, duplicates the *lpVtbl* member of *IEnumRECT* in its own structure, thereby making a pointer to IMPIENUMRECT polymorphic with a pointer to *IEnumRECT*. This duplicates what happens automatically with C++ classes and is common in C-based OLE 2 code.

Creating the *RECTEnumerator* Object

When you choose the Create command from the Enum menu of either ENUMC or ENUMCPP, you generate a call (see IDM_ENUMCREATE in the WM_COMMAND *switch*) to *CreateRECTEnumerator*. This creation function creates the object and returns the *IEnumRECT* interface pointer in an *out-parameter*—that is, the caller passes the address in which *CreateRECTEnumerator* stores the interface pointer. This technique is used everywhere in OLE 2 to allow standardization of almost all return values into a type named HRESULT, described in the later section "HRESULT and SCODE." To avoid further complicating your life now with HRESULT, we'll stick with a BOOL return type.

Note that specific functions to create specific types of object are rare in OLE 2. Most often you use a class factory object (and *IClassFactory::CreateInstance*), which eliminates the need for most, but not all, API functions such as *CreateRECTEnumerator*. As we'll see in Chapter 4, implementations of *IClassFactory::CreateInstance* look very much like *CreateRECTEnumerator*, in either language.

In this example, the ENUMC and ENUMCPP programs are both user and implementor of the same object. Both programs use an internal function, *CreateRECTEnumerator*, to obtain an *IEnumRECT* pointer to the *RECTEnumerator* object. This demonstrates the typical fashion through which a user obtains an interface pointer by calling an API function. Internally, the *CreateRECTEnumerator* creates the function table for the *IEnumRECT* interface and then allocates and initializes the object itself.

In C++, the *new* operator applied to the *CImplEnumRECT* class automatically allocates memory for the object and creates the function table. All you have to do is initialize the object. Because the *CImplEnumRECT* class

5. The jargon name *Vtbl* means *virtual function table*, which is always referred to in this book as simply a function table.

inherits from *IEnumRECT*, you can typecast the pointer from *new* to an *LPENUMRECT*, which turns it into a pointer to only the interface. So in C++, it's highly convenient to implement objects as C++ objects, although the pointers you return are always interface pointers.

In C, you must manually fill the function table, manually allocate the object's memory, and then initialize it exactly as in C++. The function *IMPIEnumRECT_Constructor* handles all this for you and lets you use it in place of the *new* operator in C++. This constructor function first creates the function table by storing function pointers in a global array of type *IEnumRECTVtbl*. (This needs to happen only once for all instances of the object.) Only the implementation of this object knows that the function table actually exists in a global variable such as this. The object's user sees only the table but has no knowledge about where that table lives. In any case, *IMPIEnumRECT-_Constructor* then allocates the object's structure and stores a pointer to the function table in the *lpVtbl* member of the object. Finally, it performs the same initialization as in C++.

Using an *IEnumRECT* Pointer

You will also notice that *CreateRECTEnumerator* calls the object's *AddRef* function before returning the pointer. This rule of reference counting, one of several, is explained in "Reference Counting." However, this one call, along with calls to the other *IEnumRECT* functions in ENUMC and ENUMCPP, demonstrates the calling differences between C and C++. Given an interface pointer, a C++ user calls member functions through the pointer as with any other C++ object pointer:

```
//C++ call to interface member function
pIEnumRect->AddRef();
```

This will land in *CImpIEnumRECT::AddRef* just as any other C++ call would. The *this* pointer inside the member function is identical to *pIEnumRECT*, through which the function was called.

In C, we have a more complicated story. First, any member function call made through an interface pointer must be indirect through the *lpVtbl* member before it gets at the function (an indirection done automatically in C++):

```
//C call to interface member function
pIEnumRect->lpVtbl->AddRef(pIEnumRect);
```

To ensure that the implementation of *IEnumRECT::AddRef* invoked here knows which object is being accessed, C users must pass the same interface pointer as the first parameter to the function. This mimics the behavior of the *this* pointer that is automatic in C++. Because this extra parameter is necessary, the function prototypes in IENUM0.H for the C interface had to include the pointer type as the first parameter.

The two lines of preceding code illustrate why C++ is more *convenient,* but no more *functional,* than C in using Windows Objects. The C user will always need the extra indirection and the extra parameter, which can quickly add up to a lot of extra code. By no means, however, does that small fact render it impossible to write C code for OLE 2. An object implementor in C needs only to provide for creating the function table manually. But aside from these few differences, programming in OLE 2 is identical in either language.

Reference Counting

The implementation of the *RECTEnumerator* object is illustrative, but not useful. To build the bridge between illustrative objects and useful objects, we need more information that applies to all the remaining chapters of this book. One of the most important subjects is reference counting, which is a set of rules that control an object's lifetime.

If you are an object, your reference counting requires that you live a unique life in which you are not allowed to rest eternally unless all your acquaintances have also passed on. (I say "unique life" because if everyone lived this way, we'd all be immortal. But an object user does not have a reference count and therefore does not live such a life.) At birth, you form an acquaintance with your mother, and as you live your life, you meet new people and form new acquaintances. Whenever you form a new relationship, you increment your reference count. Whenever an acquaintance dies, you are released of that relationship, and you decrement your reference count. Only when all such relationships end are you allowed your personal journey to the afterlife. That means that for you, the object, your reference count is zero, and you are allowed to free your memory.

You might have noticed a potential problem with this. If you are an object as well as an object user, and the object you are using just so happens to be the user that is using your object, you have a seeming paradox of mutual immortality on your hands. Neither party can die because each has an acquaintance with the other, or what is known as a circular reference count. In such cases...free the other object, as well. In other words, the Almighty End User strikes one object down with a lightning bolt from the sky, thereby breaking the circular reference. In such cases, you have to remember the Almighty End User, who does things such as close an application. This act overrides the relationship rule; the object in the application that's closing brutally terminates all connections to it in such a way that its reference count is reduced to zero, which might free the other object as well.

The rules governing reference counting can be distilled into two fundamental principles:

- Creation of a new interface pointer to an object must be accompanied by an *AddRef* call to the object through that new pointer.
- Destruction of an interface pointer (that is, when the pointer goes out of scope) must be accompanied by a *Release* call through that pointer before it can be destroyed.

This means that whenever you assign one pointer to another in some piece of code, you should use *AddRef* for the new copy (the left operand) of the pointer. Before that pointer is overwritten, it must have *Release* called for it. All *AddRef* and *Release* calls made through interfaces affect the reference count of the entire object, which is shared among all interfaces on that object. Consider the following code:

```
LPSOMEINTERFACE     pISome1;
LPSOMEINTERFACE     pISome2
LPSOMEINTERFACE     pCopy;

//A function that creates the pointer uses AddRef on it.
CreateISomeObject(&pISome1);    //Some1 ref count=1
CreateISomeObject(&pISome2);    //Some2 ref count=1

pCopy=pISome1;                  //Some1 count=1
pCopy->AddRef();                //AddRef new copy, Some1=2

[Do things]

pCopy->Release();               //Release before overwrite, Some1=1
pCopy=pISome2;                  //Some2=1
pCopy->AddRef();                //Some2=2

[What kinds of things do you do]

pCopy->Release();               //Release before overwrite, Some2=1
pCopy=NULL;

[Things that make us go]

pISome2->Release();     //Release when done, Some2=0, Some2 freed.
pISome1->Release();     //Release when done, Some1=0, Some1 freed.
```

An object's lifetime is controlled by all *AddRef* and *Release* calls on all its interfaces combined. Reference counting for a specific interface is useful in debugging to verify that your user is counting properly, but it is the object reference count that matters. According to the first fundamental principle of reference counting, any function that returns a pointer to an interface must call *AddRef* through that pointer. Functions that create an actual object and return the first pointer to an interface on that object are such functions, like *CreateISomeObject* in the preceding example. Now anytime you create a new copy of a pointer, you must also call *AddRef* through that new copy because you have two different references, two different pointer variables, to the same object that are independent. Then according to the second principle of reference counting, all *AddRef* calls must be matched with a *Release* call. So before your pointer variables are destroyed (by an explicit overwrite or by going out of scope), you must call *Release* through that pointer. This includes calling *Release* through any pointer copy (through which you called *AddRef*) as well as through the pointer you obtained from the function that created the object. Functions that create objects and return interface pointers are the functions that actually create the pointers. Such functions fill the *out-parameters* from which the caller receives the pointer. Therefore, it is the creator, not the caller, that is responsible for the first *AddRef* on the object by means of the interface pointer it initially returns.

My Kingdom for Some Optimizations!

The stated rules and their effect on the code shown earlier probably seem rather fascist. Well, they are, but that doesn't mean there's no underground movement.

When you know the lifetimes of all interface pointers to the same object, you can bypass the majority of *AddRef* and *Release* calls. There are two manifestations of such knowledge: nested lifetimes and overlapping lifetimes.

In the preceding code, every instance of *pCopy* is nested within the lifetimes of *pISome1* and *pISome2*—that is, the copy lives and dies within the lifetime of the original. After *CreateISomeObject* is called, both objects have a reference count of one. The lifetimes of their pointers is bounded by these create calls and the final *Release* calls made through those pointers. Because we know these lifetimes, we can eliminate any other *AddRef* and *Release* calls to copies of those pointers:

```
LPSOMEINTERFACE     pISome1;
LPSOMEINTERFACE     pISome2;
LPSOMEINTERFACE     pCopy;
```

```
CreateISomeObject(&pISome1);    //Some1 ref count=1
CreateISomeObject(&pISome2);    //Some2 ref count=1

pCopy=pISome1;                  //Some1=1, pCopy nested in Some1's life

[Do things]

pCopy=pISome2;                  //Some2=1, pCopy nested in Some2's life

[Do other things]

pICopy=NULL;                    //No Release necessary

[Do anything, then clean up]

pISome2->Release();     //Release when done, Some2=0, Some2 freed.
pISome1->Release();     //Release when done, Some1=0, Some1 freed.
```

Overlapping lifetimes are those in which the original pointer dies after the copy is born but before the copy itself dies. If the copy is alive at the original's funeral, it can inherit ownership of the reference count on behalf of the original:

```
LPSOMEINTERFACE     pISome1;
LPSOMEINTERFACE     pCopy;

CreateISomeObject(&pISome1);    //Some1 ref count=1

pCopy=pISome1;      //Some1=1, pCopy nested in Some1's life
pISome1=NULL;       //Pointer destroyed, pCopy inherits count, Some1=1

pCopy->Release(); //Release inherited ref count, Some1=0, Some1 freed.
```

With these optimizations, reference counting can be reduced to four specific rules, in which an *AddRef* for a new copy of a pointer is necessary (and thus must have a *Release* call made through it when destroyed):

- Functions that return a new interface pointer in an *out-parameter* or as a return value must call *AddRef* for the object through that pointer before returning.
- Functions that accept an *in-out parameter* must call *Release* for the *in-parameter* before overwriting it and must call *AddRef* for the *out-parameter*. Callers of these functions must call *AddRef* for the passed pointer to maintain a separate copy if the function is known to call *Release* for that pointer.
- If two pointers to the same object have unrelated lifetimes, *AddRef* must be called for each.
- Call *AddRef* for each local copy of a global pointer.

In all cases, some piece of code must call *Release* for every *AddRef* on a pointer. In the first of the preceding cases, the caller of a function that returns a new pointer (such as *CreateISomeObject*) becomes responsible for that new object. When the caller has finished with the object, it must call *Release.* If the object's reference count is decreased to zero because of this, the object may be destroyed at the discretion of the implementor, but from the user's point of view, the object is gone. If you fail to use *Release* for a reference count, you generally doom the object to the boredom of useless immortality—memory might not be freed, or the DLL or EXE supplying that object might not unload. Be humane to your objects: Be sure to release them.

Call-Use-Release

The first optimized reference counting rule exposes a common pattern in OLE 2 programming. To use an object, you will call some function that returns a pointer to an interface. That function will call *AddRef* on behalf of this new pointer. You then use that pointer for as long as you want. When you have finished with it, you call *Release* through that pointer to let the object know you no longer need it.

The same object might, in fact, be in use through other pointers, even in another process. As far as you're concerned, you call *Release* to free the reference count for which you are responsible, and you know that after that time you cannot access that object again because it might have freed itself. If there are other outstanding pointers to that object elsewhere, however, the object is still in memory, but you are oblivious to that fact.

This pattern, which I refer to as *Call-Use-Release,* is common in OLE 2 programming. There are many functions you call to obtain pointers with a reference count, and there are many different things to do with those pointers (which is why this book is so thick). But regardless of how you got the pointer or what you did with it, you must call *Release* through it when you are finished.

The final *Release* can do more than simply free the object—"free the object" can imply many other actions. For example, Compound File objects discussed in Chapter 5 might close a file; a memory manager object we'll see in Chapter 4 will free any allocations it has made; a compound document object we'll implement in Chapter 10 might close down an application. Because the *Release* member function can be overloaded in this manner, you will notice an absence of "close" API functions in OLE 2. There is a function to open a Compound File, but there is no function to close it—the API provides the initial *AddRef,* and closure is handled in the final *Release.*

IUnknown, the Root of All Evil

From the preceding discussion, you can isolate two fundamental interface and object operations: reference counting and pointer creation. The interface named *IUnknown*, which all Windows Objects support, encapsulates these two ideas in three member functions:

Function	Result
QueryInterface	Returns a pointer to the requested interface on the same object. *QueryInterface* is considered a function that creates a pointer, so it calls *AddRef* through any pointer it returns.
AddRef	Increments the object's reference count, returning the current count.
Release	Decrements the object's reference count, returning the new count, and can free the object when the reference count reaches zero.

Because *AddRef* and *Release* behave exactly as described in the previous section, we won't examine them further here. Instead, we'll look more closely at *QueryInterface.*

QueryInterface is more than simply the fundamental creator of interface pointers, although it does always return a pointer to a different interface on the same object. *QueryInterface* allows you to access each separate function table supported by an individual object. How you obtain the *first* interface pointer on the object is one thing—*QueryInterface* allows you to get to all other interface pointers on the same object *after* creation.

QueryInterface allows an object user to discover an object's capabilities at runtime, instead of having to incorporate specific knowledge about objects at compile-time. You learn capabilities by asking for additional interfaces that the object supports, a process called *interface negotiation.* When you create an arbitrary object, you'll always get back an interface pointer that looks like an *IUnknown* pointer because all other interfaces incorporate *IUnknown.* So if you are able to get an object, you can *always* call *QueryInterface.*

With an *IUnknown* pointer, you can now determine whether the object supports a particular feature by calling *QueryInterface.* For example, to determine whether the object supports data transfer, call *QueryInterface* asking for an *IDataObject* interface (see Chapter 6). To determine whether the object is a Compound Document object, meaning that it can be treated in a standard way for editing capabilities, call *QueryInterface* for *IOleObject* (see Chapters 9 and 10). *IOleObject* describes only an embedded object, so if you want to determine whether it supports linking, call *QueryInterface* for *IOleLink* (see Chapter 12). To go even further, you can ask the object whether it supports in-place activation by calling *QueryInterface* for *IOleInPlaceObject.* (See Chapters 15 and 16.)

When you call *QueryInterface* for a new pointer, you not only learn whether the object is capable of the set of functions implied by that interface, but you receive back the interface pointer through which you access those functions. This means that you cannot possibly attempt to use certain features of an object if it does not support those features because you can never get the appropriate interface pointer from the object. In other words, if you speak a different language than I do, we cannot communicate; only when we establish a common language can we express our ideas (functions) to one another. Furthermore, it is impossible for me to offend you verbally unless I speak in your language; or in Windows Objects terms, I am not able to pass the wrong object to a function that does not understand that object because I must use the language of the object to perform any function on it.

Applications benefit from being able to make decisions dynamically about how to treat an object based on that object's capabilities, instead of rigidly compiling such behavior. Let's say I work at the United Nations in New York City and I speak English and German. I walk into a room with 10 international delegates with whom I need to discuss a few issues. I go up to one of the delegates and ask "Do you speak English?" This query is met with an affirmative, "Yes." Great, now we can talk. Partway through our conversation, I find that I simply cannot express one of my ideas in English, but I know I could express it in German—some languages have words without equivalents in other languages. So I ask, "Sprechen Sie Deutsch?" to which the other person responds "Ja." Because my partner also speaks German, I can now express my idea in that language. If German were not in my partner's repertoire, we would be limited to speaking English only.

My ability to communicate with anyone is limited not by the number of languages I speak, but by the languages the other person and I have in common. This means that my level of communication varies from person to person. With some people, I can converse in two languages; with others, I might converse in only one, or I might not be able to converse at all. The key points are that I learn this when I meet the person and that my knowing many languages allows me to speak with many more people, not just with people who speak exactly the same set of languages.

How does this apply to objects? The *QueryInterface* mechanism allows an object, or a user of objects, to implement or to be able to use as many interfaces as desired without any fear of restricting your ability to use objects or be used by some object user. For example, a compound document object can implement full in-place activation capabilities without restricting itself to being useful only to in-place container applications. A non-in-place container can still use that object as a non-in-place object, and in such a case, the in-place activation interfaces are ignored entirely.

I've often been asked why there is not a function that returns a list of all the interfaces an object supports. The answer is that such a function would be, for the most part, useless. What would you do programmatically with such information? Although it might be useful in some very esoteric circumstances, you never really need to know whether an object supports an interface unless you intend to perform some function through that interface. So you ask for it via *QueryInterface*. Furthermore, the list of interfaces that an object of a specific class supports is constant only within a specific object's lifetime and might vary between different instantiations of objects of the same class. Therefore, you cannot assume that if Object 1 of class X supports these interfaces, Object 2 of class X does as well. You must also not assume that if objects of class X once supported interface Y, they always will, because the object might change in the meantime. Because having some list of interfaces doesn't get you far and because the capability to obtain such a list is outright dangerous, *QueryInterface* is the only way to learn about an object's capabilities.

QueryInterface vs. Inheritance

Use of *QueryInterface* is superior to use of C++ base classes and C++ inheritance for two reasons. First, given an arbitrary C++ object pointer to some base class object, you really have no way to determine whether that pointer is actually referring to some derived class object instead—you have no way to examine the virtual function table to see exactly what kind of object you have. Therefore, you are *always and forever* restricted to dealing with that object on the base class's terms. Using *QueryInterface*, on the other hand, allows you to get at any function table you want from the base *IUnknown* interface. Given any *IUnknown*, you can find out how rich the object actually is. You can get from the base to more specific interfaces.

The second major advantage of *QueryInterface* is that unless an object supports an interface, you cannot call member functions that the object does not support. This is not true of C++ objects. Take, for example, the base object class *CObject* in Microsoft's Foundation Classes. A *CObject* might be capable of serializing itself to a storage device (such as a file); to ask the question "Can you serialize yourself?", you call the member function *IsSerializable.* If the answer is positive, you can then call another function, *Serialize,* to actually perform the task.

That's nice, but a user of a *CObject* is in no way barred from calling *Serialize* at any time. In other words, serialization capability is not tightly coupled to the question of whether the object can actually serialize. It is therefore possible to call *Serialize* on an object that does not support it, with unpredictable results. The *QueryInterface* mechanism, on the other hand, does tightly couple the question and the capability. You must ask the object via *QueryInterface* whether it supports a particular functionality, and only if it does are you provided the interface through which to call such functions. Given an arbitrary *IUnknown* object, you cannot possibly ask it to serialize itself without first asking for an interface that knows about serialization. If the object does not support the capability, you cannot get the interface. Therefore, you cannot call unsupported functions, and you eliminate the possibility of unpredictable behavior.

QueryInterface Properties and Interface Lifetimes

There are a number of rules in the OLE 2 Design Specifications concerning the behavior of *QueryInterface.* The first and most important rule is that any call to *QueryInterface* asking for *IUnknown* through any interface on the object must always return the *exact same pointer value.* The specific reasoning for this is that given two arbitrary interface pointers, you can determine whether they belong to the same *object* by asking each for an *IUnknown* pointer and comparing the actual pointer values. If they match, application of this rule allows both interface pointers refer to the same object.

The second rule is that after an object is instantiated, the interfaces it supports are static. This means that if *QueryInterface* succeeded for a particular interface at one point in the object's lifetime, an identical call to *QueryInterface* at a later time will also work. This does not mean that the exact pointer *values* returned from both calls will be identical—it means only that the interface is always available. Note that the static set of available interfaces applies to a specific object instantiation, not an object class—that is, two objects of the same type might not both support the same interfaces, but during the lifetime of each, the interfaces they each support will remain static.

The third rule is that the *QueryInterface* operation must be reflexive, symmetric, and transitive, as described in the following table (in which *IInterface1, Interface2,* and *Interface3* are hypothetical):

QueryInterface Property	Meaning
Reflexive	*pInterface1->QueryInterface(IInterface1)* must succeed.
Symmetric	If *pInterface2* was returned from *pInterface1->QueryInterface(IInterface2)*, then *pInterface2->QueryInterface(IInterface1)* must also succeed.
Transitive	If *pInterface2* was obtained from *pInterface1->QueryInterface(IInterface2)* and *pInterface3* was obtained from *pInterface2->QueryInterface(IInterface2)*, then *pInterface3->QueryInterface(IInterface1)* must succeed.

In all these cases, "must succeed" is not so strong as to imply that these cannot fail under the most catastrophic situations. In addition, these properties do not mean that the same pointer *value* is always returned for the interface, with the exception of *IUnknown.*

The final rule has to do with the lifetime of a particular *interface pointer,* as opposed to the lifetime of the entire object. The rule is that as long as the object is alive, all interface pointers obtained on that object must remain valid, even if the *Release* function has been called through those pointers. Consider the following code:

```
LPSOMEINTERFACE     pSome;
LPOTHERINTERFACE    pOther;

CreateSomeObject(&pSome);                    //Object ref count is 1
pSome->QueryInterface(IOtherInterface, &pOther);  //ref count is 2
pOther->Release();                                //ref count is 1
/*
 * Since the object is still alive, pOther is still a valid
 * interface pointer although Release has been called through it.
 */

pSome->Release();            //ref count is 0, object destroyed.

//pSome and pOther are now invalid.
```

When we first obtain the *pSome* pointer, the object will have a reference count of one. The object will therefore remain alive as long as the reference count remains above zero. When we query for *pOther,* the object will have a reference count of two. When we call *pOther->Release* the object will still have a positive reference, meaning that *pOther* will still be valid, even though we called *Release* through it. That is, we can still call member functions through *pOther.* This is because the interface is alive as long as the object is alive. Only when we call *pSome->Release* and reduce the object's reference count to zero will the object be destroyed, thus invalidating all interface pointers on that object.

In later chapters, we'll see a few circumstances in which this rule becomes important. For now, this illustrates why interface-level reference counting is useful only for debugging purposes. A zero reference count on an interface means neither that the interface is invalid nor that the object is invalid. The only important reference count is the one on the entire object, which all implementations of *AddRef* and *Release* on all interfaces of that object must return.

Some Data Types and Calling Conventions

If you look in OLE 2's include file, COMPOBJ.H, you will find *IUnknown* declared as follows:

```
DECLARE_INTERFACE(IUnknown)
    {
    STDMETHOD(QueryInterface) (THIS_ REFIID riid
        , LPVOID FAR* ppvObj) PURE;
    STDMETHOD_(ULONG,AddRef) (THIS)  PURE;
    STDMETHOD_(ULONG,Release) (THIS) PURE;
    };
```

Offhand, this might look very odd, but there are a number of macros shown here that are used in many other aspects of OLE 2.

DECLARE_INTERFACE, STDMETHOD, STDMETHOD_, THIS, THIS_, and PURE are all macros that hide the differences between C and C++ interface definitions as well as those among Win16, Win32, and Macintosh implementations. When this interface declaration is compiled in C++, the result is similar to the definition of *IEnumRECT* in IENUM0.H; the same goes for a C compilation. For complete details about how these macros expand, see the comments in the COMPOBJ.H file in your OLE 2 SDK.

Note also that interfaces shown in the ENUMC program are not exactly what is generated through these macros because real OLE 2 interfaces differ in calling convention and return type. The following sections look at these, as well as the REFIID type, in more detail.

STDMETHOD and Associates

The STDMETHOD macro expands into HRESULT STDMETHODCALLTYPE. HRESULT is a special return value type discussed in the next section, "HRESULT and SCODE." STDMETHODCALLTYPE is defined under Microsoft Windows 3.1 as *__export __far __cdecl* and under Windows NT as *__export __cdecl.* The *cdecl* type was necessary to support generation of the proper stack frame for member function calls, portability of C code from 16-bit to 32-bit, and interoperability between C and C++ implementations. The OLE 2 architects would have preferred to have used a more efficient calling convention (such as PASCAL) but were unable due to these constraints.

The STDMETHOD_ (<type>) macro allows a variation on the return type from HRESULT into any other type. *AddRef* and *Release,* for example, return the new reference count instead of an HRESULT. In this sense, they are fairly unique: Most other interface members in all of OLE 2 return HRESULTs, including *QueryInterface.*

Under C++, both STDMETHOD macros include the *virtual* keyword. The PURE macro also compiles under C++ as *=0* to generate pure virtual members in the interface declarations. Of course, C compilations include neither (pure compiles to nothing).

Because the two possible STDMETHOD macros generate the *virtual* and *=0* signatures, they are not used when implementing interface functions, only when declaring one. Instead, you use STDMETHODIMP or STDMETHODIMP_(<type>), which does nothing more than eliminate the *virtual* keyword in C++ compilations but still generate either an HRESULT or a <type> return value along with STDMETHODCALLTYPE.

HRESULT and SCODE

OLE 2 introduces a new return type used by *QueryInterface* and almost every other interface member function: HRESULT, or handle to a result. Conceptually, an HRESULT is a *status code,* or *SCODE,* that describes what occurred and a handle that can be used to obtain additional information about an error or how to recover from it. The intention is that over time, interfaces will return very detailed information that can describe a suggested course of action when failure occurs.

The HRESULT and SCODE types are both 32-bit values containing a severity flag, a facility code, and an information code, as shown in Figure 3-9 on the next page. The Context field is what distinguishes an HRESULT from an SCODE because the Context is always zero in an SCODE but it could contain a handle to additional information in an HRESULT.[6] An SCODE is created or dissected with various macros in the OLE 2 include file SCODE.H. such as MAKE_SCODE. Some of the more commonly used SCODE values are shown in Table 3-1 on the next page. The Facility field of an SCODE

6. In OLE 2, the Context field in an HRESULT is always zero, but this will change in the future.

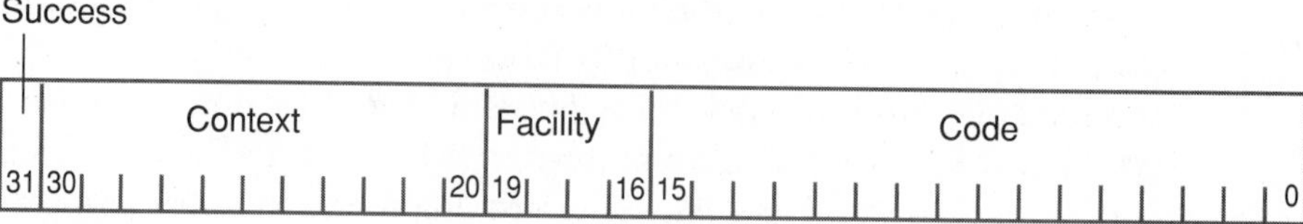

Success 1 bit: 0 Success, 1 Error
Context 11 bits: 0 in SCODE
Facility 4 bits: Indicates which group of status codes this belongs to.
Code 16 bits: Describes the error.

Figure 3-9.
Structure of an HRESULT and an SCODE.

describes the source of the error, which might be in the marshaling of the function call, in the interface function itself, or elsewhere. Any SCODE prefixed with *S_* carries information and means *success,* whereas an SCODE prefixed with *E_* means *failure* and carries a code describing the failure. Many other SCODE symbols defined in the OLE 2 header files are prefixed with other labels, such as *OLE_*, to identify the specific subtechnology generating the error. *OLE_*, for example, means Compound Documents.

Value	Meaning
S_OK	Function succeeded. Also used for functions that semantically return boolean information that succeeds with a TRUE result.
S_FALSE	Function that semantically returns boolean information that succeeds with a FALSE result.
E_NOINTERFACE	*QueryInterface* could not return a pointer to the requested interface.
E_NOTIMPL	Member function contains no implementation.
E_FAIL	Unspecified failure.
E_OUTOFMEMORY	Function failed to allocate necessary memory.

Table 3-1.
Common SCODE values.

Because the HRESULT and SCODE types are not straight equivalents, OLE 2 provides a few functions (implemented in version 2 as macros) that provide conversions between an HRESULT and an SCODE, both of which you'll use often in your own implementations. To create an HRESULT from an SCODE, use the function *ResultFromScode(SCODE)*. To dig an SCODE out of an HRESULT, use the function *GetScode(HRESULT)*, which is also a macro.

Although this seems like a pain, especially on the receiving end of an HRESULT, the most common case allows you to bypass these functions altogether. If a function works completely, it can return the predefined HRESULT called NOERROR, the equivalent of an HRESULT containing S_OK. The code receiving the HRESULT can use one of two macros to determine the success or failure of the function (*hr* stands for an HRESULT):

Macro	Result
SUCCEEDED(*hr*)	Tests the high bit of the HRESULT and returns TRUE if that bit is clear. This will return TRUE for any S_ SCODE and FALSE for any E_ SCODE.
FAILED(*hr*)	Tests the high bit of the HRESULT and returns TRUE if that bit is set. This will return TRUE for any E_ SCODE and FALSE for any S_ SCODE.

Using SUCCEEDED and FAILED is preferred to comparing an HRESULT to NOERROR directly because some codes, such as S_FALSE or STG_S_CONVERTED (see Chapter 5) mean that the function actually succeeded and is returning more information than that simple fact. A test such as *(NOERROR!=hr)* will be TRUE when an HRESULT contains S_FALSE, whereas the *FAILED(hr)* macro will be FALSE. When a function returns either the S_OK code or S_FALSE code, you *should* compare the HRESULT to NOERROR because a macro such as SUCCEEDED will return TRUE for both codes. The *GetScode* function is necessary only when you want to find the exact reason for failure instead of simply the fact that the function did fail.

Globally Unique Identifiers: GUIDs, IIDs, CLSIDs

Every interface is defined by an *interface identifier*, or IID (as in IID-_IUnknown), which is a special case of a universally unique identifier, or UUID. The universally unique identifier is also known as the globally unique identifier, or GUID (pronounced *goo-id*). GUIDs are 128-bit values created with a DEFINE_GUID macro (see INITGUID.H in the OLE 2 SDK). Every interface and object class uses a GUID for identification. As described in the OLE 2 SDK, Microsoft will allocate one or more sets of 256 GUIDs for your exclusive use when you request them, or if you have a network card in your machine, you can run a tool named UUIDGEN.EXE that will provide you with a set of 256 GUIDs based on the time of day, the date, and a unique number contained in your network card. The chance of this tool generating duplicate GUIDs is about the same as two random atoms in the universe colliding to form a small avocado. In other words, don't worry about it.

> All the code shown in this book uses GUIDs prefixed with *000211*, which are allocated to the author. Do not use these GUIDs for your own products.

OLE 2 defines IIDs for every standard interface along with class identifiers (CLSID) for every standard object class. When we call any function that asks for an IID or a CLSID, we pass a *reference* to an instance of the GUID structure that exists in our process space using the types REFIID or REFCLSID. When passing an IID or a CLSID in C, you must use a pointer—that is, pass *&IID_** or *&CLSID_**, where REFIID and REFCLSID are typed as *const* pointers to IID or CLSID. In C++, because a reference is a natural part of the language, you drop the *&*. We will see more specifics about the definition and use of GUIDs in Chapter 4 and beyond.

Finally, to compare two GUID, IID, or CLSID values for equality, use the *IsEqualGUID, IsEqualIID*, and *IsEqualCLSID* functions defined in COMPOBJ.H. There the latter two are simply more readable aliases for *IsEqualGUID*. If you are programming in C++, take a look at COMPOBJ.H, which defines an overloaded "==" operator for the GUID type that, of course, applies equally well to the IID and CLSID types. In this book, I'll use the appropriate *IsEqual...* function to keep the code more usable for C programmers.

OLE 2 Interfaces and API Functions

OLE 2 defines no fewer than 62 interfaces, many of which it implements and uses internally. Those of importance to applications are shown in Figure 3-10, grouped by the technology area to which they apply. Remember that higher technologies build on the lower technologies, as discussed in Chapter 1.

This picture might look a little intimidating at first. Many interfaces are shown, but applications have to implement only a handful. For the basic compound document container applications we'll see in Chapter 9, you need to implement only *IOleClientSite* and *IAdviseSink*. Although you implement only a few, you *use* many more, thereby contributing to the magnitude of Figure 3-10. In addition, some of the interfaces shown are useful only as base interfaces for others. Rarely, if ever, will you use or implement a simple base class by itself.

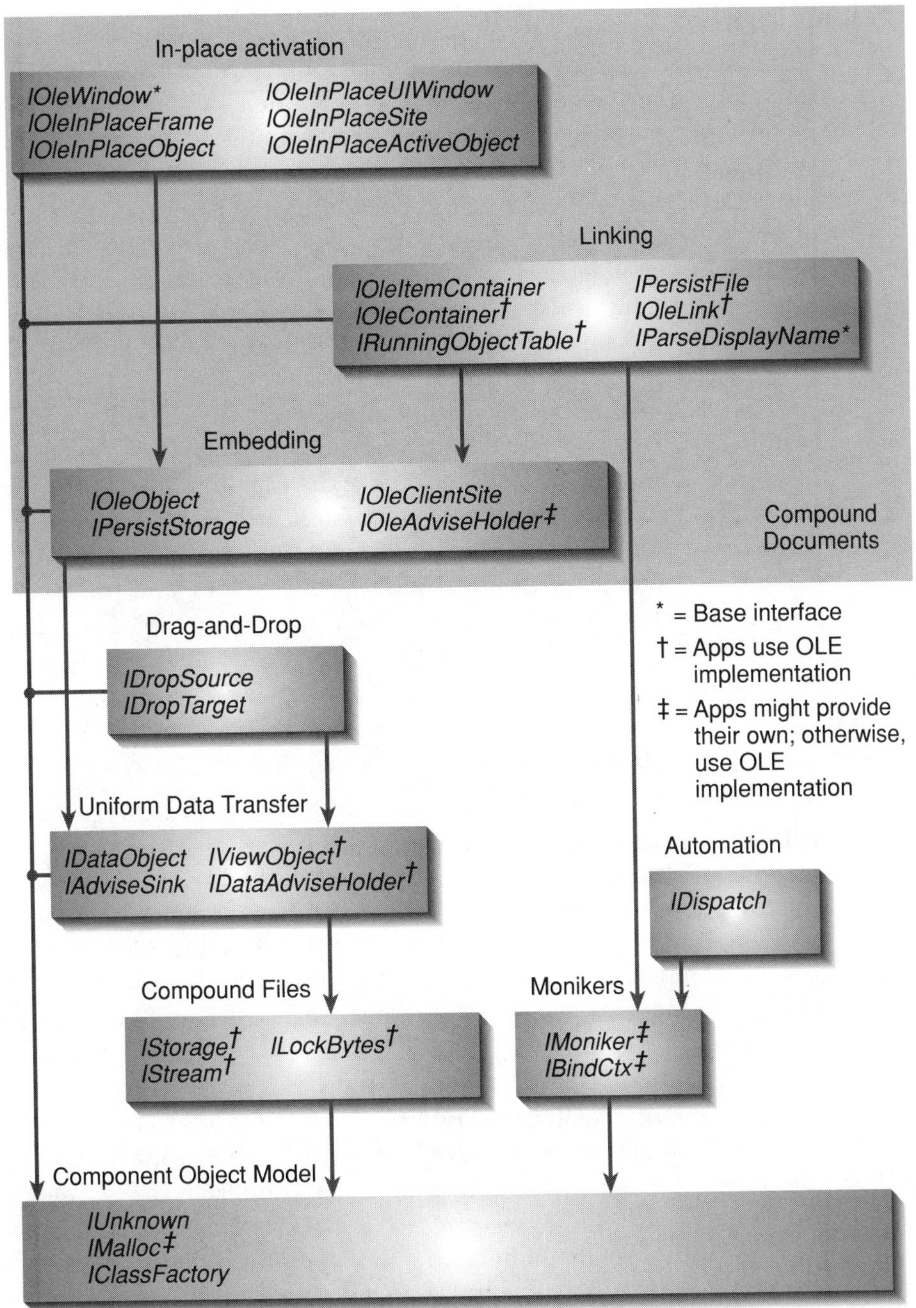

Figure 3-10.
Interesting interfaces in OLE 2 technologies.

Custom Interfaces

Although OLE 2 defines many standard interfaces, objects can define and implement their own interfaces as long as their potential users are implemented to be aware of those interfaces. To reiterate a point, the interfaces that make up compound documents aim to eliminate the need for custom interfaces in particular scenarios. By eliminating custom interfaces from an object, you greatly reduce the amount of specialized code needed in a potential user of that object. The Polyline object we start developing in Chapter 4 begins its life with a custom interface, but throughout this book we'll convert many pieces of it to use standard Compound Document interfaces, leaving truly custom functions in a custom interface.

The big restriction on custom interfaces is that unless you provide for custom marshaling as well, you can use such interfaces only on objects implemented in DLLs that do not require marshaling. Providing custom marshaling is not a simple task, and I recommend that you wait until Microsoft provides generic marshaling code so that all you need to do is provide it with a description of your function parameters, their types, and the way in which they are marshaled. If you absolutely must use the capability now, study the information in the OLE 2 SDK, primarily that concerning the *IMarshal* interface and related functions. Custom marshaling is not covered in this book.

Interfaces vs. API Functions

In developing with OLE 2, you'll soon notice that you use relatively few API functions to achieve your goals. Instead, you call many interface functions. Almost everything an OLE 2 application needs to do can be accomplished by obtaining a pointer to an interface and calling its member functions. Interfaces, in fact, make up more of the so-called "Application Programming Interface" for a user of an object and define the implementation for an object itself instead of using more archaic mechanisms such as explicitly named exports, callback functions, and messages. There are only a few truly fundamental API functions in OLE 2, and most are concerned with creating objects or manipulating things such as class IDs.

The majority of the hundred or so OLE 2 API functions are actually "wrappers" for sequences of commonly used interface calls. Some are the equivalent of calling *QueryInterface* for a specific interface, calling a member function with default parameters, and releasing that interface (Call-Use-Release again). Such wrappers are provided to simplify application development in most cases; their use is seldom required, but you can benefit from the convenience. Even then, typical compound document containers or objects, even with full in-place activation and drag-and-drop implementation, will generally use about 20 of these API functions. Some you might use for very specific reasons; others, although they exist, you probably will never use.

If you are familiar with the OLE 1 API, you'll find that many operations that were API functions in OLE 1, such as *OleSetHostNames*, are replaced by an interface call in OLE 2, such as *IOleObject::SetHostNames*. Many more should become apparent as we implement features using OLE 2.

A major advantage of defining new functions as interfaces is that people outside Microsoft can publish a new interface by providing an include file that defines the interface and possibly by providing a marshaling DLL if they want that interface to be implementable in an EXE. This means no update of the operating system is required to accommodate your functions, and you and others can immediately start using those interfaces without waiting for Microsoft to revise the system.

What Is a Windows Object? (Reprise)

A Windows Object is any object, in whatever form it manifests itself, that supports at least one interface, *IUnknown*. A Windows Object must be able to provide a separate function table for each interface it supports. The implementation of *IUnknown* members in each supported interface must be aware of the entire object because it must be able to access all other interfaces in the object and it must be able to affect the object's reference count.

C++ multiple inheritance is a convenient way to provide multiple function tables for each interface as the compiler generates them automatically. Because each implementation of a member function is already part of your object class, each automatically has access to everything in the object.

However, because this book is intended to help both C and C++ programmers, I will take a different approach. The object class itself will simply inherit from *IUnknown* and implement these functions to control the object as a whole. Each interface supported by this object is implemented in a separate C++ class that singly inherits from the interface it is implementing. These "interface implementations" are instantiated with the object and live as long as the object lives.

The *IUnknown* members of these interface implementations always delegate to some other *IUnknown* implementation, which in most cases is the overall object's *IUnknown*. Each interface implementation also holds a "back pointer'' to the object in which the implementations are contained so that they are able to access information centrally stored in the object. In C++, this generally requires that each interface implementation class be a *friend* of the object class. It is also highly useful to maintain an interface-level reference count for debugging.

You might still have one question: What about inheritance for Windows Objects? Can one Windows Object inherit from another? The truth is that there is no inheritance mechanism because inheritance is a way to achieve code that you can reuse. The Windows Object mechanism for reuse is called *aggregation.* But, alas, we are beginning to discuss the finer details of implementation. So with that, we can close this chapter.

Summary

An object in object-oriented terms is a self-contained unit of data and functions to manipulate that data. A Windows Object is a special manifestation of this definition that presents its functions as separate groups called interfaces. Windows Objects differ from C++ objects in construction and use, but they are more powerful than C++ objects because they can live anywhere on the system and still be as usable to an application as if they were incorporated into that application. The most fundamental question that forms a theme for this book is how to obtain the first interface pointer for a variety of objects and what you can do with that pointer after you obtain it.

The most basic functions of all interface pointers are concerned with reference counting and with obtaining other interface pointers to the same object. These functions are collected in an OLE 2 interface named *IUnknown.* Later chapters in this book deal with more specific types of objects, their special interfaces, how you obtain those interface pointers, and what you can do with them.

Implementations and users of objects written in C and C++ differ only slightly. Calling a member function by means of a C pointer requires an extra dereference through a pointer to an interface function table and passage of an extra parameter to simulate C++'s *this* pointer. C objects must manually construct the function tables for their interfaces. Although C++ is more convenient, it is not the required language of OLE 2.

A type of object called an enumerator provides functions through *IEnum* interfaces to iterate over a list of elements. Because Windows Objects are portable across process boundaries, an enumerator object is used to pass lists of information across those same boundaries as well as to pass the functions to iterate over that list.

OLE 2 interface members use a specific *cdecl* calling convention, and the OLE 2 header files define a number of macros to isolate machine specifics from the definitions of interfaces. Most interface members also return a type called an HRESULT, which contains detailed error information.

OLE 2 defines a number of standard interfaces but allows those objects to be implemented in DLLs to define and implement custom interfaces. If you provide custom marshaling, a topic not covered in this book, you can also provide custom interfaces from objects implemented in EXEs as well. Although OLE 2 defines many interfaces, applications need only worry about a handful, depending on the features those applications want to implement.

CHAPTER FOUR

COMPONENT OBJECTS (THE COMPONENT OBJECT MODEL)

Arthur: Camelot!
Galahad: Camelot...
Launcelot: Camelot...
Patsy: It's only a model....
Arthur: Sh!

From *Monty Python and the Holy Grail*

Almost everyone who has tried to present all the material in OLE 2 to an audience in a comprehensible way has tried to portray "The Component Object Model" as a "feature." I'm certainly guilty of trying this once, but when I did, I had never seen so many glazed looks in my life. Those who didn't have glazed expressions seemed to be saying "So what? What can you do with a model?" To clear the air and to redeem myself somewhat, this chapter is about using and implementing very general Windows Objects that involve the fundamental API functions and interfaces *specified* in the Component Object Model and *implemented* in COMPOBJ.DLL, referred to in this book as the Component Object library.

The Component Object Model—the specification—is mostly about interfaces, reference counting, and *QueryInterface* (that is, the basic standardization of a Windows Object). The Component Object library—the implementation—is a number of fundamental API functions, also specified in the model, that provide for object creation and management, as well as code that handles marshaling of interface function calls across process boundaries. This implementation provides one answer to the ultimate question posed in

Chapter 3 in the form of a "component object." A component object is a Windows Object identified by a unique class identifier (CLSID) that associates an object with a particular DLL or EXE in your file system. To obtain a pointer to a component object, you pass a CLSID to one of two Component Object library API functions. The library in turn locates and loads the code implementing that object, instantiates the object, and asks the object for an interface pointer to return to you. Note that compound document objects are merely special cases of the more general component object, so the discussion here is relevant if you are interested in implementing a compound document object server.

Before diving into the subject of using and implementing component objects, we must first discuss a few requirements of all applications (EXEs) that either use or implement objects. Applications (which define a task) must initialize the Component Object library before using any other OLE 2 API functions (from any OLE 2 DLL), and part of this initialization has to do with memory management within the application's task. Because both operations are crucial and are used in all remaining sample applications in this book, initialization and memory management will be the first two topics of this chapter.

The code using a component object, which we can refer to as a *component user,* calls the library only to obtain that first pointer to an object identified by a CLSID. The overall impact on such a component user is minimal, as this chapter will demonstrate. The component user need not be concerned about where the code for the object is actually located or how the object is implemented. The greater impact is on the implementation of a component object that allows the library to locate, load, and instantiate it, based on a CLSID. To accommodate such a capability, you must implement a standard structure around the object—one structure for EXEs, another structure for DLLs. In addition, you must store information in the registration database under your object's CLSID, which identifies the name of your object and where it lives. The Component Object library uses this information to find your object and connect it to its component user.

This chapter will demonstrate a simple object implemented in both a DLL and an EXE, as well as a user of those objects. We will also implement Cosmo's Polyline object as a component object in a DLL that we'll carry forward through subsequent chapters as we add more OLE 2 features.

This chapter closes with a discussion about Windows Object reusability through a mechanism called *aggregation*. One object, called the *aggregate*, internally creates instances of other objects, possibly exposing the interfaces of those objects as an interface on the aggregate. Aggregation accomplishes code reuse as C++ inheritance does but without the problems of inheritance. Although the topic is appropriate to discuss here, we won't actually put it to use until later chapters. You might, however, find it a useful mechanism around which to design reuse of code in your own applications.

So, to explain what the Component Object Model is, we really need to analyze the model's impact on applications in general, on the user of a component object, and on the implementation of a component object. The specifications of the Component Object Model provide the foundation for how Windows will evolve from an API-based system to an object-oriented system, a romantic walk through the lush gardens of Camelot. But that could be another whole topic in itself, so we'll stick to implementation details; it is, after all, only a model.

Where the Wild Things Are (with Apologies to Maurice Sendak)

There are component users and component objects, both of which can reside in any piece of code, EXE and DLL alike. The system features provided in OLE 2 are themselves both objects and users, all of which live in DLLs. The implementation portion of the Component Object library is considered part of the OLE 2 system features.

Whether an object user lives in an EXE or a DLL is of little importance—EXEs have a little more work, as described in the next section, because they define a task. In any case, regardless of where an object user lives, we can illustrate the relationship between object and user, as shown in Figure 4-1 on the next page. Note that the word "server" in this figure applies to the module that services an object, either an EXE or a DLL.

Because an EXE object requires marshaling support, performance is typically slower than with a DLL object. But there is one major benefit to having this marshaling support: A 16-bit DLL (and any objects it implements) cannot be loaded into a 32-bit process space of the object user, nor can a 32-bit DLL be loaded into a 16-bit process space. The marshaling code in COMPOBJ.DLL, however, knows how to pass parameters between 16-bit and 32-bit processes, thereby allowing an object user in one space to communicate with an object in another space.

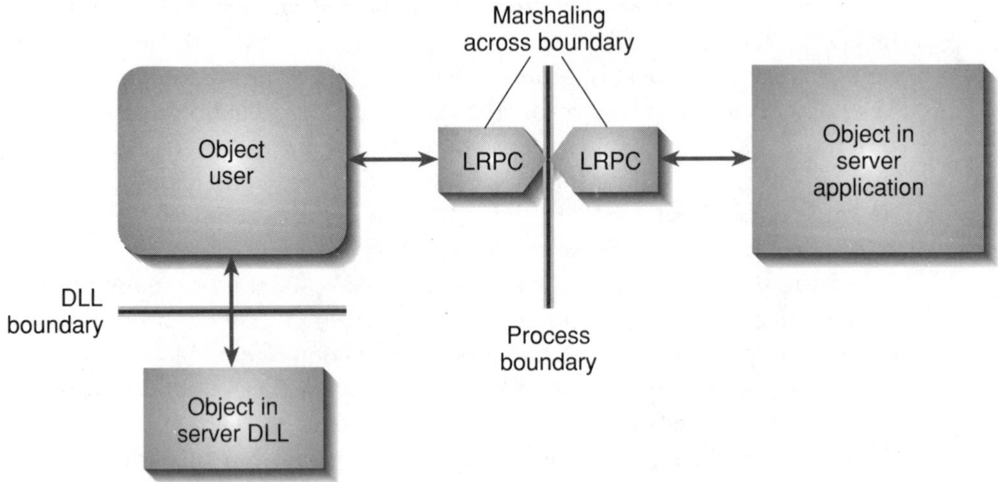

Figure 4-1.
Component users (in DLLs or EXEs) see other component objects either in DLLs or in other EXEs. The Component Object library lives between the user and an EXE object to provide marshaling. There is no mediator between the user and a DLL object.

The Component Object library is the agent responsible for getting at the first object interface pointer in any series of communications between object and user. It worries about making sure the right piece of object code is in memory whenever something else wants to use that object. However, once the initial object has been created and is handed to the user, the object and the user can create other objects themselves and pass them to their partners. The Component Object library is only there for marshaling and memory management (if even necessary) and is otherwise out of the picture. The objects we implement in this chapter require a certain structure and registration such that any user can instantiate an object through the Component Object library API. Because this API is used underneath much of the Compound Document API (those functions prefixed with *Ole*, as in *OleCreate*), all compound document objects are also objects that fit this model—they simply have a more precisely defined behavior. However, the Component Object library is highly useful for creating component software, and Windows itself is headed in this direction: not to be a Compound Document system, but to be a Component Object system.

Compound Document Terminology

A number of the terms generally used in discussions of compound documents are used in this chapter to discuss much more generic concepts. The following list provides the crucial compound document terms and describes how they apply to the information in this chapter:

Container A user of compound document objects. A container exposes site objects to the compound document objects they contain, but those site objects are not separately addressable components and are passed to the contained object only at run-time. However, site objects are Windows Objects.

Server (sometimes just object) An implementor of an object, either a DLL or an EXE. A server may implement a component object or a compound document object and expose both through identical structures usable by the Component Object library.

In-Process Server or DLL Server A server of objects specifically implemented in a DLL.

Server Application or EXE Server A server of objects specifically implemented in an EXE. Sometimes called an *object application.*

Object Handler A lightweight DLL server containing a partial implementation of an object that is fully implemented elsewhere in an EXE. Handlers are not expected to implement complete objects (especially not editing capabilities) and are intended for redistribution. Structurally they are identical to DLL servers.

The New Application for Windows Objects

Any and all applications that plan to *use or implement* Windows Objects (not just component objects) must ensure that the Component Object library is properly initialized before attempting to use other OLE 2 API functions. In addition, applications running under Windows 3.1 that intend to use objects implemented in other applications must make special considerations for Lightweight Remote Procedure Call (LRPC) use of *PostMessage.* An object or an object user in a DLL need not be concerned with any of these requirements that apply only to the application that defines a task. For applications (EXEs), here are the steps for initialization:

1. Call the Windows API *SetMessageQueue(96)* to set your application's message queue size to 96, if possible. This is the recommended size for LRPC handling. This function is not necessary in Win32 because Win32 message queues size dynamically.
2. Verify the library build version by calling *CoBuildVersion* or *OleBuildVersion.*
3. Call *CoInitialize* or *OleInitialize* on startup.
4. Call *CoUninitialze* or *OleUninitialize* when shutting down to allow the DLL objects to be freed if and only if step 3 worked.

NOTE: *CoBuildVersion, CoInitialize,* and *CoUninitialize* have counterparts with *Ole* prefixes: *OleBuildVersion, OleInitialize,* and *OleUnintialize.* The *Co...* functions control your access to Component Object library functions. If you use any clipboard, drag-and-drop, Compound Document, or Automation related API functions, you must use the *Ole...* functions instead of their *Co...* counterparts. The *Ole...* versions simply perform a few more specific operations and call the *Co...* versions. Compound Document applications, containers included, *always* use the *Ole...* versions.

Absolutely all of the sample applications in this book that compile EXEs include these four steps. Most of the samples in this chapter, as well as those in Chapters 5 and 6, use the *Co...* variants. All samples in Chapter 7 and beyond will use the *Ole...* functions because those samples will in turn depend on the "extras" provided by the *Ole...* functions. The first sample in the later section "Memory Management and Allocator Objects" will demonstrate each of these steps. In the meantime, let's look at each step in detail and examine why each is necessary.

Enlarge the Message Queue

OLE 2's LRPC implementation works on top of the Windows API function *PostMessage.* In a nutshell, when the user of an object in another application calls one of the object's member functions, the function generates an LRPC call, which in actuality is a *PostMessage* from the one application process space into the other. To handle all the possible *PostMessage* traffic, Microsoft recommends that all OLE 2 applications with even the slightest chance of engaging in LRPC calls call *SetMessageQueue* set to *96* on startup, if possible. Something like the following should, in fact, be your very first step inside *WinMain* to ensure that no messages yet exist in your queue because *SetMessageQueue* will destroy anything already there:

```
int PASCAL WinMain(HINSTANCE hInst, HINSTANCE hInstPrev
    , LPSTR pszCmdLine, int nCmdShow)
    {
    [variables, but NO code]
    int       cMsg=96;

   #ifndef WIN32
    //Enlarge the queue as large as we can starting from 96
    while (!SetMessageQueue(cMsg) && (cMsg-=8));
   #endif

    [Initialization code, message loop, etc.]
    }
```

If you don't enlarge your message queue sufficiently, the Component Object library could reject some LRPC calls when your queue is full. Enlarging your message queue provides sufficient space for LRPC traffic.

Verify the Library Build Version

Before using any other Component Object API (*Co*...) function, an application should call *CoBuildVersion(void)* to get major and minor build numbers in a returned DWORD. If you are planning to go on to use OLE 2's data transfer, Compound Document, or Automation technologies, you must instead call *OleBuildVersion(void)*, which returns a similar DWORD. The high-order word of the return value is a major version number, and the low-order word is the minor version number.

An application can run against only one major version of the libraries, but it can run against any minor version. The version numbers you can run against are compiled into your application as the symbols *rmm* (major) and *rup* (minor) defined in OLE2VER.H. (There is also a *rmj* symbol, which might look like the "major" number but is unfortunately not used this way.) Note that these numbers are not product release numbers—that is, in OLE 2 these are not *2* and *0*. Do not depend on any interpretation of these numbers. With these numbers, you must compare your *rmm* to the major version of the libraries, and if they do not match, you must fail loading your application as shown on the next page.

```
#include <compobj.h>    //For Ole... functions, use OLE2.H
#include <ole2ver.h>

...

DWORD    dwVer;

dwVer=CoBuildVersion();    //Or OleBuildVersion

if (rmm==HIWORD(dwVer))
    {
    //Major versions match.

    if (rup <= LOWORD(dwVer))
        {
        //Library is newer than or as old as the app; use normally.
        }
    else
        {
        /*
         * App was written for newer libraries. Disable features
         * that depend on API or bug fixes in newer libraries
         * or simply fail altogether.
         */
        }
    }
else
    //Major version mismatch; fail loading application.
```

Minor version numbers are useful to applications that want to know whether the libraries they've loaded contain a particular function or have a specific bug fix. Let's say minor version 12 of OLE 2 added a function that improves performance over minor version 11. If I load the minor version 11 libraries, I cannot attempt to call that version 12 function. If, however, I find that I am running against minor version 12, I can take advantage of what's available.

Call *CoInitialize* or *OleInitialize*

On startup, an application must call *CoInitialize* or *OleInitialize* before calling any other function in either of their respective libraries. You must use *OleInitialize* for any feature other than component objects and compound files, including all data transfer, drag-and-drop, compound documents, and even Automation. Component Object library and Compound File API functions can be used after only *CoInitialize*:

```
if (FAILED(CoInitialize(NULL)))     //Or OleInitialize
    [Fail loading the application].

m_fInitialized=TRUE;
```

Both functions identically take a pointer to an *allocator object* that supports the *IMalloc* interface. Through this object, all other parts of this application and the DLLs that live in this application's task can allocate task local memory (as opposed to shared memory). If NULL is passed, as shown in the preceding example, OLE uses a default allocator in COMPOBJ.DLL. Any code in this application or in a DLL loaded into this task can call the *CoGetMalloc* API function to retrieve an *IMalloc* pointer to this same allocator. We'll see this in more detail in the section "Memory Management and Allocator Objects."

Any code within the same task can call *CoInitialize* multiple times; in such circumstances, the *IMalloc* passed to the first *CoInitialize* wins. This allows any code (usually that in a DLL) to call *CoInitialize* to ensure that it can use the Component Object library even if the application that loaded the DLL did not make the call.[1]

When *CoInitialize* is called more than once in the same task, it will return an HRESULT with S_FALSE—a code that does not mean failure but that means nothing happened. As we have seen, the FAILED() macro will return FALSE for S_FALSE just as it will for S_OK, so the preceding code fragment is valid for all uses of *CoInitialize.*

An application must remember whether *CoInitialize* or *OleInitialize* worked (in a variable such as *m_fInitialized*) so that it knows whether to call *CoUninitialize* or *OleUninitialize* when it shuts down. In other words, every ...*Uninitialize* call must be matched one-to-one with an ...*Initialize* call.

Call *CoUninitialize* or *OleUninitialize*

After an application has finished with the libraries, it must call *CoUninitialize* if it previously called *CoInitialize,* or it must call *OleUninitialize* if it previously called *OleInitialize.* Neither function takes any parameters. You should remember whether the ...*Initialize* call succeeded and call ...*Uninitialize* only if it did—that is, balance the calls as you would balance *GlobalAlloc* and *GlobalFree.*

1. Microsoft recommends that DLLs always pass NULL to *CoInitialize.* Note also that because your DLL's *LibMain* is called before the application's *WinMain, CoInitialize* will never have been called by that time. It's best to defer any dependencies on the task allocator until after *LibMain,* if possible.

Internally, *OleUninitialize* cleans up the specifics from *OleInitialize* and calls *CoUninitialize.* This latter function will call another *CoFreeAllLibraries,* which forcibly and unconditionally unloads all object DLLs that were loaded on behalf of the application. That's why you must be careful when you call *CoUninitialize.* You might have use for *CoFreeAllLibraries* yourself if your application's debugging version has the ability to suddenly terminate and unload (say, on an assert failure), which might not normally call *CoUninitialize.*

Memory Management and Allocator Objects

Up to now, the only system-supported memory management functions have been the various *Local...* and *Global...* Windows API functions (*LocalAlloc, LocalFree, GlobalAlloc, GlobalFree,* and so on). OLE 2 introduces a new object-oriented technique to deal with memory management through the use of *allocator objects.* Within any given task—that is, within a process space in which a single EXE is running—there is a single task allocator object and a single shared allocator object. The application can implement the task allocator, or it can use the default task allocator implemented in the Component Object library. The shared allocator is not replaceable—the implementation in the Component Object library is always used to ensure that memory is truly shareable.

You specify the task allocator through the only parameter to *CoInitialize* or *OleInitialize.* This parameter is an *IMalloc* pointer to whatever allocator object defined memory management in the task. A NULL pointer means "use the default task allocator," whereas a non-NULL pointer means "use this application-implemented task allocator."

An allocator object implements the *IMalloc* interface, defined in COMPOBJ.H. The *IMalloc* interface describes most of the same functions that Windows provides for local and global memory, such as *LocalAlloc, LocalFree,* and *LocalCompact.* For specific details on each member function, see the *OLE 2 Programmer's Reference,* but it's fairly easy to guess at how to use each function in this interface based on their signatures alone. (*IUnknown* members have been removed from the following listing for brevity; you will see them explicitly in the include file.)

```
DECLARE_INTERFACE_(IMalloc, IUnknown)
    {
    STDMETHOD_(void FAR*, Alloc) (THIS_ ULONG cb) PURE;
    STDMETHOD_(void FAR*, Realloc) (THIS_ void FAR * pv, ULONG cb) PURE;
```

```
    STDMETHOD_(void, Free) (THIS_ void FAR * pv) PURE;
    STDMETHOD_(ULONG, GetSize) (THIS_ void FAR * pv) PURE;
    STDMETHOD_(int, DidAlloc) (THIS_ void FAR * pv) PURE;
    STDMETHOD_(void, HeapMinimize) (THIS) PURE;
    };

typedef       IMalloc FAR * LPMALLOC;
```

At any time, any piece of code in the application or any DLL loaded into this task (including the OLE 2 libraries) can and will call *CoGetMalloc* to obtain an *IMalloc* pointer to the task allocator object. In other words, a task allocator is a Windows Object, and you use the API function *CoGetMalloc* to obtain the first interface pointer. In this case, your application might be the object implementor and OLE 2 might be the object user. It works both ways.

All the OLE 2 libraries always use the task allocator for all non-shared memory needs. Some OLE 2 functions will allocate memory using the task allocator then pass a pointer to that memory to your application where you become responsible to free it. In such cases you must free the memory when you no longer need it by calling *CoGetMalloc* to obtain the task allocator's *IMalloc* pointer, pass the memory pointer to *IMalloc::Free*, and finish up by calling *IMalloc::Release.*

The first parameter to *CoGetMalloc* is either MEMCTX_TASK or MEMCTX_SHARED, depending on which allocator object you want. The second parameter is a pointer to an LPMALLOC variable that receives the *IMalloc* pointer.

The default task allocator is based on multiple local heap management (or far local heaps). This allocator allows you to allocate more than 64 KB because there are multiple heaps, but each allocation is as efficient as a local allocation because you use only one selector per heap instead of one per allocation (as *GlobalAlloc* does). The only limitation is that any single allocation must be smaller than 64 KB. The shared allocator provides memory that different processes can independently access and is built on the same type of multiple local heap management as the default task allocator. Likewise, all shared allocations must be 64 KB or smaller.

The *Malloc* program (CHAP04\MALLOC), shown in Listing 4-1, exercises the functions in both the standard task allocator (it does not implement its own allocator) and the shared allocator. It is an application that is most interesting in a debugger, and it does indicate success or failure of its operations in message boxes. (Yes, a most advanced user interface.)

MALLOC.H

```
/*
 * IMalloc Demonstration Chapter 4
 *
 * Copyright (c)1993 Microsoft Corporation, All Rights Reserved
 */

#ifndef _MALLOC_H_
#define _MALLOC_H_

#include <BOOK1632.H>

//Menu Resource ID and Commands
#define IDR_MENU                            1

#define IDM_IMALLOCCOGETMALLOCTASK          100
#define IDM_IMALLOCCOGETMALLOCSHARED        101
#define IDM_IMALLOCRELEASE                  102
#define IDM_IMALLOCALLOC                    103
#define IDM_IMALLOCFREE                     104
#define IDM_IMALLOCREALLOC                  105
#define IDM_IMALLOCGETSIZE                  106
#define IDM_IMALLOCDIDALLOC                 107
#define IDM_IMALLOCHEAPMINIMIZE             108
#define IDM_IMALLOCEXIT                     109

//MALLOC.CPP
LRESULT FAR PASCAL EXPORT MallocWndProc(HWND, UINT, WPARAM
    , LPARAM);

#define CALLOCS 10

/*
 * Application-defined classes and types.
 */

class __far CAppVars
    {
    friend LRESULT FAR PASCAL EXPORT MallocWndProc(HWND, UINT
        , WPARAM, LPARAM);

    protected:
        HINSTANCE  m_hInst;            //WinMain parameters
        HINSTANCE  m_hInstPrev;
        UINT       m_nCmdShow;
```

Listing 4-1. *(continued)*

The IMalloc program, which exercises task and shared allocator objects.

Listing 4-1. *continued*

```
        HWND        m_hWnd;             //Main window handle
        LPMALLOC    m_pIMalloc;         //IMalloc interface
        BOOL        m_fInitialized;     //Did CoInitialize work?

        ULONG       m_rgcb[CALLOCS];    //Sizes to allocate
        LPVOID      m_rgpv[CALLOCS];    //Allocated pointers

    public:
        CAppVars(HINSTANCE, HINSTANCE, UINT);
        ~CAppVars(void);
        BOOL FInit(void);

        void FreeAllocations(BOOL);
    };

typedef CAppVars FAR *LPAPPVARS;

#define CBWNDEXTRA              sizeof(LONG)
#define MALLOCWL_STRUCTURE      0

#endif //_MALLOC_H_
```

MALLOC.CPP

```
/*
 * IMalloc Demonstration Chapter 4
 *
 * Copyright (c)1993 Microsoft Corporation, All Rights Reserved
 */

#include <windows.h>
#include <ole2.h>
#include <initguid.h>
#include <ole2ver.h>
#include "malloc.h"

int PASCAL WinMain(HINSTANCE hInst, HINSTANCE hInstPrev
    , LPSTR pszCmdLine, int nCmdShow)
    {
    MSG         msg;
    LPAPPVARS   pAV;
    int         cMsg=96;
```

(continued)

Listing 4-1. *continued*

```
    #ifndef WIN32
     while (!SetMessageQueue(cMsg) && (cMsg-=8));
    #endif

     pAV=new CAppVars(hInst, hInstPrev, nCmdShow);

     if (NULL==pAV)
         return -1;

     if (pAV->FInit())
         {
         while (GetMessage(&msg, NULL, 0,0 ))
             {
             TranslateMessage(&msg);
             DispatchMessage(&msg);
             }
         }

     delete pAV;
     return msg.wParam;
     }

LRESULT FAR PASCAL EXPORT MallocWndProc(HWND hWnd, UINT iMsg
    , WPARAM wParam, LPARAM lParam)
    {
    LPAPPVARS       pAV;
    LPVOID          pv;
    ULONG           cb;
    UINT            i;
    BOOL            fResult=TRUE;
    HRESULT         hr;

    pAV=(LPAPPVARS)GetWindowLong(hWnd, MALLOCWL_STRUCTURE);

    switch (iMsg)
        {
        case WM_NCCREATE:
            pAV=(LPAPPVARS)((LONG)((LPCREATESTRUCT)lParam)
            ->lpCreateParams);

            SetWindowLong(hWnd, MALLOCWL_STRUCTURE, (LONG)pAV);
            return (DefWindowProc(hWnd, iMsg, wParam, lParam));

        case WM_DESTROY:
            PostQuitMessage(0);
            break;
```

(continued)

Listing 4-1. *continued*

```
        case WM_COMMAND:
            switch (LOWORD(wParam))
                {
                case IDM_IMALLOCCOGETMALLOCTASK:
                    pAV->FreeAllocations(TRUE);

                    hr=CoGetMalloc(MEMCTX_TASK, &pAV->m_pIMalloc);
                    fResult=SUCCEEDED(hr);

                    MessageBox(hWnd, ((fResult)
                        ? "CoGetMalloc(task) succeeded."
                        : "CoGetMalloc(task) failed.")
                        , "Malloc", MB_OK);

                    break;

                case IDM_IMALLOCCOGETMALLOCSHARED:
                    pAV->FreeAllocations(TRUE);
                    hr=CoGetMalloc(MEMCTX_SHARED, &pAV->m_pIMalloc);
                    fResult=SUCCEEDED(hr);

                    MessageBox(hWnd, ((fResult)
                        ? "CoGetMalloc(shared) succeeded."
                        : "CoGetMalloc(shared) failed.")
                        , "Malloc", MB_OK);

                    break;

                case IDM_IMALLOCRELEASE:
                    pAV->FreeAllocations(TRUE);
                    break;

                case IDM_IMALLOCALLOC:
                    if (NULL==pAV->m_pIMalloc)
                        break;

                    pAV->FreeAllocations(FALSE);

                    for (i=0; i < CALLOCS; i++)
                        {
                        LPBYTE    pb;
                        ULONG     iByte;

                        cb=pAV->m_rgcb[i];
                        pAV->m_rgpv[i]=pAV->m_pIMalloc->Alloc(cb);
```

(continued)

Listing 4-1. *continued*

```
                //Fill the memory with letters.
                pb=(LPBYTE)pAV->m_rgpv[i];

                if (NULL!=pb)
                    {
                    for (iByte=0; iByte < cb; iByte++)
                        *pb++=('a'+i);
                    }

                fResult &= (NULL!=pAV->m_rgpv[i]);
                }

            MessageBox(hWnd, ((fResult)
                    ? "IMalloc::Alloc succeeded."
                    : "IMalloc::Alloc failed.")
                    , "Malloc", MB_OK);

            break;

        case IDM_IMALLOCFREE:
            pAV->FreeAllocations(FALSE);

            MessageBox(hWnd, "IMalloc::Free finished."
                , "Malloc", MB_OK);
            break;

        case IDM_IMALLOCREALLOC:
            if (NULL==pAV->m_pIMalloc)
                break;

            for (i=0; i < CALLOCS; i++)
                {
                LPBYTE      pb;
                ULONG       iByte;

                pAV->m_rgcb[i]+=128;

                //Old memory is not freed if Realloc fails.
                pv=pAV->m_pIMalloc->Realloc(pAV->m_rgpv[i]
                    , pAV->m_rgcb[i]);

                if (NULL!=pv)
                    {
```

(continued)

Listing 4-1. *continued*

```
                    pAV->m_rgpv[i]=pv;

                    //Fill the new memory
                    //with something we can see.
                    pb=(LPBYTE)pAV->m_rgpv[i];
                    cb=pAV->m_rgcb[i];

                    if (NULL!=pb)
                        {
                        for (iByte=cb-128; iByte
                            < cb; iByte++)
                            {
                            *pb++=('a'+i);
                            }
                        }
                    }
                else
                    fResult=FALSE;
                }

            MessageBox(hWnd, ((fResult)
                ? "IMalloc::Realloc succeeded."
                : "IMalloc::Realloc failed.")
                , "Malloc", MB_OK);

            break;

        case IDM_IMALLOCGETSIZE:
            if (NULL==pAV->m_pIMalloc)
                break;

            for (i=0; i < CALLOCS; i++)
                {
                cb=pAV->m_pIMalloc->GetSize(pAV->m_rgpv[i]);

                /*
                 * We test that the size is *at least*
                 * what we wanted.
                /*
                fResult &= (pAV->m_rgcb[i] <= cb);
                }

            MessageBox(hWnd, ((fResult)
                ? "IMalloc::GetSize matched."
```

(continued)

Listing 4-1. *continued*

```
                    : "IMalloc::GetSize mismatch."), "Malloc"
                    , MB_OK);

                break;

            case IDM_IMALLOCDIDALLOC:
                if (NULL==pAV->m_pIMalloc)
                    break;

                /*
                 * DidAlloc may return -1 if it does not know if
                 * it actually allocated something. In that
                 * case, we just blindly & in a -1 with no effect.
                 */
                for (i=0; i < CALLOCS; i++)
                    {
                    fResult &= pAV->m_pIMalloc->DidAlloc(pAV
                        -> m_rgpv[i]);
                    }

                MessageBox(hWnd, ((fResult)
                    ? "IMalloc::DidAlloc is TRUE."
                    : "IMalloc::DidAlloc is FALSE.")
                    , "Malloc", MB_OK);

                break;

            case IDM_IMALLOCHEAPMINIMIZE:
                if (NULL!=pAV->m_pIMalloc)
                    pAV->m_pIMalloc->HeapMinimize();

                MessageBox(hWnd
                    , "IMalloc::HeapMinimize finished."
                    , "Malloc", MB_OK);

                break;

            case IDM_IMALLOCEXIT:
                PostMessage(hWnd, WM_CLOSE, 0, 0L);
                break;
            }
        break;

    default:
        return (DefWindowProc(hWnd, iMsg, wParam, lParam));
    }
```

(continued)

Listing 4-1. *continued*

```
    return 0L;
    }

CAppVars::CAppVars(HINSTANCE hInst, HINSTANCE hInstPrev
    , UINT nCmdShow)
    {
    UINT        i;
    ULONG       cb;

    m_hInst        =hInst;
    m_hInstPrev    =hInstPrev;
    m_nCmdShow     =nCmdShow;

    m_hWnd         =NULL;
    m_pIMalloc     =NULL;
    m_fInitialized=FALSE;

    //100 is arbitrary.  IMalloc can handle larger.
    cb=100;

    for (i=0; i < CALLOCS; i++)
        {
        m_rgcb[i]=cb;
        m_rgpv[i]=NULL;
        cb*=2;
        }

    return;
    }

CAppVars::~CAppVars(void)
    {
    FreeAllocations(TRUE);

    if (m_fInitialized)
        CoUninitialize();

    return;
    }

BOOL CAppVars::FInit(void)
    {
    WNDCLASS    wc;
    DWORD       dwVer;

    //Make sure COMPOBJ.DLL is the right version
    dwVer=CoBuildVersion();
```

(continued)

Listing 4-1. *continued*

```
    if (rmm!=HIWORD(dwVer))
        return FALSE;

    //Call CoInitialize so that we can call other Co... functions
    if (FAILED(CoInitialize(NULL)))
        return FALSE;

    m_fInitialized=TRUE;

    if (!m_hInstPrev)
        {
        wc.style          = CS_HREDRAW | CS_VREDRAW;
        wc.lpfnWndProc    = MallocWndProc;
        wc.cbClsExtra     = 0;
        wc.cbWndExtra     = CBWNDEXTRA;
        wc.hInstance      = m_hInst;
        wc.hIcon          = LoadIcon(m_hInst, "Icon");
        wc.hCursor        = LoadCursor(NULL, IDC_ARROW);
        wc.hbrBackground  = (HBRUSH)(COLOR_WINDOW + 1);
        wc.lpszMenuName   = MAKEINTRESOURCE(IDR_MENU);
        wc.lpszClassName  = "MALLOC";

        if (!RegisterClass(&wc))
            return FALSE;
        }

    m_hWnd=CreateWindow("MALLOC", "IMalloc Object Demo"
        , WS_OVERLAPPEDWINDOW, 35, 35, 350, 250, NULL, NULL
        , m_hInst, this);

    if (NULL==m_hWnd)
        return FALSE;

    ShowWindow(m_hWnd, m_nCmdShow);
    UpdateWindow(m_hWnd);

    return TRUE;
    }

void CAppVars::FreeAllocations(BOOL fRelease)
    {
    UINT    i;

    if (NULL==m_pIMalloc)
        return;
```

(continued)

Listing 4-1. *continued*

```
    for (i=0; i < CALLOCS; i++)
        {
        if (NULL!=m_rgpv[i])
            m_pIMalloc->Free(m_rgpv[i]);

        m_rgpv[i]=NULL;
        }

    if (fRelease)
        {
        m_pIMalloc->Release();
        m_pIMalloc=NULL;
        }

    return;
    }
```

Using the Heapwalker application in the Windows SDK, we can see where OLE 2 allocates each type of memory—task and shared—using its own allocator objects. As shown in Figure 4-2, task memory is allocated from multiple heaps belonging to the MALLOC application task.

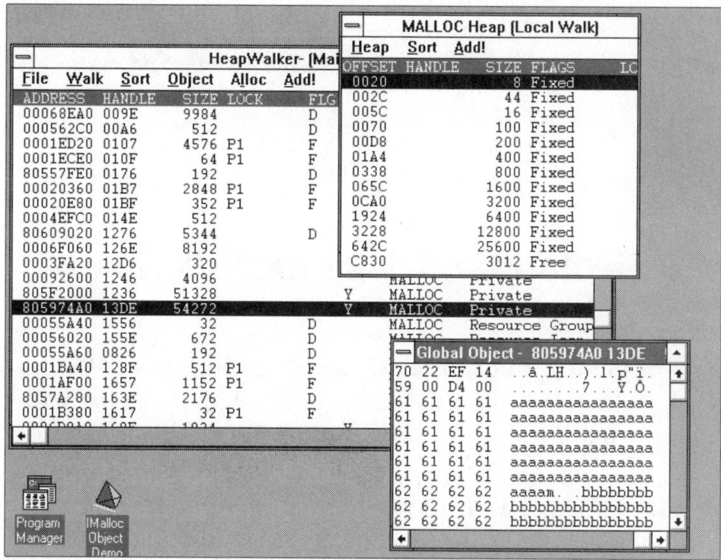

Figure 4-2.
Using Local Walk on the heap shows allocated blocks. The blocks are filled with letters to show their location in a hexadecimal dump.

When this memory is freed, the heaps are not necessarily freed, but the space inside those heaps are freed, as shown in Figure 4-3.

Shared memory is allocated on behalf of COMPOBJ.DLL, as shown in Figure 4-4, again using the same heap management technique that the standard task allocator uses. Freeing memory generates the same results for the task allocator, as shown in Figure 4-3.

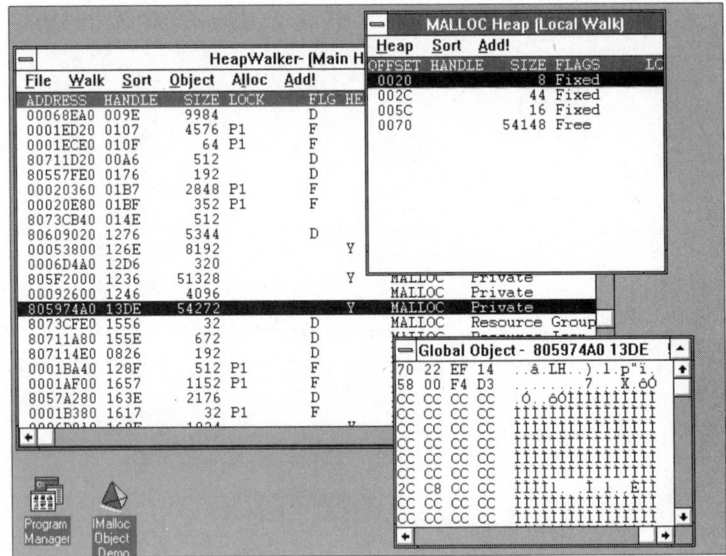

Figure 4-3.
Using Local Walk on the heap, after freeing the memory, shows free space in the heaps. Freed blocks are filled with 0xCC.

Component Objects from Class Identifiers: A Component User

Let's suppose I'm an application and I know there exists a Windows Object named Koala (which is, in fact, the name of an object we'll implement in the later section "Implementing a Component Object and Server"). I can identify the Koala object using the CLSID "00021102-0000-0000-C000-000000000046." (Whoa! That's a long name there! Remember that CLSIDs are 128 bits: This string is the hexadecimal representation of those bits.) Koalas are nice; they come with an include file that defines a CLSID_Koala constant. Let's say I also know that the Koala object supports the interface

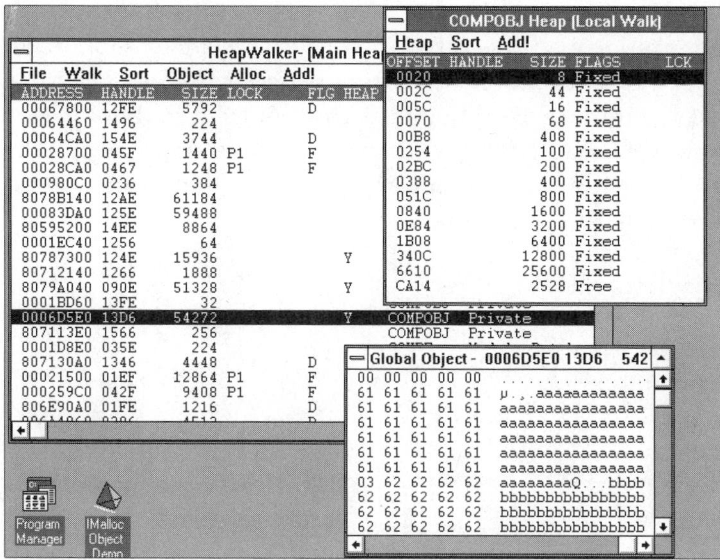

Figure 4-4.

Using Local Walk on the heap shows allocated blocks exactly as the task allocator does, but owned by COMPOBJ.DLL instead of by the application.

IPersist, which is a very simple interface capable only of returning the CLSID of its object. Given this knowledge, how do I create a Koala object with this CLSID and obtain a pointer to its *IPersist* interface?

This question should ring a harmonic with the ultimate question posed in Chapter 3, so let's look at the answer. For the benefit of those readers who will be writing compound object container applications, I want to mention that the API functions and interface functions that we use to instantiate a component object are used within more complex API functions that we'll use in Chapter 9 to instantiate a compound document object. Again, compound document objects are more refined and specialized component objects; what we discuss here is simply the logical equivalent of calling the C++ *new* operator. If you are in a hurry to implement a compound document container, you can skip to the next chapter after you finish reading this section.

The OBJUSER program, in Listing 4-2, implements a component user of the Koala component objects that we'll implement in the next section. Koala implements the *IPersist* interface only, but by virtue of implementing one interface, it also implements *IUnknown*: *IPersist* includes all *IUnknown* member functions plus one other named *GetClassID*, which returns (what else?) the CLSID of the object. *IPersist* is a base interface in OLE 2 for a number of other interfaces, and rarely is it used by itself. I chose *IPersist* for this demonstration because it has standard marshaling support already in COMPOBJ.DLL. This built-in support means we can implement marshaling in both DLLs and EXEs without any extra work. I also did not use another OLE 2 interface because most other interfaces have more member functions we would have to implement and would have raised more questions than we're prepared to deal with now.

OBJUSER.H

```
/*
 * Koala Object User Chapter 4
 *
 * Definitions and structures.
 *
 * Copyright (c)1993 Microsoft Corporation, All Rights Reserved
 */

#ifndef _OBJUSER_H_
#define _OBJUSER_H_

#include <bookguid.h>

//Menu Resource ID and Commands
#define IDR_MENU                    1

#define IDM_OBJECTUSEDLL            100
#define IDM_OBJECTUSEEXE            101
#define IDM_OBJECTCREATECOGCO       102
#define IDM_OBJECTCREATECOCI        103
#define IDM_OBJECTRELEASE           104
#define IDM_OBJECTGETCLASSID        105
#define IDM_OBJECTEXIT              106

//OBJUSER.CPP
LRESULT FAR PASCAL EXPORT ObjectUserWndProc(HWND, UINT, WPARAM
    , LPARAM);

class __far CAppVars
    {
    friend LRESULT FAR PASCAL EXPORT ObjectUserWndProc(HWND
        , UINT, WPARAM, LPARAM);
```

Listing 4-2. *(continued)*
The OBJUSER program, which uses Koala objects.

Listing 4-2. *continued*

```
    protected:
        HINSTANCE  m_hInst;          //WinMain parameters
        HINSTANCE  m_hInstPrev;
        UINT       m_nCmdShow;

        HWND       m_hWnd;           //Main window handle
        BOOL       m_fEXE;           //Menu selection

        LPPERSIST  m_pIPersist;      //IPersist interface
        BOOL       m_fInitialized;   //Did CoInitialize work?

    public:
        CAppVars(HINSTANCE, HINSTANCE, UINT);
        ~CAppVars(void);
        BOOL FInit(void);
    };

typedef CAppVars FAR *LPAPPVARS;

#define CBWNDEXTRA              sizeof(LONG)
#define OBJUSERWL_STRUCTURE     0

#endif //_OBJUSER_H_
```

OBJUSER.CPP

```
/*
 * Koala Object User Chapter 4
 *
 * Copyright (c)1993 Microsoft Corporation, All Rights Reserved
 */

#define INITGUIDS
#include <windows.h>
#include <ole2.h>
#include <ole2ver.h>
#include "objuser.h"

int PASCAL WinMain(HINSTANCE hInst, HINSTANCE hInstPrev
    , LPSTR pszCmdLine, int nCmdShow)
    {
    MSG         msg;
    LPAPPVARS   pAV;
```

(continued)

Listing 4-2. *continued*

```
    int       cMsg=96;

   #ifndef WIN32
    //Enlarge the queue as large as we can starting from 96
    while (!SetMessageQueue(cMsg) && (cMsg-=8));
   #endif

    pAV=new CAppVars(hInst, hInstPrev, nCmdShow);

    if (NULL==pAV)
        return -1;

    if (pAV->FInit())
        {
        while (GetMessage(&msg, NULL, 0,0 ))
            {
            TranslateMessage(&msg);
            DispatchMessage(&msg);
            }
        }

    delete pAV;
    return msg.wParam;
    }

LRESULT FAR PASCAL EXPORT ObjectUserWndProc(HWND hWnd, UINT iMsg
    , WPARAM wParam, LPARAM lParam)
    {
    HRESULT         hr;
    LPAPPVARS       pAV;
    CLSID           clsID;
    LPCLASSFACTORY  pIClassFactory;
    DWORD           dwClsCtx;

    pAV=(LPAPPVARS)GetWindowLong(hWnd, OBJUSERWL_STRUCTURE);

    switch (iMsg)
        {
        case WM_NCCREATE:
            pAV=(LPAPPVARS)((LONG)((LPCREATESTRUCT)lParam)
                ->lpCreateParams);

            SetWindowLong(hWnd, OBJUSERWL_STRUCTURE, (LONG)pAV);
            return (DefWindowProc(hWnd, iMsg, wParam, lParam));
```

(continued)

Listing 4-2. *continued*

```
        case WM_DESTROY:
            PostQuitMessage(0);
            break;

        case WM_COMMAND:
            switch (LOWORD(wParam))
                {
                case IDM_OBJECTUSEDLL:
                    pAV->m_fEXE=FALSE;
                    CheckMenuItem(GetMenu(hWnd), IDM_OBJECTUSEDLL
                        , MF_CHECKED);
                    CheckMenuItem(GetMenu(hWnd), IDM_OBJECTUSEEXE
                        , MF_UNCHECKED);
                    break;

                case IDM_OBJECTUSEEXE:
                    pAV->m_fEXE=TRUE;
                    CheckMenuItem(GetMenu(hWnd), IDM_OBJECTUSEDLL
                        , MF_UNCHECKED);
                    CheckMenuItem(GetMenu(hWnd), IDM_OBJECTUSEEXE
                        , MF_CHECKED);
                    break;

                case IDM_OBJECTCREATECOGCO:
                    if (NULL!=pAV->m_pIPersist)
                        {
                        pAV->m_pIPersist->Release();
                        pAV->m_pIPersist=NULL;
                        CoFreeUnusedLibraries();
                        }

                    dwClsCtx=(pAV->m_fEXE) ? CLSCTX_LOCAL_SERVER
                         : CLSCTX_INPROC_SERVER;

                    hr=CoGetClassObject(CLSID_Koala, dwClsCtx, NULL
                        , IID_IClassFactory
                        , (LPLPVOID)&pIClassFactory);

                    if (SUCCEEDED(hr))
                        {
                        //Create the Koala by asking for IID_IPersist
                        pIClassFactory->CreateInstance(NULL
                            , IID_IPersist
                            , (LPLPVOID)&pAV->m_pIPersist);
```

(continued)

Listing 4-2. *continued*

```
                //Release the class factory when done.
                pIClassFactory->Release();
                }

            break;

        case IDM_OBJECTCREATECOCI:
            if (NULL!=pAV->m_pIPersist)
                {
                pAV->m_pIPersist->Release();
                pAV->m_pIPersist=NULL;
                CoFreeUnusedLibraries();
                }

            //Simpler creation: Use CoCreateInstance
            dwClsCtx=(pAV->m_fEXE) ? CLSCTX_LOCAL_SERVER
                : CLSCTX_INPROC_SERVER;

            CoCreateInstance(CLSID_Koala, NULL, dwClsCtx
                , IID_IPersist
                , (LPLPVOID)&pAV->m_pIPersist);

            break;

        case IDM_OBJECTRELEASE:
            if (NULL==pAV->m_pIPersist)
                break;

            pAV->m_pIPersist->Release();
            pAV->m_pIPersist=NULL;

            CoFreeUnusedLibraries();
            break;

        case IDM_OBJECTGETCLASSID:
            if (NULL==pAV->m_pIPersist)
                break;

            hr=pAV->m_pIPersist->GetClassID(&clsID);

            if (SUCCEEDED(hr))
                {
                LPSTR       psz;
                LPMALLOC    pIMalloc;
```

(continued)

Listing 4-2. *continued*

```
                    //String from CLSID uses task Malloc
                    StringFromCLSID(clsID, &psz);
                    MessageBox(hWnd, psz, "Object Class ID"
                        , MB_OK);

                    CoGetMalloc(MEMCTX_TASK, &pIMalloc);
                    pIMalloc->Free(psz);
                    pIMalloc->Release();
                    }
                else
                    {
                    MessageBox(hWnd
                        , "IPersist::GetClassID call failed"
                        , "Koala Demo", MB_OK);
                    }

                break;

            case IDM_OBJECTEXIT:
                PostMessage(hWnd, WM_CLOSE, 0, 0L);
                break;
            }
        break;

    default:
        return (DefWindowProc(hWnd, iMsg, wParam, lParam));
    }

    return 0L;
    }

CAppVars::CAppVars(HINSTANCE hInst, HINSTANCE hInstPrev
    , UINT nCmdShow)
    {
    m_hInst         =hInst;
    m_hInstPrev     =hInstPrev;
    m_nCmdShow      =nCmdShow;

    m_hWnd          =NULL;
    m_fEXE          =FALSE;

    m_pIPersist     =NULL;
    m_fInitialized=FALSE;
    return;
    }
```

(continued)

Listing 4-2. *continued*

```
CAppVars::~CAppVars(void)
    {
    if (NULL!=m_pIPersist)
        m_pIPersist->Release();

    if (IsWindow(m_hWnd))
        DestroyWindow(m_hWnd);

    if (m_fInitialized)
        CoUninitialize();

    return;
    }

BOOL CAppVars::FInit(void)
    {
    WNDCLASS    wc;
    DWORD       dwVer;

    dwVer=CoBuildVersion();

    if (rmm!=HIWORD(dwVer))
        return FALSE;

    if (FAILED(CoInitialize(NULL)))
        return FALSE;

    m_fInitialized=TRUE;

    if (!m_hInstPrev)
        {
        wc.style          = CS_HREDRAW | CS_VREDRAW;
        wc.lpfnWndProc    = ObjectUserWndProc;
        wc.cbClsExtra     = 0;
        wc.cbWndExtra     = CBWNDEXTRA;
        wc.hInstance      = m_hInst;
        wc.hIcon          = LoadIcon(m_hInst, "Icon");
        wc.hCursor        = LoadCursor(NULL, IDC_ARROW);
        wc.hbrBackground  = (HBRUSH)(COLOR_WINDOW + 1);
        wc.lpszMenuName   = MAKEINTRESOURCE(IDR_MENU);
        wc.lpszClassName  = "OBJUSER";

        if (!RegisterClass(&wc))
            return FALSE;
        }

    m_hWnd=CreateWindow("OBJUSER", "Koala Component Object Demo"
        , WS_OVERLAPPEDWINDOW, 35, 35, 350, 250, NULL, NULL
        , m_hInst, this);
```

(continued)

Listing 4-2. *continued*

```
    if (NULL==m_hWnd)
        return FALSE;

    ShowWindow(m_hWnd, m_nCmdShow);
    UpdateWindow(m_hWnd);

    CheckMenuItem(GetMenu(m_hWnd), IDM_OBJECTUSEDLL, MF_CHECKED);
    CheckMenuItem(GetMenu(m_hWnd), IDM_OBJECTUSEEXE, MF_UNCHECKED);

    return TRUE;
    }
```

OBJUSER's only interesting output is a message box that shows the CLSID retrieved from the object when you make a call to *IPersist::GetClassID*. Otherwise, you should step through this program in a debugger to really understand what is happening. In any case, the first two items on the Koala Object menu control whether you use the object implemented in an application or in a DLL. Either way, the rest of the functions remain the same. You can instantiate objects in one of two ways: You can use either *CoCreateInstance* or *CoGetClassObject* and *IClassFactory::CreateInstance*; you can also call the object's *Release* function and generate a call to *IPersist::GetClassID*, which displays the object's CLSID as a string in a message box. What a hot user interface!

Note that to run OBJUSER, you must have both compiled versions of the Koala object: DKOALA.DLL (CHAP04\DKOALA) and EKOALA.EXE (CHAP04\EKOALA). After you run MAKEALL.BAT for this chapter, both files will be in the BUILD directory on your disk. You must then let the Component Object library know where they are located by merging the CHAP04\CHAP04.REG file[2] with your current Registration Database using the Windows 3.1 RegEdit program. This will create entries for CLSID_Koala indicating where DKOALA.DLL and EKOALA.EXE are located. This is one of the powerful features of such registration: The object user is isolated from the need to locate the module that implements the object. The Registration Database essentially maps the CLSID to the path of the appropriate DLL or EXE.

For OBJUSER and any other component user, the following three steps instantiate and manage a component object. (Note that OBJUSER also performs the four steps outlined in the earlier section "The New Application for Windows Objects" because it's an EXE and defines a task.)

---

2. Note that this registration file does not contain full pathnames. Normally, all path entries in the Registration Database should contain full pathnames to modules. However, because there are so many modules to deal with in this book and because you might have installed them anywhere on your machine, the REG files given here do not include pathnames. That is why I recommended in Chapter 2 that you add the BUILD directory in the sample code to your PATH.

1. Use *#include <initguid.h>* in one source file of the compilation after including COMPOBJ.H to create a code segment containing CLSIDs and IIDs.
2. Create an object based on a CLSID using one of two routes:
   - If you need only one object, call *CoCreateInstance* with the CLSID and the IID of the interface you want on the object.
   - If you need more than one object, call *CoGetClassObject* to obtain a class factory (an *IClassFactory* pointer) for the CLSID, and call *IClassFactory::CreateInstance* as often as you want with the IID of the interface you want on the object. Call *IClassFactory::Release* when you have finished.
3. Use the object through the interface pointer, call *Release* through that pointer when finished, and call *CoFreeUnusedLibraries.*

The first step affects only your build environment and compilation, but it does not really matter in programming. The second step is the real meat of our discussion; it shows exactly how to instantiate a component object. The third step deals with how you manage and free the object through your interface pointer.

#include <initguid.h> and Precompiled Headers

Anything that ever references any GUID, be it a CLSID or an IID, must include the file INITGUID.H once, and only once, in the entire compilation of your module. This includes all component users and all objects (component objects or not) and means that you should use *#include <initguid.h>* in one, and only one, file of your application after including COMPOBJ.H. Including INITGUID.H ensures that all your GUIDs are defined and that they end up in a discardable code segment instead of in your data segment, which is preferred because defined GUIDs are always constant. INITGUID.H also allows you to use the DEFINE_GUID or DEFINE_OLEGUID macro for defining your own IDs as shown in the BOOKGUID.H file in the INC directory.

If you typically use a central include file for all files in your project, wrap an *#ifdef* statement around the *#include.* The samples in this book have such a statement in the shared BOOKGUID.H file in the INC directory:

```
#ifdef INITGUIDS
#include <initguid.h>
#endif
```

Only one file in each sample project uses *#define INITGUIDs.* Note that there is a similar symbol, INITGUID, used in COMPOBJ.H for similar purposes. However, you cannot use this symbol itself because COMPOBJ.H will not later pull in another necessary include file (COGUID.H)—that is, you will not be able to compile.

Including INITGUID.H only once is a trick when you are using precompiled headers, but you will appreciate it when we start including the lengthy OLE 2 header files. Create the precompiled header in a file that does not include INITGUID.H—the samples using precompilation all use the file PRECOMP.CPP, which contains only one *#include* statement. You can then use the precompiled header from this step to compile with all files *except* the one in which you *want* to include INITGUID.H. You should compile that single file without using the precompiled header to pull in the extra file.

Instantiate a Component Object

The Component Object library provides two fundamental object creation functions: *CoCreateInstance* and *CoGetClassObject* combined with *IClassFactory::CreateInstance.* Which functions you use depends on how many objects you need at a given time.

NOTE: Compound Document container applications do not directly use the *CoCreateInstance* or *CoGetClassObject* function to create compound document objects. Instead, they use functions such as *OleCreate* that internally use *CoCreateInstance,* as discussed in Chapter 9. If you plan to implement containers, you still should understand how compound document objects are created through these mechanisms.

To create a single object given a CLSID, use *CoCreateInstance,* which internally uses *CoGetClassObject,* as described a little later. The following code demonstrates this call and is adapted from OBJUSER, modifying the symbols and their locations for ease of explanation:

```
HRESULT     hr;
DWORD       dwClsCtx;
LPPERSIST   pIPersist;
LPUNKNOWN   pUnkOuter=NULL;

//fEXE controls where the object lives based on a menu selection.
dwClsCtx=(fEXE) ? CLSCTX_LOCAL_SERVER : CLSCTX_INPROC_SERVER;

CoCreateInstance(CLSID_Koala, pUnkOuter, dwClsCtx
    , IID_IPersist, (LPLPVOID)&pIPersist);
```

First note the naming of pointers to interfaces, as shown with LPPERSIST and LPUNKNOWN. OLE 2 follows a convention in which a far pointer to an interface of type *IInterface FAR* * is typed as LPINTERFACE—that is, the interface name sans *I* is appended in all caps to an *LP*. Thus LPUNKNOWN is an *IUnknown FAR* * and LPPERSIST is an *IPersist FAR* *. In addition, note that *LPLPVOID* is defined in BOOKGUID.H as *LPVOID FAR* *. *LPLPVOID* is simply a more convenient shorthand that I use in the code in this book.

CoCreateInstance takes five parameters, the names of which vary with the object class and interfaces you are using in your own implementation. Those shown here are similar to those in the OBJUSER program:

Parameter	Meaning
CLSID_Koala	REFIID: A reference (a real C++ reference) to the class identifier of the object you want to create. In this example, we are creating a Koala object implemented in the later section "Implementing a Component Object and Server." Note that in C, because there is no concept of a reference, you must precede this value with the *&* operator, thus: *&CLSID_Koala.*
pUnkOuter	LPUNKNOWN: A pointer to the controlling unknown if the object is being created as part of an aggregate. See the section "Object Reusability" later in this chapter for more information.
dwClsCtx	DWORD: Flags indicating the context in which the object is allowed to run, which can be any combination of CLSCTX-_LOCAL_SERVER (object in EXE), CLSCTX_INPROC-_SERVER (object in DLL), or CLSCTX_INPROC_HANDLER (object handler DLL). OBJUSER chooses to run either a DLL-based or an EXE-based object depending on a menu option stored in the *fExe* variable.
IID_IPersist	REFIID: A reference to the interface identifier you want to obtain for this object. If the object does not support this interface, *CoCreateInstance* will fail. Note that, as with the class identifier, C programs must again prepend the *&* operator to an *IID.*
&pIPersist	LPVOID FAR * (or LPLPVOID): A pointer to the location in which *CoCreateInstance* is to store the interface pointer on return. If *CoCreateInstance* fails, the contents of this variable will be set to NULL. Otherwise, *CoCreateInstance* will also call *AddRef* through the pointer before returning.

Note that when more than one CLSCTX_... flag is specified, the libraries will attempt to load them in the order CLSCTX_INPROC_SERVER, CLSCTX_INPROC_HANDLER, and then CLSCTX_LOCAL_SERVER;

that is, the libraries always look for a DLL first (for better performance), trying another EXE only as a last resort.

CoCreateInstance internally executes a three-step process to create the new object, which can be written in pseudocode as follows:

```
BEGIN
    Obtain a class factory (IClassFactory) for the desired class.
    Call IClassFactory::CreateInstance to create the object.
    Call IClassFactory::Release.
END
```

The first step, obtaining a *class factory* (also called a class object), is the exact purpose of the other relevant API function, *CoGetClassObject.* A class factory is an object that implements the *IClassFactory* interface, as defined in COMPOBJ.H:

```
DECLARE_INTERFACE_(IClassFactory, IUnknown)
    {
    [IUnknown methods included]

    //IClassFactory methods
    STDMETHOD(CreateInstance) (THIS_ IUnknown FAR* pUnkOuter, REFIID riid
        , LPVOID FAR * ppvObject) PURE;
    STDMETHOD(LockServer) (THIS_ BOOL fLock) PURE;
    };
```

For cases in which you want to create only one object of this class, *CoCreateInstance* suffices. However, if you want to create more than one object at a time, call *CoGetClassObject* to retrieve a class factory for the class, call *IClassFactory::CreateInstance* as many times as necessary, and call *IClassFactory::Release* when you have finished. The following code shows an implementation equivalent to the previous code but uses *CoGetClassObject* instead:

```
HRESULT             hr;
DWORD               dwClsCtx;
LPPERSIST           pIPersist;
LPUNKNOWN           pUnkOuter=NULL;
LPCLASSFACTORY      pIClassFactory;

dwClsCtx=(fEXE) ? CLSCTX_LOCAL_SERVER
    : CLSCTX_INPROC_SERVER;

hr=CoGetClassObject(CLSID_Koala, dwClsCtx, NULL
    , IID_IClassFactory, (LPLPVOID)&pIClassFactory);

if (SUCCEEDED(hr))
```

(continued)

```
{
//Create the Koala by asking for IID_IPersist
pIClassFactory->CreateInstance(pUnkOuter
    , IID_IPersist, (LPLPVOID)&pIPersist);

//We've finished with the class factory, so release it.
pIClassFactory->Release();
}
```

This code is almost the exact implementation of *CoCreateInstance* inside the component object library: The parameters you pass to *CoCreateInstance* are simply passed to *CoGetClassObject* and *IClassFactory::CreateInstance*. The extra parameters to *CoGetClassObject* are a NULL (a reserved LPVOID that should always be NULL), the interface ID you want on the class object (always *IID_IClassFactory* in OLE 2 but perhaps with more options in the future), and a location in which to store the pointer to the class object.

Remember that because *CoGetClassObject* is a function that creates a new interface pointer (reference counting rule #1 in the section "Reference Counting" in Chapter 3), you are responsible for calling *Release* through that pointer when you have finished, as shown in the preceding code.

NOTE: If you want to hold the class factory object for a longer time, you must call *IClassFactory::LockServer(TRUE)*. A reference count on a class factory does not guarantee that the server will stay in memory and that you could use the class factory later. For these reasons, read the later section "Provide an Unloading Mechanism" under "Implementing a Component Object and Server." In short, if a class factory reference count could be used to keep a server in memory, the server could shut down only when its reference count reached zero. In the case of an EXE server, that reference can reach zero only if the server is being shut down. Catch-22. You must therefore use *LockServer(TRUE)* when you hold onto a class factory and *LockServer(FALSE)* after you release it. Besides, if the server is locked, retrieving another class factory is cheap.

Manage the Object and Call *CoFreeUnusedLibraries*

What you do with an object after you have obtained an interface pointer is entirely dependent on the object itself and is really what most of the chapters in the book are about. You must, in any case, be absolutely sure to call *Release* through that interface pointer when you have finished with the object. Otherwise, you doom the object to live in memory for all eternity—or until the universe collapses (power off or the jolly three-finger reset).

Releasing the object is not the only consideration, however. When you initially instantiate an object implemented in a DLL, COMPOBJ.DLL loads that DLL into memory using the function *CoLoadLibrary*. When the DLL is no longer needed, COMPOBJ.DLL calls *CoFreeLibrary*. Both functions map to *LoadLibrary* and *FreeLibrary* under Windows but are named differently for portability to other platforms, such as the Apple Macintosh.

However, the Component Object library does not know when an object in a DLL is destroyed because once it has facilitated loading and instantiating that object, communication between the component object and the component user is direct, completely bypassing everything in the library. Therefore, a DLL might remain loaded in memory even when it has no objects to service. Over time, many DLLs might be loaded and chew up valuable memory. The Component Object library needs a cue to free those DLLs that are no longer needed. This is very much like discardable global memory, in which memory allocated and freed will stay in memory until discarded, even if no one is using that memory.

For this reason, all object users should periodically call *CoFreeUnusedLibraries*, primarily immediately after you use *Release* on an object for good. In this function, COMPOBJ.DLL can ask each DLL loaded in your task whether it can be unloaded. If the DLL answers "yes," *CoFreeLibrary* is called to free the memory the DLL occupies. *CoFreeUnusedLibraries* does not, however, affect other EXEs because EXEs unload themselves when they are no longer servicing any objects. Using *CoFreeUnusedLibraries* is something like calling *GlobalCompact(-1)*, which will purge memory of all unreferenced discardable memory segments.

NOTE: The OLE 2 implementation of *CoFreeUnusedLibraries* does nothing. However, your user code should still call the function after destroying an object so that when the function is implemented, your code will work correctly.

Implementing a Component Object and a Server

Let's now implement a simple Koala Component Object with the *IPersist* interface, where just the object itself is shown in the source code in Listing 4-3. Koala implements the *IPersist* interface because that interface has standard OLE 2–provided marshaling support, meaning that we can freely place this object in a DLL or an EXE, as we'll actually demonstrate. In real-world use, *IPersist* is never implemented alone because it always serves as a base class for a few other interfaces.

KOALA.H

```
/*
 * Koala Object DLL/EXE Chapter 4
 *
 * Classes that implement the Koala object independent of whether
 * we live in a DLL or an EXE
 *
 * Copyright (c)1993 Microsoft Corporation, All Rights Reserved
 */

#ifndef _KOALA_H_
#define _KOALA_H_

#include <windows.h>
#include <ole2.h>        //ole2.h has IPersist, compobj.h doesn't

#include <bookguid.h>

//Type for an object-destroyed callback
typedef void (FAR PASCAL *LPFNDESTROYED)(void);

//Forward class references
class __far CImpIPersist;
typedef class CImpIPersist FAR *LPIMPIPERSIST;

/*
 * The Koala object is implemented in its own class with its own
 * IUnknown to support aggregation. It contains one CImpIPersist
 * object that we use to implement the externally exposed interfaces.
 */

class __far CKoala : public IUnknown
    {
    //Make any contained interfaces friends
    friend class CImpIPersist;

    protected:
        ULONG           m_cRef;         //Object reference count
        LPUNKNOWN       m_pUnkOuter;    //Controlling unknown
        LPFNDESTROYED   m_pfnDestroy;   //Function closure call
        LPIMPIPERSIST   m_pIPersist;    //Contained interface
```

Listing 4-3. *(continued)*

Implementation of the Koala object structured to live in either a DLL or an EXE.

Listing 4-3. *continued*

```
    public:
        CKoala(LPUNKNOWN, LPFNDESTROYED);
        ~CKoala(void);

        BOOL FInit(void);

        //Non-delegating object IUnknown
        STDMETHODIMP         QueryInterface(REFIID, LPLPVOID);
        STDMETHODIMP_(ULONG) AddRef(void);
        STDMETHODIMP_(ULONG) Release(void);
    };

typedef CKoala FAR *LPCKoala;

/*
 * Interface implementations for the CKoala object.
 */

class __far CImpIPersist : public IPersist
    {
    private:
        ULONG           m_cRef;
        LPCKoala        m_pObj;         //Back pointer to the object
        LPUNKNOWN       m_punkOuter;    //Controlling unknown

    public:
        CImpIPersist(LPCKOALA, LPUNKNOWN);
        ~CImpIPersist(void);

        //IUnknown members that delegate to m_pUnkOuter.
        STDMETHODIMP         QueryInterface(REFIID, LPLPVOID);
        STDMETHODIMP_(ULONG) AddRef(void);
        STDMETHODIMP_(ULONG) Release(void);

        //IPersist members
        STDMETHODIMP         GetClassID(LPCLSID);
    };

#endif //_KOALA_H_
```

(continued)

Listing 4-3. *continued*

KOALA.CPP

```
/*
 * Koala Object DLL/EXE Chapter 4
 *
 * Implementation of the CKoala and CImpIPersist objects that works
 * in either an EXE or a DLL
 *
 * Copyright (c)1993 Microsoft Corporation, All Rights Reserved
 *
 */

#include "koala.h"

CKoala::CKoala(LPUNKNOWN pUnkOuter, LPFNDESTROYED pfnDestroy)
    {
    m_cRef=0;
    m_pUnkOuter=pUnkOuter;
    m_pfnDestroy=pfnDestroy;

    //NULL any contained interfaces initially.
    m_pIPersist=NULL;

    return;
    }

CKoala::~CKoala(void)
    {
    //Free contained interfaces.
    if (NULL!=m_pIPersist)
        delete m_pIPersist;     //Interface does not free itself.

    return;
    }

BOOL CKoala::FInit(void)
    {
    LPUNKNOWN       pIUnknown=(LPUNKNOWN)this;

    if (NULL!=m_pUnkOuter)
        pIUnknown=m_pUnkOuter;

    //Allocate contained interfaces.
    m_pIPersist=new CImpIPersist(this, pIUnknown);
```

(continued)

Listing 4-3. *continued*

```
    return (NULL!=m_pIPersist);
    }

STDMETHODIMP CKoala::QueryInterface(REFIID riid, LPLPVOIDppv)
    {
    *ppv=NULL;

    /*
     * The only calls for IUnknown are either in a nonaggregated
     * case or when created in an aggregation, so in either case,
     * always return our IUnknown for IID_IUnknown.
     */
    if (IsEqualIID(riid, IID_IUnknown))
        *ppv=(LPVOID)this;

    /*
     * For IPersist, we return our contained interface. For EXEs, we
     * have to return our interface for IPersistStorage as well
     * since OLE 2 doesn't support IPersist implementations by
     * themselves (assumed only to be a base class). If a user
     * asked for an IPersistStorage and used it, they would crash--
     * but this is a demo, not a real object.
     */
    if (IsEqualIID(riid, IID_IPersist)
        || IsEqualIID(riid, IID_IPersistStorage))
        *ppv=(LPVOID)m_pIPersist;

    //AddRef any interface we'll return.
    if (NULL!=*ppv)
        {
        ((LPUNKNOWN)*ppv)->AddRef();
        return NOERROR;
        }

    return ResultFromScode(E_NOINTERFACE);
    }

STDMETHODIMP_(ULONG) CKoala::AddRef(void)
    {
    return ++m_cRef;
    }

STDMETHODIMP_(ULONG) CKoala::Release(void)
    {
```

(continued)

Listing 4-3. *continued*

```
    ULONG       cRefT;

    cRefT=--m_cRef;

    if (0==m_cRef)
        {
        /*
         * Tell the housing that an object is going away so that it
         * can shut down if appropriate.
         */
        if (NULL!=m_pfnDestroy)
            (*m_pfnDestroy)();

        delete this;
        }

    return cRefT;
    }

CImpIPersist::CImpIPersist(LPCKoala pObj, LPUNKNOWN pUnkOuter)
    {
    m_cRef=0;
    m_pObj=pObj;
    m_pUnkOuter=pUnkOuter;
    return;
    }

CImpIPersist::~CImpIPersist(void)
    {
    return;
    }

STDMETHODIMP CImpIPersist::QueryInterface(REFIID riid
    , LPVOID FAR *ppv)
    {
    return m_pUnkOuter->QueryInterface(riid, ppv);
    }

STDMETHODIMP_(ULONG) CImpIPersist::AddRef(void)
    {
    ++m_cRef;
    return m_pUnkOuter->AddRef();
    }
```

(continued)

Listing 4-3. *continued*

```
STDMETHODIMP_(ULONG) CImpIPersist::Release(void)
    {
    --m_cRef;
    return m_pUnkOuter->Release();
    }

STDMETHODIMP CImpIPersist::GetClassID(LPCLSID pClsID)
    {
    *pClsID=CLSID_Koala;
    return NOERROR;
    }
```

The Koala object is implemented to support aggregation and to be identically usable in either a DLL or an EXE server, but not without some impact. In addition, remember that we can call *CoGetMalloc* at any time to obtain access to shared or task memory, although the implementation of Koala shown here does not have occasion to use this feature.

To support aggregation, as we'll see in the later section "Object Reusability," the object must be aware of a *controlling unknown*, if there is one, that is cognizant of all interfaces supported by the aggregate object. The object itself, implemented by using the *CKoala* C++ class,[3] implements *IUnknown* but contains the *interface implementation* of *IPersist* in another C++ object named *CImpIPersist*. In aggregation, the interface implementations must always delegate all their *IUnknown* calls to the object that controls that interface's lifetime. When the object is not aggregated and when the *pUnkOuter* passed to *CKoala::CKoala* is NULL, *CKoala* passes its own *IUnknown* implementation to *CImpIPersist* instead. When the Koala object is aggregated, *CKoala* will receive a non-NULL *pUnkOuter*, which it passes to *CImpIPersist*. In either case, the *IPersist* interface implementation will always delegate *IUnknown* calls to a full object, performing only trivial reference counting on the interface for debugging purposes. If this seems confusing, be patient; we'll see this in more detail later.

The only interesting function of *CImpIPersist* is *GetClassID*, which simply returns the CLSID defined by the Koala object. However, the implementation of *CKoala*, the entire object, has a few more interesting features. First, note that although we hold onto a copy of the *pUnkOuter* pointer, we do *not* call *AddRef* through it. We do this to avoid a problem with circular reference counts: If we did call *AddRef* on *pUnkOuter*, the outer object could not free

3. Remember that a C++ class is a *convenient* way to create interface function tables. *CKoala* is never exposed to anything outside its DLL or EXE, period. It exposes only its *IUnknown* and *IPersist* interface function tables.

itself unless our object is freed first. But the outer object will not free our object unless it's freeing itself. The solution to this conundrum is to realize that our object's lifetime is entirely contained within the lifetime of the outer object, so we don't have to make the extra *AddRef* call, and at the same time avoid the circular reference count.

Second, we supply a two-phase instantiation process for use by the class factory we provide later. The *CKoala* constructor initializes only variables, whereas *FInit* performs any operations that are prone to failure, so the caller can determine whether a failure did occur. Because instantiating the *CImpIPersist* interface implementation might fail, we defer that action until *FInit* is called.

Next, the *QueryInterface* implementation in *CKoala*, which knows all the interfaces implemented in this object, makes a special case for the *interface* called *IPersistStorage*. When a user such as OBJUSER asks the DLL implementation for an interface identified with *IID_IPersist*, that IID comes directly into *QueryInterface*. However, when OBJUSER asks for *IID_IPersist* and the object lives in an EXE, that request goes through the marshaling layer in COMPOBJ.DLL. The OLE 2 implementation of this marshaling does not single out *IPersist* and will always ask the object for *IPersistStorage* even if the user asked only for *IPersist*. So we also check for *IPersistStorage* here. Of course, you must avoid this in real applications because the user might actually have asked for *IPersistStorage* but received only an *IPersist*. But as I pointed out earlier, *IPersist* is never useful when implemented alone—it's used here only for demonstration.

The final feature of the Koala object allows it to notify its server—either a DLL or an EXE—when the object is destroyed in *Release* by calling an "object destroyed" function in the server. This is a special technique I created to isolate the object from any specifics about its DLL or EXE server—it's not part of the OLE 2 specifications. When the object is created, the class factory passes the address of the "object destroyed" function to the object. In the case of both DKOALA and EKOALA, the function is named (what else?) *ObjectDestroyed*, and a pointer to that function is of type LPFNDESTROYED. (See KOALA.H.) When the object frees itself in its *Release* function, it calls *ObjectDestroyed*, in which the server decrements the count of objects it's currently servicing. If the object lives in a DLL, that DLL might be able to then mark itself as unloadable: if the object lives in an EXE and it was the last object, the EXE might shut down on this notification. This technique effectively lets the server worry about unloading and shutting down, keeping the object isolated. Of course, this is my technique—feel free to create your own.

With the object isolated from any concern about where it lives, we can now concentrate on seeing how you expose that object from a DLL or an EXE, which share these four steps to manage an object although their exact implementations of each step differ:

1. Register the CLSIDs and server pathnames for every class implemented in the server in the Registration Database.
2. Implement the class factory for each object class supported by the server. A single DLL or EXE server can handle any number of classes.
3. Expose the class factory to the Component Object library.
4. Provide a shutdown or an unloading mechanism when there are no more objects or lock counts on the server.

The DLL housing of Koala, DKOALA.DLL, is shown in Listing 4-4, and the EXE housing, EKOALA.EXE, is shown in Listing 4-5. Note that the Koala object implementation itself, shown in Listing 4-3, is identical in both the CHAP04\DKOALA and CHAP04\EKOALA directories in the sample code. When you run the OBJUSER program using each of these servers, you will notice a difference in the response time of calling the object's *GetClassID*. When you are using a DLL server, the response is quick because the call goes directly to the object implementation. When you are using an EXE server, the response is slower because the *GetClassID* call must be worked through the marshaling process.

DKOALA.H

```
/*
 * Koala Object DLL Chapter 4
 *
 * Definitions, classes, and prototypes for a DLL that
 * provides Koala objects to any other object user.
 *
 * Copyright (c)1993 Microsoft Corporation, All Rights Reserved
 */

#ifndef _DKOALA_H_
#define _DKOALA_H_

//Get the object definitions
#include "koala.h"

void FAR PASCAL ObjectDestroyed(void);

//DKOALA.CPP
VOID FAR PASCAL WEP(int);

//This class factory object creates Koala objects.
```

Listing 4-4. *(continued)*
The DKOALA.DLL implementation to house the Koala object.

Listing 4-4. *continued*

```
class __far CKoalaClassFactory : public IClassFactory
    {
    protected:
        ULONG           m_cRef;

    public:
        CKoalaClassFactory(void);
        ~CKoalaClassFactory(void);

        //IUnknown members
        STDMETHODIMP         QueryInterface(REFIID, LPLPVOID);
        STDMETHODIMP_(ULONG) AddRef(void);
        STDMETHODIMP_(ULONG) Release(void);

        //IClassFactory members
        STDMETHODIMP         CreateInstance(LPUNKNOWN, REFIID
                                 , LPLPVOID);
        STDMETHODIMP         LockServer(BOOL);
    };

typedef CKoalaClassFactory FAR *LPCKoalaClassFactory;

#endif //_DKOALA_H_
```

DKOALA.CPP

```
/*
 * Koala Object DLL Chapter 4
 *
 * Example object implemented in a DLL. This object supports
 * IUnknown and IPersist interfaces; it doesn't know anything more
 * than how to return its class ID, but it demonstrates how an
 * object is presented inside a DLL.
 *
 * Copyright (c)1993 Microsoft Corporation, All Rights Reserved
 */

//Do this once in the entire build
#define INITGUIDS

#include "dkoala.h"

//Count number of objects and number of locks.
ULONG       g_cObj=0;
ULONG       g_cLock=0;
```

(continued)

Listing 4-4. *continued*

```
[LibMain and WEP omitted from listing]

HRESULT EXPORT FAR PASCAL DllGetClassObject(REFCLSID rclsid
    , REFIID riid, LPVOID FAR *ppv)
    {

    if (!IsEqualCLSID(rclsid, CLSID_Koala))
        return ResultFromScode(E_FAIL);

    //Check that we can provide the interface
    if (!IsEqualIID(riid, IID_IUnknown)
        && !IsEqualIID(riid, IID_IClassFactory))
        return ResultFromScode(E_NOINTERFACE);

    //Return our IClassFactory for Koala objects
    *ppv=(LPVOID)new CKoalaClassFactory();

    if (NULL==*ppv)
        return ResultFromScode(E_OUTOFMEMORY);

    //AddRef the object through any interface we return
    ((LPUNKNOWN)*ppv)->AddRef();

    return NOERROR;
    }

STDAPI DllCanUnloadNow(void)
    {
    SCODE   sc;

    //Our answer is whether there are any object or locks
    sc=(0L==g_cObj && 0==g_cLock) ? S_OK : S_FALSE;
    return ResultFromScode(sc);
    }

/*
 * ObjectDestroyed
 *
 * Purpose:
 *  Function for the Koala object to call when it is destroyed.
 *  Because we're in a DLL, we only track the number of objects here,
 *  letting DllCanUnloadNow take care of the rest.
```

(continued)

Listing 4-4. *continued*

```
 */

void FAR PASCAL ObjectDestroyed(void)
    {
    g_cObj--;
    return;
    }

CKoalaClassFactory::CKoalaClassFactory(void)
    {
    m_cRef=0L;
    return;
    }

CKoalaClassFactory::~CKoalaClassFactory(void)
    {
    return;
    }

STDMETHODIMP CKoalaClassFactory::QueryInterface(REFIID riid
    , LPLPVOID ppv)
    {
    *ppv=NULL;

    //Any interface on this object is the object pointer.
    if (IsEqualIID(riid, IID_IUnknown)
        || IsEqualIID(riid, IID_IClassFactory))
        *ppv=(LPVOID)this;

    /*
     * If we actually assign an interface to ppv we need to AddRef
     * it because we're returning a new pointer.
     */
    if (NULL!=*ppv)
        {
        ((LPUNKNOWN)*ppv)->AddRef();
        return NOERROR;
        }

    return ResultFromScode(E_NOINTERFACE);
    }

STDMETHODIMP_(ULONG) CKoalaClassFactory::AddRef(void)
    {
    return ++m_cRef;
```

(continued)

Listing 4-4. *continued*

```
    }

STDMETHODIMP_(ULONG) CKoalaClassFactory::Release(void)
    {
    ULONG           cRefT;

    cRefT=--m_cRef;

    if (0L==m_cRef)
        delete this;

    return cRefT;
    }

STDMETHODIMP CKoalaClassFactory::CreateInstance(LPUNKNOWN pUnkOuter
    , REFIID riid, LPVOID FAR *ppvObj)
    {
    LPCKoala            pObj;
    HRESULT             hr;

    *ppvObj=NULL;
    hr=ResultFromScode(E_OUTOFMEMORY);

    //Verify that a controlling unknown asks for IUnknown
    if (NULL!=pUnkOuter && !IsEqualIID(riid, IID_IUnknown))
        return ResultFromScode(E_NOINTERFACE);

    //Create the object, passing function to notify on destruction
    pObj=new CKoala(pUnkOuter, ObjectDestroyed);

    if (NULL==pObj)
        return hr;

    if (pObj->FInit())
        hr=pObj->QueryInterface(riid, ppvObj);

    //Kill the object if initial creation or FInit failed.
    if (FAILED(hr))
        delete pObj;
    else
        g_cObj++;

    return hr;
    }

STDMETHODIMP CKoalaClassFactory::LockServer(BOOL fLock)
```

(continued)

Listing 4-4. *continued*

```
    {
    if (fLock)
        g_cLock++;
    else
        g_cLock--;

    return NOERROR;
    }
```

EKOALA.H

```
/*
 * Koala Object Chapter 4
 *
 * Definitions, classes, and prototypes for an application that
 * provides Koala objects to any other object user.
 *
 * Copyright (c)1993 Microsoft Corporation, All Rights Reserved
 */

#ifndef _EKOALA_H_
#define _EKOALA_H_

//Get the object definitions
#include "koala.h"

//EKOALA.CPP
LRESULT FAR PASCAL EXPORT KoalaWndProc(HWND, UINT, WPARAM, LPARAM);

class __far CAppVars
    {
    friend LRESULT FAR PASCAL EXPORT KoalaWndProc(HWND, UINT
        , WPARAM, LPARAM);

    protected:
        HINSTANCE       m_hInst;            //WinMain parameters
        HINSTANCE       m_hInstPrev;
        LPSTR           m_pszCmdLine;
        UINT            m_nCmdShow;

        HWND            m_hWnd;             //Main window handle
```

Listing 4-5. *(continued)*
The EKOALA.EXE implementation to house the Koala object.

Listing 4-5. *continued*

```
        BOOL            m_fInitialized;     //Did CoInitialize work?
        LPCLASSFACTORY  m_pIClassFactory;   //Our class factory
        DWORD           m_dwRegCO;          //Registration key

    public:
        CAppVars(HINSTANCE, HINSTANCE, LPSTR, UINT);
        ~CAppVars(void);
        BOOL FInit(void);
    };

typedef CAppVars FAR LPAPPVARS;

#define CBWNDEXTRA              sizeof(LONG)
#define KOALAWL_STRUCTURE       0

void FAR PASCAL ObjectDestroyed(void);

//This class factory object creates Koala objects.

class __far CKoalaClassFactory : public IClassFactory
    {
    protected:
        ULONG           m_cRef;

    public:
        CKoalaClassFactory(void);
        ~CKoalaClassFactory(void);

        //IUnknown members
        STDMETHODIMP         QueryInterface(REFIID, LPLPVOID);
        STDMETHODIMP_(ULONG) AddRef(void);
        STDMETHODIMP_(ULONG) Release(void);

        //IClassFactory members
        STDMETHODIMP         CreateInstance(LPUNKNOWN, REFIID
                                 , LPLPVOID);
        STDMETHODIMP         LockServer(BOOL);
    };

typedef CKoalaClassFactory FAR *LPCKoalaClassFactory;

#endif //_EKOALA_H_
```

(continued)

Listing 4-5. *continued*

EKOALA.CPP

```
/*
 * Koala Object EXE Chapter 4
 *
 * Object implemented in an application. This object supports
 * IUnknown and IPersist interfaces; it doesn't know anything more
 * than how to return its class ID, but it demonstrates how an
 * object is presented inside an EXE.
 *
 * Copyright (c)1993 Microsoft Corporation, All Rights Reserved
 */

//Do this once in the entire build
#define INITGUIDS

#include <ole2ver.h>
#include "ekoala.h"

//Count number of objects and number of locks.
ULONG       g_cObj=0;
ULONG       g_cLock=0;

//Make window handle global so that other code can cause a shutdown
 HWND        g_hWnd=NULL;

int PASCAL WinMain(HINSTANCE hInst, HINSTANCE hInstPrev
    , LPSTR pszCmdLine, int nCmdShow)
    {
    MSG         msg;
    LPAPPVARS   pAV;
    int       cMsg=96;

   #ifndef WIN32
    //Enlarge the queue as large as we can starting from 96
    while (!SetMessageQueue(cMsg) && (cMsg-=8));
   #endif

    pAV=new CAppVars(hInst, hInstPrev, pszCmdLine, nCmdShow);

    if (NULL==pAV)
        return -1;

    if (pAV->FInit())
```

(continued)

Listing 4-5. *continued*

```
        {
        while (GetMessage(&msg, NULL, 0, 0))
            {
            TranslateMessage(&msg);
            DispatchMessage(&msg);
            }
        }

    delete pAV;
    return msg.wParam;
    }

LRESULT FAR PASCAL EXPORT KoalaWndProc(HWND hWnd, UINT iMsg
    , WPARAM wParam, LPARAM lParam)
    {
    LPAPPVARS   pAV;

    pAV=(LPAPPVARS)GetWindowLong(hWnd, KOALAWL_STRUCTURE);

    switch (iMsg)
        {
        case WM_NCCREATE:
            pAV=(LPAPPVARS)((LONG)((LPCREATESTRUCT)lParam)
                ->lpCreateParams);

            SetWindowLong(hWnd, KOALAWL_STRUCTURE, (LONG)pAV);
            return (DefWindowProc(hWnd, iMsg, wParam, lParam));

        case WM_DESTROY:
            PostQuitMessage(0);
            break;

        default:
            return (DefWindowProc(hWnd, iMsg, wParam, lParam));
        }

    return 0L;
    }

/*
 * ObjectDestroyed
 *
 * Purpose:
 *  Function for the Koala object to call when it gets destroyed.
 *  We destroy the main window if the proper conditions are met for
 *  shutdown.
```

(continued)

Listing 4-5. *continued*

```
 */

void FAR PASCAL ObjectDestroyed(void)
    {
    g_cObj--;

    //No more objects and no locks, shut the app down.
    if (0==g_cObj && 0==g_cLock && IsWindow(g_hWnd))
        PostMessage(g_hWnd, WM_CLOSE, 0, 0L);

    return;
    }

CAppVars::CAppVars(HINSTANCE hInst, HINSTANCE hInstPrev
    , LPSTR pszCmdLine, UINT nCmdShow)
    {
    //Initialize WinMain parameter holders.
    m_hInst     =hInst;
    m_hInstPrev =hInstPrev;
    m_pszCmdLine=pszCmdLine;
    m_nCmdShow  =nCmdShow;

    m_hWnd=NULL;
    m_dwRegCO=0;
    m_pIClassFactory=NULL;
    m_fInitialized=FALSE;
    return;
    }

CAppVars::~CAppVars(void)
    {
    //Opposite of CoRegisterClassObject; class factory ref is now 1
    if (0L!=m_dwRegCO)
        CoRevokeClassObject(m_dwRegCO);

    //This should be the last Release, which frees the class factory.
    if (NULL!=m_pIClassFactory)
        m_pIClassFactory->Release();

    if (m_fInitialized)
        CoUninitialize();

    return;
    }
```

(continued)

Listing 4-5. *continued*

```
BOOL CAppVars::FInit(void)
    {
    WNDCLASS    wc;
    HRESULT     hr;
    DWORD       dwVer;

    //Fail if we've run outside CoGetClassObject
    if (lstrcmpi(m_pszCmdLine, "-Embedding"))
        return FALSE;

    dwVer=CoBuildVersion();

    if (rmm!=HIWORD(dwVer))
        return FALSE;

    if (FAILED(CoInitialize(NULL)))
        return FALSE;

    m_fInitialized=TRUE;

    if (!m_hInstPrev)
        {
        wc.style          = CS_HREDRAW | CS_VREDRAW;
        wc.lpfnWndProc    = KoalaWndProc;
        wc.cbClsExtra     = 0;
        wc.cbWndExtra     = CBWNDEXTRA;
        wc.hInstance      = m_hInst;
        wc.hIcon          = NULL;
        wc.hCursor        = NULL;
        wc.hbrBackground  = (HBRUSH)(COLOR_WINDOW + 1);
        wc.lpszMenuName   = NULL;
        wc.lpszClassName  = "Koala";

        if (!RegisterClass(&wc))
            return FALSE;
        }

    m_hWnd=CreateWindow("Koala", "Koala", WS_OVERLAPPEDWINDOW
        , 35, 35, 350, 250, NULL, NULL, m_hInst, this);

    if (NULL==m_hWnd)
        return FALSE;

    g_hWnd=m_hWnd;
```

(continued)

Listing 4-5. *continued*

```
    /*
     * Create our class factory and register it for this application
     * using CoRegisterClassObject. We are able to service more than
     * one object at a time so we use REGCLS_MULTIPLEUSE.
     */
    m_pIClassFactory=new CKoalaClassFactory();

    if (NULL==m_pIClassFactory)
        return FALSE;

    //Because we hold on to this, we should AddRef it.
    m_pIClassFactory->AddRef();

    hr=CoRegisterClassObject(CLSID_Koala
        , (LPUNKNOWN)m_pIClassFactory, CLSCTX_LOCAL_SERVER
        , REGCLS_MULTIPLEUSE, &m_dwRegCO);

    if (FAILED(hr))
        return FALSE;

    return TRUE;
    }

CKoalaClassFactory::CKoalaClassFactory(void)
    {
    m_cRef=0L;
    return;
    }

CKoalaClassFactory::~CKoalaClassFactory(void)
    {
    return;
    }

STDMETHODIMP CKoalaClassFactory::QueryInterface(REFIID riid
    , LPVOID FAR *ppv)
    {
    *ppv=NULL;

    //Any interface on this object is the object pointer.
    if (IsEqualIID(riid, IID_IUnknown)
        || IsEqualIID(riid, IID_IClassFactory))
        *ppv=(LPVOID)this;

    if (NULL!=*ppv)
        {
        ((LPUNKNOWN)*ppv)->AddRef();
```

(continued)

Listing 4-5. *continued*

```
        return NOERROR;
        }

    return ResultFromScode(E_NOINTERFACE);
    }

STDMETHODIMP_(ULONG) CKoalaClassFactory::AddRef(void)
    {
    return ++m_cRef;
    }

STDMETHODIMP_(ULONG) CKoalaClassFactory::Release(void)
    {
    ULONG           cRefT;

    cRefT=--m_cRef;

    if (0L==m_cRef)
        delete this;

    return cRefT;
    }

STDMETHODIMP CKoalaClassFactory::CreateInstance(LPUNKNOWN pUnkOuter
    , REFIID riid, LPVOID FAR *ppvObj)
    {
    LPCKoala            pObj;
    HRESULT             hr;

    *ppvObj=NULL;
    hr=ResultFromScode(E_OUTOFMEMORY);

    //Verify that a controlling unknown asks for IUnknown
    if (NULL!=pUnkOuter && !IsEqualIID(riid, IID_IUnknown))
        return ResultFromScode(E_NOINTERFACE);

    //Create the object, telling it to notify us when it's gone.
    pObj=new CKoala(pUnkOuter, ObjectDestroyed);

    if (NULL==pObj)
        {
        //Starts shutdown if no other objects
        g_cObj++;
        ObjectDestroyed();
        return hr;
        }
```

(continued)

Listing 4-5. *continued*

```
    if (pObj->FInit())
        hr=pObj->QueryInterface(riid, ppvObj);

    g_cObj++;

    /*
     * Kill the object if initial creation or FInit failed. If
     * the object failed, we handle the g_cObj increment above
     * in ObjectDestroyed.
     */
    if (FAILED(hr))
        {
        delete pObj;
        ObjectDestroyed();  //Handle shutdown cases.
        }

    return hr;
    }

STDMETHODIMP CKoalaClassFactory::LockServer(BOOL fLock)
    {
    if (fLock)
        g_cLock++;
    else
        {
        g_cLock--;

        //No more objects and no locks, shut the app down.
        if (0==g_cObj && 0==g_cLock && IsWindow(g_hWnd))
            PostMessage(g_hWnd, WM_CLOSE, 0, 0L);
        }

    return NOERROR;
    }
```

Register CLSIDs

Every component object class (but not all types of Windows Objects) must have a unique CLSID associated with it in the Registration Database. The registration entries for a simple object, such as we're implementing here, are few; as you create objects with more features that support linking and embedding, there will be much more information to add, as described in Chapter 10. For purposes of the sample code, the necessary entries are contained in the file CHAP04\CHAP04.REG, which you can add to your Registration Database by using the REGEDIT program in Windows. Creating a REG file is the preferred method of registering objects and applications because it can be done at install time instead of programmatically at run-time, which is tedious, to say the least. The online help in the OLE 2 SDK contains more information about storing information in the Registration Database.

The required entries fall under the CLSID key, where OLE 2 stores information about all classes under your spelled-out CLSID, as you can see in the REGEDIT program and as shown in Figure 4-5 on the next page. OLE 2 also stores information about its standard interfaces and the code that handles parameter marshaling under the Interface key. The following steps describe the necessary registration for DLL-based and EXE-based objects:

1. From HKEY_CLASSES_ROOT (the root key of the entire Registration Database), create the entry *CLSID\{class ID}=<name>*, where {*class ID*} is the value of your CLSID spelled out and *<name>* is a human-readable string for your object. The Koala object has the class ID string {00021102-0000-0000-C000-000000000046} which is not something many, except for a few odd individuals, consider readable. The *<name>* of the Koala object is "Koala Object Chapter 4."
2. Create an entry under the CLSID entry in step 1 to point to the object code:
   - For DLL objects, register *InprocServer=<path to DLL>*.
   - For EXE objects, register *LocalServer=<path to EXE>*.
   - For DLL object handlers, register *InprocHandler=<path to DLL>*.

   Note that these entries should always contains full pathnames so that you do not depend on your DLLs or EXEs being on the MS-DOS path. Your application's install program should update the paths when it knows where the installation occurred.[4]
3. (Optional) If you want to allow a user to look up your CLSID based on a text string, make an entry under HKEY_CLASSES_ROOT of *<ProgID>=<name>*, where *<ProgID>* is a short name without spaces or punctuation, and *<name>* is the human-readable name, identical to that in step 1, of your object. Under this key, create another entry, CLSID=*{class ID}*, in which *{class ID}* is also the same as in step 1. In

4. The sample code with this book does, however, break this rule because the installation program on the companion disks is not capable of modifying all the .REG files in each CHAPxx directory to contain a full pathname. Instead, each DLL and EXE is registered without a full pathname and therefore depends on them being in the path.

this example, *<ProgID>* is *Koala* and *<name>* is "Koala Object Chapter 4." Note that you can also create a symmetric key under the object's CLSID in the form of *ProgID = <PRogID>*.

Entries of the type created in step 3 will be required for Compound Document objects that should appear in the Insert Object dialog box inside a container application. But that is a subject for a later chapter. Without those entries from steps 1 and 2, however, the *CoGetClassObject* API function (which *CoCreateInstance* uses, remember) will not be able to locate your object implementation. Note also that the same DLL or EXE can serve multiple CLSIDs, and in such cases you must make a similar entry under each CLSID you support with the *InprocServer* and *LocalServer* keys, although they can all contain the same path to the same server.

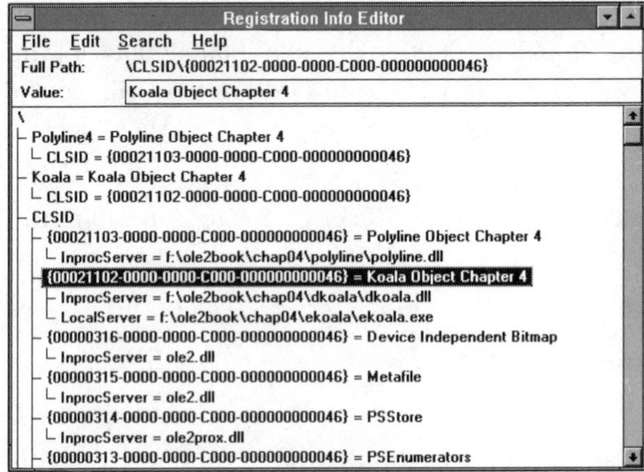

Figure 4-5.
The populated CLSID section of the Registration Database, showing the entries for Koala.

Implement the Class Factory

Telling the Component Object library where your object code lives is one thing; you still need to provide for creating objects once that code has been loaded, so the next step is to create a class factory that implements the *IClassFactory* interface. After we implement this class factory, we can provide the code to expose it outside the server. This is somewhat like implementing a window procedure in order to call *RegisterClass* because you have to store a pointer to your window procedure in the WNDCLASS before you call *RegisterCall.* Both sample implementations, DLL and EXE, use a C++ class of *CKoalaClassFactory* for this purpose, and the two are almost identical. The only differences between the DLL and EXE implementations of *CKoalaClassFactory* have to do with the unloading mechanisms, which we'll discuss later. For now, let's concentrate on those identical parts that instantiate a *CKoala* object.

All implementations of *IClassFactory::CreateInstance* are identical, and each implementation contains three major points of interest. First, the first parameter to *CreateInstance* is *pUnkOuter,* which is the controlling unknown for the object we've been asked to create, if our new object is becoming part of an aggregate. When we instantiate the object using *new CKoala,* we pass this *pUnkOuter* down to the object so that it can delegate properly. (Again, see "Object Reusability" for more details.) When an object is aggregated, the outer object *must* ask for an *IUnknown* interface on the new object. To enforce this rule, we check that *IID_IUnknown* is asked for when *pUnkOuter* is not NULL.

Next, in addition to passing *pUnkOuter* to *new CKoala,* we also pass a pointer to an independent function named *ObjectDestroyed.* When the final call to *Release* for the Koala object is about to free the object, it will call this function. This allows the object to isolate itself from the nature of its server housing (DLL or EXE) and allow that housing to act appropriately on the event. You can see again in the *CKoala::Release* function in Listing 4-3 how and when this function is called. We'll examine what *ObjectDestroyed* does in both servers in the later section "Provide an Unloading Mechanism."

Finally, if the object is successfully instantiated, we still need to initialize it through an internal *FInit* implemented in the *CKoala* object. *FInit* is not a standard feature of OLE 2 objects and is used here to support a convenient two-phase creation model common in C++ coding. *FInit* performs all operations that might fail and is thus able to communicate success or failure back to the class factory during instantiation. If this second initialization step succeeds, *CreateInstance* asks the object's *QueryInterface* to return the appropriate interface pointer, which has the convenient effect of calling that pointer's *AddRef* as required. Remember that *CreateInstance,* as a function returning a new pointer, must return the pointer with a reference count on the caller's behalf. Furthermore, *CreateInstance* increments a global object count, which the server can use to determine unloading conditions. If the initialization fails, *CreateInstance* deletes the object and returns an out-of-memory error to the caller.

IClassFactory also has a member named *LockServer,* which either increments or decrements a lock count on the DLL or EXE in which the class factory lives. *LockServer* provides a method through which a user can keep a DLL or an EXE in memory even if that server is not servicing any objects and has no outstanding reference counts on its class factory. This allows a user to optimize loading and reloading of servers, keeping the code in memory even when it's not immediately necessary. Such optimizations can greatly increase performance when a user deals with a very large server EXE or DLL.

The implementation of *LockServer* in the DLL and EXE versions differs slightly, again to handle the differences in unloading mechanisms (although we could isolate these differences as well). Their commonality is to either increment or decrement a global lock counter, which is used in different ways by the server's unloading mechanism.

Expose the Class Factory

The major difference between DLL and EXE servers is in how they expose their class factories, primarily because an EXE defines a task, whereas a DLL doesn't. Your class factory is an object, and the Component Object library needs to obtain its *IClassFactory* pointer. It does so either by calling a function that you export from an object DLL (that is, an API function that you implement) or by requiring you to call a Component Object library API function from your own code in an EXE. In either case, an API function is used to get the class factory pointer from your code to OLE 2's code.

DLL Server

The DLL exposure mechanism is the simplest, so let's start there. Every DLL server must export a function named *DllGetClassObject* with the following form:

```
HRESULT __export FAR PASCAL DllGetClassObject(REFCLSID rclsid,
    REFIID riid, LPVOID FAR *ppv);
```

The *__export* is a matter of convenience—if your compiler does not support *__export*, you can still list the function in the EXPORTS section of your DEF file. In addition, the macro STDAPI defined in COMPOBJ.H expands to *HRESULT __export FAR PASCAL* if you want to use it. In the sample code, you will see *EXPORT* instead of *__export*. *EXPORT* is a macro in BOOK1632.H (in the INC directory) that compiles to __export for Windows 3.1 and to nothing for Windows NT.

When a user calls *CoCreateInstance* or *CoGetClassObject* and passes CLSCTX_INPROC_SERVER, the Component Object library will look in the Registration Database for the *InprocServer* for the given CLSID, call *CoLoadLibrary* to get that server into memory, and then call *GetProcAddress* looking for *DllGetClassObject*. The Component Object library then calls *DllGetClassObject* with the CLSID and IID requested by the component user. Your export then creates the appropriate class factory for the CLSID and returns the appropriate interface pointer for IID, which is usually *IClassFactory*. By calling this function in your DLL, the Component Object library obtains a pointer to your class factory object; essentially, *DllGetClassObject* is an API function you implement for OLE 2. This is exactly like exporting the WEP function from a DLL so that Windows can locate and call it.

NOTE: Because *DllGetClassObject* is passed a CLSID, a single DLL can provide different class factories for any number of different classes—that is, a single module can be the server for any number of object types. OLE2.DLL is an example of such a server; it provides most of the internally used object classes of OLE 2 from one DLL.

All implementations of *DllGetClassObject* should validate that it can support the requested CLSID as well as the requested interface for the class factory, which can be either *IUnknown* or *IClassFactory*. If both checks succeed, it then instantiates the class factory object (in this case, using *CKoalaClassFactory*). Remember that, as a function that creates a new interface pointer to an object, *DllGetClassObject* must use *AddRef* on the new object before returning, as shown in the following code:

```
if (!IsEqualCLSID(rclsid, CLSID_Koala))
    return ResultFromScode(CO_E_CLASSNOTREG);

//Check that we can provide the interface
if (!IsEqualIID(riid, IID_IUnknown)
    && !IsEqualIID(riid, IID_IClassFactory))
    return ResultFromScode(E_NOINTERFACE);

//Return our IClassFactory for Koala objects
*ppv=(LPVOID)new CKoalaClassFactory();

//Don't forget to AddRef the object through any interface we return
((LPUNKNOWN)*ppv)->AddRef();
```

Notice that this code, like all the sample code described in this book, creates all objects with an initial reference count of zero, thereby requiring a call to *AddRef* before returning an interface pointer to that object. This is simply the design approach taken in this book to reinforce the idea that a new interface pointer that you return to an external object user must have *AddRef* called through it so that the user can simply call *Release* when finished with the object to free it. You could, of course, set the reference count in your own objects to 1 in their constructors and avoid the explicit *AddRef* call shown here.

EXE Server

Exposing a class factory from an EXE is somewhat different because an EXE has a *WinMain*, a message loop, and a window that define its lifetime. The real difference between an EXE and a DLL in interacting with a Component Object library is that, with a EXE, instead of having the library call an exported function such as *DllGetClassObject*, you pass your class factory object (that is, an *IClassFactory* pointer) to the *CoRegisterClassObject* API function, but only under the appropriate circumstances.

The Component Object library informs an EXE that it is being used to service objects through the command-line flag *-Embedding* (which is left over from OLE 1). This flag is simply appended to the path entry for this local server in the Registration Database, so if you register your EXE with flags yourself, look for this at the end of the command line. Checking this flag is the first priority in EKOALA's initialization. If this flag is not present, the end user has attempted to run the application as a stand-alone from the shell. Because this application doesn't live for any purpose other than to service objects, it fails to load if *-Embedding* is not present.

The next few steps in *CAppVars::FInit* are the same as those required of any OLE 2 application: They use *CoBuildVersion* and *CoInitialize* because we are using Component Object library API functions. After such initialization, we create a window for this task, but the window remains hidden; in all cases in which *-Embedding* is on the command line, the server window should remain hidden until explicitly asked to show itself. For this demonstration, the EKOALA program has no need to ever show its window because it has no user interface.

If we get past the initialization stage, we must then create the class factory object and pass it to *CoRegisterClassObject* in the same way we are accustomed to calling the Windows API function *RegisterClass.* With *RegisterClass,* you create a WNDCLASS structure, fill in the *lpfnWndProc* field with a pointer to your window's message procedure, and pass a pointer to that WNDCLASS to *RegisterClass.* Your window procedure is not actually called until someone (you or a user) creates a window of your registered class. With *CoRegisterClassObject,* you create a class factory object with an *IClassFactory* interface and pass a pointer to that interface to *CoRegisterClassObject,* but the interface functions such as *CreateInstance* are not called until someone creates a component object of your class.[5]

---

5. In reality, calling *CoRegisterClassObject* immediately generates a number of calls to your *IClassFactory::AddRef* because the Component Object library is holding onto your *IClassFactory* pointer. Thus your object is called before it ever creates an object, unlike your window procedure.

Creating the class factory is simply a matter of allocating the object's data structure and function table, which is conveniently handled in C++ with the *new* operator, as follows:

```
//Return our IClassFactory for Koala objects
m_pIClassFactory=new CKoalaClassFactory();

if (NULL==m_pIClassFactory)
    return FALSE;

//Because we hold on to this, we should AddRef it
m_pIClassFactory->AddRef();
```

The additional *AddRef* ensures that the application controls the lifetime of the class factory because the *CKoalaClassFactory* constructor initializes its reference count to zero. Because the application makes the first *AddRef*, it will have to make the last *Release*, which allows the class factory to destroy itself.

After we have created the class factory, we must inform the Component Object library about it by using *CoRegisterClassObject* because we have yet to yield from this task in our message loop. The Component Object library does not have a chance to call us, as happens in a DLL.

```
hr=CoRegisterClassObject(CLSID_Koala, (LPUNKNOWN)m_pIClassFactory
    , CLSCTX_LOCAL_SERVER, REGCLS_MULTIPLEUSE, &m_dwRegCO);

if (FAILED(hr))
    return FALSE;    //Registration failed.

[Class factory successfully registered]
```

CoRegisterClassObject takes the CLSID of the class factory we're providing, a pointer to the class factory, the context in which we're running (CLSCTX-_LOCAL_SERVER), a flag indicating how this class factory can be used, and a pointer to a DWORD in which *CoRegisterClassObject* returns a registration key that the object will need later, during shutdown.

NOTE: If your EXE is the server for multiple classes, you must call *CoRegisterClassObject* for each supported CLSID, just as you would call *RegisterClass* for each window class you support. The Component Object library will launch your object when any user requests any CLSID you support, but it cannot tell you through *WinMain* which CLSID that was. So you must register a class factory for each CLSID you placed in the Registration Database.

The fourth parameter to *CoRegisterClassObject* specifies how many objects can be created using this class factory: REGCLS_SINGLEUSE or

REGCLS_MULTIPLEUSE. If you specify single use, OLE will launch another instance of your application each time a user calls *CoGetClassObject.* If you specify multiple use, one instance of the application can service any number of objects. When you register a class with REGCLS_MULTIPLEUSE and CLSCTX_LOCAL_SERVER, the Component Object library also registers the class as CLSCTX_INPROC_SERVER. If you need to separately control whether the class factory is registered for local servers and in-process servers, use the flag REGCLS_MULTI_SEPARATE, which is available in OLE version 2.01 and later but not in the first release of OLE 2, version 2.00.

To demonstrate single-use vs. multi-use servers, run two instances of the OBJUSER program, choose Use EXE Object from the Koala Object menu of each instance, and use one of the Create commands from the menu. Now watch the modules that load and unload by using tools such as Heapwalker (in the Windows SDK) or WPS (in the OLE 2 SDK). Because EKOALA registers itself as multiple use, only one instance will be loaded to service both objects. Now change EKOALA so that it registers as single use and run two OBJUSERs again, using the same commands. This time two instances of EKOALA will run, each servicing only one object.

Also note that *CoRegisterClassObject* is not a function that can be called only from within an EXE. For all OLE cares, a DLL can call this function if it wants to expose a class factory outside of its implementation of *DllGetClassObject* or in lieu of *DllGetClassObject* altogether. The use flags should always be REGCLS_MULTIPLEUSE in such situations.

Provide an Unloading Mechanism

Because the mechanisms we use to expose a class factory from the two kinds of servers differ, the mechanisms for indicating when the server is no longer needed also differ. An unloading mechanism is not a consideration for normal Windows applications because they are almost always controlled by the user. OLE 2 allows DLLs and EXEs that serve objects to be controlled by another piece of component user code. Because the end user doesn't close applications, you must use a programmatic technique to accomplish the same end.

The bottom line is that a server is no longer needed when there are no lock counts from *IClassFactory::LockServer* and there are no objects currently being serviced. However, because the EXE server has a window, it must destroy its main window, cause a call to *PostQuitMessage,* exit the message loop, and quit the application. DLLs have no idea of how to "quit" (that is, there is no message loop to exit), so they mark themselves as "unloadable."

DLL Server

Again, let's start with the DLL because in this case the unload mechanism is trivial. As we have seen, the DLL server increments and decrements a global[6] lock count in *IClassFactory::LockServer* and increments the object count in *IClassFactory::CreateInstance.* When any Koala object is destroyed, we want to decrement the object count, a process that is handled in the *ObjectDestroyed* function we provided to the Koala object:

```
void FAR PASCAL ObjectDestroyed(void)
    {
    g_cObj--;
    return;
    }
```

The DLL never tells anyone to unload it; instead, the Component Object Model will periodically ask it "Can you unload now?" by calling an export *DllCanUnloadNow* using the following form:

```
STDAPI DllCanUnloadNow(void)
    {
    SCODE   sc;

    //Our answer is whether there are any object or locks
    sc=(0L==g_cObj && 0==g_cLock) ? S_OK : S_FALSE;
    return ResultFromScode(sc);
    }
```

The implementation shown here will answer "yes" when both object and lock counts are zero and "no" otherwise. If this function answers "yes," the libraries will internally call *CoFreeLibrary* to reverse the call the function made to *CoLoadLibrary* from within *CoGetClassObject.*

NOTE: The function that should call *DllCanUnloadNow* is *CoFreeUnusedLibraries,* which, as we've seen, is called periodically by an object user. However, the OLE 2 implementation of *CoFreeUnusedLibraries* does nothing, so you will never see a call to *DllCanUnloadNow.* However, *CoFreeUnusedLibraries* will be implemented in the near future, so implement *DllCanUnloadNow* as if it were always called anyway.

---

6. I confess! I used global variables! I normally try hard to avoid any use of global variables, as you probably do. In this case, however, having a few globals simplified both DLL and EXE implementation. You might also see me declare a global instance handle when appropriate because instance handles are really application-wide and might be needed deep in a long chain of function calls. In any case, global variables in this and other sample applications are prefixed with *g_* for clear identification. Please forgive my transgressions!

Also note that there has been no mention of class factory reference counts in any of this discussion because such reference counts are not used to keep the DLL in memory. Object user code wanting to hold a class factory must also call *LockServer* (as described earlier, in "Implementing a Component Object and Server"). Although a reference count could easily prevent a DLL from unloading, it's impossible to use this technique in an EXE, as the following section illustrates.

Congratulations! You're a proud parent! After implementing *DllCanUnloadNow*, you now have a complete DLL object server into which you can put more and more complex objects and interfaces, continuing to use the same mechanisms. The framework for DLL-based objects developed here will be used for more complex DLL objects later in this book. I certainly hope you will be able to use it for incredible objects of your own.

EXE Server

Instead of being asked when your object can be unloaded, as in the DLL case, an EXE server must initiate shutdown itself when it detects the following conditions: No objects are being serviced, and there is a zero lock count. This detection complicates use of EXE servers when we deal with compound documents because we throw in another condition regarding end-user control. (See the section titled "Call Initialization Functions at Startup and Shutdown" in Chapter 10.) When these two conditions are met, we need to start shutdown by posting a WM_CLOSE message to the main window. The two places where we must add a check are in *IClassFactory::LockServer* and in the *ObjectDestroyed* function, which the Koala object will call after it's freed:[7]

```
STDMETHODIMP CKoalaClassFactory::LockServer(BOOL fLock)
    {
    if (fLock)
        g_cLock++;
    else
        {
        g_cLock--;

        //No more objects and no locks, shut the app down.
        if (0==g_cObj && 0==g_cLock && IsWindow(g_hWnd))
            PostMessage(g_hWnd, WM_CLOSE, 0, 0L);
        }
```

(continued)

7. Another way to implement *LockServer(FALSE)* is to artificially increment the object count (g_cObj++) and call *ObjectDestroyed*, which decrements that artificial count and starts shutdown as appropriate. This approach centralizes the closure conditions in *ObjectDestroyed* and is used in samples in later chapters.

```
    return NOERROR;
    }

void FAR PASCAL ObjectDestroyed(void)
    {
    g_cObj--;

    //No more objects and no locks, shut the app down.
    if (0==g_cObj && 0==g_cLock && IsWindow(g_hWnd))
        PostMessage(g_hWnd, WM_CLOSE, 0, 0L);

    return;
    }
```

To facilitate message posting, I sinned again in EKOALA by storing its window handle as a global variable. This slight bit of what you might consider "cheating" works cleanly and easily without your having to pass the window handle around. Such a global variable guarantees that any code in this application could start a shutdown with the same mechanism. We might also use *PostAppMessage*, but that requires some changes to the application's message loop, which wouldn't be any cleaner.

By posting WM_CLOSE, we start shutdown of EKOALA exactly as if an end user had closed it from the system menu. In the process of shutting down, EKOALA destroys the main window (*DefWindowProc*'s handling of WM_CLOSE), exits *WinMain* (by calling *PostQuitMessage* in WM_DESTROY), and ends up in *CAppVars::~CAppVars*. This destructor first calls *CoRevokeClassObject*, which unregisters the class factory you passed to *CoRegisterClassObject* identified by the DWORD key that *CoRegisterClassObject* returned. If you registered multiple class factories for different CLSIDs, you must revoke each one here. *CoRevokeClassObject* will call *Release* for any reference count that the Component Object library was holding on the class factory. Furthermore, because we called *AddRef* ourselves before *CoRegisterClassObject* (remember that, long ago?), we must now match it with a *Release*. This will reduce the class factory's reference count to zero, causing it to free itself. Finally, because we called *CoInitialize*, we need to remember to call *CoUninitialize*.

CoRevokeClassObject is the reason why a Component User cannot use a class factory's reference count to keep a server—either a DLL or an EXE—in memory. If a positive reference count could keep the class factory in memory, we could not shut the application down until the reference count reached zero and the class factory was destroyed. The reference count will never reach zero unless we call *CoRevokeClassObject*, but we call *CoRevokeClassObject* only when we shut down after our window is gone, we've exited the message loop, and we're on the nonstop express to oblivion. So we can't revoke until we're shutting down and we can't shut down until we revoke. Aaaugh! Fourth down and 100 yards to go...so we punt: Officially, a positive reference count on a class factory cannot be used to keep a server in memory, so a Component User must rely on *LockServer*, not the class factory reference count, to prevent shutdown. Our salvation is that this is one of the various special cases of reference counting in all of OLE 2.

Object Handlers

An object handler is a lightweight DLL server used to provide a partial implementation of a full EXE object, thereby reducing the need to launch the EXE to service that object. Because DLL objects generally load faster and need no parameter marshaling, use of handlers generally increases overall performance. Object handlers used in conjunction with a compound document object provide for data transfer and object rendering (directly to screen or printer) but not for editing, making handlers ideal in cases of licensing for redistribution with a document, in much the same way TrueType fonts in Windows 3.1 can be saved with a document, given the proper license. Chapter 11 will examine Object Handlers for specific use with compound documents.

If an object user calls *CoGetClassObject* with CLSCTX_INPROC_HANDLER ¦ CLSCTX_LOCAL_SERVER, the handler is loaded first and all calls to the object's interfaces are sent to the DLL. If a full DLL object exists as well, OLE will use that DLL first if the CLSCTX_INPROC_SERVER flag is specified.

When a handler discovers that it cannot provide the requested function to the caller, it can delegate that call to a full implementation of the object in an EXE server. However, the handler cannot simply call *CoCreateInstance* with CLSCTX_LOCAL_SERVER to launch the EXE and obtain a pointer to an object in that EXE. Instead the handler must instantiate what is called the *default handler* (OLE2.DLL) for the same object CLSID through the mechanism known as *aggregation,* as we'll see shortly. The handler then delegates the function call to the object in the default handler, which launches the EXE as appropriate. When the object in the handler wants to free itself, it also frees the default handler object, which, in turn, closes the EXE as necessary.

Of course, this is not without restrictions: The EXE object can support only standard interfaces with built-in marshaling support, and there is limited communication between the handler and the application. Furthermore, the handler must ensure that data is synchronized between itself and the application. Most often, however, a handler exists to provide speedy rendering of specific data formats and delegates requests for more esoteric formats to the application.

Finally, the only differences between DLL object handlers and DLL object servers are their intended use and expected performance. Technically and structurally, the handler is identical to a DLL server. All discussion in this chapter dealing with DLL servers applies equally to DLL handlers. The most significant differences are in how the two are used and how they should be designed, which is a topic for Chapter 11.

Cosmo's Polyline as a DLL Object

The Koala object that supports the *IPersist* interface is pretty boring and, well, useless. To demonstrate an object much more useful and exciting, the CHAP04\POLYLINE directory in the sample code contains an implementation of Cosmo's *CPolyline* class as a Windows Object in a DLL. The source code for POLYLINE.DLL (which compiles into POLY04.DLL) is a little too long to show here, however. This implementation shows that a much more complicated object, such as Polyline, can fit into exactly the same housing (DLL or EXE) as a simple object, such as Koala.

The member functions of the original *CPolyline* from Chapter 2 are converted into a custom interface, *IPolyline4*, defined in INC\IPOLY4.H and shown in Listing 4-6. (The *4* in these names stands for Chapter 4 because we'll be making modifications to the interface in later chapters.) Note that because all interface functions should return HRESULT whenever possible, some return values in the original *CPolyline* are converted into *out-parameters* in the interface. IPOLY4.H also defines the interface *IPolylineAdviseSink4*, through which a Cosmo document receives notifications from Polyline. This replaces the *CPolylineAdviseSink* class that Cosmo used before.

If you look in Polyline's sources, you'll notice that the core implementation of Polyline has not changed significantly from what was in Cosmo. In addition, the DLLPOLY.CPP file is only a slight modification of the DKOALA.CPP file: a few name changes, a class registered in *LibMain*, and a

IPOLY4.H

```
/*
 * Polyline Object Chapter 4
 *
 * Definition of an IPolyline interface for a Polyline object used
 * in the Cosmo implementation. This interface is custom and is
 * only supported from DLL-based objects.
 *
 * Copyright (c)1993 Microsoft Corporation, All Rights Reserved
 */

#ifndef _IPOLY4_H_
#define _IPOLY4_H_

//Versioning.
#define VERSIONMAJOR                2
#define VERSIONMINOR                0
#define VERSIONCURRENT              0x00020000

#define CPOLYLINEPOINTS             20

//Version 2 Polyline structure
typedef struct __far tagPOLYLINEDATA
    {
    WORD        wVerMaj;                    //Major version number
    WORD        wVerMin;                    //Minor version number
    WORD        cPoints;                    //Number of points
    BOOL        fReserved;                  //Previously fDrawEntire
    RECT        rc;                         //Rectangle of figure
    POINT       rgpt[CPOLYLINEPOINTS];      //Points on a 0-32767 grid

    //Version 2 additions
    COLORREF    rgbBackground;              //Background color
    COLORREF    rgbLine;                    //Line color
    int         iLineStyle;                 //Line style
    } POLYLINEDATA, *PPOLYLINEDATA, FAR *LPPOLYLINEDATA;

#define CBPOLYLINEDATA   sizeof(POLYLINEDATA)

//We use the OLE 2 macro to define a new interface
#undef  INTERFACE
#define INTERFACE IPolylineAdviseSink4
```

Listing 4-6. *(continued)*
IPolyline4 *and* IPolylineAdviseSink4 *custom interfaces.*

Listing 4-6. *continued*

```
/*
 * When someone initializes a polyline and is interested in receiving
 * notifications of events, they provide one of these objects.
 */

DECLARE_INTERFACE_(IPolylineAdviseSink4, IUnknown)
    {
    //IUnknown members
    STDMETHOD(QueryInterface) (THIS_ REFIID, LPLPVOID) PURE;
    STDMETHOD_(ULONG, AddRef)  (THIS) PURE;
    STDMETHOD_(ULONG, Release) (THIS) PURE;

    //Advise members.
    STDMETHOD_(void, OnPointChange)     (THIS) PURE;
    STDMETHOD_(void, OnSizeChange)      (THIS) PURE;
    STDMETHOD_(void, OnDataChange)      (THIS) PURE;
    STDMETHOD_(void, OnColorChange)     (THIS) PURE;
    STDMETHOD_(void, OnLineStyleChange) (THIS) PURE;
    };

typedef IPolylineAdviseSink4 FAR *LPPOLYLINEADVISESINK;

#undef  INTERFACE
#define INTERFACE IPolyline4

DECLARE_INTERFACE_(IPolyline4, IUnknown)
    {
    //IUnknown members:
    STDMETHOD(QueryInterface) (THIS_ REFIID, LPLPVOID) PURE;
    STDMETHOD_(ULONG, AddRef)  (THIS) PURE;
    STDMETHOD_(ULONG, Release) (THIS) PURE;

    //IPolyline members

    //File-related members:
    STDMETHOD(ReadFromFile) (THIS_ LPSTR) PURE;
    STDMETHOD(WriteToFile)  (THIS_ LPSTR) PURE;

    //Data transfer members:
    STDMETHOD(DataSet)       (THIS_ LPPOLYLINEDATA, BOOL, BOOL) PURE;
    STDMETHOD(DataGet)       (THIS_ LPPOLYLINEDATA) PURE;
    STDMETHOD(DataSetMem)    (THIS_ HGLOBAL, BOOL, BOOL, BOOL) PURE;
    STDMETHOD(DataGetMem)    (THIS_ HGLOBAL FAR *) PURE;
    STDMETHOD(RenderBitmap) (THIS_ HBITMAP FAR *) PURE;
    STDMETHOD(RenderMetafile) (THIS_ HMETAFILE FAR *) PURE;
    STDMETHOD(RenderMetafilePict) (THIS_ HGLOBAL FAR *) PURE;
```

(continued)

Listing 4-6. *continued*

```
    //Manipulation members:
    STDMETHOD(Init)    (THIS_ HWND, LPRECT, DWORD, UINT) PURE;
    STDMETHOD(New)     (THIS) PURE;
    STDMETHOD(Undo)    (THIS) PURE;
    STDMETHOD(Window) (THIS_ HWND FAR *) PURE;

    STDMETHOD(SetAdvise) (THIS_ LPPOLYLINEADVISESINK) PURE;
    STDMETHOD(GetAdvise) (THIS_ LPPOLYLINEADVISESINK FAR *) PURE;

    STDMETHOD(RectGet) (THIS_ LPRECT) PURE;
    STDMETHOD(SizeGet) (THIS_ LPRECT) PURE;
    STDMETHOD(RectSet) (THIS_ LPRECT, BOOL) PURE;
    STDMETHOD(SizeSet) (THIS_ LPRECT, BOOL) PURE;

    STDMETHOD(ColorSet) (THIS_ UINT, COLORREF
        , COLORREF FAR *) PURE;
    STDMETHOD(ColorGet) (THIS_ UINT, COLORREF FAR *) PURE;

    STDMETHOD(LineStyleSet) (THIS_ UINT, UINT FAR *) PURE;
    STDMETHOD(LineStyleGet) (THIS_ UINT FAR *) PURE;
    };

typedef IPolyline4 FAR *LPPOLYLINE;

//Error values for data transfer functions
#define POLYLINE_E_INVALIDPOINTER   \
    MAKE_SCODE(SEVERITY_ERROR, FACILITY_ITF, 1)
#define POLYLINE_E_READFAILURE      \
    MAKE_SCODE(SEVERITY_ERROR, FACILITY_ITF, 2)
#define POLYLINE_E_WRITEFAILURE     \
    MAKE_SCODE(SEVERITY_ERROR, FACILITY_ITF, 3)

//Color indices for color member functions
#define POLYLINECOLOR_BACKGROUND    0
#define POLYLINECOLOR_LINE          1

#endif //_IPOLY4_H_
```

DLL instance handle passed to the *CPolyline* constructor. Oh yes, *CPolyline* still exists, but it is now more like the *CKoala* object in the previous examples. The member functions of the *CPolyline* of Chapter 2 have been moved to the interface implementation *CImpIPolyline.*

As we move forward in this book, we'll incrementally replace specific members of *IPolyline4* with those of another interface. In the next chapter, for example, we'll remove the two file-related functions from *IPolyline5*, replacing them with an *IPersistStorage* interface on the object. In Chapter 6, we'll replace the data transfer and graphics rendering functions in *IPolyline6* with the *IDataObject* interface. Beyond that, we'll add compound document features, including in-place activation, to Polyline. However, all these additions come in the form of other interfaces, which will not interfere with Polyline's operation as a component object.

The version of Cosmo that uses the component Polyline object, Component Cosmo, is provided in CHAP04\COCOSMO and requires only a few modifications. When you run Component Cosmo, however, you will notice absolutely no changes in the user interface or in any behavior. Component Cosmo merely changed from being the user of a local C++ object, *CPolyline*, to being a Component User of the Polyline Windows object through the *IPolyline4* interface.

Object Reusability

So what about inheritance?

Windows Objects themselves and the classes they identify through CLSIDs have no notion of *implementation inheritance* whatsoever. One Windows Object does not inherit the implementation of another Windows Object. But Windows Objects are still *reusable* through two mechanisms, *containment* and *aggregation*. These mechanisms have several significant benefits over inheritance, which is why the Component Object Model has significant benefits over models that rely heavily on inheritance.

In the Component Object Model, inheritance is simply considered a tool that is useful for implementing classes in C++, as well as for defining interfaces. In your implementation of an object, either you can use multiple inheritance from all the interfaces you support, or you can contain implementations of each interface the object supports, in which each interface implementation inherits a single interface. That's really what an interface is for: to help the *implementor* of an object but not the object *user*. Inheritance greatly enhances programmer productivity, but does the user really care how the object was implemented? The answer is definitely "NO"—object users are *supposed* to be entirely ignorant of the object's implementation, especially when the implementation exists in other pieces of code that you did not implement or for which you don't have the source, such as Windows itself.

The single most significant problem of inheritance is that two unrelated pieces of code work on the instance of an object. If I have a base class B and a derived class D, which inherits from B, an instantiation of class D is only one data structure in memory. If B contains virtual functions that D does not override or if the implementation of D explicitly calls a member function in B (that is, using *B::<member function>*), we again have two pieces of code working on the same memory. But class B does not know the expected behavior of class D, so how on earth can D force the correct behavior of its objects? The answer is that D must know what B is going to do on that object so that it knows when to override a virtual function in B and when exactly to explicitly call B's functions. This is exactly the same problem as trying to figure out when to call *DefWindowProc* for any given message: We've merely replaced the word *message* with *virtual function*. In any case, because B cannot know about the implementation of D, D must know about the implementation of B, which causes D to violate its status as a user of B.

Systems built on inheritance have the key problem that they must ship all their source code in order to be usable. Take a look at application frameworks such as the Microsoft Foundation Classes: Source code is shipped with the product, so you know how to inherit from any given class and can duplicate behavior as appropriate. Sure, inheritance works well in building large, complex systems because it's a much better way to manage source code than creating a large stockpile of sample source files. It certainly works well when you control and have access to all the source code for all classes. It certainly helped me to develop the sample applications in this book. But it does not work for reusing objects implemented in the operating system itself, for which either source code is not available or you did not originally implement the object yourself.

The Component Object Model avoids all these problems but retains reusability through its mechanisms of containment and aggregation, which we are finally in a position to explore in detail. Both mechanisms achieve reusability literally by using, instead of inheriting, the implementation of another object. The object we're using remains entirely self-contained and operates on its own instance of data. Our own object, which is called the *aggregate,* works on its own instance of data and calls the other object as necessary to perform specific functions in which we can pass it the data on which to operate.

Let's say I have an object named Animal that knows only of itself and exists as an atomic entity (like the Koala object). I can illustrate this object as a block with circular jacks for each interface: *IUnknown* and *IAnimal* (with members such as *Eat, Sleep*, and *Procreate*). Again, by convention, *IUnknown* is always shown on top, with all other interfaces shown to the side, as follows:

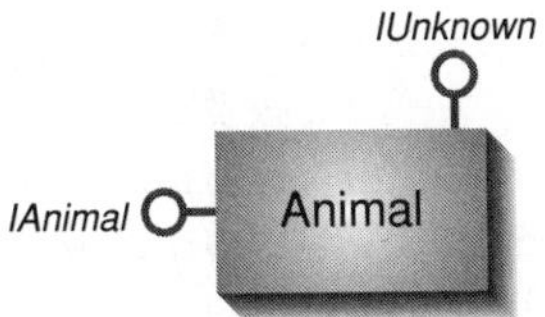

A user of this object with a pointer to either interface can use *QueryInterface* to get a pointer to the other. The implementation of *IAnimal* knows about the object's *IUnknown* and vice versa. Now I want to create a more complicated Koala object that will expose interfaces *IUnknown*, *IAnimal*, and *IMarsupial* (maybe with members such as *CarryYoungInPouch* and *LiveInAustralia*) with a more complicated picture:[8]

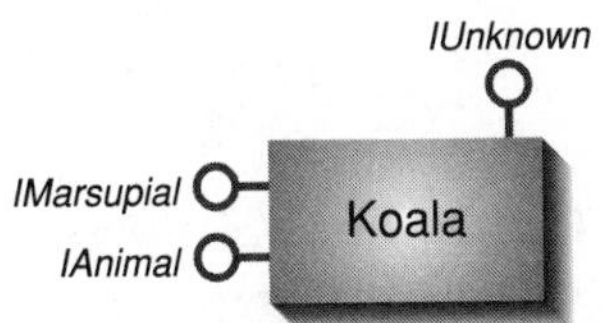

When I implement Koala, I know that Animal exists and I want to reuse Animal's implementation. I can use Animal and its implementation of *IAnimal* in the following two ways, neither of which changes how the external world sees Koala:

- Containment: Koala completely contains an Animal object and implements its own version of *IAnimal* to expose externally. This makes Koala a simple user of Animal, and Animal need not care. Koala never calls *IAnimal::QueryInterface.*
- Aggregation: Koala exposes Animal's *IAnimal* interface directly as Koala's *IAnimal.* This requires that Animal know that its interface is exposed for something other than itself, such that *QueryInterface, AddRef,* and *Release* behave as a user expects.

---

8. Instinct tells you that *IMarsupial* should inherit from *IAnimal* because a marsupial is just another kind of animal. The Windows Object notion of interfaces, however, means that through a pointer to *IMarsupial*, you deal with the object as a marsupial but not generally as anything else. If you want to treat it the same as any other animal, call *IMarsupial::QueryInterface-(IID_IAnimal)* for the appropriate interface. As a real life example, consider Compound Document objects that are all treated through *IOleObject*, regardless of whether they are linked or embedded. A linked object can be viewed as a further refinement of an embedded object, so you might expect that an interface such as *IOleLink* for linked objects would inherit from *IOleObject*. But it doesn't. You use *QueryInterface* through *IOleObject* for *IOleLink. QueryInterface* is the mechanism for getting at more functions on the same object.

Case 1: Object Containment

Complete containment of Animal is necessary when I need to change some aspect of my implementation of *IAnimal*. Because all external calls to that interface will enter Koala first, Koala can override specific functions or simply pass that call to Animal's implementation. The internal structure of Koala will appear something like this:

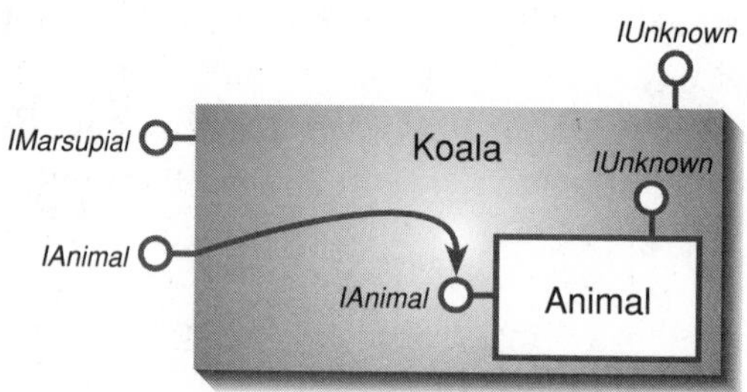

In this case, Animal always operates on its own data unless Koala explicitly passes other data to it (which is also true in aggregation). In other words, by default the two objects work on different data, and only by conscious design of an interface would the two be able to communicate. This is much different from inheritance, in which working on the same data is the default and it takes conscious effort to create separate data instances.

To build this sort of structure, Koala calls *CoCreateInstance* on *CLSID_Animal* when Koala itself is created, passing a NULL for *pUnkOuter* and asking for *IID_IAnimal*. Koala maintains this *IAnimal* pointer until the Koala object is destroyed, at which time Koala calls *IAnimal::Release* to free the Animal object. Whenever Koala's *IAnimal* implementation wants to reuse Animal's *IAnimal* implementation, Koala simply calls the appropriate member function on Animal.

Reusing an object through containment is much like using a Windows list box to manage a list of information. For example, the Patron program in Chapter 2 maintains a list box in such a way that each item is a pointer to a page in the document. The list box provides all the memory management to maintain the list, removing that burden from the application. But Patron never makes the list box visible, so nothing outside of Patron knows that it's using a list box in this manner. Containment is the same, in that the aggregate object uses specific services of the contained object without ever showing the outside world that it is using the contained object in this capacity.

This technique is the simplest way to reuse another's implementation of an interface. However, you do not always care to override *any* functions in such an interface, wanting only to pass every call through to the object you're using. You could, of course, implement stubs for every *IAnimal* function that only calls the contained object, but you would rather simply expose that interface directly and eliminate any need for such stubs. That technique is aggregation.

Case 2: Object Aggregation

Aggregation on Animal is useful when Koala does not want to change any aspect of how it appears through the *IAnimal* interface—that is, Koala has no need simply to implement a bunch of Animal stubs that only delegate to a contained Animal object. Therefore, Koala wants to expose the *IAnimal* interface of the Animal object directly, turning it into Koala's *IAnimal*. This yields an internal structure like the following:

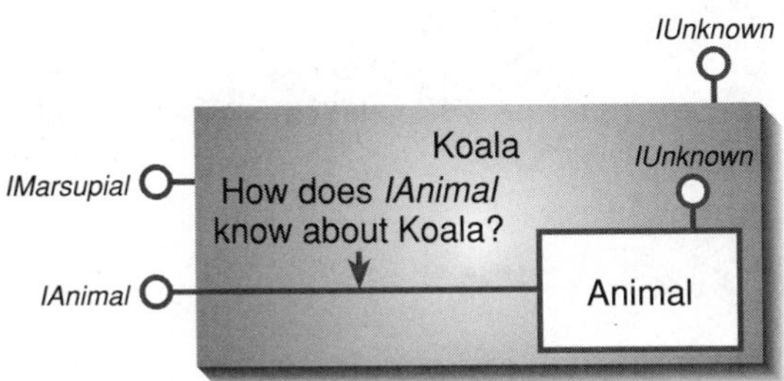

Here's the problem. Because Animal's *IAnimal* is exposed directly, users of Koala will expect that *IAnimal::QueryInterface(IID_IMarsupial)* will return a pointer to Koala's *IMarsupial*. But Animal was not written to know anything about *IMarsupial*, let alone know anything about the Koala object. How can it know the identity of the outer object and its interfaces?

The answer is that when Koala creates Animal, Koala passes its *IUnknown* pointer to the Animal class factory *CreateInstance* as the *pUnkOuter* parameter. (Note that Animal holds onto this pointer but does not—repeat, not—call *AddRef* through it.) In this fashion, Koala identifies itself as the *controlling unknown* of the aggregate. Furthermore, Koala must always ask for Animal's *IUnknown* when creating Animal as part of an aggregate. Note that an object might not support aggregation, in which case it fails *CreateInstance* when a non-NULL *pUnkOuter* is specified.

This sets up a contract between the aggregate object (Koala) and the aggregatee (Animal) in such a way that Animal *must* implement an instance of *IUnknown* that is separate from all other interfaces. This *IUnknown* can return interface pointers to all other interfaces on Animal, and so Koala can ask Animal's *IUnknown* for any of Animal's interfaces and expose those interfaces as if they belonged to Koala. Now the *QueryInterface, AddRef,* and

Release functions in any of Animal's interfaces—besides Animal's separate *IUnknown*—don't do anything to Animal. Instead these functions call the same functions in Koala's controlling unknown because these functions affect the object as a whole *as seen from the outside*. From the outside, Animal's interfaces appear as if they were interfaces on Koala, and so they must act like interfaces on Koala. This means that *AddRef* and *Release* affect Koala's reference count and that *QueryInterface* can return pointers to any interface exposed from Koala.

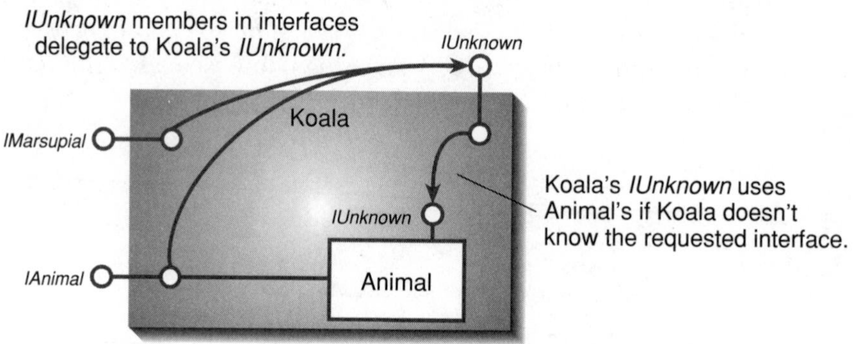
IUnknown members in interfaces delegate to Koala's *IUnknown*.
IUnknown
Koala
IMarsupial
IUnknown
Koala's *IUnknown* uses Animal's if Koala doesn't know the requested interface.
IAnimal
Animal

The *pUnkOuter* parameter passed to Animal's *IClassFactory::CreateInstance* must be available to all interfaces in Animal except for Animal's *IUnknown* itself. Typically this means that Animal stores *pUnkOuter* in its object structure:

```
STDMETHODIMP CAnimalClassFactory(LPUNKNOWN pUnkOuter, ...)
    {
    LPUNKNOWN   pObj;
    ...
    pObj=new CAnimal(pUnkOuter, ...);     //Create the object
    ...
    pObj->FInit();                        //Initialize object
    ...
    }

CAnimal::CAnimal(LPUNKNOWN pUnkOuter, ...)
    {
    ...
    m_pUnkOuter=pUnkOuter;    //Save the controlling unknown
    ...
    }
```

Note that when CAnimal saves *pUnkOuter* in this example, it does not call *AddRef* through that pointer. This is because Animal's lifetime is entirely defined by Koala's lifetime, so the *AddRef* is unnecessary and dangerous: If Animal held a reference to Koala, Koala could not free itself until Animal released that reference. But Animal will not release that reference until it frees itself, and that will not happen until Koala releases its reference on Animal, which only happens if Koala is freeing itself. If we had to choose between death and spinning around in this endless reference loop, we'd keep circling until death became the favorable alternative. To avoid such problems, the aggregatee (Animal, in this case) is specifically required to *not* call *AddRef* through *pUnkOuter*.

Now Animal's *IUnknown* must not delegate to the controlling unknown; instead it must return only those interfaces known to Animal, and it must only affect Animal's reference count. This *IUnknown* implementation essentially controls Animal's lifetime:

```
STDMETHODIMP CAnimal::QueryInterface(REFIID riid, LPLPVOID ppv)
    {
    *ppv=NULL;

    if (IsEqualIID(riid, IID_IUnknown))
        *ppv=(LPVOID)(LPUNKNOWN)this;

    if (IsEqualIID(riid, IID_IAnimal))
        *ppv=(LPVOID)m - pIAnimal;

    if (NULL!=*ppv)
        {
        ((LPUNKNOWN)*ppv)->AddRef();
        return NOERROR;
        }

    return ResultFromScode(E_NOINTERFACE);
    }
```

In this code, *m_pIAnimal* is a pointer to Animal's implementation of the *IAnimal* interface, which it creates in *CAnimal::FInit*:

```
BOOL CAnimal::FInit(void)
    {
    LPUNKNOWN       pIUnknown=(LPUNKNOWN)this;

    if (NULL!=m_pUnkOuter)
        pIUnknown=m_pUnkOuter;
```

(continued)

```
    //Allocate contained interfaces.
    m_pIAnimal=new CImpIAnimal(this, pIUnknown);

    return (NULL!=m_pIAnimal);
    }
```

Animal here plays a nasty trick on its interface implementation, which, as you may recall, must delegate to the controlling unknown if Animal is being aggregated but must affect Animal outside of aggregation. To handle this, Animal always passes some *IUnknown* to the interface implementation. Under aggregation, it's the controlling unknown. Without aggregation, Animal passes its own *IUnknown* as the controlling unknown to the interface. The interface, in turn, blindly delegates all *IUnknown* calls to whatever controlling unknown it was given, as follows:

```
CImpIAnimal::CImpIAnimal(LPVOID pObj, LPUNKNOWN pUnkOuter)
    {
    ...
    m_punkOuter=pUnkOuter;
    ...
    }

STDMETHODIMP CImpIAnimal::QueryInterface(REFIID riid, LPLPVOID ppv)
    {
    return m_pUnkOuter->QueryInterface(riid, ppv);
    }

STDMETHODIMP_(ULONG) CImpIAnimal::AddRef(void)
    {
    return m_pUnkOuter->AddRef();
    }

STDMETHODIMP_(ULONG) CImpIAnimal::Release(void)
    {
    return m_pUnkOuter->Release();
    }
```

So let's say there is no aggregation; the *m_pUnkOuter* to which *CImpIAnimal* delegates is the *IUnknown* implemented in *CAnimal.* This *IUnknown* implementation will return pointers for *IUnknown* and *IAnimal,* as shown before.

If there is an aggregate object, *m_pUnkOuter* points to the controlling unknown, so the calls to this *IUnknown* from the *IAnimal* interface bypass Animal's *IUnknown* and end up in Koala's *IUnknown.* In this controlling unknown, Koala handles *AddRef* and *Release* calls as if they were made through one of its own interfaces. As for *QueryInterface,* the controlling unknown can handle it in one of three ways:

- If the requested interface is implemented by the aggregate object, return a pointer to that interface directly.
- If the requested interface is implemented in the contained object and exposed as one of the aggregate's interfaces, delegate the *QueryInterface* to the contain object's *IUnknown.*
- If the aggregate object does not recognize the reqeusted interface it may either blindly delegate the request to the contained object or fail, depending on the goals of the aggregate object.

The *QueryInterface* of an aggregate's controlling unknown, such as the one Koala would implement, would therefore appear follows:

```
STDMETHODIMP CKoala::QueryInterface(REFIID riid, LPLPVOIDppv)
    {
    *ppv=NULL;

    if (IsEqualIID(riid, IID_IUnknown))
        *ppv=(LPVOID)this;

    if (IsEqualIID(riid, IID_IMarsupial))
        *ppv=(LPVOID)m_pIMarsupial;

    if (IsEqualIID(riid, IID_IAnimal))
        return m_pIUnknownAnimal->QueryInterface(riid, ppv);

    if (NULL!=*ppv)
        {
        ((LPUNKNOWN)*ppv)->AddRef();
        return NOERROR;
        }

    return ResultFromScode(E_NOINTERFACE);
    }
```

Here, *m_pIUnknownAnimal* is the *IUnknown* pointer we requested when creating the Animal object. The *IUnknown* implementation on an object such as *CAnimal* in this example is always the last stop for a *QueryInterface*, an *AddRef*, or a *Release* call. Animal's *IUnknown* never worries about aggregation in and of itself because it has to be the controlling unknown for its own object. Only if the Animal object itself contained more primitive objects would it do any further delegation, but in no way will it pass any request to a higher unknown.

If the requested interface was not *IUnknown, IMarsupial,* or *IAnimal,* what should Koala do? Koala has two choices, depending on how it's using the Animal object. First, Koala might be using Animal as what I call a "helper" object. A helper object is used to provide very specific services to higher aggregate objects where the aggregate objects expose only very specific interfaces from the helper object iself. The preceding code uses the Animal object in this fashion. This is similar to using a hidden list box control in an application to perform list management. You never show the list box, but you are using it as a helper for your implementation.

The second way in which Koala might use Animal is where Koala's *IUnknown* would itself delegate *QueryInterface* calls for any unrecognized interface to Animal's IUnknown. This approach would replace the *return ResultFromScode(...)* call in the preceding code with *m_pIUnknownAnimal->QueryInterface(...)).* By doing so, Koala is not aware of all the interfaces that it might expose as its own. For example, if Animal implemented an additional interface called *IPrimate,* Koala would look like both a marsupial and a primate at the same time. This type of aggregation is useful only when Koala is essentially subclassing the Animal object by adding an interface of its own. This is exactly like subclassing a Windows edit control in such a way that your subclass procedure changes the behavior of the edit control for a few specific messages but blindly passes all other messages to the original message procedure of the control. The aggregate object in this case is only a thin shell around the contained object.

To wrap up our discussion about aggregation, I want to mention one more point. In its role as the aggregate object, Koala might want to cache specific interface pointers it obtains by calling Animal's *IUnknown::QueryInterface.* If it does so, it must do something strange: It must immediately call *Release* through the pointer as follows, where *m_pIUnknownAnimal* is the Animal's *IUnknown* and *m_pIAnimal* is a variable in the Koala object:

```
HRESULT    hr;

[Code that created m_pIUnknownAnimal]

//Cache a pointer to Animal's IAnimal
m_pIAnimal=NULL;

hr=m_pIUnknownAnimal->QueryInterface(IID_IAnimal
    , (LPLPVOID)&m_pIAnimal);

if (SUCCEEDED(hr))
    m_pIAnimal->Release();
```

After executing this code, *m_pIAnimal* will be either NULL (in which case, we could not cache the pointer) or non-NULL. But we called *Release* already, right? Doesn't that invalidate the pointer? Actually, it doesn't because we are still holding onto *m_pIUnknownAnimal*, and so the object itself is still valid, which means that all its interface pointers, including the one we just called *Release* through, also remain valid. Although this seems strange, think about the consequences. Animal's *IUnknown::QueryInterface* will call *IAnimal::AddRef* before returning the pointer to Koala. But *IAnimal* has Koala's *IUnknown* as the controlling unknown, so the *AddRef* call will increment Koala's reference count, which will not be decremented until Koala calls *m_pIAnimal->Release*. If Koala did not make the call here, it would be able to make the call only when it was freeing itself, but it could never get there because of this extra reference count. So, once again, to avoid the problems of circular references, the aggregate object must call *Release* through any pointers obtained from the contained object's *IUnknown*.

Summary

A first requirement of all OLE 2 applications is that they use a message queue of size 96 (under Windows 3.1) and that they provide for initializing the OLE 2 libraries if, in fact, the application can run with the version of those libraries that currently exists on the machine. Checking versions is accomplished through the *CoBuildVersion* and *OleBuildVersion* functions, whereas initialization occurs through *CoInitialize* and *OleInitialize*. On shutdown, an application must also call *CoUninitialize* or *OleUninitialize* to reverse the corresponding ...*Initialize* call. These requirements are presented in this chapter because all later samples must comply with them.

Part of library initialization involves defining a task allocator object, one that implements the *IMalloc* interface, which is used for all task memory allocations. An OLE 2 application can either implement its own or use an OLE 2-provided allocator that works on the technique of multiple local heaps. OLE 2 always implements a similar shared allocator that can provide memory shareable between applications. Although applications can change the task allocator, they cannot change the shared allocator. While the application is running, any other piece of code (such as the OLE 2 libraries) can call *CoGetMalloc* to obtain a pointer to either the task or shared allocator objects.

The Ultimate Question presented in Chapter 3 asked how you obtain a pointer, given knowledge and the identification of a specific Windows Object. This chapter deals with the specific case in which you identify a Windows Object, given a CLSID, and use the function *CoCreateInstance* to instantiate an object of that class. Such an object is called a *component object*, and the application using it is called a *component user*. *CoCreateInstance* internally uses *CoGetClassObject*, which obtains a class factory object (*IClassFactory*) for the CLSID and calls *IClassFactory::CreateInstance* to perform the actual instantiation. What you do with the object once you have an interface pointer to it is your own business, although there are a few considerations when you release the object, such as calling *CoFreeUnusedLibraries* to purge unused DLLs from memory.

Implementations of component objects that can be loaded and called by functions such as *CoCreateInstance* and *CoGetClassObject* have different structural requirements, depending on whether the object lives in a DLL or an EXE. A DLL exports a function named *DllGetClassObject*, which provides the API function through which *CoGetClassObject* obtains a pointer to the DLL's class factory for a given CLSID. EXEs, on the other hand, must pass a pointer to their class factory to the *CoRegisterClassObject* function for each supported CLSID. The two module types also differ in their shutdown conditions. Whereas the Component Object library asks a DLL whether that DLL can be unloaded, an EXE must initiate its own shutdown when the proper conditions are met—that is, it must destroy its main window and exit its message loop. As examples, this chapter implements an object named Koala that supports the *IPersist* interface in both a DLL and an EXE and then separates the Polyline object of the sample Cosmo application into a component object and shows a modification of Cosmo, called Component Cosmo, which uses the component Polyline object.

Object reusability in OLE 2 is achieved through mechanisms called *containment* and *aggregation*, not through inheritance. The inheritance mechanism works well for source code management but generally requires that you have the source code available for any classes from which you inherit. Because of source code availability and a host of other problems, OLE 2 works on mechanisms other than inheritance that provide the same reusability of code, but it avoids the problems with traditional techniques. There is, however, some impact on the implementation of an object that wants to allow itself to be reusable via containment and aggregation.

SECTION II

OBJECT-ORIENTED SYSTEM FEATURES: FILES AND DATA TRANSFER

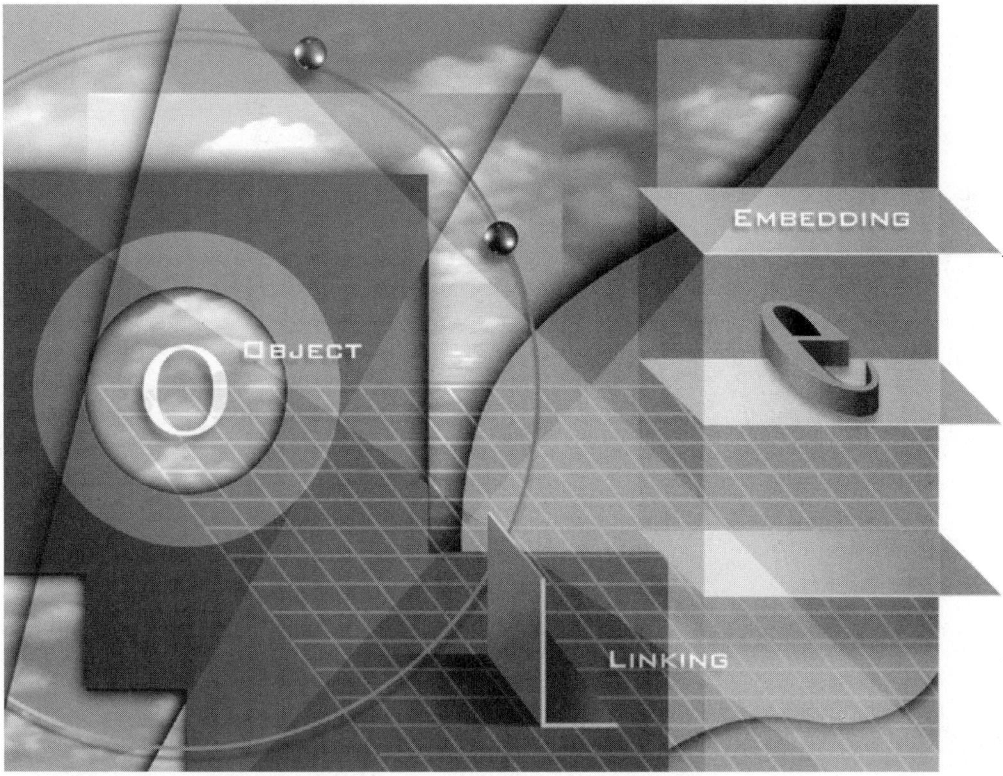

CHAPTER FIVE

STRUCTURED STORAGE AND COMPOUND FILES

Seems like every time you turn around these days, there's another API to read and write files, such as the addition of memory-mapped file I/O under Windows NT. Every mechanism available is concerned only with the functions you can use to create any sort of arbitrary structure within a disk file. In other words, all of the available file I/O techniques are completely ignorant of the file structure as the functions blindly obey their masters and read or write data as they are told. What is missing from the whole picture is any sort of standard for exactly *where* individual data structures (those defined by the application) are stored *within* a particular file, regardless of the underlying file system. Such a standard exists and is specified in OLE 2 as the *Structured Storage Model.* The implementation of this standard is provided in OLE 2 as *Compound Files.* Both will become incorporated into future versions of the Windows operating system.

Structured Storage describes how to create a "file system within a file" and how to expose that structure through two types of objects called *storages* and *streams.* A storage object within a file acts like a directory and holds other storage and stream objects. A storage object can also be opened in a transacted mode, so changes are not written to the underlying disk file until you commit them. A stream object within a storage acts like a file that contains any data you want. Storage and stream objects greatly simplify storage of complex information within a single file on a physical storage device and inherently support powerful and very desirable features, such as incremental saves. Structured Storage defines the way in which storages and streams are written to the device and the layout of a storage object. It does not, however, restrict the data structures you write into streams.

What? Microsoft is asking me to change my file format? Have those people had too much espresso or something? Such was a common response I heard when Microsoft first presented the idea of Structured Storage, which defines a standardized technique for structuring blocks of data within the confines of a single disk file regardless of the underlying file system. While not trying to change what structures you can actually store in those blocks, Structured Storage *does* change where those blocks actually exist on disk.

What good is this standardization? Given an arbitrary disk file conforming to the Structured Storage Model, any other piece of code that also knows the model might be able to open that file and examine its contents. If that file contains a stream with a standardized data structure for something such as "Summary Information" containing title, subject, author, and keywords, any application familiar with that structure could open the file and determine the title and subject of the document, determine who wrote it, and possibly search the list of keywords. In the model we have today, only the application that originally wrote the file or an application with intimate knowledge about the file format can open and browse the contents of that file. Structured Storage enables anything, including the system shell, to perform the same browsing functions, given standardized streams. To the end user, this eliminates a host of application-specific techniques used to find information in files, consolidating these techniques into one uniform systemwide interface through which some tool might browse files. By using such a tool, an end user could enter a query such as "Find all the documents I wrote that have the word *vegetarian* in the title," and the tool would go off and find all files that contained such information. For the applications programmer, this replaces the need to write full browsing with the freedom to write files containing a specific stream and enables any vendor to write a browsing tool. Microsoft is working on standard stream layouts that use a specification known as *property sets.* Information on property sets is included in the OLE 2 SDK.

Standardization is one thing; implementation is another. How can we all be assured that we'll all implement the Structured Storage standards in our files the same way? Well, we can't be, so Microsoft has provided an implementation of Structured Storage called Compound Files, contained in OLE 2's STORAGE.DLL. Compound files implement storage and stream objects on top of the FAT file system under Windows 3.1 and on top of FAT and NTFS under Windows NT. You can use compound files as you would any other set of file I/O API functions, and in fact, the way in which you manipulate a stream object corresponds directly to the way in which we manipulate a file handle today, as this chapter will demonstrate. To your application, the data in a stream always appears contiguous, although that data might not actually be stored contiguously within the file itself. This is no different from how file systems such as FAT let you look at a file as a contiguous block of bytes by means of a file handle, even though the actual bytes are scattered across the disk in disparate sectors.

Ages ago, applications had to concern themselves with the absolute sectors in which they stored their data, which was painful, to say the least. File systems came along and allowed applications to treat files as a single block, not as separate sectors. What a blessing! Today the structures within files themselves are becoming as painful to maintain as absolute sectors used to be, and so OLE 2, by means of compound files, is providing the equivalent of a file system within a file to redeem you from the burden of maintaining seek offsets a-plenty. The first section of this chapter is intended to convince you that problems exist and that Structured Storage solves those problems. Following that discussion is a review of the features and capabilities of OLE 2's implementation of storage and stream objects.

If you've discerned the theme of this book, you know there are storage and stream objects. So how do you obtain pointers to those objects? What are the interfaces those objects support? What can you do with those objects? You will find your answers in this chapter as we explore how to make simple use of compound files, followed by more complex usage, leading finally to a discussion of how these objects relate to the rest of OLE 2 and, in particular, to compound document containers and objects.

If you choose to use compound files, you will, of course, change your absolute file format on disk, although there is no need for your internal data structures to change at all. For almost all applications, compound files are optional. The only portions of code that must use them are OLE 2 compound objects and containers: A container must give every object its own piece of storage from which to load and save itself. However, this does not mean you must use compound files for your container's own native storage: You can create a storage object on top of a block of bytes somewhere in your own file or you can create a storage object in memory for an embedded object and then write the contents of that memory to your own files whenever you want. Compound document objects must be able to load and save embedded object data by means of storage and streams, but that does not change any aspect of your application's disk file format.

One of the major programmatic benefits of compound files is that you can use them as shareable data transfer media—that is, a storage object (a piece of a compound file) can be marshaled to another process. This means that, instead of always transferring data through global memory, you can transfer data through a pointer to data on disk without having to actually load any data into memory. The only process that needs to actually pull the data into memory is the process that needs to edit and manipulate that data. In other words, only one copy needs to exist in memory at any time. The process that manipulates the data furthermore has incremental access to the storage, improving performance even more. This capability can be used for data transfer, as we'll see in Chapter 6, and is used for compound document object transfer, as we'll see in Chapters 9 through 11.

Microsoft was originally motivated to define Structured Storage to improve the performance of compound document scenarios and for the tremendous end user benefit of shell-level document browsing. Other innovations for dealing with traditional files do little to simplify how you maintain a complex structure within a particular file. Memory-mapped file I/O under Windows NT merely changes the expression of that complexity from a file handle into a pointer with some benefit, of course, but with about the same amount of pain. Structured Storage is the one technology that truly solves the problems of file structure, just as the file system solved the problems of disk structure.

Motivation

A man and his 16-year-old daughter were traveling through Seattle on their way back from a long hiking trip in Alaska's Denali National Park. During the entire trip, the man had to live on the horrible, plastic taste of cheap instant coffee. Still, he put up with it because he enjoyed the extra caffeine boost that allowed him to keep up with his daughter. While in Seattle, the man remembered the lore about the Emerald City's espresso habits, recalling the infamous OLE 2 Starbuck's demo he had seen a few months earlier. Espresso carts were parked on every corner, so he didn't have any trouble finding one quickly. As he ordered a latté, he knew darn well that the tasty caffeine bomb would give him the jitters, but he really wanted one nonetheless. He would have enjoyed it too, if his daughter had not asked a simple but probing question, one that would change pleasure to guilt and one for which he had no answer. She asked with a menacing stare, "What exactly does that *do* for you?"

Similarly, what does Structured Storage, and OLE 2's implementation of compound files, *do* for you? In a manner of speaking, compound files give you the energy boost of caffeine without the jitters. In no way are you required to indulge: This section will, however, encourage you to "start the habit," so to speak, as we explore how we can add file I/O capabilities to the Patron sample, which to this point has no provision for such operations.

Patron Files with the Jitters

Patron is designed to have a document made of pages, in which each page will eventually serve as the residence for any number of bitmaps, metafiles, and compound document objects—the tenants. It needs a file layout for each document that describes those contents. If we were to implement Patron using traditional file I/O, we would create a layout with three primary structures:

- The file header structure contains the definition of how many pages are in the document, the printer configuration (a serialized DEVMODE structure), and an offset to the first page.
- Each page structure contains a header specifying how many tenants (metafiles, bitmaps, compound document objects, and so on) live on the page, an offset of the next page, and a variable-length list of offsets to the tenants. All page structures are stored sequentially in the file before writing any tenants.
- Tenant structures contain header information such as the length of the record in the file and the type of tenant, followed by a serialization of the tenant's actual data.

Such structures would result in the layout shown in Figure 5-1 on the following page.

Certainly this sort of layout is manageable, albeit tedious. When we write a file in this format, we would first write the file header, then all the page headers, and then all the tenants. Writing the file header is simple because we know its size and can easily calculate the offset of the first page to store in this header. Before writing the page headers, we need to build the entire list in memory to determine the total size of the page list and store the appropriate tenant offsets in each page structure. When we have this list, we write it all out to disk at once and then write each tenant in turn. Besides a little tedium in calculating all the offsets, this code would be simple enough and performance would be good because all the pages are at the front of the file and we only have to do potentially large seeks when accessing a particular tenant.

Let's say now that the end user deletes a page. We have two alternatives the next time the end user saves. One is to rewrite the entire file, which is typically the easiest option. The other is to mark the deleted page in the file

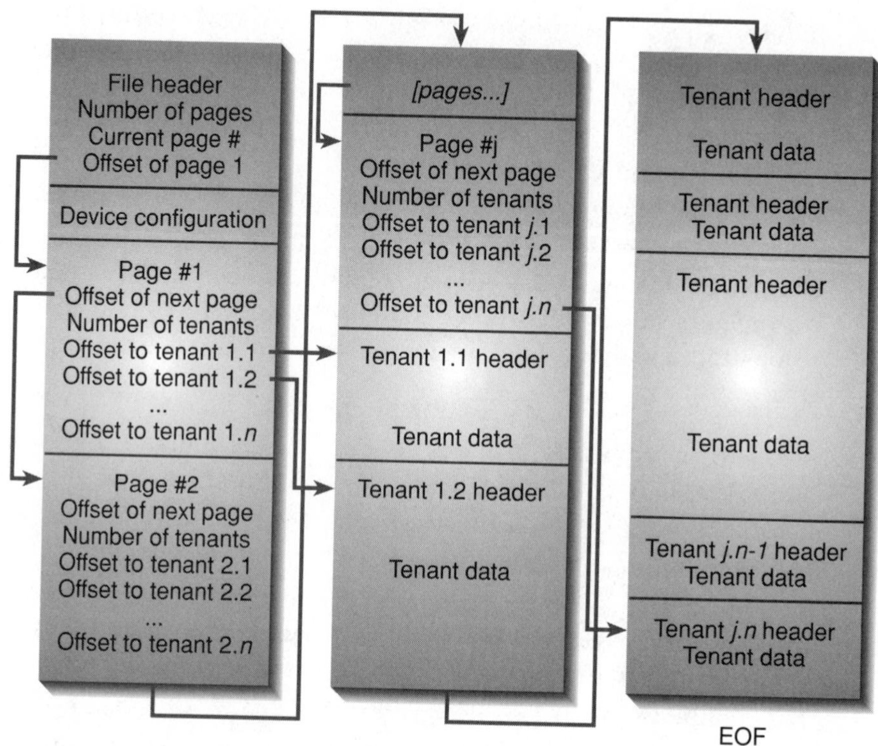

Figure 5-1.
A possible Patron file with traditional file I/O.

as unused and to mark all the tenant spaces that were deleted as unused as well. This would not reduce the file size but would allow a very quick save.

Now the end user adds a page in the middle of the document and adds a few tenants to that page. If this new page structure can fit in an unused page block created from one previously deleted, we could attempt to incrementally write the new document, storing the new page structure over the deleted one and modifying the stored seek offset of the previous page to point to this new one. If there are no open spaces for this new page, we can append the page structure to the end of the file, store it in free space from a deleted tenant, or choose to rewrite the entire file. Choosing either of the first two options defeats the purpose of originally storing page structures in sequence before storing any tenants. Choosing the last option is potentially slow because Patron files housing bitmaps and metafiles, and compound document objects can become huge.

At this point, we do what engineers call "compromise" and weigh the possible options: We can have incremental saves with file fragmentation, or we can have efficient files for reading with slower-than-molasses saves. In a performance-driven market, we generally choose incremental saves so that the save timings look great in the trade magazine reviews. Get a few developers to put in some overtime and you'll have a wonderfully elaborate scheme of managing free space in your files as best you can, just as you would handle free space in any memory manager. You would allow "fast saves" or "full saves," the latter of which would fully defragment the file by performing a full rewrite. Cool. We just turned a problem into a couple of "features" by writing a great deal of file management code. That's all well and good, but the effort to write such code might have required you to sacrifice other important features of your application. Next version, I guess.

Realize that investing enormous effort in providing for file defragmentation does not really buy you a whole lot until the end user defragments the hard disk. Even though your application sees the file as defragmented, the actual physical location of the bytes on the disk is generally random because the file system isolates you from physical sector locations. All that effort you expended to defragment your file structures doesn't really improve performance significantly; when the disk itself is fragmented, a 128-byte seek in your file might equate to a 128-MB seek on disk, and a 10-MB seek in your file might actually only seek 10 KB on disk.

File defragmentation is only a way to compress the file or reduce the file size to the minimum. Otherwise, the file might grow larger and larger, wasting more and more space on the user's hard disk. Implementing your own defragmentation serves no purpose other than to check for this continual growth.

So although all the work you put into solving this problem really tasted good, like a latté, you still get the jitters. The code really doesn't solve everything you originally set out to accomplish.

The Decaffeinated Alternative

If we could afford the luxury, we would save an enormous amount of time by having Patron simply write its files in a directory tree instead of in one huge file. There would be not merely one file for a given document—if users attempted to copy a document to another disk, they would have to do a more involved backup of many files and directories. But again, if we could accomplish it, using a directory tree would be much, much simpler to implement:

- The file becomes the "root" directory for the storage. This is not necessarily the root directory on a disk because this root might be a subdirectory somewhere on the disk, but as far as Patron is concerned, it's the root of the file. In this directory, we store a file that contains the number of pages in this document, the printer configuration, and the name of the first page. This is the same type of information that we would store in a file header.

- Each page is itself a subdirectory off the root, with a name such as PAGE*nnnn.nnn*, which would allow up to 10 million pages per document. Within each page subdirectory is a file containing the page information, which could include the names of tenants, just as a single file format would store offsets.
- Each tenant would have an entire file to itself, or better yet, an entire subdirectory off the page in which we could write as many files as necessary to save that tenant.

This scheme would create the layout shown in Figure 5-2.

This implementation has promise (again at the sacrifice of file portability). When we add a page, we merely need to create another directory off

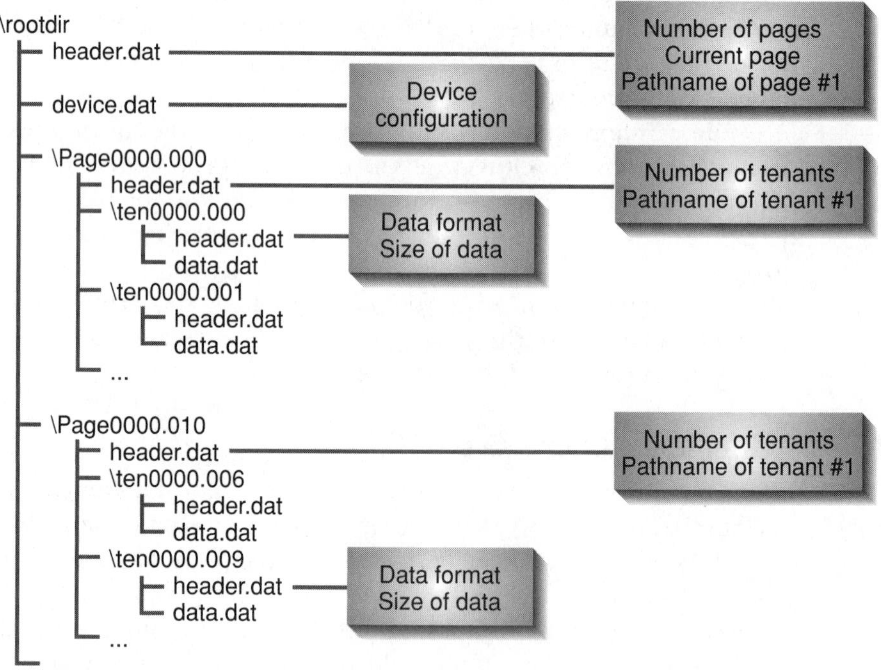

Figure 5-2.
A possible Patron storage scheme using directories.

the root and write a file containing page information. We never have to worry about rewriting the entire storage; there is simply no need because we let the file system worry about actual placement of the new files and directories. When we delete a page, we delete the directory and all its contents, returning the space to the file system, which manages reuse of that space for us. Therefore, we have no need to provide for defragmentation, instead allowing the end user to choose his or her own tool.

In addition, adding a tenant to a page is as simple as creating a subdirectory off the page and writing all the tenant information into as many files as is convenient in that new directory. The page itself doesn't even need to keep track of the tenants itself because it can simply ask the file system for a list of subdirectories in the form, for example, *TEN*.**.

All elements—the file header, the pages, and each tenant—individually benefit from incremental saves. Changing the size of a particular file in this storage model or changing the number of subdirectories of another directory does not affect any other aspect of the entire storage. There is never a need for rewriting the entire storage (except for saving under a new name). Applications that store bitmaps and metafiles can appreciate this because those kinds of data tend to become very large.

Of course, the FAT file system can slow to a crawl with too many files or subdirectories in a single directory because it uses a sequential search through the directory sectors. More advanced file systems such as NTFS use binary search algorithms to locate files faster, so depending on your needs, you would choose the appropriate file system on which to base your storage. But this is a solution that's about as satisfying as a decaffeinated latté.

Energy Boosts Without the Jitters: Compound Files

Up to now we've had two choices: Drink caffeinated coffee and risk the jitters or drink decaf and miss out on that energy hit that got you drinking coffee in the first place. What we really want is an energy-boosting coffee with no side effects, or in OLE 2 terms, we want the efficiency and benefits of using a directory structure such as the file system but we want to keep that structure within a single file in order to allow document portability. We want a powerful file system implemented within a file. We want OLE 2's Structured Storage Model.

Structured Storage in itself is not implementation but rather a specification of how storage is exposed to the system and the applications.[1] The OLE

1. These specifications, along with a reference implementation, are available from Microsoft for those who want to port this technology to other platforms, such as UNIX and OS/2. Microsoft has implemented compound files on the Mac with Mac OLE 2.

2–provided implementation of the model is called compound files. This model sits on top of the actual file system and takes full advantage of that system. Compound files provide all the free-space management for you, just like any other file system, exposing your files to your application as two objects: streams and storages. The former implements an interface called *IStream*, the latter an interface called *IStorage*. Streams are the logical equivalent of disk files; storages are the equivalent of directories.

Using streams and storages, we'll implement Patron's file I/O with a structure similar to the one shown in Figure 5-3. Directories have become storages, files have become streams. Best of all, instead of this entire structure living in separate pieces in the file system, it lives within a single file that an end user can copy the same way they copy any other single file.

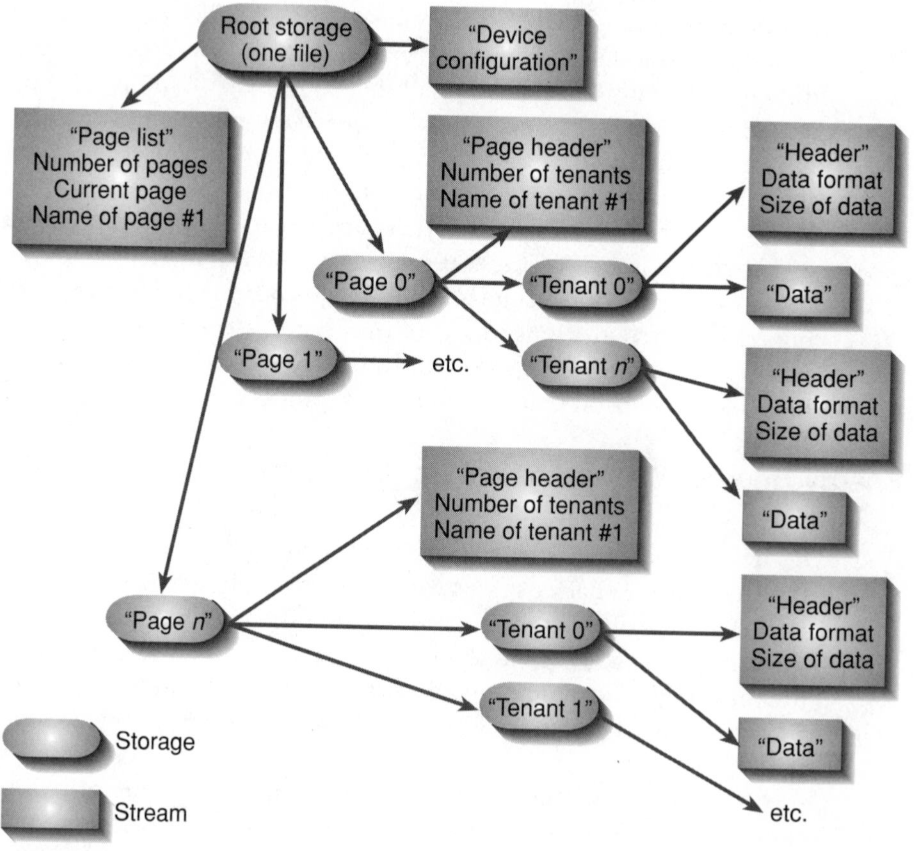

Figure 5-3.
Patron's storage scheme, using compound files.

Features of Compound Files

The design of Structured Storage, and specifically the compound file implementation, provides a number of significant features that applications can exploit to their benefit. You need to be familiar with these features before you can apply them in practice:

- Stream, Storage, and LockBytes Objects: Units of data, directories, and byte arrays on the physical device.
- Element Naming: Storages and streams can have names up to 31 characters long.
- Access Modes: Storages can be opened in transacted mode so that changes are buffered until committed (flushed).
- Incremental Access: Modifications to any element do not require a complete file rewrite and elements can be read as little as necessary.
- Shareable Elements: Storages and streams can be passed to other processes.

Again, use of compound files is completely optional for all but OLE 2 container applications, and even those can skirt the issue (but with a little cost to overall performance). However, many applications can greatly simplify their storage management by building on top of compound files, implementing an incremental save feature with little code or a feature to revert changes to a document without having to manage any previous state yourself. That code now exists in the compound file implementation.

Stream, Storage, and *LockBytes* Objects

Structured Storage is defined in terms of three objects: a stream contains data like a file; a storage contains streams and storages like a directory; and a *LockBytes* presents some physical device as a generic byte array. These objects are combined in the Structured Storage Model, as shown in Figure 5-4 on the following page.

All three objects are Windows Objects, as described in Chapter 3—that is, all three implement one or more interfaces and provide separate function tables for each.[2] A *LockBytes* object supports the *ILockBytes* interface. To obtain a pointer, you can either call an OLE 2 API function for standard implementations, or you can implement your own, in which case how you obtain the pointer is up to you. A storage object implements the *IStorage* interface to

2. Really, I'm not trying to pound this into your head...well, maybe.

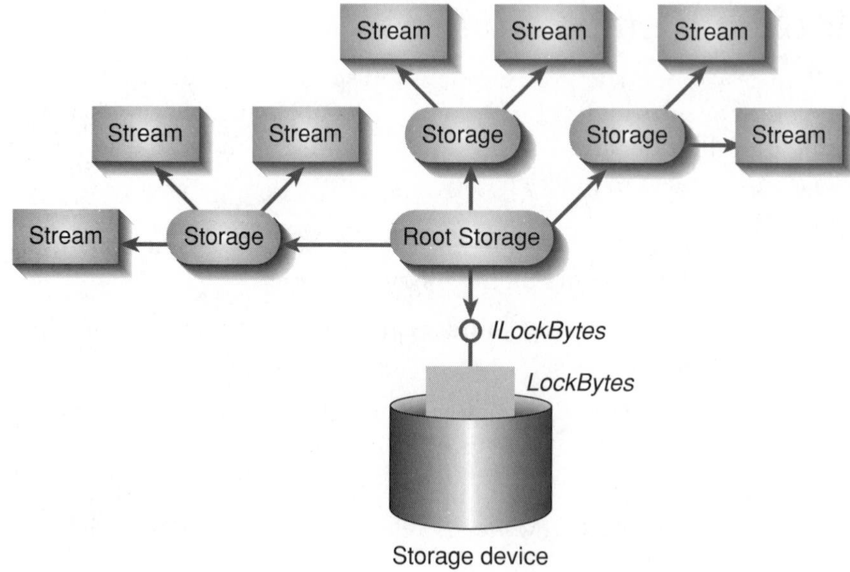

Figure 5-4.
LockBytes *sits on a device, a root storage builds on* LockBytes, *and streams and storages live inside any other storage.*

which you obtain a pointer by calling one of a number of other API functions or by calling an *IStorage* member function in an existing storage object. Some of the API functions create a storage object on the default file system, whereas others allow you to create a storage object on top of a specific *LockBytes* such as one built on memory. Those storage objects that are attached to a real file system entity also support an interface called *IRootStorage*, which is used primarily in low-memory save situations. In any case, a stream object implements the *IStream* interface, and such a pointer is generally obtained by calling a member function in the *IStorage* interface.

The later section "Compound File Objects and Interfaces" describes the exact API functions through which you obtain interface pointers; describes the *ILockBytes*, *IStorage/IRootStorage*, and *IStream* interfaces; and highlights the differences between the specification of Structured Storage (that is, the interfaces) and the compound file implementation in OLE 2. Note also that all storage-related interfaces are defined in STORAGE.H and are derived from *IUnknown*; complete details, some of which are outside the scope of this book, are described in the *OLE 2 Programmer's Reference*.

Element Naming

Each storage or stream is identified by a name, which can be up to 31 characters long, with the exception of a root storage associated with a disk file, which can have a name as long as the file system allows. The name of a root storage must obey the restrictions of the file system, but the name can contain any characters above ASCII 32 except ., \, /, :, and !. ASCII 3 is earmarked for the exclusive use of the owner of the storage *above* the storage in which the elements with such names are located. That is, if you opened a root storage and created a substorage within that root storage, any element, storage, or stream that you create in the substorage that has ASCII 3 as the first character in the name is exclusively under your control. Whoever or whatever manages the substorage in which these ASCII 3–named elements exist will not touch those elements. This allows you to store you own information in a storage that you give to someone else for their own storage needs.

A compound file stores the name as provided by the caller, with no conversion to uppercase or lowercase, although all comparisons made on the names under Windows 3.1 are case insensitive. The actual names of elements in compound files are generally not intended to be shown directly to an end user and therefore need not be localized. When such an arrangement becomes necessary in a future release of Windows, there will be a standard place to store a localized user-readable name.

Access Modes

Stream and storage objects support access modes as does a traditional file, indicated through STGM_... flags. A stream is always restricted by the access mode of its parent storage. Many of these access modes translate directly into OF_... flags that OLE 2's compound file implementation passes directly down to the Windows *OpenFile* function, as follows:

Structured Storage Flag	Definition Using *OpenFile* Flags
STGM_READ (default)	OF_READ
STGM_WRITE	OF_WRITE
STGM_READWRITE	OF_READWRITE
STGM_SHARE_DENYNONE	OF_SHARE_DENY_NONE
STGM_SHARE_DENYREAD	OF_SHARE_DENY_READ
STGM_SHARE_DENYWRITE	OF_SHARE_DENY_WRITE
STGM_SHARE_EXCLUSIVE	OF_SHARE_EXCLUSIVE
STGM_CREATE	OF_CREATE

As with *OpenFile*, you can use OR with any of these flags, which would produce the same effect on the compound file as it would on any traditional file.

OLE 2's compound files support a few other flags that have special functions above what traditional file I/O offers, as follows:

Structured Storage Flag	Function
STGM_DIRECT (default)	Opens the element for direct access.
STGM_TRANSACTED	Opens the element such that changes are buffered and not saved until the element is committed. OLE 2 supports transactioning only on storages, but a direct stream in a transacted storage is transacted as far as the physical file is concerned.
STGM_FAILIFTHERE (default)	Fails to create an element of a given name if one having that name already exists.
STGM_CONVERT (storages only)	Allows an application to convert any traditional file to a storage that contains a single stream named CONTENTS, in which the stream contains the exact data as the original file. This allows an application to use Compound File API functions to open any file, only concerning itself with the differences after the file is opened as a storage. If the file is opened with STGM_DIRECT, the old file is immediately converted on disk, and therefore STGM_CONVERT always requires STGM_WRITE.
STGM_DELETEONRELEASE	Deletes the file from the disk when a *Release* on the storage object managing that file reduces the reference count to zero. This flag is highly useful for temporary files.
STGM_PRIORITY	Allows an application to open a direct, read-only storage or stream for a short time to quickly read some data. This flag internally tells STORAGE.DLL to avoid extra buffering and processing, making the operation much faster. For more information, see *OLE 2 Programmer's Reference.*

Transacted Storages

The most interesting, and certainly the most powerful, of these modes is STGM_TRANSACTED. When you open a storage in transacted mode, the compound file implementation does not make any changes to the actual disk file (or *LockBytes*) until you commit those changes (see *IStorage::Commit*).

When a transacted storage is committed, the modified elements are merged with the original elements into a buffer (usually a temporary file), and when all merging is complete the contents of the temporary file are quickly written to disk so that an out-of-memory condition will not result in damage to the original file, merely in loss of changes. Changes are also lost when the transacted storage is released (*IStorage::Release*) or reverted (*IStorage::Revert*) without first committing that storage. In the case of *Revert,* the storage is returned to the state it was in when it was opened.

Any storage object can be opened in transacted mode, regardless of the mode of its parent storage. If you open a root storage with STGM_DIRECT, you can open a substorage with STGM_TRANSACTED and only that substorage is transacted. In other words, only when the substorage is committed will there be any change in the outer file opened in direct mode.

When multiple levels of storages are opened in transacted mode, committing changes notifies the immediate parent of the committed storage. This in turn becomes a transacted change in that parent—that is, the changes percolate upward. Only when the highest transacted storage is committed are all those changes actually saved permanently.

Transacted changes reflect any operations you might perform on a storage by means of the *IStorage* interface. For example, newly created storages or streams are created in memory and are not reflected on disk until the outermost commit occurs. Likewise, moving, renaming, or destroying elements has no permanent effect on the physical device until that final commit. Another interesting feature of a transacted storage is that you can open a storage as read-only transacted and manipulate that storage as if it were read/write. The only operation you are barred from performing is a commit.

Use of transacted storage enables easier file sharing. Two or more different applications or different users on a network can open the same transacted storage with read/write permissions but not with exclusive access. When the application commits that storage (that is, when the user saves), the application tells the storage to commit only if no one else has committed changes to that storage in the meantime. This prevents dangerous situations in which one save would otherwise wipe out the changes saved by someone else. Because storages do not automatically merge independent changes, you would need to load the saved version and reconcile any differences between it and the version the user tried to save.

Opening a transacted root storage using OLE 2's STORAGE.DLL uses at least three file handles—one for the file, one for a temporary file in which changes are recorded, and one preallocated handle for low-memory save situations. If you use transacted root storages side-by-side with C run-time file open functions, you will quickly run out of file handles in your application task. In that case, avoid using the C run-time functions and use the Windows function *OpenFile* instead.

Transacted mode enables a new technique in application design. Because most changes made to storages and streams are recorded in memory or in temporary files, writing directly to a transacted storage or stream might be only slightly slower than writing directly to memory. For any block of bytes that you would normally access using a memory pointer, you could use a stream. By doing so, you gain a number of benefits:

- Writing past the end of the stream automatically expands the stream instead of causing a UAE.
- Saving the data requires a simple commit on the storage in which the stream lives instead of copying the data from your own memory structures into the stream before you do the commit.
- Undo is a simple matter of reverting changes. You can implement multiple levels of Undo by duplicating the streams at appropriate intervals, letting the compound file implementation worry about memory allocation and copying the data.

In some cases, of course, when a memory structure contains fields such as pointers, it makes no sense to save persistently, so you would still need a translation from the memory structure to the file structure at commit time. However, for even small structures that are persistent representations, this technique can save you from keeping the same data in a memory structure—when you need it, load it from a stream; when you change it, write it to the stream. Good examples of such structures are LOGFONT and DEVMODE.

Incremental Access

An incremental save feature is one of the end user's favorite time-savers. Instead of rewriting the entire file every time the user chooses Save from the File menu, the application saves only the bits that actually changed. For example, adding one tenant to a page in Patron should save only a modification of the page header and the information for the new tenant instead of rewriting the entire page or the entire file. As we explored earlier in this chapter, providing such a feature can mean a lot of design and coding work on your part if you stick with traditional file I/O for your storage.

Making simple changes to a few values in a structure has always been a cheap incremental operation when only that structure needs modification. However, when you shrink, enlarge, move, add, or delete elements, things can get extremely tedious if you are managing free space on your own. Because compound files isolate you from the details about the allocating or freeing space in the file, your modifications to one element do not affect any other element.

When a compound file needs to expand a stream to accommodate more data, it finds the required amount of space somewhere in the file (either in previously freed regions or at the end of the file) and reserves the space as part of the original stream. The data and the actual location of the original stream remain the same as the stream *expands* into the newly allocated region. Because no other stream or storage is affected by this expansion, there is no need to make any further changes to the physical file. In the same manner, if you add a new stream or storage to an existing storage, the space for that new element as well as any space needed to update the storage's directory is either recycled from free space or allocated at the end of the file. No other elements need to move or change in any way to accommodate the new addition. Deleting an element is a simple matter of marking that space as free, allowing it to be overwritten at a later time by any other element.

Compound files make incremental saves the norm and full (compact) saves the exception. In normal operation, a compound file will eventually become fragmented internally, which can make the file larger than necessary. A full save operation copies all the data from the existing file into a new file, which defragments all the streams and storages, greatly reducing the wasted space in the file. As an example of how this is done, we'll implement a File Manager extension, called Smasher, in the "Compound File Defragmentation" section at the end of this chapter.

Compound files not only provide for incremental saves, they provide for more generic incremental *access*. This is most important for compound document objects that are given a storage object from which they can incrementally read their data as necessary. This approach eliminates having to load all the compound document object's data into memory before the object can begin editing. With incremental access, the compound document object can optimize how much it needs to load at any given time.

Shareable Elements

A most important characteristic of Structured Storage, a characteristic that benefits data transfer and compound document implementation, is that pointers to storages and streams can be marshaled across process boundaries. This means that you can use a storage or stream object to transfer data between applications instead of continually being forced to use global memory. With a storage or stream object, the data can live on the disk until it becomes necessary to whoever consumes that data; at that time, the consumer can load the data directly from the disk through the object.

We will explore the implications of this benefit in later chapters. Chapter 6, for example, shows how OLE 2's Uniform Data Transfer mechanisms can all use compound file elements to transfer literally anything. Something such as a large bitmap that always lives on disk is best transferred in a way that lets it remain on disk; because data transfer can use compound files as a transfer medium in addition to many other media, the source of the data can choose the best medium for transport.

Chapters 9 and 10 show how a storage object is used to transfer embedded object data between compound document containers and servers. Structured Storage was originally created to solve a specific problem of OLE 1, in which all embedded object data had to be loaded into global memory, exchanged via DDE messages, and possibly copied at the receiving end. This approach resulted in multiple copies of the data existing at the same time, which brought many a system to its knees when large bitmaps were involved. Embedded objects in the OLE 1 model always had to read and write their data to global memory and pass it to the container that was responsible for placing it on disk. When the container reloaded the object, it had to read the entire object data from disk into memory and pass the data to the object. All this was very slow and inefficient.

With Structured Storage, OLE 2 containers create an *IStorage* instance for each embedded object. Creating any new storage uses little memory, and if the storage is direct and lives on disk, very little memory will ever be used. In any case, a container hands that storage to the embedded object, which becomes solely responsible for loading and saving itself to that storage. This effectively transfers data directly between the embedded object and the container's document file, bypassing container code completely. Because the embedded object has the entire storage to itself, it benefits from incremental access—it needs to load only what is necessary to display or edit the data, and it benefits from incremental saves as does any other storage user.

Compound File Objects and Interfaces

As mentioned earlier, compound files are built on three objects: storages, streams, and *LockBytes*, which support the *IStorage* (or possibly *IRootStorage*), *IStream*, and *ILockBytes* interfaces, respectively. Each object handles specific functions within the compound file implementation. The interfaces actually specify more functionality than is implemented in OLE 2, so the following sections will point out the features that are not available in OLE 2. Note that when these sections list various storage-related API functions, those prefixed with *Stg* are found in STORAGE.DLL and prototyped in STORAGE.H; all others are found in OLE2.DLL (or COMPOBJ.DLL) and prototyped in OLE2.H (or COMPOBJ.H).

Storage Objects and the *IStorage* Interface

A storage object is like a directory in that it can contain any number of storages (subdirectories) and any number of streams (files), but in and of itself it does not hold any data. Each storage object supports the *IStorage* interface, described in Table 5-1. Because any substorage is a storage in itself, just as a subdirectory is always a directory, substorages might themselves contain more storages and more streams, ad nauseam, until you deplete your available disk space. Each storage has access rights (read, write, share, and so on), a feature that MS-DOS directories lack. A storage object can enumerate its elements; copy, move, rename and delete elements; and change the dates and times of an element. A storage gives you a programmatic equivalent of COMMAND.COM functions, which is generally lacking in traditional file I/O libraries.

IStorage Member	MS-DOS Equivalent	Description
Release	(none)	Closes the storage. For a root storage, closes the compound file it represents. If the storage is opened in transacted mode, the last *Release* also implies a *Revert*. Also deletes a storage opened with STGM-_DELETEONRELEASE.
CreateStream	Copy	Creates and opens a stream within the storage.
OpenStream	Copy	Opens an existing stream.

Table 5-1.
The IStorage *interface.*

(continued)

Table 5-1. *continued*

IStorage Member	MS-DOS Equivalent	Description
CreateStorage	Mkdir, Chdir	Creates and opens a new substorage.
OpenStorage	Chdir	Opens an existing storage.
CopyTo	Copy	Copies the entire contents from the storage into another storage. The layout of the destination storage might differ.
Commit	(none)	Ensures that all changes made to the storage (opened in transacted mode) are reflected to the parent storage or to the device. Committing a direct storage flushes all disk buffers.
Revert	(none)	Discards any changes made to the storage (opened in transacted mode) since the last *Commit.*
EnumElements	Dir	Returns an *IEnumSTATSTG* object that enumerates the substorages and streams directly contained in the storage.
MoveElementTo	Copy(+Del)	Copies or moves a substorage or a stream from the storage into another storage.
DestroyElement	Del, Deltree[3]	Removes a specified substorage or stream from within the storage. If a substorage is destroyed, all elements contained within it are also destroyed.
RenameElement	Ren	Changes the name of a stream or substorage.
SetElementTimes	(none)	Sets the modification, last access, and creation date and time of a substorage or stream, subject to file system support.
SetClass	(none)	Associates a CLSID with the storage, which can be retrieved by using *Stat.* Allows anyone to know who might be able to manipulate the contents of the storage.

3.MS-DOS version 6.

(continued)

Table 5-1. *continued*

IStorage Member	MS-DOS Equivalent	Description
SetStateBits	Attrib	Marks the storage with various flags defining how other agents might be able to treat this storage.
Stat	(varies)	Retrieves statistics for the storage, such as name, create, modify, access times, and so on.

Compound File Implementation of Storages

OLE 2 implements complete storages that support transactioning. All member functions of *IStorage* work as specified, with the exception of *SetStateBits,* which has no behavior. The data for a storage might not be contiguous inside the file itself.

How you obtain an *IStorage* pointer for a storage object depends on whether you want a root storage object or a substorage below another storage object. For the latter, you call *IStorage::CreateStorage* or *IStorage::OpenStorage.* For root storages, OLE 2 offers four API functions, two of which can create a new compound file and two that open an existing file:

API Function	Description
StgCreateDocfile[4]	Opens a new compound file, given a filename, in the form of a root storage on the default file system *LockBytes.* This function will generate a temporary file if no filename is provided. If the file already exists, this function might either fail or overwrite the existing file, depending on the flags you pass.
StgCreateDocfileOnILockBytes	Opens a new compound file on a given *LockBytes* object but otherwise acts like *StgCreateDocfile.*
StgOpenStorage	Opens an existing compound file given a filename or creates a new file, as will *StgCreateDocfile.*
StgOpenStorageOnILockBytes	Opens an existing compound file that exists in the given *LockBytes* but otherwise acts like *StgOpenStorage.*

4. The name *Docfile* is an archaic term for a compound file and has been preserved in these function names for compatibility with early beta releases of OLE 2.

There are three additional API functions in STORAGE.DLL that are frequently used with the preceding set:

API Function	Description
StgIsStorageFile	Tests whether a given file is a compound file.
StgIsStorageLockBytes	Tests whether a given *LockBytes* contains a compound file.
StgSetTimes	Provides the *SetElementTimes* equivalent for a root storage without having to open the storage.

A root storage obtained with one of the preceding *Stg...* API functions will support an interface called *IRootStorage* in addition to *IStorage.* You can obtain a pointer to this interface by calling *IStorage::QueryInterface* with *IID-_IRootStorage. IRootStorage* contains one member function (besides *IUnknown,* of course), called *SwitchToFile,* which is described later in "Low Memory Save As Operations."

When you have a pointer to an *IStorage* interface, you generally use that storage object by calling *IStorage* member functions to create other substorages or streams and to manage elements within the storage. The *CreateStream, OpenStream, CreateStorage,* and *OpenStorage* members are the most optimized, whereas other members are not. For example, you will gain much better performance by storing a table of your storage's elements in a stream rather than relying on *EnumElements.* You should also make judicious use of *MoveElementTo, RenameElement,* and *DestroyElement,* being sure that you make few calls to these functions during performance-critical operations.

A number of the *Stg...* API functions and interface functions have some extra parameters to deal with transaction optimizations when a storage object (root or otherwise) is opened by using STGM_TRANSACTED. The optimizations allow an application to exclude specific elements of a storage from being in transacted mode even though the entire storage is opened in transacted mode. By excluding such elements, you reduce the overall amount of memory necessary to record changes to your data. For more information, refer to the *OLE 2 Programmer's Reference.* The topic of optimizations and exclusions is not treated in this chapter.

You can also pass an *IStorage* pointer to a few other functions in OLE2.DLL that help applications and objects storing their data in compound files to mark those files in such a way that an external agent could look at that storage and get an idea of who might be able to load or edit the contents. We'll see where to call some of these API functions later when we make use of compound files:

API Function	Description
WriteClassStg	Serializes a CLSID into an OLE-controlled stream within a given storage, where the CLSID identifies the application or object writing other data.
ReadClassStg	Loads the CLSID previously written by *WriteClassStg*.
WriteFmtUserTypeStg	Serializes a clipboard format and a user-readable name describing the format of the contents of the storage. This could be used by another application to determine whether it could open your streams and read the contents.
ReadFmtUserTypeStg	Reads the clipboard format and the string previously written by *WriteFmtUserTypeStg*.

Stream Objects and the *IStream* Interface

A stream is the equivalent of a standard file, except that it is exposed through the *IStream* interface, shown in Table 5-2 on the following page. An *IStream* pointer to a stream in a compound file is always obtained by using *IStorage::CreateStream* or *IStorage::OpenStream*, although there are also a few OLE 2 API functions for using an independent stream object outside of a compound file:

API Function	Description
CreateStreamOnHGlobal	Builds a stream object on a piece of global memory.
GetHGlobalFromStream	Returns the global memory handle used in a stream created by using *CreateStreamOnHGlobal*.

These functions in OLE2.DLL are generally used to serialize some data to a stream that we can pass to another process. In those situations, the stream is used as a generic transfer medium and not for file-related storage.

Many stream functions equate directly to existing file functions, so most code that uses functions such as *_lread* and *_lwrite* is easily rewritten to handle a stream. Each stream in and of itself has access rights (read, write, share, and so on) and a single seek pointer just as files have. However, because a stream object does not use a file handle, you can open a stream and leave it open with no penalty to the underlying file system.

IStream Member	File Equivalent[5]	Description
Release	*_lclose*	Closes the stream for the user of the *IStream* pointer through which it's called if the reference count is zero.
Read	*_lread*	Reads a given number of bytes from the current seek pointer into memory.
Write	*_lwrite*	Writes a number of bytes from memory to the stream starting at the current seek pointer.
Seek	*_llseek*	Moves the seek pointer to a new offset from the beginning of the stream, from end of the stream or from the current position.
SetSize	*_chsize*	Preallocates space for the stream but does not preclude writing outside that stream (see below).
CopyTo	*_fmemcpy*	Copies the number of bytes from the current seek pointer in the stream to the current seek pointer in another stream (or a clone of the same stream).
Commit	(none)	Publishes all changes to a transacted stream to its parent storage (if the stream was opened in transacted mode) or flushes all internal buffers (if the stream was opened in direct mode). Transacted streams are not implemented in OLE 2.
Revert	(none)	Discards any changes made to the stream (opened in transacted mode) since the last *Commit* (not implemented in OLE 2).
LockRegion	*_locking*	Restricts access to a byte range in the stream instead of the stream as a whole (not supported in OLE 2).
UnlockRegion	*_locking*	Frees restrictions set with *LockRegion* (not supported in OLE 2).

Table 5-2.

The IStream *interface.*

5.Both Windows API and C run-time functions are shown here.

Table 5-2. *continued*

IStream Member	File Equivalent	Description
Stat	*_stat*	Retrieves statistics for the stream such as the name, the size, and so on.
Clone	*_dup*	Creates a new stream object with an independent seek pointer that references the same actual bytes.

The *Read, Write,* and *Seek* members of *IStream* are the most optimized for performance in the entire compound file implementation. Other operations such as *CopyTo* and *SetSize* are potentially expensive and should be used with caution.

As another optimization, *SetSize* is a function you can use to set the initial size of a stream to optimize stream allocation and to have a good chance that the stream is physically contiguous in the compound file. You are not required to use it, however, because if you just so happen to write off the end of the stream, the stream object will find more space in the compound file into which it then automatically expands.

Inside a compound file, the data contained in a stream is not necessarily contiguous, as the physical location of the contents of an MS-DOS file on a hard disk might be in widely separated sectors. From the point of view of the code using the stream, the data is contiguous—you let the stream implementation worry about exact placement.

Compound File Implementation of Streams

OLE 2 does not implement stream transactioning nor region locking—that is, *Revert, LockRegion,* and *UnlockRegion* are no-ops, and *Commit* only has the effect of flushing internal buffers. In addition, the *IStream* interface allows streams to be 2^{64} bytes—that is, a single read or write could transfer 2^{64} bytes at a time and the seek pointers are a 64-bit value. OLE 2's implementation is limited to 2^{32}-byte transfers and uses a 32-bit seek pointer.

Finally, seeking backward in a stream is potentially very slow because OLE 2's implementation uses a singly-linked list to manage discontiguous blocks of space in the file that make up the stream.

LockBytes Objects and the *ILockBytes* Interface

All root storage objects (and only root storage objects) are built on top of a byte array represented by a *LockBytes* object that implements the *ILockBytes* interface, shown in Table 5-3. A *LockBytes* isolates the root storage from any concern about how the bytes actually get to their final destination on whatever storage device the *LockBytes* accesses. For example, a *LockBytes* built on the file system writes bytes to a file; a *LockBytes* built on global memory writes data to some memory block.

ILockBytes Member	Description
ReadAt	Reads a number of bytes from a given location in the byte array. If there are not enough bytes on the device to satisfy the request, *Read* returns what can be read.
WriteAt	Writes a number of bytes to a given location in the byte array, expanding the allocations on the device to accommodate the request.
Flush	Ensures that any internal buffers in *LockBytes* are written to the physical device.
SetSize	Preallocates a specific amount of space on the device.
LockRegion	Locks a range of bytes on the device for write access or exclusive access.
UnlockRegion	Reverses a *LockRegion* call.
Stat	Fills a STATSTG structure with information about *LockBytes*, which in turn reflects information about the device.

Table 5-3.
The ILockBytes *interface.*

Compound File Implementation of *LockBytes*

OLE 2's *LockBytes* implementation supports the entire interface, region locking included. A *LockBytes* object that writes to the default file system is used inherently when you create a compound file with *StgCreateDocfile* or *StgOpenStorage*. The specific implementation of this *LockBytes* is not available for use outside this context. OLE 2 also provides a standard *LockBytes* built on global memory that you manage through two API functions in OLE2.DLL:

API Function	Description
CreateILockBytesOnHGlobal	Creates a *LockBytes* object in a piece of global memory that either this function or the caller can allocate.
GetHGlobalFromILockBytes	Returns the global memory handle in use by a *LockBytes* from *CreateILockBytesOnHGlobal*.

If you need to create a compound file on a device other than the file system or global memory, you can implement your own *LockBytes*. For example, you might want to send the data across a network to a database without ever having to bother the storage object about the details. In this case, you implement your *LockBytes* however you want to (as long as you can provide an *ILockBytes* function table) and call *StgCreateDocfileOnILockBytes* or *StgOpenStorageOnILockBytes* to obtain an *IStorage* pointer. This *IStorage* is indistinguishable from any *IStorage* built on a different *LockBytes*.

Although the read and write mechanisms in a *LockBytes* are similar to those in a stream, a *LockBytes* maintains no seek pointer and is instead always told where to read from or where to write. In addition, the actual physical location of the bytes might not be contiguous; they might span multiple physical files, multiple global memory allocations, multiple database fields, and so on. The purpose of the *LockBytes* object is to isolate any storage and stream objects from the physical aspects of the byte device.

The *Stat* Member Function and STATSTG

Each interface contains a member function called *Stat*, which is essentially identical to the standard ANSI C run-time *_stat* function. *Stat* returns its information in a STATSTG structure: the name of the element, creation and modification times, the type of object (storage, stream, and so on), the access mode under which the object is opened, and whether the object supports region locking, as described through various interfaces:

```
typedef struct FARSTRUCT tagSTATSTG
    {
    char FAR            *pwcsName;            //Name of element
    DWORD                type;                //Type of element
    ULARGE_INTEGER       cbSize;              //Size of element
    FILETIME             mtime;               //Last mod date/time
    FILETIME             ctime;               //Creation date/time
    FILETIME             atime;               //Last access date/time
    DWORD                grfMode;             //Mode element opened in
    DWORD                grfLocksSupported;   //Support region locking?
    CLSID                clsid;               //CLSID of the element
    DWORD                grfStateBits;        //Current state
    DWORD                reserved;
    } STATSTG;
```

This structure is also used to enumerate elements within a storage, as shown in the next section, through an interface called *IEnumSTATSTG*. The *OLE 2 Programmer's Reference* has complete details on the STATSTG structure.

Container Applications and *ILockBytes*

A compound document container application can use the *ILockBytes* interface to preserve an old file format while retaining the ability to supply *IStorage* pointers to be embedded as required. First, the application can implement an *ILockBytes* interface that represents a specific portion of a file into which the container wants to save the object. It can then call *StgCreateDocfileOnILockBytes* to obtain an *IStorage* pointer through which it can save a compound document object, or it can call *StgOpenStorageOnILockBytes* to obtain a storage from which to load the compound document object. Another way to preserve an old file format is to call *CreateILockBytesOnHGlobal* followed by *StgCreateDocfileOnILockBytes*, which creates a storage object in memory. After saving the compound document object to this storage, the container can call *GetHGlobalFromILockBytes*, get a pointer to that memory by calling *GlobalLock*, and write the contents of that memory into its own file format. When the container wants to reload that object, it loads the file block into memory and calls *CreateILockBytesOnHGlobal* and *StgOpenStorageOnILockBytes* to obtain the storage object from which to load the compound document object. Use of an *ILockBytes* to represent a section of your file is preferable to creating a storage in memory because compound document objects can potentially be very large and therefore require more memory than is available.

However, one important point to remember about using this structure is that STORAGE.DLL allocates the string pointed to by *pwcsName* using the task allocator from *CoGetMalloc*. You, as the user of the STATSTG structure, are responsible for freeing that string using the task allocator yourself:

```
[Code to get a STATSTG structure in the st variable]
LPMALLOC    pIMalloc;

CoGetMalloc(MEMCTX_TASK, &pIMalloc);
pIMalloc->Free((LPVOID)st.pwcsName);
pIMalloc->Release();
```

Note that, if your call to *CoInitialize* worked on startup, calls to *CoGetMalloc* will not fail if you always pass MEMCTX_ task and a valid pointer to your LPMALLOC variable. Therefore, there is no need in this code fragment to check the return value of *CoGetMalloc*.

Compound Files in Practice

Now that we've thoroughly beaten into the deep earth all the interfaces and API functions related to compound files, we can look at how to actually apply it all to implementing file functions in an application. For this chapter, I have modified the Chapter 2 version of Cosmo to write its data into a compound file, demonstrating the simplest use of compound files: open, read or write, and then close. This version of Cosmo also retains compatibility with old versions of its files by using the conversion feature of compound files, allowing it to treat old files as storages.

I have also added compound file support to Patron, which has a much more complicated storage scheme, because we implement part of the storage model shown earlier, in Figure 5-3 on page 214. Because Patron files exercise transactioning and incremental saves, they will, over time, become fragmented. A program called Smasher, which is really a File Manager Extension DLL, is presented at the end of this chapter to demonstrate how to defragment a compound file.

This chapter also shows a modification of the object DLL version of Cosmo's Polyline to deal with storage; the changes made here apply directly to an implementation of Polyline as a compound document object in Chapter 11. This implementation will show exactly what is required of a compound document object, be it in a server DLL or a server EXE, as far as storage is concerned.

Note that in all these cases, Cosmo, Patron, and Polyline can be considered component users as they use storage objects as component objects. The only difference between them and a program like OBJUSER in Chapter 4 is that they use the function *StgCreateDocfile* instead of *CoCreateInstance* to instantiate an object.

For some applications, you might want to use compound files as a standalone technology because of its power, without using any other OLE 2 technologies, such as component objects, data transfer, or compound documents. At a minimum, compound file usage requires COMPOBJ.DLL and STORAGE.DLL. The latter's necessity is obvious, but the former is a little obscure. COMPOBJ.DLL is required because functions such as *IStorage::Stat* will internally call *CoGetMalloc* (see the earlier section "The *Stat* Member Function and STATSTG"). Therefore, an application that uses compound files must call *CoBuildVersion* and *CoInitialize* on startup and *CoUninitialize* on shutdown, as explained in "The New Application for Windows Objects" in Chapter 4. However, because storage objects always live in DLLs, no marshaling will occur, so a *SetMessageQueue(96)* call is not necessary.

Simple Storage: Cosmo

Let's start off with small modifications to Cosmo, as shown in Listing 5-1. The changes are simple. Instead of opening a regular file with which to read or write data, we open a root storage. Instead of using file I/O functions such as *_lread* and *_lwrite*, we obtain a stream pointer and use *IStream* member functions. The simplest uses of compound files can be reduced to a few calls to API functions and interface members.

DOCUMENT.CPP

```
[Other code unaffected]

/*
 * CCosmoDoc::ULoad
 *
 * Purpose:
 *  Loads a given document without any user interface overwriting
 *  the previous contents of the Polyline window.  We do this by
 *  opening the file and telling the Polyline to load itself from
 *  that file.
 *
 * Parameters:
 *  fChangeFile     BOOL indicating if we're to update the window
 *                  title and the filename from using this file.
 *  pszFile         LPSTR to the filename to load, NULL if the file
 *                  is new and untitled.
 *
 * Return Value:
 *  UINT            An error value from DOCERR_...
 */

UINT CCosmoDoc::ULoad(BOOL fChangeFile, LPSTR pszFile)
    {
    HRESULT         hr;
    LPSTORAGE       pIStorage;

    if (NULL==pszFile)
        {
        //For a new untitled document, simply rename ourselves.
        Rename(NULL);
        m_lVer=VERSIONCURRENT;
```

Listing 5-1.
Modifications to the Cosmo program for simple use of compound files.

(continued)

Listing 5-1. *continued*

```
        return DOCERR_NONE;
        }

    /*
     * If not a Compound File, open the file using STGM_CONVERT in
     * transacted mode to see old files as a storage with one stream
     * called "CONTENTS" (which is conveniently the name we use
     * in the new files).  We must use STGM_TRANSACTED here or else
     * the old file will be immediately converted on disk:  we only
     * want a converted image in memory from which to read.  In
     * addition, note that we need STGM_READWRITE as well since
     * conversion is inherently a write operation.
     */

    pIStorage=NULL;

    if (NOERROR!=StgIsStorageFile(pszFile))
        {
        hr=StgCreateDocfile(pszFile, STGM_TRANSACTED | STGM_READWRITE
            | STGM_CONVERT | STGM_SHARE_EXCLUSIVE, 0, &pIStorage);

        if (FAILED(hr))
            {
            //If denied write access, try to load the old way
            if (STG_E_ACCESSDENIED==GetScode(hr))
                m_lVer=m_pPL->ReadFromFile(pszFile);
            else
                return DOCERR_COULDNOTOPEN;
            }
        }
    else
        {
        hr=StgOpenStorage(pszFile, NULL, STGM_DIRECT | STGM_READ
            | STGM_SHARE_EXCLUSIVE, NULL, 0, &pIStorage);

        if (FAILED(hr))
            return DOCERR_COULDNOTOPEN;
        }

    if (NULL!=pIStorage)
        {
        m_lVer=m_pPL->ReadFromStorage(pIStorage);
        pIStorage->Release();
        }
```

(continued)

Listing 5-1. *continued*

```
    if (POLYLINE_E_READFAILURE==m_lVer)
        return DOCERR_READFAILURE;

    if (POLYLINE_E_UNSUPPORTEDVERSION==m_lVer)
        return DOCERR_UNSUPPORTEDVERSION;

    if (fChangeFile)
        Rename(pszFile);

    //Importing a file makes things dirty.
    FDirtySet(!fChangeFile);

    return DOCERR_NONE;
    }

/*
 * CCosmoDoc::USave
 *
 * Purpose:
 *  Writes the file to a known filename, requiring that the user has
 *  previously used FileOpen or FileSaveAs to provide a filename.
 *
 * Parameters:
 *  uType           UINT indicating the type of file the user
 *                  requested to save in the File Save As dialog.
 *  pszFile         LPSTR under which to save.  If NULL, use the
 *                  current name.
 *
 * Return Value:
 *  UINT            An error value from DOCERR_...
 */

UINT CCosmoDoc::USave(UINT uType, LPSTR pszFile)
    {
    LONG        lVer, lRet;
    UINT        uTemp;
    BOOL        fRename=TRUE;
    HRESULT     hr;
    LPSTORAGE   pIStorage;

    if (NULL==pszFile)
        {
        fRename=FALSE;
```

(continued)

Listing 5-1. *continued*

```
        pszFile=m_szFile;
        }

    /*
     * Type 1 is the current version, type 2 is version 1.0 of the
     * Polyline so we use this to send the right version to
     * CPolyline::WriteToFile.
     */

    switch (uType)
        {
        case 0:         //From Save, use loaded version.
            lVer=m_lVer;
            break;

        case 1:
            lVer=VERSIONCURRENT;
            break;

        case 2:
            lVer=MAKELONG(0, 1);    //1.0
            break;

        default:
            return DOCERR_UNSUPPORTEDVERSION;
        }

    /*
     * If the version the user wants to save is different from the
     * version that we loaded and m_lVer is not zero (new doc),
     * then inform the user of the version change and verify.
     */

    if (0!=m_lVer && m_lVer!=lVer)
        {
        char        szMsg[128];

        wsprintf(szMsg, PSZ(IDS_VERSIONCHANGE), (UINT)HIWORD(m_lVer)
            , (UINT)LOWORD(m_lVer), (UINT)HIWORD(lVer)
            , (UINT)LOWORD(lVer));

        uTemp=MessageBox(m_hWnd, szMsg, PSZ(IDS_DOCUMENTCAPTION)
            , MB_YESNOCANCEL);

        if (IDCANCEL==uTemp)
            return DOCERR_CANCELLED;
```

(continued)

Listing 5-1. *continued*

```
        //If user won't upgrade versions, revert to loaded version.
        if (IDNO==uTemp)
            lVer=m_lVer;
        }

    /*
     * For version 1 files, use the old code. For new files, use
     * storages instead.
     */

    if (lVer==MAKELONG(0, 1))
        lRet=m_pPL->WriteToFile(pszFile, lVer);
    else
        {
        hr=StgCreateDocfile(pszFile, STGM_DIRECT | STGM_READWRITE
            | STGM_CREATE | STGM_SHARE_EXCLUSIVE, 0, &pIStorage);

        if (FAILED(hr))
            return DOCERR_COULDNOTOPEN;

        //Mark this as one of our class.
        WriteClassStg(pIStorage, CLSID_Cosmo2Figure);

        //Write user-readable class information.
        WriteFmtUserTypeStg(pIStorage, m_cf
            , PSZ(IDS_CLIPBOARDFORMAT));

        lRet=m_pPL->WriteToStorage(pIStorage, lVer);
        pIStorage->Release();
        }

    if (POLYLINE_E_NONE!=lRet)
        return DOCERR_WRITEFAILURE;

    //Saving makes us clean.
    FDirtySet(FALSE);

    //Update the known version of this document.
    m_lVer=lVer;

    if (fRename)
        Rename(pszFile);

    return DOCERR_NONE;
    }
```

To write a simple file with a single stream, Cosmo performs the following steps, in which steps 1, 2, and 6 occur in *CCosmoDoc::USave* (DOCUMENT.CPP) and steps 3, 4, and 5 occur in *CPolyline::WriteToStorage* (POLYLINE.CPP), a new function added to *CPolyline* to handle storage objects, in addition to *WriteToFile*, which deals in file handles:

1. *StgCreateDocfile*, using *STGM_DIRECT ¦ STGM_CREATE*, creates a new compound file, overwriting any file that already exists. This returns an *IStorage* pointer for this new file. Because we use STGM_DIRECT, there is no need to later call *IStorage::Commit*.
2. *WriteClassStg* and *WriteFmtUserTypeStg* set various flags on the storage and save standard class information.
3. *IStorage::CreateStream*, using the name "CONTENTS," returns an *IStream* pointer.
4. *IStream::Write* saves the data, passing a pointer to the data and the size of the data to go into the stream.
5. *IStream::Release* closes the stream, matching *IStorage::CreateStream*.
6. *IStorage::Release* closes the storage, matching *StgCreateDocfile*.

In a similar fashion, Cosmo makes the following calls to open and read the previously saved data during a File Open operation. Steps 1, 2, 3, and 7 happen in *CCosmoDoc::ULoad* and steps 4, 5, and 6 happen in *CPolyline::ReadFromStorage*, which handles storage objects, as opposed to happening in *CPolyline::ReadFromFile*:

1. *StgIsStorageFile* determines whether the filename refers to a compound file created by the OLE 2 (or compatible) implementation of Structured Storage. This function looks for a signature at the beginning of the disk file to determine whether the file can be read as a compound file.
2. If the file is a compound file, *StgOpenStorage* opens the storage for reading and returning an *IStorage* pointer. Otherwise, *StgCreateDocfile*, using STGM_TRANSACTED ¦ STGM_CONVERT, opens a non-compound file as a storage object returning an *IStorage* pointer.
3. At the application's option, *ReadClassStg* loads the CLSID previously saved from *WriteClassStg*, and *IsEqualCLSID* compares the expected class to the one in the file. If the two don't match, you didn't write this file, and you can read any way you want.

4. *IStorage::OpenStream* on the name "CONTENTS" returns an *IStream* pointer to the data.

5. *IStream::Read* loads the data from the file into the memory structures.

6. *IStream::Release* closes the stream, matching the *IStorage::OpenStream* call.

7. *IStorage::Release* closes the storage, matching the *StgOpenStorage* or *StgCreateDocfile* call.

The most interesting aspects of this code are the use of the STGM_CONVERT flag when dealing with an old file format and the correspondence between stream operations and traditional file operations, which are the topics of the next two sections. Note also that, although Cosmo writes a CLSID to the storage, it does not check this during File Open using *ReadClassStg* because I want Cosmo and Component Cosmo (CoCosmo, modified for storage objects a little later) to retain file compatibility. Because the two applications write different CLSIDs into their storages, we skip the *ReadClassStg* step. Using *ReadClassStg* is simply an extra check that you can perform to validate a file before loading potentially large amounts of data.

Pulling Rabbits from a Hat with STGM_CONVERT

Cosmo is capable of reading and writing two different versions of its files; in Chapter 2, both formats were typical MS-DOS files. For this chapter and those beyond, Cosmo will maintain its version 2 file format in a compound file instead, but it will remain compatible with old files (both the version 1 files and the version 2 files generated by the Chapter 2 version of Cosmo). Cosmo still retains the capability to write an old *file* format, simply by virtue of preserving the old code. However, reading files of either format has changed significantly.

We could approach the problem of reading multiple formats in one of two ways. The first would be to test the file using *StgIsStorageFile* and if that test fails, open and read that file using traditional file I/O functions. Doubtless you already have code that handles such an operation, and I encourage you to keep it if it works well. The second approach, which I've used in Cosmo to demonstrate the technique, is to use the STGM_CONVERT flag.

When Cosmo sees a non-compound file while loading, it calls *StgCreateDocfile*, passing STGM_CONVERT instead of STGM_CREATE. The STGM_CONVERT flag causes OLE 2 to open the file as if it were a storage object containing a single stream named "CONTENTS."

```
LPSTORAGE    pIStorage;
HRESULT      hr;

hr=StgCreateDocfile(pszFile, STGM_TRANSACTED | STGM_READWRITE
    | STGM_CONVERT | STGM_SHARE_EXCLUSIVE, 0, &pIStorage);

if (FAILED(hr))
    {
    if (STG_E_ACCESSDENIED==GetScode(hr))
        [Try loading the file using traditional file I/O.]
    }
```

If this operation succeeds, the HRESULT returned from *StgCreateDocfile* will contain *STG_S_CONVERTED*, which is not equal to NOERROR but which does not mean an error occurred. Therefore, using the FAILED macro is a valid test for errors.

When using *StgCreateDocfile* for conversion, I purposely passed STGM_TRANSACTED | STGM_READWRITE but never bothered to commit anything. The semantics of STGM_CONVERT in *StgCreateDocfile* mean "convert the file now." If you use STGM_DIRECT in this case, the old file will be immediately overwritten with a compound file. By specifying STGM_TRANSACTED, you create the conversion *in* temporary storage, leaving the original disk image unaffected. If you called *IStorage::Commit* on such a transacted storage, you would then change the actual file on the disk. Because conversion is a potential write operation, you must specify at least STGM_WRITE, along with STGM_CONVERT. If the file is marked as read-only, however, *StgCreateDocfile* will fail with STG_E_ACCESSDENIED. In such a situation, you can default to loading the file with old code that requires only read-only access.

When we have opened this old file as a compound file, we have a storage object (an *IStorage* pointer) through which we can treat the file as if it were a compound file. As shown in Listing 5-1 beginning on page 234, Cosmo passes an *IStorage* from either *StgCreateDocfile* or *StgOpenStorage* to the Polyline to read its data from the stream. It is not a coincidence that Cosmo's version 2 file format is a storage containing a single stream named "CONTENTS"—that naming allows Polyline to ignore how the data actually lives on the file system.

Streams vs. Files

The earlier section "Stream Objects and the *IStream* Interface" attempted to show that there is a strong parallel between traditional file I/O functions (in both the Windows API and the C run-time library) and the member functions of the *IStream* interface. In the Polyline implementation, we can see these similarities by comparing the *ReadFromFile* function used in the Chapter 2 implementation of Cosmo to the *ReadFromStorage* function used in the new version. (Note that *ReadFromFile* is still used in the new version of Cosmo when the file is marked read-only, restricting our use of STGM_CONVERT.) The two functions, *ReadFromFile* and *ReadFromStorage*, are shown here side by side to illustrate the utter similarities between the two implementations:

```
LONG CPolyline::ReadFromFile
    (LPSTR pszFile)
    {
    OFSTRUCT        of;
    HFILE           hFile;
    POLYLINEDATA    pl;
    UINT            cb=-1;
    UINT            cbExpect=0;


    if (NULL==pszFile)
        return POLYLINE_E_READFAILURE;

    hFile=OpenFile(pszFile,&of,OF_READ);




    if (HFILE_ERROR==hFile)
        return POLYLINE_E_READFAILURE;

    cb=_lread(hFile, (LPSTR)&pl
        , 2*sizeof(WORD));

    _llseek(hFile, 0L, 0);


    if (2*sizeof(WORD)!=cb)
        {
        _lclose(hFile);
        return POLYLINE_E_READFAILURE;
        }

    [Code here to calculate cbExpect
     based on the version number]
```

```
LONG CPolyline::ReadFromStorage
    (LPSTORAGE pIStorage)
    {
    HRESULT         hr;
    LPSTREAM        pIStream;
    POLYLINEDATA    pl;
    ULONG           cb=-1;
    ULONG           cbExpect=0;
    LARGE_INTEGER   li;

    if (NULL==pIStorage)
        return POLYLINE_E_READFAILURE;

    hr=pIStorage->OpenStream("CONTENTS", 0
        , STGM_DIRECT | STGM_READ
        | STGM_SHARE_EXCLUSIVE, 0
        , &pIStream);

    if (FAILED(hr))
        return POLYLINE_E_READFAILURE;

    hr=pIStream->Read((LPVOID)&pl
        , 2*sizeof(WORD), &cb);

    LISet32(li, 0);
    pIStream->Seek(li, STREAM_SEEK_SET, NULL);

    if (FAILED(hr) || 2*sizeof(WORD)!=cb)
        {
        pIStream->Release();
        return POLYLINE_E_READFAILURE;
        }

    [Code here to calculate cbExpect
     based on the version number]
```

```
cb=_lread(hFile, (LPSTR)&pl
    , cbExpect);
_lclose(hFile);

if (cbExpect!=cb)
    return POLYLINE_E_READFAILURE;

DataSet(&pl, TRUE, TRUE);
return MAKELONG(pl.wVerMin
    , pl.wVerMaj);
}
```

```
hr=pIStream->Read((LPVOID)&pl
    , cbExpect, &cb);
pIStream->Release();

if (cbExpect!=cb)
    return POLYLINE_E_READFAILURE;

DataSet(&pl, TRUE, TRUE);
return MAKELONG(pl.wVerMin
    , pl.wVerMaj);
}
```

The first difference is that a call to *OpenFile* is replaced by a call to *OpenStream*; we now treat the storage in which the data lives just as we treated the file system before. All of the old file I/O functions called with the file handle are then replaced by calls through the *IStream* pointer. A second general difference is the calling convention imposed by the use of *IStream* members. Remember that interface members generally return an HRESULT, thereby requiring you to pass pointers to variables in which those functions return additional information. So instead of a function such as *_lread*, which returns the number of bytes read, we have *IStream::Read*, which returns an HRESULT and fills another variable with the number of bytes read. Other than that, these two functions are semantically equivalent.

The preceding code also shows a difference in seeking within a file as opposed to a stream. The Structured Storage definition of *IStream* allows storages and streams to contain up to 264 addressable bytes of data. Because a stream can be that large, you have to use the LARGE_INTEGER (STORAGE.H) type to pass the seek offset, which is that unfamiliar code in *ReadFromStorage*:

```
LARGE_INTEGER   li;

LISet32(li, 0);
pIStream->Seek(li, STREAM_SEEK_SET, NULL);
```

A LARGE_INTEGER has two fields: a DWORD *LowPart* field and a LONG (signed) *HighPart* field. The *LISet32* macro sets *LowPart* to the value specified and performs sign-extension into *HighPart*. There is also a ULARGE_INTEGER, which is composed of two DWORD parts with an associated *ULISet32* macro. The third parameter to the preceding *IStream::Seek* could be a ULARGE_INTEGER, which receives the seek offset in the stream before the call. Passing a NULL simply means you're not interested.

The *CreateStream*, *OpenStream*, *Read*, *Write*, and *Seek* members of *IStorage* and *IStream* are the most commonly used, and the most performance optimized functions in the entire compound file implementation of OLE 2. For simple storage uses such as Cosmo, these and only a few others, such as *IStream::Seek*, might be all you need. Other members are used for more complicated storage models, such as that of Patron.

Complex Compound Files: Patron

English grammar defines a number of sentence structures. A simple sentence expresses one idea, such as "The rabbit sat in his form.[6]" Compound sentences express more than one independent idea, such as "The rabbit sat in his form, and the photographer set up his camera." In such a sentence, there is only a vague notion of concurrency, but no hard evidence. A complex sentence defines such a relationship, as in "The rabbit sat in his form while the photographer set up his camera." A complex-compound sentence is more on the order of "Although the rabbit felt trepidation about most humans, it calmly sat in its form, and the photographer continued to set up his camera."

If we relate these ideas to elements in OLE 2's Structured Storage Model, we can see how these descriptions of sentences apply to compound files. The simplest use of the model is writing a single stream into a file. When you use a root storage that contains one stream, you've made a compound file (sentence), in which the two elements are related mostly by virtue of them living in the same place at the same time. When we add more streams in the root storage, we make things more complex—the meaning of the data in one stream might be defined partially or completely by the context of the data in another stream. As we use even more complex structures, we add substorages alongside these streams, which generally don't need any dependency on the streams but do occupy space in the same file. This is the notion of complex compound files.

For Patron, we'll implement the storage model shown in Figure 5-5, which is the same as that shown in Figure 5-3 on page 214 but without the page header streams or tenant storages because we haven't yet added the capability to create tenants. Each Patron file is a root storage, underneath which live a stream containing the device configuration (printer parameters) and a stream containing the list of pages in the file DWORD identifies, in which the list of IDs stored in the page list defines which ID is page 1, page 2, and so on. Each page is then stored as a substorage, below the root storage, in which the name of the page storage is "Page *XX*", where *XX* is the ID in ASCII. At this time, these storages will not contain any other streams or storages, but they will provide the structure in which we can store tenants, such as bitmaps and

6. A rabbit's resting place.

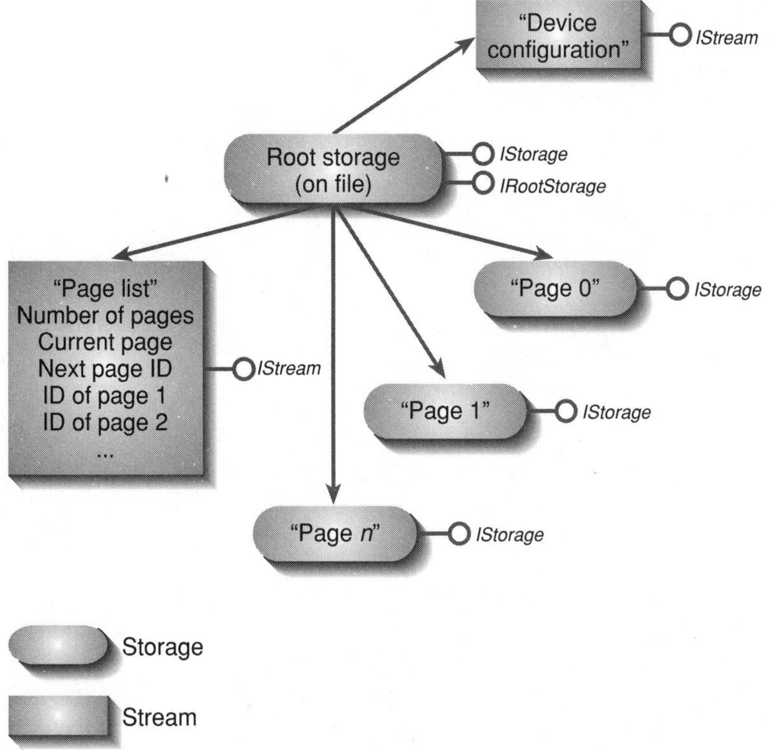

Figure 5-5.
Exact layout of Patron's compound files, as described in this chapter.

metafiles (as we'll see in Chapter 7) and compound document objects (as we'll see starting in Chapter 9).

To accommodate file I/O, Patron has undergone considerable modifications and additions, as shown in Listing 5-2 on the following page. For the most part, Patron follows the sequence of steps described for Cosmo in the preceding section, with the exception that not everything happens at the same time or in the same place. Changes made to DOCUMENT.CPP handle opening and saving the compound file—that is, implementing File New, File Open, File Save, and File Save As from the main window's point of view (*CPatronDoc::ULoad* and *CPatronDoc::USave*). The document-level code manages only the root storage and thus passes that storage to the *CPages* object, which maintains the actual page list. All stream and substorage creation happens on the *CPages* level. Still, if you follow the code, you will see that Patron generally creates a root storage, writes streams into it (as well as into substorages), calls functions such as *WriteClassStg* to identify the file, and calls *IStorage::Release* to close the file.

DOCUMENT.CPP

```
[Other code unaffected]

CPatronDoc::~CPatronDoc(void)
    {
    if (NULL!=m_pPG)
        delete m_pPG;

    if (NULL!=m_pIStorage)
        m_pIStorage->Release();

    return;
    }

UINT CPatronDoc::ULoad(BOOL fChangeFile, LPSTR pszFile)
    {
    RECT            rc;
    HRESULT         hr;
    LPSTORAGE       pIStorage;
    CLSID           clsID;
    DWORD           dwMode=STGM_TRANSACTED | STGM_READWRITE
                        | STGM_SHARE_EXCLUSIVE;

    if (NULL==pszFile)
        {
        //Create a new temp file.
        hr=StgCreateDocfile(NULL, dwMode | STGM_CREATE
            | STGM_DELETEONRELEASE, 0, &pIStorage);

        //Mark this as our class since we check with ReadClassStg.
        if (SUCCEEDED(hr))
            WriteClassStg(pIStorage, CLSID_PatronPages);
        }
    else
        {
        hr=StgOpenStorage(pszFile, NULL, dwMode, NULL, 0, &pIStorage);
        }

    if (FAILED(hr))
        return DOCERR_COULDNOTOPEN;
```

Listing 5-2.
The Patron program, using compound files for storage.

(continued)

Listing 5-2. *continued*

```
//Check if this is our type of file and exit if not.
hr=ReadClassStg(pIStorage, &clsID);

if (FAILED(hr) || !IsEqualCLSID(clsID, CLSID_PatronPages))
    {
    pIStorage->Release();
    return DOCERR_READFAILURE;
    }

//Attempt to create our contained Pages window.
m_pPG=new CPages(m_hInst);
GetClientRect(m_hWnd, &rc);

if (!m_pPG->FInit(m_hWnd, &rc, WS_CHILD | WS_VISIBLE
    , ID_PAGES, NULL))
    {
    pIStorage->Release();
    return DOCERR_READFAILURE;
    }

if (!m_pPG->FIStorageSet(pIStorage, FALSE
    , (BOOL)(NULL==pszFile)))
    {
    pIStorage->Release();
    return DOCERR_READFAILURE;
    }

m_pIStorage=pIStorage;

Rename(pszFile);

//Do initial setup if new file, otherwise Pages handles things.
if (NULL==pszFile)
    {
    //Go initialize the Pages for the default printer.
    if (!PrinterSetup(NULL, TRUE))
        return DOCERR_COULDNOTOPEN;

    //Go create an initial page.
    m_pPG->PageInsert(0);
    }
```

(continued)

Listing 5-2. *continued*

```
        FDirtySet(FALSE);
        return DOCERR_NONE;
        }

UINT CPatronDoc::USave(UINT uType, LPSTR pszFile)
        {
        HRESULT     hr;
        LPSTORAGE   pIStorage;

        //Save or Save As with the same file is just a commit.
        if (NULL==pszFile
            || (NULL!=pszFile && 0==lstrcmpi(pszFile
            , m_szFile)))
            {
            WriteFmtUserTypeStg(m_pIStorage, m_cf
                , PSZ(IDS_CLIPBOARDFORMAT));

            //Ensure that pages are up to date.
            m_pPG->FIStorageUpdate(FALSE);

            //Commit everything.
            m_pIStorage->Commit(STGC_ONLYIFCURRENT);

            FDirtySet(FALSE);
            return DOCERR_NONE;
            }

       /*
        * When we're given a name, open the storage, creating it new
        * if it does not exist or overwriting old one. Then CopyTo
        * from the current to the new, Commit the new, Release the old.
        */

       hr=StgCreateDocfile(pszFile, STGM_TRANSACTED | STGM_READWRITE
           | STGM_CREATE | STGM_SHARE_EXCLUSIVE, 0, &pIStorage);

       if (FAILED(hr))
           return DOCERR_COULDNOTOPEN;

       WriteClassStg(pIStorage, CLSID_PatronPages);
       WriteFmtUserTypeStg(pIStorage, m_cf, PSZ(IDS_CLIPBOARDFORMAT));

       //Ensure that all pages are up to date.
       m_pPG->FIStorageUpdate(TRUE);
```

(continued)

Listing 5-2. *continued*

```
    //This also copies the CLSID we stuffed in here at file creation.
    hr=pIStorage->CopyTo(NULL, NULL, NULL, pIStorage);

    if (FAILED(hr))
        {
        pIStorage->Release();
        return DOCERR_WRITEFAILURE;
        }

    pIStorage->Commit(STGC_ONLYIFCURRENT);

    /*
     * Revert changes on the original storage. If this was a temp
     * file, it's deleted since we used STGM_DELETEONRELEASE.
     */

    m_pIStorage->Release();

    //Make this new storage current.
    m_pIStorage=pIStorage;
    m_pPG->FIStorageSet(pIStorage, TRUE, FALSE);

    FDirtySet(FALSE);
    Rename(pszFile);      //Update caption bar.

    return DOCERR_NONE;
    }
```

PAGES.H

```
class __far CPage
    {
    private:
        DWORD       m_dwID;            //Persistent DWORD identifier
        LPSTORAGE   m_pIStorage;       //Substorage for this page

    public:
        CPage(DWORD);
        ~CPage(void);

        DWORD   GetID(void);
        BOOL    FOpen(LPSTORAGE);
```

(continued)

Listing 5-2. *continued*

```
        void    Close(BOOL);
        void    Update(void);
        void    Destroy(LPSTORAGE);
    };

typedef CPage FAR *LPCPage;

/*
 * Structures to save with the document describing the device
 * configuration and pages that we have. This is followed by
 * a list of DWORD IDs for the individual pages.
 */

typedef struct __far tagDEVICECONFIG
    {
    DEVMODE     dm;
    char        szDriver[CCHDEVICENAME];
    char        szDevice[CCHDEVICENAME];
    } DEVICECONFIG, FAR *LPDEVICECONFIG;

typedef struct __far tagPAGELIST
    {
    UINT        cPages;
    UINT        iPageCur;
    DWORD       dwIDNext;
    } PAGELIST, FAR *LPPAGELIST;
...
class __far CPages : public CWindow
    {
    [Existing members omitted from this listing]
        ...
        LPSTORAGE   m_pIStorage;            //Root storage
        //m_hDevMode, m_szDriver, m_szDevice removed
    ...
    public:
        [Existing members omitted from this listing]
        ...
        BOOL        FIStorageSet(LPSTORAGE, BOOL, BOOL);
        BOOL        FIStorageUpdate(BOOL);
    ...
    };
```

(continued)

Listing 5-2. *continued*

```
typedef CPages FAR *LPCPages;

//Fixed names of streams in the Pages IStorage
#define SZSTREAMPAGELIST        "Page List"
#define SZSTREAMDEVICECONFIG    "Device Configuration"
```

PAGES.CPP

```
CPages::CPages(HINSTANCE hInst) : CWindow(hInst)
    {

    [Other code omitted from listing]

    m_pIStorage=NULL;
    return;
    }

CPages::~CPages(void)
    {
    //Ensure memory cleaned up in list; do final IStorage::Release.
    FIStorageSet(NULL, FALSE, FALSE);

    [Other code omitted from listing]

    return;
    }
...
/*
 * CPages::FIStorageSet
 *
 * Purpose:
 *  Provides the document's IStorage to the pages for its own use.
 *  If this is a new storage, we initialize it with streams that we
 *  want to always exist. If this is an open, we create
 *  our page list from the PageList string we wrote before.
 *
 * Parameters:
 *  pIStorage       LPSTORAGE to the new or opened storage. If
 *                  NULL, we just clean up and exit.
```

(continued)

Listing 5-2. *continued*

```
 *  fChange          BOOL indicating whether this was Save As
 *                   operation, meaning that we have the structure
 *                   already and just need to change the value of
 *                   m_pIStorage.
 *  fInitNew         BOOL indicating whether this is a new storage or
 *                   one opened from a previous save.
 */

BOOL CPages::FIStorageSet(LPSTORAGE pIStorage, BOOL fChange
    , BOOL fInitNew)
    {
    DWORD            dwMode=STGM_DIRECT | STGM_READWRITE
                         | STGM_SHARE_EXCLUSIVE;
    HRESULT          hr;
    LPCPage          pPage;
    BOOL             fRet=FALSE;
    ULONG            cbRead;
    PAGELIST         pgList;
    LPSTREAM         pIStream;
    LPMALLOC         pIMalloc;
    LPDWORD          pdwID;
    UINT             i;

    //If we're changing saved roots, simply open current page again.
    if (fChange)
        {
        if (NULL==pIStorage)
            return FALSE;

        m_pIStorage->Release();
        m_pIStorage=pIStorage;
        m_pIStorage->AddRef();

        FPageGet(m_iPageCur, &pPage, TRUE);
        return TRUE;
        }

    if (NULL!=m_hWndPageList)
        {
        //On new or open, clean out whatever it is we have.
        for (i=0; i < m_cPages; i++)
            {
            if (FPageGet(i, &pPage, FALSE))
                delete pPage;
            }
```

(continued)

Listing 5-2. *continued*

```
        SendMessage(m_hWndPageList, LB_RESETCONTENT, 0, 0L);
        }

    if (NULL!=m_pIStorage)
        m_pIStorage->Release();

    m_pIStorage=NULL;

    //If we're only cleaning up, we're done.
    if (NULL==pIStorage)
        return TRUE;

    m_pIStorage=pIStorage;
    m_pIStorage->AddRef();

    //If this is a new storage, create the streams we require.
    if (fInitNew)
        {
        //Page list header
        hr=m_pIStorage->CreateStream(SZSTREAMPAGELIST, dwMode
            | STGM_CREATE, 0, 0, &pIStream);

        if (FAILED(hr))
            return FALSE;

        pIStream->Release();

        //Device configuration
        hr=m_pIStorage->CreateStream(SZSTREAMDEVICECONFIG, dwMode
            | STGM_CREATE, 0, 0, &pIStream);

        if (FAILED(hr))
            return FALSE;

        pIStream->Release();
        return TRUE;
        }

    /*
     * We're opening an existing file:
     *  1) Configure for the device we're on.
     *  2) Read the page list and create page entries for each.
     */

    ConfigureForDevice();
```

(continued)

Listing 5-2. *continued*

```
//Read the page list.
hr=m_pIStorage->OpenStream(SZSTREAMPAGELIST, NULL, dwMode
    , 0, &pIStream);

if (FAILED(hr))
    return FALSE;

if (SUCCEEDED(CoGetMalloc(MEMCTX_SHARED, &pIMalloc)))
    {
    pIStream->Read((LPVOID)&pgList, sizeof(PAGELIST), &cbRead);
    m_cPages  =pgList.cPages;
    m_iPageCur=pgList.iPageCur;
    m_dwIDNext=pgList.dwIDNext;

    fRet=TRUE;
    cbRead=pgList.cPages*sizeof(DWORD);

    if (0!=cbRead)
        {
        pdwID=(LPDWORD)pIMalloc->Alloc(cbRead);

        if (NULL!=pdwID)
            {
            pIStream->Read((LPVOID)pdwID, cbRead, &cbRead);

            for (i=0; i < m_cPages; i++)
                fRet &=FPageAdd(-1, *(pdwID+i), FALSE);

            pIMalloc->Free((LPVOID)pdwID);
            }
        }

    pIMalloc->Release();
    }

pIStream->Release();

if (!fRet)
    return FALSE;

FPageGet(m_iPageCur, &pPage, TRUE);

InvalidateRect(m_hWnd, NULL, FALSE);
UpdateWindow(m_hWnd);
```

(continued)

Listing 5-2. *continued*

```
    return TRUE;
    }

BOOL CPages::FIStorageUpdate(BOOL fCloseAll)
    {
    LPCPage         pPage;
    LPSTREAM        pIStream;
    LPMALLOC        pIMalloc;
    LPDWORD         pdwID;
    ULONG           cb;
    HRESULT         hr;
    PAGELIST        pgList;
    BOOL            fRet=FALSE;
    UINT            i;

    //We only need to close the current page--nothing else is open.
    if (FPageGet(m_iPageCur, &pPage, FALSE))
        {
        pPage->Update();

        if (fCloseAll)
            pPage->Close(FALSE);
        }

    //We don't hold anything else open, so write the page list.
    hr=m_pIStorage->OpenStream(SZSTREAMPAGELIST, NULL, STGM_DIRECT
        | STGM_READWRITE | STGM_SHARE_EXCLUSIVE, 0, &pIStream);

    if (FAILED(hr))
        return FALSE;

    if (SUCCEEDED(CoGetMalloc(MEMCTX_SHARED, &pIMalloc)))
        {
        pgList.cPages=m_cPages;
        pgList.iPageCur=m_iPageCur;
        pgList.dwIDNext=m_dwIDNext;

        pIStream->Write((LPVOID)&pgList, sizeof(PAGELIST), &cb);

        cb=m_cPages*sizeof(DWORD);
        pdwID=(LPDWORD)pIMalloc->Alloc(cb);
```

(continued)

Listing 5-2. *continued*

```
        if (NULL!=pdwID)
            {
            for (i=0; i < m_cPages; i++)
                {
                FPageGet(i, &pPage, FALSE);
                *(pdwID+i)=pPage->GetID();
                }

            pIStream->Write((LPVOID)pdwID, cb, &cb);
            pIMalloc->Free((LPVOID)pdwID);
            fRet=TRUE;
            }

        pIMalloc->Release();
        }

    pIStream->Release();

    return fRet;
    }
...
UINT CPages::PageInsert(UINT uReserved)
    {
    LPCPage     pPage;

    if (0!=m_cPages)
        {
        //Close the current page, committing changes.
        if (!FPageGet(m_iPageCur, &pPage, FALSE))
            return 0;

        pPage->Close(TRUE);
        }

    [Other code omitted from listing]
    }

UINT CPages::PageDelete(UINT uReserved)
    {
    LPCPage     pPage;

    if (!FPageGet(m_iPageCur, &pPage, FALSE))
        return -1;
```

(continued)

Listing 5-2. *continued*

```
    //Delete the page in both the storage and in memory.
    SendMessage(m_hWndPageList, LB_DELETESTRING, m_iPageCur, 0L);

    pPage->Destroy(m_pIStorage);

    [Other code omitted from listing]
    }

UINT CPages::CurPageSet(UINT iPage)
    {
    UINT    iPageNew
    UINT    iPagePrev=m_iPageCur;
    LPCPage  pPage;

    [Code to adjust page number omitted from listing]

    //Close the old page, committing changes.
    if (!FPageGet(iPagePrev, &pPage, FALSE))
        return -1;

    pPage->Close(TRUE);
    ...
    //Open the new page.
    FPageGet(m_iPageCur, &pPage, TRUE);

    InvalidateRect(m_hWnd, NULL, FALSE);
    UpdateWindow(m_hWnd);
    return iPagePrev;
    }
...
BOOL CPages::DevModeSet(HGLOBAL hDevMode, HGLOBAL hDevNames)
    {
    LPDEVNAMES      pdn;
    LPSTR           psz;
    DEVICECONFIG    dc;
    LPDEVMODE       pdm;
    LPSTREAM        pIStream;
    HRESULT         hr;
    ULONG           cbWrite;
    BOOL            fRet=FALSE;

    if (NULL==hDevMode || NULL==hDevNames)
        return FALSE;
```

(continued)

Listing 5-2. *continued*

```
    hr=m_pIStorage->OpenStream(SZSTREAMDEVICECONFIG, 0, STGM_DIRECT
        | STGM_WRITE | STGM_SHARE_EXCLUSIVE, 0, &pIStream);

    if (FAILED(hr))
        return FALSE;

    pdm=(LPDEVMODE)GlobalLock(hDevMode);

    if (NULL!=pdm)
        {
        dc.dm=*pdm;
        GlobalUnlock(hDevMode);
        psz=(LPSTR)GlobalLock(hDevNames);

        if (NULL!=psz)
            {
            pdn=(LPDEVNAMES)psz;
            lstrcpy(dc.szDriver, psz+pdn->wDriverOffset);
            lstrcpy(dc.szDevice, psz+pdn->wDeviceOffset);

            pIStream->Write((LPVOID)&dc, sizeof(DEVICECONFIG)
                , &cbWrite);
            GlobalUnlock(hDevNames);
            fRet=TRUE;
            }
        }
    pIStream->Release();
    if (!fRet)
        return FALSE;

    GlobalFree(hDevNames);
    GlobalFree(hDevMode);

    return ConfigureForDevice();
    }

HGLOBAL CPages::DevModeGet(void)
    {
    HGLOBAL     hMem;
    LPDEVMODE   pdm;
    ULONG       cbRead;
    LPSTREAM    pIStream;
    HRESULT     hr;
```

(continued)

Listing 5-2. *continued*

```
    hr=m_pIStorage->OpenStream(SZSTREAMDEVICECONFIG, 0, STGM_DIRECT
        | STGM_READ | STGM_SHARE_EXCLUSIVE, 0, &pIStream);

    if (FAILED(hr))
        return FALSE;

    hMem=GlobalAlloc(GHND, sizeof(DEVMODE));

    if (NULL!=hMem)
        {
        pdm=(LPDEVMODE)GlobalLock(hMem);
        pIStream->Read((LPVOID)pdm, sizeof(DEVMODE), &cbRead);
        GlobalUnlock(hMem);
        }

    pIStream->Release();
    return hMem;
    }

BOOL CPages::ConfigureForDevice(void)
    {
    POINT           ptOffset, ptPaper;
    RECT            rc;
    HDC             hDC;
    DEVICECONFIG    dc;
    HRESULT         hr;
    LPSTREAM        pIStream;
    ULONG           cbRead;

    //Read the DEVMODE and driver names from the header stream.
    hr=m_pIStorage->OpenStream(SZSTREAMDEVICECONFIG, 0, STGM_DIRECT
        | STGM_READ | STGM_SHARE_EXCLUSIVE, 0, &pIStream);

    if (FAILED(hr))
        return FALSE;

    pIStream->Read((LPVOID)&dc, sizeof(DEVICECONFIG), &cbRead);
    pIStream->Release();

    hDC=CreateIC(dc.szDriver, dc.szDevice, NULL, &dc.dm);

    [Other code omitted from listing]
    }
```

(continued)

Listing 5-2. *continued*

```
BOOL CPages::FPageGet(UINT iPage, LPCPage FAR *ppPage, BOOL fOpen)
    {
    if (NULL==ppPage)
        return FALSE;

    if (sizeof(LPCPage)==SendMessage(m_hWndPageList, LB_GETTEXT
        , iPage, (LONG)(LPVOID)ppPage))
        {
        if (fOpen)
            (*ppPage)->FOpen(m_pIStorage);

        return TRUE;
        }

    return FALSE;
    }


BOOL CPages::FPageAdd(UINT iPage, DWORD dwID, BOOL fOpenStorage)
    {
    LPCPage     pPage;
    LRESULT     lr;

    pPage=new CPage(dwID);

    if (NULL==pPage)
        return FALSE;

    if (fOpenStorage)
        pPage->FOpen(m_pIStorage);

    if (0xffff==iPage)
        iPage--;

    //Now try adding to the list box.
    lr=SendMessage(m_hWndPageList, LB_INSERTSTRING, iPage+1
        , (LONG)pPage);

    if (LB_ERRSPACE==lr)
        {
        if (fOpenStorage)
            pPage->Close(FALSE);
```

(continued)

Listing 5-2. *continued*

```
        delete pPage;
        return FALSE;
        }

    return TRUE;
    }
```

PAGE.CPP

```
[Header omitted]

CPage::CPage(DWORD dwID)
    {
    m_dwID     =dwID;
    m_pIStorage=NULL;
    return;
    }

CPage::~CPage(void)
    {
    Close(FALSE);
    return;
    }

DWORD CPage::GetID(void)
    {
    return m_dwID;
    }

BOOL CPage::FOpen(LPSTORAGE pIStorage)
    {
    BOOL        fNULL=FALSE;
    HRESULT     hr=NOERROR;
    DWORD       dwMode=STGM_TRANSACTED | STGM_READWRITE
                    | STGM_SHARE_EXCLUSIVE;
    char        szTemp[32];

    if (NULL==m_pIStorage)
        {
        fNULL=TRUE;
```

(continued)

Listing 5-2. *continued*

```
        if (NULL==pIStorage)
            return FALSE;

        /*
         * Attempt to open the storage under this ID. If none,
         * create one. In either case, the IStorage is either
         * saved in pPage or released.
         */

        wsprintf(szTemp, "Page %lu", m_dwID);

        hr=pIStorage->OpenStorage(szTemp, NULL, dwMode, NULL, 0
            , &m_pIStorage);

        if (FAILED(hr))
            {
            hr=pIStorage->CreateStorage(szTemp, dwMode, 0, 0
                , &m_pIStorage);
            }
        }
    else
        m_pIStorage->AddRef();

    if (FAILED(hr))
        {
        if (fNULL)
            m_pIStorage=NULL;

        return FALSE;
        }

    return TRUE;
    }

void CPage::Close(BOOL fCommit)
    {
    if (NULL==m_pIStorage)
        return;

    if (fCommit)
        Update();
```

(continued)

Listing 5-2. *continued*

```
    if (0==m_pIStorage->Release())
        m_pIStorage=NULL;

    return;
    }

void CPage::Update(void)
    {
    if (NULL!=m_pIStorage)
        m_pIStorage->Commit(STGC_ONLYIFCURRENT);

    return TRUE;
    }

void CPage::Destroy(LPSTORAGE pIStorage)
    {
    char            szTemp[32];

    if (NULL!=pIStorage)
        {
        if (NULL!=m_pIStorage)
            m_pIStorage->Release();

        wsprintf(szTemp, "Page %lu", m_dwID);
        pIStorage->DestroyElement(szTemp);

        m_pIStorage=NULL;
        }

    return;
    }
```

The Root Storage and Temporary Files

Patron always keeps the root storage open: If the file is untitled (from a File New command), Patron uses a temporary compound file created by passing a NULL to *StgCreateDocfile.* Note the STGM_DELETEONRELEASE flag, which should be the default for temporary files:

```
hr=StgCreateDocfile(NULL, STGM_TRANSACTED | STGM_READWRITE
    | STGM_SHARE_EXCLUSIVE | STGM_CREATE | STGM_DELETEONRELEASE
    , 0, &m_pIStorage);
```

If the file already exists on disk (opened with the File Open command), Patron opens it with *StgOpenStorage* and keeps that storage open. One of these two functions is called from *CPatronDoc::ULoad* in DOCUMENT.CPP, depending on whether the user chose File New or File Open.

Keeping a storage open in this manner is as expensive as keeping an open file using traditional file I/O: The Windows 3.1 implementation of compound files uses a file handle for each open root storage, although all substorages and streams require no additional MS-DOS resources. If you are able to tolerate the cost of keeping the root storage open, you have the benefit of keeping anything else you want open. The only cost is memory and a few file handles.

This temporary storage will be created with a pseudo-random name in the directory of your TEMP environment variable. If you specify STGM_DELETEONRELEASE, the OLE 2 libraries will keep the files cleaned out. If, however, your application crashes before releasing a temporary file or if you fail to call *IStorage::Release* the final time, you will end up with a number of these orphaned TEMP files. I suggest that you check for such files periodically during your development work.

Temporary files are also interesting in the File Save As case, which is dealt with in the later section "File Save As Operations."

Managing Substorages

As mentioned earlier, Patron manages a substorage for each page in the overall document. This, of course, means somewhat more complex code when pages are created or destroyed.

Whenever Patron creates a new page in the document, it calls *IStorage::CreateStorage* by using the name "Page *XX*," in which *XX* is the ASCII code for a DWORD page index. The code shown here is taken from PAGE.CPP in the function *CPage::FOpen,* which either creates a new substorage for a new page or opens the substorage for an existing page by using *IStorage::OpenStorage*:

```
BOOL CPage::FOpen(LPSTORAGE pIStorage)
    {
    HRESULT         hr=NOERROR;
    DWORD           dwMode=STGM_TRANSACTED | STGM_READWRITE
                        | STGM_SHARE_EXCLUSIVE;
    char            szTemp[32];

    //m_dwID is page ID (not page number) stored persistently.
    wsprintf(szTemp, "Page %lu", m_dwID);

    hr=pIStorage->OpenStorage(szTemp, NULL, dwMode, NULL, 0
        , &m_pIStorage);
```

```
if (FAILED(hr))
    {
    hr=pIStorage->CreateStorage(szTemp, dwMode, 0, 0
        , &m_pIStorage);
    }
...
```

The page identifier, *m_dwID*, is assigned when a new page is created. Each Patron document creates the first page with an ID of zero and increments the ID for each page thereafter. The next usable ID is stored persistently in the file, so the IDs continue to increment throughout the life of the document. The ordering of the pages is written into another stream as a sequence of these IDs, reflecting the positions in the document where the pages were created. IDs are not recycled when a page is destroyed, but the DWORD counter would overflow only if you sat there and created one page every second until the year 2129. I desperately hope this software is obsolete by then!

Speaking of destroying a page, this operation requires a call to *IStorage::DestroyElement* to counter the *IStorage::CreateStorage* in the preceding code. The function *CPage::Destroy* takes care of this in Patron:

```
//pIStorage is the document's root storage.
void CPage::Destroy(LPSTORAGE pIStorage)
    {
    char        szTemp[32];

    if (NULL!=pIStorage)
        {
        wsprintf(szTemp, "Page %lu", m_dwID);
        pIStorage->DestroyElement(szTemp);
        }

    return;
    }
```

The *CPage* class is a simple structure used to manage the open storage and the identifier for a page. Because it maintains its ID, we keep the code to generate a page number from that ID down in the *CPage* implementation.

Multilevel Commits

Patron opens its files in transacted mode, so it must call *IStorage::Commit* on its open storage before closing the document. Until that time, all changes, including new and deleted pages, are volatile. In other words, all these changes are only stored temporarily, and turning off your machine would only commit them to the Great Big Bit Bucket in the Sky.

Of course, we would like to commit those changes to the actual disk file instead during a File Save operation. A File Save As operation is a little different and is treated in the next section. To save changes to a file that we opened previously, we only have to call *IStorage::Commit* on the root to send all changes to disk. The catch is, however, that we have to be sure that every substorage opened in transacted mode has also been committed.

Whenever a change is made to a substorage (either a modification to an STGM_DIRECT storage or a *Commit* on an STGM_TRANSACTED storage), that change is published only to the immediate storage in which it's contained. For example, let's say I have storages A, B, and C in a compound file, like this:

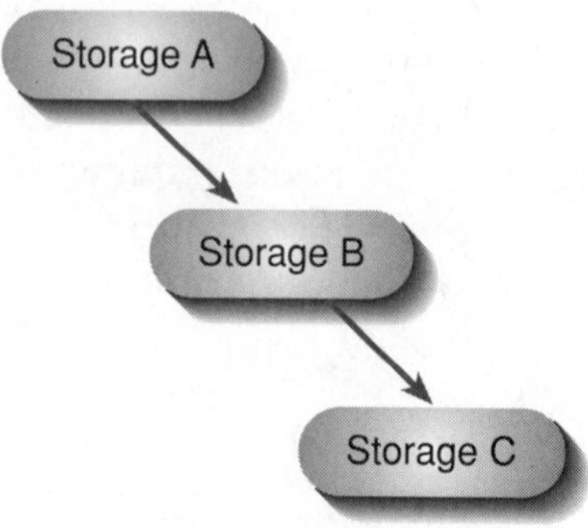
Storage A
Storage B
Storage C

If I change storage C, only storage B is aware of those changes:

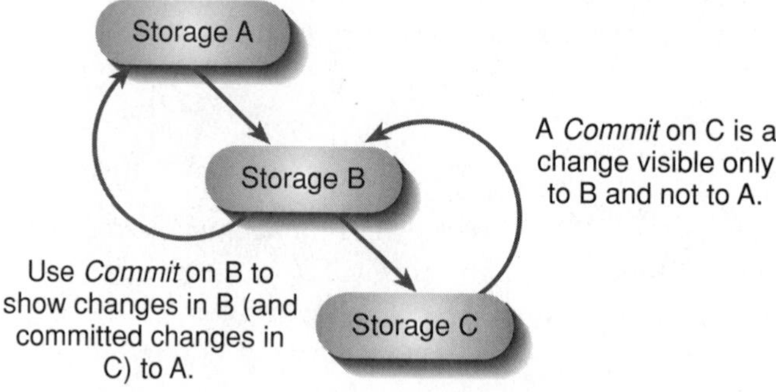
Storage A
Storage B
A *Commit* on C is a change visible only to B and not to A.
Use *Commit* on B to show changes in B (and committed changes in C) to A.
Storage C

If storage B is direct, it immediately publishes the change in C to storage A. If storage A is direct, those changes are immediately written to disk. If storage B is transacted, however, changes in C are not published to storage A until storage B is committed, just as changes to storage B (including commits) are not published to the actual disk until storage A is committed.

So the whole trick with multiple levels of transacted storages is to walk through the whole chain, being sure everything that needs committing gets committed, and then commit the root storage to actually save all the changes permanently. Patron handles this by telling the current page to commit, writing any streams that might require modification, and committing the root storage. Patron does not worry about committing any other pages because as the user switches between pages (see *CPages::FCurPageSet*), Patron calls *IStorage::Commit* and *IStorage::Release* on the current page before opening the next page. This means that when we want to commit the outermost storage, we have to commit only the current page instead of walking through all the pages to commit each in turn. This whole policy of managing pages might not be the best design, and has some consequences down the road when we deal with compound documents because switching pages will close the current page and open the new one. In this sense, switching pages is almost like closing and opening another document.

A commit can happen in a few different ways, based on one of four flags passed to *IStorage::Commit*:

Flag	Description
STGC_DEFAULT	No special semantics; simply commit changes.
STGC_ONLYIF-CURRENT	In a file-sharing scenario, this flag prevents one process from overwriting changes made in another process because the first process opened the storage. If our changes are not current, *IStorage::Commit* returns the code STG_E_NOTCURRENT on which you can attempt to merge changes or inform the user to take appropriate action.
STGC_OVERWRITE	Attempts to overwrite the entire existing file, resulting in smaller file sizes. During this operation, the state of the file is in limbo: If the machine were turned off during the process, the file would contain parts of both old and new versions. This flag is not recommended for general use.
STGC_DANGEROUSLY-COMMITMERELY-TODISKCACHE	OLE 2 designers never said they couldn't be verbose. This flag to *Commit* allows compound files to write the changes to an existing disk cache, such as Microsoft Windows' SmartDrv version 4, instead of writing to the cache and then forcing a flush of that cache (Int 21h Fn68h). Default behavior, in order to get very robust saves, is to flush the cache immediately to avoid risky disk buffering. If you want better performance for saves, you can risk using this flag, which is not any worse than using traditional file I/O as it stands today.

A sibling function to *IStorage::Commit* is *IStorage::Revert*, which dumps all the changes kept in memory or on disk for a transacted storage made since the last *Commit*. Any open substorage and stream inside a reverted storage must be closed (by calling *Release*) and reopened; otherwise, all attempts at using them will fail. In addition, if you use *Release* and *IStorage* without committing it first, you imply *Revert*—that is, you discard changes. Therefore, it is not necessary to call *Revert* on an operation such as File Close.

File Save As Operations

The use of temporary files has the interesting problem of getting all the data from that temporary file into another file with a user-specified name, such as when executing a File Save As command. Applications typically do this by creating the new file and copying the data from the temporary file into this new file, deleting the temporary file at the end of the transfer.

Compound files are no different. As we've seen already, you can use *StgCreateDocfile* to create a temporary compound file for you, as Patron does. The question is how to copy the data from the temporary file into the final destination file. One very painful way would be to somehow load all the streams and storages into memory and then write them out to the new storage. *Ouch!* I'm not sure about you, but I would not enjoy taking a few years to write this code.

Anticipating this, the OLE 2 architects kindly included *IStorage::CopyTo*, the Structured Storage Model that takes whatever data is in one storage object—regardless of whether it's a root or substorage—and copies that data into another storage. Patron uses this method when saving any file under a new name, which encompasses renaming temporary files as well as doing a Save As on an already known file.

The first step is to open the new destination file by using *StgCreateDocfile* and the STGM_CREATE flag; use of this flag means "Create the file if it's not already there, and if it is there, overwrite it completely." Most applications will use this method in Save As operations. When this new storage is open, call *CopyTo* in your currently open storage, passing the new destination storage as the fourth parameter:

```
m_pIStorage->CopyTo(NULL, NULL, NULL, pIStorage);
```

The other three parameters have to do with stream exclusion and STGM_PRIORITY, which are not covered in this book. Remember also that, if you opened the new storage with STGM_TRANSACTED, you must call *Commit* to actually save the changes to the new disk file.

When you have changed the file in which your current data lives, you generally want to keep that new file open as the active document. For this reason, you should close all substorages and streams in the original storage before *CopyTo* and reopen them later in the context of the new root storage. Otherwise, you might end up talking to the wrong file or to a file that no longer exists. Not good. Patron handles this through its policy of keeping only the current page open (a process that, as we have seen, cleans up the commit procedure somewhat) so that when it does copy from one storage to another, it merely has to close the current page, do the *CopyTo*, switch root storages, and then reopen the page. When designing your use of compound files, keep this in mind.

Low-Memory Save As Operations

When memory is low, the typical Save As operation might fail. So you are left with a bunch of uncommitted changes to the file you originally opened.

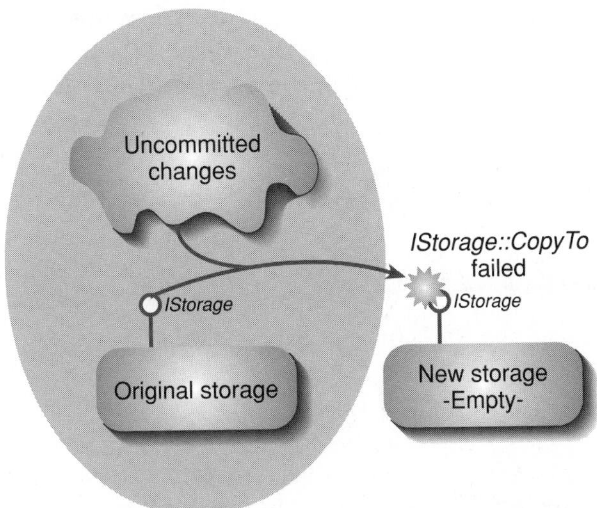

Current state of data is split between unchanged parts in the original storage and changed parts in memory.

In such a situation, you want to be able to take all uncommitted changes that live in memory and all unchanged parts of the storage that still live on disk and write them all to a new storage without taking up any more memory. In other words, you want to make a copy of the original disk file to the new file and then commit the changes into that new file.

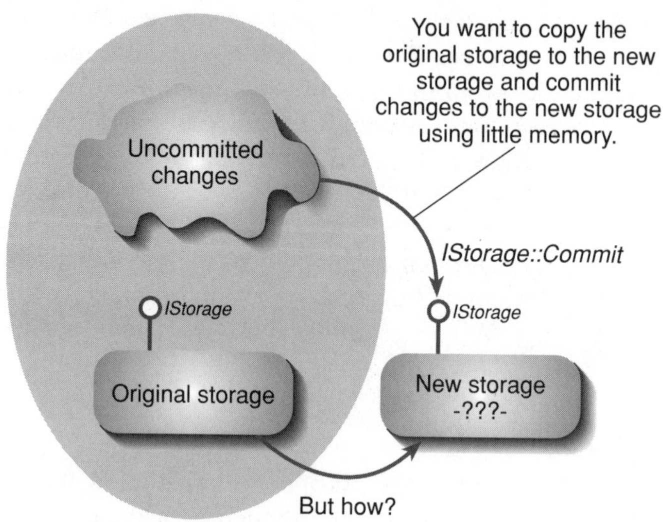

A special interface called *IRootStorage* supports just this functionality. You can obtain a pointer to this interface by calling *IStorage::QueryInterface*, with *IID_IRootStorage* on a storage object from *StgOpenStorage* or *StgCreateDoc-*

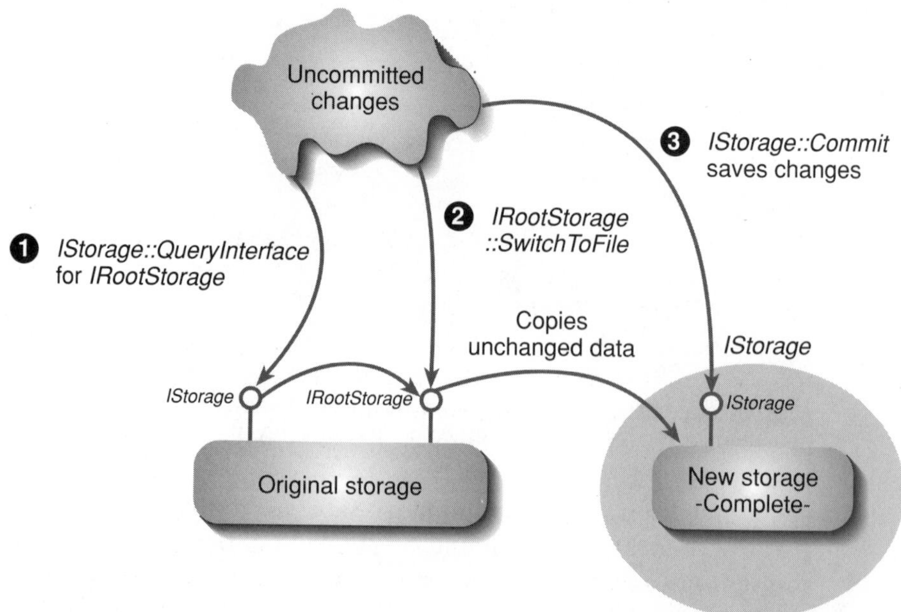

file. IRootStorage has one member function: *SwitchToFile(LPSTR pszNewFile)*, in which *pszNewFile* is the name of the new file to associate with the storage object. This effectively makes a disk copy of the original file and internally associates your *IStorage* object with that new file. You can now call *IStorage::Commit* to save changes to that new file, shown at the bottom of the preceding page.

Streams as Memory Structures

A great use for stream objects is run-time management of certain structures that eventually have to end up in your disk file. These are structures that can be persistently saved—that is, they contain no pointers or other references to values determined only at run-time. Because you will need to write some of these structures to disk anyway, it makes sense to keep them in the file in the form of streams instead of duplicating the structures in memory. Instead of having to worry about saving the structure to disk when the time comes, you can simply commit because the structures are already in a stream inside your storages.

The best candidates for this sort of treatment are structures that define a configuration for your application that is not likely to change often, because reading and writing a stream is considerably slower than performing quick pointer dereferences in memory. Some examples are a LOGFONT structure that describes the current font you are using and a DEVMODE structure that defines the printer setup for the document.

Patron saves the latter structure, DEVMODE, in a stream called "Device Configuration" that lives off the document's root storage. When a new document is created, this stream is filled with the configuration of the default printer. When the user later chooses Printer Setup, Patron first reads the contents of this stream to recreate a DEVMODE structure to pass to the common dialog box function *PrintDlg*. When *PrintDlg* returns, Patron writes the new configuration to the stream and reinitializes the display for the new parameters. Because the data lives in a stream, Patron doesn't need to perform any other steps during a File Save operation.[7]

Streams are a powerful means of managing structures, especially those that change size frequently. A common problem with memory structures is that you have to continually reallocate them as your data grows, and reallocation

7. I want to point out that Patron does not handle the case where a document created for one printer, with a specific DEVMODE, is taken to another machine without that printer installed. What will happen is that Patron will try to *CreateIC* on that information which will fail to find the driver specified in the DEVMODE. As a result, the user gets blasted with one of those ugly "Cannot find MSHPPCL5.DRV" messages. If you encounter this, remember: It's just a sample.

always requires a little more code than we'd like. A stream, on the other hand, will expand itself to accommodate a write beyond its current boundaries. In other words, the reallocation code we all hate to write is hidden down in the stream implementation.

Other OLE 2 Technologies and Structured Storage

OLE 2 makes much more use of Structured Storage and compound files than we have so far exercised in this chapter. As we'll see in Chapter 6, you can use Structured Storage as a data transfer medium much as you use global memory today. The later chapters that deal with compound documents use Structured Storage to allow compound document objects to write themselves directly into a storage object provided by the container. If the object is given a storage that already exists within the container's disk file, the object is saving itself *directly* to that file and has full incremental access to that structure because the container gives the object a storage for that object's exclusive use.

The most general use of compound-file related interfaces in OLE 2 is to provide objects with a way to answer the question "can you serialize yourself to an *x*?" where *x* might be a storage, a stream, or a file. As we learned in Chapter 3, asking such questions is the same as calling *QueryInterface* and asking for an interface that contains the functions you would like to use if you get a positive answer to your question. *QueryInterface* is the question, and the *IPersistStorage, IPersistStream,* and *IPersistFile* interfaces are the potential answers for their respective types. If you want to try serializing an object to a stream, ask it for *IPersistStream.* If it gives you one, then it's obliged to support the member functions of that interface. If it does not provide such an interface, then it's telling you that it doesn't know how to serialize itself in that way, and you cannot possibly ask it to do so.

The DLL implementation of Polyline discussed in Chapter 4 had two functions in its custom *IPolyline* interface: *ReadFromFile* and *WriteToFile.* The Component Cosmo program used these functions essentially to serialize the Polyline object. For this chapter, I have eliminated the two file-oriented functions in *IPolyline* and instead have implemented the *IPersistStorage* interface on the Polyline object itself—so that now this object supports multiple interfaces. The implementation is described in the following sections. I chose *IPersistStorage* for the object because Component Cosmo in this chapter used compound files for its file I/O, and when we turn Polyline into a compound document object in Chapter 11 we will need an implementation of *IPersistStorage.* The *IPersistFile* interface is used for servicing linked objects, so although I'll mention it here, I won't discuss any implementation until Chapter 13. The *IPersistStream* interface is not used very often in applications, so no examples in this book have a need to implement it.

The remainder of this section is split into three parts. The first describes the *IPersistStorage, IPersistStream,* and *IPersistFile* interfaces. The second details how an application such as Component Cosmo *uses* the *IPersistStorage* interface, a procedure that applies to understanding compound document container applications. The last section discusses the implementation of *IPersistStorage* on the Polyline object, an approach that will provide a good foundation for compound document work in later chapters. In this chapter, we'll cover the basics of how to use and implement objects that know how to save themselves, but there will be changes when compound documents are involved.

NOTE: The *IPersist, IPersistStorage,* and *IPersistFile* interfaces are defined in OLE2.H. However, Component Cosmo still uses *CoInitialize* and *CoUninitialize* instead of the *Ole...* variants because use of compound files and the *IPersist...* interfaces need only the *Co...* variants.

The *IPersistStorage, IPersistStream,* and *IPersistFile* Interfaces

When an object answers the question "Can you save yourself to some element," it responds with a pointer to one of three *IPersist...* interfaces. All three interfaces derive from the *IPersist* interface we discussed and implemented in the Koala object of Chapter 4. *IPersist* contributes only one member function, *GetClassID,* to the three interfaces introduced here. All the interfaces then provide information related to serialization as well as provide the actual capabilities to perform serialization. You should use them if you want to provide serialization capabilities from your own object because they are standard and published interfaces. Note that the member functions shown in Table 5-4 beginning on the following page apply only to transferring data to and from a storage medium. They imply no user interface and have no direct relationship to File menu commands. Therefore, members such as *Load* mean "Load the data," but they do not imply "Execute a File Open operation."

The two methods usually used to obtain a pointer to any one of these interfaces are to request it in a call to *IClassFactory::CreateInstance* (*CoCreateInstance* also) or to ask for it by using *QueryInterface* on some other interface pointer. All three interfaces have built-in marshaling support.

IPersistStorage	***IPersistStream***	***IPersistFile***
GetClassID	*GetClassID*	*GetClassID*
Description: Returns the CLSID of the object. A user can call this function to determine whether an object identified by the interface might be able to load a storage, stream, or file marked with another CLSID (such as with *WriteClassStg*).		
IsDirty	*IsDirty*	*IsDirty*
Description: Replies whether the object should be saved in its present state, returning SCODE S_OK if the object *is* dirty and S_FALSE if not. (An object is considered dirty if any part of its data has changed since the last time it was saved.)		
Load	*Load*	*Load*
Description: Instructs the object to load itself from a storage object, from a stream object, or from a file. Objects implementing *IPersistStorage* or *IPersistStream* usually use *AddRef* for the storage or stream object to hold on to it for incremental access. An *IPersistStorage* object will see only one *Load* call in its lifetime and will exclude the use of *InitNew*.		
Save	*Save*	*Save*
Description: Instructs the object to save itself to the element passed to this function. For *IPersistStorage*, this function is also told whether the storage object is the same as the one previously passed to *Load*, in which case the object can perform an incremental save. For *IPersistStream*, the object is told whether to reset its dirty flag. For *IPersistFile*, the object is told whether it should consider this saved file the current file or whether it should simply save a copy and forget the name.		
Save-Completed		*Save-Completed*
Description: Instructs an object that a call to *Save* is finished. See the next section "A Heavy Dose of Protocol with *IPersistStorage*" for more details.		
InitNew		
Description: When a new object is initially created, the user is contractually obligated to provide an *IStorage* in which the object can write incremental changes. The object can ignore this call or hold on to the *IStorage* with an *AddRef* for incremental access. The object can receive only one *InitNew* call in its lifetime, and use of this function precludes use of *Load*—that is, *InitNew* and *Load* are mutually exclusive.		
HandsOffStorage		
Description: Instructs the object to release any reference count it is maintaining on its storage object. The user is contractually obligated to call this only immediately after a *Save* and before a *SaveCompleted*.		

Table 5-4.
Member functions of IPersistStorage, IPersistStream, *and* IPersistFile. *(continued)*

Table 5-4. *continued*

IPersistStorage	*IPersistStream*	*IPersistFile*
	GetSizeMax	
	Description: Asks the object to return the size the stream would be if *Save* were called immediately.	
		GetCurFile
		Description: Provides the caller with the current file known to the object.

A Heavy Dose of Protocol with *IPersistStorage*

By nature, Structured Storage supports not only the capability for incremental saves but also full incremental access. This poses a few problems because many different agents can, at any given time, have various storages and streams open and uncommitted when the agent controlling the root storage wants to do a complete save, such as to a new file.

As a basis for our discussion, let's assume we have an application in control of a root storage, which in turn contains a substorage, given an object that the application is using. The object itself supports the *IPersistStorage* interface so that the application can communicate information about storage, as follows:

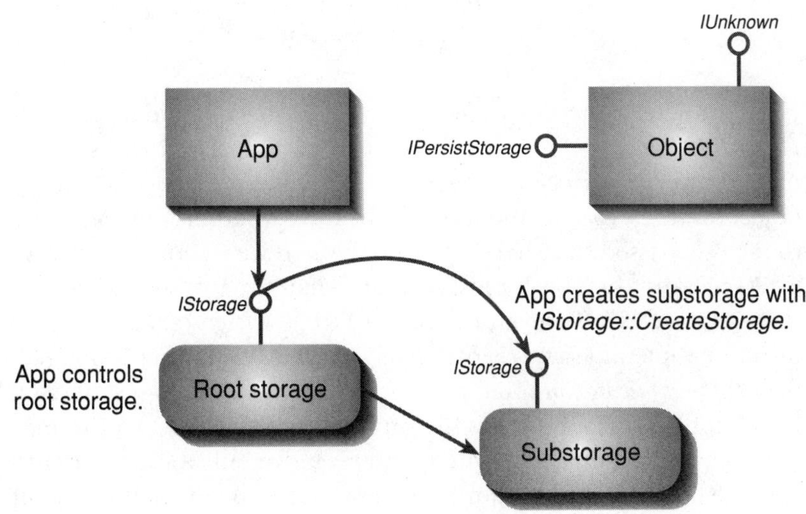

When the application creates a new file, it will create a temporary file for the root storage and create the substorage for the object. In this case, the application is required to call the object's *IPersistStorage::InitNew* function, passing the substorage's *IStorage* pointer to the new instance. Inside *InitNew*, the object can retain the *IStorage* pointer by calling *IStorage::AddRef* and saving the pointer in some variable. Similarly, when the application opens an existing file, it will reopen the substorage (with *IStorage::OpenStorage* on the root) and pass that substorage to the object's *IPersistStorage::Load*, in which the object again can retain the pointer. In either case (*InitNew* or *Load*), the object is given an *IStorage* pointer, which it can access incrementally as much as desired throughout the object's lifetime, as follows:

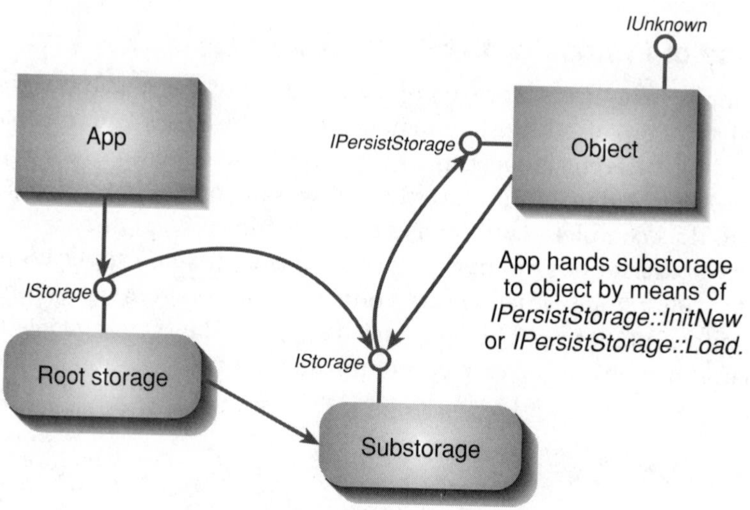

At a later time, the object will be told to save its data through a call to *IPersistStorage::Save*. *Save* is called either to perform a full save or an incremental save; in both cases, the object is given the *IStorage* pointer to a storage object in which to save and a flag indicating whether that *IStorage* is identical to the one passed to either *InitNew* or *Load*. If we're doing a full save, this flag is FALSE, and the object must recreate whatever structure it needs inside the storage object. If, however, the flag is TRUE, which means we're supposed to do an incremental save, *IPersistStorage::Save* is contractually obliged to save its data *without failing due to out-of-memory conditions*. This last statement has some heavy implications: It means that in order to fulfill this requirement, the object *must not* attempt to create new streams or substorages from within *Save* because creating them requires memory. This means that in its implementation of both *Load* and *InitNew*, the object must not only hold onto the *IStorage*

pointer, but it must also create any streams and substorages that it might need in a subsequent incremental save and hold onto those pointers as well. This is to ensure that even under very low memory conditions, the object will still be able to save. For an end user, being able to save data is everything. Of course, if you are not interested in having your application be that robust, you can freely ignore this advice. But if there's one place where you should be sure that your application is robust, it's a low-memory save situation.

In any case, after the object's *InitNew* or *Load* functions have been called, the object is in what is called the *free-access normal state,* in which the object can read and write to and from the storage object as necessary. In this normal mode, any additional calls to *InitNew* and *Load* are illegal, so you should fail, with the return code of E_UNEXPECTED.

Now one of two things might happen to the object: The application can call either *Save* or *HandsOffStorage*. As mentioned already, *Save* instructs the object to perform either an incremental or a full save. After *Save* is called, the object enters into a zombie (also termed "no-scribble") state. When the object is zombified, it cannot perform any incremental writes to the storage, although it can still read from the storage—most editing operations on this object will, in general, fail. One does not converse well with zombies. When the application will again allow the object to perform incremental writes, it calls the object's *SaveCompleted* function, which allows the object to return to normal state, as follows:

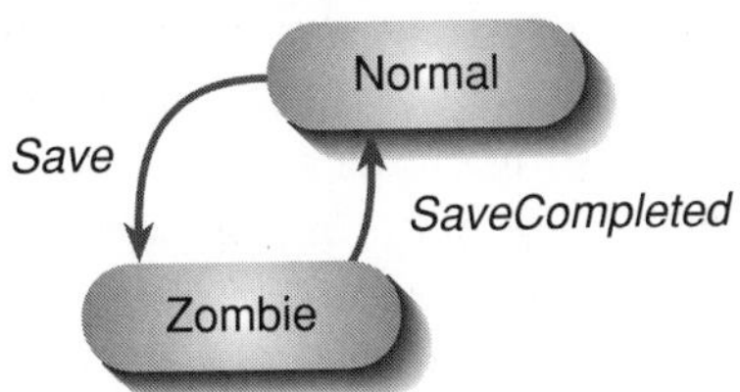

When the application wants to perform a full save, it requires that the object is not holding onto an open *IStorage*—that is, the application cannot rename or delete its root file when an object is holding onto a piece of that file. In such situations, the application will call *HandsOffStorage*. If the application calls *HandsOffStorage* without first calling *Save*, the object must shrug its shoulders, heave a heavy sigh, and blindly *Release* its held *IStorage*. However, whoever called *HandsOffStorage* must also return an *IStorage* pointer to you through *SaveCompleted* that has the same contents as the storage you had at the time of *HandsOffStorage*. In other words, you don't lose anything.

When the application calls *HandsOffStorage*, the object enters hands-off state, in which it cannot read *or* write to a storage simply because it has to call

Release on any storage on which it would even attempt such operations. Because the object has no hold on the storage, the application is free to party all over its root storage. When the application has finished partying, it must call *SaveCompleted* on the object. This call brings the object from hands-off mode to normal mode.

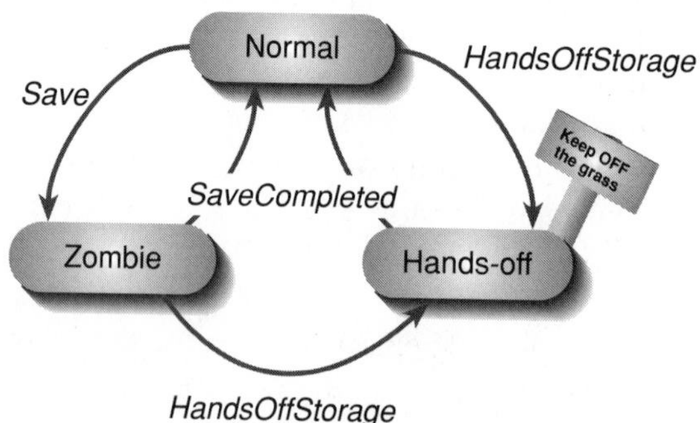

The application must always pass an *IStorage* pointer in the *SaveCompleted* call, regardless of the object's current state. The storage object identified by this pointer must always contain the structure expected by the object because the object now must retain the new storage pointer. The storage may or may not be the same as the one passed to *InitNew*, *Load*, or *Save*. If the object still has an *IStorage* pointer after *Save*, it should call *Release* through that pointer and reopen what it needs in the new one passed to *SaveCompleted*.

All of this protocol can be reduced to simple checklists for both the user of the object and the object itself. Such requirements are provided in the following two sections. Note that *IPersistFile* also has *SaveCompleted* but not *HandsOffStorage*, meaning that you must treat *IPersistFile* as you would *IPersistStorage*, ignoring the *HandsOffStorage* implications, which obviously do not apply.

Of Component Users and *IPersistStorage*: Component Cosmo

The preceding section outlined some of the responsibilities of an object user when dealing with an object through *IPersistStorage*. The Component Cosmo application is a user of the Polyline object, so because we're replacing custom file I/O members in Polyline with *IPersistStorage*, CoCosmo must follow the protocol. CoCosmo is gradually becoming a container exclusively for Polyline objects and most of the discussion in this section is pertinent to container applications. The important code changes made to CoCosmo are shown in the following code fragments, so full code listings are not provided here.

For convenience, CoCosmo always retains a pointer to the Polyline's *IPersistStorage*, first obtaining the pointer by means of *QueryInterface* after creation and releasing that pointer when freeing the object as a whole. This approach saves CoCosmo from having to use *QueryInterface* for *IPersistStorage* in the middle of a load or save operation. In the following code, *m_pIPersistStorage* is of type LPPERSISTSTORAGE:

```
BOOL CCosmoDoc::FInit(...)
    {
    ...

    hr=CoCreateInstance(CLSID_Polyline5, NULL, CLSCTX_INPROC_SERVER
        , IID_IPolyline5, (LPVOID FAR *)&m_pPL);

    if (FAILED(hr))
        return FALSE;

    hr=m_pPL->QueryInterface(IID_IPersistStorage
        , (LPLPVOID)&m_pIPersistStorage);

    if (FAILED(hr))
        return FALSE;

    ...
    }
```

When loading a file or creating a new one, CoCosmo follows its responsibilities and provides an *IStorage* pointer to the Polyline's *IPersistStorage::Load* or *IPersistStorage::InitNew*. In both cases, CoCosmo also holds onto the open *IStorage* pointer itself regardless of what Polyline does with it. CoCosmo has to maintain the pointer because Polyline might as well (and it does), which means that CoCosmo cannot reopen it again later with read-write permissions before calling *IPersistStorage::Save*. So as the following code shows, we save the pointer after calling *StgCreateDocfile* (for a new file) or *StgOpenStorage* (for an existing file):

```
//For new files
hr=StgCreateDocfile(NULL, STGM_DIRECT | STGM_READWRITE
    | STGM_CREATE | STGM_DELETEONRELEASE
    | STGM_SHARE_EXCLUSIVE, 0, &pIStorage);

if (FAILED(hr))
    return DOCERR_COULDNOTOPEN;

m_pIPersistStorage->InitNew(pIStorage);

...
```

```
//For existing files
hr=StgOpenStorage(pszFile, NULL, STGM_DIRECT | STGM_READWRITE
    | STGM_SHARE_EXCLUSIVE, NULL, 0, &pIStorage);

if (FAILED(hr))
    return DOCERR_COULDNOTOPEN;

hr=m_pIPersistStorage->Load(pIStorage);
m_pIStorage=pIStorage;
```

When saving, CoCosmo calls *IPersistStorage::Save,* passing either the existing *IStorage* saved from loading the document (for File/Save) or a new *IStorage* from *StgCreateDocfile* when writing a new file (File/Save As). When we call *Save,* we have to indicate whether or not this is a new storage through the second parameter, a BOOL called *fSameAsLoad.* After calling *Save,* we have to complete our side of the protocol by calling *SaveCompleted* with a NULL if *fSameAsLoad* was TRUE. If we created a new file, we need to call the new *IStorage* pointer. Within *SaveCompleted,* the object will reinitialize its internally held pointers:

```
LPSTORAGE           pIStorage;
BOOL                fSameAsLoad;

//If Save or Save As under the same name, do Save.
if (NULL==pszFile || 0==lstrcmpi(pszFile, m_szFile))
    {
    fRename=FALSE;
    pszFile=m_szFile;

    fSameAsLoad=TRUE;
    }
else
    {
    hr=StgCreateDocfile(pszFile, STGM_DIRECT | STGM_READWRITE
        | STGM_CREATE | STGM_SHARE_EXCLUSIVE, 0, &pIStorage);

    if (FAILED(hr))
        return DOCERR_COULDNOTOPEN;

    //Tell the object to save into this new storage
    fSameAsLoad=FALSE;

    //Update our variable
    m_pIStorage->Release();
    m_pIStorage=pIStorage;
    }
```

```
hr=m_pIPersistStorage->Save(m_pIStorage, fSameAsLoad);

if (SUCCEEDED(hr))
    {
    hr=m_pIPersistStorage->SaveCompleted(fSameAsLoad
        ? NULL : m_pIStorage);
    }
```

Of Component Objects and *IPersistStorage*: Polyline

Our good friend Polyline is on the road to becoming a full compound document object in a DLL, and part of the implementation of such an object is to support *IPersistStorage.* A number of changes had to be made to Polyline. The change most significant to our current discussion is the addition of IPERSTOR.CPP, shown in Listing 5-3. The other changes, mostly minor, occur in other files and handle the fact that Polyline now has two interfaces, *IPolyline* and *IPersistStorage*. The implementation of the latter is contained in the *CImpIPersistStorage* class implemented in Listing 5-3. Note that the IPOLY5.H file in the INC directory is a modification of IPolyline. I have removed the file-related members *ReadFromFile* and *WriteToFile* because their semantics are replaced with *IPersistStorage.*[8]

IPERSTOR.CPP

```
/*
 * Polyline Component Object Chapter 5
 *
 * Implementation of the IPersistStorage interface exposed on the
 * Polyline object.
 *
 * Copyright (c)1993 Microsoft Corporation, All Rights Reserved
 */

#include "polyline.h"

CImpIPersistStorage::CImpIPersistStorage(LPCPolyline pObj
    , LPUNKNOWN pUnkOuter)
    {
    m_cRef=0;
    m_pObj=pObj;
```

Listing 5-3. *(continued)*
The IPersistStorage *interface implementation for the Polyline object.*

8. *IPersistFile* was not used because Polyline will eventually become a compound document object, in which *IPersistStorage* is required. We also want to demonstrate compound files in this chapter, which *IPersistStorage* uses but *IPersistFile* does not necessarily use.

Listing 5-3. *continued*

```
    m_pUnkOuter=pUnkOuter;
    return;
    }

CImpIPersistStorage::~CImpIPersistStorage(void)
    {
    return;
    }

STDMETHODIMP CImpIPersistStorage::QueryInterface(REFIID riid
    , LPLPVOID ppv)
    {
    return m_pUnkOuter->QueryInterface(riid, ppv);
    }

STDMETHODIMP_(ULONG) CImpIPersistStorage::AddRef(void)
    {
    ++m_cRef;
    return m_pUnkOuter->AddRef();
    }

STDMETHODIMP_(ULONG) CImpIPersistStorage::Release(void)
    {
    --m_cRef;
    return m_pUnkOuter->Release();
    }

STDMETHODIMP CImpIPersistStorage::GetClassID(LPCLSID pClsID)
    {
    *pClsID=m_pObj->m_clsID;
    return NOERROR;
    }

STDMETHODIMP CImpIPersistStorage::IsDirty(void)
    {
    return ResultFromScode(m_pObj->m_fDirty ? S_OK : S_FALSE);
    }

STDMETHODIMP CImpIPersistStorage::InitNew(LPSTORAGE pIStorage)
    {
    HRESULT     hr;

    //This should not happen
    if (NULL!=m_pObj->m_pIStorage)
```

(continued)

Listing 5-3. *continued*

```
        return ResultFromScode(E_UNEXPECTED);

    /*
     * The rules of IPersistStorage mean we hold onto the IStorage
     * and pre-create anything we'd need in Save(...,TRUE) for
     * low-memory situations.  For us this means creating our
     * "CONTENTS" stream and holding onto that IStream as
     * well as the IStorage here (requiring an AddRef call).
     */

    hr=pIStorage->CreateStream("CONTENTS", STGM_DIRECT
        | STGM_CREATE | STGM_READWRITE | STGM_SHARE_EXCLUSIVE
        , 0, 0, &m_pObj->m_pIStream);

    if (FAILED(hr))
        return hr;

    //Initialize class information.
    WriteClassStg(pIStorage, m_pObj->m_clsID);
    WriteFmtUserTypeStg(pIStorage, m_pObj->m_cf
        , (*m_pObj->m_pST)[IDS_USERTYPE]);

    pIStorage->AddRef();
    m_pObj->m_pIStorage=pIStorage;

    return NOERROR;
    }

STDMETHODIMP CImpIPersistStorage::Load(LPSTORAGE pIStorage)
    {
    POLYLINEDATA    pl;
    ULONG           cb;
    LPSTREAM        pIStream;
    HRESULT         hr;

    //This should not happen
    if (NULL!=m_pObj->m_pIStorage)
        return ResultFromScode(E_UNEXPECTED);

    if (NULL==pIStorage)
        return ResultFromScode(STG_E_INVALIDPOINTER);

    //We don't check CLSID to remain compatible with other chapters.

    hr=pIStorage->OpenStream("CONTENTS", 0, STGM_DIRECT
        | STGM_READWRITE | STGM_SHARE_EXCLUSIVE, 0, &pIStream);
```

(continued)

Listing 5-3. *continued*

```
    if (FAILED(hr))
        return ResultFromScode(STG_E_READFAULT);

    //Read all the data into the POLYLINEDATA structure.
    hr=pIStream->Read((LPVOID)&pl, CBPOLYLINEDATA, &cb);

    if (FAILED(hr) || CBPOLYLINEDATA!=cb)
        {
        pIStream->Release();
        return hr;
        }

    /*
     * We don't call pIStream->Release here because we may need
     * it for a low-memory save in Save.  We also need to
     * hold onto a copy of pIStorage, meaning AddRef.
     */
    m_pObj->m_pIStream=pIStream;

    pIStorage->AddRef();
    m_pObj->m_pIStorage=pIStorage;

    m_pObj->m_pIPolyline->DataSet(&pl, TRUE, TRUE);
    return NOERROR;
    }

STDMETHODIMP CImpIPersistStorage::Save(LPSTORAGE pIStorage
    , BOOL fSameAsLoad)
    {
    POLYLINEDATA    pl;
    ULONG           cb;
    LPSTREAM        pIStream;
    HRESULT         hr;

    if (NULL==pIStorage)
        return ResultFromScode(STG_E_INVALIDPOINTER);

    /*
     * If we're saving to a new storage, create a new stream.
     * If fSameAsLoad it TRUE, then we write to the
     * stream we already allocated.  We should NOT depends on
     * pIStorage with fSameAsLoad is TRUE.
     */

    if (fSameAsLoad)
        {
```

(continued)

Listing 5-3. *continued*

```
        LARGE_INTEGER   li;

        /*
         * Use pre-allocated streams to avoid failures due
         * to low-memory conditions.  Be sure to reset the
         * stream pointer if you used this stream before!!
         */
        pIStream=m_pObj->m_pIStream;
        LISet32(li, 0);
        pIStream->Seek(li, STREAM_SEEK_SET, NULL);

        //This matches the Release below.
        pIStream->AddRef();
        }
    else
        {
        hr=pIStorage->CreateStream("CONTENTS", STGM_DIRECT
            | STGM_CREATE | STGM_WRITE | STGM_SHARE_EXCLUSIVE
            , 0, 0, &pIStream);

        if (FAILED(hr))
            return hr;

        //Only do this with new storages.
        WriteClassStg(pIStorage, m_pObj->m_clsID);
        WriteFmtUserTypeStg(pIStorage, m_pObj->m_cf
            , (*m_pObj->m_pST)[IDS_USERTYPE]);
        }

    //DataGet makes no allocations; it's just a memory copy.
    m_pObj->m_pIPolyline->DataGet(&pl);

    hr=pIStream->Write((LPVOID)&pl, CBPOLYLINEDATA, &cb);
    pIStream->Release();

    return (SUCCEEDED(hr) && CBPOLYLINEDATA==cb) ?
        NOERROR : ResultFromScode(STG_E_WRITEFAULT);
    }

STDMETHODIMP CImpIPersistStorage::SaveCompleted(LPSTORAGE pIStorage)
    {
    HRESULT     hr;
    LPSTREAM    pIStream;
```

(continued)

Listing 5-3. *continued*

```
    /*
     * If pIStorage is NULL, then we don't need to do anything
     * since we already have all the pointers we need for Save.
     * Otherwise we have to release any held pointers and
     * reinitialize them from pIStorage.
     */

    if (NULL!=pIStorage)
        {
        hr=pIStorage->OpenStream("CONTENTS", 0, STGM_DIRECT
            | STGM_READWRITE | STGM_SHARE_EXCLUSIVE, 0
            , &pIStream);

        if (FAILED(hr))
            return hr;

        if (NULL!=m_pObj->m_pIStream)
            m_pObj->m_pIStream->Release();

        m_pObj->m_pIStream=pIStream;

        if (NULL!=m_pObj->m_pIStorage)
            m_pObj->m_pIStorage->Release();

        m_pObj->m_pIStorage=pIStorage;
        m_pObj->m_pIStorage->AddRef();
        }

    return NOERROR;
    }

STDMETHODIMP CImpIPersistStorage::HandsOffStorage(void)
    {
    //Release held pointers
    if (NULL!=m_pObj->m_pIStream)
        {
        m_pObj->m_pIStream->Release();
        m_pObj->m_pIStream=NULL;
        }

    if (NULL!=m_pObj->m_pIStorage)
        {
        m_pObj->m_pIStorage->Release();
        m_pObj->m_pIStorage=NULL;
        }

    return NOERROR;
    }
```

You can see that most of the implementation is fairly simple. *GetClassID* and *IsDirty* are trivial, and *InitNew, SaveCompleted,* and *HandsOffStorage* need only to manage *IStorage* and *IStream* pointers for use in *Save.* These three functions demonstrate how you should maintain these pointers so that you do not need to create any new objects in *Save* under a low-memory scenario.

Polyline's *IPersistStorage::Load* function simply opens the "CONTENTS" stream, reads the data, makes the data current, and holds onto the *IStream* pointer in case we need it in *Save.* Note that because *IStorage::OpenStream* returns an *IStream* pointer with a reference count, we do not need an extra call to *AddRef* when we store that pointer in *m_pIStream.* Note also that *Load* does not concern itself with version 1 Cosmo files, so we can keep this code simple.

The implementation of *IPersistStorage::Save* is the interesting part. This function is called with a flag, *fSameAsLoad,* which tells us whether we are being asked to save into the same storage given to *InitNew* or *Load.* If we are, we already have the appropriate *IStream* pointer, which we saved in those two functions and into which we can write our current data. If you look carefully at the implementation of *Save* when *fSameAsLoad* is TRUE, you will notice that no memory is allocated, fulfilling the requirement that under low-memory conditions, we will not fail due to a lack of memory. When *fSameAsLoad* is FALSE, however, we cannot use the storage and stream pointers saved in *InitNew* and *Load*; instead we save to the storage object passed to *Save.* If we are to use that new storage as the "current" storage, we need to be sure that it will be passed to *SaveCompleted,* where we release any pointers we have been holding and reinitialize those variables from the new storage in preparation for another *Save* call later.

Compound Document Objects and Persistent Storage

All OLE 2 embedded objects must implement *IPersistStorage* as one of the three fundamental compound document object interfaces. Polyline will eventually become such an object, so it makes sense at this time to implement this portion of compound document requirements. An embedded object should not expect that the *IStorage* it receives by means of *IPersistStorage* is actually on disk, nor can it assume anything about how the storage was opened (although it can find out by using *IStorage::Stat*). Any embedded object must follow the protocol described here, regardless of the context in which it's being used.

The resulting storages created with Component Cosmo and Polyline here are identical to those generated by the version of Cosmo shown in this chapter. The only difference is that we write a different CLSID, format, and user type into the storage than Cosmo does. You can use the DFVIEW.EXE tool in the OLE 2 SDK to peek into these files and verify my claims.

Compound File Defragmentation

Because compound files inherently provide incremental saves, the physical size of a compound file on disk will typically be larger than necessary. This is because the size of the file is determined by the amount of space between the first and last sectors used by that file. This is like calculating free space on your hard disk by the location of the first and last files on it instead of by the amount of actual unused sectors: you could have two 1-KB files on a 1-GB disk, but because both are located at opposite ends of the drive, the disk is considered full.

Although this does not actually happen on hard disks, it can happen within the confines of a compound file: There might be plenty of unused space inside the file itself, but the size of that file as reported by the operating system is defined by the first and last sectors used, regardless of the internal allocation. Although free space is recycled when you write data to the compound file, there is always this possibility of internal fragmentation and larger-than-necessary files, as shown in Figure 5-6.

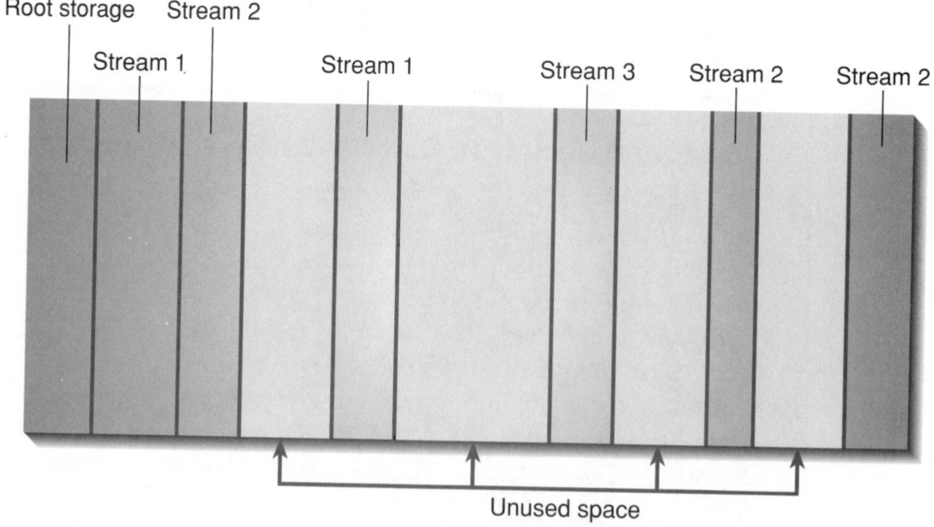

Figure 5-6.
A fragmented compound file that takes up more room than necessary on the file system.

A number of tools are commercially available to defragment your hard drive. The Smasher, utility shown in Listing 5-4, is such a tool for a compound file. Smasher is implemented as a File Manager Extension DLL that is compatible with the File Manager of both Windows 3.1 and Windows for Workgroups 3.1. In the latter system, Smasher also contributes a toolbar button, which is an additional feature of the Windows for Workgroups File Manager. Note that Smasher is written in C++, although most of it looks like straight C: The interface member calls use *pInterface->MemberFunction(...)* instead of *pInterface->lpVtbl->MemberFunction(pInterface,...)*. Other than that, there are no C++ specifics in this code.

SMASHER.CPP

```
/*
 * File Manager Extension DLL to demonstrate compound file
 * defragmentation.
 *
 * Copyright (c)1993 Microsoft Corporation, All Rights Reserved
 */

#include <windows.h>
#include <ole2.h>
#include "wfext.h"                  //Windows for Workgroups version
#include "smasher.h"

HINSTANCE   g_hInst;
BOOL        fInitialized;

//Toolbar to place on Windows for Workgroups File Manager
EXT_BUTTON btns[1]={{IDM_SMASH, IDS_SMASHHELP+1, 0}};

HANDLE FAR PASCAL LibMain(HINSTANCE hInstance, WORD wDataSeg
    , WORD cbHeapSize, LPSTR lpCmdLine)
    {
    //Remember our instance.
    g_hInst=hInstance;

    if (0!=cbHeapSize)
        UnlockData(0);

    return hInstance;
    }
```

Listing 5-4. *(continued)*
The Smasher extension for File Manager, which defragments a compound file.

Listing 5-4. *continued*

```
void FAR PASCAL WEP(int bSystemExit)
    {
    return;
    }

/*
 * FMExtensionProc
 *
 * Purpose:
 *  File Manager Extension callback function, receives messages from
 *  File Manager when extension toolbar buttons and commands are
 *  invoked.
 *
 * Parameters:
 *  hWnd            HWND of File Manager.
 *  iMsg            UINT message identifier.
 *  lParam          LONG extra information.
 */

HMENU FAR PASCAL FMExtensionProc(HWND hWnd, UINT iMsg, LONG lParam)
    {
    HMENU                hMenu=NULL;
    HRESULT              hr;
    LPMALLOC             pIMalloc;
    LPFMS_LOAD           pLoad;
    LPFMS_TOOLBARLOAD    pTool;
    LPFMS_HELPSTRING     pHelp;

    switch (iMsg)
        {
        case FMEVENT_LOAD:
            pLoad=(LPFMS_LOAD)lParam;
            pLoad->dwSize=sizeof(FMS_LOAD);

            /*
             * Check if host did CoInitialize by trying CoGetMalloc.
             * If it doesn't work, we'll CoInitialize ourselves.
             */
            hr=CoGetMalloc(MEMCTX_TASK, &pIMalloc);

            if (SUCCEEDED(hr))
                pIMalloc->Release();
            else
```

(continued)

Listing 5-4. *continued*

```
            {
            hr=CoInitialize(NULL);

            if (FAILED(hr))
                return NULL;

            fInitialized=TRUE;
            }

        //Assign the pop-up menu name for the extension.
        LoadString(g_hInst, IDS_SMASH, pLoad->szMenuName
            , sizeof(pLoad->szMenuName));

        //Load the pop-up menu.
        pLoad->hMenu=LoadMenu(g_hInst
            , MAKEINTRESOURCE(IDR_MENU));
        return pLoad->hMenu;

    case FMEVENT_UNLOAD:
        if (fInitialized)
            CoUninitialize();
        break;

    case FMEVENT_TOOLBARLOAD:
        /*
         * File Manager loaded our toolbar extension, so fill
         * the TOOLBARLOAD structure with information about our
         * buttons. This is only for Windows for Workgroups.
         */

        pTool=(LPFMS_TOOLBARLOAD)lParam;
        pTool->lpButtons= (LPEXT_BUTTON)&btns;
        pTool->cButtons = 1;
        pTool->cBitmaps = 1;
        pTool->idBitmap = IDR_BITMAP;
        break;

    case FMEVENT_HELPSTRING:
        //File Manager is requesting a status-line help string.
        pHelp=(LPFMS_HELPSTRING)lParam;

        LoadString(g_hInst, IDS_SMASHHELP+pHelp->idCommand
            , pHelp->szHelp, sizeof(pHelp->szHelp));
```

(continued)

Listing 5-4. *continued*

```
            break;

        case IDM_SMASH:
            SmashSelectedFiles(hWnd);
            break;
        }

    return hMenu;
    }

BOOL SmashSelectedFiles(HWND hWnd)
    {
    FMS_GETFILESEL  fms;
    UINT            cFiles;
    UINT            i;
    LPSTR           pszErr;
    HRESULT         hr;
    STATSTG         st;
    OFSTRUCT        of;
    LPMALLOC        pIMalloc;
    LPSTORAGE       pIStorageOld;
    LPSTORAGE       pIStorageNew;

    /*
     * Retrieve information from File Manager about the selected
     * files and allocate memory for the paths and filenames.
     */

    //Get the number of selected items.
    cFiles=(UINT)SendMessage(hWnd, FM_GETSELCOUNT, 0, 0L);

    //Nothing to do, so quit.
    if (0==cFiles)
        return TRUE;

    //Get error string memory.
    hr=CoGetMalloc(MEMCTX_TASK, &pIMalloc);

    if (FAILED(hr))
        return FALSE;

    pszErr=(LPSTR)pIMalloc->Alloc(1024);
```

(continued)

Listing 5-4. *continued*

```
/*
 * Enumerate selected files and directories with the
 * FM_GETFILESEL message. For each file, check if it's
 * a compound file (StgIsStorageFile), and if not, skip it.
 *
 * If it is a compound file, create a temp file and CopyTo
 * from old to new. If this works, we reopen the old file
 * in overwrite mode and CopyTo back into it.
 */

for (i = 0; i < cFiles; i++)
    {
    SendMessage(hWnd, FM_GETFILESEL, i, (LONG)(LPSTR)&fms);

    //Skip non-storages.
    hr=StgIsStorageFile(fms.szName);

    if (FAILED(hr))
        {
        wsprintf(pszErr, SZERRNOTACOMPOUNDFILE
            , (LPSTR)fms.szName);
        MessageBox(hWnd, pszErr, SZSMASHER, MB_OK
            | MB_ICONHAND);
        continue;
        }

    /*
     * Create a temporary file.  We don't use DELETEONRELEASE
     * in case we have to save it when copying over the old
     * file fails.
     */
    hr=StgCreateDocfile(NULL, STGM_CREATE | STGM_READWRITE
        | STGM_DIRECT | STGM_SHARE_EXCLUSIVE, 0, &pIStorageNew);

    if (FAILED(hr))
        {
        MessageBox(hWnd, SZERRTEMPFILE, SZSMASHER, MB_OK
            | MB_ICONHAND);
        continue;
        }

    //Open the existing file as read-only.
    hr=StgOpenStorage(fms.szName, NULL, STGM_DIRECT | STGM_READ
        | STGM_SHARE_DENY_WRITE, NULL, 0, &pIStorageOld);
```

(continued)

Listing 5-4. *continued*

```
        if (FAILED(hr))
            {
            pIStorageNew->Release();
            wsprintf(pszErr, SZERROPENFAILED, (LPSTR)fms.szName);
            MessageBox(hWnd, pszErr, SZSMASHER, MB_OK | MB_ICONHAND);
            continue;
            }

        /*
         * Compress with CopyTo. Because the temp is opened in
         * direct mode, changes are immediate.
         */
        hr=pIStorageOld->CopyTo(NULL, NULL, NULL, pIStorageNew);
        pIStorageOld->Release();

        if (FAILED(hr))
            {
            pIStorageNew->Release();
            MessageBox(hWnd, SZERRTEMPFILECOPY, SZSMASHER, MB_OK
                | MB_ICONHAND);
            continue;
            }

        //Temp file contains defragmented copy, try copying back.
        hr=StgOpenStorage(fms.szName, NULL, STGM_DIRECT
            | STGM_CREATE | STGM_WRITE | STGM_SHARE_EXCLUSIVE,
            NULL, 0, &pIStorageOld);

        if (FAILED(hr))
            {
            pIStorageNew->Stat(&st, 0);
            pIStorageNew->Release();

            wsprintf(pszErr, SZERRTEMPHASFILE, (LPSTR)st.pwcsName);
            pIMalloc->Free((LPVOID)st.pwcsName);

            MessageBox(hWnd, pszErr, SZSMASHER, MB_OK
                | MB_ICONHAND);
            continue;
            }

        //Copy over the old file.
        pIStorageNew->CopyTo(NULL, NULL, NULL, pIStorageOld);
        pIStorageOld->Release();
```

(continued)

Listing 5-4. *continued*

```
        //Delete the temporary file.
        pIStorageNew->Stat(&st, 0);
        pIStorageNew->Release();

        OpenFile(st.pwcsName, &of, OF_DELETE);
        pIMalloc->Free((LPVOID)st.pwcsName);
        }

    pIMalloc->Free((LPVOID)pszErr);
    pIMalloc->Release();

    return TRUE;
    }
```

Smasher's implementation is simple. First it calls *StgIsStorageFile* to check that the file is actually a compound file. Next it creates a temporary file for the defragmented copy, after which it opens the file to defragment. It then calls *CopyTo* from the original file to the temporary file, which performs the defragmentation, as shown in Figure 5-7 on the following page. It is *IStorage::CopyTo* that actually performs the defragmentation—Smasher merely tells it when.

Smasher then reopens the original file with write permissions and uses *CopyTo* to write the defragmented data from the temporary file into the new file under the original name. When this is done, Smasher closes the files and deletes the temporary one.

There are two other important points about Smasher. First, in order to delete the temporary file, it has to have a filename to pass to *OpenFile(..., OF_DELETE)*. It can obtain this filename by calling *Stat* on the temporary file, which fills a STATSTG structure pointing to the filename in *pwcsName*. As mentioned earlier, we are responsible for this string, which we must pass to the task allocator's *Free* when we have finished. We also use this task allocator to get 1 KB of scratch memory in which to generate error messages, so the function *SmashSelectedFiles* calls *CoGetMalloc* early on to obtain the allocator matching that call, with *IMalloc::Release* at the end.

Now remember again that *CoGetMalloc* returns the task allocator from *CoInitialize*. Well, File Manager is not a "Windows Object" application, and therefore it has not called *CoInitialize*. That does not stop us, however, from calling it ourselves in this DLL, which happens in the FMEVENT_LOAD case of *FMExtensionProc*. In this case, we first try *CoGetMalloc* to test whether File Manager has already called *CoInitialize*, as it will in the future. If it has not, we can go ahead and call *CoInitialize(NULL)*, making sure to match that call in FMEVENT_UNLOAD with *CoUninitialize*.

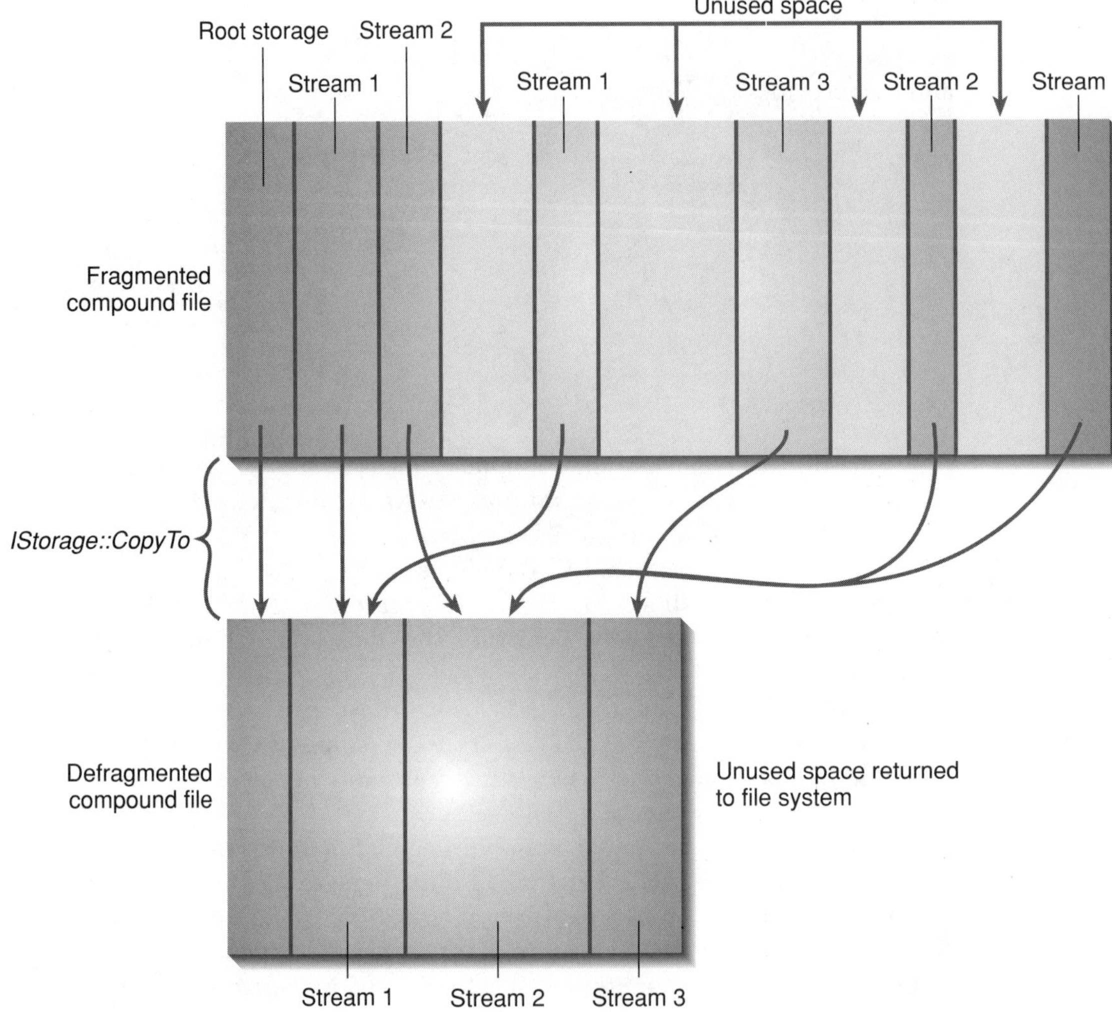

Figure 5-7.
IStorage::CopyTo *inherently defragments all storages and streams in the process of copying one compound file to another. Unused space is returned to the file system.*

If you would like more information about File Manager Extensions, please refer to your Windows 3.1 Software Development Kit.

Summary

Structured Storage is a model designed to sit on top of an existing file system and that provides shareable storage elements, which can greatly improve performance of many large data transfers as well as simplify the implementation of features such as incremental saves. The model describes a "file system within a file," with storage objects that act like directories and stream objects that act like files. Applications benefit from structuring data into a directory and file model (thereby reducing many of the uses of seek offsets) but still maintain the data within a single entity on the file system. The actual storage device is hidden from storage and stream objects by a *LockBytes* object.

The OLE 2 implementation of this model, compound files, not only can apply anywhere you would normally use traditional file I/O but also can open new possibilities for managing your application's data structures. Compound files also offer support for transactioning to further reinforce the strength of this storage model over traditional file usage. Compound files are an important part of OLE 2, as they are used in data transfer as well as in compound document implementations. Three standard interfaces define functions for objects that want to support serialization to a storage object, a stream object, or a file.

One drawback to using compound files is a potential for larger disk files that can become internally fragmented, but compound files provides its own method for defragmentation. It is therefore easy to write a defragmentation tool, as shown in this chapter.

CHAPTER SIX

UNIFORM DATA TRANSFER USING DATA OBJECTS

Have you ever flown up in an airplane and thought about all the little houses down there? If you look at them really close, they're just little piles of people's stuff.

Comedian George Carlin

Back in the early stages of Chapter 3, I defined a generic object as an instantiation of a class, in which that class is the definition of a data structure and the functions that manipulate that structure. A Windows Object, to be precise, could be seen by the user of that object only as the functions, collected into interfaces. But like all other objects, Windows Objects do have data associated with them—the object's "stuff." The question is, will that object let you look at its stuff?

A *data object*, or the *source* of data, is a general term for any Windows Object that you treat by means of the single standard data transfer interface: *IDataObject*. If a Windows Object supports this interface, you can call that object a data object and treat it as you would anything else you can call a data object. So what we mean by "data object" is different from the storage and stream objects we saw in the last chapter. To further reinforce this fact, there really isn't one single way for the object user, or *consumer* of the data, to obtain an *IDataObject* pointer to any given object; to be honest, you can obtain such a pointer by a variety of mechanisms of which two, clipboard and drag-and-drop, are the subjects of the next two chapters.

That leaves us in this chapter to define what data objects are and how they behave by means of the semantics of the *IDataObject* interface. As we'll see, all of the functionality currently distributed among the Windows API functions for the clipboard, DDE, and OLE version 1 (a data transfer mechanism) are collected together into one uniform *IDataObject* interface. So no matter what mechanism you use to obtain the pointer to a data object, you can then treat that source of data in a very standard way, which is exactly why I coined the term *Uniform Data Transfer.* OLE 2 standardizes the use of a data object, separating it from what I call a *transfer protocol.*

A transfer protocol is a mechanism for transferring an *IDataObject* pointer from the source of the data to the consumer of the data. More generically, the protocol is a mechanism to transfer information about the data—that is, to set up a standardized conversation between the source and the consumer so that they agree on the data under scrutiny. Up to this time, the actual transfer of real, tangible data has been tightly bound with the protocol used to discuss the data. In OLE 2, the functions of requesting (or setting) data are divorced from all protocols, which overall simplifies and homogenizes your application's data dealings.

Another problem with existing Windows API functions for data transfer is that both source and consumer must limit their conversations about the data to a single UINT clipboard format that describes only the data structure. In addition, the only standard medium in which that data structure can reside is global memory—no standards exist for storing and communicating data in files or other types of storage. OLE 2 introduces two new data structures that essentially provide a better clipboard format and a better global memory handle, enabling far richer description of data than a UINT can provide and far more media on which to transfer that data than a single HGLOBAL can provide. Because these structures are essential for both source and consumer, they will be an early topic, followed by an implementation of a data object as a component object.

The consumer of a data object might also be interested in notifications when the data changes in the source—that is, the consumer might want to establish a link with the source. Watch it! This idea is different from a *linked compound document object.* In this context, a link is simply a notification connection established between the source and user, not a reference to data that exists in another file, which deals with compound document links, covered in Chapters 12 and 13. OLE 2 provides an interface called *IAdviseSink* and a few member functions in the *IDataObject* interface to enable both "hot" data links (data is sent with the notification) and "warm" data links (only a notification of change is sent) such as those you can create today with DDE. In this chapter, we will look only at two member functions of *IAdviseSink.* The others must wait until we discuss compound documents. Because data objects and DDE have similarities along these lines, the last section of this chapter will discuss the important similarities and differences between these two expressions of data transfer.

Any given data object that is implemented in a DLL and that knows how to render its data in specific formats might also know how to draw a graphical representation on a device context. This chapter will also take a look at an interface called *IViewObject*, which contains this functionality, and will explain a few things about a data cache that lives inside OLE 2. Because *IViewObject* cannot be marshaled, it can be implemented only in DLLs. In any case, much of this discussion will become more significant when we deal with compound documents, but what we can exploit now is the default *IViewObject* implementation inside OLE2.DLL that knows how to draw bitmaps and metafiles. In addition, OLE2.DLL knows how to serialize the same presentations to a storage object. This chapter will demonstrate how you can freeload off OLE 2 in order to handle these normally complex functions, exchanging the tedium of painting and file I/O for bitmaps and metafiles by using a few calls to OLE 2 API functions and interfaces.

Again, this chapter will answer the question about how you obtain a pointer to a data object, but only a data object that is also a component object. How to obtain a data object representing the clipboard—that is, the OLE 2 clipboard protocol—is the subject of Chapter 7. How to obtain a data object involved through the OLE 2 drag-and-drop protocol is the subject of Chapter 8. Data objects also come up when we deal with compound documents in Chapters 9 through 11. So as you can see, there are many scenarios in which you might find yourself with a data object pointer, but you can always treat those pointers the same way. No matter how high you are flying, no matter how complex your scenario, Uniform Data Transfer and the *IDataObject* interface let you see every object down below as just a little pile of stuff.

What Is a Data Object?

Somewhere something, some Windows Object, has some data, and you want to retrieve renderings of that data. But again, how do you obtain an *IDataObject* pointer to some arbitrary source? In Chapter 4, we saw Component Objects that were identified by a CLSID and instantiated by means of functions such as *CoCreateInstance* and *IClassFactory::CreateInstance*. That is only one of the four methods by which you can obtain a pointer, as listed in the section "The Ultimate Question to Life, the Universe, and Objects" in Chapter 3. Chapter 5 looked at storage and stream objects in compound files that were obtained either by explicit API functions in STORAGE.DLL or by calling a member function in the *IStorage* interface.

In reality, you might obtain an *IDataObject* pointer by means of any of the four methods. Which one you use depends greatly on the context in which you identify the source of the data you want. In some cases, as will be demonstrated in this chapter, the data object might be its own entity, identified with a CLSID. In this case, it's not that the CLSID identifies some magical "data object" but that it identifies some object for which *IDataObject* is the primary interface.

For example, a stand-alone data object in a DLL might be the best way to expose data collection functions of a very specialized piece of hardware that you might install on your computer. Normally a board of this sort would be shipped with a DLL that exports highly customized API functions through which you could access the data. With OLE 2, such a board could ship with a Component Object in a DLL with its own CLSID so that anyone interested in accessing the data would need only to call *CoCreateInstance* with the CLSID to connect to the data source and would use the member functions of *IDataObject* to actually retrieve the data. The result? Fewer new API functions for everyone to design, implement, and learn. Furthermore, a component data object such as this, in which no outside application has any dependency on specific API functions, *is replaceable at will.* Component objects that deal exclusively through standard or well-published interfaces are truly plug-and-play components!

But I digress—I really wanted to point out that a data object can be a very specialized object or it can be simply the expression of some other type of object, such as a compound document object, as a source of data. In this case, you might obtain a pointer to *IDataObject* through *QueryInterface.* A data object might also be the object representation of some store of data, such as the clipboard, and for such cases, you might call a specific OLE 2 API function to obtain the *IDataObject* pointer. When that data is not specifically stored somewhere but is being dumped on you as in a drag-and-drop operation, you might receive the *IDataObject* pointer as a parameter to a member function that you implement yourself.

So as you can see, data objects are simply expressions of data sources through *IDataObject.* But before we get into the specifics of the interface itself, let's look at how OLE 2 allows you to describe data and the media through which you can transfer data by means of two new structures, FORMATETC and STGMEDIUM, which are defined in DVOBJ.H in the OLE 2 SDK. Note that generally DVOBJ.H contains all the definitions relevant to this chapter.

New and Improved Ultra-Structures!

The following is a paid commercial announcement.

> *Hello, friends, Ole' Bob Data here. Are you cranky because the only way to describe data is by using a lousy little clipboard format? Are you irritable because the only way to exchange data is by using a crummy global memory handle? Are you tired of wait-*

> *ing around while you try to copy a 30-MB, 24-bit, device-independent bitmap, listening to your disk chug like Grandma's old Hoover?! Well, friends, I can end your misery forever. What I have here can end hard disk swapping that sounds like a Studebaker lug nut in a meat grinder! It's New and Improved Ultra-Structures, free with every purchase of OLE 2 and free with every copy of a data object! No longer do you just say "bitmap"! No longer do you just say "metafile"! Be free! Be fresh! Send me your paycheck! Tell your data object not only that you want a bitmap but that you want it to be just a thumbnail sketch! Tell your data object not only that you want a metafile but that you want it created for a PostScript device! Tell your data object that you want every known translation of the Bible, the Koran, and the collected thoughts of Mao Tse-tung, and not just as a lousy temperamental piece of global memory but in a compound file!!! The choice is yours! How much would you be willing to pay? Five API functions? Twenty API functions? A hundred new API functions? NO! These are yours free with your qualified use of a data object! Available at a data object supplier near you.*
>
> Taxlicensinganddestinationchargesapplicablebutvoidwhereprohibitedanddoesnotincludedealerprepmarkuportheoverheadofpayingforridiculousadvertisementslikethisorthetendollarsaminuteweautomaticallychargetoeverycreditcardinyournamejustforlisteningtous.

Now back to our scheduled programming.

All versions of Windows since version 1 back in 1985 have described standardized data transfers (that is, the clipboard and DDE) using a simple clipboard format and a global memory handle. When you copy data to the clipboard, you call *SetClipboardData*, passing a clipboard format and a global memory handle. To paste, you call *GetClipboardData* with a clipboard format and again get back a global memory handle. DDE is restricted in the same fashion: WM_DDE_DATA messages carry with them only a global memory handle containing the data and an item that describes what might be in that memory.

OLE 1 suffered greatly by restricting itself to global memory data transfers. As happens with the clipboard and DDE, many copies of the same data generally sat in memory at any given moment. Small data sets are never a problem, but when an OLE 1 server supplied an object containing a large 24-bit DIB, that data had to be contained both in a metafile and in the object's native data and then shuffled to the container application using DDE, during which time another copy might be made. The container itself had to store that object's data somewhere in memory and eventually in its own disk file. This led to highly inefficient use of memory and poor performance. Something had to change.

Not only did the OLE 2 architects have to contend with the efficiency problem, but they were also faced with adding the drag-and-drop data protocol for transfer of any arbitrary data wherever the clipboard could be used.

They must have asked themselves, "Should we just do this through clipboard formats and global memory? Should OLE 2's compound document protocol continue to be hampered by multiple copies of the same data in different places? Could we let OLE 2 remain incapable of describing the device for which data was created?"

This mess simply couldn't continue to frustrate developers, and thus it became necessary to expand on the idea of data in global memory described by a clipboard format, an expansion that can still work with most of the code you already have for dealing with the clipboard or other transfer protocols. Enter two new structures, FORMATETC and STGMEDIUM.

FORMATETC (pronounced "format et cetera") is a generalization, and an improvement, of the clipboard format, and contains a rich description of data. The name comes from the idea that it contains a clipboard format and, well, some more stuff—the et cetera:

- *cfFormat* (UINT): The clipboard format identifying the structure of the data. This can be a standard format, such as CF_TEXT, or a registered format that both source and consumer register.
- *ptd* (LPTARGETDEVICE): Information about the device, such as a screen or printer, for which the data was rendered, contained in a TARGETDEVICE structure that looks and acts similar to a DEVNAMES structure. The structure itself is simply a header for a variable-length block of data, and each offset in the structure points to a specific piece of information in the block:

```
typedef struct FARSTRUCT tagDVTARGETDEVICE
    {
    DWORD   tdSize;
    WORD    tdDriverNameOffset;
    WORD    tdDeviceNameOffset;
    WORD    tdPortNameOffset;
    WORD    tdExtDevmodeOffset;
    BYTE    tdData[1];    //Contains the names and DEVMODE
    } DVTARGETDEVICE;
```

  tdSize always holds the size of the entire structure, including all additional bytes that occur after the DVTARGETDEVICE header. This simplifies copying the structure when necessary. In addition, each of the other *td... Offset* fields is an offset from the start of the entire structure, not from the start of *tdData*. This is so that a zero in one of the offsets means "not present" or a NULL value for that name.

- *dwAspect* (DWORD): How much detail is contained in the rendering? The full content (DVASPECT_CONTENT), as would normally be shown in some kind of document? A thumbnail sketch (DVASPECT_THUMBNAIL), as would be used in a print preview or document preview window, or an icon (DVASPECT_ICON), as would be appropriate for small presentations such as in e-mail messages? Or a full "printer document" (DVASPECT_DOCPRINT) that includes all page numbers, headers, footers, just as if the data were printed as a document from its native application?
- *lindex* (LONG): Identifier for the "piece" of the data when the data must be split across page boundaries. An *lindex* of –1 identifies the entire data and is the most common value. Otherwise, *lindex* only has meaning in DVASPECT_CONTENT, in which it identifies a piece of data for extended layout negotiation, and in DVASPECT_DOCPRINT, in which it identifies the page number.

  NOTE: Page-layout capabilities are not supported in OLE version 2, but they will be implemented in future versions of the libraries. Therefore, the *lindex* in any FORMATETC should always be –1. The debug OLE 2 libraries will display assertion failures if you forget.

- *tymed* (DWORD): The medium in which the data lives. See the following discussion of STGMEDIUM.

Obviously, filling out an array like this every time you want to describe a data format will grow tedious. You would have to create five lines of code simply to fill the structure. For this reason, I have defined two macros in INC\BOOKGUID.H (which is included in all the samples after Chapter 2) that facilitate filling a FORMATETC: *SETFormatEtc*, which allows you to set every field in a FORMATETC structure explicitly, and *SETDefFormatEtc*, which allows you to set *cfFormat* and *tymed* while filling the other fields with defaults:

```
#define SETFormatEtc(fe, cf, asp, td, med, li)   \
    {\
    (fe).cfFormat=cf;\
    (fe).dwAspect=asp;\
    (fe).ptd=td;\
    (fe).tymed=med;\
    (fe).lindex=li;\
    };

#define SETDefFormatEtc(fe, cf, med)   \
    {\
```

(continued)

```
(fe).cfFormat=cf;\
(fe).dwAspect=DVASPECT_CONTENT;\
(fe).ptd=NULL;\
(fe).tymed=med;\
(fe).lindex=-1;\
};
```

I encourage you to use these macros to make your life easier when programming data objects. You frequently need to fill FORMATETC structures, and these macros conveniently reduce the filling to one line. The OLE 2 SDK also has a file named OLESTD.H that defines similar macros called SETFORMATETC and SETDEFFORMATETC. I use my own definitions because many of the samples in this book do not have occasion to use anything else in OLESTD.H but will generally use BOOKGUID.H.

FORMATETC is only half of the picture, of course, because it describes only what is contained in some actual rendering of the data. We still need some reference to that data, so STGMEDIUM ("storage medium") is a generalization of the global memory handle and holds a mixture of different data references:

- *tymed* (DWORD): An identifier for the type of medium used: global memory (TYMED_HGLOBAL), disk file (TYMED_FILE), storage object (TYMED_ISTORAGE), stream object (TYMED_ISTREAM), GDI object (TYMED_GDI), METAFILEPICT (TYMED_MFPICT), or undefined (TYMED_NULL).
- *hGlobal-lpszFileName-pStg-pStm* (union of HGLOBAL, LPSTR, LPSTORAGE, and LPSTREAM): A reference to the actual data, the meaning of which is defined by *tymed.* Medium types TYMED_HGLOBAL, TYMED_GDI, and TYMED_MFPICT store their memory or GDI handles in *hGlobal.* TYMED_FILE stores a pointer to the filename in *lpszFileName,* and TYMED_ISTORAGE and TYMED_ISTREAM store pointers to their objects in *pStg* and *pStm,* respectively.
- *pUnkForRelease* (LPUNKNOWN): The *IUnknown* interface of some object that knows how to free the allocations in the STGMEDIUM. If non-NULL, the owner of the rendering (typically, the consumer) must call *pUnkForRelease->Release()* to free the data. This is handled through the function *ReleaseStgMedium* (see below).

The FORMATETC and STGMEDIUM structures open up a wide range of possibilities in data transfer and solve a number of the key problems with previous protocols and data transfer techniques. The most fundamental benefit of these richer descriptions is that data no longer *has* to live in global memory. If the data is best suited to live in a disk file, you can describe that fact by using TYMED_FILE. If the data is best suited to living in a storage or stream object, you can express that by using TYMED_ISTORAGE or TYMED-_ISTREAM. For example, very large bitmaps that do not fit in memory can be kept by the source application in a storage object (that is, a compound file) on disk. When another application wants a copy of a bitmap, the source can copy that data to a new temporary compound file (by using *StgCreateDocfile(NULL, ...)* and *IStorage::CopyTo*) and pass the new *IStorage* pointer in an STGMEDIUM structure. The consumer receives the marshaled *IStorage* pointer and can incrementally access that bitmap as necessary. So in all, very little memory is used; instead, transfer uses more available disk space. Furthermore, such large data will typically end up on disk anyway, so it makes sense to put the data there in the first place.

Consumers of data (that is, of an STGMEDIUM) usually become responsible to free the data after they have finished with it. One potential difficulty with the richness of STGMEDIUM is figuring out how to free whatever might be in it. Already you should have the image of a big *switch(stm.tymed)* statement floating in your head, which would call the appropriate API function, depending on the actual data reference in the structure. Don't bother—OLE 2 provides a single API function to perform cleanup on any STGMEDIUM: *ReleaseStgMedium*. The actual call made to free the STGMEDIUM varies with the medium type:

tymed	Freeing Mechanism
Any	If *pUnkForRelease* is not NULL, *pUnkForRelease->Release()* is always called.
TYMED_HGLOBAL	*GlobalFree(hGlobal).*
TYMED_FILE	*OpenFile(lpszFileName, &of, OF_DELETE)* along with *CoGetMalloc(MEMCTX_TASK, &pIMalloc), pIMalloc->Free-(lpszFileName),* and *pIMalloc->Release().* That is, the filename is assumed to be allocated with the task allocator.
TYMED_ISTORAGE	*pStg->Release().*
TYMED_ISTREAM	*pStm->Release().*
TYMED_GDI	*DeleteObject((HGDIOBJ)hGlobal).*
TYMED_MFPICT	*LPMETAFILEPICT pMFP;* *pMFP=GlobalLock(hGlobal);* *DeleteMetaFile(pMFP->hMF);* *GlobalUnlock(hGlobal)* *GlobalFree(hGlobal).*

Providing the *ReleaseStgMedium* API is exactly why the *tymed* fields of both STGMEDIUM and FORMATETC differentiate between handles for global memory, GDI objects, and metafile pictures: Only with such precise identification can *ReleaseStgMedium* know how to perform cleanup correctly.

Data Objects and the *IDataObject* Interface

Any agent that can be considered a source of data can describe its data by providing a data object on which is implemented the *IDataObject* interface. A data object is one view of a Compound Document object, as we'll see in Chapters 9 through 11, but any and all code that in one way or another has data to share can describe that data as a data object through *IDataObject.* The great benefit of doing this is that once you have a *single* data object around, you can use that data object in any transfer protocol, be it clipboard, drag-and-drop, or compound document. As a source, you will centralize the code that renders data into this data object. As a consumer, you will centralize the code necessary to check whether the data available from a data object is actually usable and centralize the code used to paste that data. Such centralization reduces the overall amount of code you must implement, as well as reducing the number of different API functions for dealing with each protocol.

Centralization is possible because the *IDataObject* interface combines the functionality of the existing data transfer protocols, thereby providing more functionality in an OLE2 data transfer than is available for any other existing protocol. The definition of the *IDataObject* interface is as follows (the ubiquitous *IUnknown* members are omitted):

```
DECLARE_INTERFACE_(IDataObject, IUnknown)
    {
    [IUnknown methods included]

    //IDataObject methods
    STDMETHOD(GetData) (THIS_ LPFORMATETC pformatetcIn,
        LPSTGMEDIUM pmedium ) PURE;
    STDMETHOD(GetDataHere) (THIS_ LPFORMATETC pformatetc,
        LPSTGMEDIUM pmedium ) PURE;
    STDMETHOD(QueryGetData) (THIS_ LPFORMATETC pformatetc ) PURE;
    STDMETHOD(GetCanonicalFormatEtc) (THIS_ LPFORMATETC pformatetc,
        LPFORMATETC pformatetcOut) PURE;
    STDMETHOD(SetData) (THIS_ LPFORMATETC pformatetc,
        STGMEDIUM FAR * pmedium, BOOL fRelease) PURE;
    STDMETHOD(EnumFormatEtc) (THIS_ DWORD dwDirection,
        LPENUMFORMATETC FAR* ppenumFormatEtc) PURE;
```

```
STDMETHOD(DAdvise) (THIS_ FORMATETC FAR* pFormatetc, DWORD advf,
    LPADVISESINK pAdvSink, DWORD FAR* pdwConnection) PURE;
STDMETHOD(DUnadvise) (THIS_ DWORD dwConnection) PURE;
STDMETHOD(EnumDAdvise) (THIS_ LPENUMSTATDATA FAR* ppenumAdvise) PURE;
};

typedef     IDataObject FAR* LPDATAOBJECT;
```

Many of the member functions have equivalents in specific Windows API functions; keep in mind, however, that data objects are used to describe data transferred by means of *any* protocol, and thus they provide the ability to treat data in a uniform fashion regardless of how you obtained the *IDataObject* pointer. The following list describes each *IDataObject* member in a little more detail and lists the similar (but not always exact) functionality that currently exists in the clipboard, DDE, and OLE 1 transfer protocols. Drag-and-drop is not present in this list because it's a new feature provided in OLE 2 and is simply another way to perform a clipboard-like transfer.

- *GetData* renders the data described by a FORMATETC and returns it in the STGMEDIUM, which then becomes the caller's responsibility.

Protocol	Similar Windows API Function or Message
Clipboard	*GetClipboardData*
DDE	WM_DDE_REQUEST, WM_DDE_DATA
OLE 1	*OleGetData*

- *SetData* provides data to the source described by a FORMATETC and referenced by an STGMEDIUM. The data object is responsible for releasing the data if the *fRelease* flag is TRUE.

Protocol	Similar Windows API Function or Message
Clipboard	*SetClipboardData*
DDE	WM_DDE_POKE
OLE 1	*OleSetData*

- *GetDataHere* allows the caller to provide an already allocated medium into which the data object should render the data. For example, if the caller provides an *IStream* object and asks for CF_BITMAP, the object should serialize its bitmap into that stream instead of allocating a new stream on its own as it would do in *GetData*. This capability is not present in any other existing data transfer mechanisms.

- *QueryGetData* answers whether the data object is capable of rendering data described by a specific FORMATETC structure. The caller can be as specific as desired. *QueryGetData* returns NOERROR for "yes" or S_FALSE for "no," so *don't* use the SUCCEEDED or FAILED macros to test return values; compare directly with NOERROR.

Protocol	Similar Windows API Function or Message
Clipboard	*IsClipboardFormatAvailable*
DDE	None (perhaps handled through WM_DDE_CONNECT, ADVISE)
OLE 1	None

- *GetCanonicalFormatEtc* provides a different but logically equivalent FORMATETC structure, allowing the caller to determine whether a rendering it has already obtained is identical to what would be obtained by calling *GetData* with a different FORMATETC. Use of this function can eliminate unnecessary calls to *GetData.* Note that the *tymed* field in the FORMATETC structure is irrelevant here, so it should be ignored. There is no equivalent to this function in any existing protocol.
- *EnumFormatEtc* instantiates and returns a FORMATETC enumerator object through which the caller can determine all available FORMATETCs that the object can possibly provide. There must be a unique element in the enumeration for each *cfFormat, dwAspect,* and *ptd* variation, although you can combine TYMED_... values in *tymed.* The enumerator object implements the single *IEnumFORMATETC* interface, and the caller is responsible for calling *IEnumFORMATETC::Release* when it has finished to allow the object to free itself. The caller can ask for an enumerator for either direction, *GetData* or *SetData.* See the next section, "FORMATETC Enumerators and Format Ordering," for more details on this enumerator.

Protocol	Similar Windows API Function
Clipboard	*EnumClipboardFormats* (get direction only)
DDE	None
OLE 1	None

- *DAdvise*[1] sets up an advisory connection between the data object and a caller, providing an advise sink, in which the caller indicates the data of interest in a FORMATETC. The data object calls *IAdviseSink::OnDataChange* when a change occurs, possibly sending the data along with the notification.

Protocol	Similar Windows Message
Clipboard	None
DDE	WM_DDE_ADVISE
OLE 1	None

- *DUnadvise* terminates an advisory connection previously established with *DAdvise*.

Protocol	Similar Windows Message
Clipboard	None
DDE	WM_DDE_UNADVISE
OLE 1	None

- *EnumDAdvise* returns an enumerator with the *IEnumSTATDATA* interface. There is no equivalent to this function in any existing protocol. For more information, see the *OLE 2 Programmer's Reference*.

You can see from the preceding list that no single existing protocol supports the full range of functionality that OLE 2 data objects provide for all the protocols. This is not to say that any arbitrary data object you obtain from a clipboard transfer will actually implement every member function. Some data objects, such as a static bitmap on the clipboard, will refuse any advisory connections. Others might not support any *SetData* calls. But you are always allowed to try to learn the data object's capabilities through error return values. With existing protocols, you are not even allowed to play a little.

The next few sections deal with how to both implement and use a general data object implemented as a component object. The samples shown in these sections contain more code than is relevant for this immediate discussion because they also serve the later discussion of notification in the section "Advising and Notification with Data Objects."

---

1. The *D* in the function names identify these functions as belonging to *IDataObject*. Prior to the release of OLE2, both *IDataObject* and *IOleObject* had the member functions *Advise*, *Unadvise*, and *EnumAdvise*, which played havoc on objects that used multiple inheritance. To ensure that the names will not conflict, *IDataObject*'s members are *DAdvise*, *DUnadvise*, and *EnumDAdvise*, whereas those in *IOleObject* remain *Advise*, *Unadvise*, and *EnumAdvise*.

FORMATETC Enumerators and Format Ordering

IDataObject::EnumFormatEtc is responsible for creating and returning an *IEnumFORMATETC* pointer on a FORMATETC enumerator to the caller, in which that enumerator knows either the formats obtainable from *IDataObject::GetData* or the formats that can be sent to *IDataObject::SetData.* These enumerators share the same member functions as all *IEnum...* interfaces: *Next, Skip, Reset,* and *Clone.* They merely deal with FORMATETC structures instead of some other type.

As we saw in Chapter 3, an enumerator is simple to implement, given an array of the structures it should enumerate. *IEnumFORMATETC* is, in fact, just about the only enumerator interface that most applications will have occasion to implement because the exact sequence and contents of the FORMATETCs enumerated are application-specific. Even so, such an enumerator, given a pointer to an array of structures and a count of structures, can be reduced to a reasonably standard implementation, as shown in the *CEnumFormatEtc* object in Listing 6-1. The code shown is contained in the INTERFAC directory as IENUMFE.H and IENUMFE.CPP, which provide a full enumerator implementation that you can simply drop into your own code and use without any modifications except for the *#include* at the top of IENUMFE.CPP.

IENUMFE.H

```
/*
 * Definitions of a template IDataObject interface implementation.
 *
 * Copyright (c)1993 Microsoft Corporation, All Rights Reserved
 */

#ifndef _IENUMFE_H_
#define _IENUMFE_H_

/*
 * IEnumFORMATETC object that is created from
 * IDataObject::EnumFormatEtc. This object lives on its own,
 * that is, QueryInterface only knows IUnknown and IEnumFormatEtc,
 * nothing more. We still use an outer unknown for reference
 * counting, because as long as this enumerator lives, the data
 * object should live, thereby keeping the application up.
 */
```

Listing 6-1.

The IENUMFE.H and IENUMFE.CPP implementations of an IEnumFORMATETC *object.*

(continued)

Listing 6-1. *continued*

```
class __far CEnumFormatEtc;
typedef class CEnumFormatEtc FAR *LPCEnumFormatEtc;

class __far CEnumFormatEtc : public IEnumFORMATETC
    {
    private:
        ULONG           m_cRef;         //Object reference count
        LPUNKNOWN       m_pUnkRef;      //IUnknown for ref counting
        ULONG           m_iCur;         //Current element
        ULONG           m_cfe;          //Number of FORMATETCs in us
        LPFORMATETC     m_prgfe;        //Source of FORMATETCs

    public:
        CEnumFormatEtc(LPUNKNOWN, ULONG, LPFORMATETC);
        ~CEnumFormatEtc(void);

        //IUnknown members that delegate to m_pUnkOuter.
        STDMETHODIMP         QueryInterface(REFIID, LPVOID FAR *);
        STDMETHODIMP_(ULONG) AddRef(void);
        STDMETHODIMP_(ULONG) Release(void);

        //IEnumFORMATETC members
        STDMETHODIMP Next(ULONG, LPFORMATETC, ULONG FAR *);
        STDMETHODIMP Skip(ULONG);
        STDMETHODIMP Reset(void);
        STDMETHODIMP Clone(IEnumFORMATETC FAR * FAR *);
    };

#endif //_IENUMFE_H_
```

IENUMFE.CPP

```
/*
 * Standard implementation of a FORMATETC enumerator with the
 * IEnumFORMATETC interface that will generally not need
 * modification.
 *
 * Copyright (c)1993 Microsoft Corporation, All Rights Reserved
 */

#include "ienumfe.h"
```

(continued)

Listing 6-1. *continued*

```
/*
 * CEnumFormatEtc::CEnumFormatEtc
 * CEnumFormatEtc::~CEnumFormatEtc
 *
 * Parameters (Constructor):
 *  pUnkRef         LPUNKNOWN to use for reference counting.
 *  cFE             ULONG number of FORMATETCs in pFE.
 *  prgFE           LPFORMATETC to the array over which to enumerate.
 */

CEnumFormatEtc::CEnumFormatEtc(LPUNKNOWN pUnkRef, ULONG cFE
    , LPFORMATETC prgFE)
    {
    UINT        i;

    m_cRef=0;
    m_pUnkRef=pUnkRef;

    m_iCur=0;
    m_cfe=cFE;
    m_prgfe=new FORMATETC[(UINT)cFE];

    if (NULL!=m_prgfe)
        {
        for (i=0; i < cFE; i++)
            m_prgfe[i]=prgFE[i];
        }

    return;
    }

CEnumFormatEtc::~CEnumFormatEtc(void)
    {
    if (NULL!=m_prgfe)
        delete [] m_prgfe;

    return;
    }

STDMETHODIMP CEnumFormatEtc::QueryInterface(REFIID riid
    , LPLPVOID ppv)
    {
    *ppv=NULL;
```

(continued)

Listing 6-1. *continued*

```
    /*
     * Enumerators are separate objects, not the data object, so
     * we only need to support our IUnknown and IEnumFORMATETC
     * interfaces here with no concern for aggregation.
     */
    if (IsEqualIID(riid, IID_IUnknown)
        || IsEqualIID(riid, IID_IEnumFORMATETC))
        *ppv=(LPVOID)this;

    if (NULL!=*ppv)
        {
        ((LPUNKNOWN)*ppv)->AddRef();
        return NOERROR;
        }

    return ResultFromScode(E_NOINTERFACE);
    }

STDMETHODIMP_(ULONG) CEnumFormatEtc::AddRef(void)
    {
    ++m_cRef;
    m_pUnkRef->AddRef();
    return m_cRef;
    }

STDMETHODIMP_(ULONG) CEnumFormatEtc::Release(void)
    {
    ULONG       cRefT;

    cRefT=--m_cRef;

    m_pUnkRef->Release();

    if (0==m_cRef)
        delete this;

    return cRefT;
    }

STDMETHODIMP CEnumFormatEtc::Next(ULONG cFE, LPFORMATETC pFE
    , ULONG FAR * pulFE)
    {
    ULONG               cReturn=0L;
```

(continued)

Listing 6-1. *continued*

```
    if (NULL==m_prgfe)
        return ResultFromScode(S_FALSE);

    if (NULL!=pulFE)
        *pulFE=0L;

    if (NULL==pFE || m_iCur >= m_cfe)
        return ResultFromScode(S_FALSE);

    while (m_iCur < m_cfe && cFE > 0)
        {
        *pFE++=m_prgfe[m_iCur++];
        cReturn++;
        cFE--;
        }

    if (NULL!=pulFE)
        *pulFE=(cReturn-cFE);

    return NOERROR;
    }

STDMETHODIMP CEnumFormatEtc::Skip(ULONG cSkip)
    {
    if (((m_iCur+cSkip) >= m_cfe) || NULL==m_prgfe)
        return ResultFromScode(S_FALSE);

    m_iCur+=cSkip;
    return NOERROR;
    }

STDMETHODIMP CEnumFormatEtc::Reset(void)
    {
    m_iCur=0;
    return NOERROR;
    }

STDMETHODIMP CEnumFormatEtc::Clone(LPENUMFORMATETC FAR *ppEnum)
    {
    LPCEnumFormatEtc    pNew;

    *ppEnum=NULL;

    //Create the clone.
    pNew=new CEnumFormatEtc(m_pUnkRef, m_cfe, m_prgfe);
```

(continued)

Listing 6-1. *continued*

```
    if (NULL==pNew)
        return ResultFromScode(E_OUTOFMEMORY);

    pNew->AddRef();
    pNew->m_iCur=m_iCur;

    *ppEnum=pNew;
    return NOERROR;
    }
```

You'll notice first that the class used to implement this enumerator is named *CEnumFormatEtc.* We're implementing a fairly independent object with one interface, so this is not something we classify as an interface implementation. This enumerator object maintains its own reference count, an index of the current element, a count of elements, and an array of FORMATETCs that define the elements. The count and the array are provided by the data object through the *CEnumFormatEtc* constructor; the enumerator makes a snapshot copy of the FORMATETC array. Note that the only difference between a *GetData* enumerator and a *SetData* enumerator would be the actual FORMATETCs enumerated; the data object, when creating either enumerator, can simply pass the appropriate array and count to the *CEnumFormatEtc* constructor.

The enumerator's *QueryInterface* only knows *IUnknown* and *IEnumFORMATETC*; it should *not* know *IDataObject* or any other interface. This does not mean, however, that the enumerator is *entirely* independent, because it makes little sense to have an enumerator around when the data object that created it has already been destroyed (that is, the enumerator has lost its context). Therefore, the enumerator takes a third parameter to its constructor, an LPUNKNOWN to use for reference counting, but not for *QueryInterface.* This *IUnknown* should be the controlling unknown that is used by the data object's *IDataObject* interface implementation itself, as we'll see in the next section. When the enumerator gets an *AddRef* or a *Release,* it also calls *AddRef* or *Release* on this reference-counting *IUnknown.* This approach guarantees that the data object that defines the context of the enumerator will remain at least as long as the enumerator itself remains. Of course, this is simply my design; I'm sure others are equally valid.

As mentioned in the previous section, *IDataObject::EnumFormatEtc* is the logical equivalent of the *EnumClipboardFormats* API function in Windows. Therefore, the order of formats enumerated through *IEnumFORMATETC* should be exactly the same as the order in which you would place data on the clipboard using *SetClipboardData*, typically ranging from high-fidelity formats to low-fidelity formats. This usually results in a sequence starting with your private data formats, then other standard interchange formats, followed by picture or graphic formats such as CF_METAFILEPICT and CF_BITMAP. As we'll see in later chapters, OLE 2 introduces a number of new clipboard formats for compound document use that you wedge between your existing formats because some OLE 2 formats are better descriptions of data than something like CF_BITMAP.

So let's see a data object that uses *CEnumFormatEtc*.

Component Data Objects

Implementing a data object is generally the same as implementing some general object with an *IDataObject* interface. The object might have more interfaces as well, but the one of importance here is *IDataObject*. The code shown in Listing 6-2 is an implementation of a data object in both DLL (CHAP06\DDATAOBJ) and EXE (CHAP06\EDATAOBJ) using the same module housing we implemented for the Koala objects in Chapter 4. Note that both DDATAOBJ and EDATAOBJ use the same *CEnumFormatEtc* class shown in Listing 6-1, so that code is not repeated here. Also, the internal functions *RenderText*, *RenderBitmap*, and *RenderMetafilePict* (private members of the *CDataObject* class) are not shown. You can find them in the RENDER.CPP file in the sample code.

DATAOBJ.CPP

```
/*
 * Data Object Chapter 6
 *
 * Implementation of CDataObject and CImpIDataObject that work
 * in either an EXE or DLL.
 *
 * Copyright (c)1993 Microsoft Corporation, All Rights Reserved
 *
 */

#include "dataobj.h"

extern HINSTANCE   g_hInst;
```

Listing 6-2. *(continued)*

A data object implementation. DATAOBJ.CPP contains the object, and IDATAOBJ.CPP contains the interface implementation.

Listing 6-2. *continued*

```
DWORD               g_dwID=0;

//Names of data sizes
static char  * rgszSize[3]={"Small", "Medium", "Large"};

CDataObject::CDataObject(LPUNKNOWN pUnkOuter
    , LPFNDESTROYED pfnDestroy, UINT iSize)
    {
    UINT        i;

    m_cRef=0;
    m_pUnkOuter=pUnkOuter;
    m_pfnDestroy=pfnDestroy;
    m_iSize=iSize;

    m_hWndAdvise=NULL;
    m_dwAdvFlags=ADVF_NODATA;

    //NULL any contained interfaces initially.
    m_pIDataObject=NULL;
    m_pIDataAdviseHolder=NULL;

    //Initialize the FORMATETCs arrays we use for EnumFormatEtc
    m_cfeGet=CFORMATETCGET;

    //These macros are in bookguid.h
    SETDefFormatEtc(m_rgfeGet[0], CF_METAFILEPICT, TYMED_MFPICT);
    SETDefFormatEtc(m_rgfeGet[1], CF_BITMAP, TYMED_GDI);
    SETDefFormatEtc(m_rgfeGet[2], CF_TEXT, TYMED_HGLOBAL);

    for (i=0; i < DOSIZE_CSIZES; i++)
        m_rghBmp[i]=NULL;

    return;
    }

CDataObject::~CDataObject(void)
    {
    UINT        i;

    for (i=0; i < DOSIZE_CSIZES; i++)
        {
        if (NULL!=m_rghBmp[i])
            DeleteObject(m_rghBmp[i]);
        }
```

(continued)

Listing 6-2. *continued*

```
    if (NULL!=m_pIDataAdviseHolder)
        m_pIDataAdviseHolder->Release();

    if (NULL!=m_pIDataObject)
        delete m_pIDataObject;

    if (NULL!=m_hWndAdvise)
        DestroyWindow(m_hWndAdvise);

    return;
    }

BOOL CDataObject::FInit(void)
    {
    LPUNKNOWN       pIUnknown=(LPUNKNOWN)this;
    UINT            i;
    char            szTemp[80];
    UINT            cy;

    if (NULL!=m_pUnkOuter)
        pIUnknown=m_pUnkOuter;

    //Allocate contained interfaces.
    m_pIDataObject=new CImpIDataObject(this, pIUnknown);

    if (NULL==m_pIDataObject)
        return FALSE;

    //Load sample bitmaps
    for (i=0; i < DOSIZE_CSIZES; i++)
        {
        m_rghBmp[i]=LoadBitmap(g_hInst, MAKEINTRESOURCE(i+IDB_MIN));

        if (NULL==m_rghBmp[i])
            return FALSE;
        }

    [Code to create an "Advise" window for sending notifications]
    [see "Advising and Notifications with Data Objects"]

    return TRUE;
    }

STDMETHODIMP CDataObject::QueryInterface(REFIID riid, LPLPVOID ppv)
    {
    *ppv=NULL;
```

(continued)

Listing 6-2. *continued*

```
    if (IsEqualIID(riid, IID_IUnknown))
        *ppv=(LPVOID)this;
    if (IsEqualIID(riid, IID_IDataObject))
        *ppv=(LPVOID)m_pIDataObject;
    if (NULL!=*ppv)
        {
        ((LPUNKNOWN)*ppv)->AddRef();
        return NOERROR;
        }

    return ResultFromScode(E_NOINTERFACE);
    }

STDMETHODIMP_(ULONG) CDataObject::AddRef(void)
    {
    return ++m_cRef;
    }

STDMETHODIMP_(ULONG) CDataObject::Release(void)
    {
    ULONG       cRefT;

    cRefT=--m_cRef;

    if (0==m_cRef)
        {
        if (NULL!=m_pfnDestroy)
            (*m_pfnDestroy)();

        delete this;
        }

    return cRefT;
    }

/*
 * AdvisorWndProc
 *
 * Purpose:
 *  Standard window class procedure.
 */
```

(continued)

Listing 6-2. *continued*

```
LRESULT FAR PASCAL __EXPORT AdvisorWndProc(HWND hWnd, UINT iMsg
    , WPARAM wParam, LPARAM lParam)
    {
    LPCDataObject   pDO;
    DWORD           i;
    DWORD           iAdvise;
    DWORD           dwTime;
    DWORD           dwAvg;
    char            szTime[128];
    char            szTitle[80];
    HCURSOR         hCur, hCurT;

    pDO=(LPCDataObject)GetWindowLong(hWnd, 0);

    switch (iMsg)
        {
        case WM_NCCREATE:
            pDO=(LPCDataObject) ((LONG)((LPCREATESTRUCT)lParam)
                ->lpCreateParams);

            SetWindowLong(hWnd, 0, (LONG)pDO);
            return (DefWindowProc(hWnd, iMsg, wParam, lParam));

        case WM_CLOSE:
            //Forbid task manager from closing us.
            return 0L;

        case WM_COMMAND:
            [Code to call IAdviseSink::OnDataChange many times.]
            [See "Advising and Notifications with Data Objects"]
            break;

        default:
            return (DefWindowProc(hWnd, iMsg, wParam, lParam));
        }

    return 0L;
    }
```

(continued)

Listing 6-2. *continued*

IDATAOBJ.CPP

```
/*
 * Data Object Chapter 6
 *
 * Implementation of the IDataObject interface for CDataObject.
 *
 * Copyright (c)1993 Microsoft Corporation, All Rights Reserved
 */

#include "dataobj.h"

CImpIDataObject::CImpIDataObject(LPCDataObject pObj
    , LPUNKNOWN pUnkOuter)
    {
    m_cRef=0;
    m_pObj=pObj;
    m_pUnkOuter=pUnkOuter;
    return;
    }

CImpIDataObject::~CImpIDataObject(void)
    {
    return;
    }

STDMETHODIMP CImpIDataObject::QueryInterface(REFIID riid
    , LPLPVOID ppv)
    {
    return m_pUnkOuter->QueryInterface(riid, ppv);
    }

STDMETHODIMP_(ULONG) CImpIDataObject::AddRef(void)
    {
    ++m_cRef;
    return m_pUnkOuter->AddRef();
    }

STDMETHODIMP_(ULONG) CImpIDataObject::Release(void)
    {
    --m_cRef;
    return m_pUnkOuter->Release();
    }

STDMETHODIMP CImpIDataObject::GetData(LPFORMATETC pFE
    , LPSTGMEDIUM pSTM)
    {
```

(continued)

Listing 6-2. *continued*

```
    UINT            cf=pFE->cfFormat;

    //Check the aspects we support.
    if (!(DVASPECT_CONTENT & pFE->dwAspect))
        return ResultFromScode(DATA_E_FORMATETC);

    switch (cf)
        {
        case CF_METAFILEPICT:
            if (!(TYMED_MFPICT & pFE->tymed))
                break;

            return m_pObj->RenderMetafilePict(pSTM);

        case CF_BITMAP:
            if (!(TYMED_GDI & pFE->tymed))
                break;

            return m_pObj->RenderBitmap(pSTM);

        case CF_TEXT:
            if (!(TYMED_HGLOBAL & pFE->tymed))
                break;

            return m_pObj->RenderText(pSTM);

        default:
            break;
        }

    return ResultFromScode(DATA_E_FORMATETC);
    }

STDMETHODIMP CImpIDataObject::GetDataHere(LPFORMATETC pFE
    , LPSTGMEDIUM pSTM)
    {
    return ResultFromScode(E_NOTIMPL);
    }

STDMETHODIMP CImpIDataObject::QueryGetData(LPFORMATETC pFE)
    {
    UINT            cf=pFE->cfFormat;
    BOOL            fRet=FALSE;

    //Check the aspects we support.
    if (!(DVASPECT_CONTENT & pFE->dwAspect))
        return ResultFromScode(DATA_E_FORMATETC);
```

(continued)

Listing 6-2. *continued*

```
    switch (cf)
        {
        case CF_METAFILEPICT:
            fRet=(BOOL)(pFE->tymed & TYMED_MFPICT);
            break;

        case CF_BITMAP:
            fRet=(BOOL)(pFE->tymed & TYMED_GDI);
            break;

        case CF_TEXT:
            fRet=(BOOL)(pFE->tymed & TYMED_HGLOBAL);
            break;

        default:
            fRet=FALSE;
            break;
        }

    return fRet ? NOERROR : ResultFromScode(S_FALSE);
    }

STDMETHODIMP CImpIDataObject::GetCanonicalFormatEtc
    (LPFORMATETC pFEIn , LPFORMATETC pFEOut)
    {
    *pFEOut=pFEIn;
    pFEOut->ptd=NULL;
    return ResultFromScode(DATA_S_SAMEFORMATETC);
    }

STDMETHODIMP CImpIDataObject::SetData(LPFORMATETC pFE
    , STGMEDIUM FAR *pSTM, BOOL fRelease)
    {
    return ResultFromScode(DATA_E_FORMATETC);
    }

STDMETHODIMP CImpIDataObject::EnumFormatEtc(DWORD dwDir
    , LPENUMFORMATETC FAR *ppEnum)
    {

    switch (dwDir)
        {
        case DATADIR_GET:
            *ppEnum=(LPENUMFORMATETC)new CEnumFormatEtc(m_pUnkOuter
                , m_pObj->m_cfeGet, m_pObj->m_rgfeGet);
```

(continued)

Listing 6-2. *continued*

```
            break;

        case DATADIR_SET:
            *ppEnum=NULL;
            break;

        default:
            *ppEnum=NULL;
            break;
        }

    if (NULL==*ppEnum)
        return ResultFromScode(E_FAIL);
    else
        (*ppEnum)->AddRef();

    return NOERROR;
    }

STDMETHODIMP CImpIDataObject::DAdvise(LPFORMATETC pFE, DWORD dwFlags
    , LPADVISESINK pIAdviseSink, LPDWORD pdwConn)
    {
    HRESULT         hr;

    if (NULL==m_pObj->m_pIDataAdviseHolder)
        {
        hr=CreateDataAdviseHolder(&m_pObj->m_pIDataAdviseHolder);

        if (FAILED(hr))
            return ResultFromScode(E_OUTOFMEMORY);
        }

    hr=m_pObj->m_pIDataAdviseHolder->Advise((LPDATAOBJECT)this, pFE
        , dwFlags, pIAdviseSink, pdwConn);

    return hr;
    }

STDMETHODIMP CImpIDataObject::DUnadvise(DWORD dwConn)
    {
    HRESULT         hr;

    if (NULL==m_pObj->m_pIDataAdviseHolder)
        return ResultFromScode(E_FAIL);
```

(continued)

Listing 6-2. *continued*

```
    hr=m_pObj->m_pIDataAdviseHolder->Unadvise(dwConn);

    return hr;
    }

STDMETHODIMP CImpIDataObject::EnumDAdvise(LPENUMSTATDATA FAR
    *ppEnum)
    {
    HRESULT         hr;

    if (NULL==m_pObj->m_pIDataAdviseHolder)
        return ResultFromScode(E_FAIL);

    hr=m_pObj->m_pIDataAdviseHolder->EnumAdvise(ppEnum);
    return hr;
    }
```

Both DDATAOBJ and EDATAOBJ actually support three different CLSIDs; each CLSID represents a different data set. Each class has its own CLSID but uses exactly the same entries for *InProcServer* and *LocalServer* in the Registration Database. Each object provides text, a bitmap, and a metafile in different sizes, as shown in the following table:

CLSID	Text (Characters)	Bitmap (*x***y*)	Metafile (*FillRect* Records)
CLSID_DataSmall	64	16*16	16
CLSID_DataMedium	1024	64*64	128
CLSID_DataLarge	16,384	256*256	1024

The text contains a repeating sequence of characters (starting at ASCII 32), the bitmap is a sampling of a few bitmaps lying around my hard drive, and the metafile is composed of bands of different blue-shaded rectangles. The large metafile produces an effect similar to that generated by the Windows SDK setup tools or the title screen of WinHelp. The functions in RENDER.CPP generate these renderings.

DDATAOBJ and EDATAOBJ are good examples of implementing multiple classes in a single module. In DDATAOBJ, the *DllGetClassObject* function uses the same class factory implementation for all three classes, differentiating them only by an extra parameter to the class factory constructor.

```
HRESULT EXPORT FAR PASCAL DllGetClassObject(REFCLSID rclsid
    , REFIID riid, LPVOID FAR *ppv)
    {
    if (!IsEqualIID(riid, IID_IUnknown)
        && !IsEqualIID(riid, IID_IClassFactory))
        return ResultFromScode(E_NOINTERFACE);

    *ppv=NULL;

    if (IsEqualCLSID(rclsid, CLSID_DataObjectSmall))
        *ppv=(LPVOID)new CDataObjectClassFactory(DOSIZE_SMALL);

    if (IsEqualCLSID(rclsid, CLSID_DataObjectMedium))
        *ppv=(LPVOID)new CDataObjectClassFactory(DOSIZE_MEDIUM);

    if (IsEqualCLSID(rclsid, CLSID_DataObjectLarge))
        *ppv=(LPVOID)new CDataObjectClassFactory(DOSIZE_LARGE);

    if (NULL==*ppv)
        return ResultFromScode(E_OUTOFMEMORY);

    ((LPUNKNOWN)*ppv)->AddRef();
    return NOERROR;
    }
```

The *DOSIZE_...* values are defined for these samples as 0, 1, and 2 and are used to identify the data set in the data object. The EDATAOBJ program creates three class factories on startup—one for each data size—and registers each class factory separately, maintaining a registration key for each.

```
for (i=0; i < DOSIZE_CSIZES; i++)
    {
    m_rgpIClassFactory[i]
        =(LPCLASSFACTORY)new CDataObjectClassFactory(i);

    if (NULL==m_rgpIClassFactory[i])
        return FALSE;

    m_rgpIClassFactory[i]->AddRef();
    }

hr=CoRegisterClassObject(CLSID_DataObjectSmall
    , (LPUNKNOWN)m_rgpIClassFactory, CLSCTX_LOCAL_SERVER
    , REGCLS_MULTIPLEUSE, &m_rgdwRegCO[0]);
```

```
hr2=CoRegisterClassObject(CLSID_DataObjectMedium
    , (LPUNKNOWN)m_rgpIClassFactory, CLSCTX_LOCAL_SERVER
    , REGCLS_MULTIPLEUSE, &m_rgdwRegCO[1]);

hr3=CoRegisterClassObject(CLSID_DataObjectLarge
    , (LPUNKNOWN)m_rgpIClassFactory, CLSCTX_LOCAL_SERVER
    , REGCLS_MULTIPLEUSE, &m_rgdwRegCO[2]);

if (FAILED(hr) || FAILED(hr2) || FAILED(hr3))
    return FALSE;
```

In both DLL and EXE implementations, the class factories identically create the data object by using a class *CDataObject* object and passing the *DOSIZE_...* value to identify the data set. Except for these changes, the DLL and EXE housings are the same as those used in Chapter 4.

Some *CDataObject* Features

The data object has a number of interesting features worth mentioning briefly. First, each data object carries an array of FORMATETCs that describe the data obtainable from *GetData* only, because *SetData* is not supported in *CDataObject.* Filling out such an array can be tedious, so here we make use of our *SETFormatEtc* and *SETDefFormatEtc* macros in INC\BOOKGUID.H:

```
//Initialize the FORMATETCs arrays we use for EnumFormatEtc
m_cfeGet=CFORMATETCGET;

SETDefFormatEtc(m_rgfeGet[0], CF_METAFILEPICT, TYMED_MFPICT);
SETDefFormatEtc(m_rgfeGet[1], CF_BITMAP, TYMED_GDI);
SETDefFormatEtc(m_rgfeGet[2], CF_TEXT, TYMED_HGLOBAL);
```

When *EnumFormatEtc* is called, *CDataObject* passes the count of FORMATETCs (*m_cfeGet*) and the pointer to the FORMATETC array (*m_rgfeGet*) to the *CEnumFormatEtc* constructor. (See Listing 6-1.) The enumerator copies the array and maintains it internally until it is destroyed. Ownership of the enumerator itself belongs to whoever called *EnumFormatEtc.*

The second most interesting part of our data object implementation is that the object creates its own window, regardless of whether it lives in a DLL or an EXE. Each is a small overlapped window with a thin border and no system menu—only a caption, a minimize box, and a menu. The menus for these windows are used for demonstrating notifications, as discussed in the section "Advising and Notification with Data Objects," so we won't belabor them here. These windows do not have a system menu because they should always be present when the data object itself is present. For that reason, the window procedure for the window class eats WM_CLOSE so that the windows cannot be removed through the Task Manager or with a malevolent Alt+F4.

Implementing *IDataObject*

The *IDataObject* implementation for our data object is contained in the file IDATAOBJ.CPP, as shown in Listing 6-2. You will also find a skeletal *IDataObject* implementation and class definition in the INTERFACE\IDATAOBJ.* files. Most of the implementation is straightforward, and in fact some member functions don't need implementations at all. Let's therefore simply point out the interesting parts, leaving specific details about less-used members to the *OLE 2 Programmer's Reference.*

IDataObject::GetData (as well as *GetDataHere* and *SetData*) must not only check the clipboard format desired by the caller but all other fields in the FORMATETC. In particular, you must ensure that you render the requested aspect, if possible, and comply with the requested storage medium, if possible. If you do not render specifically for any device, you can ignore the *ptd* field altogether. You need to check that field only if you make any special cases for particular devices. If you cannot comply with the FORMATETC, return an HRESULT containing DATA_E_FORMATETC. If you try to render the data and allocations fail, FORMATETC will return STG_E_MEDIUMFULL. You can see this in the code in RENDER.CPP.

It's important that your implementation of *GetData* fill the *entire* STGMEDIUM structure. It's easy to forget to fill the *tymed* field and to set the *pUnkForRelease* field to NULL unless you are using it otherwise. Both are easy to forget, and if you don't fill the *tymed* field properly, OLE 2 will not know how to marshal the data to another process.

GetDataHere, by definition, tries to render data into a caller-allocated storage medium but does not attempt to reallocate space itself. Generally the only storage mediums you need to support in this function are TYMED_ISTORAGE, TYMED_ISTREAM, and TYMED_FILE, which reallocate themselves automatically to handle whatever data you put in them. OLE 2's implementations of *GetDataHere* outright fail when passed any other TYMED_ value; *GetDataHere* really exists to support these three disk-based mediums, so if you don't support these mediums you don't need to support this function. If you do, return STG_E_MEDIUMFULL if writing to such storage fails. Note also that our implementation of *GetDataHere* returns E_NOTIMPL instead of DATA_E_FORMATETC to let callers know we just don't do this, as opposed to telling them they sent the wrong FORMATETC. Telling callers that they have a problem when we don't implement a function is likely to drive them stark raving mad.

QueryGetData is similar in structure to *GetData* because your implementation executes most of the same checks on the FORMATETC passed to it, but instead of rendering the data, you return NOERROR if you have the format or S_FALSE if you don't. (Again, don't use SUCCEEDED or FAILED to test the return value.) All other checks on the aspect, target device, and storage medium are the same.

GetCanonicalFormatEtc is easy to implement if you never do any device-specific renderings: Simply copy the input FORMATETC to the output FORMATETC, store a NULL in the output FORMATETC *ptd* field, and return an HRESULT with DATA_S_SAMEFORMATETC. Note that this is not a failure SCODE because it contains information (thus the *_S_*). Now be sure *not* to compare the return value of *GetCanonicalFormatEtc* to NOERROR to test success; use the SUCCEEDED or FAILED macro instead. This function should ignore the *tymed* fields in both FORMATETCs because they have no relevance to us here.

EnumFormatEtc simply creates one of our *CEnumFormatEtc* objects, passing to it the count and array of FORMATETCs that our *GetData* function supports. *EnumFormatEtc* takes a parameter described as the *data direction*, which is either *Get* or *Set*. If the caller asks for a *Set* enumerator, we return E_FAIL because we don't allow *SetData* at all.

Finally, you might notice a number of API function calls in the *DAdvise*, *DUnadvise*, and *EnumDAdvise* implementations—these functions make use of an object called the *Data Advise Holder* for reasons that will become (thankfully) obvious in the later section "Advising and Notification with Data Objects."

A (Component) Data Object User

Through one of a number of protocols, a piece of code that we can classify as a data consumer obtains an *IDataObject* pointer to a data object. The interface members available through that pointer represent all data manipulation API functions for the consumer, such as retrieving data or checking that formats are available. The DATAUSER program, shown in Listing 6-3 on the next page, obtains three data objects using *CoCreateInstance*: one for the small data set (*CLSID_DataObjectSmall*), one for the medium set (*CLSID_DataObjectMedium*), and one for the large data set (*CLSID_DataObjectLarge*). Initially, DATAUSER instantiates the three data objects from DDATAOBJ.DLL by specifying CLSCTX_INPROC_SERVER in *CoCreateInstance*.

You might notice that DATAUSER's file IADVSINK.CPP has been left out of Listing 6-3. That particular file is described in the next section, "Advising and Notification with Data Objects."

DATAUSER.CPP

```
/*
 * Data Object User Chapter 6
 *
 * Copyright (c)1993 Microsoft Corporation, All Rights Reserved
 */

#define INITGUIDS
#include "datauser.h"

//These are for displaying clipboard formats textually.
static char * rgszCF[13]={"Unknown", "CF_TEXT", "CF_BITMAP"
                 , "CF_METAFILEPICT", "CF_SYLK", "CF_DIF"
                 , "CF_TIFF", "CF_OEMTEXT", "CF_DIB", "CF_PALETTE"
                 , "CF_PENDATA", "CF_RIFF", "CF_WAVE"};

static char szSuccess[]    ="succeeded";
static char szFailed[]     ="failed";
static char szExpected[]   ="expected";
static char szUnexpected[] ="unexpected!";

int PASCAL WinMain(HINSTANCE hInst, HINSTANCE hInstPrev
    , LPSTR pszCmdLine, int nCmdShow)
    {
    MSG         msg;
    LPAPPVARS   pAV;
    int         cMsg=96;

   #ifndef WIN32
    while (!SetMessageQueue(cMsg) && (cMsg-=8));
   #endif

    pAV=new CAppVars(hInst, hInstPrev, nCmdShow);

    if (NULL==pAV)
        return -1;

    if (pAV->FInit())
        {
        while (GetMessage(&msg, NULL, 0,0 ))
            {
            TranslateMessage(&msg);
            DispatchMessage(&msg);
            }
```

Listing 6-3. *(continued)*

The DATAUSER program, which uses the Component Data Objects implemented in the previous section.

Listing 6-3. *continued*

```
        }

    delete pAV;
    return msg.wParam;
    }

LRESULT FAR PASCAL EXPORT DataUserWndProc(HWND hWnd, UINT iMsg
    , WPARAM wParam, LPARAM lParam)
    {
    HRESULT         hr;
    LPAPPVARS       pAV;
    HMENU           hMenu;
    FORMATETC       fe;
    WORD            wID;

    pAV=(LPAPPVARS)GetWindowLong(hWnd, DATAUSERWL_STRUCTURE);

    switch (iMsg)
        {
        case WM_NCCREATE:
            pAV=(LPAPPVARS)((LONG)((LPCREATESTRUCT)lParam)
                ->lpCreateParams);

            SetWindowLong(hWnd, DATAUSERWL_STRUCTURE, (LONG)pAV);
            return (DefWindowProc(hWnd, iMsg, wParam, lParam));

        case WM_DESTROY:
            PostQuitMessage(0);
            break;

        case WM_PAINT:
            pAV->Paint();
            break;

        case WM_COMMAND:
            SETDefFormatEtc(fe, 0, TYMED_HGLOBAL | TYMED_GDI
                | TYMED_MFPICT);

            hMenu=GetMenu(hWnd);
            wID=LOWORD(wParam);

            switch (wID)
                {
                case IDM_OBJECTUSEDLL:
                    if (!pAV->m_fEXE)
                        break;
```

(continued)

Listing 6-3. *continued*

```
                pAV->m_fEXE=FALSE;
                pAV->FReloadDataObjects(TRUE);
                break;

            case IDM_OBJECTUSEEXE:
                if (pAV->m_fEXE)
                    break;

                pAV->m_fEXE=TRUE;
                pAV->FReloadDataObjects(TRUE);
                break;

            case IDM_OBJECTDATASIZESMALL:
            case IDM_OBJECTDATASIZEMEDIUM:
            case IDM_OBJECTDATASIZELARGE:
                CheckMenuItem(hMenu
                    , IDM_OBJECTDATASIZESMALL,  MF_UNCHECKED);
                CheckMenuItem(hMenu
                    , IDM_OBJECTDATASIZEMEDIUM, MF_UNCHECKED);
                CheckMenuItem(hMenu
                    , IDM_OBJECTDATASIZELARGE,  MF_UNCHECKED);
                CheckMenuItem(hMenu, wID,  MF_CHECKED);

                //Kill old advise.
                if (NULL!=pAV->m_pIDataObject
                    || 0!=pAV->m_dwConn)
                    {
                    pAV->m_pIDataObject->DUnadvise(pAV
                        ->m_dwConn);
                    }

                if (IDM_OBJECTDATASIZELARGE==wID)
                    pAV->m_pIDataObject=pAV->m_pIDataLarge;
                else if (IDM_OBJECTDATASIZEMEDIUM==wID)
                    pAV->m_pIDataObject=pAV->m_pIDataMedium;
                else
                    pAV->m_pIDataObject=pAV->m_pIDataSmall;

                //Setup new advise.
                fe.cfFormat=pAV->m_cfAdvise;
                pAV->m_pIDataObject->DAdvise(&fe, ADVF_NODATA
                    , pAV->m_pIAdviseSink, &pAV->m_dwConn);

                break;
```

(continued)

Listing 6-3. *continued*

```
        case IDM_OBJECTQUERYGETDATA:
            if (NULL==pAV->m_pIDataObject)
                break;

            fe.tymed=TYMED_HGLOBAL | TYMED_GDI
                | TYMED_MFPICT;

            pAV->TryQueryGetData(&fe, CF_TEXT, TRUE, 0);
            pAV->TryQueryGetData(&fe, CF_BITMAP, TRUE, 1);
            pAV->TryQueryGetData(&fe, CF_DIB, FALSE, 2);
            pAV->TryQueryGetData(&fe, CF_METAFILEPICT
                , TRUE, 3);
            pAV->TryQueryGetData(&fe, CF_WAVE, FALSE, 4);
            break;

        case IDM_OBJECTGETDATATEXT:
        case IDM_OBJECTGETDATABITMAP:
        case IDM_OBJECTGETDATAMETAFILEPICT:
            if (NULL==pAV->m_pIDataObject)
                break;

            //Clean up whatever we currently have.
            pAV->m_cf=0;
            ReleaseStgMedium(&pAV->m_stm);

            if (IDM_OBJECTGETDATATEXT==wID)
                SETDefFormatEtc(fe, CF_TEXT, TYMED_HGLOBAL);

            if (IDM_OBJECTGETDATABITMAP==wID)
                SETDefFormatEtc(fe, CF_BITMAP, TYMED_GDI);

            if (IDM_OBJECTGETDATAMETAFILEPICT==wID)
                {
                SETDefFormatEtc(fe, CF_METAFILEPICT
                    , TYMED_MFPICT);
                }

            hr=pAV->m_pIDataObject->GetData(&fe
                , &(pAV->m_stm));

            if (SUCCEEDED(hr))
                pAV->m_cf=fe.cfFormat;
```

(continued)

Listing 6-3. *continued*

```
                InvalidateRect(hWnd, NULL, TRUE);
                UpdateWindow(hWnd);
                break;

            case IDM_OBJECTEXIT:
                PostMessage(hWnd, WM_CLOSE, 0, 0L);
                break;

            case IDM_ADVISETEXT:
            case IDM_ADVISEBITMAP:
            case IDM_ADVISEMETAFILEPICT:
                if (NULL==pAV->m_pIDataObject)
                    break;

                //Terminate the old connection
                if (0!=pAV->m_dwConn)
                    {
                    pAV->m_pIDataObject->DUnadvise(pAV
                        ->m_dwConn);
                    }

                CheckMenuItem(hMenu, pAV->m_cfAdvise
                    +IDM_ADVISEMIN, MF_UNCHECKED);
                CheckMenuItem(hMenu, wID, MF_CHECKED);

                //New format is wID-IDM_ADVISEMIN
                pAV->m_cfAdvise=(UINT)(wID-IDM_ADVISEMIN);
                fe.cfFormat=pAV->m_cfAdvise;
                pAV->m_pIDataObject->DAdvise(&fe, ADVF_NODATA
                    , pAV->m_pIAdviseSink, &pAV->m_dwConn);

                break;

            case IDM_ADVISEGETDATA:
                pAV->m_fGetData=!pAV->m_fGetData;
                CheckMenuItem(hMenu, wID, pAV->m_fGetData
                    ? MF_CHECKED : MF_UNCHECKED);
                break;

            case IDM_ADVISEREPAINT:
                pAV->m_fRepaint=!pAV->m_fRepaint;
                CheckMenuItem(hMenu, wID, pAV->m_fRepaint
                    ? MF_CHECKED : MF_UNCHECKED);
                break;
```

(continued)

Listing 6-3. *continued*

```
                default:
                    break;
                }
            break;
        default:
            return (DefWindowProc(hWnd, iMsg, wParam, lParam));
        }
    return 0L;
    }

CAppVars::CAppVars(HINSTANCE hInst, HINSTANCE hInstPrev
    , UINT nCmdShow)
    {
    m_hInst       =hInst;
    m_hInstPrev   =hInstPrev;
    m_nCmdShow    =nCmdShow;

    m_hWnd        =NULL;
    m_fEXE        =FALSE;

    m_pIAdviseSink =NULL;
    m_dwConn       =0;
    m_cfAdvise     =0;
    m_fGetData     =FALSE;
    m_fRepaint     =FALSE;

    m_pIDataSmall =NULL;
    m_pIDataMedium=NULL;
    m_pIDataLarge =NULL;
    m_pIDataObject=NULL;

    m_cf=0;
    m_stm.tymed=TYMED_NULL;
    m_stm.lpszFileName=NULL;      //Initializes union to NULL
    m_stm.pUnkForRelease=NULL;

    m_fInitialized=FALSE;
    return;
    }

CAppVars::~CAppVars(void)
    {

    //This releases the data object interfaces and advises
    FReloadDataObjects(FALSE);
```

(continued)

Listing 6-3. *continued*

```
    ReleaseStgMedium(&m_stm);

    if (NULL!=m_pIAdviseSink)
        m_pIAdviseSink->Release();

    if (IsWindow(m_hWnd))
        DestroyWindow(m_hWnd);

    if (m_fInitialized)
        CoUninitialize();

    return;
    }

BOOL CAppVars::FInit(void)
    {
    WNDCLASS    wc;
    DWORD       dwVer;
    BOOL        fRet;

    dwVer=CoBuildVersion();

    if (rmm!=HIWORD(dwVer))
        return FALSE;

    if (FAILED(CoInitialize(NULL)))
        return FALSE;

    m_fInitialized=TRUE;

    [Register and create the main window]

    m_pIAdviseSink=new CImpIAdviseSink(this);

    if (NULL==m_pIAdviseSink)
        return FALSE;

    m_pIAdviseSink->AddRef();

    CheckMenuItem(GetMenu(m_hWnd), IDM_OBJECTUSEDLL, MF_CHECKED);
    CheckMenuItem(GetMenu(m_hWnd), IDM_OBJECTDATASIZESMALL
        , MF_CHECKED);
```

(continued)

Listing 6-3. *continued*

```
    //Load the initial objects
    fRet=FReloadDataObjects(TRUE);
    m_pIDataObject=m_pIDataSmall;

    return fRet;
    }

/*
 * CAppVars::FReloadDataObjects
 *
 * Purpose:
 *  Releases the old data objects we're holding on to and reloads
 *  the new ones from either EXE or DLL depending on m_fEXE.
 *
 * Parameters:
 *  fReload         BOOL indicating if we are to recreate everything
 *                  or just release the old ones (so we can use this
 *                  from the destructor).
 *
 * Return Value:
 *  BOOL            TRUE if there are usable objects in us now.
 */
BOOL CAppVars::FReloadDataObjects(BOOL fReload)
    {
    HRESULT     hr1, hr2, hr3;
    DWORD       dwClsCtx;
    HCURSOR     hCur, hCurT;
    HMENU       hMenu;
    UINT        uTempD, uTempE;

    //Clean out any data we're holding
    m_cf=0;
    ReleaseStgMedium(&m_stm);

    //Turn off whatever data connection we have
    if (NULL!=m_pIDataObject && 0!=m_dwConn)
        m_pIDataObject->DUnadvise(m_dwConn);

    if (NULL!=m_pIDataLarge)
        m_pIDataLarge->Release();

    if (NULL!=m_pIDataMedium)
        m_pIDataMedium->Release();
```

(continued)

Listing 6-3. *continued*

```
if (NULL!=m_pIDataSmall)
    m_pIDataSmall->Release();

m_pIDataObject=NULL;
CoFreeUnusedLibraries();

//Exit if we just wanted to free.
if (!fReload)
    return FALSE;

hCur=LoadCursor(NULL, MAKEINTRESOURCE(IDC_WAIT));
hCurT=SetCursor(hCur);
ShowCursor(TRUE);

dwClsCtx=(m_fEXE) ? CLSCTX_LOCAL_SERVER : CLSCTX_INPROC_SERVER;

hr1=CoCreateInstance(CLSID_DataObjectSmall, NULL, dwClsCtx
    , IID_IDataObject, (LPLPVOID)&m_pIDataSmall);

hr2=CoCreateInstance(CLSID_DataObjectMedium, NULL, dwClsCtx
    , IID_IDataObject, (LPLPVOID)&m_pIDataMedium);

hr3=CoCreateInstance(CLSID_DataObjectLarge, NULL, dwClsCtx
    , IID_IDataObject, (LPLPVOID)&m_pIDataLarge);

ShowCursor(FALSE);
SetCursor(hCurT);

//If anything fails, recurse to clean up...
if (FAILED(hr1) || FAILED(hr2) || FAILED(hr3))
    return FReloadDataObjects(FALSE);

//Reset the state of the menus for Small, no advise, no options.
hMenu=GetMenu(m_hWnd);
CheckMenuItem(hMenu, IDM_OBJECTDATASIZESMALL,  MF_CHECKED);
CheckMenuItem(hMenu, IDM_OBJECTDATASIZEMEDIUM, MF_UNCHECKED);
CheckMenuItem(hMenu, IDM_OBJECTDATASIZELARGE,  MF_UNCHECKED);

m_pIDataObject=m_pIDataSmall;
CheckMenuItem(hMenu, m_cfAdvise+IDM_ADVISEMIN, MF_UNCHECKED);

uTempE=m_fEXE  ? MF_CHECKED : MF_UNCHECKED;
uTempD=!m_fEXE ? MF_CHECKED : MF_UNCHECKED;

CheckMenuItem(hMenu, IDM_OBJECTUSEDLL, uTempD);
CheckMenuItem(hMenu, IDM_OBJECTUSEEXE, uTempE);
```

(continued)

Listing 6-3. *continued*

```
    CheckMenuItem(hMenu, IDM_ADVISEGETDATA, MF_UNCHECKED);
    CheckMenuItem(hMenu, IDM_ADVISEREPAINT, MF_UNCHECKED);

    m_fGetData=FALSE;
    m_fRepaint=FALSE;

    //Cannot request data using async advises, so disable these.
    uTempE=m_fEXE  ? MF_DISABLED | MF_GRAYED : MF_ENABLED;
    EnableMenuItem(hMenu,  IDM_ADVISEGETDATA, uTempE);
    EnableMenuItem(hMenu, IDM_ADVISEREPAINT, uTempE);

    return TRUE;
    }

/*
 * CAppVars::TryQueryGetData
 *
 * Purpose:
 *  Centralized function call and output code for displaying results
 *  of various IDataObject::QueryGetData calls.
 *
 * Parameters:
 *  pFE             LPFORMATETC to test.
 *  cf              UINT specific clipboard format to stuff in pFE
 *                  before calling. If zero, use whatever is
 *                  already in pFE.
 *  fExpect         BOOL indicating expected results
 *  y               UINT line on which to print results.
 *
 * Return Value:
 *  None
 */

void CAppVars::TryQueryGetData(LPFORMATETC pFE, UINT cf
    , BOOL fExpect, UINT y)
    {
    char        szTemp[80];
    LPSTR       psz1;
    LPSTR       psz2;
    UINT        cch;
    HRESULT     hr;
    HDC         hDC;
```

(continued)

Listing 6-3. *continued*

```
    if (0!=cf)
        pFE->cfFormat=cf;

    hr=m_pIDataObject->QueryGetData(pFE);
    psz1=(NOERROR==hr) ? szSuccess : szFailed;
    psz2=((NOERROR==hr)==fExpect) ? szExpected : szUnexpected;

    hDC=GetDC(m_hWnd);
    SetTextColor(hDC, GetSysColor(COLOR_WINDOWTEXT));
    SetBkColor(hDC, GetSysColor(COLOR_WINDOW));

    if (CF_WAVE < cf || 0==cf)
        {
        cch=wsprintf(szTemp, "QueryGetData on %d %s (%s)."
            , cf, psz1, psz2);
        }
    else
        {
        cch=wsprintf(szTemp, "QueryGetData on %s %s (%s)."
            , (LPSTR)rgszCF[cf], psz1, psz2);
        }

    //Don't overwrite other painted display.
    SetBkMode(hDC, TRANSPARENT);
    TextOut(hDC, 0, 16*y, szTemp, cch);

    ReleaseDC(m_hWnd, hDC);

    return;
    }

/*
 * CAppVars::Paint
 *
 * Purpose:
 *  Handles WM_PAINT for the main window by drawing whatever
 *  data we have sitting in the STGMEDIUM at this time.
 *
 * Parameters:
 *  None
 *
 * Return Value:
 *  None
 */
```

(continued)

Listing 6-3. *continued*

```
void CAppVars::Paint(void)
    {
    ...
    GetClientRect(m_hWnd, &rc);
    hDC=BeginPaint(m_hWnd, &ps);

    //May need to retrieve the data with EXE objects
    if (m_fEXE)
        {
        if (TYMED_NULL==m_stm.tymed && 0!=m_cf)
            {
            SETDefFormatEtc(fe, m_cf, TYMED_HGLOBAL
                | TYMED_MFPICT | TYMED_GDI);

            if (NULL!=m_pIDataObject)
                m_pIDataObject->GetData(&fe, &m_stm);
            }
        }

    switch (m_cf)
        {
        case CF_TEXT:
            [Lock m_stm.hGlobal and call DrawText]
            break;

        case CF_BITMAP:
            [Select m_stm.hGlobal into a memory DC and call BitBlt]
            break;

        case CF_METAFILEPICT:
            [Lock m_stm.hGlobal and call PlayMetafile]
            break;

        default:
            break;
        }

    EndPaint(m_hWnd, &ps);
    return;
    }
```

While running, DATAUSER keeps one of its three objects as the current one, on which all calls are made. By default, this will be the small data set object. To change the current object, you can use DATAUSER's Data Object menu, which provides the following additional functions:

- Switch between DLL objects and EXE objects. To switch, you release the current objects, create the new ones by using *CoCreateInstance* with CLSCTX_INPROC_SERVER (DLL) or CLSCTX_LOCAL_SERVER (EXE), and reset the state of the application.
- Change which of the three objects is current—small, medium, or large.
- Call *QueryGetData* on the current object for the formats CF_TEXT, CF_BITMAP, CF_DIB, CF_METAFILEPICT, and CF_WAVE, displaying the result (and whether that was the *expected* result) in DATAUSER's window. This is the equivalent of calling *IsClipboardFormatAvailable* for such a data transfer, except that you must pass a FORMATETC instead of a single clipboard format. The call is isolated in a function, *CAppVars::TryQueryGetData.*
- Call *GetData* on the current object to retrieve one of the data formats supported by the data objects. DATAUSER releases its old data (*ReleaseStgMedium*) and holds onto the new data to use in repaints. This is similar to calling *GetClipboardData,* except that you can describe your desired data using a FORMATETC and you receive the data back in an STGMEDIUM structure. After the data is returned, you become responsible for it. A typical session with DATAUSER is shown in Figure 6-1, in which the background of the window is painted with the metafile from the large data set.

DATAUSER also has an Advise menu, through which it sets up advisory connections with the current object.

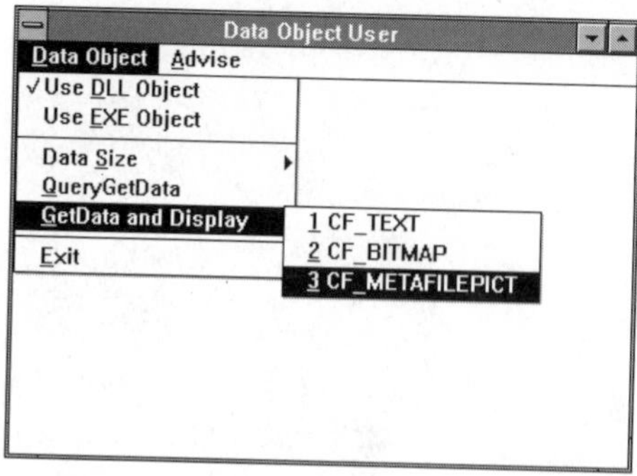

Figure 6-1.
The DATAUSER program, painted with a large metafile and showing the Data Object menu.

Notice that you have a *tymed* field in both the FORMATETC and the STGMEDIUM that you pass in this call. When calling *SetData*, be sure that these two are identical.

Advising and Notification with Data Objects

I'm frequently asked how fast data updates can be sent from a data object to the user of that object. DATAUSER and both data object implementations were constructed not only to demonstrate data objects but also to answer this question. The *IDataObject* interface has three member functions that deal with notifications: *DAdvise*, *DUnadvise*, and *EnumDAdvise*.[2]

The overall notification mechanism of OLE 2 is used not only for data objects but for two other object types as well. The agent that is interested in being asynchronously notified about data changes implements an object with the *IAdviseSink* interface:[3]

```
DECLARE_INTERFACE_(IAdviseSink, IUnknown)
    {
    [IUnknown methods included]

    //IAdviseSink methods
    STDMETHOD_(void,OnDataChange)(THIS_ FORMATETC FAR* pFormatetc,
        STGMEDIUM FAR* pStgmed) PURE;
    STDMETHOD_(void,OnViewChange)(THIS_ DWORD dwAspect, LONG lindex) PURE;
    STDMETHOD_(void,OnRename)(THIS_ LPMONIKER pmk) PURE;
    STDMETHOD_(void,OnSave)(THIS) PURE;
    STDMETHOD_(void,OnClose)(THIS) PURE;
    };
typedef     IAdviseSink FAR* LPADVISESINK;
```

This is a significant change from the way Windows has handled notification, or callbacks, up to this point. Traditionally, any time you wanted some sort of notification (be it a window procedure, a dialog box procedure, an enumeration of clipboard formats or metafile records, a DDE message, and so forth), you were required to pass a pointer to a *single* function in your code to some other Windows API function, usually sandwiched between calls to *MakeProcInstance* and *FreeProcInstance*. For example, to invoke a typical dialog box, you had to pass a pointer to your dialog procedure to a function such as *DialogBox*.

---

2. Again, the names containing *D* identify those functions as belonging to *IDataObject* to eliminate confusion with *IOleObject::Advise*, *IOleObject::Unadvise*, and *IOleObject::EnumAdvise*.
3. There is also an interface called *IAdviseSink2*, which was added late in the development cycle of OLE 2 and Microsoft could not change *IAdviseSink* itself. This interface has one additional member, called *OnLinkSourceChange*, which is not important to applications.

```
DLGPROC     pfn;

pfn=(DLGPROC)MakeProcInstance((FARPROC)AboutProc, hInstance);
DialogBox(hInstance, MAKEINTRESOURCE(IDD_ABOUT), hWnd, pfn);
FreeProcInstance((FARPROC)pfn);
```

A dialog box procedure or any other window procedure is merely a notification sink in which the notifications are in the form of messages. In OLE 2, we want to expose the equivalent type of functionality for notification sinks through Windows Objects. Therefore, instead of passing a single callback function to an API function, you pass an interface pointer to the object—that is, a pointer to an *array of callback functions*—from which you want to receive notifications. Instead of one callback and a notification code, there is one member function of the advise sink object for each type of notification. This has the obvious advantage that each member function can have a different set of parameters and as many parameters as necessary to describe the event, instead of forcing everything into the extreme bottleneck of *wParams* and *lParams*. Instead of one function that is associated with the connection and with all events, there is one object associated with the connection and one member function in that object's interface associated with each event.

As an interesting aside, your trusted window procedure will eventually evolve into a bunch of member functions on something like your Window Procedure object (a Windows Object, of course). The Microsoft Foundation Classes already provide this mechanism today through their C++ class called *CFrameWnd*, for which you define a message map that associates today's messages, such as WM_SIZE, with a member function in the class, such as *OnSize*. Again, the benefits of the object-oriented approach are that the parameters to *OnSize* can be separate variables for the new *cx* and *cy* instead of being packed into *lParam* and that within *OnSize* you have a *this* pointer, which you can use to access immediately all your window-related variables. In contrast, you generally have to use *GetWindowWord* or *GetWindowLong* to retrieve variables associated with a particular *hWnd* within a message procedure.

All of this is why so much attention has been given to the "notification" technology of OLE 2. Notification represents a significant departure from—and an improvement over—the old ways of traditional Windows programming. It also shows why the Microsoft Foundation Classes help you adjust to this new style of programming; however, the Microsoft Foundation Classes are based on C++ classes, not on Windows Objects, and they must still be considered a tool, rather than the native representation of Windows' system capabilities.

Enough lecture—let's get back to some code. The only two members of *IAdviseSink* that are of interest to us now are *OnDataChange* and *OnViewChange.* (For details on the latter, see the later section "View Objects and the *IViewObject* Interface.") The other members are related to compound document objects, which we'll see in later chapters. But for now, any general piece of code that wants data change notifications implements a stand-alone object with an *IAdviseSink* implementation. Again, the INTERFAC directory on the companion disk that accompanies this book provides a generic *CImpIAdviseSink.* The DATAUSER application uses a slightly modified version of this code to implement *IAdviseSink* as an interface on its application object, *CAppVars.* The code for DATAUSER's *IAdviseSink* interface implementation is shown in Listing 6-4.

IADVSINK.CPP

```
/*
 * Data Object User Chapter 6
 *
 * Implementation of the IAdviseSink interface.
 *
 * Copyright (c)1993 Microsoft Corporation, All Rights Reserved
 */

#include "datauser.h"

CImpIAdviseSink::CImpIAdviseSink(LPAPPVARS pAV)
    {
    m_cRef=0;
    m_pAV=pAV;
    return;
    }

CImpIAdviseSink::~CImpIAdviseSink(void)
    {
    return;
    }

STDMETHODIMP CImpIAdviseSink::QueryInterface(REFIID riid
    , LPLPVOID ppv)
    {
    *ppv=NULL;
```

(continued)

Listing 6-4.
The IADVSINK.CPP file from DATAUSER, implementing the IAdviseSink *interface for the application.*

Listing 6-4. *continued*

```
    //Any interface on this object is the object pointer.
    if (IsEqualIID(riid, IID_IUnknown)
        || IsEqualIID(riid, IID_IAdviseSink))
        *ppv=(LPVOID)this;

    if (NULL!=*ppv)
        {
        ((LPUNKNOWN)*ppv)->AddRef();
        return NOERROR;
        }

    return ResultFromScode(E_NOINTERFACE);
    }

STDMETHODIMP_(ULONG) CImpIAdviseSink::AddRef(void)
    {
    return ++m_cRef;
    }

STDMETHODIMP_(ULONG) CImpIAdviseSink::Release(void)
    {
    ULONG   cRefT;

    cRefT=--m_cRef;

    if (0==cRefT)
        delete this;

    return cRefT;
    }

/*
 * IAdviseSink::OnDataChange
 *
 * Purpose:
 *  Notifies the advise sink that data changed in a data object.
 *  On this message you may request a new data rendering and update
 *  your displays as necessary. Any data sent to this function is
 *  owned by the caller, not by this advise sink.
 *
 *  All Advise Sink methods are asynchronous and therefore we
 *  should attempt no synchronous calls from within them to an EXE
 *  object. If we do, we'll get RPC_E_CALLREJECTED as shown below.
 *
```

(continued)

Listing 6-4. *continued*

```
 * Parameters:
 *  pFEIn           LPFORMATETC describing format that changed
 *  pSTM            LPSTGMEDIUM providing the medium in which the
 *                  data is provided.
 *
 * Return Value:
 *  None
 */

STDMETHODIMP_(void) CImpIAdviseSink::OnDataChange(LPFORMATETC pFE
    , LPSTGMEDIUM pSTM)
    {
    BOOL        fUsable=TRUE;
    UINT        cf;
    STGMEDIUM   stm;

    /*
     * We first check that the changed data is, in fact, a format
     * we're interested in, either CF_TEXT, CF_BITMAP, or
     * CF_METAFILEPICT, then only in the aspects we want. We check
     * if pSTM->tymed is TYMED_NULL or something else. If NULL, we
     * just exit so the data object can time ADVF_NODATA trans-
     * actions. Otherwise we verify that the data is useful and
     * repaint. If there is data in pSTM we are responsible for it.
     */

    //Ignore the m_fGetData flag for EXE objects (we can't GetData)
    if (!m_pAV->m_fGetData && !m_pAV->m_fEXE)
        return;

    //See if we're interested
    cf=pFE->cfFormat;

    if ((CF_TEXT!=cf && CF_BITMAP!=cf && CF_METAFILEPICT!=cf)
        || !(DVASPECT_CONTENT & pFE->dwAspect))
        return;

    //Check media types
    switch (cf)
        {
        case CF_TEXT:
            fUsable=(BOOL)(TYMED_HGLOBAL & pFE->tymed);
            break;
```

(continued)

Listing 6-4. *continued*

```
        case CF_BITMAP:
            fUsable=(BOOL)(TYMED_GDI & pFE->tymed);
            break;

        case CF_METAFILEPICT:
            fUsable=(BOOL)(TYMED_MFPICT & pFE->tymed);
            break;

        default:
            break;
        }

    if (!fUsable)
        return;

    if (NULL==m_pAV->m_pIDataObject)
        return;

    /*
     * When dealing with EXE objects, invalidate ourselves
     * after setting TYMED_NULL in our STGMEDIUM that causes
     * CAppVars::Paint to request new data. We cannot call
     * GetData in here because this is an async call when we're
     * dealing with an EXE.
     */
    if (m_pAV->m_fEXE)
        {
        ReleaseStgMedium(&(m_pAV->m_stm));
        m_pAV->m_cf=cf;
        m_pAV->m_stm.tymed=TYMED_NULL;

        InvalidateRect(m_pAV->m_hWnd, NULL, TRUE);
        return;
        }

    if (FAILED(m_pAV->m_pIDataObject->GetData(pFE, &stm)))
        return;

    //Get rid of old data and update.
    ReleaseStgMedium(&(m_pAV->m_stm));

    m_pAV->m_cf=cf;
    m_pAV->m_stm=stm;
```

(continued)

Listing 6-4. *continued*

```
    InvalidateRect(m_pAV->m_hWnd, NULL, TRUE);

    if (m_pAV->m_fRepaint)
        UpdateWindow(m_pAV->m_hWnd);

    return;
    }

/*
 * Other IAdviseSink members not important to DATAUSER.
 */

STDMETHODIMP_(void) CImpIAdviseSink::OnViewChange(DWORD dwAspect
    , LONG lindex)
    {
    return;
    }

STDMETHODIMP_(void) CImpIAdviseSink::OnRename(LPMONIKER pmk)
    {
    return;
    }

STDMETHODIMP_(void) CImpIAdviseSink::OnSave(void)
    {
    return;
    }

STDMETHODIMP_(void) CImpIAdviseSink::OnClose(void)
    {
    return;
    }
```

Establishing an Advisory Connection

When you are interested in knowing when data changes, you need to follow a few straightforward steps:

1. Implement the *IAdviseSink* interface on an appropriate object. This may be a site in which the data lives, the document into which the data is integrated, or the application as a whole. *IAdviseSink* should live wherever you want to see the notifications. The only member function you need worry about at this point is *OnDataChange*.

2. When you want to set up an advise, pass the *IAdviseSink* pointer to *IDataObject::DAdvise* along with the FORMATETC describing the data you're interested in and the flags indicating how you want the advise to happen. *DAdvise* will return a DWORD key to identify your connection. In *Advise*, the data object will call *AddRef* on your advise sink.
3. When you want to terminate the connection, pass the key from *DAdvise* to *DUnadvise*. The data object will call *Release* on your advise sink.

An advise connection in OLE 2 is always associated with the *dwAspect* that is contained in the FORMATETC passed to *DAdvise*. If the data object does not support that aspect, it can refuse the connection; otherwise, it uses that aspect to determine when it needs to send a notification. In other words, the advise sink will see *OnDataChange* called only when a data change affects an aspect, not when any data change happens.

DATAUSER instantiates its *IAdviseSink* interface implementation on startup before creating any objects:

```
m_pIAdviseSink=new CImpIAdviseSink(this);

if (NULL==m_pIAdviseSink)
    return FALSE;

m_pIAdviseSink->AddRef();
```

An Object User Providing an Object?

DATAUSER's implementation of the *IAdviseSink* interface on *its C-AppVars* class is the first instance we've seen thus far showing how the user of one Windows Object on occasion needs to implement a Windows Object of its own. In this case, the user of the data object implements the advise sink object and then hands that advise sink object to the data object. The data object, in turn, becomes a user of that advise sink object, and it obtains the pointer exclusively through a call to one of its *own* member functions (*IDataObject::DAdvise*). Such a pattern is common in OLE 2 applications in which such applications are both object users and object implementors. How we classify applications into categories such as containers and servers depends on what interfaces and objects those applications implement and how they expose them. In any case, all such objects implemented in any type of application are still Windows Objects.

The extra *AddRef* on the interface accounts for the pointer in *m_pIAdviseSink* because the *CImplIAdviseSink* itself initializes its reference count to zero. When DATAUSER wants to establish an advise, it fills a FORMATETC and calls *DAdvise* for the current data object:

```
m_pIDataObject->DAdvise(&fe, ADVF_NODATA, m_pIAdviseSink, &m_dwConn);
```

where *m_pIDataObject* is the current object; *fe* is a FORMATETC structure containing DVASPECT_CONTENT; ADVF_NODATA is one of a number of inclusive advise flags, shown in Table 6-1 on the next page; *m_pIAdviseSink* is the advise sink object in which we've implemented *OnDataChange*; and *&m_dwConn* is the address in which the data object should store the connection key. When we later terminate the connection, we merely pass this key to *DUnadvise*:

```
m_pIDataObject->DUnadvise(m_dwConn);
```

DATAUSER passes ADVF_NODATA to *IDataObject::DAdvise* to prevent the data object from rendering the data and sending it to the *IAdviseSink::OnDataChange* function in the LPSTGMEDIUM parameter. By default, data objects will go ahead and provide the updated data, so if you normally would ask for the data every time it changed, you can omit this flag and have the data given to you automatically.

DATAUSER allows you to control when and how it handles the *OnDataChange* notifications through its Advise menu, as shown in Figure 6-2 on the next page. (The image is the large bitmap.) The three format items indicate which format DATAUSER will work with in *OnDataChange*. By default, *OnDataChange* will do nothing, enabling us to test how many notifications per second are possible with a do-nothing advise sink. The other two menu items turn on options for *OnDataChange* when using the DLL DATAOBJECT. Get Data On Change causes *OnDataChange* to call *IDataObject::GetData* for every notification (to test the speed of rendering the data), and Paint On Change will go the extra step of forcing a full window repaint on each notification. (DATAUSER always invalidates the window but doesn't always call *UpdateWindow*.) These two options together would allow us to watch dynamic changes to the data as they occur, although the data objects we have for this chapter don't bother changing the data at all. Because DATAUSER allows menu control over when or whether the data is actually rendered for each notification, it initially passes ADVF_NODATA to *IDataObject::DAdvise* to prevent the data objects from automatically re-rendering the data on every *OnDataChange*. In this way, we can measure the performance of notifications with and without *GetData* calls.

Flag	Meaning
ADVF_NODATA	Prevents the data object from sending data along with the *OnDataChange* notification. This is equivalent to a DDE "warm link"; absence of this flag is equivalent to a DDE "hot link." In any case, when ADVF_NODATA is used, the *tymed* field of the LPSTGMEDIUM passed to *OnDataChange* will usually contain TYMED_NULL. Some data objects might still send data and *tymed* will contain another value, and in that case, *OnDataChange* is still responsible for the STGMEDIUM. Be sure to check.
ADVF_ONLYONCE	Automatically terminates the advisory connection after the first call to *OnDataChange*. It is not necessary to call *DUnadvise* when you use this flag. You can still, however, call *DUnadvise* if you have not yet received a notification.
ADVF_PRIMEFIRST	Causes an initial *OnDataChange* call even when the data has not changed from its present state. If you combine ADVF_PRIMEFIRST with ADVF_ONLYONCE, you create a single asynchronous *IDataObject::GetData* call.
ADVF_DATAONSTOP	When provided with ADVF_NODATA, causes the last *OnDataChange* sent from the data object (before that object was destroyed) to actually provide the data—that is, *pSTM->tymed* will be a value other than TYMED-_NULL. This flag is meaningless without ADVF-_NODATA.

Table 6-1.
The advise flags usable with IDataObject::DAdvise.

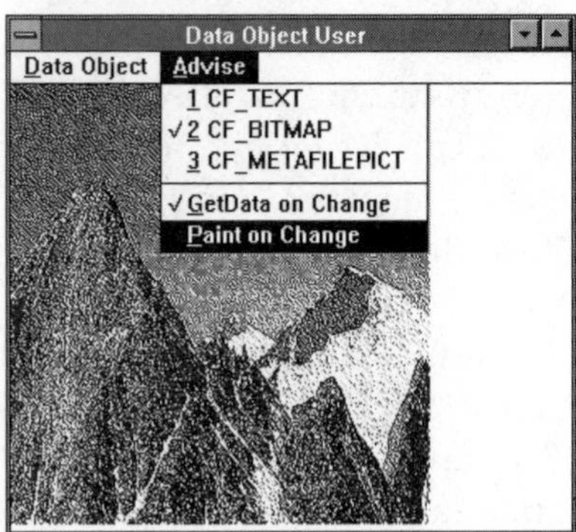

Figure 6-2.
The DATAUSER program, painted with a large bitmap, showing the Advise menu options.

Sending Notifications as a Data Object

To provide for notification within the implementation of a data object, you must implement *DAdvise*, *DUnadvise*, and *EnumDAdvise* of *IDataObject*. But there is a catch. OLE 2 specifies that any data object can receive *multiple* calls to *DAdvise* and that the data object is then responsible for sending notifications to each and every one of those advise sinks. In other words, the data object is responsible for tracking the advise sinks, as shown here:

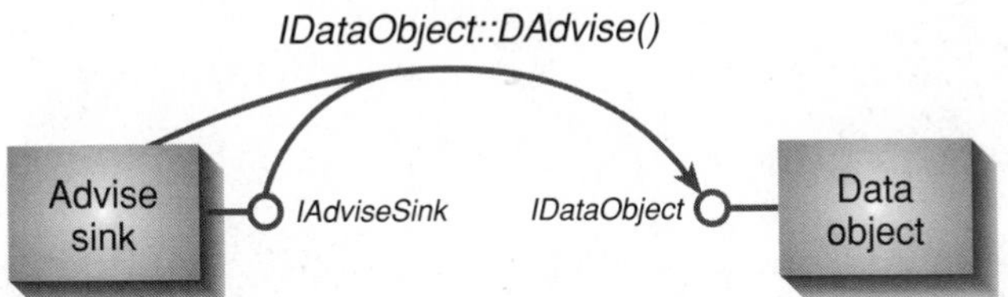

In addition, the data object must determine whom to notify when a particular aspect changes. It must go back through its list of advise sinks, find those that asked for a specific aspect, and call those *IAdviseSink::OnDataChange* functions. All of this can be a royal pain, so OLE 2 provides an object called the data advise holder, which implements an interface called *IDataAdviseHolder*:

```
DECLARE_INTERFACE_(IDataAdviseHolder, IUnknown)
    {
    [The omnipresent IUnknown methods included]

    //IDataAdviseHolder methods
    STDMETHOD(Advise)(THIS_ LPDATAOBJECT pDataObject, FORMATETC FAR* pFetc
        ,DWORD advf, LPADVISESINK pAdvise, DWORD FAR* pdwConnection) PURE;
    STDMETHOD(Unadvise)(THIS_ DWORD dwConnection) PURE;
    STDMETHOD(EnumAdvise)(THIS_ LPENUMSTATDATA FAR* ppenumAdvise) PURE;

    STDMETHOD(SendOnDataChange)(THIS_ LPDATAOBJECT pDataObject,
        DWORD dwReserved, DWORD advf) PURE;
    };

typedef      IDataAdviseHolder FAR* LPDATAADVISEHOLDER;
```

The data advise holder trivializes implementation of a data object's *Advise* members. When the data object sees its first *DAdvise* (or when it is initially created), it can create a data advise holder and delegate the initial *DAdvise* request to the holder.

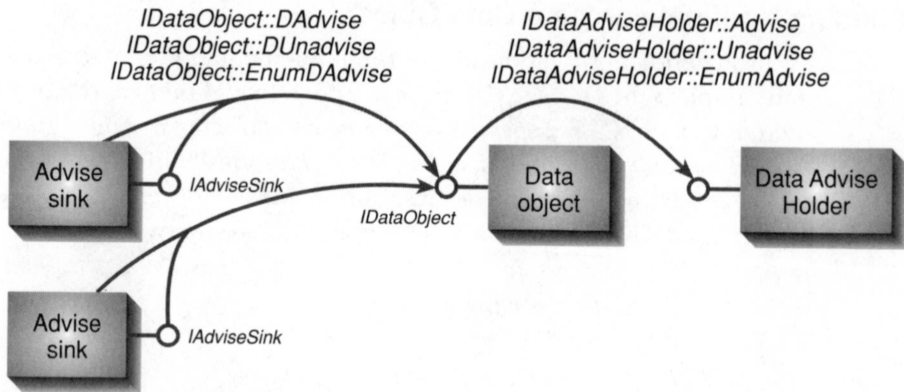

From that point on, the data object delegates *DUnadvise* and *EnumDAdvise* calls to the same data advise holder, which will manage all the advise sinks for you.

```
STDMETHODIMP CImpIDataObject::DAdvise(LPFORMATETC pFE, DWORD dwFlags
    , LPADVISESINK pIAdviseSink, LPDWORD pdwConn)
    {
    HRESULT         hr;

    if (NULL==m_pObj->m_pIDataAdviseHolder)
        {
        hr=CreateDataAdviseHolder(&m_pObj->m_pIDataAdviseHolder);

        if (FAILED(hr))
            return ResultFromScode(E_OUTOFMEMORY);
        }

    hr=m_pObj->m_pIDataAdviseHolder->Advise((LPDATAOBJECT)this, pFE
        , dwFlags, pIAdviseSink, pdwConn);

    return hr;
    }

STDMETHODIMP CImpIDataObject::DUnadvise(DWORD dwConn)
    {
    HRESULT         hr;

    if (NULL==m_pObj->m_pIDataAdviseHolder)
        return ResultFromScode(E_FAIL);

    return m_pObj->m_pIDataAdviseHolder->Unadvise(dwConn);
    }
```

```
STDMETHODIMP CImpIDataObject::EnumDAdvise(LPENUMSTATDATA FAR *ppEnum)
    {
    HRESULT         hr;

    if (NULL==m_pObj->m_pIDataAdviseHolder)
        return ResultFromScode(E_FAIL);

    return m_pObj->m_pIDataAdviseHolder->EnumAdvise(ppEnum);
    }
```

When the data object wants to send notifications, it asks the data advise holder to perform the honors by calling *IDataAdviseHolder::SendOnDataChange*. To this function, you pass a pointer to the data object (so that the holder can call *GetData* as necessary), a zero (a reserved value), and any combination of the flags shown in Table 6-1 on page 354. The flags passed here determine which advise sinks will be notified. Only those sinks that requested at least these same flags will be notified. By passing ADVF_NODATA, you can prevent the holder from asking you for data before it notifies interested advise sinks. What you end up with by using the data advise holder is some loss of performance (for a few more function calls) but great convenience.

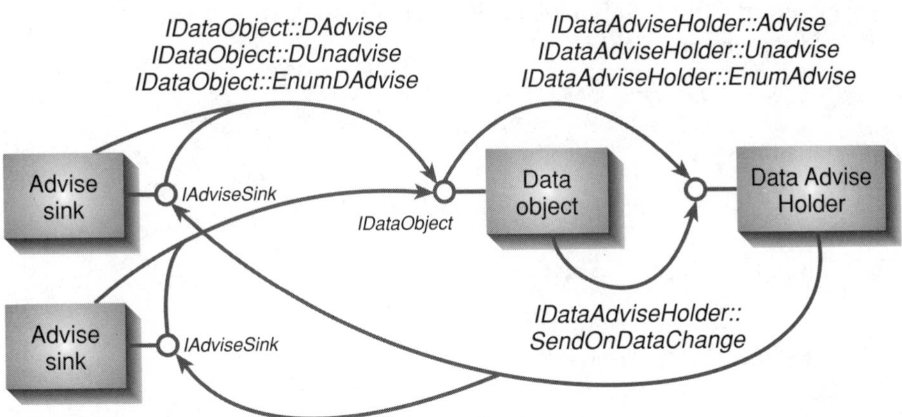

The data objects, in both DLL and EXE, create small Advisor windows, one for each instantiated object, as shown in Figure 6-3 on the next page. Each Advisor window sports an Iterations menu that allows you to fire off a number of continuous notifications from 16 through 572. (That is, $16*n^2$, in which n progresses from 1 through 6.) These Advisor windows are created from within the data objects themselves—there is no problem creating a window from within a DLL in this manner.

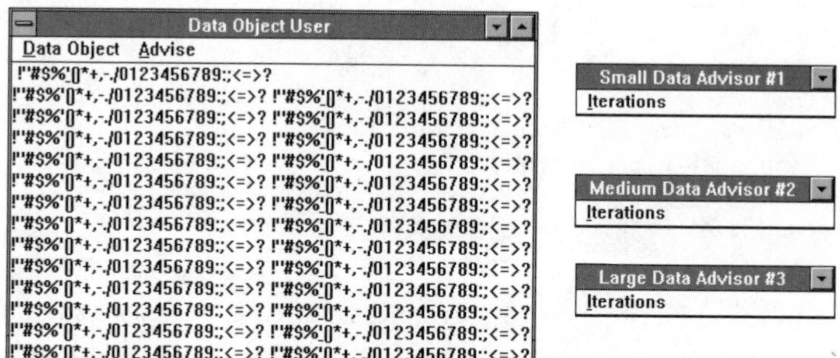

Figure 6-3.
The DATAUSER program, with Advisor windows from each of the three data objects in use.

Whenever you select one of the numbers from the Iterations menu, the object enters a loop in its *AdvisorWndProc* (in the case of the WM_COMMAND message, omitted from Listing 6-1). Within this loop, it calls the *IDataAdviseHolder::SendOnDataChange* a given number of times and then reports the number of milliseconds it took for all the calls, along with an average time for each call:

```
DWORD   dwTime, dwAvg;
char    szTime[128], szTitle[80];
UINT    i;

[In a WM_COMMAND message case]

if (NULL==m_pIDataAdviseHolder)
    break;

dwTime=GetTickCount();

i=0;
while (TRUE)
    {
    pDO->m_pIDataAdviseHolder->SendOnDataChange(pDO
        ->m_pIDataObject, 0, ADVF_NODATA);

    if (++i >= iAdvise)
        break;
    }
```

```
dwTime=GetTickCount()-dwTime;
dwAvg=dwTime/iAdvise;

wsprintf(szTime, "Total\t=%lu ms\n\rAverage\t=%lu ms"
    ,dwTime, dwAvg);

GetWindowText(hWnd, szTitle, sizeof(szTitle));
MessageBox(hWnd, szTime, szTitle, MB_OK);
```

I encourage you to play with both DLL and EXE data objects to see how fast DATAUSER can receive notifications from both on your particular machine. You will notice immediately that notifications from the EXE object are slower, simply due to the LRPC layer in between and how the presence of that layer affects notification. In addition, I've been told that the data advise holder implementation is not the fastest thing in the world, so if you're heavily reliant on real-time performance, you might want to implement your own holder or, if possible, eliminate the holder altogether. The latter is the better choice if you know exactly how many advises will be asked of your application and what sort of notification rates are necessary.

Special Considerations for Remoted Notifications

When a data object lives in an EXE, as opposed to in a DLL, there are some significant performance penalties due to the marshaling of the *IAdviseSink::OnDataChange* calls between the data object and the user. Blasting data rapidly in the preceding code works fine for a DLL but will eventually cause the message queue in the consumer application to overflow if you exceed the size of that application's message queue (which is why OLE 2 applications should generally use a message queue size of 96). To prevent this from happening and to give the advise sink application a chance to catch up, the EXE version of our data object, EDATAOBJ, has a slight modification in the loop shown in the preceding code. Note that this explicit yielding is necessary only under Windows 3.1, not under Windows NT because the latter is a preemptive system to begin with:

```
i=0;
while (TRUE)
    {
   #ifdef EXEDATAOBJECT
   #ifndef WIN32
    MSG      msg;

    if (PeekMessage(&msg, NULL, 0, 0, PM_REMOVE))
        {
```

(continued)

```
        TranslateMessage(&msg);
        DispatchMessage(&msg);
        }
    else
#endif
#endif
        {
        pDO->m_pIDataAdviseHolder->SendOnDataChange(pDO
            ->m_pIDataObject, 0, ADVF_NODATA);

        if (++i >= iAdvise)
            break;
        }
    }
```

When a call to *IAdviseSink::OnDataChange* is made from one application to another—that is, across a process boundary where marshaling is necessary—the Component Object library generates an asynchronous call. Most other marshaled function calls are synchronous, but notifications among applications are designed as asynchronous because the source application generally doesn't want to wait around for possible consumers to use that data. This is not, however, without some impact on the consumer's implementation of *IAdviseSink*—for that we need to look specifically at an *OnDataChange* implementation.

Inside the Advise Sink

The DATAUSER program implements an advise sink object by using the *IAdviseSink* interface, but because DATAUSER hands a pointer to this object only to *IDataObject::DAdvise,* it needs to implement only the single *IAdviseSink::OnDataChange* member.

You might have already noticed while running DATAUSER that it has two items on the Advise menu (in addition to those items that allow you to select the advise format): GetData On Change and Paint On Change, which change DATAUSER's behavior inside *OnDataChange* as follows:

- When you toggle GetData On Change, you toggle the *m_fGetData* flag in the instantiated *CAppVars* (C++) object. If this flag is not set inside *IAdviseSink::OnDataChange,* DATAUSER returns immediately and executes the member function as quickly as possible:

```
STDMETHODIMP_(void) CImpIAdviseSink::OnDataChange(...)
    {
    if (!m_pAV->m_fGetData)
        return;
    ...
```

- If *m_fGetData* is set, DATAUSER checks the format of the data specified in the FORMATETC parameter to *OnDataChange*, and if DATAUSER can use it, the application fires off a call to *IDataObject::GetData*, stores that data in the *CAppVars* object, and invalidates (but does not update) the main window to cause an eventual repaint:

  ```
  if (m_pAV->m_fRepaint)
      InvalidateRect(m_pAV->m_hWnd,NULL,TRUE);
  ```

  This is precisely why DATAUSER sets up an advise with ADVF_NODATA: The *m_fGetData* flag determines whether the data object should render the data on each notification.

- When you toggle Paint On Change, you toggle the *CAppVars* member *m_fRepaint*. This flag has no effect if *m_fGetData* is not set; only when *OnDataChange* has retrieved the data and invalidated the window, *m_fRepaint* determines whether to immediately call *UpdateWindow*:

  ```
  if (m_pAV->m_fRepaint)
      UpdateWindow(m_pAV->m_hWnd);
  ```

Now we have a slight complication when we are using the EXE version EDATAOBJ: Notifications are asynchronous, whereas a notification from a DLL is always synchronous (because it's a direct function call in all cases, no remoting). The complication, which will be familiar you if you've worked in OLE 1, is that during an asynchronous call, the callee (in this case, *IAdviseSink::OnDataChange*) cannot make any other function calls that might require remoting. So if we are using the EXE-based data object, our *IAdviseSink* implementation cannot call *IDataObject::GetData* from within our *OnDataChange*. Bummer.

To account for this, DATAUSER disables the GetData On Change and Paint On Change menu items when you are using EXE data objects—that is, when the *CAppVars* member *m_fEXE* is TRUE. The implementation of *IAdviseSink::OnDataChange* uses *m_fEXE* to decide whether it should call *IDataObject::GetData*. So first, because *m_fGetData* is meaningless when *m_fEXE* is TRUE, the preceding code for dealing with *m_fGetData* requires a slight modification:

```
if (!m_pAV->m_fGetData && !m_pAV->m_fEXE)
    return;
```

If our application is within an asynchronous *OnDataChange* call and it does attempt to call *IDataObject::GetData*, it'll get a return SCODE of RPC-_E_CANTCALLOUT_INASYNCCALL, which tells it exactly what's going on. Therefore, DATAUSER has to implement somewhat different behavior when data changes so that the actual call to *IDataObject::GetData* is delayed until after our application has exited *IAdviseSink::OnDataChange*:

```
if (m_pAV->m_fEXE)
    {
    ReleaseStgMedium(&(m_pAV->m_stm));  //Clean up any old data.
    m_pAV->m_cf=cf;
    m_pAV->m_stm.tymed=TYMED_NULL;

    InvalidateRect(m_pAV->m_hWnd, NULL, TRUE);
    return;
    }
```

This code in itself means very little until you examine the top of the *CAppVars::Paint* function in DATAUSER.CPP:

```
hDC=BeginPaint(m_hWnd, &ps);

 if (m_fEXE)
    {
     if (TYMED_NULL==m_stm.tymed && 0!=m_cf)
         {
         SETDefFormatEtc(fe, m_cf
             , TYMED_HGLOBAL | TYMED_MFPICT | TYMED_GDI);

         if (NULL!=m_pIDataObject)
             m_pIDataObject->GetData(&fe, &m_stm);
         }
     }

[Other code to perform painting]
```

What happens here is that in *IAdviseSink::OnDataChange*, DATAUSER stores the clipboard format that changed in the *CAppVars* object but also stores a TYMED_NULL to indicate that it actually has no data on hand with which to paint. Because *OnDataChange* still invalidates the window, we'll eventually see a WM_PAINT message, but that message will occur outside the asynchronous LRPC call. Therefore, our WM_PAINT handling in the preceding code can call *IDataObject::GetData* if it sees that our application is using the EXE data object and that the application doesn't already have data on hand (*m_stm.tymed* is TYMED_NULL). This call to *GetData* will succeed, so the application can then repaint with that updated data.

IDataObject as a Standard for Object Data Transfer

As I've mentioned already, *IDataObject* is the standardized interface for data exchange. It therefore makes sense for any object capable of performing any type of data transfer to do as much as it can through *IDataObject* instead of through custom interfaces. We can see this in practice with the Polyline component object we've been developing. The versions of the *IPolyline* interface up to this point (those in Chapters 4 and 5) contain a number of custom data transfer functions:

```
DECLARE_INTERFACE_(IPolyline5, IUnknown)
    {
    [Other members]

    STDMETHOD(DataSet)       (THIS_ LPPOLYLINEDATA, BOOL, BOOL) PURE;
    STDMETHOD(DataGet)       (THIS_ LPPOLYLINEDATA) PURE;
    STDMETHOD(DataSetMem)    (THIS_ HGLOBAL, BOOL, BOOL, BOOL) PURE;
    STDMETHOD(DataGetMem)    (THIS_ HGLOBAL FAR *) PURE;
    STDMETHOD(RenderBitmap)  (THIS_ HBITMAP FAR *) PURE;
    STDMETHOD(RenderMetafile) (THIS_ HMETAFILE FAR *) PURE;
    STDMETHOD(RenderMetafilePict) (THIS_ HGLOBAL FAR *) PURE;

    [Other members]
    }
```

In other words, *IPolyline* has so far had separate functions for exchange of its native data in both *Get* and *Set* directions: *DataSet* and *DataGet* operate on a pointer medium (which is used internally in the Polyline, for the most part); *DataSetMem* and *DataGetMem* operate on an HGLOBAL medium. This interface has also maintained three separate member functions to render specific formats. But because we can express any data format through a FORMATETC and because we can express storage mediums such as HGLOBAL and HBITMAP, we can replace all of these functions by implementing *IDataObject* on Polyline, just as we replaced the specific file storage functions with *IPersistStorage* in Chapter 5, modifying Component Cosmo appropriately.

In addition, Polyline has been traveling along with another interface, *IPolylineAdviseSink*, with members such as *OnDataChange*, *OnPointChange*, and so on. Here, as well, we remove the *OnDataChange* member from this interface and replace it with the standard *IAdviseSink*. Therefore, anyone using this object who is unaware of the custom *IPolyline* and *IPolylineAdviseSink* interfaces can still ask for data change notifications by using the standard interfaces.

Overall, the changes to both Polyline and its user, Component Cosmo, are as follows, with the revised *IPolyline* interface, *IPolyline6*, defined in INC\IPOLY6.H. I won't give code listings here because none of the code explains anything that hasn't already been covered in both DATAUSER and DDATAOBJ:

- Polyline has two additional files, IDATAOBJ.CPP and IENUMFE.CPP, which implement *IDataObject* (on the *CPolyline* object) and *IEnumFORMATETC.* CoCosmo adds IADVSINK.CPP, in which it receives *OnDataChange* notifications from the Polyline. CoCosmo implements the *IAdviseSink* as part of its *CCosmoDoc* object and has removed the *OnDataChange* member from its implementation of *IPolylineAdviseSink.*
- Polyline internally maintains a *DataAdviseHolder* object for tracking *IAdviseSink* pointers that it sees through *IDataObject::DAdvise.* Where it used to call *IPolylineAdviseSink::OnDataChange,* it now calls *IDataAdviseHolder::SendOnDataChange.*
- The *IPolyline::DataSet* and *IPolyline::DataGet* members, because they are used internally by the Polyline object in its *IPersistStorage* implementation, have been moved out of the public interface into private member functions of the C++ *CPolyline* class.
- Polyline now uses a registered clipboard format to identify its native data. The string is defined as SZPOLYLINECLIPFORMAT in INC\IPOLY6.H (''Polyline Figure'').
- The internal *CPolyline* class carries FORMATETC arrays for both *IDataObject::GetData* and *IDataObject::SetData. GetData* handles Polyline's native format in TYMED_HGLOBAL, CF_METAFILEPICT in TYMED_MFPICT, and CF_BITMAP in TYMED_GDI, in that order. *SetData* handles only Polyline's native format in TYMED _HGLOBAL. These structures are initialized in *CPolyline::CPolyline.*
- Component Cosmo implements a set of *IUnknown* members on its *CCosmoDoc* class in order to support the interface implementation of *IAdviseSink.*
- All of Component Cosmo's clipboard handling in *CCosmoDoc::RenderFormat* and *CCosmoDoc::FPaste* now work through the *IDataObject* interface on its Polyline object. Because ComponentCosmo maintains only an *IPolyline6* pointer at all times, it obtains the *IDataObject* pointer when necessary through *QueryInterface.*

All these changes again move Polyline closer to becoming a compound document object in Chapter 11. With both *IPersistStorage* and *IDataObject* in place, Polyline is already halfway toward that goal. With implementations of *IOleObject* and *IViewObject*, it will be embeddable in any compound document container and still be usable by Component Cosmo because containers will communicate with Polyline through standard interfaces, whereas Component Cosmo, which knows Polyline intimately, will continue to communicate through the custom *IPolyline* interface. This again reinforces a great benefit of interfaces and the *QueryInterface* mechanism: Polyline can support two different types of users (component users with inside knowledge, and a compound document container with no extra knowledge) by implementing additional interfaces that do not interfere with one another.

View Objects and the *IViewObject* Interface

A view object is similar to a data object in that it's almost always simply another way of treating some other more complex object. For that reason, you almost invariably obtain an *IViewObject* pointer by calling *QueryInterface* on another object. In this case, a view object is any object that you can use by means of an *IViewObject* interface pointer, an arrangement that allows you to ask the object to draw itself or otherwise manage details about its graphical presentations. The interface exists so that an object user can ask an object to render directly onto a device instead of into a transfer medium:[4]

```
DECLARE_INTERFACE_(IViewObject, IUnknown)
    {
    [IUnknown methods included]

    STDMETHOD(Draw) (THIS_ DWORD dwDrawAspect, LONG lindex,
                     void FAR * pvAspect, DVTARGETDEVICE FAR * ptd,
                     HDC hicTargetDev, HDC hdcDraw,
                     const LPRECTL lprcBounds, const LPRECTL lprcWBounds,
                     BOOL (CALLBACK * pfnContinue) (DWORD),
                     DWORD dwContinue) PURE;

    STDMETHOD(GetColorSet) (THIS_ DWORD dwDrawAspect, LONG lindex,
                     void FAR* pvAspect, DVTARGETDEVICE FAR * ptd,
                     HDC hicTargetDev, LPLOGPALETTE FAR* ppColorSet) PURE;

    STDMETHOD(Freeze)(THIS_ DWORD dwDrawAspect, LONG lindex,
                     void FAR* pvAspect, DWORD FAR* pdwFreeze) PURE;
    STDMETHOD(Unfreeze) (THIS_ DWORD dwFreeze) PURE;
```

(continued)

4. Note that OLE versions 2.01 and later define an *IViewObject2* interface, which has an addition member function called *GetExtent*. We'll see this again in Chapter 11.

```
    STDMETHOD(SetAdvise) (THIS_ DWORD aspects, DWORD advf,
                LPADVISESINK pAdvSink) PURE;
    STDMETHOD(GetAdvise) (THIS_ DWORD FAR* pAspects, DWORD FAR* pAdvf,
                LPADVISESINK FAR* ppAdvSink) PURE;
    };

typedef      IViewObject FAR* LPVIEWOBJECT;
```

Asking an object "Can you draw yourself on an *hDC* that I provide?" is the same as calling *QueryInterface* with *IID_IViewObject.* If the object is not capable or if the object is in an EXE, the answer will be "No." If, however, you are given the *IViewObject* pointer, you can do a number of things with it, the most common of which will be to ask the object to draw itself. When the object is asked to draw, it's responsible for leaving the *hDC* in the same state as it was received, which is what common sense would dictate. If you need to change the mapping mode or any other aspect about the *hDC,* be sure to use *SaveDC* on entry to *IViewObject::Draw* and *RestoreDC* on exit.

You might have noticed already that three of the parameters to *IViewObject::Draw* are an aspect (*dwAspect*), a piece index (*lindex*), and a pointer to a target device structure (*ptd*). These are three of the same fields in a FORMATETC and are used pretty much in the same way to identify the data you want to draw, much as you identify the data to render through *IDataObject::GetData.* There is no clipboard format nor is there a storage medium involved with *Draw,* however, because we are not trying to get the data ourselves but rather want it placed on an *hDC,* which can be thought of here as identifying both the format and the medium.

WARNING

IViewObject, although it is a standard interface, does not have marshaling support. It is not possible to move an *IViewObject* pointer across a process boundary under Windows. The primary problem is that the *hDC* parameter to *IViewObject::Draw* cannot be passed to another process because device contexts are meaningful only in the context of one process. Therefore, *IViewObject* can be implemented only from objects in server DLLs or object handlers. In the case in which an object in a server EXE requires the use of *IViewObject,* it must provide an object handler DLL to work in conjunction with the server EXE, as shown in Chapter 11.

IViewObject::Draw

The *Draw* member function in *IViewObject* probably has the longest parameter list in all of OLE 2 because it encompasses such rich functionality. It allows you to tell an object exactly what to draw, where to draw it, and how to draw it; it even lets you supply a callback function (yes, we still use a few of them) if you want to have the ability to break out of long repaints. Because this function covers so much ground, let's first examine the simplest use of it, which would be in the following form:

```
pIViewObject->Draw(DVASPECT_CONTENT, -1, NULL, NULL, 0, hDC, &rcl
    , NULL, NULL, 0);
```

This line of code means "Draw the full rendering of the object (*DVASPECT_CONTENT, −1*) on a rectangle (*rcl*) on this *hDC*." The object will draw whatever is meant by its "full representation" directly to the given *hDC*, scaled to the rectangle you provide. Always express the rectangle in the units of the current mapping mode in the *hDC*. The *hDC* can be the screen, a printer, a metafile, or a memory device context; the object will behave appropriately. So an object that typically generates bitmaps can implement this function with a simple *StretchBlt* call, or if it normally uses a metafile, it would call *PlayMetafile* after setting the extents properly for your rectangle.

Whenever a view object user changed the size of the object's display area, the view object user would simply repaint the object, passing a different rectangle to *Draw*. When it drew the object on the screen while processing WM_PAINT, it would pass the *hDC* from *BeginPaint*; if it were printing whatever document contained the object, it would pass the *hDC* from a *CreateDC* call on the printer device. You might also have a reason to choose a different aspect as the first parameter, such as DVASPECT_THUMBNAIL if you were drawing the object in a print preview mode, or DVASPECT_ICON if you preferred a small, compact presentation. So, in the most simple uses of *IViewObject::Draw*, you are concerned with the following four parameters:

- *dwAspect (DWORD)*: One of DVASPECT_CONTENT, DVASPECT_THUMBNAIL, DVASPECT_ICON, or DVASPECT_DOCPRINT with identical definitions as the same field in FORMATETC. The view object is not, however, required to support all of these aspects.
- *lindex (LONG)*: The index of the piece of data, as in FORMATETC. In OLE 2, this should always be −1.
- *hDC (HDC)*: The device context on which to draw. This value must not be NULL.

- *lprcBounds (RECTL FAR *)*: A pointer to RECTL that contains the rectangle in which the object should draw, scaling the presentation as necessary to fit this rectangle. This parameter cannot be NULL. Be sure not to pass a pointer to a typical Windows RECT structure under Windows 3.1—a RECTL is twice as large, so passing a RECT is living dangerously. Under Windows NT, a RECT is identical to a RECTL.

Note also that a *pvAspect* parameter exists to provide further information for a specific *dwAspect.* Under OLE 2, this parameter is not used because none of the standard aspects support additional information of this nature. Therefore, this parameter is always NULL.

OLE 2 provides the API function *OleDraw,* which streamlines this most common case of calling *IViewObject::Draw. OleDraw* is defined in OLE2.H and lives in OLE2.DLL. The exact implementation of the function is not hard to guess or reproduce:

```
STDAPI OleDraw(LPUNKNOWN pUnknown, DWORD dwAspect, HDC hdcDraw
    , LPCRECT lprcBounds);
    {
    HRESULT       hr;
    LPVIEWOBJECT pIViewObject;

    if (NULL!=pUnknown)
        {
        hr=pUnknown->QueryInterface(IID_IViewObject
            , (LPLPVOID)&pIViewObject);

        if (SUCCEEDED(hr))
            {
            pIViewObject->Draw(DVASPECT_CONTENT, -1, NULL, NULL, 0
                , hDC, lprcBounds, NULL, NULL, 0);

            pIViewObject->Release();
            }
        }

    return;
    }
```

OleDraw is provided as an API function because you normally don't hold onto an *IViewObject* pointer for any other reason, and it would be cumbersome if you always had to use *QueryInterface* every time you wanted to draw normally. However, there are many times when you want more control over the exact rendering and *OleDraw* becomes a straight jacket. In such cases, you are always free to use *QueryInterface* for *IViewObject* and call *Draw* yourself. Let's look at some of the cases where you might want more control.

Rendering for a Specific Device

Many applications, especially high-end graphics and desktop publishing packages, are concerned about getting the best possible output as well as the fastest possible output on a printer. These applications then will want to tell all view objects about the intended device when calling *Draw*. Two parameters of *Draw* handle this consideration:

- *ptd (LPDVTARGETDEVICE)*: A pointer to a target device structure identical to the one in FORMATETC that describes the exact device, generally a printer, for which the object is to render its image. A NULL means "the display."
- *hicTargetDev (HDC)*: An *information* context for the target device described by *ptd* from which the object can extract device metrics and test the capabilities of that device. If the *ptd* parameter is NULL, the object should not use this parameter, regardless of its actual value.

There are two primary cases in which you might pass non-NULL values to these functions. The first and most obvious is when *hDC* is a printer device context and you want the objects to render as accurately as possible for that printer. In this case, you can describe the printer device in *ptd* and pass either an information context you have on hand or the same *hDC* to which you are printing as the *hicTargetDev* parameter. You must pass something in *hicTargetDev*, so you tell the object that you are, in fact, going to a printer, because in the case of printing, you will *always* have an *hDC* that can be treated as an information context. An example of when you would use both parameters is when you are printing to, say, a PostScript printer, and you want to let any object you're printing optimize for PostScript. The object, knowing this fact and knowing that *hDC* is a real printer DC, might choose to send PostScript commands directly to the printer (by means of the Windows *Escape* function) instead of calling GDI functions. The result will be highly optimized output for the printer and generally better performance.

The second case applies to situations such as print preview modes, in which the application wants to draw the object on the screen but wants the object to act as if it were drawing to the printer. In this case, *ptd* will point to a valid DVTARGETDEVICE structure, but *hicTargetDev* is NULL, meaning that the object should call GDI functions on *hDC* to draw what it would show on the given device. For example, if the object would normally show a magenta shading on the screen, it might not want to draw the same shading on a printer that does not support color. By telling the object about your intended target device, you enable it to choose either to eliminate the shading or to draw in black-and-white dithering on a black-and-white device.

Drawing into a Metafile

A metafile device context is a rather special beast when it comes to drawing the object at a specific location within that metafile. The object in this case needs to know both the window extents and the window origin if it has any hope of drawing its representation in the correct context of the metafile *hDC*.

To accommodate metafiles, the *lprcWBounds* parameter contains the window extent and the window origin, not a real rectangle. The window origin is the point (*lprcWBounds->left, lprcWBounds->top*). The horizontal window extent is in *lprcWBounds->right* and the vertical window extent is in *lprcWBounds->bottom*. Objects in DLLs that implement *IViewObject::Draw* should account for these values if the caller provides them. By "account for them," I mean that you should scale or place your graphics appropriately: Do not call *SetWindowOrgEx* or *SetWindowExtEx*; if you do, you will place records into the metafile that could affect other records that you do not own. You should use only these values to correctly place whatever GDI calls you happen to make, which for the most part means you can ignore them altogether and simply use *lprcBounds*.

You *do* have to pay attention when your implementation is playing a metafile as its method for generating the presentation (for example, a metafile editor). For instance, the OLE 2 default handler usually implements *IViewObject::Draw* by pulling a metafile from its internal cache and drawing that on the *hDC*. However, each record in its cached metafile assumes a specific origin, usually (0,0), so for OLE 2 to draw that metafile into another metafile, it must play one record at a time and modify the scaling and the origin coordinates for each record so that it is displayed properly in the outer metafile. So *lprcWBounds* is required to be able to place one metafile within another. Only when you play a metafile in your own *IViewObject::Draw* implementation do you need to worry about this parameter.

Aborting Long Repaints

The two other parameters to *IViewObject::Draw* give an application the ability to break out of a long repaint or an otherwise lengthy operation:

- *pfnContinue (BOOL (CALLBACK *) (DWORD))*: A pointer to a callback function that is called periodically during a painting process. The function returns TRUE to continue drawing or FALSE to abort the operation, which causes *Draw* to return DRAW_E_ABORT.
- *dwContinue (DWORD)*: An extra 32-bit value to pass as the parameter to *pfnContinue*. Typically, this value would be a pointer to some application-defined structure needed inside the callback function.

A typical user of a view object might implement a function that would test the status of the Esc key to determine whether to continue the painting, allowing end users to terminate torturous long repaints for ridiculously complicated drawings:

```
BOOL CALLBACK DrawAbort(DWORD dwContinue)
    {
    return (GetAsyncKeyState(VK_ESCAPE) < 0);
    }
```

How often the callback function is actually called depends on the implementation of the view object, of course, as well as the actual means to draw the data. As a general guideline, call the function once for every 16 operations. (An *operation* is either a GDI call or the playing of a metafile record.) If you know you are drawing more than one large bitmap, call the function after each *BitBlt* or *StretchBlt*. If you are transferring only one bitmap or you know that your operation is quite fast, you can ignore this function altogether.

Other *IViewObject* Member Functions

Of course, there are member functions in *IViewObject* other than *Draw* that are, on the average, used far less often than *Draw*. This section will describe *GetColorSet*, *Freeze*, and *Unfreeze*. *SetAdvise* and *GetAdvise* are described in the next section, "*IViewObject* and Notification."

IViewObject::GetColorSet allows the user of a view object to obtain the logical palette that the object would use when drawn so that the object user can try to match that palette as closely as possible. *GetColorSet* takes the same *dwAspect*, *lindex*, *pvAspect*, *ptd*, and *hicTargetDev* parameters as *Draw* does. If the object uses a palette, it should fill the LOGPALETTE structure pointed to by *ppColorSet* with the colors it would use if *Draw* were called with the same parameters; otherwise, it should return S_FALSE. In general, the palette here should be identical to what the object might pass to the Windows API functions *SetPaletteEntries* and *CreatePalette*.

Freeze and *Unfreeze* (which I've always thought should have been called *Thaw*) let the object user control whether the object is allowed to change its visual representation on subsequent calls to *Draw. Freeze* works on one aspect at a time; freezing DVASPECT_CONTENT still allows *Draw* called with DVASPECT_ICON to change the actual presentation. Calling *Freeze* returns a DWORD key, which you later pass to *Unfreeze* to bring the object back from the Ice Age.

Freezing a view object can be thought of as creating a bitmap copy of the current view of the object and always using that bitmap to show the object. Underneath, the actual data might have changed, but the image does not. Because we're always using the snapshot bitmap to show the object, calls to *Draw* don't show any changes.

IViewObject and Notification

The final two members of *IViewObject, SetAdvise* and *GetAdvise*, work with *IAdviseSink::OnViewChange* independently of *IAdviseSink::OnDataChange*. For the most part, *OnViewChange* should be used by an advise sink to determine when an object's presentation changes, as opposed to determining whether its underlying data has changed—which might, in fact, not change anything about the actual display of that data. For example, if a data object is attached to a spreadsheet, a change in one of the cells precipitates only a view change for DVASPECT_CONTENT if that cell is visible in the full content rendering. A change to the spreadsheet does not, however, change DVASPECT_ICON because the icon, and its label, are quite unrelated to the actual data underneath them. A change to the actual spreadsheet filename, on the other hand, might change the icon aspect (if the filename is the icon's label) but not the content aspect, which shows only the spreadsheet cells.

Notifications from a view object are commonly used from a Compound Document container that needs to know when to repaint a Compound Document object. Therefore, containers will call *IViewObject::SetAdvise* with the aspect shown for that object (be it content, icon, and so on), advise flags (the same *ADVF_...* flags as as are used by *IDataObject::DAdvise*), and a pointer to the container's *IAdviseSink* interface. Whenever that aspect, and that aspect only, changes, the advise sink will be notified through *OnViewChange*, in which case, the container will generally force a repaint on the object and a call to *IViewObject::Draw.*

The only advise flags that are relevant here are *ADVF_PRIMEFIRST* and *ADVF_ONLYONCE*: The former will immediately generate an *OnViewChange* in your *IAdviseSink* and the latter will release your advise sink as soon as *OnViewChange* is called once. Of course, you can pass a zero for the flags.

What Happens if Multiple Users Ask for a *SetAdvise* on the Same *IViewObject*?

A common concern is that two users of the same view object will conflict when attempting to set up advise connections with that view object. If the view object itself supports only one connection at a time, will there be a conflict? Well, yes and no. Remember first that a view object can exist only in a DLL, never in an EXE, because *IViewObject* is an "unmarshalable" interface (due to the non-shareable *hDC* parameter). Therefore, each user of this view object will have a different instance of the object—a different pointer and a different piece of memory for that object. If a single user has multiple pieces of code within it that want to use the same object, there's the potential for conflict, in which case it's left to the application programmer to manage the advise connections.

You might wonder about a situation in which you have an advise established on an object through both the *IDataObject* interface and the *IViewObject* interface on that object. Which *IAdviseSink* member will be called first? The answer is undefined because it depends completely on the object's implementation. You should therefore not try to depend on any particular ordering of the notifications.

A view object might not, of course, support any advises, in which case *IViewObject::SetAdvise* will return NOTIFY_E_ADVISENOTSUPPORTED. Even when advising is supported, view objects maintain only one advise sink pointer at a time. There is no *ViewAdviseHolder* as there is a *DataAdviseHolder*. Therefore, a call to *SetAdvise* will terminate notifications for whoever previously called *SetAdvise*; a call with a NULL *IAdviseSink* will simply terminate the current connection. For this reason as well, you can call *GetAdvise* to retrieve the current *IAdviseSink* pointer to which the object is sending notifications.

Freeloading from OLE2.DLL

I want to skip ahead a little bit and show a trick using the view object implementation inside OLE2.DLL, but to do that, we need to look at Compound Documents a little. OLE2.DLL, besides providing all the *Ole*... API functions, is also known as the *default handler*—that is, the object handler that is always used for a compound document object if a specific handler does not exist. Compound document objects are seen generically as some sort of locked box, and inside that box is the object's native data; the object's server is the only agent that has the key to the box. Compound documents are all about putting these little boxes into documents and moving them around within the documents in which they exist.

The big deal is that only the server who originally created the object knows how to unlock the box to generate a picture for the object. The server is the only code that can draw anything to actually *show* or print in a document. Everything's cool as long as the server is around when you want to view or print that document, but because the little box moves around with its container document and because that document might move from machine to machine, the object eventually will become detached from its server. So the document is left with this box of goo with nothing to show for it because there's nothing around that knows how to open the box.

For this reason, OLE 2 maintains one or more cached presentations for every object, at the discretion of the container. That is, the container controls what is and is not cached. By default, OLE caches a metafile rendered for the screen for every object it handles (that is, for every object using OLE2.DLL as a handler). Whenever the container asks for a presentation to be cached for an object, OLE asks the object's server to render that presentation and tucks it away for later use. When the container saves the object, it generates a call to the implementation of *IPersistStorage::Save* in the handler. If the handler is OLE2.DLL, all presentations in the cache are also saved. When the container reloads the object, it generates a call to *IPersistStorage::Load*, which pulls those presentations out of storage and into the cache. Furthermore, whenever the object is loaded (that is, its presentation cache has been initialized), the container can call *IViewObject::Draw*, which tells the default handler to take the best presentation it can find in the cache and draw it to an *hDC*.

I'm bringing this up because in the next chapter I want to make the Patron sample capable of containing ordinary bitmaps and metafiles before we go so far as to contain compound document objects in Chapter 9. Many word processors and other document-oriented applications also share this capability or a desire for it, because sometimes you have a picture lying around on disk that you want to integrate into a document, and you might not have an application that knows anything about such a presentation. But when I thought about adding the feature to Patron, I started feeling a tad queasy: I would have to write code first to draw metafiles and bitmaps (not too bad) and then to save that data in a disk file and load it back in again. I don't know about you, but serializing graphics to a file and figuring out how to load them in again is a certain degree of tedium I avoid like the plague.

Then I suddenly realized that in OLE2.DLL's role as the default handler, it had to somewhere contain the code to do exactly what I needed: drawing and serialization. I simply had to figure out how to convince that DLL to do my work for me. It was a struggle at first, until I found two entries in the Registration Database that struck me:

```
{00000316-0000-0000-C0000-000000000046} = Device Independent Bitmap
    InprocServer=ole2.dll
{00000315-0000-0000-C0000-000000000046} = Metafile
    InprocServer=ole2.dll
```

What I found is that OLE2.DLL is a DLL server for what are called *static compound document objects,* which are presentations without any known source. As a DLL server for any compound document object, OLE2.DLL is responsible for providing *IDataObject, IViewObject,* and *IPersistStorage* interfaces, among others, on such objects. What came out of my experiment to see whether I could make use of all this neat functionality was the program called Freeloader (FREELOAD.EXE), shown in Figure 6-4. This handy little application can copy or paste any metafile or bitmap from the clipboard and load or save it to a Compound File with the FRE extension. Freeloader is a simple application built on the sample code CLASSLIB (as are Patron and Cosmo), in which each document can contain one graphic. The only code relevant to our discussion here is in the DOCUMENT.CPP file, shown in Listing 6-5 on the next page.

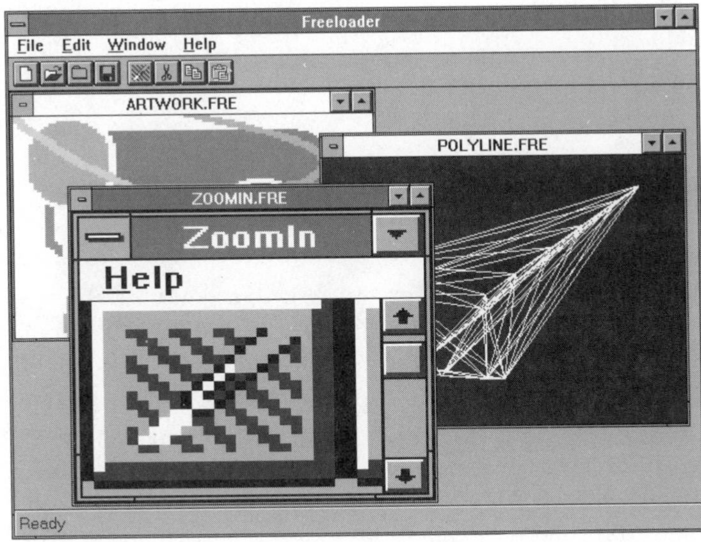

Figure 6-4.
The FREELOADER program, with three open presentations.

DOCUMENT.CPP

```
/*
 * Freeloader Chapter 6
 *
 * Implementation of the CFreeloaderDoc derivation of CDocument.
 * We create a default handler object and use it for drawing, data
 * caching, and serialization.
 *
 * Copyright (c)1993 Microsoft Corporation, All Rights Reserved
 */

#include "freeload.h"

CFreeloaderDoc::CFreeloaderDoc(HINSTANCE hInst)
    : CDocument(hInst)
    {
    m_pIStorage=NULL;
    m_pIUnknown=NULL;
    m_dwConn=0;
    return;
    }

CFreeloaderDoc::~CFreeloaderDoc(void)
    {
    ReleaseObject();

    if (NULL!=m_pIStorage)
        m_pIStorage->Release();

    return;
    }

/*
 * CFreeloaderDoc::ReleaseObject
 *
 * Purpose:
 *  Centralizes cleanup code for the object and its cache.
 */

void CFreeloaderDoc::ReleaseObject(void)
    {
```

Listing 6-5.

The DOCUMENT.CPP file of the Freeloader program, which handles compound files and clipboard operations with graphic presentations.

(continued)

Listing 6-5. *continued*

```
    LPOLECACHE      pIOleCache;
    HRESULT         hr;

    if (0!=m_dwConn)
        {
        hr=m_pIUnknown->QueryInterface(IID_IOleCache
            , (LPLPVOID)&pIOleCache);

        if (SUCCEEDED(hr))
            {
            pIOleCache->Uncache(m_dwConn);
            pIOleCache->Release();
            }
        }

    if (NULL!=m_pIUnknown)
        m_pIUnknown->Release();

    CoFreeUnusedLibraries();

    m_dwConn=0;
    m_pIUnknown=NULL;
    return;
    }

[FMessageHook catches WM_PAINT to call IViewObject::Draw ]
[ULoad and USave save and load objects through the       ]
[IPersistStorage interface, keeping the root storage open]
[at all times and following the rules for using the      ]
[IPersistStorage interface as described in Chapter 5.    ]

BOOL CFreeloaderDoc::FClip(HWND hWndFrame, BOOL fCut)
    {
    BOOL            fRet=TRUE;
    static UINT     rgcf[3]={CF_METAFILEPICT, CF_DIB, CF_BITMAP};
    const UINT      cFormats=3;
    UINT            i;
    HGLOBAL         hMem;

    if (NULL==m_pIUnknown)
        return FALSE;

    if (!OpenClipboard(hWndFrame))
        return FALSE;

    //Clean out whatever junk is in the clipboard.
    EmptyClipboard();
```

(continued)

Listing 6-5. *continued*

```
    for (i=0; i < cFormats; i++)
        {
        hMem=RenderFormat(rgcf[i]);

        if (NULL!=hMem)
            {
            SetClipboardData(rgcf[i], hMem);
            fRet=TRUE;
            break;
            }
        }

    //Free clipboard ownership.
    CloseClipboard();

    //If we're cutting, clean out the cache and the object we hold.
    if (fRet && fCut)
        {
        ReleaseObject();
        InvalidateRect(m_hWnd, NULL, TRUE);
        UpdateWindow(m_hWnd);
        FDirtySet(TRUE);
        }

    return fRet;
    }

HGLOBAL CFreeloaderDoc::RenderFormat(UINT cf)
    {
    LPDATAOBJECT        pIDataObject;
    FORMATETC           fe;
    STGMEDIUM           stm;

    if (NULL==m_pIUnknown)
        return NULL;

    //We only have to ask the data object (cache) for the data.
    switch (cf)
        {
        case CF_METAFILEPICT:
            stm.tymed=TYMED_MFPICT;
            break;

       case CF_DIB:
            stm.tymed=TYMED_HGLOBAL;
            break;
```

(continued)

Listing 6-5. *continued*

```
        case CF_BITMAP:
            stm.tymed=TYMED_GDI;
            break;

        default:
            return NULL;
        }

    stm.hGlobal=NULL;
    SETDefFormatEtc(fe, cf, stm.tymed);

    m_pIUnknown->QueryInterface(IID_IDataObject
        , (LPLPVOID)&pIDataObject);
    pIDataObject->GetData(&fe, &stm);
    pIDataObject->Release();

    return stm.hGlobal;
    }

BOOL CFreeloaderDoc::FQueryPaste(void)
    {
    return IsClipboardFormatAvailable(CF_BITMAP)
        || IsClipboardFormatAvailable(CF_DIB)
        || IsClipboardFormatAvailable(CF_METAFILEPICT);
    }

BOOL CFreeloaderDoc::FPaste(HWND hWndFrame)
    {
    UINT                cf=0;
    BOOL                fRet=FALSE;
    HRESULT             hr;
    DWORD               dwConn;
    LPUNKNOWN           pIUnknown;
    LPOLECACHE          pIOleCache;
    LPPERSISTSTORAGE    pIPersistStorage;
    FORMATETC           fe;
    STGMEDIUM           stm;
    CLSID               clsID;

    if (!OpenClipboard(hWndFrame))
        return FALSE;

    /*
     * Try to get data in order of metafile, dib, bitmap. We set
     * stm.tymed up front so if we actually get something, a call
     * to ReleaseStgMedium will clean it up for us.
     */
```

(continued)

Listing 6-5. *continued*

```
    stm.tymed=TYMED_MFPICT;
    stm.hGlobal=GetClipboardData(CF_METAFILEPICT);

    if (NULL!=stm.hGlobal)
        cf=CF_METAFILEPICT;

    if (0==cf)
        {
        stm.tymed=TYMED_HGLOBAL;
        stm.hGlobal=GetClipboardData(CF_DIB);

        if (NULL!=stm.hGlobal)
            cf=CF_DIB;
        }

    if (0==cf)
        {
        stm.tymed=TYMED_GDI;
        stm.hGlobal=GetClipboardData(CF_BITMAP);

        if (NULL!=stm.hGlobal)
            cf=CF_BITMAP;
        }

    CloseClipboard();

    //Didn't get anything? Then we're finished.
    if (0==cf)
        return FALSE;

    //This now describes the data we have.
    SETDefFormatEtc(fe, cf, stm.tymed);

    if (CF_METAFILEPICT==cf)
        clsID=CLSID_FreeMetafile;
    else
        clsID=CLSID_FreeDib;

    hr=OleCreateDefaultHandler(clsID, NULL
        , IID_IUnknown, (LPLPVOID)&pIUnknown);

    if (FAILED(hr))
        {
        ReleaseStgMedium(&stm);
        return FALSE;
        }
```

(continued)

Listing 6-5. *continued*

```
    pUnknown->QueryInterface(IID_IPersistStorage
        , (LPLPVOID)&pIPersistStorage);
    pIPersistStorage->InitNew(m_pIStorage);
    pIPersistStorage->Release();

    //Now that we have the cache object, shove the data into it.
    pIUnknown->QueryInterface(IID_IOleCache
        , (LPLPVOID)&pIOleCache);
    pIOleCache->Cache(&fe, ADVF_PRIMEFIRST, &dwConn);

    hr=pIOleCache->SetData(&fe, &stm, TRUE);
    pIOleCache->Release();

    if (FAILED(hr))
        {
        ReleaseStgMedium(&stm);
        pIUnknown->Release();
        return FALSE;
        }

    //Now that that's all done, replace our current with the new.
    ReleaseObject();
    m_pIUnknown=pIUnknown;
    m_dwConn=dwConn;

    FDirtySet(TRUE);

    InvalidateRect(m_hWnd, NULL, TRUE);
    UpdateWindow(m_hWnd);
    return TRUE;
    }
```

The most interesting functions in DOCUMENT.CPP are those dealing with the clipboard: *CFreeloaderDoc::FClip*, *CFreeloaderDoc::RenderFormat*, and *CFreeloaderDoc::FPaste*. The *ULoad* and *USave* functions are written according to the *IPersistStorage* contract between an object and the object user, and because we already nailed shut the coffin on that topic in Chapter 5, I won't resurrect it. *FMessageHook* is interesting only in that it shows a real working example of calling *IViewObject::Draw*, pretty much in the simple use for which *OleDraw* would suffice. I'm using *IViewObject* explicitly here for demonstration. *OleDraw* would be perfectly sufficient.

In all truth, *FClip* and *RenderFormat* look perfectly innocent as well. *FClip* simply places a format or two on the clipboard, and *RenderFormat* simply asks the object in the document for a metafile or bitmap through *IDataObject*. The question is, again, "How on earth did we originally obtain the pointer to the object?" The answer lies in *FPaste*.

The first half of *FPaste* looks like a reasonably normal piece of Windows code that gets a graphics image off the clipboard. The only slightly odd thing is that I'm storing the data handle directly into a STGMEDIUM (because it's there). I also initialize a FORMATETC with the description of what data I actually pasted. Then I do something weird:

```
HRESULT         hr;
LPUNKNOWN       pIUnknown;
CLSID           clsID;
UINT            cf;

...

//cf is the format we got from the clipboard.
if (CF_METAFILEPICT==cf)
    clsID=CLSID_FreeMetafile;
else
    clsID=CLSID_FreeDib;

hr=OleCreateDefaultHandler(clsID, NULL, IID_IUnknown
    , (LPLPVOID)&pIUnknown);
```

OleCreateDefaultHandler is a special function designed to create an object within OLE2.DLL to service the given CLSID. Because OLE2.DLL is also registered as the handler for two CLSIDs called *CLSID_StaticMetafile* and *CLSID_StaticDib*, *OleCreateDefaultHandler* is actually equivalent to calling *CoCreateInstance* with CLSCTX_INPROC_HANDLER. In Freeloader, I defined two different names, *CLSID_FreeMetafile* and *CLSID_FreeDib*, which have the same values as those with Static names.[5] *OleCreateDefaultHandler* is meant to be called from another specific application handler in order for that specific handler to delegate calls to the default handler. We'll see this API function put to its proper use in Chapter 11. For now, let's see how we can further talk it into doing our dirty work for us, which requires two simple steps.

First we have to fulfill our contractual obligations to the object's *IPersistStorage* by calling *IPersistStorage::InitNew* with some storage object. When

5. Both of these CLSIDs are defined in the standard OLEGUID.H include files as *CLSID_StaticMetafile* and *CLSID_StaticDib* but are not included in either OLE2.LIB or COMPOBJ.LIB. Therefore, you must define these for yourself as was done in FREELOAD.H: *DEFINE_OLEGUID(CLSID_FreeMetafile, 0x00000315, 0, 0)*; and *DEFINE_OLEGUID(CLSID_FreeDib, 0x00000316, 0, 0)*. You *must* change the names in your own definitions to avoid conflicts between those you define and those in OLEGUID.H. If you use the same names, either you get link errors with unresolved externals or you create an extra data segment in your EXE that limits you to running only one instance of your application.

the document was first opened, *CFreeloaderDoc::ULoad* was called, which either created or opened a root storage. This storage remains open for the lifetime of the document window, so we can simply pass it to *InitNew* here.

All that remains now is to somehow take the data we obtained from the clipboard and get the object to remember it and maintain it for us. To do this, we must stuff that data into the object's cache by using the *IOleCache* interface, which object handlers must implement for all compound document objects:

```
HRESULT      hr;
LPOLECACHE   pIOleCache;

...

pIUnknown->QueryInterface(IID_IOleCache, (LPLPVOID)&pIOleCache);
pIOleCache->Cache(&fe, ADVF_PRIMEFIRST, &dwConn);

hr=pIOleCache->SetData(&fe, &stm, TRUE);
pIOleCache->Release();
```

The *IOleCache* interface has a number of member functions, only two of which are of interest to us here. *Cache* instructs the object (that is, the handler) to hold onto renderings for a specific FORMATETC. *SetData* is our way of actually handing some data to the object, which the object places in the cache.

Well, that's really all there is to it. Now that we have some data in the cache, we can call *IViewObject::Draw* to display that data on the screen or to dump it to a printer. We could also call *IDataObject::GetData* to get that graphic back again ourselves as in *CFreeloaderDoc::FClip*. We can also call *IPersistStorage::Save* to serialize that data to a storage. To reload the data from the storage, we need only to re-create the object and call *IPersistStorage::Load*, which internally will call *IOleCache::SetData* for us. You can see loading in *CFreeloaderDoc::ULoad*, which creates the object using *CoCreateInstance* simply to show the equivalence between that and *OleCreateDefaultHandler*.

If you ask me, this was much simpler than the code I could have written. All compliments of OLE 2.

IDataObject and DDE

Way back in the early stages of this chapter, we saw how the member functions of *IDataObject* were very similar, in some cases identical, to functions available through other transfer protocols. As we'll see in Chapter 7, the Windows clipboard API functions are entirely subsumed by a few new OLE 2 API functions and *IDataObject*. Chapters 8 and 9 address the drag-and-drop and Compound Document protocols. But where's DDE in all this?

IDataObject and *IAdviseSink* encompass the same functionality as DDE does, with the exception of DDE execute, which is more than matched by OLE Automation. The following table shows the parallels between DDE messages and *IDataObject* member functions:

DDE Message	*IDataObject* Member Function
WM_DDE_POKE	*IDataObject::SetData*
WM_DDE_REQUEST	*IDataObject::GetData*
WM_DDE_ADVISE	*IDataObject::DAdvise*
WM_DDE_UNADVISE	*IDataObject::DUnadvise*
WM_DDE_DATA	*IAdviseSink::OnDataChange*

On the surface, it appears that one could write a simple mapping layer to expose a DDE conversation through *IDataObject* or to generate DDE messages from events in an *IDataObject* and an *IAdviseSink*. When I first began writing this book, I intended to include a DLL to do exactly this, coming full circle with the notion of Uniform Data Transfer by showing how you might isolate yourself from any DDE awareness. But there are some significant differences that I will outline only briefly here. I will not attempt to offer solutions; that is the job of later OLE revisions and third-party vendors.

The first difference is that DDE is inherently asynchronous, and DDE applications have come to depend on this fact. OLE 2 interface functions are inherently synchronous, with the exception of *IAdviseSink* calls from a data object in an EXE. If you call *IDataObject::DAdvise* with ADVF_ONLYONCE ¦ ADVF_PRIMEFIRST, you can get the equivalent of an asynchronous *IDataObject::GetData*, but that's a special case.

The second difference is how to obtain an *IDataObject* pointer that represents the data you want. Under DDE, you initiate a conversation when attempting to reach a specific service and topic, such as the service "Excel" and the topic "NASDAQ.XLS." OLE 2's mechanisms allow you to do pretty much the same in a more roundabout fashion—that is, you can call *CoCreateInstance* on Microsoft Excel's CLSID asking for *IPersistFile* and then call *IPersistFile::Load("NASDAQ.XLS")*, followed by a *QueryInterface* on *IPersistFile* for *IDataObject* (assuming, of course, that Microsoft Excel knows that this is how such a connection sequence would happen). So, in the same way you would have a DDE conversation handle, you now have an *IDataObject* representing the entire NASDAQ.XLS spreadsheet.

This brings up the third difference. With a DDE conversation, you can request data specifying an item name and a clipboard format. This causes the

DDE server to locate the data identified by the item name dynamically and to render that data in the requested format. With an *IDataObject* pointer, however, you can specify the format you want in FORMATETC, but how can you identify the item? The problem here is that *IDataObject* doesn't have a standard field in which the caller can specify the subset of data. The *lindex* field of FORMATETC could fill this void, but it's intended to be used for object layout negotiation and not as a general placeholder for something such as an atom (which DDE uses to hold an item name).

All of this means that there is no standard protocol to replace DDE with *IDataObject*. DDE will eventually be eliminated, simply from disuse. For now, you might have to support data transfer through both DDE and *IDataObject*, and only when all applications talk data objects will you be able to purge yourself of the messaging protocol. So, although the capability exists to replace DDE, there simply are not yet standards in place as to how various important data service applications provide data objects. And how can you facilitate data exchange between applications without standards? You can't, and so I'll talk no further about DDE transfers in the context of OLE 2. We can concentrate better on the existing standards of clipboard, drag-and-drop, and compound document exchanges.

Summary

A data object is any other type of object as seen through *IDataObject*-colored glasses. *IDataObject* is a standard OLE 2 interface that combines all the data transfer capabilities of the existing transfer protocols in Windows: clipboard, DDE, and OLE 1, as well as providing the transfer functions for drag-and-drop operations.

A significant improvement in data transfer provided in OLE 2 data objects is the ability to describe data not only by using a clipboard format but also by using a target device, an indication of how much detail is contained in the rendering, and the storage device on which the data lives. Before OLE 2, all data transfers had to go through global memory, which was not suitable for all kinds of data. OLE 2 opens up transfers to use not only global memory but also storage on disk, either in a traditional file or in storage or stream objects.

Implementing a data object is a matter of implementing the *IDataObject* interface on top of the data set it represents. Through a pointer to *IDataObject*, the object user can request data, set data, enumerate or query available formats, and set up an advisory connection between the data object and an advise sink object implemented by the object user with the *IAdviseSink* interface. This shows that the user of the data object is the implementor of an advise sink object and that the implementor of a data object is also the user of an advise sink object. Object use and object implementation occur everywhere, and this is the first real example of how objects are used in two-way communication.

Through *IAdviseSink*, the user of a data object can receive notifications when specific data formats in the data object change. Advisory connections can be established with a variety of options, such as whether the object should send data with the notification.

Alongside data objects are view objects, which again are any objects as seen through the *IViewObject* interface. This interface allows you to ask an object to draw itself and otherwise manage visual presentations of its data. With some special tricks, you can also get OLE2.DLL to maintain a view object for any given metafile or bitmap so that you can use the view object to draw those graphics, eliminating sometimes tedious code from your own application. In this case as well, you can even coax OLE2.DLL to save and load those graphics to and from a compound file.

The *IDataObject* interface and DDE have many parallels but some important differences, which prevent a complete replacement of DDE with data objects. Such a replacement is, however, forthcoming, and sooner or later it will become integrated into Windows. When that happens, the full circle of Uniform Data Transfer will close, and you will be able to use any existing protocol—be it clipboard, DDE, drag-and-drop, or compound documents—to move a data object pointer between a source of data and a consumer of data. After that pointer has been communicated, neither side needs to care how that communication took place.

CHAPTER SEVEN

CLIPBOARD TRANSFERS USING DATA OBJECTS

What do you do with a data object?
What do you do with a data object?
What do you do with a data object?
Put it on the clipboard!

Version 2 of an old sea chantey

As we saw in Chapter 6, data objects encompass the functionality of all the existing data transfer protocols. Using raw data objects by themselves to exchange data between applications is rich enough to describe anything you could do with existing Windows APIs, and more. This chapter, in particular, will look at how you can use data objects to implement your clipboard operations. Unless you are going to implement compound document features, using OLE 2 to interact with the clipboard is entirely optional.

Conceptually the operations are simple: To place data on the clipboard, you pass an *IDataObject* pointer to OLE2.DLL, which asks that data object about its supported formats and calls *IDataObject::GetData* when a consumer actually wants some data. To retrieve data from the clipboard, you call an OLE2.DLL function that returns an *IDataObject* pointer through which you can request data (using *GetData*) and so forth. In other words, the consumer of the data is the user of an *IDataObject* pointer, which it retrieves by calling a specific function.

Simple? On the surface, yes, but it seems like overkill to have to create an entire data object and an *EnumFORMATETC* object to do something as simple as copy a small piece of text to the clipboard. Because this is a major consideration for almost every developer I know, the first part of this chapter will address just how much of a data object you need for clipboard transfers as well as provide the implementation of a DLL component object that greatly simplifies creation of a data object for such transfers.

I'll apply this data transfer object DLL for implementations in both Cosmo and Patron. Cosmo is the simplest one through which we can demonstrate use of the three OLE 2 clipboard APIs, which replace use of the Windows clipboard API functions. Just as we paralleled file I/O to *IStream* member functions in Chapter 5, here we can parallel traditional clipboard API functions to use of the OLE 2 API function and a data transfer object.

For Component Cosmo, we'll take a slightly different approach: Instead of creating a separate data transfer object, Cosmo creates a copy of a Polyline object, which holds a snapshot of the same data as the current polyline. We can then simply throw the Polyline's *IDataObject* on the clipboard. In essence, this is the same as doing exactly what we do with the data transfer object, but on a more application-specific basis.

Finally, we'll implement clipboard operations for Patron, enabling it to copy and paste bitmaps and metafiles using the Freeloader code implemented in Chapter 6. All the work we do here will set Patron up for drag-and-drop features in Chapter 8 and for changes to become a compound document container in Chapter 9. The additions to Patron in this chapter will be significant—we implement the idea of tenants on each page.

Note again that unless you are interested in compound documents you are not required to use OLE 2 data objects to perform clipboard operations. OLE 2 offers an alternate way to deal with the clipboard using data objects, but you can continue to use API functions for existing data formats. Data object transfers become important when we deal with drag-and-drop and compound documents. For drag-and-drop, as we'll see in the next chapter, you can reuse a lot of the code you create for clipboard operations in this chapter. With the clipboard code in place, drag-and-drop implementation can be almost trivial. Data objects will be *required* for compound document implementations in Chapters 9 and 10, so if you're planning to pursue these goals, I suggest that you work these clipboard changes into your code now. This will save you a considerable amount of work later and will reduce the amount of information that you have to absorb all at once. Finally, if your application is merely going to be a source of data (that is, it will consume no external data, as a data collection does) and you are not interested in compound documents or drag-and-drop, any data transfer using data objects could be overkill. Don't feel compelled to change your code "just because." Find a reason first.

With that little bit of preaching out of the way, let's move directly to OLE 2 functions, interfaces, and code examples for clipboard operations.

The OLE 2 Clipboard Protocol

As described in Chapter 6, a data transfer protocol in the OLE 2 sense is a mechanism for communicating a data object pointer—that is, an *IDataObject* pointer—from the source of the data to a consumer of the data. The clipboard is one such mechanism, and to support it, OLE 2 provides three clipboard-related API functions in OLE2.DLL:

API Function	Description
OleSetClipboard	Places an *IDataObject* pointer on the clipboard. The given data object is tied to all the data that you want to copy. This function will call *AddRef* through the *IDataObject* pointer.
OleGetClipboard	Retrieves an *IDataObject* pointer that represents the data available on the clipboard. This function will call *AddRef* through the pointer before returning, so the consuming application must call *Release* when it is finished with the pointer.
OleFlushClipboard	Clears the clipboard, calling *Release* on the data object to reverse the *AddRef* from *OleSetClipboard.*

The overall mechanism of a clipboard data transfer in OLE 2 is shown in Figure 7-1 on the next page. The source application creates a data object, as well as the enumerator for FORMATETCs, and calls *OleSetClipboard.* In turn, OLE (that is, OLE2.DLL) calls *OpenClipboard, IDataObject::AddRef,* and *IDataObject::EnumFormatEtc.* For each enumerator format, it calls the Windows API *SetClipboardData(formatetc.cfFormat, NULL)* to mark that format as available on the clipboard without actually rendering the data and then calls *CloseClipboard.* When any other piece of code calls *GetClipboardData* for any of these formats, the Windows clipboard handler generates a WM_RENDERFORMAT message. But to what window?

The window that receives this message is actually owned by OLE2.DLL, which keeps it hidden at all times. This window is created when you first call *OleInitialize,* which is why you must use *OleInitialize* when using OLE 2 clipboard support rather than the simpler *CoInitialize.*

When this window receives WM_RENDERFORMAT, only then does it generate calls to *IDataObject::QueryGetData* (to make sure about the format) and *IDataObject::GetData.* In other words, OLE 2 provides delayed clipboard rendering by means of data objects. This does, however, have an impact on data sources, because delayed rendering means that you must make a snapshot of your current data and put it into the data object, regardless of whether you are implementing a Cut or Copy operation. I'll treat this subject in a little more detail in a bit.

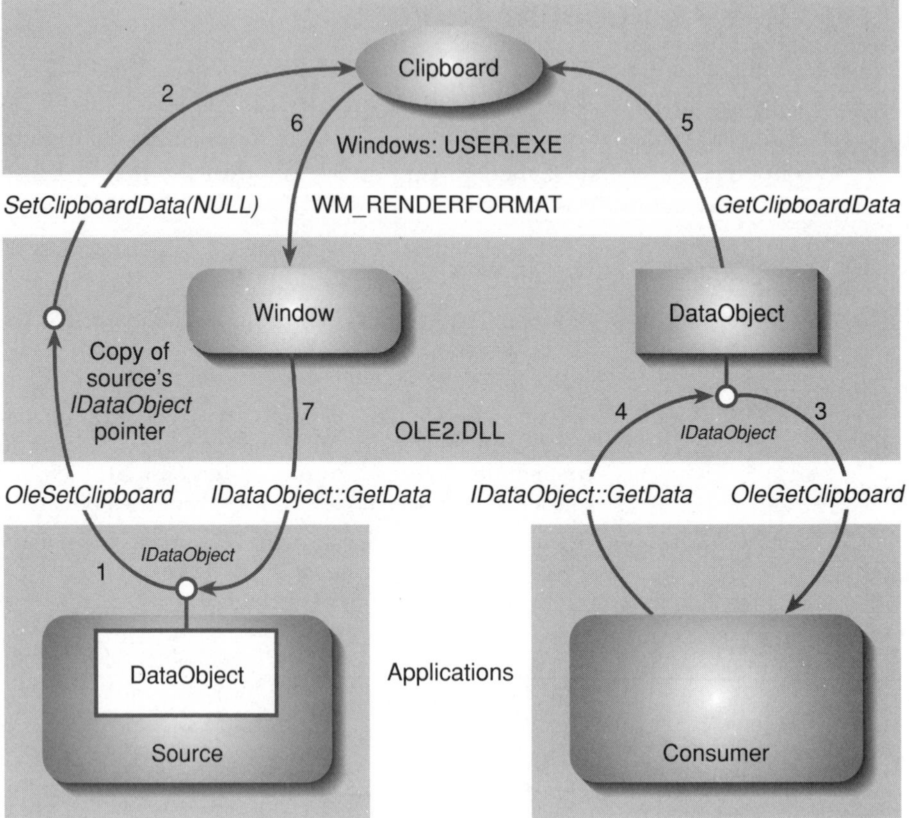

Figure 7-1.
The OLE 2 clipboard mechanisms involving the API functions OleGetClipboard *and* OleSetClipboard *as well as an* IDataObject *implementation.*

The consumer of data does not, of course, have to deal with the complications of delayed rendering. A consumer makes a single call to *OleGetClipboard* to obtain a pointer to an *IDataObject* interface. The pointer returned, however, is not the same data object that a source placed there because data might have been placed on the clipboard by an application that does not know OLE 2. *OleGetClipboard* instead returns an OLE2.DLL-owned data object pointer that represents the data on the clipboard, regardless of how that data got there. In any case, after the consumer calls *OleGetClipboard,* it can call the *IDataObject* members *EnumFormatEtc, QueryGetData,* and *GetData,* as it would call the Windows API functions *EnumClipboardFormats, IsClipboardFormatAvailable,* and *GetClipboardData.* Only a call to *IDataObject::GetData* will generate WM_RENDERFORMAT messages and thus a *GetData* call to the real source data object. As far as a data consumer is concerned, changing from clipboard handling using the Windows API functions to using the *OleGetClipboard* and the *IDataObject* interfaces takes minimal effort, as we shall see.

I should mention here that the clipboard data object implemented in OLE2.DLL is quite limited in that it implements only *IDataObject::GetData*, *IDataObject::GetDataHere* (for limited formats), *IDataObject::QueryGetData*, and *IDataObject::EnumFormatEtc*.[1] All other functions return either OLE_E_NOTSUPPORTED (*SetData* and advise functions) or in the case of *GetCanonicalFormatEtc*, NOERROR. In addition, *QueryInterface* will acknowledge only *IUnknown* and *IDataObject*, so forget any hopes that the data object here will know how to draw or save itself. You need to implement that sort of functionality by using the techniques demonstrated in the Freeloader example in Chapter 6.

But All I Want to Do Is Copy Some Simple Data!

I imagine at this point that you might be screaming or cursing because clipboard data transfers under OLE 2 seem to have become much more complex than you would like. To copy even the simplest piece of data to the clipboard—say, a short, but passionate, string such as "Why is Microsoft doing this to me?"—involves an implementation of a data object, an implementation of a FORMATETC enumerator, and the complexity of taking a snapshot of the data involved in the operation to handle delayed rendering. Ouch! Whatever happened to *OpenClipboard*, *SetClipboardData*, and *CloseClipboard*?

Well, in all reality, it has never been *quite* that simple, because somewhere along the way you have to allocate global memory that contains the data you want to copy. For instance, before calling *SetClipboardData* with the preceding example string, you would probably have some function to make a global memory copy of that string:

```
HGLOBAL CopyStringToHGlobal(LPSTR psz)
    {
    HGLOBAL     hMem;
    LPSTR       pszDst;

    hMem=GlobalAlloc(GHND, (DWORD)(lstrlen(psz)+1));
```

(continued)

1. I noticed in my work on Patron for this chapter that *EnumFormatEtc* will fail on the *IDataObject* interface on a static object—that is, an object of *CLSID_StaticMetafile* or *CLSID_StaticDib* as used in Freeloader in Chapter 6.

```
    if (NULL!=hMem)
        {
        pszDst=GlobalLock(hMem);
        lstrcpy(pszDst, psz);
        GlobalUnlock(hMem);
        }

    return hMem;
    }
```

With that, the code to copy some text to the clipboard would be as follows:

```
HGLOBAL     hMem;

hMem=CopyStringToHGlobal("Why is Microsoft doing this to me?");

if (NULL!=hMem)
    {
    if (OpenClipboard(hWndMain))
        {
        SetClipboardData(CF_TEXT, hMem);
        CloseClipboard();
        }
    else
        GlobalFree(hMem);  //We must clean up.
    }

...
```

Under OLE 2, we would like to write code that looks like the following, which shows a strong resemblance to the code shown earlier:

```
LPDATAOBJECT        pIDataObject;
HRESULT             hr;
FORMATETC           fe;
STGMEDIUM           stm;

stm.tymed=TYMED_HGLOBAL;
stm.hGlobal=CopyStringToHGlobal("Why is Microsoft doing this to me?");

if (NULL!=stm.hGlobal)
    {
    hr=FunctionToCreateADataTransferObject(&pIDataObject)

    if (SUCCEEDED(hr))
```

```
        {
        SETDefFormatEtc(fe, CF_TEXT, TYMED_HGLOBAL);
        pIDataObject->SetData(&fe, &stm);
        OleSetClipboard(pIDataObject);
        pIDataObject->Release();
        }
    else
        GlobalFree(stm.hGlobal);
    }

...
```

This code shows how we would *like* to translate our existing Windows code into OLE 2 code. *SetClipboardData* with a clipboard format and a memory handle turns into an *IDataObject::SetData* with a FORMATETC and a STGMEDIUM followed by *OleSetClipboard. CloseClipboard* turns into an *IDataObject::Release* call. But what's the *FunctionToCreateADataTransferObject*? That's not in the *OLE 2 Programmer's Reference.*

That's right, although in my opinion it's a key feature left out of the OLE 2 implementation that would greatly simplify clipboard transfers using data objects. A function like this would create a data object in which we could stuff data renderings (that is, a FORMATETC and a STGMEDIUM) to copy to the clipboard. It would assume ownership of each rendering and maintain its own reference count, making sure to call *ReleaseStgMedium* for each rendering when its own reference count was reduced to zero.

But alas, OLE 2 does not provide such a useful tool, so I implemented one for this book, in the form of a component object DLL.

A Data Transfer Component Object

An object that would simplify clipboard transfers is essentially a data cache with an *IDataObject* interface slapped on top of it. I had considered a number of ways to do this, but what I really wanted was a data object that I could grab using something like *CoCreateInstance.* Just such an object, housed in DATATRAN.DLL, is shown in Listing 7-1 on the next page and found in the sample code under CHAP07\DATATRAN. The file DATATRAN.CPP is omitted from this listing because it contains only functions such as *DllGetClassObject* and *DllCanUnloadNow,* as well as an archetypal class factory implementation, exactly the same as the one in Chapter 4. In addition, IENUMFE.CPP is omitted because it's as much the same as the implementation in Listing 6-1. Note that you must merge CHAP07\CHAP07.REG with your Registration Database to make DATATRAN operate properly.

DATAOBJ.CPP

```
/*
 * Data Transfer Object for Chapter 7
 *
 * Implementation of the CDataObject
 * for the Data Transfer Component Object.
 * Copyright (c)1993 Microsoft Corporation, All Rights Reserved
 */

#include "dataobj.h"

extern HINSTANCE g_hInst;

CDataObject::CDataObject(LPUNKNOWN pUnkOuter
    , LPFNDESTROYED pfnDestroy)
    {
    m_cRef=0;
    m_pUnkOuter=pUnkOuter;
    m_pfnDestroy=pfnDestroy;

    m_hList=NULL;

    m_pIDataObject=NULL;

    return;
    }

CDataObject::~CDataObject(void)
    {
    if (NULL!=m_pIDataObject)
        delete m_pIDataObject;

    Purge();

    if (NULL!=m_hList)
        DestroyWindow(m_hList);

    return;
    }

BOOL CDataObject::FInit(void)
    {
    LPUNKNOWN       pIUnknown=(LPUNKNOWN)this;
```

Listing 7-1. *(continued)*

Code that implements the DATATRAN component object and the IDataObject *interface.*

Listing 7-1. *continued*

```
    if (NULL!=m_pUnkOuter)
        pIUnknown=m_pUnkOuter;

    //Allocate contained interfaces.
    m_pIDataObject=new CImpIDataObject(this, pIUnknown);

    if (NULL==m_pIDataObject)
        return FALSE;

    m_hList=CreateWindow("listbox", "renderings"
        , WS_POPUP | LBS_OWNERDRAWFIXED,0, 0, 100, 100
        , HWND_DESKTOP, NULL, g_hInst, NULL);

    if (NULL==m_hList)
        return FALSE;

    return TRUE;
    }

/*
 * CDataObject::Purge
 *
 * Purpose:
 *  Cleans out all entries in our listbox.
 */

void CDataObject::Purge(void)
    {
    UINT        i, cItems;
    LPRENDERING pRen;
    DWORD       cb;

    if (NULL==m_hList)
        return;

    cItems=(UINT)SendMessage(m_hList, LB_GETCOUNT, 0, 0L);

    for (i=0; i < cItems; i++)
        {
        cb=SendMessage(m_hList, LB_GETTEXT
            , i, (LPARAM)(LPVOID)&pRen);

        if (sizeof(LPRENDERING)==cb)
            {
```

(continued)

Listing 7-1. *continued*

```
            /*
             * Release the data completely being sure to reinstate
             * the original pUnkForRelease.
             */
            pRen->stm.pUnkForRelease=pRen->pUnkOrg;
            ReleaseStgMedium(&pRen->stm);
            delete pRen;
            }
        }

    SendMessage(m_hList, LB_RESETCONTENT, 0, 0L);
    return;
    }

STDMETHODIMP CDataObject::QueryInterface(REFIID riid
    , LPLPVOID ppv)
    {
    *ppv=NULL;

    if (IsEqualIID(riid, IID_IUnknown))
        *ppv=(LPVOID)this;

    if (IsEqualIID(riid, IID_IDataObject))
        *ppv=(LPVOID)m_pIDataObject;

    if (NULL!=*ppv)
        {
        ((LPUNKNOWN)*ppv)->AddRef();
        return NOERROR;
        }

    return ResultFromScode(E_NOINTERFACE);
    }

STDMETHODIMP_(ULONG) CDataObject::AddRef(void)
    {
    return ++m_cRef;
    }

STDMETHODIMP_(ULONG) CDataObject::Release(void)
    {
    ULONG       cRefT;
```

(continued)

Listing 7-1. *continued*

```
    cRefT=--m_cRef;

    if (0==m_cRef)
        {
        if (NULL!=m_pfnDestroy)
            (*m_pfnDestroy)();

        delete this;
        }

    return cRefT;
    }
```

IDATAOBJ.CPP

```
/*
 * Data Transfer Object for Chapter 7
 *
 * Implementation of the IDataObject interface for CDataObject.
 *
 * Copyright (c)1993 Microsoft Corporation, All Rights Reserved
 */

#include "dataobj.h"

CImpIDataObject::CImpIDataObject(LPCDataObject pObj
    , LPUNKNOWN pUnkOuter)
    {
    m_cRef=0;
    m_pObj=pObj;
    m_pUnkOuter=pUnkOuter;
    return;
    }

CImpIDataObject::~CImpIDataObject(void)
    {
    return;
    }

STDMETHODIMP CImpIDataObject::QueryInterface(REFIID riid
    , LPLPVOID ppv)
```

(continued)

Listing 7-1. *continued*

```
    {
    return m_pUnkOuter->QueryInterface(riid, ppv);
    }

STDMETHODIMP_(ULONG) CImpIDataObject::AddRef(void)
    {
    ++m_cRef;
    return m_pUnkOuter->AddRef();
    }

STDMETHODIMP_(ULONG) CImpIDataObject::Release(void)
    {
    --m_cRef;
    return m_pUnkOuter->Release();
    }

/*
 * CImpIDataObject::GetData
 * CImpIDataObject::QueryGetData
 * CImpIDataObject::SetData
 * CImpIDataObject::EnumFormatEtc
 *
 * Substantial member functions.
 */

STDMETHODIMP CImpIDataObject::GetData(LPFORMATETC pFE
    , LPSTGMEDIUM pSTM)
    {
    UINT        i, cItems;
    LPRENDERING pRen;
    DWORD       cb;
    HWND        hList;

    if (NULL==m_pObj->m_hList || NULL==pFE || NULL==pSTM)
        return ResultFromScode(DATA_E_FORMATETC);

    hList=m_pObj->m_hList;
    cItems=(UINT)SendMessage(hList, LB_GETCOUNT, 0, 0L);

    for (i=0; i < cItems; i++)
        {
        cb=SendMessage(hList, LB_GETTEXT, i, (LPARAM)(LPVOID)&pRen);
```

(continued)

Listing 7-1. *continued*

```
        if (sizeof(LPRENDERING)==cb)
            {
            /*
             * Check if the requested FORMATETC is the same as one
             * that we already have. If so, copy that STGMEDIUM
             * to pSTM and AddRef ourselves for pUnkForRelease.
             */
            if (pFE->cfFormat==pRen->fe.cfFormat
                && (pFE->tymed & pRen->fe.tymed)
                && pFE->dwAspect==pRen->fe.dwAspect)
                {
                *pSTM=pRen->stm;
                AddRef();
                return NOERROR;
                }
            }
        }

    return ResultFromScode(DATA_E_FORMATETC);
    }

STDMETHODIMP CImpIDataObject::GetDataHere(LPFORMATETC pFE
    , LPSTGMEDIUM pSTM)
    {
    UINT        i, cItems;
    LPRENDERING pRen;
    DWORD       cb;
    HWND        hList;

    if (NULL==m_pObj->m_hList || NULL==pFE || NULL==pSTM)
        return ResultFromScode(DATA_E_FORMATETC);

    //We only support IStorage
    if (!(TYMED_ISTORAGE & pFE->tymed))
        return ResultFromScode(DATA_E_FORMATETC);

    hList=m_pObj->m_hList;
    cItems=(UINT)SendMessage(hList, LB_GETCOUNT, 0, 0L);

    for (i=0; i < cItems; i++)
        {
        cb=SendMessage(hList, LB_GETTEXT, i, (LPARAM)(LPVOID)&pRen);
```

(continued)

Listing 7-1. *continued*

```
            if (sizeof(LPRENDERING)==cb)
                {
                /*
                 * When we find a matching FORMATETC, we know we're
                 * only looking for IStorage (we checked above), so
                 * use IStorage::CopyTo to make the copy.
                 */
                if (pFE->cfFormat==pRen->fe.cfFormat
                    && (pFE->tymed & pRen->fe.tymed)
                    && pFE->dwAspect==pRen->fe.dwAspect)
                    {
                    pSTM->tymed=TYMED_ISTORAGE;
                    return pRen->stm.pstg->CopyTo(NULL, NULL
                        , NULL, pSTM->pstg);
                    }
                }
            }

        return ResultFromScode(DATA_E_FORMATETC);
        }

    STDMETHODIMP CImpIDataObject::QueryGetData(LPFORMATETC pFE)
        {
        UINT        i, cItems;
        LPRENDERING pRen;
        DWORD       cb;
        HWND        hList;

        if (NULL==m_pObj->m_hList || NULL==pFE)
            return ResultFromScode(S_FALSE);

        hList=m_pObj->m_hList;
        cItems=(UINT)SendMessage(hList, LB_GETCOUNT, 0, 0L);

        for (i=0; i < cItems; i++)
            {
            cb=SendMessage(hList, LB_GETTEXT, i, (LPARAM)(LPVOID)&pRen);

            if (sizeof(LPRENDERING)==cb)
                {
                /*
                 * Check if the requested FORMATETC is the same as one
                 * that we already have.
                 */
```

(continued)

Listing 7-1. *continued*

```
            if (pFE->cfFormat==pRen->fe.cfFormat
                && (pFE->tymed & pRen->fe.tymed)
                && pFE->dwAspect==pRen->fe.dwAspect)
                {
                return NOERROR;
                }
            }
        }

    return ResultFromScode(S_FALSE);
    }

STDMETHODIMP CImpIDataObject::SetData(LPFORMATETC pFE
    , STGMEDIUM FAR *pSTM, BOOL fRelease)
    {
    LPRENDERING     prn;

    //We have to remain responsible for the data.
    if (!fRelease)
        return ResultFromScode(E_FAIL);

    //If we're handed NULLs, that means clean out the list.
    if (NULL==pFE || NULL==pSTM)
        {
        m_pObj->Purge();
        return NOERROR;
        }

    /*
     * Here we take the rendering we're given and attach it to the
     * end of the list. We save the original pSTM->pUnkForRelease
     * and replace it with our own such that each 'copy' of this
     * data of actually just a reference count.
     */

    prn=new RENDERING;

    if (NULL==prn)
        return ResultFromScode(E_OUTOFMEMORY);

    prn->fe=*pFE;
    prn->stm=*pSTM;
    prn->pUnkOrg=pSTM->pUnkForRelease;
    prn->stm.pUnkForRelease=(LPUNKNOWN)this;
```

(continued)

Listing 7-1. *continued*

```
    SendMessage(m_pObj->m_hList, LB_ADDSTRING
        , 0, (LONG)(LPVOID)prn);
    return NOERROR;
    }

STDMETHODIMP CImpIDataObject::EnumFormatEtc(DWORD dwDir
    ,LPENUMFORMATETC FAR *ppEnum)
    {
    LPCEnumFormatEtc    pEnum;

    *ppEnum=NULL;

    /*
     * From an external point of view there are no SET formats,
     * because we want to allow the user of this component object
     * to be able to stuff ANY format in via Set. Only external
     * users will call EnumFormatEtc and they can only Get.
     */

    switch (dwDir)
        {
        case DATADIR_GET:
             pEnum=new CEnumFormatEtc(m_pUnkOuter);
             break;

        case DATADIR_SET:
        default:
            pEnum=NULL;
            break;
        }

    if (NULL==pEnum)
        return ResultFromScode(E_FAIL);
    else
        {
        //Let the enumerator copy our format list.
        if (!pEnum->FInit(m_pObj->m_hList))
            {
            delete pEnum;
            return ResultFromScode(E_FAIL);
            }

        pEnum->AddRef();
        }
```

(continued)

Listing 7-1. *continued*

```
    *ppEnum=pEnum;
    return NOERROR;
    }

/*
 * CImpIDataObject::GetCanonicalFormatEtc
 * CImpIDataObject::DAdvise
 * CImpIDataObject::DUnadvise
 * CImpIDataObject::EnumDAdvise
 *
 * Trivial member functions.
 */

STDMETHODIMP CImpIDataObject::GetCanonicalFormatEtc
    (LPFORMATETC pFEIn , LPFORMATETC pFEOut)
    {
    return ResultFromScode(DATA_S_SAMEFORMATETC);
    }

//No advise support for this sort of data transfer.
STDMETHODIMP CImpIDataObject::DAdvise(LPFORMATETC pFE
    , DWORD dwFlags, LPADVISESINK pIAdviseSink, LPDWORD pdwConn)
    {
    return ResultFromScode(E_FAIL);
    }

STDMETHODIMP CImpIDataObject::DUnadvise(DWORD dwConn)
    {
    return ResultFromScode(E_FAIL);
    }

STDMETHODIMP CImpIDataObject::EnumDAdvise(LPENUMSTATDATA FAR
    *ppEnum)
    {
    return ResultFromScode(E_FAIL);
    }
```

DATATRAN is a component object DLL, like those described in Chapter 4. It implements a class factory object along with the *DllGetClassObject* and *DllCanUnloadNow* exports (DATATRAN.H and DATATRAN.CPP). The object is implemented using a C++ class called *CDataObject* (DATAOBJ.H, .CPP), which holds a pointer to the *IDataObject* implementation from *CImpIDataObject* (IDATAOBJ.CPP). We also use the same *CEnumFormatEtc*, which we implemented in Chapter 6 (IENUMFE.CPP).

To this object we need to assign a CLSID, defined in BOOKGUID.H as *CLSID_DataTransferObject.* Again, the file CHAP07\CHAP07.REG will create the appropriate Registration Database entries for this DLL, which acts as an "InprocServer" for the object class.

So now if we're writing code that wants to use this object, we can call *CoCreateInstance* as the "SomeFunctionToCreateADataTransferObject" using *CLSID_DataTransferObject* and *IID_IDataObject. CoCreateInstance* will load DATATRAN.DLL, call *DllGetClassObject,* and call our *CDataTransferClassFactory::CreateInstance* as we would expect, where the class factory instantiates an object of class *CDataObject* and calls its *FInit* function.

CDataObject::FInit performs two functions: It creates an interface implementation of *IDataObject,* and it creates a list box (by means of *CreateWindow*) in which this object will track whatever data renderings it currently holds. This list box is created as LBS_OWNERDRAWFIXED because we'll be using it only to store pointers to a structure called RENDERING:

```
typedef struct _far tagRENDERING
    {
    FORMATETC       fe;             //The format
    STGMEDIUM       stm;            //The actual data
    LPUNKNOWN       pUnkOrg;        //The real owner
    } RENDERING, FAR *LPRENDERING;
```

This structure, found in DATAOBJ.H, contains the FORMATETC of the rendering, the STGMEDIUM referencing the data, and an LPUNKNOWN for reasons that will become clear in a moment.

DATATRAN allocates its RENDERING structures in the implementation of *IDataObject::SetData* and stores the pointers to the structures in the list box. It simply copies the FORMATETC and STGMEDIUM structures passed to *SetData* into the RENDERING, with one exception. It replaces the *pUnkForRelease* field of the STGMEDIUM with its own *IUnknown* so that DATATRAN now owns the data. However, it must still preserve the original *pUnkForRelease* in the *pUnkOrg* of the rendering so that it can restore the STGMEDIUM to its original form before freeing it. In any case, when DATATRAN has filled the RENDERING, it adds the pointer to the list with a simple LB_ADDSTRING message, which puts the rendering at the end of the list. Therefore, anything that calls DATATRAN's *SetData* more than once should make those calls with the same format order they would use to call *SetClipboardData.*

Implementations of functions such as *QueryGetData* and *EnumFormatEtc* are fairly simple because you already have the formats in a list, and you can leave empty implementation of the advise functions and *GetCanonicalFormatEtc. QueryGetData* needs only to walk through the list box item by item looking for a match. *EnumFormatEtc* still needs to create an enumerator object, but in initializing that object you pass the list box so that the enumerator can walk the list and create its array of FORMATETC structures.

That leaves *GetData* and *Release* as the only remaining points of interest in this component object. *GetData* walks through the list looking for a match on the requested FORMATETC. (*GetDataHere* is the same as *GetData* except that it is restricted to *IStorage* mediums. This is necessary for compound document objects in later chapters.) If it finds the requested rendering, it doesn't make a copy of the actual data; instead it copies the rendering's STGMEDIUM into the out-parameter for the caller. What's strange is the odd *AddRef* call here. Remember that the STGMEDIUM we provide to the caller here contains our own *IUnknown* in *pUnkForRelease.* That means whenever the data is no longer necessary, OLE will call *ReleaseStgMedium,* and we'll receive a call to *Release.* As far as the consumer is concerned, it's freed the data and its memory, but in actuality we're reference counting each rendering. Only when we reset or free the entire data object will we actually free the data.

This shows a very good use for *pUnkForRelease* besides being able to control how the data is freed. In this case, we're overriding the *ownership* of the data, taking over from the real source. Just before we want to actually free the data (as far as we're concerned) with *ReleaseStgMedium,* we restore original ownership. This is done in the function *CDataObject::Purge* (an internal function in this class) that cleans up all the RENDERING allocations in the list box. *Purge* is called twice: first when *SetData* is called with NULL pointers and the second time when the data object itself is destroyed.

If You Already Have a Data Object...Component Cosmo

You might run into a situation in which an object you already have has an *IDataObject* interface on it. For example, the Polyline object used by Component Cosmo already implements *IDataObject.* Therefore, it's unnecessary to create or use a whole new object (and class) simply to handle data transfers. It makes more sense to use that existing implementation.

Remember, however, that you must make some sort of snapshot of the data you want to attach to the data object. For Component Cosmo, it means that we cannot merely take the *IDataObject* pointer for its current Polyline and throw that up on the clipboard. If we did, we would have a potential for extreme end-user confusion. End-users will expect that the data they would later paste is exactly the same as the data they copied. If Component Cosmo places the visible Polyline's *IDataObject* on the clipboard, that data object is really live data instead of a snapshot of the data because any change made to the

Polyline would be reflected in a later Paste operation. What the user saw at the time of the copy would not be what the user later sees at the time of the Paste operation. Not good.

Component Cosmo instead instantiates a new hidden Polyline object as the Data Transfer object. CoCosmo creates this new object with the same dimensions as the visible one and copies the current Polyline's data into it. A perfect snapshot. Then it can toss the new hidden Polyline's *IDataObject* to the clipboard, as shown in the following code, taken from CHAP07\COCOSMO\DOCUMENT.CPP:

```
//DOCUMENT.CPP from CHAP07\COCOSMO
BOOL CCosmoDoc::FClip(HWND hWndFrame, BOOL fCut)
    {
    LPPOLYLINE                pPL;
    LPDATAOBJECT              pDataSrc, pDataDst;
    FORMATETC                 fe;
    STGMEDIUM                 stm;
    BOOL                      fRet=TRUE;
    HRESULT                   hr;
    RECT                      rc;

    //Create a transfer Polyline Object
    hr=CoCreateInstance(CLSID_Polyline6, NULL, CLSCTX_INPROC_SERVER
        , ID_IPolyline6, (LPLPVOID)&pPL);

    if (FAILED(hr))
        return FALSE;

    //Make the new transfer Polyline same size as the current one.
    m_pPL->RectGet(&rc);

    if (FAILED(pPL->Init(m_hWnd, &rc, WS_CHILD, ID_POLYLINE)))
        {
        pPL->Release();
        return FALSE;
        }

    //Copy the data.
    m_pPL->QueryInterface(IID_IDataObject, (LPLPVOID)&pDataSrc);

    SETDefFormatEtc(fe, m_cf, TYMED_HGLOBAL);
    fRet=SUCCEEDED(pDataSrc->GetData(&fe, &stm));
    pDataSrc->Release();

    if (!fRet)
```

```
        {
        pPL->Release();
        return FALSE;
        }

    pPL->QueryInterface(IID_IDataObject, (LPLPVOID)&pDataDst);
    pPL->Release();

    pDataDst->SetData(&fe, &stm, TRUE);

    fRet=SUCCEEDED(OleSetClipboard((LPDATAOBJECT)pDataDst));
    pDataDst->Release();

    if (!fRet)
        return FALSE;

    if (fCut)
        {
        m_pPL->New();
        FDirtySet(TRUE);
        }

    return TRUE;
    }
```

You will notice that the preceding code handles both Cut and Copy operations with identical vigor. The only difference between Cut and Copy is that a Cut operation removes the affected data from whatever document it came from. This means that in a Cut operation Component Cosmo clears out the visible Polyline by calling its *New* member. The point that should be clear from this, however, is that you still need to create a snapshot of the data regardless of whether you are doing a Cut or a Copy.

If You Already Have Extensive Clipboard-Handling Code

Certainly there are those applications, one of which might be yours, that have a great deal of highly optimized clipboard code already in place, especially if you already have a scheme to handle delayed rendering and snapshot copies of your data. If that's the case, I encourage you to implement a data object on top of your existing code. That is, the implementation of functions such as *IDataObject::GetData* calls other functions within your code, perhaps the same ones you call when handling the WM_RENDERFORMAT message.

This technique allows you to preserve all your existing code or perhaps only to restructure it to make it more generally accessible.

Simple Data Source and Consumer: Cosmo

Now that we have the necessary means to simplify clipboard operations—that is, DATATRAN.DLL—we can use the Cosmo application to demonstrate how to convert existing clipboard code into OLE 2 clipboard code. This involves a few steps for startup/shutdown and for the operations of Copy/Cut, Paste, and enabling the Edit/Paste menu item. Each of the following sections lists these steps along with implementations of these operations.

Startup/Shutdown

The requirements for startup and shutdown ensure that OLE will create its clipboard-handling window and that this window and all OLE2.DLL-owned data renderings are properly freed.

1. At startup, call *OleInitialize* instead of *CoInitialize.* This ensures that OLE will create its clipboard-handling window.
2. During shutdown, first call *OleFlushClipboard* to generate a *Release* to the data transfer object to match the *AddRef* from *OleSetClipboard.* The data object should be destroyed at this time. Also call *OleUninitialize* instead of *CoUninitialize* to ensure cleanup of OLE's clipboard window.

The implementation in Cosmo's COSMO.CPP is as follows:

```
//COSMO.CPP

BOOL CCosmoFrame::FInit(LPFRAMEINIT pFI)
    {
    DWORD       dwVer;

    //We need OLE versions of Initialize for Clipboard
    dwVer=OleBuildVersion();

    if (rmm!=HIWORD(dwVer))
        return FALSE;

    if (FAILED(OleInitialize(NULL)))
        return FALSE;

    m_fInitialized=TRUE;
    return CFrame::FInit(pFI);
    }
```

```
CCosmoFrame::~CCosmoFrame(void)
    {
    UINT        i;

    for (i=0; i<5; i++)
        DeleteObject(m_hBmpLines[i]);

    OleFlushClipboard();

    if (m_fInitialized)
        OleUninitialize();

    return;
    }
```

Copy/Cut

A Copy or a Cut operation, as you probably know, is the process of gaining access to the clipboard, copying the data renderings, and releasing the clipboard. The OLE 2 way of executing this process is a little different because there is no analog, per se, of opening or closing the clipboard. Instead, there's the single *OleSetClipboard* call. The steps for Copy and Cut in the following list are implemented in Cosmo as shown on the next page.

1. Create a data transfer object such as DATATRAN and attach the appropriate data to that object. This is similar to calling *OpenClipboard* (although a window handle is not required) and calling *SetClipboardData* for each format you want to copy. Note also that *EmptyClipboard* is unnecessary here because OLE automatically calls this function from within *OleSetClipboard.*
2. Pass the data transfer object to *OleSetClipboard,* which will call *AddRef* on the data object and call its *EnumFormatEtc* to find out what formats to place on the actual Windows clipboard.
3. Release the data transfer object because you are finished with your *IDataObject* pointer. The object will not be destroyed because of the *AddRef* called in *OleSetClipboard.* This is like calling *CloseClipboard.*
4. (Cut only.) Remove the affected data from the current document.

Cosmo performs these steps in its *CCosmoDoc::FClip* function, as shown in the following code. At least half of the code, and the entire structure of the function, required no modification from the version of CoCosmo in Chapter 6. What changes there are deal primarily with creating a data object and placing data in it before placing that data object on the clipboard. Cosmo uses DATATRAN.DLL to create the data object and uses its *CCosmoDoc::RenderFormat* function to create the renderings to give to DATATRAN.

```
//DOCUMENT.CPP from CHAP07\COSMO
BOOL CCosmoDoc::FClip(HWND hWndFrame, BOOL fCut)
    {
    BOOL            fRet=TRUE;
    HGLOBAL         hMem;
    UINT            i;
    static UINT     rgcf[3]={0, CF_METAFILEPICT, CF_BITMAP};
    const UINT      cFormats=3;

    static DWORD    rgtm[3]={TYMED_HGLOBAL, TYMED_MFPICT, TYMED_GDI};
    LPDATAOBJECT    pIDataObject;
    HRESULT         hr;
    STGMEDIUM       stm;
    FORMATETC       fe;

    hr=CoCreateInstance(CLSID_DataTransferObject, NULL
        , CLSCTX_INPROC_SERVER, IID_IDataObject
        , (LPLPVOID)&pIDataObject);

    if (FAILED(hr))
        return NULL;

    rgcf[0]=m_cf;

    for (i=0; i < cFormats; i++)
        {
        //Copy private data first.
        hMem=RenderFormat(rgcf[i]);

        if (NULL!=hMem)
            {
            stm.hGlobal=hMem;
            stm.tymed=rgtm[i];
            stm.pUnkForRelease=NULL;

            SETDefFormatEtc(fe, rgcf[i], rgtm[i]);
            pIDataObject->SetData(&fe, &stm, TRUE);
            }
        }

    fRet=SUCCEEDED(OleSetClipboard(pIDataObject));
    pIDataObject->Release();
```

```
    //Delete our current data if copying succeeded.
    if (fRet && fCut)
        {
        m_pPL->New();
        FDirtySet(TRUE);
        }

    return fRet;
    }
```

Enabling Edit/Paste

Any programmer who has ever implemented any Paste functionality in an application has gone through the rite of processing WM_INITMENUPOPUP and deciding whether to enable the Paste menu item, depending on the available formats on the clipboard. This user interface does not change with OLE 2; what does change is how you can implement it using data objects.

I want to stress the phrase "can implement," because OLE 2 does not excuse you from using any of the existing API functions to implement this feature or Paste, for that matter. This is simply an alternate way of doing it. The advantage is that after you write a piece of code that determines whether you can paste from any given data object, you'll have a piece of code that can determine the "pastability" of data from the clipboard or from a drag-and-drop operation, as we'll see in Chapter 8.

So, as you can see in the following code, the OLE 2 method for checking formats is only a matter of asking the data object to do the following:

1. Call *OleGetClipboard* to retrieve an *IDataObject* pointer for the clipboard.
2. Call *IDataObject::QueryGetData* for each format you would pass to *IsClipboardFormatAvailable*. If querying on any of your pastable formats succeeds, you should enable the Edit/Paste menu item. Only if none of those formats are available should you disable the item.
3. Call *IDataObject::Release* when you are finished.

```
BOOL CCosmoDoc::FQueryPaste(void)
    {
    LPDATAOBJECT    pIDataObject;
    BOOL            fRet;
```

(continued)

```
    if (FAILED(OleGetClipboard(&pIDataObject)))
        return FALSE;

    fRet=FQueryPasteFromData(pIDataObject);
    pIDataObject->Release();
    return fRet;
    }

BOOL CCosmoDoc::FQueryPasteFromData(LPDATAOBJECT pIDataObject)
    {
    FORMATETC       fe;

    SETDefFormatEtc(fe, m_cf, TYMED_HGLOBAL);
    return (NOERROR==pIDataObject->QueryGetData(&fe));
    }
```

Cosmo's *FQueryPaste* function, which used to call *IsClipboardFormatAvailable,* now retrieves the *IDataObject* pointer for the clipboard, passes it to a new function, *FQueryPasteFromData,* to determine pastability, and then releases that pointer. The real core of the code lives in *FQueryPasteFromData,* which is one call to *IDataObject::QueryGetData.*

At this point, I strongly encourage you to implement a new function such as *FQueryPasteFromData*—that is, one that takes a data object pointer as a parameter and returns whether there's any usable data there. Again, my reason for this encouragement is that with such a function in place, you can pass any data object to it, whether you got the pointer from *OleGetClipboard,* from a drag-and-drop operation, or from a *QueryInterface* on some other interface pointer. In addition, it gives you a single point in which to make changes to handle other formats that involve compound documents, as we'll do in later chapters.

Paste

Paste is pretty much the same operation as checking pastability except that instead of calling *IDataObject::QueryGetData* we call *IDataObject::GetData* with the following steps:

1. Obtain a data object pointer by calling *OleGetClipboard,* which will call *AddRef* through the pointer before returning.
2. Call *IDataObject::GetData* to retrieve your preferred FORMATETC. Because you are the owner of this data, be sure to call *ReleaseStgMedium* when you are finished copying the data. Be sure to use *ReleaseStgMedium* because the data object may have filled *pUnkForRelease* in order to control the data. Note also that you should not

hold onto this data; instead you should copy it as necessary. This is no different from the requirement of data obtained from the clipboard today using *GetClipboardData.*

3. Call *IDataObject::Release* to match the *AddRef* in *OleGetClipboard.*

These steps are implemented in Cosmo, as shown in the following code:

```
BOOL CCosmoDoc::FPaste(HWND hWndFrame)
    {
    LPDATAOBJECT    pIDataObject;
    BOOL            fRet;

    if (FAILED(OleGetClipboard(&pIDataObject)))
        return FALSE;

    fRet=FPasteFromData(pIDataObject);
    pIDataObject->Release();

    return fRet;
    }

BOOL CCosmoDoc::FPasteFromData(LPDATAOBJECT pIDataObject)
    {
    FORMATETC       fe;
    STGMEDIUM       stm;
    BOOL            fRet;

    SETDefFormatEtc(fe, m_cf, TYMED_HGLOBAL);
    fRet=SUCCEEDED(pIDataObject->GetData(&fe, &stm));

    if (fRet && NULL!=stm.hGlobal)
        {
        m_pPL->DataSetMem(stm.hGlobal, FALSE, FALSE, TRUE);
        ReleaseStgMedium(&stm);
        FDirtySet(TRUE);
        }

    return fRet;
    }
```

As we did for *FQueryPaste, FPaste* here simply obtains the data object pointer from *OleGetClipboard* and passes it to *FPasteFromData.* Again, I encourage you to split off the code that actually performs the paste into a function that takes a data object; we can reuse this function to implement a drop (essentially a Paste) in a drag-and-drop operation.

Paste Special and a Functional Patron

It's finally time to bring together the storage enhancements we made to Patron in Chapter 5 and the freeloading technique developed in Chapter 6 to make Patron an application that finally does something that could be considered useful. Because the changes are extensive, I will not show the complete code listings here—instead I will pull in important fragments for the sake of the discussion. Besides adding a number of functions to the *CPatronDoc*, *CPages*, and *CPage* classes, I've added two more nontrivial source files, TENANT.CPP and PAGEMOUS.CPP. All of this primarily supports the pasting of metafiles and bitmaps into a page as tenants, which OLE 2 will kindly draw and serialize for us. The result is that Patron finally shows something visible, as shown in Figure 7-2. All that's left is for us to provide storage for each tenant, to ensure that each tenant is saved to a file and that we can reload it again, and to provide the ability to copy or cut a tenant back to the clipboard.

Patron also contains a few user-interface components, such as mouse hit-testing that selects a tenant, a menu item to delete a tenant, and code to draw resizing handles on the selected object. Because we draw resizing handles, we have to hit-test those regions of the tenant and provide for giving visual feedback during a resize operation, as shown in Figure 7-3. Because the goal of this book is to discuss OLE 2 and not to describe exactly how you implement an application of this nature, I will not go into much detail about these non-OLE features in Patron.

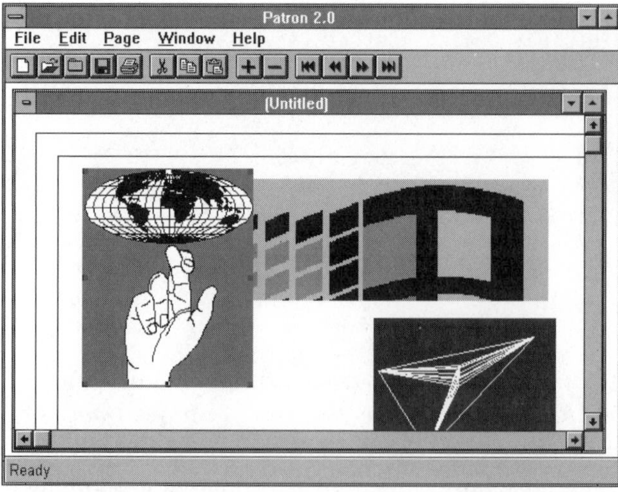

Figure 7-2.
Patron with a number of tenants on a page.

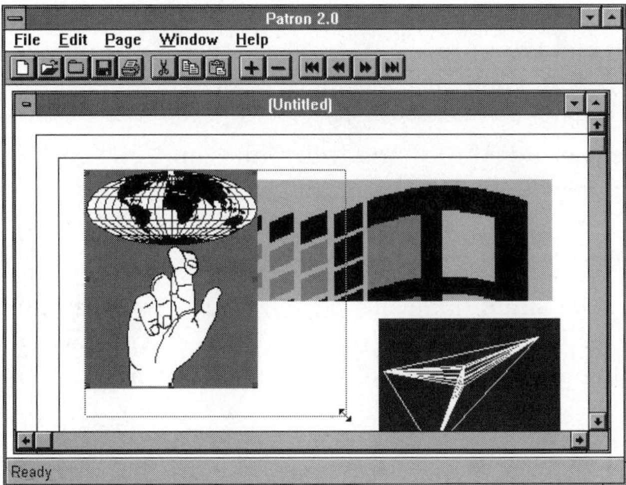

Figure 7-3.
Resizing a tenant in Patron.

However, the other most noticeable feature of Patron is its addition of a Paste Special dialog box that allows you to paste either a bitmap or a metafile. By default, Patron will prefer to paste a metafile rather than a bitmap, but with Paste Special the end user can choose the format. The Paste Special dialog box, as it appears in Figure 7-4, is implemented in the OLE2UI library

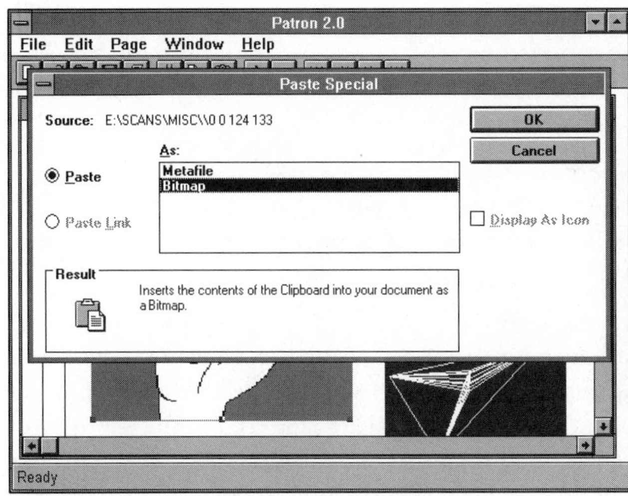

Figure 7-4.
The Paste Special dialog box in Patron.

shipped with the OLE 2 SDK. This dialog box not only supports traditional Paste Special commands but is also expandable to handle things like embedded and linked objects. We'll take advantage of such features in Chapters 9 and 12. Because this dialog box is an integral part of the OLE 2 user interface specifications, we'll spend a little extra time with it up front and then finish off this short chapter with brief discussions about other Patron modifications.

The Paste Special Dialog Box and the OLE2UI Library

I begged and pleaded and it finally happened: When I worked with OLE 1 a while back, I figured that the hardest part about implementing an OLE 1 container (called a client then) was providing all the user interface. All those dialog boxes! When I began working with OLE 2, I tried hard to convince others that Microsoft should implement common dialog boxes for OLE 2. Although I initially met stiff resistance ("not enough resources"), it eventually made sense to everyone—I was going to have to implement these dialog boxes anyway, the OLE 2 sample code would have to provide the dialog boxes, and various Microsoft product groups, including product support, were going to have to implement them. So a number of us, me included, got together to divide the work up. From that effort came OLE2UI, which will save you a tremendous amount of time in providing the proper OLE 2 interface.

Not only does OLE2UI provide dialog boxes, but it also provides a number of other useful functions to make your OLE 2 programming life easier. I have purposely avoided their use until now because I prefer that you gain an understanding of what's really happening before you use a function that hides such information from you. In any case, to use the OLE2UI library, we must now include *<ole2ui.h>* to gain all the necessary definitions, structures, and function prototypes necessary.

NOTE: Patron attempts to link to a build of OLE2UI named BOOKUI.DLL through BOOKUI.LIB. The BUILD and LIB directories in the sample code for this book contain builds of both BOOKUI.DLL and BOOKUI.LIB, respectively.

In addition, applications using the library are required to call *OleUIInitialize*, passing your instance handle before using any other function in the library, and they are required to call *OleUIUnInitialize* when the library is no longer needed. These calls are made from the same code as in PATRON.CPP, where we also call *OleInitialize* and *OleUninitialize*. Be careful with *OleUIUnInitialize* in early OLE 2 versions: The *I* in *Initialize* is capitalized, which is inconsistent with *OleUninitialize*, where the *i* is lowercase.

Our first real encounter with this great timesaving library is the Paste Special dialog box, which you invoke by filling an OLEUIPASTESPECIAL structure (shown in the following code, taken from OLE2UI.H) and by calling *OleUIPasteSpecial*. On return, the dialog box will indicate which format was chosen from the dialog box. Patron uses this format to determine whether to create an object using *CLSID_FreeDib* or *CLSID_FreeMetafile* (the CLSIDs that identify OLE2's bitmap and metafile-handling code). The real trick here is filling the OLEUIPASTESPECIAL structure:

```
//From OLE 2's OLE2UI.H
typedef struct tagOLEUIPASTESPECIAL
    {
    //These IN fields are standard across all OLEUI dialog functions.
    DWORD           cbStruct;         //Structure Size
    DWORD           dwFlags;          //IN-OUT:  Flags
    HWND            hWndOwner;        //Owning window
    LPCSTR          lpszCaption;      //Dialog caption bar contents
    LPFNOLEUIHOOK   lpfnHook;         //Hook callback
    LPARAM          lCustData;        //Custom data to pass to hook
    HINSTANCE       hInstance;        //Instance for customized template
    LPCSTR          lpszTemplate;     //Customized template name
    HRSRC           hResource;        //Customized template handle

    //Specifics for OLEUIPASTESPECIAL.

    //IN fields
    LPDATAOBJECT    lpSrcDataObj;           //Source IDataObject* (on the
                                            //clipboard) for data to paste

    LPOLEUIPASTEENTRY arrPasteEntries;      //Array of OLEUIPASTEENTRYs
                                            //of the acceptable formats.
    int             cPasteEntries;          //Number of OLEUIPASTEENTRYs

    [These are not important for this chapter]
    UINT         FAR *arrLinkTypes;
    int             cLinkTypes;

    //OUT fields
    int             nSelectedIndex;        //User-selected arrPasteEntries
    BOOL            fLink;                 //Paste or Paste Link selected?
    HGLOBAL         hMetaPict;             //Icon and icon title
    } OLEUIPASTESPECIAL, *POLEUIPASTESPECIAL, FAR *LPOLEUIPASTESPECIAL;
```

Paste Special needs to present a list box containing text descriptions of all the formats available for pasting, allowing the application to control which specific formats are possible. So first, in order for Paste Special to know what's on the clipboard, you must fill the *lpSrcDataObj* field of the OLEUIPASTE-SPECIAL dialog box with whatever you get from *OleGetClipboard*:

```
OLEUIPASTESPECIAL   ps;

_fmemset(&ps, 0, sizeof(ps));

if (FAILED(OleGetClipboard(&ps.lpSrcDataObj)))
    return FALSE;
```

You must also fill in the *cbStruct* field of the OLEUIPASTESPECIAL structure (used to verify versions) and the window that owns (is the parent of) the dialog box in *hWndParent*:

```
ps.cbStruct=sizeof(ps);
ps.hWndOwner=hWndFrame;
```

In the *dwFlags* field, you can specify any of the flags PSF_SHOWHELP, PSF_SELECTPASTE, PSF_SELECTPASTELINK, and PSF_CHECKDIS-PLAYASICON, the latter two of which we'll use later. To use this dialog box for simple pasting, specify the PSF_SELECTPASTE flag (including PSF _SHOWHELP if you want):

```
ps.dwFlags=PSF_SELECTPASTE;
```

What's left is to describe the formats we can possibly paste and to provide text descriptions for those formats. This is accomplished by filling the *cPasteEntries* and *arrPasteEntries* fields with the number of allowable formats and a pointer to an array of OLEUIPASTEENTRY structures:

```
OLEUIPASTEENTRY      rgPaste[4];

ps.arrPasteEntries=rgPaste;
ps.cPasteEntries=4;
```

Each OLEUIPASTEENTRY structure contains four fields that describe the format and provide the necessary user interface strings for each format:

```
//From OLE 2's OLESTD.H
typedef struct tagOLEUIPASTEENTRY
    {
    FORMATETC  fmtetc;
    LPCSTR     lpstrFormatName;
    LPCSTR     lpstrResultText;
    DWORD      dwFlags;
    DWORD      dwScratchSpace;
    } OLEUIPASTEENTRY, *POLEUIPASTEENTRY, FAR *LPOLEUIPASTEENTRY;
```

The following table lists the meanings of the parameters in the preceding code:

Parameter	Description
fmtetc	The FORMATETC for this entry.
lpstrFormatName	A text description of the FORMATETC. For example, if *fmtetc* contains CF_DIB, an appropriate string is "Device-Independent Bitmap." Note that the specific storage medium, target device, and aspect of the FORMATETC should not be reflected in this description.
lpszResultText	A string that describes the result of the Paste Special operation. Typically this is the word "a" prepended to the format description. For example, a FORMATETC containing CF_DIB should be accompanied by a string of "a Device-Independent Bitmap."
dwFlags	Flags indicating what operations are allowed on this particular format. The only one of relevance here is OLEUI-PASTE_PASTEONLY, which indicates that the only operation allowed on this format within the dialog box is a Paste. The dialog box also has Paste Link and Display As Icon options, which are disabled with the PASTEONLY flag.
dwScratchSpace	Reserved.

Patron can paste any of four formats. The preferred format is a structure called PATRONOBJECT (see PAGES.H), which contains information about a tenant's location within a page in such a way that a Copy or Paste between Patron documents places the object in the same place, if possible. This is followed in preference by CF_METAFILEPICT, CF_DIB, and CF_BITMAP. Therefore, Patron fills in an array of four OLEUIPASTEENTRY structures:

```
SETDefFormatEtc(rgPaste[0].fmtetc, m_cf, TYMED_HGLOBAL);
rgPaste[0].lpstrFormatName="Patron Object";
rgPaste[0].lpstrResultText="a Patron Object";
rgPaste[0].dwFlags=OLEUIPASTE_PASTEONLY;

SETDefFormatEtc(rgPaste[1].fmtetc,CF_METAFILEPICT,TYMED_MFPICT);
rgPaste[1].lpstrFormatName="Metafile";
rgPaste[1].lpstrResultText="a Metafile";
rgPaste[1].dwFlags=OLEUIPASTE_PASTEONLY;

SETDefFormatEtc(rgPaste[2].fmtetc, CF_DIB, TYMED_HGLOBAL);
rgPaste[2].lpstrFormatName="Device-Independent Bitmap";
rgPaste[2].lpstrResultText="a Device-Independent Bitmap";
rgPaste[2].dwFlags=OLEUIPASTE_PASTEONLY;
```

(continued)

```
SETDefFormatEtc(rgPaste[3].fmtetc, CF_BITMAP, TYMED_GDI);
rgPaste[3].lpstrFormatName="Bitmap";
rgPaste[3].lpstrResultText="a Bitmap";
rgPaste[3].dwFlags=OLEUIPASTE_PASTEONLY;
```

Finally, when we have this structure filled, we can call *OleUIPasteSpecial*:

```
uTemp=OleUIPasteSpecial(&ps);

if (OLEUI_OK==uTemp)
    {
    fRet=FPasteFromData(ps.lpSrcDataObj
        , &rgPaste[ps.nSelectedIndex].fmtetc
        , TENANTTYPE_STATIC, NULL, 0L);
    }

ps.lpSrcDataObj->Release();
return fRet;
```

If the function returns OLEUI_OK, the user pressed the OK button and we can actually perform a Paste with the selected format, which the dialog box stores in the *nSelectedIndex* field of OLEUIPASTESPECIAL. Note again that Patron is using a "Paste From Data" function, which takes a data object and effectively does a Paste from the specified FORMATETC. Finally, we have to remember to release the data object we obtained from *OleGetClipboard*.

Tenant Creation, Paste

The difference between Paste Special and the typical Paste operation is that Paste does not allow specific selection of the pasted format. For Paste, Patron goes through a series of checks to find the best format on the clipboard by calling *IDataObject::QueryGetData*, and after it finds a format, it uses the same *FPasteFromData* function that Paste Special uses. The function that checks for the available format is identical to what we want for enabling the Paste menu item. Patron's *FQueryPasteFromData* does just that, and it returns the best FORMATETC it found on the clipboard:

```
BOOL CPatronDoc::FQueryPasteFromData(LPDATAOBJECT pIDataObject
    , LPFORMATETC pFE, LPTENANTTYPE ptType)
    {
    FORMATETC       fe;
    HRESULT         hr;

    if (NULL!=(LPVOID)ptType)
        *ptType=TENANTTYPE_STATIC;
```

```
    //Any of our specific data here?
    SETDefFormatEtc(fe, m_cf, TYMED_HGLOBAL);
    hr=pIDataObject->QueryGetData(&fe);

    if (NOERROR!=hr)
        {
        //Try metafile, DIB, then bitmap, setting fe each time
        SETDefFormatEtc(fe, CF_METAFILEPICT, TYMED_MFPICT);
        hr=pIDataObject->QueryGetData(&fe);

        if (NOERROR!=hr)
            {
            SETDefFormatEtc(fe, CF_DIB, TYMED_HGLOBAL);
            hr=pIDataObject->QueryGetData(&fe);

            if (NOERROR!=hr)
                {
                SETDefFormatEtc(fe, CF_BITMAP, TYMED_GDI);
                hr=pIDataObject->QueryGetData(&fe);
                }
            }
        }

    if (NOERROR==hr && NULL!=pFE)
        *pFE=fe;

    return (NOERROR==hr);
    }
```

Patron's implementation of Paste, in *CPatronDoc::FPaste*, calls *FQueryPasteFromData* to first find the best format and then calls *CPatronDoc::FPasteFromData* to do the real operation. Note again, as I have mentioned before, that it is extremely valuable to implement a function to do your Paste operation from a data object, because when we implement drag-and-drop in the next chapter, this sort of function will be extremely useful:

```
BOOL CPatronDoc::FPaste(HWND hWndFrame)
    {
    LPDATAOBJECT    pIDataObject;
    BOOL            fRet=FALSE;
    FORMATETC       fe;
    TENANTTYPE      tType;

    if (NULL==m_pPG)
        return FALSE;
```

(continued)

```
    if (FAILED(OleGetClipboard(&pIDataObject)))
        return FALSE;

    //Go get the type and format we *can* paste, then actually paste it.
    if (FQueryPasteFromData(pIDataObject, &fe, &tType))
        fRet=FPasteFromData(pIDataObject, &fe, tType, NULL, 0L);

    pIDataObject->Release();
    return fRet;
    }

BOOL CPatronDoc::FPasteFromData(LPDATAOBJECT pIDataObject
    , LPFORMATETC pFE, TENANTTYPE tType, LPPATRONOBJECT ppo
    , DWORD dwData)
    {
    BOOL                fRet;
    HRESULT             hr;
    PATRONOBJECT        po;
    STGMEDIUM           stm;

    if (NULL==pFE)
        return FALSE;

    //If we're not given any placement data, see if we can retrieve it
    if (pFE->cfFormat==m_cf && NULL==ppo)
        {
        hr=pIDataObject->GetData(pFE, &stm);

        if (SUCCEEDED(hr))
            {
            ppo=(LPPATRONOBJECT)GlobalLock(stm.hGlobal);

            po=*ppo;
            ppo=&po;
            GlobalUnlock(stm.hGlobal);
            ReleaseStgMedium(&stm);
            }
        }

    fRet=m_pPG->TenantCreate(tType, (LPVOID)pIDataObject, pFE
        , ppo, dwData);

    if (fRet)
        {
        //Disable Printer Setup once we've created a tenant.
        if (m_fPrintSetup)
            m_fPrintSetup=FALSE;
```

```
        FDirtySet(TRUE);
        }

    return fRet;
    }
```

The *FPasteFromData* function first checks to see whether it was given explicit placement data for whatever it pastes—that is, a point for the upper left corner of the object on the page, where (0,0) is the upper left of the printable region, and both x- and y-extents, which define the complete object's rectangle. I separated the point and the extents so that they could be manipulated independently—changing the size of an object doesn't necessarily change the upper left corner, and moving an object doesn't necessarily change the extents.

In any case, during Pastes from the clipboard the *ppo* parameter to this function will always be NULL, which means if the clipboard holds Patron Object data, the application pastes the best available graphic format, placing that graphic at the coordinates in the PATRONOBJECT structure on the clipboard. You'll find that all code in this chapter's version of Patron passes NULL as *ppo*: It's there in preparation for the drag-and-drop feature we'll add in the next chapter. In all honesty, I had implemented this differently on my first pass through this chapter's code, and after finding it deficient for Chapter 8, I came back here and changed this code to suit the Chapter 8 change. I hope it gives you a little insight if you are designing something similar.

Whew! That's been a mouthful, but now let's look at what actually creates this thing we call a tenant. A tenant is an object of my C++ class *CTenant* that has member functions such as *Open, Load, Update, Destroy, Select, Activate, Draw,* and *SizeSet,* just to name a few. This tenant object will also become a site object in Chapter 9, in that it will maintain information for a compound document object. But we're most of the way there already—a tenant in this chapter holds onto some object with an *IUnknown* pointer, asks that object to draw by using *IViewObject,* and uses the OLE2.DLL functions of *OleSave* and *OleLoad* to save the object and its presentations to a piece of storage.

The storage for each tenant is a uniquely named storage object created below the storage object for the page. You can see this happening in the function *CTenant::FOpen,* which will either open the storage of a given name if it exists or, failing that, will create a new storage of that name. To keep unique names, each page maintains a DWORD tenant ID counter, which it saves to its storage along with a list of tenants, just as the *CPages* implementation saves lists of pages to its storage object one level higher.

When Patron needs to create a tenant, a request that usually starts from the document level, the creation request is passed from the document to *CPages*, and then to the current *CPage* that allocates a new tenant (*new CTenant*, in *FTenantAdd*) and asks that tenant to actually perform the necessary functions to obtain an *IUnknown* pointer, which the tenant then stores. This happens in *CTenant::UCreate*, which is the only piece of code that knows how to take something like a data object pointer and create an object out of whatever is there. Exactly what it does is determined by the TENANTTYPE (see TENANT.H) parameter passed to it. For this chapter, the type is always TENANTTYPE_STATIC, so *UCreate* generally uses the same technique as Chapter 6's Freeloader to create a static object. In later chapters, we'll add more types of tenants, such as compound document embedded objects for which we'll call *OleCreate* to create the object.

Saving and Loading Tenants

In Chapter 5, we added basic compound file functions to Patron so that a document could maintain a list of pages. We set up a mechanism so that each page's storage was committed when you switched away from it and opened again when you switched to that page. When we saved the compound file, we wrote a Page List stream off the root storage that contained the number of pages in the document, the currently viewed page, the next ID to use for a page, and the list of pages—that is, the list of page IDs from which Patron can recreate the name of the page's storage.

For this chapter, we just extend the same idea to each page, where a page maintains a list of tenants and writes a stream containing the number of tenants, the next tenant ID, and a list of tenant IDs that exist in the page. We make the name of the tenant's storage come from the tenant ID, just as we do for the pages. Managing the storages, however, is a little different. When the page is open, all the tenants on that page are also considered "loaded"—that is, Patron has a pointer to the object in that tenant. When you switch away from the page, each tenant's storage is committed before the page's storage is committed. Still, nothing is written to the disk because we have yet to commit the root storage. But as far as each page is concerned, we don't have to try to keep pointers to any tenant that has been modified; instead, we save those objects to storage when closing the page and reload them, from memory, when the page is reopened.

In Chapter 6's Freeloader, we explicitly used the object's *IPersistStorage* interface to affect the saving and loading of the objects and their presentations. Patron instead uses the two functions *OleSave* and *OleLoad*, OLE2.DLL

API function wrappers, which reproduce exactly, and I mean exactly (I looked), the sequence of operations that we performed in Freeloader. *OleSave* saves all the presentations in the cache and stores the object's class ID to its storage. *OleLoad* reinitializes the cache from the saved presentations and creates a pointer to the object, so when we reload a tenant and its object we do not use *UCreate.* That latter function is exclusively for first-time creation of the object residing in the tenant.

Patron's whole storage scheme really shows off the power of transactioned storage. By simple virtue of having the root storage transacted, we can write the rest of the application to think that its data is always on disk—that is, when we create a new object in a tenant, we immediately save that object to its storage. (See the *OleSave* call in *CTenant::CreateStatic.*) When any tenant is asked to update itself in its storage, it writes a small stream containing its FORMATETC and position information and then calls *OleSave* to write all the messy data, followed by a *Commit.* In all, the storage management on the tenant level is minimal, and the page only needs to insure that each tenant is given the chance to update itself before the page closes.

The most beautiful part of this storage mechanism is that we have now in place everything we need to handle storage for a compound document object. When we enable this feature in Patron in Chapter 9, you'll see that we need no modifications to our storage model.

Copy and Cut

The final feature that I would like to discuss is that of Copy and Cut operations for the currently selected tenant. I will not be discussing exactly how I implemented the sizing functionality because that's just a lot of straight Windows programming that's pretty clear from the source code itself. A discussion of it here would distract from discussing OLE 2. I will admit that the sizing code took about three times as long to write and debug as any other part of this application that is using OLE 2. I don't really want to sedate you with the details.

Patron uses the same technique developed in Cosmo at the beginning of this chapter. The data for the object is stuffed into one of our Data Transfer component objects, and it is that object we put on the clipboard. The entire Copy and Cut operations start in *CPatronDoc::FClip,* which simply calls *CPages::TenantClip,* which calls the current page's *CPage::TenantClip.* Inside this last function, the page calls its internal *TransferObjectCreate* function. *TransferObjectCreate* places two data formats in the data transfer object. The first is a PATRONOBJECT structure that describes where the object lives on the page. If we later paste back into a Patron document, we can use this data to try to put the tenant in the same place it was in the source. We'll use this as well in Patron's drag-and-drop implementation in the next chapter. In addition to this placement data, we include the graphical presentation we're using for the object in the tenant. A rendering of this graphic is readily available through the object's *IDataObject::GetData.* Mostly harmless, I would say, and when *TransferObjectCreate* is finished, *CPage::TenantClip* calls *OleSetClipboard* and possibly destroys the selected tenant if we're doing a Cut operation.

Note that I created the separate *TransferObjectCreate* function because we'll want to use it again next chapter when we need a data object as a drag-and-drop source. This is why there's the *pptl* parameter to *TransferObjectCreate,* which describes the offset from the top left of the tenant's rectangle where it was picked up in the drag-and-drop operation.

What that really means is that we've come to the end of this chapter and are ready to dive into the drag-and-drop transfer protocol with data objects.

Summary

OLE 2 provides three API functions that allow applications to replace their current clipboard-handling code with the use of data objects. OLE 2 only requires the use of its clipboard handling in drag-and-drop and compound document scenarios, so applications that have little need to be involved with compound documents or will not implement drag-and-drop need not be too concerned with this new mechanism.

However, any potential source of data that will also want to become a drag-and-drop data source, as well as a clipboard data source, will need to implement a data object for use in that operation. If you are planning to go this route, it's beneficial for you to convert your current clipboard code into OLE 2 data object transfers, because most of the code you write is just as useful on a data object obtained from a drag-and-drop operation as from a clipboard Paste operation.

The first of the three API functions is *OleSetClipboard,* which places on the clipboard a data object pointer, as well as the names of the actual data formats that data object knows about as determined from *IDataObject::EnumFormatEtc.* OLE 2 will not actually render the data, (that is, call *IDataObject::GetData*) until a data consumer asks for it. Therefore, the source application must be written to handle what is known as delayed rendering, which typically requires that the application uses snapshots of the data copied or cut and holds onto it until the clipboard is cleared.

The consumer of data calls *OleGetClipboard* to retrieve an *IDataObject* pointer representing the data on the clipboard. Through this data object pointer the consumer can retrieve data or ask about the availability of formats—that is, implement Paste functionality. I recommend here that you create a function to paste, or query pasting, from any arbitrary data object because such code centralizes the operation and enables you to use it regardless of the protocol you used to get the *IDataObject* pointer in the first place.

The other API is *OleFlushClipboard*, which will clean any existing data object off the clipboard. This is generally called at the close of an application. In addition, applications that want to use OLE 2's clipboard facilities must now call *OleInitialize* and *OleUninitialize* instead of *CoInitialize* and *CoUninitialize*. The *Ole...* versions create a hidden clipboard window that OLE 2 uses to generate calls to a source's *IDataObject::GetData*. *OleUninitialize*, of course, destroys this one-per-task window.

It might seem like overkill to have to create a data object merely for the purpose of copying one lousy little piece of text, and I agree. Therefore, this chapter implements a component object to simplify OLE 2 clipboard operations, making them reflect the way you probably use the clipboard today. This is, of course, only one possible solution, and at least two other possibilities are presented here.

For this chapter, the clipboard-handling code in both Cosmo and Component Cosmo are replaced with the OLE 2 techniques. Patron is blessed with procreative ability—that is, it can now paste real graphics from the clipboard, resize them, print them, and save and load them from Compound Files. This sets Patron up well for becoming a Compound Document container in Chapter 9. Patron also introduces the OLEUI library, which contains many useful functions for application development.

CHAPTER EIGHT

DRAG-AND-DROP OPERATIONS USING DATA OBJECTS

When I first started to work with Object Linking and Embedding, I watched a number of videotapes from OLE version 1 seminars and demonstrations in a four-month crash effort to attain OLE enlightenment. At one point, when I was getting bored out of my skull, I decided to fast-forward through some of the demos. What I noticed during that fit of impatience was how often the presenter would select some data, pull down the Edit menu to choose Cut or Copy, switch to another application, and then pull down the Edit menu to choose Paste. Not a big deal, I imagined. After all, the clipboard has been the most common technique used to transfer data between source and consumer applications, and that sequence of operations is simply what works.

I gradually realized, as others were doing at the same time, that the much more efficient way of performing the same Cut/Copy-Paste operations was to use a drag-and-drop technique. In drag-and-drop, you (the end user) select some data in the source application, *pick* it up with a mouse click, *drag* that picked-up data from the source application's window to the consumer application's window, and *drop* that data into the consumer.

This sequence of operations, which I call *pick-drag-drop,* does exactly what you today accomplish with the clipboard through the select-Cut/Copy-Paste sequence. The big difference is that drag-and-drop is direct and immediate—the entire data transfer operation happens all at once. Clipboard transfers are most useful when you want to store data on the clipboard for an undetermined amount of time, and that data might never be consumed. With drag-and-drop, the source and consumer are linked together for the transfer without having the clipboard in between. In fact, drag-and-drop does not affect the contents of the clipboard in any way.

OLE 2 drag-and-drop, like OLE 2's use of the clipboard, works through data objects. Drag-and-drop is, therefore, just another way to move a data object pointer—that is, a pointer to *IDataObject*—from the source application to the consumer application. To facilitate this pointer exchange, the source application implements an object called the *drop source,* which provides an *IDropSource* interface. The consumer application, which in drag-and-drop context is called a *target* application, implements a *drop target* object, which provides the interface *IDropTarget.* The first section in this chapter explains how these two objects are managed, how OLE 2 becomes aware of them, and how they communicate in a drag-and-drop operation.

Using the Cosmo application, I'll then show how to implement simple drag-and-drop features into an application. This example will show how little you can get away with to benefit from this OLE 2 feature, as we'll implement only minimal user interface. This minimal implementation will lead into a more complicated implementation in Patron, which will use drag-and-drop not only to accept data from other applications but also to move tenants around within a single page or between different open documents. Patron makes special considerations for scrolling a page during a drag-and-drop operation and provides more precise user feedback than Cosmo does.

I want to again stress that if you are going to implement drag-and-drop, you first convert your clipboard-handling code from Windows API functions into OLE 2 API functions and make specific functions that paste or test pasting from any given data object, as demonstrated in Chapter 7. Those efforts pay off here to the extent that a drag-and-drop implementation can be done in a matter of days, if not hours, depending on your desired level of complexity. (C'mon, Kraig, you think we *desire* complexity?) People watching your demonstrations on fast-forward video won't know what hit them.

Sources and Targets: The Drag-and-Drop Transfer Model

Let's begin with a typical situation in which the end user has two applications running and wants to transfer a selection of data from the source application into the consumer application, as represented in Figure 8-1. (In reality, the two "applications" could be two different documents in the same application, or they could be one document of one application.) In any case, we can label one place as the source and the other place as the consumer. The source

Figure 8-1.
The state of things before a drag-and-drop operation: The source has a data object attached to the affected data. There are not necessarily two separate applications; the source and consumer could be the same document in one application or perhaps two documents in the same application. With OLE 2 in the middle, who knows the difference?

of the data must implement a data object to represent the data being transferred. This can be exactly the same data object that you would create for a clipboard transfer.

So our problem now is getting that *IDataObject* pointer from the source to the target by using drag-and-drop. To be the source of a drag-and-drop operation, an application must implement an object with the *IDropSource* interface, as shown in Figure 8-2. The drop source object is a stand-alone object—that is, its *QueryInterface* function used on it will understand only *IDropSource* and *IUnknown*. *IDropSource* has only two member functions (besides *IUnknown* members):

Function	Description
QueryContinueDrag	Determines what conditions cause a drop or cancellation of the operation.
GiveFeedback	Sets the mouse cursor depending on an "effect" flag that indicates what would happen if the data were dropped at the current location. Can also provide other user interfaces within the source application.

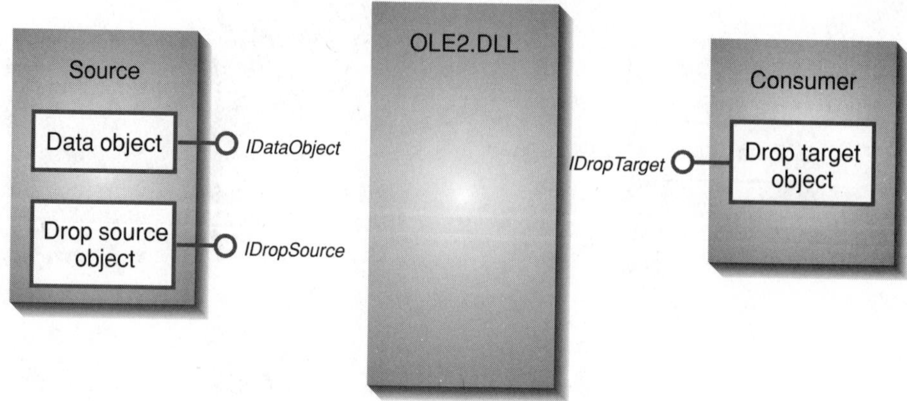

Figure 8-2.
Objects necessary in both the source and consumer to facilitate a drag-and-drop operation.

The consumer, in order to accept any data from a drag-and-drop operation, must implement a stand-alone object with the *IDropTarget* interface, as also shown in Figure 8-2.

The drop target object is generally part of the consumer's document as a whole—that is, the drop target object is identified as belonging to a specific window. To attach the object to the document window, the consumer passes the *IDropTarget* pointer to the OLE 2 API function *RegisterDragDrop*, as shown in Figure 8-3. *RegisterDragDrop* takes an HWND and an *IDropTarget* pointer and internally saves that pointer (after an *AddRef*, of course) as a property on the *hWnd*. At this point, the window is open to accept data. When the consumer no longer wants to be a drop target, it calls the OLE 2 API function *RevokeDragDrop*, using the same HWND that was passed to *RegisterDragDrop*. Internally, OLE 2 removes the property and releases the *IDropTarget* pointer.

The *IDropTarget* interface has four member functions, aside from *IUnknown* members:

Function	Description
DragEnter	Indicates that the mouse entered the window registered with this interface. The target generally initializes state variables that are meaningful during this operation and provides some visual indication of what might happen on a drop.

(continued)

Function	Description
DragOver	Indicates that the mouse moved within the window or that the keyboard state changed. The target indicates what would happen if a drop occurred here using an "effect" flag, as well as any visual feedback in its document but does not control the mouse cursor.
DragLeave	Indicates that the mouse left the window. The target cleans up any state from *DragEnter* or *DragOver*, including any visual feedback.
Drop	Indicates that the source's *IDropSource::QueryContinueDrag* said "drop," so the target must paste the data and perform cleanup as in *DragLeave*.

NOTE: The *IDropTarget* member functions are passed a POINTL structure containing the current mouse position in *screen* coordinates. Be sure to call *ScreenToClient* before hit-testing the mouse position against other client-area coordinates.

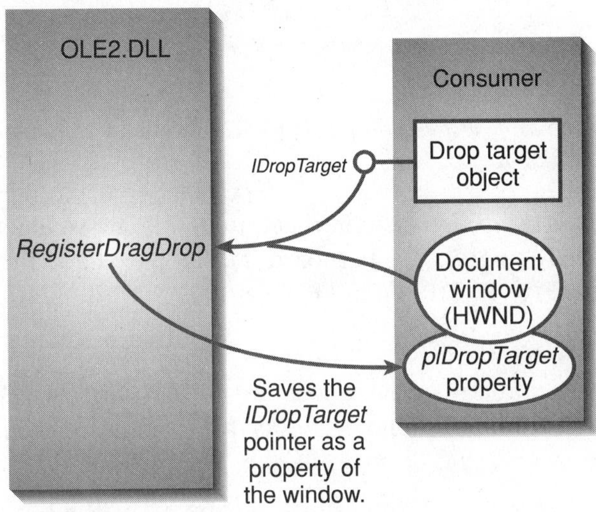

Figure 8-3.
A consumer registers itself as a drop target by passing a window handle and a pointer to its IDropTarget *interface to* RegisterDragDrop.

The table is now set for the operation to commence. The source application must provide some means for starting a drag-and-drop operation, which is typically a WM_LBUTTONDOWN on a particular region of the selected data, such as the outer edge of a rectangle. When this event occurs, the source passes its *IDropSource* and *IDataObject* pointers to the OLE 2 API function *DoDragDrop*, as shown in Figure 8-4.

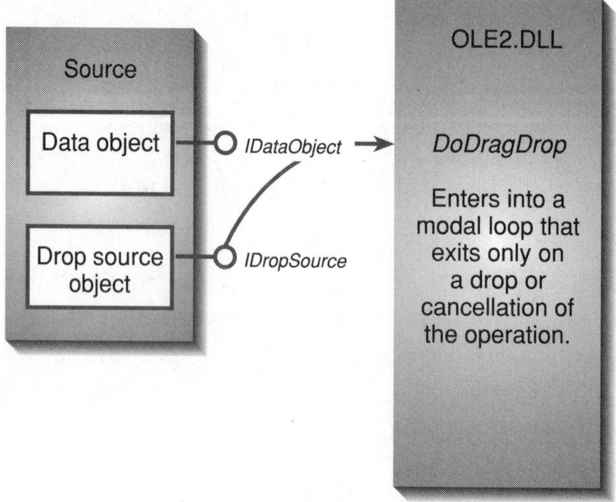

Figure 8-4.
A source starts a drag-and-drop operation by passing its IDataObject *and* IDropSource *to* DoDragDrop.

Internally, *DoDragDrop* enters a loop that watches the movements of the mouse and changes in the state of the keyboard. The loop executes the following series of commands, as illustrated in Figure 8-5:

1. The loop calls the Windows API function *WindowFromPoint*, using the current coordinates of the mouse cursor. If *WindowFromPoint* returns a valid window handle, it checks that window for the property containing an *IDropTarget* pointer.
2. If there is an *IDropTarget* pointer for this window, the loop calls *IDropTarget::DragEnter* with the *IDataObject* pointer from the source (marshaled, if necessary). The target can check the available formats in the data object and return an "effect" code that indicates what would happen if a drop occurred here—for example, Copy (Copy-Paste), Move (Cut-Paste), or nothing at all. If there is not an *IDropTarget* for the window, *DoDragDrop* assumes that nothing would happen here.

3. Given the "effect" code from the target under the current cursor position (which is nothing if there is no target), *DoDragDrop* calls *IDropSource::GiveFeedback*, which is responsible for changing the mouse cursor to an appropriate shape and providing whatever feedback is appropriate in the source depending on the effect.

4. Now, whenever the mouse moves, it might leave the confines of one window and enter another. Whenever the mouse moves out of a target window, *DoDragDrop* calls *IDropTarget::DragLeave* and then calls the *IDropTarget::DragEnter* of the new target under the mouse. If the mouse moves but does not change windows, the current target's *IDropTarget::DragOver* is called.

5. The *DragEnter-DragOver-DragLeave* loop continues as long as there is no change in the keyboard or mouse button state. Whenever there is a state change, however, *DoDragDrop* calls *IDropSource::QueryContinueDrag*, which determines whether to continue the operation, cancel it, or indicate a drop. Canceling the operation is done whenever the user presses the Esc key, and dropping is typically indicated for an event such as WM_LBUTTONUP because WM_LBUTTONDOWN typically starts the operation in the first place. Any other change allows the operation to continue. In addition, the current *IDropTarget::DragOver* is called for a keyboard state change even if the mouse does not move. By checking the key state, the target indicates whether it would do either a Move (no key down) or a Copy (Ctrl key down) if a drop happened here—that is, it returns a new effect flag. *DoDragDrop* then passes this new effect flag to *IDropSource::GiveFeedback*, which again changes the mouse cursor.

6. If *IDropSource::QueryContinueDrag* indicates that the operation should be canceled, *DoDragDrop* calls *IDropTarget::DragLeave* and finally exits with an HRESULT containing DRAGDROP_S_CANCEL. If *QueryContinueDrag* says "drop," *DoDragDrop* instead calls *IDropTarget::Drop* (which does the Paste) and exits with an HRESULT of NOERROR. *DoDragDrop* also returns the last effect code so that the source knows whether it needs to cut the affected data (say, in a move).

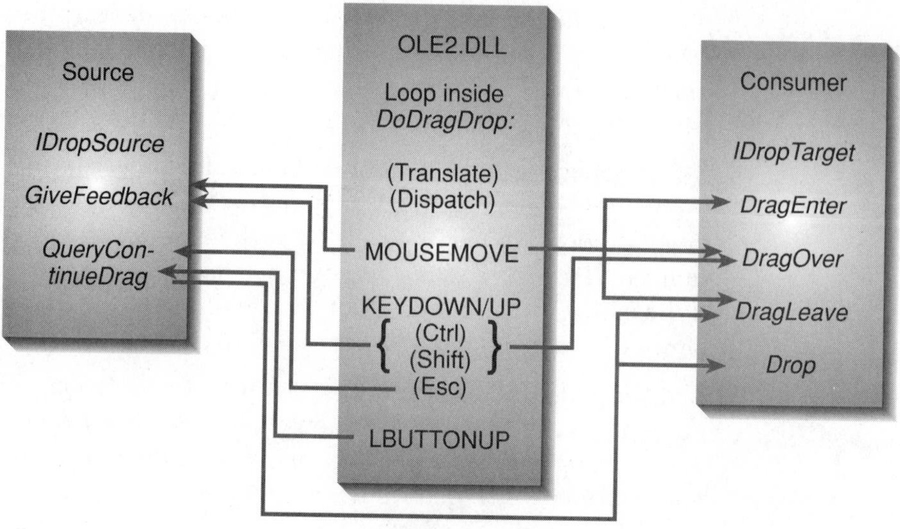

Figure 8-5.
Execution of DoDragDrop *to perform the entire drag-and-drop operation.*

Notice that the source always maintains control over the cursor during an OLE 2 drag-and-drop operation because the source is where the user is looking when the operation starts. This means that the cursor will stay reasonably stable during the entire operation—that is, the cursor will not change much from its original state in the source. If the target controlled the cursor instead, every time it entered a different target window, it would change, potentially in radical ways. The cursor that indicates a drag-and-drop in one target might be similar or identical to the cursor that indicates a completely different operation in another target. This is very disconcerting to an end user, who will probably be confused as to what happened to the data. By giving cursor control to the source, the cursor stays much more stable as a drag-and-drop crosses many potential targets. The end user is initially looking at the cursor in the source, so the cursor should stay as close as possible to that original image throughout the operation.

One potential problem is that the current visible area in the target document might not be where the end user wants to drop the data. How, then, if *DoDragDrop* is eating keyboard and mouse messages, can the end user scroll the target document? The answer is that OLE 2 specifies that within each target window is an "inset region" of a set number of pixels within the border of the window, as shown in Figure 8-6. If the mouse stays within an inset region for a given length of time, the target should start scrolling the document. If the mouse then leaves this region, the target stops scrolling.

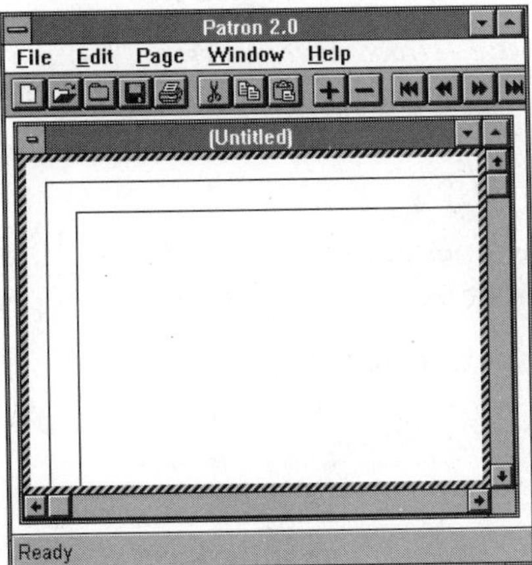

Figure 8-6.
The inset region within a consumer document window.

This is not much different from the automatic scrolling that happens when you scroll something like an edit control while selecting text or when you select items in a list box. However, the difference in OLE 2 is that when the mouse goes outside the window, scrolling stops. The reason OLE 2 drag-and-drop is specified in this manner is that a common operation is dragging data between applications. Therefore, scrolling whenever the mouse is off the edge of any target document would cause almost every document in every application to scroll wildly. Although this event certainly would conform to the Second Law of Thermodynamics, entropy is not user friendly.[1] So OLE 2 requires that the mouse be in the inset region to affect scrolling. The time delay is also specified so that a quick drag outside one window doesn't start scrolling just because the mouse passed through the inset region. The end user must hold the mouse in the inset region for a short time, usually on the order of a few tenths of a second, for scrolling to begin.

---

1. OK, OK, so you didn't take Thermodynamics in college. The law states that the amount of entropy, S (disorder, chaos), in the universe is increasing—that is, $\Delta S > 0$.

From all this we can extract the specific responsibilities for both source and target in a drag-and-drop scenario. These are as follows:

The Source

1. Provides the *IDataObject* pointer for the affected data.
2. Implements an object with the *IDropSource* interface. A drop source object does not need to be instantiated until the source calls *DoDragDrop* and can be freed immediately after the operation is finished.
3. Calls *DoDragDrop* to start the operation and implements *IDropSource::QueryContinueDrag* to determine when to end the operation.
4. Sets the appropriate mouse cursors for various effects in *IDropSource::GiveFeedback.*

The Target

1. Implements an object with the *IDropTarget* interface.
2. Registers the *IDropTarget* object with an appropriate window handle using *RegisterDragDrop.* Typically, this is done when creating or opening a document.
3. Determines whether data is acceptable in *IDropTarget::DragEnter.* Determines the effect of a drop in *IDropTarget::DragEnter* and *IDropTarget::DragOver* and provides user interface feedback appropriate to the effect. Because user feedback is optional, I recommend that you skip implementing it until other target operations are working (that is, steps 1, 2, 5, and 6).
4. Scrolls the target document (if appropriate) when the cursor has been in an inset region long enough. As with step 3, you can initially skip this step, and in some cases it will never be a consideration. Concentrate on this step after all others, including 3, have been addressed.
5. Performs a Paste on *IDropTarget::Drop.*
6. Removes the *IDropTarget* pointer by calling *RevokeDragDrop* when the window is no longer a target, typically when the document is closed.

So let's see these responsibilities in code.

A Step-by-Step Drag-and-Drop Implementation: Cosmo

To demonstrate basic drag-and-drop implementation, let's now add the feature to the Cosmo application (as well as to Component Cosmo, although I won't show any of its code here because it's identical to Cosmo). Because Cosmo's idea of a document contains only one Polyline figure, we don't have to worry about scrolling. Furthermore, providing some user feedback to indicate the drop target is easy because we can simply draw an inverted outline around the Polyline. The 8-pixel border we already have around the Polyline makes a perfect region from which to start a drag; therefore, we don't have to do any extra work to figure out when and where a pick (the event that starts a drag-and-drop operation) happens.

A Cosmo document in this example will be both source and target for its private data format. This will typically be the case in your application as well, because you can probably copy and paste your own data. In drag-and-drop, not only can you Copy-Paste within your own document, but the same exact implementation works between multiple documents in your same application as well as between different documents in multiple instances of the application. Drag-and-drop simply does not care: A source is a source, and a target a target, independent of their relationship to one another, be it identical, sibling, distant cousin, or complete stranger.

Cosmo's drag-and-drop implementation follows seven steps, three for the target and four for the source. You'll notice that the steps implement the target side first. This is intentional because I want Cosmo to drag-and-drop to itself with its private data. To test Cosmo as a drag-and-drop source, I need at least one acceptable consumer, and Cosmo is the only application that accepts its own data. Therefore, we follow simple target implementation first.

The target steps

1. Design and implement the necessary code to provide user feedback that indicates the result of a drop. This should be done first so that step 2 can use it.
2. Implement the *IDropTarget* interface for a drop target object of the consumer. All four member functions must be fully implemented; part of their implementation is to use the code from step 1 to provide the user interface.

3. Use the *RegisterDragDrop* and *RevokeDragDrop* functions to manage the lifetime of the drop target object implemented in step 2. These function calls are also accompanied by a special required use of *CoLockObjectExternal.*

The source steps

1. Design the user interface that is necessary for the source while dragging. This procedure can be as simple as changing the mouse cursor, which OLE 2 will perform for you.
2. Determine how a drag-and-drop operation starts (what I call the "pick" event) and what terminates it (either cancellation or a drop).
3. Implement the *IDropSource* interface on a drop source object. This implementation can be trivial for most circumstances.
4. Call *DoDragDrop* when the pick event occurs, and possibly cut the selected data from the source if the operation was a move instead of a copy.

Each of these steps is treated in a separate section later. The code basis for the steps is shown in Listing 8-1, as are modifications to Cosmo's COSMO.H and DOCUMENT.CPP, as well as two new files, IDROPTGT.CPP and IDROPSRC.CPP, which implement the drop target and drop source objects, respectively. (You will find these latter two in the INTERFAC directory.)

COSMO.H

```
[Unmodified sections omitted from listing]

...

class __far CCosmoDoc : public CDocument
    {
    ...

    //These need access to FQueryPasteFromData, FPasteFromData
    friend class CDropTarget;
    friend class CDropSource;
```

Listing 8-1. *(continued)*

Modifications and additions to the Cosmo application to handle drag-and-drop.

Listing 8-1. *continued*

```
    protected:
        ...

        class CDropTarget FAR *m_pDropTarget;  //Registered target.
        BOOL                  m_fDragSource;   //Source==target?

    protected:
        ...
        LPDATAOBJECT    TransferObjectCreate(BOOL)
        void            DropSelectTargetWindow(void);

    ...
    }
...

//Drag-and-drop interfaces we need in the document
class __far CDropTarget : public IDropTarget
    {
    protected:
        ULONG           m_cRef;
        LPCCosmoDoc     m_pDoc;

        LPDATAOBJECT    m_pIDataObject;  //From DragEnter

    public:
        CDropTarget(LPCCosmoDoc);
        ~CDropTarget(void);

        //IDropTarget interface members
        STDMETHODIMP QueryInterface(REFIID, LPLPVOID);
        STDMETHODIMP_(ULONG) AddRef(void);
        STDMETHODIMP_(ULONG) Release(void);

        STDMETHODIMP DragEnter(LPDATAOBJECT, DWORD, POINTL,LPDWORD);
        STDMETHODIMP DragOver(DWORD, POINTL, LPDWORD);
        STDMETHODIMP DragLeave(void);
        STDMETHODIMP Drop(LPDATAOBJECT, DWORD, POINTL, LPDWORD);
    };

typedef CDropTarget FAR *LPCDropTarget;

class __far CDropSource : public IDropSource
    {
```

(continued)

Listing 8-1. *continued*

```
    protected:
        ULONG               m_cRef;
        LPCCosmoDoc         m_pDoc;

    public:
        CDropSource(LPCCosmoDoc);
        ~CDropSource(void);

        //IDropSource interface members
        STDMETHODIMP QueryInterface(REFIID, LPLPVOID);
        STDMETHODIMP_(ULONG) AddRef(void);
        STDMETHODIMP_(ULONG) Release(void);

        STDMETHODIMP QueryContinueDrag(BOOL, DWORD);
        STDMETHODIMP GiveFeedback(DWORD);
    };

typedef CDropSource FAR *LPCDropSource;
```

DOCUMENT.CPP

```
[Unmodified code omitted from listing]

CCosmoDoc::CCosmoDoc(HINSTANCE hInst)
    : CDocument(hInst)
    {
    m_pPL=NULL;
    m_pPLAdv=NULL;
    m_uPrevSize=SIZE_RESTORED;

    m_pDropTarget=NULL;
    m_fDragSource=FALSE;
    return;
    }
...
BOOL CCosmoDoc::FInit(LPDOCUMENTINIT pDI)
    {
    ...

    m_pDropTarget=new CDropTarget(this);

    if (NULL!=m_pDropTarget)
        {
```

(continued)

Listing 8-1. *continued*

```
        m_pDropTarget->AddRef();
        CoLockObjectExternal((LPUNKNOWN)m_pDropTarget, TRUE, FALSE);
        RegisterDragDrop(m_hWnd, (LPDROPTARGET)m_pDropTarget);
        }

    return TRUE;
    }

BOOL CCosmoDoc::FMessageHook(HWND hWnd, UINT iMsg, WPARAM wParam
    , LPARAM lParam, LRESULT FAR *pLRes)
    {

    [Handling of WM_SIZE]

    if (WM_LBUTTONDOWN==iMsg)
        {
        LPDROPSOURCE    pIDropSource;
        LPDATAOBJECT    pIDataObject;
        HRESULT         hr;
        SCODE           sc;
        DWORD           dwEffect;

        /*
         * The document has an 8 pixel border around the polyline
         * window where we'll see mouse clicks. A left mouse button
         * click here means the start of a drag-and-drop operation.
         *
         * Because this is a modal operation, this IDropSource
         * is entirely local.
         */

        pIDropSource=(LPDROPSOURCE)new CDropSource(this);

        if (NULL==pIDropSource)
            return FALSE;

        pIDropSource->AddRef();
        m_fDragSource=TRUE;

        //Go get the data and start the ball rolling.
        pIDataObject=TransferObjectCreate(FALSE);
```

(continued)

Listing 8-1. *continued*

```
    if (NULL!=pIDataObject)
        {
        hr=DoDragDrop(pIDataObject, pIDropSource
            , DROPEFFECT_COPY | DROPEFFECT_MOVE, &dwEffect);

        pIDataObject->Release();
        sc=GetScode (hr);
        }
    else
        sc=E_FAIL;

        /*
         * When we return from DoDragDrop, either cancel or drop.
         * First toss the IDropSource we have here, then bail out
         * on cancel, and possibly clear our data on a move drop.
         */

        pIDropSource->Release();

        /*
         * If dropped on the same document (determined using
         * this flag), dwEffect will be DROPEFFECT_NONE (see
         * IDropTarget::Drop in IDROPTGT.CPP). In any case,
         * reset this since the operation is done.
         */

        m_fDragSource=FALSE;

        if (DRAGDROP_S_DROP==sc && DROPEFFECT_MOVE==dwEffect)
            {
            m_pPL->New();
            FDirtySet(TRUE);
            }

        //On a canceled drop or a copy don't do anything else
        return TRUE;
        }

    if (WM_DESTROY==iMsg)
        {
        /*
         * We have to revoke the drop target here because the window
         * will be destroyed and the property forcefully removed
         * before we could do this in the destructor.
         */
        if (NULL!=m_pDropTarget)
            {
            RevokeDragDrop(m_hWnd);
```

(continued)

Listing 8-1. *continued*

```
            CoLockObjectExternal((LPUNKNOWN)m_pDropTarget
                , FALSE, TRUE);
            m_pDropTarget->Release();
            }
        }

    return FALSE;
    }

...

LPDATAOBJECT CCosmoDoc::TransferObjectCreate(BOOL fCut)
    {
    HGLOBAL         hMem;
    UINT            i;
    HRESULT         hr;
    STGMEDIUM       stm;
    FORMATETC       fe;
    LPDATAOBJECT    pIDataObject=NULL;
    const UINT      cFormats=3;
    static UINT     rgcf[3]={0, CF_METAFILEPICT, CF_BITMAP};
    static DWORD    rgtm[3]={TYMED_HGLOBAL, TYMED_MFPICT
                        , TYMED_GDI};

    hr=CoCreateInstance(CLSID_DataTransferObject, NULL
        , CLSCTX_INPROC_SERVER, IID_IDataObject
        , (LPLPVOID)&pIDataObject);

    if (FAILED(hr))
        return NULL;

    rgcf[0]=m_cf;

    for (i=0; i < cFormats; i++)
        {
        //Copy private data first.
        hMem=RenderFormat(rgcf[i]);

        if (NULL!=hMem)
            {
            stm.hGlobal=hMem;
            stm.tymed=rgtm[i];
            stm.pUnkForRelease=NULL;
```

(continued)

Listing 8-1. *continued*

```
                SETDefFormatEtc(fe, rgcf[i], rgtm[i]);

                pIDataObject->SetData(&fe, &stm, TRUE);
                }
            }

    return pIDataObject;     //Caller now responsible
    }

/*
 * CCosmoDoc::DropSelectTargetWindow
 *
 * Purpose:
 *  Creates a thin inverted frame around a window that we use to
 *  show the window as a drop target. This is a toggle function:
 *  It uses XOR to create the effect, so it must be called twice to
 *  leave the window as it was.
 */

void CCosmoDoc::DropSelectTargetWindow(void)
    {
    HDC         hDC;
    RECT        rc;
    UINT        dd=3;
    HWND        hWnd;

    hWnd=m_pPL->Window();
    hDC=GetWindowDC(hWnd);
    GetClientRect(hWnd, &rc);

    //Frame this window with inverted pixels

    //Top
    PatBlt(hDC, rc.left, rc.top, rc.right-rc.left, dd, DSTINVERT);

    //Bottom
    PatBlt(hDC, rc.left, rc.bottom-dd, rc.right-rc.left
        , dd, DSTINVERT);

    //Left excluding regions already affected by top and bottom
    PatBlt(hDC, rc.left, rc.top+dd, dd, rc.bottom-rc.top-(2*dd)
        , DSTINVERT);
```

(continued)

Listing 8-1. *continued*

```
    //Right excluding regions already affected by top and bottom
    PatBlt(hDC, rc.right-dd, rc.top+dd, dd, rc.bottom-rc.top-(2*dd)
        , DSTINVERT);

    ReleaseDC(hWnd, hDC);
    return;
    }
```

IDROPSRC.CPP

```
/*
 * Cosmo Chapter 8
 *
 * Implementation of a DropSource object.
 *
 * Copyright (c)1993 Microsoft Corporation, All Rights Reserved
 */

#include "cosmo.h"

CDropSource::CDropSource(LPCCosmoDoc pDoc)
    {
    m_cRef=0;
    m_pDoc=pDoc;
    return;
    }

CDropSource::~CDropSource(void)
    {
    return;
    }

STDMETHODIMP CDropSource::QueryInterface(REFIID riid, LPLPVOID ppv)
    {
    *ppv=NULL;

    if (IsEqualIID(riid, IID_IUnknown)
        || IsEqualIID(riid, IID_IDropSource))
        *ppv=(LPVOID)this;

    if (NULL!=*ppv)
        {
```

(continued)

Listing 8-1. *continued*

```
        ((LPUNKNOWN)*ppv)->AddRef();
        return NOERROR;
        }

    return ResultFromScode(E_NOINTERFACE);
    }

STDMETHODIMP_(ULONG) CDropSource::AddRef(void)
    {
    return ++m_cRef;
    }

STDMETHODIMP_(ULONG) CDropSource::Release(void)
    {
    ULONG           cRefT;

    cRefT=--m_cRef;

    if (0L==m_cRef)
        delete this;

    return cRefT;
    }

/*
 * CDropSource::QueryDragContinue
 *
 * Purpose:
 *  Determines whether to continue a drag operation or cancel it.
 *
 * Parameters:
 *  fEsc            BOOL indicating that the Esc key was pressed.
 *  grfKeyState     DWORD providing states of keys and mouse buttons
 *
 * Return Value:
 *  HRESULT         DRAGDROP_S_CANCEL to stop the drag,
 *                  DRAGDROP_S_DROP to drop the data where it is,
 *                  or NOERROR to continue.
 */

STDMETHODIMP CDropSource::QueryContinueDrag(BOOL fEsc
    , DWORD grfKeyState)
```

(continued)

Listing 8-1. *continued*

```
    {
    if (fEsc)
        return ResultFromScode(DRAGDROP_S_CANCEL);

    if (!(grfKeyState & MK_LBUTTON))
        return ResultFromScode(DRAGDROP_S_DROP);

    return NOERROR;
    }

/*
 * CDropSource::GiveFeedback
 *
 * Purpose:
 *  Provides cursor feedback to the user because the source task
 *  always has the mouse capture. We can also provide any other
 *  type of feedback above cursors if we want.
 *
 * Parameters:
 *  dwEffect        DWORD effect flags returned from the last target
 *
 * Return Value:
 *  HRESULT         NOERROR if you set a cursor yourself or
 *                  DRAGDROP_S_USEDEFAULTCURSORS to let OLE do
 *                  the work.
 */

STDMETHODIMP CDropSource::GiveFeedback(DWORD dwEffect)
    {
    return ResultFromScode(DRAGDROP_S_USEDEFAULTCURSORS);
    }
```

IDROPTGT.CPP

```
/*
 * Cosmo Chapter 8
 *
 * Implementation of the IDropTarget interface.
 *
 * Copyright (c)1993 Microsoft Corporation, All Rights Reserved
 */
```

(continued)

Listing 8-1. *continued*

```
#include "cosmo.h"

CDropTarget::CDropTarget(LPCCosmoDoc pDoc)
    {
    m_cRef=0;
    m_pDoc=pDoc;

    m_pIDataObject=NULL;
    return;
    }

CDropTarget::~CDropTarget(void)
    {
    return;
    }

STDMETHODIMP CDropTarget::QueryInterface(REFIID riid, LPLPVOID ppv)
    {
    *ppv=NULL;

    if (IsEqualIID(riid, IID_IUnknown)
        || IsEqualIID(riid, IID_IDropTarget))
        *ppv=(LPVOID)this;

    if (NULL!=*ppv)
        {
        ((LPUNKNOWN)*ppv)->AddRef();
        return NOERROR;
        }

    return ResultFromScode(E_NOINTERFACE);
    }

STDMETHODIMP_(ULONG) CDropTarget::AddRef(void)
    {
    return ++m_cRef;
    }

STDMETHODIMP_(ULONG) CDropTarget::Release(void)
    {
    ULONG           cRefT;

    cRefT=--m_cRef;
```

(continued)

Listing 8-1. *continued*

```
    if (0L==m_cRef)
        delete this;

    return cRefT;
    }

/*
 * CDropTarget::DragEnter
 *
 * Purpose:
 *  Indicates that data in a drag operation has been dragged over
 *  our window that's a potential target. We are to decide if it's
 *  something we're interested in or not.
 *
 * Parameters:
 *  pIDataSource    LPDATAOBJECT providing the source data.
 *  grfKeyState     DWORD flags: states of keys and mouse buttons.
 *  pt              POINTL coordinates in the document client space.
 *  pdwEffect       LPDWORD into which we'll place the
 *                  appropriate effect flag for this point.
 *
 * Return Value:
 *  HRESULT         NOERROR
 */

STDMETHODIMP CDropTarget::DragEnter(LPDATAOBJECT pIDataSource
    , DWORD grfKeyState, POINTL pt, LPDWORD pdwEffect)
    {
    HWND        hWnd;

    m_pIDataObject=NULL;

    if (!m_pDoc->FQueryPasteFromData(pIDataSource))
        {
        *pdwEffect=DROPEFFECT_NONE;
        return NOERROR;
        }

    //Default is move
    *pdwEffect=DROPEFFECT_MOVE;

    if (grfKeyState & MK_CONTROL)
        *pdwEffect=DROPEFFECT_COPY;
```

(continued)

Listing 8-1. *continued*

```
    m_pIDataObject=pIDataSource;
    m_pIDataObject->AddRef();

    hWnd=m_pDoc->Window();
    BringWindowToTop(hWnd);
    UpdateWindow(hWnd);
    m_pDoc->DropSelectTargetWindow();

    return NOERROR;
    }

/*
 * CDropTarget::DragOver
 *
 * Purpose:
 *  Indicates that the mouse was moved inside the window represented
 *  by this drop target. This happens on every WM_MOUSEMOVE, so this
 *  function should be very efficient.
 *
 * Parameters:
 *  grfKeyState     DWORD providing current keyboard/mouse states
 *  pt              POINTL where the mouse currently is.
 *  pdwEffect       LPDWORD to store the effect flag for this point.
 *
 * Return Value:
 *  HRESULT         NOERROR
 */

STDMETHODIMP CDropTarget::DragOver(DWORD grfKeyState, POINTL pt
    , LPDWORD pdwEffect)
    {
    if (NULL==m_pIDataObject)
        {
        *pdwEffect=DROPEFFECT_NONE;
        return NOERROR;
        }

    //We can always drop, return effect flags based on keys
    *pdwEffect=DROPEFFECT_MOVE;

    if (grfKeyState & MK_CONTROL)
        *pdwEffect=DROPEFFECT_COPY;
```

(continued)

Listing 8-1. *continued*

```
    return NOERROR;
    }

/*
 * CDropTarget::DragLeave
 *
 * Purpose:
 *  Informs the drop target that the operation has left its window.
 *
 * Return Value:
 *  HRESULT         NOERROR
 */

STDMETHODIMP CDropTarget::DragLeave(void)
    {
    if (NULL==m_pIDataObject)
        return NOERROR;

    m_pDoc->DropSelectTargetWindow();
    m_pIDataObject->Release();
    return NOERROR;
    }

/*
 * CDropTarget::Drop
 *
 * Purpose:
 *  Instructs drop target to paste data that was just now
 *  dropped on it.
 *
 * Parameters:
 *  pIDataSource    LPDATAOBJECT from which we'll paste.
 *  grfKeyState     DWORD providing current keyboard/mouse state.
 *  pt              POINTL at which the drop occurred.
 *  pdwEffect       LPDWORD to store what you do with the data.
 *
 * Return Value:
 *  HRESULT         NOERROR
 */

STDMETHODIMP CDropTarget::Drop(LPDATAOBJECT pIDataSource
    , DWORD grfKeyState, POINTL pt, LPDWORD pdwEffect)
    {
    BOOL        fRet=TRUE;
```

(continued)

Listing 8-1. *continued*

```
    *pdwEffect=DROPEFFECT_NONE;

    if (NULL==m_pIDataObject)
        return ResultFromScode(E_FAIL);

    m_pDoc->DropSelectTargetWindow();
    m_pIDataObject->Release();

    //No point in drag-and-drop to ourselves (for Cosmo, at least)
    if (m_pDoc->m_fDragSource)
        return ResultFromScode(E_FAIL);

    fRet=m_pDoc->FPasteFromData(pIDataSource);

    if (!fRet)
        return ResultFromScode(E_FAIL);

    *pdwEffect=DROPEFFECT_MOVE;

    if (grfKeyState & MK_CONTROL)
        *pdwEffect=DROPEFFECT_COPY;

    return NOERROR;
    }
```

Design and Implement Drop Target User Feedback

There are many ways by which you can indicate what might happen if a drop happens in your document. For example, a word processor might show a shaded caret at the point where text would be dropped.

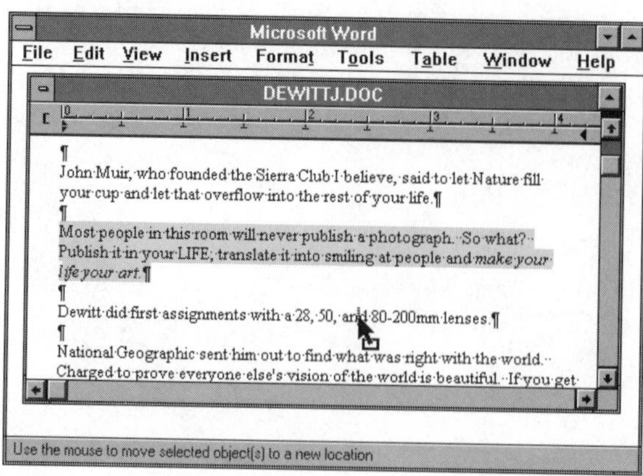

An application such as Patron, which pastes graphics, might show a rectangle of the exact size and at the location the dropped data would occupy.

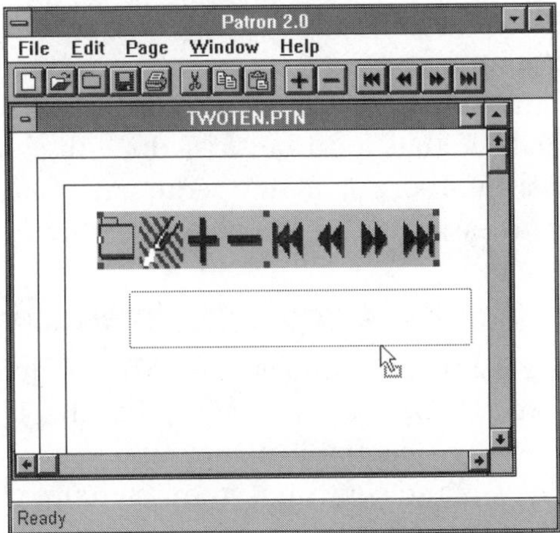

For Cosmo, pasting any Polyline data obliterates the existing data in the window with the new data. Therefore, we can just highlight the Polyline window itself with inverted lines.

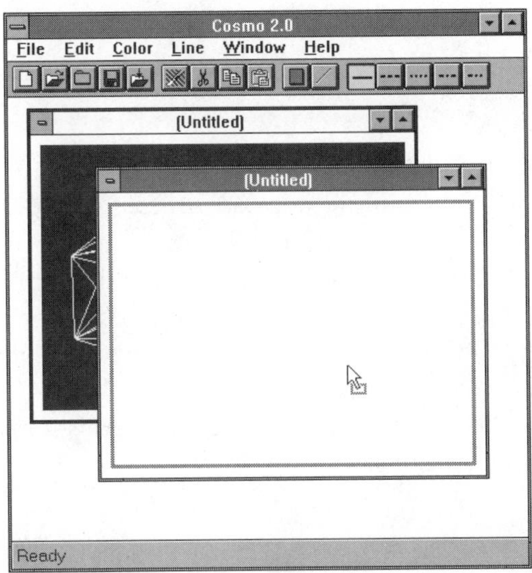

This feedback is generated in the new function *CCosmoDoc::DropSelectTargetWindow*, which simply inverts a 3-pixel frame around the window. This function is a toggle: After we turn on this feedback with a function such as *IDropTarget::DragEnter*, we have to remember to turn it off with *IDropTarget::DragLeave* or *IDropTarget::Drop*.

This *DropSelectTargetWindow* function (and whatever type of function you need to implement with it) has two purposes. First it needs to determine where to place the feedback. For Cosmo, I can simply use the rectangle of the Polyline window, but for applications such as word processors, you might need to calculate the line and character nearest the mouse cursor. For a spreadsheet, you would have to determine the closest range of cells. The second purpose then is to draw the visuals at that location, as I do with *PatBlt* and DSTINVERT. Normally we use some sort of XOR operation so that we can show it and remove it quickly and easily, but it's always your choice.

Implement a Drop Target Object and the *IDropTarget* Interface

Cosmo implements a drop target through its class *CDropTarget,* defined in COSMO.H and implemented in IDROPTGT.CPP. Note that this is not an interface implementation; it is a full object implementation because it implements an independent *QueryInterface* and controls its own reference count. In addition, this object frees itself in *Release* on a zero reference.

The only data fields in this drop target object (besides a reference count and a back pointer to the document in which this object lives) is an LPDATAOBJECT, a pointer to an *IDataObject*:

```
class __far CDropTarget : public IDropTarget
    {
    protected:
        ULONG               m_cRef;
        LPCCosmoDoc         m_pDoc;

        LPDATAOBJECT        m_pIDataObject;  //From DragEnter

...
```

This data object pointer is used to store a data object that our application is given in *IDropTarget::DragEnter* so that if we need to examine the data again during *IDropTarget::DragOver,* which does not receive a data object pointer, we know what data object is involved.

Implementation of each member function in *IDropTarget* is very specific and is covered in the following sections.

IDropTarget::DragEnter

This function, as explained earlier, is called whenever the mouse moves into the window for which we registered this specific instance of *IDropTarget*. *DragEnter* receives the following parameters:

Parameter	Description
pIDataSource	(LPDATAOBJECT): A pointer to the data object involved in this operation.
grfKeyState	(DWORD): A mixture of Windows' MK_ flags containing the current state of the keyboard—that is, any combination of MK_LBUTTON, MK_RBUTTON, MK_SHIFT, MK_CONTROL, and MK_MBUTTON.
pt	(POINTL): The current location of the mouse, in screen coordinates.
pdwEffect	(LPDWORD): A pointer to a DWORD in which the function stores the following effect flag that a drop would have: DROPEFFECT_NONE: No drop can happen here. DROPEFFECT_COPY: A copy should occur. DROPEFFECT_MOVE: A cut should occur. DROPEFFECT_LINK: A Paste Link will occur. DROPEFFECT_SCROLL: The target document is scrolling.

With these parameters, you implement *DragEnter* as follows:

1. Use *pIDataSource->EnumFormatEtc* and *pIDataSource->QueryGetData* to determine whether the data object has usable data. The conditions for a drop are generally the same as for pasting. If pasting isn't possible, store DROPEFFECT_NONE in **pdwEffect* and return NOERROR.
2. Determine whether you can drop on the point in *pt.* If not, store DROPEFFECT_NONE in **pdwEffect* and return NOERROR.
3. If you can drop at *pt,* determine what effect will occur and store that flag in **pdwEffect.*
4. If you want to access *pIDataSource* in *DragOver,* save it here and call *pIDataSource->AddRef.*
5. Provide user feedback and return NOERROR.

You will notice that your application generally returns NOERROR even if it cannot accept the data involved. OLE 2 drag-and-drop works so that if your application is a registered target, its *DragEnter* is always called when the mouse moves into it, and your application *DragOver* is always called regardless of what it returned as an effect here in *DragEnter.* That is, returning DROPEFFECT_NONE does not prevent further *DragOver* calls.

For step 1, Cosmo simply calls its *CCosmoDoc::FQueryPasteFromData* function, which we implemented in Chapter 7. As you might recall, I strongly encouraged you to write a function that given any data object pointer would determine whether you could paste (that is, drop) from it. If you have such a function, this step is simple:

```
if (!m_pDoc->FQueryPasteFromData(pIDataSource))
    {
    *pdwEffect=DROPEFFECT_NONE;     //Drop not possible with this data
    return NOERROR;
    }
```

Cosmo does nothing for step 2 because any point in the document is valid for dropping. Other applications, such as Patron, are more stingy as to valid drop points, so I'll defer further discussion of this step until then.

Step 3 is fairly standard: The OLE 2 user interface specifications state that a drag-and-drop by default means "move"—that is, Cut and Paste. If, however, the Ctrl key is down, it means "copy"—that is, Copy and Paste. To implement this, set **pdwEffect* to DROPEFFECT_MOVE by default and overwrite it with DROPEFFECT_COPY if *grfKeyState* contains MK_CONTROL:

```
*pdwEffect=DROPEFFECT_MOVE;

if (grfKeyState & MK_CONTROL)
    *pdwEffect=DROPEFFECT_COPY;
```

The Shift key (that is, MK_SHIFT) is used to effect a Paste Link instead of simply a Paste when the drop occurs. But we won't deal with linking until Chapter 12, so I'll again defer discussion of this feature until then. That leaves us with two steps to go. Step 4, copying *pIDataSource,* means saving the pointer and calling *AddRef* through it, as good citizens do:

```
m_pIDataObject=pIDataSource;
m_pIDataObject->AddRef();
```

This is not necessary if you are not going to use the data object in your *IDropTarget::DragOver* implementation because OLE will pass this same pointer to *IDropTarget::Drop* when the drop occurs.

Finally, for step 5 we merely have to give some visual indication of the drop target. Cosmo uses its *CCosmoDoc::DropSelectTargetWindow* for this purpose, but to ensure that the document is visible, it first calls *BringWindowToTop* to force it in the user's face:

```
hWnd=m_pDoc->Window();
BringWindowToTop(hWnd);
UpdateWindow(hWnd);
m_pDoc->DropSelectTargetWindow();

return NOERROR;
```

This use of *BringWindowToTop* has a nice effect: When you drag across any number of document windows in Cosmo, each one is brought to the top as the mouse moves into it. That means the end user can effectively switch document windows (as if he or she had used the Window menu in an MDI application) during this operation with only the mouse.

IDropTarget::DragOver

This function is called very frequently from within the *DoDragDrop* function. Not only is it called whenever the mouse moves and whenever the keyboard state changes (for the Ctrl and Shift keys and the mouse buttons), but it is also called for every iteration through the internal loop in *DoDragDrop*. This latter behavior is necessary to support scrolling in a target document, as we'll see later when I discuss Patron's drag-and-drop implementation.

In any case, your implementation of *DragOver* should be as optimized as possible to ensure that the drag-and-drop operation is crisp. This function generally performs hit-testing on the mouse coordinates, provides any user feedback for the drop target, and returns the effect flag applicable to the current mouse position and keyboard state. OLE 2 passes only three parameters to this function: *grfKeyState*, *pt*, and *pdwEffect*. These have the same types and uses as the same-named parameters in *DragEnter* (again, *pt* is in screen coordinates). You'll notice that OLE does not pass a data object pointer here, so if you want your application to do something like *IDataObject::QueryGetData* as the mouse moves, you must save a copy of the pointer from *DragEnter*.

I would encourage you at most to use *IDataObject::QueryGetData* in your implementation here and not to call *IDataObject::GetData* because the latter might be too expensive to ensure a smooth operation. If your implementation of this function is too slow, the user will see choppy mouse movements and a slow response when dragging into your application. The user is naturally apt to compare your application's response to other applications and, finding yours slower, will probably wonder why.

In any case, *IDropTarget::DragOver* can be implemented in three steps:

1. Check whether dropping is allowable at *pt*, given *grfKeyState* and whatever information you want to obtain from the data object.

2. If you determine that a drop is allowable, store the effect flag in **pdwEffect* and provide some sort of visual indication in your window of the result of a drop. If the Ctrl key is down, the effect should be to copy instead of move (cut). This is also the time to check for scrolling possibilities, as we'll see with Patron later.

3. Return NOERROR.

Cosmo executes one quick trick to see if it's even interested in this *DragOver* notification. Remember that even if you return DROPEFFECT_NONE from *DragEnter* (or even if you returned an error in your HRESULT), OLE will still call your *DragOver* here. Therefore, Cosmo uses NULL as its saved *IDataObject* pointer in *DragEnter*, and if it's still NULL in *DragOver*, *DragEnter* must have initially returned DROPEFFECT_NONE. Therefore, we can simply return that same effect here, making for a very fast response in this function:

```
if (NULL==m_pIDataObject)
    {
    *pdwEffect=DROPEFFECT_NONE;
    return NOERROR;
    }
```

Otherwise, Cosmo merely checks the keyboard state again, as in *DragEnter*, and returns DROPEFFECT_MOVE or DROPEFFECT_COPY. Because any point in a Cosmo document is a valid drop point, there's no need to change the user feedback visuals here. So we're finished:

```
*pdwEffect=DROPEFFECT_MOVE;

if (grfKeyState & MK_CONTROL)
    *pdwEffect=DROPEFFECT_COPY;

return NOERROR;
```

IDropTarget::DragLeave

All good things come to an end, so as far as a particular target is concerned the drag-and-drop operation initiated with *DragEnter* is over when the mouse leaves the target window. In addition, the operation is over if the source instructed OLE to cancel the whole thing. In either of these cases, OLE calls *IDropTarget::DragLeave* to give the target a chance to clean up whatever state it happens to be in. Note that if a drop occurs, however, *IDropTarget::Drop* is called. (See the next section.)

DragLeave takes no parameters, so it's fairly straightforward to understand what we must do here:

1. Remove any UI feedback in your window for potential drop results.
2. Release any *IDataObject* held from *DragEnter*.
3. Return NOERROR.

As far as Cosmo is concerned, it needs only to reverse the call to *CCosmoDoc::DropSelectTargetWindow* and to release the data object pointer it's holding. Again, if Cosmo decides it cannot use the data on *DragEnter*, its stored *IDataObject* pointer becomes NULL and therefore implementation is trivial:

```
if (NULL==m_pIDataObject)
    return NOERROR;

m_pDoc->DropSelectTargetWindow();
m_pIDataObject->Release();
```

IDropTarget::Drop

This function is called only when *DoDragDrop* has called *IDropSource::QueryContinueDrag* and that source function has returned DRAGDROP_S_DROP. OLE then calls this function, passing the same parameters as it did to *IDropTarget::DragEnter*. (Once again, *pt* is in screen coordinates.) The value of *pIDataSource* will be exactly the same as in *DragEnter*, but the values of the other parameters will likely change (unless the mouse did not move).

This function must reanalyze the data and the drop point and, seeing that the data is useful and the drop point is valid, must try to perform a Paste operation, returning the effect flag for what actually happened. This result requires the following steps:

1. Remove any UI feedback in your window for potential drop results and release any held *IDataObject* pointer, as in *DragLeave*.
2. Check whether a drop is valid at this point (*pt*) and whether you can use the formats available in *pIDataSource*. If you cannot drop here, store DROPEFFECT_NONE in **pdwEffect and* return an HRESULT with E_FAIL.
3. Perform a Paste operation from the data available in *pIDataSource*, returning DROPEFFECT_NONE in **pdwEffect* and an HRESULT with E_FAIL if the Paste does not work.

4. Otherwise, store the appropriate effect in **pdwEffect* and return NOERROR.

The first step here is to perform exactly the same cleanup as we did in *DragLeave*, so I won't belabor that point. The fourth step for Cosmo is the same old story of checking the Ctrl key and storing either DROPEFFECT_MOVE or DROPEFFECT_COPY in **pdwEffect*.

Cosmo both checks whether it can paste and actually does the Paste, if possible, by calling its function *CCosmoDoc::FPasteFromData*:

```
fRet=m_pDoc->FPasteFromData(pIDataSource);

if (!fRet)
    {
    *pdwEffect=DROPEFFECT_NONE;
    return ResultFromScode(E_FAIL);
    }
```

Again, I encourage you to make a nice function that performs a Paste given any data object, as I suggested in Chapter 7. With such a function, pasting from *IDropTarget::Drop* is trivialized.

Cosmo's implementation of *Drop* also has one other oddity:

```
if (m_pDoc->m_fDragSource)
    return ResultFromScode(E_FAIL);
```

This code handles the situation in which the document that is the drop target object is associated with the exact same document that is also the drop source. Drag-and-drop is essentially a system modal operation—that is, only one such operation can happen in the system at any given time because it captures the mouse. Therefore, when we start a drag from a Cosmo document, we set its *m_fDragSource* flag to indicate that this document is the source. If a drop occurs on the same document, the drop target can check this flag (because it belongs to the same document) and if TRUE, fails the drop—that is, nothing happens. It makes little sense to drag-and-drop the same data to the same location from whence it comes, so this code handles that special case.

Register and Revoke the Drop Target Object

The last thing to do to make Cosmo a drop target is to ensure that the drop target object (that is, its *IDropTarget* pointer) is registered with OLE. That means that when the document is ready to accept a drop, typically on creation, it must instantiate its drop target object and call *RegisterDragDrop*:

```
m_pDropTarget=new CDropTarget(this);

if (NULL!=m_pDropTarget)
    {
    m_pDropTarget->AddRef();
    CoLockObjectExternal((LPUNKNOWN)m_pDropTarget, TRUE, FALSE);
    RegisterDragDrop(m_hWnd, (LPDROPTARGET)m_pDropTarget);
    }
```

The *hWnd* passed to *RegisterDragDrop* is the handle of the document window to which the drop target is related. If we fail to create the drop target or if *RegisterDragDrop* fails, it's really of no consequence; it simply means that our application won't be a target. Therefore, I don't see enough reason to fail document creation if it cannot be a drop target. It can always use the clipboard.

Now what in tarnation is that little *CoLockObjectExternal* all about? This seems incredibly out of place here in drag-and-drop code. In my opinion, this is a design fault in OLE2.DLL, but I've been told that you must use this heavy-duty locking function on any object that sits around for a long time and has an interface that is frequently used for short periods of time. *IDropTarget* is just such an interface. (Those with linking are affected as well, as we'll see in Chapters 12 and 13.) If you don't do this locking trick, after you register your drop target it will receive one drop and only one drop, because after that first operation OLE internally loses track of the *IDropTarget* pointer. Therefore, the next time *DoDragDrop* attempts to call your *IDropTarget::DragEnter*, it finds a bogus pointer and terminates the entire operation. Urk. *CoLockObjectExternal* prevents the loss of the pointer. Really. Trust me. It works. I can't say why. Try taking it out of Cosmo and see what happens.

Anyway, we have to execute the reverse of all this when we no longer want the document to be a target, typically when the document is destroyed. This means calling *RevokeDragDrop* as a reversal to *RegisterDragDrop*, using *CoLockObjectExternal* with opposite flags, and releasing the drop target object:

```
if (NULL!=m_pDropTarget)
    {
    RevokeDragDrop(m_hWnd);
    CoLockObjectExternal((LPUNKNOWN)m_pDropTarget, FALSE, TRUE);
    m_pDropTarget->Release();
    }
```

Design and Implement Drop Source User Feedback

Congratulations, you are now more than halfway to a drag-and-drop implementation. Implementing the drop target side of the picture is much more work than implementing the source side: The source has half the number of interface functions and one-third the number of API functions to deal with. In fact, you almost don't have to think to implement this part if you've already implemented OLE 2 clipboard handling. You already have a nice convenient function for creating a data transfer object, right?

That aside for a moment, the first step is to determine for a source what, if any, user feedback you want it to provide. You might, for example, want to visually indicate that your selection will be copied instead of moved. Most of what you need, however, is encompassed in the one requirement of a source: to show the appropriate cursor, based on the effect flags generated in the target:

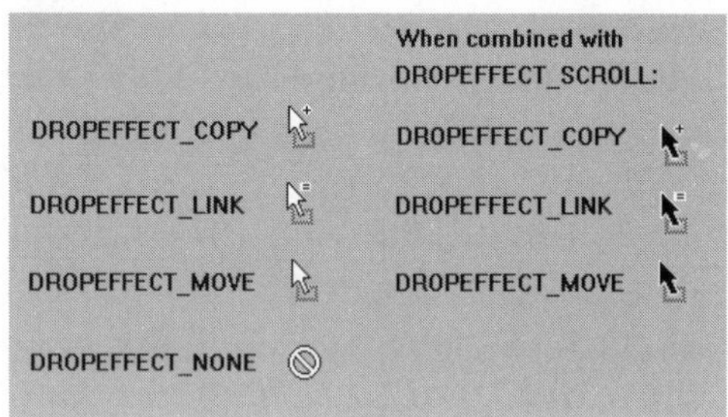

Changing the cursor is the responsibility of your *IDropSource::GiveFeedback* implementation, and as we'll see, OLE2.DLL will do all of the work for you.

If you feel that these cursors by themselves are not sufficient to describe what's happening, you can do what you want. For example, you could draw a big skull and crossbones across the selected data for DROPEFFECT_MOVE and draw a camera for DROPEFFECT_COPY.

Determine the Pick Event

What I describe as the pick event is the mouse click or the keystroke that puts the source into drag-and-drop mode—that is, the event that causes a call to *DoDragDrop*. I bring this up here because you have to know what starts your drag-and-drop operation in order to implement *IDropSource*, whose *QueryContinueDrag* member function determines when to stop the operation.

Most often, the pick event will be a WM_LBUTTONDOWN message on some meaningful point. Cosmo, for example, has an 8-pixel border around the Polyline window that I define as the pick area—any mouse movement down here starts the drag-and-drop. Conveniently, I don't have to do any hit-testing because this region is the only portion of the document window's client area that shows—the rest is covered by the Polyline window. Therefore, my pick event is any WM_LBUTTONDOWN in the document window.

Now that I know what starts a drag-and-drop, I know that something like a WM_LBUTTONUP will end it—that is, will try to affect a drop, if possible. But to control that I need to implement *IDropSource*, which I must also do before attempting to call *DoDragDrop*.

Implement a Drop Source Object and the *IDropSource* Interface

COSMO.H defines a C++ object class called *CDropSource*, implemented in IDROPSRC.CPP. Again, this object stands alone, like the drop target: It controls its own *QueryInterface* (which knows *IDropSource* and *IUnknown*) and frees itself when *Release* decrements the reference count to zero. This object needs no data members except a reference count, but I have also included a back pointer to the document out of habit.

For Cosmo, implementation is trivial. First, *IDropSouce::QueryContinueDrag* is called with two parameters:

Parameter	Description
fEsc	Indicates that the Esc key is down, usually meaning cancel the drag-and-drop operation.
grfKeyState	Contains the status of the Shift and Ctrl keys, as well as the mouse buttons.

You then use these parameters to determine whether to cancel the operation, continue, or drop the data:

1. If *fEsc* is TRUE, cancel by returning an HRESULT with DRAGDROP_S_CANCEL. Return the same value for any other canceling condition.
2. Test the opposite condition of the pick event. If you started the operation on a mouse click, test that button state in *grfKeyState*.

If the opposite state is TRUE, cause a drop by returning an HRESULT with DRAGDROP_S_DROP.

3. Otherwise, continue dragging by returning NOERROR.

Cosmo's implementation, which will probably be the most common in all applications, is only a few short lines, where a left mouse button down was the pick event:

```
if (fEsc)
    return ResultFromScode(DRAGDROP_S_CANCEL);

if (!(grfKeyState & MK_LBUTTON))
    return ResultFromScode(DRAGDROP_S_DROP);

return NOERROR;
```

Now if you think that's trivial, *IDropSource::GiveFeedback*, which takes only a DWORD *dwEffect* flag, is even simpler when all you want to change is the mouse cursor (your only requirement here). To do that, simply tell OLE2.DLL to do it for you:

```
return ResultFromScode(DRAGDROP_S_USEDEFAULTCURSORS);
```

You are, of course, free to do anything else you want here. If you need to know where the mouse is, call *GetCursorPos.* Just remember, however, that this is called just as often as *IDropTarget::DragOver*, so keep this function as fully optimized as possible.

Call *DoDragDrop*

Finally, we are ready to make it all work by starting the drag-and-drop operation. The source in this scenario performs the following steps when the pick event occurs, such as in processing WM_LBUTTONDOWN in Cosmo:

1. Instantiate a drop source object. If this fails, the operation fails.
2. Set a flag indicating that this document is currently the source of the drag to prevent unnecessary action if the user drops onto the same document.
3. Create the data object to use in the transfer.
4. Call *DoDragDrop*, passing the data object pointer, the *IDropSource* pointer, the allowable effects, and a pointer to a DWORD in which to store the final effect. *DoDragDrop* will not return until your

IDropSource::QueryContinueDrag says DRAGDROP_S_CANCEL or DRAGDROP_S_DROP. The return value of *DoDragDrop* is the same as the return for *QueryContinueDrag*.

5. Clean up your data object and your drop source object because they are no longer needed. Also reset the source flag set in step 2.
6. If and only if *DoDragDrop* returned DRAGDROP_S_DROP and if the final effect flag was DROPEFFECT_MOVE, delete the data that was used in this operation. Be sure to set your dirty flag here as well because you are modifying the source document.

   Cosmo's implementation looks like this, which can be found inside *CCosmoDoc::FMessageHook*:

```
if (WM_LBUTTONDOWN==iMsg)
    {
    LPDROPSOURCE     pIDropSource;
    LPDATAOBJECT     pIDataObject;
    HRESULT          hr;
    SCODE            sc;
    DWORD            dwEffect;

    pIDropSource=(LPDROPSOURCE)new CDropSource(this);

    if (NULL==pIDropSource)
        return FALSE;

    pIDropSource->AddRef();
    m_fDragSource=TRUE;

    pIDataObject=TransferObjectCreate(FALSE);

    if (NULL!=pIDataObject)
        {
        hr=DoDragDrop(pIDataObject, pIDropSource
            , DROPEFFECT_COPY | DROPEFFECT_MOVE, &dwEffect);

        pIDataObject->Release();
        sc=GetScode(hr);
        }
    else
        sc=E_FAIL;

    pIDropSource->Release();
    m_fDragSource=FALSE;
```

(continued)

```
    if (DRAGDROP_S_DROP==sc && DROPEFFECT_MOVE==dwEffect)
        {
        m_pPL->New();      //Clears the current Polyline
        FDirtySet(TRUE);
        }

    return TRUE;
    }
```

And with all that accomplished, we can now move or copy Polyline figures between different documents in one instance of Cosmo or between documents in different instances of Cosmo. But there is one final note to make before looking at a more complicated implementation in Patron.

DoDragDrop internally executes a large loop that first calls various member functions of *IDropSource* and *IDropTarget*, and then it calls *PeekMessage* to look for and remove any keyboard or mouse (including nonclient) messages without yielding. If there is a message, the loop continues immediately. What can happen here is that if you have a fast keyboard repeat on your machine and you hold down a key such as Ctrl during an operation, you could generate WM_KEYDOWN messages for VK_CONTROL more often than *DoDragDrop* can remove them. In other words, the time it takes to execute one loop inside *DoDragDrop* could be longer than your keyboard repeat time, so every time *DoDragDrop* looks for a message, one is there, and it continues to sit in the loop. This could mean that when you drag from a source to a target with the Ctrl key held down and then let up on the mouse button, a drop doesn't happen! *DoDragDrop* is stuck inside its loop until you release the Ctrl key, in which case a Move happens instead of a Copy. You can even click the mouse button again to no avail. This problem will be addressed in future versions of OLE.

Intermission

Ole MacDonald's document was
E-I-E-I-E-OLE
In it was a data source and
E-I-E-I-E-OLE
(With) drag-and-drop here
And drag-and-drop there
And drag-and-drops going everywhere…
Ole MacDonald's document was
E-I-E-I-E-OLE!

Sung to "Ode to Joy" theme, Beethoven Ninth Symphony, fourth movement
Lyrics inspired by Robert Fulghum

Advanced Drag-and-Drop: Feedback and Scrolling in Patron

If you've been playing with the version of Patron we developed in Chapter 7, you've probably noticed that it's highly useful except for one major flaw: There's no way to move a tenant around on a page except by enlarging it from one corner and shrinking it from the opposite one. That's hardly what I'd call a usability feature. No doubt, as someone such as Donald Norman[2] would point out, it's rather absurd to ask a user to perform two *sizing* tasks where one *moving* task would be more appropriate.

With OLE 2 drag-and-drop, you can now move a tenant in one swift stroke. This essentially means making a page both a drop source and a drop target and actually doing something when a drag-and-drop happens on the same page. In such a case, the page can simply change the rectangle for a tenant and repaint the screen. But while we're at it, we might as well be able to drop a graphic from another application onto a page or to drag tenants between pages in any open Patron document, in the same application or otherwise. This is exactly why I didn't bother to implement any kind of Move functionality for Patron in Chapter 7.

Patron implements all the same steps as we did for Cosmo earlier, instantiating drop target and drop source objects, calling the appropriate API functions, and so on. The entire implementation of *CDropSource* is exactly the same as in Cosmo, except that I eliminated the extra back pointer in the drop source object. My implementation of *IDropTarget* is generally the same, except for some extensive additions to handle drawing more user feedback and scrolling the page during a drag-and-drop operation. For these two interfaces, I've added two files, IDROPSRC.CPP and IDROPTGT.CPP, to Patron, as well as a third, DRAGDROP.CPP, which contains a few support functions. In addition, I had to make a modification to Patron's *CPage::OnLeftDown* function (PAGEMOUS.CPP) to start the drag-and-drop operation. Because the code is too lengthy to list here, I will include the important fragments in the discussions that follow.

---

2. Read *The Design of Everyday Things*, formerly *The Psychology of Everyday Things*, by Donald Norman, Basic Books, Inc., New York.

Patron has three main augmentations to drag-and-drop in Cosmo. The first is that not all points in Patron's documents are "droppable" because some are off the page boundaries or within the unusable page margins. Therefore, Patron will have to hit-test the mouse coordinates passed to *IDropTarget::DragEnter*, *IDropTarget::DragOver*, and *IDropTarget::Drop*. Second, Patron shows more detailed user feedback: When a tenant is dragged around on a page, Patron displays an outline of that tenant, showing the exact rectangle that tenant would occupy when dropped. This applies to any tenant that might be dropped on the page, regardless of whether that tenant came from the same document or another instance of Patron. The third change is that Patron provides for scrolling the page while a drag-and-drop operation is happening.

Patron's notion of the pick region is also more complex than Cosmo's, so let's examine that first before dealing with the more complex features.

Tenant Pick Regions and Drop Sourcing

In Patron, I've defined the outer rectangular boundary of any tenant as the pick region, excluding those areas already occupied by sizing handles. The width and height of the region are the same as the dimensions of sizing handles.

In Chapter 7, we added the *CPage::OnNCHitTest (PAGEMOUS.CPP)* function to determine when the mouse was over a sizing handle. We used the return value from this function in *CPage::SetCursor* to show an appropriate mouse cursor for each sizing handle. For this chapter, we need to first modify *OnNCHitTest* to check for the boundary and then modify *SetCursor* to show a four-pointed arrow (obtained from BTTNCUR.DLL), which means "move."

When *OnNCHitTest* determines that the mouse is within a pick region, it stores the code HTCAPTION in *CPage::m_uHTCode*, which is later used by *SetCursor* to show the cursor in the preceding illustration. In addition, if *m_uHTCode* contains HTCAPTION when WM_LBUTTONDOWN is processed in *CPage::OnLeftDown,* Patron drops (pun intended) into the new function *CPage::DragDrop.* This function creates the data object for use in the operation using *CPage::TransferObjectCreate,* which we added in Chapter 7 to handle clipboard operations. It then calls *DoDragDrop,* and when that function returns, it handles the Move or Copy operations appropriately.

One special case in *CPage::DragDrop* is the one in which a tenant is moved within the same page. Here I use the same trick as in Cosmo, setting a flag *m_fDragSource* to indicate that this document is the current drag-and-drop source. I also have a flag called *m_fMoveInPage,* which is initially FALSE. Now take a look in *IDROPTGT.CPP* at *IDropTarget::Drop.* If *m_fDragSource* is set and the last effect was DROPEFFECT_MOVE, we can set *m_fMoveInPage* to TRUE. In all other cases, it remains FALSE.

```
//In CPage::DragDrop
m_pPG->m_fDragSource=TRUE;
m_pPG->m_fMoveInPage=FALSE;
hr=DoDragDrop(...);

//In CDropTarget::Drop
if (m_pDoc->m_pPG->m_fDragSource && !(grfKeyState & MK_CONTROL))
    {
    *pdwEffect=DROPEFFECT_MOVE;
    m_pDoc->m_pPG->m_fMoveInPage=TRUE;
    m_pDoc->m_pPG->m_ptDrop=po.ptl;
    return NOERROR;
    }
```

When *DoDragDrop* returns and *m_fMoveInPage* is TRUE, we have only to change the tenant's rectangle, repainting the old position and making sure that the new position is properly clipped to the page boundaries. This helps you avoid unnecessarily creating a new tenant in the new position using the data from the original tenant, and then destroying the original tenant:

```
//In CPage::DragDrop
if (m_pPG->m_fMoveInPage)
    {
    m_pTenantCur->Invalidate();

    [Code to calculate the new rect and clip it to the page boundaries]

    m_pTenantCur->RectSet(&rcl, TRUE);
    m_pTenantCur->Repaint();
    return TRUE;
    }
```

If the data object is from a different source (*m_fDragSource* is FALSE) or if we're copying a tenant within the same page (by holding down the Ctrl key during the operation), *IDropTarget::Drop* calls *CPatronDoc::FPasteFromData.* Regardless of where the data came from, *FPasteFromData* will create a new tenant with the graphic in the data object. What works so beautifully here is that *FPasteFromData* doesn't know the difference between copying a tenant already on the current page and copying a graphic coming from a completely different application. Therefore, we don't have to make any special cases to copy a tenant within the same page.

```
//In CDropTarget::Drop
m_pDoc->m_pPG->m_fMoveInPage=FALSE;
fRet=m_pDoc->FQueryPasteFromData(pIDataSource, &fe, &tType);

if (fRet)
    {
    po.fe=(m_pDoc->m_cf==fe.cfFormat) ? m_fe : fe;
    fRet=m_pDoc->FPasteFromData(pIDataSource, &fe, tType, &po, 0);
    }

if (!fRet)
    return ResultFromScode(E_FAIL);

*pdwEffect=DROPEFFECT_MOVE;

if (grfKeyState & MK_CONTROL)
    *pdwEffect=DROPEFFECT_COPY;

return NOERROR;
```

Finally, *CPage::DragDrop* must be sensitive to whether the operation was a Copy or a Move (that is, a Move from a source other than the same page). When a Move occurs, the tenant must be removed from the current page, so *DragDrop* calls *CPage::TenantDestroy*:

```
if (DROPEFFECT_MOVE==dwEffect)
    {
    TenantDestroy();
    return TRUE;
    }
```

More Advanced Drop Target Hit-Testing

The implementation of Cosmo earlier in this chapter had no real considerations for undroppable points in a document. Essentially, everywhere was valid. Patron documents, however, show a page surrounded by unusable page margins and a border completely outside the page. Because these are unusable locations, nothing can be dropped there.

The function *CPages::UTestDroppablePoint* in DRAGDROP.CPP handles this more complex hit-testing, returning a code from the UDROP_... values I've defined in PAGES.H. (These are not part of OLE 2.) For now, the only values of interest are UDROP_NONE (can't drop here) and UDROP_CLIENT (drop is allowed). The other values are related to scrolling and are discussed in the later section "Scrolling the Page." *UTestDroppablePoint* returns UDROP_CLIENT if the point it's given is within the intersection of the document's client area and the client-relative rectangle of the usable page regions. Otherwise, it returns UDROP_NONE.

```
UINT CPages::UTestDroppablePoint(LPPOINTL pptl)
    {
    POINT       pt;
    RECT        rc, rcT, rcC;
    UINT        uRet;

    POINTFROMPOINTL(pt, *pptl);
    ScreenToClient(m_hWnd, &pt);

    CalcBoundingRect(&rc, FALSE);

    GetClientRect(m_hWnd, &rcC);
    IntersectRect(&rcT, &rc, &rcC);

    //Check for at least a client area hit.
    if (!PtInRect(&rcT, pt))
        return UDROP_NONE;

    uRet=UDROP_CLIENT;

    [Code here for scrolling considerations]

    return uRet;
    }
```

UTestDroppablePoint is first called from *IDropTarget::DragEnter* to set the initial effect. It's then called on entry into *IDropTarget::DragOver* to set the effect as well as to determine whether further checks for feedback and scrolling are necessary. (See the next sections.) Finally, it's called again from *IDropTarget::Drop* to ensure that our application doesn't attempt to perform a Paste on an invalid drop point.

A Feedback Rectangle

The Chapter 7 version of Patron defined a private clipboard format called "Patron Object," which contained necessary information about the original position of an object within a page:

```
typedef struct tagPATRONOBJECT
    {
    POINTL      ptl;          //Location of object
    POINTL      ptlPick;      //Pick point from drag-and-drop operation
    SIZEL       szl;          //Extents of object (absolute)
    FORMATETC   fe;           //Actual object format
    } PATRONOBJECT, FAR *LPPATRONOBJECT;
```

If Patron found this data on the clipboard, it would attempt to paste whatever graphic (metafile, DIB, or bitmap) that was on the clipboard at the location described in this structure. For drag-and-drop, we'll use this same structure to find out how large the graphic is when we see it as a drop target. In other words, whenever a target application sees a data object in *IDropTarget::DragEnter,* it can check whether this format is present. If it is, it knows exactly how large to draw a feedback rectangle. If it's not, it punts: It shows some sort of feedback, although the representation obviously will not be true to the size of the graphic. This approach lets you avoid having the application render the graphic merely to determine its size.

NOTE: There is a structure called OBJECTDESCRIPTOR defined in OLE2UI.H that does most of what Patron's PATRONOBJECT structure provides, except that OBJECTDESCRIPTOR lacks a point that describes the location of the object. This is why Patron has its own structure instead of using the OLE standard. In Chapter 9, we'll use OBJECTDESCRIPTOR as a backup format in case PATRONOBJECT is not there because we could still get the extents and formats from it, just not the position information. We'll wait until Chapter 9 because OBJECTDESCRIPTOR usually travels with information about an embedded compound document object.

As for being a drop source, Patron defines the edge of a tenant's rectangle (excluding those areas with sizing handles) as the pick region. When the end user picks up a tenant, we want the feedback rectangle to be shown with the same relative position to the mouse cursor as it had when the user picked it up:

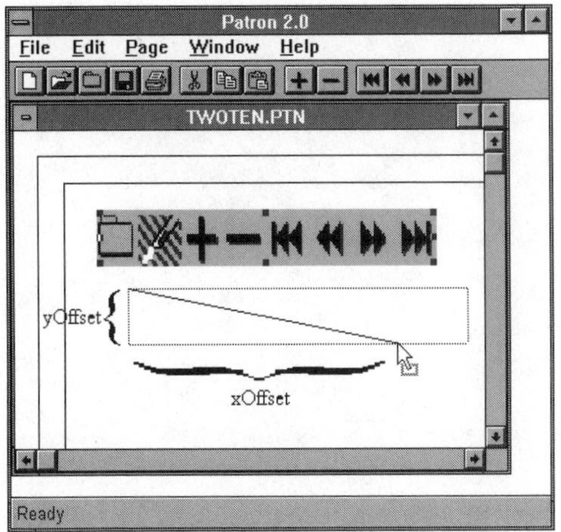

In order for Patron to know this relative location on any tenant, it stores (as a source) the offset of the mouse cursor from the upper left corner of the tenant in the *ptlPick* field of the preceding PATRONOBJECT structure. The function *CPage::TransferObjectCreate (PAGE.CPP)*, which we created in Chapter 7, was designed with this in mind. All uses of this function for clipboard transfers store (0,0) in *ptlPick*. When we create a data object for a drag-and-drop transfer (in *CPage::DragDrop*), we pass *CPage::TransferObjectCreate* the real coordinates to store in *ptlPick* (with all other calls in Patron to *TransferObjectCreate* passing a NULL):

```
//In CPage::DragDrop, x & y are mouse coordinates
m_pTenantCur->RectGet(&rcl, TRUE);
ptl.x=x+m_pPG->m_xPos-rcl.left;
ptl.y=y+m_pPG->m_yPos-rcl.top;
pIDataObject=TransferObjectCreate(&ptl);
```

Therefore, as a drop target, Patron will see these coordinates and can then place the feedback rectangle relative to the mouse so that it looks the same as when it was picked up. In *CDropTarget::DragEnter*, Patron will look for the PATRONOBJECT structure first to determine the real size of the tenant:

```
if (fe.cfFormat==m_pDoc->m_cf)  //m_cf registered using "Patron Object"
    {
    if (SUCCEEDED(pIDataSource->GetData(&fe, &stm)))
        {
        LPPATRONOBJECT  ppo;
        RECT            rc;
```

(continued)

```
            ppo=(LPPATRONOBJECT)GlobalLock(stm.hGlobal);

            SetRect(&rc, (int)ppo->szl.cx, -(int)ppo->szl.cy, 0, 0);
            RectConvertMappings(&rc, NULL, TRUE);
            SETSIZEL(m_szl, rc.left, rc.top);

            m_ptPick=ppo->ptlPick;
            m_fe=ppo->fe;

            GlobalUnlock(stm.hGlobal);
            ReleaseStgMedium(&stm);
            }
        }
    else
        {
        SETSIZEL(m_szl, 30, 30);
        m_ptPick.x=0;
        m_ptPick.y=0;
        m_fe.cfFormat=0;
        }
```

During the drag-and-drop operation, *m_ptPick* will contain the offset of the feedback rectangle from the mouse, and *m_szl* will contain the dimensions of the rectangle. If the PATRONOBJECT structure is not available, we default to a small rectangle to at least show something. *CDropTarget::DragEnter* is the first to use *m_ptPick* and is also the first to call a new function, *CPages::DrawDropTargetRect*, passing to it the upper left corner of the rectangle as well as the rectangle dimensions. (See DRAGDROP.CPP, which seems to call this Windows function *DrawFocusRect*). The upper left corner is simply the mouse coordinates minus the offset of the pick point:

```
//In CDropTarget::DragEnter
pt.x-=m_ptPick.x;
pt.y-=m_ptPick.y;

m_ptLast=pt;
m_fFeedback=TRUE;
m_pDoc->m_pPG->DrawDropTargetRect(&pt, &m_szl);
```

DrawDropTargetRect is a toggle function because it calls *DrawFocusRect*, which is an XOR operation. Therefore, in order to remove it from inside the other *CDropTarget* functions, we have to remember where the rectangle is and whether it's currently visible. That's the purpose of *m_ptLast* and *m_fFeedback*. Early in *DragOver*, *DragLeave*, and *Drop*, we remove the old rectangle if it's showing:

```
if (m_fFeedback)
    ppg->DrawDropTargetRect(&m_ptLast, &m_szl);
```

DragOver does not make this call if the mouse position did not change—that is, if the new mouse coordinates (offset for the pick location) match *m_ptLast*:

```
//In CDropTarget::DragOver
if ((pt.x-m_ptPick.x==m_ptLast.x) && (pt.y-m_ptPick.y==m_ptLast.y))
    return NOERROR;
```

This optimization is necessary because *CDropTarget::DragOver* will be called repeatedly even if the mouse position does not change. Without this special case, the feedback rectangle would continually and annoyingly flicker, even when the mouse didn't move.

Scrolling the Page

I saved this topic for last simply because it involves a few tricks. To be honest, it took me about six working days to figure out Patron's scrolling code. I hope my experience will save you some time because, on the surface, scrolling seems simple enough; it's described in less than half a page in the OLE 2 specifications.[3] It boils down to two parts:

1. The target defines an inset region, or hot zone, within the boundaries of its document *window* (not the usable page area). Any time the mouse cursor is within this region, the target uses an OR in DROPEFFECT_SCROLL with whatever other effect flag is appropriate.
2. When the cursor has remained in the inset region for a given length of time, scrolling starts and continues until the mouse leaves the inset region. That is, you can move the mouse within the inset region and scrolling continues.

The first part is what precipitates the additional code in *CPages::UTestDroppablePoint*, as described before. Not only does this function test whether a point is on a droppable region on the page, but it also checks whether the point is within the inset region on all sides of the window.

3. See OLE 2 Design Specification, 15 April 1993, page 282. Note that there are some inaccuracies in this part of the spec. For instance, it uses DRAGEFFECT_.... instead of DROPEFFECT_... and incorrectly uses *IDropTarget::GiveFeedback*, which should be *IDropSource::GiveFeedback*.

But first we need to learn the inset width in pixels, which is done in *CPages::CPages*:

```
m_uScrollInset=GetProfileInt("windows", "DragScrollInset"
    , DD_DEFSCROLLINSET);
```

Until there's another revision of Windows itself, there will not be an entry for *DragScrollInset* in WIN.INI unless an end user adds one manually, so the inset region will be DD_DEFSCROLLINSET, defined in OLE2.H as 11. *UTestDroppablePoint* then uses *m_uScrollInset* to check whether the mouse coordinates are within the inset region of the pages window:

```
UINT    uRet;
RECT    rcC;

GetClientRect(m_hWnd, &rcC);

[Code to store UDROP_NONE or UDROP_CLIENT in uRet]

//Scroll checks happen on client area
if (PtInRect(&rcC, pt))
    {
    //Check horizontal inset
    if (pt.x <= rcC.left+(int)m_uScrollInset)
        uRet |= UDROP_INSETLEFT;
    else if (pt.x >= rcC.right-(int)m_uScrollInset)
        uRet |= UDROP_INSETRIGHT;

    //Check vertical inset
    if (pt.y <= rcC.top+(int)m_uScrollInset)
        uRet |= UDROP_INSETTOP;
    else if (pt.y >= rcC.bottom-(int)m_uScrollInset)
        uRet |= UDROP_INSETBOTTOM;
    }
```

The additional UDROP_INSET... flags shown here (which again, are specific to Patron and not defined in OLE 2) are all mutually inclusive with UDROP_NONE and UDROP_CLIENT, meaning that Patron will still scroll even if the cursor is over a point where no drop is allowed. UDROP_INSETLEFT and UDROP_INSETRIGHT are both inclusive with both UDROP_INSETTOP and UDROP_INSETBOTTOM, but LEFT is mutually exclusive with RIGHT and TOP is mutually exclusive with BOTTOM. This means that Patron can scroll both horizontally and vertically at the same time if the mouse is within both horizontal and vertical inset regions. Patron will not, however, attempt to scroll up and down, or left and right, at the same time. That would be an interesting sight!

As mentioned before, *UTestDroppablePoint* is called each time in *CDropTarget::DragEnter*, *CDropTarget::DragOver*, and *CDropTarget::Drop*. The important call is the one in *DragOver*, where the variable *uRet* contains the current UDROP_... combination and *m_uLastTest* (in the current *CPages* structure) contains the code from the last cycle through *DragOver* (or the one from *DragEnter*, as the case may be). So, on any pass through *DragOver*, we know whether the cursor was outside the inset region and moved in, whether it was in the inset region and moved out, or whether we haven't changed from the last pass, in or out of the region.

These cases are handled a little later in *CDropTarget::DragOver*, which is invariably tied to the second part of scrolling: the delay. The delay exists because OLE 2 drag-and-drop is a mechanism for dragging from any arbitrary source to any arbitrary target, and that involves a mouse motion across the edges of windows. As mentioned earlier, if scrolling began as soon as the mouse hit an inset region, it would be almost impossible for the end user to drag out of a window without scrolling it a little. Therefore, the mouse must remain in the inset region for a short period of time before scrolling begins. This delay, in milliseconds, is also a new OLE 2 addition to WIN.INI which you again retrieve with *GetProfileInt*:

```
m_uScrollDelay=GetProfileInt("windows", "DragScrollDelay"
    , DD_DEFSCROLLDELAY);
```

The default value for DD_DEFSCROLLDELAY is unfortunately defined as 50 milliseconds (ms), which as you probably know, is shorter than the 55-ms timer resolution in Windows. Therefore, you can't really time this value, and my experience with trying suggests that it's too short anyway when you don't have any mouse acceleration. I recommend that you create a line in WIN.INI that reads *DragScrollDelay=200* for testing purposes.

In any case, you now have the problem of timing subsequent calls to *DragOver* to detect when the delay has elapsed. There are two ways to do this: Use a timer, or use *GetTickCount*. A timer might seem the easiest way to go first, but it's really a pain because the code to handle the timer expiration will be in a different function (NOT fun for C++ programmers) and because a WM_TIMER message (or a call to a timer process) will be generated only if you have a chance to pass through your message loop. As I found out, my message loop might not always run when I'm inside *DoDragDrop*—especially when I'm dragging within the same document, which does not yield—so my message loop is locked down in *DispatchMessage* on WM_LBUTTONDOWN. Therefore, I will receive no messages, no timer events.

That left me with the better alternative anyway, which keeps all the timing within *CDropTarget::DragOver.* When I first detect that I have entered the inset region, I call the Windows function *GetTickCount* to read the current system time, storing it in a variable *m_dwTimeLast.* OK, fine. The next time through *DragOver,* I may or may not still be in the inset region. If I am, I call *GetTickCount* and subtract from it the time I read when I first moved into the region, and if the difference is greater than the delay time, I can start scrolling. Otherwise, if I have moved out of the inset region, I reset *m_dwTimeLast* to zero (meaning "no scroll under any circumstances"). This is all wrapped up in some repetitive-looking code in *DragOver,* where *uLast* is the value in *m_uLastTest* and *ppg* is the current *CPages* pointer:

```
if ((UDROP_INSETHORZ & uLast) && !(UDROP_INSETHORZ & uRet))
    ppg->m_uHScrollCode=0xFFFF;

if (!(UDROP_INSETHORZ & uLast) && (UDROP_INSETHORZ & uRet))
    {
    ppg->m_dwTimeLast=GetTickCount();
    ppg->m_uHScrollCode=(0!=(UDROP_INSETLEFT & uRet))
        ? SB_LINELEFT : SB_LINERIGHT; //Same as UP & DOWN codes.
    }

if ((UDROP_INSETVERT & uLast) && !(UDROP_INSETVERT & uRet))
    ppg->m_uVScrollCode=0xFFFF;

if (!(UDROP_INSETVERT & uLast) && (UDROP_INSETVERT & uRet))
    {
    ppg->m_dwTimeLast=GetTickCount();
    ppg->m_uVScrollCode=(0!=(UDROP_INSETTOP & uRet))
        ? SB_LINEUP : SB_LINEDOWN;
    }

if (0xFFFF==ppg->m_uHScrollCode && 0xFFFF==ppg->m_uVScrollCode)
    ppg->m_dwTimeLast=0L;

//Set the scroll effect on any inset hit.
if ((UDROP_INSETHORZ | UDROP_INSETVERT) & uRet)
    *pdwEffect |= DROPEFFECT_SCROLL;
```

This first block of code shows how Patron handles each case in which we moved into or out of an inset region—that is, the conditions changed—as well as where it uses OR in DROPEFFECT_SCROLL. The *CPages* variables *m_uHScrollCode* and *m_uVScrollCode* contain the code to send with WM_HSCROLL and WM_VSCROLL messages, where 0xFFFF is my flag to mean "no scrolling."

CDropTarget::DragOver then checks for expiration of the time delay, and if it has elapsed, it sends the appropriate scroll messages:

```
if (ppg->m_dwTimeLast!=0
    && (GetTickCount()-ppg->m_dwTimeLast) > (DWORD)ppg->m_uScrollDelay)
    {
    if (0xFFFF!=ppg->m_uHScrollCode)
        {
        m_fPendingRepaint=TRUE;
        SendMessage(ppg->m_hWnd, WM_HSCROLL, ppg->m_uHScrollCode, 0L);
        }

    if (0xFFFF!=ppg->m_uVScrollCode)
        {
        m_fPendingRepaint=TRUE;
        SendMessage(ppg->m_hWnd, WM_VSCROLL, ppg->m_uVScrollCode, 0L);
        }
    }
```

This will send both WM_HSCROLL and WM_VSCROLL messages in the same pass through *DragOver*, if necessary. This now brings us to the final area of consideration: repainting. In Patron, we want drag-and-drop scrolling to be fast, not requiring a repaint on every scroll. With many tenants on a page, especially ones with bitmaps, each scroll would be painfully slow. To prevent the repaints, we need the *m_fPendingRepaint* flag that's FALSE unless a scroll has occurred, in which case it's set to TRUE. This flag is used in *DragOver, DragLeave,* and *Drop* to repaint the page when scrolling has stopped. The last two cases are obvious: moving out of the window or dropping stops scrolling. In *DragOver,* however, we have to determine whether the last *SendMessage* did, in fact, change the scroll position of the page. Therefore, before executing the preceding code, we save the current scroll positions in some local variables:

```
xPos=ppg->m_xPos;
yPos=ppg->m_yPos;
```

Then, after we have possibly sent WM_...SCROLL messages, we check the previous scroll positions against the new ones. If they are the same, and there's a pending repaint, we then repaint:

```
if (xPos==ppg->m_xPos && yPos==ppg->m_yPos && m_fPendingRepaint)
    {
    UpdateWindow(ppg->m_hWnd);
    m_fPendingRepaint=FALSE;
    }
```

DragLeave and *Drop* always call *UpdateWindow* if *m_fPendingRepaint* is TRUE.

There is one last consideration that caused me much consternation. When I first implemented Patron's drag-and-drop scrolling, I tested it mostly by moving tenants around on the same page or between different documents in the MDI version. Everything worked great. Then I tried to drag something in from another application, like Cosmo. Things fell apart because there was LRPC going on, there were plenty of yields happening, and my message loop had a chance to iterate. This didn't happen before because there's no yielding when both source and target are the same application!

The result was that Patron would receive WM_PAINT messages, because scrolling, of course, invalidates regions of my client area. Normally this would not have been a problem except for my little feedback rectangle. This is what happened: My *CDropTarget::DragOver* was called, I removed the previous feedback rectangle, I scrolled the page, and then I drew the new feedback rectangle over a possibly invalid region of the window. When WM_PAINT came along, it repainted that invalid region, erasing parts of my feedback rectangle. Then I came back into *DragOver* and attempted to erase the old feedback rectangle again. Because part of it was already gone and because my rectangle drawing is based on an XOR, I ended up with rectangle fragments on the screen. U-G-L-Y. I tried a number of things, such as ignoring the WM_PAINT messages (which didn't work at all, as I should have known), and finally arrived at a solution after a few more days of going nowhere. I maintain a flag in *CPages::m_fDragRectShown* that is modified only in *DrawDropTargetRect*: TRUE if the rectangle is visible, FALSE otherwise. If this flag is set when processing WM_PAINT (*PagesWndProc* in PAGEWIN.CPP), I call *DrawDropTargetRect* to erase the current rectangle, do the painting as usual, and then call *DrawDropTargetRect* again to reinstate the feedback. Now everything came out clean, and I could finally move Patron into Chapter 9. Yes, even authors struggle with some aspects of programming for Windows!

Summary

OLE 2's drag-and-drop mechanism is a streamlining of clipboard operations. Instead of selecting data in the source application, choosing Copy or Cut, switching to the consumer application, and selecting Paste, the end user can simply pick the data up in the source application, drag it to the target, and drop it, all in one swift stroke. You can, as with the clipboard, transfer any data using drag-and-drop because the mechanism uses a data object.

The two agents in a drag-and-drop operation are the source and the target, which may or may not be within the same application, the same document, or different applications. Because OLE 2 sits between source and target, the two are unaware of each other. Therefore, a target consumes data from any source, even if that source is itself (effectively a Copy-Paste to itself), and a source provides data without knowing the eventual target. Applications can, of course, maintain state flags to detect operations in which the source and target documents are identical.

The source of the drag-and-drop operation is responsible for providing the data object with the data, for implementing a drop source object with the *IDropSource* interface, for calling the *DoDragDrop* API in OLE2.DLL, and for handling the impact of a Move (Cut) operation where the data in the source is removed after it has been transferred to the target.

The target of a drag-and-drop operation is responsible for implementing a drop target object with the *IDropTarget* interface, which is typically part of a document. This drop target object is registered for the document window using the OLE 2 API function *RegisterDragDrop* when the document is available as a target. When the document is no longer available, it must remove the drop target object by calling *RevokeDragDrop*. In addition, the document must call *CoLockObjectExternal* to ensure that OLE 2 does not internally lose track of the drop target object. Once registered, the drop target waits around for calls into its *IDropTarget* interface. When a call arrives, the drop target determines whether it can use the data, decides what will happen if the data is dropped at the current mouse coordinates, provides user feedback as to what might happen, and possibly scrolls the target document.

Both Cosmo and Patron applications are modified in this chapter to support drag-and-drop. Cosmo is a simple case, but Patron has a number of complexities due to more advanced features, such as scrolling. Drag-and-drop in Cosmo allows convenient transfer of its figures between instances of itself as well as convenient transfers of metafiles and bitmaps of those figures into other applications. Drag-and-drop in Patron not only allows it to accept graphics from other applications (such as Cosmo) but also allows us to add the capability to move a tenant within a page or between separate documents or instances of Patron. Adding the ability to drag-and-drop compound document objects will be the icing on the cake, as we'll see in the next chapter.

SECTION III

COMPOUND DOCUMENTS: OLE

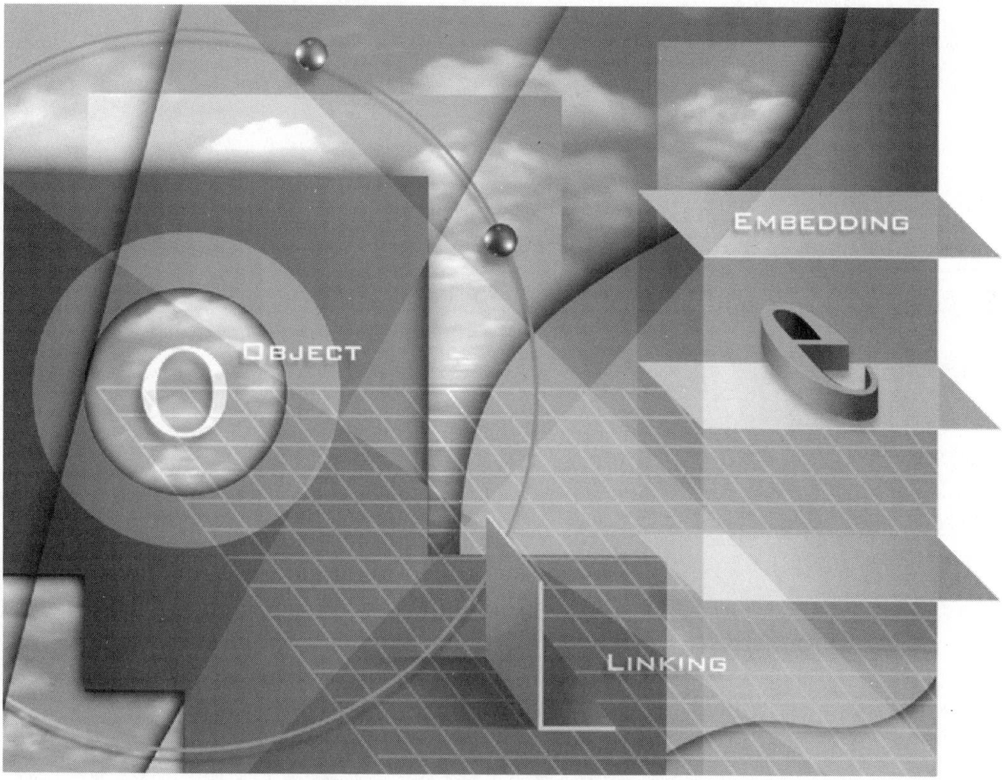

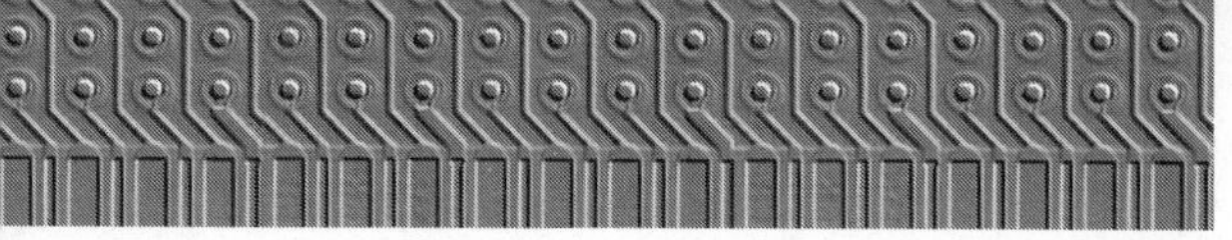

CHAPTER NINE

COMPOUND DOCUMENTS AND EMBEDDED CONTAINERS

There are things, and there are places to put things.
Tony Williams, Microsoft OLE architect

In our kitchen, my wife and I have about 150 resealable plastic storage units in all shapes and sizes, from tiny ones that hold barely a quarter cup to ones that should hold enough salad to feed a cast of thousands. (OK, so I'm exaggerating slightly.) Some are square, some are round, some have such unusual shapes that they can't be stacked in our freezer. Some are clear, some are bold "Seventies" colors (such as avocado), and some are recycled yogurt containers that say "Sell by June 1, 1962." (OK, so I'm exaggerating again.) Some we obtained as gifts from Mom, some we bought ourselves, and at least one I found at a campground in the Cascade Mountains. (No, I'm *not* exaggerating.)

Besides the ubiquitous plastic, there are boxes, bins, pots, jugs, jars, cans, bags, baskets, bottles, and small paper packets containing powders with ingredient lists long enough to choke a Toastmaster. What lives inside these various storage units is just as diverse. Some contain dry goods such as assortments of beans, lentils, split peas, whole-wheat stone-ground flour, rye flour, brown rice, couscous, millet, Wheat Chex, and spinach grown according to the California Organic Foods Act of 1990. Others, in the refrigerator, hold at least five different kinds of soups, last week's radishes, tomorrow's lunch, and usually some sort of edible yet unidentifiable leftover.

The problem with kitchen storage is that the stuff you want to put in a given container might not necessarily fit the container. Carrots, for example, do not lend themselves to storage in an egg carton. What we would really like is that any container, no matter how bizarre, have at least a basic set of attributes that allow it to contain any kind of stuff, regardless of how otherwise bizarre that container might be. In addition, we would really like to have foods that all share a basic set of attributes that allow them to fit into any of these standardized containers, regardless of how otherwise fantastic the food.

I doubt this will ever happen with food, but the same problem exists in computing when we are trying to integrate data from different applications into one centralized place, which we call a compound document. It has always been relatively easy to create some kind of functional interface in two different applications that allow them to communicate and exchange their data. When the two applications are made for each other, each with intimate knowledge about the other, they fit together as well as eggs fit in an egg carton. But just as an egg carton really doesn't work well to store anything but eggs, such a specialized interface in a computer program is not very useful to applications other than the one for which it was written.

What we need is the ability to program the container—the application that collects and stores information—so that it can use any information from any source without having to know any intimate details about that other application. We also need to have the source application provide or serve data to any other application, again without having to know anything about the others. What we need are standards for implementing both the container application and the server application, as they're called, so that they can communicate without knowing any details about each other. If a container application could treat all servers in the world identically, just as a server identically treats all containers, data would be shareable among all.

The standard is called Object Linking and Embedding,[1] which is also referred to as Compound Documents (with capital *C* and *D*). (Whenever I now use the term *compound documents*—sans capitals—I mean compound documents in the OLE 2 sense.) In the compound document model, there are embedded and linked objects, which are the units of exchange between whatever agent appears as the container and whatever agent appears as the server of those objects. All three pieces—object, container, and server—implement their parts of the standard by means of specific interfaces, and I mean OLE 2 Interfaces with a big *I*. Anything that implements the container interfaces, for example, can act in the capacity of a compound document container, regardless of what else it implements. The same is true for the server and object interfaces. This means that we can, by analogy, fit lasagna noodles into a vinegar bottle without any trouble whatsoever. We can't do that in the kitchen, but, hey, this is just software...anything is possible.

The standard is so rich that it's going to take us from here through Chapter 16 to explain it all, from embedding, to linking, to in-place activation, so we'll start in this chapter with a full step-by-step treatment of how you

1. The fact that the product name of OLE 2 is so hard-wired to relate to compound documents is unfortunate, and this explains why we have the more generic Windows Objects to collectively describe all the technologies.

write an application that can contain embedded objects, using Patron as the example. We start with containers because the container is the most active agent—that is, it provides the most user interface and really drives the servers and objects. After we have developed a container, we will look at embedded object servers in Chapters 10 and 11. Chapter 10 describes servers in EXEs, and Chapter 11 covers servers in DLLs, including what we call object handlers.

The other third of the OLE acronym—linking—is deferred until Chapters 12 and 13. Chapter 12 covers linking containers, and Chapter 13 covers linked object servers. Some containers and servers will never be concerned with linking, so I've separated it out in this manner to keep our discussion about embedding as uncluttered as possible.

After we get past linking and embedding, we'll look at a few compatibility and conversion features for both containers and servers in Chapter 14. That takes us up to in-place activation in Chapters 15 and 16. But before any of this, we need to look at how all the pieces of compound documents—containers, object handlers, servers in DLLs and EXEs, and OLE 2 itself—fit together.

Compound Document Mechanisms

The OLE 2 standard for compound documents involves not only the container application but also at least one DLL and possibly another application. To make sense of what we'll be doing in this and subsequent chapters, we must explore how these pieces work together.

A compound document object can be in any one of three states: passive, loaded, or running. A *passive* object exists entirely on disk—that is, it does not occupy any memory. In such a state, the object cannot be displayed in any way, and there are, of course, no pointers anywhere in memory to that object because there is no memory to point to. To get a pointer to an interface on that object, it must be *loaded,* which means that it does occupy some memory, that there is at least one pointer to it, and that it can be displayed, printed, or activated. When activated, the object is put into the running state and can be either hidden or visible. When running and visible, the object can interact with the end-user to allow editing or other manipulation. A visible running object might also activate itself in place, in which case we call it an active object, but that's simply the same as running visible with a lot more user interface.

In any given state, there are specific modules in memory. By modules, I mean the container application, the OLE 2 libraries, an object handler, and the object's server. The following sections describe exactly what's loaded into memory at any given time.

The Passive State

When an end user first launches an application that is an OLE 2 container, memory holds the container application and some of the OLE 2 libraries, typically COMPOBJ.DLL and OLE2.DLL, as shown in Figure 9-1. Let's assume that at this point there is also a document on disk in a compound file, and that there is a storage object within that compound file that contains all the information about an object, including the object's native data and possibly a cached presentation (a metafile or bitmap) for that object. We'll conveniently forget about how the object got there in the first place, but we'll come back to that later.

At this point, the object is comatose (in the passive state), and the only loaded modules are the container application and the OLE 2 libraries. The container has called only a few functions, such as *OleBuildVersion* and *OleInitialize* in OLE2.DLL, which requires that OLE2.DLL be in memory. OLE2.DLL calls functions in COMPOBJ.DLL, which is loaded as well. So the only activity at this point is a few function calls between the container and the OLE 2 libraries. STORAGE.DLL is not yet in use because the container has yet to access the compound file.

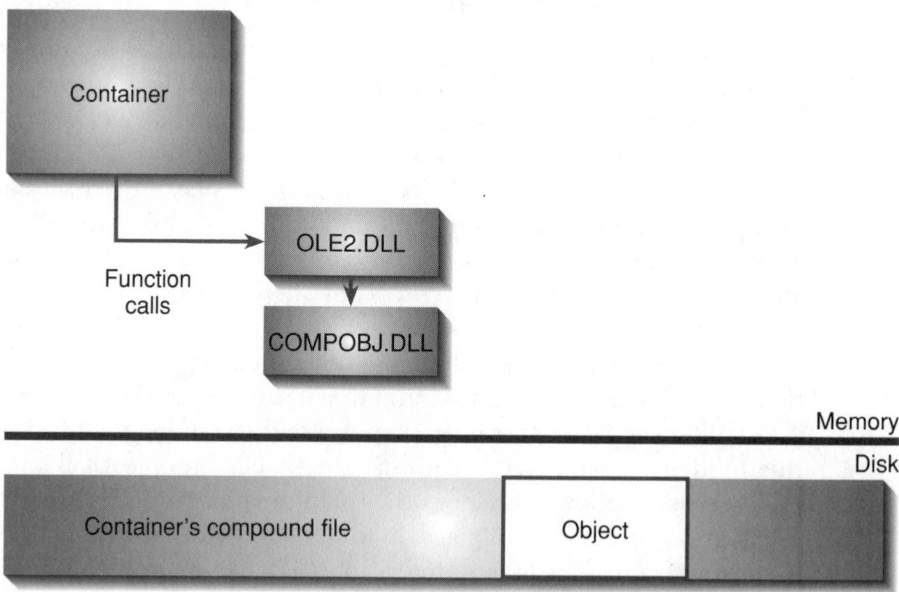

Figure 9-1.
When a container application first starts, generally memory contains only some OLE 2 DLLs and the container application itself.

The Loaded State

Now the end user opens the compound file using the container's File Open command. The container calls a function such as *StgOpenStorage*, which pulls in STORAGE.DLL and begins reading data from the file, as shown in Figure 9-2. At some point, the container will encounter the object within the file, at which time it will call the *OleLoad* function in OLE2.DLL, passing the *IStorage* pointer to the object in the compound file, as shown in Figure 9-3 on the next page. The container also passes the ID of the first interface pointer it wants on the loaded object, usually *IUnknown* or *IOleObject* (an interface we'll be using in this chapter and implementing in Chapter 10).

Now things become interesting. *OleLoad* wakes the object from the passive state into the loaded state, and a number of things happen. First, *OleLoad* calls *ReadClassStg* on the still disk-based object to determine the CLSID (which will have been put there by a previous call to *OleSave*). Using that CLSID, it calls our old friend *CoCreateInstance* with the parameters *CLSCTX_INPROC_HANDLER* ¦ *CLSCTX_INPROC_SERVER*. As we learned in Chapter 4, *CoCreateInstance* (through *CoGetClassObject*) will go out to the Registration Database and attempt to find the entry for the CLSID. There it

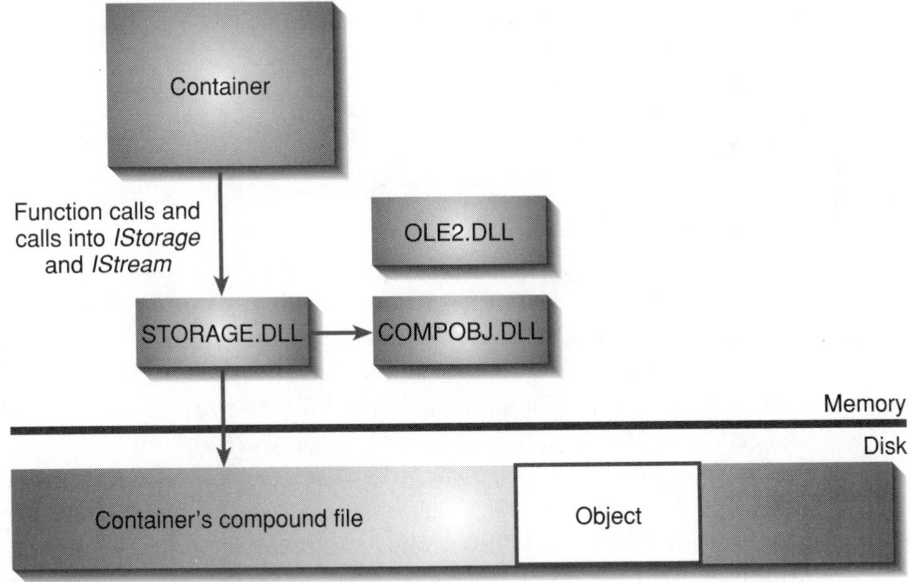

Figure 9-2.
When a container reads from a compound file, STORAGE.DLL must be loaded into memory to access that file. STORAGE.DLL uses services provided in COMPOBJ.DLL as well.

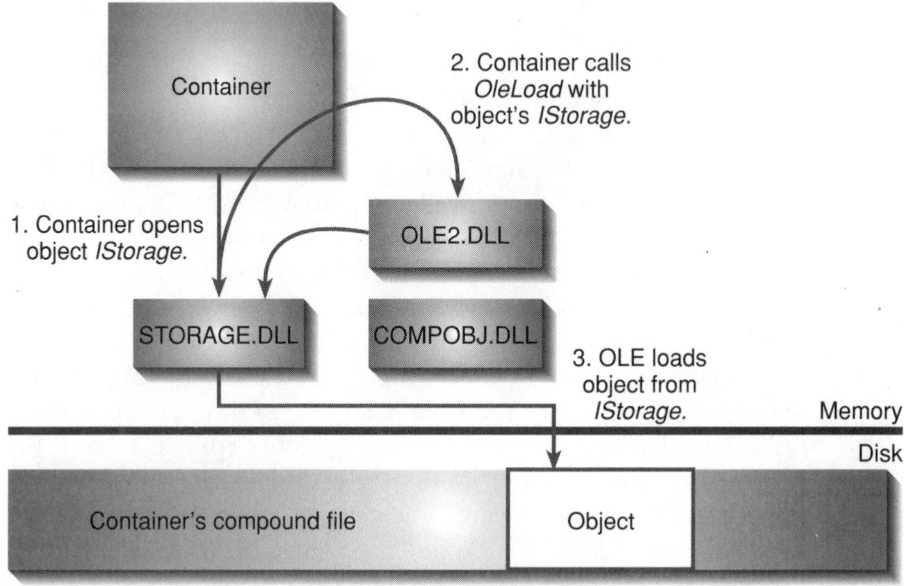

Figure 9-3.
When a container encounters an object in its compound file, it calls OleLoad *to bring that object into the loaded state.*

will find an entry for *InProcServer* (which it checks for first), an entry for *InProcHandler*, or no entry at all, in which case *OleLoad* (not *CoCreateInstance*) uses a default handler.

Case 1: *InProcServer*

The first possibility inside *OleLoad* is that the Registration Database has an entry under the *CLSID\InProcServer* key. In this case, the *InProcServer* is solely responsible for providing the complete implementation of the object, as we'll see in Chapter 11. The *InProcServer* is structured with the *DllGetClassObject* export and contains an implementation of *IClassFactory*, as shown in Figure 9-4. *OleLoad*, by virtue of calling *CoCreateInstance*, loads this DLL into memory in the container's process space and asks its *IClassFactory* to create a new object. *OleLoad* specifically asks *CoCreateInstance* to return a pointer to the object's *IOleObject* interface, regardless of the container's requested interface, so if the container asked for something else, *OleLoad* uses *QueryInterface* on that first pointer to the interface the container wanted and returns the intended pointer to the container.

The interface pointer now known to the container references an object that exists inside the *InProcServer*, not inside OLE2.DLL. Any calls through that pointer will enter the *InProcServer* first. The compound document object provided by the server must implement at least the *IOleObject*, *IDataObject*, *IViewObject*, *IPersistStorage*, and *IOleCache* interfaces, as shown in Figure 9-4. These interfaces, as we will see in Chapters 10 and 11, are what make any object appear to any container as a basic embedded compound document object.

Case 2: *InProcHandler*

If there is not an entry for *InProcServer* or if there is an error in loading the DLL listed in the Registration Database, *CoCreateInstance* attempts to load the DLL listed under the *CLSID\InProcHandler* key. (If it fails, the process advances to case 3.) An object handler looks exactly the same as an *InProcServer*, complete with the *DllGetClassObject* export and an implementation of a class factory. As far as the loaded state is concerned, there is no difference

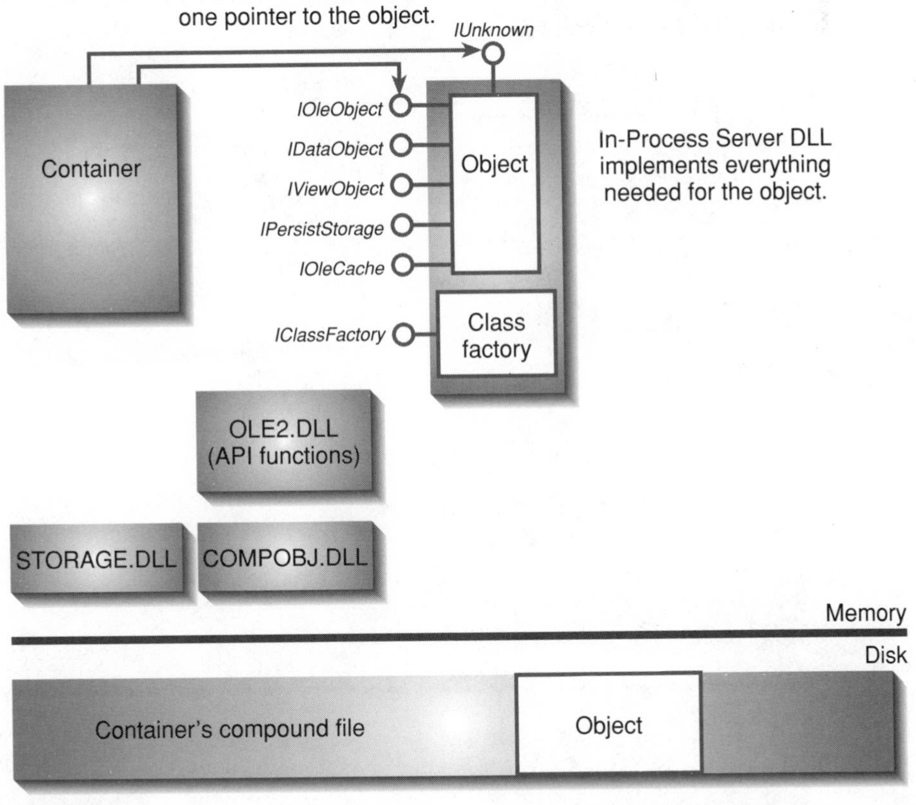

Figure 9-4.
When an InProcServer *exists for the object's CLSID, the* OleLoad *function loads that DLL and returns a pointer to the container application that points into that DLL.*

between an object handler and an *InProcServer*, as you can see by comparing Figures 9-4 and 9-5. The handler implements objects with at least the same interfaces as the *InProcServer*, so from the container's point of view, there is absolutely no difference.

Case 3: The Default Handler

If there are any errors loading an *InProcServer* or an *InProcHandler*, *OleLoad* calls *OleCreateDefaultHandler* to load the default handler, which is, in fact, OLE2.DLL. Because OLE2.DLL is already in memory (albeit acting in a different capacity, as merely a library of functions), loading the default handler always works. Servers generally register OLE2.DLL as their *InProcHandler* if they do not use a more specific handler.

The default handler itself looks no different from any other handler or any other *InProcServer* as far as the container is concerned, so for illustration, simply replace the words *In-Process Handler* in Figure 9-5 with *Default Handler (OLE2.DLL)*, and you have the whole picture.

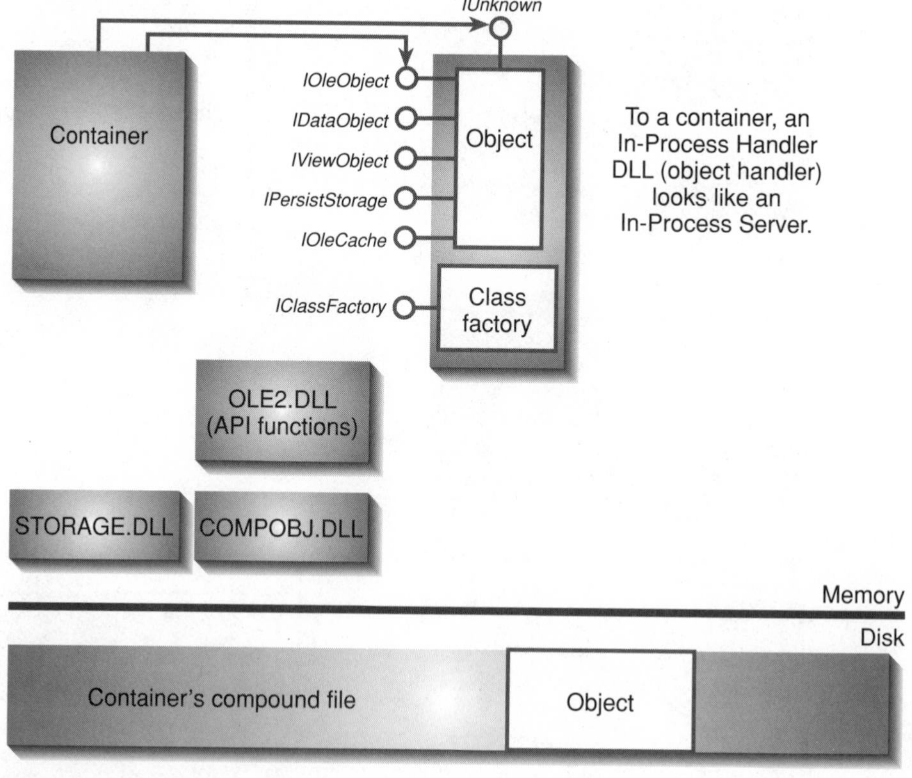

Figure 9-5.
To a container, an InProcHandler *looks exactly like an* InProcServer.

This is not, however, the only time you can load OLE2.DLL in its capacity as the default handler. As we learned in Chapter 6 with the Freeloader application, the default handler has a lot of nice functionality within it to draw and serialize graphics and to maintain cached presentations for an object, among other capabilities. In fact, OLE2.DLL is chock full of code that is useful to implementors of servers and handlers—so much code, in fact, that servers and handlers will commonly call *OleCreateDefaultHandler* (or other similar functions) to create an instance of (that is, an aggregate on top of) the default handler. To this instance of the default handler, in-process servers and handlers will delegate specific interface member functions that need no customization, or they will directly expose some of the default handler's interfaces as their own, as shown in Figure 9-6. In this case, handlers are

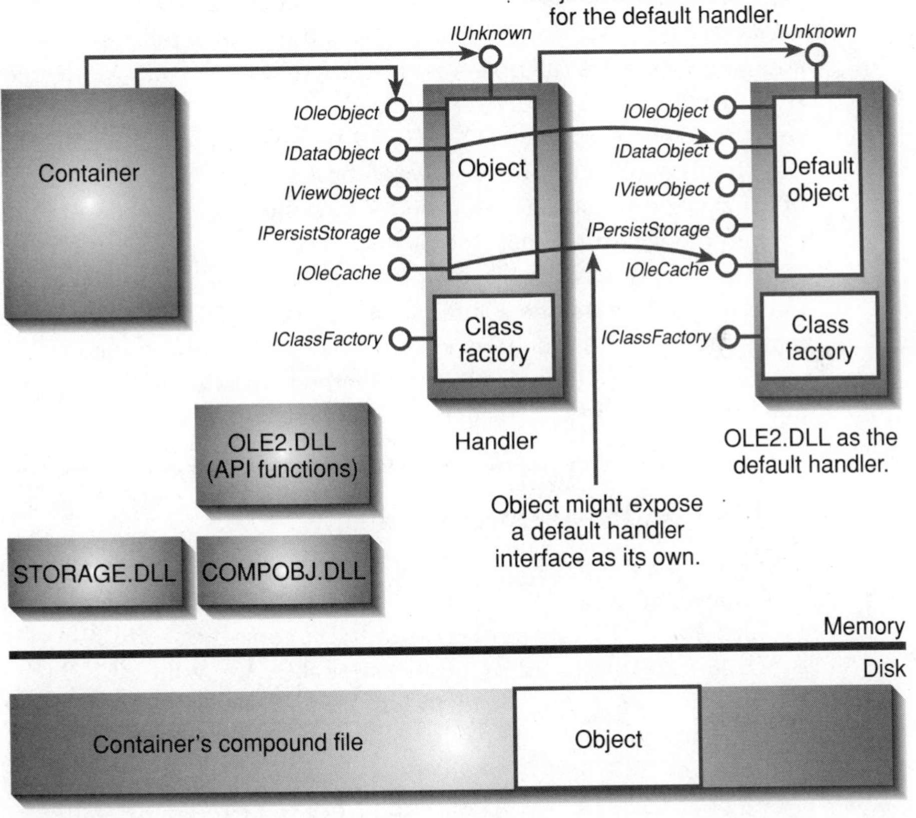

Figure 9-6.
Handlers aggregate on the default handler to expose interfaces that need no customization.

much like bank tellers: As far as customers (or containers) are concerned, the tellers do everything for the customers, but behind the scenes, the tellers are delegating much of the processing and handling of customer accounts to other people the customer never sees. The customer probably knows those other people are there, but the customer also has no way of knowing or articulating what tellers do and what everyone else does.

As we'll see in detail in Chapter 11, the *InProcHandler* that you implement delegates much of its functionality to the default handler, whereas *InProcServer* delegates only a little. The distinction between a handler and a server, in fact, is mostly in how much each delegates.

Loading the Object: All Cases

Before *OleLoad* actually returns the container's requested interface pointer, it calls *QueryInterface* on the new object, asking for *IPersistStorage*, and calls *IPersistStorage::Load*, passing to the object the *IStorage* pointer provided by the container. As far as the object is concerned, it loads whatever is necessary to operate by calling member functions in *IStorage* and *IStream*, which access the compound file through STORAGE.DLL, as shown in Figure 9-7. The object then holds onto a copy of the *IStorage* pointer (after calling *IStorage::AddRef*, of course) for the object's lifetime, as described in Chapter 5 in "Other OLE 2 Technologies and Structured Storage."

At this point, the object is officially "loaded," and *OleLoad* returns an interface pointer to the container application. *OleLoad* is only one of the many ways in which a container obtains the first pointer to a compound document object, as we'll explore in this chapter. In any case, the container can now ask the object to perform tasks, such as drawing itself.

16-Bit and 32-Bit Interoperability

OLE 2 on Windows NT, as well as on Win32s/Windows 3.1, presents some interesting problems for *InProcServer* and *InProcHandler* modules. 16-bit OLE 2 running for a 16-bit container cannot load 32-bit DLLs into that 16-bit process space. Likewise, 32-bit OLE 2 for a 32-bit container cannot load 16-bit DLLs. At the time of this writing, there are no solutions to this other than avoiding DLLs altogether. An eventual solution would be to write both 16-bit and 32-bit handlers or users of *InProcServer* and store their respective paths under different keys in the Registration Database.

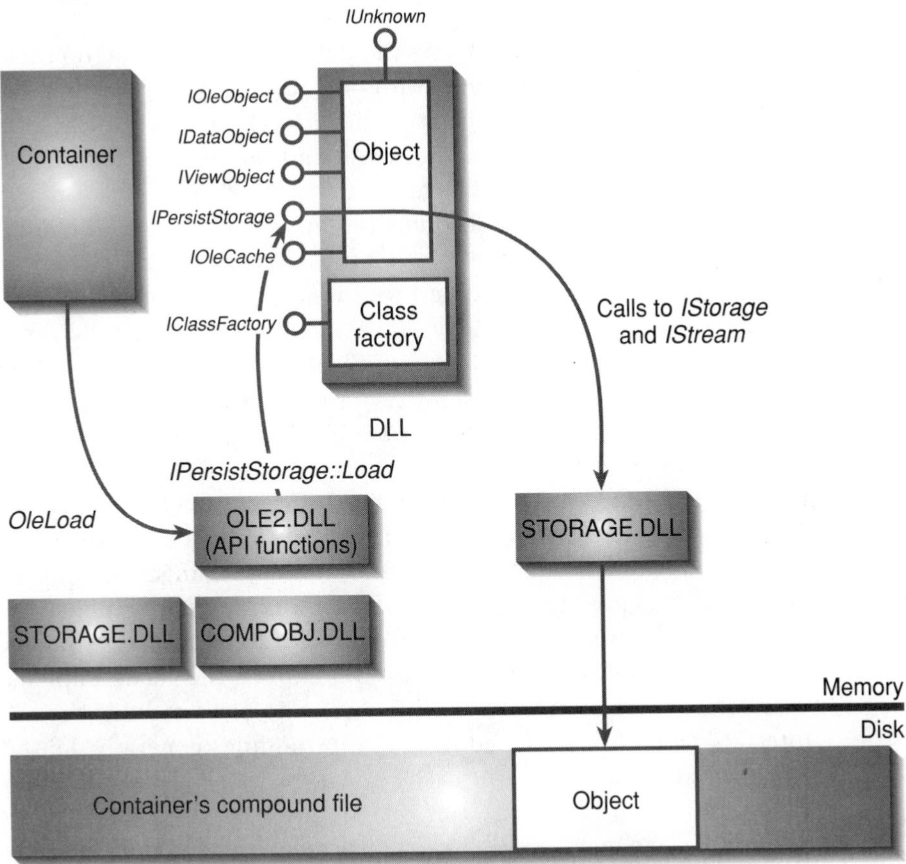

Figure 9-7.
Handlers and users of InProcServer *access the object's data on disk through the* IStorage *pointer provided by the container.*

Drawing the Object

The vast majority of compound document containers will be interested in showing a graphic of the object after loading. It would be pretty silly to load a word processor document to see its text but to be faced with large black holes where there should be charts or other types of object pictures. So a container application eventually calls *QueryInterface* for *IViewObject* and calls *IViewObject::Draw.* (Remember that the *OleDraw* function does this internally.) This call, of course, first enters the *IViewObject* implementation inside the loaded *InProcServer* or *InProcHandler*, but there are a number of things that might happen here.

First, the server or handler might draw the object directly on the *hDC* passed to *IViewObject::Draw* using the data loaded from the object's storage. In this case, drawing is finished with one quick function call to a DLL. Both *InProcServer* and *InProcHandler* modules can choose to implement *IViewObject:Draw* for whatever aspects they want, and they can depend on the default handler to draw the other aspects.

This brings us to the second case, in which the default handler has to come up with a way to draw the object. Unfortunately, the default handler's interpolation skills are weak, and thus it cannot use the object's native data sitting out in storage to render an image. So the default handler likes to keep an object photo album that has pictures of each aspect requested by the container; when the container asks to see the object in a particular aspect, the default handler can show one of the photographs in the album. OLE 2's photo album is called the *cache*, a piece of code in OLE2.DLL that implements the *IDataObject*, *IViewObject*, *IPersistStorage*, and *IOleCache* interfaces. The cache maintains presentations in memory and on disk (in the container's compound file) so that it can draw and exchange the presentations. Technically, all handlers and in-process servers must implement the *IOleCache* interface, but rarely do you find it necessary to implement your own. Both modules generally delegate all *IOleCache* calls to the cache implemented in OLE2.DLL or aggregate on OLE 2's cache to expose the cache's *IOleCache* interface as their own. In addition, both modules generally delegate other interface function calls to the cache or expose those other interfaces directly, as shown in Figure 9-8.

The cache manages one or more presentations of the object within the object's *IStorage* on disk. *IOleCache* is the mechanism through which a container specifies what should be in the cache. The cache's *IPersistStorage* interface is how OLE moves presentations to and from disk, and the *IDataObject* interface is how you can ask the cache to return a memory copy of a presentation. Right now, all you need to know is that these presentations first got here when the object was initially created; again, we don't want to get involved with the details yet. So imagine, for example, that there is only one presentation in the cache—a metafile containing DVASPECT_CONTENT and a NULL target device (meaning it was rendered for the screen).

When the container asks to draw DVASPECT_CONTENT on the screen, it calls *IViewObject::Draw* as it always would. One way or another, this request works its way into the default handler's implementation of *IViewObject::Draw.* Not knowing anything about the object, the default handler has to go see whether there's a suitable presentation in the cache by calling the

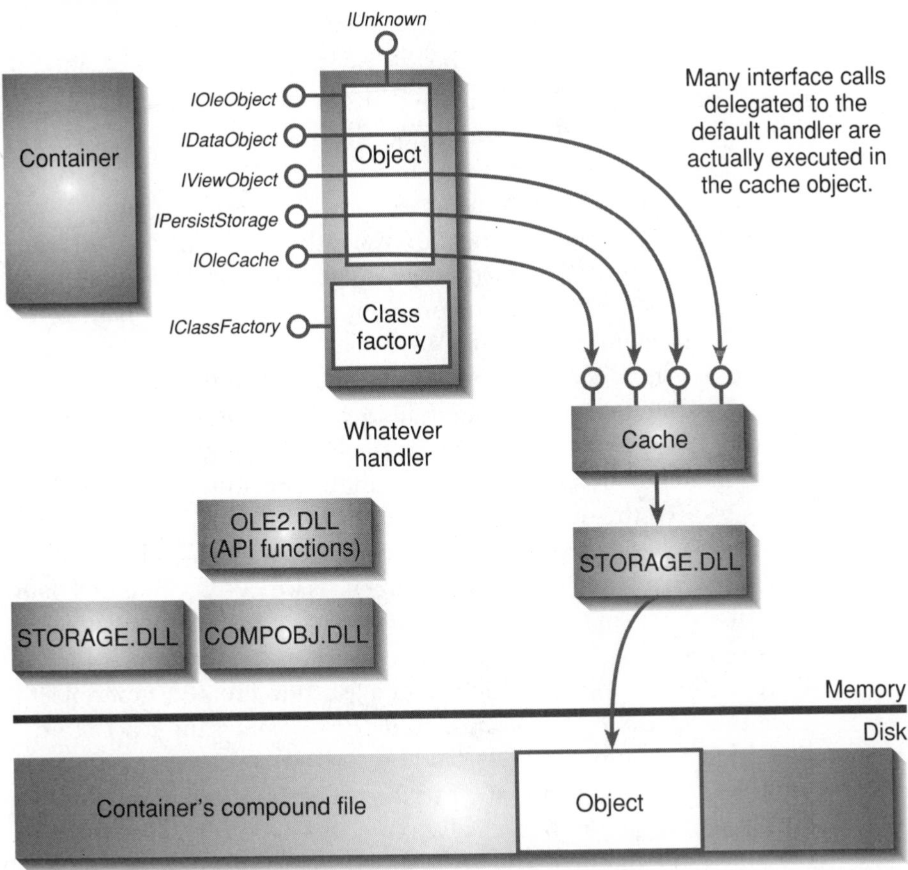

Figure 9-8.
An IOleCache *interface exposed on a handler or on the default handler is usually the* IOleCache *interface implemented on the cache itself.*

cache's *IDataObject::GetData.* In this example, the cache will locate the content metafile with a NULL target device, which is suitable, so it loads that presentation from storage and returns it to the default handler, which in turn draws that metafile to the *hDC* passed to *IViewObject::Draw.*

This brings us to the third case, in which the container asks *IViewObject::Draw* to render some really funky FORMATETC. When the default handler asks the cache for a presentation, the cache responds, "Nope, ain't got none of those." The handler could now choose to fail outright, but that would be terribly rude. Instead, it elects to put the object into the running state, which is the last resort for getting a presentation.

The Running State

This third state of an object means that there is "one-stop shopping" available for anything you want to do with the object, and if the capability is not there, it's not available anywhere. So either an *InProcServer* or what we know as a *LocalServer* (a server implemented as an EXE) could be considered Alice's Restaurant for objects ("You can get anything you want, at..."). When an *InProcServer* exists, there is no difference between the loaded and running states. When an *InProcServer* is not available, the object is loaded when a handler is present and is running only when the *LocalServer* has been launched. But when is it launched?

When no *InProcServer* is available, the handler attempts to do everything possible to avoid having to launch the *LocalServer* in order to service a request. However, there will eventually be some request outside the capabilities of the handler, as in the example in the previous section in which the container wanted the object to draw a funky FORMATETC. The handler, having tried so hard to avoid this moment, capitulates into calling *CoCreateInstance* with CLSCTX_LOCALSERVER, which, as we saw in Chapter 4, launches the EXE listed under the *CLSID\LocalServer* key in the Registration Database. This server must call *CoRegisterClassObject* on startup to provide OLE 2 with its *IClassFactory* pointer, which is then asked to create a new object that must have the *IOleObject*, *IDataObject*, and *IPersistStorage* interfaces to qualify as a compound document object.[2] When *CoCreateInstance* returns to the default handler with the appropriate interface pointer to that new object, the default handler makes a number of calls to put this new object into the same state as the one in the handler. Yes, we do have two instances of an object of the same CLSID, and they must now be synchronized. So the handler calls the new object's *IPersistStorage::Load*, as shown in Figure 9-9, again passing the same *IStorage* pointer. After the object has had a chance to load its data, the handler calls *IDataObject::GetData*, passing the FORMATETC it could not render itself. If the object fails this *GetData*, drawing simply doesn't happen, but if it succeeds, the handler gets the rendering and draws it to the container's *hDC*.

The other common case in which an object must be put into the running state is when the container calls *IOleObject::DoVerb*. (Up to this point, we've called this process *activating* the object.) *DoVerb* asks the object to execute an action such as playing a wave file or showing the object's data in a

2. Note again that the *LocalServer* cannot implement *IViewObject* because the hDC parameters in *IViewObject::Draw* cannot be marshaled.

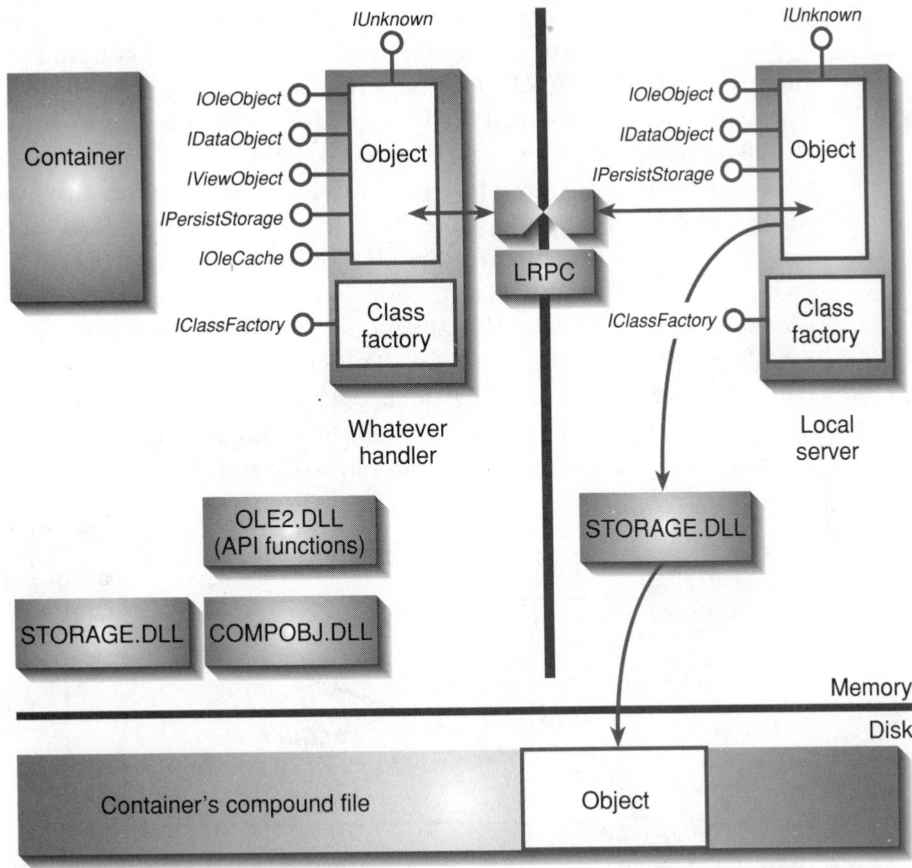

Figure 9-9.
After the object is put into the running state by the handler, OLE 2 launches the LocalServer *EXE, which provides a complete implementation of the object.*

window in which the end user can make modifications. (OLE refers to this kind of action as a *verb*. Typical verbs are Edit and Play, but the range of verbs is limited only by the imagination.) Because the definition of a verb is the sole responsibility of the object and its server, there is absolutely no chance that the default handler will know what to do with it. (Some custom handlers might know how to execute certain verbs, but for the most part, handlers do not implement this function.) So eventually the request again works into the default handler, which launches the *LocalServer* to provide the request. And again, if an *InProcServer* is loaded, it is responsible for implementing this function because an *InProcServer* usually exists without a *LocalServer*.

Eventually, either programmatically or through user action, the *LocalServer* shuts down, which takes the object from the running state back into the loaded state. If the handler again needs the services of the *LocalServer,* it must relaunch the EXE and restart the whole process. The transitions between all three states—passive, loaded, and running—are illustrated in Figure 9-10. Note that the function *OleLoad* moves from passive to loaded, and the final *Release* on the object created by *OleLoad* moves from loaded to passive. An object ultimately moves from loaded to running hidden by means of the *OleRun* function, which is called from within the default handler's implementation of *IOleObject::DoVerb* (as well as a few other interface members). *DoVerb,* called with OLEIVERB_SHOW, moves the object from running hidden to running visible. *DoVerb* called with OLEIVERB_HIDE moves the object from running visible to running hidden. *IOleObject::Close* moves any object from running (regardless of visibility) to loaded once again.

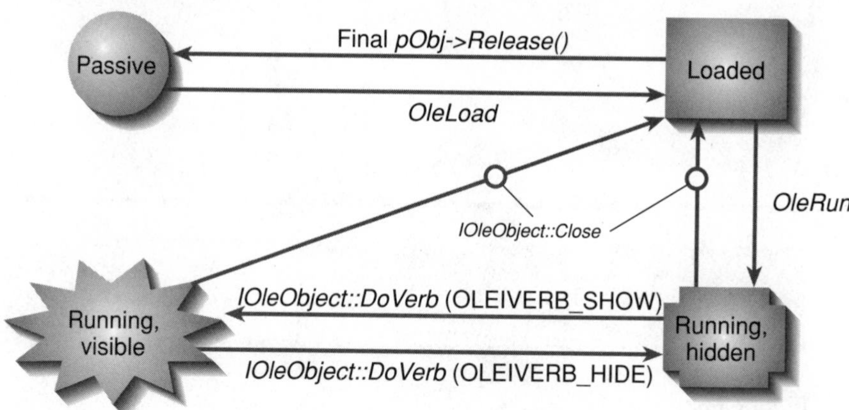

Figure 9-10.
Various function calls and events that cause state transitions.

Mommy, Daddy, Where Do New Objects Come From?

Um, well, ah, you see, there's, ah, a stork. Yeah. The Object Stork.

Sure, such an explanation might work for a four-year-old, but I don't think it works for programmers, so there must be a better explanation. Container applications create new objects using the function *OleCreate,* which a container typically calls after invoking the Insert Object dialog box and after the user has selected a name and pressed OK. (See Figure 9-14 on page 528.) You cannot say the object is in the passive state before the application calls *OleCreate* because there is not yet an object. *OleCreate* creates a new object that

OLE 1 and OLE 2 Interoperability

OLE 2 provides an OLE 1 compatibility layer, which sits between a container and a server application (EXE) so that one application can be written to OLE 1 and another to OLE 2 without either knowing the difference. Essentially OLE 2 translates the OLE 1 interfaces on one side into OLE 2 interfaces on the other. Therefore, OLE 2 containers have full access to all OLE 1 servers, and all OLE 2 servers are usable from OLE 1 containers. This allows you to upgrade your application to OLE 2 and know that you will not alienate OLE 1 applications.

But truthfully, the situation is not perfect, because of these handler things. Because an OLE 2 container talks directly to a handler, it cannot use an OLE 1 handler. (This is not too unfortunate because there are very few OLE 1 handlers. Windows 3.1 Paintbrush is one of the few.) Likewise, an OLE 2 handler or *InProcServer* cannot be used by an OLE 1 container. The differences between version 1 and version 2 designs simply do not allow it, so if you are considering a handler or an *InProcServer* at this point, you might need, for at least a while, to maintain both OLE 1 and OLE 2 versions of your DLLs.

is immediately in the loaded state—that is, a handler or an *InProcServer* has been loaded for it. Instead of OLE 2 calling *IPersistStorage::Load* as it does in *OleLoad*, it calls *IPersistStorage::InitNew.* After the object has been created, the handler will launch the *LocalServer* for the same reasons as before. As we'll see, containers will usually call *IOleObject::DoVerb* shortly after calling *OleCreate* to immediately bring the object up for editing.

Containers can also create new objects from a data object (on the clipboard or from a drag-and-drop operation) when either a CF_EMBEDSOURCE or a CF_EMBEDDEDOBJECT format is available. Both these formats are an *IStorage* containing the object's native data as it would appear on disk but with no presentation caches, so the existence of these formats essentially means that an object exists in the passive state inside the data object. When a container performs a Paste operation or accepts a drop, it can call *OleCreateFromData*, which does almost everything *OleLoad* does except that the data passed to *IPersistStorage::Load* comes from the data object instead of from the container's document file. But again, *OleCreateFromData* moves the object from the passive state into the loaded state.

The Structure of a Container Application

Now that we understand how compound documents generally work and what each state of an object implies, we can start our exploration of containers capable of managing embedded objects. The previous section explained how objects look to a container: They always have the *IOleObject, IDataObject, IPersistStorage, IViewObject,* and *IOleCache* interfaces, regardless of how many servers, handlers, or caches are in use. That's the object's part of the compound document standard, so now it's time to see the container's part.

Compound documents affect a container application on all levels. I define these levels as *application, document, page,* and *site,*[3] where the site is a place on a page, a page is part of a document (in some cases, the page is the document, or there is no distinction between a document and the pages in the document, so the structures merge[4]), and the document is managed by the application, which might have more than one document open at any given time. Patron is a good example of this structure—Patron (the application) loads documents consisting of pages on which tenants (the sites) reside. Each site is a place for one object. Each site is responsible for implementing the *IOleClientSite* and *IAdviseSink* interfaces in order to use an embedded object—that is, in order to fulfill the container's side of the standard, as shown in Figure 9-11.

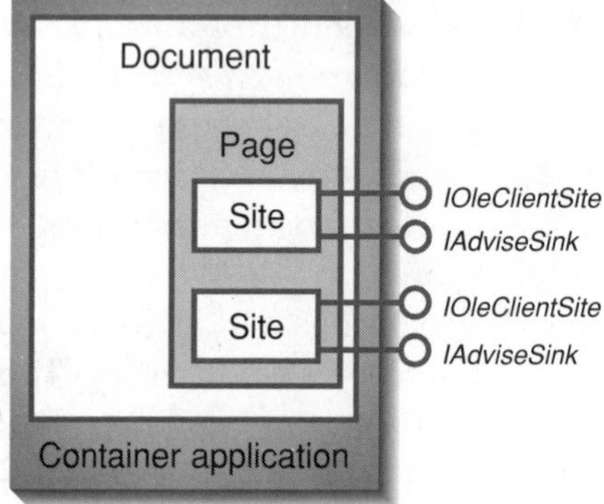

Figure 9-11.
The general structure of container applications.

3. In the Microsoft Foundation Classes version 2, these are called App, Document, View, and Item (in view).
4. A word processor generally doesn't have a separate notion of pages because it will be constantly repaginating. Spreadsheets also define pages only when printing. However, databases can view a database as the document, with specific forms or tables as the pages and specific fields in those forms or tables as the sites.

Let me illustrate this with what I call The Allegory of the Cookie Jar,[5] which will serve as a useful example in later chapters as well. An object is like a batch of cookies. Different cookies have their own form and taste, just as different objects have different classes and behavior. Cookies are great by themselves right out of the oven, but eventually we need to store the batch somewhere or they'll quickly become stale or be devoured by a rabid pack of specter hounds (other members of the household). Where we decide to store these cookies depends on how we later want to get at them. For this chapter, we have Embedded Cookies, which must always be stored inside a cookie jar. In Chapter 12, we'll see Linked Cookies, for which you will put a treasure map in the jar that tells someone where they really are. In the same way, an embedded object must always be stored at some container site. Our cookie jar can thus be called a site.

On the outside of this cookie jar is generally some sort of representation of the cookies inside. For our purposes, let's imagine a high-tech cookie jar with a video camera on the inside that transmits a picture of the current cookies to a small screen on the outside, letting us at any time see exactly what's in the jar.[6] This is equivalent to always having a presentation for an object that reflects the object's current native data. Having a broken video camera or a loss of power is like having a handler that cannot find a suitable presentation or cannot find a server that can render one. So we have a cookie jar that always shows what's in it, just as we have a site that always displays a picture of the object it maintains.

That's all well and good, but the cookie jar itself also needs a place where it can reside, such as a shelf or a countertop, just as a site needs a page in which to live. But even the shelf needs a place, such as the kitchen, just as a page needs a document. And what good is a kitchen without a house around it? By the same token, what good is a document without an application that knows how to open it?

What I call a document, a page, and a site will, of course, vary from application to application. In a database, for example, the database is the document, the page is a table or a record, and the site is a specific field in that record or table. Whatever the application, you can generally find structures that fit this model. This brings us to where we can see what we need to do at each level to create a compound document container.

---

5. With apologies, of course, to Plato and his allegory of the cave.
6. Note that cookie jars in OLE 2 do not have locking lids. That's left to future revisions, which implement object security.

Embedding Containers Step by Step

The remainder of this chapter will follow modifications I made to Patron to make it become a container for embedded objects. There are changes at many levels, and much of the necessary work involves user interface. If we return to our cookie jar for a moment, the cookies need to define user interface only to account for how they look, feel, and taste—very cookie-oriented sort of stuff. The cookie jar has to define how it opens and how it looks from the outside. In the same manner, the shelf on which the cookie jar rests has its own interface of color and dimension, just as the kitchen and the house have to define their own characteristics. So, in much the same way most of the user interface in a house is shown in rooms, shelves, and storage devices, most of the user interface in embedding compound documents falls to the container.

Nevertheless, we can reduce implementation to the following sequence of steps. Each step is designed so that you can at least compile after coding the step, and in most cases you also have something you can run and test. I strongly recommend that you test as much as you can in the early steps because the later ones build on these foundations:

1. Call *SetMessageQueue(96)* (Windows 3.1 only), *OleBuildVersion*, *OleInitialize*, and *OleUninitialize*, as described in "The New Application for Windows Objects" in Chapter 4.
2. Define what is to be a site in your application and manage unique *IStorage* instances with each site as sites are created and destroyed.
3. Make your sites Windows Objects and implement the *IOleClientSite* and *IAdviseSink* interfaces on the sites, as well as adding variables to manage embedded objects in these sites.
4. Implement a function to shade the site when the object it contains is transformed to and from the running state.
5. Invoke the Insert Object dialog box, call *OleCreate* to create a new embedded object, and call a number of follow-up functions to initialize the object after creation.
6. Draw and print the object's presentations.
7. Activate the object on a double-click, add a menu that lists the object's verbs, and activate the object when this menu is selected. Optionally, implement simple right mouse button pop-up menus on the object.

8. Call *OleCreateFromData* to create an embedded object from a data object (from the clipboard from a drag-and-drop operation). Optionally, invoke the Paste Special dialog box to allow the user to select the exact format to paste from the clipboard.
9. Provide new data formats to copy an embedded object back to the clipboard or to source it in a drag-and-drop operation.
10. Delete objects from the document. Remember to use *CoFreeUnusedLibraries* after deleting an object.
11. Save and load documents containing embedded objects.
12. (Optional) Handle iconic presentation aspects and control the cache as necessary.

After following these 12 steps in your own application, you'll end up with an embedding container that can communicate with both OLE 1 and OLE 2 servers.

Call Initialization Functions at Startup and Shutdown

As mentioned in Chapter 4 and as implemented in containers in Chapter 9, all applications that use Windows Objects must call *SetMessageQueue(96)* (under Windows 3.1 only), *OleBuildVersion*, and *OleInitialize* at startup and *OleUninitialize* (and possibly *OleFlushClipboard*) at shutdown. As containers, our applications use both storage objects and embedded compound document objects, among others.

Remember that *OleInitialize*, as opposed to *CoInitialize*, is necessary to work with compound documents. If you have been using *CoInitialize* to this point, switch now to *OleInitialize*. You can also compile and run to verify that these are all being called at the right time.

Define Sites and Manage Site Storage

Before going any further, you need to decide what exactly you want to act as a site in your container application. A site has a one-to-one correspondence with an embedded object, so for every object you want to be contained, you'll need to instantiate a site. If you plan to embed only a single object, you need only one site. Patron's sites are its *tenants*, implemented by its C++ class *CTenant*. Invariably, you too will need a data structure or C++ class to use in this regard, so now is the time to create one if you don't have anything like it yet.

Because Patron is essentially embedding bitmaps and metafiles already, much of what we need to make it a container is already present. One of the most important requirements of a site is that each site manages an *IStorage* instance that is for the exclusive use of this site and any embedded object it contains. Patron, again, already has a storage for each tenant, which it passes to a function such as *OleSave* (or more accurately *IPersistStorage::Save*) so that the object can save its data appropriately.

As a container, your application absolutely must provide every embedded object with some unique instance of *IStorage.* I say *some* because the object never knows or cares where that storage actually exists. If you decided back in Chapter 5 that you could use compound files for your application's documents, you need only to create substorages within that document for each site. If, however, you need to preserve an older file format, you have two options. The first option is to implement the *ILockBytes* interface on top of a block of bytes within your file where you want the object stored. This block must be able to grow arbitrarily large, although the actual bytes do not have to be physically contiguous. Remember from Chapter 5 that the purpose of the *ILockBytes* interface is to hide discontiguous blocks of bytes, exposing instead a continuous byte array. With this option, you should instantiate a separate *LockBytes* object for each object you want to embed and call *StgCreateDocfileOnILockBytes* to obtain the storage in which to save the object.

The second option is to create a memory *IStorage* for an object and to write the contents of that memory to a location in your disk file. This technique is simpler to implement because you don't need to create a *LockBytes* object, and it is simpler to use because you don't need to worry about dynamically allocating disk space from within an *ILockBytes* implementation. However, it builds the object's storage in global memory before ever touching the disk, and as a result it is much less likely to work under low memory conditions. In any case, the following steps, which are, of course, unnecessary if you are using compound files for all your storage needs, describe how to save and load objects using this technique:

1. Call *CreateILockBytesOnHGlobal* with a NULL memory handle. OLE 2 will allocate memory for you and return an *ILockBytes* pointer.
2. Call *StgCreateDocfileOnILockBytes* to obtain an *IStorage* pointer.
3. Store whatever object data is necessary in the *IStorage.* Saving objects is covered in a section later in this chapter (we need something to save first) and generally means calling *OleSave.*
4. When you are ready to write to your file, call *GetHGlobalFromILockBytes* to obtain the handle to the memory containing the object data.

5. Call *GlobalSize* to determine the length of the data, use *GlobalLock* on the handle, write the data to your file, and then use *GlobalUnlock* on the handle. Remember to write the size of this data somewhere in your file so that you know how much memory to allocate when you want to load the object again. When you have finished, call *IStorage::Release* to release the *ILockBytes* and release the memory in one swift stroke.

In the other direction, you again have five steps:

1. Read the size of the data block from your file and allocate that much global memory.
2. Call *CreateILockBytesOnHGlobal*, passing the memory that was allocated in step 1.
3. Call *StgOpenStorageOnILockBytes* to obtain an *IStorage* pointer that can access the object data.
4. Read the necessary data from the storage—that is, call *OleLoad.*
5. When you no longer need the storage, remember to call *IStorage-::Release.* Generally, you will keep this storage around as long as the object is in the loaded state.

The OLE2UI library has a function called *OleStdCreateIStorageOnHGlobal*, which wraps *CreateILockBytesOnHGlobal* and *StgCreateDocfileOnILockBytes* or *StgOpenStorageOnILockBytes* functions. Calling the library, of course, is equivalent to calling these functions yourself. Use whatever works best for you.

Regardless of how you decide to treat storage, you want to be sure that each site has a storage available when the site is created and that you properly clean up that storage when the site is closed or destroyed. If you wanted to test the process of committing the storage when the site is closed, you could write some bogus stream of garbage into the storage and verify by using a tool such as the OLE 2 SDK's DFVIEW.EXE to be sure that the data was actually making it into the disk file.

Back in Chapter 5, I briefly mentioned that any stream or storage that has a name prefixed with ASCII 3 (the value 3, not the character 3) is for the exclusive use of the owner of the parent storage, and now I can put that into context. When you hand an embedded object a storage, it (as well as OLE 2) has full control over everything within that storage with the exception of any element whose name starts with ASCII 3. Therefore, if you want to write a stream of site-related information into the storage that you pass to functions such as *OleSave* and *OleLoad*, prepend "*\0x03*" to the element's name, or who knows what could happen. This essentially marks those elements as "container only," as illustrated in Figure 9-12.

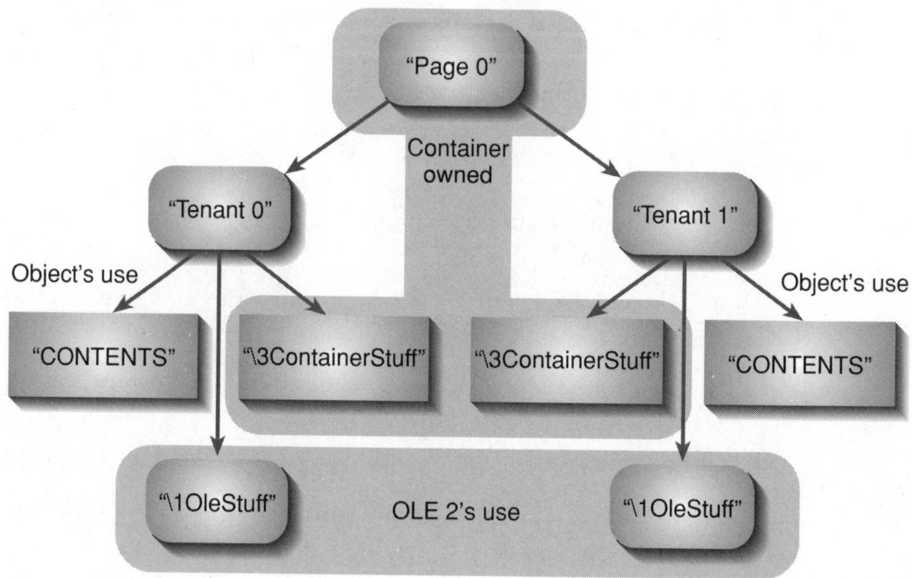

Figure 9-12.
All elements in a storage prefixed with "\0x03" *are for exclusive use of a container application, even if that storage is passed to an embedded object for its use as well.*

OLE itself will also store various streams within the object's storage, each with a name prefixed with a character lower than ASCII 32, excluding ASCII 3. If you look at such a storage in DFVIEW.EXE, you will generally see at least three OLE-managed streams:

Storage	Stream
"*\1CompObj*"	The CLSID of the object written with *WriteClassStg*. *ReadClassStg* opens this stream to retrieve the CLSID.
"*\1Ole*"	Contains information about the object, such as whether it's linked or embedded. This is the most critical stream for compound documents.
"*\2OlePres0000*"	The primary cached presentation for this object. If there are no cached presentations, this stream will not be present.
"*\2OlePresxxxx*"	Additional cached presentations.

You can again compile and verify your storage operation. In addition, if you know you are going to want to write specific site-related information into the site's storage (which Patron does not do, by the way), now is a great time to implement the necessary structures in your code to handle those streams, even if they don't yet contain useful information. Just be sure to prefix their names with an *"\0x03"*.

Implement Site Interfaces and Add Site Variables

"Sites do not live on storage alone," the maxim goes, "they need interfaces as well." To qualify a site as a place for an embedded object, the site must now become a Windows Object with two interfaces: *IOleClientSite* and *IAdviseSink*. Having these interfaces makes the site and its application appear as a container to the outside world, as shown in Figure 9-11 on page 504.

Of course, by virtue of implementing one of these interfaces, you will have an implementation of *IUnknown*. To illustrate these two interfaces and what a site object actually needs to hold an embedded object, let's look at Patron's *CTenant* implementation as revised for this chapter. First, I moved all tenant-related definitions into TENANT.H, as shown in Listing 9-1. You'll see that I've added two interface implementation classes—*CImplOleClientSite* and *CImplAdviseSink*—defined a few new symbols, and added a number of new variables and functions to *CTenant*.

TENANT.H

```
[Unmodified sections omitted from listing]

class __far CImpIOleClientSite : public IOleClientSite
    {
    protected:
        ULONG               m_cRef;
        class CTenant FAR * m_pTen;
        LPUNKNOWN           m_pUnkOuter;

    public:
        CImpIOleClientSite(class CTenant FAR *, LPUNKNOWN);
        ~CImpIOleClientSite(void);

        STDMETHODIMP QueryInterface(REFIID, LPLPVOID);
        STDMETHODIMP_(ULONG) AddRef(void);
        STDMETHODIMP_(ULONG) Release(void);
```

Listing 9-1. *(continued)*
Site-related definitions and classes for the container version of Patron.

Listing 9-1. *continued*

```
        STDMETHODIMP SaveObject(void);
        STDMETHODIMP GetMoniker(DWORD, DWORD, LPMONIKER FAR *);
        STDMETHODIMP GetContainer(LPOLECONTAINER FAR *);
        STDMETHODIMP ShowObject(void);
        STDMETHODIMP OnShowWindow(BOOL);
        STDMETHODIMP RequestNewObjectLayout(void);
    };

typedef CImpIOleClientSite FAR *LPIMPIOLECLIENTSITE;

class __far CImpIAdviseSink : public IAdviseSink
    {
    protected:
        ULONG               m_cRef;
        class CTenant FAR * m_pTen;
        LPUNKNOWN           m_pUnkOuter;

    public:
        CImpIAdviseSink(class CTenant FAR *, LPUNKNOWN);
        ~CImpIAdviseSink(void);

        STDMETHODIMP QueryInterface(REFIID, LPLPVOID);
        STDMETHODIMP_(ULONG) AddRef(void);
        STDMETHODIMP_(ULONG) Release(void);

        STDMETHODIMP_(void)  OnDataChange(LPFORMATETC, LPSTGMEDIUM);
        STDMETHODIMP_(void)  OnViewChange(DWORD, LONG);
        STDMETHODIMP_(void)  OnRename(LPMONIKER);
        STDMETHODIMP_(void)  OnSave(void);
        STDMETHODIMP_(void)  OnClose(void);
    };

typedef CImpIAdviseSink FAR *LPIMPIADVISESINK;

...

//Tenant types (not persistent, but determined at load time)
typedef enum
    {
    TENANTTYPE_NULL=0,
    TENANTTYPE_STATIC,
    TENANTTYPE_EMBEDDEDOBJECT,
    TENANTTYPE_EMBEDDEDFILE,
    TENANTTYPE_EMBEDDEDOBJECTFROMDATA
    } TENANTTYPE, FAR *LPTENANTTYPE;
```

(continued)

Listing 9-1. *continued*

```
//State flags
#define TENANTSTATE_DEFAULT      0x00000000
#define TENANTSTATE_SELECTED     0x00000001
#define TENANTSTATE_OPEN         0x00000002

class __far CTenant : public IUnknown
    {
    friend CImpIOleClientSite;
    friend CImpIAdviseSink;

    private:
        HWND            m_hWnd;         //Pages window
        DWORD           m_dwID;         //Persistent DWORD ID
        DWORD           m_cOpens;       //Count calls to FOpen

        BOOL            m_fInitialized; //Something here?
        LPUNKNOWN       m_pObj;         //The object here
        LPSTORAGE       m_pIStorage;    //Substorage for tenant

        FORMATETC       m_fe;           //Used to create the object
        DWORD           m_dwState;      //State flags
        RECTL           m_rcl;          //Space of this object

        class CPages FAR *m_pPG;        //Pages window

        TENANTTYPE      m_tType;            //Type identifier
        ULONG           m_cRef;             //We're an object now!
        LPOLEOBJECT     m_pIOleObject;      //IOleObject on m_pObj
        LPVIEWOBJECT    m_pIViewObject;     //IViewObject on m_pObj

        //Our interfaces
        LPIMPIOLECLIENTSITE m_pIOleClientSite;
        LPIMPIADVISESINK    m_pIAdviseSink;

    protected:
        BOOL    FObjectInitialize(LPUNKNOWN, LPFORMATETC, DWORD);
        HRESULT CreateStatic(LPDATAOBJECT, LPFORMATETC
            , LPUNKNOWN FAR *);
```

(continued)

Listing 9-1. *continued*

```
    public:
        CTenant(DWORD, HWND, CPages FAR *);
        ~CTenant(void);

        //Gotta have an IUnknown for delegation.
        STDMETHODIMP QueryInterface(REFIID, LPLPVOID);
        STDMETHODIMP_(ULONG) AddRef(void);
        STDMETHODIMP_(ULONG) Release(void);

        DWORD   GetID(void);
        UINT    GetStorageName(LPSTR);
        UINT    UCreate(TENANTTYPE, LPVOID, LPFORMATETC, LPPOINTL
                     , LPSIZEL, LPSTORAGE, LPPATRONOBJECT, DWORD);

        BOOL    FLoad(LPSTORAGE, LPFORMATETC, LPRECTL);
        BOOL    FOpen(LPSTORAGE);
        void    Close(BOOL);
        BOOL    Update(void);
        void    Destroy(LPSTORAGE);

        void    Select(BOOL);
        void    ShowAsOpen(BOOL);
        void    ShowYourself(void);
        void    AddVerbMenu(HMENU, UINT);
        void    CopyEmbeddedObject(LPDATAOBJECT, LPFORMATETC
                     , LPPOINTL);
        void    NotifyOfRename(LPSTR, LPVOID);

        BOOL    Activate(DWORD);
        void    Draw(HDC, DVTARGETDEVICE FAR *, HDC, int, int
                     , BOOL, BOOL);
        void    Repaint(void);
        void    Invalidate(void);

        void    ObjectGet(LPUNKNOWN FAR *);
        void    FormatEtcGet(LPFORMATETC, BOOL);
        void    SizeGet(LPSIZEL, BOOL);
        void    SizeSet(LPSIZEL, BOOL);
        void    RectGet(LPRECTL, BOOL);
        void    RectSet(LPRECTL, BOOL);
    };

typedef CTenant FAR *LPCTenant;

...
```

Tenants have a number of new variables that I find necessary for maintaining an embedded object in this site:

Variable	Description
m_tType	(TENANTTYPE) Describes what lives at this site, either a static object or an embedded object. This will expand in later chapters to include other types, such as linked objects.
m_cRef	(ULONG) Reference count for the tenant that implements an *IUnknown* interface and deletes itself when this reference count is zero.
m_pIOleObject	(LPOLEOBJECT) A pointer to the object that lives at this site. This is an interface you use rather than implement.
m_pIViewObject	(LPVIEWOBJECT) A secondary pointer object obtained from *QueryInterface* on *m_pIOleObject.* This is another interface you use rather than implement.
m_pIOleClientSite	(LPIMPIOLECLIENTSITE) A pointer to the tenant's implementation of *IOleClientSite.*
m_pIAdviseSink	(LPIMPIADVISESINK) A pointer to the tenant's implementation of *IAdviseSink.*

Patron initializes all these to zero or NULL in *CTenant::CTenant.* In *CTenant::FOpen,* Patron creates the two interface implementations, storing the pointers in *m_pIOleClientSite* and *m_pIAdviseSink.* In *CTenant::Close,* Patron releases all the object's interface pointers. Finally it uses *CTenant::~CTenant* to delete its own interface implementations.

Both interface implementations delegate all *IUnknown* calls to the tenant, which now inherits from and implements *IUknown.* The tenant's *QueryInterface* knows *IUknown, IOleClientSite,* and *IAdviseSink*:

```
STDMETHODIMP CTenant::QueryInterface(REFIID riid, LPLPVOID ppv)
    {
    *ppv=NULL;

    if (IsEqualIID(riid, IID_IUnknown))
        *ppv=(LPVOID)this;

    if (IsEqualIID(riid, IID_IOleClientSite))
        *ppv=(LPVOID)m_pIOleClientSite;

    if (IsEqualIID(riid, IID_IAdviseSink))
        *ppv=(LPVOID)m_pIAdviseSink;
```

(continued)

```
if (NULL!=*ppv)
    {
    ((LPUNKNOWN)*ppv)->AddRef();
    return NOERROR;
    }

return ResultFromScode(E_NOINTERFACE);
}
```

In addition, *AddRef* and *Release* now control the tenant's lifetime, where *Release* will call *delete this* when the reference count is zero. Because of this, any other piece of code that uses a tenant, primarily that code in PAGE.CPP that has pointers such as *pTenant*, now calls *pTenant->Release* instead of *delete pTenant*, as you can see in a function such as *CPage::Close*. (You can find the matching *AddRef* in *CPage::FTenantAdd*.)

There are also a number of new functions in *CTenant*: *FObjectInitialize*, *ShowAsOpen*, *ShowYourself*, *AddVerbMenu*, *CopyEmbeddedObject*, and *NotifyOfRename*, which are used to implement some of the additional container requirements we'll see in later sections. Some of these are called directly from the implementations of *IAdviseSink* and *IOleClientSite*.

Implement *IAdviseSink*

Container sites need an implementation of *IAdviseSink* solely for receiving *IAdviseSink::OnViewChange* notifications. All other member functions need only to be stubbed, as shown in Patron's implementation of *IAdviseSink* in Listing 9-2.

IADVSINK.CPP

```
/*
 * Implementation of the IAdviseSink interface for Patron's tenants.
 *
 * Copyright (c)1993 Microsoft Corporation, All Rights Reserved
 */

#include "patron.h"

CImpIAdviseSink::CImpIAdviseSink(LPCTenant pTenant
    , LPUNKNOWN pUnkOuter)
    {

    m_cRef=0;
```

Listing 9-2. *(continued)*
Patron's implementation of IAdviseSink *on container sites.*

Listing 9-2. *continued*

```
    m_pTen=pTenant;
    m_pUnkOuter=pUnkOuter;
    return;
    }

CImpIAdviseSink::~CImpIAdviseSink(void)
    {
    return;
    }

STDMETHODIMP CImpIAdviseSink::QueryInterface(REFIID riid
    , LPLPVOID ppv)
    {
    return m_pUnkOuter->QueryInterface(riid, ppv);
    }

STDMETHODIMP_(ULONG) CImpIAdviseSink::AddRef(void)
    {
    ++m_cRef;
    return m_pUnkOuter->AddRef();
    }

STDMETHODIMP_(ULONG) CImpIAdviseSink::Release(void)
    {
    --m_cRef;
    return m_pUnkOuter->Release();
    }

/*
 * IAdviseSink::OnDataChange
 *
 * Unused since we don't IDataObject::Advise.
 */

STDMETHODIMP_(void) CImpIAdviseSink::OnDataChange(LPFORMATETC pFEIn
    , LPSTGMEDIUM pSTM)
    {
    return;
    }

/*
 * CImpIAdviseSink::OnViewChange
 *
```

(continued)

Listing 9-2. *continued*

```
 * Purpose:
 *  Notifes the advise sink that presentation data changed in the data
 *  object to which we're connected providing the right time to update
 *  displays using such presentations.
 *
 * Parameters:
 *  dwAspect        DWORD indicating which aspect has changed.
 *  lindex          LONG indicating the piece that changed.
 */

STDMETHODIMP_(void) CImpIAdviseSink::OnViewChange(DWORD dwAspect
    , LONG lindex)
    {
    //Repaint only if this is the right aspect
    if (dwAspect==m_pTen->m_fe.dwAspect)
        m_pTen->Repaint();

    m_pTen->m_pPG->m_fDirty=TRUE;
    return;
    }

STDMETHODIMP_(void) CImpIAdviseSink::OnRename(LPMONIKER pmk)
    {
    return;
    }

STDMETHODIMP_(void) CImpIAdviseSink::OnSave(void)
    {
    return;
    }

STDMETHODIMP_(void) CImpIAdviseSink::OnClose(void)
    {
    return;
    }
```

Your implementation of *OnViewChange* needs only to repaint your site and to set your document's dirty flag, in whatever way you do that. *OnViewChange* is called whenever something changes in a *running* object—that is, whenever the end user generally modifies the object in some way, by adding more graphics, typing more text, and so on. When you repaint the site, you'll generate a call to *IViewObject::Draw* (via *OleDraw*), which will cause in-process servers or handlers to redraw the object or will cause the default handler to ask the running local server for a rendering, which it can then draw in your site. By means of this mechanism, any change made to the object in the server is reflected in your site. Note that an OLE 1 server does not send notifications on every modification, so in this case you won't see updates as frequently.

You might wonder why we don't use *OnDataChange* to detect changes instead of having this extra *OnViewChange*. Because a container is interested in displaying the object's presentation, it really wants to know when that *presentation* changes. It might be true that a data change in the object does not necessarily precipitate such a view change. The converse is also true: A view change might not necessarily mean a data change. *OnDataChange* is useful only when the container knows a little more about the object and its data formats and is stepping a little outside the basic notion of embedded objects, and the container knows nothing about the object. For example, a chart server can act like a normal object server when used with any container, but when it is used with the same vendor's spreadsheet, the end user might have more ways to link together data in the spreadsheet with the presentation in the chart. In that sense, the two modules are talking on a higher level than is specified in compound documents alone.

All of the other member functions—*OnClose*, *OnRename*, and *OnSave*—are important for the default handler and its management of linked objects. Remember that the handler always sits between the container and a *LocalServer*, so all notifications from that server pass through the handler on their way to the container, meaning that the handler itself might take action on such notifications. Note that an *InProcServer* does not generally service linked objects, so there is always a handler in the linked case. Again, that's a topic for a later chapter.

Implement *IOleClientSite*

The container implements the *IOleClientSite* interface so that an object can inform the container of specific events or ask the container to perform specific operations. The *IOleClientSite* member functions are shown in the following table:

IOleClientSite Member	Description
SaveObject	Requests that the container call *OleSave* to ensure that the object's data is saved to its *IStorage*. This is commonly called immediately before a server shuts down.
GetMoniker	Requests a container-defined moniker that references the object in this site. (See Chapters 12 and 13.)

(continued)

IOleClientSite Member	Description
GetContainer	Requests an *IOleContainer* interface pointer through which the object can see what else is in the container's document. This interface is implemented as part of a document, not as part of a site. (See Chapter 13.)
ShowObject	Asks the container to ensure that the object in this site is visible within the container's window.
OnShowWindow	Informs the container that the object in the server either is becoming visible in another window, so that the user can edit it, or is being hidden. On receiving this function, the container either draws hatching on the site or removes hatching from the site.
RequestNewObjectLayout	Asks the container to make more space for the object in the container's document. (Unsupported in OLE 2.)

Of these six member functions (besides *IUnknown,* of course), you will need to implement only three to support embeddings: *SaveObject, ShowObject,* and *OnShowWindow.* In fact, even *SaveObject* is the only functionally essential member; the other two are used strictly to implement user interface and do not interfere with the embedding aspects. As for the other three, we'll need to implement *GetMoniker* and *GetContainer* to support linking in Chapters 12 and 13. We'll never have to implement *RequestNewObjectLayout* until OLE itself is updated because OLE 2 does not support any use of this function. With that, let's look at the specific requirements of each of the three necessary functions in Patron's implementation, as shown in Listing 9-3. A template implementation of *IOleClientSite* can be found in INTERFAC\ICLISITE.CPP for your use.

ICLISITE.CPP

```
/*
 * Implementation of the IOleClientSite interface for
 * Patron's tenants.
 *
 * Copyright (c)1993 Microsoft Corporation, All Rights Reserved
 */

#include "patron.h"
```

Listing 9-3.
Patron's implementation of IOleClientSite.

(continued)

Listing 9-3. *continued*

```
CImpIOleClientSite::CImpIOleClientSite(LPCTenant pTenant
    , LPUNKNOWN pUnkOuter)
    {
    m_cRef=0;
    m_pTen=pTenant;
    m_pUnkOuter=pUnkOuter;
    return;
    }

CImpIOleClientSite::~CImpIOleClientSite(void)
    {
    return;
    }

STDMETHODIMP CImpIOleClientSite::QueryInterface(REFIID riid
    , LPLPVOID ppv)
    {
    return m_pUnkOuter->QueryInterface(riid, ppv);
    }

STDMETHODIMP_(ULONG) CImpIOleClientSite::AddRef(void)
    {
    ++m_cRef;
    return m_pUnkOuter->AddRef();
    }

STDMETHODIMP_(ULONG) CImpIOleClientSite::Release(void)
    {
    --m_cRef;
    return m_pUnkOuter->Release();
    }
/*
 * CImpIOleClientSite::SaveObject
 *
 * Purpose:
 *  Requests that the container call OleSave for the object that
 *  lives here. Typically this happens on server shutdown.
 */

STDMETHODIMP CImpIOleClientSite::SaveObject(void)
    {
    //Since we're set up with the tenant to save, this is trivial.

    m_pTen->Update();
    return NOERROR;
    }
```

(continued)

Listing 9-3. *continued*

```
STDMETHODIMP CImpIOleClientSite::GetMoniker(DWORD dwAssign
    , DWORD dwWhich, LPMONIKER FAR *ppmk)
    {
    *ppmk=NULL;
    return ResultFromScode(E_NOTIMPL);
    }

STDMETHODIMP CImpIOleClientSite::GetContainer(LPOLECONTAINER FAR
    *ppContainer)
    {
    *ppContainer=NULL;
    return ResultFromScode(E_NOTIMPL);
    }

/*
 * CImpIOleClientSite::ShowObject
 *
 * Purpose:
 *  Tells the container to bring the object fully into view as much
 *  as possible, that is, scroll the document.
 */

STDMETHODIMP CImpIOleClientSite::ShowObject(void)
    {
    m_pTen->ShowYourself();
    return NOERROR;
    }

/*
 * CImpIOleClientSite::OnShowWindow
 *
 * Purpose:
 *  Informs the container if the object is showing itself or
 *  hiding itself. This is done only in the opening mode and allows
 *  the container to know when to shade or unshade the object.
 *
 * Parameters:
 *  fShow           BOOL indicating that the object is being shown
 *                  (TRUE) or hidden (FALSE).
 */

STDMETHODIMP CImpIOleClientSite::OnShowWindow(BOOL fShow)
    {
    //All we have to do is tell the tenant of the open state change.
    m_pTen->ShowAsOpen(fShow);
```

(continued)

Listing 9-3. *continued*

```
    return NOERROR;
    }

STDMETHODIMP CImpIOleClientSite::RequestNewObjectLayout(void)
    {
    return ResultFromScode(E_NOTIMPL);
    }
```

As you can see from the listing, this implementation of *IOleClientSite* delegates just about everything to some of the functions added in *CTenant.* We'll look at *OnShowWindow* in the next section, but let's examine *SaveObject* and *ShowObject* right away.

SaveObject simply tells the container to save the object in this site. In short, that means the following steps:

1. Call *QueryInterface* on the object, asking for *IPersistStorage.*
2. Call *OleSave,* passing the *IPersistStorage* and the *IStorage* in which to save the object.
3. Call *IPersistStorage::SaveCompleted.*
4. Call *IPersistStorage::Release.*

These are the four steps taken in Patron's function *CTenant::Update,* which we've been using since Chapter 7 and which requires no modification here:

```
BOOL CTenant::Update(void)
    {
    LPPERSISTSTORAGE    pIPS;

    if (NULL!=m_pIStorage)
        {
        m_pObj->QueryInterface(IID_IPersistStorage
            , (LPLPVOID)&pIPS);
        OleSave(pIPS, m_pIStorage, TRUE);
        pIPS->SaveCompleted(NULL);
        pIPS->Release();

        m_pIStorage->Commit(STGC_ONLYIFCURRENT);
        }

    return FALSE;
    }
```

ShowObject tells the container to bring the object (that is, the site) into view if at all possible. An object calls this function when it's opened for editing in a separate window so that the object in the container's site is visible alongside the object in the server's editing window. This is very nice for end users to see both their editing session and the context around that object in the container.[7] Of course, because *ShowObject* has to do only with user interface, it's not necessary for the actual function of embedding. If it's too much trouble or not applicable to your container, feel free to ignore it altogether.

Implementing *ShowObject* means one thing: Make the object visible. How you actually do that will be specific to the nature of your application, document, page, and site, of course. In Patron, *ShowObject* calls *CTenant::ShowYourself*:

```
void CTenant::ShowYourself(void)
    {
    RECTL           rcl;
    RECT            rc;
    POINT           pt1, pt2;

    //Scrolling deals in device units; get our rectangle in those.
    RectGet(&rcl, TRUE);

    //Get the window rectangle offset for the current scroll pos.
    GetClientRect(m_hWnd, &rc);
    OffsetRect(&rc, m_pPG->m_xPos, m_pPG->m_yPos);

    //Check if the object is already visible. (macro in bookguid.h)
    SETPOINT(pt1, (int)rcl.left,  (int)rcl.top);
    SETPOINT(pt2, (int)rcl.right, (int)rcl.bottom);

    if (PtInRect(&rc, pt1) && PtInRect(&rc, pt2))
        return;

    //Check if the upper left is within the upper left quadrant
    if (((int)rcl.left > rc.left
        && (int)rcl.left < ((rc.right+rc.left)/2))
        && ((int)rcl.top > rc.top
        && (int)rcl.top < ((rc.bottom+rc.top)/2)))
        return;

    //These are macros in INC\BOOK1632.H
    SendScrollPosition(m_hWnd, WM_HSCROLL, rcl.left-8);
    SendScrollPosition(m_hWnd, WM_VSCROLL, rcl.top-8);
    return;
    }
```

7. Of course, full in-place activation is a much stronger way to express this same feature, but that takes a lot more work. This is a small courtesy in comparison, and one that is much easier to provide.

A good rule of thumb here is to avoid scrolling if at all possible, so *ShowYourself* first checks to see whether the site's rectangle (which is the same as the object's in the container) is already visible—that is, both upper left and lower right corners are already visible in the page window. If so, nothing needs to happen, and we can exit the routine. If this first check fails, either the site is not visible at all or the site is too big to be entirely shown in the window. So, if the upper left corner of the site is in the upper left quadrant of the window, it must be true that the site is not completely visible but that enough is visible that we would still want to avoid scrolling. If this second check fails, *ShowYourself* capitulates and scrolls the window so that the upper left corner of the site is visible just below the upper left corner of the window. The *SendScrollPosition* macros (defined in INC\BOOK1632.H) send WM_...SCROLL messages with SB_THUMBPOSITION messages, which are processed in *PagesWndProc* of PAGEWIN.CPP.

After coding both *IAdviseSink* and *IOleClientSite* interfaces and the rest of your site objects, you can compile and ensure that the interfaces are created and destroyed as necessary. Because you can't yet create an object that calls these interface functions, you might want to write some test code that would call each interface function so that you can test that *IAdviseSink::OnViewChange* repaints and sets a dirty flag, that *IOleClientSite::SaveObject* calls *OleSave*, that *IOleClientSite::ShowObject* actually scrolls the site into view, and that any other conditions exist that might be meaningful. After one more step to implement *IOleClientSite::OnShowWindow*, we're ready to put an object in this site and have these functions called for real.

Implement Site Shading

The user interface specifications for an OLE 2 application ask that when an object is "open"—generally, in its running state and visible in a server window—the container site be shaded with a hatch pattern, as shown in Figure 9-13. Conveniently, we have *IOleClientSite::OnShowWindow* to tell us when to

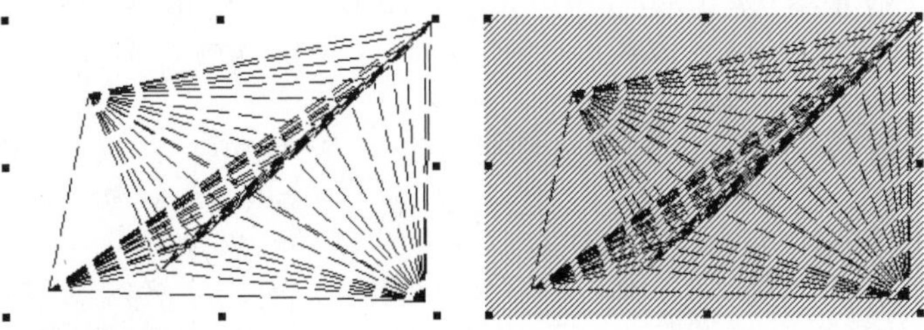

Figure 9-13.
A typical appearance of a site with a loaded object and shaded with an open object. The sizing handles are optional.

shade and unshade the site: The functions-only parameter—a BOOL *fShow*—says the object is now open (TRUE) or not open (FALSE).

Patron's implementation of *OnShowWindow* calls *CTenant::ShowAsOpen*, passing *fShow* as the only parameter:

```
void CTenant::ShowAsOpen(BOOL fOpen)
    {
    BOOL            fWasOpen;
    DWORD           dwState;
    RECT            rc;
    HDC             hDC;

    fWasOpen=(BOOL)(TENANTSTATE_OPEN & m_dwState);

    dwState=m_dwState & ~TENANTSTATE_OPEN;
    m_dwState=dwState | ((fOpen) ? TENANTSTATE_OPEN : 0);

    //If this was not open, then just hatch, otherwise repaint.
    if (!fWasOpen && fOpen)
        {
        RECTFROMRECTL(rc, m_rcl);
        RectConvertMappings(&rc, NULL, TRUE);
        OffsetRect(&rc, -(int)m_pPG->m_xPos, -(int)m_pPG->m_yPos);

        hDC=GetDC(m_hWnd);
        OleUIDrawShading(&rc, hDC, OLEUI_SHADE_FULLRECT, 0);
        ReleaseDC(m_hWnd, hDC);
        }

    if (fWasOpen && !fOpen)
        Repaint();

    return;
    }
```

This function first checks to see whether any state change has actually occurred—that is, if the object is already open and the application is being asked to show it as open again, there's nothing to do, nor is there when the object is not open and is told it's not open. If the states differ, there are two possible courses of action.

First, if the change is from loaded to open (running), we need to draw the hatch pattern across the site rectangle. The OLE2UI library provides a convenient function for hatching, *OleUIDrawShading*, which takes the rectangle to shade, the *hDC* on which to draw, some flags from OLEUI_SHADE_... values, and a width (the zero in the preceding code). There are three possible (and exclusive) flags you can pass that affect how the function shades in or around the rectangle:

Flag	Description
	OLEUI_SHADE_FULLRECT: Shades the entire rectangle. The width parameter is ignored.
	OLEUI_SHADE_BORDERIN: Shades the width inside the border of the rectangle.
	OLEUI_SHADE_BORDEROUT: Shades the width outside the border of the rectangle.

The OLEUI_SHADE_BORDER... flags are used for in-place activation and are not used here. Also note that OLE2UI.H defines another flag, OLEUI_SHADE_USEINVERSE, which is a no-op: *OleUIDrawShading* doesn't do anything with it. If it did, it might draw a hatch pattern using an XOR ROP code. Instead, *OleUIDrawShading* always draws the hatch pattern in black, using *PatBlt* with a hatch pattern brush and the ROP *0x00A000C9*, which performs the logical AND between the black pattern and whatever is on *hDC*—that is, it draws a black hatch pattern regardless of what's underneath.

Because this hatching is destructive, going from an open state into a loaded state requires that we repaint the entire object to remove the hatching. Fortunately for Patron, *CTenant::Repaint* does exactly that. You will generally need to do the same or implement your own version of *OleUIShadeBorder* that uses the inverse process. (Remember that you have the code for this function in the OLE 2 SDK.)

Invoke the Insert Object Dialog Box

We've finally arrived at the point at which all the necessary container pieces are in place and we can create a new object to occupy a site. In other words, we have some sort of object that we can call a site and that has *IOleClientSite* and *IAdviseSink* interfaces, and we have a storage object that we can give to the object in this site. What's left is to somehow obtain the CLSID of an embeddable object and call the *OleCreate* function to obtain our first pointer to that new object. The way in which you determine the CLSID is up to you, depending on your application and its use. For most cases, however, the standard Microsoft-recommended way is to invoke the Insert Object dialog box. This dialog box allows the user to create a new embedded object based on a CLSID when the user has selected Create New, as shown in Figure 9-14, or to create an embedded object that contains a copy of a file[8] when the user has selected Create From File, as shown in Figure 9-15. In Chapter 12, we'll also be able to create a link to a file using this same dialog. The OLE2UI library provides an implementation of this dialog box through the *OleUIInsertObject* function, which we'll make use of here.

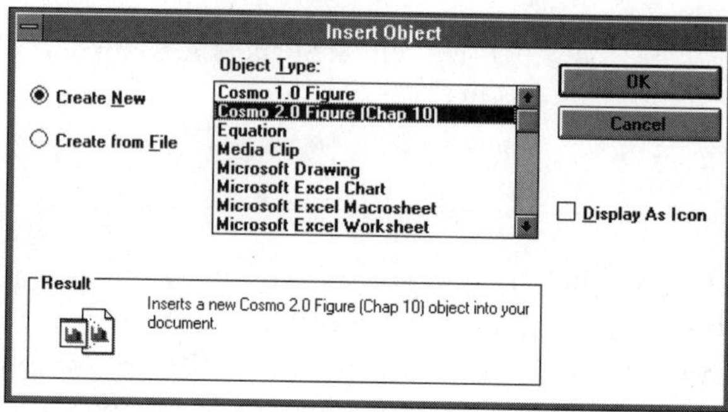

Figure 9-14.
The Insert Object dialog box, with Create New selected.

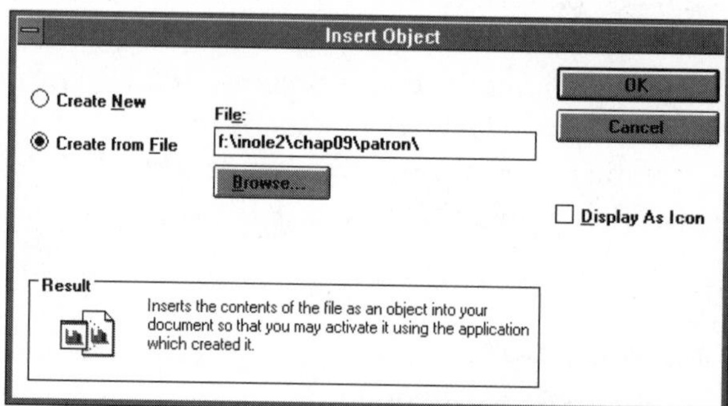

Figure 9-15.
The Insert Object dialog box, with Create From File selected.

8. In OLE 1, this capability was provided by the Packager server. Packager's functions are now incorporated into OLE 2 itself.

The list of names in the list box shown in Figure 9-14 are enumerated from the Registration Database for any entry that appears as follows:

```
\
<ProgID> = <User-readable name of this type of object>
    CLSID = {xxxxxxxx-xxxx-xxxx-xxxx-xxxxxxxxxxxx}
    Insertable
```

Any key that has the *Insertable* subkey has its user-readable name in the list box. When the user selects that name and presses OK, the container application receives the CLSID for this entry from the Registration Database. The container can instruct the dialog box to verify that an *InProcServer* or a *LocalServer* exists for that CLSID, which takes considerably more time to invoke the dialog box.

Dealing with the Insert Object dialog box will require small modifications at almost every level of your container application:

1. Add a menu item on the Edit menu that has the string *Insert Object...* or, if you have an Insert menu already, add an item with the string *Object....* This item should be enabled whenever you have an open document.
2. When the user selects the Insert Object command, invoke the dialog box to retrieve the CLSID (for Create New) or the filename (for Create From File).
3. Call *OleCreate* (for Create New) or *OleCreateFromFile* (for Create From File), and store the returned pointer with your site object.
4. Initialize the object by calling a number of miscellaneous functions and interface members on the object.
5. If you do not support iconic aspects (see the last section in this chapter), you can tell the dialog box to remove the Display As Icon check box with OLE 2.01 or later. The Insert Object dialog box in the first release of OLE 2.0 did not have this feature, so if you have that release, you must change the dialog box template or hook the dialog box procedure to disable the feature.

Adding the menu item should not be much trouble; basically, add a *#define* and a MENUITEM in your RC file (remember the ellipsis on *Insert Object...*):

```
//In Patron's RESOURCE.H
#define IDM_EDITINSERTOBJECT        (IDM_CUSTOMEDITMIN+2)

//In PATRON.RC
MENUITEM "&Insert Object...",        IDM_EDITINSERTOBJECT
```

That was the simple step. The others are more involved.

Call *OleUIInsertObject*

When Patron's frame window procedure detects a WM_COMMAND message with IDM_EDITINSERTOBJECT, it calls the active document's *FInsertObject* function, which I added new to this chapter's version of Patron:

```
BOOL CPatronDoc::FInsertObject(HWND hWndFrame)
    {
    OLEUIINSERTOBJECT   io;
    DWORD               dwData=0;
    char                szFile[CCHPATHMAX];
    UINT                uTemp;
    BOOL                fRet=FALSE;

    if (NULL==m_pPG)
        return FALSE;

    _fmemset(&io, 0, sizeof(io));

    io.cbStruct=sizeof(io);
    io.hWndOwner=hWndFrame;

    szFile[0]=0;
    io.lpszFile=szFile;
    io.cchFile=sizeof(szFile);

    io.dwFlags=IOF_SELECTCREATENEW | IOF_DISABLELINK;

    uTemp=OleUIInsertObject(&io);

    if (OLEUI_OK==uTemp)
        {
        TENANTTYPE      tType;

        LPVOID          pv;
        FORMATETC       fe;

        SETDefFormatEtc(fe, 0, TYMED_NULL);

        if (io.dwFlags & IOF_SELECTCREATENEW)
            {
            tType=TENANTTYPE_EMBEDDEDOBJECT;
            pv=(LPVOID)&io.clsid;
            }
        else
            {
            tType=TENANTTYPE_EMBEDDEDFILE;
            pv=(LPVOID)szFile;
            }
```

```
        if ((io.dwFlags & IOF_CHECKDISPLAYASICON)
            && NULL!=io.hMetaPict)
            {
            fe.dwAspect=DVASPECT_ICON;
            dwData=(DWORD)(UINT)io.hMetaPict;
            }

        fRet=m_pPG->TenantCreate(tType, pv, &fe, NULL, dwData);

        //Free this regardless of what we do with it.
        if (NULL!=io.hMetaPict)
            OleUIMetafilePictIconFree(io.hMetaPict);

        if (fRet)
            {
            //Disable Printer Setup once we've created a tenant.
            m_fPrintSetup=FALSE;
            FDirtySet(TRUE);
            }
        }

    return fRet;
    }
```

To call *OleUIInsertObject*, we must first initialize an OLEUIINSERTOBJECT structure. This structure contains the usual fields for the size of the structure (*cbStruct*) and the parent window (*hWndOwner*) as well as others for hooking and template customization that are common to all the dialog boxes in the library. For our purposes, we need to fill in a few other Insert-Object-specific fields: *lpszFile* points to a buffer to receive a filename in the Create From File case, *cchFile* is the length of the *lpszFile* buffer, and *dwFlags* describes various options for this dialog box. In our case, we use the IOF_CREATENEW flag to select the Create New option button initially (the standard) and the IOF_DISABLELINK flag, which removes a Link check box that would otherwise appear when the Create From File option button is selected. (We'll remove this flag later, of course.) We can then call *OleUIInsertObject* and let the dialog box do what dialog boxes do.

The return value from *OleUIInsertObject* indicates whether the user pressed OK or Cancel. The Cancel case is uninteresting, so let's look at the return of OLEUI_OK. When this happens, *dwFlags* in the OLEUIINSERTOBJECT structure will first contain the identity of the option button that was selected on closing the dialog box: IOF_CREATENEW or IOF_CREATEFROMFILE. In Patron, we use this identity to determine the type of object to create and what data is necessary for a tenant to create the object. For Create New, the type is a straight embedded object, and we want to use the selected

CLSID that is in the *clsid* field in the structure; for Create From File, the type is an embedded object from a file, and we want to use the filename from the dialog box (which was written to *lpszFile*). The code that looks at IOF_DISPLAYASICON has to do with iconic aspects of the object, a topic we'll discuss at the end of this chapter, so we'll ignore it for now.

After Patron determines what type of object to create, it issues the order to create the object by calling *CPages::TenantCreate*, which passes through to *CPage::TenantCreate*, which in turn creates a new tenant and tells the tenant to create the object, as we'll see in a moment.

Note that there may be a memory handle in the *hMetaPict* field of the structure on return from *OleUIInsertObject*, and it is your responsibility to clean up this field by calling *OleUIMetafilePictIconFree*, as shown earlier. Regardless of what else happens, be sure you do this to avoid memory leaks.

Call *OleCreate* or *OleCreateFromFile*

Patron's object creation involves both creating a tenant in *CPage::TenantCreate* and creating the object in *CTenant::UCreate*. The *CPage* code is responsible for placing the tenant on the page and ensuring that it's repainted and selected properly. This code has not changed appreciably from what we first wrote in Chapter 7. Our main focus is on the changes to *CTenant::UCreate*:

```
UINT CTenant::UCreate(TENANTTYPE tType, LPVOID pvType
    , LPFORMATETC pFE, LPPOINTL pptl, LPSIZEL pszl
    , LPSTORAGE pIStorage, LPPATRONOBJECT ppo, DWORD dwData)
    {
    HRESULT             hr;
    LPUNKNOWN           pObj;
    UINT                uRet=UCREATE_GRAPHICONLY;

    [Unmodified code to validate params and obtain placement data from ppo]

    //Now create an object based specifically on the type.
    switch (tType)
        {
        case TENANTTYPE_NULL:
            break;

        case TENANTTYPE_STATIC:
            hr=CreateStatic((LPDATAOBJECT)pvType, pFE, &pObj);
            break;

        case TENANTTYPE_EMBEDDEDOBJECT:
            hr=OleCreate(*((LPCLSID)pvType), IID_IUnknown
```

```
            , OLERENDER_DRAW, NULL, NULL, m_pIStorage
            , (LPLPVOID)&pObj);
        break;

    case TENANTTYPE_EMBEDDEDFILE:
        hr=OleCreateFromFile(CLSID_NULL, (LPSTR)pvType
            , IID_IUnknown, OLERENDER_DRAW, NULL, NULL
            , m_pIStorage, (LPLPVOID)&pObj);
        break;

    case TENANTTYPE_EMBEDDEDOBJECTFROMDATA:
        hr=OleCreateFromData((LPDATAOBJECT)pvType, IID_IUnknown
            , OLERENDER_DRAW, NULL, NULL, m_pIStorage
            , (LPLPVOID)&pObj);
        break;

    default:
        break;
    }

//If creation didn't work, get rid of the element FOpen created.
if (FAILED(hr))
    {
    Destroy(pIStorage);
    return UCREATE_FAILED;
    }

FObjectInitialize(pObj, pFE, dwData);

//We depend here on m_pIOleObject having been initialized.
if ((0==pszl->cx && 0==pszl->cy))
    {
    SIZEL   szl;

    //Try to get the real size of the object, default to 2"*2"
    SETSIZEL((*pszl), 2*LOMETRIC_PER_INCH, 2*LOMETRIC_PER_INCH);

    if (SUCCEEDED(m_pIOleObject->GetExtent(pFE->dwAspect, &szl)))
        {
        //Convert HIMETRIC to our LOMETRIC mapping
        if (0!=szl.cx && 0!=szl.cy)
            SETSIZEL((*pszl), szl.cx/10, szl.cy/10);
        }
    }

return uRet;
}
```

There are three new ways a tenant can now create an object: *OleCreate*, *OleCreateFromFile*, and *OleCreateFromData*. The first, *OleCreate*, creates a new embedded object from a CLSID. We pass to it the CLSID from the Insert Object dialog box, the interface we want (*IUnknown*), a render option (OLERENDER_DRAW), a pointer to a FORMATETC (NULL in this case because we're using OLERENDER_DRAW), a pointer to an *IOleClientSite* interface (NULL because we'll give it to the object later), the storage for this object (*m_pIStorage*), and the address in which to store the interface pointer that we requested.

The second way to create an object, *OleCreateFromFile*, creates a new embedded Packager-type object from the contents of a file and takes all the same parameters except that the CLSID is now CLSID_NULL and the additional filename.

In either case, what we get back is the first interface pointer to this new object to whatever interface we asked for, in this case *IUnknown*. The third way to create an object, *OleCreateFromData*, we'll see later.

If *OleCreate*... worked, Patron continues by initializing the object and obtaining the initial size. Because the initialization sequence involves a number of functions and because it's the same as when we load an object from a file later on, I've centralized the code in *CTenant::FObjectInitialize*. I strongly recommend that you do the same.

Initialize the Object

After creating (or loading) an object, we'll perform the following initialization steps:

1. Save the type of the object: static or embedded. We will use this later to determine whether we can activate the object.
2. Call *IViewObject::SetAdvise* to establish a connection between the object and our *IAdviseSink::OnViewChange* for the aspect of the object we display. Most often the aspect is DVASPECT_CONTENT, but later in this chapter we'll enable our container to deal with DVASPECT_ICON as well.
3. Pass the *IOleClientSite* pointer to the object by calling *IOleObject::SetClientSite*. This is the only way in which the object knows its site. We could also pass the *IOleClientSite* pointer to an *OleCreate*... function, but we also need to call *SetClientSite* when loading an object with *OleLoad*, and *OleLoad* does not take such a parameter. So, to keep it all central (as well as explicit), we do it here.

4. Call *IOleObject::Advise* with a pointer to our *IAdviseSink* so that the object can inform the handler of events such as *OnClose* and *OnSave*. This is necessary for proper operation of the handler, but it really doesn't do much for our application.

5. Call the weird function *OleSetContainedObject* in OLE2.DLL, which basically makes OLE 2 work correctly with your container. Failure to call this function will generally leave a few extra reference counts on your site object through the *IOleClientSite* interface. Don't worry. Be happy. Just do it.

6. Provide the object with strings for its user interface requirements by sending your application and document names to *IOleObject::SetHostNames*. Patron does this through *CTenant::NotifyOfRename*, which passes "Patron 2.0" (or "Untitled") as the application name and the short eight-character filename and the three-character extension of the document. The object will generally use the document name in window titles and on menus when it opens editing windows, as we'll see in Chapter 10.

You can see these steps in Patron's *CTenant::FObjectInitialize*:

```
BOOL CTenant::FObjectInitialize(LPUNKNOWN pObj, LPFORMATETC pFE
    , DWORD dwData)
    {
    HRESULT         hr;
    LPPERSIST       pIPersist=NULL;
    DWORD           dw;
    LPCDocument     pDoc;
    char            szFile[CCHPATHMAX];

    if (NULL==pObj || NULL==pFE)
        return FALSE;

    m_pObj=pObj;
    m_fe=*pFE;
    m_dwState=TENANTSTATE_DEFAULT;

    /*
     * Determine the type: Static or Embedded. If Static,
     * this will have CLSID_FreeMetafile or CLSID_FreeDib.
     * Otherwise it's Embedded. Later we'll add a case for links.
     */
    m_tType=TENANTTYPE_EMBEDDEDOBJECT;
```

(continued)

```
if (SUCCEEDED(pObj->QueryInterface(IID_IPersist
    , (LPLPVOID)&pIPersist)))
    {
    CLSID   clsid;

    pIPersist->GetClassID(&clsid);

    if (IsEqualCLSID(clsid, CLSID_FreeMetafile)
        || IsEqualCLSID(clsid, CLSID_FreeDib))
        m_tType=TENANTTYPE_STATIC;

    pIPersist->Release();
    }

m_pIViewObject=NULL;
hr=pObj->QueryInterface(IID_IViewObject
    , (LPLPVOID)&m_pIViewObject);

if (FAILED(hr))
    return FALSE;

m_pIViewObject->SetAdvise(pFE->dwAspect, 0, m_pIAdviseSink);

//We need an IOleObject most of the time, so get one here.
m_pIOleObject=NULL;
pObj->QueryInterface(IID_IOleObject
    , (LPLPVOID)&m_pIOleObject);

//Follow up object creation with advises and so forth.
if (FAILED(hr))
    return FALSE;

/*
 * We could pass m_pIOleClientSite in an OleCreate... call, but
 * because this function could be called after OleLoad, we still
 * need to do this here, so it's always done here...
 */
m_pIOleObject->SetClientSite(m_pIOleClientSite);
m_pIOleObject->Advise(m_pIAdviseSink, &dw);

OleSetContainedObject((LPUNKNOWN)m_pIOleObject, TRUE);

/*
 * For IOleObject::SetHostNames we need the application name
 * and the document name (which is passed in the object
 * parameter). The design of Patron doesn't give us nice
 * structured access to the name of the document we're in, so
```

```
     * I grab the parent of the Pages window (the document) and
     * send it DOCM_PDOCUMENT which returns us the pointer.
     * Roundabout, but it works.
     */

    pDoc=(LPCDocument)SendMessage(GetParent(m_hWnd), DOCM_PDOCUMENT
        , 0, 0L);

    if (NULL!=pDoc)
        pDoc->FilenameGet(szFile, CCHPATHMAX);
    else
        szFile[0]=0;

    NotifyOfRename(szFile);

    if ((DVASPECT_ICON & pFE->dwAspect) && NULL!=dwData)
        {
        DWORD       dw=DVASPECT_CONTENT;
        BOOL        fUpdate;

        OleStdSwitchDisplayAspect(m_pIOleObject, &dw, DVASPECT_ICON
            , (HGLOBAL)(UINT)dwData, TRUE, FALSE, NULL, &fUpdate);
        }

    return TRUE;
    }
```

Some of this is included in an OLE2UI function called *OleStdSetupAdvises,* which may or may not be useful to your application. As for the preceding Patron code, the stuff at the end that deals with DVASPECT_ICON is, again, a subject for the end of this chapter. In addition to the initialization steps mentioned earlier, this function also initializes *CTenant*'s *m_pIOleObject* and *m_pIViewObject* fields using *QueryInterface.* I hold onto these interface pointers for the lifetime of the object simply because we need them in a variety of places and we can avoid excess *QueryInterface* calls. *IPersistStorage* is not included here because I use it only once, in *CTenant::Update.*

Finally, when you create a new embedded object, there are two more steps to follow that I did not include in the preceding list because you execute them only after using the Insert Object dialog box and not after loading an object or creating one with data from the clipboard (after which Patron calls *CTenant::FObjectInitialize*):

1. Invoke *IOleObject::DoVerb* with OLEIVERB_SHOW. (See the later section "Activate Objects and Add the Object Menu.")
2. Save the object by using *OleSave* and *IPersistStorage::SaveCompleted.*

Both of these are called from *CPage::TenantCreate* for a new object from *OleCreate* or *OleCreateFromFile.* Calling *IOleObject::DoVerb* (which happens in *CTenant::Activate*) with OLEIVERB_SHOW instructs the object to show itself in a window, ready for editing. Saving the object immediately afterward saves the initial editing state of the object when it's open. This is most important for working well with OLE 1 servers, which might not update themselves before closing.

Here I would suggest that you compile your code, work out those errors, and verify that objects are, in fact, created and that all the initialization flows smoothly. However, things won't look like much until we can display the objects.

Draw and Print Objects

Showing some sort of presentation for the object is, of course, one of the most important aspects of a container's user interface. This really boils down to calling *OleDraw* or *IViewObject::Draw* whenever you repaint the site, exactly as Patron has been doing in *CTenant::Draw.* Remember that if the object is still open when you repaint, you need to be sure that you draw the shading as described earlier. This is why Patron's tenants have a state flag to mark them as open: so that repaints will produce the proper results.

Creating an Object Based on a Selection: *IOleObject::InitFromData*

For certain compound document objects (particularly ones you write yourself or those written to work more closely with your container), you might elect, after calling *OleCreate,* to initialize the object based on a selection of other data in your container. For example, in a spreadsheet application acting as a container, the user can select a range of cells and create a new chart object. The spreadsheet can package the current selection in an *IDataObject* and pass that to the newly created chart's *IOleObject::InitFromData,* along with an *fCreation* flag set to TRUE. The chart can then display the data immediately, without any further user action.

In containers such as word processors and spreadsheets that have their own data, I strongly encourage you to use this function and to document the formats you send in order to enable third-party add-on packages that are designed specifically to add value to your application.

Printing is no different, although you do not generally shade the object and you generally want to pass a non-NULL target device to the drawing functions to give the objects a chance to render themselves specifically for that device. Most custom handlers, for example, exist only to optimize an object's output for specific printers. It's important that you let them do their job.

It's a good idea here to quickly test that objects in your sites repaint appropriately when you receive notifications such as *IAdviseSink::OnViewChange*. When they do, you can see your sites being updated as changes are made in the object's server.

Activate Objects and Add the Object Verb Menu

Creating new objects and displaying or printing them give us nothing more than a static bitmap or metafile. One of the most important features of compound documents under OLE is that you can activate the object—that is, you can ask it to execute one of its verbs and thus perform some action, such as playing a sound or displaying its data for editing. This ability for activation is the only thing that separates an embedded or linked object from a static one. But in some way or another, you have to allow the end user to select the actions available for that object, which vary from object to object. For this reason, the OLE 2 user interface defines two methods to allow end users to invoke verbs.

Resizing Objects: *IOleObject::SetExtent*, and *IOleObject::GetExtent*

In the course of managing objects, your container might need to resize the site in which the object lives, as Patron does. In such a situation, you might want to call *IOleObject::SetExtent* to let it know the exact size of its display. The object can then optimize its output for that size. On the other hand, the container might not want to be ultimately responsible for the object's size, in which case it can call *IOleObject::GetExtent* to ask the object how large it would like to be. Patron calls *GetExtent* after creating a new object to set the initial size of the site, but thereafter it will always tell the object the new extents when the site is resized by calling *SetExtent*. These new extents affect only a running object or an object in a handler, and the server or handler might ignore the extents altogether. In other words, any extents you pass to *SetExtent* are not guaranteed to be returned from a subsequent call to *GetExtent*, nor do they necessarily change the object in any way.

The first method is to execute what is known as the primary, or default, verb when the object is double-clicked with the left mouse button. The exact meaning of this primary verb is defined by the object, not by the container, so the container blindly tells the object to execute without any knowledge of what will happen. The second method, of which the container is equally ignorant, is to provide a menu item on its own Edit menu that lists all the available verbs for the currently selected object. When the end user selects one of these menu items, the container again blindly tells the object to execute a verb. However, the container can ask the object to perform known actions by using predefined verbs, although these options are generally not shown directly to the end user.

All verbs are a simple integer index. Verbs with values less than zero are predefined verbs defined in the OLE 2 specifications:

Verb	Description
OLEIVERB_SHOW	(–1) Instructs the object to show itself.
OLEIVERB_OPEN	(–2) Instructs the object to open itself in its own window for editing. This applies mostly to in-place activation. For an object that is not capable of in-place activation, this is identical to OLEIVERB_SHOW.
OLEIVERB_HIDE	(–3) Instructs the object to hide its editing window.
OLEIVERB_UIACTIVATE	(–4) For in-place activation. (See Chapter 15.)
OLEIVERB_INPLACEACTIVATE	(–5) For in-place activation. (See Chapter 15.)
OLEIVERB_DISCARDUNDOSTATE	(–6) For in-place activation. (See Chapter 15.)

As is apparent in this table, a number of these verbs deal only with in-place activation. We'll see in-place activation in later chapters, so we can ignore them for now.

In addition to the negative values, OLE 2 also defines zero as the primary verb:

Verb	Description
OLEIVERB_PRIMARY	(0) Instructs the object to execute its default action.

All other positive verb indexes are object-specific, so all verbs that are zero or above are complete enigmas to the container and can be invoked only at the request of an end user, as mentioned earlier. Executing this verb is a matter of calling *IOleObject::DoVerb* with the index of the verb and with a few other parameters. Whenever Patron needs to execute a verb on an object, it asks the tenant to do so through *CTenant::Activate*:

```
BOOL CTenant::Activate(LONG iVerb)
    {
    RECT        rc, rcH;
    HCURSOR     hCur;

    //Can't activate statics.
    if (TENANTTYPE_STATIC==m_tType)
        {
        MessageBeep(0);
        return FALSE;
        }

    RECTFROMRECTL(rc, m_rcl);
    RectConvertMappings(&rc, NULL, TRUE);
    XformRectInPixelsToHimetric(NULL, &rc, &rcH);

    hCur=SetCursor(LoadCursor(NULL, MAKEINTRESOURCE(IDC_WAIT)));
    ShowCursor(TRUE);

    m_pIOleObject->DoVerb(iVerb, NULL, m_pIOleClientSite, 0
        , m_hWnd, &rcH);

    SetCursor(hCur);
    ShowCursor(FALSE);

    return FALSE;
    }
```

Because you cannot activate static objects, Patron simply beeps when any attempt is made to activate one. Otherwise, it needs to prepare itself to call *IOleObject::DoVerb*, which takes a number of parameters:

Parameter	Description
iVerb	(LONG) Index of the verb to execute.
lpMsg	(LPMSG) Pointer to the MSG structure describing the event that invoked the verb (such as a mouse click). Inclusion of this is optional for non-in-place containers, so you can generally pass NULL for now.[9]

(continued)

9. The message is important for in-place objects such as buttons that would want to know whether they should show themselves in a pressed or an unpressed state. Presumably, for such an object, a container would call *DoVerb* on both button-up and button-down messages, which would allow the object to look and act like any other button.

Parameter	Description
pActiveSite	(LPOLECLIENTSITE) Pointer to the *IOleClientSite* that invoked this verb. In some specialized cases, it might not be the one in which the object is contained.
lindex	(LONG) Index of the piece of the object on which this verb was invoked. Always 0 in OLE 2, meaning "the whole object."
hWndParent	(HWND) Handle of whatever window immediately contains the site.
lprcPosRect	(LPCRECT) Rectangle in client coordinates describing the boundaries of the object in *hWndParent*.

The *hWndParent* and *lprcPosRect* parameters specifically support multimedia objects that an end user might want to play in place but not edit. Video clips are a good example. Such objects will either want to temporarily place their own window in the container or want to draw directly to the container's *hDC* while playing the video. In the first case, the object can use *hWndParent* as the parent for the temporary window and *lprcPosRect* to position that window. In the second case, the object can call *GetDC(hWndParent)* and draw inside *lprcPosRect* on that *hDC*. Note that the object can munge the container's window like this only temporarily—that is, while executing a verb. It can't hold onto the *hDC* nor can it leave a window in the container outside *DoVerb*. If the object requires a more permanent fixture in the container, it must implement in-place activation, which is described in Chapter 16.

With that, we can now look at the specific cases in which Patron calls *CTenant::Activate*. After you have added those cases that are important to your application, you can compile and test activation by creating new objects with the Insert Object dialog box, making initial edits, closing the server window, and then reactivating the object to edit the data again. Note that if a server window is already open, activating the object will generally switch the focus to that window because most servers call *SetFocus* on themselves inside *IOleObject::DoVerb*.

Mouse Double-Clicks

In Patron, a WM_LBUTTONDBLCLK on a page comes into *PagesWndProc* (PAGEWIN.CPP) and is dispatched to *CPage::OnLeftDoubleClick*. Note that before this happens, Patron will have processed WM_LBUTTONDOWN and selected the tenant under the mouse if there was one so that the tenant is now the current one. *CPage::OnLeftDoubleClick* (PAGEMOUS.CPP) is simple: It checks to see whether there is a tenant under the current mouse position (determined previously in *CPage::OnNCHitTest*), and if there is one, it calls *CTenant::Activate* on it with OLEIVERB_PRIMARY:

```
BOOL CPage::OnLeftDoubleClick(UINT uKeys, UINT x, UINT y)
    {
    if (HTNOWHERE!=m_uHTCode)
        return m_pTenantCur->Activate(OLEIVERB_PRIMARY);

    return FALSE;
    }
```

The way in which you invoke *DoVerb(OLEIVERB_PRIMARY)* on the object in your site is, of course, your choice. Note that when we implement in-place activation later, we'll change this function to also send a MSG structure with WM_BUTTONDBLCLK to the tenant (and the object). If you plan to go that far, you might want to incorporate passing the message right away. I simply chose not to, at this point, to keep new code to a minimum.

Object Verb Menu

Double-clicking lets the user execute only one verb on the object, even when the object has multiple verbs. For example, a sound object will generally have a primary verb that plays the sound and a secondary verb that edits the sound (in a server window). Other objects could have even more verbs. To present all these to the end user, OLE 2 specifies that these verbs appear on the container's Edit menu in one of two ways:

- If the object has only one verb, create a menu item with the string *<verb> <object name>*.
- If the object has multiple verbs, create a cascading menu item with the string *<object name>* in such a way that its pop-up menu contains a separate item for each verb.

For example, an Equation object might have the single verb Edit, and so the container's menu should appear as follows:

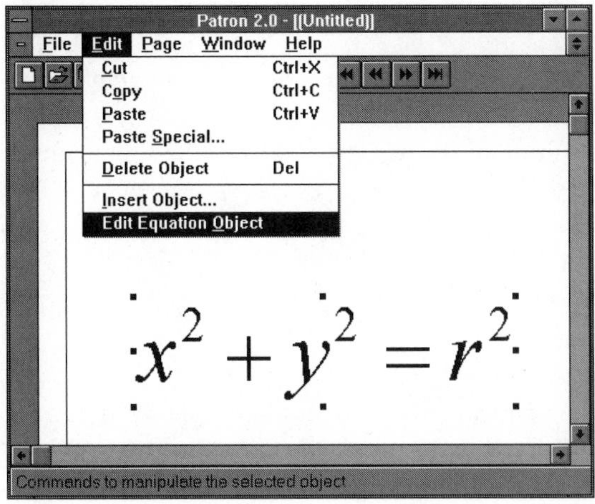

Something like a Sound Recorder's Sound object has two verbs, Play and Edit, and so the container's menu should appear as follows:

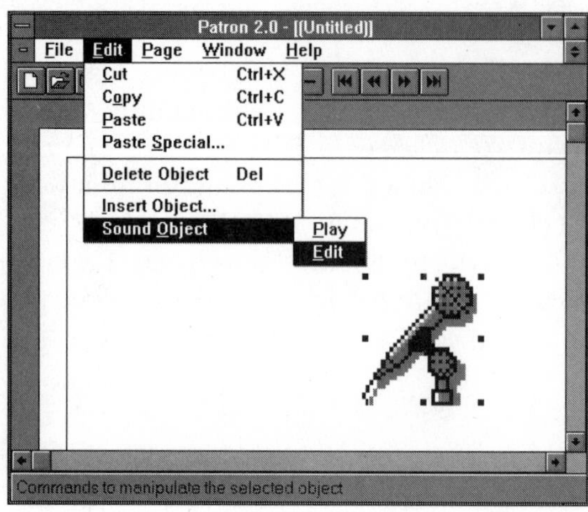

The OLE2UI library provides a function called *OleUIAddVerbMenu* to create this menu item using the object's *IOleObject::EnumVerbs* function. The new menu item may or may not be cascaded, depending on how many verbs are registered for that object. Implementing the verb menu yourself is no picnic, so I recommend that you avoid the pain, at least initially, of dealing with it yourself. In any case, the *OleUIAddVerbMenu* takes a number of parameters:

Parameter	Description
lpObj	(LPOLEOBJECT) Points to the *IOleObject* interface of the currently selected object.
lpszShortType	(LPSTR) Pointer to the object's short descriptive name as defined by the object itself. The container can pass NULL, in which case this function uses a name for the object from the Registration Database, which is generally what you want.
hMenu	(HMENU) Handle of the container's Edit menu or the menu to modify. This should *not* be your top-level menu, but the handle to your Edit pop-up menu, *GetSubMenu.*
uPos	(UINT) Position of the item to modify in the Edit menu.
idVerbMin	(UINT) Starting WM_COMMAND identifier to use for the verbs.
bAddConvert	(BOOL) Flag indicating whether to add a Convert... item to this menu. See Chapter 14.
idConvert	(UINT) WM_COMMAND identifier for the Convert menu item. See Chapter 14.
lphMenu	(HMENU FAR *) Pointer to an HMENU to receive the handle of the pop-up menu added if there are multiple verbs for this object.

The most important parameter here is *idVerbMin* because when the user selects a verb from this menu, this parameter will generate a WM_COMMAND message to your top-level menu with an identifier of *<verb index>* + *idVerbMin*. So, by subtracting *idVerbMin*, you can get to the real verb indexes (0, 1, 2, and so on) to pass to *IOleObject::DoVerb*. Also, be sure that you define a reasonably large range of menu identifiers for assignment to verbs to avoid any conflict with other menu identifiers (such as those for MDI child windows) and to allow the number of verbs on the menu to be quite large. Patron defines a range of 100 values for verbs in RESOURCE.H.

So there are two parts to this story: creating the menu and processing the items. Patron creates the menu based on the currently selected tenant in the *CPatronDoc::FQueryObjectSelected* function. This function is called whenever the frame window detects a WM_INITPOPUPMENU message on the Edit menu. On the document level, this function does nothing more than pass the message on down to the page level, through *CPages::FQueryObjectSelected* and finally to *CPage::FQueryObjectSelected*:

```
BOOL CPage::FQueryObjectSelected(HMENU hMenu)
    {
    HMENU       hMenuTemp;

    if (NULL!=m_pTenantCur)
        {
        m_pTenantCur->AddVerbMenu(hMenu, MENUPOS_OBJECT);
        return TRUE;
        }

    OleUIAddVerbMenu(NULL, NULL, hMenu, MENUPOS_OBJECT
        , IDM_VERBMIN, FALSE, 0, &hMenuTemp);

    return FALSE;
    }
```

If there is no currently selected tenant, the application calls *OleUIAddVerbMenu* with NULL pointers. This call creates a grayed and disabled menu item with only the word *Object* in it, as described by the OLE 2 user interface guidelines in the OLE 2 SDK. If there is a selected tenant, this function asks it to call *OleUIAddVerbMenu* because only the tenant knows the object pointer:

```
void CTenant::AddVerbMenu(HMENU hMenu, UINT iPos)
    {
    HMENU       hMenuTemp;
    LPOLEOBJECT pObj=m_pIOleObject;
```

(continued)

```
    //If we're static, say we have no object.
    if (TENANTTYPE_STATIC==m_tType)
        pObj=NULL;

    OleUIAddVerbMenu(pObj, NULL, hMenu, iPos, IDM_VERBMIN
        , FALSE, 0, &hMenuTemp);

    return;
    }
```

Here again, we call *OleUIAddVerbMenu* with NULL pointers for a static object because those menu items can have no verbs. IDM_VERBMIN is the starting verb index, which has no other defined menu identifiers above it.

We had to go through a number of layers (document, pages, page, tenant) to create this menu, and it's no different for processing the WM_COMMAND messages the menu generates. This processing in Patron starts up in *CPatronFrame::OnCommand*, which is called on WM_COMMAND messages:

```
LRESULT CPatronFrame::OnCommand(HWND hWnd, WPARAM wParam, LPARAM lParam)
    {
    [Other code omitted]

    pDoc=(LPCPatronDoc)m_pCL->ActiveDocument();

    if (NULL!=pDoc && (IDM_VERBMIN <= wID)&& (IDM_VERBMAX >= wID)
        {
        pDoc->ActivateObject(wID-IDM_VERBMIN);
        return 0L;
        }

    [Other command handling here.]
    }
```

The call to *CPatronDoc::ActivateObject* and to the verb index passes unmolested to *CPages::ActivateObject*, *CPage::ActivateObject*, and finally *CTenant::Activate*. I didn't say Patron had the world's most elegant design!

One other side note: If your application has a status line, you might want to have it display status information for these verbs as the user selects them from the menu. Patron does this by watching for WM_MENUSELECT messages in *CPatronFrame::FMessageHook* with the appropriate identifiers. If it detects a selection of the pop-up verb menu itself (as opposed to an item with a verb), it displays no message (as described by the user interface guidelines in the OLE SDK). If it sees the selection of a verb item, it displays the string *Commands to manipulate the selected object.* If you want, you can try to follow the "OLE User Interface Guidelines" chapter in the *OLE 2 Programmer's Reference* and display a more precise message string more like *<Verb> the <object name>*

object. However, because you control neither the actual verb strings nor the object name (and can't interpret them), you can create strings such as "Edit Drawing the Acme Drawing Object object" quite easily. Besides that, you would need to worry about how to localize such a string, which is not easy in situations where language uses verbs that are expressed in more than one word or where you are running a container written for one language with an object written for a different one. In addition, because you will create the string inside the WM_MENUSELECT message of your frame window, you have to be able to get at the object pointer itself to ask for its name, and go read the Registration Database to get the verb string. Personally, I don't see much benefit in adding this amount of complexity, so Patron sticks to a single, simple string.

The Right Mouse Button Pop-Up Menu

The "OLE User Interface Guidelines" chapter in the *OLE 2 Programmer's Reference* also recommends that you display a small menu over an object in a container when the end user single-clicks the right mouse button.[10] This menu generally appears with various commands from your Edit menu, such as Cut, Copy, and an object's verbs, along with optional commands such as Delete and Convert. None of the strings on this menu should have keyboard mnemonics because the menu is a mouse-only feature.

Patron creates a menu with Cut, Copy, Delete Object, and a verb command on it when it detects a WM_RBUTTONDOWN in *PagesWndProc (PAGEWIN.CPP)* by calling *CPage::OnRightDown*:

```
BOOL CPage::OnRightDown(UINT uKeys, UINT x, UINT y)
    {
    HMENU           hMenu;
    HMENU           hMenuRes;
    HINSTANCE       hInst;
    HWND            hWndFrame, hWndT;
    POINT           pt;
    UINT            i, cItems;

    //Select the tenant under the mouse, if there is one.
    if (!FSelectTenantAtPoint(x, y))
        return FALSE;
```

(continued)

10. You might have seen marketing material from Microsoft that touts the right mouse pop-up menu feature as something "supported in OLE 2." The fact is that Windows itself supports floating pop-up menus of this kind through the *TrackPopupMenu* API function—OLE 2 merely documents some guidelines as to what should appear in the menu. So don't be confused when you find no specific OLE 2 functions to support such menus. It's simply Windows.

```
/*
 * Get the top-level window to which menu command will go. This
 * will be whatever parent doesn't have a parent itself...
 */
hWndT=GetParent(m_hWnd);

while (NULL!=hWndT)
    {
    hWndFrame=hWndT;
    hWndT=GetParent(hWndT);
    }

/*
 * Build a popup menu for this object with Cut, Copy, Delete,
 * and object verbs.
 */
hInst=GETWINDOWINSTANCE(m_hWnd);    //Macro in BOOK1632.H
hMenuRes=LoadMenu(hInst, MAKEINTRESOURCE(IDR_RIGHTPOPUPMENU));

if (NULL==hMenuRes)
    return FALSE;

//Resource-loaded menus don't work, so we'll copy the items.
hMenu=CreatePopupMenu();
cItems=GetMenuItemCount(hMenuRes);

for (i=0; i < cItems; i++)
    {
    char        szTemp[80];
    int         id, uFlags;

    GetMenuString(hMenuRes, i, szTemp, sizeof(szTemp)
        , MF_BYPOSITION);
    id=GetMenuItemID(hMenuRes, i);

    uFlags=(0==id) ? MF_SEPARATOR : MF_STRING | MF_ENABLED;
    AppendMenu(hMenu, uFlags, id, szTemp);
    }

DestroyMenu(hMenuRes);

//Munge the Object menu item
m_pTenantCur->AddVerbMenu(hMenu, MENUPOS_OBJECTONPOPUP);

SETPOINT(pt, x, y);
ClientToScreen(m_hWnd, &pt);
```

```
TrackPopupMenu(hMenu, TPM_LEFTALIGN | TPM_RIGHTBUTTON
    , pt.x, pt.y, 0, hWndFrame, NULL);

DestroyMenu(hMenu);
return FALSE;
}
```

This function essentially checks to see whether there is an object below the mouse pointer, and if there is, it creates a menu using items from a resource-template menu (which is a top-level menu, meaning *LoadMenu* cannot be used with *TrackPopupMenu*). It then adds the object's verbs using *CTenant::AddVerbMenu* and displays it with *TrackPopupMenu,* with the following result. All command identifiers on this menu are identical to those on the top-level menu, so no other modifications are necessary to support this feature.

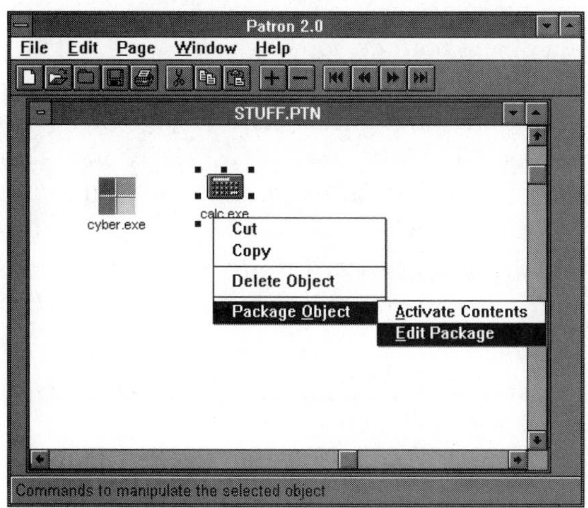

Create Objects from the Clipboard and Drag-and-Drop Transfers

Creating a new object using the Insert Object dialog box is only one of the ways to get an object into a container. It is also possible to paste an object by using data from the clipboard or to accept an embedded object dropped on your container. Again, because both the clipboard and drag-and-drop operations operate from a single *IDataObject,* the discussion here applies identically to both.

First, there are two new clipboard formats that a container must register by using *RegisterClipboardFormat.*

Format	Description
CF_EMBEDDED-OBJECT	An *IStorage* containing the object's native data.
CF_OBJECT-DESCRIPTOR	An OBJECTDESCRIPTOR structure in global memory that contains the object's size, aspect (iconic, content, and so on), class, and other information in which a potential consumer might be interested.[11]

The CF_... values are not integers as they are with Windows-defined formats. Instead they are strings defined in OLE2.H that you must register, as Patron does, in the *CPatronDoc* constructor:

```
m_cfEmbeddedObject  =RegisterClipboardFormat(CF_EMBEDDEDOBJECT);
m_cfObjectDescriptor=RegisterClipboardFormat(CF_OBJECTDESCRIPTOR);
```

Now, given any data object pointer, you can determine whether there's an embedded object available by calling *OleQueryCreateFromData*, passing the *IDataObject* pointer. This function basically checks for the existence of CF_EMBEDDEDOBJECT or CF_EMBEDSOURCE (a format identical to CF_EMBEDDEDOBJECT but under a different name) as well as OLE 1 embedded object formats such as *Native* and *OwnerLink*. But what *OleQuery-CreateFromData* does inside is of no concern to us; we can use the function to enable pasting and dropping, as we can see in *CPatronDoc-::FQueryPasteFromData*:

```
BOOL CPatronDoc::FQueryPasteFromData(LPDATAOBJECT pIDataObject
    , LPFORMATETC pFE, LPTENANTTYPE ptType)
    {
    FORMATETC  fe;
    HRESULT    hr, hr2;
    [Other tests]

    hr2=OleQueryCreateFromData(pIDataObject);

    if (NOERROR==hr2)
        {
        if (NULL!=pFE)
            {
            /*
```

11. CF_OBJECTDESCRIPTOR is similar to the general format for the problem we had to solve in Chapter 8's version of Patron, in which we wanted a graphic on the clipboard to be accompanied by data that indicates the size and placement of the object. Patron's private format contains both data items, whereas CF_OBJECTDESCRIPTOR contains only extents (because placement data is generally meaningless between different applications). Patron will still look for its own format and then look for CF_OBJECTDESCRIPTOR as a backup.

```
                 * Default to content. FPaste will use
                 * CF_OBJECTDESCRIPTOR to figure the actual aspect.
                 */
                SETDefFormatEtc(*pFE, m_cfEmbeddedObject
                    , TYMED_ISTORAGE);
                }

            if (NULL!=(LPVOID)ptType)
                *ptType=TENANTTYPE_EMBEDDEDOBJECTFROMDATA;

            [Other tests]
            }

    ...
    }
```

If Patron sees an available embedded object, it remembers that fact by storing a FORMATETC containing the embedded object clipboard format. This information is used in pasting as well as dropping, which calls *CPatronDoc::FPasteFromData.* I don't want to show this lengthy function here, so I will show only some of its features. First, *FPasteFromData* looks for the CF_OBJECTDESCRIPTOR format, which describes the aspect of the object. This is necessary to paste objects that are displayed as icons. Also, in the same way that we implemented it in Chapter 7, this function generates a call to the current page to create a new tenant. Doing so tells the tenant to create a new object. If we're pasting an embedded object, it sets the tenant type to TENANTTYPE_EMBEDDEDOBJECTFROMDATA.

Eventually this type reaches *CTenant::UCreate.* Instead of calling *OleCreate* as we did for Insert Object, *CTenant::UCreate* now calls *OleCreateFromData,* which does nearly the same as *OleCreate* except that it takes an *IDataObject* pointer instead of a CLSID as its basis for the creation. All other parameters to *OleCreateFromData* are exactly the same as those for *OleCreate*:

```
//In CTenant::UCreate:

case TENANTTYPE_EMBEDDEDOBJECTFROMDATA:
    hr=OleCreateFromData((LPDATAOBJECT)pvType, IID_IUnknown
        , OLERENDER_DRAW, NULL, NULL, m_pIStorage
        , (LPLPVOID)&pObj);
    break;
```

The interface pointer we receive from this function call is indistinguishable from a pointer returned in *OleCreate,* so from here, we treat this new object using the exact same initialization steps. Note, however, that unlike Insert Object, pasting or dropping an object does not immediately activate it, so do not immediately call *IOleObject::DoVerb,* as we did before.

If you are using the Paste Special dialog box, you will need to add a new entry so that it can now list an available object on the clipboard. This new entry should have the format CF_EMBEDDEDOBJECT and the flag OLEUIPASTE_PASTE:

```
SETDefFormatEtc(rgPaste[1].fmtetc, m_cfEmbeddedObject
    , TYMED_ISTORAGE);
rgPaste[1].lpstrFormatName="%s Object";
rgPaste[1].lpstrResultText="%s Object";
rgPaste[1].dwFlags=OLEUIPASTE_PASTE;
```

Be careful to use OLEUIPASTE_PASTE, not OLEUIPASTE_PASTEONLY. If you use the latter (as we did for other static formats), you will not see this entry in the dialog box at all. This can increase your job stress by a few orders of magnitude. Believe me. It took me six hours to figure this out.

Also, note that no matter where you put this entry in your array of pasteable formats, the Paste Special dialog box will always list embedded objects first. If you don't agree with this behavior, you will need to create your own version of the dialog box based on the sample code in the OLE 2 SDK. (See the SDK's SAMP\OLE2UI\PASTESPL.C.)

Copy and Source Embedded Objects

It's sure nice to have cookies in a cookie jar, but that's not the only place you might want to store cookies. You might want to be able to move some of them from one container to another. Similarly, if end users can paste an embedded object into a container, they will probably expect to be able to copy or cut those same objects from a container and put them into another container. (It would be nice to *copy* cookies, huh?) To do this for our application, we have to include CF_EMBEDDEDOBJECT (and CF_OBJECTDESCRIPTOR) whenever we create a data object for a clipboard operation or as a drag-and-drop source. It might seem as if you could simply use *QueryInterface* on the embedded object for its *IDataObject* and use the result for a data transfer, but this is not a good idea. Instead of copying the object, you are passing a pointer to the real object, which could result in unpredictable things happening to it that are outside the control of the container. So you truly need to duplicate the whole object.

This affects Patron in *CPage::TransferObjectCreate*, which is called whenever we need a data object for some transfer operation. The only modification here is to include a call to *CTenant::CopyEmbeddedObject* (after we've copied higher priority formats), which creates both of the new formats and stuffs them into our transfer object:

```
void CTenant::CopyEmbeddedObject(LPDATAOBJECT pIDataObject
    , LPFORMATETC pFE, LPPOINTL pptl)
    {
    LPPERSISTSTORAGE    pIPS;
    STGMEDIUM           stm;
    FORMATETC           fe;
    HRESULT             hr;
    UINT                cf;
    POINTL              ptl;

    //Can only copy embeddings.
    if (TENANTTYPE_EMBEDDEDOBJECT!=m_tType)
        return;

    if (NULL==pptl)
        {
        SETPOINTL(ptl, 0, 0);
        pptl=&ptl;
        }

    /*
     * Create CF_EMBEDDEDOBJECT. This is simply an IStorage with a
     * copy of the embedded object in it. The not-so-simple part is
     * getting an IStorage to stuff it in. For this operation we'll
     * use a temporary compound file.
     */

    stm.tymed=TYMED_ISTORAGE;
    hr=StgCreateDocfile(NULL, STGM_TRANSACTED | STGM_READWRITE
        | STGM_CREATE | STGM_SHARE_EXCLUSIVE | STGM_DELETEONRELEASE
        , 0, &stm.pstg);

    if (FAILED(hr))
        return;

    m_pObj->QueryInterface(IID_IPersistStorage, (LPLPVOID)&pIPS);

    if (NOERROR==pIPS->IsDirty())
        {
        OleSave(pIPS, stm.pstg, FALSE);
        pIPS->SaveCompleted(NULL);
        }
    else
        m_pIStorage->CopyTo(0, NULL, NULL, stm.pstg);

    pIPS->Release();
```

(continued)

```
//stm.pstg now has a copy, so stuff it away.
cf=RegisterClipboardFormat(CF_EMBEDDEDOBJECT);
SETDefFormatEtc(fe, cf, TYMED_ISTORAGE);

if (SUCCEEDED(pIDataObject->SetData(&fe, &stm, TRUE)))
    *pFE=fe;
else
    stm.pstg->Release();

//Create CF_OBJECTDESCRIPTOR which OLE2UI handles.
stm.tymed=TYMED_HGLOBAL;

/*
 * You want to make sure that if this object is iconic, that you
 * create the object descriptor with DVASPECT_ICON instead of
 * the more typical DVASPECT_CONTENT. Also remember that
 * the pick point is in HIMETRIC.
 */
XformSizeInPixelsToHimetric(NULL, (LPSIZEL)pptl, (LPSIZEL)&ptl);
stm.hGlobal=OleStdGetObjectDescriptorDataFromOleObject
    (m_pIOleObject, NULL, m_fe.dwAspect, ptl);

cf=RegisterClipboardFormat(CF_OBJECTDESCRIPTOR);
SETDefFormatEtc(fe, cf, TYMED_HGLOBAL);

if (FAILED(pIDataObject->SetData(&fe, &stm, TRUE)))
    stm.pstg->Release();

return;
}
```

Pasting into an Object: *IOleObject::InitFromData*

If an object is currently selected in a container when performing Edit/Paste, you can elect to paste into the object itself instead of into your container. To do so, pass the *IDataObject* from the clipboard or through a drag-and-drop operation to *IOleObject::InitFromData* with the *fCreation* parameter set to FALSE. The call will return S_FALSE if the object cannot accept the data to paste, in which case you can paste it as you normally would. If the object returns E_FAIL, it tried but could not paste the data, so display an appropriate error message. The object will use the *fCreation* flag to distinguish this call from the other use of *InitFromData* during creation because this time the object knows it's not initializing, it's pasting.

Creating CF_EMBEDDEDOBJECT really means creating an *IStorage* and saving the object in it. The storage used here is a temporary disk file with STGM_DELETEONRELEASE because the object is potentially so large that a memory storage is a bad idea. After we have this new storage, we get an *IPersistStorage* interface for the object and call *IPersistStorage::IsDirty*. If the object is not dirty, a *CopyTo* from the object's storage into the new storage used in the transfer is sufficient because the data is current. If the object is dirty, however, we must call *OleSave*, followed by *IPersistStorage::SaveCompleted*, to make sure that the current state of the object is what's copied. You want no surprises for the end user.

The OLE2UI library has a function to create the CF_OBJECTDESCRIPTOR format: *OleStdGetObjectDescriptorFromOleObject*. This function allocates and fills an OBJECTDESCRIPTOR structure with information that it can obtain from an *IOleObject* pointer. We still have to provide the object's user-readable name (a NULL here, in which case the function asks the object for a name), the aspect (which in Patron's case might be either content or icon), and a pick point (POINTL, in HIMETRIC) for drag-and-drop operations.

With these other two formats in the data object, another container can create embedded objects that can use this data. Patron itself uses the data when it copies an object during drag-and-drop operations (with the Ctrl key pressed), which results in two independent embedded objects that just happen to contain exactly the same data until one or the other is modified.

Close and Delete Objects

We would quickly fill our hard disks with large documents if we could never remove objects from them. So we now must add some way to delete an object from a document. This is similar to, but not exactly the same as, closing an object when the document is being closed and the object still exists—that is, the object moves from the loaded state to the passive state. Deleting an object means taking it from the running or loaded state into outright nonexistence.

Closing an embedded object requires two actions: making sure the object's storage is committed and calling *IOleObject::Close*. The latter signals the object's local server to completely shut down and purge itself from memory if there are no other containers using it. But as far as our container is concerned, this object is now in the passive state, so we must call *OleLoad* to bring it back to loaded.

IOleObject::Close takes one parameter, called the Save option, which instructs the object how to proceed:

Save Option	Description
OLECLOSE_SAVE-IFDIRTY	If the object is not dirty, it can simply shut down. Otherwise, the object should call *IOleClientSite::SaveObject* first and then shut down. This is the most common flag.
OLECLOSE_NOSAVE	The object should simply shut down, discarding all changes. This is a common flag when an object is destroyed.
OLECLOSE_PROMPT-SAVE	If the object is not dirty, it can shut down. Otherwise, it will prompt the user with a Yes/No/Cancel message box, asking whether the user wants to save the object. If you use this flag, you might get a return value of OLE_E-_PROMPTSAVECANCELLED, in which case, you should not close the object. Use of this flag is rare.

If you are destroying an object (as Patron does when selecting Delete Object from the Edit menu), you still call *IOleObject::Close,* but with OLECLOSE_NOSAVE. This is in addition to destroying the storage element for this object, which your site manages. Finally, after destroying an object, you should call *CoFreeUnusedLibraries* as a matter of habit.

When you test closing and destroying objects, try it with and without the object's server actually running. When it is running, be sure that the server shuts down completely and is no longer in memory. If it stays in memory (and you are using a reliable server), you might not be releasing a reference count somewhere, or you might have a lock on the server's class factory (*IClassFactory::LockServer*).

Save and Load the Document with Embedded Objects

At some point, it would be nice to save all the objects we've been creating and editing so that we can reload them at a later time. We've pretty much covered all the steps of saving an object in a document: providing an *IStorage,* calling *OleSave* when asked through *IOleClientSite* or when closing the object, calling *IPersistStorage::SaveCompleted,* and commiting the *IStorage* when you have finished because Patron does so in *CTenant::Update*:

```
BOOL CTenant::Update(void)
    {
    LPPERSISTSTORAGE    pIPS;
```

```
    if (NULL!=m_pIStorage)
        {
        m_pObj->QueryInterface(IID_IPersistStorage
            , (LPLPVOID)&pIPS);
        OleSave(pIPS, m_pIStorage, TRUE);
        pIPS->SaveCompleted(NULL);
        pIPS->Release();

        m_pIStorage->Commit(STGC_ONLYIFCURRENT);
        }

    return FALSE;
    }
```

On a larger scale, Patron's document saving starts in *CPatronDoc::USave*, which first asks *CPages* to update, which in turn asks the currently open *CPage* to update which in turn asks each tenant to update using the preceding code. After all that, the document commits itself, and because it is the owner of the root storage, that commit writes the file to disk. Little of this storage code has changed from previous versions of Patron in previous chapters.

Patron, by the way, is designed—and I won't argue that this is the best design—to keep only the current page open. That means when you switch pages, all open/running objects on the old page are closed back to the passive state and all objects on the new page are opened into the loaded state.

Loading a document in Patron starts with opening a root storage for the document and initializing the pages. Then Patron opens the current page by using *CPage::FOpen*. This, in turn, re-creates all the tenants on the page, but instead of calling *CTenant::UCreate*, Patron calls *CTenant::FLoad*, telling it the object's storage, what is in this storage, and the rectangle occupied by the tenant on the page:

```
BOOL CTenant::FLoad(LPSTORAGE pIStorage, LPFORMATETC pFE, LPRECTL prcl)
    {
    HRESULT         hr;
    LPUNKNOWN       pObj;

    if (NULL==pIStorage || NULL==pFE || NULL==prcl)
        return FALSE;

    //Fail if this is called for an already living tenant.
    if (m_fInitialized)
        return FALSE;

    m_fInitialized=TRUE;
```

(continued)

```
    //Open the storage for this tenant.
    if (!FOpen(pIStorage))
        return FALSE;

    hr=OleLoad(m_pIStorage, IID_IUnknown, NULL, (LPLPVOID)&pObj);

    if (FAILED(hr))
        {
        Destroy(pIStorage);
        return FALSE;
        }

    FObjectInitialize(pObj, pFE, NULL);

    RectSet(prcl, FALSE);
    return TRUE;
    }
```

Most of this is unchanged from previous versions. *OleLoad* brings passive objects into the loaded state and returns an interface pointer. Now, however, to support embedded objects, we call *FObjectInitialize* to perform the same initialization sequence as was required after *OleCreate* and then to position the object on the page before repainting (by virtue of opening a new window, which generates a WM_PAINT message). So we're doing the same steps of querying for *IOleObject* and *IViewObject* interfaces, setting up advises, and communicating our *IOleClientSite* and *IAdviseSink* interfaces to the object. The difference between this and creating a new object is that we do not immediately activate the object. It would be crazy for a user to open one innocent little document and be hit with a barrage of editing windows!

There is still one small modification to Patron's file I/O that you can find in *CPatronDoc::Rename*—an override of the *CDocument::Rename* function in CLASSLIB. This is called whenever the user chooses File Save As or otherwise changes the name of a document:

```
void CPatronDoc::Rename(LPSTR pszFile)
    {
    //We don't need to change the base class, just augment...
    CDocument::Rename(pszFile);
    m_pPG->NotifyTenantsOfRename(pszFile);
    return;
    }
```

Here we call through *CPages::NotifyTenantsOfRename* to *CPage::NotifyTenantsOfRename*, which informs each tenant of the new document name:

```
void CPage::NotifyTenantsOfRename(LPSTR pszFile, LPVOID pvReserved)
    {
    LPTENANT    pTenant;
    UINT        i;

    for (i=0; i < m_cTenants; i++)
        {
        if (FTenantGet(i, &pTenant, FALSE))
            pTenant->NotifyOfRename(pszFile, LPVOID pvReserved);
        }

    return;
    }
```

Down in *CTenant::NotifyOfRename,* we need to tell any *loaded or running* objects of the new host names by calling *IOleObject::SetHostNames* again.

```
void CTenant::NotifyOfRename(LPSTR pszFile, LPVOID pvReserved)
    {
    char        szObj[40];
    char        szApp[40];

    if (NULL==m_pIOleObject)
        return;

    if (0==*pszFile)
        {
        LoadString(m_pPG->m_hInst, IDS_UNTITLED, szObj
            , sizeof(szObj));
        {
    else
        {
        GetFileTitle(pszFile, szObj, sizeof(szObj));

       #ifndef WIN32
        //Force filenames to uppercase in DOS versions.
        AnsiUpper(szObj);
       #endif
        }

    LoadString(m_pPG->m_hInst, IDS_CAPTION, szApp, sizeof(szApp));
    m_pIOleObject->SetHostNames(szApp, szObj);
    return;
    }
```

If you leave out this small part, your current document name will not be reflected in open server windows, which is, of course, not very user friendly.

After making these additions to your code, you should verify (by using a tool such as DFVIEW.EXE in the OLE 2 SDK) that all your objects are indeed inside the compound file and that what you expect to be there is actually there. You should then reopen the file and attempt to activate each object. Then make some changes, save the file again, close it, reopen it, and make sure that those changes were actually saved. If all is well, accept my congratulations—you have built yourself a basic embedding container. You are now ready for more advanced container features, which we'll see in Chapters 12, 13, and 14. But there is just one more option you might want to add now.

Handle Iconic Presentations (Cache Control)

Finally we're at the last step, which is optional but highly recommended: support of iconic aspects on objects. I will admit that when I first looked at this feature, I was so intimidated that I wanted to defer it to a later chapter as some sort of avoidance strategy. After whacking myself in the head a few times with the 40-ounce Louisville Slugger I keep in my office, I got myself to do it for this chapter. And it really didn't turn out to be all that hard.

The trick to iconic aspects is really a special case of the more general issue of controlling what's cached for an object. Back in Chapter 6, when we first used *OleSave* to serialize bitmaps and metafiles (see "Freeloading from OLE2.DLL"), we learned that OLE 2 maintains a presentation cache for each object that we can control through the *IOleCache* interface. This interface is always provided from an object handler, and generally the one used is the one in OLE2.DLL. Through it, a container can tell OLE 2 not to save any presentations or to save one that is different from the default DVASPECT_CONTENT rendering.

This is exactly what we want to do with an iconic presentation, or DVASPECT_ICON. So where do we get the iconic representations? They come either from the Paste Special or the Insert Object dialog box when the user has selected the Display From Icon check box or from a Paste or drop operation. The iconic representation is not a handle to an icon; instead, it is a special metafile that contains both the icon and a label stored in such a way that the OLE2UI library can re-extract the icon and label from this metafile. The reason it's all packaged up in a metafile is so that containers can throw such a representation into the cache and forget about it.

Icon handling affects a number of places in the code we've developed in this chapter, so let me just run down the list of small modifications that are necessary for Paste Special (as well as Paste or drop) and Insert Object:

1. In Paste Special, add OLEUIPASTE_ENABLEICON for the CF_EMBEDDEDOBJECT entry. This enables the Display As Icon check box in the dialog box when this format is selected.

2. If you previously disabled or removed the Display As Icon check box in the Insert Object dialog box, enable it now.
3. On return from Paste Special or Insert Object, the *hMetaPict* field of their respective structures might contain a non-NULL handle. It is your responsibility, regardless of anything else you do, to clean up this memory by calling *OleUIMetafilePictIconFree.*
4. If Display As Icon is checked on return from Paste Special or Insert Object, the *dwFlags* fields in their respective structures will contain PSF_CHECKDISPLAYASICON (Paste Special) or IOF_CHECK-DISPLAYASICON (Insert Object). This is your signal to use DVASPECT_ICON to display the object rather than DVASPECT_CONTENT.
5. When pasting an object using Paste or a drop, examine the CF_OBJECTDESCRIPTOR data that should accompany the object. If there is no such data, the data cannot be an iconic object. Otherwise, the *dwDrawAspect* field in the structure will contain the DVASPECT_... value to use. If this is set, you must ask the data object for its CF_METAFILEPICT in DVASPECT_ICON, which will be the iconic representation. If you fail to use DVASPECT_ICON, you'll get an error.
6. After creating an iconic object from Paste, drop, Paste Special, or Insert Object, you have to be sure that the correct aspect presentation is cached by calling *OleStdSwitchDisplayAspects.* This function calls *IOleCache::Cache* for DVASPECT_ICON and sends it the icon metafile from the dialog box or from Paste. It will also free any other currently cached formats and establish a view object advise link with DVASPECT_ICON.
7. When saving and reloading an object, remember that it's iconic if you later need to copy it to the clipboard or source it in a drag-and-drop operation—its aspect must then be part of the CF_OBJECT-DESCRIPTOR structure. However, after you have set the cache for DVASPECT_ICONIC, *OleSave* and *OleLoad* will ignorantly save and load whatever is in the cache.
8. Remember to pass DVASPECT_ICON to *IViewObject::Draw* or *OleDraw.* If you forget, your objects will draw blanks, and these functions will return OLE_E_BLANK.

9. Be forewarned that you will receive very few *IAdviseSink-::OnViewChange* notifications for iconic objects because most changes to an object happen to DVASPECT_CONTENT.

Any of these steps that require differentiation between content and icon aspects apply equally well when you want to manage other aspects. In all cases, after you tell the cache what to do, *OleSave* and *OleLoad* do the appropriate thing. It's mostly a matter of your structures indicating the correct aspect.

The one missing piece of this icon story is how one either changes the icon at a later time or switches back to viewing DVASPECT_CONTENT for the object. The answer lies in a more involved feature called *Object Conversion*, which is a subject for Chapter 14. If, for now, you want to provide for simply changing the icon and label, you can invoke the *OleUIChangeIcon* dialog box in the OLE2UI library. This function takes an icon metafile on input and returns a new icon metafile on output. You can then use *IOleCache::SetData* to change the currently cached metafile to this new image. There's not much else to say about this process because there are no user interface standards for using the Change Icon dialog box.

Summary

Support for Compound Documents is a primary technology in OLE 2 that allows a container application to embed and link objects from any OLE 1 or OLE 2 server application. By implementing their part of the compound document standard, containers and servers need not have any knowledge about each other, which leads to the ability to integrate data from arbitrary sources into a container document.

An object in a container document can have one of three states: passive, loaded, or running. A passive object exists entirely on disk and is not visible, printable, or available for any manipulation. When an end user opens the document in which the object lives and the container application loads the object, it transitions to the loaded state, in which it can be seen and printed but not edited or otherwise manipulated in any way. Only when the object is activated does it transition to the running state, in which the user can perform any number of actions on that object, such as playing or editing the data.

All three object states are associated with particular modules being in memory. These modules can be the container application, various OLE 2 libraries, an object handler DLL, an In-Process Server DLL, or a local server EXE. Handlers, In-Process Servers, and local servers all have their place in the compound document picture and each has specific responsibilities.

This chapter focuses on the compound document container module and how it must be structured to place embedded objects in its documents. This chapter gives detailed step-by-step instructions for adding the code necessary to support this feature, including initializing and shutting down applications, creating and managing sites, creating site interfaces and storage, creating new objects, initializing objects, drawing and printing objects, closing and deleting objects, dealing with objects by using the clipboard and drag-and-drop operations, and saving and loading documents with objects. Also covered is the optional step of supporting iconic aspects for objects.

CHAPTER TEN

COMPOUND DOCUMENTS AND EMBEDDED OBJECT SERVERS (EXEs)

COO-KIES!
Cookie Monster

In Chapter 9, I made the comparison between embedded objects and a batch of cookies in a cookie jar, and I described how, figuratively, to create the cookie jar. That left us with the question of how to bake cookies. At least some of us, I'm sure, have at one time or another gotten out all the ingredients—flour, sugar, eggs, butter, shortening, baking soda, salt, and vanilla (maybe also an obscene number of chocolate chips)—to mix up and bake a batch of cookies. (OK, I'll admit that once or twice I didn't bother to bake them.) We later remove them from the oven, let them cool, and put them in the cookie jar.

Baking cookies is a good analogy for what's involved in creating an OLE 2 server for embedded objects. As bakers, we first create the cookies by mixing the dough, and then we manage the cookies by baking, cooling, and storing them. As bakers, we are cookie "servers." In the case of embedded objects, a server application must create objects and then manage those objects. Object creation, as we saw in Chapter 4, is the responsibility of a class factory. Object management is the responsibility of everything else in the application. As we saw in previous chapters, a C++ object is a very convenient way to manage a Windows Object, but you can accomplish the same thing in a language such as C with well-designed data structures.

This chapter deals exclusively with EXE servers, or Local Servers, which implement the embedded object parts of the compound document picture discussed in Chapter 9. Any server components that are implemented in DLLs—that is, in-process servers and object handlers—are covered in the next chapter because they have their own structures and their own unique issues. That leaves us here to discuss the specific structure of a server application and where to implement certain interfaces. Using Cosmo as an example, we'll follow a step-by-step guide to adding basic server features in the form of a class factory and the objects that it creates.

Because OLE 2 defines such a rich compound document technology, we will not be able to cover every possibility for embedded objects; I'll leave some functions of some interfaces to your own exploration. There are so many recipes for objects that we'd go crazy trying to look at them all at once. We need to start with the OLE equivalent of your basic sugar cookie. That will be enough to satisfy a container as well as a furry, blue, ball-eyed maniac from Sesame Street.

The Structure of a Server Application

In "Compound Document Mechanisms" in Chapter 9, we saw that a server, in order to fit the compound document standard, must provide objects that implement the *IOleObject*, *IDataObject*, and *IPersistStorage* interfaces, as shown in Figure 10-1. In addition, the server must provide a class factory that implements the *IClassFactory* interface because that class factory is responsible for creating the server's objects.

Each of the three object interfaces has its own specific purpose in the compound document picture. *IPersistStorage* is the interface through which the object is told about its *IStorage* in the container's document, in which the object loads and saves its native data. *IDataObject* is the interface through

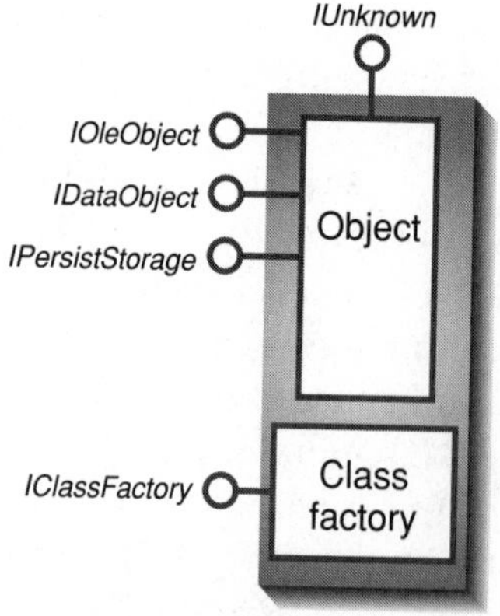

Figure 10-1.
The server side of compound documents.

which the handler, generally OLE2.DLL, asks for presentations to cache, such as a metafile or a bitmap. Handlers can also ask the data object for an advisory connection so that they know when the data has changed in the server, in such a way that the cache might need updating. Containers also can ask the data object for an advisory connection, or they might request a copy of specific data other than a graphic format.

IOleObject is the interface that in general handles all other parts of the standard. If you read all of Chapter 9, you saw that containers use a large number of the member functions in this interface. For the most part, this interface provides containers with a wide variety of operations that the object supports, the most important of which is the action of executing a verb.

Becoming an embedding server will therefore affect your application on a number of levels, just as container modifications affect that class of applications. Server applications have levels that I describe as Application, Document, and Object, as shown in Figure 10-2. The application is the agent that loads and saves documents, and those documents can provide one or more objects. For example, a spreadsheet application can open a specific spreadsheet document, and that document can contain a wide variety of cell ranges, where each cell range is a potential object. Simpler applications, such as drawing tools (of which Cosmo is a low-tech example), have one object (the drawing) per document and might not care to distinguish between document and object at all.

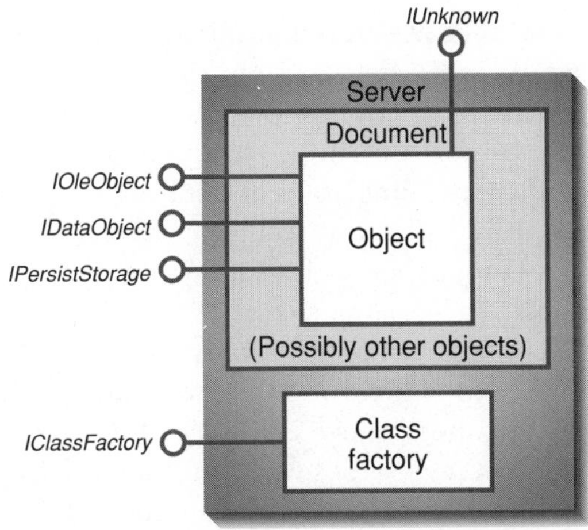

Figure 10-2.
The structure of a server application.

The application is where you implement the class factory for the server. The objects that this class factory creates might, in fact, be documents, and the document itself creates an object inside itself. This is the case when a single document can contain more than one object. For example, a spreadsheet might contain any number of cells, and any selection of cells within that spreadsheet might constitute an object. In the Cosmo example, each document maintains one object—that is, a compound document object—with the appropriate interfaces to make that object useful to a compound document container. These objects need not be tightly integrated with the existing editing windows or with objects already present in your application. For example, Cosmo's editing window, Polyline, is implemented in the C++ class *CPolyline*, but this is not what Cosmo exposes as a compound document object. Instead it implements a new C++ class, *CFigure*, that has the appropriate *IOleObject*, *IDataObject*, and *IPersistStorage* interfaces. *CFigure* makes use of the existing *CPolyline* implementation, to the point that we need to make only a few minor additions to *CPolyline* itself. In other words, the Figure is a compound document object wrapper around the internal Polyline.

Before diving into implementation, let's first look at a few issues that require a little thought.

Linking Support and Mini-Servers vs. Full-Servers

Although support for embedded objects is only half the overall linking and embedding picture, some applications have no need to support linking nor do they need to run stand-alone. Such servers are called mini-servers and can run only within the context of embedding—that is, the only way to run the server is to create an object it manipulates by means of a container's Insert Object dialog box (and later, by activating the object again). Those applications that support linking and embedding are called full-servers.

Mini-servers work well for small visual data, such as font effects or a simple drawing. Because they support only embedding, mini-servers should not require a great deal of storage—each object from a mini-server takes up space in the container's document. Simple drawings, for example, can be stored in a metafile of a few hundred bytes. On the other hand, a 24-bit DIB might take megabytes. A server whose native data is small can therefore be either a mini-server or a full-server, but those that can potentially generate very large stores of data should always be full servers. Give the end user the choice of whether to link or to embed when storage space is a factor.

Because a mini-server cannot run by itself, there is no opportunity for it to load, edit, and save any sort of file. Because it cannot generate files, there is nothing to which anyone can link, and therefore mini-servers do not support linking. Full-servers, on the other hand, because they can run as stand-alone, have some concept of files and therefore can provide links. Most existing applications that you might consider making a server probably read and write their own files already and should thus become full-servers. If, however, you are designing a new type of editable object, a mini-server might be the best route.

Version Numbers

If you ever plan to release a new version of your application, which just about all of us do, you will want to use version numbers in all instances of data that might be stored on disk. This includes the data you store as an embedded object because that data ultimately ends up in a container's disk file. A later version of your server might be asked to load and edit an old version of your data that's been sitting undisturbed in a container's compound document for years. By having access to a version number in this embedded object, your new server can convert the old data into the new data. Typically, the first few bytes in an object's storage should contain a version number because that will be the first thing you want to read before attempting to load data. Cosmo, for example, uses the version number to know how many bytes to read, as later versions of its storage contain more than older ones.[1]

Installation

Implementing a compound document server will require some modifications to your installation program—that is, whatever copies your application from floppy disks (or CD-ROM), to the end user's hard disk. This installation program will need to create a number of entries in the Registration Database that provide OLE and other applications with information about your particular compound document objects.

The best way to accomplish this generally is to use the Registration Database Editor, RegEdit, to create a .REG file with the appropriate entries (for example, CHAP10\CHAP10.REG in the sample code). Your installation program should first copy this file to the installation directory. Next, it should call the Windows API function *WinExec* with the command line *regedit -s <path to .REG file>*. This command will merge the contents of your .REG file with the exiting Registration Database. Finally, use the SHELL.DLL functions such as *RegOpenKey* and *RegSetValue* to update the *LocalServer*, *InProcServer*, and *InProcHandler* entries for your application. What is most important here is that you store *full path names* as the values for these entries so that you do not depend on your installation directory being part of the system path, so that you don't clutter other system directories, and so that you don't use precious space in the user's PATH command to point to your single application.

1. I am referring to my OLE 1 version of Cosmo, given in CHAP02\COSMO10.

Embedding Servers Step by Step

The remainder of this chapter will follow modifications I made to Cosmo so that it could become an embedded object server. Unlike container applications, a server has very little user interface to contend with; instead, most of the work is functional and deals with rendering and exchanging data. In other words, the server has to define how a cookie looks, how it tastes, what kind of ingredients it needs, and how to mix together all those ingredients. However, it does not have to worry about cookie jars, counters, kitchens, and houses in which such cookie jars would sit. Its only concerns are the cookies.

These steps assume that you already have some sort of application working that you now want to make an embedded object server. If you are writing a new server application, I recommend reviewing these steps and then writing the application without embedding support, returning here to go through the step-by-step process. This approach will let you first concentrate on your application's specifics with knowledge about how embedding will affect various areas. In other words, don't try to implement everything at once, and don't be too concerned about tightly integrating embedded object support from the beginning.

About a third of the steps in this implementation deal with the class factory portion of a server—that is, what's necessary to launch the server and create an object. The steps dealing with the object are primarily concerned with the three object interfaces and a small bit of user interface. The final steps are concerned with additional features important to creating a full-server, as well as some MDI and SDI differences. The steps, like those for the container in Chapter 9 if you've read them, are designed so that you can compile and test something after each step. Again, I strongly recommend that you test your implementations of the early steps before moving on, because the later steps use the earlier ones as a foundation. What you'll see is that by leaving out much of the implementation at the beginning, you naturally simulate a number of failure conditions.

1. Call *SetMessageQueue(96)* (Windows 3.1 only), *OleBuildVersion*, *OleInitialize*, and *OleUninitialize*, as described in "The New Application for Windows Objects" in Chapter 4.
2. Create compound document entries in the Registration Database.
3. Implement a class factory and register. Some applications will register the class only when they detect *-Embedding* on the command line during startup. Include a shutdown mechanism as described in Chapter 4 under "Implementing a Component Object and Server."

4. Implement an object with *IUnknown* but no other interfaces, and modify other code in your application to create and manage this object.
5. Implement the *IPersistStorage* interface for the object. Much of this code can use any existing functions that read and write your data to *IStorage* objects.
6. Implement the *IDataObject* interface for the object. If you have already written code to handle the clipboard by means of a data object, this implementation will be quite straightforward.
7. Implement the *IOleObject* interface for the object. This includes code to execute object verbs. This is the largest of all interfaces, although it has various functions that need not be implemented at all and others that are downright trivial.
8. Modify your server's user interface when editing an embedded object to eliminate or disable various menu commands, as well as when changing the window's caption bar to reflect the embedding state. This also affects your implementation of File/Save As and File/Close.
9. Send notifications of data change, closure, saving, and renaming at various times in the object's life.
10. (Full-servers) Augment your server's clipboard code to provide CF_EMBEDSOURCE and CF_OBJECTDESCRIPTOR so that you could copy from your server and paste an embedded object into a container.
11. (Optional, Full-servers) Provide alternate user interface for MDI applications, which adds another shutdown condition.

After following these steps for your own application, you'll end up with an embedding server fully usable by OLE 1 and OLE 2 containers, including any you implemented in Chapter 9.

Call Initialization Functions at Startup and Shutdown

As mentioned in Chapter 4 and implemented in containers in Chapter 9, all applications that use Windows Objects must call *SetMessageQueue(96)* (Windows 3.1 only), *OleBuildVersion*, and *OleInitialize* on startup and *OleUnintialize* (and possibly *OleFlushClipboard*) on shutdown. As a server, your application not only uses storage objects but also advises sinks and site objects in your container.

I want to point out again that *OleInitialize*, as opposed to *CoInitialize*, is necessary to work with compound documents. If you have been using *CoInitialize* to this point, switch now to *OleInitialize*. You can also compile and run your code to verify that these are all called at the right time.

Create Registration Database Entries

In Chapter 4, we created a number of basic Registration Database entries in such a way that *CoGetClassObject* could locate and load the DLL or EXE that serviced an object of a particular CLSID. These entries are still required, but for compound documents, there are a number of additions. Therefore, the first task for embedding servers is to obtain a CLSID for its use. For Cosmo we'll use {0021107-000-0000-C000-000000000046}, which is defined in INC\BOOKGUID.H as CLSID_Cosmo2Figure. We use this because all the compound files that Cosmo generates from Chapter 5 on are already marked with this CLSID. We'll simply use it now for our object CLSID as well.

REMINDER: All CLSIDs beginning with 000211xx have been allocated for the author's exclusive use—that is, they're mine. In other words, be sure to obtain your own CLSIDs for use in your server by running the UUIDGEN.EXE program provided in the OLE 2 SDK. You can also obtain CLSIDs by contacting Microsoft directly, as is described in the OLE 2 SDK.

Let's review those entries from Chapter 4. Here *<classID>* is your CLSID value spelled out as in "{0021107-000-0000-C000-000000000046}". The first set of entries went under the key *<ProgID>*, where *<ProgID>* is a short name without spaces or punctuation, like an OLE 1 class name (\ means HKEY_CLASSES_ROOT):[2]

```
\
    <ProgID> = <Main Descriptive Object Name>
        CLSID = <class ID>
```

Here *<MainDescriptive Object Name>* is a user-readable name that will appear in the Insert Object dialog box in container applications and other user interface areas. Besides this basic entry, we also had entries under CLSID (shown for a server EXE):

```
\
    CLSID
        <class ID> = <Main Descriptive Object Name>
            LocalServer = <Path to server EXE>
```

---

2. A good technique to follow to avoid ProgID conflicts as well as to create a unique identifier, is to use *<App><VersionNumber><ObjectType>* as in *Cosmo2Figure*. The application name can also identify your company for even less possibility of conflicts.

For a compound document server like this chapter's version of Cosmo, the first set of entries (for *ProgID*) contains the following:

```
\
    Cosmo2Figure = Cosmo 2.0 Figure (Chap 10)
        CLSID = {0021107-000-0000-C000-000000000046}
        Insertable
        protocol
            StdFileEditing
                server=<Path to Cosmo EXE>
                verb
                    0 = &Edit
```

The new entry with the key *Insertable* (with no value) marks this object as one that can appear in a container's Insert Object dialog box. Only those classes registered with *Insertable* will be shown in that dialog box. The other entries under *protocol\StdFileEditing* are for OLE 1 compatibility; they are, in fact, the same entries used by OLE 1 servers. By this small amount of registration, an OLE 2 server is usable from an OLE 1 container.

The second set of entries under CLSID grows tremendously for compound document servers:

```
\
    CLSID
        {0021107-000-0000-C000-000000000046}= Cosmo 2.0 Figure (Chap 10)
            LocalServer = <Path to Cosmo EXE>
            InProcHandler = OLE2.DLL
            ProgID = Cosmo2Figure
            Insertable
            DefaultIcon = <Path to Cosmo EXE>,0
            verb
                0 = &Edit,0,2
                -1 = Show,0,0
                -2 = Open,0,0
                -3 = Hide,0,1
            AuxUserType
                2 = Cosmo 2.0
                3 = Cosmo 2.0 from Chapter 10
            MiscStatus = 16
                1 = 17
            DataFormats
                GetSet
                    0 = Polyline Figure,1,1,3
                    1 = Embed Source,1,8,1
                    2 = 3,1,32,1
                    3 = 2,1,16,1
```

Obviously, there is a lot of new stuff here, so let's take the innovations on one at a time, skipping the *LocalServer* and *InProcHandler* entries, which we already understand.

Key	Subkeys and Values
ProgID	Provides the name of the key under which other entries can be found. This value must match the *ProgID* registered elsewhere.
Insertable	Marks the object as one that can appear in a container's Insert Object dialog box. This is redundant with the *Insertable* that appears under the *ProgID* entries for the server, and both should always appear together.
DefaultIcon	A path to a module and an index of the icon in that module to use by default when the user checks Display As Icon in the Insert Object and Paste Special dialog boxes of a container. If no entry is given here or if the path is invalid, the dialog boxes will show a default icon (a sheet of paper with an edge folded down, your standard "document" icon).
AuxUserType	This key has no value itself but instead has subkeys of the format *<form number>* = *<string>*, where *<form number>* is either 2 or 3 (but never 1 for reasons known only to the gods[3]) and <string> is some user-readable name of the object. Form number 2 should always be a short name that describes the type of the object, as in *Cosmo 2*. Try to keep this string under 10 characters. Form number 3 is a longer application name such as *Cosmo 2 from Chapter 10*, which is used specifically in the OLE2UI Paste Special dialog box.
MiscStatus	Can have one value called the "default" status and can optionally have subkeys, each of which has the form *<aspect>* = *<status>*, where *<aspect>* is a DVASPECT value and *<status>* is an integer flag. The status values come from the OLEMISC enumeration in OLE2.H and can be any combination of the values in the enumeration. In the example above, *1 = 17* marks DVASPECT_CONTENT with the flag OLEMISC_RECOMPOSEONRESIZE, which means the object would like to redraw itself if a content presentation is resized in a container, and the flag OLEMISC_CANTLINKINSIDE, which means the object does not support some advanced linking features that we'll see in Chapter 13.

I left descriptions of *verb* and *DataFormats* off the preceding table because they are somewhat detailed. These, as well as many of the other entries, are registered so that OLE 2 and a container application can determine

3. Actually, number 1 is always the string after the *<class ID>* in this set of entries, and so we don't need to store it here.

specific capabilities of an object without having that object running. For example, when a container loads an object, it wants to display the list of verbs the user can invoke on that object, and only when the user does select a verb is the object put into the running state. It would be silly to run the object just to determine the verbs because the user might look at the verbs and decide not to invoke them at all. In addition, a good number of functions in the *IOleObject* interface return the same information you register here. By registering these values, you can trivialize the implementation of these member functions, as we will see later.

The "verb" key itself has no value. It simply has a number of subkeys below it; each subkey and its value is of the format *<verb number>* = *<name>*,*<menu flags>*,*<verb flags>*. Verb numbers are those defined with OLEIVERB prefixes OLE2.H as well as any server-defined values. Those with negative numbers are predefined verbs, such as OLEIVERB_HIDE (-3), OLEIVERB_OPEN (-2), and OLEIVERB_SHOW (-1); those with 0 or positive numbers are defined by the application. (Number 0 is defined as OLEIVERB_PRIMARY as well.)

Each verb number key has three components in its value: verb name, menu flags, and verb flags. First, the name of the verb is a string that will appear in a container's menus. The OLE 2 user interface recommends that all verbs numbered 0 and above include a mnemonic character in these names—that is, one character prefixed with an ampersand, as in *&Edit.* Next, "menu flags" is a combination of various MF_... values from windows.h. Most often this is MF_STRING ¦ MF_ENABLE ¦ MF_UNCHECKED, which translates into a 0 (hence the entries shown previously). Generally, containers use this value to control enabling of the verb menu items,[4] so don't register values that make no sense, such as MF_BITMAP or MF_OWNERDRAW. Finally, "verb flags" is a combination of values from the OLEVERBATTRIB enumeration in OLE2.H. In OLE 2, this enumeration contains two bits: OLEVERBATTRIB_NEVERDIRTIES (value of 1) indicates that executing this verb on an object does not have the possibility of modifying the data, and OLEVERBATTRIB_ONCONTAINERMENU (value of 2) indicates whether a container should show this verb in its menus. According to the OLE 2 specification, Open, Show, and Hide should never use this latter flag, but you should still register them with either a 0 or 1 value for the verb flags. For Cosmo, Open and Show allow modifications, whereas Hide does not (of course not!). The other verb, Edit, can be shown on container menus and also

4. Chapter 9 doesn't include any mention of these "menu flags" or "verb flags." The OLE2UI function *OleUIAddVerbMenu* takes these flags into consideration, so that a container application doesn't have to think about them.

has the possibility of modification. A verb such as Play (on a sound or video object) would have a value of 3 because it appears on menus but doesn't allow modification.

DataFormats is another special entry that describes all the different clipboard formats that an object of this class can exchange. *DataFormats* can have one or more subkeys, the first is key 0, the second key 1, and so on. These values determine only the priority of the formats and have no meaning otherwise. So the format with the highest fidelity (such as your application-specific format) should have key 0, and the key number for better graphic formats such as a metafile should have a lower value than a bitmap has.

ALERT: Intimidating Paragraph Ahead!

Each value for the subkeys has four elements: format, aspect, medium, and flag. The first is the number of the clipboard format, if there is a CF_... symbol for it in WINDOWS.H, or the string name of the format if it's registered. In Cosmo's preceding registration, the first two entries have registered formats of "Polyline Figure" and "Embed Source" (the latter is an *IStorage* with the objects data), whereas the last two have values of 3 (CF_METAFILEPICT) and 2 (CF_BITMAP). The next element, the aspect, is the combination of any DVASPECT values where –1 means "all aspects." All the sample entries are registered with a value of 1 for DVASPECT_CONTENT. If, for example, we could also provide CF_METAFILEPICT with DVASPECT_ICON (defined as 4), the value would be 5 (DVASPECT_ICON ¦ DVASPECT_CONTENT). The third component contains all the types of storage mediums in which the server can render the format. This value can be any combination from the TYMED enumeration in DVOBJ.H. For "Polyline Figure," for example, we have a 1, which is TYMED_HGLOBAL. "Embed Source" is 8 for TYMED_ISTORAGE, CF_METAFILEPICT is 32 for TYMED_MFPICT, and CF_BITMAP is 16 for TYMED_GDI. If we could render something in two mediums, such as TYMED_ISTORAGE ¦ TYMED_ISTREAM, the value would be 12. Finally, the "flag" for each format is a combination of DATADIR values from the (what else?) DATADIR enumeration in DVOBJ.H. If you can ask the object for the format, that's a "Get" direction and has the value 1 (DATADIR_GET). If you can send the object the format but not retrieve it, use 2 (DATADIR_SET). If the object can exchange the format in both directions (as with "Polyline Figure") use the combined value of 3.

A primary benefit of this registration is to prevent OLE 2 from having to run your application to learn such information when a container wants to see whether your object supports exchange using a specific format. In fact, OLE2.DLL as the default handler will implement *IDataObject::EnumFormatEtc* using this information, which is much less bother than launching your server. Even if your application is running, you can still tell OLE 2 to implement the enumerator for you based on these entries by returning OLE_S_USEREG from *EnumFormatEtc.* Making these entries is much easier than implementing an enumerator.

With all your entries in the Registration Database, your application will now appear in a container's Insert Object dialog box. If you select your server's name in the dialog box (and choose OK), OLE 2 will find the path in the Registration Database and launch your application. Of course, nothing else will work, but you can at least verify that this part of the process is working. So now let's see what we should do on startup when our application is launched.

Implement and Register a Class Factory

In Chapter 4, we learned how to implement a class factory in a simple EXE server called EKoala. The "Koala" objects that this class factory created were pretty simple: They had only the one *IPersist* interface. We learned how to register the class factory from an EXE server by calling the *CoRegisterClassObject* function in COMPOBJ.DLL, and we learned how to provide an unloading mechanism that would ensure that the server shut down properly when there were no more objects to serve.

An embedding server in the compound document scenario is really the same thing as a very simple server such as EKoala. The difference is solely in what sort of object the server provides. In the case of EKoala, we had an object with one functional interface and no user interface. An embedded object, on the other hand, has at least three interfaces—*IOleObject, IPersistStorage,* and *IDataObject*—and does require some user interface through which the end user can make changes to that object. But because the difference is in the *object,* most parts of the *server* that deal with the class factory are the same as before. We can see these difference in changes made to Cosmo on the "application" (or server) level, as shown in Listing 10-1 on the next page. These changes include modifications to COSMO.H and COSMO.CPP, as well as the addition of two new files, COSMOOLE.H and ICLASSF.CPP.

The C++ object we use to implement our embedded objects is called *CFigure,* which we'll see in the next section. The class factory is thus called *CFigureClassFactory.* Because most of this latter class is the same as other class factories we've seen, the code listing does not show its definition or any of its implementation outside of its *CreateInstance* member. (The only additions to the class itself are a pointer variable to the *CCosmoFrame* called *m_pFR* and a BOOL member called *m_fCreated.*) In addition, the listing does not show parts of COSMO.CPP that are identical to other server code we've seen, but note that we've added one more global flag *g_fUser,* which provides an additional condition in the *ObjectDestroyed* function. We'll see why shortly.

COSMO.H

```
[Other lines omitted]

class __far CCosmoFrame : public CFrame
    {
    friend class CFigureClassFactory;
    friend class CFigure;    //For UI purposes.

    private:
        ...

        BOOL            m_fEmbedding;      //-Embedding found?
        DWORD           m_dwRegCO;         //Registration key
        LPCLASSFACTORY  m_pIClassFactory;

    protected:
        ...

        virtual void       ParseCommandLine(void);

        ...

    public:
        ...

        virtual void       UpdateEmbeddingUI(BOOL, LPCDocument
                               , LPCSTR, LPCSTR);
    };
```

COSMO.CPP

```
[Other globals omitted from listing]

//Indicate if the user has control
BOOL        g_fUser=TRUE;

[Other code omitted from listing]
```

Listing 10-1.

Changes and additions to Cosmo on the "application" or "server" level to support embedded objects.

(continued)

Listing 10-1. *continued*

```
/*
 * ObjectDestroyed
 *
 * Purpose:
 *  Function for the Cosmo Figure object to call when it gets
 *  destroyed. We destroy the main window if the proper conditions
 *  are met for shutdown.
 */

void FAR PASCAL ObjectDestroyed(void)
    {
    g_cObj--;

    //No more objects, no locks, no user control, shut the app down.
    if (0L==g_cObj && 0L==g_cLock && IsWindow(g_hWnd) && !g_fUser)
        PostMessage(g_hWnd, WM_CLOSE, 0, 0L);

    return;
    }

CCosmoFrame::CCosmoFrame(HINSTANCE hInst, HINSTANCE hInstPrev
    , LPSTR pszCmdLine, int nCmdShow)
    : CFrame(hInst, hInstPrev, pszCmdLine, nCmdShow)
    {
    ...
    char    szTemp[256];
    ...
    m_fInitialized=FALSE;
    m_fEmbedding=FALSE;

    //This function is in OLE2UI
    ParseCmdLine(m_pszCmdLine, &m_fEmbedding, szTemp);
    g_fUser=!m_fEmbedding
    m_dwRegCO=0;
    m_pIClassFactory=NULL;

    return;
    }

CCosmoFrame::~CCosmoFrame(void)
    {
    UINT            i;

    //Reverse CoRegisterClassObject, takes class factory ref to 1
    if (0L!=m_dwRegCO)
```

(continued)

Listing 10-1. *continued*

```
        CoRevokeClassObject(m_dwRegCO);

    //Should be last Release, which frees the class factory.
    if (NULL!=m_pIClassFactory)
        m_pIClassFactory->Release();

    ...

    return;
    }

BOOL CCosmoFrame::FInit(LPFRAMEINIT pFI)
    {
    HRESULT     hr;

    [OleInitialize et. al omitted from listing]

    ...

    if (m_fEmbedding)
        {
        m_pIClassFactory=new CFigureClassFactory(this);

        if (NULL==m_pIClassFactory)
            return FALSE;

        //Because we hold on to this, we should AddRef it.
        m_pIClassFactory->AddRef();

        hr=CoRegisterClassObject(CLSID_Cosmo2Figure
            , (LPUNKNOWN)m_pIClassFactory, CLSCTX_LOCAL_SERVER
            , REGCLS_SINGLEUSE, &m_dwRegCO);

        if (FAILED(hr))
            return FALSE;
        }

    return CFrame::FInit(pFI);
    }

/*
 * CCosmoFrame::FPreShowInit
 *
 * Purpose:
 *  Called from FInit before initially showing the window.  We do
 *  whatever else we want here, modifying m_nCmdShow as necessary
 *  which affects ShowWindow in FInit.
 */

BOOL CCosmoFrame::FPreShowInit(void)
```

(continued)

Listing 10-1. *continued*

```
    {
    [Other code omitted]

    //Save the window handle for shutdown if necessary.
    g_hWnd=m_hWnd;

    //If we're -Embedding, don't show the window initially.
    if (m_fEmbedding)
        m_nCmdShow=SW_HIDE;

    return TRUE;
    }

/*
 * CCosmoFrame::ParseCommandLine
 *
 * Purpose:
 *  Allows the application to parse the command line and take action
 *  after the window has possibly been shown. For a compound
 *  document server we need to just make sure that if -Embedding
 *  is there that we take no file action. FPreShowInit has already
 *  handled the window visibility.
 */

void CCosmoFrame::ParseCommandLine(void)
    {
    //If -Embedding was there, prevent any attempt to load a file.
    if (m_fEmbedding)
        return;

    CFrame::ParseCommandLine();
    return;
    }
```

ICLASSF.CPP

```
[Other code omitted]

CFigureClassFactory::CFigureClassFactory(LPCCosmoFrame pFR)
{
m_cRef=0L;
m_pFR=pFR;
m_fCreated=FALSE;
return;
CFigureClassFactory::~CFigureClassFactory(void)
```

(continued)

Listing 10-1. *continued*

```
    {
    return
    }
    ...

STDMETHODIMP CFigureClassFactory::CreateInstance(LPUNKNOWN pUnkOuter
    , REFIID riid, LPLPVOID ppvObj)
    {
    LPCCosmoDoc         pDoc;
    HRESULT             hr;

    *ppvObj=NULL;

    //Great idea to protect yourself from multiple creates here.
    if (m_fCreated)
        return ResultFromScode(E_UNEXPECTED);

    m_fCreated=TRUE;
    hr=ResultFromScode(E_OUTOFMEMORY);

    //We don't support aggregation
    if (NULL!=pUnkOuter)
        return ResultFromScode(CLASS_E_NOAGGREGATION);

    //Try creating a new document, which creates the object.
    pDoc=(LPCCosmoDoc)m_pFR->m_pCL->NewDocument(TRUE, m_pFR->m_pAdv);

    if (NULL==pDoc)
        {
        //This will cause shutdown as object count will go to zero.
        g_cObj++;
        ObjectDestroyed();
        return hr;
        }

    //Insure the document is untitled, then get requested interface.
    pDoc->ULoad(TRUE, NULL);
    pDoc->m_pFigure->FrameSet(m_pFR);
    hr=pDoc->m_pFigure->QueryInterface(riid, ppvObj);

    //Closing the document will destroy the object and cause shutdown.
    if (FAILED(hr))
        {
        m_pFR->m_pCL->CloseDocument(pDoc);
        return hr;
        }

    return NOERROR;
    }
```

The following two sections explain what all of this is for, with the exception of the function *UpdateEmbeddingUI*, which will be covered in "Modify the Server's User Interface" later on.

The Class Factory for Embedded Objects

There are only a few differences between the class factory in Listing 10-1 and those we've seen for component objects. The first difference is that the class factory's constructor in Listing 10-1 is given a pointer to the application's frame structure. We need this in Cosmo because *IClassFactory::CreateInstance* will ask the frame and its client window to create a new document that will contain a new object. This is somewhat different from before, but it is necessary because the object we're creating here involves user interface, and therefore we need some way to create a window in which to display that object.

The second difference is that in our implementation of *IClassFactory::CreateInstance*, we need to remember whether this class factory has already created one object through the variable *m_fCreated*. I included this here because we're going to register this class factory for single use with REGCLS_SINGLEUSE, but that flag determines only whether COMPOBJ.DLL will launch another instance of your EXE from *CoGetClassObject*. If someone obtains a pointer to our class factory through a single *CoGetClassObject* call, they could potentially call our *CreateInstance* more than once. For simplicity, we want our application to service only a single embedded object from one instance of Cosmo, so we prevent the outside world from asking our application for more. There are a few complications in servicing multiple embedded objects (mostly with user interface) that are covered in the last section of this chapter, "(Optional) MDI Servers, User Interface, and Shutdown."

You'll also notice that if the value of *pUnkOuter* passed to *CreateInstance* is non-NULL, we fail, with E_NOAGGREGATION. Whether you allow aggregation or not is up to you, but I see little point in supporting it here, so my version fails if someone attempts to aggregate. This, of course, makes the actual object implementation rather atheistic because it never acknowledges the existence of a higher unknown.

If you are adding code to an application, as you read this you can implement all the parts of the class factory shown here for Cosmo except the part of *IClassFactory::CreateInstance* that instantiates an object because you don't have an object yet. For now, start shutdown as appropriate (Cosmo does this by calling *ObjectDestroyed*) and return *ResultFromScode(E_OUTOFMEMORY)*, which is a good simulation of what might happen if real object creation failed. Note that in such a failure situation, your server should free itself from memory by exiting *WinMain* one way or another. Cosmo does this by calling its own *ObjectDestroyed* function.

Startup with *-Embedding*

Back in Chapter 4, I mentioned that when a server is launched to service an object, COMPOBJ.DLL will send *-Embedding* on the command line as an indication. There is no difference for an embedded object server, so Cosmo detects the presence of the flag in its function frame constructor and sets its *m_fEmbedding* flag appropriately, using the *ParseCmdLine* function in the OLE2UI library:

```
ParseCmdLine(m_pszCmdLine, &m_fEmbedding, szTemp);
```

ParseCmdLine checks for *-Embedding* as well as */Embedding* and removes all white space from the command line before parsing. Checking for both - and / variations and ignoring white space are essential to work with OLE 1 containers, which might send such variations.

Immediately after Cosmo calls *ParseCmdLine* to set *m_fEmbedding*, it sets the new global variable *g_fUser* to *!m_fEmbedding*. The *g_fUser* variable is a new condition for shutdown in *ObjectDestroyed*. When you run Cosmo stand-alone, open a document, and close that document, the *ObjectDestroyed* function will be called because the object that was in the document was destroyed. Without the flag that says our application is running under user control, *ObjectDestroyed* would close the application. This is a rather unexpected user interface. So we add the *g_fUser* flag to prevent that from happening. Only when our application is running in the compound document scenario do we want this flag to be FALSE, in which case closing the document will, in fact, shut down the server correctly.

In any case, *m_fEmbedding* is later used in *CosmoFrame::PreShowInit* and *CCosmoFrame::ParseCommandLine*, which are called in this order. (Both are overrides of default implementation in CLASSLIB's *CFrame*.) *PreShowInit* first saves the window handle in *g_hWnd* so that the *ObjectDestroyed* function can post it a WM_CLOSE for shutdown. In addition, *PreShowInit* checks to see whether *m_fEmbedding* is set. If so, it forces the initial *ShowWindow* parameter to SW_HIDE, irrespective of its original value. This ensures that the server's main window—and thus all other child windows within it—remain hidden until the server is specifically told to show those windows. This is part of the compound document contract: The server can be asked to silently load an object and provide an updated rendering (say, a metafile) of the object's data. By silently, I mean that the server is launched, asked for the rendering, and immediately closed without ever having shown itself. If the server is launched and later is asked to edit the object, it can show itself, as we will see later in "Implement *IDataObject* and *IOleObject* Interfaces."

The *ParseCommandLine* function is called from CLASSLIB's *CFrame::FInit* function at the end of all other initialization with the purpose of loading any document that was listed on the command line. We need to override this function so that if *m_fEmbedding* is set, we do not attempt to load anything. Otherwise, we would attempt to load a file called *-Embedding*, which will invariably fail and throw up a terribly confusing message box, which says *Cannot load file.* Now there's something I'd call user unfriendly, especially if this were all happening in the context of the Insert Object dialog box in a container application.

The other place we use *m_fEmbedding* is in *CCosmoFrame::Finit*, where it determines whether we can create and register a class factory. If the end user launches Cosmo from the shell, *-Embedding* is not present, so we don't need to worry about servicing an embedded object. Therefore, we have no need for the class factory. In addition, Cosmo uses REGCLS_SINGLEUSE in such a way that OLE 2 will launch another instance for each embedded object the end user wants to manipulate.

The bottom line is that handling *-Embedding* involves five steps:

1. On startup, look for *-Embedding* on the command line and set a flag to indicate its presence or absence.
2. Set your "user control" flag to FALSE if your flag is true or to TRUE if your flag is false.
3. If your flag is TRUE, create and register your class factory. Otherwise, only register the class factory if you can handle multiple objects.
4. If your flag is TRUE, do not initially show your application window. Otherwise, obey the *nCmdShow* parameter passed to *WinMain*.
5. If your flag is TRUE, prevent the rest of your application's code from trying to load *-Embedding* as an initial file.

NOTE: If your application is an MDI application that can service multiple objects in a single instance of the application, you might want to create and register a class factory even when *-Embedding* does not appear on the command line. See "(Optional) MDI Servers, User Interface, and Shutdown" later for more details.

When you're finished adding the class factory and placing the code to handle *-Embedding*, you can compile and test the code so that you're sure you detect *-Embedding* properly, and you can register your class factory as well when appropriate. An easy way to test this is to run your program using

Program Manager's (or File Manager's) File/Run command, which allows you to add command-line arguments. You can toss *-Embedding* there and see what happens. If all goes well, you'll have your application in memory but hidden, in which case you have no way to close the thing unless you purge it with a tool such as WPS.EXE (in the OLE 2 SDK). But, hey, you know that it works.

You can also test your unloading mechanism by using Insert Object in a container. In this situation, your application again is launched with *-Embedding* (for real, this time), and if you're testing your code with a fake *-Embedding* you'll know that your initialization and class factory registration works fine. So after your application is launched, you should see a call to *IClassFactory::CreateInstance*. Because you failed to create an object and you have no other locks or objects, your shutdown should kick in and purge your application from memory.

Implement an Initial Object with *IUnknown*

Having a class factory is pretty pointless unless you have an object for it to create, so the next step is to begin implementing your embedded object. I say "begin implementing" because it will be a little less painful to implement the object in pieces rather than attempt to implement the entire thing at once. So let's implement an object with just the *IUnknown* interface so that we can compile and test to see that the object is indeed created and that we close it properly.

As mentioned before, Cosmo's object is implemented using a C++ class called *CFigure*, with the parts of its implementation important for this discussion, as shown in Listing 10-2. COSMOLE.H contains the definition of *CFigure* and interface implementation classes for *IPersistStorage*, *IDataObject*, and *IOleObject*, which I have omitted from the listing. FIGURE.CPP contains the implementation of *CFigure*. All of the extra functions in *CFigure* and the use of many of the class's variables will be shown in the context of the other interfaces that use them, so only those relevant to our immediate discussion are shown here.

COSMOLE.H

```
/*
 * Include file containing all compound document related
 * definitions.
 *
 * Copyright (c)1993 Microsoft Corporation, All Rights Reserved
 */
```

Listing 10-2. *(continued)*

The implementation of Cosmo's Figure object.

Listing 10-2. *continued*

```
[Class factory-related parts shown in Listing 10-1]

//FIGURE.CPP
//This is what the class factory creates

#define CFORMATETCGET   5
...
class __far CFigure : public IUnknown
    {
    friend class CImpIPersistStorage;
    friend class CImpIDataObject;
    friend class CImpIOleObject;

    protected:
        ULONG                m_cRef;
        LPCCosmoFrame        m_pFR;      //Frame (for UI changes)
        LPCCosmoDoc          m_pDoc;     //What holds real polyline
        LPCPolyline          m_pPL;      //Copy of m_pDoc->m_pPL

        BOOL                 m_fEmbedded;
        LPFNDESTROYED        m_pfnDestroy;

        LPCStringTable       m_pST;      //Object strings

        //Things for IPersistStorage
        LPIMPIPERSISTSTORAGE m_pIPersistStorage;
        LPSTORAGE            m_pIStorage;
        LPSTREAM             m_pIStream;

        //Things for IDataObject
        LPIMPIDATAOBJECT     m_pIDataObject;         //Implemented
        LPDATAADVISEHOLDER   m_pIDataAdviseHolder;   //Used

        UINT                 m_cf;                   //pDoc->m_cf
        ULONG                m_cfeGet;
        FORMATETC            m_rgfeGet[CFORMATETCGET];

        //Things for IOleObject
        LPIMPIOLEOBJECT      m_pIOleObject;          //Implemented
        LPOLEADVISEHOLDER    m_pIOleAdviseHolder;    //Used
        LPOLECLIENTSITE      m_pIOleClientSite;      //Used

    public:
        CFigure(LPFNDESTROYED, LPCCosmoDoc);
        ~CFigure(void);
```

(continued)

Listing 10-2. *continued*

```
        //Nondelegating IUnknown:  we don't support aggregation here.
        STDMETHODIMP QueryInterface(REFIID, LPLPVOID);
        STDMETHODIMP_(ULONG) AddRef(void);
        STDMETHODIMP_(ULONG) Release(void);

        BOOL FInit(void);
        void FrameSet(LPCCosmoFrame);
        BOOL FIsDirty(void);
        BOOL FIsEmbedded(void);
        void SendAdvise(UINT);
    };

typedef CFigure *LPCFigure;

[Remainder of file relevant to interfaces]
```

FIGURE.CPP

```
/*
 * Implementation of the CFigure object for Cosmo.
 *
 * Copyright (c)1993 Microsoft Corporation, All Rights Reserved
 */

#include "cosmo.h"

CFigure::CFigure(LPFNDESTROYED pfnDestroy, LPCCosmoDoc pDoc)
    {
    m_cRef=0;
    m_pfnDestroy=pfnDestroy;

    m_pFR=NULL;     //We get this later through FrameSet.
    m_pDoc=pDoc;
    m_pPL=pDoc->m_pPL;

    m_fEmbedded=FALSE;

    //NULL any contained interfaces initially.
    m_pIPersistStorage=NULL;
    m_pIDataObject=NULL;
    m_pIDataAdviseHolder=NULL;
    m_pIOleObject=NULL;
    m_pIOleAdviseHolder=NULL;
    m_pIOleClientSite=NULL;
```

(continued)

Listing 10-2. *continued*

```
    m_cf=pDoc->m_cf;

    //These are for IDataObject::QueryGetData
    m_cfeGet=CFORMATETCGET;

    SETDefFormatEtc(m_rgfeGet[0], pDoc->m_cf, TYMED_HGLOBAL);
    SETDefFormatEtc(m_rgfeGet[1], pDoc->m_cfEmbedSource
        , TYMED_ISTORAGE);
    SETDefFormatEtc(m_rgfeGet[2], pDoc->m_cfObjectDescriptor
        , TYMED_HGLOBAL);
    SETDefFormatEtc(m_rgfeGet[3], CF_METAFILEPICT, TYMED_MFPICT);
    SETDefFormatEtc(m_rgfeGet[4], CF_BITMAP, TYMED_GDI);

    return;
    }

CFigure::~CFigure(void)
    {
    //Free contained interfaces.
    if (NULL!=m_pIOleObject)
        delete m_pIOleObject;

    if (NULL!=m_pIDataObject)
        delete m_pIDataObject;

    if (NULL!=m_pIStorage)
        m_pIStorage->Release();

    if (NULL!=m_pIStream)
        m_pIStream->Release();

    if (NULL!=m_pIPersistStorage)
        delete m_pIPersistStorage;

    //Free strings.
    if (NULL!=m_pST)
        delete m_pST;

    return;
    }

STDMETHODIMP CFigure::QueryInterface(REFIID riid, LPLPVOID ppv)
    {
    *ppv=NULL;

    if (IsEqualIID(riid, IID_IUnknown))
        *ppv=(LPVOID)this;
```

(continued)

Listing 10-2. *continued*

```
    if (IsEqualIID(riid, IID_IPersist)
        || IsEqualIID(riid, IID_IPersistStorage))
        *ppv=(LPVOID)m_pIPersistStorage;

    if (IsEqualIID(riid, IID_IDataObject))
        *ppv=(LPVOID)m_pIDataObject;

    if (IsEqualIID(riid, IID_IOleObject))
        *ppv=(LPVOID)m_pIOleObject;

    if (NULL!=*ppv)
        {
        ((LPUNKNOWN)*ppv)->AddRef();
        return NOERROR;
        }

    return ResultFromScode(E_NOINTERFACE);
    }

STDMETHODIMP_(ULONG) CFigure::AddRef(void)
    {
    return ++m_cRef;
    }

STDMETHODIMP_(ULONG) CFigure::Release(void)
    {
    ULONG       cRefT;

    cRefT=--m_cRef;

    if (0L==m_cRef)
        {
        if (NULL!=m_pfnDestroy)
            (*m_pfnDestroy)();
        }

    return cRefT;
    }

/*
 * CFigure::FInit
 *
 * Purpose:
 *  Performs any initialization of a CFigure that's prone to failure
 *  that we also use internally before exposing the object outside.
 */
```

(continued)

Listing 10-2. *continued*

```
BOOL CFigure::FInit(void)
    {
    m_pST=new CStringTable(m_pDoc->m_hInst);

    if (NULL==m_pST)
        return FALSE;

    if (!m_pST->FInit(IDS_FIGUREMIN, IDS_FIGUREMAX))
        return FALSE;

    //Allocate contained interfaces.
    m_pIPersistStorage=new CImpIPersistStorage(this
        , (LPUNKNOWN)this);

    if (NULL==m_pIPersistStorage)
        return FALSE;

    m_pIDataObject=new CImpIDataObject(this, (LPUNKNOWN)this);

    if (NULL==m_pIDataObject)
        return FALSE;

    m_pIOleObject=new CImpIOleObject(this, (LPUNKNOWN)this);

    if (NULL==m_pIOleObject)
        return FALSE;

    return TRUE;
    }

/*
 * CFigure::FrameSet
 *
 * Purpose:
 *  Provides the compound document object with access to the frame
 *  of this application for UI purposes.
 */

void CFigure::FrameSet(LPCCosmoFrame pFR)
    {
    m_pFR=pFR;
    return;
    }
```

As you can see, the figure itself has a nondelegating *IUnknown* implementation to which all the interfaces will delegate. I mentioned before that this object does not support aggregation, which manifests itself through the fact that the *CFigure::FInit* always passes itself (the *this* pointer) as the *IUnknown* to which the interfaces delegate. In previous examples that did support aggregation, this might have been the outer unknown had there been one.[5]

Most of what's shown in this listing makes little sense until we see exactly where a figure object is created and manipulated. In Listing 10-1, you can see that the *CreateInstance* function of our class factory doesn't actually create an object; it creates a document window (*CCosmoDoc*), just as if the user had selected File/New from Cosmo's menu. *CCosmoDoc* has been modified for this chapter to have a variable called *m_pFigure*, which is a pointer to a single *CFigure* object it manages. This gives a one-to-one correspondence between a *CFigure* object that serves as an embedded object and the *CPolyline* object that Cosmo uses to display and edit its data. So by creating a new document, which calls *new CCosmoDoc* and *CCosmoDoc::FInit* (DOCUMENT.CPP) we create a new figure object (although you might not need the explicit document yourself):

```
CCosmoDoc::CCosmoDoc(HINSTANCE hInst)
    : CDocument(hInst)
    {
    ...

    m_pFigure=NULL;

    return;
    }

CCosmoDoc::~CCosmoDoc(void)
    {
    ...

    /*
     * The AddRef here preserves a reference count on the object
     * even after our call to CoDisconnectObject.  When we then
     * Release that reference count, we'll free the object and
     * start shutdown.  If the object was destroyed before we
```

(continued)

5. Note also that I didn't bother to change the interface implementations themselves; other code we've already implemented always passed the object pointer and the controlling unknown to the interface implementation, where the controlling unknown was either the object or a real outer unknown. I decided not to change the interface implementations here just to remain consistent with all other implementations. I've often heard that readers prefer consistency above sheer elegance, so here ya go.

```
     * are destroyed, it will NULL out m_pFigure for us (see
     * CFigure::Release in FIGURE.CPP)
     */

    if (NULL!=m_pFigure)
        {
        m_pFigure->AddRef();
        CoDisconnectObject((LPUNKNOWN)m_pFigure, 0L);
        m_pFigure->Release();   //Starts shutdown if necessary.
        }

    return;
    }

BOOL CCosmoDoc::FInit(LPDOCUMENTINIT pDI)
    {
    [Other initialization]

    m_pFigure=new CFigure(ObjectDestroyed, this);

    if (NULL==m_pFigure)
        return FALSE;

    //We created an object, so count it.
    g_cObj++;

    if (!m_pFigure->FInit())
        return FALSE;

    return TRUE;
    }
```

It might seem strange that I play some tricks with reference counting here on the figure object, but I do it to centralize all the shutdown code into *CFigure::Release* (and ultimately *ObjectDestroyed*). When we create the figure using *new*, it has a reference count of zero (as set in *CFigure::CFigure*). So if creation succeeds, we should use *AddRef* on it to set a reference count of one and increment the global object count, which we do in *CCosmoDoc::FInit* instead of the class factory's *CreateInstance*. Let's say now that the call to *m_pFigure->FInit()* shown previously fails, and *CCosmoDoc::FInit* returns FALSE, which eventually calls the document's destructor. Here, instead of calling *delete m_pFigure*, it calls *m_pFigure->Release*, which will reduce the reference count to zero, which will call *ObjectDestroyed*. This function will decrement the global object count to zero, see that there are no locks, that there is no user control, and that the frame window is still valid, and then post a WM_CLOSE, which shuts the whole application down and purges it from memory. In this way, I keep all the shutdown code in one place and one place only.

You probably also noticed that funny *CoDisconnectObject* call on *m_pFigure.* This function ensures that just before we release the object that might shut the application down there are no external connections to it. As we make this call in the document's destructor, we are on a nonstop, one-way flight to oblivion as far as this object is concerned. So we have to tell OLE 2 that after this there is nothing, and to make sure that no other agent tries to get at this object. *CoDisconnectObject* is just the ticket, although it seems rather brutal. In any case, you must call this function when closing the document that holds your object. It's the only way to remove all other reference counts on your object. Otherwise, we have a circular reference situation as we first saw in Chapter 4 in which your object holds reference counts on external objects that also hold reference counts on your object. In Chapter 4, we mentioned that some intervention was necessary to break this circular referencing. In this case, the end user will close the document or application, which forces a call to *CoDisconnectObject,* which breaks all the external connections on the object, allowing it to free itself.

Again, the rest of the *CFigure* implementation supports the other interfaces we need on this object: *IPersistStorage, IDataObject,* and *IOleObject,* which are the subjects of the next three sections. But because you have an *IUnknown* implementation here already, you have, of course, a Windows Object. You can now test your server again in the context of a container's Insert Object dialog box. This time, instead of failing inside *CreateInstance,* you can actually instantiate an object and return successfully. You will probably see a number of *QueryInterface* calls on this object, asking for the other three expected interfaces. Because we don't have those interfaces yet, things won't be working right and your server might be left in memory. So it's time to start adding those interfaces.

Implement the *IPersistStorage* Interface

The best choice for the first interface to implement on an embedded object is *IPersistStorage,* exactly the *IPersistStorage* interface we discussed in Chapter 5, with all the same contractual obligations. Through this interface, the embedded object is told to initialize its storage, save or load itself from a storage, and get its grubby hands off the storage when the container wants to perform a File Save As with the object still open.[6]

6. Patron, as a container, does not keep objects running when performing a File Save or Save As, so it does not call *IPersistStorage::HandsOffStorage.*

For all intents and purposes, there is nothing special about the implementation of this interface that we don't already know, but it's worthwhile to point out that this interface is used only for embedded objects; linked objects have no use for it. (They use *IPersistFile* instead.) In any case, to be a server of embedded objects, your application must have an implementation of *IPersistStorage* like the one shown for Cosmo in Listing 10-3.

IPERSTOR.CPP

```
/*
 * Implementation of the IPersistStorage interface that we expose on
 * the CFigure compound document object.  This ties into the
 * functionality of CPolyline.
 *
 * Copyright (c)1993 Microsoft Corporation, All Rights Reserved
 */

#include "cosmo.h"

CImpIPersistStorage::CImpIPersistStorage(LPCFigure pObj
    , LPUNKNOWN pUnkOuter)
    {
    m_cRef=0;
    m_pObj=pObj;
    m_pUnkOuter=pUnkOuter;
    return;
    }

CImpIPersistStorage::~CImpIPersistStorage(void)
    {
    return;
    }

STDMETHODIMP CImpIPersistStorage::QueryInterface(REFIID riid
    , LPLPVOID ppv)
    {
    return m_pUnkOuter->QueryInterface(riid, ppv);
    }

STDMETHODIMP_(ULONG) CImpIPersistStorage::AddRef(void)
    {
    ++m_cRef;
```

Listing 10-3. *(continued)*
Cosmo's IPersistStorage *implementation.*

Listing 10-3. *continued*

```
    return m_pUnkOuter->AddRef();
    }

STDMETHODIMP_(ULONG) CImpIPersistStorage::Release(void)
    {
    --m_cRef;
    return m_pUnkOuter->Release();
    }
STDMETHODIMP CImpIPersistStorage::GetClassID(LPCLSID pClsID)
    {
    *pClsID=CLSID_Cosmo2Figure;
    return NOERROR;
    }

STDMETHODIMP CImpIPersistStorage::IsDirty(void)
    {
    //CFigure::FIsDirty returns the document's dirty flag.
    return ResultFromScode(m_pObj->FIsDirty() ? S_OK : S_FALSE);
    }

STDMETHODIMP CImpIPersistStorage::InitNew(LPSTORAGE pIStorage)
    {
    HRESULT     hr;

    //This should not happen
    if (NULL!=m_pObj->m_pIStorage)
        return ResultFromScode(E_UNEXPECTED);

    /*
     * The rules of IPersistStorage mean we hold onto the IStorage
     * and pre-create anything we'd need in Save(...,TRUE) for
     * low-memory situations.  For us this means creating our
     * "CONTENTS" stream and holding onto that IStream as
     * well as the IStorage here (requiring an AddRef call).
     */

    hr=pIStorage->CreateStream("CONTENTS", STGM_DIRECT
        | STGM_CREATE | STGM_READWRITE | STGM_SHARE_EXCLUSIVE
        , 0, 0, &m_pObj->m_pIStream);

    if (FAILED(hr))
        return hr;

    //Initialize class information.
    WriteClassStg(pIStorage, CLSID_Cosmo2Figure);
```

(continued)

Listing 10-3. *continued*

```
    WriteFmtUserTypeStg(pIStorage, m_pObj->m_cf
        , (*m_pObj->m_pST)[IDS_USERTYPE]);

    pIStorage->AddRef();
    m_pObj->m_pIStorage=pIStorage;

    return NOERROR;
    }

STDMETHODIMP CImpIPersistStorage::Load(LPSTORAGE pIStorage)
    {
    HRESULT     hr;
    LONG        lRet;
    LPSTREAM    pIStream;

    //This should not happen
    if (NULL!=m_pObj->m_pIStorage)
        return ResultFromScode(E_UNEXPECTED);

    if (NULL==pIStorage)
        return ResultFromScode(STG_E_INVALIDPOINTER);

    hr=pIStorage->OpenStream("CONTENTS", 0, STGM_DIRECT
        | STGM_READWRITE | STGM_SHARE_EXCLUSIVE, 0, &pIStream);

    if (FAILED(hr))
        return ResultFromScode(STG_E_READFAULT);

    lRet=m_pObj->m_pPL->ReadFromStream(pIStream);

    if (lRet < 0)
        return ResultFromScode(STG_E_READFAULT);

    /*
     * We don't call pIStream->Release here because we may need
     * it for a low-memory save in Save.  We also need to
     * hold onto a copy of pIStorage, meaning AddRef.
     */
    m_pObj->m_pIStream=pIStream;

    pIStorage->AddRef();
    m_pObj->m_pIStorage=pIStorage;

    return NOERROR;
    }

STDMETHODIMP CImpIPersistStorage::Save(LPSTORAGE pIStorage
    , BOOL fSameAsLoad)
```

(continued)

Listing 10-3. *continued*

```
    {
    LONG        lRet;
    HRESULT     hr;
    LPSTREAM    pIStream;

    if (NULL==pIStorage)
        return ResultFromScode(STG_E_INVALIDPOINTER);

    /*
     * If we're saving to a new storage, create a new stream.
     * If fSameAsLoad is TRUE, then we write to the
     * stream we already allocated.  We should NOT depends on
     * pIStorage with fSameAsLoad is TRUE.
     */
    if (fSameAsLoad)
        {
        LARGE_INTEGER   li;

        /*
         * Use pre-allocated streams to avoid failures due
         * to low-memory conditions.  Be sure to reset the
         * stream pointer if you used this stream before!!
         */
        pIStream=m_pObj->m_pIStream;
        LISet32(li, 0);
        pIStream->Seek(li, STREAM_SEEK_SET, NULL);

        //This matches the Release below.
        pIStream->AddRef();
        }
    else
        {
        hr=pIStorage->CreateStream("CONTENTS", STGM_DIRECT
            | STGM_CREATE | STGM_WRITE | STGM_SHARE_EXCLUSIVE
            , 0, 0, &pIStream);

        if (FAILED(hr))
            return hr;

        WriteFmtUserTypeStg(pIStorage, m_pObj->m_cf
            , (*m_pObj->m_pST)[IDS_USERTYPE]);
        }

    lRet=m_pObj->m_pPL->WriteToStream(pIStream, VERSIONCURRENT);
    pIStream->Release();
```

(continued)

Listing 10-3. *continued*

```
    if (lRet >= 0)
        return NOERROR;

    return ResultFromScode(STG_E_WRITEFAULT);
    }

STDMETHODIMP CImpIPersistStorage::SaveCompleted(LPSTORAGE pIStorage)
    {
    HRESULT     hr;
    LPSTREAM    pIStream;

    /*
     * If pIStorage is NULL, then we don't need to do anything
     * since we already have all the pointers we need for Save.
     * Otherwise we have to release any held pointers and
     * reinitialize them from pIStorage.
     */

    if (NULL!=pIStorage)
        {
        hr=pIStorage->OpenStream("CONTENTS", 0, STGM_DIRECT
            | STGM_READWRITE | STGM_SHARE_EXCLUSIVE, 0
            , &pIStream);

        if (FAILED(hr))
            return hr;

        if (NULL!=m_pObj->m_pIStream)
            m_pObj->m_pIStream->Release();

        m_pObj->m_pIStream=pIStream;

        if (NULL!=m_pObj->m_pIStorage)
            m_pObj->m_pIStorage->Release();

        m_pObj->m_pIStorage=pIStorage;
        m_pObj->m_pIStorage->AddRef();
        }

    return NOERROR;
    }

STDMETHODIMP CImpIPersistStorage::HandsOffStorage(void)
    {
    //Release held pointers
    if (NULL!=m_pObj->m_pIStream)
        {
```

(continued)

Listing 10-3. *continued*

```
            m_pObj->m_pIStream->Release();
            m_pObj->m_pIStream=NULL;
            }

        if (NULL!=m_pObj->m_pIStorage)
            {
            m_pObj->m_pIStorage->Release();
            m_pObj->m_pIStorage=NULL;
            }

        return NOERROR;
        }
```

There are only a few interesting features to point out in this small piece of code. First, the *FIsDirty* function in the *CFigure* class exists solely to implement *IPersistStorage::IsDirty* because of C++ access restrictions. *CFigure* is marked as a friend of *CCosmoDoc*, which holds the dirty flag in a protected member *m_fDirty* so that only *CFigure* functions can access it. Because *CImpIPersistStorage* is a friend only of *CFigure* and not of *CCosmoDoc*, the interface has to call the object, which in turn can look up the dirty state. You might wonder why this *IPersistStorage* implementation does not simply call the public *CCosmoDoc::FIsDirty* function. The reason is that due to the notifications we'll be sending out from this server, an embedded object is never considered dirty as far as the user interface is concerned, and *CCosmoDoc::FIsDirty* is a function for the user interface. Later, we'll modify this function to always return "not dirty" when we're editing an embedded object. *IPersistStorage::IsDirty* is not so much a part of a user interface as it is a way for a container to know whether it needs to ask our application to save before closing the object, a process that does not necessarily involve the user interface. (See *IOleObject::Close.*)

I also want to point out that to assist in Cosmo's implementation of *IPersistStorage*, I added two new functions to the *CPolyline* class: *ReadFromStream* and *WriteToStream.* These two functions are the guts of what has been the *CPolyline* functions *ReadFromStorage* and *WriteToStorage*, which we implemented in Chapter 5. These two new functions are so much like the previously presented functions, in fact, that *ReadFromStorage* and *WriteToStorage* now merely open or create the appropriate stream to pass to *ReadFromStream* and *WriteFromStream.* I have separated the stream functionality of *CPolyline* from the storage functionality because we are contractually obliged in *IPersistStorage::Save* to not fail due to memory constraints. That means that Save cannot create new streams when writing data, which means we cannot simply call a function such as

CPolyine::WriteToStorage as the implemenation of *IPersistStorage::Save*. Instead we must pre-create the streams we'll need in Save from within *InitNew* and *Load*, as shown in Listing 10-3, and pass those streams to these new stream-related CPolyline functions.

What you will notice is that the impact on *CPolyline* is minimal, and had I seen the need for stream-related functions a little sooner, we might not have had to make any changes to *CPolyline* at all. In any case, this shows how a compound document object implementation can build upon whatever editor you might already have in your application.

After you have an implementation of *IPersistStorage* and you again launch your server through a container's Insert Object dialog box, you see that your object creates and initially asks for the *IOleObject* interface. If your application fails that, you'll be asked for *IUnknown* and then *IPersistStorage*. After you return that interface, you'll see a call to *IPersistStorage::InitNew*, which tells you that your application is being used from Insert Object. But for now, we cannot test *Load*, *Save*, *SaveCompleted*, or *HandsOffStorage* because we don't have a complete object and because the container will never get to the point of asking us to save. But you can at least make sure this all compiles and that your server still runs. (It's also a good idea to see whether the server runs stand-alone as well, if you allow it.)

Implement the *IDataObject* Interface

We saw in Chapter 9 how the default handler, OLE2.DLL, maintains a presentation cache in the container's storage. But somehow OLE2.DLL must obtain the presentations to cache in the first place. For that reason, all embedded objects must implement an *IDataObject* interface that at a minimum can provide CF_METAFILEPICT or CF_DIB (or CF_BITMAP) through *IDataObject::GetData* and *IDataObject::QueryInterface*. At least one of these formats is required to maintain some sort of basic cache for the object.

Besides providing presentations, an object will generally want to support its native clipboard format through both *GetData* and *SetData*. A container that knows more about your object might ask for your application's data or might give your application some data to integrate into it. If you don't foresee any reason why someone would want to use *GetData* or *SetData* for your private format, you have no reason to support it in this implementation of *IDataObject*. (You will, however, still want to support it on the clipboard through the *IDataObject* you use in such operations, but that is a different object and a different *IDataObject* from the one on the embedded object). One case in which you will have to support at least *GetData* on a native format is when you have your own object handler, such that the object handler can synchronize its copy of an object's format with the server's. But that is a topic for Chapter 11.

Besides graphic and native formats, you should also support the CF_EMBEDSOURCE format (which is the registered string "Embed Source"), which is an *IStorage* containing exactly the same data you would write to an *IStorage* in *IPersistStorage.* In fact, Cosmo's implementation of *IDataObject,* shown in Listing 10-4 along with parts of *CCosmoDoc* that are used by the *IDataObject* implementation, ultimately uses the same *CPolyline::WriteToStorage* to implement *IDataObject::GetData* and *GetDataHere* as it uses to implement *IPersistStorage::Save.*

IDATAOBJ.CPP

```
/*
 * Implementation of the IDataObject interface.
 *
 * Copyright (c)1993 Microsoft Corporation, All Rights Reserved
 */

#include "cosmo.h"

CImpIDataObject::CImpIDataObject(LPCFigure pObj
    , LPUNKNOWN pUnkOuter)
    {
    m_cRef=0;
    m_pObj=pObj;
    m_pUnkOuter=pUnkOuter;
    return;
    }

CImpIDataObject::~CImpIDataObject(void)
    {
    return;
    }

STDMETHODIMP CImpIDataObject::QueryInterface(REFIID riid
    , LPLPVOID ppv)
    {
    return m_pUnkOuter->QueryInterface(riid, ppv);
    }

STDMETHODIMP_(ULONG) CImpIDataObject::AddRef(void)
    {
    ++m_cRef;
    return m_pUnkOuter->AddRef();
    }
```

Listing 10-4.

Implementation of the IDataObject *interface for Cosmo's* CFigure *class.*

(continued)

Listing 10-4. *continued*

```
STDMETHODIMP_(ULONG) CImpIDataObject::Release(void)
    {
    --m_cRef;
    return m_pUnkOuter->Release();
    }

/*
 * CImpIDataObject::GetData
 *
 * Purpose:
 *  Retrieves data described by a specific FormatEtc into a StgMedium
 *  allocated by this function. Used like GetClipboardData.
 */

STDMETHODIMP CImpIDataObject::GetData(LPFORMATETC pFE
    , LPSTGMEDIUM pSTM)
    {
    UINT            cf=pFE->cfFormat;
    BOOL            fRet=FALSE;

    //Another part of us already knows if the format is good.
    if (NOERROR!=QueryGetData(pFE))
        return ResultFromScode(DATA_E_FORMATETC);

    if (CF_METAFILEPICT==cf || CF_BITMAP==cf || m_pObj->m_cf==cf)
        {
        if (CF_METAFILEPICT==cf)
            {
            pSTM->tymed=TYMED_MFPICT;
            }
        else
            pSTM->tymed=TYMED_HGLOBAL;

        pSTM->pUnkForRelease=NULL;
        pSTM->hGlobal=m_pObj->m_pDoc->RenderFormat(cf);
        fRet=(NULL!=pSTM->hGlobal);
        }
    else
        fRet=m_pObj->m_pDoc->FRenderMedium(cf, pSTM);

    return fRet ? NOERROR : ResultFromScode(DATA_E_FORMATETC);
    }

/*
 * CImpIDataObject::GetDataHere
```

(continued)

Listing 10-4. *continued*

```
 *
 * Purpose:
 *  Renders the specific FormatEtc into caller-allocated medium
 *  provided in pSTM.
 */

STDMETHODIMP CImpIDataObject::GetDataHere(LPFORMATETC pFE
    , LPSTGMEDIUM pSTM)
    {
    UINT        cf;
    LONG        lRet;

    /*
     * The only reasonable time this is called is for CF_EMBEDSOURCE
     * and TYMED_ISTORAGE (and later for CF_LINKSOURCE). This means
     * the same as IPersistStorage::Save.
     */

    cf=RegisterClipboardFormat(CF_EMBEDSOURCE);

    //Aspect is unimportant to us here, as is lindex and ptd.
    if (cf==pFE->cfFormat && (TYMED_ISTORAGE & pFE->tymed))
        {
        //We have an IStorage we can write into.
        pSTM->tymed=TYMED_ISTORAGE;
        pSTM->pUnkForRelease=NULL;
        lRet=m_pObj->m_pPL->WriteToStorage(pSTM->pstg
            , VERSIONCURRENT);

        if (lRet >= 0)
            return NOERROR;

        return ResultFromScode(STG_E_WRITEFAULT);
        }

    return ResultFromScode(DATA_E_FORMATETC);
    }

/*
 * CImpIDataObject::QueryGetData
 *
 * Purpose:
 *  Tests if a call to GetData with this FormatEtc will provide
 *  any rendering; used like IsClipboardFormatAvailable.
 */
```

(continued)

Listing 10-4. *continued*

```
STDMETHODIMP CImpIDataObject::QueryGetData(LPFORMATETC pFE)
    {
    UINT            cf=pFE->cfFormat;
    UINT            i;

    //Check the aspects we support.
    if (!(DVASPECT_CONTENT & pFE->dwAspect))
        return ResultFromScode(S_FALSE);

    for (i=0; i < m_pObj->m_cfeGet; i++)
        {
        if (pFE->cfFormat==m_pObj->m_rgfeGet[i].cfFormat
            && pFE->tymed & m_pObj->m_rgfeGet[i].tymed)
            {
            return NOERROR;
            }
        }

    return ResultFromScode(S_FALSE);
    }

STDMETHODIMP CImpIDataObject::GetCanonicalFormatEtc
    (LPFORMATETC pFEIn, LPFORMATETC pFEOut)
    {
    return ResultFromScode(DATA_S_SAMEFORMATETC);
    }

/*
 * CImpIDataObject::SetData
 *
 * Purpose:
 *  Places data described by a FormatEtc and living in a StgMedium
 *  into the object. The object may be responsible to clean up the
 *  StgMedium before exiting.
 */

STDMETHODIMP CImpIDataObject::SetData(LPFORMATETC pFE
    , STGMEDIUM FAR *pSTM, BOOL fRelease)
    {
    LONG            lRet;

    /*
     * Data can only come from global memory containing a
     * POLYLINEDATA structure that we send to the Polyline's
     * DataSetMem.
     */
```

(continued)

Listing 10-4. *continued*

```
    if ((pFE->cfFormat!=m_pObj->m_cf)
        || !(DVASPECT_CONTENT & pFE->dwAspect)
        || (TYMED_HGLOBAL!=pSTM->tymed))
        return ResultFromScode(DATA_E_FORMATETC);

    lRet=m_pObj->m_pPL->DataSetMem(pSTM->hGlobal, FALSE, TRUE
        , TRUE);

    if (fRelease)
        ReleaseStgMedium(pSTM);

    return (POLYLINE_E_NONE==lRet) ?
        NOERROR : ResultFromScode(DATA_E_FORMATETC);
    }

STDMETHODIMP CImpIDataObject::EnumFormatEtc(DWORD dwDir
    , LPENUMFORMATETC FAR *ppEnum)
    {
    return ResultFromScode(OLE_S_USEREG);
    }

STDMETHODIMP CImpIDataObject::DAdvise(LPFORMATETC pFE, DWORD dwFlags
    , LPADVISESINK pIAdviseSink, LPDWORD pdwConn)
    {
    HRESULT         hr;

    if (NULL==m_pObj->m_pIDataAdviseHolder)
        {
        hr=CreateDataAdviseHolder(&m_pObj->m_pIDataAdviseHolder);

        if (FAILED(hr))
            return ResultFromScode(E_OUTOFMEMORY);
        }

    hr=m_pObj->m_pIDataAdviseHolder->Advise((LPDATAOBJECT)this, pFE
        , dwFlags, pIAdviseSink, pdwConn);

    return hr;
    }

STDMETHODIMP CImpIDataObject::DUnadvise(DWORD dwConn)
    {
    if (NULL==m_pObj->m_pIDataAdviseHolder)
        return ResultFromScode(E_FAIL);
```

(continued)

Listing 10-4. *continued*

```
    return m_pObj->m_pIDataAdviseHolder->Unadvise(dwConn);
    }

STDMETHODIMP CImpIDataObject::EnumDAdvise(LPENUMSTATDATA FAR
    *ppEnum)
    {
    if (NULL==m_pObj->m_pIDataAdviseHolder)
        return ResultFromScode(E_FAIL);

    return m_pObj->m_pIDataAdviseHolder->EnumAdvise(ppEnum);
    }
```

DOCUMENT.CPP

```
...

CCosmoDoc::CCosmoDoc(HINSTANCE hInst): CDocument(hInst)
    {
    [Other initialization omitted]

    //Registers clipboard formats for embedded objects.
    m_cfEmbedSource=RegisterClipboardFormat(CF_EMBEDSOURCE);
    m_cfObjectDescriptor=RegisterClipboardFormat
        (CF_OBJECTDESCRIPTOR);

    [Other code omitted]
    return;
    }
...
/*
 * CCosmoDoc::FRenderMedium
 *
 * Purpose:
 *  Like RenderFormat, this function creates a specific data format
 *  based on the cf parameter. Unlike RenderFormat, we store the
 *  result in a STGMEDIUM in case it has a medium other than
 *  TYMED_GLOBAL. For convenience we'll centralize all compound
 *  document formats here, hGlobal or not.
 *
 * Parameters:
 *  cf              UINT clipboard format of interest.
 *  pSTM            LSTGMEDIUM to fill. We only fill the union
 *                  and tymed.
```

(continued)

Listing 10-4. *continued*

```
 * Return Value:
 *  BOOL         TRUE if we could render the format
 *               , FALSE otherwise.
 */

BOOL CCosmoDoc::FRenderMedium(UINT cf, LPSTGMEDIUM pSTM)
    {
    if (NULL==pSTM)
        return FALSE;

    if (cf==m_cfEmbedSource)
        {
        pSTM->pstg=OleStdCreateStorageOnHGlobal(NULL, TRUE
            , STGM_DIRECT | STGM_READWRITE | STGM_SHARE_EXCLUSIVE);

        if (NULL==pSTM->pstg)
            return FALSE;

        //Now save the data to the storage.
        WriteClassStg(pSTM->pstg, CLSID_Cosmo2Figure);
        WriteFmtUserTypeStg(pSTM->pstg, m_cf
            , PSZ(IDS_CLIPBOARDFORMAT));

        if (POLYLINE_E_NONE!=m_pPL->WriteToStorage(pSTM->pstg
            , VERSIONCURRENT))
            {
            pSTM->pstg->Release();
            return FALSE;
            }

        pSTM->tymed=TYMED_ISTORAGE;
        return TRUE;
        }

    if (cf==m_cfObjectDescriptor)
        {
        SIZEL   szl, szlT;
        POINTL  ptl;
        RECT    rc;

        m_pPL->SizeGet(&rc);
        SETSIZEL(szlT, rc.right, rc.bottom);
        XformSizeInPixelsToHimetric(NULL, &szlT, &szl);

        SETPOINTL(ptl, 0, 0);
```

(continued)

Listing 10-4. *continued*

```
        pSTM->hGlobal=OleStdGetObjectDescriptorData
            (CLSID_CosmoFigure, DVASPECT_CONTENT, szl, ptl
            , OLEMISC_RECOMPOSEONRESIZE, PSZ(IDS_OBJECTDESCRIPTION)
            , NULL);

        pSTM->tymed=TYMED_HGLOBAL;
        return (NULL!=pSTM->hGlobal);
        }

    return FALSE;
    }
```

First note that the function *CCosmoDoc::FRenderFormat,* which generates bitmaps, metafiles, and native data, is unchanged from previous versions of Cosmo. Again, the implementation of this interface, specifically *IDataObject::GetData,* is *using* the existing code instead of modifying it. Likewise, the implementation of *IDataObject::SetData* uses *CPolyline::DataSet* to support native data imports.

However, we do have to add a little more code to *CCosmoDoc,* first by registering the OLE 2 clipboard formats of CF_EMBEDSOURCE and CF_OBJECTDESCRIPTOR in the constructor, and second by adding the *FRenderMedium* function to create those formats. Creating CF_OBJECTDESCRIPTOR is a matter of calling the OLE2UI function *OleStdGetObjectDescriptorData,* which will conveniently allocate and fill the structure for us.

CF_EMBEDSOURCE is a little more interesting, however. This format, again, is an *IStorage* containing the object's native data, exactly like *IPersistStorage::Save.* To create the *IStorage,* Cosmo uses the OLE2UI function *OleStdCreateIStorageOnHGlobal,* which internally calls *CreateILockBytesOnHGlobal* and *StgCreateDocfileOnILockBytes.* Cosmo uses a memory *IStorage* because it knows its data is small, using somewhere on the order of 2 KB for the entire storage. If you have much larger data, I strongly encourage you weigh the tradeoffs between a memory *IStorage* and a disk-based *IStorage* because at some point a memory *IStorage* will begin using virtual memory, which is on the disk anyway—dealing with the disk through both *IStorage* and swapping layers will be much slower than simply going to a disk-based *IStorage* directly. But regardless of what you do with storage, notice that in Cosmo, after we obtain the *IStorage,* we call *CPolyline::WriteToStorage* exactly as we called it from *IPersistStorage::Save.* Furthermore, our implementation of *IDataObject::GetDataHere* does exactly the same thing, calling *CPolyline::WriteToStorage* on whatever *IStorage* is provided by the caller.

So why do I make such a big point of matching *IPersistStorage::Save* and *IDataObject::GetData* on CF_EMBEDSOURCE? Because the data you render for CF_EMBEDSOURCE can be used by a container application to create a new object of your class. When that container later activates that object, it will launch your server and ask your *IPersistStorage::Load* to read from that very same storage. Because *IPersistStorage::Save* and *IPersistStorage::Load* must be compatible, your rendering of CF_EMBEDSOURCE also must be compatible.

That leaves us with the easy stuff in *IDataObject*, such as *QueryGetData*, which is implemented here by cycling through an array of FORMATETCs kept in *CFigure*. *GetCanonicalFormatEtc* is its typically trivial self, and the three amigos—*DAdvise*, *DUnadvise*, and *EnumDAdvise*—are implemented by using the *DataAdviseHolder* provided by OLE 2. So now you're saying, "The only member function left is *EnumFormatEtc*, and I have to implement another object for that, right?" Well, not any more, because now we can use the FORMATETC enumerator implemented in the default handler, OLE2.DLL, which will enumerate whatever formats we list under our *CLSID\DataFormats\GetSet* in the registration database. All we have to do to obtain this freebie implementation is return OLE_S_USEREG. What really happens is that when something over in the container's process calls *IDataObject::EnumFormatEtc*, the call first reaches the object handler. If this is the default handler (generally the case, even when custom handlers are present), it first attempts to call *EnumFormatEtc* on a running server. If the server is not running, or it is running but returns OLE_S_USEREG, the default handler will create the enumerator based on Registration Database entries. If you want control and want to implement the enumerator yourself, go right ahead. I won't stop you. This simple return value is just the quickest and easiest way to provide this necessary functionality.

The best you can do for testing after implementing this interface is to be sure everything compiles because a container will not make use of this interface unless it can also use *IOleObject*, which is next on our list to implement. If you really want to test your interface, you can, of course, write a simple object user such as DATAUSER in Chapter 6 to call *CoCreateInstance* on your CLSID and ask for *IDataObject*. That works perfectly well, because this object you're implementing looks exactly like any other component object with the *IDataObject* interface. In fact, you could make only minor changes to DATAUSER to turn it into a quick and dirty test application for your *IDataObject* interface here.

Implement the *IOleObject* Interface

The *IOleObject* interface is the big prize winner of all OLE 2 interfaces for having the most member functions—21, excluding those in *IUnknown*. In some ways, *IOleObject* looks like the interface from hell, a dumping ground for every function that just didn't seem to have any better home. Intimidating? You bet! Is it a problem? Not really. For the most part, the member functions in this interface have either trivial or optional implementations. Only about 15 of the member functions require some implementation in one way or another, and 12 of those 15 are trivial to implement or use defaults from the registration database. The remaining six (of the 21) functions are either entirely optional or completely useless for embedded object themselves. Some will, however, become important when we provide support for linked objects in Chapter 13.

All 21 member functions and their responsibilities are shown in Table 10-1 on the next page. Cosmo's *CImplOleObject* implementation is shown in Listing 10-5 on page 614. You'll find the definition of *CImplOleObject* in COSMOLE.H, and it is pretty much the same old, boring sort of interface implementation that we've seen for all the others. *IOleObject* is really the main interface of an embedded object, in that it forms the bulk of the functions presented to a container application. If you've read all of Chapter 9, you have already seen where many of these functions are called.

Note that unimplemented functions return E_NOTIMPL, and those that use Registration Database defaults return OLE_S_USEREG. The interesting member functions of the other groups that have at least some implementation in the code in Listing 10-5 are discussed in the following three sections.

Trivial Functions

Let's look at the simple implementations first, because we'll need some of the information from these functions to implement the more complex ones. The functions in this set are *SetClientSite, GetClientSite, Update, IsUpToDate, GetExtent, GetUserClassID*, and the triumvirate of *Advise, Unadvise*, and *EnumAdvise.*

SetClientSite illustrates one of the rare times when an object is handed the first pointer to some other object on a silver platter. This is, in fact, the only way through which the embedded object gets an *IOleClientSite* pointer to the container's site object. You must hold onto this pointer for the lifetime of your object, meaning you need to save it in a variable somewhere. And what does holding onto an interface pointer mean? Use *AddRef* on it, of course. In addition, on the off chance that your application receives multiple calls to *SetClientSite*, release whatever pointer you are currently holding before overwriting it with the new one. Although I haven't seen multiple calls actually happen, it's very possible, and it's good defensive programming to be sure you release before you overwrite.

IOleObject member	Description
Requires real programming:	
SetHostNames	Provides the object with the name of its container application and the name of the document in which the object lives. On this call the object changes its user interface to reflect its embedded state. This function is called only on embedded objects.
Close	Instructs the object to close itself, possibly saving in the process and possibly asking the end user to verify the save. This will also destroy the object, which might cause server shutdown.
DoVerb	Executes an action on the object that can include hiding or showing the object's editing window.
Trivial implementations:	
SetClientSite	Provides the object with an *IOleClientSite* pointer to its container site. This is the only way in which the object can obtain any pointer to the container, and this is the first container pointer it sees. The object must hold onto this pointer (meaning call *AddRef*) to send notifications later on.
GetClientSite	Returns the last *IOleClientSite* pointer seen in *SetClientSite*, with *AddRef* applied, of course.
Update	Ensures that the object is up-to-date. Embedded objects are generally considered up-to-date.
IsUpToDate	Checks to see whether the object is up-to-date. The answer is always "yes" for embedded objects.
GetExtent	Retrieves the current size of the object. You implement this simply by copying your object's horizontal and vertical dimensions (in HIMETRIC units) into a SIZEL structure.
Advise	Provides an *IAdviseSink*, which the object notifies through *OnSave*, *OnClose*, and *OnRename*. This function can be delegated to a holder available from *CreateOleAdviseHolder*.
Unadvise	Terminates a connection from *Advise*, which can also be delegated to an *OleAdviseHolder*.
EnumAdvise	Enumerates the connections made through *Advise* and can be delegated to an *OleAdviseHolder*.
GetUserClassID	Returns the CLSID of the object that users think they're editing, even if your application is not the real server for that class. (We'll see this in Chapter 14.)

Table 10-1.
The IOleObject *interface.*

(continued)

Table 10-1. *continued*

IOleObject member	Description
Default implementations using the Registration Database (return OLE_S_USEREG):	
EnumVerbs	Returns an enumerator for OLEIVERB values.
GetUserType	Returns a pointer to a user-readable string, which can be taken from the *AuxUserType* entries in the Registration Database.
GetMiscStatus	Returns a set of OLEMISC flags for the given aspect, which can be taken from the registered values under *MiscStatus.* The most common values are OLEMISC_RECOMPOSEONRESIZE, which indicates that the object would like to redraw its presentation if scaled, and OLEMISC_ONLYICONIC, which indicates that there is no useful view of this object other than an iconic one, and OLEMISC_CANTLINKINSIDE, which indicates that you are not implementing *SetMoniker* and *GetMoniker* (see Chapter 13).
Completely optional:	
SetExtent	Instructs the object to change its size, usually to match the size of the object in the container's view.
InitFromData	Provides the object with an *IDataObject* pointer from which it can initialize itself, essentially performing a Paste into the object. This is provided in addition to *IDataObject::SetData* because it does not require the caller to know server-specific clipboard formats.
GetClipboardData	Asks the object for an *IDataObject* pointer, which would be exactly what the server would place on the clipboard for this object.
SetColorScheme	Provides the object with a preferred color palette that it should use if possible.
Important only for linking:	
SetMoniker	Provides the object with a name in a moniker. This is only used in linking scenarios, as described in Chapter 13.
GetMoniker	Asks the object for a moniker describing itself with or without information about its container as well.

GetClientSite is the direct sibling of *SetClientSite,* which simply needs to copy the last *IOleClientSite* pointer from *SetClientSite* into the out parameter **ppSite.* In addition, it is a function that returns a new copy of a pointer, so be sure to use *AddRef* on the *IOleClientSite* again.

IOLEOBJ.CPP

```
/*
 * Implementation of the IOleObject interface for Polyline.
 *
 * Copyright (c)1993 Microsoft Corporation, All Rights Reserved
 */

#include "cosmo.h"

CImpIOleObject::CImpIOleObject(LPCFigure pObj, LPUNKNOWN pUnkOuter)
    {
    m_cRef=0;
    m_pObj=pObj;
    m_pUnkOuter=pUnkOuter;
    return;
    }

CImpIOleObject::~CImpIOleObject(void)
    {
    return;
    }

STDMETHODIMP CImpIOleObject::QueryInterface(REFIID riid
    , LPLPVOID ppv)
    {
    return m_pUnkOuter->QueryInterface(riid, ppv);
    }

STDMETHODIMP_(ULONG) CImpIOleObject::AddRef(void)
    {
    ++m_cRef;
    return m_pUnkOuter->AddRef();
    }

STDMETHODIMP_(ULONG) CImpIOleObject::Release(void)
    {
    --m_cRef;
    return m_pUnkOuter->Release();
    }
...
/*
 * CImpIOleObject::SetHostNames
 *
```

Listing 10-5. *(continued)*
Implementation of the IOleObject *interface for Cosmo's* CFigure *class.*

Listing 10-5. *continued*

```
 * Purpose:
 *  Provides the object with names of the container application and
 *  the object in the container to use in object user interface.
 *
 * Parameters:
 *  pszApp          LPCSTR of the container application.
 *  pszObj          LPCSTR of some name useful in window titles.
 */

STDMETHODIMP CImpIOleObject::SetHostNames(LPCSTR pszApp
    , LPCSTR pszObj)
    {
    m_pObj->m_fEmbedded=TRUE;
    m_pObj->m_pFR->UpdateEmbeddingUI(TRUE, m_pObj->m_pDoc
        , pszApp, pszObj);
    return NOERROR;
    }

/*
 * CImpIOleObject::Close
 *
 * Purpose:
 *  Forces the object to close down its user interface and unload.
 *
 * Parameters:
 *  dwSaveOption    DWORD describing the circumstances under which
 *                  object is being saved and closed.
 */

STDMETHODIMP CImpIOleObject::Close(DWORD dwSaveOption)
    {
    HWND        hWnd;
    BOOL        fSave=FALSE;

    hWnd=m_pObj->m_pDoc->Window();

    if (OLECLOSE_SAVEIFDIRTY==dwSaveOption && m_pObj->FIsDirty())
        fSave=TRUE;

    if (OLECLOSE_PROMPTSAVE==dwSaveOption && m_pObj->FIsDirty())
        {
        UINT        uRet;

        uRet=MessageBox(hWnd, (*m_pObj->m_pST)[IDS_CLOSECAPTION]
            , (*m_pObj->m_pST)[IDS_CLOSEPROMPT], MB_YESNOCANCEL);
```

(continued)

Listing 10-5. *continued*

```
        if (IDCANCEL==uRet)
            return ResultFromScode(OLE_E_PROMPTSAVECANCELLED);

        if (IDYES==uRet)
            fSave=TRUE;
        }

    if (fSave)
        {
        m_pObj->SendAdvise(OBJECTCODE_SAVEOBJECT);
        m_pObj->SendAdvise(OBJECTCODE_SAVED);
        }

    //We get directly here on OLECLOSE_NOSAVE.
    PostMessage(hWnd, WM_CLOSE, 0, 0L);
    return NOERROR;
    }
...
/*
 * CImpIOleObject::DoVerb
 *
 * Purpose:
 *  Executes an object-defined action.
 *
 * Parameters:
 *  iVerb           LONG index of the verb to execute.
 *  pMSG            LPMSG describing the event causing the
 *  pActiveSite     activation. LPOLECLIENTSITE to the site involved.
 *  lIndex          LONG the piece on which execution is happening.
 *  hWndParent      HWND of window in which to play in-place.
 *  pRectPos        LPRECT of the object in hWndParent where the
 *                  object can play in-place if desired.
 */

STDMETHODIMP CImpIOleObject::DoVerb(LONG iVerb, LPMSG pMSG
    , LPOLECLIENTSITE pActiveSite, LONG lIndex, HWND hWndParent
    , LPCRECT pRectPos)
    {
    HWND            hWnd, hWndT;

    //Find the uppermost window
    hWndT=GetParent(m_pObj->m_pDoc->Window());
```

(continued)

Listing 10-5. *continued*

```
    while (NULL!=hWndT)
        {
        hWnd=hWndT;
        hWndT=GetParent(hWndT);
        }

    switch (iVerb)
        {
        case OLEIVERB_HIDE:
            ShowWindow(hWnd, SW_HIDE);
            m_pObj->SendAdvise(OBJECTCODE_HIDEWINDOW);
            break;

        case OLEIVERB_PRIMARY:
        case OLEIVERB_OPEN:
        case OLEIVERB_SHOW:
            ShowWindow(hWnd, SW_SHOWNORMAL);
            SetFocus(hWnd);
            m_pObj->SendAdvise(OBJECTCODE_SHOWOBJECT);
            m_pObj->SendAdvise(OBJECTCODE_SHOWWINDOW);
            break;

        default:
            return ResultFromScode(OLEOBJ_S_INVALIDVERB);
        }

    return NOERROR;
    }
...
/*
 * CImpIOleObject::SetClientSite
 * CImpIOleObject::GetClientSite
 *
 * Stores or retrieves the container's IOleClientSite pointer.
 */

STDMETHODIMP CImpIOleObject::SetClientSite
    (LPOLECLIENTSITE pIOleClientSite)
    {
    if (NULL!=m_pObj->m_pIOleClientSite)
        m_pObj->m_pIOleClientSite->Release();

    m_pObj->m_pIOleClientSite=pIOleClientSite;
    m_pObj->m_pIOleClientSite->AddRef();
    return NOERROR;
    }
```

(continued)

Listing 10-5. *continued*

```
STDMETHODIMP CImpIOleObject::GetClientSite(LPOLECLIENTSITE FAR
    * ppSite)
    {
    //Be sure to AddRef the new pointer you are giving away.
    *ppSite=m_pObj->m_pIOleClientSite;
    m_pObj->m_pIOleClientSite->AddRef();

    return ResultFromScode(E_NOTIMPL);
    }
...
STDMETHODIMP CImpIOleObject::Update(void)
    {
    //We're always updated since we don't contain.
    return NOERROR;
    }

STDMETHODIMP CImpIOleObject::IsUpToDate(void)
    {
    //We're always updated since we don't contain.
    return NOERROR;
    }

STDMETHODIMP CImpIOleObject::GetUserClassID(LPCLSID pClsID)
    {
    *pClsID=CLSID_Cosmo2Figure;
    return NOERROR;
    }
...
/*
 * CImpIOleObject::GetExtent
 *
 * Purpose:
 *  Retrieves the size of the object in HIMETRIC units.
 *
 * Parameters:
 *  dwAspect        DWORD of the aspect requested
 *  pszl            LPSIZEL into which to store the size.
 */

STDMETHODIMP CImpIOleObject::GetExtent(DWORD dwAspect, LPSIZEL pszl)
    {
    RECT            rc;
    SIZEL           szl;
```

(continued)

Listing 10-5. *continued*

```
    if (!(DVASPECT_CONTENT & dwAspect))
        return ResultFromScode(E_FAIL);

    m_pObj->m_pPL->RectGet(&rc);
    szl.cx=rc.right-rc.left;
    szl.cy=rc.bottom-rc.top;

    XformSizeInPixelsToHimetric(NULL, &szl, pszl);
    return NOERROR;
    }

STDMETHODIMP CImpIOleObject::Advise(LPADVISESINK pIAdviseSink
    , LPDWORD pdwConn)
    {
    if (NULL==m_pObj->m_pIOleAdviseHolder)
        {
        HRESULT     hr;

        hr=CreateOleAdviseHolder(&m_pObj->m_pIOleAdviseHolder);

        if (FAILED(hr))
            return hr;
        }

    return m_pObj->m_pIOleAdviseHolder->Advise(pIAdviseSink
        , pdwConn);
    }

STDMETHODIMP CImpIOleObject::Unadvise(DWORD dwConn)
    {
    if (NULL!=m_pObj->m_pIOleAdviseHolder)
        return m_pObj->m_pIOleAdviseHolder->Unadvise(dwConn);

    return ResultFromScode(E_FAIL);
    }

STDMETHODIMP CImpIOleObject::EnumAdvise(LPENUMSTATDATA FAR *ppEnum)
    {
    if (NULL!=m_pObj->m_pIOleAdviseHolder)
        return m_pObj->m_pIOleAdviseHolder->EnumAdvise(ppEnum);

    return ResultFromScode(E_FAIL);
    }
...
STDMETHODIMP CImpIOleObject::EnumVerbs(LPENUMOLEVERB FAR *ppEnum)
```

(continued)

Listing 10-5. *continued*

```
    {
    //Trivial implementation if you fill the regDB.
    return ResultFromScode(OLE_S_USEREG);
    }
...
STDMETHODIMP CImpIOleObject::GetUserType(DWORD dwForm
    , LPSTR FAR * ppszType)
    {
    return ResultFromScode(OLE_S_USEREG);
    }
...
STDMETHODIMP CImpIOleObject::GetMiscStatus(DWORD dwAspect
    , LPDWORD pdwStatus)
    {
    return ResultFromScode(OLE_S_USEREG);
    }
...
/*
 * CImpIOleObject::InitFromData
 *
 * Purpose:
 *  Initializes the object from the contents of a data object.
 *
 * Parameters:
 *  pIDataObject    LPDATAOBJECT containing the data.
 *  fCreation       BOOL indicating if this is part of a new
 *                  creation. If FALSE, the container is trying
 *                  to paste here.
 *  dwReserved      DWORD reserved.
 */

STDMETHODIMP CImpIOleObject::InitFromData(LPDATAOBJECT pIDataObject
    , BOOL fCreation, DWORD dwReserved)
    {
    BOOL    fRet;

    /*
     * If we get a data object here, try to paste from it. If
     * you've written clipboard code already, this is a snap.
     * We don't really care about fCreation or not since pasting
     * in us blasts away whatever is already here.
     */
    fRet=m_pObj->m_pDoc->FPasteFromData(pIDataObject);
    return fRet ? NOERROR : ResultFromScode(E_FAIL);
    }
```

(continued)

Listing 10-5. *continued*

```
/*
 * CImpIOleObject::GetClipboardData
 *
 * Purpose:
 *  Returns an IDataObject pointer to the caller representing what
 *  would be on clipboard if server did an Edit/Copy using
 *  OleSetClipboard.
 *
 * Parameters:
 *  dwReserved      DWORD reserved.
 *  ppIDataObj      LPDATAOBJECT FAR * into which to store the
 *                              pointer.
 */

STDMETHODIMP CImpIOleObject::GetClipboardData(DWORD dwReserved
    , LPDATAOBJECT FAR * ppIDataObj)
    {
    /*
     * Again, if you have a function to create a data object for the
     * clipboard, this is a simple implementation. The one we have
     * does all the compound document formats already.
     */
    *ppIDataObj=m_pObj->m_pDoc->TransferObjectCreate(FALSE);
    return (NULL!=*ppIDataObj) ? NOERROR : ResultFromScode(E_FAIL);
    }
...
/*
 * CImpIOleObject::SetExtent
 *
 * Purpose:
 *  Sets the size of the object in HIMETRIC units.
 *
 * Parameters:
 *  dwAspect        DWORD of the aspect affected.
 *  pszl            LPSIZEL containing the new size.
 */

STDMETHODIMP CImpIOleObject::SetExtent(DWORD dwAspect, LPSIZEL pszl)
    {
    RECT            rc;
    SIZEL           szl;

    if (!(DVASPECT_CONTENT & dwAspect))
        return ResultFromScode(E_FAIL);
```

(continued)

Listing 10-5. *continued*

```
    XformSizeInHimetricToPixels(NULL, pszl, &szl);

    //This resizes the window to match the container's size.
    SetRect(&rc, 0, 0, (int)szl.cx, (int)szl.cy);
    m_pObj->m_pPL->SizeSet(&rc, TRUE);

    return NOERROR;
    }
...
STDMETHODIMP CImpIOleObject::SetColorScheme(LPLOGPALETTE pLP)
    {
    return ResultFromScode(E_NOTIMPL);
    }

STDMETHODIMP CImpIOleObject::SetMoniker(DWORD dwWhich, LPMONIKER pmk)
    {
    return ResultFromScode(E_NOTIMPL);
    }
...
STDMETHODIMP CImpIOleObject::GetMoniker(DWORD dwAssign
    , DWORD dwWhich, LPMONIKER FAR * ppmk)
    {
    return ResultFromScode(E_NOTIMPL);
    }
```

Update and *IsUpToDate* are a pair of functions that a container can use to be sure that the presentation it has in its cache matches the current state of the object. *IsUpToDate* asks "Are you current" whereas *Update* tells your application "Make yourself current." I mentioned earlier in Table 10-1 that embedded objects are always up to date. This is because embedded objects must always notify the container's *IAdviseSink* (which is actually in the handler) when data changes and this mechanism always keeps the cache updated. These functions really exist to support linked objects in cases where the current visible state of the object might not, in fact, reflect the current contents of another file. So we might have to launch an application to load the file and give us a new presentation. We'll see these again in Chapter 12 when we deal with linking.[7]

7. If the embedded object itself is a container for other objects, it must recursively call *IOleObject::Update* and *IOleObject::IsUpToDate* on all contained objects. This is not, however, a topic covered in this book.

GetExtent asks the object "How big is this aspect?" by asking the object to fill a SIZEL structure with the horizontal and vertical dimensions of the object in HIMETRIC units that are sensitive to the requested aspect. These extents are in absolute units—that is, the vertical value is not negative as it would be if you were dealing in the MM_HIMETRIC *mapping mode.* Because there is no *hDC* anywhere in sight, there is no conception of a mapping mode in this function. Cosmo implements this by retrieving the rectangle of the current Polyline window (in pixels) and using the OLE2UI function *XformSizeInPixelsToHimetric* to convert the values before returning.

GetUserClassID is a rather odd fellow that you can use to support object conversion and emulation through a container's Convert dialog box, which we'll see in Chapter 14. In the conversion/emulation scenario, your server and object might be editing an object of a CLSID that is different from your usual one (but only if your application registered itself as being able to work with that CLSID). In such a situation, the CLSID that users think they are working on is not the default CLSID of your server. This function gives the container (and OLE 2) a way of knowing what the object actually is. Because we are not going to look at conversion and emulation until Chapter 14, implementation here is simple: Fill the out parameter **pClsID* with your server's CLSID.

You can implement the last three functions dealing with notifications in the same fashion we implemented their counterparts in *IDataObject*: Use an *advise holder.* A container will call *Advise* with its *IAdviseSink* pointer in order to get *OnSave, OnRename,* and *OnClose* notifications from the object. Usually these are of interest to the object handler to support linking, but we really don't see that from the server side of things. Therefore, we have to ignorantly squirrel away every *IAdviseSink* we see in *IOleObject::Advise* so that we can notify them later. This is why we need the advise holder to reduce the implementation down to simple steps:

1. In *Advise,* if you do not already have an advise holder, call *CreateOleAdviseHolder,* which returns (in an out-parameter) a pointer to an *IOleAdviseHolder* interface, which has a reference count of one.

2. In *Advise, Unadvise,* and *EnumAdvise,* if you have an *IOleAdviseHolder* pointer available, delegate the call directly to its member functions of the same name.

3. When destroying the object, remember to call *IOleAdviseHolder::Release* to free the holder created in *Advise.*

After you implement *SetClientSite,* the three *IOleObject* advising functions, and the three advising functions in *IDataObject,* you have three pointers: to

IOleClientSite, IOleAdviseHolder, and *IDataAdviseHolder.* You send various notifications and requests to the container through these three, as described in "Send Notifications" later in this chapter. Using these notifications, we allow the container to update its cache and presentations, to save the object when appropriate, and to control its user interface properly.

Required Functions

In this set, we'll find *DoVerb, Close,* and *SetHostNames* the three most important members of *IOleObject* (in that order). First and most important is *DoVerb,* which asks an object to execute an action. If *DoVerb* didn't exist, activation wouldn't exist, so it is really the crux of compound documents. As we'll see in Chapters 15 and 16, it is through this function that the whole process of in-place activation begins.

As discussed before, *DoVerb* is what takes an object from the loaded state to the running state or to transition between the running visible and running hidden states. This function receives a number of parameters, the first of which, *iVerb,* is the number of the verb to execute, which can be either a server-defined verb or a predefined verb.[8] Each predefined verb has a specific implementation:

Implementation	Description
OLEIVERB_SHOW	Calls *ShowWindow(hWnd, SW_SHOW),* where *hWnd* is your main application window (for single-object servers) or the document window containing the object (if your application is an MDI server). In the latter case, you might need to show the frame window if it is not yet visible itself. After *ShowWindow,* call *SetFocus(hWnd)* followed by calls to *IOleClientSite::ShowObject* and *IOleClientSite::OnShowWindow(TRUE),* where the *IOleClientSite* pointer is the one you save from *SetClientSite,* not the one passed to this function (which is for in-place activation). Cosmo last handles these two calls through *CFigure::SendAdvise.*
OLEIVERB_OPEN	Outside of in-place activation, this has the same semantics as OLEIVERB_SHOW.
OLEIVERB_HIDE	Calls *ShowWindow(hWnd, SW_HIDE),* where *hWnd* is your main application window (if your application is editing one object only) or your document window (if you are editing multiple objects in multiple documents). Follow this with a call to *IOleClientSite::OnShowWindow (FALSE),* where *IOleClientSite* is the one you saved in *SetClientSite.*

8. Not all predefined verbs are shown here because some are relevant only to in-place activation.

Aside from these three verbs, which have the values –1, –2, and –3 (and which you must implement), you will see verbs with values of 0 and higher and possibly some negative ones less than –3. If any verb index makes no sense to you, return OLE_E_INVALIDVERB. Otherwise, the exact meaning of the verb is something only you know, in which case you perform whatever action is appropriate. For Cosmo, its single verb Edit (which is also the primary verb of index 0 or OLEIVERB_PRIMARY) only needs to show the window containing an editable Polyline figure. In this case, our primary verb is exactly the same as OLEIVERB_SHOW. Another type of object, such as a sound that has a Play verb, would only play the sound and not actually show any windows, nor would it call anything in *IOleClientSite.*

The other parameters to *DoVerb* provide more information to the object that it can use to modify its behavior. *lpMsg* tells the object what message (such as WM_LBUTTONDBLCLK) actually caused the *DoVerb* call from the container. This information is mostly important for a type of in-place object we call "inside-out," which is a topic of Chapters 15 and 16. The *IOleClientSite* pointer *pActiveSite* is again used in other special cases that are not yet important in our discussion. *lindex* is always 0 in OLE 2, meaning "the entire object." It is reserved for future enhancements to OLE. Finally, *hWndParent* and *pRectPos* are useful to objects, such as video, that temporarily play in the context of the container without having to implement full in-place activation. The object is allowed to *temporarily* create a window inside *hWndParent* in which to play or to call *GetDC(hWndParent),* and it is allowed to draw directly onto the container's window. The *pRectPos* parameter provides you with the position of your object (that is, the container's site) in *hWndParent.* Although you can create a window that is larger than this rectangle, you should *never* draw outside that rectangle on the container's *hDC.* What is most important to note here is that anything you do with these two parameters must be temporary—that is, what you do must not persist outside your execution of *DoVerb.* If you need more persistent windows in the container, you must implement in-place activation for your object.

The next most important member of *IOleObject* is *Close,* which moves an object from the running state into the loaded state—that is, it moves the object in the direction opposite the one called for by *DoVerb. Close* is also called when the container either closes the document in which this object lives (meaning it's going back to the passive state, not simply the loaded state) or when the user has deleted the object from the container altogether, taking us far beyond the passive state to just plain nonexistent. In any case, the object is generally required to execute two steps:

1. Close the document that's showing this object. If there are no other objects being edited in this instance of your application and no other conditions are met, this should start the shutdown process. As we saw before, closing a Cosmo document destroys the object, which will call *ObjectDestroyed*, which in turn begins shutdown if appropriate.
2. When you destroy the window that displays the object, inform the container that the object is no longer visible by calling *IOleClientSite-::OnShowWindow(FALSE)*. This shows the end user that the object is reverting back to the loaded state by removing the shading from the container's site.

There's a reason why I said these "two" steps are "generally" required: the *dwSaveOption* parameter to this function, which can be one of three values, adds two steps:

Value	Description
OLECLOSE-_SAVEIFDIRTY	If you are not dirty, allows you to save yourself and then close.
OLECLOSE-_NOSAVE	Simply closes.
OLECLOSE-_PROMPTSAVE	Displays a message box with a message on the order of "This object has been changed. Do you want to update *<container document>* before closing?"[9] with Yes, No, and Cancel buttons. If the user chooses Yes, save yourself and close. If the user chooses No, simply close. On Cancel, return OLE_E-_PROMPTSAVECANCELLED without doing anything else. The *<container document>* string is passed in *IOleObject-::SetHostNames* as we'll see shortly.

The process of saving has two steps, which must be executed before the preceding steps 1 and 2 (which is why these are numbered i and ii):

i. If your object has been modified, call *IOleClientSite::SaveObject*. The *IOleClientSite* pointer through which you call is the most recent one passed to *SetClientSite*. If you have no pointer, you cannot make the call, of course, and any lack of functionality is the container's fault. In Cosmo this is accomplished by calling your own *CFigure::Send-Advise* with OBJECTCODE_SAVEDOBJECT.

9. I could find no standard for this in any OLE 2 documentation. This message is a slight modification from OLE 1 guidelines, where the word *closing* is used in place of *proceeding*.

ii. If you called *IOleClientSite::SaveObject*, call *IAdviseSink::OnSave* for every *IAdviseSink* you've seen in *IOleObject::Advise*. If you are using an advise holder, call *IOleAdviseHolder::SendOnSave*. Again, Cosmo handles this through *CFigure::SendAdvise* with OBJECTCODE-_SAVED.

The final required function we implement in *IOleObject* is *SetHostNames*, which informs the object that it's being embedded in a container and is a signal to the server to show the appropriate user interface for embedding. At this point in our development, it's not necessary to fully implement this function, so we'll come back to this later in "Modify the Server's User Interface," after we take a short look at the optional functions in *IOleObject*.

Optional Functions

The four functions in this group—*SetExtent, InitFromData, GetClipboardData,* and *SetColorScheme*—are not required for standard operation of compound documents, so you can implement them as suits your fancy.

SetExtent adds a nice touch to the interaction between a container and server, so I do recommend that you implement it. A container will call this function when it resizes an object in one of its documents. If it's appropriate for your server, you can use this to change the size (that is, reduce or enlarge) of the object in your editing window. Cosmo, for example, scales the Polyline window (and the document window in which it lives) in such a way that it's as close to the size of the container's site as possible (and within reason). *SetExtent* works best for graphical objects, but it does not work so well for text or table objects where scale is much less important than the textual or numerical data. *SetExtent* is also sensitive to the display aspect that is passed in the *dwAspect* parameter.

InitFromData allows a container to do one of two things: either paste into your object directly or provide initial data during creation. This function is passed an *IDataObject* pointer, which you can use to retrieve the data, and the flag *fCreation*, which indicates the scenario in which this function is being called. If *fCreation* is FALSE, you should integrate the data in the data object with your current data as if Edit/Paste had been performed in the server itself. If *fCreation* is true, the container is attempting to create a new instance of your object based on a selection in the container that is described by the data object. For example, a spreadsheet application might pass a range of selected cells to a new chart object in a format that the chart object registered for the *Set* direction under *DataFormats\GetSet* in the Registration Database. Cosmo happens to treat both cases identically by passing the data object to

CCosmoDoc::FPasteFromData. Again, I highly recommend that you make a function that pastes data from any arbitrary data object such as those you can get from the clipboard, from drag-and-drop, or from a function such as *InitFromData.*

GetClipboardData goes the other direction from the one called for by *InitFromData,* asking the object for an *IDataObject* pointer that is identical to the one the server would place on the clipboard if the user performed an Edit/Copy operation. This allows a caller to get a snapshot of the object, as opposed to the *IDataObject* interface on the object itself, which always reflects the most recent data. Therefore, if you implement this function you have to return an *IDataObject* pointer for an object whose data will not change. Cosmo has the handy function *CCosmoDoc::TransferObjectCreate,* which does the job for us.

Finally, *SetColorScheme* provides the object with the container's recommended palette. The object might choose to ignore this without any dire consequences, but if you can, try to use the colors provided.

But It Still Doesn't Work

After implementing and compiling this mammoth interface, you have almost all of the server side complete. Now when you use Insert Object from a container, it will launch your application, obtain your class factory, create an object, and fire off calls such as *IPersistStorage::InitNew, IOleObject::SetClientSite, IOleObject::GetExtent, IOleObject::SetHostNames,* and *IOleObject::DoVerb,* and your window will appear ready for editing. If you have implemented *IOleObject::Close,* complete with a call to *IOleClientSite::SaveObject;* when you close your application, you see a call to *IPersistStorage::Save.* When you activate the object from the container (with a quick double-click), you see a call to *IPersistStorage::Load,* followed by the same calls to *IOleObject* as before. Your application should at this point again be visible, with the previously saved data ready for editing.

What is not happening is that there is no presentation in the container or that whatever presentation is there is not being updated when you make changes in the server as OLE 2 servers should. In addition, when you close your application, you probably get a prompt that says, "Document has changed, do you want to save." If you say "yes," you get a File Save dialog box. Well, that's not part of the OLE 2 interface for embedded object servers. In fact, there's nothing else to tell you that you are working with an embedded object (as opposed to an untitled file). To solve both these problems, we have to modify the application for embedded object UI as well as to round out the notifications we send to the container.

Modify the Server's User Interface

I will admit it. I seriously loathe writing user interface code because it's the one place that you cannot be the least bit wrong without someone noticing. In addition, user interface specifications seldom identify who is responsible for doing what, and sometimes they don't articulate all possible cases. I guess that's why they're called "guidelines." The situation in which you execute *IOleObject::DoVerb* and show a server window is one such case that is not very well defined. Neither the OLE 2 Design Specification nor the OLE 2 SDK shows what an embedded object server is supposed to look like; both documents concentrate solely on in-place activation. Such is life for us in the trenches, shooting in the dark at an unknown and unseen target.

So what I'm describing here is not something I could call "official." It is pieced together from what I've seen other applications doing. That's how we get standards in the first place, isn't it?

All the following changes should take place when your *IOleObject::SetHostNames* is called because that function tells you that your application is an embedded object, and it tells you the names of the container application and container document that you need to make these changes. *SetHostNames* is always called before *DoVerb,* so these changes should be in effect before you show an editing window:

1. Remove the New, Open, Close, and Save commands from your File menu, as well as any toolbar buttons that invoke the same commands.
2. Change the name of the Save As command on the File menu to Save Copy As. You can usually keep the same command identifier for this modified item. You might also want to remove any toolbar button for this function, but that's up to you. Save Copy As essentially creates an Export function that does not remember the filename after the copy is written. In addition, if you have an Import function, as Cosmo does, you can leave that on the menu and toolbar. If you have a status line, you might also want to change the message displayed for this item (which Cosmo does not do, mind you).
3. Change File/Exit to File/Exit And Return To *<container document>*, where *<container document>* is the string pointed to by the *pszObj* parameter of *SetHostNames.* Again, you might want to change any toolbar and status line UI to accommodate this. (I know that it seems silly that the parameter containing the document name is called *pszObj,* or *pszContainerObj* in the OLE 2 documentation, but, hey, it's only software—call it anything you like.)

4. Change your title bar to read "*<object type>* in *<container document>*" where *<object type>* is the user-readable name of your object such as "Cosmo 2 Figure" and *<container document>* is the *pszObj* parameter from *SetHostNames.* If your application is an SDI application or if it is MDI but the document is maximized, this string appears in the main application window's title bar prefixed with "*<application name>* -." If your application is an MDI application without a maximized document window, the frame caption remains the same and this string appears in the document's title bar.[10]

Cosmo makes these changes by calling *CCosmoFrame::UpdateEmbeddingUI* because the frame controls the menus and the GizmoBar. This is why our *CFigure* class needed to have a pointer to the frame that it received through *CFigure::FrameSet. UpdateEmbeddingUI* is actually capable of switching between an embedding state and a non-embedding state in case I ever decide to allow it to service multiple objects as well as other non-object documents, as described in "(Optional) MDI Servers, User Interface, and Shutdown."

```
void CCosmoFrame::UpdateEmbeddingUI(BOOL fEmbedding, LPCDocument pDoc,
    LPCSTR pszApp, LPCSTR pszObj)
    {
    HMENU               hMenu;
    char                szTemp[256];

    //First let's play with the File menu.
    hMenu=m_phMenu[0];

    //Remove or add the File New, Open, and Save items
    if (fEmbedding)
        {
        DeleteMenu(m_phMenu[0], IDM_FILENEW,    MF_BYCOMMAND);
        DeleteMenu(m_phMenu[0], IDM_FILEOPEN,   MF_BYCOMMAND);
        DeleteMenu(m_phMenu[0], IDM_FILECLOSE,  MF_BYCOMMAND);
        DeleteMenu(m_phMenu[0], IDM_FILESAVE,   MF_BYCOMMAND);

        //Save As->Save Copy As
        ModifyMenu(m_phMenu[0], IDM_FILESAVEAS, MF_BYCOMMAND
            , IDM_FILESAVEAS, PSZ(IDS_SAVECOPYAS));


}
    else
        {
```

(continued)

10. MDI automatically handles the maximized document case by concatenating the frame window's caption with the - character and the document's caption.

```
        InsertMenu(m_phMenu[0], 0, MF_BYPOSITION, IDM_FILENEW
            , PSZ(IDS_NEW));
        InsertMenu(m_phMenu[0], 1, MF_BYPOSITION, IDM_FILEOPEN
            , PSZ(IDS_OPEN));
        InsertMenu(m_phMenu[0], 2, MF_BYPOSITION, IDM_FILESAVE
            , PSZ(IDS_SAVE));
        InsertMenu(m_phMenu[0], 3, MF_BYPOSITION, IDM_FILECLOSE
            , PSZ(IDS_SAVE));

        //Save Copy As->Save As
        ModifyMenu(m_phMenu[0], IDM_FILESAVEAS, MF_BYCOMMAND
            , IDM_FILESAVEAS, PSZ(IDS_SAVEAS));
        }

    //Change "Exit" to "Exit & Return to xx" or vice-versa for SDI
    if (fEmbedding)
        wsprintf(szTemp, PSZ(IDS_EXITANDRETURN), (LPSTR)pszObj);
    else
        lstrcpy(szTemp, PSZ(IDS_EXIT));

    ModifyMenu(m_phMenu[0], IDM_FILEEXIT, MF_STRING, IDM_FILEEXIT
        , szTemp);
    DrawMenuBar(m_hWnd);

    //Now let's play with the gizmobar.
    m_pGB->Show(IDM_FILENEW,   !fEmbedding);
    m_pGB->Show(IDM_FILEOPEN,  !fEmbedding);
    m_pGB->Show(IDM_FILECLOSE, !fEmbedding);
    m_pGB->Show(IDM_FILESAVE,  !fEmbedding);

    //Enable what's left appropriately.
    UpdateGizmos();

    //Now play with the title bar.

    //IDS_EMBEDDINGCAPTION is MDI/SDI sensitive in COSMO.RC.
    wsprintf(szTemp, PSZ(IDS_EMBEDDINGCAPTION), pszObj);

    /*
     * Remember that in MDI situations Windows takes care of
     * the frame window caption bar when the document is maximized.
     */
#ifdef MDI
    SetWindowText(pDoc->Window(), szTemp);
#else
    SetWindowText(m_hWnd, szTemp);
#endif

    return;
    }
```

When Cosmo is in the embedding state, it appears as shown in Figure 10-3. Note that the Import command is still on the File menu and toolbar.

Because we modified the appearance of certain menu items, we also need to modify the behavior of those commands. First, to change Save As to Save Copy As, you can either implement a new function or modify your existing save function. In either case, Save Copy As is the same as a Save As except that you don't use the filename as the "active document" or anything to that effect. In other words, you write the file and forget it, not changing any other part of your user interface to reflect the filename. It's simply a way for the user to make a disk copy of the object.

In Cosmo, we simply modify *CCosmoDoc::USave* so that a Save Copy As does not make the document "clean," as a normal Save As would, and so that we don't store the filename in the document's structure or change the caption bar. *USave* determines that we're in an embedding state by calling *CFigure::FIsEmbedded* (which returns the value of *CFigure*'s *m_fEmbedded* flag, set to TRUE in *IOleObject::SetHostNames*). You can see these changes in CHAP10\COSMO\DOCUMENT.CPP, which is not shown here.

We also changed Exit to Exit And Return To *<container document>*. By itself, there's no big change to the process of closing a document and closing the application. But when running normally, Cosmo always checks to see whether the document is dirty when it closes the document before exiting the application. If it is, Cosmo asks the user to save the document to a file.

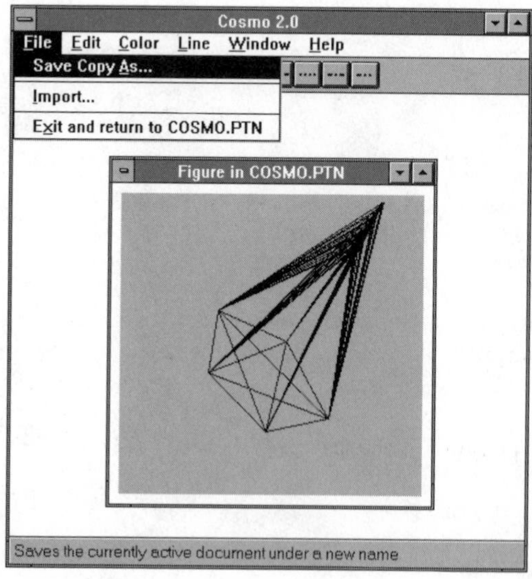

Figure 10-3.
Cosmo, sporting its embedded object user interface.

Because saving the object as a file makes no sense in the case of embedding (we removed File Save altogether), we need to prevent this prompt. So we modify *CCosmoDoc::FDirtyGet* to return FALSE if we're in the embedded state, which effectively prevents prompting:

```
BOOL CCosmoDoc::FDirtyGet(void)
    {
    if (m_pFigure->FIsEmbedded())
        return FALSE;

    return m_fDirty;
    }
```

Now you are probably asking, "What if the object really is dirty? How do we make sure the container saves the object before we destroy it?" We need to tell the container to save the object when we're closing the document holding the object by calling *IOleClientSite::SaveObject*, which is done in the *CCosmoDoc* destructor:

```
CCosmoDoc::~CCosmoDoc(void)
    {
    m_pFigure->SendAdvise(OBJECTCODE_SAVEOBJECT);

    ...
    }
```

And because I know you're getting sick of this *CFigure::SendAdvise* function, it's about time we looked at it and its notifications in general. If you want, you can compile and test your application here to see that your user interface is set appropriately when *SetHostNames* is called and that your Save Copy As functionality works correctly. However, it won't work correctly with the container until you tell it everything that's going on.

Send Notifications

In dealing with a server, I classify a number of different interface function calls as "notifications," although they are not all notifications in the strictest asynchronous sense. True notifications are calls to an *IAdviseSink* interface, and therefore asynchronous. All other "notification" calls, such as *IOleClientSite::SaveObject*, are completely synchronous. Nevertheless, I find it very convenient to lump these all together as 'notifications' in an embedding server. That enables us to make one function for our object, which will send the right notification to the right interface. That function is *CFigure::SendAdvise*, as shown on the next page.

```
//COSMOLE.H
//Codes for CFigure::SendAdvise
//......Code......................Method called in CFigureSendAdvise...
#define OBJECTCODE_SAVED          0  //IOleAdviseHolder::SendOnSave
#define OBJECTCODE_CLOSED         1  //IOleAdviseHolder::SendOnClose
#define OBJECTCODE_RENAMED        2  //IOleAdviseHolder::SendOnRename
#define OBJECTCODE_SAVEOBJECT     3  //IOleClientSite::SaveObject
#define OBJECTCODE_DATACHANGED 4  //IDataAdviseHolder::SendOnDataChange
#define OBJECTCODE_SHOWWINDOW     5  //IOleClientSite::OnShowWindow(TRUE)
#define OBJECTCODE_HIDEWINDOW     6  //IOleClientSite::OnShowWindow(FALSE)
#define OBJECTCODE_SHOWOBJECT     7  //IOleClientSite::ShowObject

//FIGURE.CPP
/*
 * CFigure::SendAdvise
 *
 * Purpose:
 * Calls the appropriate IOleClientSite or IAdviseSink member
 *  function for various events such as closure, renaming, saving, etc.
 */

void CFigure::SendAdvise(UINT uCode)
    {
    switch (uCode)
        {
        case OBJECTCODE_SAVED:
            if (NULL!=m_pIOleAdviseHolder)
                m_pIOleAdviseHolder->SendOnSave();

            break;
        case OBJECTCODE_CLOSED:
            if (NULL!=m_pIOleAdviseHolder)
                m_pIOleAdviseHolder->SendOnClose();

            break;

        case OBJECTCODE_RENAMED:
            //Call IOleAdviseHolder::SendOnRename (later)
            break;

        case OBJECTCODE_SAVEOBJECT:
            if (FIsDirty() && NULL!=m_pIOleClientSite)
                m_pIOleClientSite->SaveObject();

            break;

        case OBJECTCODE_DATACHANGED:
            //No flags are necessary here.
```

```
            if (NULL!=m_pIDataAdviseHolder)
                {
                m_pIDataAdviseHolder->SendOnDataChange
                    (m_pIDataObject, 0, 0);
                }

            break;

        case OBJECTCODE_SHOWWINDOW:
            if (NULL!=m_pIOleClientSite)
                m_pIOleClientSite->OnShowWindow(TRUE);

            break;

        case OBJECTCODE_HIDEWINDOW:
            if (NULL!=m_pIOleClientSite)
                m_pIOleClientSite->OnShowWindow(FALSE);

            break;

        case OBJECTCODE_SHOWOBJECT:
            if (NULL!=m_pIOleClientSite)
                m_pIOleClientSite->ShowObject();

            break;
        }

    return;
    }
```

What this function really does for us is eliminate the need to check for NULL pointers anywhere else and to distill all "notifications" down to one function and one parameter. We then don't have to remember which interface out of *IAdviseSink*, *IOleClientSite*, *IOleAdviseHolder*, and *IDataAdviseHolder* we use to send which notification to the container.

We've seen a number of places in this chapter already where we send various notifications and so we can collect them all into one list in Table 10-2 on the next page. The only ones we haven't covered so far are all those for closing a document and for data changes.

You'll notice that we don't use or implement OBJECTCODE_RENAMED anywhere because it's used only for linking and requires a moniker that we won't add until Chapter 13. In addition, you'll notice that the server never calls *IAdviseSink::OnViewChange* because a local server never implements *IViewObject*. Instead, the object handler watches *IAdviseSink::OnDataChange* and generates *OnViewChange* notification from that.

Event	Notifications (in the order shown)
Closing a document *(CCosmoDoc::~CCosmoDoc)*	*IOleClientSite::SaveObject* *IOleClientSite::OnShowWindow(FALSE)*; *IOleAdviseHolder::SendOnClose* (all of this before *CoDisconnectObject)*
Data changes *(CCosmoDoc::FDirtySet)*	*IDataAdviseHolder::SendOnDataChange*
IOleObject::Close (if saving)	*IOleClientSite::SaveObject* *IOleAdviseHolder::SendOnSave*
IOleObject::DoVerb (HIDE)	*IOleClientSite::OnShowWindow(FALSE)*
IOleObject::DoVerb (SHOW) (includes any verb that shows)	*IOleClientSite::ShowObject* *IOleClientSite::OnShowWindow(TRUE)*

Table 10-2.
When to send notifications from an embedding server.

I need to point out that you might need to optimize when you actually send *OnDataChange* to advise sinks. The preceding table describes this situation as anytime data changes in your application. To reflect that in a container, OLE must call your *IDataObject::GetData* to request a new presentation. If your presentation is complex—say, a metafile with 5000 records—this operation will not be fast. In such cases, you might want to defer sending the notification for a specific time after the most recent change—say, one or two seconds. This would allow end users to make rapid changes without having to continually wait for you to generate a new presentation, and only when they stop making changes will you actually find the time to send an *OnDataChange*. You can also consider making updates part of your idle time processing. If you do defer the *OnDataChange* notification in any way, send one immediately upon shutdown to ensure that OLE can get a final presentation from you.

And now, as the stork would say, "Congratulations! You're a mother!" Well, at least a mother of an embedded object server that is fully functional with a container application. At this point, you should be able to run Insert Object from a container to launch your server, make changes in the object, and see those changes reflected in a shaded object site. If changes are not being reflected in the container, either it's displaying a different aspect than the one you are changing, or when your *IDataObject::GetData* is asked for CF_METAFILEPICT or CF_BITMAP, you're returning the wrong STGMEDIUM. In developing Cosmo, I tore my hair out for a while trying to figure out why the container was not reflecting changes, and it was because the *tymed* I was storing in *GetData*'s STGMEDIUM was TYMED_HGLOBAL instead of TYMED_MFPICT for the CF_METAFILEPICT format. Subtle, but ever so important.

If the container site is not shading itself, you might not be calling *IOleClientSite::OnShowWindow* at the appropriate times, or the container itself might be at fault. To determine whether you are doing it correctly, try your server with a dependable container such as Chapter 9's version of Patron and the samples shipped with the OLE 2 SDK.

When you close your server, you should see no prompts asking to save unless you get OLECLOSE_PROMPTSAVE in *IOleObject::Close.* In this case and in the case when you delete the running object from a container, your server should be completely purged from memory. If not, your shutdown conditions are not being met, and you are not closing your main window and exiting *WinMain.* If you are shutting down completely, you should see your object in a container document. Double-clicking on that object should again launch your server but this time you are asked to reload that saved object and edit that data instead.

The last two sections in this chapter deal briefly with the clipboard and MDI servers. The first is mostly a consideration for a full-server but is optional with a mini-server. The second section is, of course, only important for full-servers that want to service multiple embedded objects possibly with other non-embedded documents open.

(Full-Servers) Add OLE 2 Clipboard Formats

If you read through Chapter 9, you will already know that one way a container might create an object is if it is pasted from the clipboard or it was used in a drag-and-drop operation using the *OleCreateFromData* function. (If you didn't know this, now you do.) For this to happen, something has to put embedded object data up on the clipboard in the first place, and that's left to a server application, regardless of whether it's running to service an embedded object or running stand-alone.

Embedded object data is made of two formats: CF_EMBEDSOURCE and CF_OBJECTDESCRIPTOR, which are exactly the same two formats we supported in the embedded object's implementation of *IDataObject.* The difference here is that we also need to provide these formats in the data object we place on the clipboard whenever we happen to do a Copy or Cut. A mini-server might not have any clipboard user interface, which is why such a feature is generally for full-servers.

In Cosmo, this means a modification to *CCosmoDoc::TransferObjectCreate*, which is used in calling *OleSetClipboard*, in drag-and-drop operations, and as we saw in this chapter, in calls from *IOleObject::GetClipboardData*. Creating the two formats we're adding here is done in *CCosmoDoc::FRenderMedium*, exactly the function we used in implementing the object's *IDataObject::GetData* function. Again, these formats should be placed in the data object after your private data but before any presentations.

I want to mention that when you call *OleSetClipboard* with a data object that contains CF_EMBEDSOURCE, OLE2.DLL will create the OLE 1 formats "Native" and "OwnerLink" and place those on the clipboard as well. This allows OLE 1 containers to also paste in your object, a fact of which you remain blissfully ignorant.

(Optional) MDI Servers, User Interface, and Shutdown

If you would like to support multiple objects in one instance of your application through an MDI interface, you have a few additional issues to consider and differences in procedure to absorb from those we've covered in this chapter. These are especially important for applications that can run only a single instance.

1. Only full-servers can use MDI because mini-servers are always single-object servers.
2. Register your class factory with REGCLS_MULTIPLEUSE and remove any code in *IClassFactory::CreateInstance* that prevents creation of multiple objects.
3. When modifying your user interface on *IOleObject::SetHostNames*, save the container's application and document string with your document (for step 4). Do not remove File New and File Open, but remove File Close and File Save and modify the File Save As and File Exit items as described earlier. File New and File Open simply create new file-based documents as they always have, which does not interfere with the document holding the embedded object.
4. If you have multiple documents open, you need to switch your user interface between the embedded and non-embedded states as you change document windows. That means that switching to an embedded object document installs the embedded object UI, and switching to a normal document reinstates your normal UI. Because you will be switching the UI, you should hold on to the strings from *IOleObject::SetHostNames* because this function will not be called again.

5. Do not shut down when the last embedded object document is closed if the user has at any time in the life of this application used File/New or File/Open. Invoking either function passes control of the application to the user. Generally, this means you should set your "user control" flag to TRUE on any File/New or File/Open. When you test for shutdown in a function such as *ObjectDestroyed*, don't close if this flag is TRUE. You should also be sure that you only close when the *last* object is closed—that is, your object count is truly zero.
6. Hiding an object through *IOleObject::DoVerb(OLEIVERB_HIDE)* should hide only its document window unless that's the only object. If it is, you also hide the frame window. If another object is created before the existing one is shown again, you must show the frame window and the new document but not the existing document. In addition, whenever the visible document is closed and there is still a hidden document, hide the frame window again so that the whole server is in the state expected by the container that sent OLEIVERB_HIDE.

NOTE: You will find that I did not implement these MDI features in Cosmo, even though Cosmo can compile into an MDI application. My reason is that Microsoft is slowly moving away from encouraging the MDI interface, although support for MDI applications will remain in Windows for a long time to come. Microsoft is moving away from MDI because the document-centric user interface possible with in-place activation can eliminate all document management from applications making it the sole responsibility of the system shell. At that point, individual applications don't need MDI. We'll see why in more detail at the end of Chapter 16.

Summary

A server application's support for the compound document standard means adding code to expose a class factory that creates embedded objects. These objects support the *IPersistStorage*, *IDataObject*, and *IOleObject* interfaces, which make them embeddable in any container application that is also written to its part of the compound document standard. Neither server nor embedded object need any specific knowledge about any container and will work transparently with any OLE 1 or OLE 2 container application.

There are two kinds of server applications: mini-servers and full-servers. The former can manipulate only one object per instance of the application and does not support linking. It can have a dialog-box-type user interface as well. Full-servers are those applications that can also run stand-alone and save and load their own files; thus, they can support multiple objects per instance and provide linking support, as discussed later in Chapter 13. The possible features for both types are a little different, but the implementation is the same.

This chapter focuses on the compound document server application (EXE) and how to implement its class factory and the embedded objects that the class factory creates. This chapter gives detailed step-by-step instructions for adding the necessary pieces, including application initialization and shutdown; Registration Database entries, the class factory, and shutdown mechanisms; the embedded object with *IUnknown*; the *IPersistStorage*, *IDataObject*, and *IOleObject* interfaces; embedded object user interface; and notifications that communicate events and requests to the container. In addition, a server might want to provide additional clipboard formats in clipboard and drag-and-drop operations and might want to support multiple objects as an MDI application.

CHAPTER ELEVEN

IN-PROCESS OBJECT HANDLERS AND SERVERS

Style and structure are the essence of a book; great ideas are hogwash.

Vladimir Nabokov (1899–1977)
Russian-American novelist

Follow this silver watch with your eyes. Back and forth it moves. Moving ...moving...you are feeling sleepy. You are feeling hungry. When I count to three, you will forget about any lengthy chapter introduction and awake starving for information about these handler things. One. Two. Two and a half...

The Structure of In-Process Modules

In all truth, in-process servers and object handlers are structurally identical. The idea that the two are somehow mystically different *is* hogwash. Both are DLLs that export *DllGetClassObject* and *DllCanUnloadNow* like any other DLL component, as described in Chapter 4. Both must implement a class factory and keep track of how many objects they have created so that they can provide the proper unloading mechanisms. Both implement the same interfaces on their objects (*IOleObject*, *IDataObject*, *IPersistStorage*, *IViewObject*, and *IOleCache*) so that they appear as embedded objects from a container's point of view, as shown in Figure 11-1 on the next page. The container remains safely ignorant of who or what implements the embedded object.

Indeed, the only things separating embedded objects (that is, objects from in-process servers and object handlers) from those of a more generic component object (in some other DLL) are the interfaces the object supports. To create a component object, you can choose to implement whatever interfaces you want because you define how that object can be used. For embedded objects, the OLE 2 Design Specification dictates how the object will be used, so you don't have total freedom in choosing your interfaces.

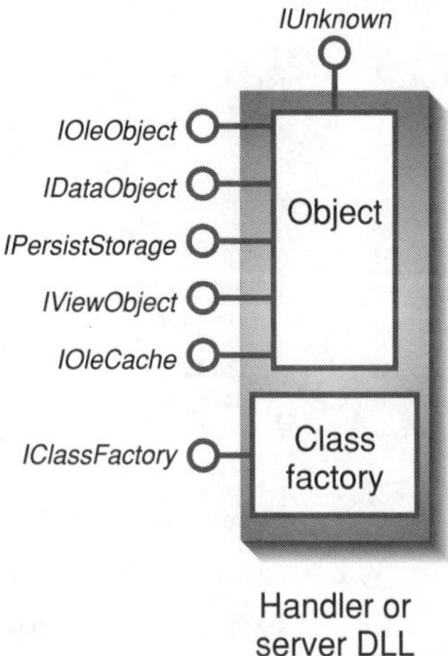

Figure 11-1.
The structure of any in-process embedded object component is the same no matter whether it is a particular handler, the default handler, or an in-process server.

So exactly what is the difference between an object handler and an in-process server? The difference lies in the completeness of implementation of their respective objects. It's the same as the difference between the lowest-price economy car and the most expensive European luxury sports car—both have the same basic car structure: a body, a chassis, four wheels, a steering column, an engine and transmission, and some seats inside. To make the most basic lowest-priced car on the market, you have to be extraordinarily careful about what you put in this car so that no part is any more expensive than is necessary. Likewise, to make the most luxurious car, you spare no expense whatsoever. It is a fact that there is always a better car than the lowest economy model and that there is no better or more complete car than the top-of-the-line luxury automobile.

An object handler is like the economy car: as small as possible, as inexpensive as possible (to load into memory, that is), and as minimal in its number of features as possible to qualify as a car. In other words, the handler implements as little as possible to get into the market, simply overriding specific member functions of specific interfaces and delegating all others to the default handler (which might ultimately end up in a local server). An in-process server is like a luxury car: There is no higher power to which to delegate requests on its interfaces; the in-process handler implements all of it.

I can tell by the look on your face that you are starting to feel the same way about these object DLLs as you would if your only choice were between a

$4,500 car and a $45,000 car. Relax—you have more choices because we *do* want to sell you a car for a little more than what you think you can afford, just as any good car dealer would. Although the basic, most minimal handler is at one end of the spectrum and the complete in-process server is at the other, there are many options in between. Just as there are many models of cars to choose from between the two extremes, there are many choices for DLL object implementations. Every feature you add to the minimal handler brings you one step closer to luxury, and somewhere in the middle, the picture becomes very fuzzy as to whether your application is truly a handler or an in-process server, as shown in Figure 11-2. At any point between the two extremes, your product is still a car. (Below the low end, your product ceases to be useful as a car; above the high end, you are dabbling in unauthorized experimental sciences.)

Figure 11-2.
Between the minimalist handler and the complete in-process server lie many possibilities for handler/servers, all of which still have the same structure.

There is one more point to all this that is comparable to luxury tax. At some point in car prices, luxury tax might kick in: Suddenly you're paying an extra 10 percent. This is not a gradual change but a very sudden one. In the context of handlers and in-process servers, there comes a point where a handler is overqualified to be a handler and must be called an in-process server. The dividing line is at the point where the handler still depends on the existence of a local server. In other words, when the handler no longer delegates any features or calls to the default handler that would require a local server, the handler is a qualified in-process server.

That is the difference: A handler is designed to work in conjunction with a local server, whereas an in-process server operates exclusive of a local server. Handlers are designed to be smaller on disk and therefore faster to load and to provide only a few basic features. The handler can cut corners all it wants, and if a container wants something more, it will require the local server. An in-process server is meant to be larger and to implement the object completely so that a local server is never necessary and a container can get from the DLL whatever it wants.

This is not to say that an in-process server cannot take advantage of certain services provided in OLE2.DLL, the default handler. In both server and handler cases, we will primarily use the OLE2.DLL implementation of the cache and specific member functions of the *IOleObject* and *IDataObject* interfaces that OLE2.DLL will implement for us using information in the Registration Database. The trick is to know exactly when OLE2.DLL, in its capacity as the default handler, will try to launch a local server to fulfill a request, which is the topic of "Delegating to the Default Handler" later in this chapter. But before we get into the implementation details, we need to look at the pros and cons of DLL-based objects.

NOTE: The release of OLE version 2.01 (Fall 1993) provides additional support for implementing in-process servers beyond what was provided in OLE version 2.00 (April 1993). The primary change is that an in-process server can use the caching services of OLE2.DLL without *ever* running the risk of launching a local server. OLE version 2.00 requires you to use the default handler to implement caching in an in-process server; OLE 2.01 lets you bypass the default handler and get directly at the same cache implementation. The point at which a handler becomes a server is when it stops using the default handler and starts using only OLE 2's cache implementation. In this chapter, however, I always use the term "default handler" to designate the useful functionality in OLE2.DLL, even where you are no longer dealing with handlers specifically. Where applicable, I will also note additional differences between OLE 2.00 and OLE 2.01.

...three! Wait, don't tell me you just slept through all that!

Why Use a Handler?

There are two main reasons for implementing an object handler to work with your local server: speed and document portability. First, an object handler can generally satisfy most of the requests a container might make of an object, such as drawing an object on a specific device or making a copy of the object in another *IStorage*. Object handlers might also be capable of reloading a linked file and providing an updated presentation to the container. An object handler does not, however, provide any sort of editing facilities for the object itself: It might be able to play a sound, for example, but it cannot provide the user interface and functionality to change the sound. Therefore, the handler has much less code than might be present in a server because most of the code in an application is usually a result of editing features. Imagine how small a word processor would be if all it had to do was read and display text, but never edit it. That's the idea of a handler. So the speed advantage comes from the fact that the handler is a small DLL optimized to perform specific actions, such as drawing and rendering presentations. Because it's a DLL, it is loaded much faster into a container's process space than another EXE could be launched, and because no LRPC is involved, calls to the handler are much faster than calls to a local server. In addition, because a handler knows (at a minimum) how to draw the object from its native data, there is no reason to cache a metafile or bitmap for the object, thus making the container's compound files smaller (saving at least 2 KB per object). In general, therefore, the existence of a handler greatly improves the performance of an object and its container.

The second benefit is a little less tangible. To explain what I mean by portability, let me use the following scenario: One user on one machine has created an embedded object of class X, using the local server for class X, and the user has saved that object in a container's file. In this case, a cached screen presentation in the object's *IStorage* along with its native data is available. Let's also say that a cached presentation for a PostScript printer is available as well.

Now let's say this document is sent to other users, who do not have the local server for class X on their machines because they have no use for editing the object, only for viewing and for printing it. Because there are cached presentations for this object in the container's file, these users can open those files and view or print the object. However, this assumes that the cached presentations are compatible with the output devices these users want to send them to. If they have only 16-color displays and the cached presentation uses 256 colors, the screen display might be ugly. If their printer is only dot matrix, the only possible presentation to send to such a printer is the one for the screen because we know that PostScript data sent to a dot-matrix printer does not get you anywhere. In either case, the output quality is poor.

There are two solutions to this. First, you could sell these secondary users copies of the local server, but why would they want to pay for extra copies merely to print? You wouldn't want to let them freely copy your server either. So that solution won't work. A different solution is much better: Provide an object handler that can render a presentation for an object's data reasonably well on any display or printer, and allow your customers to freely distribute this handler. It's a small piece of code that can be used only to display and to print objects; you don't need to let people freely copy your full application. Furthermore, because a handler is generally very small, users can put it on a floppy disk along with a document so that the recipient of the document has the necessary tools for optimized output. This is a big advantage for you—your objects always show up nicely regardless of where they're created and where they're displayed. That's the document portability factor.

The bottom line is that object handlers improve object performance and can be confidently licensed for free distribution to optimize output wherever the object happens to travel. Because a handler does not include editing capabilities (which would qualify it for luxury tax), people still have an incentive to purchase your full server.

Just as an aside, you could include some free advertising in an object handler that would encourage people to buy your full product, much as shareware includes messages that suggest registration. A handler typically could pass *IOleObject::DoVerb* to the default handler, which would try to launch the local server. If that failed, the handler could display a message that says "Since you'd really like to edit this object, why don't you call our toll-free number right now and have your credit card handy so that we can get this product into your hands by tomorrow morning for the incredibly low price of $149.95!"

Why Use an In-Process Server?

An in-process server provides all the benefits that an in-process handler provides, except that loading time is generally slower because the DLL is larger. Nonetheless, there is no LRPC and no need for cached presentations, so the other speed benefits apply. Also, as you can with a handler, you can license an in-process server DLL for redistribution if you see fit, or you can have it pop up registration or purchase notices.

The primary benefit of an in-process server is that all the speed and portability advantages of a handler and all the editing capabilities of a local server are stored inside a single disk entity—truly one-stop shopping for an embedded object. Such a DLL is a great choice for control-like objects using in-place activation. In-process server DLLs are also great choices for objects that the user can edit inside a dialog-box type of user interface[1] because they will look like part of the container application instead of a separate

1. As examples, two OLE 1 servers from Microsoft—Note-It and Word-Art—appeared as dialog boxes in the container application. They looked to be part of the container and not a separate application.

application. In any case, when your user interface for editing is simple, consider an in-process server.

Why Not Use an In-Process Server?

The biggest reason to avoid DLLs can be summed up in two words: limited interoperability. When you write any part of an OLE 2 embedded object in a DLL, you limit yourself to using objects only from OLE 2 containers (because an OLE 1 container can't make any sense of an OLE 2 DLL), and you limit yourself to working only with containers that were written for the same 16-bit or 32-bit environment you are using. That is, if you write a 16-bit handler (native for Windows 3.1), your application will not work with a 32-bit application under Windows NT. The converse is true as well—only 32-bit DLLs work with 32-bit containers. The only solution to these problems for the time being is to write multiple versions of your DLLs: one for OLE 1,[2] one for OLE 2, and both for 16-bit and 32-bit versions. Yep, that's a pain, but that's part of the price we must pay as the operating systems evolve.

The other issues that might put DLLs out of your reach are various technical implementation issues. DLLs, because they have no message loop themselves, have a problem handling, for example, keyboard accelerators or MDI interfaces that would normally require changes to a message loop. Overall, there are simply a number of things that you cannot do from a DLL, and if you must have one of them, a DLL is not for you. In implementing the Polyline example for this chapter, I ran into such problems. I originally planned to make the Polyline in-process server look pretty much like Cosmo when it opened an object for editing, including menus and so forth, but the lack of accelerators meant menus were only marginally useful. So I was forced to come up with a different user interface altogether based on a dialog box. Although this works well, it is different, and that difference might be reason enough for you to avoid an in-process server yourself.

One of the other technical issues involving an in-process server specifically (but not a handler) is that because there is nothing that can ever run stand-alone (as a local server EXE can), there is no easy way of providing linked objects. You cannot run a DLL by itself, so how do you create files, especially when the embedded object user interface we saw in Chapter 10 eliminates most vestiges of "file" from the server? If your data is potentially large, an in-process server might not be your best choice—users might balk at their container files growing outrageously large because you don't let them create linked objects.

2. See *Object Linking and Embedding Programmer's Reference* for version 1 (Microsoft Press, 1992).

Delegating to the Default Handler

We programmers generally do not like to make extra work for ourselves—if code has already been written somewhere, we use it. I'm not saying we're lazy; we simply like to be as resourceful as possible in finding reusable code. That's why a language such as C++ was invented in the first place and why OLE 2 has the code-reuse mechanism of aggregation.

In writing handlers and in-process servers, we will aggregate on the default handler in order to reuse quite a lot of its functionality, just as Patron has been freeloading its presentation display and caching functionality for a number of chapters now. Aggregation in our case means calling the function *OleCreateDefaultHandler*, getting a number of interface pointers to that default handler object, and delegating interface calls to that object whenever we have no need to implement it ourselves.

NOTE: Under OLE version 2.01, an in-process server should use the new *CreateDataCache* function in place of *OleCreateDefaultHandler*. *CreateDataCache* takes the same parameters as *OleCreateDefaultHandler* (although in a different order), supports the same interfaces (*IOleCache*, *IOleObject*, *IDataObject*, and *IPersistStorage*) and ensures that nothing will cause OLE2.DLL to attempt to launch a local server. However, under OLE version 2.00, you must still use *OleCreateDefaultHandler*, as this book will demonstrate. Anywhere you see *OleCreateDefaultHandler*, you can insert *CreateDataCache* instead.

Regardless of which version of OLE 2 you are dealing with, there is nothing special or tricky about delegating interface functions to OLE 2.DLL.

When we implemented a local server in Chapter 10, we were doing exactly the same thing, only from the other side. For example, we implemented *IOleObject::EnumVerbs* by returning *ResultFromScode(OLE_S_USEREG)*, which forces the default handler to implement the function using the verbs for our CLSID in the Registration Database. This worked because the container always calls the handler first, and if the handler sees a running server, it asks the server. If the server says "Just use the Registration Database instead," the default handler does just that. When we implement a handler or an in-process server now, we get the call from the container first and we delegate it to the default handler object. That object in turn checks to see whether a local server is running, and if not, it simply uses the Registration Database to fulfill the request. For a function such as *IOleObject::EnumVerbs*, the default handler does the same when the server is running and returns OLE_S_USEREG as when the server is not running at all, and that's what we can exploit.

But then the question is "How do I know when the default handler will implement something, and how do I know when it will try to launch a local server?" There is no simple answer. Instead we have to look at each member function of the interfaces we will use in the default handler. The next sections list all the functions in *IOleObject*, *IDataObject*, *IPersistStorage*, *IViewObject*, and *IOleCache* and what the default handler (and the cache, which sits underneath the default handler) will do with each one. There are only a few specific instances in which the default handler or cache will attempt to launch a local server. If you implement a handler, you will want to use this functionality because you need to work with the local server to provide the full object implementation. From an in-process server, however, there is no local server to execute, so you will want to make sure you avoid those calls completely.[3]

The tables in the following sections form a guide to implementing handlers and in-process servers starting with "Implementing an Object Handler." As we'll see, there are some cases in which we can simply expose the default handler's interface as our own (such as *IOleCache*), some cases in which we delegate some or most of an interface's calls (such as *IOleObject*), and other cases in which we don't delegate them at all (as with *IViewObject*). *IOleCache* is not listed in a table because it's an all-or-nothing case: Either you implement it completely without delegation, or you don't implement it at all.[4]

Except where noted, all of the actions in the following sections assume that a local server is not running. Those that launch the server are marked by an asterisk.

IOleObject

There are only two member functions in *IOleObject* that will always attempt to run the local server and delegate directly to its *DoVerb* and *Update*. All others either have minimal implementations or simply return an HRESULT, as shown in Table 11-1 on the next page. Note also that the default handler saves the information from *Advise*, *Unadvise*, *EnumAdvise*, *SetClientSite*, *GetClientSite*, and *SetHostNames* so that if and when it launches a local server, it can forward that information.

---

3. This is, again, an irrelevant question if you are using OLE 2.01 and *CreateDataCache* from an in-process server; none of its member functions in any interface will attempt to launch a local server. However, this is always a consideration for an in-process handler.

4. One exception to this rule is that you can reduce the amount of storage your object requires by implementing an *IOleCache* interface for the sole purpose of catching calls to *IOleCache::Cache* that are passed a NULL pointer in its FORMATETC parameter. What you are doing with this approach is preventing the cache from storing a default presentation in the object's storage. Usually this is a waste of resources because an object handler usually exists to generate presentations. However, a default presentation is useful if the compound document is viewed on another machine without your handler—without your drawing code—present. In that case, the default presentation at least shows something to the end user instead of a gaping black hole. It's your decision whether you want to spend the extra time overriding OLE 2's *IOleCache* interface for this one purpose or whether you want to use extra space in your storage.

Member function	Action
Advise	Calls *CreateOleAdviseHolder* if one has not yet been created. In either case, delegates to *IOleAdviseHolder::Advise*, which does not run the server in any case.
Close	Returns NOERROR.
*DoVerb**	Runs and delegates to the server.
EnumAdvise	Delegates to *IOleAdviseHolder*. Does not run the server.
EnumVerbs	Creates an enumeration based on the verb entries for the CLSID in the Registration Database and returns NOERROR.
GetClientSite	Returns the last *IOleClientSite* seen in *SetClientSite* and NOERROR.
GetClipboardData	Returns OLE_E_NOTRUNNING.
GetExtent	Attempts to locate the requested aspect in the cache and returns the size of that presentation if available. Otherwise, returns NOERROR.
GetMiscStatus	Retrieves the value from the CLSID's *MiscStatus* entries in the Registration Database and returns NOERROR.
GetMoniker	Calls *IOleClientSite::GetMoniker* if *SetClientSite* has been called with a valid *IOleClientSite* pointer. Otherwise, returns E_UNSPEC.
GetUserClassID	Returns the CLSID passed to *OleCreateDefaultHandler* and NOERROR.[5]
GetUserType	Retrieves a string from the CLSID's *AuxUserType* entries in the Registration Database and returns NOERROR.
InitFromData	Returns OLE_E_NOTRUNNING.
IsUpToDate	Returns OLE_E_NOTRUNNING.
SetClientSite	Saves the *IOleClientSite* pointer in an internal variable and returns NOERROR.
SetColorScheme	Returns OLE_E_NOTRUNNING.
SetExtent	Returns OLE_E_NOTRUNNING.
SetHostNames	Stores the strings in atoms and returns NOERROR.
SetMoniker	Returns NOERROR.
Unadvise	Delegates to *IOleAdviseHolder*. Will not run the server.
*Update**	Runs and delegates to the server.

*Launches the local server

Table 11-1.
Actions for the IOleObject *interface on a nonrunning object.*

5. This also includes the CLSID passed to *CreateDataCache* in OLE version 2.01. In addition, if there is an entry under the *TreatAs* or *AutoTreatAs* keys under the object's CLSID in the Registration Database, the CLSID stored as the value of either key is returned. This has to do with object conversion and emulation, as described in Chapter 14.

IDataObject

The default handler's implementation of *IDataObject* in OLE 2 depends on what's available in the cache. What really happens is that the default handler delegates to the *IDataObject* of the cache. The default handler's *IDataObject* implementation is described in Table 11-2, and those of the cache are given in Table 11-3.

Member function	Action
DAdvise	Delegates to cache, which returns OLE_E_ADVISENOTSUPPORTED.
DUnadvise	Delegates to cache, which returns OLE_E_NOCONNECTION.
EnumDAdvise	Delegates to cache, which returns OLE_E_ADVISENOTSUPPORTED.
EnumFormatEtc	Creates an enumerator based on the CLSID's entries under *DataFormats\GetSet* in the Registration Database.
GetCanonicalFormatEtc	Returns OLE_E_NOTRUNNING.
GetData	Delegates to the cache.
GetDataHere	Delegates to the cache.
QueryGetData	Returns OLE_E_NOTRUNNING.
SetData	Returns OLE_E_NOTRUNNING.

Table 11-2.
Actions for the IDataObject *interface on a nonrunning object.*

Member function	Action
DAdvise	Returns OLE_E_ADVISENOTSUPPORTED.
DUnadvise	Returns OLE_E_NOCONNECTION.
EnumDAdvise	Returns OLE_E_ADVISENOTSUPPORTED.
EnumFormatEtc	Returns E_NOTIMPL.
GetCanonicalFormatEtc	Returns E_NOTIMPL.
GetData	Attempts to find the data in the cache. If it can't, attempts to find an already running server and to retrieve the data from there. Otherwise, returns OLE_E_NOTRUNNING.
GetDataHere	Same as for *GetData*.
QueryGetData	Returns OLE_E_NOTRUNNING.
SetData	Returns OLE_E_NOTRUNNING.

Table 11-3.
Actions for the cache's IDataObject *interface for a nonrunning object.*

IPersistStorage (on the Cache)

In no case will the cache run the server to support *IPersistStorage.* The cache deals exclusively with cached presentations and does not affect the object's native data. If you want to use the cache to store, say, iconic presentations, you always need to call the default *IPersistStorage* members from your own *IPersistStorage* after manipulating your native data, with the exception of *GetClassID,* which it is pointless to delegate. The default handler's *IPersistStorage* implementation is shown in Table 11-4.

Member function	Action
GetClassID	Returns the CLSID passed to *CreateDefaultHandler* and NOERROR.
IsDirty	Returns S_OK if the cache's *IAdviseSink* has seen an *OnViewChange.* Otherwise, returns S_FALSE.
InitNew	Returns NOERROR, but saves and uses *AddRef* on the *IStorage.*
Load	Loads information describing the presentations area that is available in the cache. No data is actually loaded until required in the cache's *IDataObject* implementation. The return value might contain an error code. This happens regardless of the running state of a server.
Save	Saves any presentations that have changed since the call to *Load* as well as an information block describing what is cached. Return value might contain an error code. This happens regardless of the running state of a server.
SaveCompleted	Releases and replaces any held *IStorage* pointers as necessary and returns NOERROR.
HandsOffStorage	Releases any held *IStorage* pointers and returns NOERROR.

Table 11-4.
Actions for the cache's IPersistStorage *interface for a nonrunning object. The default handler delegates all calls to the cache.*

IViewObject

In most cases, a handler or an in-process server will implement all of *IViewObject* for at least some display aspects. For others, such as DVASPECT_ICON, you can delegate to the cache through the default handler, which will try to perform the action on a presentation in the cache. The default handler's *IViewObject* never runs the local server. If you implement a member function for an aspect, you do not need to call the default. The default handler's *IViewObject* implementation is shown in Table 11-5.

Member function	Action
Draw	Attempts to draw using a presentation from the cache. Otherwise, returns OLE_E_BLANK.
GetColorSet	Tries to determine the color set from the metafile or bitmap in the cache. Returns OLE_E_BLANK if there is no presentation. Otherwise, returns NOERROR or S_FALSE, depending on success of the function.
Freeze	Adds the aspect to an internal list that affects the behavior of *Draw* and returns NOERROR if successful or OLE_E_BLANK if not. Returns VIEW_S_ALREADY-_FROZEN if this is a repeat request.
Unfreeze	Removes an entry from the internal list of frozen aspects and frees any duplicate presentation. Returns OLE_E-_NOCONNECTION if the aspect was not frozen. Otherwise, returns NOERROR.
SetAdvise	Saves the *IAdviseSink* in such a way that the cache calls its *OnViewChange* when the cache itself is notified from the server through the cache's own *IAdviseSink*. Returns NOERROR.
GetAdvise	Returns the last *IAdviseSink* from *SetAdvise* and returns NOERROR.

Table 11-5.
Actions for the cache's IViewObject *interface for a nonrunning object.*

Implementing an Object Handler

This section deals with implementation details for a basic handler using CHAP11\HCOSMO (Handler for Cosmo) as an example. It will not provide as much detail of the step-by-step process as in the last two chapters simply because most of the interfaces we need to implement in a handler we've already discussed. In addition, we've already seen (way back in Chapter 4) how to make an object in a DLL, including the class factory. Nevertheless, the following list outlines the steps to create the minimal object handler. Anything you do beyond this is a bonus.

1. Implement *DllGetClassObject*, *DllCanUnloadNow*, your class factory, and your basic object with an *IUnknown* interface. You may or may not want to support aggregation, and there is no requirement to do so. In all ways, a handler is structured exactly like a component object DLL.

2. Store the path of the handler under your CLSID in the Registration Database under the key *InprocHandler*. In Chapter 10, we stored "OLE2.DLL" under *InprocHandler* because we should always have an entry and OLE2.DLL is the default handler.

3. When creating your object, create a default handler object and obtain pointers to its *IOleObject*, *IPersistStorage*, and *IViewObject* interfaces.

4. Delegate *QueryInterface* calls for any interface you are not implementing to the default handler *IUnknown*, including *IDataObject* and *IOleCache*.

5. Implement all of *IPersistStorage*, but call the default handler anyway to ensure maintenance of the cache.

6. Implement *IOleObject::GetExtent*, delegating all *IOleObject* calls to the default handler. *GetExtent* might not even be needed for your type of data, in which case you can still delegate.

7. Implement all of *IViewObject* for supported aspects; otherwise, delegate to the default handler.

I will not bother to discuss steps 1 and 2 because they should already be a familiar process for you—the code for step 3 in HCosmo is in HCOSMO.CPP, where *IClassFactory::CreateInstance* creates a C++ object of the class *CFigure* that holds all the necessary interfaces. The *CFigure* class is defined in HCOSMO.H as follows:

```
class __far CFigure : public IUnknown
    {
    //Make any contained interfaces your friends
    //so they can get at private functions
    friend class CImplOleObject;
    friend class CImplViewObject;
    friend class CImplPersistStorage;
    friend class CImplAdviseSink;

    private:
        ULONG               m_cRef;
        LPUNKNOWN           m_pUnkOuter;
        LPFNDESTROYED       m_pfnDestroy;

        POLYLINEDATA        m_pl;           //Our actual data.
        UINT                m_cf;           //Obj clipboard format.
        CLSID               m_clsID;        //Current CLSID
```

```
        LPSTORAGE           m_pIStorage;    //Cached for Save
        LPSTREAM            m_pIStream;

        //These are default handler interfaces we use
        LPUNKNOWN           m_pDefIUnknown;
        LPOLEOBJECT         m_pDefIOleObject;
        LPVIEWOBJECT        m_pDefIViewObject;
        LPPERSISTSTORAGE    m_pDefIPersistStorage;
        LPDATAOBJECT        m_pDefIDataObject;

        //Implemented interfaces
        LPIMPIOLEOBJECT       m_pIOleObject;
        LPIMPIVIEWOBJECT      m_pIViewObject;
        LPIMPIPERSISTSTORAGE m_pIPersistStorage;
        LPIMPIADVISESINK      m_pIAdviseSink;

        //Advise sink we get in IViewObject
        LPADVISESINK        m_pIAdvSinkView;
        DWORD               m_dwAdviseFlags;
        DWORD               m_dwAdviseAspects;
        DWORD               m_dwFrozenAspects;

        //Copies of frozen aspects
        POLYLINEDATA        m_plContent;
        POLYLINEDATA        m_plThumbnail;

    protected:
        void        Draw(HDC, LPRECT, DWORD, DVTARGETDEVICE FAR *
                        , HDC, LPPOLYLINEDATA);
        void        PointScale(LPRECT, LPPOINT, BOOL);

    public:
        CFigure(LPUNKNOWN, LPFNDESTROYED, HINSTANCE);
        ~CFigure(void);

        BOOL        FInit(void);

        //Non-delegating object IUnknown
        STDMETHODIMP QueryInterface(REFIID, LPLPVOID);
        STDMETHODIMP_(ULONG) AddRef(void);
        STDMETHODIMP_(ULONG) Release(void);
    };

typedef CFigure FAR *LPCFigure;
```

Note that HCOSMO.H also contains definitions of all the *CImpl...* classes that are friends of *CFigure.* These are like all the other interface implementations we've already seen, so I won't repeat their descriptions here. Most of the variables in *CFigure* are set initially to NULL or zero, except for *m_pUnkOuter* and *m_pfnDestroy*, which are set from the parameters to the constructor; *m_clsID*, which is set to *CLSID_Cosmo2Figure2;* and *m_cf*, which is set to the return value from *RegisterClipboardFormat* on the string "Polyline Figure." This clipboard format matches that used in all Cosmo applications. In addition, the *CFigure* destructor will call *Release* on any interface that we're using and call *delete* for any interface we implement, as is normal in cleanup. You can see these in FIGURE.CPP.

Now let's concentrate specifically on the rest of *CFigure*, inside the handler, and what it must do. Working through these steps works best if you already have created a compound document in some container that has an object of the class you want to handle.

Obtain a Default Handler *IUnknown*

When initializing the handler object, you need to obtain at least an *IUnknown* pointer to a default handler object set up for your CLSID so that you can take advantage of the many services provided by OLE2.DLL. To obtain the pointer, call *OleCreateDefaultHandler*, passing your CLSID and a pointer to your object's *IUnknown* (because the default handler must be aggregated). You need to pass your CLSID so that the default handler can implement various functions using the entries in the Registration Database under that CLSID. You must pass your *IUnknown* as the controlling unknown because we are aggregating the default handler.

After you have this *IUnknown*, you should call *QueryInterface* for *IOleObject*, *IPersistStorage*, and *IViewObject* pointers (and also perhaps *IDataObject*) to which you can later delegate. This is much more efficient than calling *QueryInterface*, delegating the function, and calling *Release* every time you need to delegate. In HCosmo this is handled in *CFigure::FInit*, called from *IClassFactory::CreateInstance*. *FInit* first allocates the interface implementations for this object and then calls *OleCreateDefaultHandler*, followed by a series of *QueryInterface* calls:

```
BOOL CFigure::FInit(void)
    {
    LPUNKNOWN        pIUnknown=(LPUNKNOWN)this;
    HRESULT          hr;
    DWORD            dwConn;
    FORMATETC        fe;

    if (NULL!=m_pUnkOuter)
        pIUnknown=m_pUnkOuter;
```

```
//First create our interfaces.
m_pIOleObject=new CImpIOleObject(this, pIUnknown);

if (NULL==m_pIOleObject)
    return FALSE;

m_pIViewObject=new CImpIViewObject(this, pIUnknown);

if (NULL==m_pIViewObject)
    return FALSE;

m_pIPersistStorage=new CImpIPersistStorage(this, pIUnknown);

if (NULL==m_pIPersistStorage)
    return FALSE;

m_pIAdviseSink=new CImpIAdviseSink(this, pIUnknown);

if (NULL==m_pIAdviseSink)
    return FALSE;

/*
 * Get an IUnknown on the default handler, passing pIUnknown
 * as the controlling unknown.  The extra reference count is to
 * prevent us from going away accidentally.
 */
m_cRef++;

hr=OleCreateDefaultHandler(CLSID_Cosmo2Figure, pIUnknown
    , IID_IUnknown, (LPLPVOID)&m_pDefIUnknown);

if (FAILED(hr))
    return FALSE;

//Now try to get other interfaces to which we delegate
hr=m_pDefIUnknown->QueryInterface(IID_IOleObject
    , (LPLPVOID)&m_pDefIOleObject);

if (FAILED(hr))
    return FALSE;

m_pDefIOleObject->Release();

hr=m_pDefIUnknown->QueryInterface(IID_IViewObject
    , (LPLPVOID)&m_pDefIViewObject);
```

(continued)

```
if (FAILED(hr))
    return FALSE;

m_pDefIViewObject->Release();

hr=m_pDefIUnknown->QueryInterface(IID_IDataObject
    , (LPLPVOID)&m_pDefIDataObject);

if (FAILED(hr))
    return FALSE;

m_pDefIDataObject->Release();

hr=m_pDefIUnknown->QueryInterface(IID_IPersistStorage
    , (LPLPVOID)&m_pDefIPersistStorage);

if (FAILED(hr))
    return FALSE;
m_pDefIPersistStorage->Release();
m_cRef--;

//Set up an advise on native data so we can keep in sync
SETDefFormatEtc(fe, m_cf, TYMED_HGLOBAL);
m_pDefIDataObject->DAdvise(&fe, 0, m_pIAdviseSink, &dwConn);

return TRUE;
}
```

Whoa! What are all those calls to *Release* doing in there? Good question, and I'm glad you asked. All of this additional code makes reference counting work correctly when you are aggregating on another object, and it is a technique described in the OLE 2 Design Specification. In aggregation, as we saw in Chapter 4, the aggregatee (in this case, the default handler) has a lifetime controlled by the outer unknown (in this case, our handler). This has two implications.

First, the default handler does not call *AddRef* on the *IUnknown* pointer that we pass to *OleCreateDefaultHandler,* even though it holds onto that pointer (an official violation of reference counting rules). Therefore, our actual reference count is unmodified when we obtain the default handler's *IUnknown,* and we can simply use *Release* on that pointer in our destructor. If *AddRef* was called in *OleCreateDefaultHandler,* we would never reach a zero reference count in our *Release* because we'd have to call *Release* on the default handler's *IUnknown,* which we do only in our destructor (because there's nowhere else to put it).

Second, anytime we call *QueryInterface* on the default handler's *IUnknown* for another one of its interfaces, we call *AddRef* ourselves because each of those interfaces will delegate its *IUnknown* calls to our outer unknown.

If we do not immediately call *Release* on these interfaces we obtain, we'll never free ourselves because our destructor is the only place we could otherwise call *Release* on those reference counts.

How can we get away with releasing pointers in this way? The OLE 2 Design Specification states that when we are holding the *IUnknown* of an aggregated object, the aggregatee must ensure the validity of all interfaces on that aggregated object, even if there are no reference counts on those interfaces themselves (which is why we don't have interface reference counting in the first place). So, even though we call *Release* on those pointers, the pointers are still valid because we have the *IUnknown* from *OleCreateDefaultHandler.*

Otherwise, everything about this code should look familiar by now, except for the part at the end, which sets up a data advise with the *IDataObject* interface in the default handler. This connection is used to synchronize the handler and a local server when one is launched, as discussed later in "Synchronized Swimming with Your Local Server." Note that I don't save the connection key from *DAdvise* because I won't need to call *DUnadvise* until I release the *m_pDefIDataObject,* which will terminate the connection for me.

Expose Default Handler Interfaces in *QueryInterface*

You want to hold onto the default handler's *IOleObject, IViewObject,* and *IPersistStorage* pointers for delegation, but why hold on to its *IUnknown*? Remember that when we aggregate on any object, as described at the end of Chapter 4, we first are required to ask for an *IUnknown* pointer when creating the object—*OleCreateDefaultHandler* eventually calls *IClassFactory::CreateInstance* with a non-NULL *pUnkOuter,* which requires that *riid* passed to *CreateInstance* is *IID_IUnknown.* Second, the outer object controlling the aggregation is required to delegate *QueryInterface* calls to the aggregated object when the object does not implement that interface. We can see this in *CFigure::QueryInterface*:

```
STDMETHODIMP CFigure::QueryInterface(REFIID riid, LPLPVOID ppv)
    {
    *ppv=NULL;

    /*
     * The only calls we get here for IUnknown are either in a non-
     * aggregated case or when we're created in an aggregation, so
     * in either we always return our IUnknown for IID_IUnknown.
     */
    if (IsEqualIID(riid, IID_IUnknown))
        *ppv=(LPVOID)this;

    if (IsEqualIID(riid, IID_IPersist)
        || IsEqualIID(riid , IID_IPersistStorage))
        *ppv=(LPVOID)m_pIPersistStorage;
```

(continued)

```
    if (IsEqualIID(riid, IID_IOleObject))
        *ppv=(LPVOID)m_pIOleObject;

    if (IsEqualIID(riid, IID_IViewObject))
        *ppv=(LPVOID)m_pIViewObject;

    if (NULL!=*ppv)
        {
        ((LPUNKNOWN)*ppv)->AddRef();
        return NOERROR;
        }

    /*
     * Only expose default handler interfaces--you don't want to
     * just delegate to the default handler's QueryInterface as
     * it may return an interface you do not expect...like
     * IViewObject2 when you only know IViewObject.
     */

    if (IsEqualIID(riid, IID_IDataObject)
        || IsEqualIID(riid, IID_IOleCache))
        return m_pDefIUnknown->QueryInterface(riid, ppv);

    return ResultFromScode(E_NOINTERFACE);
    }

STDMETHODIMP_(ULONG) CFigure::AddRef(void)
    {
    return ++m_cRef;
    }

STDMETHODIMP_(ULONG) CFigure::Release(void)
    {
    ULONG       cRefT;

    cRefT=--m_cRef;

    if (0L==m_cRef)
        delete this;

    return cRefT;
    }
```

Because your object is implementing *IPersistStorage*, *IOleObject*, and *IViewObject* itself, it returns its interface pointers from *QueryInterface* (as well as from *CFigure*'s *IUnknown*). If asked for some other interface for which the handler exposes one of the default handler's interfaces, it hands the request to the default handler's *IUnknown.* So when asked, for example, for *IDataObject* or *IOleCache,* the handler will return its interfaces directly, which means that as far as the container (the user of this object) is concerned, those interfaces belong to it. Again, the container does not know that your object is aggregating the default handler, and it simply sees all the necessary embedded object interfaces as if your object were implementing them. Through this simple act of delegating *QueryInterface,* your object exposes default handler interfaces as its own.

This exposure is the entire reason why we must give a controlling unknown to *OleCreateDefaultHandler.* Any *QueryInterface* call to a pointer returned from the default handler, with the exception of *IUnknown,* will enter *CFigure::QueryInterface,* allowing you the chance to show your interface implementation. You must trust that the default handler's *IUnknown* will not delegate the controlling unknown, as is required.

Note also that because *CFigure* is the embedded object, not an interface implementation, it destroys itself when the reference count is zero, as shown in the preceding code in *CFigure::Release.*

WARNING

This is one situation in which you do not want to blindly delegate *QueryInterface* to the default handler (the contained object) as discussed in Chapter 4 under "Object Reusability." This is because the default handler might implement more recent revisions of a particular interface so that if the container asks for the revised interface instead of the original one, it will get a pointer to the interface in the default handler, which will then bypass your handler completely. A good example of the danger here is the interface *IViewObject2,* which was added in OLE version 2.01 and is supported by that revision of the default handler. If your handler implements only *IViewObject* (because you want to control rendering) but blindly delegates to the default handler's *QueryInterface,* when a container asks for *IViewObject2,* it will always get the *IViewObject2* interface on OLE 2's cache. If the container then calls *IViewObject2::Draw,* your handler would never be called. If, however, you write your *QueryInterface* to delegate the call to the default handler only for specific interfaces, the same query for *IViewObject2* would fail, prompting the container to ask instead for *IViewObject* over which you *do* have control.

If you want to compile and test something at this point, you can omit the code in the preceding example that instantiates interface implementations as well as that which returns those pointers from *QueryInterface*. Then your object's *QueryInterface* delegates all requests to the default handler (not something you always would want to do), essentially making your handler nothing more than a reference counter for the default handler object. But you can verify that your *DllGetClassObject* and class factory are working correctly and that all other operations of your embedded object class in a container are normal—that is, you should not see any difference between having your handler registered as the *InprocHandler* and having OLE2.DLL listed there. Your handler is merely a simple layer between the container and the default handler.

Implement *IPersistStorage*

We now have an exciting opportunity to start changing specific pieces of each interface to suit our purposes. *IPersistStorage* is the best place to start because it's always called first in an embedded object scenario and is one that we can implement without any other impact on the operation of the container or default handler.

When you want to override any member function of an interface, you must have entry points for the entire interface in your code. I recommend that you start off with a template interface implementation, in which each function simply delegates to the default handler's interface, as shown in the following example code for *IPersistStorage*. (NOTE: This is not part of HCosmo; it is simply an example.) This code assumes that the interface implementation has a controlling unknown to which it delegates all *IUnknown* members (*m_pUnkOuter*) and has access to the default *IPersistStorage* pointer. In this case, that is *m_pObj->m_pDefIPersistStorage*, where *m_pObj* is a *CFigure* pointer:

```
STDMETHODIMP CImpIPersistStorage::QueryInterface(REFIID riid
    , LPLPVOID ppv)
    {
    return m_pUnkOuter->QueryInterface(riid, ppv);
    }

STDMETHODIMP_(ULONG) CImpIPersistStorage::AddRef(void)
    {
    ++m_cRef;
    return m_pUnkOuter->AddRef();
    }

STDMETHODIMP_(ULONG) CImpIPersistStorage::Release(void)
    {
```

```
    --m_cRef;
    return m_pUnkOuter->Release();
    }

STDMETHODIMP CImpIPersistStorage::GetClassID(LPCLSID pClsID)
    {
    return m_pObj->m_pDefIPersistStorage->GetClassID(pClsID);
    }

STDMETHODIMP CImpIPersistStorage::IsDirty(void)
    {
    return m_pObj->m_pDefIPersistStorage->IsDirty();
    }

STDMETHODIMP CImpIPersistStorage::InitNew(LPSTORAGE pIStorage)
    {
    return m_pObj->m_pDefIPersistStorage->InitNew(pIStorage);
    }

STDMETHODIMP CImpIPersistStorage::Load(LPSTORAGE pIStorage)
    {
    return m_pObj->m_pDefIPersistStorage->Load(pIStorage);
    }

STDMETHODIMP CImpIPersistStorage::Save(LPSTORAGE pIStorage
    , BOOL fSameAsLoad)
    {
    return m_pObj->m_pDefIPersistStorage->Save(pIStorage, fSameAsLoad);
    }

STDMETHODIMP CImpIPersistStorage::SaveCompleted(LPSTORAGE pIStorage)
    {
    return m_pObj->m_pDefIPersistStorage->SaveCompleted(pIStorage);
    }

STDMETHODIMP CImpIPersistStorage::HandsOffStorage(void)
    {
    return m_pObj->m_pDefIPersistStorage->HandsOffStorage();
    }
```

You can now integrate this "pass-through" interface implementation into your code and compile and test again. Because you are not doing anything but calling the default handler, there should be no effect on the container or on any other operation of the embedded object.

To this pass-through implementation, you can now add your own implementation of *IPersistStorage*, with all the contractual obligations of that interface, including holding onto open streams in case of a low-memory call to

IPersistStorage::Save. The following *IPersistStorage* implementation from HCosmo looks so much like the one for the full Cosmo appilication we saw in Chapter 10 that all the similarities have been removed, leaving the calls to the default handler's implementation of *IPersistStorage*:

```
STDMETHODIMP CImpIPersistStorage::GetClassID(LPCLSID pClsID)
    {
    *pClsID=m_pObj->m_clsID;
    return NOERROR;
    }

STDMETHODIMP CImpIPersistStorage::IsDirty(void)
    {
    /*
     * Since we don't edit, we have no idea if this data is dirty.
     * Delegate to the default handler in case it wants to ask the
     * server.
     */
    return m_pObj->m_pDefIPersistStorage->IsDirty();
    }

STDMETHODIMP CImpIPersistStorage::InitNew(LPSTORAGE pIStorage)
    {
    [Code to initialize the figure and save pre-created pointers]

    m_pObj->m_pDefIPersistStorage->InitNew(pIStorage);
    return NOERROR;
    }

STDMETHODIMP CImpIPersistStorage::Load(LPSTORAGE pIStorage)
    {
    [Code to load the object and save IStorage/IStream pointers]

    m_pObj->m_pDefIPersistStorage->Load(pIStorage);
    return NOERROR;
    }

STDMETHODIMP CImpIPersistStorage::Save(LPSTORAGE pIStorage
    , BOOL fSameAsLoad)
    {
    ...

    /*
     * If the server is running, don't do the save ourselves since
     * we'd end up writing the storage twice with possible conflicts.
     */
    if (OleIsRunning(m_pObj->m_pDefIOleObject))
        {
        return m_pObj->m_pDefIPersistStorage->Save(pIStorage
```

```
            , fSameAsLoad);
        }

    [Code to save to new storage or to an existing one.]

    m_pObj->m_pDefIPersistStorage->Save(pIStorage, fSameAsLoad);

    [Return success based on whether we succeeded in writing data]
    }


STDMETHODIMP CImpIPersistStorage::SaveCompleted(LPSTORAGE pIStorage)
    {
    [Other code to release old pointers and save new ones]

    m_pObj->m_pDefIPersistStorage->SaveCompleted(pIStorage);
    return NOERROR;
    }


STDMETHODIMP CImpIPersistStorage::HandsOffStorage(void)
    {
    [Code to release held pointers]

    m_pObj->m_pDefIPersistStorage->HandsOffStorage();
    return NOERROR;
    }
```

Now you are probably wondering why we still have all these calls to the default handler's *IPersistStorage* implementation. Well, Henry Jones Sr. would remind us that "There is more in the diary than just the map." To which we would respond, "OK, Dad, tell me."[6] There is more in the storage than just our object—there are cached presentations. If the container has obtained an *IOleCache* pointer and has called *IOleCache::SetData*, somewhere down in the bowels of the default handler that presentation is waiting to be serialized to storage. If we never pass calls to our *IPersistStorage* functions through to the default handler, it would never have a chance to work with its presentations, and it would never have the chance to manage its copies of the *IStorage* and *IStream* pointers (especially for low-memory save conditions). So unless you want to implement all caching functions so that you do not rely on the default handler's cache, you must give the default handler the opportunity to manage storage whenever you are given the opportunity yourself.

This brings up the question of what the preceding code is doing with return values from OLE 2's implementation. For the most part, we ignore

6. From *Indiana Jones and the Last Crusade, ©1989 LucasFilm Ltd.*

them completely, except in those cases where we use the default implementation completely. We ignore these return values because what really matters is whether the operation succeeded on our own data. The default handler's return values describe whether the operation succeeded on the cache. If the cache failed, but your object succeeded in saving its own data, should that fail the entire function? Not in most cases—the cache is a bonus, and your data is what's important, especially because handlers are designed to generate presentations from native data in the first place. However, you might attach more importance to the success of the cache functions, in which case you should pay more attention to the actual return values.

NOTE: If a handler implements *IViewObject::Draw* for any given aspect in such a way that it never delegates *Draw* to the default handler, the cache will *never* contain a presentation for that aspect. Your handler is entirely responsible for generating presentations for that aspect. If a compound document is taken to another machine, where not even your handler is present, the object will appear blank in the container. This is another reason why you should license handlers for free redistribution.

Finally, I want to explain that use of *OleIsRunning (OLE2.H)* in *Save*. The *OleIsRunning* function returns a BOOL, telling us whether the server for this CLSID is running for the object pointed to in the only parameter to the function (which *must* be an *IOleObject* pointer). If the server is running, the handler completely delegates to the default handler, which saves the cache and calls the server's *IPersistStorage::Save*. This ensures that we don't save our data twice (a waste of time) and that what we save in the handler does not conflict with what the server decides to save. This is especially important if the server is incrementally accessing the storage and has already written some changes there, changes that a *Save* in the handler might obliterate. We want to avoid conflicts with the running server, so *OleIsRunning* is just what we need here.

Implement *IOleObject::GetExtent*

I have some bad news: The minimal handler has to override the *GetExtent* function in *IOleObject*, which means you have to provide pass-throughs for the other 20 members. What a pain. We never said life was fair. But you can use HCosmo's IOLEOBJ.CPP as a template for doing this if you have structured your code similarly to mine.[7]

7. For this reason OLE version 2.01 defines the *IViewObject2* interface to be identical with *IViewObject* with an additional member *GetExtent* to eventually eliminate the need to separately override all of *IOleObject* merely to implement *IOleObject::GetExtent*. Because *IViewObject2* was not part of OLE 2.00, you will still need to implement an *IOleObject* interface and implement *GetExtent* until nothing in existence uses *IViewObject* anymore—that is, until anyone who wants the extent of your object always asks through *IViewObject2* and never through *IOleObject*.

GetExtent is a required override because a container might depend on this function to determine the size of its site in which it displays your object when loading a compound document. The entry for *GetExtent* in Table 11-1 mentioned that for this function the default handler tries to determine the size of the data based on presentations in the cache. But as we saw in discussing *IPersistStorage* just now, there are generally no cached presentations for those aspects for which you implement *IViewObject::Draw*, and so the default handler cannot implement *GetExtent* for those aspects. In HCosmo we implement *IViewObject::Draw* for DVASPECT_CONTENT and DVASPECT_THUMBNAIL, so we must provide an implementation of *GetExtent* for both of those presentations as well:

```
STDMETHODIMP CImpIOleObject::GetExtent(DWORD dwAspect, LPSIZEL pszl)
    {
    SIZEL       szl;
    LPRECT      prc;

    /*
     * We can answer for CONTENT/THUMBNAIL, but try the server for
     * others. In addition, always delegate if the server is running
     * since it has a window to define the size.
     */
    if (!((DVASPECT_CONTENT | DVASPECT_THUMBNAIL) & dwAspect)
        || OleIsRunning(m_pObj->m_pDefIOleObject))
        return m_pObj->m_pDefIOleObject->GetExtent(dwAspect, pszl);

    /*
     * The size is in the rc field of the POLYLINEDATA structure
     * which we now have to convert to HIMETRIC.
     */
    prc=&m_pObj->m_pl->rc;
    SETSIZEL(szl, prc->right-prc->left, prc->bottom-prc->top);
    XformSizeInPixelsToHimetric(NULL, &szl, pszl);
    return NOERROR;
    }
```

The POLYLINEDATA structure that makes up the object's data in HCosmo just so happens to contain a rectangle that we can use here to calculate the size of the object in HIMETRIC units (as *GetExtent* must return). In addition, notice that we delegate this call to the default handler not only when it's called with an aspect we don't draw ourselves but also when the server is running for *any* aspect. This is because a running server, because it generally implements *SetExtent* as well, has a better idea of how large the object currently is, whereas this handler only knows what's in our storage. You might also choose, if you want, to implement *SetExtent* in your handler to record what the container says is the size (then calling the default anyway) and return those extents from *GetExtent.*

You can again compile and test your *GetExtent* implementation and verify that everything else you pass through in *IOleObject* is correct.

Implement *IViewObject*

Now comes the real reason why we generally have object handlers in the first place: to optimize drawing for particular devices. Your implementation of *IPersistStorage* loads the data to draw, and your *IOleObject::GetExtent* lets the container know what sort of rectangle you generally like drawn (although the container can have its own rather individualistic ideas about your size, in which case you must obey). So now we can implement *IViewObject::Draw.*

If you implement *IViewObject::Draw,* you also need to implement *IViewObject::Freeze, Unfreeze, SetAdvise,* and *GetAdvise* for the same aspects. This makes *IViewObject* the most complicated interface in your handler, as you can see from the amount of code shown in Listing 11-1.

IVIEWOBJ.CPP

```
[Constructor, destructor, IUnknown members omitted]

STDMETHODIMP CImpIViewObject::Draw(DWORD dwAspect, LONG lindex
    , void FAR * pvAspect, DVTARGETDEVICE FAR * ptd, HDC hICDev
    , HDC hDC, const LPRECTL pRectBounds, const LPRECTL pRectWBounds
    , BOOL (CALLBACK * pfnContinue) (DWORD), DWORD dwContinue)
    {
    RECT            rc;
    POLYLINEDATA    pl;
    LPPOLYLINEDATA  ppl=&m_pObj->m_pl;

    RECTFROMRECTL(rc, *pRectBounds);

    //Delegate iconic and printed representations.
    if (!((DVASPECT_CONTENT | DVASPECT_THUMBNAIL) & dwAspect))
        {
        return m_pObj->m_pDefIViewObject->Draw(dwAspect, lindex
            , pvAspect, ptd, hICDev, hDC, pRectBounds, pRectWBounds
            , pfnContinue, dwContinue);
        }

    /*
     * If we're asked to draw a frozen aspect, use the data from
     * a copy we made in IViewObject::Freeze. Otherwise use the
```

Listing 11-1. *(continued)*
Implementation of the IViewObject *interface in HCosmo.*

Listing 11-1. *continued*

```
     * current data.
     */
    if (dwAspect & m_pObj->m_dwFrozenAspects)
        {
        //Point to the data to actually use.
        if (DVASPECT_CONTENT==dwAspect)
            ppl=&m_pObj->m_plContent;
        else
            ppl=&m_pObj->m_plThumbnail;
        }

    //Make a copy so we can modify it
    _fmemcpy(&pl, ppl, CBPOLYLINEDATA);

    /*
     * If we're going to a printer, check if it's color capable.
     * if not, then use black on white for this figure.
     */
    if (NULL!=hICDev)
        {
        if (GetDeviceCaps(hICDev, NUMCOLORS) <= 2)
            {
            pl.rgbBackground=RGB(255, 255, 255);
            pl.rgbLine=RGB(0, 0, 0);
            }
        }

    m_pObj->Draw(hDC, &rc, dwAspect, ptd, hICDev, &pl);
    return NOERROR;
    }

STDMETHODIMP CImpIViewObject::GetColorSet(DWORD dwDrawAspect
    , LONG lindex, LPVOID pvAspect, DVTARGETDEVICE FAR * ptd
    , HDC hICDev, LPLOGPALETTE FAR * ppColorSet)
    {
    return ResultFromScode(S_FALSE);
    }

STDMETHODIMP CImpIViewObject::Freeze(DWORD dwAspect, LONG lindex
    , LPVOID pvAspect, LPDWORD pdwFreeze)
    {
    //Delegate any aspect we don't handle.
    if (!((DVASPECT_CONTENT | DVASPECT_THUMBNAIL) & dwAspect))
```

(continued)

Listing 11-1. *continued*

```
        {
        return m_pObj->m_pDefIViewObject->Freeze(dwAspect, lindex
            , pvAspect, pdwFreeze);
        }

    if (dwAspect & m_pObj->m_dwFrozenAspects)
        {
        *pdwFreeze=dwAspect + FREEZE_KEY_OFFSET;
        return ResultFromScode(VIEW_S_ALREADY_FROZEN);
        }

    m_pObj->m_dwFrozenAspects |= dwAspect;

    /*
     * For whatever aspects become frozen, make a copy of the data.
     * Later when drawing, if such a frozen aspect is requested,
     * we'll draw from this data rather than from our current data.
     */
    if (DVASPECT_CONTENT & dwAspect)
        {
        _fmemcpy(&m_pObj->m_plContent, &m_pObj->m_pl
            , CBPOLYLINEDATA);
        }

    if (DVASPECT_THUMBNAIL & dwAspect)
        {
        _fmemcpy(&m_pObj->m_plThumbnail, &m_pObj->m_pl
            , CBPOLYLINEDATA);
        }

    if (NULL!=pdwFreeze)
        *pdwFreeze=dwAspect + FREEZE_KEY_OFFSET;

    return NOERROR;
    }

STDMETHODIMP CImpIViewObject::Unfreeze(DWORD dwFreeze)
    {
    DWORD       dwAspect=dwFreeze - FREEZE_KEY_OFFSET;

    //Delegate any aspect we don't handle.
    if (!((DVASPECT_CONTENT | DVASPECT_THUMBNAIL) & dwAspect))
        return m_pObj->m_pDefIViewObject->Unfreeze(dwFreeze);

    //The aspect to unfreeze is in the key.
    m_pObj->m_dwFrozenAspects &= ~(dwAspect);
```

(continued)

Listing 11-1. *continued*

```
    /*
     * Since we always kept our current data up to date, we don't
     * have to do anything here like requesting data again.
     * Because we removed dwAspect from m_dwFrozenAspects, Draw
     * will again use the current data.
     */

    return NOERROR;
    }

STDMETHODIMP CImpIViewObject::SetAdvise(DWORD dwAspects
    , DWORD dwAdvf, LPADVISESINK pIAdviseSink)
    {
    //Pass anything we don't support on through
    if (!((DVASPECT_CONTENT | DVASPECT_THUMBNAIL) & dwAspects))
        {
        return m_pObj->m_pDefIViewObject->SetAdvise(dwAspects
            , dwAdvf, pIAdviseSink);
        }

    if (NULL!=m_pObj->m_pIAdvSinkView)
        m_pObj->m_pIAdvSinkView->Release();

    m_pObj->m_dwAdviseAspects=dwAspects;
    m_pObj->m_dwAdviseFlags=dwAdvf;

    m_pObj->m_pIAdvSinkView=pIAdviseSink;

    if (NULL!=m_pObj->m_pIAdvSinkView)
        m_pObj->m_pIAdvSinkView->AddRef();

    return NOERROR;
    }

STDMETHODIMP CImpIViewObject::GetAdvise(LPDWORD pdwAspects
    , LPDWORD pdwAdvf, LPADVISESINK FAR* ppAdvSink)
    {
    if (NULL==m_pObj->m_pIAdvSink)
        return ResultFromScode(OLE_E_NOCONNECTION);

    if (NULL==ppAdvSink)
        return ResultFromScode(E_INVALIDARG);
    else
```

(continued)

Listing 11-1. *continued*

```
        {
        *ppAdvSink=m_pObj->m_pIAdvSinkView;
        m_pObj->m_pIAdvSinkView->AddRef();
        }

    if (NULL!=pdwAspects)
        *pdwAspects=m_pObj->m_dwAdviseAspects;

    if (NULL!=pdwAdvf)
        *pdwAdvf=m_pObj->m_dwAdviseFlags;

    return NOERROR;
    }
```

Let's look first at the simpler member functions before we jump into *Draw*. First, *GetColorSet* is unimportant for this handler (and for Cosmo, as well), so we simply return S_FALSE to say we don't have anything for the caller. Next, *SetAdvise* and *GetAdvise* handle a container's *IAdviseSink* pointer, to which we must send *OnViewChange* notifications when any data change occurs in our object in such a way that we would need to repaint. We delegate both of these calls to the default handler for DVASPECT_ICON and DVASPECT_DOCPRINT because we rely on the cache to handle those aspects for us in all other parts of the handler. That leaves us in *SetAdvise* to save the advise aspects, the flags, and the *IAdviseSink* pointer, to which we'll later send notifications, as described later in "Synchronized Swimming with Your Local Server." We need to hold all of these parameters so that we can return them through *GetAdvise* as shown. Remember to call *AddRef* on the *IAdviseSink* pointer when you save a copy in *SetAdvise* (and release it before overwriting it) as well as to call *AddRef* on it when returning a copy from *GetAdvise.*

NOTE: You can call *SetAdvise* with a NULL *IAdviseSink* pointer. This means that the container is terminating the connection. Be sure you don't attempt to call *AddRef* on it without checking for NULL. (I tell you this because I forgot and had a few extra UAEs to deal with.)

Freeze and *Unfreeze* are a pair that the container uses to control when a presentation is allowed to change. Note that a change in the presentation does not mean that you freeze underlying data because a freeze affects only one aspect. In HCosmo's case, a freeze on DVASPECT_CONTENT cannot freeze the data because DVASPECT_THUMBNAIL is drawn from the same data and it is not frozen. Therefore, we must make a snapshot of the frozen data so that when we're asked to draw that aspect, we use the frozen copy instead of the current data, thus still allowing the current data to change as desired. This also allows *IPersistStorage::Save* to write the current data without having to consider a frozen view aspect, which should not affect storage in any way.

Your implementation of *Freeze* must somehow remember that the aspect is frozen and make a snapshot of the data. HCosmo's code uses OR on the new aspect in which a list of currently frozen aspects exists in *CFigure*'s *m_dwFrozenAspects* and then takes a snapshot of the current data, putting it into either *CFigure*'s *m_plContent* or *m_plThumbnail* structure, depending on the aspect. *Draw* will later use all of this to determine exactly which data to present. In addition, *Freeze* must return some sort of key that can be later passed to *Unfreeze.* A good key is the aspect plus some random number to make the number meaningless to the caller. For example, I use FREEZE_KEY_OFFSET, which I define in HCOSMO.H as 0x0723.[8] When this key is later passed to *Unfreeze,* we subtract the offset to yield an aspect and remove that aspect from *m_dwFrozenAspects.* When *Draw* is subsequently called, we will see that the aspect is not frozen and will therefore draw from the current data. (We can assume *Draw* will be called because a container that thaws a view object will generally want to update immediately.)

Note also with *Freeze* that you should first check to see whether the requested aspect is already frozen and return VIEW_S_ALREADY_FROZEN if it is. However, it must still return a key, which the caller can later pass to *Unfreeze.* VIEW_S_ALREADY_FROZEN, having the *_S_*, is not an error—it simply avoids unnecessary repetition.

This brings us to *Draw,* which generally calls either *CFigure::Draw* (FIGURE.CPP) for DVASPECT_CONTENT and DVASPECT_THUMBNAIL or the default handler's *IViewObject::Draw* for any other aspect. The latter check happens first, so we can ignore those cases.

For content and thumbnail aspects, we now have to see whether they are frozen. If they are, we use the data we copied in *Freeze* instead of the current data. In Listing 11-1, *Draw* sets a pointer *ppl* initially to the current data and later, if the aspect is frozen, points *ppl* instead to the snapshot of that aspect. In this way, *Draw* can copy whatever *ppl* points to into a local POLYLINEDATA structure so that we can now do a few device optimizations. HCosmo doesn't do anything fancy with devices, but it does provide an example of how to render differently for a printer and for the screen. If the parameter *hICDev* to *Draw* is non-NULL, that means the data is going to a device other than the screen. If that is true, we check for the number of colors the device supports. If it's a black-and-white device with only two colors, we force the background color of the rendering to be white and the line color to be

8. If you can figure out where I got this number, I congratulate you on your resourcefulness. But don't expect any prizes; its meaning is entirely personal.

black, which avoids potentially ugly dithering or large black blocks on the printer. I can't say that this is the best thing to do, but hey, it's just an example.

IViewObject::Draw then calls *CFigure::Draw* with the local POLYLINEDATA structure that we potentially modified. It might be a frozen aspect, in which case the correct image is drawn, and it might be modified for a printer. In any case, *CFigure::Draw* draws the image. I won't show that function here because it's a load of GDI calls that add nothing to our insights about handlers. I do want to point out one bug I encountered when writing it, however. This code was originally taken from Cosmo's WM_PAINT handling of the Polyline window. Because Polyline was always in its own window, its client area always started at (0,0). So I did not have the code in place to handle cases in which the upper left corner was not (0,0). When I first compiled HCosmo with the *IViewObject* implementation, it continually drew in the upper left corner of the container instead of in the container's site. Not good. I had to be sure that HCosmo's implementation of the drawing code would work for any rectangle.

After implementing *IViewObject,* you now have a handler that can load, save, and display or print your object's data to a device without requiring a local server. After you have debugged your drawing code, you might want to create a compound document and copy it to another machine, where you can open it again with and without your handler installed in the Registration Database. This will give you an indication of what will happen without the handler and what is possible with it in the absence of a local server.

Synchronized Swimming with Your Local Server

So now everything looks great and is less filling too, until you activate the object and start making changes in the server. Wait a minute! The changes you make in the server are not reflected in the container as they were before. What's going on? Well, you have a handler, and whenever the container calls *OleDraw* or *IViewObject::Draw,* it's going to the handler, but the handler doesn't know about the changes you've been making. So how do you keep the handler and the running server in sync?

When we implemented a local server in Chapter 10, we sent *OnDataChange* notifications to all advise sinks that came into our *IDataObject* implementation (through *IDataAdviseHolder,* of course). Where do these notifications go? The simple answer is that they go to any advise sink with a connection to the running object. By default, the only advise sink with a connection to the running server is the cache, which asks the server through *IDataObject::GetData* for an updated presentation of whatever aspects are in the cache.

Our handler would also like to know when the data changes so that it can update its data in preparation for the next time the container calls the handler's *IViewObject::Draw*. In addition, because our handler has the container's *IAdviseSink* pointer as it was passed to *IViewObject::SetAdvise*, we must also inform the container that we have new data to draw. For this reason, we need our own implementation of *IAdviseSink::OnDataChange* (but NOT *OnViewChange* because we don't call the default handler's *IViewObject::SetAdvise* ourselves).

This is a little tricky and had me beating my head against the wall a few times. First, *IAdviseSink* is conceptually part of a different object, separate from the embedded object. What this means in practice is that your object's *QueryInterface* does *not* know about *IAdviseSink* and that your *IAdviseSink::QueryInterface* does *not* know any of the object interfaces. I'll admit that I'm doing it a little sleazily here: My handler's advise sink is managed by *CFigure*, but *CFigure::QueryInterface* and *CImpIAdviseSink::QueryInterface* do not intermix. In other words, my advise sink does not delegate *QueryInterface* to *CFigure*, although it still delegates *AddRef* and *Release* because the advise sink's lifetime is still contained within *CFigure*'s lifetime, as you can see in the following code:

```
STDMETHODIMP CImpIAdviseSink::QueryInterface(REFIID riid, LPLPVOID ppv)
    {
    if (IsEqualIID(riid, IID_IUnknown)
        || IsEqualIID(riid, IID_IAdviseSink))
        {
        *ppv=(LPVOID)this;
        AddRef();
        return NOERROR;
        }

    return ResultFromScode(E_NOINTERFACE);
    }

STDMETHODIMP_(ULONG) CImpIAdviseSink::AddRef(void)
    {
    ++m_cRef;
    return m_pUnkOuter->AddRef();
    }

STDMETHODIMP_(ULONG) CImpIAdviseSink::Release(void)
    {
    --m_cRef;
    return m_pUnkOuter->Release();
    }
```

This advise sink is, by the way, the same one I previously passed to the default handler's *IDataObject::DAdvise* in *CFigure::FInit,* asking for notifications on the registered clipboard format of "Polyline Figure." Note also that when I called *DAdvise* I did not specify ADVF_NODATA. Therefore, whenever a running Cosmo server calls *OnDataChange,* HCosmo's advise sink will see an *OnDataChange* call, whereas the STGMEDIUM passed to this call contains the most recent data from Cosmo:

```
/*
 * IAdviseSink::OnDataChange
 *
 * Purpose:
 *  Tells us that things changed in the server. We asked for data
 *  on the advise so we can copy it from here into our own structure
 *  so that on the next OnViewChange we can repaint with it.
 */

STDMETHODIMP_(void) CImpIAdviseSink::OnDataChange(LPFORMATETC pFE
    , LPSTGMEDIUM pSTM)
    {
    //Get the new data first, then notify the container to repaint.
    if ((pFE->cfFormat==m_pObj->m_cf)
        && (TYMED_HGLOBAL & pSTM->tymed))
        {
        LPPOLYLINEDATA      ppl;

        ppl=(LPPOLYLINEDATA)GlobalLock(pSTM->hGlobal);
        _fmemcpy(&m_pObj->m_pl, ppl, CBPOLYLINEDATA);
        GlobalUnlock(pSTM->hGlobal);

        /*
         * Now tell the container that the view changed, but only
         * if the view is not frozen.
         */
        if (pFE->dwAspect & m_pObj->m_dwAdviseAspects
            && !(pFE->dwAspect & m_pObj->m_dwFrozenAspects))
            {
            //Pass this on to the container.
            if (NULL!=m_pObj->m_pIAdvSinkView)
                {
                m_pObj->m_pIAdvSinkView->OnViewChange(pFE->dwAspect
                    , pFE->lindex);
                }
            }
        }

    return;
    }
```

When we get the *OnDataChange*, we check to see that the data is actually what we asked for (a good defensive measure). Then we copy it into our current data. But that is not all we're responsible for—we have a pointer to the container's advise sink that has been patiently waiting for a call to its *OnViewChange*. Therefore, in *OnDataChange*, we check to see whether the aspect that changed (in *pFE->dwAspect*) is frozen. If it is not, we call the container's *IAdviseSink::OnViewChange*. This in turn will cause the container to repaint and will call *IViewObject::Draw* in our handler, which then draws this current data.

Simple enough? It looks that way, but I want to let you know a few things that reared their ugly heads while I was writing this code. The problem I had to solve was how to get a copy of the most recent server data into the process space of the container and handler. I thought first that when I received *IViewObject::Draw*, I could reload the data from the *IStorage* passed to *InitNew* and *Load*, but that presupposed that the server was actively writing changes to the storage. Alas, it was not so with Cosmo, so I thought, "Why not ask the server to save the data for me before I repaint so that I can reload it?" Well, that's slow, for one thing, but the bigger problem was that when you receive an *OnDataChange*, you're in an asynchronous LRPC call (as notifications go). I tried to send *OnViewChange* to the container, which turned around and called *IViewObject::Draw*, still within the asynchronous call.[9] That meant that a call to the server's *IPersistStorage::Save* failed with RPC_E_CANTCALLOUT_INASYNCCALL. So that didn't work. Eventually I had to let go of the idea of reloading from the storage I saw in *IPersistStorage*. Instead I opted for the correct method—having data sent through *OnDataChange*. I did so because I also got the same error code when I attempted to call *IDataObject::GetData* from within an *IViewObject* member.

The other problem I had was the result of a bad assumption on my part. Because the container called my *IViewObject::SetAdvise*, I was responsible for calling its *IAdviseSink::OnViewChange*. I assumed that I could call the default handler's (actually, the cache's) *IViewObject::SetAdvise* with my own *IAdviseSink* and that my *IAdviseSink::OnViewChange* could then call the container's *OnViewChange*. The cache will send *OnViewChange* notifications when it sees *OnDataChange* notifications from the local server, right? True, that does happen, but it sends *OnViewChange* to my advise sink before the server's *OnDataChange* call reaches that same sink. Then what happened was that I would call the container's *OnViewChange*, which would immediately call back into my *IViewObject::Draw*, but because I had not yet seen an *OnDataChange*, I was still drawing the old data. When I finally understood the order of these

9. You could ask all containers to yield between *OnViewChange* and a repaint, but that is ludicrous and would place an absurd burden on containers.

notifications, I realized that I had to be sure that I was not calling the container's *OnViewChange* before I received an *OnDataChange* myself. Therefore, I now call *OnViewChange* from *within* my implementation of *OnDataChange.*

The final remark about this code I want to make is that you should make optimal use of the storage mediums when communicating between server and handler across *OnDataChange.* For small data structures, it's best for the data to be exchanged in TYMED_HGLOBAL, as Cosmo and HCosmo are. For larger data, take advantage of TYMED_ISTORAGE or TYMED-_ISTREAM so that very little data has to be copied in crossing the process boundary. TYMED_ISTORAGE is a great choice because it can allow incremental access in both pieces of code. Note that if you use this method, the server must open the *IStorage* with the appropriate permissions so that the handler can also access that storage.

Year-End Bonuses

If you followed the examples in the previous sections, you now have a complete, basic handler that is fully functional for rendering your object on a variety of displays without depending on the cache or a local server. Anything else you do now is an added benefit to your handler—like giving it an extra paycheck at the end of the year.

There are many possibilities for improvement. You might want to implement *IDataObject::GetData* and *GetDataHere,* for example, to further reduce the need to launch a local server. After all, you already know how to draw your data in the handler, as well as how to save it to an *IStorage,* so you'd only need to add a little code to draw into a metafile or bitmap and to save into a different *IStorage.* You might also think of ways to reduce your dependence on the cache, possibly managing it all yourself. You might also consider adding features through a custom interface, given that you have a DLL and can provide one without the need for custom marshaling. These new interfaces can do whatever you like. You can also implement a Play verb in *OleObject::DoVerb* if your object type supports that sort of concept, again greatly improving performance and reducing your need for a server.

But eventually you cross the line. You give the handler too much extra pay and it decides to go out and buy a yacht, for which it has to pay luxury tax. At that point, it ceases to rely on a local server for anything by implementing all of *IDataObject* and all of *IOleObject,* thus providing full editing services. The handler is now qualified to be an in-process server. But before it is *confirmed* as such, there are a number of points to consider. The remainder of this chapter looks specifically at those issues.

Notes on Implementing an In-Process Server

In Chapter 10, we saw how to implement a complete local server, and in the last section we saw how to implement a handler in a DLL. Now we can bring the two together into a single in-process server DLL. Because we've seen most of the implementation already, this section will highlight specific issues that I faced when modifying the Polyline object DLL to become an in-process server, as well as what I dealt with while the DLL served as the component object it has been up to this point. It will not be an implementation guide because you need only to follow the guide for the handler in the previous section (using *CreateDataCache* under OLE 2.01, of course) and then add more code to fill out the interfaces so that the default handler never attempts to launch a local server. In essence, you go to a car dealer and keep adding more options until that bare-bones economy car becomes your high-performance dream machine. You also don't need to worry about synchronizing with a running local server because there will never be one.

I want to point out up front that modifications made to Polyline to make it an in-process DLL have not affected its usefulness to Component Cosmo. In fact, the only change that is necessary for CoCosmo for this chapter to make it use the revised Polyline DLL is to change the CLSID_Polyline6 in *CCosmoDoc::FInit* to CLSID_Polyline11. Because of this, you won't find a new copy of CoCosmo in the sample code; instead, you'll find README.TXT, which explains what you need to change if you feel so inclined. If I were not using chapter numbers on Polyline's CLSID, no changes would be required. This shows that support for compound documents *does not interfere with the general operation of the object as a component object.* Although a container can now use Polyline as an in-process server for embedded objects, CoCosmo can still use exactly the same DLL and exactly the same objects as a component object with a custom interface. That's the beauty of the *QueryInterface* mechanism: An object such as Polyline can support both types of users without requiring either one to hard-code specific information. CoCosmo doesn't know anything about Polyline's *IOleObject* interface and never asks for any information. Any container will remain safely ignorant about the *IPolyline* interface—all because of the almighty *QueryInterface.*

To serve as a basis for our discussion, the important modifications and additions to Polyline (from various source files) are shown in Listing 11-2 on the next page. There is considerable code that is not shown in this listing because it is identical to what we've shown already for the handler in the previous section.

POLYLINE.H

```
...

#define PROP_SELECTOR   "Selector"
#define PROP_OFFSET     "Offset"

BOOL EXPORT FAR PASCAL PolyDlgProc(HWND, UINT, WPARAM, LPARAM);

class __far CPolyline : public IUnknown
    {
    ...

    friend BOOL EXPORT FAR PASCAL PolyDlgProc(HWND, UINT
        , WPARAM, LPARAM);
    friend class CImpIOleObject;
    friend class CImpIViewObject;

    protected:
        ...

        //These are default handler interfaces we use
        LPUNKNOWN           m_pDefIUnknown;
        LPOLEOBJECT         m_pDefIOleObject;
        LPVIEWOBJECT        m_pDefIViewObject;
        LPPERSISTSTORAGE    m_pDefIPersistStorage;
        LPDATAOBJECT        m_pDefIDataObject;

        //Implemented and used interfaces
        LPIMPIOLEOBJECT     m_pIOleObject;      //Implemented
        LPOLEADVISEHOLDER   m_pIOleAdviseHolder; //Used

        LPOLECLIENTSITE     m_pIOleClientSite;  //Used

        LPIMPIVIEWOBJECT    m_pIViewObject;     //Implemented
        LPADVISESINK        m_pIAdviseSink;     //Used
        DWORD               m_dwFrozenAspects;  //Freeze
        DWORD               m_dwAdviseAspects;  //SetAdvise
        DWORD               m_dwAdviseFlags;    //SetAdvise

        POLYLINEDATA        m_plContent;        //For freezing
        POLYLINEDATA        m_plThumbnail;      //For freezing

        HWND                m_hDlg;             //Editing window
```

Listing 11-2. *(continued)*

Important modifications and additions to Polyline to be an in-process server.

Listing 11-2. *continued*

```
        ...
    };

[Also added codes for CPolyline::SendAdvise]
[Added a CImpIOleObject class]
```

RESOURCE.H

```
[Other definitions omitted]

#define IDS_CLOSECAPTION     2
#define IDS_CLOSEPROMPT      3
#define IDS_POLYLINEMAX      3

#define IDR_ICON             1

#define IDD_EDITDIALOG       1

#define ID_UNDO              100
#define ID_COLORBACK         101
#define ID_COLORLINE         102
#define ID_GROUPCOLORS       103
#define ID_GROUPPREVIEW      104
#define ID_GROUPSTYLES       105
#define ID_GROUPFIGURE       106
#define ID_POLYLINERECT      107
#define ID_POLYLINE          108

#define ID_LINEMIN           200
#define ID_LINESOLID         200      //(ID_LINEMIN+PS_SOLID)
#define ID_LINEDASH          201      //(ID_LINEMIN+PS_DASH)
#define ID_LINEDOT           202      //(ID_LINEMIN+PS_DOT)
#define ID_LINEDASHDOT       203      //(ID_LINEMIN+PS_DASHDOT)
#define ID_LINEDASHDOTDOT    204      //(ID_LINEMIN+PS_DASHDOTDOT)
```

POLYLINE.RC

```
[Other resources omitted]

//This is the default for iconic representations.
IDR_ICON        ICON    polyline.ico
```

(continued)

Listing 11-2. *continued*

```
//This dialog is used to edit the Polyline
IDD_EDITDIALOG DIALOG 6, 18, 258, 152
STYLE DS_MODALFRAME | WS_POPUP | WS_VISIBLE
    | WS_CAPTION | WS_SYSMENU
CAPTION "Polyline"
FONT 8, "MS Sans Serif"
BEGIN
    CONTROL         "", ID_POLYLINERECT, "Static", SS_BLACKFRAME
                        , 8, 12, 134, 132
    PUSHBUTTON      "&Close", IDOK, 178, 6, 56, 14
    PUSHBUTTON      "&Undo", ID_UNDO, 178, 24, 56, 14
    PUSHBUTTON      "&Background...", ID_COLORBACK, 178, 54, 56, 14
    PUSHBUTTON      "&Line...", ID_COLORLINE, 178, 72, 56, 14
    GROUPBOX        "Colors", ID_UNDO, 158, 42, 94, 48
    GROUPBOX        "Figure", ID_GROUPFIGURE, 2, 0, 146, 148
    GROUPBOX        "Line Styles", ID_GROUPSTYLES, 158, 94, 94, 54
    CONTROL         "&Solid", ID_LINESOLID, "Button"
                        , BS_AUTORADIOBUTTON | WS_GROUP
                        , 166, 106, 32, 10
    CONTROL         "&Dash", ID_LINEDASH, "Button"
                        , BS_AUTORADIOBUTTON, 216, 106, 32, 10
    CONTROL         "Da&sh-Dot-Dot", ID_LINEDASHDOTDOT, "Button"
                        , BS_AUTORADIOBUTTON, 166, 134, 80, 10
    CONTROL         "D&ot", ID_LINEDOT, "Button", BS_AUTORADIOBUTTON
                        , 216, 120, 32, 10
    CONTROL         "D&ash-Dot", ID_LINEDASHDOT, "Button"
                        , BS_AUTORADIOBUTTON, 166, 120, 48, 10
END

STRINGTABLE
   BEGIN
    IDS_STORAGEFORMAT, "Polyline Figure"
    IDS_USERTYPE,      "Polyline Figure"
    IDS_CLOSECAPTION,  "Polyline"
    IDS_CLOSEPROMPT,   "Object has changed. Do you wish to update it?"
   END
...
```

POLYLINE.CPP

```
STDMETHODIMP CPolyline::QueryInterface(REFIID riid, LPLPVOID ppv)
    {
    *ppv=NULL;
```

(continued)

Listing 11-2. *continued*

```
    [Cases for IUnknown, IPersist(Storage), IDataObject, unmodified]

    if (IsEqualIID(riid, IID_IOleObject))
        *ppv=(LPVOID)m_pIOleObject;

    if (IsEqualIID(riid, IID_IViewObject))
        *ppv=(LPVOID)m_pIViewObject;

    //Use the default handler's cache.
    if (IsEqualIID(riid, IID_IOleCache))
        return m_pDefIUnknown->QueryInterface(riid, ppv);

    if (NULL!=*ppv)
        {
        ((LPUNKNOWN)*ppv)->AddRef();
        return NOERROR;
        }

    return ResultFromScode(E_NOINTERFACE);
    }

[AddRef, Release, and RectConvertMappings unmodified]

STDMETHODIMP CPolyline::DataSet(LPPOLYLINEDATA pplIn
    , BOOL fSizeToData, BOOL fNotify)
    {
    [Unmodified code to integrate data...]

    //Notify containers
    SendAdvise(OBJECTCODE_DATACHANGED);
    return NOERROR;
    }

[Rendering code unmodified]
[CPolyline::SendAdvise identical to Cosmo's in Chapter 10]
```

POLYWIN.CPP

```
...

LRESULT EXPORT FAR PASCAL PolylineWndProc(HWND hWnd, UINT iMsg
    , WPARAM wParam, LPARAM lParam)
    {
```

(continued)

Listing 11-2. *continued*

```
    ...
    case WM_LBUTTONDOWN:
        ...
        [Adds a point to the Polyline and repaints]
        ppl->SendAdvise(OBJECTCODE_DATACHANGED);
        break;
    ...
    }

[CPolyline::Draw modified to take a rectangle and POLYLINEDATA
 structure, but is still just a lot of GDI]

/*
 * PolyDlgProc
 *
 * Purpose:
 *  Dialog procedure for a window in which to display the Polyline
 *  for editing. This pretty much handles all editing functionality
 *  for the embedded object.
 */

BOOL EXPORT FAR PASCAL PolyDlgProc(HWND hDlg, UINT iMsg
    , WPARAM wParam, LPARAM lParam)
    {
    LPCPolyline     ppl=NULL;
    WORD            w1, w2;
    HWND            hWnd;
    RECT            rc;
    POINT           pt;
    UINT            uID, uTemp;
    UINT            cx, cy;

    w1=(WORD)GetProp(hDlg, PROP_SELECTOR);
    w2=(WORD)GetProp(hDlg, PROP_OFFSET);

    ppl=(LPCPolyline)MAKELP(w1, w2);

    switch (iMsg)
        {
        case WM_INITDIALOG:
            ppl=(LPCPolyline)lParam;
            ppl->m_hDlg=hDlg;

            SetProp(hDlg, PROP_SELECTOR, (HANDLE)SELECTOROF(ppl));
            SetProp(hDlg, PROP_OFFSET,   (HANDLE)OFFSETOF(ppl));
```

(continued)

Listing 11-2. *continued*

```
        //Center the dialog on the screen
        cx=GetSystemMetrics(SM_CXSCREEN);
        cy=GetSystemMetrics(SM_CYSCREEN);
        GetWindowRect(hDlg, &rc);
        SetWindowPos(hDlg, NULL, (cx-(rc.right-rc.left))/2
            , (cy-(rc.bottom-rc.top))/2, 0, 0, SWP_NOZORDER
            | SWP_NOSIZE);

        //Create the Polyline to exactly cover the static rect.
        hWnd=GetDlgItem(hDlg, ID_POLYLINERECT);
        GetWindowRect(hWnd, &rc);
        SETPOINT(pt, rc.left, rc.top);
        ScreenToClient(hDlg, &pt);

        //Set the polyline just within the black frame
        SetRect(&rc, pt.x, pt.y, pt.x+(rc.right-rc.left)
            , pt.y+(rc.bottom-rc.top));
        InflateRect(&rc, -1, -1);

        //Try to create the window.
        ppl->m_pIPolyline->Init(hDlg, &rc, WS_CHILD | WS_VISIBLE
            , ID_POLYLINE);

        //Set the initial line style radiobutton.
        ppl->m_pIPolyline->LineStyleGet(&uTemp);
        CheckRadioButton(hDlg, ID_LINESOLID, ID_LINEDASHDOTDOT
            , uTemp+ID_LINEMIN);

        ppl->SendAdvise(OBJECTCODE_SHOWOBJECT);
        ppl->SendAdvise(OBJECTCODE_SHOWWINDOW);

        //Disable parent to act modal
        EnableWindow(GetParent(hDlg), FALSE);
        return TRUE;

    case WM_COMMAND:
        uID=LOWORD(wParam);

        switch (uID)
            {
            case IDOK:
                RemoveProp(hDlg, PROP_SELECTOR);
                RemoveProp(hDlg, PROP_OFFSET);

                if (NULL!=ppl)
                    {
                    //Make sure we're saved
```

(continued)

Listing 11-2. *continued*

```
                ppl->SendAdvise(OBJECTCODE_SAVEOBJECT);
                ppl->SendAdvise(OBJECTCODE_SAVED);
                ppl->SendAdvise(OBJECTCODE_HIDEWINDOW);
                ppl->SendAdvise(OBJECTCODE_CLOSED);
                ppl->m_hDlg=NULL;
                }

            //Re-enable the parent
            EnableWindow(GetParent(hDlg), TRUE);
            DestroyWindow(hDlg);
            break;

        case ID_UNDO:
            if (NULL!=ppl)
                ppl->m_pIPolyline->Undo();
            break;

        case ID_COLORLINE:
        case ID_COLORBACK:
            if (NULL!=ppl)
                {
                UINT            i;
                COLORREF        rgColors[16];
                CHOOSECOLOR     cc;

                //Invoke the color chooser for either color
                uTemp=(ID_COLORBACK==uID)
                    ? POLYLINECOLOR_BACKGROUND
                    : POLYLINECOLOR_LINE;

                for (i=0; i<16; i++)
                    rgColors[i]=RGB(0, 0, i*16);

                _fmemset(&cc, 0, sizeof(CHOOSECOLOR));
                cc.lStructSize=sizeof(CHOOSECOLOR);
                cc.lpCustColors=rgColors;
                cc.hwndOwner=hDlg;
                cc.Flags=CC_RGBINIT;
                ppl->m_pIPolyline->ColorGet(uTemp
                    , &cc.rgbResult);

                if (ChooseColor(&cc))
                    {
                    //rgColor is just some COLORREF pointer
                    ppl->m_pIPolyline->ColorSet(uTemp
                        , cc.rgbResult, rgColors);
                    }
                }
            break;
```


(continued)

Listing 11-2. *continued*

```
                case ID_LINESOLID:
                case ID_LINEDASH:
                case ID_LINEDOT:
                case ID_LINEDASHDOT:
                case ID_LINEDASHDOTDOT:
                    if (NULL!=ppl)
                        {
                        ppl->m_pIPolyline
                            ->LineStyleSet(uID-ID_LINEMIN, &uTemp);
                        }

                    break;
                }
            break;

        case WM_CLOSE:
            //Close just like we hit the "Close" button.
            SendCommand(hDlg, IDOK, 0, 0);
            break;
        }
    return FALSE;
    }
```

//IOLEOBJ.CPP

```
...

STDMETHODIMP CImpIOleObject::DoVerb(LONG iVerb, LPMSG pMSG
    , LPOLECLIENTSITE pActiveSite, LONG lIndex, HWND hWndParent
    , LPCRECT pRectPos)
    {
    switch (iVerb)
        {
        case OLEIVERB_HIDE:
            if (NULL!=m_pObj->m_hDlg)
                ShowWindow(m_pObj->m_hDlg, SW_HIDE);
            break;

        case OLEIVERB_PRIMARY:
        case OLEIVERB_OPEN:
        case OLEIVERB_SHOW:
```

(continued)

Listing 11-2. *continued*

```
            //If we have a window, just make sure it's showing
            if (NULL!=m_pObj->m_hDlg)
                {
                ShowWindow(m_pObj->m_hDlg, SW_NORMAL);
                SetFocus(m_pObj->m_hDlg);
                return NOERROR;
                }

            //This stores the dialog handle in m_pObj.
            CreateDialogParam(hgInst, MAKEINTRESOURCE(IDD_EDITDIALOG)
                , hWndParent, PolyDlgProc, (LPARAM)m_pObj);
            break;

        default:
            return ResultFromScode(OLEOBJ_S_INVALIDVERB);
        }

    return NOERROR;
    }

[All others are standard implementations as we have seen before.]
```

Many of the modifications to Polyline are minor because most of the code to support embedded objects comes in the form of additions.

- The *CPolyline* class now manages additional interface pointers as well as pointers into the default handler *m_pDef<Interface>*, exactly like the *CFigure* class in HCosmo. In fact, much of Polyline's code was taken from HCosmo, so it has not been shown again in Listing 11-2. It also maintains the window handle of the dialog box we use to implement *IOleObject::DoVerb.* These additional variables are initialized to NULL in the *CPolyline* constructor and set to their real values in *CPolyline::FInit* through *QueryInterface* on an *IUnknown* as returned from *OleCreateDefaultHandler.* This is also identical to that shown earlier for HCosmo.
- RESOURCE.H now contains many more identifiers for additions to POLYLINE.RC: an icon (for the default icon), some strings we use in UI, and a dialog box used for editing the figure.

- The *SendAdvise* function added to *CPolyline* takes a notification code and calls the appropriate member function in *IOleClientSite, IOleAdviseHolder*, or *IDataAdviseHolder*. The most frequent notification that required a number of changes in Polyline is *OnDataChange* (generated by calling *CPolyline::SendAdvise* with OBJECTCODE_DATACHANGED). Any member function in *IPolyline* (IPOLYLIN.CPP) that changes data, such as *LineStyleSet* and *ColorSet*, has been modified to send data changes, as has *CPolyline::DataSet* itself. In addition, we send this code when the user clicks in the Polyline window, thus adding a point to the figure.
- Member functions of *IPersistStorage* (IPERSTOR.CPP is not shown) now, in addition to their normal operation, call the default handler's *IPersistStorage* to allow the cache to do what caches do.
- Polyline's *IDataObject* now implements *GetDataHere* for CF_EMBEDDEDOBJECT and can now delegate the implementation of *EnumFormatEtc* to the default handler, thereby eliminating all the cumbersome enumerator code.
- An implementation of *IViewObject* that was added is virtually identical to the one for HCosmo shown in Listing 11-1 and therefore is not shown here.
- CPolyline's *QueryInterface* now includes the additional interfaces (*IViewObject* and *IOleObject*) that it implements and also returns the default handler's *IOleCache* interface, but no others.
- Most of the implementation of *IOleObject* is identical to ones we have already seen, with the exception of *DoVerb*, which, oddly, invokes a dialog box. *PolyDlgProc* in POLYWIN.CPP is the dialog box procedure for the one *DoVerb* invokes.

These last two changes are the most important ones. Let me first explain the handling of *QueryInterface* on the object. When we implemented a handler, we were selectively overriding only those interfaces we needed to augment, passing everything else to the default handler. If we did not know about an interface in *QueryInterface*, we simply passed it to the default handler's *IUnknown::QueryInterface*. We had no idea what interfaces were requested or returned.

For an in-process server, you no longer want to delegate *QueryInterface* to the default handler for any interface. The simple reason is that *OleCreate* functions will fail for your CLSID if there is no local server registered. Therefore, your object cannot be inserted as a new object in a container. But, of course, there is no local server because our application is an in-process server. The default handler supports more interfaces than we want to show from a default handler, including some OLE 2 internal ones. *OleCreate* will use *QueryInterface* for one of these internal interfaces through which it attempts to run the *local* server. This will, of course, fail because there is no local server, so *OleCreate* returns REGDB_E_CLASSNOTREG. This is not at all what you would expect because you have your *InProcServer* key registered, and that's all you need. Figuring this out might make you seriously consider becoming a clam.

The bottom line is that you need to exercise more control over which interfaces you expose because an in-process server is totally responsible for what is and is not implemented. In Polyline, the in-process server passes only *QueryInterface* to the default handler for *IOleCache*. Essentially, this means that we are directly using the cache's *IOleCache*. We do use other interfaces in the handler, but we do not expose them directly. Instead, we filter calls through our own implementations first. Note that passing *QueryInterface* through, as we do here, is no more effective than using *QueryInterface* in *CPolyline::FInit*, as we do for all the other defaults, storing that pointer in a variable such as *m_pDefIOleCache* and returning that pointer when needed.

That leaves us with Polyline's implementation of *IOleObject::DoVerb*, which looks much like any other implementation except that instead of simply displaying an already existing, but hidden, window as we did in Cosmo, we have to create the whole editing user interface.

The question of user interface is an important one when you are designing an in-process server. Because you cannot run an in-process server standalone, it's not a good idea to display a window that looks like one belonging to a real stand-alone application. When I first began this chapter's modifications to Polyline, I tried to duplicate Cosmo's user interface with a frame window, a GizmoBar, menus, and the like. But there are specific technical difficulties with creating this sort of window from within a DLL. The most important is that you have no message loop to call your own. Therefore, you can have no keyboard accelerators, and you cannot use an MDI interface (which is absurd from an in-process server anyway). Keystrokes such as Alt+Backspace or Ctrl+Z, which we used in Cosmo for Undo, are meaningless, as are those for clipboard operations. In general, in-process servers don't need to mess with the clipboard because they don't run stand-alone. (But there is nothing stopping you, of course.)

The better user interface for an in-process server is that of a dialog box, which makes your object look very much like a part of the container application. Because you are invoking this dialog box from a DLL that has already been loaded, such a window will appear very soon after the end user double-clicks on the object in the container. This further reinforces the idea that the dialog box is tightly integrated into the container. Dialog boxes also give you a lot of support, such as keyboard mnemonics for controls, that you would otherwise not get without your own message loop. As you can see from the code in Listing 11-2, it didn't take much to implement such a dialog box in Polyline that provides all the editing capabilities of the full Cosmo application, simply through the interface of the dialog box shown in Figure 11-3.

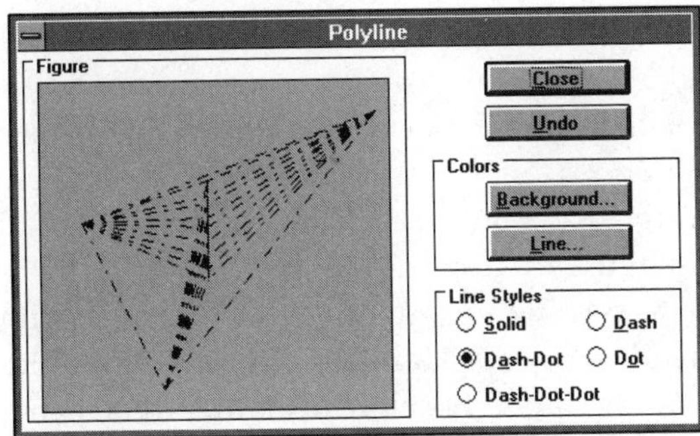

Figure 11-3.
Polyline's user interface for a dialog box for editing an embedded object.

Because we use *CreateDialogParam* to invoke this dialog box in *DoVerb,* it would normally appear as a modeless dialog box. We want to call *CreateDialogParam* so that *DoVerb* can return to the container immediately because some containers perform idle-time processing. To make the dialog box appear modal, however, we use the DS_MODALFRAME style and disable the parent window while the dialog box is displayed. Note also that we *center* the dialog box on the *screen* instead of letting it be placed relative to the container window. This is because the default placement will typically cause the dialog box to cover the container's site, and usually the first thing an end user does in this context is move the dialog box. Placing it at the center of the screen will generally keep the site visible and your server more usable.

Other than that, the dialog box processes commands the same way any other does, changing Polyline's line style or invoking the Choose Color dialog box to change background and line colors. It also sends the appropriate notifications when closing the dialog box, as we would when closing a document window in a server application. Note that we don't need to call *IOleClientSite::SaveObject* because we aren't unloading the server, we're simply closing the dialog box. We had to do this in an EXE server because the application would generally shut down when the user interface went away, and that would mean the data was lost as well. But because this is a DLL, it's going to stay in memory along with the object's most current data, data that will be used in subsequent calls to *IViewObject::Draw* and the like. When the container wants to actually save the DLL, it calls *OleSave*, which will call our *IPersistStorage::Save*, in which we'll save our current data. Therefore, no *SaveObject* call is necessary.

Summary

In-process servers and in-process handlers are structurally identical because they both export the standard component object functions of *DllGetClassObject* and *DllCanUnloadNow*. Furthermore, to work with embedded objects, they serve objects with the *IOleObject*, *IDataObject*, *IViewObject*, *IPersistStorage*, and *IOleCache* interfaces. Therefore, a container application is not cognizant of what sort of DLL module is in use for a specific object.

Handlers and DLL servers differ only to the extent that they implement the interfaces on the embedded objects. Handlers, in general, implement as little as possible to remain small, lightweight modules that can provide specific optimizations for an object. For example, they can render data more specifically for devices because handlers—like in-process servers, but unlike local servers—can implement *IViewObject* and therefore have direct access to the *hDC* on which the container wants the object displayed. As a result, the handler can obtain information about the device and optimize its output accordingly. As a simple example of this, the HCosmo DLL in this chapter, a handler for Cosmo, checks to see whether the printer is color capable, and if not, renders its data in black and white only.

In-process modules also increase performance because they eliminate much of the need to run and communicate via LRPC to a local server, and they cut out the middlemen. Because object handlers can, through *IViewObject*, provide for all rendering necessities, they can eliminate the need for a local server to render metafiles or bitmaps, and they can do away with the need to have OLE 2 cache those same presentations. The reduced dependence on the cache can greatly reduce the amount of space an object requires in a container's compound file. So not only does your application benefit from increased performance, your container does too.

Because handlers implement only select interface member functions, they usually rely on the presence of a local server to fulfill all requests on the object, especially those for editing. Handlers are designed to allow for displaying, optimized printing, and copying of objects, without the local server being anywhere in sight.

In-process servers, on the other hand, implement enough interfaces and member functions to completely eliminate the need for a local server. That means they provide for all drawing, all data transfer, all storage management, and all editing facilities. The last requirement—editing—means that the in-process server will need to display windows of some sort from within their implementation of *IOleObject::DoVerb.* However, there are some technical details that make a window shown in a DLL different from one shown from an EXE, most notably the lack of a message loop that you control. Therefore, the user interface of a dialog box is more applicable to in-process servers than to a normal overlapped application-type window.

There are also a few interoperability issues to consider when deciding whether to use a DLL module. Because DLLs written for a 16-bit world, such as Windows 3.1, cannot be loaded into a 32-bit process, as under Windows NT, you might need to provide DLLs for both or to limit yourself to whatever containers can work with you. In addition, DLLs written for OLE 2 can be used only with containers written for OLE 2. Therefore, you lose compatibility with OLE 1 containers, which OLE 2 local servers keep. Certainly there are trade-offs: Suffer in interoperability, suffer in performance, or suffer the burden of maintaining multiple versions of your code to suit the various environments you want to support.

Nonetheless, this chapter shows how to implement a basic handler and details the modifications made to the Polyline object, last seen in Chapter 6, to make it an in-process server that is complete with editing facilities.

CHAPTER TWELVE

MONIKERS AND LINKING CONTAINERS

Let's go back in time for a moment, back to the simpler days of Windows version 1 when Windows itself was as new and confusing as OLE 2 might seem today, when Windows had a grand total of 350 API functions, and programs such as Reversi were totally cool. Back in those years, there was this incredible new thing called Dynamic Data Exchange, whose acronym you know well as "DDE." An old Windows version 1 book I have in my office introduced DDE with these words:

"In a multitasking environment, applications often need to transfer data without the user specifically requesting it.... The technique you use for application-driven transfer of data is called Dynamic Data Exchange (DDE) by Microsoft. In DDE, handles to global memory objects (ooh, there's that word again) containing the data are passed via predefined message types. The message types for Dynamic Data Exchange have been established by Microsoft, along with standards specifying what information should be placed in the word and long parameters and how applications should respond to those messages. These standards are called the Dynamic Data Exchange protocol. They are scheduled to be included in the Software Development Kit documentation shortly.... It's important to note here that Dynamic Data Exchange protocols are a recent addition to Windows and are still subject to change and enhancement."[1]

DDE enabled one application to initiate communication with another application and ask that other application for some data. This question could be a onetime transaction using the WM_DDE_REQUEST message, which acts much like *IDataObject::GetData* in OLE 2, as we have seen in Chapter 6.

1. From *Programmer's Guide to Windows,* by David Durant, Geta Carlson, and Paul Yao, copyright 1987, Sybex.

The transaction might also be a more permanent advise loop set up through WM_DDE_ADVISE, much like *IDataObject::DAdvise.* Besides initiating a new conversation from scratch, an application might also paste data from the clipboard in the form of a registered clipboard format simply called Link. The data in the Link format identifies the source application of the data, the name of the document, and the item where the data lives. The application that pastes the link uses all of this information to reconnect to the source of the link at a later time to get updated data. In all cases, the data is located outside of the document containing the link, generally in another file owned and maintained by the source application.

This gives you the basic requirements for linking: a place where the data is stored and information that lets you reconnect to that place.

The problem is that in DDE, as well as with *IDataObject,* we always have to know something about the data and the source application—either we have to hard-code data structures and names of applications (as well as the names of DDEs, topics, and items) or we have to provide some sort of user interface to allow the user to enter those names. This is typically the same problem we have in all data-integration scenarios: a dependence on specific knowledge about other applications.

But as we've seen in the last three chapters, the *Embedding* aspect of Object Linking and Embedding is a standard for integrating arbitrary data into a compound document as an embedded object. As we've seen, an embedded object contains its data and presentation entirely within the confines of a container's compound file. This is the solution to the age-old problem of pasting data from the clipboard and trying to make later modifications to that data. In this chapter and the next, we'll examine the *Linking* aspect of OLE, which is the standard and generalized solution to the linking problem that first started years ago with DDE. OLE 2 provides the capability for creating a *linked* object, which like an embedded object carries a presentation with it in the container's compound file, but unlike the embedded object the actual data lives somewhere else. In our Allegory of the Cookie Jar (see Chapter 9), a linked object is like a note, or a treasure map, inside of the cookie jar that tells you where to find the cookies because they're not in the jar itself. In OLE 2, this note can essentially describe a location anywhere in the universe.

Microsoft's first attempt at solving this problem was linking support in OLE 1, which suffered from technical deficiencies and design limitations. First, the information that identified the "somewhere else" the linked data was located was strictly two-part: a document name and an item name. You could not be any more descriptive of where the cookies were than by specifying a room and an area of the room; you could not say, for example, that the cookies were in the back of the third drawer of the tall dresser on the left side of the master bedroom. That is, you could not to create a link to data that was in something like an embedded object that was itself in a container document. Such a situation required the document name, the name of the embedded object, and some name that identified what part of that object's data was linked. Second, the functions in OLE 1 that were designed to allow the container to know when the presentation for a linked object was out of data could not be implemented properly, and it was difficult to automatically reconnect to the source of the linked object even when you did know something was out of date.

Perhaps the most detrimental deficiency was that the name of a document in an OLE 1 linked object was always stored with an absolute pathname. This allowed people to do the equivalent of leaving a note in the cookie jar that said, "Cookies are on the third shelf in the pantry" and later moving the cookies to some new location without updating the note. In OLE 1, if the source document moved, the link was broken, even if all the end user did was move the entire directory tree to a different drive—like moving the entire kitchen and cookie jar into another house. The absolute path to the source became invalid because it described the wrong house, but the source was still in the same place relative to the container document holding the linked object; the cookie jar was still in the same place relative to the kitchen.

OLE 2 solves almost all of these problems, except the one in which the source file of the link moves independently from the container document because there is simply no way for OLE 2 to know when this happens. In other words, if someone wanted to be nasty, they could move the cookies from the location described by the treasure map in the cookie jar. Only after we had gone to all the trouble of painstakingly following each instruction on the map would we find that the cookies had moved. If the person who moved the cookies doesn't tell anyone where they were moved, we would have to go searching for them. This makes end users very angry. Very angry indeed. If you're not careful, they might point a PU-235 Space Modulator in the direction of your program with intent to destroy.

The potential for losing track of a link is a limitation of Windows running on MS-DOS, because you can always boot into MS-DOS from a floppy and munge the file system to your heart's content. Under later versions of Windows, especially Windows NT, in which you have to be running Windows to do anything to the file system, OLE will be able to track files even in this case so that links are never broken. In other words, OLE will be clever enough to know when anyone moves the cookies, and it will kindly update all notes describing the location of those cookies, without having to bother anyone. But that is still a little ways off, so let's focus on what we can do today.

A long time ago, DDE enabled linking in a rudimentary form. As we were warned, DDE was subject to change and enhancement, and those changes evolved first into OLE 1 (which could actually be implemented using DDE and not the OLE 1 libraries) and now into OLE 2, with only link tracking cases left to solve. But OLE 2 introduces a more important change because to support linking in any way, shape, or form, we still need to know the place where the data lives and some information that lets us reconnect to that place. To remove the limitations of DDE and OLE 1, OLE 2 allows that place to be virtually anywhere in the known universe. The information that lets us describe "anywhere" is this jolly chap called a moniker.

Will Someone Please Explain Just What a Moniker Is?

Webster's Ninth New Collegiate Dictionary (1990) defines a moniker as follows:

> **moniker** *or* **monicker** *n* [origin unknown] *slang* (1851) : name, nickname

Actually, in OLE 2 a moniker is a thing, and *thing* just happens to be a convenient synonym for (what else) an object.

A moniker is, in fact, a Windows Object that implements the *IUnknown* and *IMoniker*[2] interfaces. Just as we call an object with *IClassFactory* simply a class factory, we call an object with *IMoniker* simply a moniker. There is no magic about it. Monikers are merely another type of object in the whole Windows Objects scheme. They are generally implemented as component objects in DLLs.

But the name is most appropriate: A moniker is essentially a name that identifies the source of a particular piece of data—that is, a moniker is the information that tells us where the data is. The word *nickname* also fits because certain parts of monikers are understood by a select few, say only one or two applications.

A moniker is more than simply a name. It also has code that knows how to take that information—that reference to some data—and do what is called *binding* to that data. Binding is the process of reconnecting a linked object (which manages the moniker) to the source of data identified by the moniker. The binding process starts when the linked object calling *IMoniker::BindToObject*, which does whatever is necessary to return an interface pointer to the linked object through which that object can request an updated presentation to show the next time its container calls *IViewObject::Draw*.

2. *IMoniker* derives from *IPersistStream*. *IPersistStream* was introduced in Chapter 5.

With binding, not only does a moniker contain the map telling you how to find the treasure, but the process also brings the treasure to you! All you have to do is call *BindToObject*, and the moniker takes care of everything else.

To implement a linking container or server, you don't need to know much about the *IMoniker* interface. Usually your application will create a moniker through an OLE 2 API function, or it will indirectly call *IMoniker* functions through other actions, such as activating a linked object with *IOleObject::DoVerb*. In fact, none of the code described in this chapter needs to call any *IMoniker* function except *AddRef* and *Release*. Even in Chapter 13, where we'll discuss moniker binding and link sources, we don't need to call *IMoniker* functions directly. You need to know all the *IMoniker* interface members only if you want to develop your own moniker class, which is far beyond the scope of this book. If you are truly interested in implementing a moniker, please refer to the *OLE 2 Programmer's Reference* and the OLE 2 Design Specification for more information on the interface.

Of more interest will be the *IOleLink* interface, which is always implemented in the default handler for a linked object. However, even in that case, you need to see this interface in only a few specific circumstances. In Chapter 13, when we explore the binding mechanisms for monikers, we'll concern ourselves with implementing *IOleItemContainer* and *IPersistFile*, and we'll look at using an interface called *IRunningObjectTable*, which the OLE 2 libraries implement. For now, let's look at the different types of monikers we might encounter.

Moniker Classes

What? More classes? I thought I had finished all my classes in college! Ah, but they never told you about monikers.

There is no single type of moniker. In fact, there are a total of five different moniker classes that OLE 2 itself implements, each with a different CLSID, that you may need to work with: *Composite*, *File*, *Item*, *Anti*, and *Pointer*.[3] Monikers, by design, can be serialized to a stream, and in fact, *IMoniker* derives from *IPersistStream*. However, only composite, file, and item monikers allow serialization. Anti and pointer monikers refuse to do so. The anti moniker also refuses to bind, for reasons we'll see shortly.

Composite Monikers

A composite moniker is a collection of other types of monikers that knows how to manage the relationships between those other types. Inside the composite

3. There are two other classes, *DDECompositeMoniker* and *PackagerMoniker*, which are used internally in OLE 2. You will see them listed in the Registration Database with OLE2.DLL as their *InProcServer*.

moniker, sometimes called a generic composite, the other, simpler monikers are stored in a left-to-right order, as shown in Figure 12-1. The composite moniker is the entire treasure map that tells you where to find the cookies. (Cookies *are* treasure, right?) The moniker shows you where you have to go, in sequence, and provides instructions for each step along the way, as long as each step is unique. These steps are representative of each simpler moniker within the composite. By itself, the composite is composed of smaller, simpler monikers, just as a map is composed of smaller, simpler instructions.

Of course, like any moniker, the composite knows how to go out and find the treasure when we ask it to bind. Binding to a composite means binding to each moniker inside of it (in other words, following each step on the map). If you don't follow a step correctly, you won't find the treasure. What is most odd about binding a composite moniker is that it happens in a right-to-left order, not a left-to-right order. The reason is that you might already be somewhere along the path to the treasure map, and it would be a terrible waste of time and effort to go tromping back to the beginning of the map and follow all the instructions merely to get back to where you were originally. It's much more efficient to follow the treasure map in reverse to find the point closest to your current position from which to follow the remainder of the instructions.

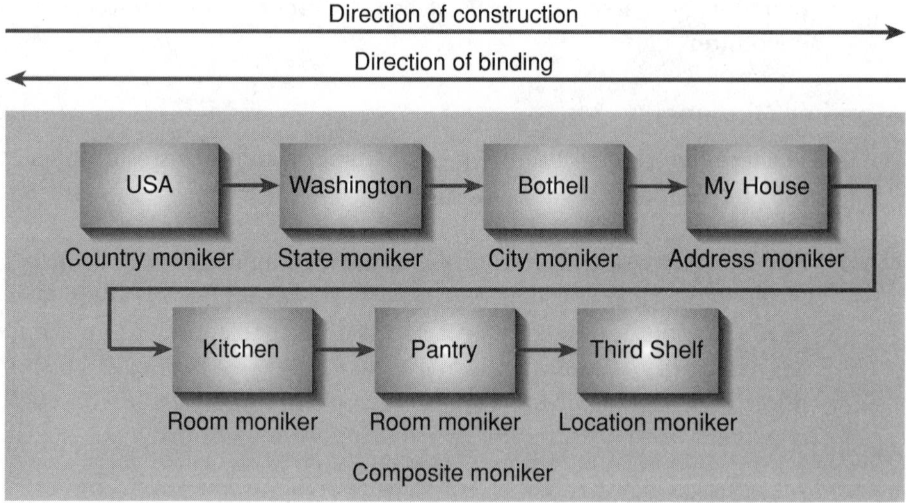

Figure 12-1.
A composite moniker stores other monikers inside it in a flat structure, with a left-to-right order.

In terms of a composite moniker, following a map in reverse is the same as binding in right-to-left order. We avoid as much binding (an expensive process) as possible. If we bound a composite moniker from left to right, we'd always be starting from the beginning of the treasure map even if we were already sitting on top of the spot marked 'X.' By binding right to left, we get to the treasure via the shortest possible route.

File Monikers

A file moniker is one such simple moniker that knows a single pathname, which might be absolute (as in C:\REPORTS\JUNE\MONTHLY.DOC) or might be relative (such as ..\JUNE\MONTHLY.DOC). Anything that the operating system can understand as a pathname (or that an application can parse into such) can be stored in a file moniker. Binding a file moniker causes it to determine the application that can handle the pathname, launch that application, and ask it to load the file by means of an *IPersistFile* interface. Binding a file moniker is like following the instructions on a treasure map that asks you to hop a plane and go to another place in the world. For example, the map might say, "Go to USA\Washington\Canyon Park\Highlands." Obviously there is a large expense of time and money in following this procedure, so you want to avoid binding file monikers as much as possible. If I'm already in the Highlands of Canyon Park in Washington State[4] I certainly don't need do anything else to get there. This is why composite monikers bind their internal monikers from right to left—it allows them to avoid taking a ride on a boomerang.

Item Monikers

An item moniker contains a source application-defined string that is comprehensible only by the application that created that string. An item moniker always works in conjunction with the moniker to its "left" in a composite moniker—that is, the item moniker depends on its left moniker. In other words, if your treasure map says, "Look on the third shelf on the right wall of the pantry in the kitchen of the house at 723 East Satori Street,"[5] you have to first get to the kitchen to find the pantry and the shelves. To get to the kitchen, you need to find and somehow get into the house at 723 East Satori. So binding to the item moniker depends on first binding to the moniker to its left. And that moniker might depend on the moniker to its left. The "third shelf in the pantry" item moniker depends on the "kitchen in the house at 723 East Satori Street" item moniker to its left, which depends on the "in USA\Washington\Canyon Park\Highlands" file moniker to its left.

---

4. This is, conveniently, where I happen to live. Don't worry. I'll watch the cookies.

5. This is NOT my address. You think I'd be crazy enough to publish it?

In programming terms, binding an item moniker means asking that moniker to find an *IOleItemContainer* interface that can resolve the name of that item into an interface pointer on the actual object (such as *IOleObject*). The item moniker's implementation of *BindToObject* is simply to call the *BindToObject* function on the moniker to its left, asking for *IOleItemContainer*. If the moniker to the left is itself an item moniker, it too will recursively call *BindToObject* on the moniker to its left, again asking for *IOleItemContainer*. This recursion continues until it reaches a moniker with no dependencies on the moniker to its left, such as a file moniker. At that point, the file moniker will launch an application, call *IPersistFile::Load*, and call *IPersistFile::QueryInterface* to obtain the *IOleItemContainer* interface requested by the item moniker immediately to the right of the file moniker. The item moniker can then call *IOleItemContainer::GetObject* to resolve its item name into another *IOleItemContainer* pointer, which it returns to the item moniker to its immediate right. This process of unwinding the recursion continues until it passes an *IOleItemContainer* pointer to the rightmost item moniker, which then calls *GetObject*, asking for the *IOleObject* pointer to return to whatever started the whole mess.

We'll see this in more detail, and in code, in Chapter 13.

Anti and Pointer Monikers

An anti moniker is a rather odd beast in that it only makes sense as part of a composite moniker, and it cannot be individually bound. Its effect is to annihilate the moniker that comes before it in the composite in such a way that the binding algorithm in the composite will ignore the one before the anti moniker. This class is necessary for design reasons because you can only append more monikers onto a composite. Creating a composite moniker is similar to writing a treasure map in permanent ink. After you write an instruction, you can't erase it—you have to scratch it out and say, "Ignore that last instruction."

A pointer moniker is the other oddball of the group of moniker classes. Although both file and item monikers identify pieces of what we call *passive storage,* or *disk-based storage,* a pointer moniker represents something in active storage—that is, in memory. A pointer moniker exists so that the user (other code, not an end user) of a moniker can bind in an identical manner to any moniker regardless of whether it references memory or disk storage. A pointer moniker internally maintains some other interface pointer so that binding it merely calls *QueryInterface* on that pointer. This is something like an instruction on the map that says, "Now turn around" or "Look down."

Custom Monikers?

With any imagination, you can probably come up with scenarios in which the five standard types of monikers would not be sufficient to fully describe the location of some data, such as a location on a network share. Here you would like to have a "NetShare Moniker" that contains a \\SERVER\SHARE designation. Binding this moniker would connect you to that share and would generally be stored as part of a composite that contained a pathname on that share and whatever else identified the data.

The longer you dream, the more examples you can imagine because a moniker, again, is simply some information, like a string or a pointer, and some code that somehow is capable of returning an interface pointer from binding to that information. Although you might find it necessary to implement your own moniker types, that subject is beyond the scope of this book. I refer you to the OLE 2 Design Specification for more details about monikers.

Where Do I Get Monikers?

A very good question. How do you write a treasure map to put in the cookie jar? This is the same question we've been asking throughout this book: "There are objects called monikers, so how do I get my first *IUnknown* or *IMoniker* pointer?"

The answer is that, depending on who you are, you might obtain moniker pointers in a variety of ways. The source of a link is usually responsible for creating monikers (writing the map) to hand to other applications to identify a piece of the source's data. In addition, a container itself needs to create a new moniker to identify a file, as we'll see later in this chapter. Whenever you have to create a new moniker, you call one or more API functions shown in Table 12-1 on the following page to obtain the first pointer to a particular type. There is one API function for each moniker class.

These functions are useful only to an application that has to create a moniker for some reason. As we'll see shortly, we will need to use *CreateFileMoniker* once for a linking container, but that's it. The linking container otherwise only passes monikers around but does not need to manipulate them in any way. For example, we'll modify the *IOleClientSite::GetMoniker* function to return the container's file moniker when asked. When we rename a document we'll need to call *IOleObject::SetMoniker*, but again, we merely pass the moniker around.

Most moniker manipulation actually happens within the OLE 2 libraries, such as when a container creates a linked object from clipboard data (a Paste Link operation) as well as in the OLE2UI library in its implementation of what is called the Links dialog box, which allows users to change or repair links. But to see all this, let's do it in the context of a container application.

Function	Description
CreateFileMoniker	Creates a file moniker given any *portion* of a pathname. That portion could be as short as a drive letter or as long as a complete path.
CreateItemMoniker	Creates an item moniker given a name to associate with the item. The application creating this moniker will later be asked to resolve it by means of an *IOleItemContainer* interface.
CreateAntiMoniker	Creates an anti moniker, which needs no extra information.
CreatePointerMoniker	Creates a pointer moniker, which wraps any existing interface pointer, passed as an LPUNKNOWN.
CreateCompositeMoniker	Creates a new composite moniker from two existing monikers, one called the "left" and one called the "right." The right is appended as a suffix on the left to form the new composite.

Table 12-1.
API functions to create monikers.

Step-by-Step Linking Container

Within the framework of the support we built for embedded objects in Chapter 9, we can now add support for linked objects as well, again using the Patron program as our example (found in CHAP12\PATRON on the companion disks that accompany this book). These steps cover how a container obtains a treasure map and what it has to do to follow the map correctly.

The first step will be to obtain the information necessary to create a linked object. We get that information from the clipboard, from a drag-and-drop operation, or from the Insert Object dialog box. With that information, we can use other variations on *OleCreate,* such as *OleCreateLinkFromData,* to create a linked object that, for the most part, acts like an embedded object.

Because the end user might want to know which objects are linked and which are embedded, we'll implement what is called the Show Objects command to identify each object by type. We can then worry about managing a file moniker for the container's document, finally implement the *IOleClientSite::GetMoniker* function, and then handle updating links and deal with the Links Dialog.

Again, we'll take a step-by-step approach to adding these features, each of which is concluded with a short description of what you can test after completing the step:

1. Enable links in the Insert Object dialog box.
2. Enable linking from clipboard and drag-and-drop operations.
3. Distinguish between linked and embedded objects with the Show Objects command.
4. Manage a file moniker for the document, call *IOleObject::SetMoniker*, and partially implement *IOleClientSite::GetMoniker*.
5. Invoke the Links Dialog, which involves implementing the *IOleUILinkContainer* interface, changing link sources, and breaking links intentionally.
6. Update links on loading a document.

After following these six steps you will have a container ready to link to any source. Some of the sample applications supplied with the OLE 2 SDK are applicable link sources. In addition, the linking facilities you implement with OLE 2 buy you compatibility with OLE 1 linking servers, so you can test with a number of OLE 1 applications.

Enable Links from Insert Object

To create any sort of linked object, we first need some information to which we can link. The Insert Object dialog box offers a link capability that allows you to create a new linked object from scratch—that is, you can tell OLE, "Draw me a treasure map for this thing and create a linked object around it." If you'll remember back in Chapter 9, we used the *IOF_DISABLELINK* flag when calling the *OleUIInsertObject* function. To support links, we can remove that flag, which causes the dialog box shown in Figure 12-2 to appear when the Create From File option button is selected.

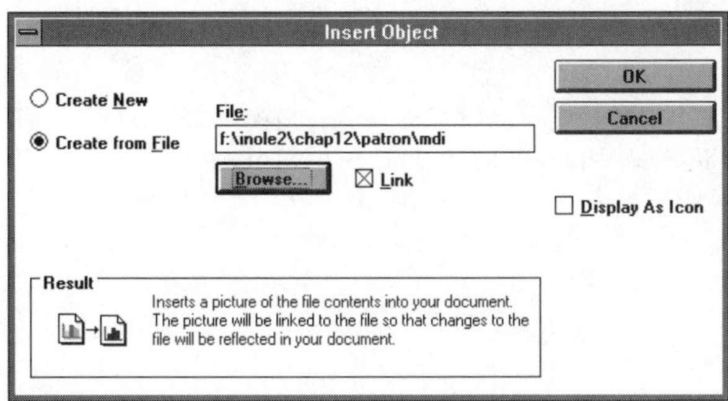

Figure 12-2.
The Insert Object dialog box with links enabled.

If the user selects the Link button in this dialog box, the *dwFlags* field in the OLEUIINSERTOBJECT structure will have the IOF_CHECKLINK bit set. Using this, we can therefore distinguish what type of object to create from the filename in the same structure's *lpszFile* field. In Patron, the *CTenant::UCreate* function actually handles the creation of the object, so we use this flag only at Patron's document level to change the type of tenant we'll create:

```
//In CPatronDoc::FInsertObject, if OK was pressed in the dialog.
if (io.dwFlags & IOF_SELECTCREATENEW)
    {
    tType=TENANTTYPE_EMBEDDEDOBJECT;
    pv=(LPVOID)&io.clsid;
    }
else
    {
    if (io.dwFlags & IOF_CHECKLINK)
        tType=TENANTTYPE_LINKEDFILE;
    else
        tType=TENANTTYPE_EMBEDDEDFILE;

    pv=(LPVOID)szFile;
    }

/*
 * tType and pv (the filename) passed to CPages::TenantCreate which
 * goes to CPage::TenantCreate and to CTenant::UCreate.
 */
```

To handle a linked object, Patron has to add only a case for TENANTTYPE_LINKEDFILE in *CTenant::UCreate* to call *OleCreateLinkToFile*:

```
//In CTenant::UCreate
switch (tType)
    {
    [Other cases]

    case TENANTTYPE_LINKEDFILE:
        hr=OleCreateLinkToFile((LPSTR)pvType, IID_IUnknown
            , OLERENDER_DRAW, NULL, NULL, m_pIStorage
            , (LPLPVOID)&pObj);
        break;

    ...
    }
```

The first parameter to *OleCreateLinkToFile* is the filename to which we want to link, and the other parameters are identical to those we pass to any other function in the *OleCreate* family. Note that the linked object in this case does not itself use the *IStorage* pointer you provide. The storage is still necessary, however, for OLE to save presentations and other data for this object.

OleCreateLinkToFile will create either a real linked object or a packager object that contains the filename. To make this decision, it tries to find an OLE server that might possibly read the file. If the file is a compound file, it tries to find a CLSID in the file by calling *GetClassFile*, which returns a CLSID written with *WriteClassStg* on a root storage. If the file is not a compound file or if there is no CLSID there, it attempts to associate the extension of the file with a *ProgID* in the Registration Database—that is, it looks for a Registration Database entry of the form

```
<extension> = <ProgID>
```

as in *.cos=Cosmo2Figure*. Using the *ProgID*, it then tries to find a CLSID marked with the 'Insertable' subkey under the ProgID\CLSID entry elsewhere in the Registration Database. If either method to retrieve a CLSID works, *OleCreateLinkToFile* attempts to launch the local server for that CLSID and have the local server create a single object from the entire contents of the file. It then requests a presentation for that linked object and notifies the container site that the view changed, which causes a repaint to show the object.

If *OleCreateLinkToFile* cannot find a CLSID, if it cannot launch the local server, or if the entire operation fails for some reason, it will create an *embedded* Package object in which the package contains the filename. When you activate this packager object, the packager attempts to run the application associated with the file as if you had double-clicked that file in File Manager. This sort of minimal linking does not qualify the package as a linked object (which is why it's embedded), and the package can be displayed only as an icon. It's more like an embedded filename. This process shows the other side of Packager. On one side, it can create objects that contain a copy of a file. In this case, we create an object that contains the pathname of a file. It's truly the packager equivalent of embedding vs. linking, simply in an utterly generic manner.

There is one subtlety that did not require any code changes to Patron for this chapter: After inserting a new linked object, you do not immediately activate it as you do with an embedded object from the Insert Object dialog box. Patron was already set to handle this at the end of *CPage::TenantCreate*.

```
//Activate new objects immediately and force a save on them
if (TENANTTYPE_EMBEDDEDOBJECT==tType)
    {
    m_pTenantCur->Activate(OLEIVERB_SHOW);
    m_pTenantCur->Update();
    }
```

Originally we added this code to avoid activating new static metafiles and bitmaps, but now it serves equally well to avoid activating linked objects upon creation as well.

I should mention here that if you ever want to programmatically determine whether a given object is linked or embedded, call *QueryInterface* and ask for *IOleLink*, an interface that allows you to manipulate information about the link itself. If you have an embedded (or static) object, *QueryInterface* will fail. Otherwise, it will return the pointer. Again, this is the advantage of the interface mechanism, whereby you cannot possibly try to manipulate a nonlinked object as a linked object because you cannot possibly obtain an *IOleLink* interface pointer for that object. Therefore, you cannot possibly ask the object to do something that will have unpredictable and possibly hazardous results.

With these few small additions, you now have a container capable of containing linked packages and of creating new linked objects to files for which a server exists. Activating the object (in fact, just about any other object manipulation) is no different from what you do for embedded objects. You can test the packager feature by using the Insert Object dialog box, selecting Create From File, checking Link, and choosing a file for which you know there is not a server but there is a file nevertheless for which a simple association might exist (a TXT file is a good candidate). This will create a new embedded package that has the filename inside it. If you choose the Edit Package verb for this object, you can see and modify the filename. If you choose the Activate Contents verb, the packager will attempt to run something that can handle TXT files, which by default will run Notepad with that file loaded.

You can also use Packager to create a link to an EXE so that when you activate the contents, you'll run that EXE. Create a container document full of such packager icons, and you can almost replace Program Manager.

To test the creation of linked objects, create and save a file by using one of the OLE 2 SDK's server samples. Enter that filename in the Insert Object dialog box and check the link. When you choose OK, the server is launched and is asked to load the file, generate a presentation for that object, and return an interface pointer to your container. Visually, this looks like an embedded object from the same server, and all your code to activate that object is completely applicable. In fact, go ahead and activate the object. You should see the server come up on your screen with the linked file loaded. As you make changes to that server file, you should see those changes reflected in your container site. You might also notice that the user interface for the server does not change from the way it looks when it runs as a stand-alone application because it's not editing an embedded object.

Enable Linking from Clipboard and Drag-and-Drop Operations

In the same way that we could create embedded objects from both clipboard and drag-and-drop operations by using *OleCreateFromData*, we can now create linked objects from those same sources by using *OleCreateLinkFromData*. This is the case when another application has—so to speak—already drawn a treasure map and left it around for us to find. To create a linked object with it, we need to modify both our drag-and-drop code and our pasting code.

We first need registered clipboard formats that we'll use in these operations: CF_LINKSOURCE and CF_LINKSRCDESCRIPTOR. Patron registers these in *CPatronDoc::CPatronDoc*.

```
m_cfLinkSource       =RegisterClipboardFormat(CF_LINKSOURCE);
m_cfLinkSrcDescriptor=RegisterClipboardFormat
    (CF_LINKSRCDESCRIPTOR);
```

Next, we create a function to check whether we can create a link from what's in a data object, such as *Patron's CPatronDoc::FQueryPasteLinkFromData*:

```
BOOL CPatronDoc::FQueryPasteLinkFromData(LPDATAOBJECT pIDataObject
    , LPFORMATETC pFE, LPTENANTTYPE ptType)
    {
    HRESULT         hr;

    if (NULL==pIDataObject)
        return FALSE;

    hr=OleQueryLinkFromData(pIDataObject);

    if (NOERROR!=hr)
        return FALSE;

    if (NULL!=pFE)
        SETDefFormatEtc(*pFE, m_cfLinkSource, TYMED_ISTREAM);

    if (NULL!=(LPVOID)ptType)
        *ptType=TENANTTYPE_LINKEDOBJECTFROMDATA;

    return TRUE;
    }
```

In Patron, this function serves two purposes. First, it uses the OLE 2 API *OleQueryLinkFromData* to see whether a call to *OleCreateLinkFromData* will work. Be careful! This query function can return NOERROR or S_FALSE. You need to distinguish between these two cases, so don't use the SUCCEEDED or FAILED macro here. Instead, compare the result directly to NOERROR to determine success.

If we find that a linked object is available from this data object, *CPatronDoc::FQueryPasteLinkFromData* fills a FORMATETC with the CF_LINKSOURCE format and the TYMED_ISTREAM medium(CF_LINKSOURCE is a moniker serialized to a stream) and returns TENANTTYPE_LINKEDOBJECTFROMDATA as the type of object we can create. Both FORMATETC and TENANTTYPE values eventually tell *CPatronDoc::FPasteFromData* and *CTenant::UCreate* to create a linked object as opposed to an embedded object. Down in *UCreate,* this information generates a call to *OleCreateLinkFromData*:

```
//In CTenant::UCreate
switch (tType)
    {
    [Other cases]

    case TENANTTYPE_LINKEDOBJECTFROMDATA:
        hr=OleCreateLinkFromData((LPDATAOBJECT)pvType
            , IID_IUnknown, OLERENDER_DRAW, NULL, NULL
            , m_pIStorage, (LPLPVOID)&pObj);
        break;

    ...
    }
```

After this, you again have a linked object that works well with all code you already have for embedded objects. Now, of course, comes the question of when we want to do all this. To help answer this question, note that CF_LINKSOURCE will be very low on the list of available clipboard formats (that's where link sources put it)—so low, in fact, that it appears after CF_EMBEDSOURCE, any presentation format, and even many disgustingly low-tech formats such as CF_TEXT. Therefore, creating a link by default—that is, simply by choosing Edit/Paste—is highly unlikely. Instead, the user has to specifically give a command to paste data as a link instead of as an embedded object or as any other format. How the user indicates this is, of course, different in clipboard and drag-and-drop operations, requires some additional user interface, and thus is the topic of the next two sections.

Paste Link and Paste Special Commands

To repeat myself, users must have an explicit command through which to paste a link, as opposed to a higher available clipboard format. There are two standard ways to present this command. The first is to enable linking in the Paste Special dialog box. If you aren't using this dialog box, you really don't care about this technique. The other way is to create an item immediately under the Paste item on your Edit menu that has the string *Paste Link.* In Patron, I've enabled this command only through the Paste Special dialog box, which causes the user to go through a little more work than a Paste Link command would. But the end results are the same. If you only want to have Paste Link on your menus, you can quickly skim the next few paragraphs until you see what to do after the Paste Special dialog box has closed.

You probably noticed before that the Paste Special dialog box has an option button with the text *Paste Link.* In Chapter 9, this was always grayed (disabled) because we did not enable linking for any of the formats we stored in the OLEUIPASTEENTRY array. Now we can enable linking, and it takes only one addition to the array and requires us to fill a few more fields of the OLEUIPASTESPECIAL structure:

```
BOOL CPatronDoc::FPasteSpecial(HWND hWndFrame)
    {
    OLEUIPASTESPECIAL   ps;
    OLEUIPASTEENTRY     rgPaste[6];
    UINT                rgcf[1];        //For ps.m_arrLinkTypes

    [Code to initialize other rgPaste[0] through rgPaste[4]]

    SETDefFormatEtc(rgPaste[5].fmtetc, m_cfLinkSource, TYMED_ISTREAM);
    rgPaste[5].lpstrFormatName=PSZ(IDS_PASTELINK);
    rgPaste[5].lpstrResultText=PSZ(IDS_PASTEASLINK);
    rgPaste[5].dwFlags=OLEUIPASTE_LINKTYPE1 | OLEUIPASTE_ENABLEICON;

    //Types we can Paste Link from the clipboard.
    rgcf[0]=m_cfLinkSource;
    ps.arrLinkTypes=rgcf;
    ps.cLinkTypes=1;

    ...

    uTemp=OleUIPasteSpecial(&ps);

    [Code continued below]
```

The Paste Special dialog box will enable the Paste Link option button if it encounters an OLEUIPASTEENTRY structure containing CF_LINK-SOURCE (like the one shown in the preceding code, in *rgPaste[5]*) and if the data object from the clipboard also provides CF_LINKSOURCE.

The next step might seem a little strange because the Paste Special dialog box is designed to handle more than one type of link information, such as (dare we say it) DDE links. You'll notice that the CF_LINKSOURCE entry in the preceding code has the flag OLEUIPASTE_LINKTYPE1. This flag indicates that this entry is attached to the first clipboard format in the OLEUI-PASTESPECIAL structure's *arrLinkTypes* field. This field is a pointer to an array of UINTs in which each element is some sort of link format. In our example, the array *rgcf* has only one entry, CF_LINKSOURCE, so we indicate the length of the array in the *cLinkTypes* field. If we wanted to support another link source format—say, an old DDE link—we would add that clipboard format to *rgcf*, increase *cLinkTypes*, and add another OLEUIPASTE-ENTRY structure with the flag OLEUIPASTE_LINKTYPE2, and so on. The Paste Special dialog box in the OLE2UI library supports up to eight link formats.

When the Paste Special dialog box comes up now, the Paste Link option button can be enabled, and selecting it displays the items available for linking as well as information about the source of the link. When you select a linked format and press OK, *OleUIPasteSpecial* returns with the *fLink* field of the OLE-UIPASTESPECIAL structure set to TRUE. (Otherwise, it's FALSE, of course.)

```
[Continued from above]

if (OLEUI_OK==uTemp)
    {
    UINT        i=ps.nSelectedIndex;
    TENANTTYPE  tType;

    if (ps.fLink)
        tType=TENANTTYPE_LINKEDOBJECTFROMDATA;
    else
        {
        if (1==ps.nSelectedIndex)
            tType=TENANTTYPE_EMBEDDEDOBJECTFROMDATA;
        else
            tType=TENANTTYPE_STATIC;
        }

    //Handle iconic aspects...from links as well
    if ((1==i || ps.fLink) && (PSF_CHECKDISPLAYASICON
        & ps.dwFlags) && NULL!=ps.hMetaPict)
        {
```

```
            rgPaste[i].fmtetc.dwAspect=DVASPECT_ICON;
            dwData=(DWORD)(UINT)ps.hMetaPict;
            }

        fRet=FPasteFromData(ps.lpSrcDataObj, &rgPaste[i].fmtetc
            , tType, NULL, dwData, FALSE);

        ...
        }
    ...
    }
```

Paste Link readers can come back into the discussion now. When we come back with *fLink* set to TRUE, which would essentially be the same condition as when the Paste Link command is used directly from a menu, we create a tenant with the type TENANTTYPE_LINKEDOBJECTFROMDATA, which, again, generates a call to *OleCreateLinkFromData.* Note also that in the Paste Special code, we enabled iconic aspects for linked objects as well. We must be sure to change the aspect used in creating the object if *fLink* is *TRUE* and PSF-_CHECKDISPLAYASICON is set in *dwFlags.*

So by virtue of user selection of Paste Link from a menu or in the Paste Special dialog box, we note that we want to create a linked object from the data object instead of any embedded object. *OleCreateLinkFromData* will safely ignore all other formats except CF_LINKSOURCE (and CF_LINKSRC-DESCRIPTOR).

Drag-and-Drop Linking Feedback

Just as we can create linked objects from data on the clipboard, we should be able to create linked objects, as a drop target, from a drag-and-drop operation. But how do we know when to link as opposed to doing any other sort of paste?

Remember that the drag-and-drop code we've built up to this point looks at the Ctrl key: If the Ctrl key is down, the operation is a Copy instead of a Move. For linking, we throw another hook into the picture: Shift+Ctrl means Link, so when you see a call to your *IDropTarget::Drop* function and both the Shift and Ctrl keys are down, you should do the exact equivalent of a Paste Link, as described in the previous section.

In addition, a drop target implementation is responsible for setting the appropriate "effect" flags, depending on whether the operation is Move, Copy, or now, Link, each of which can still be combined with the scrolling effect. When we first implemented drag-and-drop in Chapter 8, we had a number of occasions on which we tested the keyboard flags to determine whether we should use Copy or Move.

```
*pdwEffect=DROPEFFECT_MOVE;

if (grfKeyState & MK_CONTROL)
    *pdwEffect=DROPEFFECT_COPY;
```

To that, we must now add the link case:

```
*pdwEffect=DROPEFFECT_MOVE;

if (grfKeyState & MK_CONTROL)
    {
    if (ppg->m_fLinkAllowed && (grfKeyState & MK_SHIFT))
        *pdwEffect=DROPEFFECT_LINK;
    else
        *pdwEffect=DROPEFFECT_COPY;
    }
```

By default, we move the data, but if the Ctrl key is down, the end user might want to either link or copy. If the end user presses Shift+Ctrl, linking takes place; otherwise, Ctrl produces a copy. This sort of code occurs, at least in Patron's implementation of *IDropTarget* (IDROPTGT.CPP), in *IDropTarget::DragEnter*, *DragOver*, and *Drop*. When DROPEFFECT_LINK is returned from any of these functions, the drop source's *IDropSource::GiveFeedback* function shows a linking cursor. Please refer to Chapter 8 for the image of the linking cursor.

So now, what's that *ppg->m_fLinkAllowed* flag for? Patron uses this flag (and I believe you will want to as well) to remember from *IDropTarget::DragEnter* whether linking is available from the particular data object. Remember from Chapter 8 that *DragEnter* should test the data object for pastable data, and if none exists, it should save a NULL data object pointer (as opposed to saving the real one that was passed to it):

```
m_pIDataObject=NULL;

if (!m_pDoc->FQueryPasteFromData(pIDataSource, &fe, NULL))
    {
    *pdwEffect=DROPEFFECT_NONE;
    return NOERROR;
    }
```

Later the implementations of *DragOver* and *Drop* check for a NULL data object, and continually return DROPEFFECT_NONE if no data object exists. Well, we need to do the same thing for linking, but we want to disable only linking, not the entire operation. So we call the function we made to test whether we can use Paste Link from a data object, saving that result in *m_fLinkAllowed*:

```
    ppg->m_fLinkAllowed
        =(NOERROR==OleQueryLinkFromData(pIDataSource));

//We never allow it dragging in ourselves.
ppg->m_fLinkAllowed &= !ppg->m_fDragSource;
```

In this example from Patron, we also prevent paste linking to ourselves by setting the flag to FALSE if the drag-and-drop is happening within the same page. So whenever *m_fLinkAllowed* is FALSE, we prevent our code from ever returning DROPEFFECT_LINK.

Finally, when we get to the point of pasting data in *IDropTarget::Drop*, we want to be sure we use Paste Link if that's the effect we decided to use, as we can see happening in Patron:

```
/*
 * We know linking is desired if effect flag is set, so this
 * function will get the FORMATETC for linking.  Otherwise
 * FQueryPasteFromData will get the other FORMATETC to use.
 */
if (DROPEFFECT_LINK==*pdwEffect)
    {
    fRet=m_pDoc->FQueryPasteLinkFromData(pIDataSource, &fe
        , &tType);
    }
else
    fRet=m_pDoc->FQueryPasteFromData(pIDataSource, &fe, &tType);
```

Other than these changes, all your existing drag-and-drop code remains the same.

Test Your Linking

At this point, you should be able to run a server application such as one of the samples with the OLE 2 SDK, create a file, copy some data to the clipboard, and try to use Paste Link in your container by using both the clipboard and drag-and-drop. What should appear in your container is an object that looks like an embedded object from the same server. You should be able to activate it, which should bring up the server with the linked file loaded and with the linked range of data as the current selection. Again, changes made to the data in the server should be reflected in your container by virtue of your *IAdviseSink* receiving *OnViewChange* notifications.

Be sure as well to test that the correct feedback appears in a drag-and-drop operation when you hold down both Shift and Ctrl together, and verify that you are not attempting to link to your object from itself.

WARNING WARNING WARNING WARNING WARNING

There are a number of really nasty bugs in the first release (April 1993) of the OLE 2 SDK. I really had a time figuring these out. First, you might experience GP Faults in OLE2.DLL when working with monikers—there is a compiler optimization glitch deep inside the implementation of a certain *IEnumMoniker::Release* that ends up accessing an invalid pointer, and BOOM! My machine was cruel to me while this was happening. Windows decided to start giving random UAEs. Not good. Any release of the OLE 2 libraries after April 1993 contains the necessary correction.

In addition, I encountered a number of places in the OLE2UI library where string buffers were overwritten, thus trashing the stack. The primary ones are in the *FPasteSpecialInit* function in PASTESPL.C. Look for character arrays with the name *szLabel* that are OLEUI_CCHLABELMAX characters long and at least double their size, if not triple them. OLEUI_CCHLABELMAX is only 40 characters, and things begin to blow up when you have a long *File!Item!Item!Item...* moniker on the clipboard. The function tries to copy the expanded text name of that moniker into this small buffer using *lstrcpy*. BOOM! You're dead. As a backup precaution, also change any *lstrcpy* calls with *szLabel* buffers into *lstrcpyn* calls to be sure the array boundaries are not exceeded.

Finally, I encountered a similar problem with debug builds of OLE2UI that caused it to overwrite character arrays. In particular, there was one that attempted to put a moniker name with a mess of other text into an 80-character buffer using *wsprintf,* which ignorantly overwrote the array boundaries, causing yet another UAE, but only when the moniker name was long enough. If you encounter this problem, either remove the debug code or compile a retail build.

If you encounter other UAEs, these are the first places you should check. Future releases of the OLE2UI library undoubtedly will be more careful about their memory use. (And don't look at me, I only wrote the Insert Object dialog box!)

> **WARNING: POTENTIAL HAIR-PULLER!**
>
> The OLE 2 SDK's Server Outline sample has a quirky feature (that you might also find in other applications): When you copy a selection to the clipboard, the sample defines a name for that range automatically if one does not already exist. You have to *save* that file *after* you do the Copy; otherwise, that name will not be saved with the file, and the linked object you create from that data will not properly reconnect to the server. When you activate the object, your disk will churn for a while and then quit without anything else appearing on the screen. What has happened is that the Server Outline application started up, loaded the file, but failed to relocate the range for the name you linked to because that name was not saved, so Outline simply quits. You need to be sure you save the file after you or the application defines a new name. The quirky part is that Server Outline does not consider the document dirty if it creates a new name when you copy data to the clipboard, and so it will not ask you to save if you merely close the file. Avoid some headaches and save the file after you copy a selection that does not already have a persistent name.

Implement the Show Objects Command

I've mentioned a number of times now that after initial creation, a linked object looks and acts a lot like an embedded object. Both a linked object and an embedded object appear as a rectangular presentation in your container document, both can be activated, both supply verbs, and so on. As programmers, we greatly benefit from the high level of commonality between the two types of objects because that approach means less code. However, as mentioned previously, an end user might want to know exactly which type an object is, so it's a great idea to give the end user a way to distinguish between linked objects and embedded objects. This is the reason behind a Show Objects menu command, which is a rather quiet part of the OLE 2 User Interface Guidelines in the *OLE 2 Programmer's Reference* that's been largely forgotten in the concentration on in-place activation but is nevertheless important. The Show Objects command gives end users an idea of how much time it might take to activate that object.

Show Objects, which can appear on nearly any menu you deem appropriate (Edit being the default), is a state toggle. When Show Objects is off, embedded and linked objects appear only with their presentations. When the option is turned on, you need to surround embedded objects with a solid line

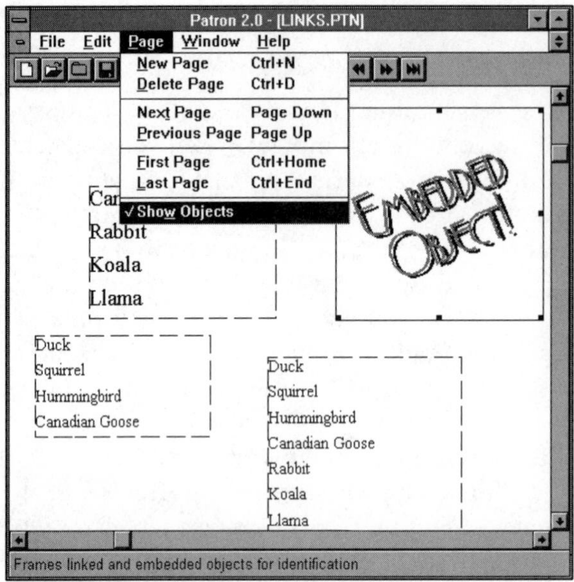

Figure 12-3.

Patron with the Show Objects command activated so that embedded objects are surrounded with a solid line and linked objects are surrounded with a dashed line.

and linked objects with a dashed line, as shown for Patron in Figure 12-3. The figure also shows the command on Patron's Page menu—in PATRON.RC this menu item is given the identifier IDM_PAGESHOWOBJECTS.

I admit that I had to make a lot of changes to all levels of Patron to enable this command, even though the code itself is simple. Down at the tenant level, I needed to add another state flag to the container sites so that when the object is drawn again it can be surrounded with the appropriate indicator:

```
//In TENANT.H, with other state flags
#define TENANTSTATE_SHOWTYPE      0x00000004

//In TENANT.CPP, function CTenant::Draw
if (TENANTSTATE_SHOWTYPE & m_dwState)
    {
    OleUIShowObject(&rc, hDC
        , (TENANTTYPE_LINKEDOBJECT==m_tType));
    }
```

The function *OleUIShowObject* in the OLE2UI library conveniently draws the solid or dashed lines for you, given the rectangle to surround, the *hDC*, and a boolean flag indicating which type of indicator to draw, TRUE being linked and FALSE being embedded.

So drawing these indicators is no problem, but we still have to tell the tenants when to toggle the TENANTSTATE_SHOWTYPE flag. This happens in the function *CTenant::ShowObjectType*, which looks a lot like the *ShowAsOpen* function we added in Chapter 9 to indicate whether the object was open for editing in a server:

```
void CTenant::ShowObjectType(BOOL fShow)
    {
    BOOL        fWasShow;
    DWORD       dwState;
    RECT        rc;
    HDC         hDC;

    fWasShow=(BOOL)(TENANTSTATE_SHOWTYPE & m_dwState);

    dwState=m_dwState & ~TENANTSTATE_SHOWTYPE;
    m_dwState=dwState | ((fShow) ? TENANTSTATE_SHOWTYPE : 0);

    /*
     * If this wasn't previously shown, just add the line,
     * otherwise repaint.
     */
    if (!fWasShow && fShow)
        {
        RECTFROMRECTL(rc, m_rcl);
        RectConvertMappings(&rc, NULL, TRUE);
        OffsetRect(&rc, -(int)m_pPG->m_xPos, -(int)m_pPG->m_yPos);

        hDC=GetDC(m_hWnd);
        OleUIShowObject(&rc, hDC
            , (TENANTTYPE_LINKEDOBJECT==m_tType));
        ReleaseDC(m_hWnd, hDC);
        }

    if (fWasShow && !fShow)
        Repaint();

    return;
    }
```

So now, of course, the question is,"Who calls this function?" For that we have to go up to the page level, where *CTenant::ShowObjectType* is called from *CPage::FOpen*, *CPage::TenantCreate*, and *CPage::ShowObjectTypes*. We'll call this last function when the user selects the Show Object menu item where the page merely has to inform all the tenants within it to show their types.

```
void CPage::ShowObjectTypes(BOOL fShow)
    {
    LPTENANT    pTenant;
    UINT        i;

    for (i=0; i < m_cTenants; i++)
        {
        if (FTenantGet(i, &pTenant, FALSE))
            pTenant->ShowObjectType(fShow);
        }

    return;
    }
```

The page also calls *CTenant::ShowObjectType* when loading an object or creating a new object because the Show Objects state is the state of the document that then has to apply to all objects within that document. So whenever we load an object from a file, as in *CPage::FOpen*, we have to remember to tell it to show its type if necessary:

```
//This is the loop that reloads all tenants on opening a page.
for (i=0; i < m_cTenants; i++)
    {
    if (FTenantAdd(-1, (pti+i)->dwID, &pTenant))
        {
        pTenant->FLoad(m_pIStorage, &(pti+i)->fe
            , &(pti+i)->rcl)
        pTenant->ShowObjectType(m_pPG->m_fShowTypes);
        }
    }
```

In the same way, we have to tell any new tenants we create on this page about the Show Objects state as well, as seen in *CPage::TenantCreate*:

```
//Toward the end of CPage::TenantCreate
...

m_pTenantCur->Select(TRUE);    [This was already here]

//Make sure this new tenant knows about showing its type.
m_pTenantCur->ShowObjectType(m_pPG->m_fShowTypes);

...
```

Because pages open and close during the life of a document, the state of Show Objects must be kept in some structure with the same document lifetime. *CPages* is just such a structure to hold such a boolean flag called *m_fShowTypes* in the preceding code. This flag is initially set to FALSE when the document is first loaded and changed in *CPages::ShowObjectTypes*:

```
void CPages::ShowObjectTypes(BOOL fShow)
    {
    if (NULL==m_pPageCur)
        return;

    m_fShowTypes=fShow;
    m_pPageCur->ShowObjectTypes(fShow);
    return;
    }
```

For the most part, this function simply passes the call through to the current page, but it also saves the state of the option for all others to look at. I put *m_fShowTypes* in *CPages* to allow the *CPage* class access to that state so that functions such as *CPage::FOpen* can tell whether the option is on or off.

In any case, both the *CPages::ShowObjectTypes* function and *m_fShowTypes* are used from the document level (I told you this affected all levels) in the function *CPatronDoc::FQueryOrShowObjectTypes*:

```
BOOL CPatronDoc::FShowOrQueryObjectTypes(BOOL fQuery, BOOL fShow)
    {
    if (fQuery)
        return m_fShowTypes;

    m_fShowTypes=fShow;
    m_pPG->ShowObjectTypes(fShow);
    return TRUE;
    }
```

This function is a two-faced swindler, hence the more complicated name. It will either return the current state of the Show Objects option for this document or pass the *change* down to the pages and tenants. Note that when changing states, I again save the current state in the *m_fShowTypes* flag in *CPatronDoc*, which is separate from the variable of the same name in *CPages*. (Both variables will always have the same value, however.)

It should be fairly clear that we'd call this function with *fQuery FALSE* and the Show Objects state in *fShow* when we select the Show Objects command from the menu, which happens in *CPatronFrame::OnCommand (PATRON.CPP)*:

```
case IDM_PAGESHOWOBJECTS:
    {
    BOOL    fTemp;

    //First get the current state, then toggle it.
    fTemp=pDoc->FShowOrQueryObjectTypes(TRUE, FALSE);
    pDoc->FShowOrQueryObjectTypes(FALSE, !fTemp);
    }
    break;
```

The other purpose of *CPatronDoc::FShowOrQueryObjectTypes* is to return the state of the command so that we can check or uncheck the menu item when processing WM_INITMENUPOPUP for the Page menu, as is done in *CPatronFrame::UpdateMenus (PATRON.CPP)*:

```
[Handling for other top-level popups]

//m_phMenu[2] in CPatronFrame has the "Page" menu.
if (m_phMenu[2]==hMenu)
    {
    [Enable or disable other Page commands]

    //Check the Show Objects command or not.
    if (NULL!=pDoc)
        fOK=pDoc->FShowOrQueryObjectTypes(TRUE, FALSE);
    else
        fOK=FALSE;

    CheckMenuItem(hMenu, IDM_PAGESHOWOBJECTS, MF_BYCOMMAND
        | ((fOK) ? MF_CHECKED : MF_UNCHECKED));

    [uTemp is MF_DISABLED | MF_GRAYED if there's no document]
    EnableMenuItem(hMenu, IDM_PAGESHOWOBJECTS, uTemp);
    }
```

In Patron, the Show Objects command is disabled if there is no current document; if there is a current document, it's always enabled and will appear either checked or unchecked, depending on the current value of *m_fShowTypes* in the document.

Testing this feature, of course, is simple—see whether the repaints happen correctly. You should test this by selecting your menu item a few times and then, with Show Objects on, create a new object and verify that the indicator is also drawn. Then turn the Show Objects option off and verify that the new object reacts accordingly. In addition, if your application closes and reloads objects during the lifetime of the document, as happens in Patron when you switch between pages, verify that newly reloaded objects reflect the state properly. Hey, I forgot to do this at first! Fortunately, it wasn't one of those bugs that took long to figure out.

Manage a File Moniker, Call *IOleObject::SetMoniker*, and Implement *IOleClientSite::GetMoniker*

Linked objects always appreciate knowing exactly where they live so that they can use a map to keep track of the relative positions between themselves in the container and the treasure (the source of the link). If they find that the treasure has moved to another known location, they'll change the map.

Remember that a linked object internally maintains two file monikers, one absolute and the other relative. The linked object (as managed inside OLE2.DLL) itself generates the relative pathname from the pathname of the container document in which the linked object lives and the pathname of the file in which the actual linked data lives. The relative pathname is simply the pathname of the source file where all common elements between the container document pathname and the source file pathname are replaced with ..\ prefixes.

For example, if the container document is *c:\reports\june\monthly.doc* and the absolute pathname of the source file is MS-DOS *c:\reports\may\sales.xls*, the relative path from the document to the source is ..\..*may\sales.xls*. The common elements *c:\reports* are stripped, and because there are two elements remaining in the container document path, you have to prepend ..\ to get up to where you can append the remaining path of the source file. Note that if the only common element between the two paths is the drive letter, the relative path to the link source is simply the absolute path, sans drive letter; that's the best OLE can do.

I mention all this to emphasize how important it is for your container to tell all linked objects about the pathname of the container document, which you do by calling *IOleObject::SetMoniker*. Instead of passing a filename of the container document, you have to pass a moniker, so somewhere you have to call *CreateFileMoniker* with the absolute pathname of the container document.

In Patron, this happens in *CPatronDoc::Rename*. In Chapter 9, we modified this function (from the default in CLASSLIB\CDOCUMNT.CPP) to call down through *CPages* and *CPage* to *CTenant::NotifyOfRename*, passing the document's filename:

```
//This is from CHAPTER 9!
void CPatronDoc::Rename(LPSTR pszFile)
    {
    CDocument::Rename(pszFile);
    m_pPG->NotifyTenantsOfRename(pszFile, NULL);
    return;
    }
```

In Chapter 9, the call to *m_pPG->NotifyTenantsOfRename* eventually ended up in *CTenant::NotifyOfRename*, which called *IOleObject::SetHostNames*. But we had this mysterious "reserved" parameter in all those functions. Mystery no more! We use this now to pass a file moniker from the document down to the tenant so that it can call *IOleObject::SetMoniker*:

```
//Chapter 12 DOCUMENT.CPP
void CPatronDoc::Rename(LPSTR pszFile)
    {
```

```
    LPMONIKER   pmk;

    CDocument::Rename(pszFile);

    //Give a moniker to linked objects in tenants.
    if (NULL!=pszFile)
        {
        CreateFileMoniker(pszFile, &pmk);
        m_pPG->NotifyTenantsOfRename(pszFile, pmk);

        //No need for us to hold on to this.
        pmk->Release();
        }

    return;
    }

//TENANT.CPP
void CTenant::NotifyOfRename(LPSTR pszFile, LPMONIKER pmk)
    {
    [Unmodified code to call IOleObject::SetHostNames]

    ...

    if (NULL!=pmk)
        {
        if (NULL!=m_pmkFile)
            m_pmkFile->Release();

        m_pmkFile=pmk;
        m_pmkFile->AddRef();

        m_pIOleObject->SetMoniker(OLEWHICHMK_CONTAINER, pmk);
        }

    return;
    }
```

Note that *CPatronDoc* has no reason to hold onto the file moniker after it hands it off to the tenants (and the objects) because each tenant uses AddRef on the moniker itself when saving a copy. We will actually need this moniker when we implement *IOleClientSite::GetMoniker* (later). But outside of *GetMoniker*, Patron has no other use for the file moniker, so the document doesn't need to maintain the pointer. Also note that the *NotifyTenantsOfRename* functions in *CPages* and *CPage* have not changed except in changing the types of the second parameter from LPVOID *pvReserved* to LPMONIKER *pmk*.

You are probably wondering why Patron calls *IOleObject::SetMoniker* to all objects in all tenants, regardless of whether they are linked, embedded, or static. As we'll see in the next chapter, embedded objects actually need to know when their container monikers change, for reasons that we won't get into now. So although it seems counterintuitive (like much of compound documents, no doubt), you do want to call *SetMoniker* for all linked *and* embedded objects. Static objects ignore the call completely, so I don't bother with extra code to check.

The first parameter to *SetMoniker* also needs a little explanation. The *SetMoniker* function is used for more than merely telling the object the container document's moniker: It can also tell the object of a relative moniker for it within the container document. (We'll see this in Chapter 13.) Passing OLEWHICHMK_CONTAINER (WHICHMK is read as "which moniker") says that the moniker in the second parameter is the container's file moniker. The other possibility is OLEWHICHMK_REL, which asks the container to return a moniker for the object relative to the container itself, meaning everything but the container document's pathname. This is called the *container-relative* moniker for the object.

You might wonder whether you need to implement *IOleClientSite::GetMoniker* here. The answer is that you have to implement this function at least for OLEWHICHMK_CONTAINER, as you can see in Patron's *IOleClientSite* implementation:

```
STDMETHODIMP CImpIOleClientSite::GetMoniker(DWORD dwAssign
    , DWORD dwWhich, LPMONIKER FAR *ppmk)
    {
    *ppmk=NULL;

    /*
     * To support linking as a container we at least have to
     * implement this for OLEWHICKMK_CONTAINER but not for any
     * others.  This allows OLE to update absolute monikers when
     * it has to use the relative moniker to locate a link source.
     */

    switch (dwWhich)
        {
        case OLEWHICHMK_CONTAINER:
            //This is just the file we're living in.
            if (NULL!=m_pTen->m_pmkFile)
                *ppmk=m_pTen->m_pmkFile;

            break;
        }
```

(continued)

```
if (NULL==*ppmk)
    return ResultFromScode(E_FAIL);

(*ppmk)->AddRef();
return NOERROR;
}
```

We need this implementation to ensure that a linked object can track a link source that moves enough to invalidate the absolute pathname but can still be found through a relative path. With your call to *IOleObject::SetMoniker* in place and your implementation of *IOleClientSite::GetMonikers,* you can perform an experiment to see how linked objects can track a link source.

First create a file from some server and save it in some subdirectory. Then create a linked object to that source and save your container document in another subdirectory that shares some common elements with the source file, but not in the same directory as the source. If you activate the object now, the server will run appropriately and load the file. No problem.

Now go to another directory or another drive and recreate the same directory structure as the one where you have the original container and source files. Copy all the files here, and then delete the original files so that any absolute pathnames in any file monikers are now invalid. Now run your container again, reload the file containing the link, and activate the linked object. Guess what? It still worked. The server still found and loaded the source file. The relative file moniker still contained a valid path because you preserved the directory structure. Under OLE 1, this experiment would have failed because you would have broken the absolute pathname. But because OLE 2 linked objects maintain two file monikers—one absolute and one relative—and because at least one is still valid, the link is not broken. This is one of the major improvements in linking in OLE 2 because users frequently move directory structures without disturbing the relative positions between container and source files.

When an OLE 2 linked object (in the default handler) finds an invalid absolute moniker but a valid relative moniker, it updates the absolute moniker to point to the new location, recreating the absolute path from the relative moniker. But to do this, OLE needs an abolute pathname to the container's file. It obtains this absolute pathname by calling *IOleClientSite::GetMoniker* with OLEWHICHMK_CONTAINER. To prove that this works, save your container document (to save the moniker) and move that file to a random location so that you invalidate the relative moniker but not the updated absolute moniker. Loading the file and activating the linked object will still work, and in the process OLE will update the relative moniker (which precipitates another call to *GetMoniker*).

Note that when such an update happens you must save the container document again. Otherwise, the new monikers in the linked object will not be saved persistently (regardless of whether you are using compound files and regardless of any direct or transactioned storage modes you are using). Beware that you are not notified of this change in any way through your *IAdviseSink* implementation. Instead you need to call the object's *IPersist::IsDirty* function to see if it needs to be saved.

The Links Dialog Box and the *IOleUILinkContainer* Interface

Now we come to what I consider the ugliest part of implementing a container application: the Links dialog box, shown in Figure 12-4. As you can see, this dialog box has a lot happening in it. It allows the user to change the source of a link, open the source of the link, force an update on the linked object, break the link completely, or to change what are known as the update options, making them either automatic or manual. An automatic link, which is the default for all newly created linked objects, is what was called a "hot link" in DDE: Changes made to the source are immediately updated in the container. A manual link, which requires the user to explicitly change settings in the Links dialog box, is the DDE "warm link," in which the user has to also explicitly tell the container when to update the presentation. This is the reason for the Update Now button in the dialog box. The Change Source button also invokes the sub-dialog box shown in Figure 12-5, which allows specific manipulation of the moniker maintained in the linked object.

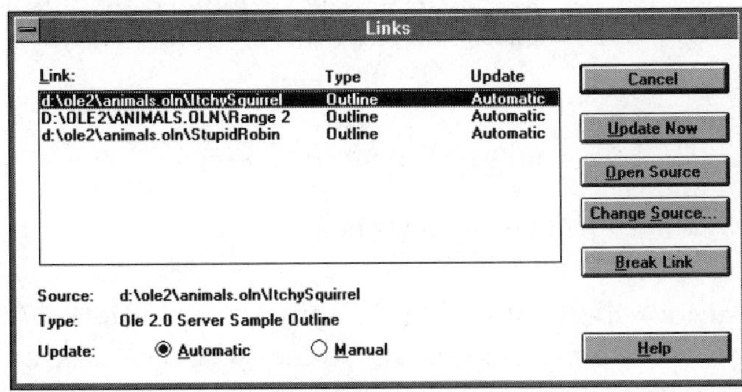

Figure 12-4.
The Links dialog box displays the links in a document, allowing the user to change options, change the link source, update the presentation, or break the link.

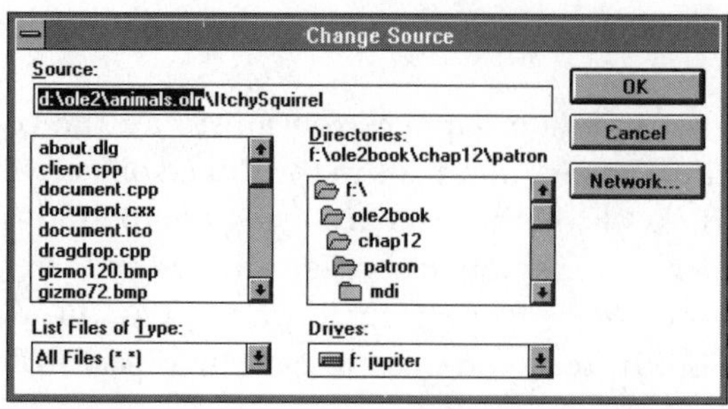

Figure 12-5.
The Change Source dialog box displays the human-readable name of the source moniker and allows the user to change specific pieces of it.

The Links dialog box is supposed to display *all* links in the current document. I find this far too harsh, especially for an application such as Patron, which does not load any objects except those on the current page. It's absurd to ask an application to figure out how to load everything in its document merely to support this one dialog box. (Loading that much could run you out of memory in a hurry too.) So I amend this to say that the Links dialog box should show all *currently loaded* links. Thus, Patron shows only the links in the current page because that's all I have loaded at one time. Spend your time on more useful features such as In-Place Activation.

When I was working with OLE 1, I called the Links dialog box the dialog box from Hell because it was, well, a real devil to implement. Fortunately for all of us working with OLE 2, the dialog box is implemented as part of the OLE2UI library through the function *OleUIEditLinks.* This function, like all the other dialog box functions, takes a structure pointer as the only parameter (in this case, a pointer to OLEUIEDITLINKS):

```
typedef struct tagOLEUIEDITLINKS
    {
    [Common elements of all OLE2UI dialog structures]

    LPOLEUILINKCONTAINERlpOleUILinkContainer;
    } OLEUIEDITLINKS, *POLEUIEDITLINKS, FAR *LPOLEUIEDITLINKS;
```

There is only one special field in this entire structure, *lpOleUILinkContainer.* Otherwise, it is simply the standard owner window, flags, and other fields common to all the OLE2UI dialog boxes. *lpOleUILinkContainer* is a pointer to the special interface *IOleUILinkContainer,* which is defined in

OLE2UI.H specifically for the Links dialog box. So we'll need to implement an object with this interface before we can invoke the dialog box.

The *IOleUILinkContainer* Interface

It might seem strange to have this interface for a dialog box, but realize that the Links dialog box is really only a control panel for a number of different functions instead of an input collecting dialog box such as File Open. Because the application generally is the only one that knows where it maintains its object pointers, the Links dialog box asks the application to perform specific tasks when specific controls are pressed in the dialog box. You can see that there is a tight correlation between the controls in the dialog box and the functions in this interface as defined in OLE2UI.H:

```
DECLARE_INTERFACE_(IOleUILinkContainer, IUnknown)
    {
    [IUnknown members omitted]

    STDMETHOD_(DWORD,GetNextLink) (THIS_ DWORD) PURE;
    STDMETHOD(SetLinkUpdateOptions) (THIS_ DWORD, DWORD) PURE;
    STDMETHOD(GetLinkUpdateOptions) (THIS_ DWORD, DWORD FAR *) PURE;
    STDMETHOD(SetLinkSource) (THIS_ DWORD, LPSTR, ULONG, ULONG FAR *
        , BOOL) PURE;
    STDMETHOD(GetLinkSource) (THIS_ DWORD, LPSTR FAR *, ULONG FAR *
        , LPSTR FAR *, LPSTR FAR *, BOOL FAR *, BOOL FAR *) PURE;
    STDMETHOD(OpenLinkSource) (THIS_ DWORD) PURE;
    STDMETHOD(UpdateLink) (THIS_ DWORD, BOOL, BOOL) PURE;
    STDMETHOD(CancelLink) (THIS_ DWORD) PURE;
    };
```

These functions are used either to initialize the list of links in the dialog or to execute a specific command when the user presses a control, as shown in Table 12-2.

For the most part, the implementations of each of these members deals with calls to *IOleObject* and the linked object interface, *IOleLink*. If you look at the *IOleLink* interface, you'll also see a strong correspondence among the dialog box, *IOleUILinkContainer*, and *IOleLink*. For example, *IOleLink* has functions called *SetUpdateOptions* and *GetUpdateOptions*, and two others called *SetSourceMoniker* and *GetSourceMoniker*.

Patron's implementation of this interface is a stand-alone object of class *CIOleUILinkContainer*, defined in PAGES.H and implemented in IUILINK.CPP as shown in Listing 12-1 on the next page. Note that I have purposely left in long header comments on each function because they are basically not documented in the OLE 2 SDK (at least at the time of this writing).

Function	When called
GetNextLink, GetUpdate-Options, GetLinkSource	All three of these functions are used to fill the dialog box. The dialog box manages a DWORD for each link in the list box, and *GetNextLink* is the function called repeatedly to obtain those DWORDs. Typically, this will be some sort of pointer. When the dialog box initially fills the list box, it will, after calling *GetNextLink*, call *GetUpdateOptions* and *GetLink-Source* to obtain additional information to create the list-box items.
SetLinkUpdateOptions	Called when the user selects the Automatic or Manual option buttons.
SetLinkSource	Called when the user makes changes in the Change Source subdialog box.
OpenLinkSource	Called when the user chooses Open Source.
UpdateLink	Called when the user chooses Update Now.
CancelLink	Called when the user chooses Break Link.

Table 12-2.
How the Links dialog box uses IOleUILinkContainer.

PAGES.H

```
class __far CIOleUILinkContainer : public IOleUILinkContainer
    {
    private:
        ULONG                       m_cRef;
        LPPAGE                      m_pPage;
        UINT                        m_iTenant;
        LPOLEUILINKCONTAINER        m_pDelIUILinks;

    public:
        BOOL                        m_fDirty;    //No reason to hide it.

    protected:
        STDMETHODIMP GetObjectInterface(DWORD, REFIID, LPLPVOID);

    public:
        CIOleUILinkContainer(LPPAGE);
        ~CIOleUILinkContainer(void);

        BOOL FInit(void);
        BOOL IsDirty(void);

        [IOleUILinkContainer member declarations omitted]
    }
```

Listing 12-1.
Patron's IOleUILinkContainer *implementation.*

(continued)

Listing 12-1. *continued*

IUILINK.CPP

```
/*
 * Patron Chapter 12
 *
 * Implementation of an object with the IOleUILinkContainer
 * interface necessary to use the Links Dialog in OLE2UI.  This
 * is implemented as a stand-alone object with access to the CPage
 * with which its associated, primarily because it is only used
 * for the one dialog.  Therefore this object has its own IUnknown.
 * In addition, we use the Links Assistant object developed in this
 * chapter to simplify our own code.
 *
 * Copyright (c)1993 Microsoft Corporation, All Rights Reserved
 */

#include "patron.h"

CIOleUILinkContainer::CIOleUILinkContainer(LPCPage pPage)
    {
    m_cRef=0;
    m_pPage=pPage;
    m_iTenant=0;
    m_pDelIUILinks=NULL;
    m_fDirty=FALSE;
    return;
    }

CIOleUILinkContainer::~CIOleUILinkContainer(void)
    {
    if (NULL!=m_pDelIUILinks)
        m_pDelIUILinks->Release();

    return;
    }

/*
 * CIOleUILinkContainer::FInit
 *
 * Purpose:
 *  Performs initialization on the object that might fail.  In
 *  particular this creates an object of CLSID_LinksAssistant that
 *  helps in implementing this interface.
 */
```

(continued)

Listing 12-1. *continued*

```
BOOL CIOleUILinkContainer::FInit(void)
    {
    HRESULT     hr;

    hr=CoCreateInstance(CLSID_LinksAssistant, NULL
        , CLSCTX_INPROC_SERVER, IID_IOleUILinkContainer
        , (LPLPVOID)&m_pDelIUILinks);

    return SUCCEEDED(hr);
    }

STDMETHODIMP CIOleUILinkContainer::QueryInterface(REFIID riid
    , LPLPVOID ppv)
    {
    *ppv=NULL;

    if (IsEqualIID(riid, IID_IUnknown)
        || IsEqualIID(riid, IID_IOleUILinkContainer))
        {
        *ppv=(LPVOID)this;
        AddRef();
        return NOERROR;
        }

    return ResultFromScode(E_NOINTERFACE);
    }

STDMETHODIMP_(ULONG) CIOleUILinkContainer::AddRef(void)
    {
    return ++m_cRef;
    }

STDMETHODIMP_(ULONG) CIOleUILinkContainer::Release(void)
    {
    ULONG           cRefT;

    cRefT=--m_cRef;

    if (0L==m_cRef)
        delete this;

    return cRefT;
    }
```

(continued)

Listing 12-1. *continued*

```
/*
 * CIOleUILinkContainer::GetNextLink
 *
 * Purpose:
 *  Called when the Links dialog is filling its listbox.  Here we
 *  need to return a key for the first link if dwLink is zero, then
 *  return the next links if it's non-zero.
 *
 * Parameters:
 *  dwLink          DWORD last returned from this function.  Zero if
 *                  this is the first call to this function.
 *
 * Return Value:
 *  DWORD           Some value that identifies this object.  Zero
 *                  stops the sequence such that this function is
 *                  no longer called.
 */

STDMETHODIMP_(DWORD) CIOleUILinkContainer::GetNextLink(DWORD dwLink)
    {
    LPCTenant       pTenant;

    //If we're told to start the sequence, set index to zero.
    if (0L==dwLink)
        m_iTenant=0;

    /*
     * On each subsequent call, find the next linked object in
     * this document and return it.  Make sure the index is
     * incremented for the next time this function is called.
     */
    for ( ; m_iTenant < m_pPage->m_cTenants; m_iTenant++)
        {
        if (m_pPage->FTenantGet(m_iTenant, &pTenant, FALSE))
            {
            if (TENANTTYPE_LINKEDOBJECT==pTenant->TypeGet())
                {
                m_iTenant++;
                return (DWORD)pTenant;
                }
            }
        }

    //If we hit the end of list, this tells the dialog to stop.
    return 0L;
    }
```

(continued)

Listing 12-1. *continued*

```
/*
 * CIOleUILinkContainer::SetLinkUpdateOptions
 *
 * Purpose:
 *  Informs the application to call IOleLink::SetUpdateOptions for
 *  the object identified by dwLink.
 *
 * Parameters:
 *  dwLink          DWORD object identifier as returned from
 *                  GetNextLink.
 *  dwOptions       DWORD containing the new options.
 *
 * Return Value:
 *  HRESULT         Return value of IOleLink::SetUpdateOptions.
 */

STDMETHODIMP CIOleUILinkContainer::SetLinkUpdateOptions(DWORD dwLink
    , DWORD dwOptions)
    {
    LPOLELINK       pIOleLink;
    HRESULT         hr;

    if (NULL==dwLink)
        return ResultFromScode(E_FAIL);

    /*
     * Your responsibility is to call the object's
     * IOleLink::SetUpdateOptions function with dwOptions.  Simple?
     *
     * For Patron we must first get the object pointer obtainable
     * from the tenant's ObjectGet function, then QI for IOleLink.
     */

    GetObjectInterface(dwLink, IID_IOleLink, (LPLPVOID)&pIOleLink);
    hr=pIOleLink->SetUpdateOptions(dwOptions);
    pIOleLink->Release();

    m_fDirty=SUCCEEDED(hr);
    return hr;
    }

/*
 * CIOleUILinkContainer::GetLinkUpdateOptions
 *
```

(continued)

Listing 12-1. *continued*

```
 * Purpose:
 *  Requests the container to call IOleLink::GetUpdateOptions for
 *  the object identified by dwLink.
 *
 * Parameters:
 *  dwLink          DWORD identifying the object
 *  pdwOptions      LPDWORD in which to store the options.
 *
 * Return Value:
 *  HRESULT         Return value of IOleLink::GetUpdateOptions
 */

STDMETHODIMP CIOleUILinkContainer::GetLinkUpdateOptions(DWORD dwLink
    , LPDWORD pdwOptions)
    {
    LPOLELINK       pIOleLink;
    HRESULT         hr;

    if (NULL==dwLink)
        return ResultFromScode(E_FAIL);

    GetObjectInterface(dwLink, IID_IOleLink, (LPLPVOID)&pIOleLink);
    hr=pIOleLink->GetUpdateOptions(pdwOptions);
    pIOleLink->Release();

    return hr;
    }

/*
 * CIOleUILinkContainer::SetLinkSource
 *
 * Purpose:
 *  Changes the moniker to which an object is linked.
 *
 * Parameters:
 *  dwLink          DWORD identifying the object in question.
 *  pszName         LPSTR to the displayable name of the source.
 *  cchName         ULONG length of the file portion of pszName
 *  pchEaten        ULONG FAR * in which to return the number of
 *                  characters used in parsing pszDisplayName.
 *  fValidate       BOOL indicating if we're to validate that the
 *                  source exists first.
```

(continued)

Listing 12-1. *continued*

```
 *
 * Return Value:
 *  HRESULT         NOERROR if successful, E_FAIL otherwise.
 */

STDMETHODIMP CIOleUILinkContainer::SetLinkSource(DWORD dwLink
    , LPSTR pszName, ULONG cchName, ULONG FAR * pchEaten
    , BOOL fValidate)
    {
    LPCTenant       pTenant=(LPCTenant)dwLink;
    HRESULT         hr;
    LPOLELINK       pIOleLink;

    if (NULL==dwLink)
        return ResultFromScode(E_FAIL);

    //This is for use in GetLinkSource, below.
    pTenant->m_fLinkAvail=FALSE;

    GetObjectInterface(dwLink, IID_IOleLink, (LPLPVOID)&pIOleLink);
    hr=m_pDelIUILinks->SetLinkSource((DWORD)pIOleLink, pszName
        , cchName, pchEaten, fValidate);
    pIOleLink->Release();

    if (FAILED(hr))
        return hr;

    //hr will be S_FALSE if link is unavailable.
    pTenant->Repaint();
    pTenant->m_fLinkAvail=(NOERROR==hr);
    m_fDirty=TRUE;
    return NOERROR;
    }

/*
 * CIOleUILinkContainer::GetLinkSource
 *
 * Purpose:
 *  Retrieves various strings and values for this link source.
 *
 * Parameters:
 *  dwLink          DWORD identifying the object affected.
 *  ppszName        LPSTR FAR * in which to return the new source
 *                  name
 *  pcchName        ULONG FAR * in which to return the length of
 *                  pszName
```

(continued)

Listing 12-1. *continued*

```
 *  ppszFullLink     LPSTR FAR * in which to return the full name of
 *                   the class of linked object.
 *  ppszShortLink    LPSTR FAR * in which to return the short name of
 *                   the class of linked object.
 *  pfSourceAvail    BOOL FAR * in which to return if this is an
 *                   available link source.
 *  pfSelected       BOOL FAR * in which to return if this object is
 *                   currently selected in the document.  This
 *                   selects the item in the listbox for this object.
 *
 * Return Value:
 *  HRESULT          NOERROR on success, error code otherwise.
 */

STDMETHODIMP CIOleUILinkContainer::GetLinkSource(DWORD dwLink
    , LPSTR FAR *ppszName, ULONG FAR *pcchName
    , LPSTR FAR *ppszFullLink, LPSTR FAR *ppszShortLink
    , BOOL FAR *pfSourceAvail, BOOL FAR * pfSelected)
    {
    HRESULT         hr;
    LPCTenant       pTenant=(LPCTenant)dwLink;
    LPOLELINK       pIOleLink=NULL;
    LPOLEOBJECT     pIOleObject=NULL;
    LPMONIKER       pmk=NULL;
    LPMONIKER       pmkFirst=NULL;
    LPBC            pbc=NULL;

    if (NULL==dwLink)
        return ResultFromScode(E_FAIL);

    //We know what this is from SetLinkSource
    *pfSourceAvail=pTenant->m_fLinkAvail;

    if (pfSelected)
        *pfSelected=pTenant->FIsSelected();
    hr=GetObjectInterface(dwLink, IID_IOleLink
        , (LPLPVOID)&pIOleLink);

    if (FAILED(hr))
        return hr;

    hr=m_pDelIUILinks->GetLinkSource((DWORD)pIOleLink, ppszName
        , pcchName, ppszFullLink, ppszShortLink, pfSourceAvail
        , pfSelected);
```

(continued)

Listing 12-1. *continued*

```
    pIOleLink->Release();
    return hr;
    }

/*
 * CIOleUILinkContainer::OpenLinkSource
 *
 * Purpose:
 *  Asks the container to call DoVerb on this object with
 *  OLEIVERB_SHOW.
 *
 * Parameters:
 *  dwLink          DWORD identifying the linked object.
 *
 * Return Value:
 *  HRESULT         Standard.
 */

STDMETHODIMP CIOleUILinkContainer::OpenLinkSource(DWORD dwLink)
    {
    LPCTenant       pTenant=(LPCTenant)dwLink;

    pTenant->Activate(OLEIVERB_OPEN);
    return NOERROR;
    }

/*
 * CIOleUILinkContainer::UpdateLink
 *
 * Purpose:
 *  Asks the container to update the link for this object.
 *
 * Parameters:
 *  dwLink          DWORD identifying the linked object.
 *  fErrorMessage   BOOL indicating if we can show errors.
 *  fErrorAction    BOOL making no sense whatsoever.
 *
 * Return Value:
 *  HRESULT         Standard.
 */

STDMETHODIMP CIOleUILinkContainer::UpdateLink(DWORD dwLink
    , BOOL fErrorMessage, BOOL fErrorAction)
```

(continued)

Listing 12-1. *continued*

```
    {
    LPCTenant       pTenant=(LPCTenant)dwLink;
    LPOLELINK       pIOleLink;
    HRESULT         hr;

    hr=GetObjectInterface(dwLink, IID_IOleLink
        , (LPLPVOID)&pIOleLink);

    if (FAILED(hr))
        return hr;

    hr=m_pDelIUILinks->UpdateLink((DWORD)pIOleLink, fErrorMessage
        , fErrorAction);

    pTenant->Repaint();
    pTenant->m_fLinkAvail=SUCCEEDED(hr);
    pIOleLink->Release();

    if (FAILED(hr))
        {
        if (fErrorMessage)
            {
            MessageBox(m_pPage->m_hWnd, "Could not update link."
                , "Patron", MB_OK);
            }
        }
    else
        m_fDirty=TRUE;

    return hr;
    }

/*
 * CIOleUILinkContainer::CancelLink
 *
 * Purpose:
 *  Requests that the container turn this linked object into a
 *  static object.
 *
 * Parameters:
 *  dwLink          DWORD identifying the linked object.
 *
```

(continued)

Listing 12-1. *continued*

```
 * Return Value:
 *  HRESULT         Standard.
 */

STDMETHODIMP CIOleUILinkContainer::CancelLink(DWORD dwLink)
    {
    LPCTenant       pTenant=(LPCTenant)dwLink;
    LPOLELINK       pIOleLink;
    HRESULT         hr;

    hr=GetObjectInterface(dwLink, IID_IOleLink
        , (LPLPVOID)&pIOleLink);

    if (FAILED(hr))
        return hr;

    //This sets the source moniker to NULL.
    m_pDelIUILinks->CancelLink((DWORD)pIOleLink);
    pIOleLink->Release();

    //Go change this object over to a static one.
    pTenant->FConvertToStatic();

    m_fDirty=TRUE;
    return NOERROR;
    }

//PROTECTED FUNCTIONS INTERNAL TO CIOleUILinkContainer

/*
 * CIOleUILinkContainer::GetObjectInterface
 * (Protected)
 *
 * Purpose:
 *  Retrieves an interface pointer for the object identified by
 *  dwLink
 *
 * Parameters:
 *  dwLink          DWORD identifying the object
 *  riid            REFIID of the interface desired.
 *  ppv             LPLPVOID into which we return the pointer.
 *
 * Return Value:
 *  HRESULT         NOERROR on success, error code otherwise.
 */
```

(continued)

Listing 12-1. *continued*

```
STDMETHODIMP CIOleUILinkContainer::GetObjectInterface(DWORD dwLink
    , REFIID riid, LPLPVOID ppv)
    {
    LPCTenant       pTenant=(LPCTenant)dwLink;
    LPUNKNOWN       pIUnknown;
    HRESULT         hr;

    pTenant->ObjectGet((LPUNKNOWN FAR *)&pIUnknown);
    hr=pIUnknown->QueryInterface(riid, ppv);
    pIUnknown->Release();

    return hr;
    }
```

As seems typical with my code, there are a few weird things in this interface implementation. First, note the extra protected function I've added, *GetObjectInterface*, which merely obtains an interface pointer from a tenant identified by the DWORD *dwLink*. For Patron, every DWORD identifier in this interface is a pointer to a *CTenant*. Because most of what we use in *IOleUILinkContainer* is a pointer to *IOleLink*, this *GetObjectInterface* function exists to clean up the code everywhere else.

Next, because this is a stand-alone object, it maintains some of its own variables, such as *m_pPage*, a pointer to the current page from which we can obtain tenant pointers; *m_iTenant*, which is used to implement *GetNextLink* (see below); and *m_fDirty*, which is a public variable in *CIOleUILinkContainer* and operates in such a way that after invoking the Links dialog box the *CPatronDoc* code can see whether anything happened in the dialog box that would make the document dirty. This is perhaps a little inelegant, but it provides an efficient way for the document to know whether any changes were made in the dialog box.

There's also *m_pDelIUILinks*, which has to do with the other strange part of this code: the call to *CoCreateInstance* by using *CLSID_LinksAssistant*. This CLSID refers to a component object that I implemented to help me, and ultimately you, implement the *IOleUILinkContainer* interface. Essentially, it provides default implementations of most of the member functions to which we can delegate, as shown in the code in Listing 12-1. Yep, we like delegation. It makes life easy. I really made this Links Assistant object because in the rush to finish the implementation of this dialog box, the developers put a greater burden on the application than is necessary: The *IOleUILinkContainer* interface should have a member function such as *GetObjectInterface* through which it can ask the application for *IOleLink* and thus provide most of the default implementation in Links Assistant automatically. Look at the *SetUpdateOptions* and *GetUpdateOptions* functions: They call only one function of *IOleLink*, which could have easily been done in the dialog box itself. But it didn't turn out that way, so this quick component object does the job from the other side. I won't show any of the code here for this object, leaving you to explore the source code in CHAP12\LNKASSIS. To use it, you have to create entries for it in the Registration Database using the CHAP12\CHAP12.REG file.

That leaves us to look at the interesting parts of the interface. First, *GetNextLink* is an iterative function that you call in order to fill the dialog box. The first call passes a 0 in *dwLink*, meaning "Return the first linked object." What it returns is again a DWORD that all the other functions are passed to identify which object is being manipulated. *GetNextLink* returns a 0 when there are no more links. Patron is concerned only with keeping an index of the current tenant to return (*m_iTenant*), and when this function is called, it gets the tenant pointer and checks to see whether it's an embedded or a linked object by means of the function *CTenant::TypeGet.* Note that Links Assistant can't implement this function, so it simply returns an error.

SetUpdateOptions and *GetUpdateOptions,* as I said before, are simple pass-throughs to the same functions in *IOleLink.* That's exactly what Links Assistant does with the calls as well, so I didn't bother to delegate in the code in Listing 12-1.

SetLinkSource is called when the user changes the source of the link. The implementation of this function is a little complex, so most of the meat is down in the Links Assistant object. If the change was successful, we set *m_fDirty* so that the rest of the application knows. We also must remember whether this change worked for the implementation of *GetLinkSource.* We do this here with a public flag in *CTenant* called *m_fLinkAvail,* which was added to *CTenant* specifically for this interface. It's part of *CTenant* because we need to maintain one value for each object, not for the *IOleUILinkContainer* interface as a whole. With this flag, we start by assuming that the new source is not valid, but if the Links Assistant succeeds in changing the source, we can mark it as available. The reason we need to remember is exposed in *GetLinkSource,* which is called whenever the Links dialog box needs to update the list box entry for an object. *GetLinkSource* returns a flag indicating whether the link source is available, which is simply *CTenant::m_fLinkAvail,* and another flag indicating whether the object is currently selected in the container, which the application determines by calling another new function *CTenant::FIsSelected.* The rest of the information needed from *GetLinkSource* is handled by the code in Links Assistant. If you say this object is unavailable, the rightmost column of the list box entry will say *Unavail.* If you say the object is selected, that entry, as well as any others that you say are selected, will be selected when the dialog box is initially displayed. The selected flag is meaningless anytime thereafter, however.

OpenLinkSource is another way of saying "activate with OLEIVERB-_OPEN." So that's what we do. *UpdateLink* is not quite as simple: Links Assistant calls *IOleObject::IsUpToDate*, and if it returns S_FALSE, Links Assistant calls *IOleObject::Update*, which might launch servers to obtain the update. Because the presentation might have changed, we should repaint the container site as well as update the tenant's *m_fLinkAvail* according to the success of the update. If the parameter *fErrorMessage* is set, we're also responsible for displaying some meaningful error message on failure.

The last function in this interface, *CancelLink*, is meant to convert a linked object to a static object—that is, it causes the object to lose the ability to be activated, and it disconnects the object entirely from its link source. The Links Assistant disconnects the object by calling *IOleLink::SetSourceMoniker-(NULL)*, which forces the linked object to forget about its source completely, although the object still maintains any cached presentations. Mind you, we want to keep those presentations because a static object still needs something to show for itself.

Removing an object's ability to be activated is handled by yet another new function *CTenant::FConvertToStatic*, which is really a load of cheap-shot implementation because I really don't convert the object to another CLSID or anything of that nature. Instead I simply change the internally maintained type of the object to a static type:

```
BOOL CTenant::FConvertToStatic(void)
    {
    m_tType=TENANTTYPE_STATIC;
    return TRUE;
    }
```

Because all other *CTenant* functions enable or disable other actions based on this type, this change effectively makes the object appear to be static, although to OLE it's still a linked object without a source. The catch in all of this is that you must remember that this object is static when you reload it. You can save a flag in your file indicating the object's status, or you can simply test the object's status when you reload it. Patron does the latter in *CTenant::FObjectInitialize*:

```
LPOLELINK     pIOleLink;

m_tType=TENANTTYPE_EMBEDDEDOBJECT;

if (SUCCEEDED(pObj->QueryInterface(IID_IPersist
    , (LPLPVOID)&pIPersist)))
```

(continued)

```
    {
    CLSID   clsid;

    pIPersist->GetClassID(&clsid);

    if (IsEqualCLSID(clsid, CLSID_FreeMetafile)
        || IsEqualCLSID(clsid, CLSID_FreeDib))
        m_tType=TENANTTYPE_STATIC;

    pIPersist->Release();
    }

if (SUCCEEDED(pObj->QueryInterface(IID_IOleLink
    , (LPLPVOID)&pIOleLink)))
    {
    LPMONIKER   pmk;

    hr=pIOleLink->GetSourceMoniker(&pmk);

    if (FAILED(hr) || NULL==pmk)
        m_tType=TENANTTYPE_STATIC;
    else
        {
        m_tType=TENANTTYPE_LINKEDOBJECT;
        pmk->Release();
        }

    pIOleLink->Release();
    }
```

When creating or loading an object (both of which call this function), Patron assumes an object is embedded. If the object is *CLSID_FreeMetafile* or *CLSID_FreeDib*, you know it's static. Otherwise, you see whether you can get *IOleLink* from it. If so, it has the *potential* to be a link, but only if the object has a source moniker. So the application calls *IOleLink::GetSourceMoniker.* If this fails or if there is a NULL moniker (as there will be after we set the source moniker to NULL), this object is indeed a link, but it is one that we canceled, so we treat it forever as static.

So that does it for implementing the *IOleUILinkContainer* interface. Now let's see where we use it.

Invoke the Links Dialog Box

After all the work to implement *IOleUILinkContainer,* actually invoking the dialog box is rather painless. But first we need a menu item for it that should appear as *Links...* on your Edit menu. This menu item should be enabled whenever there are links in the document and disabled at all other times.

Patron handles the enabling through code in *CPatronFrame::UpdateMenus*, which calls *CPatronDoc::FQueryEnableEditLinks*, which passes through to *CPages::FQueryLinksInPage* and finally into *CPage::FQueryLinksInPage*. This function checks to see whether there are any tenants of a linked type and returns the results all the way back up to *CPatronFrame::UpdateMenus*:[6]

```
//In CPatronFrame::UpdateMenus for the Edit menu case
    ...

    if (NULL!=pDoc)
        fOK=pDoc->FQueryEnableEditLinks();
    else
        fOK=FALSE;

    EnableMenuItem(hMenu, IDM_EDITLINKS
    , (fOK) ? uTempE : uTempD);

    ...

//In PAGE.CPP
BOOL CPage::FQueryLinksInPage()
    {
    LPTENANT    pTenant;
    UINT        i;
    BOOL        fRet=FALSE;

    for (i=0; i < m_cTenants; i++)
        {
        if (FTenantGet(i, &pTenant, FALSE))
            fRet |= (pTenant->TypeGet()==TENANTTYPE_LINKEDOBJECT);
        }

    return fRet;
    }
```

I also added the Links... menu item to the right mouse button pop-up menu for the objects, and so we need to use the same function to ensure that it's enabled appropriately:

```
//In PAGEMOUS.CPP, CPage::OnRightDown
[After creating the menu but before TrackPopupMenu]
i=FQueryLinksInPage() ? MF_ENABLED : MF_DISABLED | MF_GRAYED;
EnableMenuItem(hMenu, IDM_EDITLINKS, i | MF_BYCOMMAND);
```

6. OK, so I have four functions to accomplish this, and I'm sure there are nice elegant ways to reduce the number. I never said Patron was the best way to structure a general Windows application.

Whenever the command from either menu is selected, the main window sees WM_COMMAND with IDM_EDITLINKS, which calls *CPatronDoc::FEditLinks* to invoke the dialog box:

```
BOOL CPatronDoc::FEditLinks(HWND hWndFrame)
    {
    UINT                        uRet;
    OLEUIEDITLINKS              el;
    LPCIOleUILinkContainer      pIUILinks;

    _fmemset(&el, 0, sizeof(el));
    el.cbStruct=sizeof(el);
    el.hWndOwner=hWndFrame;

    if (!m_pPG->FGetUILinkContainer(&pIUILinks))
        return FALSE;

    el.lpOleUILinkContainer=(LPOLEUILINKCONTAINER)pIUILinks;
    uRet=OleUIEditLinks((LPOLEUIEDITLINKS)&el);

    //Only the IOleUILinkContainer interface will know about dirtying.
    m_fDirty=pIUILinks->m_fDirty;

    el.lpOleUILinkContainer->Release();
    return TRUE;
    }
```

This function simply fills the OLEUIEDITLINKS structure and calls *OleUIEditLinks.* On return, it merges the *m_fDirty* flag (remember, it's marked as public) in the *CIOleUILinkContainer* object with the document's dirty flag, which, of course, is used to remind users to save the document when they attempt to close it.

This function itself obtains the instantiation of *CIOleUILinkContainer* by calling *CPages::FGetUILinkContainer* because only *CPages* knows the current page, which it maintains in its *m_pPageCur* variable. It passes this variable to the *CIOleUILinkContainer* constructor:

```
BOOL CPages::FGetUILinkContainer(LPCIOleUILinkContainer FAR *ppObj)
    {
    LPCIOleUILinkContainer  pObj;

    *ppObj=NULL;

    if (NULL==m_pPageCur)
        return FALSE;

    pObj=new CIOleUILinkContainer(m_pPageCur);
```

```
    if (NULL==pObj)
        return FALSE;

    if (!pObj->FInit())
        {
        delete pObj;
        return FALSE;
        }

    pObj->AddRef();
    *ppObj=pObj;
    return TRUE;
    }
```

With all this code in place, you can finally compile and test the Links dialog box, which will probably take a little while because you need to verify the correct behavior of all the *IOleUILinkContainer* functions. If you encounter UAEs in any of this, please note that there are a number of critical bugs in earlier releases of the OLE2UI library (and one in OLE2.DLL itself) that are not your fault. See the sidebar titled "WARNING WARNING WARNING..." earlier in this chapter.

Update Links on Loading a Document

There is one last requirement you need to fulfill for your linking container application before you can consider your application complete: You need to update any automatic links when you load them. Your container knows where there's a lot of treasure, and being paranoid that someone else might find it and steal it, your container would like to know that it's all still there. So by updating all automatic links, your container can go get current, up-to-the-minute photographs of the hoard.

A container application, when loading a document (or in Patron's case, opening a page), must check to see whether the document contains any automatic links. If so, it calls the function *OleUIUpdateLinks*. This function displays a dialog box with a progress indicator, as shown in Figure 12-6.

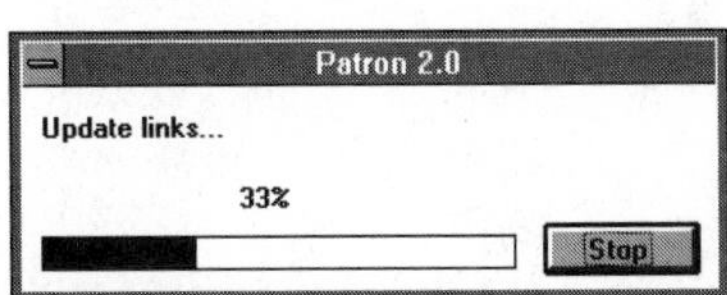

Figure 12-6.
The Update Links dialog box displayed from the OleUIUpdateLinks *function.*

The *OleUIUpdateLinks* function is a little different from other OLE2UI functions in that it doesn't take a structure pointer basically because it does not provide for customization. What it does take, however, is a pointer to an *IOleUILinkContainer* interface, an HWND of the owner window, a caption for the title bar, and a count of how many links it has to update. Let's see how Patron handles this dialog box in *CPage::FOpen* after it has loaded all tenants:

```
//In CPage::FOpen, after loading tenants from the page IStorage
...

UINT                    cLinks;
LPOLELINK               pIOleLink;
LPUNKNOWN               pIUnknown;
UINT                    uRet;
OLEUIEDITLINKS          el;
LPCIOleUILinkContainer  pIUILinks;
HWND                    hWndDoc;

...

/*
 * Update all the links in this page, showing the progress
 * indicator as it's happening.  We use the same
 * IOlUILinkContainer implementation as we do for the links
 * dialog, passing it to OleUIUpdateLinks which does everything
 * for us.
 */

//First, count the number of automatic links.
cLinks=0;

for (i=0; i < m_cTenants; i++)
    {
    if (FTenantGet(i, &pTenant, FALSE))
        {
        DWORD       dw;

        pTenant->ObjectGet(&pIUnknown);
        hr=pIUnknown->QueryInterface(IID_IOleLink
            , (LPLPVOID)&pIOleLink);
        pIUnknown->Release();

        if (FAILED(hr))
            continue;

        pIOleLink->GetUpdateOptions(&dw);
        pIOleLink->Release();
```

(continued)

```
            if (OLEUPDATE_ALWAYS==dw)
                cLinks++;
            }
        }

    //If we have any automatic links, invoke the update dialog.
    if (0==cLinks)
        return TRUE;

    //Create an IOleUILinkContainer instantiation.
    if (!m_pPG->FGetUILinkContainer(&pIUILinks))
        return TRUE;    //Guess we can't update, oh well.

    hWndDoc=GetParent(m_hWnd);
    LoadString(m_pPG->m_hInst, IDS_CAPTION, szTemp, sizeof(szTemp));

    if (!OleUIUpdateLinks(pIUILinks, hWndDoc, szTemp, cLinks))
        {
        /*
         * If updating failed, ask to show the links dialog.  NOTE:
         * OleUIPromptUser has a variable wsprintf argument list
         * after the hWnd parameter!  Use appropriate typecasting!
         */
        uRet=OleUIPromptUser(IDD_CANNOTUPDATELINK, hWndDoc
            , (LPSTR)szTemp);

        if (ID_PU_LINKS==uRet)
            {
            //Throw up the links dialog.
            _fmemset(&el, 0, sizeof(el));
            el.cbStruct=sizeof(el);
            el.hWndOwner=hWndDoc;
            el.lpOleUILinkContainer=(LPOLEUILINKCONTAINER)pIUILinks;
            OleUIEditLinks((LPOLEUIEDITLINKS)&el);
            }
        }

    m_pPG->m_fDirty=pIUILinks->m_fDirty;
    pIUILinks->Release();

    ...
```

Our first task is to count how many automatic links there are in this page (which is the document for Patron's purposes) by checking the types of all tenants in the page and incrementing the variable *cLinks* for each. If *cLinks* is zero at the end, there are no links and there's nothing we need to do. Otherwise, we instantiate the *IOleUILinkContainer* interface, using exactly the same implementation we created for the Links dialog box. This was completely intentional, but note that *OleUIUpdateLinks* will use only the *GetNextLink* and *UpdateLink* members of that interface. We also grab the window handle of the document and a caption string and finally call *OleUIUpdateLinks.*

The progress dialog box will update its thermometer bar and the displayed percentage every time it finishes updating a link. If it fails on any one of them, it will finish updating the remaining links, but it will then return FALSE instead of TRUE. A FALSE return value means the application should display the message shown in Figure 12-7, which gives the user the option of going directly to the Links dialog box to correct any problems. The OLE2UI library even has a function called *OleUIPromptUser* to create this prompt (because *MessageBox* can't do a Links... button), which returns ID_PU_LINKS if the user chooses the Links button. In response, the application invokes the Links dialog box exactly as before, passing our already created *IOleUILinkContainer* object.

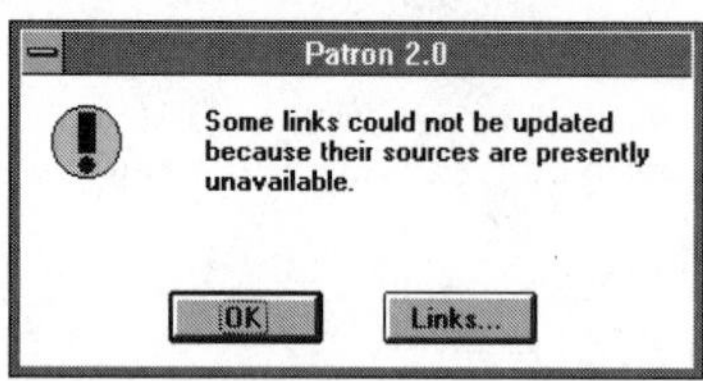

Figure 12-7.
The message displayed from OleUIPromptUser-(IDD_CANNOTUPDATELINK).

One last thing, and then you're done: Be sure to update your document's dirty flag after calling *OleUIUpdateLinks* because things might have changed that do require a save.

So now you can link to the world, no matter how complicated the moniker. If links are broken, you can repair them with the Links dialog box. Your container stays current with all automatic links by updating them as you load those objects. You want to be sure now that this last feature works and can properly invoke the Links dialog box when necessary.

In closing I'll mention one other improvement of OLE 2 over OLE 1. If you open a container document with a linked object and independently open the link source in another application, activating the linked object in the container will successfully connect to that already running source instead of launching another instance of that application, as happened in OLE 1. This is achieved through a gadget called the Running Object Table, which always knows what link sources are loaded anywhere on the system. But that's a matter for link sources to worry about, and the whole subject of link sources requires another chapter.

Summary

A link can be defined as information that refers to a source of data, where that data might live in another file managed by another application. The consumer of a link uses the information to reconnect to the link source and request updates of the data or a presentation of the data. Before Object Linking and Embedding, linking was accomplished through DDE topic and item names, but DDE had some inherent limitations as to how complex the link reference could be.

OLE 2 introduces an object class called a moniker, which manages the reference to a link source and contains code that knows how to reconnect to that source. The process of reconnection is known as binding. There are actually a number of moniker classes, of which the most important ones are file monikers, item monikers, and composite monikers. A file moniker contains a reference in the form of some pathname to a file, and binding to that file moniker means attempting to launch an application that can load that file. An item moniker contains some reference that makes sense only to some application's implementation of the *IOleItemContainer* interface, which is responsible for resolving the item name into some type of object interface pointer, such as *IOleObject.*

Binding to an item moniker in itself makes little sense because the name is meaningless outside the context of a file, so an item moniker always travels with at least a file moniker companion and might also travel with other item monikers. When more than one of these simple monikers is necessary to describe a link source, they are collected into a generic composite moniker, or simply composite. When you ask a composite moniker to bind to its source, it binds all the monikers inside it that are necessary to get to the source. If it finds an item moniker, it has to backtrack far enough to eventually find a file moniker so that it can also find an application to load the file. That same application is then responsible for providing the implementations of *IOleItemContainer.*

There are a number of OLE 2 API functions that create monikers of various sorts, such as *CreateFileMoniker,* which packages a pathname into a file moniker. *CreateFileMoniker, CreateItemMoniker,* and *CreateGenericComposite* are the three most used moniker functions.

A container that wants to support linking first has to enable itself to create linked objects, which requires only small modifications to the Insert Object dialog box and the Paste Special dialog box, and the container can optionally add a Paste Link menu command. The dialog boxes generally obtain information necessary to call either *OleCreateLinkToFile*, which creates a new linked object, or *OleCreateLinkFromData*, which creates a linked object from the information stored in a data object, such as that from the clipboard. Keeping in the best tradition of Uniform Data Transfer, the same code you write for linking from the clipboard can be used to enable linking from a drag-and-drop operation, requiring only minimal modifications to your implementation of *IDropTarget*.

A convenient feature of linked objects is that they behave exactly like embedded objects, so all your code that manages, activates, saves, and loads those objects is equally applicable and requires no modifications whatsoever. However, because the source data of a linked object does not always move with the container document, as happens for embedded objects, there is the possibility that the moniker referencing the link source will become invalid. To allow the end user to repair broken links, container applications must implement the Links dialog box, for which there is support in the OLE2UI library. This dialog box allows end users to update a linked object, cancel a link, activate the linked object, change update options, and even to change the source moniker. The Links dialog box is really a control panel for manipulating a linked object through its *IOleLink* interface.

By the same token, a container is required to automatically update links when opening a document, which is accomplished through another OLE2UI dialog box called Update Links, which displays an indicator of the percentage of links that have been updated.

To fill out its support for linking, a container application also needs to maintain a file moniker for its own document's pathname, which it sends to all objects within it, linked or embedded, by means of *IOleObject::SetMoniker*. It also needs to implement its *IOleClientSite::GetMoniker* function so that it can return the container's file moniker on request. This implementation of *GetMoniker* is critical for enabling OLE to perform some highly beneficial link tracking.

CHAPTER THIRTEEN

MONIKER BINDING AND LINK SOURCES

The history of The Valley has never lacked the dramatic element, and in this, the latest episode, it has held to its traditions. For consider the circumstances. This was to be our final season in The Valley. Six full seasons we had excavated there, and season after season had drawn a blank; we had worked for months at a stretch and found nothing, and only an excavator knows how desperately depressing that can be; we had almost made up our minds that we were beaten, and were preparing to leave The Valley and try our luck elsewhere; and then—hardly had we set a hoe to ground in our last despairing effort than we made a discovery that far exceeded our wildest dreams. Surely, never before in the whole history of excavation has a full digging season been compressed within the space of five days.

Howard Carter
from *The Discovery of the Tomb of Tutankhamen*

In the early years of the twentieth century, Egyptologists were busy scouring The Valley of the Kings in the Egyptian desert, hoping they would find previously undiscovered tombs of the pharaohs before tomb robbers plundered their rich history. The Valley had already, centuries earlier, surrendered the tombs of kings such as Rameses VI and Seti II. In the area of the tombs, Howard Carter and other archaeologists found clues that there might be other, still-hidden tombs. One such name that appeared in a few circumstances was that of boy-king Tutankhamen. By fall of 1917, Carter and his benefactor, Lord Carnavon, had decided to begin a systematic search of the rubble in the area in which they hoped to find Tutankhamen's tomb. In Carter's words, "The difficulty was to know where to begin, for mountains of rubbish thrown out by previous excavators encumbered the ground in all directions, and no sort of record had ever been kept as to which areas had been properly excavated and which had not."

Six long seasons they dug, finding nothing. All their hopes were worn out. All their work had gone for naught. All the time spent piecing together clues to figure out even where to dig had gone unrewarded. But on the morning of November 4, 1922, Carter arrived at the site to find a strange silence, a void of activity that suggested something unusual, perhaps something extraordinary. A mere 13 feet downhill from the well-known entrance to the tomb of Rameses VI his workers had uncovered a step cut in the rock. Subsequent clearing unearthed 16 steps leading down to a sealed doorway, the seal unbroken since it was applied millennia earlier. But was it the tomb he was searching for? Or was it merely the tomb of a noble? Further painstaking work revealed that Carter had indeed discovered the tomb of King Tutankhamen. The riches he found within the tomb have enabled the modern world to behold all the wonderful antiquities that had lain locked beneath the desert for over three thousand years.

In searching for the tomb, Carter had a most difficult time. While he was drawing his sketchy treasure map, he really didn't know where the treasure was. Even with his map complete, he put in many passionate years of toil trying to follow his map, searching and hoping for a tomb beneath the sand. Few of us would have such patience and perseverance—certainly not modern computer users. They simply do not want the hassle of tracking down the sources of linked objects.

Fortunately, computers are much more precise than Carter's rudimentary tools when creating and following treasure maps to the source of a link. In the best traditions of object-oriented programming, if you want a map to some treasure, you simply ask the treasure to make you one. That's precisely what happens with a link source. The source is responsible for providing monikers that other applications can use to reconnect to that source by means of the binding process. Even better, a treasure map is an object (that is, a moniker), so instead of working hard to follow the map, we simply ask the map to follow itself to the treasure. We've seen in the previous chapter how a container application makes use of a moniker in a linked object. Now we can investigate the means by which an application creates a map and how the application must structure itself to allow OLE to follow that map.

So this chapter is first about the mechanisms of moniker creation and binding, which reveal to us exactly what we have to do in a source application to support the binding process. We first look at the mechanisms of binding a simple file moniker and show the implications in modifications to Cosmo that now becomes a link source. Cosmo provides a file moniker so that containers can create a linked object that shows the entire figure contained one of Cosmo's files, because Cosmo does not have any concept of breaking a file into smaller pieces.

The chapter also deals with binding to composite monikers such as *File!Item!Item*, using Patron as an example. Wait a minute, you might be saying, Patron is a container. How can it become a link source? In this chapter, we'll enable Patron to provide links to embedded objects that it contains—that is, other containers can then link to Patron, which will render the embedded object's interface pointers. This process will involve adding a number of server-like features to Patron, blurring the distinctions between container and server. Both its document and its page objects—until now simply regular old C++ classes—become Windows Objects with at least one interface each. If you think this will be a nontrivial piece of work, you're right, but it's certainly less work than digging through rubble for six years. And to other applications, the embedded treasures you hold are in some ways as valuable as those of an Egyptian pharaoh.

Moniker Binding Mechanisms

In writing this book, I spent plenty of time trying to figure out what I was supposed to do with monikers and why I was doing such things in the first place. As I'm sure you too have done before, I was mindlessly cutting and pasting sample code. Writing the code for this chapter and Chapter 12 has helped me to understand exactly how all this works and why I had to add the code I did. In this section, I hope to explain the mechanisms of moniker binding in enough detail so that you too will understand why we need the code we add to Cosmo and Patron.

We start by examining how a source application provides a simple file moniker and how OLE binds that moniker to get back at the source later. A container application, as we saw in Chapter 12, would obtain this moniker by creating a linked object through the Insert Object dialog box or the Paste Link command.

After we understand how file moniker binding is accomplished, we can look at a more complex example in which the source moniker is a composite moniker with one file and one item moniker in the composite. To bind to this composite, we need to bind to both file and item monikers.

We can extend the example one step further to one in which there are two item monikers and a file moniker. A composite moniker potentially can contain any number of item monikers in a row. Following the process for one item and two items shows how the binding process works for any number of items. Proof by induction, no less.

A Simple Linked Object: Single File Moniker

Let's start with a simple linked object in a container application, where that linked object manages a single file moniker, which holds the pathname C:\COSMO\TOASTED\BAGEL.COS. The linked object obtained this file moniker either from the Insert Object dialog box (which can link only to entire files) or from the Paste Link command.

At some point in the lifetime of the linked object, some event will cause a call to its *IOleObject::DoVerb* function. If the server is not already running, somehow OLE (in its role as the default handler) has to get the server running, have the server load the source file, and then ask the server for an *IOleObject* pointer (to the now *running* object) to which OLE can delegate *DoVerb.* In short, OLE has to follow the moniker's treasure map to get to the object's *IOleObject* interface pointer.

Nothing is easier. OLE simply calls *IMoniker::BindToObject(IID_IOleObject...)* to get the pointer, where the moniker in question is the one stored in the linked object. Remember that linked objects actually manage both an absolute moniker and a relative moniker (as to the paths they contain) so that if *BindToObject* on the absolute one fails, it can try *BindToObject* on the relative one. In this simple case, let's look at where OLE calls *BindToObject* on the absolute file moniker that contains the filename C:\COSMO\TOASTED\BAGEL.COS.

The file moniker's *BindToObject* looks at the filename it contains and tries to associate the file with an application that might be able to load that file. It first does so by calling *GetClassFile* on that filename. *GetClassFile* first attempts to call *StgOpenStorage* and *ReadClassStg,* which tries to retrieve the CLSID previously written to a compound file using *WriteClassStg.* (This is a good example of how structured storage allows anyone to get a lot of information about a file without having to know who wrote it.) If this works, *GetClassFile* had an easy life and can simply return that CLSID.

If the file is not a compound file or if there is no CLSID written to it, *GetClassFile* attempts to find the entry in the Registration Database for the file's extension where that entry has the form,

```
<extension> = <ProgID>
```

as in *.cos* = *Cosmo2Figure.* Using the *ProgID, GetClassFile* then attempts to look up the CLSID for that *ProgID,* assuming an entry exists in the following form:

```
<ProgID>
    CLSID = {...}
```

If this still doesn't return a CLSID, *GetClassFile* fails and the file moniker's *BindToObject* fails. Otherwise, the file moniker's *BindToObject* calls *CoCreateInstance* for a local server, with that CLSID asking for an *IPersistFile* interface in return.

This means that any application that sources a file moniker by itself should expect to be launched with *-Embedding* on the command line, at which time it can create and register a class factory. That class factory will be asked to create an object and return an *IPersistFile* interface. In all, this process is the same as for any standard server, as we saw in Chapter 10. It is even the same in that the application must *not* show its window initially when *-Embedding* is present. Obviously, if any part of this process fails in the source application, the file moniker's call to *CoCreateInstance* fails, and *BindToObject* fails.

Otherwise, the file moniker has an *IPersistFile* interface and now calls *IPersistFile::Load*, passing the pathname that the moniker contains, such as C:\COSMO\TOASTED\BAGEL.COS. This simply asks the source application to reload that file. Again, if the source fails to load it, the binding fails. And if failure occurs, the linked object will attempt to bind to the relative moniker, which starts this whole process over again but eventually passes a relative pathname to *Load* instead.

So now we have a running (but hidden) server that has loaded the source file referenced by the file moniker. But are we finished? Nope. Remember that all this binding started with a linked object that wanted an *IOleObject* pointer to which it could delegate a *DoVerb* call, so somehow the file moniker has to get from the *IPersistFile* interface pointer it has now to an *IOleObject* interface.

In this case, the course is clear: *QueryInterface.* When a source provides a single file moniker as the source of a link, the OLE 2 Design Specification states that the server's (source's) object on which *IPersistFile* was implemented must be the same compound document object that implements *IOleObject, IPersistStorage,* and *IDataObject.* The data that makes up the object is all the data in the document. Therefore, in the source, we have an object attached to a document that appears to the outside world, as that shown in Figure 13-1 on the next page.

So the file moniker will call *IPersistFile::QueryInterface(IID_IOleObject...)*, followed by *IPersistFile::Release.* (The file moniker has no use for *IPersistFile* anymore.) If *QueryInterface* works, the file moniker returns the *IOleObject* pointer to the linked object, which then has a pointer to which it delegates the container's original call to *DoVerb.* This, of course, causes the server to perform its designated task, a task such as showing its editing window.

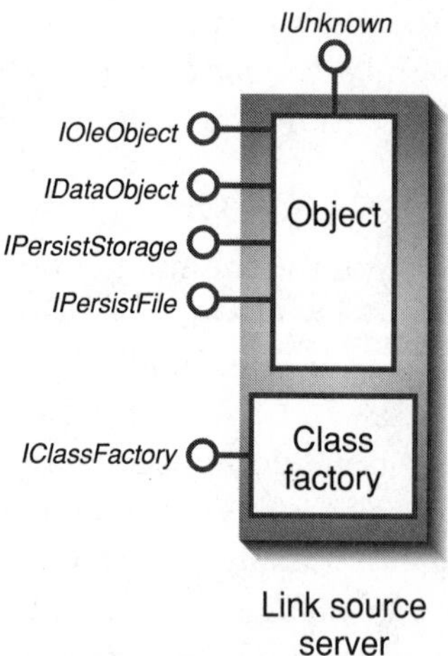

Figure 13-1.
A link source that is an entire document appears with the IOleObject, IPersistStorage, IDataObject, *and* IPersistFile *interfaces. The server implements a class factory object with the* IClassFactory *interface, as it does for embedded objects. Note that* IPersistStorage *is not used when this object is used for linking.*

Map followed, treasure found. We can see from all this that a simple server that describes a link source with a file moniker must essentially add the *IPersistFile* interface to whatever object could already be embedded. In fact, this is pretty much the only modifications necessary to support linking if your application already supports embedding, as we'll see with Cosmo.

Note that in servicing a linked object, the server's *IOleObject::SetHostNames* is never called—that is, the default handler does not delegate this call to the server for a linked object as it does for an embedded object. Therefore, the server never changes its user interface to reflect an embedded object editing session. Instead, the server simply appears as if the user had run it from Program Manager. The user can then make whatever changes are desired, but the user must manually save the server file and close the server when finished to move the object back into the loaded state.

A Linked Object with a Composite *File!Item* Moniker

It will not always be the case that the source data for a linked object can be described simply with a file moniker. Take, for example, a spreadsheet, in which any range of cells within the entire spreadsheet can be the source of an individual linked object, as shown in Figure 13-2. To establish a link to a range

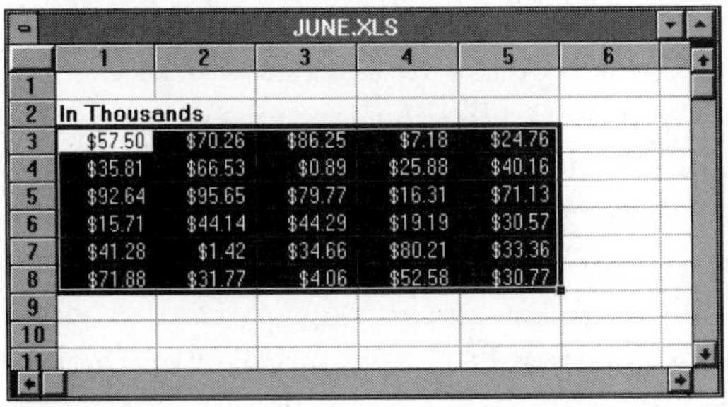

JUNE.XLS

	1	2	3	4	5	6
1						
2	In Thousands					
3	$57.50	$70.26	$86.25	$7.18	$24.76	
4	$35.81	$66.53	$0.89	$25.88	$40.16	
5	$92.64	$95.65	$79.77	$16.31	$71.13	
6	$15.71	$44.14	$44.29	$19.19	$30.57	
7	$41.28	$1.42	$34.66	$80.21	$33.36	
8	$71.88	$31.77	$4.06	$52.58	$30.77	
9						
10						
11						

Figure 13-2.
A spreadsheet has cell ranges, any of which can be the source of a linked object.

of cells in the spreadsheet, we therefore need a moniker that describes both the file and the range of cells. That's why we have composite monikers.

All of this starts out when the end user of the spreadsheet application selects a range of cells and *copies*—not *cuts*—them to the clipboard. (Cutting would delete the cells from the spreadsheet, so there would be nothing to link to.) Presumably, the application will first copy embedded object data and then will copy other formats, such as metafiles and plain text. To support linking, it now also needs to copy the CF_LINKSOURCE and CF_LINKSRCDESCRIPTOR formats. The latter format is nearly the same structure as CF_OBJECTDESCRIPTOR except that it applies to CF_LINKSOURCE instead of to CF_EMBEDSOURCE. CF_LINKSOURCE contains whatever moniker identifies the source, such as a composite moniker created with the following code:

```
LPMONIKER     pmkFile;
LPMONIKER     pmkRange;
LPMONIKER     pmkComp;

//Note:  Production code should check for error returns.
CreateFileMoniker(pszCurrentFile, &pmkFile);
CreateItemMoniker("!", pszRange, &pmkItem);
CreateGenericComposite(pmkFile, pmkItem, &pmkComp);
pmkItem->Release();
pmkFile->Release();

//pmkComp now has the composite moniker File!Item
```

In this example, *pszCurrentFile* is the filename in which the cell range exists—let's say it's C:\SALES\1993\JUNE.XLS. If a server does not yet have a filename, it will not copy link source information because there is no definite source yet. But if there is a filename, we can create a simple file moniker for it.

The *pszRange* variable then is a string that defines the selection being copied, such as "R1C3:R5C8". We pass this string to *CreateItemMoniker* along with a delimiter string that will serve to separate the filename from the range name when we pack this item moniker into a composite with the file moniker. The delimiter must be a character not used in the item name. A "!" is common because it's hardly ever used in filenames and has a sordid history in DDE.

With the file and item monikers, we can now create the composite, in which the file moniker is on the left and the item moniker on the right, using *CreateGenericComposite.* This function will use *AddRef* on both file and item monikers, so be sure to use *Release* on your holds on them when you no longer need them. This composite moniker is what the server places on the clipboard (using a data object, of course) in the CF_LINKSOURCE format. Note that when a server calls *OleSetClipboard* with a data object that knows CF_LINKSOURCE, it generates the OLE 1 format of *ObjectLink* to enable linking with OLE 1 containers.

Now as far as a container and linked objects are concerned, this link looks no different from any other link—it's merely a linked object that we know manages some sort of moniker. Without knowing any better, the container will, at some point, call the linked object's *IOleObject::DoVerb.* After the linked object heaves a heavy sigh and utters "Here we go again...," it reluctantly calls *IMoniker::BindToObject,* again asking for *IOleObject.* It treats this moniker *no* differently. If the linked object gets a pointer back, it again delegates the *DoVerb* call.

So again, the linked object has asked whatever moniker it manages to follow its own treasure map and return us the goodies. This time, we have a composite moniker, which itself knows that it has a file moniker and an item moniker within it. The composite's *BindToObject* then starts by calling the *item* moniker's *BindToObject,* asking for the same interface that was requested from the composite, in this case *IOleObject.*

Remember that composite binding happens from right to left, following the map backward from the treasure to our current location so that we avoid having to execute any extra steps on the map. So if binding to the rightmost item moniker works, there's no reason to bind to anything to the left of it. But an item moniker is *always* dependent on the moniker to its left, whereas a file moniker is not. So when the composite binds to the item moniker, the item moniker in turn asks the file moniker to its left to bind (using *BindToObject*) to satisfy the item's dependency.

Earlier we saw that when a linked object asks a file moniker to bind, it asks the moniker to return an *IOleObject* pointer. In this example, the agent asking the file moniker to bind is an item moniker and not the linked. The item moniker is not interested in the *IOleObject* pointer; instead, it asks the file moniker to bind and return an *IOleItemContainer* pointer that can resolve the name of the item into an *IOleObject* pointer to return to the linked object.

This means that as a server, the object on which you implement *IPersistFile*—independent of everything else it does—must also support the *IOleItemContainer* interface.

Specifically, after the item moniker receives this interface back from the file moniker's *BindToObject*, it then calls *IOleItemContainer::GetObject*, passing the string name of the item stored in the item moniker and the interface it wants in return—in this case, *IOleObject*. The string is exactly what the source application passed to *CreateItemMoniker*. (The delimiter is not passed because *GetObject* does not need it.) The source's implementation of *GetObject* must somehow translate this name into an interface pointer, as requested by the caller. This process will generally require some sort of parsing.

This object is considered a piece of the document but is not the whole document—that is, the object returned is *not* the same one on which *IOleItemContainer* is implemented. For example, the spreadsheet application which has by now loaded C:\SALES\1993\JUNE.XLS takes the name "R1C3:R5C8," and from *GetObject*, it locates those cells and creates a compound document object around them, complete with *IOleObject*, *IDataObject*, and *IPersistStorage*.

So we can see that a different structure is required in the source application, as shown in Figure 13-3. Instead of simply having a class factory and a

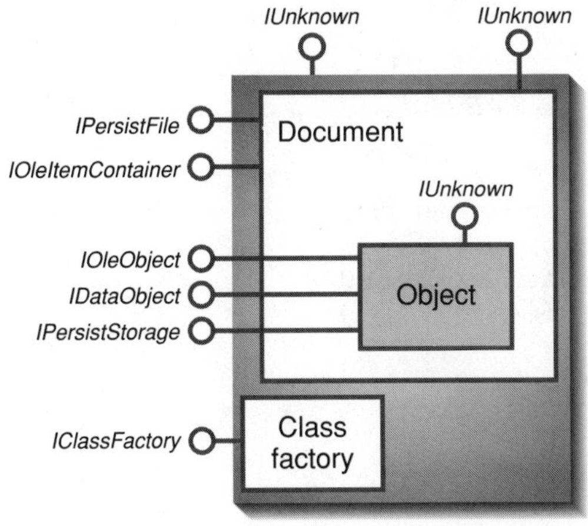

Figure 13-3.
A server that supports linking to ranges within a document appears different from one that links only to the whole document, primarily because of the relationship between the linked ranged themselves and the document that now must support the IOleItemContainer *interface.*

linked object, it now has a class factory, a document object with *IPersistFile* and *IOleItemContainer*, and compound document objects within that document with the standard object interfaces.

So the linked object will receive back its *IOleObject* pointer and delegate *DoVerb*, which causes the server to show itself as usual. The server must also ensure that the data in the document to which this object applies is initially selected when the document becomes visible. The end user can make changes to the whole file and must manually save the file and close the server to transition the object from the running state back to loaded. Note that only changes made to the range attached to the linked object causes the server to send *OnDataChange* notifications because only that range is visible in the container's linked object. This chapter, however, does not show any code that demonstrates this type of notification.

Binding a Composite *File!Item!Item!Item!Item...* Moniker

As I stated in Chapter 12, OLE 1 and DDE could use only file or document names and a single item name to identify the source of the data. I also said that monikers went beyond that, so I imagine you would like some proof.

A composite moniker, as we have seen, can itself contain many smaller monikers. Creating a more composite moniker with two item names simply means more calls to *CreateGenericComposite*:

```
LPMONIKER     pmkFile;
LPMONIKER     pmkItem1;
LPMONIKER     pmkItem2;
LPMONIKER     pmkComp0;
LPMONIKER     pmkComp;

//Note:  Production code should check for error returns.
CreateFileMoniker(pszFile, &pmkFile);
CreateItemMoniker("!", pszItem1, &pmkItem1);
CreateItemMoniker("!", pszItem2, &pmkItem2);

CreateGenericComposite(pmkFile, pmkItem1, &pmkComp0);
CreateGenericComposite(pmkComp0, pmkItem2, &pmkComp);

pmkComp0->Release();
pmkItem2->Release();
pmkItem1->Release();
pmkFile->Release();

//pmkComp now has the composite moniker File!Item1!Item2
```

This code first creates the *File!Item1* moniker in *pmkComp0* and then creates *pmkComp* by appending *pmkItem2* to the end of *pmkComp0* to produce *File!Item1!Item2* (and of course we release all the intermediates).

Again, we'll eventually come to a point where a linked object tells the composite treasure map to bind to the object, asking for an *IOleObject* pointer. Like all other good composites, the moniker will begin binding its internal components from right to left. In this case, binding starts with the Item2 moniker. As we've seen, all item monikers are dependent on the moniker to their left, so Item2's *BindToObject* will always call *BindToObject* on the moniker to its left, asking for an *IOleItemContainer* interface.

Because Item1, the moniker to the left of Item2 in this example, is itself an item moniker, it recursively calls the moniker to *its* left, *again* asking for an *IOleItemContainer* pointer. The object implementing this interface for Item2 will generally be a completely different object than whatever implements the same interface for *Item1*. Be careful not to confuse the fact that there are two objects here but both have *IOleItemContainer* interfaces.

When Item1 calls *BindToObject(IID_IOleItemContainer)* to the moniker to its left, it ends up talking to the file moniker. We saw this interaction between an item moniker and a file moniker in the last section: The item moniker gets its interface pointer and then calls (the document's) *IOleItemContainer::GetObject* to resolve its item name into another interface pointer.

But here's the difference: Remember that Item2 asked Item1's *BindToObject* to itself return an *IOleItemContainer* interface. That means that when Item1 calls the document's *IOleItemContainer::GetObject* it asks for *another IOleItemContainer* interface pointer in return. Funky! But that's what Item1 was asked to do, so it blindly follows instructions like a good little lemming and does it. If the document's *GetObject* can resolve the name of Item1 into this second *IOleItemContainer* pointer, Item2 finally asks the second one's *GetObject* to resolve the name in Item2 into an *IOleObject* pointer, which it returns to the composite who returns it to the linked object, which then delegates the *DoVerb* call that started this whole mess.

Whew! Let's stop for a minute to catch our collective breath. (Huffing and Panting.)

What we can learn from this complex example is that in general, any file moniker requires some document object with an *IPersistFile* interface to resolve the filename into some other interface pointer. Any item moniker requires an *IOleItemContainer* interface to resolve its item name into an interface pointer. When these are mixed together in a composite moniker, the rightmost item moniker always asks the moniker to its left to bind to an *IOleItemContainer* interface, which it then asks to resolve the item name into whatever interface pointer was requested. Each item moniker recursively calls *BindToObject(IID_IOleItemContainer)* to the moniker to its left, again asking *IOleItemContainer::GetObject* for another *IOleItemContainer* interface, ad nauseam. This all stops, of course, when we reach the Pepto Bismol file moniker, which ends our bout with indigestion by not having any dependencies on the left.

Knowing these two facts tells us much of what we have to do to our source to support linking. In the container Patron, we'll make a source of links to embedded objects that will provide a three-part composite moniker for enabling linking to an embedded object. The rightmost item moniker will be the name of the tenant in which the object lives. The tenant itself needs to know what page it lives on, and therefore the second (middle) item moniker is the name of the page in which the linked tenant sits. Of course, we need to know the document in which this page lives, so the leftmost part of the composite moniker will be a file moniker created from the pathname of the current document. The structure that outsiders will see in Patron is shown in Figure 13-4.

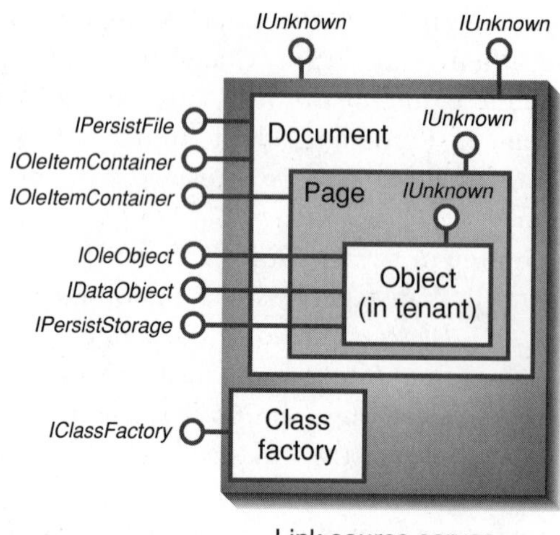

Figure 13-4.
The appearance of Patron as a link source for embedded objects it contains on a page.

Bind Contexts

I want to mention these briefly so that you are not too confused when you see them come up in some interface member functions. A bind context is an object that implements the *IBindCtx* interface. A bind context is passed through a binding process that affects all the monikers involved. It allows each moniker to store information relevant to this particular binding, or context. Primarily it's used to store variables that tell a moniker if it's already been bound in this context so that it can eliminate redundant work as well as stop infinite loops caused by circular linking. In other words, it's possible in OLE 2 to have a chain of links in which the original source eventually becomes a consumer of a linked object that is dependent on that original source. Thus that application is circularly linked to itself. Monikers use the bind context to prevent eternal binding in such circumstances.

As far as an application is concerned, you won't see or use bind contexts much. At most you might need to create one temporarily by using *CreateBindCtx* because you have to pass it to another function—for example, *MkParseDisplayName.* Some interface member functions that we'll see later in this chapter receive a pointer to an *IBindCtx* (type LPBC or LPBINDCTX) as a parameter in case those functions are interested.

The Running Object Table

Before we get into implementation details, we need to look at another new OLE 2 mechanism that solves a different problem in linking. All the preceding discussion assumes that the link source was not running at the time of binding. But what if it *is* running? How then do we connect?

OLE 2 solves this little problem with an object called the *running object table,* which implements an interface called *IRunningObjectTable.* Mysterious, huh? This object tracks all link sources that are *currently* running in servers. At any time, you can ask the running object table whether a link source with a given moniker is currently running or you can ask it to enumerate the monikers for all running objects. You can obtain the *IRunningObjectTable* pointer to this object by calling *GetRunningObjectTable.* Be sure to call *Release* through that pointer when you are finished with it, as always.

All link sources, be they containers or servers, are responsible for registering monikers for their running objects in the running object table by passing the appropriate monikers to *IRunningObjectTable::Register.* Other pieces of code that have a moniker can check to see whether whatever that moniker references is running by calling *IRunningObjectTable::IsRunning.* If the object is running, they can call *IRunningObjectTable::GetObject* to retrieve another interface pointer, which might cause some binding to happen to the object.

When a link source closes anything that it previously registered, it then calls *IRunningObjectTable::Revoke,* passing an identifier that *Register* returned to it earlier. So only when the object is running will its moniker be held in the running object table and available for others to connect to. OLE specifically uses this approach when a container loads a document that contains linked objects. When the container calls *OleLoad,* OLE2.DLL reads the linked object's moniker from storage and checks to see whether the linked object is running by calling *IsRunning.* If it is, OLE2.DLL automatically reconnects the container's site with that linked object in such a way that OLE2.DLL can request an immediate update as well as reflect additional changes in the object as modifications are made in the server.

One case that is not addressed by the running object table is the one in which the container has already loaded linked objects at the time a server loads the source of those links. Under OLE 2, those linked objects are not automatically reconnected to that running server, even though the server registers the source monikers as running. It requires that the container activates the object at which time the connection is reestablished. The problem is that under OLE 2 the container has no idea when to activate an object for this purpose. The OLE 2 Design Specification describes something called the *Alert Object Table* in which loaded linked objects would be registered as waiting for their sources to appear in such a way that when the running object table registered the moniker, the reconnection would happen automatically. However, the alert object table is not implemented in OLE 2, so you do not currently have the benefit of such automatic reconnection. It will be added in the future.

The code we'll see in this chapter shows the few instances in which your application will actually need to use the running object table by calling *Register* and *Revoke.* Generally, we will not be using the other member functions. Besides being useful for internal uses, the additional member functions exist to accommodate much more sophisticated uses of the running object table, which far exceed what we can cover in this book.

A Simple Link Source: Cosmo

Let's see some of this talk in action! For this chapter, I have modified the Cosmo application to be a link source for objects made up of the entire contents of a Cosmo document (that is, one figure). It doesn't make sense to try linking to anything else because Cosmo does not address individual lines. The changes required to support linking are not that extensive, as the following steps indicate:

1. When opening a file, create a file moniker and register it with the running object table. Remember to revoke the moniker from the table when closing the document. Also re-create and reregister the file moniker when the document is renamed, which also means that you need to send the *OnRename* notification to any advise sinks obtained through *IOleObject::Advise.*
2. Register the CF_LINKSOURCE and CF_LINKSRCDESCRIPTOR formats and include them with data you copy to the clipboard, but not when you perform a Cut. The same data object can apply to a drag-and-drop operation in which you want to be sure you don't delete data on a drag-and-drop link.
3. Implement the *IPersistFile* interface to load the document on request, a process that includes registering it in the running object table as if the end user had opened it.
4. Implement *IOleObject::SetMoniker* and *IOleObject::GetMoniker.*

We'll keep the tradition we've established in previous chapters by taking each step in turn, seeing how we can compile and test something after each.

NOTE: The release of the OLE libraries version 2.01 (Fall 1993) requires that DLL servers and object handlers that support linking-to-embedding themselves must also implement (or at least expose) two additional interfaces, *IRunnableObject,* and *IExternalConnection,* to allow such linking to work properly. This book does not give an example of implementing these interfaces in a DLL server such as Polyline, and you will not find a revision of Polyline for this chapter because this book was going into print before these libraries were completed. Please refer to the OLE 2.01 SDK documentation for more information on these interfaces and the considerations for linking under OLE 2.01.

Create, Register, and Revoke a File Moniker

For managing a file moniker and its registration in the running object table, Cosmo has added two variables to its *CCosmoDoc* class:

```
LPMONIKER               m_pMoniker;
DWORD                   m_dwRegROT;
```

m_pIMoniker will hold a moniker for the currently loaded file, and *m_dwRegROT* will hold the last key from *IRunningObjectTable::Register.* Initially set the moniker to NULL and the key to zero, as usual.

You generally need only to have a file moniker on hand when you have a known filename, so if you are operating on a new, untitled file you don't need to register anything. If you load a document from a known file or if you save a new document to a known filename, you must then create and register the moniker. For this purpose, the *CCosmoDoc* class now overrides the default *CDocument::Rename* function in CLASSLIB:

```
void CCosmoDoc::Rename(LPSTR pszFile)
    {
    LPMONIKER   pmk;

    //We don't need to change the base class, just augment...
    CDocument::Rename(pszFile);

    /*
     * Get rid of the old moniker. The OldStd function
     * sets the key to zero.
     */
    if (0L!=m_dwRegROT)
        OleStdRevokeAsRunning(&m_dwRegROT);

    if (NULL!=m_pMoniker)
        {
        m_pMoniker->Release();
        m_pMoniker=NULL;
        }

    if (NULL!=pszFile)
        {
        CreateFileMoniker(pszFile, &pmk);

        if (NULL!=pmk)
            {
            m_pMoniker=pmk;      //pmk AddRef'd in CreateFileMoniker
            OleStdRegisterAsRunning((LPUNKNOWN)m_pFigure, m_pMoniker
                , &m_dwRegROT);

            m_pFigure->SendAdvise(OBJECTCODE_RENAMED);
            }
        }

    return;
    }
```

If, on entry to this function, we already have a registered moniker, *m_dwRegROT* is nonzero. If so, we want to revoke it from the running object table because we no longer have that file loaded. The preceding code calls the function *OleStdRevokeAsRunning* in the OLE2UI library, which is a convenient way of saying the following:

```
//What little functions like OleStdRevokeAsRunning do
LPRUNNINGOBJECTTABLE    pROT;

GetRunningObjectTable(0, &pROT);
pROT->Revoke(dwRegROT);
pROT->Release()=RegROT=0;
```

Of course, it would be just as easy to call these three functions yourself. Anyway, after revoking the previously registered moniker, we also want to release any previously held moniker so that we can get to the part that actually creates the moniker in the first place. In the preceding code from Cosmo, we create a file moniker with *CreateFileMoniker* only if we have a non-NULL filename—that is, if we have a known file. *CreateFileMoniker*, as a function that returns a new pointer to an interface, calls *AddRef* on the moniker before returning, so we don't need to call *AddRef* another time before copying it into a permanent variable such as *m_pMoniker*. With this new moniker, we can then register it in the running object table by calling *OleStdRegisterAsRunning*, also in the OLE2UI library. This function takes three parameters: an IUnknown pointer identifying the object, a moniker, and a pointer to the DWORD in which to return the key:

```
//OleStdRegisterAsRunning
LPRUNNINGOBJECTTABLE    pROT;

GetRunningObjectTable(0, &pROT);

if (0!=*pdwRegROT)
    pROT->Revoke(*pdwRegROT);

pROT->Register(NULL, pIUnknown, pMoniker, pdwRegROT);
pROT->Release();
```

OleStdRegisterAsRunning conveniently revokes any previously registered moniker if you pass the previous key. I do not use this feature in Cosmo merely to be explicit about what's actually happening with the registration.

Now whenever anyone else in the system attempts to bind to a moniker, the moniker will call *IRunningObjectTable::IsRunning* to first check whether the object is already running. If it is, the moniker merely has to ask the running object table for the *IUnknown* registered for that moniker (*IRunningObjectTable::GetObject*) and call *QueryInterface* to obtain the correct interface pointer to return to whatever asked the moniker to bind in the first place. You can see why this mechanism is much more efficient than launching an application.

The other interesting thing in all this code is the little call to *CFigure::SendAdvise* with OBJECTCODE_RENAMED. This ends up sending an *OnRename* notification:

```
//A case in CFigure::SendAdvise, FIGURE.CPP
case OBJECTCODE_RENAMED:
    //Update the moniker copy we have.
    m_pMoniker=m_pDoc->m_pMoniker;

    if (NULL!=m_pIOleAdviseHolder)
        m_pIOleAdviseHolder->SendOnRename(m_pMoniker);

    break;
```

Besides notifying interested advise sinks, the figure that we use to implement the object in Cosmo holds a copy of the moniker for use in implementing *IOleObject::GetMoniker* later. Note that because this object has a one-to-one association to the document it lives in and because the object lifetime is defined by the document, there's no reason to call *AddRef* on the copy of the moniker we keep in *CFigure::m_pMoniker*. It's simply one of those reference counting optimizations.

The *OnRename* notification is really important only for the default handler's implementation of a linked object. It uses this notification to update its own internally held moniker in such a way that it always has the latest information.

Although all this code will not produce any useful results, it's a good idea to compile and test it to make sure that you are handling your monikers correctly, creating them whenever your filename changes on File/New, File/Open, or File/Save As, registering and revoking them properly, and sending *OnRename* notifications. Be sure that you are releasing the monikers you create when you no longer need them. They are objects, and they do occupy memory.

Provide Link Source Formats in Data Transfer

With the simple addition of CF_LINKSOURCE and CF_LINKSRCDESCRIPTOR formats to our data transfer objects, we enable all other applications to link to our object. First, we need to register both these formats and save those registered values:

```
m_cfLinkSource=RegisterClipboardFormat(CF_LINKSOURCE);
m_cfLinkSrcDescriptor=RegisterClipboardFormat
    (CF_LINKSRCDESCRIPTOR);
```

As mentioned in Chapter 12, CF_LINKSOURCE is a moniker serialized to a stream, a task that the moniker handles itself because *IMoniker* derives from *IPersistStream.* CF_LINKSRCDESCRIPTOR is the same format as CF_OBJECTDESCRIPTOR but applies to the object identified in CF_LINKSOURCE. CF_OBJECTDESCRIPTOR, if you remember, applies to the object identified with CF_EMBEDSOURCE. Therefore, the description information for linked and embedded objects can be different.

To support these additional formats, I added them to the list of formats supported in *CCosmoDoc::TransferObjectCreate.* When Cosmo wants to place the formats in the data transfer object, it calls *CCosmoDoc::FRenderMedium* which handles them with the following code:

```
BOOL CCosmoDoc::FRenderMedium(UINT cf, LPSTGMEDIUM pSTM)
    {
    [Case for CF_EMBEDSOURCE]

    /*
     * CF_OBJECTDESCRIPTOR and CF_LINKSRCDESCRIPTOR are the same
     * formats, but only copy link source if we have a moniker.
     */
    if (cf==m_cfLinkSrcDescriptor && NULL==m_pMoniker)
        return FALSE;

    if (cf==m_cfObjectDescriptor || cf==m_cfLinkSrcDescriptor)
        {
        SIZEL   szl, szlT;
        POINTL  ptl;
        RECT    rc;
        LPSTR   psz=NULL;

        m_pPL->SizeGet(&rc);
        SETSIZEL(szlT, rc.right, rc.bottom);
        XformSizeInPixelsToHimetric(NULL, &szlT, &szl);

        SETPOINTL(ptl, 0, 0);

        //Include the moniker display name now, if we have one.
        if (m_pMoniker)
            {
            LPBC    pbc;

            CreateBindCtx(0, (LPBC FAR*)&pbc);
            m_pMoniker->GetDisplayName(pbc, NULL, &psz);
            pbc->Release();
            }
```

(continued)

```
        pSTM->hGlobal=OleStdGetObjectDescriptorData
            (CLSID_Cosmo2Figure, DVASPECT_CONTENT, szl, ptl
            , OLEMISC_RECOMPOSEONRESIZE, PSZ(IDS_OBJECTDESCRIPTION)
            , psz);

        pSTM->tymed=TYMED_HGLOBAL;
        return (NULL!=pSTM->hGlobal);
        }

    if (cf==m_cfLinkSource)
        {
        if (NULL!=m_pMoniker)
            {
            FORMATETC   fe;
            HRESULT     hr;

            pSTM->tymed=TYMED_NULL;
            SETDefFormatEtc(fe, cf, TYMED_ISTREAM);
            hr=OleStdGetLinkSourceData(m_pMoniker
                , (LPCLSID)&CLSID_Cosmo2Figure, &fe, pSTM);

            return SUCCEEDED(hr);
            }
        }

    return FALSE;
    }
```

Note that we don't bother copying either format when we don't have a moniker—you can't get something from nothing. In addition, CF_LINKSRCDESCRIPTOR shares the same code with CF_OBJECT-DESCRIPTOR, and to both we now include that the display name of the moniker. The display name is simply a user-readable text string of the entire moniker. If the moniker is a composite, the display name is the concatenation of the strings in each simple moniker. Also, the function *CreateBindCtx* is only required to call *IMoniker::GetDisplayName.* If you are interested in bind contexts, refer to the OLE 2 SDK for more details.

The OLE2UI library has a convenient function, *OleStdGetLinkSource-Data,* for creating CF_LINKSOURCE from any moniker and a CLSID (to identify the server), rendering it into a STGMEDIUM. (See "Warning" on the next page.)

As for the placement of these formats on the clipboard, they should always go at the end, even below simple formats such as CF_TEXT. The reason is that linking almost never happens by default when a container pastes. It almost always happens when the user explicitly asks the container to use a Paste Link. So to keep the link formats out of the way, they get bottom spot on the totem pole.

WARNING

I found that in calling *OleStgGetLinkSourceData* I had to pass the STGMEDIUM with TYMED_NULL already set in the *tymed* field (for reasons I do not know, so don't ask) and that I had to pass a FORMATETC with CF_LINKSOURCE and TYMED_ISTREAM already set. Why this function can't figure that out itself is a matter for national debate, but it will certainly fail to do what you want if you fail to set the mediums correctly. This is another one of those things I struggled with for a long time, and I'd hate to see you do the same. If you don't like it, you have the OLE2UI code, so go ahead and modify it to suit your needs.

Through this simple action of providing these formats, you open yourself up to all kinds of abuse. After you get things to compile, run your server stand-alone, create a file with some junk in it, save that file, and then copy it all to the clipboard. If all goes well, you will create CF_LINKSOURCE and CF_LINKSRCDESCRIPTOR and copy them to the clipboard via your data object. Note that if you look at the clipboard contents using the Windows clipboard viewer, you will see only *Link Source Descriptor* listed and not *Link Source.* (Both, however, will appear in the OLE 2 SDK's Data Object Viewer tool.) The existence of CF_LINKSRCDESCRIPTOR is a cue to functions such as *OleCreateLinkFromData* that CF_LINKSOURCE is actually available, but you have to explicitly ask the data object for it—OLE doesn't bother to place that format on the clipboard proper.

Also note that *OleSetClipboardData* will create the OLE 1 format *ObjectLink* from your OLE 2 formats, thus enabling OLE 1 containers to link. You should try a Paste Link into containers for both versions of OLE, and both should end up with valid linked objects. After doing Paste Link, close the server application.

Now you have a linked object of your class in a container. What the heck. Go ahead and activate it. If you're using a compound file for the server and you've called *WriteClassStg* or if you've registered an entry for your extension in the Registration Database, your server should be launched with *-Embedding* on the command line, and your class factory should be asked for an *IPersistFile* interface. But you don't have one, so your application has to fail for the time being. (Make sure you fail well!) Nevertheless, you can ensure that your application is getting launched properly and that it is getting to the point of needing the *IPersistFile* interface. Because that's now a pressing need, let's implement it.

Implement the *IPersistFile* Interface

To handle a linking server that gives only simple file monikers, the *IPersistFile* interface should be implemented on the same object as *IOleObject*, *IDataObject*, and *IPersistStorage*. For Cosmo I added another interface implementation class, *CImpIPersistFile*, that is implemented as part of the *CFigure* class. Therefore, *QueryInterface* on *CFigure* (and thus any other interface) can return an *IPersistFile* pointer. This is especially important as our implementation of *IClassFactory::CreateInstance* will now ask *CFigure* for *IPersistFile* when binding the file moniker.

As you can probably guess, the implementation of this interface holds few surprises. The implementation for Cosmo is shown in Listing 13-1 in which functions such as *Load* and *Save* simply make use of existing functionality elsewhere in the application.

IPERFILE.CPP

```
/*
 * Cosmo Chapter 13
 *
 * Implementation of the IPersistFile interface for Cosmo
 *
 * Copyright (c)1993 Microsoft Corporation, All Rights Reserved
 */

#include "cosmo.h"

CImpIPersistFile::CImpIPersistFile(LPCFigure pObj
    , LPUNKNOWN pUnkOuter)
    {
    m_cRef=0;
    m_pObj=pObj;
    m_pUnkOuter=pUnkOuter;
    return;
    }

CImpIPersistFile::~CImpIPersistFile(void)
    {
    return;
    }

STDMETHODIMP CImpIPersistFile::QueryInterface(REFIID riid
    , LPLPVOID ppv)
    {
```

Listing 13-1. *(continued)*
The implementation of IPersistFile *on the figure objects in Cosmo.*

Listing 13-1. *continued*

```
    return m_pUnkOuter->QueryInterface(riid, ppv);
    }

STDMETHODIMP_(ULONG) CImpIPersistFile::AddRef(void)
    {
    ++m_cRef;
    return m_pUnkOuter->AddRef();
    }

STDMETHODIMP_(ULONG) CImpIPersistFile::Release(void)
    {
    --m_cRef;
    return m_pUnkOuter->Release();
    }

STDMETHODIMP CImpIPersistFile::GetClassID(LPCLSID pClsID)
    {
    *pClsID=CLSID_Cosmo2Figure;
    return NOERROR;
    }

STDMETHODIMP CImpIPersistFile::IsDirty(void)
    {
    return ResultFromScode(m_pObj->FIsDirty() ? S_OK : S_FALSE);
    }

STDMETHODIMP CImpIPersistFile::Load(LPCSTR pszFile, DWORD grfMode)
    {
    UINT        uRet;

    uRet=m_pObj->m_pDoc->ULoad(TRUE, (LPSTR)pszFile);
    return (DOCERR_NONE==uRet) ? NOERROR
        : ResultFromScode(STG_E_READFAULT);
    }

STDMETHODIMP CImpIPersistFile::Save(LPCSTR pszFile, BOOL fRemember)
    {
    UINT        uRet;
    BOOL        fTemp;

    /*
     * We set CFigure::m_fEmbedding here to TRUE if we don't want to
     * remember this file, as that cons USave into ignoring this
     * filename. This is not something you have to do in your own
     * code the same way, but be sure to pay attention to fRemember.
     */
```

(continued)

Listing 13-1. *continued*

```
    fTemp=m_pObj->m_fEmbedded;
    m_pObj->m_fEmbedded=!fRemember;
    uRet=m_pObj->m_pDoc->USave(0, (LPSTR)pszFile);

    m_pObj->m_fEmbedded=fTemp;

    return (DOCERR_NONE==uRet) ? NOERROR
        : ResultFromScode(STG_E_WRITEFAULT);
    }

STDMETHODIMP CImpIPersistFile::SaveCompleted(LPCSTR pszFile)
    {
    return NOERROR;
    }

STDMETHODIMP CImpIPersistFile::GetCurFile(LPSTR FAR * ppszFile)
    {
    LPMALLOC     pIMalloc;
    LPSTR        psz;
    UINT         uRet;

    *ppszFile=NULL;

    if (FAILED(CoGetMalloc(MEMCTX_SHARED, &pIMalloc)))
        return ResultFromScode(E_FAIL);

    psz=(LPSTR)pIMalloc->Alloc(OLEUI_CCHPATHMAX);
    pIMalloc->Release();

    uRet=m_pObj->m_pDoc->FilenameGet(psz, OLEUI_CCHPATHMAX);

    //If we have no filename, return the prompt for File Open/Save.
    if (0==uRet)
        lstrcpy(psz, (*m_pObj->m_pST)[IDS_EXTENSION]);

    *ppszFile=psz;
    return (0==uRet) ? ResultFromScode(S_FALSE) : NOERROR;
    }
```

The only tricky aspect of *Save* is that you might or might not be asked to make the file current—that is, to do a Save As instead of a Save. To handle this in Cosmo, I fiddled with the *m_fEmbedded* flag in *CFigure* because when it's set, the *CCosmoDoc::USave* function doesn't try to remember the filename, which is the behavior we want in *IPersistFile::Save* when *fRemember* is FALSE.

I also want to mention *IPersistFile::GetCurFile.* This function has either of two responsibilities: It can either return the current filename or, if there is no filename, it can return the search string to use in a File Open dialog box. Allocate both string buffers with the shared allocator—that is, the *IMalloc* returned from *CoGetMalloc(MEMCTX_SHARED, ...).*

After you have implemented *IPersistFile,* you should now be able to fully activate a linked object in a container. That activation should launch your server, get a pointer to your *IPersistFile,* call *IPersistFile::Load,* call *IPersistFile::QueryInterface* asking for *IOleObject,* and then call *IOleObject::DoVerb(OLEIVERB_PRIMARY).* The *DoVerb* call, as usual, should display your window and allow editing, as appropriate.

Implement *IOleObject::SetMoniker* and *IOleObject::GetMoniker*

With the implementation of *IPersistFile,* you have what appears to be a complete linking server, but you also want to fill out the implementation of *IOleObject,* specifically implementing *SetMoniker* and *GetMoniker.*

SetMoniker is important only if you do not have the OLEMISC_CANTLINKINSIDE flag registered for your class as first mentioned in Chapter 10. The absence of this flag means that containers, such as the version of Patron described in this chapter, can allow others to link to your embedded object. It really doesn't have anything to do with the functionality of your server, but it is important if you want to provide complete linking capabilities. In fact, providing this courtesy really doesn't even touch your own server's moniker, as you can see from Cosmo's implementation:

```
STDMETHODIMP CImpIOleObject::SetMoniker(DWORD dwWhich, LPMONIKER pmk)
    {
    LPMONIKER       pmkFull;
    HRESULT         hr=ResultFromScode(E_FAIL);

    /*
     * For an embedded object we might be living in a container that
     * has given us away as a link. This is our indication to
     * register the full moniker for this object that we obtain from
     * IOleClientSite::GetMoniker(OLEWHICHMK_FULL).
     */

    if (0L!=m_pObj->m_dwRegROT)
        {
        OleStdRevokeAsRunning(&m_pObj->m_dwRegROT);
        m_pObj->m_dwRegROT=0L;
        }
```

(continued)

```
    if (NULL!=m_pObj->m_pIOleClientSite)
        {
        hr=m_pObj->m_pIOleClientSite->GetMoniker
            (OLEGETMONIKER_ONLYIFTHERE, OLEWHICHMK_OBJFULL
            , &pmkFull);
        }

    if (SUCCEEDED(hr))
        {
        OleStdRegisterAsRunning((LPUNKNOWN)m_pObj, pmkFull
            , &m_pObj->m_dwRegROT);
        pmkFull->Release();
        }

    return hr;
    }
```

This says that *SetMoniker* is a cue to the object, in this case an embedded object, to register as running what is known as its full moniker. The full moniker for an embedded object is the full name by which your application is called in your container. For example, if this object were embedded (not linked, mind you) in the version of Patron we're going to implement, the full moniker might be *c:\patron\stuff.ptn!Page 2!Tenant 4* because the embedded object itself knows no other file. This moniker is always available from your container's *IOleClientSite::GetMoniker* if it supports this sort of functionality.

GetMoniker might seem a little more concrete in the context of this section. *GetMoniker* always returns the full moniker to the object, no matter whether it's linked or embedded. If the object is linked, it returns your file moniker (or whatever moniker your object has). If your application is embedded, it returns the full moniker assigned by your container, as you can see in the following code:

```
STDMETHODIMP CImpIOleObject::GetMoniker(DWORD dwAssign, DWORD dwWhich
    , LPMONIKER FAR * ppmk)
    {
    HRESULT         hr=ResultFromScode(E_FAIL);

    *ppmk=NULL;

    /*
     * When we support linking we either return our file moniker if
     * we're linked, or our full moniker from the container if we're
     * embedded.
     */
```

```
if (NULL!=m_pObj->m_pMoniker)
    {
    *ppmk=m_pObj->m_pMoniker;        //Document file moniker
    m_pObj->m_pMoniker->AddRef();
    }
else
    {
    //Get the full container:object moniker if we're embedded
    if (NULL!=m_pObj->m_pIOleClientSite)
        {
        hr=m_pObj->m_pIOleClientSite->GetMoniker
            (OLEGETMONIKER_ONLYIFTHERE, OLEWHICHMK_OBJFULL
            , ppmk);
        }
    }

return (NULL!=*ppmk) ? NOERROR : hr;
}
```

And with those two implementations, you are now the proud owner of a simple linking server. Although it might be a feature you want, you might also want to link to ranges of data—if your application is something like a spreadsheet. That means you need to implement the *IOleItemContainer* interface, which we can see in the context of a container that links to embedded objects.

Complex Linking and Linking to Embeddings

The steps given in the previous section describe completely how an application would provide a file moniker and the necessary code to bind to that file through the *IPersistFile* interface. But for more complicated applications, a single file moniker is not enough to describe the source of a link. For example, a spreadsheet would typically need to include a cell range as well as the file in the link source by creating a composite moniker that contains a file moniker and an item moniker. A word processor might allow linking to a specific part of a document defined between two "bookmarks" or other persistent markers in the document. A database might need to enable linking to an individual record or form in a whole database. In all these cases, a simple file moniker is not sufficient.

The other case in which a file moniker is too simple is when a container, such as Patron, needs to allow other containers to link to objects embedded within its own documents. In such a situation, the container needs to identify the document by means of a file moniker, the current page by means of an item moniker, and the name of the tenant that manages the embedded object by means of a second item moniker.

This section will first explain the motivations for providing linking to embeddings and then will show how Patron implemented the feature.

Although we are using an advanced link sourcing container (Patron) for our discussion, everything applies equally well to servers that provide more complex links as well. The only difference is that, for Patron, we'll need to add new code for the class factory and make objects out of more parts of the application. If you are making complex linking modifications to an application that is already a server, you will not have to add as much code.

Why Linking to Embedding?

Consider a typical word processor with an open report containing an embedded table with the latest sales figures, as shown in Figure 13-5.

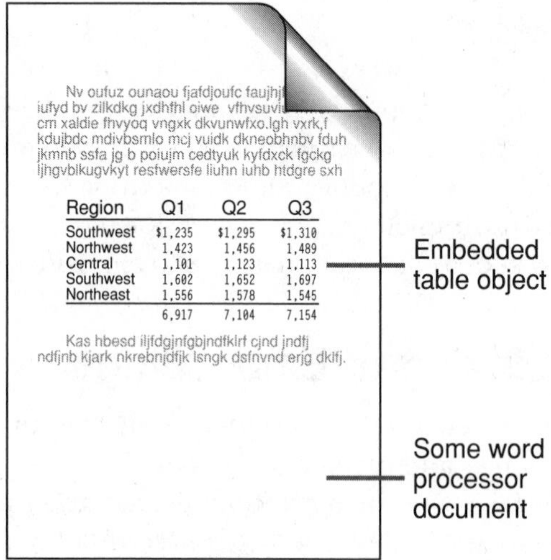

Figure 13-5.
A typical word processor document that contains an embedded table object.

Because the table is an embedded object, its data exists only in the storage for that embedded object. Now let's say you want to add a chart to this report that shows the numbers in that table graphically. You could create a new chart object and manually reenter all the numbers in the table to fill out the chart, but that would be boring. What you would really like to be able to do is automatically link the chart to the numbers in the table, as shown in Figure 13-6.

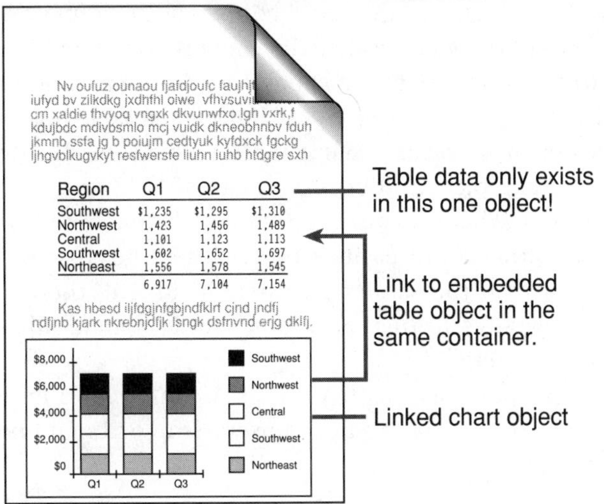

Figure 13-6.
End users would like to be able to link an embedded chart object to an embedded table object that contains the data necessary to create the chart.

The problem, of course, is that the numbers exist only in the embedded object for the table. How is the chart supposed to get at those numbers? The answer is that the chart needs help from the container. The chart needs the container to provide link source information to that embedded table object.

Generally, the user will select the table in the container and do an Edit/Copy operation. The user will then create and activate the new chart and do an Edit/Paste Link into that new chart object. The way in which the chart object manages the moniker it gets from Paste Link is its own choice. It could create a linked object by using *OleCreateLinkToFile* itself, but because it's really not interested in a presentation of the table, it will more likely persistently store the moniker. At any time later, the chart can call *IMoniker::BindToObject* and ask for the *IDataObject* interface, which the table, as an embedded object, will be more than happy to provide. By using *IDataObject*, the chart can then use *GetData* to find out about the format that it can use to create the chart graphics. The chart object also has the option of calling *IMoniker::BindToStorage*, which will give it access to the object's *IStorage*, thus reducing the amount of memory necessary to copy and transfer the data.

In either case, the chart application has a link to the information in the table, and when the user closes the chart, the container document will then have two objects: the embedded table and the linked chart. If users then make changes to the data in the table, they can update the linked chart object to reflect those changes. Such an update would happen automatically when the container reloaded the document because the chart is a linked object.

Without the linking-to-embedding capability, the user could not possibly create a chart on the same data used by the embedded table object, simply because there is no way for it to access that data. In such a case, the user would have to use a *linked* table object and create a chart that linked to the same source as the table object. That uses only one source of data, but there's still a separate linked file and that link is easily broken. When the chart is linked to an embedded object within the same container document, the chances of breaking the link are small, and such an event would happen only through direct and conscious user action.

So although implementing this feature as a container is entirely optional, it's a nice one to provide for your end users. Implementation involves the following steps:

1. Create and manage the composite moniker.
2. Source the composite moniker in clipboard and drag-and-drop operations.
3. Assign a CLSID to the container and implement a class factory for that CLSID so that the class factory creates "document" objects with the *IPersistFile* interface.
4. Implement the *IOleItemContainer* interface for each item moniker in the composite moniker you created and sourced in steps 1 and 2.

Create and Manage the Composite Moniker

As we deal with any source of a link, we must create and manage some sort of moniker that describes the link source. In the earlier discussion in this chapter concerned with simple file monikers, we saw how a source application (which I am now using freely to mean both servers and linking-to-embedding containers) creates and registers a file moniker. Any application that uses a file moniker should create and register that moniker independently of any composite monikers it will create with that file moniker. So Patron, for example, calls *CreateFileMoniker* and *OleStdRegisterAsRunning* in its *CPatronDoc::Rename* function:

```
void CPatronDoc::Rename(LPSTR pszFile)
    {
    LPMONIKER   pmk;
```

```
    //We don't need to change the base class, just augment...
    CDocument::Rename(pszFile);

    /*
     * Get rid of the old moniker. The OldStd function sets the
     * key to zero.
     */
    if (0L!=m_dwRegROT)
        OleStdRevokeAsRunning(&m_dwRegROT);

    if (NULL==pszFile)
        return;

    CreateFileMoniker(pszFile, &pmk);

    if (NULL!=pmk)
        {
        OleStdRegisterAsRunning((LPUNKNOWN)this, pmk, &m_dwRegROT);

        //Give a moniker to linked objects in tenants.
        m_pPG->NotifyTenantsOfRename(pszFile, pmk);

        //No need for us to hold on to this.
        pmk->Release();
        }

    return;
    }
```

As before, Patron is still notifying all tenants of the new filename, but now it registers the moniker itself. Because Patron does not use the file moniker by itself anywhere else in *CPatronDoc,* it does not hold onto a copy here as Cosmo did earlier. If your application is a server that supports linking to the entire document as well as to selections within the document, you'll probably want to hold the moniker pointer.

Again, the LPUNKNOWN passed to *IRunningObjectTable::Register* (through *OleStdRegisterAsRunning*) as the interface that OLE will use when someone binds to this file moniker. Note that when the file moniker is registered as running, OLE will never ask for the *IPersistFile* interface on this object because there is no need to reload the file that's already loaded. If you ever give out the file moniker by itself in a CF_LINKSOURCE format, the object might be asked for an *IOleObject* interface pointer. Patron does not support this, but a server might.

In our container, Patron, we make a call to *CPages::NotifyTenantsOfRename,* which, as we saw in Chapter 12, works its way down to each tenant that just called *IOleObject::SetMoniker.* To support linking to embeddings, this notification of a new file moniker is a cue to build other monikers as well as the composite moniker that leads to the embedded object.

In *CPage::NotifyTenantsOfRename,* we now store the file moniker (for use later) and create an item moniker for the page using *CreateItemMoniker*:

```
void CPage::NotifyTenantsOfRename(LPSTR pszFile, LPMONIKER pmk)
    {
    LPTENANT    pTenant;
    UINT        i;
    LPMONIKER   pmkPage;
    char        szTemp[32];

    //Save the file moniker
    if (NULL!=m_pmkFile)
        m_pmkFile->Release();

    m_pmkFile=pmk;
    m_pmkFile->AddRef();

    //Create a page moniker to send to the tenants.
    GetStorageName(szTemp);
    CreateItemMoniker("!", szTemp, &pmkPage);

    for (i=0; i < m_cTenants; i++)
        {
        if (FTenantGet(i, &pTenant, FALSE))
            pTenant->NotifyOfRename(pszFile, pmk, pmkPage);
        }

    //If anything held onto this, they AddRef'd
    pmkPage->Release();
    return;
    }
```

The page item moniker is only temporary and is used to tell each tenant, by using *CTenant::NotifyOfRename,* the exact page the tenant lives in, as well as the exact document that contains the page. The document file moniker and the page item moniker are the last two parameters to *CTenant::NotifyOfRename.*

Here we see our first use of *CreateItemMoniker.* This function takes the string to use for the item and the LPMONIKER pointer in which to return the new moniker. It also takes a string to use as a delimiter—that is, a string that does not occur elsewhere in the item name. This delimiter string is used internally in OLE's composite moniker implementation to know where one item moniker ends and where another begins.

If we press on further down into *CTenant::NotifyOfRename*, we see some additions as well. Before, we simply called *IOleObject::SetMoniker* with OLEWHICHMK_CONTAINER and held onto the file moniker so that we could implement *IOleClientSite::GetMoniker* for the container moniker. Now, we add a call to tell the object of the relative moniker as well. The relative moniker of the object in the container in Patron is the composite moniker generated from a page item moniker (with a name such as "Page 2") and a tenant item moniker (with a name such as Tenant 1):

```
//In CTenant::NotifyOfRename
if (NULL!=pmkFile && NULL!=pmkPage)
    {
    LPMONIKER    pmkTenant=NULL;
    LPMONIKER    pmkRel=NULL;
    HRESULT      hr;

    //Create the moniker for this tenant.
    GetStorageName(szObj);
    hr=CreateItemMoniker("!", szObj, &pmkTenant);

    if (SUCCEEDED(hr))
        {
        //Create the relative moniker, i.e. no pathname.
        hr=CreateGenericComposite(pmkPage, pmkTenant, &pmkRel);
        pmkTenant->Release();

        if (SUCCEEDED(hr))
            m_pIOleObject->SetMoniker(OLEWHICHMK_OBJREL, pmkRel);

        //Hold on to the relative moniker
        if (NULL!=m_pmk)
            m_pmk->Release();

        m_pmk=pmkRel;
        }
    }

[Other code does Release both m_pmk and m_pmkFile]
```

In this code, the tenant creates a tenant item moniker with which it builds a composite for itself that it holds in a newly added variable *CTenant::m_pmk*. *NotifyOfRename* calls *IOleObject::SetMoniker* with OLEWHICHMK_OBJREL, which, as we've seen in the previous sections of this chapter, is a cue to the server application to call our *IOleClientSite::GetMoniker* asking for OLEWHICHMK_OBJFULL (not OBJREL) and register that moniker. Through this action, the object itself registers itself as running by using our composite moniker that contains the container portion, the file moniker, and the object relative portion, the page and tenant, together in the full composite.

As a container, then, we need to augment our *IOleClientSite::GetMoniker* function to handle all three moniker cases:

```
STDMETHODIMP CImpIOleClientSite::GetMoniker(DWORD dwAssign, DWORD dwWhich
    , LPMONIKER FAR *ppmk)
    {
    *ppmk=NULL;

    switch (dwWhich)
        {
        case OLEWHICHMK_CONTAINER:
            //This is just the file we're living in.
            if (NULL!=m_pTen->m_pmkFile)
                *ppmk=m_pTen->m_pmkFile;

            break;

        case OLEWHICHMK_OBJREL:
            //This is everything but the filename.
            if (NULL!=m_pTen->m_pmk)
                *ppmk=m_pTen->m_pmk;

            break;

        case OLEWHICHMK_OBJFULL:
            //Concatenate the file and relative monikers for this one.
            if (NULL!=m_pTen->m_pmkFile && NULL!=m_pTen->m_pmk)
                {
                CreateGenericComposite(m_pTen->m_pmkFile
                    , m_pTen->m_pmk, ppmk);
                }

            break;
        }

    if (NULL==*ppmk)
        return ResultFromScode(E_FAIL);

    (*ppmk)->AddRef();
    return NOERROR;
    }
```

This code shows why Patron's tenants hold onto the file and relative monikers—in that way, we have everything available to return those monikers as well as the full moniker, which is simply the composite of the file moniker and the relative moniker.

Most of the preceding code applies equally to a server application that wants to provide linking to a range of data in a document. Think of Patron's tenants as a range in a page, and think of a page as a range in a document, which is why Patron has two item monikers in the composite assigned to the object. If your application is a spreadsheet, for example, one item moniker for a cell range would be sufficient to describe the selection, in which case you have a simpler moniker to manage.

You can easily compile at this point and verify that you are correctly building the composite moniker and releasing it when necessary. You should also confirm that you are properly registering and revoking the file moniker for the document. With all that working, you can now turn your attention to giving those monikers away as CF_LINKSOURCE format.

Source the Composite Moniker

In our discussion of Cosmo earlier in this chapter, we saw how to present a moniker in the CF_LINKSOURCE format and how to provide the CF-_LINKSRCDESCRIPTOR format in clipboard and drag-and-drop operations. Patron does pretty much those same things in its function *CTenant::CopyLinkedObject*, which is called from *CPage::TransferObjectCreate* in any drag-and-drop or clipboard operation:

```
void CTenant::CopyLinkedObject(LPDATAOBJECT pIDataObject
    , LPFORMATETC pFE, LPPOINTL pptl)
    {
    STGMEDIUM           stm;
    FORMATETC           fe;
    HRESULT             hr;
    UINT                cf;
    POINTL              ptl;
    LPMONIKER           pmk;
    LPSTR               psz=NULL;
    DWORD               dwStat;

    //If we don't have a full moniker, no linking allowed
    if (NULL==m_pmk)
        return;

    //If the object doesn't support this, return.
    dwStat=0;
    m_pIOleObject->GetMiscStatus(m_fe.dwAspect, &dwStat);

    if (OLEMISC_CANTLINKINSIDE & dwStat)
        return;
```

(continued)

```
[Code to initialize ptl for the drag-and-drop pick point]

/*
 * We need to get CF_LINKSOURCE, but the server may not be
 * running, in which case we just grab the moniker and CLSID
 * for this object and call OleStdGetLinkSrcData.
 */

m_pIOleObject->GetUserClassID(&clsID);
hr=m_pIOleObject->GetMoniker(0, OLEWHICHMK_OBJFULL, &pmk);

if (FAILED(hr))
    return;

if (FAILED(hr))
    return;

//Set these tymeds or brain-dead OleStdGetLinkSourceData fails.
stm.tymed=TYMED_NULL;
cf=RegisterClipboardFormat(CF_LINKSOURCE);
SETDefFormatEtc(fe, cf, TYMED_ISTREAM);
hr=OleStdGetLinkSourceData(pmk, &clsID, &fe, &stm);

[Set CF_LINKSOURCE in the data transfer object]

...

stm.hGlobal=OleStdGetObjectDescriptorDataFromOleObject
    (m_pIOleObject, NULL, m_fe.dwAspect, ptl);

//Better set these properly or errors occur.
stm.tymed=TYMED_HGLOBAL;
stm.pUnkForRelease=NULL;

[Set CF_LINKSRCDESCRIPTOR in the data transfer object]
return;
}
```

For the most part, this is exactly what a server needs to do when it copies a composite moniker. However, there are two conditions for containers that must be met before it can copy link source information. First, the container document must have a known filename and a full moniker for the object in it. In Patron, this condition is met if the tenant has a value in *m_pmk* that is the full moniker we need. The second condition is that the object itself must support linking-to-embedding, which means it implements *IOleObject::SetMoniker* properly, in such a way that it will register the full moniker in the running object table. If a server does not implement *SetMoniker*, it will have the OLEMISC_CANTLINKINSIDE flag set in its status as returned from *IOleObject::GetMiscStatus*. This is the most important condition for the object to meet when it is sourcing links to embeddings as a container.

When you get ready to copy the CF_LINKSOURCE format, you want to first ensure that the moniker you use is the *full* moniker for the object. It's easy enough to obtain this: Call *IOleObject::GetMoniker* by using OLEWHICHMK_OBJFULL, which will probably merely call back to your *IOleClientSite::GetMoniker* with the same flag. But because you cannot be assured that it will always remain that way, make the call by means of *IOleObject*. The other point here is to ensure that the CLSID you tag this data with must be the CLSID of the object, not any CLSID of the container might define. That way, the consumer of this link can show the user exactly what is being linked, which is the object, not the container.

Finally, note that Patron is using another utterly verbose function—*OleStdGetObjectDescriptorDataFromOleObject*—which does almost the same as *OleStdGetObjectDescriptorData* except that it is based on information obtainable from an *IOleObject* pointer instead of from all the parameters you pass it. In using this function, you still need to tell it the aspect of the object and the drag-and-drop pick point, if applicable. Also note that this function only returns an HGLOBAL—it does not fill a STGMEDIUM that you will probably need in other parts of your code, so be sure to fill out any STGMEDIUM in which you save the returned handle.

With that, you can compile, create some embedded objects in a document, save that document (so that you have a known filename), and copy an object to the clipboard. Any container application, your own included, can then create a new linked object with Paste Link. Now close the source application, and activate the linked object. Nothing happened, huh? Maybe the disk crunched a little, or maybe you got a UAE, but things definitely didn't work right. That's because we haven't added the other necessary code to support composite moniker binding. We need to add *IPersistFile* and *IOleItemContainer* interfaces.

Implement a Class Factory for Document Objects with *IPersistFile*

This step will be pretty simple for a server application because it should already have a class factory and the whole structure for servicing objects. In a container now, we also have to support the entire class factory structure to make our application a link source.

When you source a complex moniker—that is, a composite with at least File and Item monikers within it—the file moniker binds to what we call a *document object,* one that implements the *IPersistFile* interface but does not implement the other compound document object interfaces such as *IOleObject, IPersistStorage,* and *IDataObject.* In the simple example using Cosmo, the document object and the compound document object were one and the same, so all these interfaces ended up on the same object. When the source is only a portion of a document, there is a document object that knows how to load files and also how to find objects within that document.

If you have a server application that supports linking to the entire document (by means of a simple file moniker) and you also want to link to a selection within that document, you have all the necessary class factory and document objects already. In that case, go ahead and skip to the last two paragraphs in this section. There's a little surprise for you there.

For Patron, however, we have no such structures, so we must first add all the pieces of an EXE server: Registration Database entries, lock and object counters, and unloading mechanism, a class factory, and some object for that class factory to create. The Registration Database entries that are necessary for a linking-to-embedding container are like those of a *component object,* not a *compound document object*—that is, you need only the entries under *<ProgID>* = *<Descriptive Name>* and the *ProgID, InprocHandler,* and *LocalServer* entries under CLSID. Of course, you need to assign a CLSID to your container. This should be the same CLSID that you write to your files (if you are using compound files) so that the file moniker can know who to launch by calling *GetClassFile.* If you are not using compound files, you must rely on the *<extension>* = *<ProgID>* entry and the CLSID listed under your *ProgID.* Patron's entries are included in CHAP13\CHAP13.REG.

If you look at the sources in CHAP13\PATRON, you will notice that there are numerous additions to PATRON.CPP to handle the unloading mechanism as well as registering the class factory and parsing *-Embedding* out of the command line, in which case Patron does not initially show its window, as any good server would. There is also the addition of the file ICLASSF.CPP, which contains the class factory implementation. All of this code should look very familiar by now because it is the standard stuff we implement in anything that can serve objects.

What is interesting is that in Patron, the objects we serve from the class factory are those of the *CPatronDoc* class, which we must now turn into Windows Objects instead of normal C++ objects. So *CPatronDoc* now has a reference count and an *IUnknown* implementation, as you can see in DOCUMENT.CPP. Notice that instead of calling *delete this* in Release when the reference count is zero, it instead posts a WM_CLOSE message to itself. This was simply to accommodate all the other code in Patron and CLASSLIB that has until now expected the document to be closed through some user action and does not expect the *CPatronDoc* object to merely be deleted.

Now this document object implements the *IPersistFile* interface, most of which looks pretty much the same as we've seen before in Listing 13-1 for Cosmo. The following code shows only Patron's Load and Save implementation, which can conveniently use functions in *CPatronDoc* to do the work:

```
STDMETHODIMP CImpIPersistFile::Load(LPCSTR pszFile, DWORD grfMode)
    {
    UINT        uRet;

    uRet=m_pDoc->ULoad(TRUE, (LPSTR)pszFile);
    return (DOCERR_NONE==uRet) ? NOERROR
        : ResultFromScode(STG_E_READFAULT);
    }

STDMETHODIMP CImpIPersistFile::Save(LPCSTR pszFile, BOOL fRemember)
    {
    UINT        uRet;

    /*
     * Since we don't want to mess with changing USave (which would
     * require changes to CLASSLIB (urk) we instead save fRemember
     * in the document before calling USave which supresses the call
     * to CPatronDoc::Rename if FALSE.
     */

    m_pDoc->m_fRename=fRemember;
    uRet=m_pDoc->USave(0, (LPSTR)pszFile);
    m_pDoc->m_fRename=TRUE;

    return (DOCERR_NONE==uRet) ? NOERROR
        : ResultFromScode(STG_E_WRITEFAULT);
    }
```

I wanted to show Save because I did something sleazy here. In implementing Save, I wanted to use my already existing code in *CPatronDoc::USave*, which until now has always called *CPatronDoc::Rename* whenever it saved a file. Well, *IPersistFile::Save* has this little *fRemember* flag that tells us not to remember anything about the filename we're saving when it's FALSE. So I had to prevent the call to *Rename* from within *USave*. Because I didn't want to change the function signature on *USave* (that approach would play havoc with its use from all the code in CLASSLIB, which up to now is what has always been the sole agent calling this function), I instead added the *m_fRename* flag to *CPatronDoc*, and in *USave* I do not call *Rename* if the flag is FALSE. By default, this flag is always TRUE, and only when *fRemember* in *IPersistFile::Save* is

FALSE will it ever be FALSE, and even then we reset it to TRUE after *USave*. This is a pretty foolish way to communicate with a function, standing somewhere on the evolutionary line that leads from rats to wolverines and eventually to politicians, but no one knows where for sure.

When all of these changes compile, go back to the container in which you created a link to an embedded object in your container and activate that linked object. Just as happens for a linked object server, you should see your container launched with *-Embedding* on the command line and, if all goes well, OLE will call your *IClassFactory::CreateInstance* function, asking for *IPersistFile*. In that case, you can create a document and take hold of the *IPersistFile* pointer on it. When you return from *CreateInstance*, you will see a call to *IPersistFile::Load*, which then does its thing.

But what happens next shows us the last step in providing this feature. When we merely supplied a simple file moniker as the link source, OLE called *IPersistFile::QueryInterface* asking for *IOleObject* or some other compound document object type of interface. Now, because the linked object manages a composite moniker with a file *and* at least one item moniker, OLE instead asks for a pointer to an *IOleItemContainer* interface. This interface is what can resolve an item name (that you previously passed to *CreateItemMoniker*) into a pointer to compound document object interface such as *IOleObject*.

Implement *IOleItemContainer* for Each Item Moniker

Every time you append an item moniker onto a composite, you are eventually going to need a separate implementation of the *IOleItemContainer* interface to resolve the item name into an object. If you source monikers such as *File!Item*, you will need one *IOleItemContainer*. If you source *File!Item!Item*, you will need two implementations of the interface, and so on.

The *IOleItemContainer* interface is basically responsible for returning information about objects within the containment unit they represent, such as a document or a page. In addition, they are capable of resolving the name of an item, usually one that's stored in an item moniker, into another interface pointer on an object in this container:

```
DECLARE_INTERFACE_(IOleItemContainer, IOleContainer)
    {
    [IUnknown members]

    //From IParseDisplayName
    STDMETHOD(ParseDisplayName) (THIS_ LPBC lpbc, LPSTR lpszDisplayName,
        ULONG FAR* pchEaten, LPMONIKER FAR* ppmkOut) PURE;
```

```
    //From IOleContainer
    STDMETHOD(EnumObjects) (THIS_ DWORD grfFlags, LPENUMUNKNOWN FAR *
        ppenumUnknown) PURE;
    STDMETHOD(LockContainer) (THIS_ BOOL fLock) PURE;

    //Specific to IOleItemContainer
    STDMETHOD(GetObject) (THIS_ LPSTR lpszItem, DWORD dwSpeedNeeded,
        LPBINDCTX pbc, REFIID riid, LPVOID FAR* ppvObject) PURE;
    STDMETHOD(GetObjectStorage) (THIS_ LPSTR lpszItem, LPBINDCTX pbc,
        REFIID riid, LPVOID FAR* ppvStorage) PURE;
    STDMETHOD(IsRunning) (THIS_ LPSTR lpszItem) PURE;
    };
```

You can see that *IOleItemContainer* is derived from *IOleContainer*, which is derived from *IParseDisplayName*, which is derived from, of course, *IUnknown*. Because of this, be sure that your *QueryInterface* implementations that know *IOleItemContainer* respond equally to *IOleContainer* and *IParseDisplayName*:

```
if (IsEqualIID(riid, IID_IOleItemContainer)
    || IsEqualIID(riid, IID_IOleContainer)
    || IsEqualIID(riid, IID_IParseDisplayName))
    [Return your IOleItemContainer interface pointer]
```

The *ParseDisplayName* member function is responsible for turning a user-readable name of an item into a moniker. For our uses, I've not found a need to implement it, nor have I found a need to implement the *EnumObjects* function. *LockContainer* is important, however. It acts exactly like *IClassFactory::LockServer*—that is, it increments or decrements a lock count on the container in such a way that when locked, the application is not allowed to shut down.

The three member functions specific to *IOleItemContainer* are *GetObject*, *GetObjectStorage*, and *IsRunning*, all of which must be implemented for any application that sources a complex moniker. *GetObject* is really the most important because it is the function that takes an item name in the *lpszItem* parameter and is required to locate the object described by that name and return the requested interface pointer for it. Furthermore, it is required to return the interface pointer on a *running* object, not simply a loaded one, so we'll see that we call *OleRun* inside the implementation of *GetObject* to meet that requirement.

Before we look at code, let me mention that this interface is implemented on whatever you consider to be the unit that contains the object named in the item. In other words, if you have a cell selection in a spreadsheet, the selection of cells defines the object and the spreadsheet defines the document that contains those cells. If you source a *File!Item* moniker for this selection, the document must first implement *IPersistFile*, but then it also must implement *IOleItemContainer* because the document is one level above the cell range selection. The cell range itself is the object, and the document manages that object. Therefore, the document is the agent that knows the names of all objects within it.

In Patron, we have an even more complex situation. The document object we discussed in the last section implements *IPersistFile* for the file moniker, but then it also implements its version of *IOleItemContainer.* This interface knows how to resolve a *page* name such as *Page 2* into some other interface pointer. Now comes the interesting part: Because the moniker that Patron gave away was *File!Item!Item,* the document's *IOleItemContainer* interface is asked to resolve the item name (in this case a page name) into *another IOleItemContainer* interface. This interface implementation is different from the one on the document, and is responsible for resolving the item name for a tenant into the actual interface pointer (such as *IOleObject*) on the embedded object.

In Patron, I have defined one interface implementation called *CImpIOleItemContainer (PATRON.H),* which maintains a flag to know which container object it's implemented, for either *CPatronDoc* or *CPage.* (The existence of this interface on *CPage* has necessitated that *CPage* is now a Windows Object with an *IUnknown,* so any code, especially that in *CPages,* that used to call *delete pPage* now calls *pPage->Release(),* which will free the page when the reference count reaches zero.)

```
class __far CImpIOleItemContainer : public IOleItemContainer
    {
    protected:
        ULONG               m_cRef;
        class CPage FAR    *m_pPage;
        LPCPatronDoc        m_pDoc;         //Convenient naming & types
        LPUNKNOWN           m_pUnkOuter;
        BOOL                m_fDoc;         //Document or page?

    private:
        BOOL          FTenantFromName(LPSTR, LPCTenant FAR *);

    public:
        CImpIOleItemContainer(LPVOID, LPUNKNOWN, BOOL);
        ~CImpIOleItemContainer(void);

        STDMETHODIMP QueryInterface(REFIID, LPLPVOID);
        STDMETHODIMP_(ULONG) AddRef(void);
        STDMETHODIMP_(ULONG) Release(void);
```

```
        STDMETHODIMP ParseDisplayName(LPBC, LPSTR, ULONG FAR *
            , LPMONIKER FAR *);
        STDMETHODIMP EnumObjects(DWORD, LPENUMUNKNOWN FAR *);
        STDMETHODIMP LockContainer(BOOL);
        STDMETHODIMP GetObject(LPSTR, DWORD, LPBINDCTX, REFIID
            , LPLPVOID);
        STDMETHODIMP GetObjectStorage(LPSTR, LPBINDCTX, REFIID
            , LPLPVOID);
        STDMETHODIMP IsRunning(LPSTR);
    };
```

This class's constructor takes a BOOL parameter indicating which object it's a part of, and the LPVOID parameter then is either a *CPatronDoc* pointer or a *CPage* pointer. In this way, I have to define this interface implementation only once, and I need only one set of entry points for the member functions, and the functions themselves act differently depending on their value of *m_fDoc*, as shown in Listing 13-2.

IOLECONT.CPP

```
/*
 * Patron Chapter 13
 *
 * Implementation of the IOleItemContainer interface for Patron's
 * CPage and CPatronDoc alike, using the constructor parameter fDoc
 * to differentiate.
 *
 */

#include <stdlib.h>
#include "patron.h"

CImpIOleItemContainer::CImpIOleItemContainer(LPVOID pObj
    , LPUNKNOWN pUnkOuter, BOOL fDoc)
    {
    m_cRef=0;
    m_fDoc=fDoc;

    if (fDoc)
        {
        m_pDoc=(LPCPatronDoc)pObj;
        m_pPage=NULL;
        }
```

Listing 13-2. *(continued)*
The IOleItemContainer *interface implementation for both documents and pages in Patron.*

Listing 13-2. *continued*

```
    else
        {
        m_pDoc=NULL;
        m_pPage=(LPCPage)pObj;
        }

    m_pUnkOuter=pUnkOuter;
    return;
    }

CImpIOleItemContainer::~CImpIOleItemContainer(void)
    {
    return;
    }

STDMETHODIMP CImpIOleItemContainer::QueryInterface(REFIID riid
    , LPLPVOID ppv)
    {
    return m_pUnkOuter->QueryInterface(riid, ppv);
    }

STDMETHODIMP_(ULONG) CImpIOleItemContainer::AddRef(void)
    {
    ++m_cRef;
    return m_pUnkOuter->AddRef();
    }

STDMETHODIMP_(ULONG) CImpIOleItemContainer::Release(void)
    {
    --m_cRef;
    return m_pUnkOuter->Release();
    }

/*
 * CImpIOleItemContainer::ParseDisplayName
 *
 * Purpose:
 *  Inherited member of IParseDisplayName that takes a string name
 *  and turns out a moniker for it.
 *
 * Parameters:
 *  pbc             LPBC to the binding context
```

(continued)

Listing 13-2. *continued*

```
 *  pszName         LPSTR to the name to parse.
 *  pchEaten        ULONG FAR * into which to store how many
 *                  characters we scanned in the display name.
 *  ppmk            LPMONIKER FAR * in which to return the moniker.
 *
 * Return Value:
 *  HRESULT         NOERROR if successful, error code otherwise.
 */

STDMETHODIMP CImpIOleItemContainer::ParseDisplayName(LPBC pbc
    , LPSTR pszName, ULONG FAR * pchEaten, LPMONIKER FAR *ppmk)
    {
    *ppmk=NULL;
    return ResultFromScode(E_NOTIMPL);
    }

STDMETHODIMP CImpIOleItemContainer::EnumObjects(DWORD dwFlags
    , LPENUMUNKNOWN FAR *ppEnum)
    {
    *ppEnum=NULL;
    return ResultFromScode(E_NOTIMPL);
    }

STDMETHODIMP CImpIOleItemContainer::LockContainer(BOOL fLock)
    {
    /*
     * This is pretty much the same implementation as
     * IClassFactory::LockServer, and we can use the same lock
     * count to accomplish our goal.
     */

    if (fLock)
        g_cLock++;
    else
        {
        g_cLock--;
        g_cObj++;
        ObjectDestroyed();
        }

    return NOERROR;
    }
```

(continued)

Listing 13-2. *continued*

```
/*
 * CImpIOleItemContainer::GetObject
 *
 * Purpose:
 *  Returns the requested interface pointer on an object in this
 *  container.
 *
 * Parameters:
 *  pszItem         LPSTR to the item we must locate.
 *  dwSpeed         DWORD identifying how long the caller is willing
 *                  to wait.
 *  pcb             LPBINDCTX providing the binding context.
 *  riid            REFIID of the interface requested.
 *  ppv             LPLPVOID into which to return the object.
 *
 * Return Value:
 *  HRESULT         NOERROR if successful, error code otherwise.
 */

STDMETHODIMP CImpIOleItemContainer::GetObject(LPSTR pszItem
    , DWORD dwSpeed, LPBINDCTX pbc, REFIID riid, LPLPVOID ppv)
    {
    DWORD       dw;
    char        szTemp[40];     //Local assumes SS==DS
    HRESULT     hr=ResultFromScode(E_FAIL);
    LPCPage     pPage;
    LPCTenant   pTenant;
    LPUNKNOWN   pObj;
    UINT        i, iCur;

    *ppv=NULL;

    if (m_fDoc)
        {
        /*
         * The item name should be "Page n", so we'll do it the
         * easy way:  call atol on pszItem+5 (we always know that
         * we'll have "Page " there since we put it there (see
         * CPage::GetStorageName).
         */

        lstrcpy(szTemp, (LPSTR)(pszItem+5));
        dw=atol(szTemp);
```

(continued)

Listing 13-2. *continued*

```
        i=m_pDoc->m_pPG->IPageGetFromID(dw, &pPage, FALSE);

        if (-1==i)
            return hr;

        /*
         * If we're asked for immediate speed, only do this if the
         * page is already current, i.e. everything is loaded.
         */
        iCur=m_pDoc->m_pPG->CurPageGet();

        if (BINDSPEED_IMMEDIATE==dwSpeed && iCur!=i)
            return ResultFromScode(MK_E_EXCEEDEDDEADLINE);

        m_pDoc->m_pPG->CurPageSet(i);

        //This will have changed to be the current page now.
        if (NULL!=m_pDoc->m_pPG->m_pPageCur)
            hr=m_pDoc->m_pPG->m_pPageCur->QueryInterface(riid, ppv);
        }
    else
        {
        if (FTenantFromName(pszItem, &pTenant))
            {
            pTenant->ObjectGet(&pObj);

            /*
             * If we're asked for immediate or moderate, only work
             * if the object is already running.
             */
            hr=IsRunning(pszItem);  //This is the function below

            if ((BINDSPEED_IMMEDIATE==dwSpeed
                || BINDSPEED_MODERATE==dwSpeed) && NOERROR!=hr)
                hr=ResultFromScode(MK_E_EXCEEDEDDEADLINE);
            else
                {
                //IMPORTANT:  Make sure this object is running first
                OleRun(pObj);
                hr=pObj->QueryInterface(riid, ppv);
                }

            pObj->Release();
            }
```

(continued)

Listing 13-2. *continued*

```
        else
            hr=ResultFromScode(MK_E_NOOBJECT);
        }

    return hr;
    }

/*
 * CImpIOleItemContainer::GetObjectStorage
 *
 * Purpose:
 *  Similar to get Object in that we have to locate the object
 *  described by a given name, but instead of returning any old
 *  interface we return a storage element.
 *
 * Parameters:
 *  pszItem         LPSTR to the item we must locate.
 *  pcb             LPBINDCTX providing the binding context.
 *  riid            REFIID of the interface requested. Usually
 *                  IStorage or IStream.
 *  ppv             LPLPVOID into which to return the object.
 *
 * Return Value:
 *  HRESULT         NOERROR if successful, error code otherwise.
 */

STDMETHODIMP CImpIOleItemContainer::GetObjectStorage(LPSTR pszItem
    , LPBINDCTX pbc, REFIID riid, LPLPVOID ppv)
    {
    LPCTenant   pTenant;

    *ppv=NULL;

    if (m_fDoc)
        return ResultFromScode(E_NOTIMPL);

    //Can only handle IStorage.
    if (!IsEqualIID(riid, IID_IStorage))
        return ResultFromScode(E_NOINTERFACE);

    if (FTenantFromName(pszItem, &pTenant))
        pTenant->StorageGet((LPSTORAGE FAR *)ppv);

    return (NULL!=*ppv) ? NOERROR : ResultFromScode(E_FAIL);
    }
```

(continued)

Listing 13-2. *continued*

```
/*
 * CImpIOleItemContainer::IsRunning
 *
 * Purpose:
 *  Answers if the object under the given name is currently running.
 *
 * Parameters:
 *  pszItem         LPSTR of the item to check
 *
 * Return Value:
 *  HRESULT         NOERROR if the object is running, S_FALSE
 *                  otherwise. Possibly MK_E_NOOBJECT if the name
 *                  is bogus.
 */

STDMETHODIMP CImpIOleItemContainer::IsRunning(LPSTR pszItem)
    {
    HRESULT     hr;
    LPCTenant   pTenant;
    LPUNKNOWN   pObj;
    LPOLEOBJECT pIOleObject;

    /*
     * If this is the document's container interface, the object
     * is a page and the page is always running.
     */
    if (m_fDoc)
        return NOERROR;
    else
        {
        if (FTenantFromName(pszItem, &pTenant))
            {
            //Ask the actual object if its running.
            pTenant->ObjectGet(&pObj);
            hr=pObj->QueryInterface(IID_IOleObject
                , (LPLPVOID)&pIOleObject);
            pObj->Release();

            if (SUCCEEDED(hr))
                {
                hr=(OleIsRunning(pIOleObject))
```

(continued)

Listing 13-2. *continued*

```
                    ? NOERROR : ResultFromScode(S_FALSE);
                pIOleObject->Release();
                }
            }
        else
            hr=ResultFromScode(MK_E_NOOBJECT);
        }

    return hr;
    }

/*
 * CImpIOleItemContainer::FTenantFromName
 * (Private)
 *
 * Purpose:
 *  This function which is NOT part of the interface retrieves
 *  a tenant pointer from a tenant name.
 *
 * Parameters:
 *  pszItem         LPSTR of the tenant to locate.
 *  ppTenant        LPCTenant FAR * in which to return the pointer.
 *
 * Return Value:
 *  BOOL            TRUE if successful, FALSE otherwise.
 */

BOOL CImpIOleItemContainer::FTenantFromName(LPSTR pszItem
    , LPCTenant FAR *ppTenant)
    {
    DWORD       dw;
    char        szTemp[40];

    if (m_fDoc)
        return FALSE;

    //The item name should be "Tenant xxxx", so use pszItem+7
    lstrcpy(szTemp, (LPSTR)(pszItem+7));
    dw=atol(szTemp);

    *ppTenant=NULL;

    return m_pPage->FTenantGetFromID(dw, ppTenant, FALSE);
    }
```

As mentioned before, you do not need to implement some of these functions, such as *EnumObject. LockContainer* should look very familiar: If you compare it with Patron's implementation of *IClassFactory::LockServer*, you'll see that the two are identical.

Patron's implementation of this interface for the document level is the simplest because it only needs to resolve a page name to another *IOleItemContainer* interface. First, *IsRunning* always returns NOERROR (TRUE) because if the document is loaded into Patron, the page is essentially loaded (although the objects on it are not loaded). Note that OLE will not call *IsRunning* on this interface implemented on the page. OLE only calls *IsRunning* on behalf of the last moniker in the entire composite that it is binding because OLE can predict that there is no specific server to run for the intermediate monikers. By the same token, we don't have to worry much about *GetObjectStorage* for the document implementation because OLE itself has nothing to do with the page storage, whereas it has everything to do with a tenant's storage (such as the cached presentations it stores there). So *GetObjectStorage* and *IsRunning* are not important to the document.

That leaves the document with only having to resolve the page name *pszItem* into the *IOleItemContainer* interface on the page. The page name is in the form *Page xx* because we were the ones who stuffed it in an item moniker in the first place. So we can simply parse the number from this string, match that page identifier into a page index, and switch to that page. The function *CPages::IPageGetFromID* that we call here does the matching.

Here we see how to interpret the requested "bind speed" that we're given in the *dwSpeed* parameter. This might be BINDSPEED_IMMEDIATE, BINDSPEED_MODERATE, or BINDSPEED_INDEFINITE.[1] For an immediate speed, we only succeed if the page to which the caller wants to bind is the current page. If not, we'd have to switch to a new page. In Patron, that means loading objects and possibly updating links. So unless the desired page is current, we fail to bind with MK_E_EXCEEDEDDEADLINE, which tells the caller to either put up with the failure or give us more time. If we are given more time, we can switch to the page number we were told (using *CPages::CurPageSet,* which opens the page as well and sets *CPages::m_pPageCur*) and ask that page for its *IOleItemContainer* interface. Again, this is a different instantiation of the *CImpIOleItemContainer* interface, which will have a FALSE in *m_fDoc* to identify it as belonging to the page.

After we return that second *IOleItemContainer* pointer, we'll eventually see a call back into *GetObject* again. However, this time *m_fDoc* is FALSE and

1. Under OLE 2, this is *always* BINDSPEED_INDEFINITE. Future versions might be pickier.

so we execute the half of this function that resolves the name of a tenant, such as *Tenant xx*, into an actual interface pointer on the embedded object that lives in that tenant. Because matching a tenant name to a tenant pointer is something we need to do here as well as in *GetObjectStorage* and *IsRunning* for the page, the *CImplOleItemContainer* object that we defined for Patron has an internal function *FTenantFromName*, which centralizes parsing of the tenant name by calling *CPage::FTenantGetFromID* added for this chapter.

Back in *GetObject*, after we have a tenant pointer—that is, a pointer to whatever thing manages an embedded object in our container—we can check if it's running. If it's not, specifications say we must fail binding for all but BINDSPEED_INDEFINITE, again by returning MK_E_EXCEEDED-DEADLINE. Otherwise, we *must* make sure that the object is running by calling *OleRun* and then ask it for the interface the caller requested through *QueryInterface*.

You might have noticed that we used our own implementation of *IOleItemContainer::IsRunning* from *GetObject* to see whether the object was already running. This means we can centralize the code to check for the running state in one place. Implementing *IsRunning* is simply a matter of calling *OleIsRunning* with an *IOleObject* pointer.

Finally, *GetObjectStorage* is required to return a pointer (after calling *AddRef*) to the object's storage medium. Your application might be asked to return an *IStorage* or *IStream* pointer, so you should ensure that you can provide the correct interface before going any further. In Patron, we make sure our application is asked for an *IStorage* pointer. If it is, we can simply ask the tenant identified by the item name to return the *IStorage* pointer it maintains internally using *CTenant::StorageGet*:

```
void CTenant::StorageGet(LPSTORAGE FAR *ppStg)
    {
    if (NULL==ppStg)
        return;

    *ppStg=m_pIStorage;

    if (NULL!=*ppStg)
        (*ppStg)->AddRef();

    return;
    }
```

There are two additional tasks a container needs to do before you can consider linking-to-embedding complete. Remember *IOleClientSite*? Remember *IOleClientSite::GetContainer*? This function is specified to return the

IOleItemContainer interface in which the object lives. For Patron it means that each site should be able to return the interface pointer on the page in which the tenant lives as we can see in the following code:

```
STDMETHODIMP CImpIOleClientSite::GetContainer(LPOLECONTAINER FAR
    *ppContainer)
    {
    CPAGE  pPage;

    *ppContainer=NULL;

    m_pTen->m_pPG->IPageGetFromID((DWORD)-1, &pPage, FALSE);

    if (NULL!=pPage)
        {
        return pPage->QueryInterface(IID_IOleItemContainer
            , (LPLPVOID)ppContainer);
        }

    return ResultFromScode(E_FAIL);
    }
```

The function *CPages::IPageGetFromID* conveniently returns the current *CPage* pointer to us through which we can call *QueryInterface.*

In addition, we also need to make one more change to *IOleClientSite::ShowObject.* In earlier samples, this function was responsible for bringing the object into view. Well, because this container application can now be launched with *-Embedding* on the command line, in which case it does not initially show its window, *ShowObject* must now also show the container application window, making everything visible:

```
STDMETHODIMP CImpIOleClientSite::ShowObject(void)
    {
    HWND        hWnd, hWndT;

    m_pTen->ShowYourself();

    //For linking to embedding, now show the main window.
    hWndT=GetParent(m_pTen->m_hWnd);

    while (NULL!=hWndT)
        {
        hWnd=hWndT;
        hWndT=GetParent(hWnd);
        }

    ShowWindow(hWnd, SW_SHOW);
    return NOERROR;
    }
```

I apologize that all this discussion was centered around Patron and containers that provide linking to embeddings, but the implementations of the functions in *IOleItemContainer* are pretty much the same for a server that provides linking to specific selections. In the case of a server, you will need only one implementation of *IOleItemContainer*, where you need not implement *GetObjectStorage* (OLE will not ask for it) and where *IsRunning* should always return NOERROR because the selection is always running if the document in which it lives is already loaded in a running server. Because it is always running, it will not need to pay attention to the *dwSpeed* flag in *GetObject*. You can do whatever it takes to return the requested interface pointer to the caller.

With your implementation(s) of this interface in place, you can now test full linking-to-embedding in a container application. When you activate that object, you will now see all the calls made to *IPersistFile*, including a *QueryInterface* for *IOleItemContainer*. After that, you will see a call to *IOleItemContainer::GetObject*, which should eventually (perhaps through more implementations of *IOleItemContainer*) return a pointer to a running embedded object. Make sure it's running. After you return that pointer you can expect some calls to your *IOleClientSite*, such as *ShowObject*, at which time you should show your window.

What also happens unbeknownst to your container is that OLE has established advises between the other linking container and the embedded object in the running server. When you make a change to the object in the server, you will see the object change in both your container *and* the other one. To the user, it appears that the server is updating your embedded object, which is then updating the linked object in the other container, as expected. (But your container doesn't have to worry about advising itself.)

Summary

A source of a link has two responsibilities: to create a moniker that clearly identifies the source data and to assist the OLE 2 libraries in binding that moniker. If the source is identified by only a simple file moniker, the application only needs to provide a document object that implements *IPersistFile* in order to load the linked file. Compound document object interfaces, such as *IOleObject* and *IDataObject*, must be available through *QueryInterface* through *IPersistFile*.

If the source identifies the data using a composite *File!Item* moniker, it must provide a document object with the *IPersistFile* and *IOleItemContainer* interfaces, but no others are needed. *IOleItemContainer* is then given the item moniker's name which it must resolve into a compound document object interface.

If the source identifies the data by using a composite moniker with more items, such as *File!Item!Item,* it must implement a document object with *IPersistFile* and *IOleItemContainer,* where that document's implementation of *IOleItemContainer* must be able to resolve the middle item name into another *IOleItemContainer* that is able to resolve the name of the rightmost item moniker into a compound document object interface.

And so the story goes, for as many item monikers as are tacked onto the end of a composite. A file moniker requires an *IPersistFile* interface, an item moniker requires an *IOleItemContainer* interface. Where you implement these and how they are used are covered in this chapter as we add linking capabilities to Cosmo that allow linking to its files as a whole, and to Patron, which allows linking to objects embedded within its pages. Patron has now ceased to be only a container: It's now also a server for embedded objects from other servers, but it does not have to implement all the interfaces such as *IOleObject* and *IDataObject.* If you did implement these interfaces within that same structure, however, you would have a server that could resolve composite monikers into the data source of a link.

CHAPTER FOURTEEN

CONVERSION, EMULATION, AND COMPATIBILITY WITH OLE 1

With OLE 1, one server from one vendor couldn't manipulate an embedded object that was originally created in a different server. For a long time, vendors have provided conversion utilities to read and write the files of all their competitors, but under OLE 1 there was no way to do this with embedded objects. Also end users expect that if they receive a container document that contains what appear to be spreadsheet objects, they can edit those objects with whatever spreadsheet they happened to have installed. But they can't under OLE 1, so they just stew in rage.

OLE 2 attempts to solve that problem by using the processes that are generally called *Conversion* and *Emulation.* Conversion is the process of changing the class of an embedded object from one CLSID to another in such a way that it will, from that time forward, always be considered an object of the new CLSID. There is no going back. This approach is like an application from one vendor reading a competitor's file format and then overwriting the file with its own format. After the overwrite, the original file is gone. Emulation, on the other hand, is the temporary treatment of one object class as if it were another class, but the persistent class of the object does not change. This is, to use the file example again, like an application reading a competitor's file, making changes, and saving that file in the same format. The structure of that file does not change.

In OLE 2, conversion and emulation affect both servers and containers. In this chapter, we'll look at how to write a server that can convert or emulate another object class. Specifically, we'll modify Cosmo so that it will be able to convert and emulate Polyline objects (objects created through

POLYLINE.DLL, which we developed in Chapter 11). The modifications are not extensive; they involve only the Registration Database and the server's *IPersistStorage* interface implementation. There are also ways to install a server in such a way that all objects of another class (say, those from a prior version of your application) are automatically converted.

The container is then responsible for invoking the Convert dialog box, which allows the end user to convert an object to another class or to specify that all objects of one class should be treated the same way as those of another class. In addition, this dialog box allows the end user to change the view aspect of the object from whatever it normally is to an iconic representation by using the same Display As Icon interface seen in other dialog boxes, such as Insert Object and Paste Special. We'll see all of this implemented in Patron.

Conversion of object classes between OLE 2 servers is similar to conversion from an OLE 1 embedded object to an OLE 2 embedded object. For the most part, the process is identical to conversion from another OLE 2 embedded object of a different CLSID, with some small differences. To demonstrate this process, we'll modify the OLE 2 version of Cosmo in this chapter to enable us to convert and emulate embedded objects from the OLE 1 version of Cosmo presented in Chapter 2.

Finally, we'll briefly look at a little defensive coding in Patron to prevent a few problems I've noticed when working with a few OLE 1 servers. In addition, we'll discuss some support functions that help containers convert old files that contain OLE 1 objects to a compound file that contains OLE 2 objects. This, however, will only be discussion, without any implementation in Patron. Patron did, in fact, have an OLE 1 version long ago, but the differences between the two versions are too great to convert files between them (the OLE 1 version had no page concept, as the OLE 2 version does).

The extra work to support conversion, emulation, and OLE 1 compatibility is not major, but the payoff can be very important for your end users.

The Convert Dialog Box for Containers

Let's say I'm the vendor of MySpreadsheet, which is a server of MyTable objects. Let's say you are a vendor of YourSpreadsheet, which is a server for YourTable objects. Now imagine two people, Bev and Maurice. They both use the same word processor (which is a container application) but Bev has purchased MySpreadsheet and Maurice has purchased YourSpreadsheet.

One day Bev writes a report about barnacles on boat hulls and includes some data in an embedded MyTable table object created with MySpreadsheet. This embedded object, of course, has the CLSID of MyTable and stores its data in a specific registered clipboard format, which is called MyTableFormat. This report goes to Maurice, who opens it to make a few additions to the table from his research before sending it on. However, Maurice does not have MySpreadsheet installed on his machine, so when he double-clicks on that table object, OLE fails to locate the server, and he cannot make his additions. Well, this is entirely unsuitable, wouldn't you say? Under OLE 1, Maurice was stuck—because he didn't have MySpreadsheet, there was nothing he could do to modify that object except obtain a copy of MySpreadsheet himself.

Fortunately, MySpreadsheet is an OLE 2 server and the word processor is an OLE 2 container, so Maurice simply invokes the Convert dialog box on the object, as shown in Figure 14-1. The dialog box displays information from the Registration Database on his machine to see whether there's any other application that can handle data stored in MyTableFormat (because that's what MySpreadsheet writes for MyTable objects). Now, if YourSpreadsheet were aware of MyTableFormat (as good competitors are), you will have created the appropriate entries in the Registration Database that says YourSpreadsheet can either convert objects that are stored in MyTableFormat into its own YourTable objects or emulate them. If you can convert such objects to your own format (which means you can read MyTableFormat but cannot write it), the name of your objects will appear in the dialog box when Convert To is selected. If you can emulate such objects (which means that you can both read and write MyTableFormat), your descriptive name will appear when Activate As is selected.

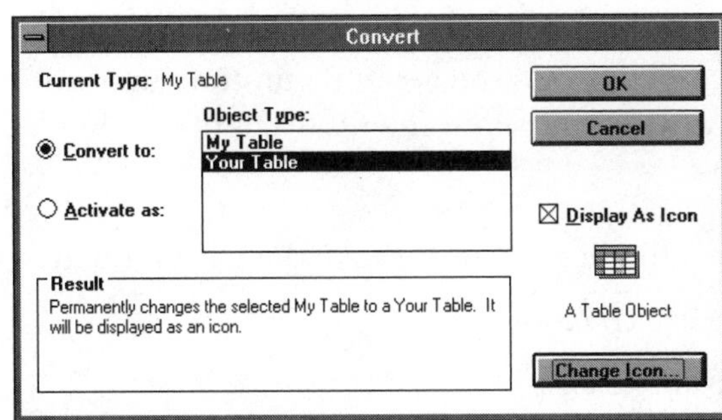

Figure 14-1.
The Convert dialog box invoked on a hypothetical MySpreadsheet object for the Conversion case.

If Maurice selects Convert To and chooses OK, the embedded object in the container will be changed from a MyTable object to a YourTable object, in which the data structure of the object's storage will be in a format known to YourSpreadsheet, such as YourTableFormat. In conversion, that object is now considered a YourTable object until it's converted to something else.

Let's say that Maurice did convert this object to YourSpreadsheet and that the document returned to Bev, who has MySpreadsheet. If MySpreadsheet is not aware of YourSpreadsheet, and MySpreadsheet is not able to convert YourTable objects into MyTable objects, Bev will not be able to manipulate that table again. If Maurice realizes this, he can instead use the Activate As option in the Convert dialog box. When he selects Activate As and presses OK, the embedded object opens for editing in YourSpreadsheet (if it can read and write MyTableFormat), but the object remains a MyTable object, meaning that when it goes back to Bev, she can still manipulate it as if nothing has happened. More accurately, she doesn't know that Maurice actually used another server to make additions to the object because he used YourSpreadsheet to emulate MySpreadsheet.

In addition, Maurice's act of selecting Activate As in the Convert dialog box created an entry in his Registration Database that says all MyTable objects that appear on his machine any time in the future will be treated as if they were YourTable objects—that is, YourSpreadsheet will always be used to emulate objects originally created with MySpreadsheet.

Basically, that's what conversion and emulation are all about. Conversion is the process of changing one embedded object of one CLSID into another, in all respects, including what's written in the object's storage. Emulation is the process of manipulating objects of one CLSID in another server, different from the one that created the object, that marked itself as capable of reading and writing those objects.

Container applications provide the general run-time user interface for these features, which involves four requirements, each of which is described in the sections that follow:

- Support a Convert menu item and invoke the Convert dialog box
- Handle the Convert To case
- Handle the Activate As case
- Handle Display As Icon changes

The fourth item might seem a little out of place because it has to do only with changing the displayed aspect of an object and has nothing to do with the server that is used to activate that object. But because it happens from the Convert dialog box, we'll invariably see the code to handle icon changes in the same places as handling the other features.

Support a Convert Menu Item and Invoke the Convert Dialog Box

To invoke the Convert dialog box, of course, we need some way for the user to say when. Because the Convert dialog box generally applies to one object, the natural place for a Convert item is on an object-specific pop-up menu. An object's verbs appear on the pop-up menu as specified in the OLE 2 User Interface Guidelines in the *OLE 2 Programmer's Reference.* So, for example, the pop-up menu for a Polyline object should now appear in Patron as shown in Figure 14-2. Note that the verb menu should appear identical, whether it is on the Edit menu or on a pop-up menu, as shown.

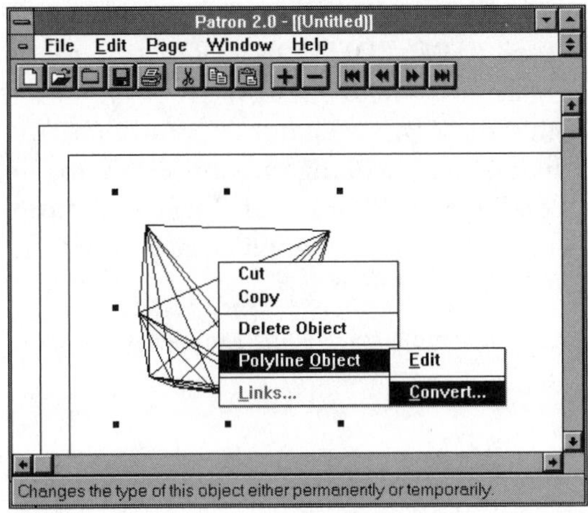

Figure 14-2.
Where the Convert menu item should appear for an object.

Adding and maintaining this menu item is easy. Remember the *OleUIAddVerbMenu function* we used back in Chapter 9 to create the verb pop-up menu in the first place? Remember its two parameters *bAddConvert* and *idConvert?* These are simply the parameters we need now. By setting *bAddConvert* to TRUE and passing a WM_COMMAND identifier in *idConvert, OleUIAddVerbMenu* will add the separator and the Convert item for us. In Patron, this affects only *CTenant::AddVerbMenu,* which now enables Convert... with the identifier of IDM_EDITCONVERT.

```
void CTenant::AddVerbMenu(HMENU hMenu, UINT iPos)
    {
    HMENU       hMenuTemp;
    LPOLEOBJECT pObj=m_pIOleObject;

    //If we're static, say we have no object.
    if (TENANTTYPE_STATIC==m_tType)
        pObj=NULL;

    OleUIAddVerbMenu(pObj, NULL, hMenu, iPos, IDM_VERBMIN
        , TRUE, IDM_EDITCONVERT, &hMenuTemp);

    return;
    }
```

Note that because the Convert item is always part of the object's verb pop-up menu, it will not be present if there is no object, so you don't need any other code to enable or disable it.

Now when Patron sees IDM_EDITCONVERT (in *CPatronFrame::OnCommand*), it will call *CPatronDoc::FConvertObject*, which calls *CPages::FConvertObject*, which calls *CPage::FConvertObject*, which finally does the honor of invoking the dialog box. Invoking the Convert dialog box is, like invoking our other OLE UI dialog box, a matter of filling a structure—in this case OLEUICONVERT—and calling the appropriate function in the OLE2UI library—in this case *OleUIConvert*:

```
BOOL CPage::FConvertObject(HWND hWndFrame, BOOL fNoServer)
    {
    HRESULT         hr;
    OLEUICONVERT    ct;
    TENANTTYPE      tType;
    FORMATETC       fe;
    UINT            uRet;
    HCURSOR         hCur;
    BOOL            fActivate=fNoServer;
    RECTL           rcl;

    if (NULL==m_pTenantCur)
        return FALSE;

    tType=m_pTenantCur->TypeGet();

    if (TENANTTYPE_STATIC==tType)
        {
        MessageBeep(0);
        return FALSE;
        }
```

```
//Get object information we may want.
m_pTenantCur->FormatEtcGet(&fe, FALSE);

//Fill the structure.
_fmemset(&ct, 0, sizeof(ct));
ct.cbStruct=sizeof(OLEUICONVERT);
ct.hWndOwner=hWndFrame;
ct.fIsLinkedObject=(TENANTTYPE_LINKEDOBJECT==tType);
ct.dvAspect=fe.dwAspect;

m_pTenantCur->ObjectClassFormatAndIcon(&ct.clsid, &ct.wFormat
    , &ct.lpszUserType, &ct.hMetaPict);

uRet=OleUIConvert(&ct);

if (OLEUI_OK==uRet)

[Code to handle the OK button goes here]

if (ct.lpszUserType)
    OleStdFreeString(ct.lpszUserType, NULL);

if (ct.hMetaPict)
    OleUIMetafilePictIconFree(ct.hMetaPict);

return TRUE;
}
```

The parameter *fNoServer* is a flag you might want to use, but it is one that Patron does not use to indicate that an attempt to invoke a verb on an object failed. If you find that it failed because the server does not exist for that object, you can dump directly into the Convert dialog box. This parameter would indicate that situation. We'll use that approach in some of the following cases.

First, we cannot convert a static object (that is, a presentation with no information about its source), so we don't invoke the dialog box in such an instance. Otherwise, we would fill the OLEUICONVERT structure with the typical structure size and owner window as well as with an indicator of whether the object is linked and information about the current aspect of the object. In addition, to support the Display As Icon feature of the dialog box, we need to obtain the CLSID, the clipboard format, the user type string, and the metafile containing the iconic aspect from the object as appropriate. Here we use *CTenant::ObjectClassFormatAndIcon* to retrieve that information, which calls *ReadClassStg* (or *IOleObject::GetClassID* if *ReadClassStg* fails) to get the CLSID, *ReadFmtUserTypeStg* (or *OleStdGetUserTypeOfClass*) to get the format and the user type, and *IDataObject::GetData* with DVASPECT_ICON for the iconic metafile. This code is merely a sequence of these calls, done in the tenant because the tenant has all the actual object pointers. The code is not important enough to show for our discussion here.

With the OLEUICONVERT structure filled, we can now call *OleUIConvert*, which displays the dialog box and returns a value indicating which button was chosen. If OK was chosen, we generally have a lot more work to do. If another button was chosen, we need to do some cleanup, first freeing the string from *ReadFmtUserTypeStg* that we stored in *ct.lpszUserType* by calling *OleStdFreeString*, and then freeing the iconic metafile by using *OleUIMetafilePictIconFree*. Note that we do these cleanup steps regardless of whether OK or Cancel was chosen.

If OK was chosen we first change the cursor to an hourglass because what we're about to do can take a while:

```
if (OLEUI_OK==uRet)
    {
    //Potentially a long operation.
    hCur=SetCursor(LoadCursor(NULL, IDC_WAIT));

    [Other operations]

    SetCursor(hCur);
    }
```

Then we can handle each of the three cases: Convert To, Activate As, and Display As Icon.

Handle the Convert To Case

If the end user selected Convert To in the dialog box and chose OK, *OleUIConvert* will return with CF_SELECTCONVERTTO in the *dwFlags* field of the OLEUICONVERT structure. If this is set, the user wants to convert the current object to a different CLSID. This process involves four steps:

1. Unload the object, taking it back to the passive state.
2. Call *OleStdDoAutoConvert*, which calls *WriteClassStg*, *WriteFmtUserTypeStg*, and *SetConvertStg*.
3. Reload the object with *OleLoad* and then force an update, which means set the document's dirty flag and force a repaint.
4. If the Convert dialog box was invoked as a result of a failed activation, activate the object now.

These steps can be seen in the following code taken from Patron's *CPage::FConvertObject*.

```
BOOL            fActivate=fNoServer;
RECTL           rcl;
...
if ((CF_SELECTCONVERTTO & ct.dwFlags)
    && !IsEqualCLSID(ct.clsid, ct.clsidNew))
    {
    LPSTORAGE   pIStorage;

    m_pTenantCur->RectGet(&rcl, FALSE);
    m_pTenantCur->StorageGet(&pIStorage);
    m_pTenantCur->Close(FALSE, FALSE);

    hr=OleStdDoConvert(pIStorage, ct.clsidNew);
    pIStorage->Release();

    if (SUCCEEDED(hr))
        {
        LPUNKNOWN    pObj;
        LPOLEOBJECT pIOleObject;

        //Reload and update.
        m_pTenantCur->FLoad(m_pIStorage, &fe, &rcl);

        m_pTenantCur->ObjectGet(&pObj);
        pObj->QueryInterface(IID_IOleObject
            , (LPLPVOID)&pIOleObject);
        pIOleObject->Update();
        pIOleObject->Release();
        pObj->Release();
        }

    m_pPG->m_fDirty=TRUE;
    }
m_pTenantCur->Repaint();
if (fActivate)
    m_pTenantCur->Activate(OLEIVERB_SHOW);
```

Closing the object is necessary because there might be a specific object handler for the new class to which we're converting and we have to make sure that handler is now loaded for this object. The process of taking the object to the passive state and then reloading it does the trick.

As mentioned in the preceding steps, *OleStdDoAutoConvert* calls *WriteClassStg* (to change the CLSID of the object from the old to the new), *WriteFmtUserTypeStg* (to ensure that these pieces of information match the CLSID), and *SetConvertStg.* This last function, which we haven't seen before, specifically marks the *IStorage* for this object as being converted to a new

CLSID. We mark the object in this way because although the CLSID, format, and user type have changed, the actual data in the *IStorage* has not changed. By calling *SetConvertStg*, we tell the server of the new CLSID to write its own data to the *IStorage* and to remove all other elements in that storage that belonged to the old CLSID, as we'll see later in "Conversion Between Servers."

After we have marked the object's storage as appropriate, we can reload the object (here, by using *CTenant::FLoad*, which calls *OleLoad*) and call *IOleObject::Update* to ensure that the presentation matches what the server of the new CLSID would want there. Of course, if we update an object, we should repaint as well as set our dirty flag.

Finally, as I mentioned in the preceding steps, you might have invoked the Convert dialog box because a call to *IOleObject::DoVerb* failed with an error code such as *REG_E_CLASSNOTREG* or *CO_E_APPNOTFOUND*, which generally means that the server for the object is not available. In this case, you'll want to invoke the Convert dialog box to let the user check for other servers that might be able to convert or emulate the object in question.[1] If the Convert dialog box was invoked for such an occasion, as indicated by the *fActivate* flag in Patron, you need to activate the object immediately after the Convert To case because the user wanted to activate the object in the first place.

Handle the Activate As Case

The Convert dialog box might also return the CF_SELECTACTIVATEAS in *dwFlags*, in which case we need to perform the following four steps:

1. Add the *TreatAs* entry in the Registration Database and call *CoTreatAsClass*, which is all handled through *OleStdDoTreatAsClass*.
2. Unload all objects of the old CLSID that you have loaded. You can do this before step 1 if necessary.
3. Reload all the unloaded objects as necessary.
4. Set your document's dirty flag to TRUE, activate the current object, and repaint.

These steps, again, are shown in the following code from Patron's *CPage::FConvertObject*.

1. Note that in the OLE 2.01 release, the OLE2UI library has an additional function, *OleUICanConvertOrActivateAs*, to determine whether the Convert dialog box will actually show anything useful to the end user. Without this function, you could invoke an empty dialog box, which might merely cause confusion. This function is not called from the version of Patron in this chapter, however, to remain compatible with the OLE 2.00 release.

```
BOOL            fActivate=fNoServer;

if (CF_SELECTACTIVATEAS & ct.dwFlags)
   {
    hr=OleStdDoTreatAsClass(ct.lpszUserType
        , ct.clsid, ct.clsidNew);

    if (SUCCEEDED(hr))
        {
        FORMATETC   feT;
        LPTENANT    pTenant;
        UINT        i;

        for (i=0; i < m_cTenants; i++)
            {
            if (FTenantGet(i, &pTenant, FALSE))
                {
                pTenant->RectGet(&rcl, FALSE);
                pTenant->FormatEtcGet(&feT, FALSE);
                pTenant->Close(FALSE, TRUE);
                pTenant->FLoad(m_pIStorage, &feT, &rcl);
                }
            }

        fActivate=TRUE;
        }
   }

m_pTenantCur->Repaint();
if (fActivate)
    m_pTenantCur->Activate(OLEIVERB_SHOW);
```

OleStdDoTreatAsClass adds an entry under the CLSID of the original object in the following form:

```
\
    CLSID
        {<CLSID of original object>} ...
            TreatAs = {<CLSID selected in dialog>}
```

This means that from now on, until the end user makes a change using the Convert dialog box again, all objects of the original CLSID will be emulated using the server for the CLSID selected in the dialog box. Note that this includes OLE 1 servers because OLE 2 registers Microsoft-assigned CLSIDs for all of the known OLE 1 servers. In any case, because the addition of the *TreatAs* key in the Registration Database affects all objects of the original CLSID, you should unload and reload all objects of that CLSID to reflect the change. It would be preferable to do this throughout the system, but that simply isn't practical under OLE 2. Patron does this unload-reload process in one nice, tight loop that iterates all tenants in the current page. Patron also could (but doesn't to avoid extra complexity) go through the same process in all other open documents in an MDI version. You might want to consider doing this yourself.

The final step, activating the current object, should always happen for the Activate As case because the user reads "Activate As" in the dialog box and so expects an activation to happen. The result text in the dialog box also tells the user that activation will happen, so it's a good idea to comply.

Handle Display As Icon Changes

You might have noticed the extra condition on the Convert To case in the preceding code that compared the old and new CLSIDs:

```
!IsEqualCLSID(ct.clsid, ct.clsidNew)
```

This check first prevents unnecessary unloading and reloading of an object in case the user said "Convert to the same object." So why does the user have the option in the first place? Because the user might want to change the display aspect of the object to or from the iconic aspect by using the Display As Icon check box. (This check box is displayed only when Convert To is selected, which is why the call to *IsEqualCLSID* appears in the code only for that case.) If the user did change the aspect, we need to reflect that change in the container.

Patron does this by calling *CTenant::FSwitchOrUpdateAspect*, which handles changes between DVASPECT_CONTENT and DVASPECT_ICON, as well as cases in which the aspect doesn't change but the icon does:

```
if ((DVASPECT_ICON==ct.dvAspect && ct.fObjectsIconChanged)
    || ct.dvAspect!=fe.dwAspect)
    {
    HGLOBAL      hMem=NULL;

    //Only pass non-NULL handle for icon aspects.
    if (DVASPECT_ICON==ct.dvAspect)
        hMem=ct.hMetaPict;

    m_pPG->m_fDirty=m_pTenantCur->FSwitchOrUpdateAspect(hMem
        , FALSE);
    }
```

The *fObjectsIconChanged* flag in the OLEUICONVERT structure indicates the latter case: The object was and still is DVASPECT_ICON, but the actual icon changed. Therefore, we need to take the new metafile for that icon and stuff it in the cache so that we can repaint with the new image. Otherwise, we might be switching from DVASPECT_CONTENT to DVASPECT_ICON or vice-versa. If we're going from content to icon, we pass the new metafile handle to the tenant; otherwise, we pass NULL, meaning that we're going to content from icon.

CTenant::FSwitchOrUpdateAspect takes advantage of a number of convenient functions in the OLE2UI library:

```
BOOL CTenant::FSwitchOrUpdateAspect(HGLOBAL hMetaIcon, BOOL fPreserve)
    {
    HRESULT     hr;
    DWORD       dwAspect;
    BOOL        fUpdate=FALSE;

    //Nothing to do if we're content already and there's no icon.
    if (NULL==hMetaIcon && DVASPECT_CONTENT==m_fe.dwAspect)
        return FALSE;

    //If we're iconic already, just cache the new icon
    if (NULL!=hMetaIcon && DVASPECT_ICON==m_fe.dwAspect)
        hr=OleStdSetIconInCache(m_pIOleObject, hMetaIcon);
    else
        {
        //Otherwise, switch between iconic and content.
        dwAspect=(NULL==hMetaIcon) ? DVASPECT_CONTENT : DVASPECT_ICON;

        /*
         * Switch between aspects, where dwAspect has the new one
         * and m_fe.dwAspect will be changed in the process.
         */
        hr=OleStdSwitchDisplayAspect(m_pIOleObject, &m_fe.dwAspect
            , dwAspect, hMetaIcon, !fPreserve, TRUE, m_pIAdviseSink
            , &fUpdate);

        if (fUpdate && SUCCEEDED(hr))
            {
            m_pIOleObject->Update();    //This repaints.
            return TRUE;
            }
        }

    //If we switched, update our extents.
    if (SUCCEEDED(hr))
        {
        SIZEL       szl;
```

(continued)

```
        m_pIOleObject->GetExtent(m_fe.dwAspect, &szl);

        if (0 > szl.cy)
            szl.cy=-szl.cy;

        //Convert HIMETRIC absolute units to our LOMETRIC mapping
        if (0!=szl.cx && 0!=szl.cy)
            SETSIZEL(szl, szl.cx/10, -szl.cy/10);

        Invalidate();              //Remove old aspect
        SizeSet(&szl, FALSE);      //Change size
        Repaint();                 //Paint the new one
        }

    return SUCCEEDED(hr);
    }
```

First, if we're merely changing the icon but not the aspect, we can simply call *OleStdSetIconInCache*, which frees the old cached presentation and caches the new one. Otherwise, we need to switch aspects, which is an arduous process of changing what we cache (by calling *IOleCache::Uncache* and *IOleCache::Cache*), storing a presentation for the new aspect in the cache, updating the presentation, and changing the advise we have on the object's *IViewObject* interface to the new aspect. All of that work is best left to *OleStdSwitchDisplayAspects*. When the aspects are switched, Patron calls *IOleObject::Update*, which generates a call to our *IAdviseSink::OnViewChange*, which repaints.

The other important task we need to perform here, at least for Patron, is to change the size of the tenant if we changed aspects. We do this so that a switch from a content aspect to an iconic aspect shows the icon in the standard icon size and so that a switch in the other direction doesn't squash the content aspect into the size of an icon. A quick call to *IOleObject::GetExtent* and a resize of the tenant does the job.

With that, you have handled all the cases that might result from the Convert dialog box.

Conversion Between Servers

Now that we know how a container is going to cause all sorts of nasty things to happen to our servers, how do we prepare for the onslaught? Server support for both conversion and emulation is actually quite straightforward, requiring you only to make some additional changes to your entries in the Registration Database—some of which are appropriate at the time you install your application—and requiring small modifications to your *IPersistStorage* implementation. But that's it. As you will see, the bark is worse than the bite.

The sample we'll use to illustrate these changes to *IPersistStorage* will be Cosmo. Note that these changes are also required for any *IPersistStorage* implementation in your own object handler, such as HCosmo. However, this book does not provide a revision of HCosmo with the modifications outlined here because those are left as an exercise for the reader. To ensure that you do not attempt to use HCosmo from Chapter 11, the CHAP14\CHAP14.REG file will remove the specific handler and reinstate OLE2.DLL as the handler for Cosmo figure objects.

Registration Database Entries for Conversion

There are three additional keys of interest to a server that you can register under your server's CLSID: *AutoConvertTo, TreatAs,* and *Conversion.* The first two are created primarily during installation when a previous version of your server (and thus objects of that previous version) exist on the machine. The other is also created at installation time but is used to specify which other object classes your server can read and possibly write. This information is then used by a container's Convert dialog box.

AutoConvertTo and *TreatAs*

The first key you might want to create at installation time is *AutoConvertTo.* During installation, you can check for the presence of a prior version of your server, and if one exists, you can ask the user whether he or she wants to automatically convert all objects from the previous server. The OLE 2 User Interface Guidelines (in the *OLE 2 Programmer's Reference*) recommends that you present a Yes/No message box with the text "Do you want to automatically upgrade all *<application prior version>* objects to *<application new version>* the next time each is activated?" If the user answers Yes, you should add the *AutoConvertTo* entry under your CLSID:

```
\
    CLSID
        {<CLSID of prior version>} ...
            AutoConvertTo = {<CLSID of new version>}
```

where the CLSID after *AutoConvertTo* is, of course, the CLSID value spelled out in text and contained between two braces. Again, because OLE 2 registers Microsoft-assigned CLSIDs for all known OLE 1 servers, *AutoConvertTo* affects those as well.

The presence of this flag means that any time the CLSID of the prior version is used in any situation, no matter whether it is Insert Object or Paste

Special, or, when activating an object, the CLSID of the new version will actually be used, the object will behave as if it were an object of the new version. This is, again, what is meant by object conversion.

You can add the second key, *TreatAs*, if the user answers No to the first question during installation. The *"OLE User Interface Guidelines"* chapter of *OLE 2 Programmer's Reference* recommends that if the user does not want to automatically convert old objects to the new version, you allow the user to always use the new server to handle the old object but without changing the version of the object itself. In this case, your installation program should present the question "Do you want to use <*application new version*> to activate existing <*application prior version*> objects without upgrading them?" in a Yes/No dialog box. If the user answers Yes, you need to add the *TreatAs* key under your CLSID:

```
\
    CLSID
        {<CLSID of prior version>} ...
            TreatAs = {<CLSID of new version>}
```

Your new server will always be used to service all objects—new or existing—of the prior CLSID, but those objects still retain the old version. If, for example, the user invokes the Insert Object dialog box in a container and selects the old server, OLE will launch your new server but will read and write the old version. This is again what is meant by object emulation—we are using a new program to emulate the behavior of a prior version.

If the end user answers No to both questions, you should not add either of these keys: The two versions of the server are considered independent. Note that the samples do not demonstrate these messages nor do they demonstrate creation of these keys because we don't have a real installation program.

Conversion

Conversion and emulation do not stop simply to deal with old versions of your own server. OLE 2 also allows you to convert and emulate objects from other servers altogether. (Your old server is merely a special type of "other server.") In this case, conversion means that your server is capable of reading another object class, but you are not capable of writing it in that same format. In other words, you must always write the object in your own format, which means conversion. Emulation, on the other hand, means that your server is capable of both reading and writing another object class, in which case your server can be used to service those objects without changing the object's original class.

To now specify which objects you can convert and which objects you can emulate, you create entries under the *Conversion* key for your server's CLSID using the following form:

```
\
    CLSID
        Conversion
            Readable
                Main = <format,format,format,format,...>
            Readwritable
                Main = <format,format,format,format,...>
```

Anything entered under *Readable* specifies which formats you can convert; those under *Readwritable* specify those you can emulate. These keys are used from a container's Convert dialog box.

So what do you use for in each format value? These are the text strings of the clipboard formats you can convert from and emulate. Why a clipboard format? Think back to our discussions of the *IPersistStorage* interface in Chapters 5, 10, and 11. There we saw that when writing our data to a storage object, we also needed to make two other function calls,

```
WriteFmtUserTypeStg(pIStorage, cf, szUserType);
```

where *pIStorage* is the storage in which we saved our object, *cf* is the registered clipboard format of our data, and *szUserType* is a human-readable description of the object. What's important to us here is the *cf* we passed to *WriteFmtUserTypeStg*: In doing so, we marked the object as having a specific data structure, and that structure is described by *cf*. Therefore, anyone else in the entire system can call *ReadFmtUserTypeStg* to retrieve the value of *cf*. OLE and the Convert dialog box use this format to find other servers in the Registration Database.

For example, we would like the version of Cosmo we create in this chapter to be able to convert and emulate objects created with the Polyline DLL server from Chapter 11. Polyline writes its objects in a format identified with the string "Polyline Figure", so Cosmo registers this under *Conversion\Readable* for conversion and *Conversion\Readwritable* for emulation:

```
Conversion
    Readable
        Main = Polyline Figure
    Readwritable
        Main = Polyline Figure
```

Now if a container invokes the Convert dialog box on a Polyline object, the dialog box will show "Cosmo 2.0 Figure" (the descriptive name of Cosmo's objects) for both the Convert To option and the Treat As option.

What we have to worry about now is how to handle these cases in the server, which affects only your implementation of *IPersistStorage*.

IPersistStorage Modifications

Overall, the modifications to *IPersistStorage* are minimal, affecting only the member functions of *GetClassID*, *Load*, and *Save*. First, *GetClassID* has to return the CLSID of the object as will be written to the storage, which is your server's actual CLSID if you are converting, but which is the CLSID of the other object if you are emulating. To know whether you are converting or emulating and to remember the CLSID we're working on, we need two additional variables accessible from the *IPersistStorage* implementation, which I've added to *CImpIPersistStorage* in COSMOLE.H:

```
class __far CImpIPersistStorage : public IPersistStorage
    {
    protected:
        [Other members]

        BOOL                    m_fConvert;  //Are we Converting?
        CLSID                   m_clsID;     //CLSID for GetClassID

    [Other members]
    }
```

Initially *m_fConvert* is set to FALSE, and *m_clsID* is set to CLSID_Cosmo2Figure. *IPersistStorage::GetClassID* is then implemented by returning *m_clsID*. Previously, we always returned CLSID_Cosmo2Figure:

```
STDMETHODIMP CImpIPersistStorage::GetClassID(LPCLSID pClsID)
    {
    *pClsID=m_clsID;
    return NOERROR;
    }
```

Now we have to examine modifications to *IPersistStorage::Load* that will change *m_fConvert* and *m_clsID*:

```
STDMETHODIMP CImpIPersistStorage::Load(LPSTORAGE pIStorage)
    {
    ...

    //This tells us if we're coming from another class storage.
    m_fConvert=(NOERROR==GetConvertStg(pIStorage));

    //This is the type of storage we're really messing with in Treat As
    if (!m_fConvert)
        ReadClassStg(pIStorage, &m_clsID);

    [Code to call CPolyline::ReadFromStream as usual]
    }
```

Before adding conversion and emulation support, this function in Cosmo simply called *CPolyline::ReadFromStream.* Now we have to determine whether our application has been asked to convert the object in the storage by calling *GetConvertStg,* which returns the value of a specific bit in the storage that is twiddled in a container's Convert dialog box when it calls *SetConvertStg.* This function returns NOERROR if we are converting the object to our own CLSID, and S_FALSE if we're not. So be careful not to use the SUCCEEDED macro here; instead compare directly to NOERROR, as shown in the preceding code.

Because our implementation of *GetClassID* has to return the CLSID of the object that we'll *write* to the storage in *Save,* we need to change *m_clsID* so that it contains the object's true CLSID instead of our own. We can obtain this information by calling *ReadClassStg,* because as we have seen, a server's implementation of *IPersistStorage::Save* is obliged to call *WriteClassStg.*

Cosmo makes no other considerations in *IPersistStorage::Load* because what the Polyline DLL server writes into a storage is exactly what Cosmo writes, so Cosmo can simply load it as if it were its own. In real-world situations, of course, you will do a lot more work to read someone else's format over which you have no control. But as far as the outside world is concerned, what's most important is the CLSID you return from *GetClassID* as well as what you now need to write back to the storage in *IPersistStorage::Save.*

In *Save,* you must write your object's own data to the storage if you are converting, but you must otherwise write the original format of the object if you are emulating. Remember that in emulation, you are being asked to service an object of another class, but you are not allowed to change its class or the format of the data in the storage.

Again, Cosmo is a simple case because its data formats in the storage are identical to those of the Polyline DLL Server, so writing a Polyline storage for emulation purposes is the same as writing our own. However, we have to make sure that the conversion is complete by taking a few extra steps:

```
STDMETHODIMP CImpIPersistStorage::Save(LPSTORAGE pIStorage
    , BOOL fSameAsLoad)
    {
    [Code to call CPolyline::WriteToStream as usual]

    //Clear the convert bit if it was set
    if (m_fConvert)
        {
        UINT        cf;
```

(continued)

```
        cf=RegisterClipboardFormat((*m_pObj->m_pST) [IDS_FORMAT]);
        WriteFmtUserTypeStg(pIStorage, cf
            , (*m_pObj->m_pST) [IDS_USERTYPE]);

        SetConvertStg(pIStorage, FALSE);
        m_fConvert=FALSE;
        }

    ...
    }
```

If we are converting, we have to make sure that the format written to the storage is ours, that the user type is ours, and the storage bit that we previously read by using *GetConvertStg* is cleared. Therefore, we first have to call *WriteFmtUserTypeStg* ourselves with our own clipboard format and our own type string, as shown in the preceding code. (Note that in the sample code, I don't use string literals as shown here.) We then have to call *SetConvertStg*, where the FALSE parameter turns off the convert bit in the storage that the container's Convert dialog box originally set. Of course, we should remember that this object is now officially converted to our own class, and therefore our *m_fConvert* flag should be FALSE.

In a real-world conversion situation (but not in emulation), you will have much more to do where I simply call *CPolyline::WriteToStream* because you'll have to restructure everything in the storage to match your server. This means that you should remove all other streams and substorages that you no longer need—that is, you should remove any elements in the storage that were required by the other object class but that you replace with others. If you don't remove these extra elements, you unnecessarily waste storage space.

One such real-world case in which you always have to do this is when updating an OLE 1 embedded object to an OLE 2 embedded object.

OLE 1 Embedded Object Conversion and Emulation

In truth, converting or emulating from an OLE 1 embedded object to an OLE 2 embedded object is merely a special case of the conversion and emulation support we've already seen. OLE2.DLL presents an OLE 1 embedded object to an OLE 2 server in an *IStorage* through *IPersistStorage::Load*, and when you are asked to save the embedded object in *IPersistStorage::Save*, you simply write it back to the *IStorage*. OLE takes care of sending that data to whatever container is concerned.

As was mentioned in the introduction to this chapter, there is an OLE 1 version of Cosmo in the sample code for Chapter 2. To mark our OLE 2 version as being able to convert and emulate the OLE 1 version, we again have to make additions to the Registration Database under Conversion. But because OLE 1 servers had no concept of how to write clipboard formats to the object's storage, what do we store under the format? The answer is that you store the OLE 1 server's short class name (not the human-readable descriptive name) as the format. These are written in addition to any other formats you support for another OLE 2 server, as shown below for version 1 of Cosmo:

```
Conversion
    Readable
        Main = Cosmo1.0,Polyline Figure
    Readwritable
        Main = Cosmo1.0,Polyline Figure
```

Now comes the fun part: modifying *IPersistStorage* to handle the OLE 1 case. First, you will need to remember that you read from a storage that contained an OLE 1 object so that you can remember to write that OLE 1 version if you are asked to emulate. Therefore, the first step in implementing this feature in Cosmo was to add a flag to *CPolyline*, as seen in POLYLINE.H:

```
class __far CPolyline : public CWindow
    {
    [Friends and private variables]

    public:
        BOOL            m_fReadFromOLE10;

    [Member functions]
    }
```

Here *m_fReadFromOLE10* is made public, so that the implementation of *IPersistStorage* can access it directly without having to make *CImpIPersistStorage* a friend of *CPolyline*. This is not the most elegant solution, but because this flag is of interest only to *IPersistStorage*, we might as well make it public.

CPolyline initially sets *m_fReadFromOLE10* to FALSE, of course. The flag is changed only when *IPersistStorage::Load* finds the storage to contain an OLE 1 object instead of the expected OLE 2 object:

```
STDMETHODIMP CImpIPersistStorage::Load(LPSTORAGE pIStorage)
    {
    [Variables and other initialization]

    hr=pIStorage->OpenStream("CONTENTS", 0, STGM_DIRECT
        | STGM_READWRITE | STGM_SHARE_EXCLUSIVE, 0, &pIStream);
```

(continued)

```
    //We might be looking for OLE 1 streams as well.
    if (FAILED(hr))
        {
        hr=pIStorage->OpenStream("\1Ole10Native", 0, STGM_DIRECT
            | STGM_READWRITE | STGM_SHARE_EXCLUSIVE, 0, &pIStream);

        if (FAILED(hr))
            return ResultFromScode(STG_E_READFAULT);

        m_pObj->m_pPL->m_fReadFromOLE10=TRUE;
        }

    lRet=m_pObj->m_pPL->ReadFromStream(pIStream);

    ...
    }
```

Here *IPersistStorage::Load* initially tries to open the "CONTENTS" stream in the storage and passes the IStream pointer to *CPolyline::ReadFromStream* if successful. If it cannot find the "CONTENTS" stream, it tries to open a stream under the name of "\1Ole10Native," which will contain the OLE 1 object. (The \1 is an ASCII 1 preceding Ole10Native. Remember from Chapter 5 that streams whose names begin with ASCII 32 or less, excluding ASCII 3, are for use by OLE.) If Load does find the OLE 1 stream, it sets *m_fReadFromOLE10* to TRUE so we can do a few chores later in *IPersistStorage::Save.*

CPolyline::ReadFromStream now has to handle this OLE 1 stream correctly:

```
LONG CPolyline::ReadFromStream(LPSTREAM pIStream)
    {
    [Variables and other initialization]

    if (m_fReadFromOLE10)
        {
        DWORD       dw;

        /*
         * Skip the DWORD length at the beginning of the
         * Ole10Native stream.
         */
        pIStream->Read((LPVOID)&dw, sizeof(DWORD), &cb);
        }

    //Read version numbers and seek back to file beginning.
    hr=pIStream->Read((LPVOID)&pl, 2*sizeof(WORD), &cb);
```

```
    //If we read OLE 1, seek back but skip the size header.
    if (m_fReadFromOLE10)
        LISet32(li, sizeof(DWORD));
    else
        LISet32(li, 0);

    pIStream->Seek(li, STREAM_SEEK_SET, NULL);

    [Read the data in the appropriate version and set it for editing.]

    ...
    }
```

What's in this "Ole10Native" stream is a DWORD containing the length of the data (the rest of the stream), followed by the OLE 1 object data as written by the OLE 1 server. Because Cosmo knows exactly how long data from its earlier version is (96 bytes), we simply skip this value here. (You might, of course, be more interested in it.) In doing so, the stream's seek pointer is positioned at the beginning of the data, which will always contain version numbers for either version 1 or version 2 data, so Cosmo then simply reads those version numbers to determine how much data to read, repositions the seek pointer to the top of the data, reads it, and sets it as the active data ready for editing.

This code looks simple because Cosmo was already set to handle data from its version 1 files. In converting files, we had the version 1 file data in a stream called "CONTENTS", as created by *StgOpenStorage* with STGM_CONVERT. In converting an embedded object, we get the data the "\1Ole10Native" stream, which, with the exception of the DWORD header, contains exactly what a version 1 converted file would contain. You might, of course, have to do much more work to read your version 1 embedded object data.

So now let's wrap up the story by looking at *IPersistStorage::Save* when we're dealing with an OLE 1 embedded object. There are again two cases here: conversion and emulation. If we are converting, we write our OLE 2 object data to the storage, setting the appropriate class, format, and type in the storage.[2] But as I mentioned before, anytime you write a different structure into the storage you need to clean up any elements that are now unused. In the conversion case, the "\1Ole10Native" stream will no longer be used because the storage now contains an OLE 2 object. Cosmo takes care of this in *IPersistStorage::Save*:

```
if (m_pObj->m_pPL->m_fReadFromOLE10 && m_fConvert && (1Ret >= 0))
    pIStorage->DestroyElement("\1Ole10Native");
```

2. Note that when your server is initially run to convert the OLE 1 object into your current version, you'll only be asked to load the object and generate a new presentation. Only when the object is next activated, modified, and closed will your *IPersistStorage::Save* be called, at which time you write your new data.

This code will probably look very similar to the code for your own application. Note that the additional condition of (*lRet>=0*) ensures that we destroy only the OLE 1 element in the storage if and only if writing the OLE 2 information worked, which this extra condition indicates.

That leaves us with looking at the final case of emulating an OLE 1 embedded object. This requires a slight change to our *IPersistStorage::Save* implementation:

```
STDMETHODIMP CImpIPersistStorage::Save(LPSTORAGE pIStorage
    , BOOL fSameAsLoad)
    {
    LONG     lVer=VERSIONCURRENT;

    ...

    if (!m_fConvert && m_pObj->m_pPL->m_fReadFromOLE10)
        lVer=0x00010000;
    ...
    [Determine the stream in which to write the data]
    lRet=m_pObj->m_pPL->WriteToStream(pIStream, lVer);
    ...
    }
```

If the *m_fConvert* flag is FALSE and we read from an OLE 1 object (which we determine by peeking into the public *m_fReadFromOLE10* flag in *CPolyline*), we know we're emulating an OLE 1 embedded object. Therefore, in *IPersistStorage::Save* we need to write to the "\1Ole10Native" stream instead of our usual "CONTENTS" stream. If *fSameAsLoad* is TRUE within *Save* and we're emulating an OLE 1 object, we can simply write the version 1 data back into the current stream that we hold open from *Load*. Otherwise, we need to create the right stream with the right name, and if it is an OLE 1 stream, we must remember to write the DWORD header in the stream indicating the size of the remaining data:

```
//In IPersistStorage::Save

if (!m_fConvert && m_pObj->m_pPL->m_fReadFromOLE10)
    {
    hr=pIStorage->CreateStream("\1Ole10Native", STGM_DIRECT
        | STGM_CREATE | STGM_WRITE | STGM_SHARE_EXCLUSIVE
        , 0, 0, &pIStream);
    }
else
    {
     hr=pIStorage->CreateStream("CONTENTS", STGM_DIRECT
         | STGM_CREATE | STGM_WRITE | STGM_SHARE_EXCLUSIVE
         , 0, 0, &pIStream);
    }
```

After creating these streams, Cosmo simply writes its data in the appropriate version to whatever is in *pIStream*. And with this, our modification of Cosmo to handle conversion and emulation is complete.

Notes on OLE 1 Compatibility for Containers

I'm including this section simply to expose you to a number of considerations for OLE 1 compatibility as far as containers are concerned. OLE 2 provides a compatibility layer so that OLE 2 containers can work with OLE 1 servers (linked or embedded objects) transparently, but the compatibility layer is not perfectly transparent. The first consideration is how to deal with OLE 1 servers that don't quite behave as expected. In my experience, I have come across only two major quirks in servers that can cause a container to behave erratically. The second consideration is important to you if you have an OLE 1 container that you want to convert into an OLE 2 container: how to read and write old files that contain OLE 1 objects. For this situation, we'll briefly look at two OLE 2 API functions that help you do such conversion.

OLE 1 Server Quirks

There are two behavioral oddities that an OLE 2 container might encounter in an OLE 1 server: It might encounter negative extents returned from *IOleObject::GetExtent*, and it might not receive an *IOleClientSite::OnShowWindow(FALSE)* call when the object closes.

First, many programmers (myself included) are extremely confused about the use of HIMETRIC units in specifying extents of objects. As we've seen in previous chapters, you use the *scaling* of the MM_HIMETRIC mapping mode to express extents, but you do not use the *mapping mode* itself. That is, when you convert a vertical extent into HIMETRIC units for the purpose of OLE, you do not negate this number as you would if you were drawing in the MM_HIMETRIC mapping mode. Therefore, all extents returned from a call such as *IOleObject::GetExtent*, and all that you send to *IOleObject::SetExtent*, must be in *absolute units*, expressed in HIMETRIC. That is, all values are positive. The confusion this caused for OLE 1 programmers resulted in a few servers specifying a negative vertical extent, so your container's call to *IOleObject::GetExtent* might come back with a negative *y* value. Patron handles this by checking for that case and changing the extent back to positive, as it should be, after calling *IOleObject::GetExtent*.

```
SIZEL    szl;

m_pIOleObject->GetExtent(dwAspect, &szl);

if (0 > szl.cy)
    szl.cy=-szl.cy;
```

This is simply a good, defensive habit for a container to practice.

The second concern is that some OLE 1 servers will not properly generate a call to your *IOleClientSite::OnShowWindow* when the object closes. Remember that we used *OnShowWindow* to add or remove the hatching on a container site depending on the *fShow* parameter to the function. Well, for some OLE 1 servers *OnShowWindow(FALSE)*, which removes the hatching, is never sent, so you're stuck with a permanently hatched object. Ugly. To protect yourself, you can build in a redundancy by using *IAdviseSink::OnClose*. Patron makes the same call to *CTenant::ShowAsOpen(FALSE)* in *OnClose* as it does in *OnShowWindow*:

```
//In ICLISITE.CPP
STDMETHODIMP CImpIOleClientSite::OnShowWindow(BOOL fShow)
    {
    m_pTen->ShowAsOpen(fShow);
    return NOERROR;
    }

//Redundancy in IADVSINK.CPP
STDMETHODIMP_(void) CImpIAdviseSink::OnClose(void)
    {
    m_pTen->ShowAsOpen(FALSE);
    return;
    }
```

Again, this is an excellent defensive programming technique.

File Conversion

If you programmed an OLE 1 container and you have now seen how to implement an OLE 2 container, you will have noticed by now that the storage models in each are quite different. OLE 2 containers treat all compound document objects as if they lived inside a storage object, and you can control where the actual bytes end up by implementing or using an alternate *LockBytes* object. OLE 1 containers, on the other hand, treated compound document objects by means of a data structure called OLESTREAM. This structure had one field, an OLESTREAMVTBL in which the container stored the pointer to two functions, *Get* and *Put*, through which the container controlled the placement of bytes within its disk file.

So how do you reconcile the two? Most complete container applications, such as word processors and spreadsheets, will need to be able to read and write files compatible with previous versions of that application. That means an OLE 2 container must be able to read objects written using OLESTREAM and must be able to write OLE 2 objects into an OLESTREAM.

OLE 2 provides two API functions to accommodate these needs: *OleConvertOLESTREAMToIStorage* and *OleConvertIStorageToOLESTREAM.* The first function is used to read an object that was written in an OLESTREAM as if it were in a storage object—that is, to enable your container to load the object simply by calling *OleLoad* as you do for anything else in a storage. The other function is used to take an object that your container knows through a storage and write it to a file through an OLESTREAM. Let's see some hypothetical code to show how this would work. Again, note that this feature is not implemented in Patron for a variety of reasons, although Patron did have an OLE 1 version in its sordid past—the differences between Patron version 1 and 2 were simply too significant to try to make conversion work.

In any case, let's look at the implementation and use of a typical OLESTREAM in an OLE 1 container. This involved the container defining its own variation of the OLESTREAM structure in which it usually put something like a file handle so that the *Get* and *Put* functions would have access to it. When the container wanted to save or load an object, it would call *OleSaveToStream* or *OleLoadFromStream,* passing a pointer to the OLESTREAM structure. (In this context, these are OLE 1 API functions and *not* the functions of the same name in OLE 2 that take *IStream* pointers.) The OLE 1 libraries would then call *Get* and *Put* as necessary to write the object into the file:

```
//The container-specific OLESTREAM structure
typedef struct
    {
    LPOLESTREAMVTBL     pvt;
    HANDLE              hFile;
    } OLE1STREAM, FAR *LPOLE1STREAM;

//The function that would write a file.
void FileSave(LPSTR pszFile)
    {
    HANDLE        hFile
    OFSTRUCT      of;
    LPOLE1STREAM  pStream;

    hFile=OpenFile(pszFile, &of, OF_CREATE | OF_WRITE);

    [Other error checking code, etc.]
```

(continued)

```
    /*
     * This is usually some function that allocates and initializes the
     * OLE1STREAM structure and its VTBL.
     */

    pStream=AllocateOLE1STREAM();
    pStream->hFile=hFile;

    [Containers typically wrote other data here]

    [This would be called for each object saved]
    OleSaveToStream(pObj, (LPOLESTREAM)pStream);

    ...

    [Cleanup]
    }

//The function that would read a file
void FileLoad(LPSTR pszFile)
    {
    HANDLE          hFile
    OFSTRUCT        of;
    LPOLE1STREAM    pStream;

    hFile=OpenFile(pszFile, &of, OF_READ);

    [Other error checking code, etc.]

    pStream=AllocateOLE1STREAM();
    pStream->hFile=hFile;

    [Containers typically read other data here]

    [This would be called for each object loaded]
    OleLoadFromStream((LPOLESTREAM)pStream, "StdFileEditing", ...);

    ...

    [Cleanup]
    }

//OLESTREAM methods
DWORD FAR PASCAL Get(LPOLE1STREAM pStream, LPBYTE pb, DWORD cb)
    {
```

```
    if (NULL==pStream->hFile)
        return 0L;

    return _hread(pStream->hFile, (void huge *)pb, cb);
    }

DWORD FAR PASCAL Put(LPOLE1STREAM pStream, LPBYTE pb, DWORD cb)
    {
    if (NULL==pStream->hFile)
        return 0L;

    return _hwrite(pStream->hFile, (void huge *)pb, cb);
    }
```

What generally happened here is that when a container saved a file, it opened the file, wrote whatever header information was necessary, and then wrote headers for objects within that file, which would position the file's seek offset at the place where the container wanted the object's data saved. It then called the OLE 1 *OleSaveToStream* for each object in the document, which would call *Put,* in which the container wrote the data to the file. In the same manner, the container would position the file's seek offset at the start of an object and call the OLE 1 *OleLoadFromStream,* which would call *Get* to retrieve that data previously written. All in all, the container controlled where the data was placed in a file by positioning the seek pointer in whatever file handle was in the OLESTREAM structure before calling the *OLE 1 OleSaveToStream.*

So to handle such files from an OLE 2 container, we have to get one of these OLESTREAM instances to look like a storage object. Presumably, you will have code in your OLE 2 container that knows how to read every other part of a file generated from the OLE 1 version of your application. Eventually, that code will come across a record in the file that says "What follows is an OLE 1 compound document object"—that is, a header on an object in that file. You need to load that object and obtain some OLE 2 *interface pointer* for it. You can't use an OLE 1 API function to do it because those functions are ignorant of interfaces, and the only function that loads an object and returns an interface pointer is *OleLoad. OleLoad* requires an *IStorage* pointer from which to load the object, so we have to call *OleConvertOLESTREAM-ToIStorage* to get the *IStorage* pointer.

To call *OleConvertOLESTREAMToIStorage,* you will have to allocate and initialize an OLESTREAM structure like the one you allocated and initialized in your OLE 1 application. Generally, you can use all the same code you had before. You then pass the OLESTREAM pointer to *OleConvertOLE-STREAMToIStorage* to obtain the *IStorage* pointer, which you can then pass to *OleLoad.*

```
void ImportOldFile(LPSTR pszFile)
    {
    HANDLE          hFile
    OFSTRUCT        of;
    LPOLE1STREAM    pStream;
    LPSTORAGE       pIStorage;
    LPUNKNOWN       pObj;

    hFile=OpenFile(pszFile, &of, OF_READ);

    [Other error checking code, etc.]

    pStream=AllocateOLE1STREAM();
    pStream->hFile=hFile;

    [Containers typically read other data here]

    ...

    [This would be called in some loop when encountering an OLE 1 object]
    OleConvertOLESTREAMToIStorage((LPOLESTREAM)pStream, &pIStorage, NULL);
    OleLoad(pIStorage, IID_IUnknown pIOleClientSite, (LPLPVOID)&pObj);
    pIStorage->Release();

    ...

    [Cleanup]
    }
```

For the most part, importing an OLE 1 object into an OLE 2 container is a matter of recycling all your OLE 1 code by replacing the call to *OleLoadFromStream* with calls to *OleConvertOLESTREAMToIStorage, OleLoad,* and of course, *IStorage::Release.* (Don't forget the *Release.*) *OleConvertOLESTREAMToIStorage* is a function that returns a new pointer to an interface and therefore has a reference count on that pointer.

The other half of the equation is to write an OLE 2 object—one for which you have an *IStorage* pointer—into an OLE 1 file using your old OLESTREAM implementation. For this, you call *OleConvertIStorageToOLESTREAM,* which goes ahead and calls the OLESTREAM's *Put* function to write the object:

```
void ExportOldObjectToFile(HFILE hFile, LPSTORAGE pIStorage)
    {
    LPOLE1STREAM  pStream;
```

```
pStream=AllocateOLE1STREAM();
pStream->hFile=hFile;

OleConvertIStorageToOLESTREAM(pIStorage, (LPOLESTREAM)pStream);

...
}
```

So overall, the majority of the work in reading and writing OLE 1 compatible files will generally be in re-creating your own data structures in the file, especially if your OLE 2 container is using compound files. When you hit a spot where you have to either save or load an OLE 1 object, you need to make only a few OLE 2 calls, as shown in the previous code.

Summary

OLE 2 provides the capability for a container to manipulate an object using servers other than the one that originally created the object. There are two ways it can do this: conversion or emulation. Conversion is the process of changing the class of the object so that it will be permanently seen as an object from a different server. Emulation is the process of using a different server to manipulate all objects of a given class and is most useful when the original server is not present on a machine but the machine does have a server that is marked as being able to read and write those other objects.

The end user accesses the conversion and emulation features by invoking the Convert dialog box on an object through an OLE2UI library helper function. Within this dialog box the user can convert an object to a new class, instruct OLE 2 to always treat objects of that class as if they came from a different server, or change the display aspect of the object in the container as well as edit any iconic representation. A container must be ready for all three of these cases, as is demonstrated in the Patron sample.

As far as a server is concerned, it has to make additional entries in the Registration Database to mark it as being able to convert or emulate other objects. The server does this by specifying which data formats it can read and write for the purposes of conversion and emulation, not by identifying specific objects through CLSIDs. Because conversion and emulation affect data formats, the server only needs to modify its *IPersistStorage* implementation to handle the other formats. This chapter shows modifications to the Cosmo server to handle objects generated from the Polyline server implemented in Chapter 11.

If an OLE 2 server had an OLE 1 version, it could register the name of the OLE 1 version as another format it can convert or emulate. For the most part, the server sees an OLE 1 embedded object as any other embedded object through *IPersistStorage*, except that the native data will always be contained in a stream named "\1Ole10Native". If the server can emulate an OLE 1 object, it must read and write data in this stream. If it converts the object, it must remember to destroy this stream when writing OLE 2 embedded object data in the storage object. Cosmo again serves as the example here.

Although OLE 2 servers only need to modify their *IPersistStorage* implementation to be compatible with an OLE 1 version, containers have a little more work in different places. First, there are some eccentricities in some OLE 1 servers that can cause a container to malfunction. A few good defensive measures, as demonstrated in Patron, can prevent a lot of confusion for your end users. In addition, if your container has an OLE 1 version, you will probably be interested in importing and exporting files created in that version. The two functions *OleConvertOLESTREAMToIStorage* and *OleConvertIStorageToOLESTREAM* are there to help, and they affect only a small part of your importing and exporting code. These are not, however, demonstrated in Patron; they are simply discussed, using the hypothetical code shown in this chapter.

SECTION IV

COMPOUND DOCUMENTS: IN-PLACE ACTIVATION

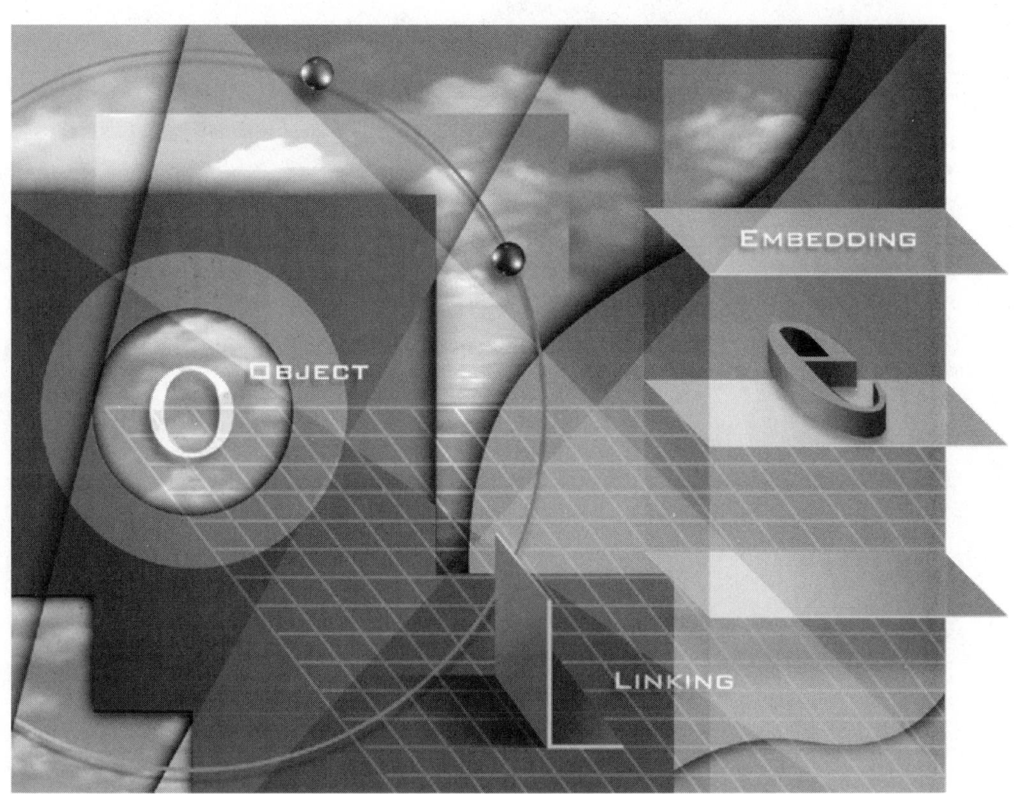

CHAPTER FIFTEEN

VISUAL EDITING: IN-PLACE ACTIVATION AND IN-PLACE CONTAINERS

Long ago, in the time of great simplicity, when the OLE 2 Design Specification was only 50 pages long, there was a new idea called ''in-situ editing.'' Instead of forcing you to edit an embedded object in a separate server window, in-situ editing, an extension of OLE 1, let you edit an object while remaining in the context of the container application. *In situ* in Latin means ''in the natural or original position.'' Simple enough.

But the marketing types at Microsoft looked at the phrase *in-situ editing*, and for good, sound intentions changed it to *in-place editing*. OK, that's cool. The change got rid of that funny Latin stuff and made the term more comprehensible to us programmers who didn't break 600 on the SAT verbal. Everyone understood and was happy to get working on it.

In a burst of pure reason, marketing figured that the word *editing* was much too specific for compound documents because certain objects, such as video objects, are more apt to be *played* in place instead of being *edited*. So, of course, the terminology had to change again, giving us *in-place activation*. But that wasn't the end of the matter.

Marketing pondered the term *in-place activation* and yearned for a new, improved term that not only would appeal more to end users, but would tie in with all of the other ''visual'' stuff from Microsoft (Visual Basic, Visual C++, and so on). The name was changed to *Visual Editing* with a prominent trademark symbol (™).

Of course, this latest term means the word *editing* has crept back in. Perhaps *Visual Editing* will be replaced by the more logical *Visual Activation.* About that time, we'll drop the word *Visual* because it's been overused by all of the other Visual products. That will leave us with *Activation.* This could eventually lead back to the term *in-situ activation* and inevitably back to *in-place activation.*

So I'm going to stick with *in-place activation* for the rest of this book, and I will often refer to the feature simply as *in-place.*

We'll start this chapter with a look at a typical session of editing an embedded object in which both the object and its container have in-place support. This will show us how both applications present themselves through additional in-place interfaces and how they work together to merge their user interfaces into something a little weird but something that has proved itself in usability testing. The process of merging user interfaces to get to the point where the end user can manipulate the object is called *in-place activation.*

When an object is in the in-place active state, or simply active state, any number of events can occur, each of which might be handled by the container or the object, according to rules of interoperability as laid out in the OLE 2 Design Specification. For example, if the end user presses an accelerator key, both applications need a chance to process the event and the specification state that the object always gets first crack. Eventually, the end user finishes manipulating the object and generally moves to work on another part of the container document. At that time, the object is deactivated, which means a transition from the active state to the running hidden state. Deactivation removes all the merged user interfaces and restores the original interface of the container.

With an understanding of how the whole in-place activation process works, we will finish this chapter by looking at the additions necessary to make Patron an in-place container. If you are interested in implementing an in-place object, you can skip ahead to Chapter 16, but you might find it helpful to at least skim the container material here. If you are interested only in containers, note that there is a section at the end of Chapter 16 that explores where in-place activation can take us.

Once again, I present this in a step-by-step fashion so that you can stop, compile, and actually run something at each step along the way. In-place support for a container requires a decent amount of work, mostly involving user-interface considerations. But I hope this guide will reduce a very complex interoperability feature into a recipe that brings back some of the simplicity of days gone by. Maybe then we'll find time to learn Latin.

Motivations and the Guts of an In-Place Session

In-place activation is all about document-centric computing—or the notion that what end users really want to do is concentrate on the task and to be free from having to remember which application from which vendor they happen to be using at the time. As my mother would say, "I just want it to work! I just want to write a letter!"

End users really want a document-centric user interface (although they usually don't say that in so many words). They want to concentrate on the task, and they want to use the best tools to get that job done without having to think too much about which tools they are using. Here's a case in point: The week before I wrote this chapter, Microsoft held a usability contest in which representatives came from other companies to create the most usable ATM—Automatic Taco Machine. No, seriously. The goal was to create an interface through which any Joe- or Jane-in-the-Street could walk up and, without ever having seen the device before, order a taco with any number of options in the least amount of time. From what I heard, contestants exploited pull-down menus, pointing devices, three-dimensional beveled button controls, and all the other glitz we're used to seeing on a desktop computer. The entry that won was a simple design with a touch screen. At a glance, you could tell that by pressing on one spot on the screen, you could order a taco, and by pressing on other places, you could specify exactly what kind of taco you wanted. No glitz. Just plain common sense.

Why did this win? Because it was, for lack of a better term, taco-centric. The purpose of the device was to allow an end user to order a taco. Period. The winning design did exactly that, no more, no less. Virtually everyone could walk up to it and get what they wanted without any help whatsoever. It's not so much that it *could* do the right thing but that it was designed in such a way that the only thing you could *possibly* do with it was the right thing. If this sort of idea interests you, Donald Norman's wonderful book, *The Design of Everyday Things* (formerly *The Psychology of Everyday Things*), is a must. Norman would be the first to point out that the other designs failed because they paid so much attention to aesthetics that usability was flushed straight down the toilet. Sure, the menus and 3-D buttons were neat, but they didn't work. They would, however, probably win some prize for artistry.

With in-place activation and document-centricity, we're talking about usability, not design elegance. Usability is what's motivating all of this—letting end users concentrate on their tasks so that using a computer is natural and fun. But because I'm not usability expert, I won't try to convince you any longer that this is a worthy goal and that in-place activation adds a great deal of value to your applications.

So let's see how it works.

Where Does It All Start?

Let's say I have a container application, such as Patron, in which I have opened a compound document. On the current page of the opened document there is a little embedded graphic—say, one from Cosmo, as shown in Figure 15-1, which I created earlier. I would now like to change that graphic, so I double-click on it to activate it. With the embedded object support we implemented in the last few chapters, the object opens up into a full Cosmo window in which I can make changes. This all happens when the container calls the object's *IOleObject::DoVerb* function.

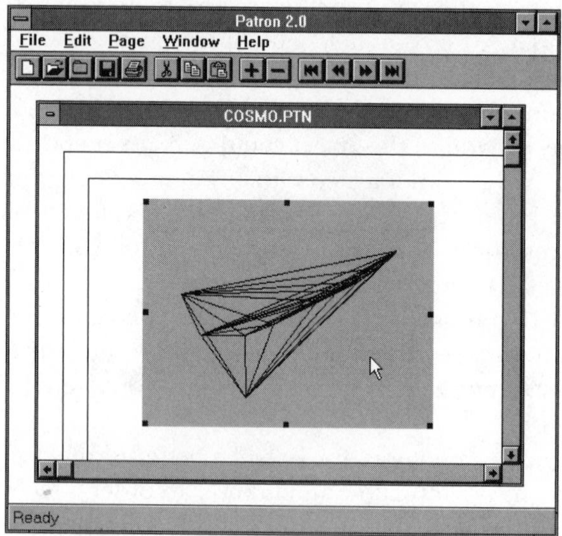

Figure 15-1.
A typical container with a typical compound document in which a typical embedded object lives.

To support embedding, as we saw in Chapters 9 and 10, the container implements the *IOleClientSite* and *IAdviseSink* interfaces, and the object implements the *IOleObject, IDataObject,* and *IPersistStorage* interfaces. To support in-place activation for embedded objects (linked objects are now allowed to activate in place), each side must implement additional interfaces, as shown in Figures 15-2 and 15-3. The existence of these interfaces tells the rest of the world that the container and object are in-place capable—that is, they understand the contractual obligations of supporting these interfaces.

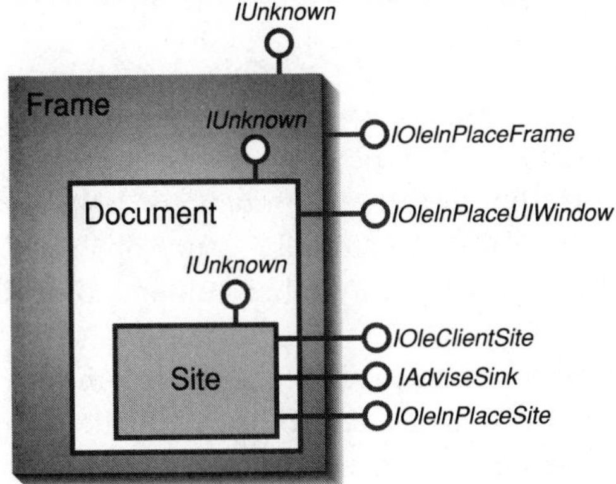

Figure 15-2.
Interfaces for an in-place capable container application.

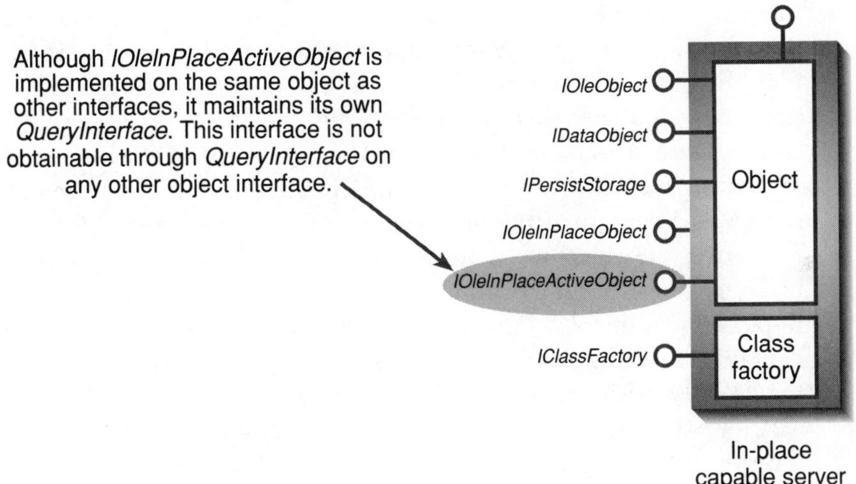

Figure 15-3.
Interfaces for an in-place capable server.

An Innocent Little *DoVerb*

Let's say the version of Patron we're running is in-place capable, as it will be after we finish this chapter. In opening a compound document and loading an object, we have not yet touched any in-place code. Patron runs along as it always has until it sends off the seemingly innocuous *IOleObject::DoVerb(OLEIVERB_PRIMARY)* call to the embedded Cosmo object. Up to this point, Patron has treated this object like any other embedded or linked object, as it should be.

Now let's say Cosmo is also in-place capable, as it becomes in the next chapter. Knowing that Cosmo has this new capability, we'll take a slightly different course of action as it begins to execute *IOleObject::DoVerb.* Instead of merely showing its windows to open the object for editing, Cosmo calls the container's *IOleClientSite::QueryInterface,* asking for *IOleInPlaceSite.* In other words, it asks, "Hey, do you talk container in-place activation?" In the lively spirit of *QueryInterface,* Patron responds, "Why yes, my good object, I do, and here's my *IOleInPlaceSite* interface to prove it." This little conversation establishes that the container can activate the object in-place and so the object can move forward with additional activation steps. Of course, if the container does not support the *IOleInPlaceSite* interface (and thus is not in-place capable), the object has no way of activating in-place,[1] and so it goes into the open state as a regular embedded object. This is a great example once again of where you can make a decision in your code based on information from *QueryInterface.* An object that has implemented full in-place support will still work with a container that implements only minimal embedding support.

After the object has determined whether the container is in-place capable, it must also ask the container whether it can currently activate the object in-place by calling *IOleInPlaceSite::CanInPlaceActivate.* This call decouples the container's general in-place support for all objects, expressed by its support for *IOleInPlaceSite,* from the ability to activate the specific object. A container will, for example, refuse to activate the embedded object in-place if the object is displayed in an aspect other than DVASPECT_CONTENT. If the container refuses to activate in-place, the specific object can always open into a separate window, as usual.

If the container says that in-place activation is allowed, the object can start the full activation process, which generally involves three steps: moving the object's editing window to the container, merging container and server menus into one shared menu, and creating editing tools (toolbars and so on) for the object in the container window.

---

1. The exceptions are video objects and the like, which can use the *hWnd* and RECT passed to *DoVerb* to temporarily *play* inside the container window.

Activating In-Place

After the object determines that it can activate in-place, it tells the container of its intentions by calling *IOleInPlaceSite::OnInPlaceActivate.* It then obtains pointers to the other two container interfaces—*IOleInPlaceUIWindow* (for the document) and *IOleInPlaceFrame,* along with some other necessary information, by calling *IOleInPlaceSite::GetWindowContext.* This is another instance when one piece of code (the object, in this case) obtains the first interface pointers to two different objects (the container's document and frame) by calling a member of a different interface altogether. The container's site, document, and frame objects are, of course, different, so *QueryInterface* on *IOleInPlaceSite* cannot possibly obtain a pointer to *IOleInPlaceFrame* or the document's *IOleInPlaceUIWindow.*

GetWindowContext also returns a position rectangle that describes where the object must initially appear in the container window and a clipping rectangle that describes the space in which the container can display anything. With this information, the object takes whatever "editing window" it has, such as Cosmo's Polyline, and physically moves it into the container window with a *SetParent* call (the Windows function), where the parent window is obtained by calling *IOleInPlaceSite::GetWindow.* The object then moves the editing window to the position rectangle and clips it to the clipping rectangle. The position rectangle is the same as the container's site in which this object lives, so the editing window appears on top of the site.

At this point, the object's editing window starts behaving like a custom control inside the container. Because it's a window, it gets whatever messages are generated by various mouse actions on it. So if the user clicks the mouse—presto! WM_LBUTTONDOWN comes into the editing window's message procedure. For Cosmo's Polyline, such a click adds a new point and new lines to the figure. From the end user's standpoint, the object is truly activated in place and ready for manipulation.

But as shown in Figure 15-4 on the next page, the only visual changes are the absence of the container's selection handles and a possible change in the mouse cursor. Compare Figures 15-1 (on page 846) and 15-4. What's different? Did anything happen? Not a whole lot—not enough to let users know that they're now supposed to be working on the figure and not on the container. We need some subtle indications that something changed. In addition, we need to allow the object to display its editing commands both in menus and toolbars.

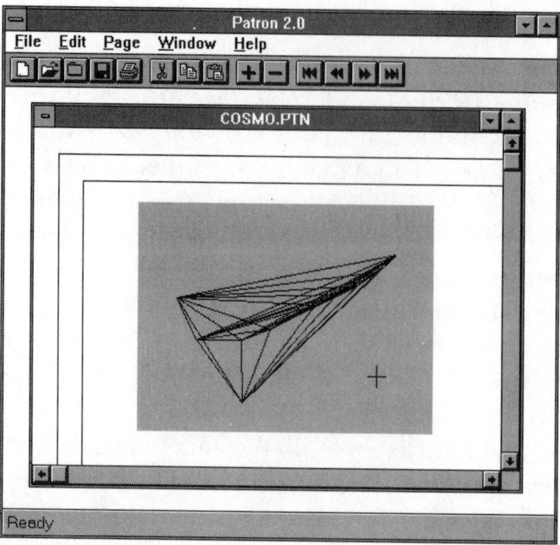

Figure 15-4.
What Patron would look like if all Cosmo did for in-place activation was to move its Polyline window into Patron. There's no magic here!

Therefore, there are four primary user interface problems that we need to solve to make in-place activation effective:

- The container's caption bar(s) does not indicate that we are editing an object.
- There is little to show the object itself as being "in-place active" as opposed to just loaded.
- The menu holds only container functions, some of which are not applicable when an object is active in place.
- The toolbar shows only container functions such as the menu.

Because the object is in control of the activation process, it is responsible for initiating the steps to address each of these issues as the following sections describe.

Caption Bars and Active Object Shading

You might have noticed that we have not yet mentioned the object's *IOleInPlaceActiveObject* interface. This interface allows the container to notify the object of important events, whereas the *IOleInPlaceObject* interface is used when the the object is not necessarily active but only running (and hidden).

The container always receives the pointers through the *SetActiveObject* member of *IOleInPlaceFrame* and *IOleInPlaceUIWindow,* which the object calls as part of the activation process. These are two of those situations in which one piece of code obtains an interface pointer through a member function of one of its own interfaces.

However, the object's *IOleInPlaceActiveObject* interface pointer is not the only parameter to *SetActiveObject.* The other is a pointer to a string for the container to use in caption bars. Generally, this string is a descriptive name of the object such as "Cosmo 2.0 Figure." In its implementations of *SetActiveObject,* the container places the string in its caption bars appropriately depending on whether it's MDI or SDI. So that takes care of the first user interface problem.

The second user interface problem we need to solve is that when an object is activated in-place, there should be some visual indication of the object's state. When the object is open, the container's side is drawn over with a hatch pattern, as we saw in Chapter 9. However, such an indicator will not work here because the object's editing window is covering the container site. What we do then is to draw a hatched border around the outside of the editing window, as shown in Figure 15-5. You might also want to include resizing handles in this hatched border.

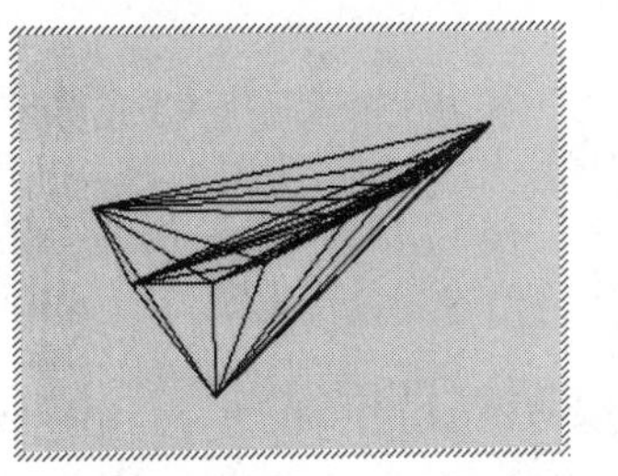

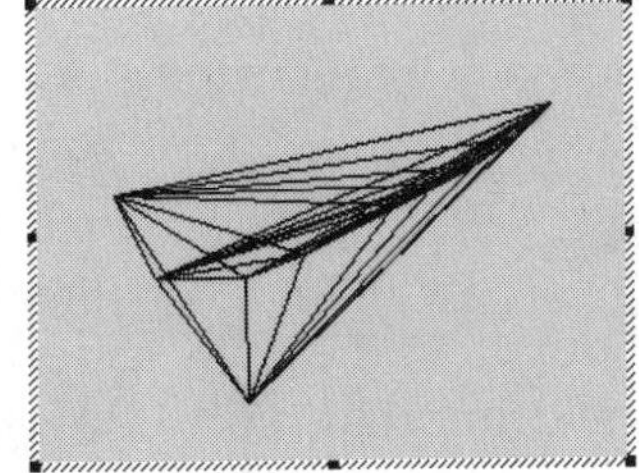

Figure 15-5.
The hatched border that an object creates around itself when activated in-place, with and without sizing handles.

As we'll see in Chapter 16, the object can conveniently create another window to do the hatching because the hatching has to appear outside the editing window itself. This extra window also helps the in-place object meet some requirements about clipping and focus. But as far as the end user is concerned, it looks as if the object grew a hatched border to identify itself as in-place active, and by this time in our activation, we've addressed the first two user interface problems, as shown in Figure 15-6 on the next page. However, there are still the nagging problems of the menu and the toolbar.

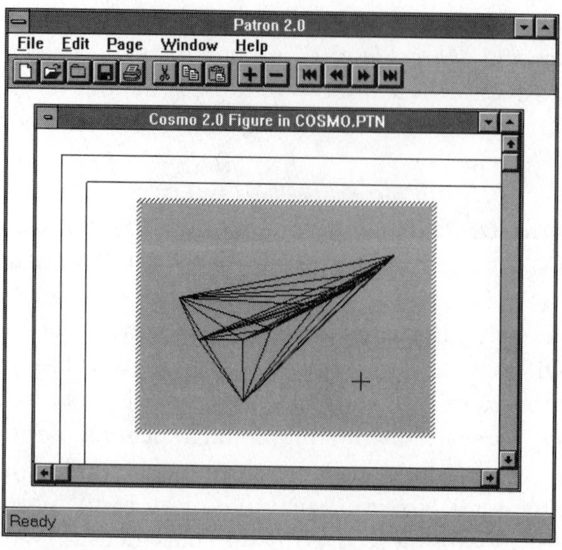

Figure 15-6.
What Patron looks like after Cosmo calls the container's SetActiveObject *functions and draws the hatched border around the editing window.*

Socially Adept Menus

I call these menus socially adept because they're good at mixing. OK, bad pun.

The next phase in integrating the object's user interface with the container's is creating a mixed, or shared, menu that the container displays on its top level window. This menu is composed of individual pieces from the normal menus of both container and server. In a nutshell, the container retains possession of anything that has to do with the application frame and with documents, so it provides the File menu, the Window menu (if MDI), and any other menus that pertain to document and container type functions. The object, on the other hand, provides the Edit menu and the Help menu and has the right to add any other menu necessary to manipulate the object while it is activated in-place.

For Patron, this means it can retain its File, Page, and Window menus, but it cannot display its Edit or Help menus. Cosmo can retain its Edit, Color, Line, and Help menus, but it cannot show its File or Window (in the MDI case) menu. But that makes sense, no? The question is how to take two menus and programmatically merge them into one menu, as shown in Figure 15-7.

How this actually works (and it does work) is that both container and object control three menu groups each, where each group can have as many individual popup menus as desired. The container controls what are called

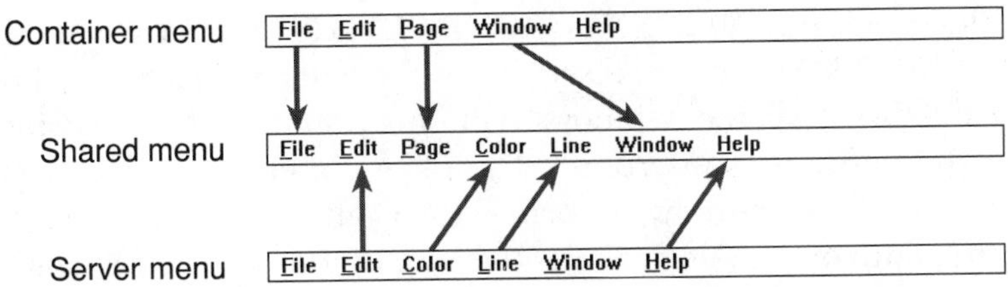

Figure 15-7.
How container and server menus can merge to create one shared menu in which the container contributes those items pertaining to documents and the server contributes those pertaining to editing the object.

the File, Container, and Window groups; the object handles the Edit, Object, and Help groups. The shared menu is the alternate combination of these groups: File, Edit, Container, Object, Window, and Help.

So if Patron, for example, assigned the File menu to the File group, Page to the Container group, and Window to the Window group, and Cosmo assigned Edit to the Edit group, Color and Line to the Object group, and Help to the Help group, the shared menu would appear exactly as shown in Figure 15-7. So both agents (container and object) ultimately control where their menus end up in the shared menu by controlling what they put in each group.

The menu itself is built from scratch; the object starts by calling the Windows API function *CreateMenu* to create a brand new empty menu. It then passes the menu to the container's *IOleInPlaceFrame::InsertMenus* along with a pointer to a structure called OLEMENUGROUPWIDTHS, which is simply an array of six integers. Inside *InsertMenus,* the container calls the Windows API function *AppendMenu* or *InsertMenu* as appropriate to build its half of the menu. After Patron executes *InsertMenus,* for example, the menu will appear as follows:

File Page Window

How does the object know where to put its menus? The container also stores the widths of each of its groups, or the number of menu items in each group, in the OLEMENUGROUPWIDTHS array. The array has six elements, and each element corresponds to the width of each of the six menu groups. The container stores the width of its File group in element 0 (zero-based arrays), the width of its Container group in element 2, and the width of the Window group in element 4. Patron (in its MDI version that we're using here) stores the value 1 in each element before returning from *InsertMenus.*

At this point, the object has the menu with the container's items already in it along with the OLEMENUGROUPWIDTHS array in which elements 0, 2, and 4 are filled in. It now inserts its own menu items between those of the container by using the Windows API function *InsertMenu* (being careful about the position of insertion). The object inserts each menu in its Edit group after the File group but before the Container group, meaning that it uses the width of the File group as the base offset, where it can start to insert the items in the Edit group. Likewise, when it inserts the items in the Object group, it not only considers the File group but also its own Edit group and the Container group. When it inserts the Help group, the object places those items after all the items in the other five groups. In all cases, the object uses the values in the OLEMENUGROUPWIDTHS array as well as knowledge about its own menu groups to calculate the correct offset at which to insert menus.

The object then completes the OLEMENUGROUPWIDTHS array by storing the number of menus in its groups in elements 1, 3, and 5. By using this array and the shared menu handle, it creates a *menu descriptor* by calling *OleCreateMenuDescriptor.* It passes that descriptor, the shared menu, and a window handle to receive messages generated from the object's menus, to *IOleInPlaceFrame::SetMenu.* At that time, the container displays the shared menu, as shown in Figure 15-8, and passes all the information along to *OleSetMenuDescriptor,* which is the key to making all this work. *OleSetMenuDescriptor*

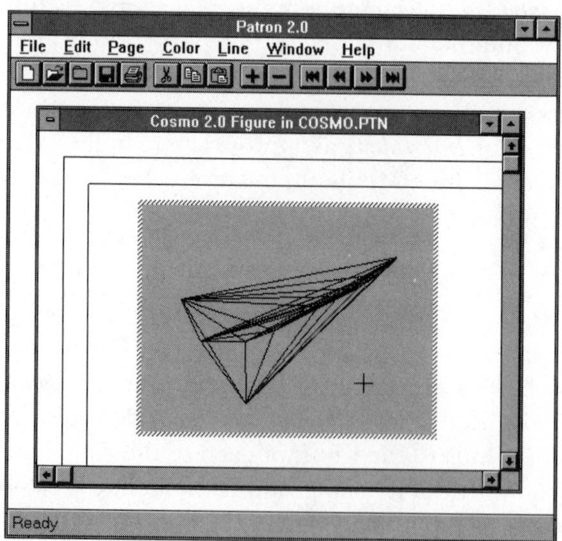

Figure 15-8.
Patron displaying a menu it shares with Cosmo.

creates a message hook on the container's main window so that it can watch the messages generated from this shared menu (WM_COMMAND, WM-_MENUSELECT, and so on) and redirect them to the server. OLE determines who owns which menu by checking the position of the menu generating the message against the group widths array stored in the descriptor.

No magic. It really does work!

A Stop by the Hardware Store

Hi there! Welcome to Hank's Hardware Heaven! We have everything*! We have plumbing. We have lighting. We have paints, wallboard, industrial appliances, and 387 types of electrical tape! You want tools? We have tools! Lots of tools! Screwdrivers, wire cutters, wrenches, tape measures, drills, sanders, planers, jigsaws, bandsaws, hacksaws, power saws, table saws, radial arm saws! We have every conceivable drill bit, every conceivable lathe tool, every...*

Oh, pipe down. Can you just point me to the toolbars?

Huh? Toolbars? Ain't got none of those... better try the object down the street.

The remaining user interface problem we need to address is that of the toolbar. If you look back to Figure 15-8, you'll notice that Patron's toolbar is still visible and accessible. For the most part that's just fine because it provides easy access to commands such as File Open, File Save, Edit Copy, and Edit Paste, as well as the commands that also appear on the Page menu. There are two problems with this, however. The first is a usability problem: The object has the user's attention, but none of its tools, if it has any to show, are visible. The second problem is more technical: Although the Edit commands are showing on the menu and the toolbar, those on the menu are dispatched to the server because the server owns the Edit menu. Those on the toolbar, however, are sent to the container because it's still the container's toolbar. And this is also a usability problem itself: Although the end user sees the same commands on the toolbar and the menu, the commands are not processed by the same code, so they will behave differently. Not good.

For these and other fine reasons, the OLE 2 specifications give ownership of toolbars to the in-place object[2] with the exception of the status line at the bottom, which is always controlled by the container (for consistency, I'm told).

This manifests itself in code by the object negotiating with the container for space in the container's frame and document windows in which the object can create tools. The object can ask for space for tools on any edge of each window. The most common case is where the object asks for space at the top or left of the frame window for a standard toolbar or tool palette.

---

2. Future revisions of OLE might provide for a shared toolbar much as we have a shared menu, but there wasn't time to design such a deep level of integration for OLE 2.

The negotiation process involves the object calling three member functions of the *IOleInPlaceUIWindow* interface (from which *IOleInPlaceFrame* inherits) for the window of interest. First, the object calls the *RequestBorderSpace* function in the appropriate interface, passing a BORDERWIDTHS structure (defined as a RECT), where the *left, right, top,* and *bottom* fields hold the amount of space the object wants to allocate from each side of the window. Here the container can decide whether it wants to surrender that space to the object, and it has every right to just say no. If the container does give up the space, the object then calls *SetBorderSpace,* at which time the container repositions its windows (like an MDI client) appropriately to make space for the object's tools. The object then calls *GetBorder* to determine the actual dimensions of the container window and creates its tools as children of the container window to fit.

Of course, moving windows around in the container like this can be disconcerting, so we'll see later in this chapter how to minimize the screen flicker that can occur. The other important usabilty point is that no matter what happens, the container should try hard to keep the object in exactly the same absolute screen position, regardless of how the windows move around. This is to minimize the distraction a user sees during the user interface switches, allowing the user to focus attention on the task at hand. This can be tricky for the container, but it is generally possible.

After the object gets space, of course, it has to create its tools as children of the window in which they are shown. At this point the object is fully activated, user interface and all. Cosmo's in-place toolbar, when displayed in Patron, is shown in Figure 15-9. One of the big considerations for doing this is that many control windows always send messages to their parent window by default. Well, the container's parent window might have no idea what to do with such messages. This can lead to all sorts of problems, so whatever controls the object placed in a container window must be capable of redirecting its messages to a window other than the parent. We'll see more of this in Chapter 16.

If a container refuses to grant an object tool space, it's not the end of the world. The object can always display those tools in a floating pop-up window if it wants because such popups don't require permission from the container. A very flexible object would generally be able to display its tools in a popup or on a toolbar on any side of a window in such a way that it would be able to work well in any container.

Besides pop-up tools and toolbars on the frame and the document window, the object is also allowed to create what are called *object adornments,* or additional tools attached to the outer edges of the editor window itself. For

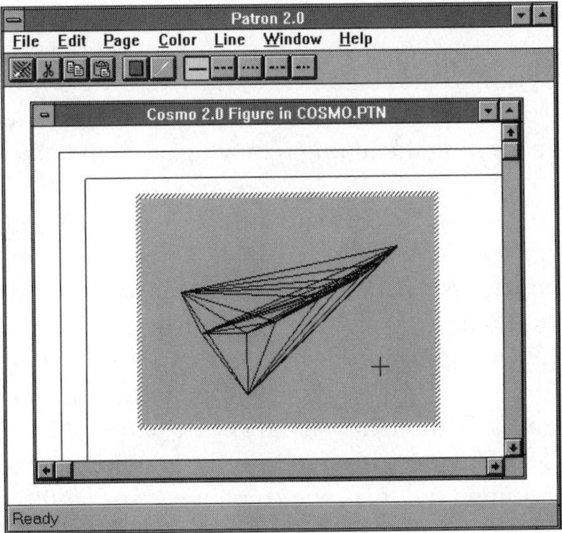

Figure 15-9.
Cosmo fully activated inside Patron.

example, table or spreadsheet objects might want to display row and column headers. A text-editing object might want to display style information to the left of the text. In such cases, the object simply makes its in-place window larger, always keeping the editing space the same size as the container site—that is, the same size as the object that is displayed in the container when the object is not active. The only restriction to these object adornments is that they are not allowed to reach outside of a clipping rectangle provided by the container under any circumstances. The object must obey out of courtesy—there are no police to stop you but end users would likely complain about the visual problems disobedience would entail.

Manipulations of an Active Object

Now that the object is fully activated in place, many events can occur that can be processed by the object, the container, or both.

First, there are mouse events. When the mouse pointer is over the in-place object's editing window, all mouse messages will go directly to that window, including WM_MOUSEMOVE, WM_SETCURSOR, and WM_LBUTTONDOWN. When the mouse pointer moves out of the object window, it first crosses over the hatching window (if you are using one, which I will recommend in Chapter 16) and onto the container's document window. At this point, the container sees the messages. So having the end user clicking around in the object window is no different from the user clicking in the same window in the server. The user clicking on the document window again outside the object, however, signals the container to deactivate the object by calling *IOleObject::InPlaceDeactivate*, at which time the object reverses everything it did in the process of activating, including removing all of the object's user interface.

The second type of event is the keyboard event. According to the OLE 2 specifications, the object always has first crack at all keystrokes. This is guaranteed first by the object always having the focus, so the container is responsible for calling the Windows API function *SetFocus* to the object window whenever the document containing that object becomes the currently active document. The container obtains the object's window handle by calling *IOleInPlaceObject::GetWindow*. Although focus takes care of normal keystrokes, it does not take care of accelerators. This requires a little special treatment on behalf of the container and server. First, the container must modify its message loop to call *IOleInPlaceActiveObject::TranslateAccelerator* before doing any of its own translation when an object is activated in place. This call actually applies only to DLL servers that would otherwise have no chance of handling accelerators because they have no message loop to call their own. When the server is an EXE, however, its message loop is actually the one in control, and it must be modified to call *OleTranslateAccelerator* after checking for accelerators itself but before calling *TranslateMessage* and *DispatchMessage*. *OleTranslateAccelerator* will call *IOleInPlaceFrame::TranslateAccelerator* if it finds that the accelerator pressed is in the container's accelerator table.

This brings up another point: Both container and server need to load and process different accelerator tables when they're involved with an active in-place object. The container will want to disable its accelerators for any menu command that is not currently available—that is, for anything outside the File, Container, and Window menu groups. Likewise, the server must do the same so that it doesn't attempt File Save or Window Tile operations as an in-place object.

Speaking of menu commands, we already saw how the container and server menus are merged and that by calling *OleSetMenuDescriptor* the container tells OLE to intercept messages that should go to the server instead. I want to point out that the object passes its main window handle (the server frame) to *IOleInPlaceFrame::SetMenu*, which the container then passes to *OleSetMenuDescriptor*. All messages generated from the server's pop-up menus on the shared menu are sent to that frame window.

One such message is WM_MENUSELECT, on which many applications change the text in their status lines. Patron and Cosmo are just such applications. However, when servicing an in-place object, Cosmo's status line is not visible. Instead, only the container's is visible. How, then, does Cosmo tell the container what to display in the status line for each menu item? The simple answer is that it calls *IOleInPlaceFrame::SetStatusText,* passing a pointer to the string to display. In this way, status line text shows up for both container and server menus. Note also that an object can determine whether the container even *has* a status line by calling *SetStatusText* with NULL and watching for failure.

A status line is one form of help that is not associated with the object's Help menu. The other form of help is context-sensitive help, initiated by pressing Shift+Fl (and possibly a menu command, as well). If the container detects this case, it calls *IOleInPlaceActiveObject::ContextSensitiveHelp* to instruct the object to enter that help mode. If the object detects the keystroke, it can call the same member function on all three of the container interfaces. Please note, however, that context-sensitive help is beyond the scope of this book and only minimal support will be discussed in this chapter and the next.

Undo is another common application feature that has some special considerations for in-place activation. For example, an Undo immediately after an in-place object has been activated should mean "deactivate," as an Undo immediately after a deactivation should be "reactivate." If the first thing an object sees after activating in place is an Undo, it calls *IOleInPlaceSite::DeactivateAndUndo*; otherwise, it calls *IOleInPlaceSite::DiscardUndoState* to let the container free memory it was holding in case *DeactivateAndUndo* was called. In the same way, if an in-place object is deactivated and the first thing that happens in the container is an Undo, it calls *IOleInPlaceObject::ReactivateAndUndo.* If anything else happens after a deactivation, the container calls *IOleObject::DoVerb(OLEIVERB_DISCARDUNDOSTATE).*

For all the usability that in-place activation brings, sometimes it's just not good enough. For example, the space an object is given in which to operate in place might be too small for the user. In some cases, the object extends past the edge of the container window. In that case, the object can call *IOleInPlaceSite::Scroll* to have the container show more of the object. This is useful for something like a spreadsheet object because the user might move the cell selection outside the visible region using the arrow keys. The user might also scroll the container document to make more room directly, in which case the container can call *IOleInPlaceObject::SetObjectRects* to let it know the new position. The object itself might also allow resizing while in place, in which case it can call *IOleInPlaceSite::OnPosRectChange* with the desired rectangle. In response, the container calls *IOleInPlaceObject::SetObjectRects* to let the object know how much it can actually resize, but it does not change the size of the container site itself. This is strictly to give the object more room to operate while activated in place, at the container's discretion.

If the object is too small, the user can open the object up into the full server window as if in-place activation never existed. This is done by somehow calling the object's *IOleObject::DoVerb* with OLEIVERB_OPEN, which causes it always to activate in another window and never to activate in place. Generally, the object will want to provide a way for this to happen, either with a menu item or with a double-click on the hatched border. The container can also use a keystroke such as Ctrl+Enter to generate the call.

Pulling the Plug: Deactivation

Invoking the Open verb is one of the many ways in which an active in-place object can be deactivated. Other ways include clicking with the mouse on the container document outside the object or performing an action in the container that would otherwise require that object to be deactivated. For example, if a container is currently open with an active in-place object and the end user drops another object onto the document, the container should deactivate the object and process the drop. Closing the document is another good time to deactivate.

The container notifies the object of deactivation by calling *IOleInPlaceObject::InPlaceDeactivate.* At this time, the object calls *IOleInPlaceSite::OnUIDeactivate,* removes (and possibly destroys) its in-place tools, disassembles the shared menu, moves the editing window back to its own document and frame windows (using *SetParent* again), calls *IOleInPlaceFrame::SetActiveObject* and *IOleInPlaceUIWindow::SetActiveObject* with NULLs (to say no more active object), calls *IOleInPlaceSite::OnInPlaceDeactivate,* and finally releases all held container interface pointers. The container, during all of this, releases the pointers it holds on the object's interfaces, but otherwise basically sits around waiting for the object to finish.

Removing its own tools is a simple matter of hiding and possibly destroying them as the object wants. It is not necessary to call the container's *SetBorderSpace* functions to "return" space to the container. *SetBorderSpace* is only for reserving what you want, and the container will reinstate its own tools on *IOleInPlaceSite::OnUIDeactivate.* You don't need to worry about the container.

Disassembling the menu is a little more work and has a lot of potential for error. The object must first remove its menu items (and *only* its items) from the shared menu. It must leave the container's menus there because the object does not know how the container manages its half of the shared menu. When the object has finished removing its items, it calls *IOleInPlaceFrame::RemoveMenus* to let the container do its own work. When the container is finished, the object can call *DestroyMenu* (the opposite of the earlier *CreateMenu* call) to finally put the menu to rest.

With all of that, the process of deactivation takes the object from the active state back to the loaded state, just as *IOleObject::Close* takes an object from the open state back to the loaded state, as we saw in Chapter 10.

Active vs. UI Active and Inside-Out Objects

I want to make a short mention about two parts of in-place activation for which I implement minimal support in our container, but which I do not otherwise explain in great detail. First, there are actually two distinct states of an active object. There's Active, which means the object has its editing window in the container's window ready for manipulation, and there's UI Active, which means the object is displaying a hatched border, has its name in the container's caption bars, and is working from its own toolbars and a shared menu. A container can choose to deactivate the UI for an object instead of deactivating the object completely by calling *IOleInPlaceObject::UIDeactivate* so that reactivating the object needs only to reactivate the UI components.

These two states exist so that there can be any number of objects in a container that are active but only one that is UI active because, well, there's only one place to put UI, and you can't have all the objects fighting over it.

So why would we want more than one active object at a time? The answer lies with things called *inside-out objects,* objects that are active as long as they are visible—end users have to double-click first before manipulating the object as they must with the typical *outside-in objects.* Basically the inside-out objects behave a little differently when selected, single-clicked, and double-clicked. For example, an inside-out object really never has a "loaded" state because being loaded means being in-place active but not UI active. Being in-place active, however, does mean that the object can be manipulated with single mouse clicks. Any number of objects can be in-place active but only the currently selected object is UI active. We'll see how to handle this at the end of the chapter.

Yes, This Actually Does Work

If you still have doubts that this actually works, and works well, go through the implementation and watch what happens.

I did, however, want to share what Microsoft learned in usability tests involving in-place activation. The company found some test subjects who were accustomed to working with Microsoft Word and Microsoft Excel. The usability testers created a simulation in which an Excel spreadsheet object would activate in place inside of Word. At first, the usability designers thought there might be some serious problems when the simulation began to switch menus and toolbars around. What they actually found was quite surprising. When subjects activated the spreadsheet object in place, they immediately recognized it as Excel and without noticing what had happened, went along using Excel's toolbar and formula bar, which had quietly appeared in place of Word's toolbar and ribbon, and using Excel's menus, which had quietly merged with Word's. Only after a number of minutes of doing their jobs (that is, manipulating the spreadsheet), the subjects began to notice that things had changed.

This was a surprise because the testers thought it would be obvious that stuff was switching around. But because the users were focusing so intently on the object they wanted to edit, they weren't even looking at the menu or the toolbar. When the object changed from a simple presentation to something that looked just like an Excel spreadsheet, their Excel training kicked right in without a hitch. This is one of the major reasons why a container application should try *really* hard to keep that object in the same place and to minimize flicker; otherwise, you give the user too much opportunity to notice the other changes taking place, which is nothing less than a disruption in their work. Disruptions are far from usable.

I hope you can see the tremendous user benefit in all of this, and I hope that you can take advantage of it in your applications. Let's see then, how to go about it for a container, as we follow Patron through its last series of modifications in this book.

In-Place Container Step-By-Step

Think of support for in-place activation as an extension to support for embedding. You really only need to make those changes in Chapter 9 to support embedding before you undertake these modifications because linking support is an entirely separate matter.

Most of what we're going to do here involves user interface because in-place activation is a UI-intensive feature. As we did with other OLE features, we have a few interfaces to implement and a number of places where we need to add a small amount of code to make everything work smoothly. Given that warning, the steps for producing in-place container support are as follows:

1. Prepare the container application to handle the effect of creating shared menus, switching toolbars, and handling accelerators while an object is active in place.
2. Implement skeletal *IOleInPlaceFrame*, *IOleUIWindow*, and *IOleInPlaceSite* interfaces.

3. Activate and deactivate the object.
4. Contribute your application's half of the shared menu.
5. Negotiate tool space, and handle window repositioning when an object requests space.
6. Give the object a chance to process accelerators before your application starts, and be sure you disable all accelerators that are not applicable during an in-place session.
7. Handle all the remaining cases in which an event occurs in the container, such as switching between documents, resizing the frame or document windows, scrolling a document, and flushing out the oddball members of the in-place container interfaces. These are all the little tweaks needed to make it all work. There are also a number of optional additions you can make to your container that will also be covered.

Again, you will be able to compile your application and test it after each step. It's probably obvious that the last step is rather nebulous. I simply lumped a number of small steps into one larger step. I did this because by this time, you have provided for all the major functionality required of your container, and you can add and test the little pieces at your leisure, one at a time if necessary.

There are also a number of notes about my "experiences" with this code. These notes are set off from the rest of the text in boxes on the pages to come. Many are notes about things that caused me to regularly beat my head into a table, wall, or other sufficiently hard surface while I was developing this code. Not all of them are about bad stuff, however—some of them are merely comments about tricky parts of the implementation. I hope they can prevent you from developing the same sort of flat spot as I inflicted on my forehead.

Prepare the Container

Instead of starting out with a big, scary "experience" box I decided to add this little section to acquaint you with some implications of in-place activation. I recommend that you think about how these implications apply to your application and how to make changes now before you get too much deeper into coding.

Limited Command Availability

When you have an active in-place object in your container, you will not have all of your menus available, you might not have your toolbar available, and you will not have first crack at accelerators. Now would be a good time to think about a few questions. What functions do you want to have available during an in-place session? Are those on menus that you will retain during the session? Are there commands that are available only on a toolbar where they will be inaccessible during the session? What accelerators correspond to menu items that you will not retain? Do you need to define separate menu and accelerator resources to load specifically during a session? Can you modify your editing toolbar in such a way that if you are allowed to retain it during a session, you can remove those commands that you do not retain?

Your answers to some of these questions might mean redesigning or modifying your existing toolbar and menu handling code, as well as how you load and manage accelerators. All of these are ways in which you expose your application's commands to the end user. If you have ways by which you expose commands other than through menus, accelerators, and toolbars, you must include those in these implications.

Implications for Mixed Menus

Almost all applications that use menus use the WM_INITMENU or WM_INITMENUPOPUP messages to enable or disable specific menu items based on a number of conditions, such as disabling Edit/Paste when there is no suitable data on the clipboard.

Typically, we've compared the index (position) of the menu to a known fixed value to determine which menu we're working with. During an in-place session when there's a shared menu, the positions of your menu items are not going to remain constant, which means you need to remove any constants from your WM_INITMENU[POPUP] handling code.

There are two ways to do this. One way is to keep around an array of integers that hold the current position for each menu you have showing. You then compare the index passed in the message to those in this array to find out which menu you are dealing with. This is an ideal technique when you are going to place new pop-up menus on the shared menu and the new menus are not already present on your normal container's menu.

The other technique uses the menu handles themselves, which are also passed with these messages. This works best when you are going to use the same pop-up menus on the shared menu as those that are in your normal menu. (Two top-level menus can have the same *hMenu* for a pop-up item.) In this case, create an array of HMENUs on startup and always compare the *hMenu* passed in the message to those in this array. If you use the same menu handles in the shared menu, you're WM_INITMENU[POPUP] code doesn't need modification for the in-place scenario.

Implications of Tool Space Negotiation

More questions to ask yourself: Can you resize whatever window occupies the client area of your frame and document windows? Can you resize them in any direction? Can you resize them while keeping the contents at the same absolute screen position? How small can they be? Is there a point at which you would restrict the border space allowed for an object? Are there spaces in the frame or document client areas that should never be overlapped by an object (especially those areas that are drawn and are not separate windows)? Do your tool windows use WS_CLIPSIBLINGS to keep them from interfering with object tools? Do you have a status line? When the frame or document window is resized, do you always resize the client to a specific position?

Grist for the mill. During an in-place session, you are responsible for respecting the space you allow an object, which means not drawing over it, keeping your client area windows inside the space left over after the object's allocations, and ensuring that you resize the client windows correctly when the frame or document is resized. Thinking about the impact of sharing space with a completely random application is well worth the trouble at this point. I also suggest that you make any necessary changes to your application now and debug them completely so that you can later concentrate solely on the in-place activation work.

Implement Skeletal In-Place Container Interfaces

As we saw in Figure 15-2, a container application must implement three additional interfaces: *IOleInPlaceSite*, which is implemented on the same site object as *IOleClientSite*; *IOleInPlaceUIWindow*, which is implemented on a document object like *IPersistFile* or *IOleItemContainer*; and *IOleInPlaceFrame*, which is implemented on the frame object, whatever that might be. Note that the frame object is not the same as the class factory object we saw for containers in Chapter 13—it is whatever C++ object structure that manages your container's frame window. Note that there are additional files in the INTERFAC directory on the sample code for these interfaces: IIPSITE.CPP, IIPSITE.H, IIPUIWIN.CPP, IIPUIWIN.H, IIPFRAME.CPP, and IIPFRAME.H.

All of these interfaces inherit from an interface called *IOleWindow*, which serves as the base class for all in-place interfaces, including the interfaces of an in-place object:

```
DECLARE_INTERFACE_(IOleWindow, IUnknown)
    {
    [IUnknown members]

    STDMETHOD(GetWindow) (THIS_ HWND FAR* lphwnd) PURE;
    STDMETHOD(ContextSensitiveHelp) (THIS_ BOOL fEnterMode) PURE;
    };
```

For all in-place interfaces, the *GetWindow* function returns whatever window is associated with the particular object; note how much this reinforces the idea that in-place activation is very user-interface oriented—every in-place interface has an associated window. *IOleInPlaceFrame::GetWindow,* for example, returns the container's frame window, whereas *IOleInPlaceUIWindow::GetWindow* returns the container's document window. Depending on how your container is implemented, *IOleInPlaceSite::GetWindow* might return the document window as well (if there is nothing else related to the site), or it might do something like Patron's implementation, which returns the Pages window that lives inside the document. In any case, *GetWindow* always returns the closest window to the object on which it is implemented.

IOleInPlaceUIWindow is a fairly general interface that augments *IOleWindow* (from which it inherits) with the tool space negotiation functions of *GetBorder, RequestBorderSpace, SetBorderSpace,* and *SetActiveObject*:

```
DECLARE_INTERFACE_(IOleInPlaceUIWindow, IOleWindow)
    {
    [IUnknown members]
    [IOleWindow members]

    STDMETHOD(GetBorder) (THIS_ LPRECT lprectBorder) PURE;
    STDMETHOD(RequestBorderSpace) (THIS_ LPCBORDERWIDTHS
        lpborderwidths) PURE;
    STDMETHOD(SetBorderSpace) (THIS_ LPCBORDERWIDTHS
        lpborderwidths) PURE;
    STDMETHOD(SetActiveObject) (THIS_ LPOLEINPLACEACTIVEOBJECT
        lpActiveObject, LPCSTR lpszObjName) PURE;
    };
```

As we saw earlier in this chapter, the three *Border* functions are concerned with tools that an object might want to place inside the window on which the interface is implemented. We won't need to worry about implementing them until we deal with tools later. The container uses *SetActiveObject,* as we have seen, to obtain a pointer to the in-place object's *IOleInPlaceActiveObject* interface, and this will be one member function we'll want to implement early on. A container document implementation will use *IOleInPlaceActiveObject* only to notify the object when the document is resized (so the object can resize its tools appropriately) and when the document changes activation (so the object can affect its user interface as you want it to).

IOleInPlaceUIWindow serves as the base class for *IOleInPlaceFrame* because the frame also needs to negotiate border space as documents do. The additional member functions deal with creating the shared menu (which is always a function of the container's frame) and functions concerned with the status line (which the container owns), modeless pop-up windows, and accelerators:

```
DECLARE_INTERFACE_(IOleInPlaceFrame, IOleInPlaceUIWindow)
    {
    [IUnknown members]
    [IOleWindow members]
    [IOleInPlaceUIWindow members]

    STDMETHOD(InsertMenus) (THIS_ HMENU hmenuShared,
        LPOLEMENUGROUPWIDTHS lpMenuWidths) PURE;
    STDMETHOD(SetMenu) (THIS_ HMENU hmenuShared, HOLEMENU holemenu, HWND
        hwndActiveObj) PURE;
    STDMETHOD(RemoveMenus) (THIS_ HMENU hmenuShared) PURE;
    STDMETHOD(SetStatusText) (THIS_ LPCSTR lpszStatusText) PURE;
    STDMETHOD(EnableModeless) (THIS_ BOOL fEnable) PURE;
    STDMETHOD(TranslateAccelerator) (THIS_ LPMSG lpmsg, WORD wID) PURE;
    };
```

As you can guess, the menu functions do not need an implementation until we create the menu. Nor do we need to implement any of the other functions until we get to those specific features much later—they are completely unnecessary to get an in-place object into the UI active state.

The *IOleInPlaceSite* interface is the one that will have the most initial implementation because it provides the critical communication path between the in-place object and the container:

```
DECLARE_INTERFACE_(IOleInPlaceSite, IOleWindow)
    {
    [IUnknown members]
    [IOleWindow members]

    STDMETHOD(CanInPlaceActivate) (THIS) PURE;
    STDMETHOD(OnInPlaceActivate) (THIS) PURE;
    STDMETHOD(OnUIActivate) (THIS) PURE;
    STDMETHOD(GetWindowContext) (THIS_ LPOLEINPLACEFRAME FAR* lplpFrame
        , LPOLEINPLACEUIWINDOW FAR* lplpDoc, LPRECT lprcPosRect
        , LPRECT lprcClipRect, LPOLEINPLACEFRAMEINFO lpFrameInfo) PURE;
    STDMETHOD(Scroll) (THIS_ SIZE scrollExtent) PURE;
    STDMETHOD(OnUIDeactivate) (THIS_ BOOL fUndoable) PURE;
    STDMETHOD(OnInPlaceDeactivate) (THIS) PURE;
    STDMETHOD(DiscardUndoState) (THIS) PURE;
    STDMETHOD(DeactivateAndUndo) (THIS) PURE;
    STDMETHOD(OnPosRectChange) (THIS_ LPCRECT lprcPosRect) PURE;
    };
```

The *CanInPlaceActivate* function, as we saw earlier, will be the first of the object calls out of all these container interfaces. We also saw that the object will call functions such as *OnInPlaceActivate* and *GetWindowContext* early on in the in-place activation process. For the most part, half these will need some implementation right away, with most of the others needing implementation only when we want to complete all the container features.

With that we can list the steps to follow as we initially add these interfaces:

1. Add each interface to its appropriate container object and modify (or, probably in the frame's case, add) the interface, along with all of its base interfaces, so that *QueryInterface* knows about it.
2. Implement the trivial *GetWindow* function of each interface.
3. Implement *SetActiveObject* in the frame and document interfaces to save the *IOleInPlaceActiveObject* pointers and to change the container's caption bars.
4. Implement *CanInPlaceActivate, OnInPlaceActivate, OnInPlaceDeactivate,* and *GetWindowContext* in *IOleInPlaceSite.*
5. Return *ResultFromScode(E_NOTIMPL)* from everything else for the time being.

EXPERIENCE: The Site Requires Access to the Frame and Document

What will become obvious as you begin your in-place container implementation is that the *IOleInPlaceSite* interface will need to call functions that affect the frame user interface and will need access to the container's *IOleInPlaceFrame* and *IOleInPlaceUIWindow* interfaces on the frame and document, respectively. This means that you will probably not be able to keep the frame, document, and site objects as independent or separate as you would like. For example, in Patron I simply had to punt—I created a global variable to hold the *CPatronFrame* pointer so that the site could get at it *(g_pFR)*. I didn't like using this approach, but I didn't want to define and implement a number of other functions merely to pass this pointer around. It's easier simply to use the pointer directly. So, another global variable. Something to keep in mind as you start working with these interfaces.

Each of these steps, with the exception of step 5, is treated in a section that follows.

Add Interfaces and Modify *QueryInterface*

This step is really to help you remember that the in-place interfaces we're adding here derive from *IOleWindow* or, in the case of *IOleInPlaceFrame*, from *IOleWindow* and *IOleInPlaceUIWindow*. So your *QueryInterface* implementations need to be sure to check for all the base interfaces:

```
//In PATRON.CPP, where CPatronFrame inherits from IOleInPlaceFrame
STDMETHODIMP CPatronFrame::QueryInterface(REFIID riid, LPLPVOID ppv)
    {
    ...

    if (IsEqualIID(riid, IID_IUnknown)
        || IsEqualIID(riid, IID_IOleWindow)
        || IsEqualIID(riid, IID_IOleInPlaceUIWindow)
        || IsEqualIID(riid, IID_IOleInPlaceFrame))
        *ppv=(LPVOID)(LPINPLACEFRAME)this;

    ...
    }

//In DOCUMENT.CPP; CPatronDoc contains an impl. of IOleInPlaceUIWindow
STDMETHODIMP CPatronDoc::QueryInterface(REFIID riid, LPLPVOID ppv)
    {
    ...

    //IUnknown implemented separately
    if (IsEqualIID(riid, IID_IOleWindow)
        || IsEqualIID(riid, IID_IOleInPlaceUIWindow))
        *ppv=(LPVOID)m_pIOleIPUIWindow;

    ...
    }

//In TENANT.CPP; CTenant contains and impl. of IOleInPlaceSite
STDMETHODIMP CTenant::QueryInterface(REFIID riid, LPLPVOID ppv)
    {
    ...

    //IUnknown implemented separately
    if (IsEqualIID(riid, IID_IOleWindow)
        || IsEqualIID(riid, IID_IOleInPlaceSite))
        *ppv=(LPVOID)m_pIOleIPSite;

    ....
    }
```

Note that *CPatronFrame* inherits from *IOleInPlaceFrame* directly because it's the only interface we have on that frame object. Therefore, it returns the *IOleInlaceFrame* pointer identically for *IUnknown*, *IOleWindow*, *IOleInPlace-UIWindow*, and *IOleInPlaceFrame*.

Implement *GetWindow* in All Interfaces

This is truly trivial because your entire implementation in all interfaces will look something like this:

```
STDMETHODIMP CPatronFrame::GetWindow(HWND FAR * phWnd)
    {
    *phWnd=m_hWnd;
    return NOERROR;
    }
```

That is, return the window that is most closely associated with the interface.

Implement *SetActiveObject* for the Frame and Document

SetActiveObject is only a little more work. First, you need to keep a copy of the in-place object's *IOleInPlaceActiveObject* pointer in both your frame structure and your document structure. In Patron, both *CPatronFrame* and *CPatronDoc* have a member *m_pIOleIPActiveObject* of type LPOLEINPLACEACTIVE-OBJECT.

SetActiveObject is called with both NULL and non-NULL pointers for the *IOleInPlaceActiveObject* interface. When passed a non-NULL pointer, release the pointer you have, save the new one, and call *AddRef* through it. When passed a NULL pointer, release the one you have and NULL your variable:

```
/*
 * From the frame's implementation of IOleInPlaceFrame.
 * pIIPActiveObj is the parameter to the function.
 */

if (NULL!=m_pIOleIPActiveObject)
    m_pIOleIPActiveObject->Release();

m_pIOleIPActiveObject=pIIPActiveObj;    //NULLs if pIIPActiveObj is NULL

if (NULL!=m_pIOleIPActiveObject)
    m_pIOleIPActiveObject->AddRef();
```

As I described earlier in this chapter, both *SetActiveObject* functions in frame and document interfaces also receive a string from the object to use in caption bars in the *pszObj* parameter. However, depending on your application, only one of these needs to affect the caption bar. If your application is an

MDI container, change the document's title bar in *IOleInPlaceUIWindow::SetActiveObject* and leave the frame window's caption bar alone in *IOleInPlaceFrame.* If your application is an SDI application, do the opposite, changing the frame window's caption in *IOleInPlaceFrame::SetActiveObject* and ignoring the string passed to *IOleInPlaceUIWindow.* You can see this in Patron's implementations (which I won't show here) where the caption-bar code in *IOleInPlaceFrame* is conditionally compiled on *#ifndef MDI* whereas the *IOleInPlaceUIWindow* implementation in the document is conditionally compiled on the opposite condition *#ifdef MDI.*

Implement Crucial *IOleInPlaceSite* Members

The four functions that you need to implement from the start in *IOleInPlaceSite* are *CanInPlaceActivate, OnInPlaceActivate, OnInPlaceDeactivate,* and *GetWindowContext.* The first three are very short, at least in Patron:

```
STDMETHODIMP CImpIOleInPlaceSite::CanInPlaceActivate(void)
    {
    if (DVASPECT_CONTENT!=m_pTen->m_fe.dwAspect)
        return ResultFromScode(S_FALSE);

    if (TENANTTYPE_EMBEDDEDOBJECT!=m_pTen->m_tType)
        return ResultFromScode(S_FALSE);

    return NOERROR;
    }

STDMETHODIMP CImpIOleInPlaceSite::OnInPlaceActivate(void)
    {
    //m_pIOleIPObject is our in-place flag.
    m_pTen->m_pObj->QueryInterface(IID_IOleInPlaceObject
        , (LPLPVOID)&m_pTen->m_pIOleIPObject);
    return NOERROR;
    }

STDMETHODIMP CImpIOleInPlaceSite::OnInPlaceDeactivate(void)
    {
    m_pTen->m_pIOleIPObject->Release();
    m_pTen->m_pIOleIPObject=NULL;
    return NOERROR;
    }
```

For most applications, *CanInPlaceActivate* will not be too complex. In Patron, we disallow in-place activation (returning S_FALSE, not an error code) only when the object is not embedded or displayed using DVASPECT-_CONTENT. You might find it necessary to disallow in-place activation for some objects based on other conditions, such as the position of the object in your document.

OnInPlaceActivate and *OnInPlaceDeactive* tell the container to put itself into or out of an in-place state. Patron needs to manage the object's *IOleInPlaceObject* pointer only in these functions, which it saves in the *m_pIOleIPObject* variable in *CTenant*. The pointer, which we need for making other function calls later, doubles as a flag to tell us whether we are handling an in-place session at the time.

GetWindowContext is the hairy beast of the group, requiring more code because there are more parameters to mess with. This function has to store pointers to the container's *IOleInPlaceFrame* and *IOleInPlaceUIWindow* interfaces in two out parameters (*ppIIPFrame* and *ppIIPUIWindow*), specify the initial position and clipping rectangles for the object (in *prcPos* and *prcClip*), and fill an OLEINPLACEFRAMEINFO structure with accelerator information:

```
STDMETHODIMP CImpIOleInPlaceSite::GetWindowContext
    (LPOLEINPLACEFRAME FAR * ppIIPFrame, LPOLEINPLACEUIWINDOW FAR
    * ppIIPUIWindow, LPRECT prcPos, LPRECT prcClip
    , LPOLEINPLACEFRAMEINFO pFI)
    {
    LPCPatronDoc    pDoc;
    RECTL           rcl;

    *ppIIPUIWindow=NULL;

    *ppIIPFrame=(LPOLEINPLACEFRAME)g_pFR;
    g_pFR->AddRef();

    pDoc=(LPCPatronDoc)SendMessage(GetParent(m_pTen->m_hWnd)
        , DOCM_PDOCUMENT, 0, 0L);

    if (NULL!=pDoc)
        {
        pDoc->QueryInterface(IID_IOleInPlaceUIWindow
            , (LPLPVOID)ppIIPUIWindow);
        }

    //Now get the rectangles and frame information
    m_pTen->RectGet(&rcl, TRUE);
    RECTFROMRECTL(*prcPos, rcl);

    //Include scroll position here.
    OffsetRect(prcPos, -(int)m_pTen->m_pPG->m_xPos
        , -(int)m_pTen->m_pPG->m_yPos);

    SetRect(prcClip, 0, 0, 32767, 32767);
```

```
#ifdef MDI
 pFI->fMDIApp=TRUE;
#else
 pFI->fMDIApp=FALSE;
#endif

 pFI->hwndFrame=g_pFR->Window();

 pFI->haccel=g_pFR->m_hAccelIP;
 pFI->cAccelEntries=CINPLACEACCELERATORS;

 return NOERROR;
 }
```

Patron simply stores the global *CPatronFrame* pointer *g_pFR* as the *IOleInPlaceFrame* pointer because *CPatronFrame* inherits from the interface (and calls *AddRef*, of course). It has to ask the document for its *IOleInPlaceUIWindow*, however, by means of *QueryInterface*.

The container is responsible for returning two rectangles here. The position rectangle tells the object exactly which rectangle it occupies in the container in *device units*. In Patron's case, this is the rectangle of the tenant implementing this site, offset for the current scroll position. The position rectangle determines the scaling of the object. The clipping rectangle, on the other hand, specifies where the object can legally display *anything*—that is, the object is a downright criminal if it dares to place anything outside the clipping rectangle. This is the law to prevent the object from overlapping parts of the container if the container so desires. Because Patron has no restrictions,[3] it stores the maximum rectangle (0–32767 in both extents) in *prcClip*, again in device units. Note that the position rectangle can be larger than or extend outside the clipping rectangle. The object will scale to the position rectangle, but it will be displayed only in the intersection of the position and clipping rectangles.

The OLEINPLACEFRAMEINFO structure that you fill here provides the server with information it requires for calling *OleTranslateAccelerator*, if we're dealing with an EXE server. DLL servers do not use this information. *OleTranslateAccelerator* generally wants to know whether your container is MDI (so that it can call *TranslateMDISysAccel* appropriately), as well as the window that will receive accelerator commands, the handle to the accelerators you want to use during an in-place session, and a count of the number of accelera-

3. Because the object's child window in the container is also clipped to the container's document window, the object will never be shown outside the container window itself.

tors in that table. (It needs this count because OLE accesses the accelerator table directly instead of by calling *TranslateAccelerator.*) For your initial implementation, you can simply store NULL in the *haccel* and *cAccelEntries* fields and fill them in later when you add accelerator support. In Patron, the *CPatronFrame* in use loads the in-place accelerator table (resource identifier IDR_INPLACEACCELERATORS) at startup and stores it in *m_hAccelIP* (which we used in the preceding code):

```
IDR_INPLACEACCELERATORS ACCELERATORS
   BEGIN
    "^N",         IDM_PAGENEWPAGE
    "^n",         IDM_PAGENEWPAGE
    "^D",         IDM_PAGEDELETEPAGE
    "^d",         IDM_PAGEDELETEPAGE
    VK_NEXT,      IDM_PAGENEXTPAGE, VIRTKEY
    VK_PRIOR,     IDM_PAGEPREVIOUSPAGE, VIRTKEY
    VK_HOME,      IDM_PAGEFIRSTPAGE, CONTROL, VIRTKEY
    VK_END,       IDM_PAGELASTPAGE, CONTROL, VIRTKEY

    //Accelerators for open the object and context-help
    VK_RETURN,    IDM_OPENOBJECT, CONTROL, VIRTKEY
    VK_F1,        IDM_ENTERCONTEXTHELP, SHIFT, VIRTKEY
    VK_ESCAPE,    IDM_ESCAPECONTEXTHELP, VIRTKEY
   END
```

Finally, be aware of *cb* field in OLEINPLACEFRAMEINFO, which you can use to check the version of the structure. This will not be a consideration until release of later versions of OLE that have a different structure size. The server is therefore required to always fill *cb* before calling *GetWindowContext,* and the container should not modify the value but use it only to check with other fields it needs to fill.

After adding all these interfaces and implementing the essential functions, you can compile to get rid of all the typos and give your container a quick run to be sure everything is running smoothly. If you insert a new object that you know is in-place capable, you can trace through your *CanInPlaceActivate, OnInPlaceActivate,* and *GetWindowContext* calls, as well as verify that *QueryInterface* works properly and that your *GetWindow* implementations are correct. With this small amount of implementation you can generally get an object activated to the point shown in Figure 15-4 on page 850, where the object's window is sitting ready in the container's document. Try it with the Cosmo sample from Chapter 16.

Activate and Deactivate the Object

Activating the object happens as it always has by calling *IOleObject::DoVerb* with object-specific verbs or those like OLEIVERB_SHOW. However, there are two important points to distinguish now.

First, OLEIVERB_OPEN will *never* activate an object in place. It's the one verb guaranteed to open an object into a server window. Just be careful how you use it.

Second, there's another parameter to *DoVerb* that we've ignored until now—*lpMSG*, a pointer to a MSG structure. A message? Why do we need the message? This parameter exists for uses in which the object is something like a button and the container calls *DoVerb(OLEIVERB_PRIMARY)* on both WM_LBUTTONDOWN and WM_LBUTTONUP messages.[4] The object can then use the message to take different actions for the same verb. A button object would depress with the mouse down, and pop back up with the mouse up. For a standard container, this means that you should always include the message that caused the call to *DoVerb*, unless it was generated from a menu selection or some other event that would have no meaning to an object (such as WM_COMMAND). I mention this because for this chapter I modified Patron to send an a WM_LBUTTONDBLCLK message to *DoVerb* when the object is activated with the mouse:

```
BOOL CPage::OnLeftDoubleClick(UINT uKeys, UINT x, UINT y)
    {
    if (HTNOWHERE!=m_uHTCode)
        {
        MSG     msg;
        DWORD   dw;

        //Include a message for in-place objects.
        msg.hwnd=NULL;
        msg.message=WM_LBUTTONDBLCLK;
        msg.wParam=(WPARAM)uKeys;
        msg.lParam=MAKELONG(x, y);
        msg.time=GetMessageTime();

        dw=GetMessagePos();
        SETPOINT(msg.pt, LOWORD(dw), HIWORD(dw));

        return m_pTenantCur->Activate(OLEIVERB_PRIMARY, &msg);
        }

    ...
    }
```

4. This is not, of course, in compliance with standard UI guidelines, but you might have a use for this some day, so it's part of *DoVerb*.

All other cases pass a NULL pointer as the second parameter because they have no meaningful message information to give.

So other than including the message, activation of an in-place object is the same as for a typical linked or embedded object. But remember now that when we opened an object before it would come back only to the loaded state when the end user closed the server. Because there is no separate server window for the end user to close, how then do we get an active object back to the loaded state?

The answer is addressed in the "OLE User Interface Guidelines" chapter of the *OLE 2 Programmer's Reference,* which state that if the end user clicks anywhere in the document outside the active object, the container deactivates that object. In Patron, this means that any WM_LBUTTONDOWN (handled in *CPage::OnLeftDown*) or WM_RBUTTONDOWN (*CPage::OnRightDown*) outside the current object in the page generates a call to *CTenant::DeactivateInPlaceObject,* which calls *IOleObject::InPlaceDeactivate* to take the object back to the loaded state:

```
void CTenant::DeactivateInPlaceObject(void)
    {
    if (NULL!=m_pIOleIPObject)
        m_pIOleIPObject->InPlaceDeactivate();

    return;
    }
```

Note how Patron uses *m_pIOleIPObject* both to know that it's currently servicing an in-place session and to provide the means through which it controls that session.

Clicking outside the object is not the only event that can cause deactivation. Basically you should deactivate if anything else happens that would create or activate a different object (such as a drag-and-drop operation) or anything that would require the object in the loaded state (such as closing the document or application). This latter case is handled in *CTenant::Close,* which calls *CTenant::DeactivateInPlaceObject* before calling *IOleObject::Close.*

After you have a method for deactivating an object, you can try activating and deactivating the object several times to be sure the changes you make will persist from one activation to the next. Now that you can activate and deactivate the object, you have a framework into which you can build the other aspects of in-place activation, such as menus, tools, accelerators, and other small considerations.

EXPERIENCE: The Server Is Still Running

An important fact to remember: After deactivating an in-place object, the server is *not* unloaded—that is, OLE keeps it running with open reference counts although the container itself has no pointers to the object. This is done so that reactivating the object again is fast because it eliminates the time to load the server. This means that the state of the server is not necessarily reset between activations, so if, while you debug your container, something becomes messed up during one activation, it will still be messed up on the next. To reset the server (and possibly your own container) you must either close and reopen the document, which will unload the server, or you can use a tool such as WPS.EXE in the OLE 2 SDK to unload directly, although this latter course is much riskier and might introduce other problems.

Mix-a-Menu: Shaken, Not Stirred

Earlier, we saw how the object and container work together to create the shared menu. To support that cooperation, we now need to implement the *InsertMenus*, *RemoveMenus*, and *SetMenu* members of *IOleInPlaceFrame*. In addition, we need to do a little work now in *IOleInPlaceSite::OnUIDeactivate* to handle the menu correctly. The following sections deal with each member function in detail.

IOleInPlaceFrame::InsertMenus

The container has the easy part in creating the shared menu—it gets to operate on an empty menu or one that holds only container menus. (The object has to work with the menu after the container plays with it.) Our first encounter with the shared menu is in *IOleInPlaceFrame::InsertMenus*, in which we need to create each menu in our File, Container, and Window groups and store the number of menus in those groups in the OLEMENUGROUPWIDTHS array we're given.

Patron's implementation of *InsertMenus* takes a menu handle from its normal top-level menu and adds it to the shared menu by calling the Windows API *InsertMenu* (singular). Note that Windows has no problem with two or more menus holding the same pop-up item.

```
STDMETHODIMP CPatronFrame::InsertMenus(HMENU hMenu
    , LPOLEMENUGROUPWIDTHS pMGW)
    {
    InsertMenu(hMenu, 0, MF_BYPOSITION | MF_POPUP, (UINT)m_phMenu[0]
        , PSZ(IDS_FILEMENU));
    InsertMenu(hMenu, 1, MF_BYPOSITION | MF_POPUP, (UINT)m_phMenu[2]
        , PSZ(IDS_PAGEMENU));

    pMGW->width[0]=1;
    pMGW->width[2]=1;

   #ifdef MDI
    InsertMenu(hMenu, 2, MF_BYPOSITION | MF_POPUP
        , (UINT)m_hMenuWindow, PSZ(IDS_WINDOWMENU));

    pMGW->width[4]=1;
   #else
    pMGW->width[4]=0;
   #endif

    return NOERROR;
    }
```

Conveniently, all of Patron's pop-up menu handles are already stored in the *CPatronFrame* array *m_phMenu*, and Patron uses strings from its string table for the item names. Because we are working on a clean menu we can use constants to specify the positions of these items, and we need to store only the width of our groups in the OLEMENUGROUPWIDTHS array. Note also that Patron uses the same *m_phMenu* array in processing WM_INITMENUPOPUP messages to determine which menu it's affecting so that the same code we've always used for enabling and disabling items (*CPatronFrame::UpdateMenus*) works without a hitch when we display this shared menu on Patron's frame window.

IOleInPlaceFrame::RemoveMenus

By the time this function is called, the object has already done the more tedious work of removing its menus from the shared menu. So when we get the menu back at this point, all we have to do is remove the items we know we added. The best way to implement this function is to walk the menu, removing any pop-up menu handle you recognize:

```
STDMETHODIMP CPatronFrame::RemoveMenus(HMENU hMenu)
    {
    int         cItems, i, j;
    HMENU       hMenuT;
```

```
    if (NULL==hMenu)
        return NOERROR;

    cItems=GetMenuItemCount(hMenu);

    for (i=cItems; i >=0; i--)
        {
        hMenuT=GetSubMenu(hMenu, i);

        for (j=0; j <= CMENUS; j++)
            {
            if (hMenuT==m_phMenu[j])
                RemoveMenu(hMenu, i, MF_BYPOSITION);
            }
        }

    //The menu should now be empty.
    return NOERROR;
    }
```

This defensive programming practice eliminates the possibility that any of our popups remain on this menu after we've finished with it because as soon as we return, the object usually calls *DestroyMenu* on the whole shared menu. If any popups still exist on it, they too are destroyed. This doesn't bode well if those popups are also on our normal menu. Because we can't ensure that the object cleans up its pop-up menus properly, we should be sure we clean up ours.

IOleInPlaceFrame::SetMenu

This frame function is the interesting one because only here does something visual actually happen. You can call *SetMenu* in one of two ways: You can pass it a valid menu handle, or you can pass it a NULL menu handle. The first case means your application is being given a shared menu to display, so the application displays it. The second case means that your application is asked to display its normal menu again, as if UI deactivation has happened. You can see this in Patron's implementation:

```
STDMETHODIMP CPatronFrame::SetMenu(HMENU hMenu
    , HOLEMENU hOLEMenu, HWND hWndObj)
    {
    HRESULT         hr;
    LPCPatronClient pCL=(LPCPatronClient)m_pCL;

    if (NULL==hMenu && NULL==hOLEMenu)
        {
        m_hWndObj=NULL;
```

(continued)

```
        //Prevent redundant calls, or debug warnings on startup.
        if (NULL==m_hMenuOrg)
            return NOERROR;

        hMenu=m_hMenuOrg;
        m_hMenuOrg=NULL;
        }
    else
        {
        m_hMenuOrg=GetMenu(m_hWnd);
        m_hWndObj=hWndObj;
        }

    pCL->SetMenu(m_hWnd, hMenu, m_hMenuWindow);
    hr=OleSetMenuDescriptor(hOLEMenu, m_hWnd, hWndObj, NULL, NULL);
    return hr;
    }
```

If you receive a non-NULL HMENU in this function, you will also get a non-NULL HOLEMENU, which is merely a value you pass through to *OleSetMenuDescriptor.* Again, this function installs a message filter on your container's frame window to watch for and redirect messages that should go to the server. The *hWndObj* window is the window to which those messages are sent.

If *hMenu* and *hOLEMenu* are NULL, that means you should reinstall your normal menu. In the preceding code, Patron saves its original menu (in the *CPatronFrame* variable *m_hMenuOrg*) when *SetMenu* is first called with a non-NULL shared menu handle in such a way that when Patron is later called with NULLs, we have the handle of the normal menu to display. Note that calling *OleSetMenuDescriptor* with NULLs will remove the message filter too.

Patron's *CPatronClient::SetMenu* function, which is my own creation, isolates the rest of Patron from MDI/SDI considerations for changing the frame's menu bar. Under SDI, we can call the Windows API function *SetMenu,* whereas we need to use WM_MDISETMENU under MDI. After both cases, we have to call *DrawMenuBar*:

```
void CPatronClient::SetMenu(HWND hWndFrame, HMENU hMenu
    , HMENU hMenuWin)
    {
   #ifdef MDI
    SendMessage(m_hWnd, WM_MDISETMENU, (WPARAM)FALSE
        , MAKELPARAM(hMenu, hMenuWin));
    SendMessage(m_hWnd, WM_MDISETMENU, (WPARAM)TRUE, 0L);
```

```
#else
 if (NULL!=hMenu)
     ::SetMenu(hWndFrame, hMenu);
#endif

 DrawMenuBar(hWndFrame);
 return;
 }
```

EXPERIENCE: Menu Destruction: Just Do It (Right)

When developing Patron and Cosmo together for this chapter and Chapter 16, I had a really weird problem—the first activation would happen just fine and the shared menu worked perfectly, but on the second activation, although everything looked OK, some of the menus would not pop down. On the third activation, I would get a bunch of cascaded menu items on the top-level menu instead of the usual horizontal menu bar. What is going on? Now this was a real head-banger. I tried all sorts of combinations, thinking it might be an MDI issue (which it was not) or that it was a problem in my object's menu construction code because if I didn't put all the object's menu items in the shared menu, the problem disappeared. The problem was actually in the menu destruction code in the object, where it was not removing one of its menu items properly. This meant that one of the popups on the shared menu (either one of the container's or one of the server's) was destroyed when I called *DestroyMenu*, and it could have been one of the container's or one of the server's. Because the now-invalid menu handle was still in use on other top-level menus, unpredictable things happened all over the place, including stack faults in USER. Urk.

It eventually boiled down to a problem in Cosmo's MAKEFILE, which did not include the MDI/SDI flag on the precompiled header command line, so the menu destruction code failed to remove the last item. If you encounter this problem while writing a container program, try modifying your *RemoveMenus* function to remove all items in the menu, regardless of where they came from. If that fixes it, the menu is not being cleaned up properly. You might then want to try a more robust *RemoveMenus* implementation. If that doesn't help, the problem is most likely in the object's code.

IOleInPlaceSite::OnUIDeactivate

We're not quite finished with the menu yet. Now we need to start implementing *IOleInPlaceSite::OnUIDeactivate*, which eventually has to call our own *IOleInPlaceFrame::SetMenu* with NULLs. This does a nice job of restoring our menu to its original state. (Any in-place menu has already been disassembled by the time *OnUIDeactivate* occurs.) We have to make this call because the object does not, and there would otherwise be no event that would tell it to restore our menu.

In Patron, this happens in the function *CPatronFrame::ShowUIAndTools* (which is not part of any interface, mind you). *CPatronFrame::Show UIAndTools* is called from the *CPatronFrame::ReinstateUI* (another noninterface function), which is called from *IOleInPlaceSite::OnUIDeactivate.* When we look at tools next and repaint optimizations a little later, we'll see what else we need to do in this function. For now, however, you can simply call *IOleInPlaceFrame::SetMenu(NULL, NULL, NULL).*

Test the Shared Menu

With these four functions implemented as described, you should now be able to activate an in-place object to the point shown in Figure 15-6, in which every UI feature is correct except for the toolbar. Your menu should have the correct ordering of the six menu groups, and if something seems out of place, you should recheck your *InsertMenus.* Selecting menu commands from the various groups should affect either the container or the object, depending on the group. If there is a problem, you should check the numbers you stored in the OLEMENUGROUPWIDTHS array because those are used to determine who owns which menu. If those are correct, the object might be at fault in which case I hope you have its source code or the phone number of its lead programmer.

Be sure to test deactivation as well to ensure that the menu is properly disassembled. Activate and deactivate a few more times to be sure. Your menu should always reappear after the object is deactivated. Also verify that any enabling and disabling of your menus happens as you expect and that all commands that you wanted on the menu (and didn't want) are there (or not there).

Negotiate Tool Space

Our next task, the next most important step that those pesky little objects are going to bug us about, is to handle tools space negotiation. As described earlier, the negotiation is generally a repeated process of the object calling *RequestBorderSpace* with a BORDERWIDTHS structure filled with your preferred space allocations, followed by a call to *SetBorderSpace* if the container agrees to the allocations sent to *RequestBorderSpace.* These functions can be called on either *IOleInPlaceFrame* or *IOleInPlaceUIWindow.* Some lazy objects will merely call *SetBorderSpace* as a quick way to check acceptance and reserve the space at the same time, so don't assume that *RequestBorderSpace* will always be called first. The object will resort to that only if you reject a call to *SetBorderSpace.* When you tell the object that it can have a certain amount of space, it will call your *GetBorder* function to ask for the rectangle in which to position those tools.

Typical support for tool space negotiation involves implementing the *GetBorder, RequestBorderSpace,* and *SetBorderSpace* functions for both the frame and the document. All of these functions work exclusively on device units and not HIMETRIC because we're dealing with windows, not graphics. There is also the matter of keeping the object in the same place on the screen when you move your windows around in *SetBorderSpace,* so we'll discuss tricks to manage that case as well. Finally, there are some factors to consider when deactivating an object to minimize the amount of flicker, especially when the action causing the deactivation is the activation of another object. The end of this section will look at the details of such optimizations.

GetBorder

This is generally simple to implement: Return your client rectangle if you have no restrictions about where an object can place tools. The rectangle represents the negotiable space from which the object can make requests for space. Anything you don't include here is strictly off limits.

Documents generally don't have many restrictions, so all the space is negotiable. Patron's *IOleInPlaceUIWindow::GetBorder* simply returns the client area of the document.

```
STDMETHODIMP CImpIOleInPlaceUIWindow::GetBorder(LPRECT prcBorder)
    {
    if (NULL==prcBorder)
        return ResultFromScode(E_INVALIDARG);

    GetClientRect(m_pDoc->m_hWnd, prcBorder);
    return NOERROR;
    }
```

The frame is a special case because the container owns the status line. If you have one, exclude the space it occupies from the *GetBorder* rectangle, as shown in Patron's *IOleInPlaceFrame* implementations:

```
STDMETHODIMP CPatronFrame::GetBorder(LPRECT prcBorder)
    {
    if (NULL==prcBorder)
        return ResultFromScode(E_INVALIDARG);
```

(continued)

```
    GetClientRect(m_hWnd, prcBorder);
    prcBorder->bottom-=CYSTATSTRIP;

    return NOERROR;
    }
```

RequestBorderSpace

Implementing this function can range from downright trivial to extravagantly complicated, depending on how picky you want to be with giving away border space. If you are not picky at all, simply return NOERROR from this function, as Patron does.

If you do have some restrictions you want to enforce, you need to check each of the values in the BORDERWIDTHS structure passed to this function. BORDERWIDTHS has the fields *left, top, right,* and *bottom,* which specify how much space the object wants on each side of the window in question (frame or document). If you can grant the space, return NOERROR; otherwise return *ResultFromScode(INPLACE_E_NOTOOLSPACE).*

SetBorderSpace

This is the function in which important things happen. If you can grant the requested space, you have to move your windows around to make room for the object's allocation, and you have to also remember those allocations so that you resize your client-area windows properly when resizing the frame or document window.

First, if you have any restrictions on space, call your own *RequestBorderSpace* function on behalf of the object. Lazy objects will not call *RequestBorderSpace* first, but that doesn't mean you cannot check the requests yourself. Like *RequestBorderSpace, SetBorderSpace* returns INPLACE_E_NOTOOLSPACE if it cannot grant the requests.

After you accept those requests, you need to remember the space allocations on all four sides and resize whichever window occupies the client area of the affected window. In Patron's *IOleInPlaceFrame* implementation, *SetBorderSpace* stores the allocations in some *CPatronFrame* variables in such a way that resizing the frame (in the WM_SIZE case of *CPatronFrame::FMessageHook*) resizes the client correctly so as to not disturb the object's tools:

```
STDMETHODIMP CPatronFrame::SetBorderSpace(LPCBORDERWIDTHS pBW)
    {
    ...

    m_cyTop    =pBW->top;
    m_cyBottom=pBW->bottom;
```

```
    m_cxLeft  =pBW->left;
    m_cxRight =pBW->right;

    ...
    }

BOOL CPatronFrame::FMessageHook(HWND hWnd, UINT iMsg, WPARAM wParam
    , LPARAM lParam, LRESULT FAR *pLRes)
    {
    ...
    int         dx, dy;
    ...

    switch (iMsg)
        {
        case WM_SIZE:
            ...

            m_fSizing=TRUE;
            dx=LOWORD(lParam);
            dy=HIWORD(lParam);

            //Change the GizmoBar and StatStrip widths to match
            m_pGB->OnSize(hWnd);
            m_pSS->OnSize(hWnd);

            //Adjust the client properly, remembering the StatStrip.
            m_pCL->OnSize(m_cxLeft, m_cyTop, dx-m_cxLeft-m_cxRight
                , dy-m_cyTop-m_cyBottom-CYSTATSTRIP);

            m_fSizing=FALSE;
            return TRUE;

        ...
        }

    ...
    }
```

You must also adjust the size of your client-area window initially if necessary. There will be situations in which the requested tool space is the same as the space your application allocates for itself without there being any in-place object. In such a case, you do not need to move any windows. Patron checks for this case by obtaining the position of the client rectangle and comparing it to where it would be after Patron grants the space. Only if there is a change does it call *CPatronClient::MoveWithoutFamily*, which is discussed in the next section.

```
STDMETHODIMP CPatronFrame::SetBorderSpace(LPCBORDERWIDTHS pBW)
    {
    RECT        rc;
    POINT       pt1, pt2;

    ...

    //Get the current offset of the client
    GetWindowRect(m_pCL->Window(), &rc);
    SETPOINT(pt1, rc.left, rc.top);
    SETPOINT(pt2, rc.right, rc.bottom);
    ScreenToClient(m_hWnd, &pt1);
    ScreenToClient(m_hWnd, &pt2);

    /*
     * Now move the client, keeping documents steady. pBW->left-pt.x
     * and pBW->top-pt.y are the deltas for the documents.
     */

    GetClientRect(m_hWnd, &rc);
    rc.left+=pBW->left;
    rc.right-=pBW->right;
    rc.top+=pBW->top;
    rc.bottom-=pBW->bottom+CYSTATSTRIP; //Remember the status line

    ///Only bother the client if necessary.
    if (!(pt1.x==rc.left && pt1.y==rc.top
        && pt2.x==rc.right && pt2.y==rc.bottom))
        {
        ((LPCPatronClient)m_pCL)->MoveWithoutFamily(&rc
            , pBW->left-pt1.x, pBW->top-pt1.y);
        }

    return NOERROR;
    }
```

Patron's *IOleInPlaceUIWindow::SetBorderSpace* is implemented in much the same way—the Pages window that is affected is moved and resized.

Finally, note that *SetBorderSpace* can be called with NULL to indicate that the object is not interested in allocating any border space whatsoever and that the container can leave its tools showing. However, you should remove any tools that do not apply during an in-place session, such as Edit menu commands.

The Jitters: Keeping the Object Rock Steady

As I explained earlier in this chapter, it's extremely important to the usability of the in-place activation that your container not move the object on the screen when activating it in place. This can be really tricky when you are moving a number of windows around. Let me illustrate a solution to this problem using Patron's *CPatronClient::MoveWithoutFamily*. This function is called when *IOleInPlaceFrame::SetBorderSpace* has been asked to allocate tool space that is different from what our application normally allocates for itself. To it we pass the rectangle that the client window should occupy as well as two deltas, which describe how much the client window is moving. *MoveWithoutFamily* uses these deltas to move each document in the client in such a way that they remain in the same place:

```
void CPatronClient::MoveWithoutFamily(LPRECT prc, int dx, int dy)
    {
    RECT            rc;
    HWND            hWndFrame;
    HWND            hWnd;
    POINT           pt;

    hWndFrame=GetParent(m_hWnd);
    SendMessage(hWndFrame, WM_SETREDRAW, FALSE, 0L);

    ShowWindow(m_hWnd, SW_HIDE);
    SetWindowPos(m_hWnd, NULL, prc->left, prc->top
        , prc->right-prc->left, prc->bottom-prc->top
        , SWP_NOZORDER | SWP_NOACTIVATE);

    //Move all children of the client
    hWnd=GetWindow(m_hWnd, GW_CHILD);

    while (NULL!=hWnd)
        {
        GetWindowRect(hWnd, &rc);
        SETPOINT(pt, rc.left, rc.top);
        ScreenToClient(m_hWnd, &pt);

        if (pt.x!=dx && pt.y!=dy && !IsZoomed(hWnd))
            {
            //Move window in the opposite direction as the client
            SetWindowPos(hWnd, NULL, pt.x-dx, pt.y-dy
                , rc.right-rc.left, rc.bottom-rc.top
                , SWP_NOZORDER | SWP_NOACTIVATE | SWP_NOSIZE);
            }

        hWnd=GetWindow(hWnd, GW_HWNDNEXT);
        }

    SendMessage(hWndFrame, WM_SETREDRAW, TRUE, 0L);
    ShowWindow(m_hWnd, SW_SHOW);

    return;
    }
```

Notice that this code uses WM_SETREDRAW on the frame window in such a way that we only repaint once. Without the redraw trick, you would see some serious jitters: When you move the client window, all the documents within it (under MDI) would move too, and you would then see each window move back to its original position. To force only one repaint, we turn off the redraw flag of the frame, move everything around, and then turn redraw back on and force a repaint by showing the client window after hiding it. This code works well even on iconic MDI windows and their titles as well as with dithered client window backgrounds. Basically, we simply loop through all the child windows of the client, moving them the same distance in the opposite direction as the client moved, thus keeping the absolute screen position the same for each document and thus for each object within the document.

EXPERIENCE: The Jitters and *DeferWindowPos*

I tried a different solution from the one on page 887, using *BeginDeferWindowPos*, *DeferWindowPos*, and *EndDeferWindowPos*. Theoretically, this should move a collection of windows all at the same time, which would be as effective as avoiding the extra repaints. However, these functions turn themselves into NOPs when the windows you build with *DeferWindowPos* are not all siblings. That is, you cannot use *DeferWindowPos* on a parent and any of its children the same time. *EndDeferWindowPos* says it worked (returns TRUE), but nothing actually happens. Because we need to move both client and document windows in Patron, I had to come up with an alternate solution.

EXPERIENCE: The Taming of the *ShowObject*

Be careful with your implementation of *IOleClientSite::ShowObject* in an in-place container. Back in Chapter 9, we implemented this function to scroll an object into view so that it was fully visible. Patron scrolls the object in this function if it's not fully visible and the upper left corner of the object is not in the upper left quadrant of the document window. This can easily ruin all the effort you put into keeping that object steady when activating in place, so if you've seen a call to *IOleInPlaceSite::OnInPlaceActivate*, don't scroll your document if any part of the object is visible. Only if the entire object is out of view should you scroll because in that way the user does need to see the object.

Repaint Optimizations

When people first tried implementing in-place activation in test applications, they found a few cases in which the flicker was horrible. Consider, for example, the case in which the container has an in-place object fully activated—user interface and all—so that the object's shared menu and tools are displayed. Now the end user immediately jumps over and double-clicks on another in-place object. Without any optimizations, the first object's tools would disappear, the container's would reappear, and then the second object would activate causing the container tools to disappear again and the new tools to show up. It would be a nice optimization for the container simply to forget about showing its tools again in the middle, thus reducing the number of repaints. This applies equally well to the shared menu because there's little point in restoring the original menu when we're immediately going to replace it again.

The OLE 2 SDK documented how to write a container to minimize repaints that affect the functions *IOleInPlaceSite::OnUIActivate* and *IOleInPlaceSite::OnUIDeactivate*, as well as suggesting a few frame-level functions to add or remove specific user-interface components. These functions in Patron are *CPatronFrame::ShowUIAndTools* (which can show or hide them) and *CPatronFrame::ReinstateUI* (again, these are Patron functions, not interface functions):

```
void CPatronFrame::ShowUIAndTools(BOOL fShow, BOOL fMenu)
    {
    //This is the only menu case...restore our original menu
    if (fMenu && fShow)
        SetMenu(NULL, NULL, NULL);

    ShowWindow(m_pGB->Window(), fShow ? SW_SHOW : SW_HIDE);

    if (fShow)
        {
        InvalidateRect(m_pGB->Window(), NULL, TRUE);
        UpdateWindow(m_pGB->Window());
        }

    m_fOurToolsShowing=fShow;
    return;
    }

void CPatronFrame::ReinstateUI(void)
    {
    BORDERWIDTHS    bw;

    ShowUIAndTools(TRUE, TRUE);
```

(continued)

```
    SetRect((LPRECT)&bw, 0, m_cyBar, 0, 0,);
    SetBorderSpace(&bw);
    return;
    }
```

The *CPatronFrame* variable *m_fOurToolsShowing* is used to determine how to resize the client window during a frame window WM_SIZE message. It initially starts TRUE and is modified only when *ShowUIAndTools* is asked to show or to hide the tools. If it's FALSE, the frame window must use the values we got in *SetBorderSpace* for resizing the client.

In any case, these functions are then used from *IOleInPlaceSite::OnUIActivate* and *IOleInPaceSite::OnUIDeactivate*:

```
STDMETHODIMP CImpIOleInPlaceSite::OnUIActivate(void)
    {
    m_pTen->m_pPG->m_fAddUI=FALSE;

    //Hide the frame tools, but not all the UI (FALSE, FALSE)
    g_pFR->ShowUIAndTools(FALSE, FALSE);
    return NOERROR;
    }

STDMETHODIMP CImpIOleInPlaceSite::OnUIDeactivate(BOOL fUndoable)
    {
    LPCDocument pDoc;
    MSG         msg;

    //If in shutdown (NULL storage), don't check messages.
    if (NULL==m_pTen->m_pIStorage)
        {
        g_pFR->ReinstateUI();
        return NOERROR;
        }

    pDoc=(LPCDocument)SendMessage(GetParent(m_pTen->m_hWnd)
        , DOCM_PDOCUMENT, 0, 0L);

    //If there's a pending double-click, delay showing our UI
    if (!PeekMessage(&msg, pDoc->Window(), WM_LBUTTONDBLCLK
        , WM_LBUTTONDBLCLK, PM_NOREMOVE | PM_NOYIELD))
        {
        //Turn everything back on.
        g_pFR->ReinstateUI();
        }
    else
        m_pTen->m_pPG->m_fAddUI=TRUE;

    SetFocus(pDoc->Window());
    return NOERROR;
    }
```

First, in *OnUIActivate* we need to remove our frame-level tools, so we can simply call the frame's *ShowUIAndTools* with FALSE parameters, which really only call *ShowWindow(SW_HIDE)* on the frame's toolbar. That sets up everything for later calls to *SetBorderSpace* to deal with the object's tools.

OnUIDeactivate is the interesting case. Here we call the frame's *ReinstateUI* function when we're closing the document and the object along with it (which in Patron is detected by the tenant's *IStorage* being NULL) or when we're deactivating and there is not a double-click message in the application's message queue. In the case of closing, be sure Patron's UI is back in place after closing a document. Checking for a double-click is the optimization we can make when the user has activated another in-place object to cause this deactivation in the first place. At least there is the potential that another in-place object will be activated. If there is a double-click, we don't want to reinstate our own UI until we know that we are not activating another object. This means that we have to set a flag *(CPages::m_fAddUI)* to check later when as process that double-click message. If it's set and we double-clicked outside of another object, only at that time do we show our UI again:

```
//In PAGEMOUS.CPP
BOOL CPage::OnLeftDoubleClick(UINT uKeys, UINT x, UINT y)
    {
    [Other processing]

    //If we've been waiting to add UI, now's the time to do all of it.
    if (m_pPG->m_fAddUI)
        {
        g_pFR->ShowUIAndTools(TRUE, TRUE);
        m_pPG->m_fAddUI=FALSE;
        }

    ...
    }
```

This effectively stops us from showing our user interface again between activation of two objects. Note that although what I've shown here applies to the frame window, it applies equally well to tools in the document window. Patron, however, doesn't address that case because it has no document tools itself.

Testing It All

With all this negotiation and repaint code completed, you can test everything again. By now, you will see an in-place object fully activated in place—user interface and all—as shown earlier in Figure 15-9, on page 857. It's a good idea to test your container with a few different in-place objects, especially those that have different border space requirements than your container so that you can be sure you are keeping the object exactly where it was originally even after you have resized your client-area windows. The more you can reduce any flashing at this point the better.

You'll want to test to be sure that full deactivation of the object happens properly, with all your tools reappearing. Be sure to check that your client area is properly resized in all cases. Try moving a document window (if you are an MDI container) around by dragging on the caption bar. If the mouse is held within the visible client-area window, you've done everything right. If you can move the mouse over any of the object's tools (or your own), your client-area window is too large. If you can't move it to the edge of those tools, the window is too small. Finally, resize the frame window to be sure the client is still resized properly by using the same test. What you will notice after resizing the frame (or the document as well) is that the object's tools are not resized to match. That's one of the little bits of polish we'll add a little later in "Round the Corners: Other Miscellany."

But first, let's handle accelerators.

Provide In-Place Accelerators and Focus

We have already encountered the first instance in which accelerators matter—in *IOleClientSite::GetWindowContext*, where the container should store a handle to its in-place accelerators table in the OLEINPLACEFRAMEINFO structure, along with the number of accelerators in that table and a window handle to which commands from that table are dispatched. These are used from the *OleTranslateAccelerator* function that an EXE server will call in its message loop.

Your first task is to determine which accelerators you want to have active during an in-place session and to create a separate table for them in your resources. Patron, for example, does not use any accelerators for its Edit menu commands (such as Shift+Ins or Ctrl+C for Edit/Copy) during in-place activation. Patron also loads the accelerators into *CPatronFrame::m_hAccelIP* on startup so that they're always available.

The container's responsibility for accelerators does not end there, however, because you cannot tell whether you are working with an in-place object from a DLL or from an EXE, so you have to accommodate both.

If you are working with a DLL object, your container's message loop is the only one around for you and the object together. To accommodate such cases, you must call *IOleInPlaceActiveObject::TranslateAccelerator* in your message loop before translating any accelerators yourself, and if the object translates the accelerator, you should not. Patron's message loop modified for this is *CPatronFrame::MessageLoop*:

```
WPARAM CPatronFrame::MessageLoop(void)
    {
    MSG     msg;

    while (GetMessage(&msg, NULL, 0,0 ))
        {
        HACCEL      hAccel=m_hAccel;

        //Always give the object first crack at translation.
        if (NULL!=m_pIOleIPActiveObject)
            {
            HRESULT     hr;

            hAccel=m_hAccelIP;
            hr=m_pIOleIPActiveObject->TranslateAccelerator(&msg);

            //If the object translated the accelerator, we're done
            if (NOERROR==hr)
                continue;
            }

        if (!m_pCL->TranslateAccelerator(&msg))
            {
            //hAccel is either the normal ones or the in-place ones.
            if (!::TranslateAccelerator(m_hWnd, hAccel, &msg))
                {
                TranslateMessage(&msg);
                DispatchMessage(&msg);
                }
            }
        }

    return msg.wParam;
    }
```

(If you are new to C++, *::TranslateAccelerator* calls the globally named Windows API. I had to do this here because *CPatronFrame* has a *Translate-Accelerator* member function, so just calling *TranslateAccelerator* by itself without the :: prefix would call our member function, which is not what we want. Don't feel bad about not knowing this—I had to ask others how to do this when writing this code.)

If *IOleInPlaceActiveObject::TranslateAccelerator* does not process the keystroke, we can resume our message loop as usual. Note that this function is set up in such a way that when we're not servicing an in-place object, we use our normal accelerators, but when we have an *IOleInPlaceActiveObject* pointer, which is the in-place session flag for Patron's frame, we use the in-place accelerators.

This message-loop modification is only applicable for DLL objects. What if the object is running from an EXE? In that case the server's message loop is also running and will call *OleTranslateAccelerator* after the server finds the accelerator uninteresting to itself. *OleTranslateAccelerator* looks for a match between the keystroke and your accelerator table, and if one is found, it will call *IOleInPlaceFrame::TranslateAccelerator*, passing the message itself as well as the already-translated command ID. You can either call the Windows *TranslateAccelerator* again (which would be redundant), or you can simply process the ID as you would any other WM_COMMAND message. Patron does the latter:

```
STDMETHODIMP CPatronFrame::TranslateAccelerator(LPMSG pMSG, WORD wID)
    {
    SCODE       sc;

    if ((IDM_PAGENEWPAGE <= wID && IDM_PAGELASTPAGE >= wID)
        || IDM_OPENOBJECT == wID || IDM_ENTERCONTEXTHELP == wID
        || IDM_ESCAPECONTEXTHELP == wID)
        {
        //wID properly expands to 32-bits
        OnCommand(m_hWnd, (WPARAM)wID, 0L);
        sc=S_OK;
        }
#ifdef MDI
    else if (TranslateMDISysAccel(m_pCL->Window(), pMSG))
        sc=S_OK;
#endif
    else
        sc=S_FALSE;

    return ResultFromScode(sc);
    }
```

EXPERIENCE: *TranslateAccelerator* Weirdness

OK, here's one I didn't figure out. I originally tried calling *::TranslateAccelerator* from within *CPatronFrame::TranslateAccelerator*, but for some reason, the WM_COMMAND message was sent to the server and not to Patron. I tried some variations on the parameters to the function, but no dice. So I punted and went with looking at the *wID* parameter directly because OLE had already translated the accelerator for me.

The *OnCommand* function is another member of *CPatronFrame*. Note that Patron also takes this opportunity to process MDI accelerators for itself because it gets no other chance. If you have an MDI container, you will want to do the same.

Before you can give all this a test, there is one more consideration that makes accelerators work properly. Whenever there's an in-place UI active object in your container, you must ensure that it has the focus, much as a control would. That ensures that keystrokes that aren't otherwise translated as accelerators end up in the object's window procedure and not your container's.

The object itself will take the focus when first activated, but there's always the chance that while it is still active, the end user will switch away from your application and back again, which will generate a WM_SETFOCUS message to your frame. In processing this message, you want to call *SetFocus* to the window associated with the *IOleInPlaceActiveObject* interface you have:

```
case WM_SETFOCUS:
    if (NULL!=m_pIOleIPActiveObject)
        {
        HWND    hWndObj;

        m_pIOleIPActiveObject->GetWindow(&hWndObj);
        SetFocus(hWndObj);
        }

    break;
```

NOTE: Avoid the temptation to pass the ill-named *hWndObj* parameter from *IOleInPlaceFrame::SetMenu* to *SetFocus* because this might be the frame window handle of the server. If that is the case, your container would never get the focus at all. If you tried to reactivate your container's frame window, you would see it briefly flash active but then become inactive again when you did this *SetFocus* call. To bypass any problems, always use the window handle from *IOleInPlaceActiveObject::GetWindow*.

Testing accelerators should not be too difficult: Activate an object and start pounding keys. Try those that the object displays in its menus as well as your own. It is also an interesting test to have a conflicting accelerator to see who wins: It should always be the object.

Round the Corners: Other Miscellany

There are still a few places to make modifications to your container so that everything works properly. This section discusses those that are required and those that are optional (marked in the following steps).

- (Required) Call *IOleInPlaceActiveObject::OnFrameWindowActivate* and *OnDocWindowActivate* when your frame and document windows receive WM_ACTIVATEAPP and WM_MDIACTIVATE messages, respectively. Switching document windows might also mean restoring your container's normal UI.
- (Required) Call *IOleInPlaceActiveObject::ResizeBorder* when either your frame or document window is resized so that the object can adjust its tools.
- (Required) *Call IOleObject::SetObjectRects* whenever you scroll the document or otherwise change the position and clipping rectangles of the object relative to the document window (the object's parent). Also implement *IOleInPlaceSite::OnPosRectChange* and *IOleInPlaceSite::Scroll.*
- (Required) Implement minimal Context-Sensitive Help support in case the server supports it, even if you don't.
- (Required) Provide minimal Undo support by calling *IOleObject::DoVerb(OLEIVERB_DISCARDUNDOSTATE)* when making a change after deactivation and by implementing *IOleInPlaceSite::DeactivateAndUndo.*
- (Optional) If you have an Undo command, call *IOleInPlaceObject::ReactivateAndUndo* if the command is given immediately after deactivation. Also implement *IOleInPlaceSite::DiscardUndoState.*
- (Optional) Provide a Ctrl+Enter accelerator to generate a call to *IOleObject::DoVerb(OLEIVERB_OPEN).*
- (Optional) If you have a status line, implement *IOleInPlaceFrame::SetStatusText.*
- (Optional) If you have modeless pop-up windows that are normally shown as part of your user interface, show or hide these when your *IOleInPlaceFrame::EnableModeless* function is called. You might also tell an object to do the same by calling *IOleInPlaceActiveObject::EnableModeless.*
- (Optional) Provide support for inside-out objects.

The following sections briefly discuss each of these.

Call *IOleInPlaceActiveObject::On[Frame ¦ Document]WindowActivate*

For the frame window, process the WM_ACTIVATEAPP message and call *OnFrameWindowActivate* if you have an *IOleInPlaceActiveObject* pointer (and therefore are servicing an in-place session):

```
//Frame window procedure
case WM_ACTIVATEAPP:
    if (NULL!=m_pIOleIPActiveObject)
        {
        m_pIOleIPActiveObject->OnFrameWindowActivate
            ((BOOL)wParam);
        }

    break;
```

The case of a document is a little more complex, especially for an MDI container because the user might be switching between one document that has an active object and another without, so you have to allow for user interface changes. First, process the WM_MDIACTIVATE message in the document as follows:

```
//Document window procedure
case WM_MDIACTIVATE:
    if (NULL!=m_pIOleIPActiveObject)
        {
        //The LOWORD on wParam makes us Win32 compatible here.
        m_pIOleIPActiveObject->OnDocWindowActivate((BOOL)LOWORD(wParam));
        }
    else
        {
        //Restore frame-level UI if we're becoming active.
        if ((BOOL)wParam)
            g_pFR->ReinstateUI();
        }

    break;
```

If there's an in-place active object in the document, you must call *OnDocWindowActivate* regardless of whether your application is becoming active or inactive, where the parameter to the function is a flag indicating which state your application is currently in. If your application becomes active, the object will reinstate its in-place interface, mixed menus and toolbars included. If your application is becoming inactive, the object will remove its user interface and will tell your application to reinstate its own by calling *IOleInPlaceHSite::OnUIDeactivate.*

If the document is becoming active but has no active in-place object in it, then you should restore your container's normal user interface. So when you switch from a document doing in-place to a document that's not, the first document, in becoming inactive, tells the object to remove its UI and the second document, in becoming active, installs the container's UI. When you switch back to the in-place document the object tells you to remove your UI by calling *IOleInPlaceSite::OnUIActivate* before installing its own.

Call *IOleInPlaceActiveObject::ResizeBorder*

When you added support for tool space negotiation earlier in this chapter, I suggested that you resize the frame or document window when an in-place object has its own tools displayed. If you did, you found that those tools did not resize with the window. Obviously. No one told the object that the frame or document window size changed. That means the container must call *IOleInPlaceActiveObject::ResizeBorder* to let the object know. The first parameter to this function is a pointer to a RECT with the new client area of the window. The second parameter is a pointer to the relevant *IOleInPlaceUIWindow* for either the frame or the document (remember that *IOleInPlaceFrame* is an *IOleInPlaceUIWindow*) so that the object's *ResizeBorder* implementation can immediately use that interface to negotiate new tools space as necessary. The second parameter to *ResizeBorder* is a BOOL indicating whether we're calling the function for the frame or document window.

So when processing WM_SIZE in both frame and document, make the *ResizeBorder* call with the proper parameters:

```
//Frame window procedure
case WM_SIZE:
    [Other processing]

    if (NULL!=m_pIOleIPActiveObject)
        {
        RECT        rc;

        GetClientRect(m_hWnd, &rc);
        m_pIOleIPActiveObject->ResizeBorder(&rc
            , (LPOLEINPLACEUIWINDOW)this, TRUE);
        }

    break;

//Document window procedure
case WM_SIZE:
    [Other processing]

    if (NULL!=m_pIOleIPActiveObject)
        {
        RECT        rc

        GetClientRect(m_hWnd, &rc);
        m_pIOleIPActiveObject->ResizeBorder(&rc, m_pIOleIPUIWindow
            , FALSE);
        }

    break;
```

WARNING

Be very careful with the last parameter (*fFrame*) to *ResizeBorder*. When I first wrote this code, my document passed a TRUE and all sorts of wild things started happening as the object was resizing its frame tools to the dimensions of the document window. It was a hard bug to find, so give your implementation a little extra care.

Call *IOleInPlaceObject::SetObjectRects* and Flush Out *IOleInPlaceSite*

Remember back when we implemented *IOleInPlaceSite::GetWindowContext*? Some of the elements we returned to the object were a position rectangle and a clipping rectangle that specified the initial location of the object in our document window. Well, that is great for initial setup, but if you scroll your document or otherwise change the position of the object window relative to the document window, you have to call *IOleInPlaceObject::SetObjectRects* with the new rectangles. Let's be sure we understand each other here: Scrolling a document window changes the position of the contents of that window relative to the document window itself. Because *ScrollWindow* (which we typically use for scrolling) also changes the position of child windows in the document, you are changing the position of the object in relation to the document. Therefore, you call *SetObjectRects*. Whenever Patron finds that it did any scrolling in the document, it calls *CPage::ScrolledWindow*, which calls each tenant's *UpdateInPlaceObjectRects* to generate the *SetObjectRects* call, taking scrolling into account:

```
void CTenant::UpdateInPlaceObjectRects(void)
    {
    RECTL       rcl;
    RECT        rc;
    RECT        rcClip;

    if (NULL!=m_pIOleIPObject)
        {
        RectGet(&rcl, TRUE);
        RECTFROMRECTL(rc, rcl);

        //Account for scrolling
        OffsetRect(&rc, -(int)m_pPG->m_xPos, -(int)m_pPG->m_yPos);
```

(continued)

```
        //We don't clip special anywhere in our window.
        SetRect(&rcClip, 0, 0, 32767, 32767);

        m_pIOleIPObject->SetObjectRects(&rc, &rcClip);
        }

    return;
    }
```

Note that by calling *CTenant::UpdateInPlaceObjectRects* for all tenants, we satisfy one of the inside-out requirments we'll see later. If you don't support inside-out objects, you only need to call this for the object in-place active object. You need to call it for all active inside-out objects, however, because they all need to reposition their windows.

I mentioned before as well that the end user might cause the document to scroll either by manipulating the document directly or by doing something in the object that would cause the object to call *IOleInPlaceSite::Scroll,* so you will want to implement that function as well:

```
STDMETHODIMP CImpIOleInPlaceSite::Scroll(SIZE sz)
    {
    int         x, y;

    x=m_pTen->m_pPG->m_xPos+sz.cx;
    y=m_pTen->m_pPG->m_yPos+sz.cy;

    SendScrollPosition(m_pTen->m_hWnd, WM_HSCROLL, x);
    SendScrollPosition(m_pTen->m_hWnd, WM_VSCROLL, y);
    return NOERROR;
    }
```

In Patron, the *SendScrollPosition* macros here cause the document to scroll, which generates the call to *SetObjectRects* as appropriate.

There is also the case in which the object doesn't want the document to scroll but wants more space for itself—that is, it wants to display itself in a rectangle larger than the container site. In such situations, the object will call *IOleInPlaceSite::OnPosRectChange* in which we have to again call *SetObjectRects*:

```
STDMETHODIMP CImpIOleInPlaceSite::OnPosRectChange(LPCRECT prcPos)
    {
    LPRECT  rcClip;

    SetRect(&rcClip, 0, 0, 32767, 32767);
    m_pIOleIPObject->SetObjectRects(prcPos, &rcClip);
    return NOERROR;
    }
```

The *prcPos* parameter to this function specifies how large the object would like to be. You can either grant the object this position (or an adjustment) by calling *SetObjectRects* with that rectangle, as Patron does, or you can ignore it altogether and call *SetObjectRects* with your site rectangle as the position. As the container, your application has the power and can restrict the size of the object as you see fit. *OnPosRectChange* is how a courteous object double-checks with you before it changes its window position.

Implement Minimal Context-Sensitive Help Support

The OLE 2 Design Specification states that all applications capable of in-place activation must provide some basic support for context-sensitive help even if they don't implement the feature in any other way. This means a container needs to add accelerators for Shift+F1 (enter mode) and ESC (exit mode) and process them as follows, where *fEnterMode* is TRUE on Shift+F1 and FALSE on ESC:

1. Call your own *IOleInPlaceFrame::ContextSensitiveHelp(fEnterMode)*.
2. If your application is an SDI application, have the frame implementation call *IOleInPlaceActiveObject::ContextSensitiveHelp(fEnterMode)*.
3. If your application is an MDI application, have the frame implementation call *IOleInPlaceUIWindow::ContextSensitiveHelp(fEnterMode)* for each document.
4. For MDI documents, have their *IOleInPlaceUIWindow* implementations call *IOleInPlaceActiveObject::ContextSensitiveHelp(fEnterMode)*.

I added the function *CPatronClient::CallContextHelpOnDocuments* for the purpose of step 3. The interface member implementations are trivial and are not shown here.

If the object detects the Shift+F1 or ESC, it will call your *IOleInPlaceSite::ContextSensitiveHelp*, which should be implemented as follows:

1. If your application is an SDI application, call your document window's *IOleInPlaceUIWindow::ContextSensitiveHelp(fEnterMode)*.
2. If your application is an MDI application, call the frame's *ContextSensitiveHelp(fEnterMode)*, which will propagate the mode to all the documents.

If your application is both a container and a server, there's the possibility that it contains an in-place active object inside its own object that is in-place active in another container. That means that whenever it is notified of a change in the context-sensitive help mode, it must notify the object it contains (if your application was notified through its *IOleInPlaceActiveObject* interface) or the container it is in (if your application was notified through its *IOleInPlaceSite* interface). Basically, this means propagating the call up or down because your application is in the middle of other objects and containers, which are expecting your application to behave as if its other half did not exist. The details of this are beyond the scope of this book, but some can be found in the *OLE 2 Programmer's Reference* and the OLE 2 Design Specification.

Provide Minimal Undo Support

Even if the container does not have an Undo command (as is the case with Patron), it still has two small responsibilities in that regard. First, implement *IOleInPlaceSite::DeactivateAndUndo* by calling *IOleInPlaceObject::InPlaceDeactivate*:

```
STDMETHODIMP CImpIOleInPlaceSite::DeactivateAndUndo(void)
    {
    m_pTen->m_pIOleIPObject->InPlaceDeactivate();
    return NOERROR;
    }
```

Second, whenever the object is deactivated, call *IOleObject::DoVerb* with OLEIVERB_DISCARDUNDOSTATE. Why do we do this? Read on. It's important if you have an Undo command of your own, or if you are just exceptionally curious.

Support Your Own Undo Command

If you have an Undo command, you will generally save some Undo information when you activate an object in place. If the first thing that happens in the in-place object is its own Undo command, it will call your *IOleInPlaceSite::DeactivateAndUndo*, at which time you deactivate the object as described in the last section and use whatever Undo information you saved to go back to whatever state is applicable. You don't want to hold onto that Undo state forever, so if the object does anything else after activation besides Undo, it will call *IOleInPlaceSite::DiscardUndoState*, which means you can free that information.

Now let's go the other direction. Let's say you just deactivated an object; and then the end user selects your Undo command. That should mean "undo the deactivation," in which case you call *IOleInPlaceObject::ReactivateAndUndo*. Note here that the object is still running and might have an Undo state saved. In that case, you want to call *IOleObject::DoVerb(OLEIVERB_DISCARDUNDOSTATE)* if you do anything else besides Undo after a deactivation to let the object know that it can let go of that saved state.

Provide an Open Accelerator

If you want to, you can add a Ctrl+Enter accelerator for in-place activation, which would generate a call to *IOleObject::DoVerb(OLEIVERB_OPEN)* to take an object from the in-place active state to the open state like a non-in-place embedded object. The object will generally also provide a way to do this on its own menus, so don't add a menu item, simply add the accelerator. Of course, you can use this accelerator all the time if you want, even outside of in place, but then you might be using it for other purposes, which is why it's not specified as a standard for opening objects in any other scenario.

Implement *IOleInPlaceFrame::SetStatusText*

If your application has a status line, you will want to implement this function to take whatever text is sent to it and display it in your application status line. OLE 2 SDK guidelines suggest that all in-place objects process their WM-_MENUSELECT messages themselves to call your *SetStatusText* function even if they don't normally have a status line in their server window. This ensures that there's always something to display in the container's status line. Patron implements this by passing the string to its *StatStrip* control:

```
STDMETHODIMP CPatronFrame::SetStatusText(LPCSTR pszText)
    {
    m_pSS->MessageSet((LPSTR)pszText);
    return NOERROR;
    }
```

If this function is called with NULL, the object is testing whether your application has a status line. If this happens in Patron, the *StatStrip* (the m_pSS variable) ignores the *MessageSet* call and the function returns NOERROR to say "Yes, we have a status line, and it works." If your application doesn't have a status line, return E_FAIL.

If your application is passed a string that is too long for its status line, your application should return S_TRUNCATED to let the object know. I'm not really sure what an object would do with this information, but it's in the OLE 2 Design Specification.

Show or Hide Modeless Pop-up Windows

Last, but not least, is the function *IOleInPlaceFrame::EnableModeless* and *IOleInPlaceActiveObject::EnableModeless.* The container and object use the other's *EnableModeless* call to show or hide floating pop-up windows at various points in the in-place session. Let's say, for example, that the object has created a floating tool palette instead of a toolbar. When the container displays a modal dialog box, it might want to keep visual distraction to a minimum by asking the object to hide those pop-up windows. In that case, it calls the active object's *EnableModeless(FALSE)* when the modal dialog box appears and *EnableModeless(TRUE)* when the dialog box disappears. In the same manner an object might ask the container to show or hide its popups when the object invokes a modal dialog box.

It is not necessary to implement or call either function—that is, you will not be impairing any functionality. It's merely a way for you to control the user interface that the end user attributes to your application.

Support Inside-Out Objects

A container's basic support for inside-out objects takes five steps:

1. When creating or loading an object, the container calls *IOleObject::GetMiscStatus* and saves the return value. The two relevant flags here are OLEMISC_INSIDEOUT and OLEMISC_ACTIVATEWHENVISIBLE. Patron performs this step and step 2 at the end of *CTenant::FObjectInitialize.*

2. If an object is OLEMISC_ACTIVATEWHENVISIBLE, the container immediately calls *IOleObject::DoVerb(OLEIVERB_INPLACEACTIVATE)* to get the object active, but not UI active.

3. When the selected object changes, the container calls *IOleInPlaceObject::UIDeactivate* if the previous selection was inside out and calls *IOleObject::DoVerb(OLEIVERB_UIACTIVATE)* on the newly selected object if that one is inside out as well. Remember that this is selection, not activation. Check Patron's *CTenant::FSelect* function.

4. When scrolling the document, call *IOleInPlaceObject::SetObjectRects* for all active inside-out objects because they all need to update their window positions accordingly. Patron does this by calling *CTenant::UpdateInPlaceObjectRects* in every tenant, letting that tenant call *SetObjectRects* if it's inside out.

5. When taking the object back to the passive state, call *IOleInPlaceObject::InPlaceDeactivate.* You will probably already be doing this with normal in-place support.

The bottom line here is that for an inside-out object, there is little distinction between loaded and active. It's only a distinction between active and UI active. If you need an inside-out object to test, use POLYLINE.DLL implemented in Chapter 16.

Summary

In-place activation, also called Visual Editing for marketing reasons, is a feature in OLE 2 that allows a container application to activate an embedded object directly inside the container's document window, without showing a separate server window. The entire process of activation is somewhat involved, depending on the level of integration the container wants to support, which includes sharing the menu bar with the object and allowing the object to create toolbars and other adornments in the container's frame or document windows. The processes by which menus and tools are integrated are controlled by specific rules that both container and server follow in implementing their in-place interfaces.

This chapter begins by describing how an entire in-place session works from a programmatic perspective (that is, what functions are called by both container and object). This provides a clear understanding of what is going on, which guides our step-by-step implementation guide for adding complete in-place support to a container application.

Most of the work happens when the object tries to go from its loaded state into the fully in-place active state, complete with a shared menu and its own tools displayed in the container window. But implementing this does not have to happen all at once, so in developing an in-place container, you can stop at many points along the activation path to compile and test small portions of the overall code. After you have enough code to activate the object, you need to provide a way to deactivate the object back to the loaded state. In addition, many events will occur during an in-place session, many of which require small bits of code in the right place in the container. Such events are scrolling or resizing a document window, detecting an accelerator key, or invoking an Undo command.

For the most part, the container is a passive agent during an in-place session; most of the code you need for in-place support goes into the three necessary interfaces, *IOleInPlaceSite*, *IOleInPlaceUIWindow*, and *IOleInPlaceFrame*. Most of what you do as well is related to user interface because in-place activation is a very user-interface-intensive feature. But it works, and Microsoft did a lot of successful usability tests on the model. I think you'll be happy with the results after you do all the work to get there. Certainly your customers will.

CHAPTER SIXTEEN

IN-PLACE ACTIVATION FOR COMPOUND DOCUMENT OBJECTS

ACTIVE INGREDIENT: Tetrahydrozoline Hydrochloride, 0.05%

Many medicines contain only a tiny amount of the key ingredient that makes you better. For example, I have on my desk this small bottle of eye drops that I grabbed out of the medicine cabinet. Of the 14.7 ml of liquid in this bottle, only a minuscule 0.00735 ml is the active ingredient. The rest is inert water that no one would pay any attention to. The water by itself does nothing. But the addition of a small amount of an active ingredient turns the liquid in the bottle into something of real value.

Computer applications are often the same way—the presence of a little feature can distinguish your application from the rest of the crowd. If your application is merely a small bottle of water, what will set it apart from the ocean of applications? A little bit of an active ingredient. Adding in-place activation capabilities to your compound document objects is just the ingredient you need. Compared to the rest of your application, a small percentage of extra code that is necessary to implement in-place support (primarily two more interfaces and some small modifications to other parts of your application) is a small price to pay. Overall, it's nothing like what we had to do to create a container application in Chapter 15. Most of the work in creating an object, as you might imagine, is in building up and tearing down the in-place user interface, such as the shared menu and the in-place tools that we discussed in the first half of the last chapter.

The primary sample for this chapter is Cosmo, modified to service in-place objects. Although Cosmo is an EXE server, nearly the same steps can be applied to a DLL server. The only exception is how you treat accelerators. To that end I've updated Polyline in this chapter to activate in place, but I've left out any menu items or tools to keep the implementation as simple as possible. Polyline is also marked (in CHAP16.REG) as an inside-out object. (This doesn't affect any of the implementation, however.) You can also make a version of CoCosmo that uses this new POLYLINE.DLL to prove that all the in-place code does not interfere with the operation of Polyline as a normal component object.

At the end of this chapter, after following a step-by-step implementation of in-place objects, we'll look at where in-place objects can go and what the implications of OLE2 might be. Basically, this is my chance to do some wild dreaming. But maybe it will also give you some idea of what you might do with this great technology in your own products so that you can be in the lead of the next generation of Windows software.

All with just a few drops of the programming equivalent of Tetrahydrozoline HCl.

In-Place Objects Step by Step

First, you need an embedded object. Got one? Great, let's make it in-place capable. As we saw in Chapter 15, an in-place object adds two interfaces—*IOleInPlaceObject* and *IOleInPlaceActiveObject*—to those that it already has—*IOleObject*, *IDataObject*, and *IPersistStorage*. In-place activation starts inside *IOleObject::DoVerb*, where your object makes a conscious decision to attempt to activate in place, so it starts bugging the container for some assistance.

Well, let's not jump in so fast. There are crocodiles in the lake. In-place activation carries some heavy implications for your object and server. So the first step in implementing in-place activation is to address these implications before adding anything related to in-place interfaces. Most of these implications have to do with the fact that you are going to be placing windows and menu items into a container application, so you have to remove all dependencies on them that exist in your server windows exclusively. This may or may not be a major issue for you, but I hope to have you thinking about it before you get in too deep.

Given that deflating remark, here's how we'll progress through this chapter:

1. Prepare your object for the implications of in-place activation.
2. Implement skeletal *IOleInPlaceObject* and *IOleInPlaceActiveObject* interfaces, and create some stubs for a few useful internal functions in your object.

3. Modify *DoVerb* to begin activation for the appropriate verbs and to provide for simple deactivation. This excludes most of the user interface.
4. Create, manage, and disassemble the shared menu.
5. Negotiate and create your in-place tools.
6. Modify your accelerators and your message loop to share the keyboard with the container.
7. Complete your implementation of the two in-place interfaces and add small fragments of code to round out your in-place object. This section, like the one we had in Chapter 15, is the catch-all for the little fish that tend to slip through big nets. Here we'll also look briefly at inside-out objects, which really aren't any different from the rest but which are fun to think about anyway.

And, as usual, each section comes with comments on what you can expect to have working after each step, so that you can stop, compile, and test.

Drivers, Prepare Your Objects

All this merging of user interface from two different applications that don't necessarily know anything at all about one another is scary. However, little of it is scary when you understand what is going on and you have prepared yourself for it. For in-place objects, you need to think about two major aspects:

1. Your menu items will be displayed in a shared menu in another application.
2. Your windows will have parents that you do not know and do not control.

Many of the issues I raise here are similar to concerns for containers that we looked at in Chapter 15, and you might find it beneficial to read the "Prepare the Container" section under "In-Place Containers Step-By-Step" in that chapter.

Implications of Mixed Menus

Number one on the list of implications is that when you activate in place, you need to share the menu with the container. That means all your application's usual menus will not be available. You are limited to menus that fall into the Edit, Object, and Help groups in the shared menu, so whatever commands you want need to be on those menus. A typical problem is how to deal with

File/Import, which is nice to have when doing editing. Consider how this might be moved to your Edit menu as an item such as Import From File.[1] Basically, you have to see whether your application needs any items on document-management menus such as File and Window in your server while activated in place. If so, now is a great time to move them.

Because some of your menu items will not be available during in-place activation, be sure that you can disable whatever accelerators apply to those items. This generally means managing a separate accelerator table in your resources that you will load when they become necessary. If you do not do this, the end user might press an accelerator key combination to try to invoke a command that does not apply to the in-place version. For example, if you invoked your File Open command while in place, the user would see it as the container's dialog box, not as the server's, and would wonder why nothing happened when he or she chose OK. Not a good idea.

When you place items on the shared menu, you still get all the appropriate messages for those items, including WM_INITMENUPOP. Typically, you will still use this message to enable or disable certain items, such as Edit/-Paste, a menu command that your object will control. But because the absolute position of each popup you might process will most likely change in the shared menu, you can no longer compare the index of the pop-up menu in this message with a constant. For example, the Edit menu is usually at index 1, so many applications have code that says "If the popped-up menu is in position 1, enable or disable the Paste command." As I mentioned in the discussion of containers, you have two ways of dealing with this. One way is to keep an array of integers that hold the current position for each menu you have showing. You then compare the index passed in the message to those in this array to find which menu you are dealing with. This is an ideal technique to use when you are going to place new pop-up menus on the shared menu that are not already present on your normal container's menu.

The other technique depends solely on the menu handles, which are passed with these messages. This technique works best when you are going to use the same pop-up menus on the shared menu as those in your normal menu. I will demonstrate this approach in this chapter. So create an array of HMENU messages on startup and always compare the hMenu passed in the message to those in this array. If you use the same menu handles in the shared menu, your WM_INITMENUPOPUP code doesn't need modification for the in-place scenario.

1. Cosmo has a File/Import command, but I didn't bother moving it for this chapter. It will simply be unavailable while the object is activated in place.

Your Parents Are Strangers

As an in-place object, your application is going to place a number of its windows in the container by using functions such as *SetParent.* The biggest issue here is that your application has no control over the parent window, so you should ask yourself a few questions. Do the windows you intend to place in the container send any messages to the parent window? Controls are excellent examples of this, and many applications' editing windows, which will ultimately end up in the container, are structured like controls that send WM_COMMAND messages to the parent. Because the container will not be expecting such commands, the results are highly unpredictable. Do your windows make assumptions about what other windows are around? Do your windows use WS_CLIPSIBLINGS? They should, because you are going to share space with unknown sibling windows and you do not want to overlap them visually. Can your windows be independently resized outside of a WM_SIZE message in another window? At some point, the container application might ask your application to take just such an action in your *IOleInPlaceActiveObject* implementation, so be prepared. How will your editing window react if it cannot be shown completely? Can it handle the clipping rectangle that the container will specify?

The biggest problem I've seen with all of this occurs when I try to put some sort of window in the container that always sends messages to the parent window. This is specifically why the *GizmoBar* and *StatStrip* tools included with this book use an "associate" window. The controls always send notification messages to the associate, not to the parent, so that the two windows can be different. You might find yourself in the situation where you are using a control that you cannot modify to work with such an associate window. In that case, you'll need to create a wrapper window that can perform the redirection. One way or another, you prevent those messages from floating freely up to the container.

You might want to see how your tools might work on the side or bottom of a window instead of always being stuck at the top, or in a floating pop-up window, although this is not as important as other considerations. When your application negotiates tool space, the container might not give it space in the most traditional places for tools, and the more flexible it is, the better chance it has of working well with an arbitrary container. If the container doesn't give your application space at the top, try the side, try the bottom, and if all that fails, float the tools in a pop-up window. The more options you give your application, the better your object will look.

Implement Skeletal In-Place Object Interfaces and Object Helper Functions

Most of the modifications you make to support in-place activation will be made directly on your object. In Cosmo's case, the object is *CFigure.* There are two primary sets of functions to add at this point: the in-place interfaces and a group of helper functions structured so that they are immediately useful to your interface implementations. You don't have to implement all of the functions yet, but at least make stubs that you can gradually fill with code as you move through your implementation.

Interfaces

The two interfaces we have to implement on the in-place object are *IOleInPlaceObject* and *IOleInPlaceActiveObject,* many of whose member functions we have seen in use in Chapter 15. Both of these interfaces inherit from *IOleWindow*:

```
DECLARE_INTERFACE_(IOleWindow, IUnknown)
    {
    [IUnknown members]

    STDMETHOD(GetWindow) (THIS_ HWND FAR* lphwnd) PURE;
    STDMETHOD(ContextSensitiveHelp) (THIS_ BOOL fEnterMode) PURE;
    };

DECLARE_INTERFACE_(IOleInPlaceObject, IOleWindow)
    {
    [IUnknown members]
    [IOleWindow members]

    STDMETHOD(InPlaceDeactivate) (THIS) PURE;
    STDMETHOD(UIDeactivate) (THIS) PURE;
    STDMETHOD(SetObjectRects) (THIS_ LPCRECT lprcPosRect
        , LPCRECT lprcClipRect) PURE;
    STDMETHOD(ReactivateAndUndo) (THIS) PURE;
    };

DECLARE_INTERFACE_(IOleInPlaceActiveObject, IOleWindow)
    {
    [IUnknown members]
    [IOleWindow members]

    STDMETHOD(TranslateAccelerator) (THIS_ LPMSG lpmsg) PURE;
    STDMETHOD(OnFrameWindowActivate) (THIS_ BOOL fActivate) PURE;
```

```
    STDMETHOD(OnDocWindowActivate) (THIS_ BOOL fActivate) PURE;
    STDMETHOD(ResizeBorder) (THIS_ LPCRECT lprectBorder
        , LPOLEINPLACEUIWINDOW lpUIWindow, BOOL fFrameWindow) PURE;
    STDMETHOD(EnableModeless) (THIS_ BOOL fEnable) PURE;
    };
```

Cosmo implements these in the files IIPOBJ.CPP and IIPAOBJ.CPP. (*IOleWindow* is not implemented by itself.) The INTERFAC directory also has templates for these interfaces.

Both *IOleInPlaceObject* and *IOleInPlaceActiveObject* are part of your object, so they should have access to all your object's variables. Note that *IOleInPlaceActiveObject* should *not*—repeat *not*—be available through *QueryInterface* on any other interface pointer. This means that the object's *QueryInterface* will know *IOleObject* but not *IOleInPlaceActiveObject*, which has its own *QueryInterface* implementation:

```
//The object's QueryInterface
STDMETHODIMP CFigure::QueryInterface(REFIID riid, LPLPVOID ppv)
    {
    ...

    //IOleWindow will be the in-place object
    if (IsEqualIID(riid, IID_IOleWindow)
        || IsEqualIID(riid, IID_IOleInPlaceObject))
        *ppv=(LPVOID)m_pIOleIPObject;


    ...
    }

//A stand-alone QueryInterface for IOleInPlaceActiveObject
STDMETHODIMP CImpIOleInPlaceActiveObject::QueryInterface(REFIID riid
    , LPLPVOID ppv)
    {
    *ppv=NULL;

    if (IsEqualIID(riid, IID_IUnknown)
        || IsEqualIID(riid, IID_IOleWindow)
        || IsEqualIID(riid, IID_IOleInPlaceActiveObject))
        *ppv=(LPVOID)this;

    if (NULL!=*ppv)
        {
        ((LPUNKNOWN)*ppv)->AddRef();
        return NOERROR;
        }

    return ResultFromScode(E_NOINTERFACE);
    }
```

OK, why are we doing this? We make this separation because we want to enforce the idea that the container should *always* obtain our application's *IOleInPlaceActiveObject* interface by our application calling its *SetActiveObject* functions. This keeps the container's copy of the pointer always current with the active in-place object. The container should never ask for the interface. This extra measure of a separate *QueryInterface* protects us from containers that might decide to query for *IOleInPlaceActiveObject.*

Note, however, that *IOleInPlaceActiveObject,* because it is being used on the same overall object, can still use the object's *AddRef* and *Release* as any other interface can. It's only the *QueryInterface* function we want to protect.

Here at the start, you don't need to implement *any* of the *IOleInPlace-ActiveObject* functions, not even *GetWindow.* Even *IOleInPlaceObject* doesn't need much implementation—I'll really only call helper functions for it that I've added to the object itself.

Helper Functions

By adding a number of helper functions to your object, you can simplify the structure of your code and keep a lot of the mess out of the interface implementations. My primary reason for doing this is that Cosmo's object, *CFigure,* has all the useful variables, and permission to poke around in other Cosmo structures. For example, we need access to the frame window's menu when creating the in-place shared menu, and I already have *CFigure* as a friend of *CCosmoFrame.* An interface implementation such as Cosmo's *CImplIOleInPlace-Object* doesn't have those same permissions. Obviously, if you are using multiple inheritance for your object, some of these extra functions will be duplicates of those in *IOleInPlaceObject.* Some of the functions are, however, useful to other code changes we'll need, so I highly recommend creating functions like those I've added to *CFigure*:

```
class CFigure : public IUnknown
    {
    ...

    public:
        ...

        HRESULT  InPlaceActivate(LPOLECLIENTSITE, BOOL);
        void     InPlaceDeactivate(void);
        HRESULT  UIActivate(void);
        void     UIDeactivate(void);
        BOOL     FInPlaceMenuCreate(void);
        BOOL     FInPlaceMenuDestroy(void);
        BOOL     FInPlaceToolsCreate(void);
```

```
        BOOL      FInPlaceToolsDestroy(void);
        BOOL      FInPlaceToolsRenegotiate(void);

        void      OpenIntoWindow(void);
        BOOL      FUndo(void);
    }
```

InPlaceDeactivate and *UIDeactivate* contain the same code you need in the *IOleInPlaceObject* functions of the same name, so the interface simply calls the same function in *CFigure*:

```
STDMETHODIMP CImpIOleInPlaceObject::InPlaceDeactivate(void)
    {
    m_pObj->InPlaceDeactivate();
    return NOERROR;
    }

STDMETHODIMP CImpIOleInPlaceObject::UIDeactivate(void)
    {
    m_pObj->UIDeactivate();
    return NOERROR;
    }
```

You can do the same in your interface now, so that we can build the code into the object's functions and basically forget about the interface.

Having an *InPlaceActivate* function is very handy because we'll need to call it from *IOleObject::DoVerb* as well as from *IOleInPlaceObject::ReactivateAndUndo*. All the functions dealing with UI, menus, and tools are split off to create strongly isolated functions for dealing with those specific features. *OpenIntoWindow* and *FUndo* are two functions that we'll use when implementing some of the small features later on.

InPlaceActivate is the only function that takes any parameters—an *IOleClientSite* pointer (generally the one passed to *IOleObject::DoVerb*) and a BOOL flag indicating that we want to activate the UI as well. The first parameter is necessary for initiating our activation. The second allows us to activate without going fully UI active, a design which works well for inside-out objects.

Add stubs for all these functions so that we can fill them later, and add the two interfaces. You can then compile and test to be sure that the interfaces are being instantiated and destroyed properly.

Implement Simple Activation and Deactivation

As described in Chapter 15, *IOleObject::DoVerb* is where in-place activation starts. First, then, we need to decide which object-specific verbs (the ones we register in the Registration Database) will possibly try to activate in place. For example, any *Play* verb will not need to activate in place because they temporarily play in the container using the HWND passed to *DoVerb.* In such cases, they do not need full in-place activation because they don't need to share menu commands or tools with the container.

Each standard verb defined with an OLEIVERB_* symbol has specific behavior as far as in-place activation is concerned, as shown in Table 16-1. The exception is OLEIVERB_PRIMARY, which, like custom verbs, has a behavior defined by the object. Note that this table also describes three new verbs that we did not discuss in Chapters 9 and 10.

Verb	Behavior
OLEIVERB_SHOW	Attempt to in-place activate. On failure, open the object into a server window as usual.
OLEIVERB_HIDE	Deactivate the object if it's currently active in place; otherwise, hide the server window as usual.
OLEIVERB_OPEN	Do *not* attempt to activate in place. Always open into a server window.
OLEIVERB_INPLACEACTIVATE	Activate in place without UI or fail if in-place activation is not possible. Generally used for inside-out objects.
OLEIVERB_UIACTIVATE	Activate in place with full UI or fail if in-place activation is not possible. Generally used for inside-out objects.
OLEIVERB_DISCARDUNDOSTATE	Free any Undo information you are holding. (See "Provide Undo Support" under "Rounding Third...and Heading for Home" later in this chapter.)

Table 16-1.
In-place activation behavior for standard verbs.

We can see how these affect Cosmo's *DoVerb* implementation, which makes use of the functions we added to *CFigure.* This sort of *DoVerb* implementation is the primary reason why it's so convenient to add helper functions to the object:

```
STDMETHODIMP CImplOleObject::DoVerb(LONG iVerb, LPMSG pMSG
    , LPOLECLIENTSITE pActiveSite, LONG lIndex, HWND hWndParent
    , LPCRECT pRectPos)
    {
    ...
```

```
switch (iVerb)
    {
    case OLEIVERB_HIDE:
        if (NULL!=m_pObj->m_pIOleIPSite)
            m_pObj->InPlaceDeactivate();
        else
            {
            ShowWindow(hWnd, SW_HIDE);
            m_pObj->SendAdvise(OBJECTCODE_HIDEWINDOW);
            }
        break;

    case OLEIVERB_PRIMARY:
    case OLEIVERB_SHOW:
        //If already IP active, nothing much to do here.
        if (NULL!=m_pObj->m_pIOleIPSite)
            return NOERROR;

        if (m_pObj->m_fAllowInPlace)
            {
            if (SUCCEEDED(m_pObj->InPlaceActivate(pActiveSite
                , TRUE))) return NOERROR;
            }

        //FALL-THROUGH

    case OLEIVERB_OPEN:
        /*
         * If we're already in-place active, deactivate and
         * prevent later reactivation.
         */

        if (NULL!=m_pObj->m_pIOleIPSite)
            {
            m_pObj->InPlaceDeactivate();
            m_pObj->m_fAllowInPlace=FALSE;
            }

        /*
         * With all the in-place stuff gone, we can go back to
         * our normal open state.
         */
        ShowWindow(hWnd, SW_SHOWNORMAL);
        SetFocus(hWnd);

        m_pObj->SendAdvise(OBJECTCODE_SHOWOBJECT);
        m_pObj->SendAdvise(OBJECTCODE_SHOWWINDOW);
        break;
```

(continued)

```
        case OLEIVERB_INPLACEACTIVATE:
            return m_pObj->InPlaceActivate(pActiveSite, FALSE);

        case OLEIVERB_UIACTIVATE:
            return m_pObj->InPlaceActivate(pActiveSite, TRUE);

        case OLEIVERB_DISCARDUNDOSTATE:
            //We don't hold a state, but if you do, free it here.
            break;

        default:
            return ResultFromScode(OLEOBJ_S_INVALIDVERB);
        }

    return NOERROR;
    }
```

Note that if our application fails to activate in place for OLEIVERB_SHOW and OLEIVERB_PRIMARY, it tries to open the object into a window as usual.

The only tricky part of this is the Open verb. The container might send this verb to our application or our application might generate the verb itself, as we'll see later. If it's asked to open when it's already active in place, we want to deactivate and open it into a window. After it's open into a window, it cannot go back to being in-place active unless the user closes the window and reactivates the object in the container. In other words, if it's opened into a window and the user double-clicks the object in the container again, it will receive OLEIVERB_PRIMARY again. But our application is already open so it shouldn't need to try to activate in place again. To prevent that, Cosmo maintains *m_fAllowInPlace* in *CFigure*, which is initially set to TRUE but which is set to FALSE after executing OLEIVERB_OPEN.

Of course, to make any of this work, we need to do a little work in our *InPlaceActivate* and *InPlaceDeactivate* helper functions.

Basic Activation (*sans* UI)

The steps for basic activation are similar to steps we used in Chapter 15:

1. Use *QueryInterface* on the *IOleClientSite* passed to *DoVerb* for *IOleInPlaceSite* to test for in-place support. If you get that interface, call *IOleInPlaceSite::CanInPlaceActivate* to test whether the specific object can activate in place. If so, call *IOleInPlaceSite->OnInPlaceActivate.*

2. *Call IOleInPlaceSite::GetWindowContext,* use the information to change the parent and position of your editing window, show the window in the container, call *IOleClientSite::ShowObject,* and use *SetFocus* on the editing window.
3. Call *IOleInPlaceFrame::SetActiveObject* and *IOleInPlaceUIWindow::SetActiveObject* to give the container your *IOleInPlaceActiveObject* pointer (because the container cannot query for it).
4. If you want to activate UI as well, call your *UIActivate* function. At this point, the function will do nothing, but you'll want to call it later, so you might as well add it now while you're thinking about it.

You can see these steps implemented in Cosmo's *CFigure::InPlaceActivate*:

```
HRESULT CFigure::InPlaceActivate(LPOLECLIENTSITE pActiveSite
    , BOOL fIncludeUI)
    {
    HRESULT                 hr;
    HWND                    hWnd, hWndHW;
    RECT                    rcPos;
    RECT                    rcClip;

    if (NULL==pActiveSite)
        return ResultFromScode(E_INVALIDARG);

    //Prevent doing this all twice
    if (NULL!=m_pIOleIPSite)
        {
        if (fIncludeUI)
            UIActivate();

        return NOERROR;
        }

    /*
     * 1. Initialization, obtaining interfaces, calling
     *     OnInPlaceActivate.
     */
    hr=pActiveSite->QueryInterface(IID_IOleInPlaceSite
        , (LPLPVOID)&m_pIOleIPSite);

    if (FAILED(hr))
        return hr;

    hr=m_pIOleIPSite->CanInPlaceActivate();
```

(continued)

```
if (NOERROR!=hr)
    {
    m_pIOleIPSite->Release();
    m_pIOleIPSite=NULL;
    return ResultFromScode(E_FAIL);
    }

m_pIOleIPSite->OnInPlaceActivate();
m_fUndoDeactivates=TRUE;

/*
 * 2. Get the window context and create a window or change the
 *     parent and position of an existing window. Servers are
 *     required to full cb in the OLEINPLACEFRAMEINFO structure.
 */
m_pIOleIPSite->GetWindow(&hWnd);
m_pFR->m_frameInfo.cb=sizeof(OLEINPLACEFRAMEINFO);

m_pIOleIPSite->GetWindowContext(&m_pIOleIPFrame
    , &m_pIOleIPUIWindow
    , &rcPos, &rcClip, &m_pFR->m_frameInfo);

/*
 * Copy container frame pointer to CCosmoFrame for accelerators.
 * No AddRef because frame never messes with it. Note also that
 * we don't do anything special with our own accelerators here
 * because we just use the same ones as always.
 */
m_pFR->m_pIOleIPFrame=m_pIOleIPFrame;

/*
 * We'll use a hatch window as the child of the container and the
 * editing window as a child of the hatch window. We already
 * created the hatch window, so now all we have to do is put it
 * in the right place and stick the Polyline in it.
 */

m_pHW->HwndAssociateSet (m_pFR->Window());
m_pHW->ChildSet(m_pPL->Window());    //Calls SetParent
m_pHW->RectsSet(&rcPos, &rcClip);    //Positions polyline

hWndHW=m_pHW->Window();
SetParent(hWndHW, hWnd);             //Move the hatch window
ShowWindow(hWndHW, SW_SHOW);         //Make us visible.
SendAdvise(OBJECTCODE_SHOWOBJECT);

//Critical for accelerators to work initially.
SetFocus(hWndHW);
```

```
//3. Set the active object
if (NULL!=m_pIOleIPFrame)
    {
    m_pIOleIPFrame->SetActiveObject(m_pIOleIPActiveObject
        , PSZ(IDS_INPLACETITLE));
    }

if (NULL!=m_pIOleIPUIWindow)
    {
    m_pIOleIPUIWindow->SetActiveObject(m_pIOleIPActiveObject
        , PSZ(IDS_INPLACETITLE));
    }

/*
 * These steps are handled in UIActivate:
 *  4. Create and install the shared menu
 *  5. Create and install any in-place tools.
 */
if (fIncludeUI)
    return UIActivate();

return NOERROR;
}
```

The first step is to call *QueryInterface* on the given *IOleClientSite* to ask for *IOleInPlaceSite.* If this fails, the container doesn't know about in-place activation, so open the object for editing as usual (back in *DoVerb,* that is). This situation shows that even when we implement all the code to support in-place activation, we can still work with any container that doesn't know what we're talking about. Again, we do not have to implement for the lowest common denominator to remain compatible with other applications; we can implement as many features as we want with full assurances that our application can be used by any container regardless of its supported features.

Cosmo uses the *CFigure* variable *m_pIOleIPSite* (and OLEINPLACESITE pointer) as its "in-place active" flag, so if Cosmo fails to activate in place after obtaining this pointer initially, we must remember to NULL the flag. One such possibility of failure is the call we make to *IOleInPlaceSite::CanInPlaceActivate.* This function tells us whether we can activate this *specific* object in place at the given time. If our application happens to be displayed in iconic form, the container will fail this call (returning S_FALSE, which is why we compare with NOERROR) so our application simply opens normally.

If our application gets past *QueryInterface* and *CanInPlaceActivate,* it can do the rest of the activation. To inform the container of our intent to continue, we call *IOleInPlaceSite::OnInPlaceActivate* so that it can save whatever state it wants. We don't care; calling that function is simply part of our contract. (For the time being, forget about the *m_fUndoDeactivates* flag; we'll discuss it later).

Our next task is to get all the information we need in order to work with the container by calling *IOleInPlaceSite::GetWindow,* which will be the parent of our editor window; and by calling *IOleInPlaceSite::GetWindowContext,* which provides us with our initial position, provides us with the other two container interfaces we need (*IOleInPlaceFrame* and *IOleInPlaceUIWindow*), and fills the OLEINPLACEFRAMEINFO structure we'll need in our message loop to handle accelerators. (Note that the object must fill the *cb* field of the OLEINPLACEFRAMEINFO structure before calling *GetWindowContext*). Because we need the frame information in the message loop, Cosmo stores it directly in its *CCosmoFrame* structure. Because our frame also needs the container's *IOleInPlaceFrame* pointer, we copy that to the *CCosmoFrame* as well. Note that we save the *IOleInPlaceUIWindow* here in *CFigure,* so some changes we make later to *CCosmoDoc* can use that interface.

Next we need to take our editing window, which in Cosmo is the Polyline referenced through *CFigure::m_pPL,* and move it into the container as a child of whatever window we get from *IOleInPlaceSite::GetWindow.* We actually don't place the Polyline window there alone. Instead we make the Polyline a child of a special hatch window. I added this hatch window for this chapter and set it up so that it is managed through the *CHatchWin* class in HATCH.H and is implemented in HATCH.CPP. (I don't show the code listings here because there's nothing very exciting in these files). *CFigure* creates a *CHatchWin* object in *CFigure::FInit,* storing the pointer in *m_pHW* for our use here.

This hatch window draws the border hatching around the object, as described in Chapter 15, using the function *OleUIDrawShading* in its WM_PAINT processing. The width of the border is read from the *OleInPlaceBorderWidth* key of WIN.INI (the default is 4):

```
m_dBorder=GetProfileInt("windows", "OleInPlaceBorderWidth"
    , DEFAULT_HATCHBORDER_WIDTH);
```

In addition, the hatch window manages the position and clipping rectangles that we obtain from the container. Basically, we make the Polyline a child of the hatch window and tell the hatch window through *CHatchWin::RectsSet* to size the Polyline within it to the position rectangle (*rcPos*) and size itself according to the intersection of the position rectangle and the clipping rectangle (*rcClip*):

```
void CHatchWin::RectsSet(LPRECT prcPos, LPRECT prcClip)
    {
    RECT    rc;
    RECT    rcPos;

    //Calculate the rectangle for the hatch window, then clip it.
    rcPos=*prcPos;
    InflateRect(&rcPos, m_dBorder, m_dBorder);
    IntersectRect(&rc, &rcPos, prcClip);

    SetWindowPos(m_hWnd, NULL, rc.left, rc.top, rc.right-rc.left
        , rc.bottom-rc.top, SWP_NOZORDER | SWP_NOACTIVATE);

    SetWindowPos(m_hWndKid, NULL, m_dBorder, m_dBorder
        , prcPos->right-prcPos->left, prcPos->bottom-prcPos->top
        , SWP_NOZORDER | SWP_NOACTIVATE);

    return;
    }
```

The cumulative effect is that the Polyline is always scaled to the position rectangle but as it is clipped to its parent. (The hatch window has WS_CLIPCHILDREN for this purpose.) As the hatch window clips itself to the clipping rectangle, the object is also clipped to the clipping rectangle while still showing the proper scaling. The hatch window keeps itself slightly larger than its child window by the hatch border width on all sides, subject, of course, to the container's clipping rectangle.

After the hatch window is positioned, with the Polyline inside it, we can move it to the container with *SetParent,* make it visible with *ShowWindow,* and call *IOleClientSite::ShowObject* to let the container know our application is visible. This last call allows the container to scroll our application into view if it is completely scrolled out of view at the time. Finally, we take the focus by calling *SetFocus* on the hatch window, which calls *SetFocus* on the Polyline. The editor window should always end up with the focus, so if we happened to put an edit control in the hatch window instead, it would end up with the focus.

The hatch window used in Cosmo (there is also a similar one in OLE2UI) is very useful when your editing window normally sends messages to its parent and you do not have the power to change it. In that case, you can have the hatch window redirect WM_COMMAND messages to an associate window. Cosmo's hatch window is already set up for this, as you can see from its window procedure in HATCH.CPP.

Object Adornments

The hatch window is a special case of what are called *object adornments,* or additional user interface elements that appear outside the position rectangle of the object but inside the clipping rectangle. A spreadsheet object might display row and column headings, for example. If you need additional space for similar adornments, you can expand whatever windows you place in the container to accommodate them, as long as those windows stay within the container's clipping rectangle and as long as the object area stays the same size as the position rectangle, at least initially. No matter what adornments you add, the hatched border should always surround the object and all adornments.

The next step is to call the *SetActiveObject* members of the container's *IOleInPlaceFrame* and *IOleInPlaceUIWindow,* which includes passing a string for the container to use in its caption bars if it wants. In Cosmo, we pass "Cosmo 2.0 Figure." At this time, you should implement both *IOleInPlaceObject::GetWindow* and *IOleInPlaceActiveObject::GetWindow* to return the window you passed to *SetParent*; in Cosmo this is the hatch window:

```
STDMETHODIMP CImpIOleInPlaceObject::GetWindow(HWND FAR * phWnd)
    {
    *phWnd=m_pObj->m_pHW->Window();
    return NOERROR;
    }

STDMETHODIMP CImpIOleInPlaceActiveObject::GetWindow(HWND FAR * phWnd)
    {
    *phWnd=m_pObj->m_pHW->Window();
    return NOERROR;
    }
```

This works out nicely because when the container gets a WM_SETFOCUS in the frame during an in-place session, it will call *SetFocus* on whatever window is returned from *IOleInPlaceActiveObject::GetWindow.* That means it will use *SetFocus* on the hatch window, which will use *SetFocus* on your editor window, which is exactly how things should happen.

As the final step, Cosmo ends *CFigure::InPlaceActivate* by calling *CFigure::UIActivate,* which builds the shared menu and negotiates with the container for tool space, as we'll see a little later.

Basic Deactivation (*sans* UI)

Deactivation basically means reversing anything we did in the activation phase, in the opposite order. Where we previously obtained an interface pointer, we release it here. Where we used *SetParent* on a window to move it to the container, we call *SetParent* here to bring it back home to the server. Deactivation involves four steps, the reverse of those steps described for activation:

1. Call your *UIDeactivate* to remove menus and tools.
2. Call the container interfaces' *SetActiveObject* functions, passing a NULL for the *IOleInPlaceActiveObject* pointer. This will instruct the container to release the pointers you passed before. This step can be done anywhere that it's convenient.
3. Call *SetParent* to move the hatch window and editing window back to the server. You should reposition the editing window back in the server document so that it will appear in the proper place if *IOleObject::DoVerb* is called with OLEIVERB_OPEN to show the server windows.
4. Call *IOleInPlaceSite::OnInPlaceDeactivate*, release the pointers obtained from *IOleInPlaceSite::GetWindowContext*, and release the *IOleInPlaceSite* pointer obtained from *QueryInterface.*

We can see these steps implemented in Cosmo's *CFigure::InPlaceDeactivate*:

```
void CFigure::InPlaceDeactivate(void)
    {
    RECT        rc;

    UIDeactivate();

    /*
     * When setting the parent back to the normal document, reposition
     * the Polyline to be at (8,8) instead of at wherever it was in
     * the container's window or our hatch window. This is so if we
     * are deactivating to open in our own window the Polyline appears
     * in the proper place in the document window.
     */

    SetParent(m_pPL->Window(), m_pDoc->m_hWnd);
    m_pHW->ChildSet(NULL);

    //Make sure the hatch window is invisible and owned by Cosmo
    ShowWindow(m_pHW->Window(), SW_HIDE);
    SetParent(m_pHW->Window(), m_pDoc->m_hWnd);
```

(continued)

```
    GetClientRect(m_pDoc->m_hWnd, &rc);
    InflateRect(&rc, -8, -8);

    SetWindowPos(m_pPL->Window(), NULL, rc.left, rc.top
        , rc.right-rc.left, rc.bottom-rc.top
        , SWP_NOZORDER | SWP_NOACTIVATE);

    if (NULL!=m_pIOleIPFrame)
        {
        m_pIOleIPFrame->SetActiveObject(NULL, NULL);
        m_pIOleIPFrame->Release();
        m_pIOleIPFrame=NULL;
        m_pFR->m_pIOleIPFrame=NULL;
        }

    if (NULL!=m_pIOleIPUIWindow)
        {
        m_pIOleIPUIWindow->SetActiveObject(NULL, NULL);
        m_pIOleIPUIWindow->Release();
        m_pIOleIPUIWindow=NULL;
        }

    if (NULL!=m_pIOleIPSite)
        {
        m_pIOleIPSite->OnInPlaceDeactivate();
        m_pIOleIPSite->Release();
        m_pIOleIPSite=NULL;
        }

    return;
    }
```

There are only two points I want to make with this code:

- The Polyline window was originally a child of a document window in Cosmo. When we set it as a child of the hatch window, its position relative to its parent changed, so when we move it back now, we have to readjust its position to the document window. If and when the server window is shown as open, the Polyline will already be positioned correctly in the document, as it should be.
- When an in-place object is activated, it is taken from the loaded state to the running state and then to the active state. In-place deactivation only brings it back to the running state. Therefore, the object still exists—that is, our *CFigure* object in Cosmo here is not released to the point where it frees itself. Therefore, it's a good idea to set any pointer you release for the last time to NULL, especially if you are using that pointer as a flag to remember whether you are servicing an in-place object.

Test Activation and Deactivation

After you can successfully compile all the code you added for this step you should be able to activate your object and have your editing window appear inside the container. You should be able to make whatever modifications you can in that window alone, and it should appear with a hatched border around it. If your window does not appear, check the window handles you are passing to *SetParent* and ensure that the window is visible. Your object name should also appear in the container's caption bar (either on the document or the frame, depending on the container) after you call *SetActiveObject.*

When you deactivate the object, usually by clicking somewhere outside of it in the container, your deactivation function should successfully remove the window from the container and clean up all the pointers appropriately. When you call *SetActiveObject* with NULLs, the caption bar in the container should revert to its normal state.

You might also, as an extra debugging measure, actually display your server window during this time, so that you can watch the editing window disappear from within the server document on activation and reappear on deactivation.

Assemble and Disassemble the Menu

After you have your basic activation and deactivation, you can start filling out your *UIActivate* and *UIDeactivate* functions. If you created all the helper functions I suggested, you can fully implement these functions now, as shown in Cosmo as follows:

```
HRESULT CFigure::UIActivate(void)
    {
    FInPlaceToolsCreate();
    FInPlaceMenuCreate();

    if (NULL!=m_pIOleIPSite)
        m_pIOleIPSite->OnUIActivate();

    return NOERROR;
    }

void CFigure::UIDeactivate(void)
    {
    if (NULL!=m_pIOleIPSite)
        m_pIOleIPSite->OnUIDeactivate(FALSE);

    FInPlaceToolsDestroy();
    FInPlaceMenuDestroy();
    return;
    }
```

The most critical parts of these functions are the calls to *IOleInPlaceSite::OnUIActivate* and *OnUIDeactivate* because the container will take action on those calls to hide or show its normal user interface in preparation for the user interface the object will display. If you've stubbed helper functions for menu creation and destruction and for tool creation and destruction, you can call those functions here with no ill effects. Of course, it's not necessary to have separate menu and tool functions—all the code could appear in *UIActivate* and *UIDeactivate*, but I find it cleaner to keep the two functions separate. It certainly makes it easier to write about.

So let's turn our focus to the *CFigure* functions, *FInPlaceMenuCreate* and *FInPlaceMenuDestroy*.

FInPlaceMenuCreate

As described in Chapter 15, the entire process of assembling the in-place shared menu can be summed up in a few tidy steps:

1. Create a new menu with the Windows API *CreateMenu*.
2. Call *IOleInPlaceFrame::InsertMenus* to have the container make its contribution, also passing it the OLEMENUGROUPWIDTHS array in which the container stores the number of items in each of its groups.
3. Call the Windows API *InsertMenu* to add your own menu items to the shared menu in the appropriate places and fill in the remainder of the OLEMENUGROUPWIDTHS array.
4. Call *OleCreateMenuDescriptor* with the menu and the OLEMENUGROUPWIDTHS array.
5. Call *IOleInPlaceFrame::SetMenu*, passing the menu handle, the menu descriptor from step 4, and the handle of the window to receive messages generated from your items on this menu, typically your frame window.

These are, of course, the exact steps executed in Cosmo's *CFigure::FInPlaceMenuCreate*:

```
BOOL CFigure::FInPlaceMenuCreate(void)
    {
    HMENU               hMenu, hMenuT;
    UINT                uTemp=MF_BYPOSITION | MF_POPUP;
    UINT                i;
    OLEMENUGROUPWIDTHS  mgw;
```

```
    for (i=0; i<6; i++)
        mgw.width[i]=0;

    //We already have popup menu handles in m_pFR->m_phMenu[]

    //Create the new shared menu and let container do its thing
    hMenu=CreateMenu();
    m_pIOleIPFrame->InsertMenus(hMenu, &mgw);

    //Add our menus remembering that the container has added its already
    InsertMenu(hMenu, (WORD)mgw.width[0]
        , uTemp, (UINT)m_pFR->m_phMenu[1], PSZ(IDS_MENUEDIT));

    //Add the Open item to the edit menu.
    AppendMenu(m_pFR->m_phMenu[1], MF_SEPARATOR, 0, NULL);
    AppendMenu(m_pFR->m_phMenu[1], MF_STRING, IDM_EDITOPEN
        , PSZ(IDS_MENUOPEN));

    InsertMenu(hMenu, (WORD)mgw.width[0]+1+(WORD)mgw.width[2]
        , uTemp, (UINT)m_pFR->m_phMenu[2], PSZ(IDS_MENUCOLOR));

    InsertMenu(hMenu, (WORD)mgw.width[0]+1+(WORD)mgw.width[2]+1
        , uTemp, (UINT)m_pFR->m_phMenu[3], PSZ(IDS_MENULINE));

#ifdef MDI
    hMenuT=m_pFR->m_phMenu[5];
#else
    hMenuT=m_pFR->m_phMenu[4];
#endif

    InsertMenu(hMenu, (WORD)mgw.width[0]+1+(WORD)mgw.width[2]+2
        + (WORD)mgw.width[4], uTemp, (UINT)hMenuT, PSZ(IDS_MENUHELP));

    //Tell OLE how many items in each group are ours.
    mgw.width[1]=1;
    mgw.width[3]=2;
    mgw.width[5]=1;

    m_hMenuShared=hMenu;
    m_hOLEMenu=OleCreateMenuDescriptor(m_hMenuShared, &mgw);

    m_pIOleIPFrame->SetMenu(m_hMenuShared, m_hOLEMenu, m_pFR->Window());
    return TRUE;
    }
```

After we call *CreateMenu* and the container's *IOleInPlaceFrame::InsertMenus,* we'll have a half-filled menu and elements 0, 2, and 4 of the OLEMENUGROUPWIDTHS structure filled with the number of items in the container's File, Container, and Window menu groups. When we add our own items to our Edit, Object, and Help groups, we have to use the widths of the container groups to properly position our own menus. Therefore, the starting positions of each of our groups are as follows, where *mgw* is the width array:

Group	Description
Edit	Starts at offset *mgw.width[0].*
Object	Starts at offset *mgw.width[0]+<number of menus in the Edit group>+mgw.width[2].*
Help	Starts at offset *mgw.width[0]+<number of menus in the Edit group>+mgw.width[2]+<number of menus in the Object group>+mgw.width[4].*

You can see this in the preceding code where our first call to *InsertMenu* specifies the position *mgw.width[0]* for the Edit menu. Because we have only one item in the Edit group, the *InsertMenu* calls for the Color and Line menu in our Object group are at positions *mgw.width[0] + 1 + mgw.width[2]* and *mgw.width[0] + 1 + mgw.width[2] + 1*, respectively. Note how additional menus in a group must be offset from the first item in that group. The last *InsertMenus* call adds the Help menu in the Help group and specifies position *mgw.width[0] + 1 + mgw.width[2] + 2 + mgw.width[4]*. We then store the values 1, 2, and 1 in elements 1, 3, and 5 of the width array because we added one menu in the Edit group, two in the Object group, and one in the Help group.

Cosmo takes advantage of a convenient ability of multiple menus to share the same pop-up handles. During an in-place session, Cosmo puts the same Edit, Color, Line, and Help menus on the shared menu that it displays on its own menu, using the same pop-up handles that are stored in its *CCosmoFrame::m_phMenu* array. This saves us from the trouble of recreating each pop-up menu all over again, but means we have to be very careful when we disassemble the menu, as we'll see shortly.

However, Cosmo makes a small addition to the Edit menu for in-place uses: an Open item, which causes the in-place active object to deactivate and open in a full window. We'll see how we process this command later, but this is a nice addition for an object to provide.

The object is responsible for maintaining the menu it creates here, so remember to save the handle with the object, as Cosmo does in *CFigure::m_hMenuShared*. The object must also save the menu descriptor, a variable of type HOLEMENU like *CFigure::m_hOLEMenu*, that it gets back from *OleCreateMenuDescriptor* so that it can destroy the descriptor later.

WARNING

If your application is an MDI multiple-use server, you should *not* modify a pop-up menu that is used from two top-level menus (that is, the shared menu and the server's normal menu) because you'll be modifying the menu anywhere it's used. Either abstain from such modifications or create a separate pop-up menu for the shared menu and make your modifications to it alone. Remember also to save this menu handle so that you can enable or disable items in it while processing WM_INITMENUPOPUP.

OleCreateMenuDescriptor creates a data structure that OLE will use to intercept messages from this menu to the server that would normally go to the container because the container displays the shared menu. OLE does this by installing a message hook on the container. When a message comes through this filter, OLE checks to see which menu generated it, looks it up in the menu descriptor, and, based on the OLEMENUGROUPWIDTHS array that both the object and container fills, either lets the message through or redirects it to the server.

But none of this happens unless you tell the container to display the menu by calling *IOleInPlaceFrame::SetMenu,* to which you must also pass the menu descriptor and the handle of the window to which you want menu messages sent. Generally, this window is your frame window because it's already set up to receive menu messages. *IOleInPlaceFrame::SetMenu* calls *OleSetMenuDescriptor* to install the message filter on its side of the universe.

You can stop here to compile and test your menu creation. When you call *IOleInPlaceFrame::SetMenu,* the menu should appear in the container, and from your items, you can expect to receive the following messages: WM_COMMAND, WM_MENUSELECT, WM_ENTERIDLE, WM_INITMENU[POPUP], WM_DRAWITEM, and WM_MEASUREITEM. The problem is, of course, that when you deactivate, you have this major resource leak because you don't have any code to remove the items and free the shared menu. So the next step is to implement disassembly code.

FInPlaceMenuDestroy

Disassembling the menu means that you basically perform the opposite of each assembly step, in the reverse order, as shown in *CFigure::FInPlaceMenuDestroy* on the next page.

1. Call *IOleInPlaceFrame::SetMenu* with NULLs.
2. Call *OleDestroyMenuDescriptor* to free the menu descriptor structure in OLE.
3. Remove each of your menu items from the shared menu.
4. Call *IOleInPlaceFrame::RemoveMenus* to let the container clean up its half.
5. Call the Windows API function *DestroyMenu* to free the menu itself.

Here's how you take the menu apart, piece by piece.

```
BOOL CFigure::FInPlaceMenuDestroy(void)
    {
    int         cItems, i, j;
    HMENU       hMenuT;

    //If we don't have a shared menu, nothing to do.
    if (NULL==m_hMenuShared)
        return TRUE;

    //Stop the container frame from using this menu.
    m_pIOleIPFrame->SetMenu(NULL, NULL, NULL);

    //Clean up what we got from OleCreateMenuDescriptor.
    OleDestroyMenuDescriptor(m_hOLEMenu);
    m_hOLEMenu=NULL;

    cItems=GetMenuItemCount(m_hMenuShared);

    /*
     * Walk backwards down the menu. For each popup, see if it matches
     * any other popup we know about, and if so, remove it from the
     * shared menu.
     */
    for (i=cItems; i >=0; i--)
        {
        hMenuT=GetSubMenu(m_hMenuShared, i);

        for (j=0; j <= CMENUS; j++)
            {
            /*
             * If the submenu matches any we have, remove, don't
             * delete. Because we're walking backwards this only
             * affects the positions of those menus after us so the
             * GetSubMenu call above is not affected.
             */
```

```
            if (hMenuT==m_pFR->m_phMenu[j])
                RemoveMenu(m_hMenuShared, i, MF_BYPOSITION);
            }
        }

    //Remove the Open item and separator from the Edit menu.
    RemoveMenu(m_pFR->m_phMenu[1], 6, MF_BYPOSITION);
    RemoveMenu(m_pFR->m_phMenu[1], 5, MF_BYPOSITION);

    if (NULL!=m_pIOleIPFrame)
        m_pIOleIPFrame->RemoveMenus(m_hMenuShared);

    DestroyMenu(m_hMenuShared);
    m_hMenuShared=NULL;
    return TRUE;
    }
```

The trick here is to *remove* each menu item you added before. I stress *remove* because you will generally be sharing menu handles between this menu and your normal server's menu, so destroying those pop-up items is not a good idea. Cosmo ensures that it removes all of its items by removing any pop-up it recognizes in the shared menu (that is, any handle that is also stored in *m_phMenu*). It also removes the extra Open item we added in the assembly phase. After we've called the *IOleInPlaceFrame::RemoveMenus* function, we can call *DestroyMenu* to free the resource. Then we're done.

WARNING

It's extremely important that you remove *all* your menu items properly before calling *DestroyMenu,* because that function also destroys any popups on that menu as well. If you experience any weirdness at all in assembling or disassembling your shared menu, comment out your call to *DestroyMenu* and see if the problem still exists.[2] If it does, you are not cleaning up your menu properly. If you missed it earlier, go back and read the box titled "EXPERIENCE: Menu Destruction: Just Do It (Right)!" in Chapter 15 for a description of what happened when I *didn't* do it right. I had one major-league hair-puller with this one, and it all turned out to be a bug in my MAKEFILE, of all things.

2. Another good idea for debug builds is to include an assertion check that *GetMenuItemCount* on the shared menu returns zero before you call *DestroyMenu.*

Test the Shared Menu

Once again, you can compile your server and verify that your shared menu is being properly assembled and disassembled. Activate and deactivate your object a number of times to ensure that all the menu items—both yours and the container's—are showing up properly. If they are not right the first time you activate your object, check your assembly code. If they're right the first time but not on subsequent activations, your disassembly code is in error. Note that if you accidentally destroy a popup with one menu handle but later use that handle again (even though it's invalid), a number of odd things can happen: (for example) no popup appears, the wrong popup appears, or a stack fault occurs in USER, depending on what that handle is pointing to.

Create and Destroy In-Place Tools

The last major piece of user interface to add before we can call our object fully activated in place are any in-place tools that we want to display during activation. This includes toolbars or toolboxes on any side of the container's frame or document window. We'll need to implement two functions: one to create and show the tools, such as *CFigure::FCreateInPlaceTools,* and one to hide and destroy them, such as *CFigure::FDestroyInPlaceTools.*

Before looking at the code, I want to remind you again that tools you create inside the container's windows are going to be child windows with unfamiliar parents. You must be sure to redirect all messages that these tools normally send to the parent because the container will not understand those messages and will likely malfunction. (Most likely, it will bomb like crazy.) In addition, remember that all your child windows for such tools must be created with WS_CLIPSIBLINGS so that they don't interfere with other container windows.

You can, of course, provide your tools in floating pop-up windows instead of in toolbars or toolboxes inside the container. If you have the opportunity, create tools that can appear either as toolbars or as floating palettes. That way, your object will be flexible enough even to work with containers that don't allow toolbars. Cosmo, however, does not provide floating palettes.

FInPlaceToolsCreate

In a nutshell, creating your in-place tools involves only three steps:

1. Negotiate tool space with the container by calling the *RequestBorderSpace* function in *IOleInPlaceFrame* for frame-level tools and in *IOleInPlaceUIWindow* for document windows. (These are the two interfaces you obtained from *IOleInPlaceSite::GetWindowContext.*)

2. When the container accepts your space requests, send those same numbers to the *SetBorderSpace* members of the appropriate interface.
3. Create your tools either as children of the container's frame or document window or as pop-up windows, and make them visible. You can use the rectangle from the *GetBorder* function of either container interface to set the initial dimensions of the tools if necessary.

Note that all units used here are device units because we're dealing with windows whose dimensions are always in device units.

CFigure::FInPlaceToolsCreate performs the preceding steps by creating an extra *GizmoBar* control at the top of the container's frame window (the most common case). In the following code, I omitted the parts that add each specific button to the GizmoBar because those are unnecessary distractions. Also note that BORDERWIDTHS is the same as a RECT, so we can get away with using *SetRectEmpty* on it:

```
BOOL CFigure::FInPlaceToolsCreate(void)
    {
    BORDERWIDTHS     bw;
    HWND             hWnd;
    UINT             uState=GIZMO_NORMAL;
    UINT             utCmd =GIZMOTYPE_BUTTONCOMMAND;
    UINT             utEx  =GIZMOTYPE_BUTTONATTRIBUTEEX;
    UINT             i;
    HBITMAP          hBmp;

    //0. We don't need anything on the document, so send zeros.
    SetRectEmpty((LPRECT)&bw);

    if (NULL!=m_pIOleIPUIWindow)
        m_pIOleIPUIWindow->SetBorderSpace(&bw);

    if (NULL==m_pIOleIPFrame)
        return FALSE;

    /*
     * 1. Make sure we can reserve space for what we need. If this
     *    fails then we just do without because the menu has
     *    everything we really need. A more willing server could
     *    put tools in popup windows as well.
     */

    if (!FInPlaceToolsRenegotiate())
        {
```

(continued)

```
        //If the container doesn't allow us any, don't ask for any.
        m_pIOleIPFrame->SetBorderSpace(&bw);
        return FALSE;
        }

    //2. Create the gizmobar using the container window as the parent
    m_pIOleIPFrame->GetWindow(&hWnd);

    //If we already have a gizmobar, just show it again.
    if (NULL!=m_pGB)
        {
        ShowWindow(m_pGB->Window(), SW_SHOW);
        return TRUE;
        }

    m_pGB=new CGizmoBar(m_pFR->m_hInst);

    if (NULL==m_pGB)
        {
        SetRectEmpty((LPRECT)&bw);
        m_pIOleIPFrame->SetBorderSpace(&bw);
        return FALSE;
        }

    m_pGB->FInit(hWnd, ID_GIZMOBAR, m_cyBar);

    [Other code to initialize the GizmoBar with buttons omitted]

    //3. Make the tools visible.
    ShowWindow(m_pGB->Window(), SW_SHOW);

    return TRUE;
    }
```

This code needs to create tools in both the container's frame and document windows, but because Cosmo does not use any document tools, it calls *IOleInPlaceUIWindow* with a BORDERWIDTHS structure full of zeros meaning "We want no space." If we call *SetBorderSpace* with a NULL pointer, however, that means "We don't want any space and you can leave your tools up to the container." An object that does nothing for the UI active state should call *SetBorderSpace* with NULLs.

But Cosmo does want to create a toolbar in the container's frame window, so we need to go through a round of border space negotiations with the container. This is handled in the separate function *CFigure::FInPlaceToolsRenegotiate.* We have this separate function because we'll need it later in *IOleInPlaceActiveObject::ResizeBorder:*

```
BOOL CFigure::FInPlaceToolsRenegotiate(void)
    {
    HRESULT         hr;
    BORDERWIDTHS    bw;

    SetRect((LPRECT)&bw, 0, m_pFR->m_cyBar, 0, 0);

    hr=m_pIOleIPFrame->RequestBorderSpace(&bw);

    if (NOERROR!=hr)
        return FALSE;

//Safety net:  RequestBorderSpace may modify values in bw
SetRect((LPRECT)&bw, 0, m_pFR->m_cyBar, 0, 0);

    m_pIOleIPFrame->SetBorderSpace(&bw);
    return TRUE;
    }
```

If this function returns FALSE, the container will not allow us space for our toolbar. In this case Cosmo merely lives without the tools because everything is still available on the shared menu. Some other objects might not want to activate in place in such a situation and should thus deactivate everything done to this point (including the shared menu) and open as a normal embedded object. Still other objects can elect to place those same tools in a floating pop-up window, which the container cannot restrict.

If the container does allow us the space we need, we can create our toolbar using the container's frame window from *IOleInPlaceFrame::GetWindow* as the parent and the appropriate dimentions from *IOleInPlaceFrame::GetBorder*. For example, Cosmo creates a GizmoBar that is the same width as the rectangle from *GetBorder* but only as high as a standard toolbar.

(An aside: Cosmo saves a copy of the in-place GizmoBar in *g_pInPlaceGB* in such a way that when the user selects a line style from the menu, the *CCosmoFrame::CheckLineSelection* function can depress the appropriate button on the in-place toolbar as it does on the normal toolbar. You will see extra code in COSMO.CPP to handle this.)

After we have created all the tools, we can make them visible, and they should appear in the container window. Because the reverse case for deactivation is so simple, let's look at that first before we compile and test.

FInPlaceToolsDestroy

Destroying in-place tools is substantially simpler than creating them because all you have to do is destroy the tool windows:

```
BOOL CFigure::FInPlaceToolsDestroy(void)
    {
```

(continued)

```
//Nothing to do if we never created anything.
if (NULL==m_pGB)
    return TRUE;

/*
 * No reason to call SetBorderSpace with an empty rectangle
 * since you call IOleInPlaceSite::OnUIDeactivate.
 */

//Destroy the gizmobar.
if (NULL!=m_pGB)
    {
    delete m_pGB;
    m_pGB=NULL;
    g_pInPlaceGB=NULL;
    }

return TRUE;
}
```

We do not need to call *SetBorderSpace* with an empty rectangle or anything like that because by now we have already called *IOleInPlaceSite::OnUIDeactivate,* and when we called it the container reinstated its own UI. By not calling *SetBorderSpace,* we avoid asking the container to resize its frame or document client area windows, as if there were no tools to show, only to later resize them again to fit the container's tools back in. That would cause a significant amount of flicker, which is best avoided simply by destroying your tools. It is appropriate to hide the tools at this time if you don't want to recreate them every time you call *IOleInPlaceSite::OnUIActivate.*

Now you can compile these changes and watch your tools appear and disappear as you activate and deactivate your object. If they don't appear, check the parent window you are using, and check to see where the tools are positioned, and check the return values from *RequestBorderSpace* and *SetBorderSpace.* If you continue to play around with your tools, try resizing the frame and document windows in the container. Ugly, huh? Your tools didn't resize with the container windows. That's because we haven't finished implementing the *IOleInPlaceActiveObject* interface yet. But first, let's finish up the last major modification—accelerator support.

Manage and Process Accelerators

As the in-place active, your application always has first crack at accelerators. If your application is an EXE server, its message loop will be the first to retrieve keystrokes headed for its window, in which case you process accelerators by calling the Windows API *TranslateAccelerator* as you always have. If your application is a DLL server, the container's message loop will call your *IOleInPlaceActiveObject::TranslateAccelerator* function before it dares to translate the accelerator itself. *IOleInPlaceActiveObject::TranslateAccelerator* is not used in an EXE server, so Cosmo leaves it empty. Note that I don't implement this in Polyline because Polyline has no accelerators.

An EXE server has two other considerations for its message loop in order to handle accelerators properly. First it must avoid calling *TranslateMDISysAccel* if the server is an MDI application because the server's Window menu is not available during an in-place session. Second it must call *OleTranslateAccelerator* to give the container a shot at the accelerators before the server dumps the message on *TranslateMessage* and *DispatchMessage.* Therefore Cosmo's message loop, *CCosmoFrame::MessageLoop,* appears as follows:

```
WPARAM CCosmoFrame::MessageLoop(void)
    {
    MSG     msg;

    while (GetMessage(&msg, NULL, 0,0 ))
        {
        //If we're in-place, don't bother with MDI accelerators
        if (NULL==m_pIOleIPFrame)
            {
            if (m_pCL->TranslateAccelerator(&msg))
                continue;
            }

        //Translate our accelerators.
        if (TranslateAccelerator(m_hWnd, m_hAccel, &msg))
            continue;

        if (NULL!=m_pIOleIPFrame)
            {
            if (NOERROR==OleTranslateAccelerator(m_pIOleIPFrame
                , &m_frameInfo, &msg))
                continue;
            }

        TranslateMessage(&msg);
        DispatchMessage(&msg);
        }

    return msg.wParam;
    }
```

Note that the *IOleInPlaceFrame* pointer (*m_pIOleIPFrame*) and the OLEINPLACEFRAMEINFO structure (*m_frameInfo*) passed to *OleTranslateAccelerator* are those obtained from *IOleInPlaceSite::GetWindowContext*, which you call when you activate the object. The OLEINPLACEFRAMEINFO structure contains the window handle of the container and a copy of its accelerator table.

NOTE: If your EXE server is MDI and multiple-use, you will have a more complex test to determine if you call *OleTranslateAccelerator*. You must call it with the *IOleInPlaceFrame* pointer and OLEINPLACEFRAMEINFO structure of the container that's involved with the in-place object in the currently active document.

You should test your code by trying all of your accelerators as well as those of the container to be sure that each side receives the appropriate keystrokes. You can also try creating an accelerator that conflicts with one of a container to ensure that you are getting that accelerator first. If not, you might be calling *OleTranslateAccelator* before calling *TranslateAccelerator* for yourself, or the container is in error.

Rounding Third...and Heading for Home

We're now on the home stretch and have only to add little bits of code to complete our in-place object implementation. This involves the following steps, some of which are required, some of which are optional:

1. (Required) Resize your tools on *IOleInPlaceActiveObject::ResizeBorder*.
2. (Required) Implement *IOleInPlaceObject::SetObjectRects* to update your editing window's position and call *IOleClientSite::OnPosRectChange* and *IOleClientSite::Scroll* if you need more room.
3. (Required) Implement *IOleInPlaceActiveObject::OnFrameWindowActivate* and *IOleInPlaceActiveObject::OnDocWindowActivate* to handle UI changes appropriately.
4. (Required) Implement minimal context-sensitive help support in case the container supports it, even if you don't.

5a. (Required) Provide Undo support by calling *IOleClientSite::DiscardUndoState* when making a change after activation and by implementing *IOleInPlaceObject::ReactivateAndUndo.*

5b. (Optional) If you have an Undo, call *IOleInPlaceSite::DeactivateAndUndo* if it's given immediately after deactivation. Also implement *IOleObject::DoVerb* for OLEIVERB_DISCARDUNDOSTATE.

6. (Required) Call *IOleInPlaceFrame::SetStatusText* with messages for your menu items even if you don't have your own status line. (This is optional if you really don't care about it.)
7. (Optional) Provide methods for opening the object into a server window from an in-place active state.
8. (Optional) If you have modeless pop-up windows that are normally shown as part of your user interface, show or hide these when your *IOleInPlaceActiveObject::EnableModeless* function is called. You can also tell the container to do the same by calling *IOleInPlaceFrame-::EnableModeless.*

Also, if you want to experiment with having your object be an inside-out object, set the OLEMISC_INSIDEOUT and OLEMISC_ACTIVATEWHEN-VISIBLE flags in the value of the *MiscStatus* key in the Registration Database (CHAP16.REG does this for Polyline) and run your object with a container that supports inside-out. You'll see that such a container treats your application a little differently when it's marked as an inside-out object.

Implement *IOleInPlaceActiveObject::ResizeBorder*

Whenever the end user resizes the container's frame window or document window, the container will call your *IOleInPlaceActiveObject::ResizeBorder* function with the frame's or document's *IOleInPlaceUIWindow* interface (remember again that *IOleInPlaceFrame* inherits from *IOleInPlaceUIWindow*) and a flag indicating which one we're dealing with. On this function, you must renegotiate space for your object's tools and resize those tools to fit in that space:

```
STDMETHODIMP CImpIOleInPlaceActiveObject::ResizeBorder(LPCRECT pRect
    , LPOLEINPLACEUIWINDOW pIUIWindow, BOOL fFrame)
    {
    //The document case is uninteresting for us.
    if (!fFrame)
        return NOERROR;

    if (!m_pObj->FInPlaceToolsRenegotiate())
        return ResultFromScode(INPLACE_E_NOTOOLSPACE);

    SetWindowPos(m_pObj->m_pGB->Window(), NULL, pRect->left, pRect->top
        , pRect->right-pRect->left, m_pObj->m_cyBar, SWP_NOZORDER);

    return NOERROR;
    }
```

This code from Cosmo first shows that because we don't have any document tools, we can simply return NOERROR if the *fFrame* parameter is FALSE. Otherwise, we need to go through the *RequestBorderSpace* and *SetBorderSpace* process again, which is handled by *CFigure::FInPlaceToolsRenegotiate*. To optimize, you can try calling *SetBorderSpace* first; only if that fails, do you need to call *RequestBorderSpace* again. Either way works—the container expects that you'll try this.

When you've renegotiated space for your tools, reposition your tools by using the rectangle passed to this function. This rectangle contains the same thing you would receive from a call to the container's *GetBorder*. In Cosmo's case, we make the toolbar the same width as would be returned from *GetBorder* but with the height in *m_pObj->m_cyBar*, which is how much space *CFigure::FInPlaceToolsRenegotiate* requested from the container at the top of the frame.

Implement *IOleInPlaceObject::SetObjectRects* and Call Container Position Functions

There will probably be situations in which your object is not fully visible in the container document and the end user will want to scroll you into view. There are two ways this can happen. The end user might scroll the container document directly or might perform some action in your object that would require your application to bring more of itself into view.

First, when the user scrolls the container document, the container will call your *IOleInPlaceObject::SetObjectRects* with a new position rectangle and a new clipping rectangle. As an object, your application has no choice other than to resize its editing window to the new position rectangle, keeping it clipped to the clipping rectangle. This is one big advantage of using something like Cosmo's hatch window, because we can simply tell it to do the resizing:

```
STDMETHODIMP CImpIOleInPlaceObject::SetObjectRects(LPCRECT prcPos
    , LPCRECT prcClip)
    {
    m_pObj->m_pHW->RectsSet((LPRECT)prcPos, (LPRECT)prcClip);
    return NOERROR;
    }
```

The *CHatchWin::SetObjectRects* function, as we have seen, resizes its child window (Cosmo's Polyline, in our case) to the position rectangle and resizes the hatch window to the intersection of the position rectangle—inflated by the hatch border—and the clipping rectangle. Therefore, the editing window shows the correct scaling but is still restricted to the clipping rectangle. Again, I remind you that you don't have a choice when *SetObjectRects* is called:

You are contractually obliged by virtue of supporting the *IOleInPlaceObject* interface to obey the wishes of the container.

However, that does not mean you have no control over the size of your object. As an object, your application can, in fact, allow the end user to resize the editing window (and the hatch window, of course) during an in-place session. This has the effect of giving the user a larger space in which to work but does *not* change the size of the container site. When the user has resized your window, calculate the new position rectangle of the editing area of the window, excluding all object adornments and the hatch border and call *IOleInPlaceSite::OnPosRectChange.* In this function, the container will determine whether it can give you this space, or at least a portion of it, and will call your *IOleInPlaceObject::SetObjectRects* in response. At that time, your application obediently resize itself. Some containers will let your object grow as much as it wants. Others will never let it grow larger than the container site itself. It's your responsibility to determine how your application will respond in these cases. You can either scale your object to fit the container's specified position rectangle, or you can add scroll bars to your in-place editing window if you cannot scale and cannot display all the object's data in the position rectangle. In any case, what you do with the position rectangle from *SetObjectRects* is your choice, as long as your application can fit into it somehow.

This brings up the second case that can cause scrolling to occur. There will be times when not all of your object is visible but the user needs to work in that nonvisible area. For example, if you have a table object with only half the cells visible, the user might use the arrow keys to move the cell selection into one of the hidden cells. In that case, your object can call *IOleInPlaceSite::Scroll,* specifying the amount you want the container document to scroll. If the container can scroll, it will do so and call your *IOleObject::SetObjectRects,* once again to let you know the new position and clipping rectangles.

Implement *IOleInPlaceActiveObject* Functions for Window Activation Changes

Try this with what we've implemented so far. Run an in-place capable MDI container and create two new, untitled documents. Into one insert your object, and activate it in place. All your UI shows up as it should. Now switch to the other empty document in the container. What happened? You will see that your user interface (shared menu and tools) is still displayed even though you are now working on a container document that does not have an active in-place object. This is not right. If you switch back to the document that has your active object, you'll probably see some flashing of the menu and tools.

What's missing here is our implementation of *IOleInPlaceActiveObject::OnDocWindowActivate.* The container will call this function any time one of its document windows with an active in-place object becomes active (for example, in the case of a highlighted caption bar) or inactive.

When your document is becoming inactive, you must call *IOleInPlaceFrame::SetActiveObject* with NULLs and hide your tools. When the document becomes active again you must pass your *IOleInPlaceActiveObject* pointer back to the frame via *IOleInPlaceFrame::SetActiveObject*, call *IOleInPlaceFrame::SetMenu*, pass the shared menu and menu descriptor you store in your object, and show your tools again:

```
STDMETHODIMP CImpIOleInPlaceActiveObject::OnDocWindowActivate
    (BOOL fActivate)
    {
    HWND        hWndGB;

    if (NULL==m_pObj->m_pIOleIPFrame)
        return NOERROR;

    hWndGB=m_pObj->m_pGB->Window();

    if (fActivate)
        {
        m_pObj->m_pIOleIPFrame->SetActiveObject(this
            , (*m_pObj->m_pST)[IDS_INPLACETITLE]);

        m_pObj->m_pIOleIPFrame->SetMenu(m_pObj->m_hMenuShared
            , m_pObj->m_hOLEMenu, m_pObj->m_pFR->Window());

        if (m_pObj->FInPlaceToolsRenegotiate())
            {
            RECT    rc;

            m_pObj->m_pIOleIPFrame->GetBorder(&rc);
            SetWindowPos(hWndGB, NULL, rc.left, rc.top
                , rc.right-rc.left, m_pObj->m_cyBar
                , SWP_NOZORDER);

            ShowWindow(hWndGB, SW_SHOW);
            }
        }
    else
        {
        m_pObj->m_pIOleIPFrame->SetActiveObject(NULL, NULL);

        //Hide our tools, but do not call SetMenu
        ShowWindow(hWndGB, SW_HIDE);
        }

    return NOERROR;
    }
```

The effect of this implementation is that you show and hide your tools at the appropriate times and tell the container when to redisplay the shared menu. Note that you do not tell the container to reinstate its own menu in the inactive case by calling *IOleInPlaceFrame::SetMenu* with NULLs. This allows the container to minimize menu switching when switching between two documents, especially between two documents that both have in-place active objects. If the document becoming active has an in-place active object, that object's *OnDocWindowActivate* function will tell the container to install a different shared menu, replacing the current shared menu. If there is not an in-place active object in that document, the container will redisplay its own normal menu, again switching menus only once. Note that when the document is becoming active, you must always call *SetMenu*. If you don't have a shared menu, pass NULL to the function.

If you have frame-level tools, you must also renegotiate and reposition your tools on activation. Switching to another document generally switches tools (to the container's or to another object's), so when switching back to your document, you must tell the container to show yours again. The repeat round of border space negotiation lets the container resize its windows to accommodate your requests once again.

You might have noticed the other function, *IOleInPlaceActiveObject::OnFrameWindowActivate*. (Aren't these names getting ridiculously long?) This function needs no implementation at the present time and is basically in the interface for consistency and possible future uses. For now, you can return NOERROR:

```
STDMETHODIMP CImpIOleInPlaceActiveObject::OnFrameWindowActivate
    (BOOL fActivate)
    {
    return NOERROR;
    }
```

Implement Minimal Context-Sensitive Help Support

Both containers and objects must provide at least some support for context-sensitive help even if they do not support that feature themselves. As an object, your application really doesn't need to do *anything*. This actually means you want to *avoid* doing certain things. First, you do not want to trap the Shift+F1 and Esc accelerators. Instead you need to let them pass through to the container. If the container wants to enter the help mode, it will do so and call your *IOleInPlaceObject::ContextSensitiveHelp* function with a TRUE parameter. When this help mode is on and you do not support such help, ignore all mouse clicks in your object—that is, provide no help.

If you support context sensitive help and *do* trap Shift+F1 and Esc, you must do the following:

1. When you detect the Shift+F1 key combination, notify the container that you are entering the mode by calling *IOleInPlaceSite::ContextSensitiveHelp(TRUE).*
2. If you detect the Esc key while in context-sensitive help mode, call *IOleInPlaceSite::ContextSensitiveHelp(FALSE).*

Essentially, you have to maintain a flag indicating the state of context-sensitive help mode and notify the container when there is a change in the mode. When help is enabled, mouse clicks and other events in your object generate messages instead of making changes to the object itself.

Provide Undo Support

Undo is another sort of function that you may or may not support and your container may or may not support. If you do not support Undo, you still need to implement *IOleInPlaceObject::ReactivateAndUndo* by reactivating your application as if it had received a *DoVerb* call. Cosmo implements this function by calling *CFigure::InPlaceActivate*:

```
STDMETHODIMP CImpIOleInPlaceObject::ReactivateAndUndo(void)
    {
    return m_pObj->InPlaceActivate(m_pObj->m_pIOleClientSite, TRUE);
    }
```

If your object has an Undo command itself, as Cosmo does, you have a little more work, but not much. First, you'll want to maintain a flag like Cosmo's *m_fUndoDeactivates,* which is initially set to TRUE in *CFigure::InPlaceActivate.*

If this flag is set when the user selects your Undo command, you should call *IOleInPlaceSite::DeactivateAndUndo,* which will cause deactivation as if the user clicked in the container document outside your object. When the Undo command is given to Cosmo (by means of Edit/Undo or by means of the Ctrl+Z or Alt+Bksp accelerator), we call *CCosmoDoc::Undo,* which calls *CFigure::FUndo.* If our *m_fUndoDeactivates* flag is TRUE, we set it to FALSE and perform the deactivation.

```
BOOL CFigure::FUndo(void)
    {
    if (!m_fUndoDeactivates)
        return FALSE;
```

```
    m_fUndoDeactivates=FALSE;
    m_pIOleIPSite->DeactivateAndUndo();
    return TRUE;
    }
```

Now we want Undo to deactivate only if it's the first thing that happens after activation. If any other changes are made to the object, we want to provide Undo as usual, meaning we should set *m_fUndoDeactivates* to FALSE. Cosmo clears the flag in *CFigure::SendAdvise* after posting an *IAdviseSink::OnDataChange* to the container because all other parts of our code call *SendAdvise* when a change is made, so this is a nice, central area to make this change. In addition, if this is the first change to the object after activation, we must call *IOleInPlaceSite::DiscardUndoState* to tell the container that we will not be calling *DeactivateAndUndo* so that it can free any state it's holding:

```
//After sending IAdviseSink::OnDataChange
if (NULL!=m_pIOleIPSite && m_fUndoDeactivates)
    m_pIOleIPSite->DiscardUndoState();

m_fUndoDeactivates=FALSE;
```

The remaining part of the Undo picture is that you might also need to hold onto some state information when you deactivate the object in preparation for use if *IOleInPlaceObject::ReactivateAndUndo* is called. If the container makes a change after deactivation and does not execute Undo, it will call *IOleObject::DoVerb(OLEIVERB_DISCARDUNDOSTATE)* to inform your application that it can free that state information. Yep, the use of *DoVerb* is a little odd, but that's how it works. Note that Cosmo does not hold any such Undo information, so it doesn't do anything with this verb.

Call *IOleInPlaceFrame::SetStatusText*

The OLE 2 UI guidelines encourage all objects to call *IOleInPlaceFrame::SetStatusText* when they process WM_MENUSELECT messages for the object's menus when active in place. This is so that if the container has a status line, there will be a consistent stream of messages when the user drags through all the menus from both container and server. This can potentially be a lot of work if you do not already work with a status line.

Cosmo has it easy because it already has WM_MENUSELECT processing that uses its StatStrip control. By calling *CStatStrip::MenuSelect*, we tell the StatStrip to show the appropriate string for the menu item described in *wParam* and *lParam*. Because the pop-up menus on the shared menu are the same as Cosmo's usual menu, the StatStrip, hidden or visible, always has the right string for Cosmo's menus. During an in-place session, we need to get the same string over to the container, so in *CCosmoFrame::FMessageHook* (called from CLASSLIB's frame window procedure), we merely ask the StatStrip for a copy of the string, which we then pass to *IOleInPlaceFrame::SetStatusText*:

```
BOOL CCosmoFrame::FMessageHook(HWND hWnd, UINT iMsg, WPARAM wParam
    , LPARAM lParam, LRESULT FAR *pLRes)
    {
    BOOL            fRet=FALSE;
    char            szText[128];

    if (WM_MENUSELECT!=iMsg)
        return FALSE;

    if (NULL==m_pIOleIPFrame)
        return FALSE;

    m_pSS->MenuSelect(wParam, lParam);
    m_pSS->MessageGet(szText, sizeof(szText));
    m_pIOleIPFrame->SetStatusText(szText);

    *pLRes=0L;
    return TRUE;
    }
```

You can see this interaction at work when you activate a Cosmo object inside the version of Patron from Chapter 15.

Provide Techniques for Opening Into a Window

I mentioned before briefly that a container can call your *IOleObject::DoVerb* with OLEIVERB_OPEN to get it to deactivate in place and open into your normal server window. I also mentioned that Cosmo adds an Open verb to its Edit menu while activated in place to do the same thing. There are two other techniques for accomplishing the same task. First is a Ctrl+Enter accelerator. If you already use that key combination for another function, it doesn't have to mean Open. If you don't want to bother with another accelerator (as Cosmo does), that's fine, too, because the container probably will provide it anyway. The other technique, which is much more exciting, is a double-click on the hatched border around your editing window. (We had to do something with that space.) A double-click here should generate a call to your own *IOleObject::DoVerb* with OLEIVERB_OPEN.

In Cosmo, *CCosmoFrame::OnCommand* handles the IDM_EDITOPEN command from the menu by calling *CCosmoDoc::OpenInPlaceObject*, which simply calls *CFigure::OpenIntoWindow*:

```
void CFigure::OpenIntoWindow(void)
    {
    if (NULL!=m_pIOleIPSite)
```

```
        {
        //Make sure we don't try to do this.
        m_fUndoDeactivates=FALSE;

        /*
         * We can get away with passing a lot of NULLs since we know
         * how we implemented DoVerb.
         */
        m_pIOleObject->DoVerb(OLEIVERB_OPEN, NULL, m_pIOleClientSite
            , -1, NULL, NULL);
        }

    return;
    }
```

DoVerb, as we have seen, will deactivate the object from its in-place state on this verb. In addition, because opening the object into a window does not *change* the object, we must clear our *m_fUndoDeactivates* flag because Undo in the open window should certainly not try in-place deactivation again.

When you double-click in the hatch border the hatch window sends a WM_COMMAND message to its associate window with the hatch window's ID and a notification code of HWN_BORDERDOUBLECLICKED (defined in HATCH.H). Cosmo treats this case in *CCosmoFrame::OnCommand* exactly as it does the IDM_EDITOPEN case.

When I implemented the Open command in Cosmo I had a couple of problems. First, the object would not be saved (via *IPersistStorage::Save*) after I opened it in a window and closed the window. The problem was that the object was not marked as dirty after such an operation. To correct this, I added the flag *m_fForceSave* to *CFigure* and set it to TRUE in *CFigure::OpenIntoWindow.* That causes it to appear as dirty when closing, which generates the proper call to *IOleClientSite::SaveObject.* The other, related problem was that the container site was blank when I opened the object into a window until that site was repainted. So in *CFigure::OpenIntoWindow* I immediately send an *OnDataChange* notification, which propagates to the container as *OnViewChange,* causing it to repaint the site.

Show or Hide Modeless Pop-up Windows

Last come the functions *IOleInPlaceActiveObject::EnableModeless* and *IOleInPlaceFrame::EnableModeless.* As I mentioned in Chapter 15, the container and object use the other's *EnableModeless* call to show or hide floating pop-up windows at various points in the in-place session. If you ever have occasion to tell the container to hide its pop-up windows, (say, when you display a modal dialog box), call *IOleInPlaceFrame::EnableModeless* with TRUE when showing the dialog box and with FALSE when closing the dialog box. The container will do the same thing to your application through *IOleInPlaceActiveObject::EnableModeless* for the same reasons. But use and implementation of these functions is entirely optional

Where In-Place Activation Can Take Us

I promised some wild dreaming, so here goes....

Let's take a typical application such as Microsoft Excel that has a frame window, three different types of document windows (Worksheet, Macrosheet, Chart, and perhaps others, depending on add-ins), and a variety of different editing windows inside those documents (cells in the Worksheet, commands in the Macrosheet, graphics in the Chart, and so on).

The frame window by itself has a simple menu with File and Help popups and two functional toolbar buttons by default (File New and File Open). When you create a new document, a document window appears, more menu items show up, and more toolbar buttons are enabled. Then, depending on what you do in that document—that is, what you are editing at the time—additional menu items and toolbars might appear.

This is starting to sound exactly like what happens when a container activates an object in place. In fact, the way in which Excel works is a perfect example of how in-place activation can be further refined. What I propose here is that any application, given enough refinement of in-place activation, can be viewed as a series of in-place capable containers and in-place objects.

Let's imagine Excel's frame as an in-place container. When you select File New, it normally prompts you for the type of document you want to create. (File Open determines this from the file itself.) For example, the version of Excel I have on my machine displayed this dialog box with five different document types, as shown in Figure 16-1. At this point, only a few toolbar buttons are enabled (New and Open); the rest are disabled.

When I select Worksheet and press OK, Excel creates a new document window in which is drawn a group of cells. I can view this as Excel in-place activating a worksheet object, which provides the document window and draws all the cells. In the process of activation, the worksheet object supplied a number of additional menu items (Edit, Formula, Format, Data, Options, and Macro) and additional toolbar buttons, all of which are now enabled. In addition, the Excel frame added a Window menu to this shared menu because it now has at least one document window to manage, as shown in Figure 16-2.

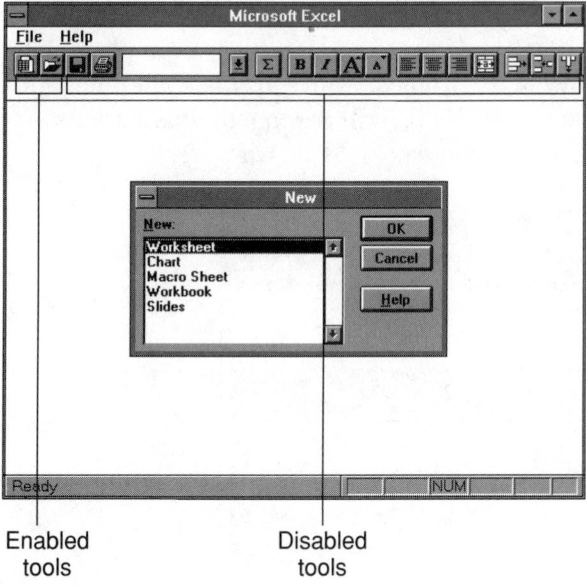

Figure 16-1.
Microsoft Excel prompting for the document type. Isn't this dialog box a little like Insert Object?

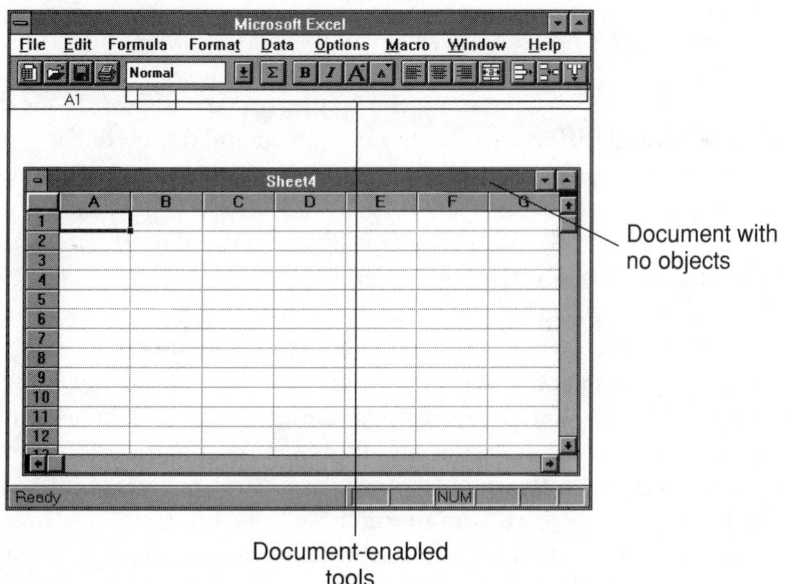

Figure 16-2.
Microsoft Excel after creating a worksheet object and activating it in place.

When I then enter something in one of the cells, I can view the worksheet object as specifically creating and activating an in-place cell object. In mixing menus, the worksheet object, which has become the container, disables a number of its own menus as well as some toolbar buttons. As for tools, the cell object creates the formula bar, as shown in Figure 16-3.

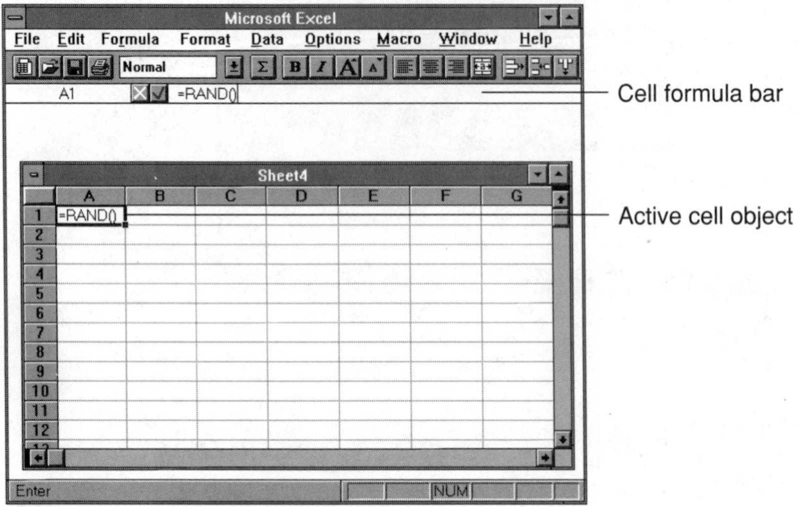

Figure 16-3.
Microsoft Excel with a cell object activated in place in the worksheet.

If I created other types of objects in the worksheet, I would see different in-place tools and different menu items enabled and disabled. For example, if I added a chart object on the worksheet, I'd get a chart toolbar at the bottom of the window, as shown in Figure 16-4. Note that the worksheet itself (and therefore the chart object) does not visibly accommodate the toolbar.

Doing all of this with the current OLE 2 specifications is not possible because although creating the menu is no problem, OLE 2 does not allow a container (Excel's frame) and an object (the worksheet) to share toolbar space. But that is exactly what's going on in Excel, and it shows one area of future refinement: shared toolbar negotiation. That, of course, will require some heavy-duty user interface standards between many industry vendors. But it should come in the next few years in future versions of OLE. This certainly seems to be the direction in which we're heading.

So what's down the road in that direction? Ideally an application such as Excel would not be lumped together into one large, multi-megabyte application but rather would be broken up into many smaller server DLLs. It would

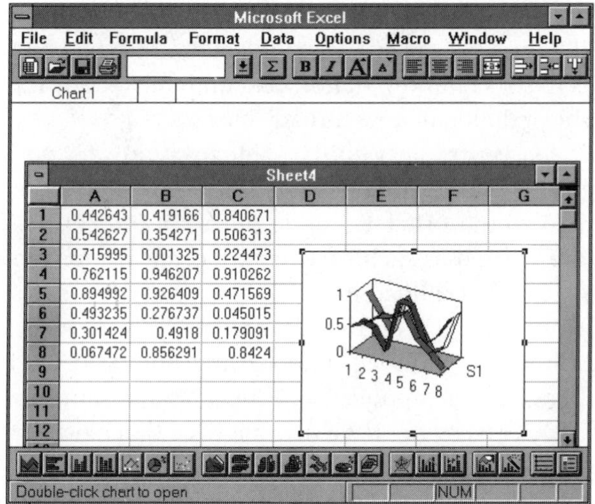

Figure 16-4.

Microsoft Excel with a chart object in the worksheet. Excel's current model is a little different from the in-place activation model because the chart is only selected at this point. If the chart were an inside-out object, selection and UI activation would mean the same thing.

start by breaking the cell, the chart, and any other editing control into an in-place object in a DLL. Excel's worksheet would then specifically create in-place activate objects of those known classes as necessary. Excel's interface would not change, however, because all of these objects create the same interface as before when they were part of the EXE.

The difference now is that in breaking these pieces into DLLs, Excel has created a host of objects that can be used in *other* containers as well via the Insert Object dialog box, thus making the entire system richer for the end user. End users now have many more tools available in all container applications instead of only in one.

Excel's next step would then be to break the document objects into separate DLLs so that the Excel frame can selectively instantiate objects of those classes and activate them in place. Excel's File New dialog box, shown in Figure 16-1, if you think about it, is simply a restricted Insert Object dialog box, is it not? Instead of showing all available objects, it shows only those that Excel knows are document objects that also have containment facilities.

OLE 2 does not have a concept of document objects, but this will probably also change in a future version. All Windows Objects will be classified as "document objects" or "editing objects," where the document objects generally provide a pop-up window like an MDI document window, whereas an editing object creates a child window inside some other document. When this distinction exists, there will be two flavors of Insert Object dialog box: one for document objects, such as Excel's File New dialog box, and one for editing objects, such as the Insert Object dialog box we already have.

At that point, Excel, as a frame, would be able to create any type of document inside itself, even if that document were written by some other vendor and originally used for some other frame application altogether. If all of Excel's documents are written as such objects too, other frame applications would be able to create an Excel document.

Now let's take this to a logical extreme. We would have a system in which there are a great number of document and editing objects in DLLs and a much smaller number of frame application EXEs. My question now is this: Who needs separate EXEs? Why not have the one EXE that exists be the ultimate container, the shell? Would it even have to be an EXE at all?

This is where compound documents are headed: There is only one application, the shell, which is the container that provides frame functionality (for example, File and Window commands). Opening a file means activating an in-place document object that can load the file and display it. That document object really provides only a template that suits specific tasks. A spreadsheet document would provide a template of cells. A word processor document would provide a template of paragraphs. A database document would provide a form. This is why you might have heard that Microsoft is beginning to discourage MDI applications—in the future, applications will not manage documents themselves; instead, they will leave that functionality to the system shell and will then need only to implement document objects.

What we've essentially created is a system in which the user chooses the task he or she wants to perform and chooses the best type of document to perform that task. When that document appears, it gives the user a structure in which to do that task. Users focus their attention on the document, on the task, on the data. They have forgotten that there was ever such a thing as an application. All they know and see—indeed, all they care about—is the work they are doing. Your job is to provide the best tools to do that work, and that is the component software of the years to come.

I think the Patron application we've developed in this book is the kind of document shell we'll see in the future. (There will be other features, like searching, of course.) If there are enough different objects to insert on a page, and the objects' presentations can be broken into pieces, wrapped around one another, shown in nonrectangular shapes, and broken across page boundaries, I could essentially create any conceivable document with Patron, just as I could with any word processor, spreadsheet, database, presentation package, or DTP application today, although it would not be as easy in

Patron as in these other applications to make the task. That's where document objects as templates come in: Each template is designed to make the specific task of writing a report, a budget sheet, a form, a newsletter, or a presentation as easy and guided as possible, helping the user decide which editing objects to use for the best results.

All of this is going to take a lot more work and many more revisions and refinements to the idea of Windows Objects and compound documents. With OLE 2, we have the beginning of a long evolution in the way we use computers and the way in which we create, use, and sell software. That's what we mean by "Information at Your Fingertips." Personally, I'm excited to think about all the possibilities, and it looks like we'll all have plenty to work on for a long time. If you are, too, please get involved with Microsoft to provide input for OLE 2 and future refinements of this great technology. There's plenty of room in the future for everyone. You just have to know how to run forward into the future.

So does the evolution still seem like heresy and misconduct?

Summary

With a very reasonable amount of work, any embedded object can be enhanced to support in-place activation. The primary enhancements to the object come in two additional interfaces, *IOleInPlaceObject* and *IOleInPlaceActiveObject*. These provide the functions through which the in-place container application notifies the object of specific event on which the object is required to take some action.

The object during an in-place session is really the active agent because it has the keyboard focus and is what the user is primarily working on. To that end, the object will frequently be calling many member functions of the container's in-place interfaces *IOleInPlaceFrame*, *IOleInPlaceUIWindow*, and *IOleInPlaceSite*. Most of those functions deal with the process of activating the object's user interface, which includes creating a shared menu and negotiating with the container for in-place tools.

The object also has specific responsibilities as far as accelerators, Undo, context-sensitive help, and other areas are concerned. Most requirements mean either implementing or modifying a member function in the object's interfaces or calling a member function in the container. Overall, the great majority of changes necessary to support in-place activation happen to the object itself. Very little is changed in the server's frame and document windows themselves.

This chapter follows the step-by-step modifications to the Cosmo application to make it a complete and up-to-spec in-place object server. The same process can be used to add such capabilities to your own application.

This chapter concludes with some thoughts about where OLE, Windows Objects, and compound documents are headed, and why all of this is so important and powerful. OLE 2 is not only the start of the evolution of Windows into an object-oriented operating system, but it is also the beginning of the transition from application-centric computing to document-centric computing, in which the end user focuses on the task and not on the application to do it. This sounds scary because we're all so used to selling applications with a tangible identity, and document-centric computing threatens that. But there is a great deal of new territory to explore and claim—so much, in fact, that we can all have a significant slice of the pie.

INDEX

Note: *Italicized* page numbers refer to figures.

D

F

K

L

N

O

P

T

U

V

W

X

KRAIG BROCKSCHMIDT

Kraig Brockschmidt is a software design engineer in Microsoft's developer relations group, where he is responsible for explaining new system technologies to independent software vendors through books, papers, articles, and seminars. His articles have appeared in *Microsoft Systems Journal* and in *Windows Tech Journal.* Brockschmidt's primary area of specialization has been Object Linking and Embedding, versions 1 and 2. He joined Microsoft in March 1988, and worked in the product support, applications, and systems divisions before moving to developer relations in November 1991. He holds a bachelor of science degree in computer engineering from the University of Washington.

The manuscript for this book was prepared and submitted to Microsoft Press in electronic form. Text files were prepared using Microsoft Word 2.0 for Windows. Pages were composed by Microsoft Press using the Magna Composition System, with text in New Baskerville and display type in Helvetica Bold. Composed pages were delivered to the printer as electronic prepress files.

Cover Illustrator
Studio MD

Cover Color Separator
Color Service, Inc.

Interior Graphic Designer
Kim Eggleston

Interior Graphic Artist
Lisa Sandburg

Principal Typographer
Lisa Iversen

Principal Editorial Compositor
Barb Runyan

Principal Proofreader/Copy Editor
Kathleen Atkins

Indexer
Shane-Armstrong Information Systems

Printed on recycled paper stock.

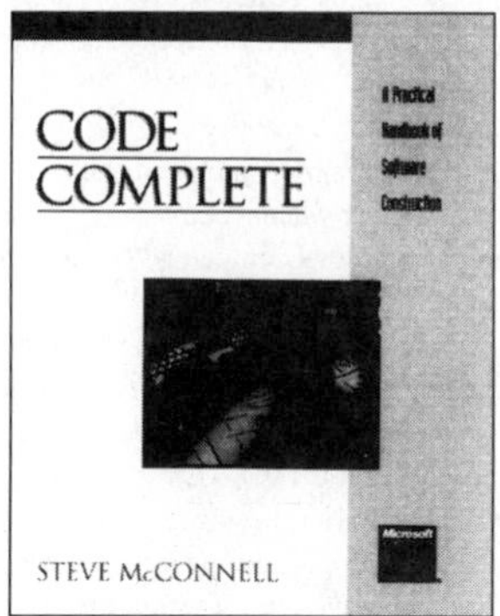

CODE
COMPLETE
STEVE McCONNELL

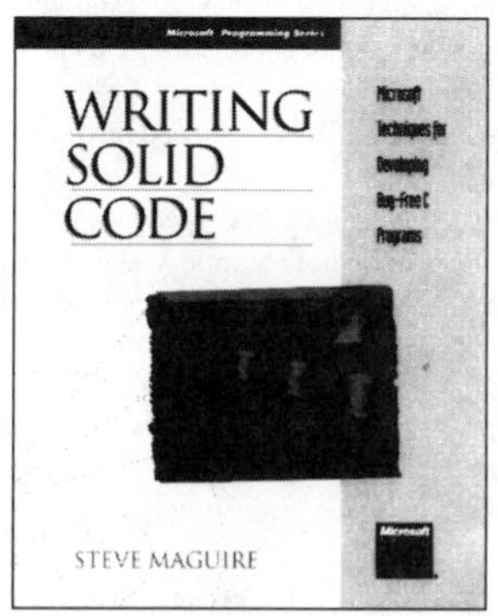

WRITING
SOLID
CODE
STEVE MAGUIRE

PROGRAMMER'S REFERENCE LIBRARY
OLE2
Programmer's Reference
VOLUME ONE
Overview and
API
Reference

IMPORTANT— READ CAREFULLY BEFORE OPENING SOFTWARE PACKET(S). By opening the sealed packet(s) containing the software, you indicate your acceptance of the following Microsoft License Agreement.

MICROSOFT LICENSE AGREEMENT

(Book Companion Disks)

This is a legal agreement between you (either an individual or an entity) and Microsoft Corporation. By opening the sealed software packet(s) you are agreeing to be bound by the terms of this agreement. If you do not agree to the terms of this agreement, promptly return the unopened software packet(s) and any accompanying written materials to the place you obtained them for a full refund.

MICROSOFT SOFTWARE LICENSE

1. GRANT OF LICENSE. Microsoft grants to you the right to use one copy of the Microsoft software program included with this book (the "SOFTWARE") on a single terminal connected to a single computer. The SOFTWARE is in "use" on a computer when it is loaded into the temporary memory (i.e., RAM) or installed into the permanent memory (e.g., hard disk, CD-ROM, or other storage device) of that computer. You may not network the SOFTWARE or otherwise use it on more than one computer or computer terminal at the same time.

2. COPYRIGHT. The SOFTWARE is owned by Microsoft or its suppliers and is protected by United States copyright laws and international treaty provisions. Therefore, you must treat the SOFTWARE like any other copyrighted material (e.g., a book or musical recording) except that you may either (a) make one copy of the SOFTWARE solely for backup or archival purposes, or (b) transfer the SOFTWARE to a single hard disk provided you keep the original solely for backup or archival purposes. You may not copy the written materials accompanying the SOFTWARE.

3. OTHER RESTRICTIONS. You may not rent or lease the SOFTWARE, but you may transfer the SOFTWARE and accompanying written materials on a permanent basis provided you retain no copies and the recipient agrees to the terms of this Agreement. You may not reverse engineer, decompile, or disassemble the SOFTWARE. If the SOFTWARE is an update or has been updated, any transfer must include the most recent update and all prior versions.

4. DUAL MEDIA SOFTWARE. If the SOFTWARE package contains both 3.5" and 5.25" disks, then you may use only the disks appropriate for your single-user computer. You may not use the other disks on another computer or loan, rent, lease, or transfer them to another user except as part of the permanent transfer (as provided above) of all SOFTWARE and written materials.

5. SAMPLE CODE. If the SOFTWARE includes Sample Code, then Microsoft grants you a royalty-free right to reproduce and distribute the sample code of the SOFTWARE provided that you: (a) distribute the sample code only in conjunction with and as a part of your software product; (b) do not use Microsoft's or its authors' names, logos, or trademarks to market your software product; (c) include the copyright notice that appears on the SOFTWARE on your product label and as a part of the sign-on message for your software product; and (d) agree to indemnify, hold harmless, and defend Microsoft and its authors from and against any claims or lawsuits, including attorneys' fees, that arise or result from the use or distribution of your software product.

DISCLAIMER OF WARRANTY

The SOFTWARE (including instructions for its use) is provided "AS IS" WITHOUT WARRANTY OF ANY KIND. MICROSOFT FURTHER DISCLAIMS ALL IMPLIED WARRANTIES INCLUDING WITHOUT LIMITATION ANY IMPLIED WARRANTIES OF MERCHANTABILITY OR OF FITNESS FOR A PARTICULAR PURPOSE. THE ENTIRE RISK ARISING OUT OF THE USE OR PERFORMANCE OF THE SOFTWARE AND DOCUMENTATION REMAINS WITH YOU.

IN NO EVENT SHALL MICROSOFT, ITS AUTHORS, OR ANYONE ELSE INVOLVED IN THE CREATION, PRODUCTION, OR DELIVERY OF THE SOFTWARE BE LIABLE FOR ANY DAMAGES WHATSOEVER (INCLUDING, WITHOUT LIMITATION, DAMAGES FOR LOSS OF BUSINESS PROFITS, BUSINESS INTERRUPTION, LOSS OF BUSINESS INFORMATION, OR OTHER PECUNIARY LOSS) ARISING OUT OF THE USE OF OR INABILITY TO USE THE SOFTWARE OR DOCUMENTATION, EVEN IF MICROSOFT HAS BEEN ADVISED OF THE POSSIBILITY OF SUCH DAMAGES. BECAUSE SOME STATES/COUNTRIES DO NOT ALLOW THE EXCLUSION OR LIMITATION OF LIABILITY FOR CONSEQUENTIAL OR INCIDENTAL DAMAGES, THE ABOVE LIMITATION MAY NOT APPLY TO YOU.

U.S. GOVERNMENT RESTRICTED RIGHTS

The SOFTWARE and documentation are provided with RESTRICTED RIGHTS. Use, duplication, or disclosure by the Government is subject to restrictions as set forth in subparagraph (c)(1)(ii) of The Rights in Technical Data and Computer Software clause at DFARS 252.227-7013 or subparagraphs (c)(1) and (2) of the Commercial Computer Software — Restricted Rights 48 CFR 52.227-19, as applicable. Manufacturer is Microsoft Corporation, One Microsoft Way, Redmond, WA 98052-6399.

If you acquired this product in the United States, this Agreement is governed by the laws of the State of Washington.

Should you have any questions concerning this Agreement, or if you desire to contact Microsoft Press for any reason, please write: Microsoft Press, One Microsoft Way, Redmond, WA 98052-6399.